DATA

Objectives, System

DATABASE MANAGEMENT
Objectives, System Functions, and Administration

Gordon C. Everest

Graduate School of Management
University of Minnesota

McGraw-Hill Book Company

New York St. Louis San Francisco Auckland Bogotá Hamburg
London Madrid Mexico Montreal New Delhi
Panama Paris São Paulo Singapore Sydney Tokyo Toronto

DATABASE MANAGEMENT
Objectives, System Functions, and Administration
INTERNATIONAL EDITION 1986

Exclusive rights by McGraw-Hill Book Co—Singapore for
manufacture and export. This book cannot be re-exported
from the country to which it is consigned by McGraw-Hill.

  6 7 8 9 0 CMO   9 4 3

This book was set in Times Roman by York Graphic Services, Inc.
The editor was Christina Mediate;
The production supervisor was Marietta Breitwieser.

Library of Congress Cataloging in Publication Data

Everest, Gordon C.
    Database management.

    (McGraw-Hill series in management information
systems)
    Includes bibliographics and index.
    1. Data base management.   2. Management information
systems. 1. Title.   II. Title: Data base management.
III. Series.
QA76.9.D3E93   1986   001.64'4   85-11404 .
ISBN 0-07-019781-4

When ordering this title use ISBN 0-07-066456-0

Printed in Singapore

To Marty, James, Rob, Mary, Sarah, and Peter
who involuntarily gave of their time
so that Daddy's puzzle could be completed,
and to Jesus Christ to whom belongs
all the honor and glory.

CONTENTS

Preface   xi

1   Managing Data in Organizations   1

Four Components of a Data Processing System   3
Data and the Database Approach   7
Managing Data Resources   13
Organizational Context for Database Management   16
The State of Database Management in Organizations   18

Part I   Overview of Database Management Systems

**2   Motivation, Objectives, and Evolution of the
Database Approach**   27

Traditional Approach to Application System Development   28
Motivations toward the Database Approach   31
Countervailing Forces Inhibiting DBMSs   34
Objectives of Database Management   36
Evolution of Database Management Systems   52

3   A Conceptual DBMS Model   73

Several Dimensions of DBMS   74
User Roles in the DBMS Environment   74
Database Management Functions   84
A Conceptual DBMS Model   88
How the DBMS Model Satisfies   97
The DBMS Environment   106

4 Logical Data Structures 119

A Taxonomy of Data Structures 120
Single Flat File Data Structure 123
Single Hierarchical Data Structure 129
Multifile Data Structure 133
Object-Relation Data Structure 143

5 User Interface, Language, and DBMS Operation 159

Evolution of the User Interface 160
Principles of Direct Manipulation 163
Types of Online Users: By Usage Mode and Dialogue Style 168
Additional Online Support 181
Types of Data Languages: Definition, Manipulation, Mapping 186
Data Languages on Data Structures 187
DBMS Modes of Operation 188

Part II Database Management System Functions

6 Database Design and Definition 197

The Process of Database Design 198
The Process of Database Definition 205
Database Definition Information 213
Importance of Formal Database Definition 242
Logical Database Design 244

7 Database Retrieval: Flat Files 257

Steps in the Retrieval Process 258
Selection 265
Projection and Derivation of Data Items 273
Ordering, Control Breaks, and Statistics 275
Formation and Presentation of Output Results 280
A General Flat File Retrieval Language 287
Graphical Presentation of Statistical Output 294
Natural Language Query Systems and Artificial Intelligence 299

8 Database Retrieval: Hierarchical and Multifile Structures 307

Development of Retrieval Languages on Hierarchical Data Structures 308
Querying a Single-Path Hierarchical Data Structure 311
Querying a Multipath Hierarchical Data Structure 323
Retrieval from a Multifile Data Structure 330

9 Database Creation and Update 339

Data Capture and Mechanization 340
Database Creation 341
Transaction Processing and Database Update 346
General Update Operations 354

10 Programming User Facilities for System Development   359

Methods of Program Access to a Database   361
COBOL Input-Output Statements   362
Program Communication with the DBMS   364
Form, Time, and Scope of Program-System Communication   371
Additional Facilities for the DBMS System Programmer   375
Converging Facilities for Programming and Nonprogramming Users   376

11 Data Independence, Data Conversion, and
Database Revision   385

Historical Evolution of the Program-Data Relationship   387
Data Independence   390
Binding, Data Independence, and Evolvability   398
Data Conversion Processes   409
Database Revision   416

12 Database Integrity: Backup and Recovery   427

Overview of Integrity Control Functions   428
The Processes of Database Backup and Recovery   430
Backup Strategies   431
Summary Chart of Traditional Backup and Recovery Strategies   439
Residual Dump Backup Strategy   441
Variables in the Backup Process   444
Process Checkpoint and Restart   446

13 Database Integrity: Quality Control and
Concurrent Update   453

Data Validation   454
Update Authorization   465
Concurrent Update Control   466
Update Synchronization   496

14 Database Integrity: Access Control and Encryption   505

Data Access Control Policies and Approaches   508
A General Model of Data Access Control   510
User Identification and Authentication   515
Authorization   529
Controlling Inferences from Statistical Data   538
Encryption   544
Threat Monitoring and Audit Trail   562

Part III Database Administration

15 Database Administration Organization, Functions, and Tools 575

History of and Need for Database Administration 576
Database Administration within the Organization 576
Organization of the Database Administration Function 586
Functions of Database Administration 589
Database Administrator Tool: The Data Dictionary 601
DBMS Performance Monitoring and Usage Statistics 610
Organizational Response to a Database Administration Role 613

16 Data Privacy and Fair Information Practices 623

Privacy and Personal Data 624
The Three Basic Rights 628
Organizations, Individuals, and Personal Data 633
Legislative Approaches to Fair Information Practices 640
Organizational Response 653

17 DBMS Selection and Acquisition 671

Beginning the Search and Evaluation Process 672
Acquisition Alternatives 679
DBMS Evaluation Process 685
Investigating DBMS Packages ("Getting Answers") 693
Selection Criteria ("Asking Questions") 697
Final Selection, Contract Negotiation, and Acquisition 704
Installation and Use 714

18 Trends to the Future in Database Management 731

DBMS Development and Usage Trends 732
Organizational Resistance to New DBMS Tools 736
Databases in a Distributed Processing Environment 738
Backend Database Management Machine 750
Emerging Standards in Database Technology 760

Index 783

PREFACE

This book is about managing data in organizations. It presumes the use of computers. Managing data involves the use of a Database Management System (DBMS) on the computer and a human Database Administrator (DBA). Hence the dual thrust of this book into both the technology of DBMS and the administrative dimension of developing, using, and controlling data resources.

Several things are different about this book:

- Takes a *broad, comprehensive* view of DBMS, going far beyond those systems which simply augment programming languages (such as COBOL) with some verbs to manipulate a database one record at a time. In this book, a DBMS includes high-level languages for defining and manipulating databases, producing reports with statistics and graphics, and handling data entry screens and menus. Such a view of DBMS encompasses what have been called "fourth generation languages" and "application development systems."
- Focus on the *functions* of database management rather than the more traditional focus on data structures—hierarchical, network, and relational.
- Strong on the *conceptual*, with a clear organization of material, and understandable explanations of some difficult technical issues in DBMS.
- Strong on the *administrative* aspects of managing data. With this emphasis, some have used the term "Information Resource Management (IRM)" to differentiate it from Database Management.
- Up-to-date with the integration of material as it relates to the use of DBMS on microcomputers, distributed systems, and database machines.

The Importance of Information

Information is the lubricant for the operations and decisions carried out in modern organizations. Through the use of "mind-amplifying" computers we are entering an era of information-intensive production. Harnessing and using information resources can make *both* labor and capital equipment more productive. Information is an increasingly valuable organizational resource that must be managed.

Today, there is substantial disparity between the needs of organizations to manage and make available their data resources and the existing state of the technology in currently available DBMSs. The disparity exists for users at all levels—clerks, managers, analysts, and computer systems personnel who develop and maintain management information systems (MIS).

Purpose and Focus

A basic goal in writing this text is to close the gap between the available DBMS technology and the needs of users. The book should:

stretch DBMS builders,
  guide DBMS documenters,
    humble DBMS vendors,
      armor DBMS buyers,
        excite DBMS users,
          encourage DBMS administrators, and
          educate DBMS students.

This text tells a modern organization how to get a handle on its data resources. The answer lies in appointing a responsible manager of these resources and using computer-based facilities for managing data. This book, then, has two major thrusts: organizational and technological—the management of data resources, and the technology of DBMS.

In 1980, Frost and Sullivan, a market analysis firm in New York, estimated the DBMS market at $137 million, increasing 30% annually to over $1 billion by 1987. Their study calls DBMS "the single most significant software product to come along since the advent of computer operating systems . . . its use in time will permeate the EDP world." A similar study by International Data Corp. (Framingham, MA) in 1983, entitled *The DBMS Marketplace,* predicted that by 1987 the market for DBMS products would climb to $1.75 billion. They further predicted that DBMS programs for desktop microcomputer would capture a 12% share of that market. In another study, Strategic Inc. of San Jose, CA, forecasted a 600% increase in the DBMS market during the 1980s, to over $4 billion by 1989.

For some readers this text will generate great expectations for DBMS. When they seek to acquire a commercially available DBMS, they may become disappointed. The material should help steer an organization away from the poor systems, and give them realistic expectations for the system they do acquire *before they actually use it.* A comparison of any DBMS against the material here will reveal its weaknesses and indicate where the organization will have to compensate for them. At least a company can avoid buying a system because it is popular or oversold. The potential of a well-designed, comprehensive DBMS can make us optimistic about the future. This book seeks to present the full potential of DBMS and the administrative challenges of using a DBMS effectively.

A comprehensive DBMS enables an organization to define and create databases, to maintain established databases with the timely capture and processing of update transactions, to retrieve data from established databases, to maintain the integrity and quality of the data, and to revise the established databases (and related processes) as needs change. A DBMS enables direct end users to access organizational data resources, provides a building block of functional capabilities used to develop information systems, and provides the tools for an organization to manage and control its data resources.

Audience

This text is aimed at professionals in business and government organizations, and students of business administration and computers preparing to develop or use information systems in organizations. It is for those who have or expect to have a responsibility for or an interest in the effective management of organizational data resources.

For persons who both use and control the use of DBMS, this text is detailed enough to foster appreciation for the more technical aspects of database management. For the technical information specialist it reviews the major objectives, functional capabilities, and organizational issues of database management. The specialist can better understand how technical problems and functional capabilities relate to management needs. The book, then, establishes common understanding between the specialist, and the users and managers of information systems.

Since the mid 1950's, several hundred DBMSs have been developed, with many still commercially available and more still being developed. Even so, all systems fall short of the model presented here. This text aims to stimulate and guide the future development of DBMSs which better serve the organizational need to manage and make available data resources. The industry must strive to perfect a tool for database management which satisfies the fundamental objectives and adequately meets the real needs of modern organizations.

Also since the mid 1950's, several thousand organizations have installed and used DBMSs with varied success. With the advent of microcomputers, this number is being multiplied many times over. This text seeks to encourage and direct the professionals who select and acquire DBMSs, who build application information systems using database management facilities, and who use DBMSs to access organizational data resources.

Premises and Assumed Background

This text is committed to the proposition that it is no longer necessary to know how data is physically stored, manipulated, and accessed before learning how to establish, query, and update databases and to manage data resources. Therefore, the text does not attempt to cover data storage structures and access methods. These methods can differ widely from one system to another and learning them can quickly bog the student down in unnecessary detail. Most users do not (at least should not) need to know how data is stored on secondary devices and accessed within the computer system. Instructors who feel their students do not adequately appreciate basic storage structure concepts may add outside readings—including a look at the storage structure for the DBMS available to the students for class projects. Understanding how COBOL stores and accesses data files can provide a useful example but would not be necessary. It would enable those who already know COBOL to relate that knowledge to the material in the text.

This text also takes the position that it is no longer necessary to know high-level programming languages (such as COBOL and FORTRAN) before learning about databases, and high-level *data* definition languages and *data* processing languages. This extends the accepted view that you need not learn assembly language programming before learning a high-level programming language. An average high-level language programmer using an optimizing compiler can usually produce better object code at less cost than can an assembly language programmer. Comprehensive, high-level data languages for defining and manipulating data, and effective DBMS, eliminate the need to learn low-level *data* languages first. Only the specialist concerned with the efficiency of a specialized process beyond the capabilities of the DBMS needs low-level languages. Unfortunately, many of today's DBMSs lack comprehensive functional capabilities and high-level data languages.

This text has been used experimentally in colleges over ten years. Students are assumed to have a background in computers and data processing (as found in an introductory text, e.g., Davis, *Computer Data Processing,* McGraw-Hill, 1973), with some appreciation for the role of information systems in organizations (as in Davis and Olson, *Management Information Systems,* McGraw-Hill, 1985).

This text seldom mentions specific DBMSs. Its focus on general concepts, functional capabilities, and languages transcends the ever changing software marketplace. Readers already familiar with a DBMS can easily relate this text to their own understanding and experience. To enhance learning, an instructor can supplement this text with the manual for an existing DBMS. The student can see a consistent, practical example of a DBMS and can use the system to design, create, query, and manipulate databases in class projects. The Instructor's Manual contains suggestions for using this text and constructing a course on data management.

Contrast with Existing DBMS Literature

To those somewhat familiar with the literature, this text will initially appear to be out of the mainstream of thought in database management technology. For example, the text is not organized around what many consider to be the major basis for classifying DBMS: hierarchical, network, and relational data structures. Readers are cautioned not to reject the approach taken here without examining the arguments and the alternative classification presented. The chosen data structure classes must be rooted in fundamental not spurious differences, and must be related to their corresponding, high-level data languages. The taxonomies developed in this text were carefully thought through. Most students of DBMS will readily accept the classifications used herein and find them superior to existing ones.

Consider how this book differs from current database management texts:

- Emphasis on concepts and principles.
- Focus on the logical aspects of data structures, with minimum discussion of physical data storage and access methods.
- Description of logical data structures which transcends the minor differences between "network" and "relational" data structures.
- Focus on high-level data languages for definition and manipulation, with little attention to low-level, one-record-at-a-time navigational languages.
- Little discussion of existing DBMSs which become obsolete quickly, or represent at best a since-improved-upon technology.
- Emphasis on the database management functions to serve the needs of end users and management.
- Broad coverage of organizational acquisition, use, and administration of DBMS.

Organization of the Chapters

After an introductory chapter, this text is organized into three parts. Chapter 1 answers the "why" and "so what can I hope to achieve" with database management technology.

Part I provides both a foundation and overview of DBMS by exploring several different definitions and classifications of DBMS.

Chapter 2 identifies several factors which motivate an organization to consider DBMS. It outlines the objectives an organization would hope to achieve by applying database technology, perhaps acquiring a DBMS, and embracing the philosophy and principles of database management. It concludes with a brief look at the evolution of the database approach to managing data in organizations.

Chapter 3 develops a conceptual model of DBMS based upon different user types, and the functions performed. This chapter also relates DBMS to other types of systems oriented to processing other forms of data, and relates a DBMS to other functions within a computer environment.

Chapter 4 differentiates DBMS based upon the underlying data structure class (or "data model") which can be defined with a DBMS.

Chapter 5 explores differences in DBMS based upon user interface, language, and modes of operation.

The casual reader or one new to the field can focus on the development of the conceptual model in Chapter 3, skimming the rest of the material in Part I. Those previously exposed to database literature or familiar with DBMS will want to read Part I in more detail to set their present state of knowledge in perspective.

Part II consists of nine chapters covering the major technological functions of a comprehensive DBMS.

Chapter 6 focuses on the design and definition of a database structure.

Chapters 7 and 8 describe database retrieval using high-level facilities, first on a single flat file, then extended in Chapter 8 to retrieve from hierarchical and multifile structures.

Chapter 9 covers the functions for getting data into the database—initial creation and ongoing update—still using high-level functional capabilities.

Chapter 10 considers the functions and interface for programming users who build an information system using the DBMS as a development tool.

Chapter 11 discusses the meaning and means of data independence, an important characteristic of DBMS providing for evolvability. Data independence implies a difference in the way data is viewed, and therefore, the need for a family of data conversion processes. Once the database has been established and used for a time, the revision process becomes increasingly important.

Chapters 12, 13, and 14 cover the DBMS functions for maintaining database integrity—backup and recovery, quality control through data validation and concurrent update control, and access control through identification, authorization, encryption, and threat monitoring.

Part III looks at the administrative side of database management.

Chapter 15 details the organization, functions, and tools of database administration.

Chapter 16 explores the legal issues pertaining to database administration, particularly the organizational response to laws relating to the right to privacy, due process, and public access.

Chapter 17 gives some guidelines for evaluating, selecting, and acquiring a DBMS.

Finally, Chapter 18 examines future developments in database technology, including distributed databases, database machines, and standards activities.

Each chapter ends with a summary, a set of exercises for students to test their own comprehension and to apply and extend the material in the chapter, and a selected, annotated bibliography for further reading. The text extensively uses figures to organize, exemplify, and summarize. Each figure with its caption should be self-explanatory. The figures and accompanying captions provide a unique and efficient way of overviewing or reviewing the major concepts in the text.

A special thanks to those who took the time to review this manuscript or portions thereof in various stages of its development: Gordon B. Davis, University of Minnesota; Donald L. Davis; James C. Emery, University of Pennsylvania, for his early encouragement; David Jefferson, NBS; Hugh F. Juergens, formerly University of Wisconsin, Madison; Salvatore March, University of Minnesota; G. M. Nijssen, University of Queensland, Australia; T. William Olle; Craig Roger; George M. Scott, University of Connecticut, Storrs; James A. Senn, Georgia State University; Ben Shneiderman, University of Maryland; James L. Smith, Northwestern College; Ronald Teichman, Pennsylvania State University; Yannis Vassiliou, New York University; Eric A. Weiss; and Gio Wiederhold, Stanford University. I am also indebted to many former graduate students at the University of Minnesota who provided detailed feedback on prior versions of this text, as well as attendees at the University of Michigan Summer Engineering Conferences. Finally, a special thanks to Nancy Rudisill and Mary Jo Gregory at York Production Services for their patience and their responsiveness to my requests.

The pioneering emphases of this text in a relatively new field make feedback very important. You are encouraged to write or call with any comments or suggestions.

Gordon C. Everest

MANAGING DATA IN ORGANIZATIONS

1.1	FOUR COMPONENTS OF A DATA PROCESSING SYSTEM	3
1.1.1	The Problem of Data	3
1.1.2	A Copernican Revolution in Data Processing	4
1.2	DATA AND THE DATABASE APPROACH	7
1.2.1	Data versus Information	9
1.2.2	Data versus "Library" Information	11
1.2.3	The Singularity of "Data"	11
1.2.4	Database	11
1.2.5	The Database Approach	12
1.3	MANAGING DATA RESOURCES	13
1.3.1	The Human Component: Database Administrator (DBA)	14
1.3.2	The Machine Component: Database Management System (DBMS)	14
1.3.3	Overview of Relationships in Database Management	15
1.4	ORGANIZATIONAL CONTEXT FOR DATABASE MANAGEMENT	16
1.4.1	Managers and Organizations	16
1.4.2	Management Information Systems	17
1.4.3	Role of the Database in an Organization	18
1.5	THE STATE OF DATABASE MANAGEMENT IN ORGANIZATIONS	18
	SUMMARY	20
	EXERCISES	21
	SELECTED REFERENCES	22
	Management Information Systems—the DBMS Context	22
	Books and Articles Generally on DBMS	22
	Serials Devoted Substantially to DBMS	26

"I know you have last year's employment statistics somewhere in the computer system. Why can't you get them for me quickly?"

"Why must I always consult a programmer to get the data I want?"

"I just want to know how many electrical engineers are in the company, where they are in the organization, and the projects they're currently working on. Why do I have to specify all this formatting information and tell the system how to search for the data?"

"It would sure be nice if I could write my own little computer program for my unique data needs; the existing facilities are so awkward and inefficient."

"Don't expect me to use the data from the corporate database. It's old and inaccurate; I can't depend on it to do my job properly."

"Why can't I simply tell the system what the data is supposed to look like and have the system ensure that the actual data conforms?"

"With all that effort just to revise the database structure and add a few more items, I'll build my own database for this new application, even though it's redundant."

Complaints of this sort are common in most organizations today and reflect a need to manage and make available data resources. A well designed, comprehensive database management system (DBMS) can fulfill these needs. The principles of database management are universal, even if an organization chooses not to use a DBMS.

Data is an important resource in the operation and management of an organization. Effective data resource management makes an organization responsive and successful. Through a base of data, the organization has an *image* of itself and its environment, its past and its future. This image stimulates and conditions the response of the organization. With a timely and accurate image, daily operations run more smoothly. People in the organization make better decisions and respond more confidently to organizational change and environmental demands.

This text looks at data within an organizational context, including both technical and administrative considerations—the machine aspects and the human aspects of data management.

Gathering and using data in organizations is not new. However, the recent use of computers has forced greater discipline on the management of data. The computer enables an organization to better respond to internal demands for data as well as external demands from governmental and public agencies. After nearly three decades, the computer industry and users have gained solid experience in using computers to process and manage data. This text synthesizes this past experience and indicates future directions for development.

This chapter introduces major database concepts and terminology. Later chapters build on this base and context for understanding. Remaining sections in this chapter discuss the meaning of data, database, the database approach, database management, database management systems, database administration, and finally, the context of DBMS—organizations, managers, and MIS.

1.1 FOUR COMPONENTS OF A DATA PROCESSING SYSTEM

A computer-based data processing system has four basic components (see Figure 1-1): machines, programs, data, and people. Machines and programs are also called "hardware" and "software."

The invention of modern computers during the late 1940s led to an industry that produced and marketed such machines.

As business organizations responded to the computer revolution, they concentrated on selecting and installing equipment, training programmers and analysts, and mechanizing existing office procedures. They devised sophisticated algorithms to extend the numerical and scientific capabilities of the new machines, developed higher-level languages to more efficiently utilize human resources, and evolved supervisory and operating systems to more efficiently use the machine. Both the computer industry and using organizations have worked hard to develop better programming techniques (to tell a computer what to do). High-level programming languages have been developed to such a degree that today the definition of a process* can be quite machine independent.

1.1.1 The Problem of Data

Data are "facts" represented by values—numbers, character strings, or symbols which carry meaning in a certain context. These values can be punched into cards, stored on secondary storage devices (such as magnetic tape or disk), or stored in the central memory of a computer. Programs direct the movement and manipulation of data within a computer system.

Since the mid-1950s computer professionals have striven to develop programming languages independent of machines and geared to users. Yet they made relatively little effort to do the same for data. Only recently has there been a significant effort toward developing machine-independent, high-level data languages. This effort has been partly fostered by the emergence of the microcomputer industry. Could the computer industry have focused on data first? Probably not. Effective computer use required an initial emphasis on programming and programming languages because without programs the computer does nothing.

Figure 1-2 illustrates the relationships between machines, programs, data, and people. Notice that data is not well decoupled from programs which use it or machines which store it. This is the problem of data in most organizations today.

Several problems stem from data dependent programs and machine dependent

---

*"Process" is used in this text in a very precise sense: a sequence of operations scheduled and executed over time. A computer *program* (or set of programs) defines a process to be carried out on a machine. A program consists of a sequence of statements or commands written in some programming language. A *procedure* defines a process to be carried out by a person. An intuitive definition of *process* is provided by Butler W. Lampson, "A Scheduling Philosophy for Multiprocessing Systems," *Communications of the ACM* (11:5), 1968 May, page 347; and an extended, formal definition is given by J. J. Horning and B. Randell, "Process Structuring," *Computing Surveys* (5:1), 1973 March, pages 5-30.

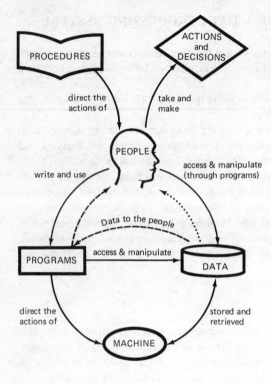

Figure 1-1. Components of a Data Processing System.

Until recently, the focus has been largely on the machine and the programs it executes, perhaps explaining the popularity of the terms "hardware" and "software."

data. Sharing data among applications and transferring data across machines and systems create data problems. When new systems are installed to replace existing hardware and/or software, organizations must transfer (convert) their existing programs and data over to the new system. People in the computer industry are predicting data conversion problems more extensive than program conversions of the past. Data is rapidly being converted to machine-processable forms. Moving to a new computer system now involves converting both programs (made easier with high-level languages) and large volumes of data. As our investment in machinable data increases, the problem of data increases the cost of shifting to new machines and to new technology, and of incorporating new application systems.

The technological development of data processing systems should eventually reconcile programs and data to serve people and meet their needs. At the same time programs and data must become mutually independent as well as machine independent (Figure 1-3). The growing interest in data, data structures, database design, high-level data languages, menu-driven facilities for the online database user, and managing data resources in organizations suggests such a trend.

1.1.2 A Copernican Revolution in Data Processing

The problem of data is causing a Copernican revolution in data processing. At first the profession seemed to focus exclusively on programs, viewing input and output of

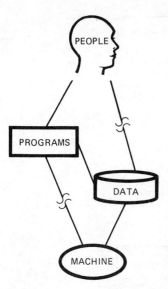

Figure 1-2. The Problem of Data.
Today, programs and programming languages are closer to people and relatively independent of the machine, while data is closely tied to both programs and the machine, and not close to the people who need it.

data as adjuncts to the program (see Figure 1-4, phase I). In certain applications some of the output could be retained and used in the next execution of the program (phase II). Even when data was saved it remained an extension of the application process and was seldom valued apart from the program which read and updated the file. The file of data saved from one run to the next was called a "master file." With increased mastery of programming, emphasis can shift to data.

The fullness of the Copernican revolution is shown in the third phase of Figure 1-4. Here the data is a valued entity, distinct from the application programs. Several different applications can draw upon the same database. This was difficult if not im-

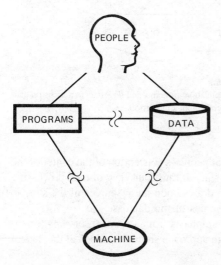

Figure 1-3. Desirable Relationships in a Data Processing System.
Programs and data are more independent of each other, and both are independent of the machine and closer to people.

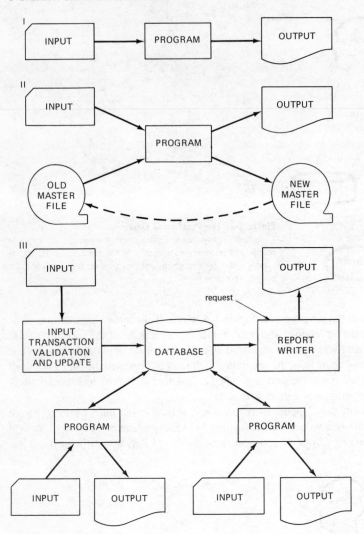

Figure 1-4. Copernican Revolution in Data Processing.
The industry is witnessing a shifting focus from application programs and *their* data to a focus on data as a resource common to, yet existing apart from, several application processes.

possible before. Just as Copernicus argued that people's conception of the center of the solar system must shift from the earth to the sun, so must our view of data processing shift from programs to data. Just as the earth draws upon the resources of the sun, so do programs and people draw upon the resources of the database.

The Copernican revolution shifts design emphasis from a *process*, or *runs*, orientation to a *file*, or *data*, orientation. The design approach should first look at the data of the application systems—the entities in the real world, their attributes, and their relationships. Then the designer can focus on the processes or operations involving people and the data. The expression of data requirements should be rooted in the basic operations of the organization and not the processing runs which will be made against the database. Design activity should focus on the definition and flow of data. Data in its many forms is the driving and coupling force in most computer-based systems. The resulting design of the database and the application system will be more stable and adaptable to new and changing application needs.

This shift is most significant in business organizations in which data is treated as a truly valuable resource. As a resource, data is to be defined, collected, managed, and used. Such an orientation demands that data be as important as "Men, Machines, Material, and Money." Adding *Messages* to represent data completes the set of important resources to any organization—the five M's. Traditionally, we speak of computer systems in terms of hardware and software. Perhaps data will acquire equal status when we begin speaking of hardware, software, and "dataware."

1.2 DATA AND THE DATABASE APPROACH

Webster's Dictionary defines data as:

> "things known or assumed;
> facts or figures from which conclusions can be inferred."*

The American National Standards Institute (ANSI) offers a dual definition for data:

1. A representation of facts, concepts, or instructions in a formalized manner suitable for communication, interpretation, or processing by humans or by automatic means.
2. Any representation such as characters or analog quantities to which meaning is or might be assigned. Generally, we perform operations on data or data items to supply some information about an entity.†

Data consists of symbols written or stored on some recording medium. The symbols represent certain things, ideas, or values, which convey information in particular contexts. In terms of structure, data consists of *values* of *attributes* of *entities* (see examples in box and Figure 1-5).

Webster's New World Dictionary, College Edition, Toronto, Canada: Nelson, Foster, and Scott, 1962, page 374.

†*American National Dictionary for Information Processing*, Washington, DC: Computer and Business Equipment Manufacturers Association (CBEMA), Report No. X3/Tr-1-77, 1977 September. The first definition of data comes from the International Standards Organization (ISO).

Entity:	EMPLOYEE		
Attributes:	EMPNO	Values:	15324
	EMPNAME		CALLAGAN, R.F.
	UNIT		2100
	JOBCODE		5210
	TITLE		SECRETARY
	BIRTHDATE		550606
	SALARY		$10,800

ENTITY:	Any concrete or abstract object or event in the organizational or user environment, often called the "real world"
ATTRIBUTE:	Something we want to know about an entity; a characteristic of interest about an entity
VALUES:	Symbols assigned to attributes of specific entities in the real world; values of attributes describe entities
RELATIONSHIP:	Some connection between entities

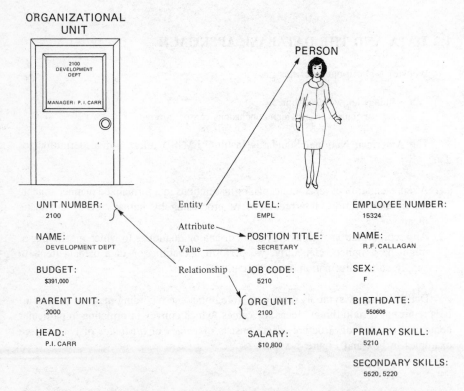

ORGANIZATIONAL UNIT

PERSON

UNIT NUMBER:
2100

NAME:
DEVELOPMENT DEPT

BUDGET:
$391,000

PARENT UNIT:
2000

HEAD:
P.I. CARR

Entity

Attribute

Value

Relationship

LEVEL:
EMPL

POSITION TITLE:
SECRETARY

JOB CODE:
5210

ORG UNIT:
2100

SALARY:
$10,800

EMPLOYEE NUMBER:
15324

NAME:
R.F. CALLAGAN

SEX:
F

BIRTHDATE:
550606

PRIMARY SKILL:
5210

SECONDARY SKILLS:
5520, 5220

Figure 1-5. An Entity-Attribute-Value-Relationship View of Data.
An organization collects information about entities—any person, object, or event, however concrete or abstract. Attributes are the characteristics of interest about entities. Values of attributes represent the actual data pertaining to specific entities in the organization or its environment. Relationships may exist between entities and are usually represented by additional attributes. For example, recording the number of the organizational unit for which an employee works establishes a relationship between these two entities.

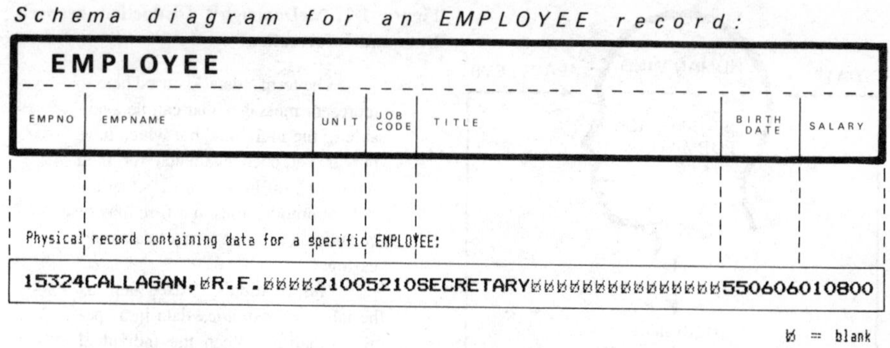

Schema diagram for an EMPLOYEE record:

```
┌─────────────────────────────────────────────────────────────────────────────┐
│  EMPLOYEE                                                                     │
│  - - - - - - - - - - - - - - - - - - - - - - - - - - - - - - - - - - - - - -  │
│  ┌──────┬─────────┬──────┬──────┬───────┬──────────────┬────────┬────────┐   │
│  │EMPNO │EMPNAME  │UNIT  │JOB   │TITLE  │              │BIRTH   │SALARY  │   │
│  │      │         │      │CODE  │       │              │DATE    │        │   │
│  └──────┴─────────┴──────┴──────┴───────┴──────────────┴────────┴────────┘   │
│                                                                               │
│  Physical record containing data for a specific EMPLOYEE:                     │
│  ┌──────────────────────────────────────────────────────────────────────┐   │
│  │15324CALLAGAN,ɃR.F.ɃɃɃɃ21005210SECRETARYɃɃɃɃɃɃɃɃɃɃɃɃɃɃ550606010800      │   │
│  └──────────────────────────────────────────────────────────────────────┘   │
└─────────────────────────────────────────────────────────────────────────────┘
```

Ƀ = blank

Figure 1-6. Schema Diagram and Physical View of an EMPLOYEE Record.
The schema diagram indicates that the record contains data about the entity EMPLOYEE. Four named attributes describe an employee. A set of values for the four attributes constitutes an *instance* of the class of employee entities. The *physical storage structure* of the data values in an employee entity record may appear as shown above.

A personnel database would have several sets of values—one set for each employee. Every set of values is described by a common definition, or *schema*, as shown on the left in the example in the box.

A *schema diagram* represents the general structure and content of the database—each entity record and the relationships between records. Figure 1-6 shows the schema diagram for a record describing the EMPLOYEE entity, and a physical *record instance* containing data values for a specific employee. Most users do not need to know how the data is actually stored. They use a *logical view* of the database—a more abstract view containing data names and essential structure of entities, attributes, and relationships. The schema diagram is a logical view of a defined database.

Here are some other kinds of data found in organizations:

Sales statistics	Competitor data	Payroll and personnel data
Forecasts	Production rates	Financial data and budgets
Economic indicators	Inventory levels	

Comparing data and information can further enhance our understanding of these terms.

1.2.1 Data versus Information

There is now a rather widely accepted distinction between data and information:

Data is the encoded representation of information.
Information is derived from data and useful in solving problems.

Information, therefore, is a potential function of data. Note the circularity which exists in these two definitions. According to the International Standards Organization (ISO) and ANSI:

Information is "the meaning that a human assigns to data by means of the known conventions used in their representation."*

*Ibid.

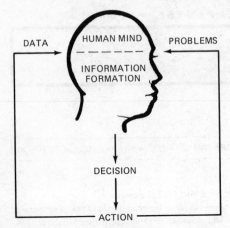

Figure and quotation from: Adrian M. McDonough, *Information Economics and Management Systems*, New York: McGraw-Hill, 1963, pages 71-72.

Figure 1-7. McDonough's Distinction between Data and Information.

The term "data" is used here to represent messages that can be available to the individual but which have not as yet been evaluated for their worth to him in a specific situation. All communications in a firm may be considered as some form of data processing.

"Information" is used here as the label for *evaluated* data in a specific situation. When the individual singles out one of his problems and finds among his data materials that help him solve the problem, he is converting or isolating information from data. Note that a given message may remain constant in content and yet, under this approach, change from data to information when it is put to use in making a decision.

McDonough offered an early distinction between data and information (see Figure 1-7). He argued that data becomes information when *evaluated* in a specific situation or applied to solving a particular problem. That is, data becomes information when *used* to make a decision. Since value derives solely from solving problems, it is meaningful to speak only of the value of information and not of the value of data. Information is formed in the human mind when data and a problem come together; the supplier and the user of information must both contribute to making the product. The supplier or supplying system cannot produce a complete product—information—without the user who is faced with a problem.

Some consider McDonough's position extreme, yet his opinion leads to a key point: data requires interpretation to derive information, and the interpretation must stem from a specific problem situation. Consequently, it is meaningless to speak of an information processing system. No matter how much data is processed, it cannot be turned into information until a manager uses it to solve a problem. For this reason, this text consistently uses the terms "*data* processing" and "*data*base management system." Perhaps MIS uses the term "information" in anticipation of management's using it to solve business problems.

Hanold draws an interesting and clarifying distinction between data and information:

> Information has to do with the communication of knowledge inspired by observation—with the interchange of thoughts and ideas proceeding from experience. . . .
> Information is different in kind from data. Information has the attribute of communication which data does not have. In the context of business, data is merely the digital shadow of haphazard events indifferently recorded. . . .

Yet information begins with data. Data is transformed into information through the infusion of purposeful intelligence. Thus, information is data refined by intelligence so that it communicates meaning or knowledge, . . .*

1.2.2 Data versus "Library" Information

Some people have used the term "information" to refer to the text or abstract of a document. This sense is used in the phrase "information storage and retrieval system." While a document is conceptually a long string of textual data, an organization's database consists of highly structured and formatted data. To make this distinction clearer, some authors refer to DBMSs as "formatted file systems." In a DBMS, strings of textual data are one possible kind of data which can be defined, stored, and processed.

1.2.3 The Singularity of "Data"

Historically, the word "data" was considered plural, and "datum" was considered singular. Some continue to use the word "data" strictly as plural. However, it is sometimes awkward to insist on "data are . . ."

> The word *data* used to be defined only as a plural of datum. It meant *facts* or *figures*. To use it with a singular verb was considered highly improper.
>
> Over a comparatively short span of years *data* has come to mean also *information*. In this sense it is logically singular. Thus, *data* is a collective, and the number of its verb may be either singular or plural depending upon whether it means *a body of information* or a lot of *separate figures*.†

Data is a *collective noun* and may be singular or plural.‡

1.2.4 Database

The following definition is used in this text (assuming automated data processing):

> A *database* is a mechanized, shared, formally defined, and centrally controlled collection of data used in an organization.

---

*Terrance Hanold, "An Executive View of MIS," *Datamation* (18:11), 1972 November, page 66.

†Joseph N. Ulman, Jr., and Jay R. Gould, *Technical Reporting*, Rev. ed., New York: Holt, Rinehart, and Winston, 1959, page 161.

‡Arguing "data" versus "datum" differently, DeWan observed that the term "data item" is rapidly gaining acceptance as meaning the smallest unit of named data in a database. The writer continues:

> Now, sit back, stare at the ceiling, . . . and let your imagination take over: You can see it now—in a few years, maybe months, somebody will get lazy and make a contraction; thus, "dat'em." Then, before you know it, we will have "datem," "dat'm," or maybe "datum." Lo! Behold! Just what every programmer has always wanted (and feared)—a singular form for "data"!

Ed DeWan, in a letter to the editor, *Datamation* (18:9), 1972 September, page 23.

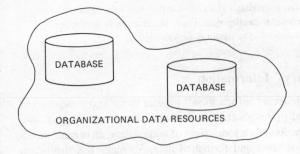

Figure 1-8. Databases in an Organization.

The mechanized, shared, formally defined, and centrally controlled collections of data within the total collection of organizational data resources.

It excludes the informal, private, or manual collections of data. Storing and processing data using a computer system forces formalization. Most important, a database exists as a separate entity within an organization and within a computer-based system. "Centrally controlled" does not imply "physically centralized." A database relates to some defined organizational unit: a whole organization or a division. Above all, some person is responsible for controlling the database. Figure 1-8 indicates that several databases may exist in an organization.

Sometimes it is useful to distinguish database from "file," the latter being an older concept used when records were stored on a sequential medium such as punched cards or magnetic tape. Direct access storage devices gave rise to new possibilities for explicitly relating data records within and between files. The systems are no longer restricted to processing records in their storage sequence but can directly access records as required. The term *file* is still useful to mean a collection of records all conforming to the same type and format description, each record describing an entity from the same entity class. A *database* then becomes a collection of interrelated records, describing entities from *one or more* entity classes.

1.2.5 The Database Approach

Since professionals have proclaimed database and DBMS technology as revolutionary, managers may regard the database approach as disruptive and may therefore avoid it; or they may think it must be embraced at any cost for their organization to remain efficient, modern, and competitive. Neither position is entirely acceptable, yet both contain some truth.

To say the database approach is entirely new reflects a lack of historical perspective. Data has always existed in organizations, and accountants have traditionally controlled it to provide information in support of operations and management. The approach may seem radically new to people in data processing, but it is not. Many electronic data processing (EDP) departments have not applied well-known, sound management practices such as accountability and control. This "radical new concept" is merely a return to good management—of an old resource.

Growing recognition of data as a valuable corporate resource has led to the establishment of organizational units such as "Information Systems and Management Services" or "Information Resource Management" which have responsibility for data processing, management information systems, and the computer. Database technology is forcing a re-examination of the goals and operation of EDP departments; in other words, it is forcing top management and users to change the way they view the EDP department.

Traditionally, EDP/MIS departments have been viewed as managing the hardware and software systems. Yet these are only the factors of production, that is, the tools. The real product of the EDP/MIS department is data to support organizational operations and management decisions. Viewing the EDP/MIS department as a service function to the organization focuses attention on the product to be delivered. The real resource being managed is data.

The database approach is rooted in an attitude of:

- Sharing valued data resources
- Releasing control of those resources to a common responsible authority
- Cooperating in the maintenance of those shared data resources

The database approach is:

- More than simply acquiring a DBMS
- More than collecting and storing data in one integrated database
- More than designating someone to centrally control the data

It involves tools to collect and manage the data, a responsible and cooperative attitude among users, and a database administrator.

An organization must not become overly optimistic. The database approach is not a panacea for information systems and the use of computers. Neither is acquiring a DBMS a panacea for managing data resources. A DBMS is only a tool; it must be made to work *in* and *for* an organization.

1.3 MANAGING DATA RESOURCES

The central idea behind managing data resources is getting a handle on organizational data resources which support operations and management decisions. Proper management of data also promotes the use of data.

PROBLEM:

- Effective management of organizational data resources

SOLUTION:

- Database Administrator (DBA), the responsible human authority
- Database Management System (DBMS), the computer-based tool

Solving the problem of data management entails both administrative and technical factors: creating an effective organizational structure and appointing a responsible authority called the Database Administrator, and using computer-based facilities (whether a full DBMS or not) along with associated operating personnel and procedures.

Many organizations need guidance in moving toward the database approach. The database administrator first seeks to define the responsibilities of the role. Then the DBA must determine what database tools to make available within the organization. When investigating commercially available systems, the organization must learn to evaluate them in light of its own needs. This text guides an organization through the database approach.

1.3.1 The Human Component: Database Administrator (DBA)

The DBA must be a manager, rather than a technician—seeking to meet the needs of people who use data. Since many users may share the same data resources, the DBA must be prepared to mediate conflicting needs and objectives, sometimes imposing a compromise solution.

FUNCTIONS OF DATABASE ADMINISTRATION

- Define, acquire, and retire data according to user needs.
- Provide tools to access and update the data and produce reports.
- Inform and assist users in planning and using data resources and database management tools.
- Maintain database integrity by protecting its existence, maintaining its quality, and controlling access to private data.
- Monitor operations for efficient performance and integrity threats.

The organizational role, functions, and tools of database administration are covered in Chapter 15.

1.3.2 The Machine Component: Database Management System (DBMS)

A *database management system (DBMS)** is a computer-based system to manage a database, or a collection of databases or files. The essential word here is "manage." Management implies the *controlled use* of a resource, that is, controlling its quality, coordinating shared use, and controlling access to authorized users.

A DBMS has many uses:

- it enables users to access and manipulate the database.
- it provides a building block in constructing data processing systems for applications requiring database access—MIS or systems for accounting, production and inventory control, or customer support.
- it helps the DBA perform certain managerial duties.

---

*The name "database management system" was chosen recognizing that different names are in use and different types of systems exist. DBMS is used in a broad sense in this text. Substantial generalization is assumed in any DBMS of interest without using "generalized." "Data" is preferred over "information" for the reasons cited earlier. "Database" is written as one word since that form prevails in the evolution of compound words in English. In this text, the word "data" is used rather than "database" when a *more general* reference to organizational data resources is intended (as implied in Figure 1-8).

Part I of this book provides an overview of DBMS, discussing in greater detail the motivation, objectives, and evolution of database management facilities; an overall conceptual model of DBMS based upon the types of users served and the functions performed; types of DBMSs based upon the underlying logical data structures; and the user interface, language, and operational environment of a DBMS. Part II covers the various functions of a DBMS.

FUNCTIONS OF A DATABASE MANAGEMENT SYSTEM

- Database Definition
- Database Creation (storing data in a defined database)
- Retrieval (query and reporting)
- Update (changing the contents of the database)
- Programming User Facilities for system development
- Database Revision and Restructuring
- Database Integrity Control
- Performance Monitoring

1.3.3 Overview of Relationships in Database Management

In a database environment, the main components, or "players," are database users, a database administrator, applications programs, and the DBMS (see Figure 1-9).

People can access the database directly using a DBMS, or they can write a program (or have a programmer write one for them, or use a previously written program)

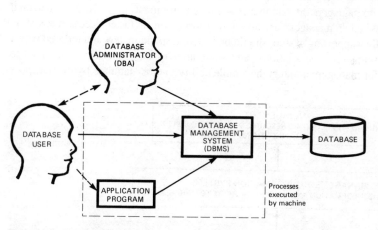

Figure 1-9. Relationships in Database Management.
Database users access the database directly using the facilities of the database management system or through a program written by themselves or someone else. (The distinction may be transparent to the nonprogramming user.) The database administrator establishes the database and the controls on people and programs using the database.

in cases requiring special or more complex processing. The DBA establishes and periodically revises the database to meet the needs of the users. The DBA establishes integrity controls. The users and the DBA communicate formally and informally about system use and database access, and about the regulations and standards in force. Application programs and the DBMS are processes executed by machine. While accessing and controlling the database, the DBMS has three distinct interfaces—with users, with the DBA, and with programs.

1.4 ORGANIZATIONAL CONTEXT FOR DATABASE MANAGEMENT

This text examines database management in the context of organizations and MIS (see Figure 1-10). It is not concerned with library reference retrieval, text processing, or military intelligence systems—although there may be overlap.

1.4.1 Managers and Organizations

In an uncertain and demanding society, managers of modern organizations need help—new and improved ways of managing human and economic resources. More data is not what managers need. They need data which is filtered, massaged, analyzed, and compared in ways they cannot predict.

As management faces new problems, information requirements change. Management can only partially perceive future information needs. When managers encounter a recurring problem, they develop procedures for delegating it to subordinates. Then they need deal only with the exceptional cases and new problems.

Not only do managers operate in a changing environment, they also have personal differences. Whether managers ask for new information or faster access to existing information, the supporting system should be able to respond in new and tailored ways. Different presentations, associations, and summaries of data can sometimes lead to new insights for management. Just the simple ability to cross-tabulate two variables—

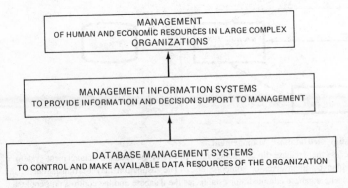

Figure 1-10. Organizational Context for Database Management.

BUSINESS INFORMATION (S = SOURCE, U = USER)	MARKETING	ADVERTISING	SALES SERVICE	ORDER ENTRY	RESEARCH	ENGINEERING	MANUFACTURING	INVENTORY CTRL	DISTRIBUTION	PURCHASING	PERSONNEL	ACCOUNTING	TREASURER	MANAGEMENT
PRODUCT DATA	SU	U	U	U	SU	SU	SU							U
CUSTOMER & CREDIT DATA	SU		SU									SU		U
FACTORY & WAREHOUSE INVENTORY DATA	U		SU				U	SU	U		U			U
ROUTINGS & RATES DATA			U					U	SU	U		U		U
FREIGHT & WAREHOUSING BILLS									SU			U		U
SALES FORECAST SUMMARIES	SU	U		U				U	U			U		U
SALES & COMPETITIVE STATISTICS	SU	U	U									U		U
SALES PERSONNEL DATA	U		SU								U	U		U
SALES EXPENSE DATA	U		SU									U		U
SALES PROMOTIONAL MATERIALS INVENTORY	U		SU									U		U
DISTRIBUTORS DATA			U	U					SU			U		U
AUTOMOBILE FLEET DATA			SU									U		U
PRODUCTION FORECAST & SCHEDULES				S			SU	U		U		U		U
MANUFACTURING PRODUCTION DATA							SU				U			U
MANUFACTURING MACHINE EFFICIENCY DATA					U	U	SU							U
MANUFACTURING LABOR EFFICIENCY DATA						U	SU							U
MANUFACTURING COSTS						U	SU			U		U		U
MATERIALS INVENTORY							SU	U	SU		U			U
MAINTENANCE SUPPLIES INVENTORY						SU	SU			U		U		U
MAINTENANCE LABOR DATA						SU	SU				U	U		U
MAINTENANCE SCHEDULES						SU	SU							U
VENDOR & CREDIT DATA										SU		SU		U
PURCHASING OPEN ORDERS										U	SU			U
PURCHASING STATISTICS						U	U			U	SU			U
PRODUCT & BRAND TEST DATA	U				SU									U
MATERIALS QUALITY CONTROL DATA					SU	U	U			U				U
MARKETING STRATEGY DATA	SU	U			U									SU
ADVERTISING EXPENSE DATA		SU										U	U	U
PAYROLL & PERSONNEL DATA											SU	U	U	U
ACCOUNTS PAYABLE DATA										SU		U	U	U
ACCOUNTS RECEIVABLE DATA				SU								U	U	U
BUDGET DATA	SU	SU	SU	SU	SU	SU	SU	SU	SU	SU	SU	SU		SU
GENERAL LEDGER & TAX DATA												SU		U
BANK POSITIONS, LINES OF CREDIT													SU	SU

Figure 1-11. General Business Information Needs.

In a typical organization, a consumer products manufacturer, for example, management is a user of *all* types of information within the organization.

Source: Diebold Research Program, *Organizing for Data Base Management*, New York: The Diebold Group, Document Number S16, 1971 December, page 10 (adapted).

any two variables—may help managers identify a repeating association, hinting at a causal relationship between the variables.

Management's information needs are diverse and ever-present. While other parts of the organization produce or use only *some* types of data, management collectively uses virtually *all* data (as vividly illustrated in Figure 1-11). Moreover, this data is heterogeneous yet interrelated—complicating the process of structuring and storing data. Storing only personnel data is much simpler than organizing and storing data on employees, departments where they work, skills they possess, and projects on which they participate.

1.4.2 Management Information Systems

Management and organizations facing constantly changing problems, diverse managerial styles, and ever-present information needs offer a challenging context for developing computer-based information systems. MIS uses computer technology to provide information and decision support to managers, helping them become more effective. Developments in the young computer industry are changing corporate management style. Computer technology, including DBMSs, is the motivating and enabling basis for the rapidly expanding field of MIS.

Davis points out that an MIS serves the changeable and often ill-defined needs of top management, while at the same time being rooted in and facilitating the daily operations of the organization, that is, the routine inquiries, update transactions, and processing:

> A *management information system* is an integrated, user-machine system for providing information to support operations, management, analysis, and decision-making functions in an organization. The system utilizes computer hardware and software; manual procedures; models for analysis, planning, control, and decision making; and a data base.*

Managers at all levels use similar data. Operating managers require data which is timely, precise, detailed, internal, and historical. Upper-level managers need data which is aggregated, external as well as internal, future-oriented as well as historical, and covering a longer time span.

There was much talk in the 1960s about the potential of computers in organizations. By the early 1970s, these high expectations had not been fulfilled. Many unsuccessful MIS developments resulted from the absence of available and well-managed data resources.

An effective MIS cannot be built without viable data management tools. Such tools were not generally *available* until the late 1960s. Moreover, most organizations did not effectively *use* DBMS technology until the mid to late 1970s. An important key to a successful MIS is the effective management of an organization's data resources.

1.4.3 Role of the Database in an Organization

An organization is traditionally viewed as a three-level pyramid—operational activities at the bottom, management planning and control activities in the middle, and strategic planning and policy-making in top management (see Figure 1-12). The corporate database (consisting of all databases in an organization) contains data relating to the organization, its operations, its plans, and its environment.

1.5 THE STATE OF DATABASE MANAGEMENT IN ORGANIZATIONS

The needs of organizations and management are changeable, diverse, and often ill-defined, yet they must be met. Added to these are outside pressures from federal taxing authorities, public auditors, federal securities agencies (like the U.S. Securities Exchange Commission), and legislators making privacy laws. Both internal and external forces demand that organizations exercise control over their data resources.

---

*Gordon B. Davis and Margrethe H. Olson, *Management Information Systems: Conceptual Foundations, Structures, and Development*, second edition, New York: McGraw-Hill Book Company, 1985, page 6.

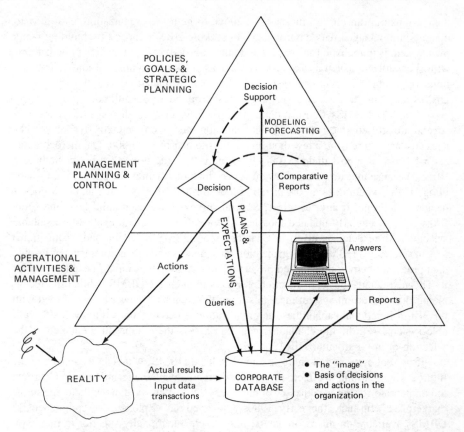

Figure 1-12. Role of the Database in an Organization.

    Decisions and actions in the organization are based upon the *image* contained in the corporate database. Managerial decisions direct the actions at the operational level and produce plans and expectations which are (should be) formally captured and stored in the corporate database. Transactions record actual results of organizational activities and environmental changes, and update the database to maintain a current image. People in the organization query the database for information to conduct the daily operations. Middle management receives reports comparing actual results to previously recorded plans and expectations. The corporate database provides data for modeling and forecasting which support top management needs. The corporate database supports all levels of an organization and is vital for operations, decision making, and the management process.

    While management seeks to control data resources, computer applications grow. When a corporation achieves comprehensive support of its operations, for instance, computer applications begin to penetrate into higher management levels. With comprehensive database support of operations, an MIS can mature as a tool for planning, control, and decision making.

    Early in the development of an MIS, an organization must appoint a DBA to manage its data resources. While an organization's move toward the database approach can be hastened by the acquisition of a DBMS, the latter is not necessary. Most commercially available DBMSs fall substantially short of ideal capabilities, making their acquisition an interim measure—a move to help the organization learn how to operate in a managed data environment. In seeking DBMS capability, building one's own system is unrealistic (due to cost and talent needed) except for large organizations with special needs, such as a very large database or large volumes of known transactions requiring rapid, online response. Roughly estimated, developing a specific DBMS may take from 2 to 5 years, and cost from $1 to $5 million.

Over 600 DBMSs (loosely defined) have been built in the past 25 years, and several are still commercially available and supported. Commercially available packages cost anywhere from a few thousand dollars to nearly $200,000. On microcomputers a DBMS may cost under $100—little more than the price of a book! Some are "free" because the computer hardware vendor includes them in the price (called "bundling"). But where does an organization look for available systems, and how does it decide which one, if any, to select? Several surveys have been published, and some firms offer a regularly updated looseleaf service describing and evaluating available systems. (More detail is given in Chapter 17 on DBMS Selection and Acquisition.)

In selecting a DBMS, an organization must understand the requirements of its own data processing environment, and project what such a system *should* be able to do for it. This text details the set of functions for a comprehensive DBMS, while fully recognizing that no current system measures up to this standard. Nevertheless, armed with this list of functional capabilities, an organization is better equipped to evaluate available systems. Furthermore, management can assess the compromise entailed in the selection of any particular DBMS.

If present systems fall short of some idealized DBMS, what can we expect in the future? After learning to effectively use the currently available technology and learning to compensate for the weaknesses of current systems, new systems will emerge in the marketplace. In fact, the early 1980s witnessed an explosion of comprehensive DBMSs available on microcomputers. Some were functionally superior to most systems available on larger computers! There are also advances taking place in hardware architectures to better support the functions of database management—functionally distinct, parallel processors and backend database machines.

SUMMARY

Data is a vital resource in an organization and must be managed. The organizational database is an essential component in a management information system. Of the four components of a data processing system, attention to data has lagged behind the development of machines and programming technology. The "Copernican revolution" in data processing is causing a shift from programs to data and a simultaneous effort to bring data closer to people. Taking a database approach requires an organization to focus on data as a valued resource. Data is separate from programs and application systems which use it.

Data is facts, figures, and values from which information is derived. Data is distinct from information which is formed in the human mind when data is evaluated and used to solve problems. A *database* is a mechanized, shared, formally defined, and centrally controlled collection of data relating to a specific organizational entity. The term "database" does not include manual, informal, or private collections of data.

A *database management system* (DBMS) is a computer-based tool used to set up a database, make it available to users within an organization, and control the integrity of those data resources. A comprehensive DBMS serves both programmers who develop application systems for end users *and* people who need ad hoc, interactive access to data resources without having to write a program.

A person filling the role of *database administrator* (DBA) designs, defines, and creates databases; provides and maintains the computer-based facilities for using the database (the DBMS); assists and trains users of the DBMS and the databases; and is responsible for the integrity of the databases.

Though a DBMS is not a panacea for the problems of getting a handle on organizational data resources, it can help an organization learn how to function in a managed data environment. People in the organization must learn how to share common data resources, release control of those resources to a database administrator, and then cooperate in the maintenance of those shared data resources.

EXERCISES

1-1. There are four components of a data processing system. Describe the *current* and the *desired* relationships among them in terms of degree of closeness or of decoupling.

1-2. What is meant by the "problem of data"?

1-3. Discuss the Copernican revolution in data processing. What is happening in the orientation of data processing?

1-4. Define and contrast data and information.

1-5. Compare McDonough's distinction between data and information with Hanold's distinction.

1-6. According to McDonough, is it meaningful to speak of the "value of data"? Explain.

1-7. Can the term "data" be used to describe collective descriptions of a set of values (such as COUNT, SUM, AVERAGE), or is the term "information" more appropriate? Explain.

1-8. Define "database." What organizational data resources are excluded from this definition?

1-9. With respect to a database, what is the difference between centrally controlled and physically centralized?

1-10. Considering both "files" and "databases" as logical collections of data (that is, ignoring the genesis of these terms), what is the major difference between them? How are the terms related?

1-11. In what sense does the database constitute the "image" of an organization?

1-12. The database approach demands that data users do what three things?

1-13. The problem of database management has both a human and a machine component to its solution. What are they?

1-14. What is a DBMS? What are its general functions?

1-15. Describe the role of a database (and its DBMS) in supporting each of the three levels of management.

1-16. Who is the database administrator? What are the general functions of database administration?

1-17. Draw a diagram of the relationships between the user of a database, the database administrator, application programs, the DBMS, and the database.

1-18. Identify three characteristics of management which make MIS a rich and challenging context within which to study database management.

1-19. What are the implications of management being a user of *all* types of information in an organization?

1-20. What steps should an organization take to move toward the database approach?

1-21. Acquiring an "off-the-shelf" DBMS might be characterized as an interim measure in the development of application systems. How can an organization take full advantage of the DBMS during this interim? Describe the consequences to an organization of having a DBMS without a DBA.

SELECTED REFERENCES

Management Information Systems—the DBMS Context

ACKOFF, Russell L., "Management Misinformation Systems," *Management Science* (14:4), 1967 December, pages B147-158; and rebuttal by Alfred Rappaport, *Management Science* (15:4), 1968 December, pages B133-136.
    A thought-provoking article challenging some of the early tenents of MIS.

BELL, Daniel, "The Social Framework of the Information Society," in *The Computer Age: A Twenty-Year View*, edited by M. L. Dertouzos and J. Moses, Cambridge, MA: MIT Press, 1979, pages 163-211.
    The sociologist who coined the term "postindustrial society" to characterize the change from an industrial-manufacturing society dependent on steam and electric power, to a postindustrial service society in which major effort is expended on the creation, organization, processsing, and dissemination of information and knowledge through the use of computers and telecommunications.

DAVIS, Gordon B. and Margrethe H. OLSON, *Management Information Systems: Conceptual Foundations, Structure, and Development*, second edition, New York: McGraw-Hill Book Company, 1985, 693 pages.
    The first edition (1974) was the first book to comprehensively cover the whole field of MIS and its conceptual foundations.

EMERY, James C., *Organizational Planning and Control Systems: Theory and Technology*, New York: Macmillan, 1969, 166 pages.
    A thorough treatment of the organizational context for management information systems.

GORRY, G. Anthony and Michael S. SCOTT MORTON, "A Framework for Management Information Systems," *Sloan Management Review*, 1971 Fall, pages 55-70.

HANOLD, Terrance, "An Executive View of MIS," *Datamation* (18:11), 1972 November, pages 65-71.
    Eloquently expressed thoughts on MIS from the then top level executive at Pillsbury.

LONG, Larry E., *Manager's Guide to Computers and Information Systems*, Englewood Cliffs, NJ: Prentice-Hall, 1983.

McDONOUGH, Adrian M., *Information Economics and Management Systems*, New York: McGraw-Hill Book Company, 1963, 321 pages.
    An early treatment of management information systems.

SPRAGUE, Ralph H. and Hugh J. WATSON, "Model Management in MIS," *AIDS Seventh Annual National Conference Proceedings*, Cincinnati, 1975 November, edited by M. W. Hopfe and H. C. Schneider, Atlanta, GA: American Institute for Decision Sciences, 1975, pages 213-215.

SPRAGUE, Ralph H. and Hugh J. WATSON, "MIS Concepts: Parts I and II," *Journal of Systems Management* (26:1 and 2), 1975 January and February, pages 34-37 and 35-40, respectively.

WETHERBE, James C., *Executive's Guide to Computer-Based Information Systems*, Englewood Cliffs, NJ: Prentice-Hall, 1983, 175 pages.

Books and Articles Generally on DBMS

ATRE, S., *Data Base: Structured Techniques for Design, Performance, and Management* with case studies, New York: Wiley, 1980.
    Good coverage of database design and modeling; physical storage, access, and performance issues; and database administration. Less theory than DATE or ULLMAN and more practical than MARTIN.

BRADLEY, James, *Introduction to Database Management in Business*, New York: Holt, Rinehart and Winston, 1983, 630 pages.

Intended for business students, this text begins with the computer's perspective on data, physical storage structures and access methods. Then the text focuses on the structure of data within the three "models"—CODASYL, relational, and hierarchical—and the manipulation of data using COBOL, SQL and System R, Query-by-Example, IMS, TOTAL, and ADABAS. The last chapter covers management of the database environment.

CARDENAS, Alfonso F., *Data Base Management Systems*, second edition, Boston, MA: Allyn and Bacon, Inc., 1985, 745 pages.

Practical orientation with chapters on database concepts, architecture, design, and administration. Most of the book describes several current systems: CODASYL, TOTAL, IMS, SYSTEM 2000, and the Relational Data Model including SQL and Query-by-Example. The second edition includes new chapters on data dictionary, database machines, and distributed databases.

CODASYL Systems Committee, *Feature Analysis of Generalized Data Base Management Systems*, New York: Association for Computing Machinery, 1971 May, 520 pages.

Following on from the Survey published in 1969, looks at individual features of a database management capability and then describes each of 10 systems in terms of that feature—a feature-by-feature analysis of 10 generalized database management systems. It is difficult reading and is intended to be more of a reference work. The systems covered are GIS(IBM), MARK IV(Informatics), NIPS(IBM for U.S. Government), TDMS(SDC), UL/1(RCA), COBOL(CODASYL), DBTG(CODASYL), IDS(Honeywell), IMS(IBM), and SC-1(Western Electric and Auerbach). Knowledge of one or more of the systems greatly helps the reader. You cannot read the report to find out about any given system. The report is a milestone in the DBMS literature.

DATE, Chris J., *An Introduction to Database Systems*, [volume I], third ed., Reading, MA: Addison-Wesley, 1981, 574 pages [fourth edition, 1986].

Somewhat advanced. Weak on overall concepts and taxonomies. Strength is the comparative treatment of three classes of data structure, data sublanguages for each of the three data models, and one illustrative system from each class—the relational data model of Codd, hierarchical structures and IMS, and the network model and the CODASYL-DBTG proposal. One of the best books published so far even though the title is somewhat misleading. Aimed more to the professional than to the student. Second edition expanded to include higher-level languages on the relational data model and additional functional capabilities of IMS.

EVEREST, Gordon C., "Managing Corporate Data Resources: Objectives and a Conceptual Model of Database Management Systems," unpublished doctoral dissertation, Wharton School, University of Pennsylvania, Philadelphia, 1974 May, 602 pages (available from Xerox University Microfilms, Ann Arbor, MI, #74-22,836).

GHOSH, Sakti P., *Data Base Organization for Data Management*, New York: Academic Press, 1977, 376 pages.

First two chapters on data structures and query languages are useful. Quite analytical with heavy use of mathematical notation throughout. Most of the text is concerned with searching and physical access methods on relatively complex data structures and in response to comprehensive queries. Intended for an advanced computer science course on the fundamental theories of database organization and the formal description of complex logical structures and queries.

HASEMAN, William D. and Andrew B. WHINSTON, *Introduction to Data Management*, Homewood, IL: Richard D. Irwin, 1977, 423 pages.

Directed to the understanding and use of DBMS in a broad organizational context. Divided into three parts: the first is an introduction to data management, the second is an extensive description of the capabilities and use of GPLAN (a CODASYL-DBTG type of DBMS extended with high-level interrogation languages; implemented by the author at Purdue University), and the third includes advanced topics of systems design tools, data conversion, relational data model, optimal data structures, and use in planning systems. Somewhat parochial in its extensive focus on GPLAN.

KATZAN, Harry, Jr., *Computer Data Management and Data Base Technology*, New York: Van Nostrand Reinhold, 1975, 347 pages.

    Good coverage but a superficial treatment. Reads too much like a disjointed collection of materials that have appeared elsewhere. Decent coverage of the more conceptual topics. Separate chapters for DBTG, relational model, GUIDE-SHARE, IDS, and IMS.

KROENKE, David, *Database Processing*, second edition, Palo Alto, CA: Science Research Associates, Inc., 1983.

    After an introductory chapter, the first part describes physical data structures and file processing. The second part describes three approaches to DBMS based upon DL/I (or IBM's IMS), CODASYL DBTG, and the relational data model. Part three describes the use of a DBMS along with several commercially available systems (only one of which is not a host language system). The last two chapters focus on the design of databases and database administration. Easy to read and understand.

LANGEFORS, Borge and Kjell SAMUELSON, *Information and Data in Systems*, New York: Mason/Charter Publishers, 1976, 124 pages.

    A succinct, introductory treatment of concepts and terminology from an important school of thought. Distinguishes data as the representation of information; the carrier of information to assist people. Chapters 1 and 2 discuss the need for information for control and decision making in organizations. Chapter 3 contains the key definitions and concepts—a theory of data, defining elementary data constructs: entity, attribute, value, and time. Terminology is different, making initial reading difficult. Chapters 4 and 5 provide a broad, conceptual discussion of how data is stored and retrieved in file systems, and processed according to algorithms.

LEFKOVITZ, David, *Data Management for On-Line Systems*, Rochelle Park, NJ: Hayden Book Co., 1979, 289 pages.

    Somewhat broader than his "file structures" book (1969). Still suffers from an obsessive focus on multilist structures, which he helped to pioneer at the University of Pennsylvania Moore School. Concepts and terminology are somewhat at odds with the general literature—a casual reading leads to confusion. These books still constitute the main reference for multilist structures, variants thereupon, their processing, and comparison with inverted structures.

LYON, John K., *The Database Administrator*, New York: John Wiley and Sons, 1976, 170 pages.

    The first book to be published on the database administrator. Focuses primarily on the design, definition, creation, and maintenance of databases. Suffers from the author's bias toward network structured databases (IDS, DBTG), but does a good job here. A better title might have been "A Designer's Handbook for Network Structured Databases." Pulls together many of the nuances and useful hints in designing network structured databases. Cursory treatment of other database administration functions such as providing high-level languages for using a database, helping users, integrity control, and ways of enhancing evolvability.

MARTIN, James, *Managing the Data-Base Environment*, Englewood Cliffs, NJ: Prentice-Hall, 1983, 766 pages.

    Stresses the importance of data to an organization. Then moves on to more detailed, technical topics such as database languages, database design, and data modelling.

MARTIN, James, *Computer Data-Base Organization*, second edition, Englewood Cliffs, NJ: Prentice-Hall, 1977, 713 pages.

    Focuses on data organization, both logical and physical. The first part of the book discusses several data structure classes (tree, plex, relational) and representative systems based on each (CODASYL-DBTG and IMS from IBM). Data independence is an underlying theme.

MARTIN, James, *Principles of Data-Base Management*, Englewood Cliffs, NJ: Prentice-Hall, 1976, 352 pages.

Intended as an easy-to-read introduction to the area and to the detailed books Martin has written on subjects within the area. Organized into four parts:

    I. Why Data Base?

       —basic, motivation, objectives, usage.

    II. Data Organization (data structures)

       —schema/subschema, hierarchical, network, relational, file addressing, scheduling, distributed databases.

    III. Data-Base Software (database management systems, languages)

       —CODASYL-DBTG, IMS, query languages, data dictionaries.

    IV. Management Considerations (administration)

       —DBA, security and privacy, integrity, MIS.

MARTIN, James, *Application Development Without Programmers*, Englewood Cliffs, NJ: Prentice-Hall, 1982, 350 pages.

Popularized the notion that application systems do not always have to be developed by writing programs in conventional programming languages. Software packages, higher-level languages, and nonprocedural techniques are rapidly becoming available which enable systems personnel or end users to develop their own application systems with greater efficiency and productivity.

McFADDEN, Fred R. and Jeffrey A. HOFFER, *Data Base Management*, Menlo Park, CA: Benjamin/Cummings Publishing, 1985, 531 pages.

Specifically aimed at the business student rather than computer science, this text seeks a balance between managerial and technical issues. It is strong on the logical and physical design and organization of data (Chapters 2-9), with a chapter on database administration, one on DBMS which includes a little on the issues of database security and integrity, and one each on network, hierarchical, and relational data structures and languages. Examples from a furniture manufacturer and a hospital are used throughout the text.

MEADOW, Charles T., *Applied Data Management*, New York: John Wiley & Sons, 1976, 300 pages.

Intended for the applications-oriented user, not the theorist. Concentration on principles rather than particular computer programs. Good coverage of the material relating to data structures and processing with additional emphases on data communications and generalized DBMS. Chapter 1 includes a mini-tutorial on computer operating systems for those who need it, 2-elementary data concepts, 3-data storage, 4-logical file structure, 5-external addressing mechanisms (hashing, indexing), 6-searching (sequential, chains, multikey, multifile), 7-updating and file maintenance, 9-DBMS, 10-user interface and languages, 11-role in information systems, 12-role in computer/communication networks, and 13-privacy, protection, and security.

NOLAN, Richard L., "Computer Data Bases: The Future is Now," *Harvard Business Review* (15:5), 1973 September-October, pages 98-114.

One of the most widely reprinted articles in the journal.

PROTHRO, Vivian C., *Information Management Systems Data Base Primer*, New York: Mason/Charter, 1976, 109 pages.

Well written at an introductory level. Discusses the features and intended usage of a database system in an effort to answer the question, "What is it and what does it do for me?" Focuses on the organizational context and usage of database management system facilities, with an exclusive focus on the application programmer's use of a host language DBMS, and the integrated design of files shared across several application systems.

ROSS, Ronald G., *Data Base Systems: Design, Implementation, and Management*, New York: American Management Associations, AMACOM, 1979, 229 pages.

Broad coverage of topics. A decent starter to understand database technology and management serving the needs of end users.

SPROWLS, Clay, *Management Data Bases*, New York: John Wiley & Sons, 1976, 382 pages.

    This text was developed in conjunction with a course taught at UCLA. It focuses predominantly on host language database management facilities for the programming user. Describes some selected systems: CODASYL, ADABAS, SYSTEM 2000, DL/1, IDMS, TOTAL.

SUNDGREN, Bo, *Theory of Data Bases*, New York: Mason/Charter Publishers, 1975, 244 pages.

    A doctoral thesis written under B. Langefors in Sweden. Introduces the "infological" approach to designing databases. Difficult to read with somewhat obscure terminology. However, for the person with substantial background in data processing, the highly conceptual approach can stimulate thoughtful ideas.

TSICHRITZIS, Dionysios C. and Frederick H. LOCHOVSKY, *Data Base Management Systems*, New York: Academic Press, 1977, 388 pages.

    Written mainly for the DBMS user rather than the designer. First four chapters give an introduction to the concepts of data structure models, languages, and DBMS facilities. This is followed by a detailed discussion of three approaches to DBMSs based upon data structure—hierarchical, network, and relational with chapters on the implementational and operational considerations. The second half of the book contains chapters describing commercially available systems—IMS, SYSTEM 2000, IDMS, TOTAL, and ADABAS. Weak on the organizational and administrative aspects of database management.

ULLMAN, Jeffrey D., *Principles of Database Systems*, second edition, Rockville, MD: Computer Science Press, 1982, 484 pages.

    Primarily aimed at computer science students, this text has a chapter on physical data organization followed by chapters on the network (CODASYL DBTG), hierarchical, and relational data "models." Then several chapters provide a more technical and mathematical treatment of database design theory (functional dependencies and decomposition), query optimization, concurrency control to guarantee data consistency, security and integrity, distributed database systems, and the universal relation as a user interface.

VASTA, Joseph, *Understanding Data Base Management Systems*, Belmont, CA: Wadsworth Publishing Co., 1985, 385 pages.

    Covers logical and physical database organization and the hierarchical, network, and relational data structures. Some chapters are followed by actual applications and case studies.

WIEDERHOLD, Gio, *Database Design*, New York: McGraw-Hill, 1977, 658 pages.

    A substantive, well-thought-through book aimed at the more advanced computer science student. The first seven chapters cover data storage structures and access methods from the viewpoint of traditional file systems. The other half of the book covers more complex data structures and the supporting representational, integrity, and performance functions needed. Uses an engineering attitude to the problems of database organization in order to combine formality with applicability. Weak on organizational and administrative aspects.

Serials Devoted Substantially to DBMS

ACM Transactions on Database Systems, published quarterly by the Association for Computing Machinery, New York, since 1976 March.

Information and Management, published bi-monthly by North-Holland Publishing Co., Amsterdam, since 1977.

Information Systems: Data Bases: Their Creation, Management, and Utilization, published quarterly by Pergamon Press, since 1974 July.

SIGMOD Record, for the ACM Special Interest Group on Management of Data, published approximately quarterly by ACM, New York, since 1969 (formerly *FDT* Bulletin of ACM-SIGFIDET from 1969 to 1976), unrefereed.

Data Base, a quarterly newsletter of SIGBDP, the ACM Special Interest Group on Business Data Processing, published by ACM, New York, since 1969, unrefereed.

MOTIVATION, OBJECTIVES, AND EVOLUTION OF THE DATABASE APPROACH

2.1	TRADITIONAL APPROACH TO APPLICATION SYSTEM DEVELOPMENT	28
2.2	MOTIVATIONS TOWARD THE DBMS APPROACH	31
2.2.1	Inability to Get Quick Answers to "Simple" Ad Hoc Requests	31
2.2.2	High Development Costs	32
2.2.3	Low Responsiveness to Change	33
2.2.4	Low Data Integrity and Quality	34
2.2.5	Inadequate Data Model of the Real World	34
2.3	COUNTERVAILING FORCES INHIBITING DBMS	34
2.4	OBJECTIVES OF DATABASE MANAGEMENT	36
2.4.1	Sharability	36
2.4.2	Availability	38
2.4.2.1	Diverse Data	38
2.4.2.2	Diverse Users	39
2.4.2.3	Diverse Modes	41
2.4.2.4	Diverse Languages	42
2.4.2.5	Diverse Usage Patterns	43
2.4.3	Evolvability	44
2.4.3.1	Changing Technology	45
2.4.3.2	Changing User Demands	45
2.4.4	Database Integrity	46
2.4.4.1	Protecting Database Existence	48
2.4.4.2	Maintaining Database Quality	50
2.4.4.3	Ensuring Data Privacy	51
2.5	EVOLUTION OF DATABASE MANAGEMENT SYSTEMS	52
2.5.1	Types of Data Systems	53
2.5.2	Dedicated Database Systems	54
2.5.3	The Historical Dichotomy in DBMS Evolution	55
2.5.4	Why the Dichotomy in DBMS Must Disappear	58
2.5.5	Historical Thought on DBMS Functions	61
	SUMMARY	64
	EXERCISES	65
	SELECTED REFERENCES	67
	APPENDIX 2A. Bibliographic Systems	69

What motivates an organization to consider the database approach? Why does it seek to acquire a DBMS? What would it expect to accomplish with a DBMS? The answers to these questions can enlighten organizations currently using or leaning toward database technology. The traditional approach to application development creates problems which often motivate a move to DBMS. This chapter examines problems in the traditional approach and motivators toward the database approach.

Discussion of basic objectives in managing organizational data resources begins with the word "management." Management of any resource implies making it *available* for use and *controlling* its use. All database management functions are rooted in the basic objectives of sharability, availability, evolvability, and integrity. Various features of a DBMS can contribute to each of these basic objectives.

One word of caution: Installing and using a DBMS does not automatically mean that an organization has adopted the database approach. Many organizations using a DBMS are still following a traditional approach to systems development. Part of the reason stems from an inadequate DBMS—one that can be used only by applications programmers. The database approach demands much more comprehensive database management tools.

Different types of DBMSs have evolved to satisfy the various motivations and objectives of database management. Early systems were either self-contained, or hosted in a conventional programming language. More recently, systems have emerged with increasingly higher level, *data-oriented* languages; additional facilities for defining and handling data display and data entry screens, menus, and help screens; and providing statistical and graphical output. These newer systems are sometimes called *fourth-generation languages*, *information resource management systems*, or *application development systems*.

The last part of this chapter reviews the historical evolution of DBMSs to meet the motivations and objectives discussed earlier. It ends showing the inadequacies of many current approaches, setting the stage for the conceptual model of DBMS introduced in the next chapter.

2.1 TRADITIONAL APPROACH TO APPLICATION SYSTEM DEVELOPMENT

A strong focus on application programs and processes characterizes the traditional approach to application system development. With a primary focus on processes, application systems often develop separately and operate independently. Figure 2-1 shows a set of application subsystems developed in a petroleum exploration and production organization.

In the traditional approach, data files are established as a by-product of application development. If the same items of data are needed in two applications, they are often kept redundantly, that is, duplicated in several application systems. Redundancy also occurs when multiple applications serve different organizational functions or manage-

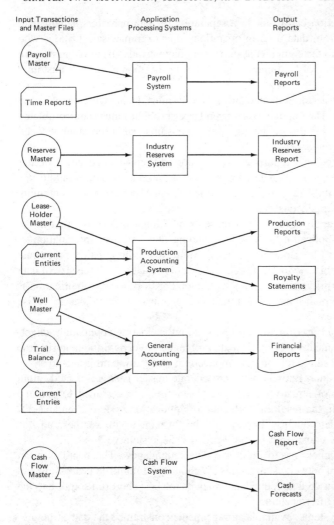

Figure 2-1. Traditional Application System Development in a Petroleum Organization.

In this abbreviated schematic of the system, relatively independent application processes have their own master files. Six master files of data are associated with five application processing subsystems. One of the master files is shared by two applications. Designing relatively independent subsystems results in redundancy and inconsistency. In the petroleum organization, different codes represent the geographical location of wells, leases, and lands. Product accounting and financial accounting each have their own location codes, while the legal department and government reports use a legal location or a latitude-longitude designation. Another inconsistency often results because product accounting is done in barrels of oil or cubic feet of gas, while financial accounting is always done in dollars. If the barrels of oil are updated one month in the product accounting system and the corresponding dollars are updated the following month in the financial accounting system, the month-end reports to top management will be inconsistent, sometimes even bizarre! Management is understandably perturbed when the reported barrels of oil produced and dollars of production from a lease for a given month do not correspond (using an approximate price per barrel to recalculate the dollars).

rial levels. Level separation can result in a separation of data used for management reporting and analysis from data used in operations. For example, salespersons who enter customer orders into the computer system every day may also be asked to prepare a summary of the number of customers visited during the month in each customer class.

To retrieve data that is stored redundantly, the user must decide which application to use to obtain the data. Data updating, an even larger problem, must be coordinated across application systems to ensure that the same data is updated in the same way and at the same time wherever it exists.

Preparing top management reports is always more difficult. Independent master files with relatively homogeneous data cannot easily represent the data relationships across files. This makes it difficult to prepare top-level management reports containing aggregates of more heterogeneous data.

Developing a new application system presents additional problems. To use the data from an existing application may require adding new items of information or restructuring an existing file. Both alternatives require rewriting existing programs. With programs tied very closely to the physical layout of the data (e.g., the size of data values or the relative position of data items within a record), program modification is very difficult, which explains the great reluctance of most organizations to revise existing files or databases.

With no attempt to use existing data directly from the existing application, developing a new application means solving the data problem all over again—capturing the data, putting it in a form suited for the new application, and writing programs to store, retrieve, and update the data. Entirely new and separate master files are created, often resulting in duplication of already stored data. Data files are designed to suit the individual application. In the resulting collection of application systems, marked differences can occur in data quality. It may also be difficult to answer new ad hoc questions not previously considered in the design of the system.

Sometimes the designers try to minimize data redundancy. The result is often excessive transfer of data between subsystems. Without good multifile processing and reporting facilities, increased data redundancy may be the best short run solution to the problem of intersystem file transfers.

In early computer systems, available storage media constrained the data structure. In the petroleum organization, all master files were stored on magnetic tape and the input data transactions on punched cards. Punched cards and magnetic tape (often viewed as a long strip of punched cards) impose a sequential structure on the file and a periodic batching discipline on its processing. In the early 1960s, direct access storage devices and online equipment expanded the possibilities for storing and processing data. Unfortunately, some systems in use today still carry the legacy of this batch processing mentality.

During the 1960s and early 1970s, several DBMSs emerged. Most systems provided facilities which augmented a conventional programming language. A host language DBMS was designed to serve application programmers. While such a system may have allowed the integration of multiple, independent data files, it still relied on traditional tools for application systems development—namely, writing programs. All too often, even with a host-language DBMS, an organization still followed the traditional approach to application systems development.

Centralized development and operation has also characterized the traditional approach. The high cost of equipment and the scarcity of skilled personnel dictated strong central execution and control of system development. As a result, users often faced unavailable or unreliable data. This led to private, manual collections of data maintained by end users. The emergence of inexpensive microcomputers (with the power and capacity of a mainframe 20 years ago!) now makes it possible for these local, private collections of data to be mechanized. Local organizational units press for decentralization believing that their information problems would be overcome if the data processing operations were locally controlled. In fact, local users often end up making many of the same mistakes made by central DP a decade earlier, rediscovering the lessons learned from past experience in the computer industry.

The above discussion reveals many symptoms of problems in data processing. Although the petroleum organization scenario may be worse than current practice in some organizations, it does illustrate many of the problems stemming from the traditional approach to application system development. Such problems motivate the database approach.

2.2 MOTIVATIONS TOWARD THE DATABASE APPROACH

Several problems may motivate management in an organization to adopt the database approach—focusing on the problem of data, and perhaps acquiring a DBMS. Difficulties may be manifest in an inability to get something done, or done economically, quickly, and accurately. Though this need may initially justify acquiring a DBMS, solving a *particular* problem or building a *particular* system must not be the sole criterion for selecting a DBMS. Management must look at the application environment and the data processing requirements from a global perspective.

Five major problems motivate a database approach:

- Inability to get quick answers to "simple" ad hoc requests
- High development costs
- Low responsiveness to change
- Low data integrity and quality
- Inadequate data model of the real world

2.2.1 Inability to Get Quick Answers to "Simple" Ad Hoc Requests

When managers can't get a quick answer to a simple request for information, they become frustrated and disillusioned with computers. Sometimes they know the data they need exists "somewhere in the computer room," but it's apparently locked up in the application programs. Data has become a frozen organizational asset. Extracting specific data from existing files is difficult, requiring one or more application programs to be designed, written, and debugged.

Many existing application systems were designed to satisfy a prescribed set of requests (specified "last year"). Executives must realize that their ad hoc request may require a different processing strategy. Clerks and operating management generally have regular, predictable processing and reporting requirements, while upper management usually has "never asked before" or "one of a kind" reporting requirements. Middle management may go away unsatisfied because an answer would cost too much or take too long; top management gets its answers even if the staff must work around the clock. Obtaining information may be costly, but a manager subpoenaed to appear at a government hearing may have no choice. Managers and employees, then, still appear to be a long way from needed data.

Effective response to ad hoc requests require (1) that the needed data already be stored, and (2) that the system have generalized query and report writing capabilities. To pull together data from separate application systems may involve extensive processing and recoding. Sometimes a programmer can write a special program to retrieve data from existing files, augment these with new data, and manipulate and format the data as requested for output. At other times, a commercially available report-writing system may do the job if the data structure isn't too complex. If the needed data does not exist in a mechanized form, additional steps are needed: a project to gather and mechanize the data, write the programs to edit and validate the input data, define and create a file, select the desired data, and process and format it into a report.

The database approach aims to build up a base of data covering all important operations and management activity. With such a database and generalized retrieval facilities, the organization can better respond to ad hoc requests.

2.2.2 High Development Costs

Long development times and high costs in the design and implementation of data-intensive applications also motivate the database approach.

Application system *development* depends primarily on *human* resources; application system *operation*, on *machine* resources. More effective use of human resources reduces the cost and lead time of system development. This depends upon:

1. having the data readily available in an established database or providing a mechanism for the definition and acquisition of data.
2. providing generalized tools to access and manipulate the database.

Generalized data management tools for building an application system should have higher-level, data-oriented languages. The industry has developed higher-level languages for the specification of *processes* (for example, COBOL, FORTRAN, BASIC, and PASCAL). Many computer languages for dealing with *data* are still very primitive. For example, they read one record at a time perhaps by finding a match on a "key." This is at a level comparable to assembly language for process specification. A good DBMS provides higher-level languages for defining and processing data. Some systems today do offer high-level *data* languages for update, retrieval, and reporting— sometimes called "fourth generation languages."

With good DBMS tools, system developers need not solve the same data problems repeatedly. Several data-related functions, such as report writing and transaction validation, are now so well understood that generalized tools have been developed to better utilize human resources, thereby reducing the lead time in systems development. To ignore the commonality in many data processing tasks is to misuse skilled staff—a substantial and increasing part of the data processing budget.

It is all too common to find an organization busily making its data processing more machine-efficient while at the same time pursuing very limited solutions to people problems. Such a policy is really unworkable. The entire industry needs to (re)evaluate and (re)establish data processing objectives that will make the best use of people and data in addition to machine time and storage space.

2.2.3 Low Responsiveness to Change

Once an application system is developed and operational, the forces of change begin. Users see how things can be done differently, government regulation or labor union agreements require application system changes, and new or changed data requirements call for a revision of the database. The consequent long lead times and high costs make change difficult if not economically infeasible. People then perceive the system to be less than responsive to changing needs.

The need to revise an established database can result in program revision, database reorganization, or both. Since programs are often tightly coupled to the definition and storage of data, any change requires a recompilation and perhaps substantial rewriting of the programs. Maintenance of existing application programs in some companies today consumes 75 percent of the time of systems analysts and programmers. Whether excessive program maintenance will motivate the database approach depends on an organization's current investment in application programs—the number of programs, their implementation language, modularity, quality of documentation, and stability. Some programs which perform input editing and validation, loading, or dumping could be replaced by a comprehensive DBMS.

Revising a database also requires *data conversion*, that is, restructuring and reorganizing the actual stored data. Changing hardware or system software may entail extensive and complex data conversion. Some organizations may not have experienced this problem yet, but once large collections of machinable (machine readable) data have been used a few years, the pressure for conversion will increase.

As with system development, system modification and database revision primarily use human resources.

SYSTEM STAGE:	development	operation	modification
PRIMARY RESOURCE:	human	machine	human

When staff time is disproportionately spent on maintenance and modification, management will look for ways to reduce people-intensive activities. Such a reduction generally requires less efficient operation or increased effort in disciplined system development.

2.2.4 Low Data Integrity and Quality

Incomplete and inaccurate data will destroy people's confidence in the database. Managers cannot make decisions using low-quality data. They will begin keeping their own private files—a needless waste of human effort. When a manager makes a bad decision because of poor data or when a firm faces bankruptcy because destroyed data cannot be reconstructed, there is strong motivation to install integrity control mechanisms, both system controls and administrative controls.

2.2.5 Inadequate Data Model of the Real World

Another motivator for DBMSs is an inability to design a database which adequately mirrors the basic entities, relationships, and events facing the organization every day. Early unit record equipment (such as punched card sorters) and most programming languages force a very simple and limiting structure on data—single, independent, and often flat files. Complex data and interfile relationships cannot be formally defined to the system. System developers and users are responsible for properly processing the data according to what they know to be the true data structure. Limited tools for defining data structures force adjustments and modifications to the natural data structure to fit the simple structure of the language. This obscures the real data structure, making it almost incomprehensible to users. Richer data structuring capabilities make it possible to integrate and interrelate data files, and to eliminate needless redundancies and inconsistencies.

2.3 COUNTERVAILING FORCES INHIBITING DBMSs

While some in an organization may want to change, the database approach faces countervailing forces and substantial cost. An organization must first assess its readiness, determine its real needs, and evaluate its capacity to adopt this approach. Some organizations may not be ready for the database approach.

A number of questions should be asked.

- Are the users ready to share common data resources, release control to a responsible authority, and cooperate in collecting and maintaining shared resources?
- Are people willing to overlook departmental walls and work together to define common requirements and establish standards for developing and using the database?
- Are users and EDP staff willing to try a new approach to application systems development and operation?

In determining real needs, an organization must not be sidetracked by the professional ambitions of staff specialists to push out the boundaries of DBMS technology or gain experience in DBMS use. Using a DBMS must be rooted in real organizational needs now and in the future.

What a corporation can do is measured in personnel, computer hardware, applications software, time, and money.

- Are there some people on the data processing staff competent and willing to use database technology?
- Is the present hardware adequate in speed and storage capacity, and sufficiently stable to support a database processing environment?
- Are the existing application systems sufficiently stable, error-free, and well documented, and is the level of the language they are written in high enough so that conversion will be relatively easy?
- Does the organization currently have the time to devote resources to the conversion and live through the growing pains?
- Does the organization have the resources to conduct a feasibility study, acquire a DBMS, maintain a support staff, train users, and convert existing programs and data?

These conditions may not prevail if EDP personnel are struggling to keep on top of the current applications. A company should be able to answer these questions affirmatively before moving to adopt the database approach. Negative answers indicate some problems which may need to be resolved first.

A database environment creates administrative burdens. When data is integrated to provide a more accurate model of reality, conflicting views and needs in a company necessitate formal mechanisms for their resolution. Increased sharing of data leads to greater security problems and to a need for quality control to maintain the confidence of users. Users, incidentally, tolerate errors more readily when they are also responsible for maintaining data quality. Problems arise when "someone else" is responsible for data quality.

In some application environments, the methods of DBMS will be too inefficient. The need to process high volumes of transactions quickly may force a company to build systems intended to process a fixed set of transactions, thus sacrificing a certain flexibility to respond to unplanned requests and changing needs. When assessing the feasibility of a DBMS, an organization must balance the increased costs of machine operation against the savings in developing and maintaining application systems and the benefits of data integrity.

Another set of inhibiting forces stems from the inadequacies of current DBMS products or the complexities of the marketplace. Some DBMSs, even with comprehensive capabilities, provide such a poor user interface that organizations are understandably reluctant to acquire such packages and subject their employees to the frustration of learning and using such systems. Some systems were originally developed for an offline ("batch") environment and are awkward to use in an online mode. Some prospective buyers see the marketplace as presenting such a bewildering array of choices that they are afraid to pick a system for fear of not picking the best. Others prefer to wait until satisfactory DBMS products appear.

It is possible for an organization to move toward the database approach without acquiring a DBMS. However, they will miss the (forced) opportunity to gain experience with these new tools and to begin cooperative activities such as common database design which crosses organizational boundaries. A better course of action is to pick a reasonably good DBMS and begin learning how to use such a system and building inhouse expertise.

An organization cannot simply acquire a DBMS, plug it in, and watch it run. *A DBMS by itself has no data*, no stored queries or report definitions, and no user application programs to act on that data. The organization must collect and store (or convert) data, must train users, and must develop report definitions and application processes to operate in the new database environment.

As DBMSs become less costly, more comprehensive in capabilities, easier to use, and available on smaller systems (minicomputers and microcomputers), the countervailing forces diminish. In spite of the cost of a DBMS, an organization's need may be so overwhelming that waiting any longer would be an expensive mistake—as it becomes increasingly expensive to develop new applications using obsolete tools and methods.

2.4 OBJECTIVES OF DATABASE MANAGEMENT*

Having considered the various factors which can motivate an organization to move toward the database approach and acquire a DBMS, what are the objectives to be accomplished with such a move? This section outlines the various objectives an organization my have in moving to the database approach.

Motivators are problems an organization faces while objectives are the desirable end results stemming from a solution to those problems. An expression of objectives serves to focus attention on the needs of the using environment and the system and administrative requirements for meeting those needs. Some objectives of database management derive directly from the assumed context of organizations and management information systems.

The proper management of any resource involves making it available for its intended purpose and controlling its use so as to maintain its integrity, ensuring that it is used as intended and that it will be available for future use. *Management* implies both control and use. Database management encompasses the control and use of data resources in an organization. *Control* involves maintaining the existence and quality of the database and restricting its use to authorized people. Control seeks to maintain database integrity. *Use* of data resources leads to the objective of availability, which includes sharing present data resources and enhancing future availability. The objectives of sharability, availability, evolvability, and integrity are related as shown in Figure 2-2.

2.4.1 Sharability

An ability to share data resources is a fundamental objective of database management. In its fullest interpretation, this means different people and different processes using the same actual data at virtually the same time.

*An earlier version of the material in this chapter appeared in *Information Systems: COINS-IV*, Proceedings of the Fourth International Symposium on Computer and Information Sciences, Miami Beach, Florida, 1972 December 14-16, edited by Julius T. Tou, New York: Plenum Press, 1974, pages 1-35. Portions reprinted with permission.

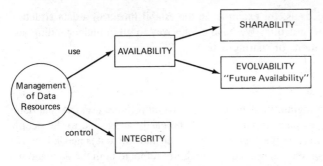

Figure 2-2. Objectives of Database Management.
The management of any resource involves both the use of that resource and the control of its use.

No person in an organization can act completely independently of everyone else in the organization. An organization brings together a variety of human talents to work together toward common goals. In working toward goals, people perform various operations and activities in varying degrees of cooperation or conflict. A database, whether or not it can be identified as a single physical entity, contains data relating to the primary and support operations of an organization. Sharing of data is a necessary first step toward a corporate database.

Since the data pertains to various aspects of the organization, it literally "belongs" to the whole organization and not to any one individual. A system which provides shared access to a corporate database is quite different from a typical time-sharing system where files are "owned" by individual users.* In organizations, shared files are the general rule and private files become the exception.

A shared database environment requires central control to coordinate the collection and use of data and to integrate the storage of data. This can result in increased consistency, reduced redundancy, and reduced effort in the capture and maintenance of data.

Rather far reaching ramifications stem from the stated objective of sharability:

- Serving different types of users with varying skill levels
- Handling different user views of the same stored data
- Combining interrelated data
- Setting standards
- Controlling concurrent updates so as to maintain data integrity
- Coordinating restart and recovery operations across multiple users

This list indicates some of the additional problems which arise in managing shared data. A central implication of sharing is that compromise will often be required be-

---

*The typical time-sharing system in university or scientific research environments permits sharing *time* on computer system resources. Time-sharing systems handle the private files of various participants in the environment. Each file has an owner, that is, a person who creates and maintains the file. Sometimes a person can use data with permission of the owner, or use data in a small "public file," which is usually read-only.

tween conflicting user needs as, for example, in the establishment of a data structure and corresponding storage structure. We have a long way to go in understanding and responding to the implications of sharing data.

2.4.2 Availability

Availability means bringing the data of an organization to the users of that data. The system which manages data resources should be easily accessible to the people within an organization—making the data available when and where it is needed, and in the manner and form in which it is needed. Availability refers to both the data and the DBMS which delivers the data.

Two dimensions of the availability objective are function and form (see Figure 2-3).

Availability functions make the database available to users: defining and creating a database, and getting data in and out of a database. These are the *direct* functions performed by a DBMS.

Form broadly encompasses the ability of the system to operate in a convenient, timely, and economic manner to store diverse data, in an environment of diverse users, operating in diverse modes, using diverse languages, and satisfying diverse patterns of usage. The next few sections examine the diversity of forms in which data resources can be made available to DBMS users.

2.4.2.1 Diverse Data

A DBMS should accommodate diversity in the data stored. Figure 2-4 depicts three dimensions of data—historical to forecast, internal to external, and financial or quantitative to qualitative and subjective. The bulk of organization data, as tradition-

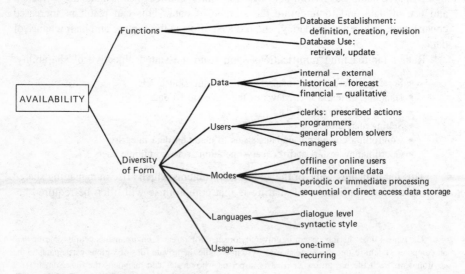

Figure 2-3. Facets of Database Availability.

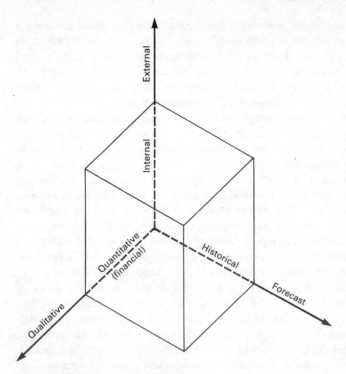

Figure 2-4. Dimensions on Data.
  Although the bulk of organizational data handled in accounting systems lies in the enclosed region of historical, internal, financial data, a DBMS must handle diversity in data.

ally handled in accounting systems, lies in the enclosed region of historical, internal, financial data. A database management system must be capable of reaching beyond this region to handle greater diversity in the data stored, including subjective data (hunches and wild guesses), fragmentary marketing intelligence data, uncertain forecasts, and aggregated data, as well as factual marketing, manufacturing, personnel, and accounting data. If the stored data varies widely in its accuracy or precision, these characteristics of the data should be explicitly recorded and stored along with the data. This can determine the degree of confidence a user can place on the data.

2.4.2.2 Diverse Users

  Potential users of a data management system are as diverse as the people in an organization. The database in an organization satisfies the information needs of people and processes in the organization. This includes chief executives, middle management, people involved in daily operations, accountants, programmers, nonprogrammers, and even simulation models and programs which control and monitor physical processes (such as manufacturing).

  Some users interface with the system in a relatively small number of prescribed ways. Examples include airline reservation agents, bank tellers, persons obtaining a stock market quotation, and retail clerks using point-of-sale cash registers with credit verification facilities. For such users, the system can be preprogrammed with the users invoking one of the several prescribed transactions and providing certain parameters. In the case of the airline reservation agent making a reservation, parameters might include customer name, flight number, day, and number of seats.

The programmer, simulation model, and process control program all interface with the database during execution. The DBMS must provide facilities for programmers to access and manipulate the database through programs they write in any one of several programming languages.

Other more general users do not wish to write programs to access the database and cannot be restricted to any set of prescribed transactions. They are general problem solvers such as marketing or financial analysts. They interface with the system by asking a broad range of questions and producing output reports in a wide variety of forms. Such users need general-purpose facilities to query, update, and manipulate data. This general problem solver includes managers facing a wide variety of problems but unable to prescribe the data they will need and the form of presentation.

The DBMS should provide facilities to meet diverse users needs. For example, accountants require data to be assigned to specific time periods according to standard classification schemes. The DBMS should be able to satisfy the need to compare data over multiple time periods, to compare actual and expected data for the same time period, and to compare data for multiple organizational units in the same period. Handling generations of data is a difficult problem seldom handled adequately in current DBMSs. For another example, the quality control engineer needs the ability to apply various statistical procedures (averages, trends, confidence levels) to portions of the database. The payroll manager wants to be able to incorporate tables and special formulas into the calculation of the payroll.

Managers may also use a DBMS. One of the ongoing debates about applying computers to management needs concerns whether or not upper-level managers will or should have any direct interface with the system. One group takes the position that the application programmer acts as an agent in responding to management requests for information.* Direct interface may not be for all managers, but it is unrealistic to assume that *no* manager will *ever* want a direct interface to the database. The DBMS should *not preclude* any direct management interface. Beyond their direct interface with the system, managers will vary in their style of operation. While providing a standard set of functional capabilities, a DBMS must provide those functions in a variety of forms to accommodate individual differences among managers.

The next chapter provides a more detailed characterization of users. The degree of diversity expands when diversity in modes, languages, and usage patterns are superimposed on the different types of users.

---

*GUIDE-SHARE Data Base Requirements Group, *Data Base Management System Requirements*, New York: SHARE, Inc., 1970 November 11, page 2.2.

2.4.2.3 Diverse Modes

Low or high availability is influenced by different operational characteristics of a system:

LOW AVAILABILITY	HIGH AVAILABILITY
The computer system is physically **remote** from the user; even if the system is next door, the administrative control procedures may make it seem remote.	The user has **ready access** to the computer room and to related personnel who can provide help when needed.
The user and the database are both **offline**.	The user and the database are **online**, connected directly to the central computer system or computer network via some form of communication link.
Input data transactions and output requests are collected at some central location for **periodic processing** against the database.	Input data and output requests are **processed immediately** upon receipt by the system.
Database is stored on **sequential storage** media, such as magnetic tape, making it very inefficient to process input data transactions or user output requests immediately upon receipt. The only economical way of processing is to batch the transactions and user requests, sort them in the same order as the master file, and process them sequentially.	Database is stored on **direct access storage** devices, making immediate processing feasible.
The users must express their requests in a **low-level** language.	Users may express their requests in a **high-level data language**.
Users must view the whole **database as stored** and use the predefined access methods.	Users can have a **logical view** of only the required portion of the database without having to be cognizant of its physical storage structure or methods of access.

While each of the operational modes on the left may be efficient or required for security reasons, they are the least conducive to real human interaction. To the user, such a system represents low availability.

Online operation provides a direct interface with the system via some type of terminal. Terminals on the market today offer considerable diversity in operational mode. At the terminal, the user can operate in a batch mode or a highly interactive mode. The nature of organizational activity will determine the operational modes required of the system. The actual mode of operation is largely a function of the configuration and operational characteristics of the whole computer system and not the DBMS. Nevertheless, the DBMS should be capable of operating in these various modes.

To put it another way, the DBMS should *not preclude* the availability of the database in any of these modes. For example, a DBMS which always processes one or more transactions (requests or updates) by reading completely through a sequential file precludes the possibility of effectively making the database available to an interrogator at an online terminal. Conversely, a DBMS that only operates online and immediately processes all inputs makes it impossible to take advantage of the efficiency in sequentially processing large, sorted batches of update transactions.

2.4.2.4 Diverse Languages

Users interface with a DBMS using different language forms and dialogue levels. The previous two dimensions of users and modes dictate some language characteristics.

For programming users, the facilities of the DBMS must be available through subroutine calls or special verbs added to the programming language. Moreover, programmers should be able to construct their calls to the DBMS dynamically. This is required when writing a generalized program and the specific data elements to be addressed are not known until the program is in execution and receives its input data.

For the user at an online terminal, a number of approaches can be taken. Morrison describes some of the alternatives as follows:

> It is highly desirable for the actual user of the system to interact with the system the way he wishes. This implies user or application oriented terminal languages. It also means temperamental matching. Some users, particularly casual users, may not want to be led by the hand (conversational mode). Other users may want to write natural language-like statements. Others may want to enter a simple, short code. Still others may want to push one or more buttons or move a light pen. A user may wish to interact actively with the algorithm. Others may wish to see the results of a completed analysis.*

In terms of *levels of dialogue*, systems operate in command mode or interactive mode. In command mode the user is in control. The system essentially waits for the user to issue a command, telling the system what to do next. In command mode, the system may execute a previously created and stored file of commands. In interactive mode, the system is in control, always requesting the user to enter some instruction or information based upon the current context of the dialogue. This system request can range from a simple prompt, to a list of acceptable user responses with explanations of what each one means. At any point the user may be able to say "help" to obtain more information concerning the function being performed or the choices being offered.

Languages may also have various *syntactic styles*. The most general syntactic style is free-form narrative, which looks like English (though it may have much more rigid rules of construction). Intermediate styles of language have values or parameters preceded with keywords, or simply listed with separators. At the other extreme is fixed position, often associated with filling in forms.

The system should provide a *choice* of language form or level of dialogue which is most natural and convenient for each individual user within their own discipline, in

---

*Paul L. Morrison, Jr., "Toward a Management Planning and Control System," *Information Processing 68*, Vol. 2, Proceedings IFIP Congress, Edinburgh, 1968 August 5-10, edited by A. J. H. Morrell, Amsterdam: North-Holland Publishing, 1969, page 1143.

each situation, and performing each function. Various users have developed and will continue to develop their own jargon, abbreviations, and other shortcuts in their language. The system should be able to accommodate these differences. Again, the DBMS should *not preclude* the possibility of accommodating a diversity of languages either in level of dialogue or style of syntax.

2.4.2.5 Diverse Usage Patterns

As a general rule, new requests to a DBMS should be satisfied quickly (and accurately) and at minimum cost.

The total effort needed to respond to a new request includes both the development effort and the execution effort. Effort can be measured in terms of elapsed time or cost. Development may entail any combination of the following: formulating queries, defining reports, defining input transactions and their processing, or writing and compiling programs to perform special applications. Execution effort is chiefly machine time to process and store the definitional information and to execute the request.

Using a DBMS can reduce application development effort (with a possible decrease in execution efficiency). Moreover, when using a DBMS, it may be possible to respond to a request in more than one way depending upon the anticipated pattern of usage. For example, a new request or application process may exhibit a pattern of DBMS usage ranging from one-time to frequently recurring. The anticipated usage pattern will often influence the development effort devoted to achieving execution efficiency and evolvability.

If development and execution effort were independent, then a system could strive to satisfy both. Unfortunately, they are generally inversely related. The tradeoff is most noticeable in a recurring request. One DBMS may be designed for efficient execution and is therefore slow and difficult to respond to new demands. Another may be designed for general purpose use at the expense of high overhead and inefficiency in satisfying recurring requests involving large volumes of data.

A viable DBMS must satisfy both types of requests: one-time requests and recurring requests. Some users will want to get an answer quickly because they are experimenting in an attempt to find a satisfactory approach. Others will know the precise requirements of the request and will take all the time necessary to set up the job for greatest efficiency in subsequent recurring execution. Some users will simply want to get the job done while others will want to exploit the DBMS tool.

To satisfy these diverse needs, the system should make it possible to first reach a feasible solution to the request with minimum development effort. After the approach proves satisfactory, the system should permit the users to fine-tune the approach to arrive at a more machine-efficient solution. One method provides both interpretation and generative execution of the original request. In interpretive mode, the system executes the request as given. In generative mode, the system takes the original request, does some extensive analysis of it, incorporates some system parameters, and finally generates object machine language code. The object code is then executed to satisfy the request. The generative approach can be much more machine efficient when handling a recurrent request.

Since there is a tradeoff between development effort and machine efficiency, a breakeven analysis should be performed based on the expected number of recurring uses. A frequently recurring request would suggest spending more development effort so as to increase execution efficiency.

From a slightly different perspective, it should be possible to do "simple jobs simply" without generating complex language instructions and without high overhead. This suggests the use of natural defaults. It also suggests the creation of separate functional modules with the expensive options removed. At the same time, users need a flexible capability to satisfy complex and sophisticated requests.

Many DBMSs have failed, fallen short of expectations, or simply become unresponsive in the eyes of users because they handled only a very narrow range of diversity.

2.4.3 Evolvability

Evolvability refers to the ability of the DBMS to change in response to growing user needs and advancing technology. Evolvability is the system characteristic that enhances future availability of the data resources. Evolvability is not the same as *expandability* or *extensibility*, which imply extending or adding to the system, which then grows ever larger. Evolvability covers expansion or contraction, both of which may occur as the system changes to fit the ever-changing needs and desires of the using environment.

Adaptability is a more advanced form of evolvability in which built-in algorithms enable a system to change itself, rather than having a change made to it. Adaptability involves purposive, self-organizing, or self-controlling behavior, that is, self-regulation toward a single criterion of success: ultimate, long-term survival.* A system exhibiting adaptive behavior actively seeks a particular state or goal by *changing itself* (or its environment) in response to a change in itself or its environment.

A DBMS may exhibit simple adaptive behavior by monitoring interactions with its environment to detect, for example, changing patterns of usage. Heavy usage of a particular part of the database may cause the DBMS to pause for a moment and set up some more efficient access mechanisms. Repeated insertion and deletion of data may automatically trigger the DBMS to reorganize the stored data when it gets too disorganized.

Evolvability implies the gradual unfolding, development, and growth of a system to better meet the needs of the using environment; and it implies change of the system in response to changing needs and technology. With the present state of technology, such change is externally administered. In the future such change may occur automatically within the system, thus exhibiting adaptive behavior.

The lack of evolvability in DBMSs (as well as traditional data processing systems) has been one of the major reasons for the notable lack of success in developing MISs and the lack of acceptance in organizations.

In discussing the previous objective of availability, no implication was intended

---

*Stafford Beer, *Cybernetics and Management*, Science Edition, New York: John Wiley & Sons, 1964, page 134.

that any system would or even should be able to meet such wide diversity. The initial DBMS in an organization should provide some minimum level of availability while possessing the essential capability to maintain data integrity. If the system is truly evolvable, it can grow with the growing needs and demands of the using environment, thus becoming increasingly available. New or enhanced avenues of availability can be added on a priority basis depending on the available resources and cost-benefit considerations.

Even if it were possible to build a DBMS satisfying all the diversity in availability, it would not obviate the need for evolvability. It is impossible to foresee all the availability requirements within the organization. New needs and desires will emerge and new technology will come that will demand changes to the DBMS. The objective of evolvability requires that the door be left open for the DBMS to respond to new demands and to take advantage of new technology.

2.4.3.1 Changing Technology

The possibility of technological advances is ever present. For example, revolutionary advances in computer architecture such as parallel, array, or pipeline processing may open up new possibilities in the use of indexes and rapid retrieval algorithms. The emergence of database machines may change how users interact with the functions of DBMS.

At the same time, gone is the day of the massive conversion in the sense the industry has come to know it—rewriting and recompiling programs and redefining and restructuring data files. Greater program evolvability is possible within the development of reasonably general and standard (at least widely accepted) high-level languages. Now that the industry is beginning to understand the basic functions of database management and to study the problem of transferability, the problem of data is beginning to be solved.

Once a system is installed and the data defined and stored according to its rules, it is very difficult to change. The organization effectively becomes "locked-in" to its use. The DBMS should be designed to minimize both the risk of technical obsolescence and the cost and disruption of redefining and restructuring the database.

2.4.3.2 Changing User Demands

In addition to handling new technology, evolvability enables the DBMS to respond to the increasing user demands. The graph in Figure 2-5 shows the relationship between system capabilities and user demands over time. The vertical axis represents a composite of increasing quality of response and availability of the data and the DBMS. The horizontal axis represents time into the future.

The upper curve, the maximum threshold of system capability, reflects what can be handled by the DBMS and the MIS/EDP department. In a sense, it is the learning curve of the people in the MIS/EDP department who are responsible for making the database available.*

---

*Typically, human learning curves have a decreasing slope (concave down). This curve actually would be a composite of human learning and technological advances. If the effect of technology dominates, then the curve could appear concave up as shown in Figure 2-5.

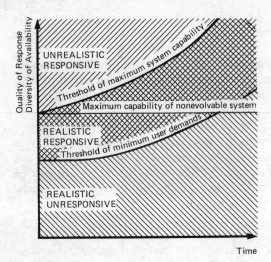

Figure 2-5. System Capabilities versus User Demands.

The graph shows two learning curves. The upper curve is for the DBMS and its support staff; the lower is for the user. A system must operate in the region of realistic system capabilities and be responsive to user demands. With a nonevolvable system and increasing user demands, users will eventually view the system as unresponsive. The system is still the same as before but the users have grown.

The lower curve represents the threshold of minimum responsiveness and availability as demanded by the people in the using environment. As before, it reflects the learning curve of the users, including management.

To survive, the system must operate somewhere in between these two curves. If the system has little or no capacity to evolve, the upper curve will be relatively flat. As the system is used, the lower curve will rise and eventually cross the threshold of technical capability of the system. Under such conditions, even though the system capability remains constant, users *see* the system as unresponsive. Unable to satisfy their growing demands, the system falls into "tolerated use" or disuse.

For a system with substantial capacity to evolve, the upper curve will rise over time. If the system actually grows and operates close to the technical threshold, it will have its maximum effect in raising the lower curve. If the system can continue to satisfy the increasing demands, the users are reinforced and stimulated to make even greater demands. As the quality of response and availability rises, so do user expectations. In such a situation the system grows to better serve the using environment. The organization can grow and profit from the better performance of the users.

2.4.4 Database Integrity

The importance and pervasiveness of the need to maintain database integrity is rooted in the reality that man is imperfect: "For all have sinned and come short of the glory of God."* If man is imperfect, so also are his constructions—his organizations, his systems, and his databases. Destruction, errors, and improper disclosure must be anticipated, and explicit mechanisms provided for handling them. In the 1970s, data integrity became a significant concern.

*Romans 3:23.

Webster's dictionary defines "integrity" as:

the quality or state of being complete; . . . and unimpaired;
wholeness; soundness; perfect condition.*

Precisely this broad meaning is intended when referring to "database integrity."†
Two premises establish database integrity as an objective of database management. First and most obvious, if the data in an organization is valuable, then measures must be instituted for protection and quality control. The principles of asset management, maintenance, and control which apply to men, machines, material, and money also apply to data (or "*messages*"!). Second, sharability raises concern for database integrity. Users cannot be expected to rely on the existence and accuracy of certain data needed in their operations until they are satisfied that integrity control measures appropriate to their needs have been established. When data is collected and maintained by a single person or a single organizational unit, they are responsible only to themselves for the integrity of the data. When sharing is fully endorsed, an organization must establish formal procedures to maintain database integrity.

In order for management to be an enthusiastic supporter and willing user of databases, formal procedures for the maintenance of database integrity are absolutely necessary. Managers cannot be expected to support and use something in which they do not have complete confidence.

Before computerization, controllers and accountants exercised stewardship over corporate data. Many procedures were highly formalized and mechanized; systems based upon generally understood and widely accepted principles were installed and used with amazing confidence.

In their enthusiasm, computer systems specialists have largely forgotten or discounted the principles and procedures of accountants. In developing DBMSs, the accountant's concept of internal control has been practically ignored. Computer specialists need such concepts to improve database integrity and enhance management confidence.

The three primary facets of database integrity are:

- Protecting the *existence* of the database
- Maintaining the *quality* of the database
- Ensuring the *privacy* of the database

This chapter discusses each of these, describes threats to database integrity, and introduces the system integrity control functions and the database administration procedures used to maintain database integrity (see Figure 2-6).

Maintaining database integrity involves both the DBMS and the database administrator. The DBMS operates during job execution. All requests to access or manipulate

---

*Webster's New World Dictionary, College Edition, Toronto, Canada: Nelson, Foster, and Scott, 1962, page 759.

†It has become prevalent among some authors to use the term "integrity" in a very restricted sense, that is, the condition that can result when two processes attempt to update the same piece of data concurrently. This is certainly one aspect of database integrity, but the word itself inherently means more.

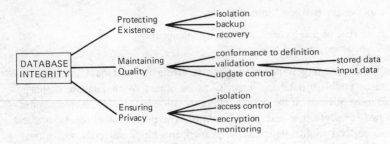

Figure 2-6. Facets of Database Integrity.

data in the database are funneled through the system. When the system responds to the request, it also verifies the authority of the requestor, ensures that any data stored or modified conforms to its definition, and executes any prescribed data backup, audit, or monitoring. The DBMS is the mechanized counterpart or agent of the DBA, carrying out his or her established policies. Conversely, the DBA directly controls the DBMS.

Historically, the responsibility for data integrity rested with the programmers and systems analysts who developed application systems of which the data files were a part. The system played a negligible role in data integrity, being primarily concerned with the storage and transfer of data and the maintenance of bit parity. Similarly, other people were seldom involved to any great extent. Responsibility for data integrity fell through the cracks, largely unassigned as an ongoing responsibility.

Increased sharing and recognition of the value of data make it important to clearly establish responsibility for data. Control over data resources is better vested in a responsible person with authority than in a programmer.

Simply building checks and controls into the processing systems is not sufficient to maintain data integrity. A machine cannot be held accountable; only a person can. Holding a person accountable increases management confidence in the database. When complaints can be directed to a person, the managers and users are more likely to use the system to obtain desired data. The DBA establishes external policies and procedures and provides certain information and parameters to guide the execution of the integrity control functions in the DBMS.

Complete or perfect integrity is impossible to achieve. A DBMS should provide viable options to realize some degree of database integrity. A higher degree of database integrity carries a higher cost. The value of the data and the cost stemming from its loss or misuse determine the extent of implementing various protective measures.

2.4.4.1 Protecting Database Existence

The existence of a database is threatened by natural acts (such as fire, flood, earthquake, and lightning) or deliberate or inadvertent human acts (such as vandalism, theft, and operator error). Preventive strategies insulate the physical database from destruction; curative strategies re-create the data whenever loss or destruction occurs.

Preventive strategies seek to protect data stored in tape or disk libraries, cards, or other media, and to protect online data from destruction through hardware and software failures, power failures, and other causes. Various preventive measures can increase physical security. In achieving this objective, the database administrator interacts closely with the manager of the computer installation who is responsible for the physical security of the entire installation, often including storage devices and data storage areas.

The possibility of loss is always greater than zero. To recover from loss or destruction of data, it is necessary to store data redundantly and preferably remotely, away from the primary location. The data stored for backup is generally some combination of copies of the database (''periodic dump''), copies (''logs'') of input data transactions, and logs of before and after images of portions of the database each time it changes.

A lost database may be re-created by recovering the most recent dump and reprocessing the input transactions logged subsequent to the dump. This results in *bringing forward* the database from some prior point at which the data was secure. Variations on this general procedure depend upon the need for complete re-creation and speed of recovery. To accomplish backup and recovery of data, the DBMS must be coordinated with the job management system which is responsible for the checkpoint and restart of programs.

The unsuccessful completion or erroneous action of an update process also requires backup and recovery facilities. The previous paragraph referred to a need to go back and *redo* the update processing. Now there is a need to *undo* the update processing back to the point at which the processing began or some logically acceptable intermediate point. This *rollback* recovers a prior state of the database. Selective rollback may be required if two or more processes were updating the database concurrently when one of them failed. The system would reverse only those changes made by the failed program.

Suppose a process was set up to post a batch of transactions to a code of accounts, and within the batch the debits equaled the credits. During the processing, a condition arises (say, an invalid transaction) making it impossible to complete processing of the batch. If the account balances cannot be restored to what they were before processing began on the batch of transactions, the integrity of the database will be lost, for in all likelihood the debits will not equal the credits. This would be unacceptable if any other process wanted to reference the code of accounts before the erroneous batch can be corrected and its processing completed. The solution is either to disallow access to the affected portion of the database until processing is completed (untenable if the delay is very long) or else restore the database to its prior state, disallowing access during rollback.

Providing a rollback mechanism is difficult. One solution considers all updates tentative and held in limbo until a signal is finally received from the process indicating that a logical update sequence has been completed. Alternatively, if before and after images have been logged for every individual change to the database and they are appropriately tagged with information sufficient to identify the source, cause, and location of the change (user, program, data, transaction, database record, etc.), then it is possible to selectively step back and undo the results of previous processing. The logging of before and after images provides the ability to backout changes to the database as well as bring forward an earlier version of the database.

2.4.4.2 Maintaining Database Quality

Given that database existence is protected, it is now necessary to maintain the quality of the stored data by:

- ensuring that it always conforms to its definition,
- validating the stored data and the input data,
- controlling the execution of update processes ensuring proper authorization, controlling concurrent update, and synchronizing update of multiple copies

Database quality can be threatened by erroneous input or improper update actions. Even if good quality-control procedures exist for input data, undetected errors can propagate, gradually degrading the quality of the stored data.

Every DBMS retains some information regarding the structure and format of the stored data. The system uses this information to properly interpret and process the stored data. Users also use this information to properly interpret the data, and to establish what to expect from the system. It may seem obvious, but, a system should ensure that the stored data always conforms to its definition—the definition as understood by the users. It is a grievous mistake for a system to permit the definition of certain data characteristics, such as alpha- or numeric-type data fields, but not ensure that all stored values conform to the declared type. This will undoubtedly lead to a loss of user confidence in a system, or unwilling tolerance of its shortcomings.

Whether a system stores a sketchy database definition or a comprehensive definition is immaterial here. A skeleton definition makes it easy for the system to check for conformance. Users are responsible for testing additional conditions which should be satisfied for the data to be valid. A comprehensive definition means more work for the system but also means higher-quality data. This can instill greater user confidence in the database and its management system.

Data validation means comparing data to an expression of what the data should look like. For stored data, the definition represents validity conditions. It can also include explicit validation criteria beyond the normal size and type declarations. A more comprehensive definition of the stored data provides a basis for better quality control.

In addition to testing data for conformance to its definition, validation of input data before it is used to update the database can increase the quality of the database. With a reduced database definition capability, input transaction validation becomes relatively more important for database integrity. It is generally easier and more efficient to validate input transactions than to continuously monitor the database against a comprehensive database definition. This may account for the greater emphasis placed on transaction validation in practice. Nevertheless, it would be wrong to conclude that input validation can be a substitute for monitoring against the database definition. The database must still conform to its definition.

Processes which change the database can disrupt the information system by destroying the quality of the database. Threats may result from multiple processes attempting to update the same data concurrently, a runaway update process, an incompletely debugged program, or an update initiated by an unauthorized user. These threats suggest the need to control the development, cataloguing, initiation, and execution of update processes.

Various levels of update may demand different levels of control. Merely adding data to a database is not generally as disruptive as changing the existing data. Tighter controls may be needed on processes which delete data, particularly whole records or files.

Not everyone in an organization should be permitted to freely update the database. Some responsible authority must tell the system *who* is permitted to initiate *what* update operations, and the system must check every requested update action to ensure that it is properly authorized.

The independent and uncontrolled execution of *concurrent update* processes can threaten the quality of the database. The solution of allowing a process to lock out concurrent update processes can lead to deadlock. Every multiuser DBMS must have some solution to the potential of deadlock.

Update synchronization is required when data is stored redundantly, in multiple copies. Besides the obvious cost of additional storage space, the major cost of data redundancy is in synchronizing updates (or tolerating inconsistent data!). These costs must be weighed against the benefits of increased availability of data, faster response to requests for data, and better recovery with the redundant data serving as backup.

2.4.4.3 Ensuring Data Privacy

Privacy is the right of individuals to be left alone, to keep their affairs confidential from others, and to choose what information about themselves to share with others. When personal data is collected and stored in a database, used within an organization, or disseminated to others, it can be used to violate the privacy rights of individuals.

The objective of data privacy requires the protection of personal data from inadvertent or unauthorized disclosure to unauthorized persons or for unauthorized purposes.

Ensuring data privacy requires both legal and technical solutions. While a DBMS can provide on-the-scene access control, it can never stop an authorized person from accessing the data and later using it for unauthorized purposes. Legal solutions provide penalties and remedies in such a situation. Legal solutions can also encourage an organization to utilize data privacy protection measures. Increased public concern in the early 1970s led to the passage of privacy legislation in states and countries around the world.

Legislation provides added impetus for implementing appropriate administrative and technical safeguards. Implementing privacy safeguards involves expenditures with no direct monetary returns. Thus, there is a negative economic incentive for industry and government agencies to police themselves and protect the privacy of data about individuals. Laws can force administrative action and stimulate the development of technically viable solution alternatives.

Various technical and administrative measures enable an organization to respond to the data privacy objective and to comply with privacy legislation. The ultimate protection of data privacy is not to collect and store sensitive data in the first place. Such solutions, while helpful, do not obviate the need for technical measures. Administrative and technical measures complement each other. Administrative protection strategies include such measures as isolation, personnel screening, and physical security. Technical protection mechanisms include access control, encryption, and monitoring. A DBMS can provide these technical protection mechanisms.

Isolation of the system storing the data reduces unauthorized access and disclosure. This relates closely to physical security which uses similar techniques. The design of a secure system is largely a matter of cost and efficiency. In the extreme, a lead and concrete wall could be built around the computer system, thus ensuring absolute protection. Of course, this is impractical since data is stored to be accessed and used. An organization should determine the value of the information, quantify the effect of unauthorized disclosure (and loss or destruction when considering overall physical security), and balance this against the cost of protective measures. More and varied avenues of access to the data increase the risk of unauthorized disclosure.

Access control via established avenues of access starts with some responsible authority telling the system *who* has access to *what* data. Upon receipt of a request for data, the system first authenticates the identification of the requestor (a person, perhaps through a program or at a particular location) and then checks to ensure that they are authorized to see the requested data.

Encryption techniques are useful when data may be exposed to inadvertent disclosure or unauthorized access during transmission or storage. Encryption is any technique that makes it difficult to interpret data being transmitted or stored. Prior to transmission or storage of data, some reversible transformation is applied to the data. When received or retrieved, the data is decoded by reversing the transformation. Encryption and decryption facilities could be made available in a DBMS for an organization to use on data which is sensitive to a violation of personal privacy or organizational secrets.

Monitoring and audit trail techniques also contribute to data integrity. If a breach of privacy or unauthorized modification takes place, it is desirable to have a past record or trace of the sequence of events that occurred. Accountants call this an audit trail. It can be helpful in later investigations to verify the current status of something or to detect where or when the unauthorized activity took place. Sometimes those who are authorized to access data abuse that right by using it for unauthorized purposes. An audit trail may make it possible to discover the offender. For additional security, the audit trail or system operation can be closely monitored for any unusual activity or threat, for example, repeated failure to provide a valid identification, or repeated interrogations attempting to incrementally access data from a statistical data bank.

2.5 EVOLUTION OF DATABASE MANAGEMENT SYSTEMS

Generalized DBMSs have evolved to better meet the motivations and objectives discussed earlier in this chapter. To better appreciate the state of the art in DBMSs, it is helpful to review how the industry got there. At each stage along the way, certain objectives were met, and others were not. The first stage led to a dichotomy of systems into host-language DBMSs and self-contained DBMSs. (The reader with no desire to review historical developments may choose to skim over this section.)

2.5.1 Types of Data Systems

The DBMS is one type of generalized system within a broader class of data systems. This section briefly describes several different types of data systems. Bibliographic systems and dedicated database systems are described in contrast to generalized DBMSs.

Data systems can be distinguished by the type of data processed. Data may be in the form of arbitrary strings of text or words, references to other sources of information, or formatted into specific items of information.

DATA SYSTEMS

Reference System	Used to store and retrieve references to items such as engineering drawings or books. Rather than storing the content of each item, the system stores subject descriptors to represent the content of each item and provide selection criteria. Sometimes the system is expanded to retrieve actual documents.
Text Processing System	Used to compose and record text in a computer and to analyze the stored text to derive meaning in the form of keywords, or to output the text for photocomposition and reproduction. Also called *word processing system.*
Bibliographic System	A combination reference and text processing system used to store and retrieve bibliographic reference information, subject descriptors, and a textual abstract of each document. Such systems are commonly called *information storage and retrieval systems.*
Database System	Used to store and retrieve formatted data for any application environment, most commonly in business organizations. The database consists of a collection of specific data item values. Sometimes called *formatted file system* or *fact retrieval system* to distinguish from text, reference, and bibliographic systems.
Dedicated Database System	A special-purpose database system, tailored to process a high volume of a prescribed set of transactions in realtime. Tailoring to a particular environment is necessary to handle the high volume of throughput; dedicating the system is feasible with a fixed set of transactions. Such systems sacrifice evolvability to obtain economic and operational feasibility.

A DBMS can be used as a reference system. A few reference systems and bibliographic systems have been developed with sufficiently generalized facilities to be used as a DBMS. Some DBMSs include a modest text processing capability by providing a textual data item as one of their generic item types.

A bibliographic system is distinctly different from (though often confused with) a generalized DBMS. First, the data structure is designed for particular data—a single file of reference citations with a series of key words or descriptor terms for each citation, and a textual abstract for each. The software to manage a bibliographic system is usually more specialized than a DBMS. It usually stores the citation file along with indexes ("inversions") on the key terms. Emphasis is on taking a profile of a researcher's request (expressed as a combination of key terms) and accurately matching it to the profiles of stored reference citations. Such systems are evaluated primarily on their ability to retrieve all the *relevant* document citations while retrieving a minimum of irrelevant citations ("noise"). Further description of bibliographic systems is found in Appendix 2A.

2.5.2 Dedicated Database Systems

Even though they maintain a database, systems dedicated to a particular application environment seldom use a generalized DBMS. They are designed to respond to a fixed set of prescribed requests. Since the information and operating requirements are stable and known in advance, the system can be tailored to the application environment, optimizing throughput and realtime response.

After a period of use, an organization often encounters considerable pressure to change and extend the dedicated system. The fixity is sometimes a delusion to satisfy some other need. Generally, the real need is realtime response with a high transaction volume and a large database. Generalized solutions seldom work here; tailoring is more cost effective. To meet the realtime requirements, these systems are specifically tailored to process a fixed set of requests in a specified manner. They cannot afford the performance degradation of generalized processing. Some systems cannot even afford the luxury of a general-purpose operating system. Nevertheless, even dedicated systems should be designed with some flexibility.

While current DBMSs may not be appropriate for realtime fixed-transaction systems, they may be used to test a design or develop a prototype for a dedicated system. A DBMS may also be important with greater management use of the system. Even though generalized systems may not be helpful, the concepts of data management and the techniques used in building a generalized DBMS can help. Furthermore, future technology may render generalized database management solutions viable for large-volume, realtime systems, particularly as more DBMS functions are incorporated into hardware (the database machine).

A dedicated database system may be large and complex, yet structured and stable compared to an MIS. Experimentation is possible to develop special systems of hardware and software dedicated to an application. In addition, a large potential market may provide economic incentive, as in supermarket checkout counters, stockmarket quotations, hospital housekeeping functions and patient records, library management systems (ordering, cataloguing, and circulation), medical testing and diagnosis, bank teller support systems, and many others. Extremely unpredictable and changeable management requirements motivate the assumed MIS context used in this text. It helps little to develop special-purpose systems for management from the ground up. Only basic underlying functions can be stabilized to some degree. Hence, this text describes the basic data-oriented functions which can support an MIS.

2.5.3 The Historical Dichotomy in DBMS Evolution

When data was first stored within a computer, facilities were needed to perform input from and output to secondary storage devices such as magnetic tape and disks. Very early computer systems provided no software facilities to move data within the system. User programs initiated and performed all data movement. The programmer had machine language instructions to transfer data between central memory and a secondary storage device. The user provided the appropriate physical storage addresses and the extent of the physical block of data to be transmitted. If any errors occurred during transmission, the user had to test for them and perform appropriate follow-up and recovery procedures. For example, if a write to magnetic tape was unsuccessful, users could backspace and try to rewrite. If that failed after repeated attempts, they could skip forward and attempt to write on a new section of the tape.

In this environment, users soon recognized the similarity of procedures from one write operation to the next, and from one program to the next. Users developed generalized input-output routines. At the same time, hardware manufacturers began to provide generalized software called by such names as *input-output control systems (IOCS)*. Such software would reread or rewrite in the event of an error, set up and manage input and output buffers, and block and deblock records so that the physical unit of data transfer in and out of the user program could differ in size from the physical unit of data transfer between the main memory and the secondary storage.

As computer systems became faster and more complex, manufacturers had to supply an operating system to control the execution of programs, and to control and coordinate the peripheral devices. This produced smoother, more continuous system operation and more efficient use of system resources. The generalized input-output routines grew more sophisticated and became known as *access methods*. Today, access methods support relatively simple data structures and treat the data as strings of bits or characters to be transmitted. The system is never cognizant of the contents of a physical unit of data (except for a key in some cases).*

Out of operating system access methods grew two distinct types of data management facilities, based upon very different philosophies about who should be served and how they should interface with the system.

One type extended the data management facilities of operating systems to encompass more of the functions of data transfer to and from secondary storage. These facilities were invoked from a program using macros, calls, or language verbs (for example, OPEN, READ, READ NEXT, SEEK, WRITE, INSERT, DELETE) to initiate data movement. Such systems aided programmers by essentially extending their programming languages. Some systems also supported backup, editing, and data conversion.

The emergence of "random access memories" or magnetic disk storage devices in the early 1960s made it much more difficult for a programmer to store and manipulate

---

*William A. Clark, "The Functional Structure of OS/360: Part III, Data Management," *IBM Systems Journal* (5:1), 1966, pages 30-51, gives an excellent discussion of access methods within the IBM/360 Operating System.

data. These devices permitted a departure from traditional sequential file processing using magnetic tape storage. Now it was possible to have multiple access paths into the data, and to store the data in more complex structures. The programmer now had difficulty representing that structure in the stored data and navigating through the structure later. Bachman significantly advanced database technology with Integrated Data Store (IDS), a comprehensive set of facilities for the programmer to store and manipulate data exclusively on direct access storage devices.*

Other developers believed that the users should have direct access to data without requiring programmers to write application software in a conventional programming language. This produced self-contained or stand-alone program packages for data retrieval, report generation, and file maintenance.

In 1959 McGee identified several generic *data* processing applications.† Sorting was fundamental to data processing and generalizable to *any* file, regardless of its data content. Other generalizable operations possessed a common feature: They all made use of a *file* of data. He detailed the functions of file maintenance, report generation, and record or file generation. These are common across application because *they relate to data, not to the application process*. McGee's paper is significant for its early recognition and design of basic database management functions. His detailed discussion remains quite representative of the self-contained systems of today (except for the focus on punched cards and magnetic tape files, the technology of the day).

During the 1960s, when many development efforts were underway, this dichotomy between systems-for-programmers and systems-for-nonprogramming-users was not clearly perceived. By the early 1970s people began to recognize the two distinct avenues of development. The CODASYL Systems Committee [1971] used the names "host-language system" and "self-contained system" to refer to the two types of systems. These terms were quite readily adopted in the industry.

Only a programmer can use a host-language system since the facilities are hosted in a programming language and accessible only through that language. A self-contained system can be used by a nonprogrammer or a programmer since a program need not be written in some conventional programming language. A self-contained system uses a new language of its own. However, it could be so complex and procedural that the user must possess the *skill* of a programmer.

Both types of system permit the definition of more complex data structures than are usually available in a programming language such as COBOL. Self-contained systems typically deal with "flat" files or hierarchical files, often processed only sequentially. On the other hand, host-language systems offer the opportunity for defining even richer data structures—multifile structures. Most host-language systems provide low-level facilities which put the burden of navigating through the structure on the programming user.

---

*Charles W. Bachman and S. B. Williams, "A General Purpose Programming System for Random Access Memories," *1964 Fall Joint Computer Conference Proceedings*, Baltimore: Spartan Books, pages 411-422.

†William C. McGee, "Generalization: Key to Successful Electronic Data Processing," *Journal of the ACM* (6:1), 1959 January, pages 1-23.

Self-contained systems are generally easier to use than host-language systems because the user *thinks* of operating on the whole file. In a host-language system the user typically thinks of records when issuing read and write commands. While some of the processing and manipulation algorithms are built-in, the self-contained systems are somewhat less flexible to use. With the full power of the host programming language available, the host-language system user has greater flexibility in dealing with the database. Whatever cannot be done in the data manipulation language can probably be done in the host programming language (which makes things easier for the DBMS designer).

Figure 2-7 illustrates the evolutionary development of data management facilities and the resulting dichotomy in DBMSs.

With few exceptions, DBMSs developed before the early 1970s were exclusively host-language or self-contained systems. Today, the majority of *available* systems are self-contained. However, on large mainframe computers, the majority of *installed* systems are host-language because they are the most widely used. Just the opposite is the case on microcomputers. The vast majority of systems available and installed are

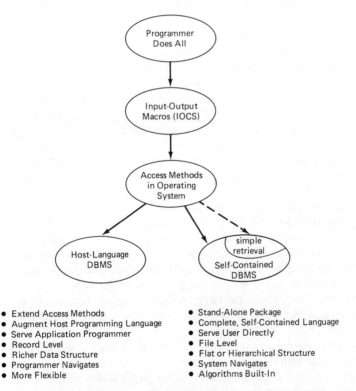

● Extend Access Methods	● Stand-Alone Package
● Augment Host Programming Language	● Complete, Self-Contained Language
● Serve Application Programmer	● Serve User Directly
● Record Level	● File Level
● Richer Data Structure	● Flat or Hierarchical Structure
● Programmer Navigates	● System Navigates
● More Flexible	● Algorithms Built-In

Figure 2-7. The Dichotomy in the Historical Evolution of Data Management Facilities.
Two distinct avenues of development grew out of the data management facilities of operating systems. Several differences characterize the dichotomy between a host-language DBMS and a self-contained DBMS.

self-contained. Almost all users of microcomputers do not know anything about conventional programming languages. Furthermore, most of them shouldn't even try since better DBMS tools are rapidly becoming available on microcomputers.

2.5.4 Why the Dichotomy in DBMS Must Disappear

In its 1971 *Feature Analysis* report, the CODASYL Systems Committee clearly laid out the distinction between host-language and self-contained systems. Furthermore, they argued that it had to disappear.

> The most significant point observed in the course of the Systems Committee's study is the difference between host language capabilities and self-contained capabilities. . . . Some members of the committee find it convenient to refer to two classes of systems—host-language systems and self-contained systems. . . . This dichotomy . . . is by no means exact, nor are the two categories mutually exclusive. . . . A generalized data base management system is potentially capable of providing generalized processing facilities for either the programming user or the nonprogramming user, or both . . . The committee is generally agreed that the difference is one which ought to disappear and is in the process of doing so. [page 16, 38, 40 passim]

The dichotomy must disappear because with only host-language and self-contained DBMSs, *none of the objectives of data management can be satisfied.*

Lack of Availability. A self-contained system does not make data directly available to users who want to write their own programs for some unique or complex processing of the data. Conversely, a host-language system does not make data available to the nonprogrammer without using the services of a programmer (which may delay getting a timely response). In the second case, *if* the programmers are skilled enough *and* the system offers the required facilities for generalized programmers, they can develop the generalized facilities to give the nonprogrammer direct access. The data resources of an organization should be available to satisfy the needs of all people and processes in the organization. Facilities for both types of user are needed.

Lack of Sharability. Suppose an organization sets out to solve the availability problem by acquiring both types of DBMS. With few exceptions, they will be incompatible with each other and with respect to a stored database. A database set up under one system will not be available to users of the other system. If the databases managed by the two systems are independent, different users cannot share the same physical database. Although data conversion may be possible between the two systems, it is prohibitively expensive. Considering the large number of organizations which have already acquired two systems, this solution to the availability problem *appears* to be realistic.

Lack of Integrity. Four levels of access to a stored database (see Figure 2-8) reveal opportunities for integrity violations. Given a stored database shown at the top of the diagram, the first level of access is direct to the physical storage medium and device. For example, if the database is stored on a reel of tape, the reel can be mounted on the tape drive of a computer system (assuming physical compatibility) and accessed directly with a specially written program. This, of course, assumes that the program

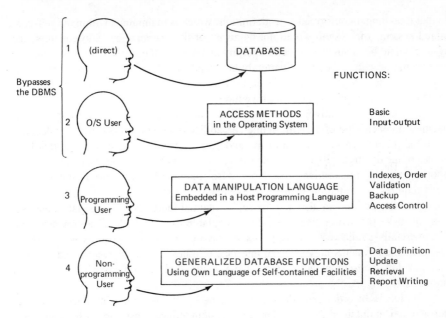

Figure 2-8. Levels of Access to a Database.
The heads indicate the levels at which a user can access the database. Each box indicates the functions used to gain such access. Besides the nonprogramming and programming users, others may circumvent the DBMS facilities and access the database through the operating system. The top one (1) indicates access by a direct dump of the database.

knows the data structure and format and can properly read the data on the tape reel. Since most of the recording conventions in today's computers are difficult to decipher, such access is practically impossible.

The second level of access utilizes the standard access methods within the operating system. At these two levels, the system merely transmits physical strings of characters, without regard to data content.

The third level of access corresponds to the programming user of a host-language system; and the fourth, to the nonprogramming user of a self-contained system. Notice that the integrity control functions are (or should be) placed at the programming user interface.

To achieve both availability and sharability, an organization has several possibilities. In a strictly self-contained system, no visible programming user interface exists—the direct availability functions and the underlying integrity control functions are combined into one package. Some self-contained systems are built using the standard access methods of the operating system. In such a case, a program may be able to access the stored database using the access methods of the operating system. To do so, however, would circumvent the integrity control functions of the self-contained system. As long as the access methods were properly used, programmers would be able to read, write, and otherwise modify the stored database. If they changed the stored data so that it no longer conformed to its definition, which is maintained within the self-contained system, the system would not be aware of the discrepancy. Subsequently, the system would be unable to correctly interpret and process the stored data. For example, alphanumeric values could inadvertently be stored in a data item defined as numeric. Such threats to integrity exist in several self-contained systems and can only be controlled by external administrative procedures.

As another alternative, an organization can maintain a duplicate copy of the database in each type of system. While sharability is satisfied, data integrity depends upon the proper synchronization of the update activities of both systems so that both copies of the database reflect the same values. Such synchronization is again dependent upon external administrative procedures. Also, maintaining separate database definitions requires coordination with each revision.

An organization can also add the self-contained facilities to a host-language system, or make the self-contained facilities available to or callable by a user program. Commercially available software packages have been enhanced in this way. Several self-contained systems now offer an interface to a host-language system and its files. Also, a few self-contained systems have made their facilities available to user programs.

Caution is in order regarding self-contained systems which interface with files defined and maintained in a host-language system. Since most current host-language systems maintain an incomplete data definition, that definition must be supplemented in the self-contained system. Now an organization must maintain two separate definitions of the *same* stored database. In some cases, the self-contained systems access the host-language system files by circumventing the integrity control mechanisms. This threatens database integrity. These incompatibilities are most likely present if the two systems are sold by different vendors. Add an independent data dictionary, and the proliferation of multiple definitions of the same database creates a serious administrative burden.

The solution? Have all access to the stored database occur through the integrity control functions. *There must be only one door to access the database.* The integrity functions must control all requests and transmissions through the door. All requests from nonprogramming and programming users alike must go through the same integrity control functions when sharing the same physical database.

Lack of Evolvability. Self-contained systems violate evolvability because the functions provided are fixed in what they do and how they do it. (Sometimes users can persuade a vendor to enhance a system.) In host-language systems, evolvability depends upon the generality of the interface with the programming user. Most programming user interfaces are intended for the application programmer who already knows (unlike the generalized programming user) the data structure and how it is to be manipulated. A generalized program obtains this information at execution time. Therefore, the generalized programming user must be able to create buffers dynamically and reference the stored data definition. No commercial DBMS fully meets this need for generality in the programming user interface.

Since it is difficult to satisfy the objectives of database management using some combination of present-day technology, a new conceptual DBMS model is needed.

Requirements for a variety of user interfaces must be coordinated in the design of DBMSs if they are to aid in developing viable MISs. A comprehensive DBMS model is presented in the next chapter. As its central feature, the DBMS model integrates facilities for both programming and nonprogramming users.

2.5.5 Historical Thought on DBMS Functions

Looking at DBMS functions, this section first reflects on past thinking about different functions, leading up to a comprehensive taxonomy. This taxonomy is the basis for the conceptual DBMS model described in the next chapter.

A clear picture of DBMS functions did not emerge until the early 1970s. A short excursion into the literature published during the formative years of database management yields the chart in Figure 2-9. Each column reflects the ideas of a key author regarding database management functions. The CODASYL Systems Committee solidified this thinking in a 1971 report. Although by no means exhaustive, this chart does reveal some important conceptual milestones in our thinking about DBMSs.

As expected, the list of database management functions grew more complete as time passed. In 1959, McGee made no mention of data definition, reflecting a time when the layout of records in a file was an integral and often obscured part of the program. By 1965, the definition of data was recognized as separable from programs. The 1969 CODASYL Systems Committee report divided definition into the logical data structure and the physical storage structure.

The term "maintenance" had a variety of meanings. McGee used it to refer only to changes in the content, or physical structure, of the database. Others included the redefinition of the logical data structure and the consequent restructuring of the physical database (Dobbs, Dixon). Maintenance has also meant data revision and conversion, excluding normal data update. Fry included logical data definition, creation, revision, and internal file generation as well — everything except retrieval and output!

Changes in database content are distinct from changes in structure. In the short run, structure remains constant relative to content. Furthermore, structure should be stable to avoid disrupting the system and confusing the people who use it. An organization requires greater control over changes to structure than changes in content. Therefore, a sharp distinction between redefinition and update is better than combining them under the term "maintenance."*

Another observation concerns the interrelatedness of retrieval and output. The process of asking a question and getting an answer seems to involve a sequence of steps: selection, extraction, processing, and output in the form of a report or a newly generated file. For some authors, retrieval referred to earlier steps in the process, and

---

*A good distinction between *structure* and *content* and their relative importance in the life of a system is given by Talcott Parsons, "An Outline of the Social System," in *Theories of Society*, edited by T. Parsons, New York: Free Press of Glencoe, 1961, pages 36ff; similarly, for a discussion of two types of impact a "message" may have on an "image"—simple change (content) and revolutionary change (structure)—see Kenneth E. Boulding, *The Image: Knowledge in Life and Society*, Ann Arbor, MI: University of Michigan Press, 1956 (Ann Arbor Paperback AA47, 1961), pages 7-8.

1959 McGee	1965 Dobbs	1967 Dowkont	1968 Dixon	1968 Olle	1968 Fry	1969 McGee	1969 CODASYL	1971 Systems Committee
	Definition	Definition	Definition	Establishment	File Generation	File Definition	Data Structure Definition	Data Definition
	File Creation	Creation				File Creation	Storage Structure Definition	Storage Structure Definition
							File Creation	File Creation
File Maintenance	Maintenance	Maintenance	Maintenance	Revision	File "Creation"	File Redefinition		
				Update	File Updating	File Updating	Update	Update
Report Generation	Retrieval	Retrieval			Retrieval	Report Writing		
		Processing		Interrogation	Output Presentation		Interrogation	Interrogation
	Presentation	Output	Use					
Record Generation					File Creation	File Writing		
								Programming Facilities
								Data Administration Functions

Maintenance

output referred to later steps. Still others called the whole process data use, report writing, or interrogation.

Only two authors included facilities for the programmer. Although Dobbs recognized the dichotomy between facilities in a host programming language and self-contained facilities for nonprogrammers, all of his functions relate to self-contained systems. Dowkont briefly mentioned processing "by conventional 'programming'" but actually meant executing user-written subroutines *from within a self-contained func-*

Figure 2-9. Summary Chart of DBMS Functions.
The historical development of DBMS thought flows from the ideas of key authors. A common vertical scale helps relate the lists of functions from each author. The CODASYL Systems Committee solidified the list of DBMS functions in their 1971 report. Several observations can be drawn from this chart:

- Expansion in the list of functions which grew more complete.
- Separation of data definition from programs in 1965.
- Confusion with the meaning of "maintenance."
- Distinction between changes in content (update) from changes in structure (revision) in 1968.
- Combination of retrieval (asking a question) and output (receiving an answer).
- Recognition of facilities for the programmer in 1971 even though host-language systems existed several years earlier.
- No explicit recognition of data integrity functions although they were mentioned with all the other functions.

CODASYL Systems Committee, *Feature Analysis of Generalized Data Base Management Systems*, New York: Association for Computing Machinery, 1971 May, 520 pages, (in Europe: British Computer Society, London, England, or IFIP Administrative Data Processing Group, Amsterdam, Netherlands; in Japan: *bit* (5:14), 1973).

CODASYL Systems Committee, *A Survey of Generalized Data Base Management Systems*, New York: Association for Computing Machinery, 1969 May, (now available only from NTIS: PB 203 142), 398 pages.

DIXON, Paul J., "Generalized Data Management—Functional Requirements," *File Organisation*, selected papers from "FILE 68"—an IAG Conference, Denmark, 1968 November 20, Amsterdam: Swets and Zeitlinger N.V., 1969, IAG Occasional Publication No. 3, pages 302-309.

DOBBS, Guy H., "State-of-the-Art Survey of Data Base Systems," Proceedings of the Second Symposium on Computer-Centered Data Base Systems, Santa Monica, 1965 September 20-21, edited by Claude Baum and L. Gorsuch, Santa Monica, CA: Systems Development Corporation, TM-2624, (NTIS: AD 625 417), 1965 December 1, pages 2-3 to 2-10).

DOWKONT, Anthony J., William A. MORRIS, and T. Dwight BUETTELL, *A Methodology for Comparison of Generalized Data Management Systems: PEGS (Parametric Evaluation of Generalized Systems)*, Sherman Oaks, CA: Informatics, Inc., (NTIS: AD 811 682), 1967 March, 286 pages.

FRY, James P., et al., *A Survey of Data Management Systems*, Washington, DC: The MITRE Corporation, (NTIS: AD 684 707), 1969 January, 206 pages.

McGEE, William C., "Generalized File Processing," in Mark I. Halpern and Christopher J. Shaw, editors, *Annual Review in Automatic Programming*, Volume 5, Oxford, England: Pergamon Press, 1969, pages 77-149.

McGEE, William C., "Generalization: Key to Successful Electronic Data Processing," *Journal of the ACM* (6:1), 1959 January, pages 1-23.

OLLE, T. William, "UL/1: A Non-Procedural Language for Retrieving Information from Data Bases," *Information Processing 68*, Volume 1, Proceedings of IFIP Congress, Edinburgh, 1968 August 5-10, edited by A. J. H. Morrell, Amsterdam: North-Holland Publishing Co., 1969, pages 572-578.

tion—not a program. Dixon explicitly included facilities for programs and for nonprogramming users.

The 1969 CODASYL *Survey* made no mention of facilities for the programmer. This led to confusion in describing systems available *only* to programmers (namely, IDS).* The subsequent *Feature Analysis* report corrected this situation by including a new chapter entitled "Programming Facilities."

Functions often overlap in a classification. Some functions can be identified correctly; others seem to cut across the obvious functions. A division of functions into the two objectives of availability and integrity seems to be a useful method of organization. Availability tools relate directly to data processing functions and users. Integrity tools relate to database administration and underlie the availability tools. None of the functional taxonomies up to 1971 gave separate and explicit recognition to integrity functions. Clearly, there is need for a consistent and comprehensive view of DBMS, its users, and its functions. This is done in the next chapter.

SUMMARY

The traditional approach to application system development focused on processes, which were considered to operate independently. It viewed data as an adjunct to the application process. This view motivated organizations toward the database approach. Motivating forces include:

- Inability to get quick answers to simple ad hoc questions
- High development costs
- Low responsiveness to change
- Low data integrity
- Inadequate database model of the real world

A DBMS can reduce development and maintenance effort, making people more productive, while sometimes decreasing machine efficiency.

The management of data resources implies making them available for use and controlling their use to ensure the integrity and future availability of data resources. The *objectives* of database management include:

- *Sharing data* resources across users and across applications
- Making data resources *available* through the functions of a DBMS operating in a timely and economic manner to store diverse data, in an environment of diverse users, operating in diverse modes, using diverse languages, to satisfy diverse usage patterns

---

*For example, under "interrogation," the *Survey* described the RETRIEVE verb of IDS, a host-language system, and the QUERY module of TDMS, a self-contained system. Moreover, for SC-1 with combined host-language and self-contained facilities, the *Survey* described two different features under a single heading. Interestingly, this was the system Dixon worked with, thus explaining his broader "database use" function in Figure 2-9. SC-1, developed jointly by Western Electric and Auerbach Corporation, was one of the first DBMSs to explicitly recognize the coexistence of facilities for both programming and nonprogramming users.

- Maintaining *evolvability* in the database and the DBMS to respond to changing technology and changing user demands in the future
- Ensuring database *integrity* by protecting the existence of data, maintaining data quality, and ensuring the privacy of sensitive data

The four objectives of sharability, availability, evolvability, and integrity serve as four concurrent themes throughout subsequent discussions of DBMS functions and administrative considerations of data management.

Data systems include reference systems, text or word processing systems, bibliographic systems, database systems (the subject of this text), and dedicated database systems. Bibliographic systems differ from DBMSs because:

1. They involve a particular data structure, typically a single file of bibliographic references augmented with subject descriptors and abstracts.
2. The functions serve the researcher as opposed to the decision maker.
3. They use specialized software.
4. Retrieval is done by matching a request with the stored document description. Relevance and recall ratios measure their effectiveness.

The early development of database management facilities began with generalized input-output routines, first incorporated into user programs, and later invoked as part of the operating system. The one avenue of development extended the facilities of the operating system (or the programming language) to aid the application programmer: host-language systems. Another avenue of development sought to bypass the programmer and provide high-level language facilities directly to the nonprogramming user: self-contained systems. This created a dichotomy in DBMSs that must disappear because it violates all four database management objectives for an organization.

A brief review of the literature describing the functions of database management leads to several important observations on DBMS evolution. Observations relate to the separation of data definition, use of the term "maintenance," changes in database content versus changes in structure, the relationship of retrieval to output, facilities for the programming user, the coexistence of facilities for programming and nonprogramming users, and the place of integrity control functions.

EXERCISES

2-1. Describe the traditional approach in application system development. What problems result from this approach?

2-2. What are the main disadvantages of separately developing application systems and their associated data files?

2-3. Why does redundancy occur in the traditional approach to application system development?

2-4. In many traditional data processing shops, there is a good deal of reluctance to the idea of revising existing data files. Discuss some of the reasons for this reluctance.

2-5. Reflect on an application with which you are familiar. Characterize the approach used to develop the system. To what extent did it attempt to integrate application areas and set up shared databases separate from the using applications?

2-6. List the five problems which may motivate an organization to move toward the database approach. Explain the significance of each one to a manager; to an organization.

2-7. Which motivating problems would be chiefly felt by the following (you may list more than one for each)?
a. top management
b. users outside of the MIS/EDP organization
c. operating personnel who interface daily with the database
d. problem analysts
e. project leaders
f. MIS management faced with limited resources
g. new people in the organization seeking to learn their way around

2-8. What is the primary resource (that is, people or machine) used in the following stages of a system life cycle?
a. development
b. operation
c. modification

2-9. What is the major effect of having low data quality in a database?

2-10. Identify the most important factors inhibiting an organization's move toward a DBMS.

2-11. What administrative burdens and requirements are placed on an organization adopting the database approach and utilizing a DBMS?

2-12. Often a DBMS can severely reduce machine efficiency. Under what circumstances would an organization still consider using a DBMS?

2-13. What trends are diminishing the impact of the countervailing forces to adopting DBMS technology?

2-14. Beginning with the general concept of management, derive the objectives of database management presented in this chapter. Explain the meaning of each objective. Is any one more important than the other? Explain.

2-15. Data nonredundancy is often put forth as an objective of database management. This would suggest that redundancy of data is always bad and to be avoided. What are some reasons why data redundancy is desirable? What are the real problems that stem from storing data redundantly? Relate your answer to the objectives discussed in this chapter. Under what conditions of usage would unlimited data redundancy be most desirable? (*Hint:* Think of the census data gathered by most central governments.)

2-16. What is the central implication of sharing data?

2-17. What are five form dimensions of availability? Describe the potential diversity of each.

2-18. What are the factors which distinguish between a low mode and a high mode of availability?

2-19. Describe a type of organization or organizational function which requires high data availability. Similarly, describe one which needs only low availability.

2-20. Should upper management have any direct interface with a database management system? Support your answer.

2-21. For a given request, the pattern of usage may range from one-time to infrequent to very frequent. How might the usage pattern influence the allocation of human and machine resources to the satisfaction of the request? Organize your answer in terms of the three stages of development, operation, and modification.

2-22. Draw the graphs for the breakeven analysis suggested in the consideration of development effort and machine efficiency depending upon the expected frequency of use (see 2.4.2.6). What labels should go on the horizontal X axis and the vertical Y axis?

2-23. What is meant by the objective of evolvability? What are the costs and benefits of a high degree of evolvability?

2-24. In what sense can a database management system become unresponsive to the needs of users, even though the system was responsive when first acquired?

2-25. What is the relationship between availability and evolvability? How does each contribute to the other?

2-26. What is the key organizational consequence of maintaining a high level of quality in organizational data resources, that is, what feeling is generated in the users?

2-27. Identify and distinguish the three primary facets of the database integrity objective.

2-28. What is the role of and relationship between the database management system and the database administrator with respect to database integrity?

2-29. Why is it important to ensure that a stored database conform to its definition? Describe two consequences of not meeting this integrity objective.

2-30. What is the benefit and the cost of storing a comprehensive definition of a stored database?

2-31. What is data privacy?

2-32. What is the importance and necessity of privacy legislation?

2-33. What are the technical and administrative data privacy protection mechanisms and how do they work together to ensure data privacy?

2-34. What is the major characteristic which distinguishes types of data systems? Briefly describe five types of data systems.

2-35. Trace the evolution of database management facilities for accessing data on a secondary storage device. Explain how each stage was a logical next step. What contribution did each step make to improved system efficiency? to improved human efficiency?

2-36. Why is it important to distinguish between changes in database content and database structure?

2-37. What were the two avenues of DBMS development that led to a dichotomy in DBMSs? What was the rationale behind each?

2-38. What are the differences between host-language and self-contained DBMSs? Who uses each type? Contrast the advantages and disadvantages of each.

2-39. Explain how the dichotomy in DBMSs does not allow an organization to meet each of the four database management objectives.

2-40. If self-contained DBMSs or host-language DBMSs by themselves make it impossible for an organization to achieve the four database management objectives, what alternative DBMS development is necessary?

2-41. Assuming an organization has acquired both a self-contained DBMS and a host-language DBMS and that they can ''talk'' to each other, what database management objectives are still not satisfied and what problems is the organization likely to face in using the two systems?

2-42. Describe the four levels of access to a database with respect to data integrity problems, and discuss possible solutions.

2-43. How does a bibliographic or document reference retrieval system differ from a DBMS?

2-44. Differentiate between a generalized database system and a dedicated database system. Is one better than the other, in general? Under what circumstances would an organization favor one over the other?

2-45. What conditions must exist (or assumptions made) to make a database system economically and operationally feasible in a high-volume, realtime environment?

2-46. List some possible applications requiring a dedicated DBMS. Describe one in detail and discuss the reasons such an organization would favor a dedicated DBMS. Draw upon your own experience, if possible.

2-47. Will generalized DBMSs be used more and more in high-volume, realtime systems in the future? Explain.

SELECTED REFERENCES

AHITUV, Niv, and Michael HADASS, ''Identifying the Need for a DBMS,'' *Journal of Systems Management*, 1980 August, pages 30-33.

     Provides a good list of symptoms within an organization which may indicate the need for a DBMS.

BACHMAN, C. W. and S. B. WILLIAMS, "A General Purpose Programming System For Random Access Memories," *1964 Fall Joint Computer Conference Proceedings*, Baltimore: Spartan Books, Inc., pages 411-422.

> An early discussion of host-language facilities to aid the application programmer in processing data stored on the then newly emerging direct access storage devices.

CANNING, Richard G., "The Current Status of Data Management," *EDP Analyzer* (12:2), 1974 February, 13 pages.

> Describes what motivated two organizations to acquire a DBMS and how each used the DBMS to satisfy their needs. Byron Jackson acquired one system to improve "the process of developing new application systems" and Arcata acquired another system to "respond more quickly to data changes requested by customers."

CODASYL Systems Committee, *Selection and Acquisition of Data Base Management Systems*, New York: Association for Computing Machinery, 1976 March.

> The first chapter, "Rationale and Qualification for a Data Base Approach," provides an extended discussion of the benefits and costs, and the motivating and inhibiting forces, of the database approach.

CODASYL Systems Committee, *Feature Analysis of Generalized Data Base Management Systems*, New York: Association for Computing Machinery, 1971 May, 520 pages, (in Europe: British Computer Society, London, England, or IFIP Administrative Data Processing Group, Amsterdam, Netherlands; in Japan: *bit* (5:14), 1973).

FRY, James P., "Managing Data is the Key to MIS," *Computer Decisions* (3:1), 1971 January, pages 6-10.

> A useful comparison of bibliographic systems, DBMSs, and dedicated "realtime, fixed-transaction systems."

FRY, James P. and Edgar H. SIBLEY, "Evolution of Data-Base Management Systems," *Computing Surveys* (8:1), 1976 March, pages 7-42.

> Discusses historical DBMS development, including the genealogy of particular systems and an extensive bibliography.

GOSDEN, John and Eugene RAICHELSON, "The New Role of Management Information Systems," in *Fourth Generation Computers: User Requirements and Transition*, edited by Fred Gruenberger, Englewood Cliffs, NJ: Prentice-Hall, 1970, pages 75-87, (NTIS: AD 691 834).

> Discusses user diversity and data diversity that must be handled in future database management systems.

HAYES, Robert M., "Information Retrieval: An Introduction," *Datamation* (14:3), 1968 March, pages 22-26.

> A professor of library science provides a useful taxonomy of information retrieval systems into database systems, reference systems, and text processing systems. He then discusses each emphasizing document reference retrieval systems.

LEFKOVITZ, David, *File Structures for On-Line Systems*, New York: Spartan Books, 1969.

> Although discussing systems design, file structures, and file processing from the viewpoint of bibliographic systems (note particularly Chapter 1, "The Information Systems Model"), this book is often cited in the database management literature because of its practical discussion of database management problems.

McGEE, William C., "Generalization: Key to Successful Electronic Data Processing," *Journal of the ACM* (6:1), 1959 January, pages 1-23.

> An early, thoughtful article on the generalization of interrogation and update functions in a database environment.

PATTERSON, Albert C., "Data Base Hazards," *Datamation* (18:7), 1972 July, pages 48-50.

ROARK, Mayford L., "Data-Base Management Systems—The Hazards of Getting Trapped," remarks made at Data-Base Seminar, AFIPS National National Computer Conference, New York, 1973 June 7.

> A perceptive link with reality and a cogent raising of questions.

APPENDIX

2A

BIBLIOGRAPHIC SYSTEMS

Bibliographic or document reference retrieval systems relate to the intellectual rather than the housekeeping activities of a library (acquisitions, cataloguing, and circulation). Although a DBMS can generally be used as a bibliographic system, such systems are different enough to warrant separate attention and classification.

A document reference retrieval system differs from a DBMS in the following ways:

- The data structure is designed for particular data, typically a single file of bibliographic citations often with subject descriptors ("keywords") and sometimes an abstract (see Figure 2A-1).
- The functions serve a researcher as opposed to a decision maker.
- The software is usually more specialized, not sufficiently generalized to meet the needs of database management.

Figure 2A-2 provides a sketch of a document reference retrieval system. The following paragraphs point out how it differs from a DBMS. First, the data and its structure are known and relatively common across all document reference retrieval systems. Furthermore, these systems may have large files—up to several million citations.

The second and most important difference is the heavy emphasis on creating an accurate profile of each document and matching it by machine to a request profile. A document profile can be created using a "controlled" thesaurus of subject descriptors. Document reference data is more difficult to search because of the complex relationships among subjects. Reference systems must include thesauri which describe relationships among subject terms, indicating other terms which are more general, more specific, similar, or synonymous. A document profile may be augmented with a textual abstract or a brief description of how the document relates to each descriptor in its profile, as shown in Figure 2A-1.

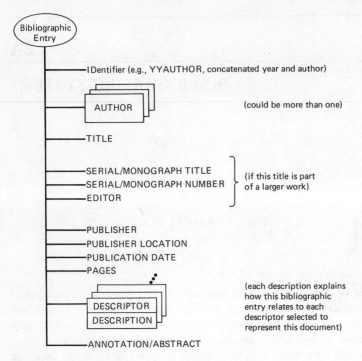

Figure 2A-1. Sample Schema for a Bibliographic Entry.

Third, users of an "information retrieval" system can best be characterized as researchers. They need to browse through the thesaurus to construct their requests. As an added service, the system may keep a profile of each researcher and automatically notify them whenever a newly entered document matches their interests. This feature is called SDI—selective dissemination of information.

In the retrieval process, the system attempts to retrieve documents which match the request. Sometimes a relevant document will not be retrieved by the system. Conversely, some retrieved documents will not be relevant. Relevance and recall ratios measure the retrieval effectiveness of a document reference retrieval system. The *relevance* measure is the ratio of the number of relevant documents retrieved to the total number of documents retrieved by a particular request. The *recall* measure is the ratio of the number of relevant documents retrieved to the total number of relevant documents stored in the system. The measure of *noise* is one minus the relevance ratio. The *omission* factor is one minus the recall ratio. These measures of retrieval effectiveness are shown in Figure 2A-3 using a Venn diagram.

The omission factor is of major concern in bibliographic systems. The problem lies in determining the set of all relevant items. The user knows the set of retrieved items and can isolate those that are relevant. The only way to find the relevant items not retrieved is to somehow examine *all* the items existing in the system. The user of

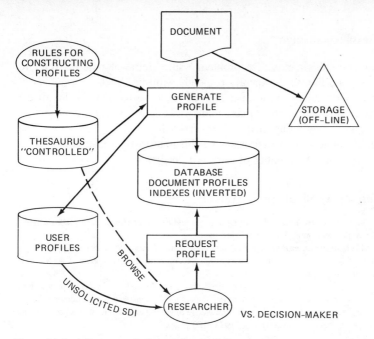

Figure 2A-2. A Document Reference Retrieval System.

When entering a document into the database, its bibliographic data is augmented with a set of relevant descriptor terms. The descriptors are selected from a thesaurus. Adding new descriptors to the thesaurus is often controlled by someone responsible for the system. A researcher, desiring a list of relevant documents from the database, constructs a request using descriptors from the thesaurus. Browsing helps the researcher become familiar with the terms used to describe documents stored in the database. The system may also maintain a profile of user interests expressed using descriptor terms. Then it can periodically notify users of newly added documents which may be of interest to them. This is called selective dissemination of information (SDI). Users are characterized as researchers in contrast with users of a DBMS who might be clerks and managers performing tasks and making decisions.

Figure 2A-3. Performance Measures of a Bibliographic System.

If a bibliographic system retrieves 50 items in response to a particular request and 30 are found to be relevant, the RELEVANCE RATIO would be 0.6 or 60%. If we estimated (or knew) that the database contained 40 relevant items, the RECALL RATIO would be 75%. While the 40% NOISE RATIO represents the inconvenience of examining and rejecting 20 retrieved items, the 25% OMISSION RATIO is worrisome. There is no practical way for the requestor to know that 10 relevant items were not retrieved. Recall and omission ratios are difficult to measure without scanning the entire database of items. Broadening the retrieval request to capture more of the omitted items raises the noise ratio.

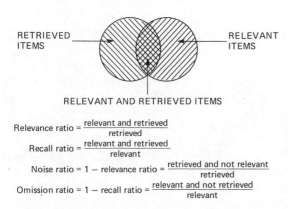

In response to a particular request:

RELEVANT AND RETRIEVED ITEMS

$$\text{Relevance ratio} = \frac{\text{relevant and retrieved}}{\text{retrieved}}$$

$$\text{Recall ratio} = \frac{\text{relevant and retrieved}}{\text{relevant}}$$

$$\text{Noise ratio} = 1 - \text{relevance ratio} = \frac{\text{retrieved and not relevant}}{\text{retrieved}}$$

$$\text{Omission ratio} = 1 - \text{recall ratio} = \frac{\text{relevant and not retrieved}}{\text{relevant}}$$

a DBMS does not face this "existence problem" since retrieval requests refer to specific stored data, and the system merely responds with the "facts."

Of course, the user's ability to formulate a good request affects the quality of the response. A broad request will retrieve many items yielding low selectivity or resolution. A narrow request, highly qualified with several selection criteria, may retrieve nothing. The user must know the thesaurus and be able to broaden or restrict incrementally the request to change the number of retrieved documents.

Books Generally on Bibliographic Systems

BECKER, Joseph and Robert M. HAYES, *Information Storage and Retrieval: Tools, Elements, Theories*, New York: John Wiley and Sons, Inc., 1963, 448 pages.

LANCASTER, F. Wilfrid, *Information Retrieval Systems*, New York: Wiley, 1968, 222 pages.

MEADOW, Charles T., *The Analysis of Information Systems*, Second Edition, Los Angeles, CA: Melville Publishing Co., 1973, 420 pages.

SALTON, Gerard, *Dynamic Information and Library Processing*, Englewood Cliffs, NJ: Prentice-Hall, 1975, 523 pages. This book synthesizes and interprets the author's extensive past research and experimental systems. He is a central contributor to the knowledge of computer-based textual processing and information retrieval systems. Publishing Co., 1973, 420 pages.

CHAPTER THREE

A CONCEPTUAL DBMS MODEL

3.1	SEVERAL DIMENSIONS OF DBMS	74
3.2	USER ROLES IN THE DBMS ENVIRONMENT	74
3.2.1	Sharability with Different Users	75
3.2.2	End User versus System Developer	75
3.2.3	Programming versus Nonprogramming Users	76
3.2.4	DBMS User Roles	78
3.2.4.1	Casual User	80
3.2.4.2	Parametric User	80
3.2.4.3	General User	81
3.2.4.4	DBMS Language Programmer	82
3.2.4.5	Conventional Application Programmer	83
3.2.4.6	DBMS System Programmer	83
3.2.5	Future Importance of User Classes	84
3.3	DATABASE MANAGEMENT FUNCTIONS	84
3.3.1	Function: Language and Program Module	86
3.3.2	A Taxonomy of Database Management Functions	86
3.4	A CONCEPTUAL DBMS MODEL	88
3.4.1	Incorporating Three Major User Interfaces	89
3.4.2	Incorporating Database Management Functions	89
3.4.3	The Database Control System (DBCS)	91
3.4.4	The Database and Its Schema	92
3.4.5	DBMS Architecture for a Shared, Evolvable Database	92
3.4.5.1	The Userschema	94
3.5	HOW THE DBMS MODEL SATISFIES	97
3.5.1	Satisfying the Motivators	97
3.5.2	Reducing Application Development Effort	97
3.5.3	Meeting the Objectives of Database Management	98
3.5.4	The Means to Evolvability: Generality; High-Level Data Languages;	99–101
	Programming User Facilities; Data Independence and Late Binding;	101–102
	Database Revision Utilities	103
3.5.5	Supportive Relationships among DBMS User Roles	104
3.6	THE DBMS ENVIRONMENT	106
3.6.1	Internal Computer System Environment	107
3.6.2	DBMS: A Tool in Building Application Systems	109
	SUMMARY	113
	EXERCISES	115
	SELECTED REFERENCES	116

This chapter develops a conceptual model of DBMS based upon users served and functions performed. The historical dichotomy in DBMSs stemmed from attempts to serve two different types of users. Some DBMSs today still serve one user type or the other, exclusively. The conceptual model presented here serves *both* types of users.

This chapter describes both types of users with three variants for each. Then there is a description of the overall model and its major functions, followed by a review of how the model satisfies the motivators and objectives discussed in the previous chapter.

3.1 SEVERAL DIMENSIONS OF DBMS

Database Management Systems can be viewed from several different perspectives:

- Historical evolution.
- Classes of users served.
- Functions performed.
- Data structures definable.
- Languages used to access and manipulate the data.
- Modes of operation.

Exploring each of these enhances our understanding of DBMSs. Each of these views can also be used independently to *classify* DBMSs. The first view was covered in the previous chapter. The user and function views are covered in this chapter and lead to the definition of the conceptual DBMS model. Chapter 4 describes a classification of DBMSs based upon definable data structures. Chapter 5 reviews different user interfaces, languages, and modes of operation.

3.2 USER ROLES IN THE DBMS ENVIRONMENT

People interface with a DBMS. They operate in various roles* requiring various levels of training. The assumed user role strongly influenced the design of DBMSs. Two primary user roles account for the dichotomy in DBMSs revealed in the previous chapter. Much can be understood about DBMS functions and operation by examining the basic user roles served.

People may be direct or indirect DBMS users. *Direct users* use the DBMS facilities directly. They may be online or offline when interacting with the DBMS. An offline user would fill out a coding form and submit it to someone else in making a

---

*To speak of roles recognizes that a given person may play different roles at different times. For a good discussion of the distinction between roles and individuals, see Talcott Parsons, "Boundary Relations Between Sociocultural and Personality Systems," in *Toward a Unified Theory of Human Behavior*," edited by Roy R. Grinker, New York: Basic Books, Inc., 1956, page 328.

The roles associated with the design and development of a DBMS are explicitly excluded from consideration. The identified roles concern the ongoing use, control, and evolution of the system within an organization.

request of the DBMS. For an online user, the response from the system may be immediate or deferred.

Indirect users are passive toward the system or go through a direct user—for example, a bank teller who looks up a customer's account balance in a daily printed listing of all account balances is an indirect user. Similarly, customers who call the utility company concerning an apparent error on their monthly statement would be indirect users of the system. They would talk to a clerk having direct access to the system. This text concerns direct DBMS users primarily.

A person acting in a user role is sometimes a direct *end user* of the data in the database; at other times the person may be responding to a request for data from another person. Often a request for data from top management initiates a chain of activities which use facilities at various levels of sophistication. More difficult requests require knowledgeable people, using more generalized and more flexible facilities in the DBMS.

A user role is distinct from an *administrative role*. A person acting in an administrative role acts as an agent for a community of users. Such persons may be direct users of the DBMS, but their primary concern for the data is custodial.

Administrative functions include: planning for the future use of the database; providing, maintaining, and enhancing the facilities of the DBMS; establishing and executing control and authorization procedures to maintain database integrity; and continuous, smooth operations. (The role of database administration is detailed later in Chapter 15.)

3.2.1 Sharability with Different Users

When data resources are mechanized and stored in a database, different users may want to use the data in carrying out their duties. Sharability means providing facilities for different types of users to access the same database (see Figure 3-1).

3.2.2 End User versus System Developer

End users of a DBMS *use* the results of their efforts with the DBMS, directly. They are consumers of the results of interacting with the DBMS. A person is also considered an end user, *from the viewpoint of the DBMS*, if they are acting for an *indirect* end user.

A system developer is a person who is using the facilities of the DBMS to build or add facilities or stored procedures which can subsequently be invoked by an end user. Of course, it is possible for the same person to build and store some procedure which they invoke later for themselves. This is one person playing two roles and points up the importance of distinguishing roles from people who fill those roles. System developers are programmers since they write programs consisting of sequences of commands stored for later execution. They concentrate on developing prestored procedures to meet needs of other users.

With the advent of desktop microcomputers, the distinction between end user and system developer becomes fuzzier. The user of a DBMS in this environment is inher-

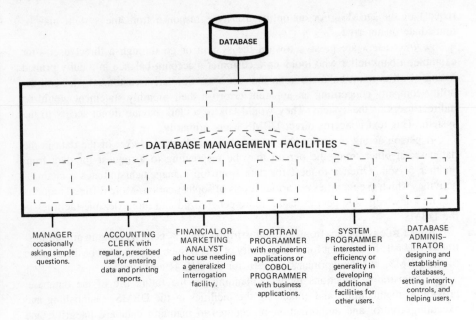

Figure 3-1. Database Sharability with Different Users.
To meet the sharability objective, different types of users should be able to access the same database.

ently online. They operate the computer. They will perform some ad hoc operations with the DBMS on the stored data. As they become more experienced in the use of the DBMS, they will want to be able to prestore frequently used sequences of operations in the DBMS. Now they become a system developer.

The more sophisticated system developer will need to be able to:

- Store predefined queries, report definitions, and data entry transaction definitions.
- Define data display and data entry screens.
- Define menus and help screens.
- Write programs in a high-level data language—a self-contained language within the DBMS consisting, in part, of high-level commands to access and manipulate the database.
- Write programs in a conventional programming language to access and manipulate the database.

3.2.3 Programming versus Nonprogramming Users

The user roles are first divided into nonprogramming users (or ad hoc end users) and programming users. System developers are always programming users since they create additional definitions or procedures which are stored for later execution.

The nonprogramming user is not necessarily a nonprogrammer. Rather, they do not write a procedural program in some programming language to use the database.

Here users are classified according to what they have to *do* as opposed to what they have to *be* (their skills, etc.). Conversely, a programming user invokes the DBMS facilities by writing and executing a program.

Nonprogramming users require facilities for ad hoc retrieval, extraction, and update. The user invokes the function and provides the required input, which could be anything from a small set of parameters to a sequence of statements written in some special-purpose language. A self-contained DBMS usually provides a special high-level language for specifying operations on the database.

When using the system, the end user normally thinks of:

- A whole file.
- An update transaction.
- A query.
- A report.

The file-processing algorithm is built into the functional modules of the system. The nonprogramming user can access and manipulate more than individual "records" one at a time—they think of processing a whole file (or even multiple related files) at once. The system provides the nonprogramming user with "file-level" rather than "record-level" services.

Nonprogramming user roles are classified into casual users, parametric users, and general users which are described in more detail later.

Programming users access the DBMS through a program written in some programming language. The language may be self-contained within the DBMS. Alternatively, it may augment a conventional programming language (such as COBOL, FORTRAN, BASIC, or PASCAL) which literally "hosts" the DBMS facilities. These users can be novice or highly sophisticated programmers with extensive knowledge of the system.

Some say the industry should not cater to the programming users—there is a critical shortage of programmers that will exist for some time. In a day when programmers are increasingly scarce and costly, systems should ease the resulting burden by serving the nonprogramming users whenever possible. There is an interesting contradiction in this statement. While it is desirable to develop systems with minimal dependence on programmers, organizations still need a system with evolvability. *Once a DBMS is built, its ability to grow and evolve depends precisely on the ability of a programmer to enhance or modify the system.*

The growth and evolution of computer software depends upon programmers. This growth is further aided by a formal and well-understood programmer interface that can be utilized by persons within the using environment. Yes, try to minimize the need for conventional programmers, but, NO, do not eliminate them entirely.

Facilities for the programming user are called data manipulation facilities because they enable manipulation of a database by a programmer: opening and closing files; fetching or storing data on direct access storage devices; and searching for, holding, or modifying particular sets of data. These facilities are requested through statements written in a program.

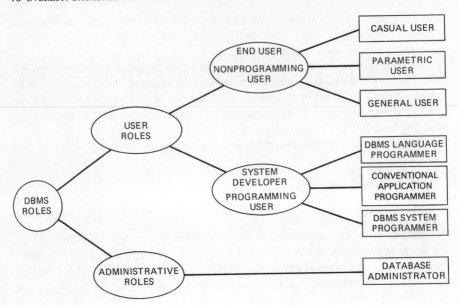

Figure 3-2. Roles in the DBMS Environment.

Programming users are divided into DBMS language programmers, conventional application programmers, and DBMS system programmers.

3.2.4 DBMS User Roles

The following sections provide a more detailed description of the six types of DBMS users previously identified. The taxonomy of user roles in the DBMS environment is shown in Figure 3-2.

The user roles form a hierarchy. Figure 3-3 shows the six user roles and nine ways they relate to each other. The differentiating factors are not all independent nor absolute. A counter argument could probably be found for each factor shown. This figure aims to give an overall feel for the hierarchical relationship of the five user roles. Some of the factors do not apply with the casual user placed before the parametric user since the result of a dialog with the casual user could be a request expressed in the DBMS command language.

3.2.4.1 Casual User

A casual user interacts with a system irregularly and occasionally. Therefore, the system cannot expect the user to be knowledgeable about the system, able to formulate a request properly, or willing to learn beforehand. They are untrained with respect to the system they use. Codd describes the casual user, user-system interaction, and a supporting facility.* He classifies "managers and housewives" as casual users.

*E. F. Codd, "Seven Steps to Rendezvous with the Casual User," in *Data Base Management*, edited by J. W. Klimbie and K. L. Koffeman, Amsterdam: North-Holland Publishing Company, 1974, pages 179-200.

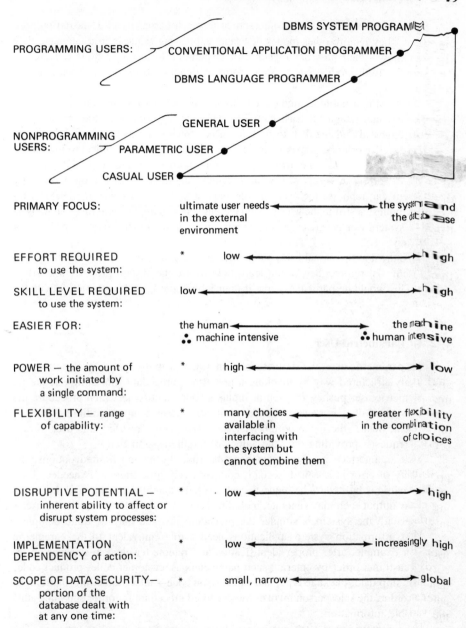

*Factors do not extend to the casual user in the hierarchy.

Figure 3-3. The Hierarchy of User Roles.
The user roles can be differentiated in a hierarchy using nine factors. None are absolute, but they do give an overall feel for role differences.

Since it is uneconomical or impractical to teach casual users a special-purpose language, they require other modes of usage: expressing requests in a language they already know——their *natural language*, or responding to menu prompts (covered in Chapter 5). Both modes require some form of dialogue between the users and the system.

When using a natural language interface, the user must know how to initiate a request and understand (at least partially) what can be done with the system—the actions requested and the data to be referenced. Such requests in a native language (such as English or French) may be inconsistent, ambiguous, and subject to interpretation. The system must be very tolerant of errors, engaging in dialogue with the user to correct mistakes, resolve ambiguities, and obtain clarification. Eventually the system can rephrase the user's initial request and ask for confirmation. The rephrased request is still in the user's language but is now complete and unambiguous so that the system can generate an equivalent request in a formal internal language for processing.

In contrast to the casual user, parametric and general users interact regularly with the system. Therefore, they would learn how to use the system properly and effectively. This would be particularly true if their job required regular interaction with the system.

3.2.4.2 Parametric User

The parametric user, the simplest role, interfaces with the system in an anticipated and highly structured way by invoking a predefined procedure. For simple requests, the parametric user pushes a button or inputs a code identifying which procedure the system is to invoke. For more complex requests, the user inputs additional data or parameters, hence, the name *parametric user*. The system restricts this user to prescribed requests, providing only the values of required parameters.

Such an interface has two main benefits: first, by having limited options, the probability of error is lessened; second, comparatively little training is needed. User understanding is limited to the requests each has been taught to invoke, and the meaning of any output each may generate, including error messages. Even though the user's interface with the system is simple, the procedure invoked may be quite complex.

Most information system applications need a role equivalent to the parametric user. For example, after proper identification at a remote terminal, a salesperson records a customer order by entering such parameters as: customer code, product code, quantity, ship date, package type, and salesperson code—all variable information. To enter an order, the salesperson invokes the prestored procedure for order entry and adds the variable information.

The parametric user often interacts with the system from an online terminal. The terminal may be highly specialized, with function keys representing specific requests or transactions. For example, a broker inputs the code for a particular stock and then pushes one of several buttons to get the high, low, close (latest sale), or volume traded for today, yesterday, last month, or last year. There may also be buttons to get earnings, dividends, yield, or price/earnings ratio.

Facilities for the parametric user are essential. In the average business where the system is serving the people well, *most* interactions with the database are via prescribed requests. In some dedicated environments, *everything* is tailored to a specific application, such as airline reservations, and nearly all interactions are prescribed.

Certain functions are well served by parametric users, one being data entry. Good data entry practice is to capture input data once, as close as possible to its source. Adding on-the-spot validation enables the data entry clerk to resubmit rejected transactions immediately. The DBMS should provide parametric user facilities to aid this process.

From the standpoint of evolvability, it is seldom possible to specify all the requests users will make. By repeating a certain activity, it becomes better understood and the interface between the users and the database can become more standardized. As the skill of users increases, the system should provide for defining new transactions and redefining existing ones, that is, to *prescribe* more interactions. More sophisticated users provide the means to respond to the changing needs of the parametric user.

3.2.4.3 General User

A general (nonprogramming) user interfaces directly with a generalized module of the DBMS for retrieval or update. By interfacing with a module having a wide range of facilities, this user gains flexibility and versatility. The user interacts with the system in an unstructured, unanticipated, and ad hoc manner. Financial or marketing analysts and auditors, for example, must be able to search the database and manipulate the output in various ways, sometimes by trial and error.

When interfacing with the generalized module, the general user must specify the task completely using the language, often high-level, of the function. The user needs to understand the language of the functional module. Both the function and its language can rest anywhere on the complexity spectrum. The user should be able to specify a simple query simply, and get output regardless of form. The user should also be able to specify, if necessary, the detailed layout of a report. A general user operating online may interactively formulate a query or construct a report by carrying on a dialogue with the system.

A self-contained DBMS serves the general user. Many such systems focus primarily on retrieval, providing limited update capability.

The parametric and general users are at opposite ends of a spectrum based on the amount of information given in a request compared with the amount given to the system in advance. The parametric user supplies the least information, while the general user must formulate a complete request writing one or more statements in a general, self-contained language. The amount and completeness that must be submitted at request time differentiates the parametric user and the general user. A user becomes more general as more complex information is provided to the system at request time. A "completely" general user interfaces with a generalized functional module and provides complete information when making requests.

3.2.4.4 DBMS Language Programmer

The DBMS language programmer uses essentially (perhaps exactly) the same facilities as the general user—namely, the self-contained language of the DBMS. Rather than issue ad hoc commands for immediate execution as the general user does, the DBMS language user writes those commands into a command file which can be stored and later executed. If the system is strictly menu driven, then there will be no command language and hence no facilities for the DBMS language programmer.

In the simplest case, the DBMS commands are written into a command file. For example:

```
PROMPT "Enter User ID":USERID
USER USERID
OPEN EMPLOYEE FILE
DESTINATION PRINTER
SELECT RECORDS WHERE TITLE = "ELEC ENGR" OR PRIMARY_SKILL = "1130"
SORT BY EMPNAME
LIST /TITLE "Electrical Engineers"/ EMPNAME, ORGUNIT, SALARY
:
```

The preceding prestored program will obtain the invoking user's ID for access control and print out all electrical engineers from the employee file ordered by employee name.

Sometimes a user needs to have control over the sequence of command execution. Some commands or group of commands may need to be executed conditionally and perhaps multiple times. For these needs the system must provide additional commands to allow the user to modify the flow of control of execution through the stored command file. The common command constructs for this include:

- IF . . . THEN . . . ELSE . . . [ENDIF]
- DO WHILE . . . or DO UNTIL . . . [ENDDO]
- GO TO . . .
- IF . . . GO TO . . .

(The GO TO constructs are not conducive to good structured programming and, therefore, do not appear in some of the newer, better-designed languages. The IF and DO constructs are completely sufficient to define any general programming sequence.)

Since the stored command file or program will be executed later, the DBMS language programmer also needs commands for displaying data and literal text (prompts and exception messages) on the screen and for capturing user input during execution. This also means that the DBMS language must provide a means for storing values in variables (registers, etc.) within the program during execution. In the preceding example, the programmer issued a prompt at the screen for the user to enter his or her ID, to accept it from the keyboard, and store it in a variable named USERID.

3.2.4.5 Conventional Application Programmer

The conventional application programmer writes programs in a conventional programming language such as COBOL, FORTAN, BASIC, or PASCAL. For purposes of this text, a conventional programming language is characterized by a low-level, one-record-at-a-time approach to accessing and manipulating data files. Such languages may be high-level with respect to *specifying processes* (when compared to assembly language or machine language), but they are distinctly *low-level* when it comes to *manipulating data* in files, or file processing.

For this type of user, the DBMS is accessed *through* a conventional programming language. That is, the facilities of the DBMS are hosted in the conventional programming language. Therefore, such systems are called "host-language DBMSs," or simply "hosted DBMSs." The facilities of the DBMS may be obtained by using special commands which have been added to the host programming language or by issuing calls to DBMS routines.

When application programmers write a program to process a database, they know its logical structure and definition (at least the needed part of the database). They can define the content of and size of working storage (buffer) and name specific files and data items in their program. Therefore, a human-oriented programming language (narrative or free form) bests suits the system developer using a DBMS.

The programming user of a hosted DBMS has available all the power and flexibility of the host programming language to manipulate data beyond what is provided in the DBMS. This provides a certain attraction to the buyers of a DBMS. They are not trapped into the limitations of the DBMS. It also provides an escape for the builder of the DBMS, for they don't have to worry about providing all needed facilities. For this reason, DBMSs which are (or were originally) exclusively host-language DBMSs tend to have less complete capabilities than those systems which are (or were originally) self-contained.

Processing efficiency is not usually an overwhelming consideration for the application programmer, at least not initially. They need some easy way to get the application system built and running for the end users. Fine-tuning can come later (if ever!).

3.2.4.6 DBMS System Programmer

Within the entire computer organization, there are different types of system programmers. The one here is a *DBMS system programmer* who develops generalized programs to interface with the DBMS, using the DBMS as given. The DBMS system programmer must not be confused with the person responsible for maintaining an installed DBMS and installing new versions from the vendor. This is an administrative role, not a user role.

Application programming users focus on the application in the organization. Systems programmers write generalized procedures to operate on any part of the database in conjunction with any application. With more sophistication, they can use more complex and versatile facilities. They better understand the implications and consequences of using the DBMS.

Application programmers and system programmers differ in their objectives. The system programmer is often more concerned with achieving greater generality or greater efficiency than the application programmer. The system programmer often enjoys intricate details, whereas the application programmer concentrates on getting the job done.

In many respects, the application and system programmers are at opposite ends of a spectrum. However, the system programmer is assumed *not* to know what database (or portion thereof) the written program will address at any given time. This information is input to the program when it is in execution. The system programmer must be able to write a program that can process any definable data structure. While writing a program, the system programmer cannot reference any specific data items or files by name. Such names, along with corresponding values and selection criteria, are available only at execution time. System programmers must write their program so that, once it receives input data, it can subsequently discover the data structure being addressed. Then, the program must be able to construct the appropriate statements which call upon the DBMS.

3.2.5 Future Importance of User Classes

Consider the relative importance of each type of user now and in the future. Codd has speculated that, in the next 20 years, casual users will emerge and become dominant. Parametric and general users will also increase while programming users will decrease (relatively, though probably not in absolute numbers). These speculations are graphically portrayed in Figure 3-4. As DBMS use penetrates further into the operation and management of organizations, more people will use them. Relatively fewer people will be skilled general users or programming users.

Codd's comments were made in 1974. Ten years later the trend is true except for the casual user. The reason is the lack of DBMSs which have any capabilities for the casual user. They are extremely difficult to build, and the few that currently exist are quite simple. Codd's forecasts are still probably true except for the time frame. The next 10 years may see the emergence of viable facilities for the casual user.

The projections have certainly been born out in the world of microcomputers, where the vast majority of available DBMSs serve nonprogramming users exclusively.

3.3 DATABASE MANAGEMENT FUNCTIONS

The functions of database management represents another useful perspective for classifying DBMSs. A comprehensive taxonomy of functions evolved in the review of the history of DBMSs in the previous chapter. The functions also cluster according to the three major DBMS roles—nonprogramming user, programming user, and database administrator.

3.3.1 Function: Language and Program Module

In describing a taxonomy of functions, it is important to distinguish function from mechanism. Dowkont lumped file creation and maintenance together because they were both "effected by the same means." As noted before, some authors consolidated

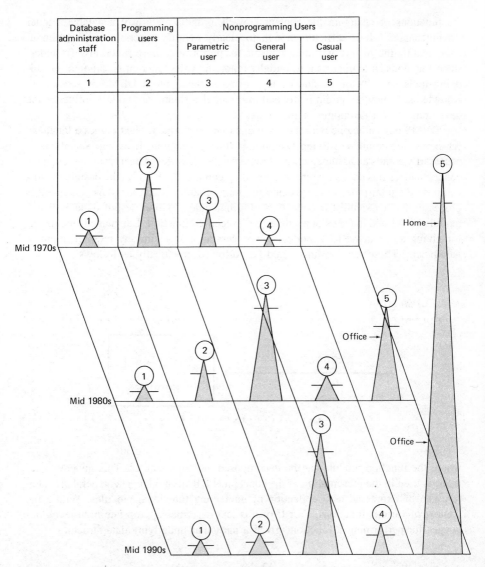

Figure 3-4. Anticipated Use of Large Integrated Databases.
In the future Codd suggests that casual users will dominate followed by parametric users of DBMSs, while programming users will diminish, relatively, in importance.

Source: E. F. Codd, "Recent Investigations in Relational Data Base Systems," presented at IFIP Congress, Stockholm, Sweden, 1974 August 5-10, 1974.

the functions of changing the content as well as the structure of a database under "maintenance." It is difficult enough to clearly identify functions per se without complicating the picture with mechanisms for performing those functions. To understand functions, it is important to initially ignore *how* the function is satisfied. Developing tools or software modules and packaging them into a DBMS is secondary. Knowledge of how a system is divided into modules should not unduly influence the development of a taxonomy of functions.

DBMS design begins with the functions to be performed. Next comes a language for expressing commands to the system to perform a function. Language specification necessarily entails an assumed class of logical data structures. The user of the language conceptualizes this data structure when writing commands. Finally, the designers must compose the total processing task into program modules. Each language statement is processed by a module (or collection of submodules). Good design dictates that a module be defined in terms of a single, well-specified function. Language is the means for giving a command to a module for processing along with any required input or parameters. These relationships could be portrayed graphically as follows:

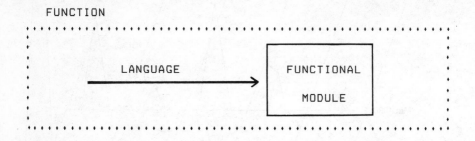

where the function module can be decomposed into submodules. This general schematic is used in the presentation of the conceptual DBMS model. The general architecture can be expressed as a collection of interacting functional modules. Within the context of various functions, Part II of this text describes appropriate high-level languages for performing a function, given a particular underlying data structure.

3.3.2 A Taxonomy of Database Management Functions

Database management functions are those that generally are or ultimately could be mechanized, that is, those functions which could be reasonably incorporated into a DBMS. This view goes beyond what is currently available. A DBMS is a collection of data-related functions. They may be included in future DBMSs; some are already features in current systems.

DBMS functions differ from DBA functions. A system performs DBMS functions while a person performs DBA functions. Database administration functions include:

people-to-people functions; design, definition, and redefinition functions; exception handling and recovery functions; and accountability functions. A DBMS provides establishment and control tools for the DBA staff to perform its duties, and retrieval and update tools which make the data available to users.

A list of possible DBMS functions may be classified in several ways. However, one observation repeatedly stands out. Some functions deal directly with the database while others seem to cut across the direct functions. Dividing the functions according to the major objectives of availability and integrity serves to place them on two levels: The integrity control functions must underlie all avenues of access to the database. On top of both of these is a level of availability forms. The user conceptually penetrates different levels when using the system (see Figure 3-5).

Figure 3-6 presents an overall taxonomy of database management functions and dictates the arrangement of chapters in Part II. This taxonomy includes all functions for using and managing data resources in an ever-changing environment where users share data resources, and where, therefore, usage must be controlled.

These functions relate to the database management objectives. The availability objective relates to the direct availability functions, to the availability interface forms, and to the underlying performance monitoring. Integrity maintenance is the other component of the underlying support functions. Database revision and programming user facilities relate to the evolvability objective (future availability).

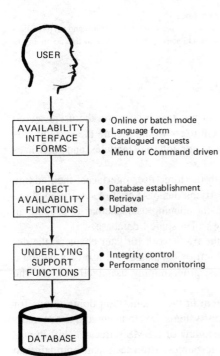

Figure 3-5. Levels between the User and the Database.

When accessing a database, the user penetrates three levels conceptually. The first level involves getting into the system, whether online or in batch mode, and expressing a request in the language of the function or invoking a previously catalogued request. The second level relates to the direct functions by which a user establishes, retrieves from, and updates a database. In the third level, integrity control and performance-monitoring functions underlie the direct availability functions to monitor and control all access to the database according to the policies established by the database administrator.

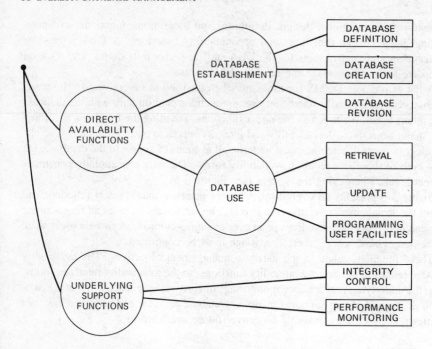

Figure 3-6. A Taxonomy of Database Management Functions.
    Establishment and use functions make a database available to users. Integrity control and performance-monitoring functions underlie the availability functions. The chapters in Part II relate to this taxonomy of functions.

3.4 A CONCEPTUAL DBMS MODEL

The conceptual DBMS model developed in this text focuses on the users served and functions performed. It shows how different users would picture the system. It is an external view of a DBMS with only the major internal modules and interfaces shown.

The DBMS model unfolds beginning with the three user interfaces, then adding functions for each interface, detailing the underlying database control system, explaining the database and its schema, and, finally, introducing userschemas to provide an architecture which permits multiple user views of a shared database.

This conceptual DBMS model provides the framework for later chapters: the design, definition, structure, creation, and revision of databases; the use of a database with high-level retrieval and update languages; programming user facilities; and the underlying integrity control functions.

The conceptual model emphasizes a system *in* the organization doing things for people. The "people problems" of information systems development and use increasingly overshadow the technical problems. This view of DBMS reflects a shift in emphasis—from technical feasibility to human resources; from technical optimality to human viability.

3.4.1 Incorporating Three Major User Interfaces

Taking a user view and expanding on the three major DBMS interfaces introduced in Chapter 1 leads to the picture shown in Figure 3-7. The nonprogramming user requires a high-level language for retrieval and update. The programming user may use the high-level language or the more flexible, record-level, navigational interface. The DBA needs special facilities for establishing the database, and setting parameters for the underlying integrity control and performance monitoring functions. In addition, the DBA, in the role of a nonprogramming user, may utilize the high-level language interface, for example, to investigate the quality or completeness of data.

3.4.2 Incorporating Database Management Functions

Adding the functional modules from the taxonomy of Figure 3-6 to the user interfaces of Figure 3-7 produces the overall conceptual DBMS model shown in Figure 3-8. This represents a high-level design for a functionally viable and complete DBMS, satisfying the objectives of database management.

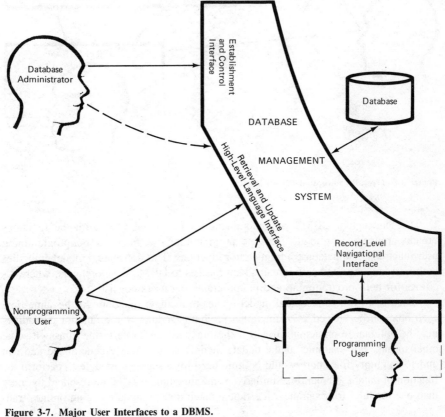

Figure 3-7. Major User Interfaces to a DBMS.

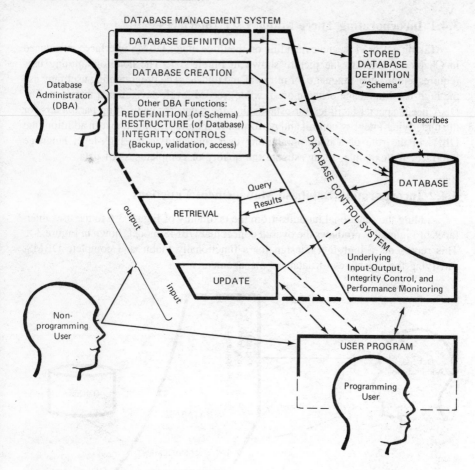

Figure 3-8. Overall Conceptual DBMS Model.

The conceptual DBMS is predominantly a functional view with the functions broadly grouped according to user type: programming user facilities, nonprogramming user functions, and database administrator functions. This conceptual model embodies both host-language and self-contained approaches to DBMS developments, where facilities for both programming and nonprogramming users coexist.

Each box in the conceptual model relates to a single function. At the same time each box can be viewed as a functional program module. Some functional modules may be optional in an actual DBMS if the function can be performed through some other means. For example, if the update module is sufficiently generalized and can update an empty file, there would be little need for a separate module to perform the function of database creation. Similarly, some functions may be represented by more than one module, for example, an efficient batch update module and an online "random'' update module. If the DBMS consisted only of a reasonably complete database control system with a reasonably generalized interface for the DBMS system programmer, it would be possible to build all the other functional modules.

3.4.3 The Database Control System (DBCS)

The database is available through, and controlled internally by, the database control system (DBCS) which is the:

- Internal, machine-oriented agent of the DBA.
- Run-time support module for programs while in execution.
- Module which receives *all* requests to access or manipulate data in the database.
- Processor for database manipulation language statements.
- Security guard which intercepts and checks *all* database requests for proper authorization and for proper syntax and semantics.
- Auditor who keeps a log of all events and changes affecting the database.

The major availability functions have several common subfunctions. Both the common availability subfunctions and the underlying support functions are packaged together to make up the DBCS. The DBCS becomes the common denominator of all interfaces with the DBMS. All functions relating to database integrity are performed or invoked by the DBCS, and all user interfaces eventually come to the single controlling door of the DBCS. The modules built on top of the DBCS extend the functional capabilities of the system and diversify the various forms and modes of interface.

The database control system ''stands'' at the only door to the database, to receive and screen all requests to access the database. Providing a single door for the availability functions, that is, collecting together the common subfunctions, is *desirable* for improved performance but is *mandatory* for integrity control. When all references to the database are funneled through one channel, it is much easier to protect and maintain the overall integrity of the database—a fundamental objective of database management.

Present-day operating systems inadequately maintain database integrity. Therefore, direct access to the database through the input-output commands of the operating system must be disallowed (see Figure 2-8). Allowing access to the database directly through the operating system bypasses the integrity control mechanisms of the DBCS. One solution is for the operating system to ''trap'' any physical-level retrieval or update request *not* emanating from the DBCS. Alternatively, the input-output channels to the secondary storage devices containing the database could be dedicated to the DBCS, no other process being permitted to initiate (data) transfers through the dedicated channels. To repeat: All access to the database must be made through the single door of the database control system.

When multiprocessing systems become commonplace, one of the processors can be dedicated to executing the functions of the DBCS. In such a system the multiple processors must be made functionally differentiable and should operate asynchronously. The logical conclusion to such an evolutionary trend would be to move the database management functions increasingly into firmware or hardware for more efficient execution on a dedicated processor—a database management machine (described more fully in Chapter 18).

3.4.4 The Database and Its Schema*

The database appears in the upper right of Figure 3-8 along with its schema. The database is defined independently of and exists apart from any particular programs which access it.

A *schema* is the definition of something. A *database schema* is the definition of a database, including such information as:

- Characteristics of data objects such as entities and attributes.
- Logical structure and relationships among those data objects.
- Validation criteria and semantic constraints.
- Physical storage representation ("format").
- Physical location on storage devices and media.
- Integrity parameters such as access authorization and backup policies.

The database schema (or simply schema) contains all necessary and sufficient information for the system to do all database processing. Of course, not all systems today meet this ideal. Some operate with a skeletal schema taking a minimum, mechanistic view of the stored database, while leaving the user responsible for processing and maintaining the data with respect to undefined characteristics.

A (database) schema is written using a data definition language (DDL). The DDL processor accepts DDL statements and creates a stored database definition. The term "schema" can refer to the source DDL version or the stored version of a database definition. Just as a high-level language for fully specifying a process is important to the development and transferability of computer software, a high-level language for separately and fully defining a database is critically important to the database approach.

3.4.5 DBMS Architecture for a Shared, Evolvable Database

When writing a program or interacting with a database, DBMS users must have some perception of the data structure and content. This is true of both programming

---

*In 1968, McGee used "schema" to refer to the definition of stored data. A file schema defines "a class of files whose members have the same 'structure' but differ from one another with respect to the values assigned to elementary items, the number of entities represented, the number of subentities possessed by a given entity, and so forth. [The term 'file schema' conveys] the notion that it is a 'pattern' or 'template' from which individual members of the class may be produced." (William C. McGee, "File Structure for Generalized Data Management," *Information Processing 68*, Proceedings of IFIP Congress, Edinburgh, 1968 August 5-10, Volume 2, edited by A. J. H. Morrell, Amsterdam: North-Holland Publishing Co., 1969, page 1236.) The term was subsequently adopted by CODASYL and is now widely used. As used in this book, the term "schema" or "database schema" encompasses more than that which can be defined by the CODASYL Data Definition Language (DDL).

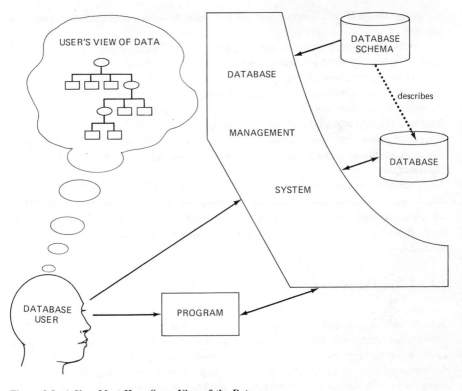

Figure 3-9. A User Must Have Some View of the Data.

Whether accessing a database online at a terminal or writing a program, a DBMS user must have some perception of the structure and content of the database: names of data objects, representation of values, and structural relationships. With only a database schema, all users must view the stored database exactly as the system does. This results in lower sharability and evolvability in the DBMS.

and nonprogramming users. They must have names to refer to data objects, some knowledge of how data item values are represented, and some sort of mental picture of the structural relationships among those data objects. This is depicted in Figure 3-9.

Ideally, the user's view should reflect the user's environment—the entities and their attributes in the organizational and operational environment and only those of interest to the user. In many DBMSs, the database schema predetermines the user's view. Users must know the exact and entire definition of the database. Moreover, they must use the precise data names in the schema and know exactly how to interpret the physical stored representation of the data. The user's view of data must coincide exactly with the database schema.

Requiring the user's view to coincide with the database schema produces real problems under two conditions: multiple users and a changing database.

With a common schema view, multiple users must be of one mind; they must all have exactly the same view of the database. However, different users have different jobs, may use different jargon, and do not need to know about *all* the data in a database.

As the database changes, so must the user views. As the database grows and gets more complex, so must the user views. The database administrator must notify all users to incorporate any change into their view of the database. Alternatively, users could ask if the database schema has changed since their last interaction with the database. If so, they could study the revised schema to change their view of the database. Prior to executing a program, the system could check to see if the database schema changed since the program was last compiled or the request was catalogued. These are all possible but not so practical ways of handling multiple users of a changing database.

To achieve a sharable, evolvable database, it would be desirable to decouple each user's view of the database from the database schema. This would enable different users and different application systems to have different views of the same database. It would also help to insulate the user views from changes in the database schema.

3.4.5.1 The Userschema

The user's view of the database is decoupled from the schema by introducing a *userschema*, also called a "subschema" or "external schema" (Figure 3-10). The userschema is a formal definition of a user's view of the database. It may include *part* of the schema; only that portion which is of interest to the user. Furthermore, it may use different data names and reflect a different structure, one that is more "natural" or compatible with the user's perceptions or application processes.

The userschema is actually another definition of data as viewed by a user or a user program. Figure 3-11 shows two possible userschemas defined on the schema for an EMPLOYEE database. It identifies (names) the data in the user view and describes its logical structure, its physical representation, and correspondence with data in the database ("mapping"). The physical description can apply to the data in a program buffer, or on the printed page or screen display of an interactive user. Often the system assumes a default physical description. The userschema is in effect for a session of interaction with the database either from a program or a user at a terminal. It is the basis for interpreting subsequent requests to access the database.

Any differences between the userschema and the database schema imply some form of data conversion when data is transferred between the user (or the user program) and the database. For example, a database item may record a measurement in metric and in floating-point while the (old) program still expects to receive data values in fixed-point, English units of measure. Data conversion can be expensive (in terms of machine efficiency) in a DBMS with a substantial userschema capability. Benefits include an easier user interface in a shared environment and a greater degree of evolvability. Additional machine resources can yield increased human productivity through reduced effort for application system development and maintenance, and user training.

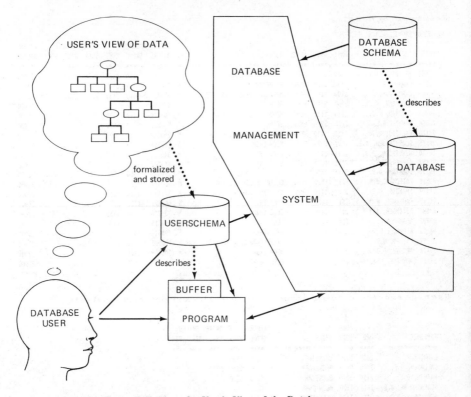

Figure 3-10. Userschema: Definition of a User's View of the Database.

Every user has some perception of the structure and content of the data being accessed at any given time. The userschema is a formal expression of the user's view of the database. It consists of:

- A logical data definition.
- Its physical representation in a program buffer, or on the screen or output page of a user's terminal.
- Its mapping to the data in the database.

The userschema may use different data names, reflect a different data structure, and refer to only portions of the database. The DBMS knows both the userschema and the database schema and can convert the data when transferred between the two according to the defined mapping. The userschema is the fundamental component of a DBMS architecture for achieving sharability and evolvability.

Database Schema:

EMPLOYEE

EMPNO	EMPNAME	UNIT	JOB CODE	LEVEL	TITLE	SEX	BIRTH DATE	PRIMARY SKILL	SSK1	SECONDARY SKILLS SSK2	SSK3	SSK4	ACTUAL SALARY
45584	PETERSON, N.M.	2000	0110	HEAD	DIVISION MANAGER	M	280607	0110	6130	6625	6040		56000
32579	LYNN, K.R.	2000	5210	EMPL	SECRETARY	F	530121	5210	5520				12000
57060	CARR, P.I.	2100	1110	HEAD	MANAGER DEVELOPMENT DEPT	M	350720	1110	1130	1135	0130	1355	48000
15324	CALLAGAN, R.F.	2100	5210	EMPL	SECRETARY	F	550606	5210	5520	5220			10800
10261	GUTTMAN, G.J.	2110	1110	HEAD	MANAGER SYSTEMS GROUP	M	301110	1110	1130	1135	0150		35000
72556	HARRIS, D.L.	2110	5210	EMPL	SECRETARY	F	550517	5210	5520				8400
24188	WALTERS, R.J.	2111	1110	HEAD	CHIEF PROPOSAL SECTION	M	260202	1110	1120				28000
21675	SCARBOROUGH, J.B.	2111	1120	EMPL	MECH ENGR	M	240914	1120					21000
18130	HENDERSON, R.G.	2111	1130	EMPL	ELEC ENGR	M	340121	1130					23000
91152	GARBER, R.E.	2111	1130	EMPL	ELEC ENGR	M	440707	1330	1130				16400
30793	COMPTON, D.R.	2111	1350	EMPL	COST ESTIMATOR	M	290328	1350	1351	1355	1130		16200
81599	FRIEDMAN, J.M.	2112	1110	HEAD	CHIEF DESIGN SECTION	M	360317	1110	1130				26000
21777	FRANCIS, G.C.	2112	1110	EMPL	SYSTEMS ENGR	M	321111	1110	1130				24000
24749	FAULKNER, W.M.	2112	1120	EMPL	MECH ENGR	M	400621	1120	1130	1330			24000
13581	FITINGER, G.J.	2112	1130	EMPL	ELEC ENGR	M	431216	1130	1355				22000
82802	APGAR, A.J.	2112	1130	EMPL	ELEC ENGR	M	500715	1130	1330				21000
63633	BLANK, L.F.	2112	1330	EMPL	DRAFTSMAN	F	491010	1330					16000
22959	BRIGGS, G.R.	2115	1110	HEAD	CHIEF PROD SPEC SECTION	M	400508	1110	1120				24000
29414	ARTHUR, P.J.	2115	1120	EMPL	MECH ENGR	M	300109	1120					22000
37113	ARNETTE, L.J.	2115	1130	EMPL	ELEC ENGR	M	450729	1130					22000
:	:	:	:	:	:	:	:	:	:	:	:	:	:

Userschema for persons interested in skill and position analysis of employees only (LEVEL ='`EMPL`'):

EMPLOYEE	ORG	JOB CODE	TITLE	PRIMARY SKILL	SSK1	SECONDARY SKILLS SSK2	SSK3	SSK4
LYNN, K.R.	2000	5210	SECRETARY	5210	5520			
CALLAGAN, R.F.	2100	5210	SECRETARY	5210	5520	5220		
HARRIS, D.L.	2110	5210	SECRETARY	5210	5520			
SCARBOROUGH, J.B.	2111	1120	MECH ENGR	1120				
HENDERSON, R.G.	2111	1130	ELEC ENGR	1130				
GARBER, R.E.	2111	1130	ELEC ENGR	1330	1130			
COMPTON, D.R.	2111	1350	COST ESTIMATOR	1350	1351	1355	1130	
FRANCIS, G.C.	2112	1110	SYSTEMS ENGR	1110	1130			
FAULKNER, W.M.	2112	1120	MECH ENGR	1120	1130	1330		
FITINGER, G.J.	2112	1130	ELEC ENGR	1130	1355			
APGAR, A.J.	2112	1130	ELEC ENGR	1130	1330			
BLANK, L.F.	2112	1330	DRAFTSMAN	1330				
ARTHUR, P.J.	2115	1120	MECH ENGR	1120				
ARNETTE, L.J.	2115	1130	ELEC ENGR	1130				
:	:	:	:	:	:	:	:	:

Userschema for analysis of salary over characteristics of age, sex, level:

NAME	UNIT	LEVEL	SEX	BDATE	SALARY
PETERSON, N.M.	2000	HEAD	M	280607	56000
LYNN, K.R.	2000	EMPL	F	530121	12000
CARR, P.I.	2100	HEAD	M	350720	48000
CALLAGAN, R.F.	2100	EMPL	F	550606	10800
GUTTMAN, G.J.	2110	HEAD	M	301110	35000
HARRIS, D.L.	2110	EMPL	F	550517	8400
WALTERS, R.J.	2111	HEAD	M	260202	28000
SCARBOROUGH, J.B.	2111	EMPL	M	240914	21000
:	:	:	:	:	:

Figure 3-11. Example Userschemas on a Database Schema.

Each of the userschemas includes a subset of the data items (columns) from the database schema. Some have different item names so the correspondence (or mapping) to the schema would have to be explicitly defined. The first userschema also has a selection expression which specifies the records of interest.

3.5 HOW THE DBMS MODEL SATISFIES

Having briefly presented the conceptual DBMS model based on users served and functions performed, it is now useful to reflect back to see how the model satisfies the motivating forces and objectives of database management.

3.5.1 Satisfying the Motivators

The five factors motivating the database approach are summarized as follows, along with the capabilities for solution found in a DBMS.

MOTIVATING PROBLEM	DBMS CAPABILITIES WHICH PROVIDE SOLUTIONS
Inability to get answers to simple, ad hoc requests	• Query language and report writer if the data is already in the organizational database • Database definition (or revision) and creation functions if the data is not already in the system
High development costs	• High-level data languages and data management functions which can be used in building application systems • Full definition of database semantics
Low responsiveness to change	• Full definition of database semantics • Independence of data in programs from the database • Database revision function and database conversion routines
Low data integrity	• Full definition of database semantics and validation criteria • Data integrity control functions to protect existence, maintain quality, and regulate access to data
Inadequate database model of the real world	• Comprehensive data definition language for a broad class of data structures including the representation of rich structures, data relationships, and all relevant data characteristics

3.5.2 Reducing Application Development Effort

A DBMS can reduce development and maintenance effort, making people more productive while sometimes decreasing machine efficiency.

With the traditional approach to system development, a typical application program reads input data, performs some processing, and produces some output (see the top of Figure 3-12). The input usually involves some editing and validation before the data can be accepted for further processing. The output phase similarly involves editing and formatting of the results before printing or storage in a master file. In most cases, the input and output activity is not unique to the application program. The editing,

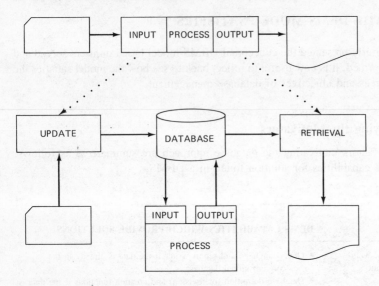

Figure 3-12. Reducing Application Development Effort.
With generalized update and retrieval facilities to replace the input and output phases of a conventional program, the remaining development effort can focus on the unique processing aspects of the application.

validating, and formatting operations can be generalized across many application programs.

A study done at a large national bank of the modeling and data analysis part of an MIS implementation found that the analytical process was labor intensive, slow, and error prone; and that 86 percent of the cost went into data gathering. Getting a handle on the data and making it available for processing in analytical models is a dominant cost of an MIS today. With comprehensive transaction processing and database update facilities, an organization can cut costs substantially.

Providing a generalized update tool which inputs data to the database and a generalized retrieval tool which produces output from the database frees the system developers to concentrate on the unique processing aspects of the application. In many application systems, after stripping the common "input, processing, and output," little unique processing remains in most of the programs. That is, with a DBMS, the application system could have been built by writing fewer special application programs. The same update and retrieval facilities can be used by all the application developers, resulting in more efficient use of personnel.

3.5.3 Meeting the Objectives of Database Management

The sharability objective is satisfied when the same system can be used by all types of users—programming and nonprogramming users alike—to access the same stored database. Sharability is enhanced when the DBMS has a userschema capability, permitting different users to have their own views of the database. Sharability is also realized when the DBMS permits multiple users to access the stored database concurrently. This is a function of the underlying database control system which must be able to handle requests from multiple concurrent users.

The availability objective is satisfied when a system provides languages (functional modules) for each type of user to access and manipulate the data in a variety of modes. This includes interactive, ad hoc query, report generation, and update. The database is more available if it is accessible with the user and the data online. The user should be able to access and process the database immediately or in deferred batch mode for greater machine efficiency. Ease of use with "user friendly" languages contributes to higher availability. A database is also more available if the users can have a logical view of the desired portion of the database and can use a high-level data language in which to express their requests. Diversity of users, data, languages, and modes of access all contribute to greater availability.

The integrity objective is never completely met but is increasingly satisfied when the system:

- Has a single controlling door of access to the database and all the underlying integrity control mechanisms are in the underlying database control system.
- Provides a backup and recovery mechanism.
- Includes a comprehensive data definition language which contains validation criteria.
- Ensures that the stored data always conforms to its definition.
- Provides comprehensive editing and validation checks on input data.
- Restricts access to the data to properly authorized individuals.

3.5.4 The Means to Evolvability

Several characteristics of a DBMS can contribute to evolvability:

- Generality.
- High-level data languages.
- Programming user facilities.
- Data independence and late binding.
- Database revision utilities.

These factors are complementary in their contribution to evolvability. A particular system may not provide any programming user facilities or database revision utilities. Within any given system, each factor may exist in varying degrees, making measurement difficult. Each of these factors is discussed briefly in the following sections, and some in greater detail in later chapters.

Achieving a high degree of evolvability is very costly in terms of development and machine operating efficiency. Future availability and present performance efficiency are, in large measure, directly conflicting goals. Performance is most efficient when all variability is assumed out in the system development process. The resulting programs are not inhibited by having to test for varying conditions; there is no interpretive processing of parameters; and there is no checking or conversion on data transfer within the system. Specialized program modules with built-in parameters can execute very efficiently. Such performance improvements are attained by sacrificing some measure of evolvability. In the long run, it will be most important to develop DBMSs that can evolve as people understand what they want and grow in the knowledge of the system.

3.5.4.1 Generality

Generality is the characteristic of something to be able to handle *variety*, to be applicable to a large number of cases, situations, inputs, or demands. Generality encompasses the notion of *completeness*, that is, the inclusion of all necessary functions within the system, or else the ability to achieve completeness through future changes and enhancements. Generality also encompasses the notion of *modularity*, that is, the unity or singleness of function within a submodule of the system. The term "generality" usually relates to computer programs or functional software modules but can also apply to the design of programming languages and data definition languages.

Several years ago McGee directed attention to the need for generality in an excellent and often referenced article: "Generalization: Key To Successful Electronic Data Processing."* He pointed to the success of generalized sort routines that would "sort *any* file, regardless of the data it contains. . . . All the programmer has to do is supply certain *parameters* which specify key elements in the sorting process." He further described his approach to providing generalized routines for file maintenance (update) and report generation.

McGee argues that most data processing applications are so complex that it is impossible to make a complete definition of system design on the first try. The design process requires experimentation and iteration. Generalization can reduce the cost and simplify experimenting with new systems and revising existing systems. It is easier to supply parameters than to rewrite the programs. Generalization can lead to better use of resources in the development of data processing operations common to many applications. Common, generalized routines can reduce the time to get a data processing application up and running.

Generality is the opposite of high specificity or tailoring in the design of a program or a data structure. In building a system, tailoring may be preferred when operating efficiency is an overriding consideration or the designers are not sure how to generalize a particular function.

The cost of generality is reduced operating efficiency. During execution, parameters must be interpreted. Inefficiency may be avoided by regenerating the object program whenever changes are made in any of the parameter values. At the 1971 ACM National Conference, Withington predicted that users might "cheerfully (accept) software overhead exceeding 90% as the price willingly paid for a degree of adaptability, flexibility and human orientation that would be incredible today."† This statement reflects increasing recognition within the industry of the importance of generality in

---

*William C. McGee, *Journal of the ACM* (6:1), 1959 January, pages 1-23.

†Alan Drattell, "Eniac to 2001: 'Economic Payoff' and 90% Overhead?" *Computerworld* (V:32), 1971 August, page 2.

software design. The developments in DBMS in the past decade have proven this statement to be true.

Goetz, vice president for proprietary software at Applied Data Research, made similar observations in assessing the reason for numerous failures in the proprietary software market. He noted that "several misjudgments combined to contribute to their downfall. . . . The products were not sufficiently generalized to service as many different clients as envisioned." He further noted that a computer program, to be a "viable proprietary software product" must be "developed to satisfy a variety of users" and "developed so that it could be enhanced."* He is calling for generality and evolvability.

Some authors use the acronym GDBMS to emphasize that they are referring to generalized DBMS. As used in this text, DBMS always assumes some measure of generality.

3.5.4.2 High-Level Data Languages

Along with generality, abstraction contributes to evolvability. Abstraction allows one to view the essentials of a structure or a process while suppressing the details of how it is performed or implemented. While high-level languages reduce the time required to design and implement databases and application processes, they also make it easier to change databases after they are created and used.

If a database can be established by simply defining its logical structure, and letting the system choose appropriate physical storage representations, then it will be easier to later revise the logical database definition. This is because fewer statements are needed to define the database. If a programmer does not have to know the detailed physical structure of the database to write a program, the resulting program need not depend upon, and *can* be insulated from, changes to the physical database structure. A high-level language to manipulate the database requires fewer statements to specify a given process acting on the database, thereby simplifying program modifications. If it is easier to change programs acting on a database, an organization is more willing and economically able to respond to user requests for change.

By contrast, a low-level language, while allowing considerable flexibility and perhaps efficiency in initially defining a data structure or a data manipulation process, makes subsequent modification much more difficult and costly.

3.5.4.3 Programming User Facilities

Even if a DBMS consists of relatively generalized functions, evolvability will be inadequate without providing facilities with which to extend the capabilities of the system.

Programming users access the database through their own programs, rather than some system-supplied functional module. By writing programs in a language of their choosing and by accessing and manipulating the database at the level of items and

---

*Martin A. Goetz, "Proprietary Software is Risky but Predictable Area," *Computerworld* (VI:4), 1972 January, page 32.

groups rather than files, it becomes possible for the DBMS to be tailored and extended in a way that makes it more responsive.

With appropriate facilities, a programming user can develop:

SPECIAL PROCESSING	*Special-purpose* application programs with special processing requirements such as decision or simulation models, linear programming, statistical measures, or tax calculations using tables
MORE GENERAL	Functional packages to perform normal retrieval or update tasks in a *more general* way than provided in the system-supplied functions
MORE EFFICIENT	Functional programs to perform normal retrieval or update *more efficiently* by avoiding inefficient generalized methods
TAILORED FUNCTIONS	*Tailored* programs to perform the normal retrieval and update functions in differing user modes such as batch, online, conversational, and even to interface with a highly stylized terminal having a restricted set of function buttons
PRESCRIBED REQUESTS	Programs to efficiently handle *prescribed* requests or predefined update transactions which occur frequently

In short, if a task needs to be done differently than in the system-supplied functions, it should be possible to develop programs which interface with the same shared database.

Evolvability is further enhanced when the system offers facilities for a programming user who writes a *generalized* program—generalized in that the programmer does not know what part of the database is to be addressed. This information is given to the program during execution. This programming user is like a system programmer writing generalized programs to deal with potentially any portion of the database.

3.5.4.4 Data Independence and Late Binding

Independence is a system characteristic wherein a component can operate correctly in spite of or without dependence upon other components. It relates to the effects on one piece of the system caused by the behavior of or change to another part. Independence is closely related to modularity or a building-block approach to systems design. Independence is a characteristic of the thing itself.

Data independence is a characteristic of a DBMS and may be possessed in varying degrees. It is a *means to evolvability* and *not an objective per se*. Fundamentally, data independence refers to the separation of data from: programs, application processes, output reports, input transactions, users, management, and the DBMS itself! In addition, data independence refers to the separation of the logical definition from the physical representation of data—from addressing and accessing mechanisms, value representation, the storage media, and the physical data transport devices. Data independence promotes compatibility across storage devices, operating systems, different machines, and machines of different vendors.

When these various aspects of data management are relatively independent, evolvability is more readily achieved. A change in one part of the system does not always lead to a propagation of changes through other parts of the system. For example, adding a new data item type to a record type should not necessitate recompilation of any programs not using the new data item. Independence reduces the disruptive effects of change. Without data independence the process of coping with change can severely inhibit the growth of a system. With more and more of the limited supply of programmers performing maintenance functions, organizations are continually deferring new applications.

Binding is the process of testing two sets of information, such as a database schema and a userschema, for any differences or variability. The data as it resides in a data area of a user program must be related to the data as it resides in the database. The binding process examines the two definitions and sets up a correspondence which is assumed to hold true thereafter. The binding process makes something constant.

Independence is never completely attainable, for at some point all the pieces of a DBMS do work together and interface with the using environment. The important question is: *When* does binding occur? The earlier that binding occurs, the less tolerant the system will be to variability and change.

Early binding assumes certain information is constant when a program is written and compiled. The information may relate to the definition of data. Then when it is necessary to revise the definition, it will be necessary to modify and recompile the program. If many programs interface with the data to be revised, the change can be very expensive and time consuming.

3.5.4.5 Database Revision Utilities

Even with high degrees of generality and data independence, changes to an established database will occur, and some will be disruptive. When changes occur in the nature of the data, in user data requirements, or in patterns of usage, a DBMS should provide mechanisms for responding to those changes. The system may be able to tolerate some changes (such as the elimination of an index to a file) perhaps at a reduced efficiency level; other changes may require special utilities.

Database revision begins with a change in the definition of an established database. If a DBMS maintains an incomplete definition of a database and something is changed which was not previously defined to the system, there is no way the system can respond to the change. For example, if a length was originally stored as measured in *feet* but the system only knew the data item to be *numeric*, the system can do nothing when the organization desires to change the stored length to be measured in *meters*. The only alternative is for someone to go through every stored record instance converting values measured in feet to meters and to go through every program appropriately changing the code which uses the length measurement in calculations and recompiling the changed programs. In summary, a comprehensive data definition facility is a prerequisite to database revision and a main contributor to evolvability.

If only the physical storage structure of the database is changed (for example, moving the stored data within the storage device, changing the blocking factor, adding or deleting indexes, reordering the stored records, or changing the access method) leaving the logical data structure unchanged, the impact on user programs would be minimized if the DBMS has a high degree of physical data independence. The system could initiate physical database reorganization utilities in response to requested changes.

Revising an established database not only requires changing the database definition but may also require several additional steps: converting the stored data to conform to the revised definition, rewriting and recompiling user application programs, revising stored user views of the database (userschemas or "subschemas"), revising catalogued queries or report definitions, and finally communicating the database revisions to people in the organization through documentation and training. A directory of system components and their interrelationships (sometimes served by a "data dictionary" facility) can help an organization isolate the specific areas of impact of a proposed change.

A comprehensive revision capability, combining generality and data independence to tolerate change and revision utilities to effect change, can greatly contribute to the evolvability of application systems built around a DBMS.

3.5.5 Supportive Relationships among DBMS User Roles

Some users are end users of the data. Some users support other users by extending the facilities of the system. Figure 3-13 depicts the interrelationships among DBMS user roles. Within this framework, the database can be made available to and shared by a variety of users—people with various needs, operating in various modes, and utilizing various skills.

The programming users can interact with the system for themselves or for others. They can develop and store a procedure which can later be invoked by another type of user. That is the meaning of the box with a broken line on the lower half in Figure 3-13.

Programming users can build interactive procedures to support the casual users (although it may be difficult for the application programmer and more so for the DBMS language programmer). All three programming users can produce facilities for the parametric user. The DBMS language programmer may be able to prestore requests written in a general language (update or retrieval) for later use by a parametric user. If a program can be stored and later invoked, the programming users can expand facilities for the parametric user.

Prescribed request information can be prestored in tables for later interpretation by a generalized request processor, or it can be embodied in a stored program (written by a programming user) to process that request type. If no information is prestored, the general user must express a complete request (query, report format, update transaction, etc.) in a system-supplied language. In effect, the system processes a *single*, very general type of request. Prestoring *several* tailored requests requires that each be as-

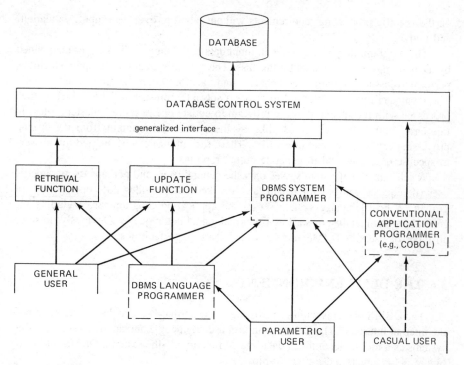

Figure 3-13. Supportive Relationships among DBMS Users.
   When not acting for themselves, a user may provide facilities or services for another type of user. The DBMS system programmer can support all other users. Only the system programmer can add generalized facilities for the general (nonprogramming) user. Any of the programming users can predefine a request for later use by a parametric user.

signed a unique identifier. Then the parametric user invokes a particular request by supplying its identifier and any required parameter values. The prestored information is like an incomplete or skeletal request which is completed by "filling in the blanks" at request time.

   The DBMS system programmer supports the general user by developing program modules to accept new or extended generalized language statements. Without facilities for the system programmer, the general user is restricted to modules already in the system. No mechanism within the using environment can create a more general, a more efficient, or a special-purpose module. The developer or vendor of the DBMS would have to specially build one.

   Providing facilities for the full spectrum of users has important consequences. Those wanting to deal simply and directly with the database can avoid programming. Those with complex processing requirements can concentrate on the programming task. When the DBMS provides generalized facilities for retrieval, report writing, update, file creation, and security and backup, the programming user can concentrate on the specific processing requirements without laboring over data input, validation, and output.

The programming user can obtain input data from ongoing files either maintained by the system or newly created for this task. The system's creation and update facilities perform necessary validation, edit checks, and transformations before storing the data. The input facility could be used to create a special "transaction" file which is then processed with the special-purpose program to update one or more "master" files. In this case, both files are treated alike by the system. The output from the special processing can generate additional files. These files in turn can be queried for answers to specific questions and to generate output reports.

A self-contained system serves only the general user, and perhaps the parametric user (if requests can be stored and later invoked). It provides little opportunity for growth. A host-language system serves the application programmer, excluding the general problem analyst or staff assistant making ad hoc requests. Obviously, to serve all types of users, a DBMS must have a full range of facilities.

3.6 THE DBMS ENVIRONMENT

The DBMS operates within an existing computer hardware and software system— the internal interface. The DBMS is in turn used by people and application processing systems as a tool to accomplish data-related functions—the external DBMS interface. Figure 3-14 depicts these relationships.

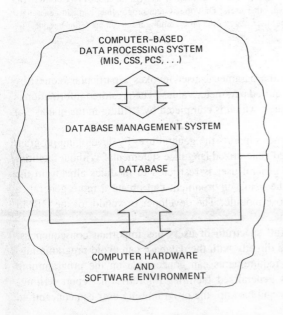

Figure 3-14. Database Management System Interfaces.

A DBMS operates within an existing computer hardware and software environment. In turn, a DBMS is a tool used in building and operating application systems, such as management information systems (MIS), customer support systems (CSS), or production control systems (PCS).

3.6.1 Internal Computer System Environment

From the viewpoint of the computer, the DBMS is generally treated like another "user" program to be managed. The DBMS interfaces with the computer operating system which manages system resources and supervises job execution. The major operating system functions of interest to a DBMS include scheduling and control of communication with the external environment, job scheduling and management, and the mechanics of data transfer with a secondary storage device.

All input to the computer system is first handled by hardware devices, such as terminal devices or card readers. The activity of these input devices is controlled by the communications control function of the operating system or sometimes a separate teleprocessing (TP) monitor. The input may be processed directly by the operating system, or it may be passed on to a program for processing. The input may go to a user application program, which in turn may call on the facilities of the DBMS, or the input may go directly to the DBMS. Figure 3-15 depicts three alternative relationships among the operating system, the DBMS, and the user program.

At the bottom of each diagram, the DBMS goes through the input-output control functions (or access methods) of the operating system to get to the data on secondary storage. The operating system controls the operation of the storage devices and handles the mechanics of data transfer. Beyond the low-level operations of channel control and data transfer, the data-handling functions could be performed by either the operating system or the DBMS. The placement of functions is a DBMS implementor's choice. Often the file system and access methods, both part of the operating system, do not do enough. At some point, the DBMS (or the user) must complete the data handling tasks:

- A file system offers access to records in a file in terms of a unique record identifier, and, in some cases, secondary keys. The DBMS usually must add the capability to access records based upon the values of data items in combination.
- A file system does not usually know (i.e., have defined to it) the contents of a record, except for one (or more) record identifiers ("keys"). The *whole* record is the smallest unit of data transfer within the system. With a full definition of records, the DBMS can access *portions* of a record for delivery to an application program.
- A file system generally provides backup, access control, and concurrency control at the file level, that is, on the basis of the file as a whole. With large files used interactively by several processes, it becomes necessary to break down the unit of control to the record level. The DBMS must maintain quality control over the stored data because a file system does not have a definition of the data items within a record.

In Figure 3-15(*a*) the DBMS is a subprogram to a user program and not under the direct control of the operating system. Each user program gets its own copy of the DBMS for its exclusive use, and, in turn, the DBMS gets exclusive use of the database to be processed by the user program. There is no capability for concurrent sharing of the same database because the multiple copies of the DBMS do not know about each other and their activities are not coordinated.

In Figure 3-15(*b*) there is only one copy of the DBMS for all user programs and the

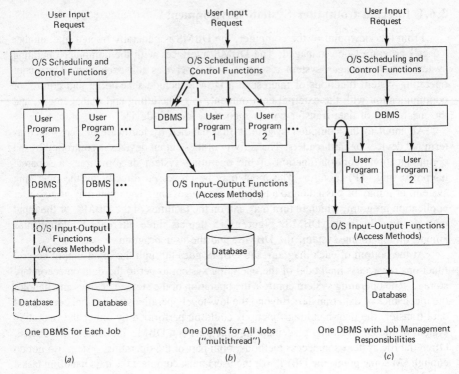

Figure 3-15. DBMS Relationships in the Computer System Environment.

Adapted from figures in Chapter 4, "Hardware and Software Support," CODASYL Systems Committee, *Selection and Acquisition of Data Base Management Systems*, New York: Association for Computing Machinery, 1976.

DBMS is under the control of the operating system. Data requests from user programs are transmitted via the operating system which handles interjob communication. The single DBMS coordinates concurrent data requests from multiple user programs. (Even with a single copy of the DBMS, some systems may still assign a database exclusively to a user program, thus avoiding the problem of handling concurrent requests to the same file.) Under this arrangement, the various functions of the DBMS can be separated and individually controlled by the operating system. In this way, parts of the DBMS can be assigned different priorities, for example, a higher priority to the DBMS module handling interactive requests from an online user.

In Figure 3-15(c) the user programs are executed under the control of the DBMS rather than the operating system. Under such an arrangement, the DBMS takes on the added burden of job management, duplicating the facilities already in the operating system for program scheduling and control, and communication.

Clearly, the arrangement in Figure 3-15(b) is preferred. The DBMS is always present to manage the database. All user requests, whether from a user program or directly from a user, come to the DBMS for processing. With a single copy, the DBMS can properly coordinate concurrent access to the database. The only problem is that the DBMS must still go through the operating system to gain access to the actual stored data. With increasing concern over data integrity, this loss of control over data access cannot be tolerated in the future. New computer system architectures must emerge to enable the DBMS to have complete control over the stored database.*

DBMSs should not include the functions related to job management, program management, or terminal management. A sketch of the relationship between database management, job management, and program management is given in Figure 3-16.

Job management deals with setting priorities, allocating computing resources, and scheduling the execution of jobs based upon received job requests.

Program management deals with maintaining a program library (which may include both source and object versions of programs), compiling programs (that is, converting source programs into executable object representations), and aiding in the process of editing and debugging programs.

Terminal management, performed by a teleprocessing monitor, deals with enabling and disabling terminals, polling terminals, sending messages to and receiving messages from terminals, and managing queues of terminal messages.

Many of the underlying activities of a DBMS must be coordinated with the job management system. For example, concurrency control relates to all resources, both computational and data resources, and deadlock can occur with a combination of data and nondata resources. The dividing line of responsibility between the DBMS and the job management system requires a much more careful study of operating systems. (Such a study is beyond the scope of this text.)

3.6.2 DBMS: A Tool in Building Application Systems

A DBMS provides a base on which to build a management information system, a production control system, a customer support system, or any application involving substantial data handling. It is a *tool* for managing data in any sort of application environment and making data available to the using environment. Breaking down a DBMS into its various functions reveals a collection of tools—tools for different types of users and tools for different kinds of applications.

Although a DBMS is used in building a management information system, it alone does not constitute an MIS.

- It does not include application decision models—but decision aids should be able to draw on the database in evaluating alternative courses of action.
- It does not include corporate simulation models—but a simulation model running in the computer should be able to access the database.
- It is not a forecasting model—but a forecasting model should be able to access the database which contains both objective and subjective data as an aid to forecast-

---

*The required architecture can be seen in Control Data Cyber machines with their peripheral processors, and the IBM 3081. All that remains is to take advantage of it in building the functions of database management.

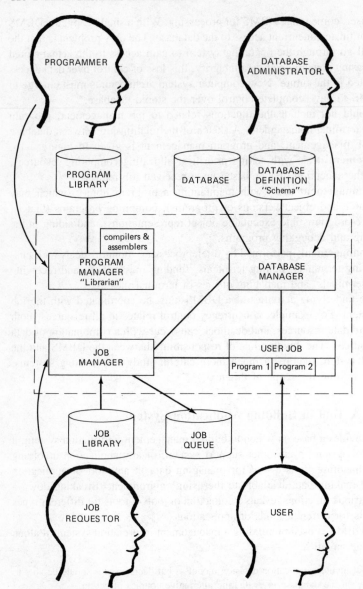

Figure 3-16. Database Management versus Job Management and Program Management.

A DBMS should not take on added tasks of job management, program management, or terminal management. A DBMS should be designed to coexist with separate modules performing these functions. The job manager receives requests to execute a job, schedules and supervises the execution of jobs, and stores the definition of frequent jobs. The program manager maintains a library of source and object programs and invokes appropriate compilers and assemblers. The terminal manager (teleprocessing monitor) handles all communication between the external environment of the computer system and the functional modules and user programs within the computer. It essentially lies over all the functions in this figure.

ing, and it should be possible later to compare forecasts to actual results and highlight the significant deviations.

- It does not include the management "military control center"—but selected data from the database should be available to such a center.
- It is not a reporting system—but it should provide the facility to define the content and format of reports and then generate those reports either periodically or on demand to reflect the data currently in the database.

While a DBMS is not an MIS, the model presented here reflects the realities of business organizations, management information systems, and decision making.

A DBMS is an application-independent tool. It is a general-purpose tool for managing data in any environment—to define, store, retrieve, update, and redefine data. Emery asks a question and provides an answer:

> How . . . can an information processing system be designed [before] the decision structure is specified? To answer this question I rely on an (unsupported) assumption about information processing systems: namely, that a properly designed system is largely neutral with respect to its specific inputs and outputs. That is, it should be able to accommodate any (reasonable) set of inputs and outputs specified by the decision structure. This assumption rests on the (again, unsupported) assertion that the cost of providing such generality will be small compared to its value.*

If Emery's stated assumptions are not substantially true, then many people have been wasting their time during the past two decades in the development of generalized database management systems. In fact, the widespread interest in and use of such systems today attests to the truth of his "unsupported" assumptions.

A DBMS by itself is like an empty box; it has form without content. There is no database, no defined update transactions, and no reports. After acquiring a DBMS, an organization first defines and creates a stored database, then defines the transactions to be processed and the reports to be produced, and develops programs to perform the special application processing for the users in the organization. A DBMS with these additions yields a database-oriented application system which can then serve the users in the organizational environment (see Figure 3-17).

The functional completeness of the DBMS determines how much additional work the user must do to build a database application system. With a DBMS providing a low level of capability (but probably a great deal of flexibility), the user must compensate by devoting more effort and resources to developing the application system. By analogy, a builder with sand, bricks, mortar, water, nails, and wood has considerable flexibility but expends much effort in building a house. With prefabricated rooms, walls, cabinets, etc., it takes much less effort to build a house. For that special room, you can still use the flexible, low-level building blocks.

Figure 3-18 gives an expanded picture of a database-oriented application system in operation. It highlights the information ("system data") needed to support the application system and guide the operation of the DBMS.

*James C. Emery, "The Design of an 'Ideal' Information System," Philadelphia: University of Pennsylvania, Wharton School, Management Science Center, Technical Paper #81166, 1966 August, pages 2-3.

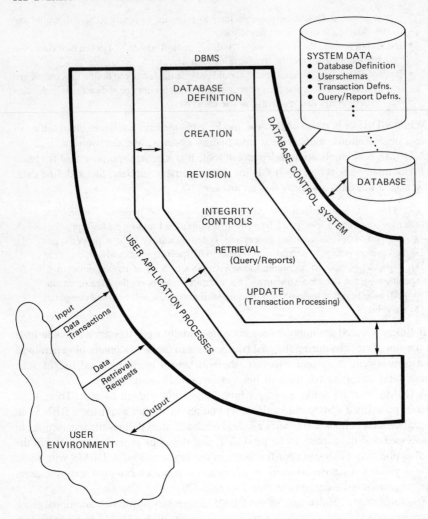

Figure 3-17. A Database Application System.

A DBMS is at the heart of a database-oriented application system. To a DBMS, add a database definition, populate the database with actual data, update transactions and output reports, and develop programs for the special application processing. Then the system is ready to serve users in the organization. The level of functional capability in the DBMS determines the amount of additional work an organization must do in building application systems. A comprehensive DBMS is the key to quick, evolutionary development of computer-based information systems.

System data:

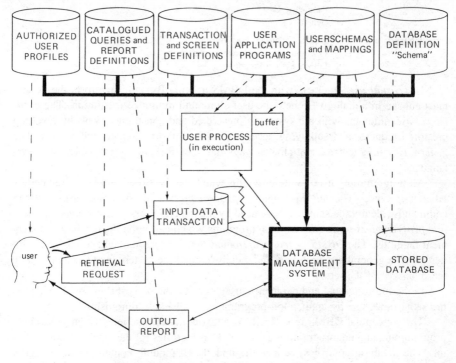

Figure 3-18. Components of a Database Application System.
   An organization supplies information ("system data") to a DBMS in building a database-oriented application system. The system data guides and directs the operation of the DBMS.

SUMMARY

This chapter presents a conceptual model of a DBMS which is functionally comprehensive and meets the four objectives of database management. The model focuses on users served and functions performed.

The concept of a user *role* permits a separation of the person from the activities and the skills needed. User roles have *direct* contact with the facilities of the DBMS. The database administrator role differs from a user role by acting as an agent for a community of users.

User roles are divided into nonprogramming and programming users—a distinction based upon whether or not the user writes a program in the DBMS command language or in a conventional programming language such as COBOL or FORTRAN. Generally, nonprogramming users would account for most system use. However, the programming user plays an important role. Once a DBMS is built, its ability to grow and evolve depends precisely on the ability of a programmer to enhance or modify its facilities.

Nonprogramming Users: Casual User
                         Parametric User
                         General User

Programming Users: DBMS Language Programmer
                         Conventional Application Programmer
                         DBMS System Programmer

The *casual user* interacts with the DBMS irregularly, and, therefore, the system must engage in a dialogue to help the user along and minimize frustration. The *parametric user* interacts with the system in prescribed and constrained ways by invoking prestored requests and supplying necessary parameters to complete the request. The *general user* interacts in unanticipated ways and, therefore, needs a flexible, high-level language.

All programming users write programs which can be stored and later executed by other user types. The *DBMS language programmer* builds programs using DBMS commands (ideally the same as those used by the general user). *Conventional application programmers* write conventional programs which call upon the database management facilities. The *DBMS system programmer* needs more generalized DBMS facilities to write generalized programs and thereby extend the system facilities available to the other types of users.

In the future, casual and parametric users may be the biggest users of DBMSs. At the same time, use by application programmers will likely diminish.

The conceptual DBMS model reflects a taxonomy of functions which serves both programming and nonprogramming users and has facilities for the database administrator. The database control system is the underlying module containing the integrity control and performance monitoring functions and which handles the internal data input and output to the database on secondary storage. The database is defined by a logically separate, stored schema.

A userschema is the formal definition of a user's view of the database. A DBMS architecture supporting userschemas allows multiple, different user views of the same database. It also insulates users and user programs from the complexity of a large database and from changes to the database.

The conceptual DBMS model meets the five motivators and four objectives presented in the previous chapter.

Internally, a DBMS interfaces with the computer hardware and operating system. The user input request enters the system through a hardware device which is under the control of the operating system. There are three alternative architectures for the relationship of the DBMS and user programs under the scheduling and control function of the operating system: the DBMS under the control of the user program, the DBMS and the user programs both equally under the control of the operating system, and the user programs under the direct control of the DBMS.

Externally, a DBMS interfaces with the application systems which use it as a tool for handling and managing data. It is an application-independent tool which can be used in building and operating any kind of application system, including a management information system. With a comprehensive DBMS, an organization defines and creates a database; defines update transactions, queries, and output reports; and develops programs for special application processing to produce a database application system. With high-level facilities, an application system can be built and made operational using less time and effort than with low-level (though flexible) building blocks.

EXERCISES

3-1. What is the importance of the "role" concept in describing DBMS users?

3-2. Olle began a 1968 ACM panel session by dividing nonprogramming users into "intelligent nonprogrammers" and "unintelligent nonprogrammers." How would the concept of a user *role* have helped him better distinguish the two types of nonprogramming users?

3-3. Differentiate between a "direct user" and an "end user."

3-4. Describe an "indirect user" of a DBMS. Find some examples from your own experience.

3-5. Differentiate between a "user role" and an "administrative role."

3-6. Differentiate between a "nonprogramming user" and a "programming user."

3-7. For each of the six user roles, briefly describe the facilities required of a DBMS. Make a table.

3-8. Explain the choice of name for the "parametric user."

3-9. In what sense are the parametric and general users at opposite ends of a spectrum?

3-10. Describe a DBMS application where parametric users would dominate. How would this application be a candidate for a dedicated DBMS as discussed in the previous chapter?

3-11. Explain the fundamental importance of providing a programming user interface for the database at a time when organizations should be trying to reduce the need for scarce and expensive programmers.

3-12. Differentiate between the conventional application programmer and the DBMS system programmer. Describe the differences you might observe between the programs written by each.

3-13. If a DBMS does not have suitable facilities for the DBMS system programmer, which of the other types of user is most seriously affected? What does this do to the evolvability of the DBMS?

3-14. Will the need for DBMS system programmer facilities increase or decrease in the future? Explain the circumstances under which the need would increase or decrease.

3-15. For each of the six user roles, describe the skill level required to use the DBMS and describe the nature of the interaction with the system (online or batch; immediate or deferred; one-way communication or a dialogue; regular or occasional, etc.).

3-16. Self-contained DBMS and host-language systems were each developed primarily for which type(s) of user?

3-17. Assuming direct DBMS use, what role would a middle manager most likely assume?

3-18. Who are the users of the future?

3-19. How do function, language, and module relate to each other in a computer system?

3-20. How do the DBMS functions presented in this chapter relate to the database management objectives of sharability, availability, evolvability, and integrity?

3-21. Contrast the nature of the DBMS interfaces with the programming user, the nonprogramming user, and the database administrator.

3-22. How would the overall conceptual DBMS model in Figure 3-8 change to reflect a host-language DBMS? a self-contained DBMS?

3-23. What is the database control system? What is its role in a DBMS?

3-24. Why is the database control system so important? (Discuss this in terms of the objectives of database management.)

3-25. In what sense are operating systems an incompatible or even hostile host to a DBMS?

3-26. What is the importance of *logically* separating the definition of the database, the "schema," from the physical stored database?

3-27. What is the function and importance of the userschema?

3-28. Does the concept of a userschema always imply a programming user? Explain.

3-29. What is the cost of having a comprehensive userschema capability? What is the cost of not having it?

3-30. Why is it misleading to call a userschema a subschema? Look at the *essential* relationship between a userschema and the schema.

3-31. Have you written a (COBOL) program that uses a data file which is also used by other programs? If so, redefine the data division so that it best fits your programming needs. Feel free to rename data items, omit unused data items, perhaps even changing the intrarecord structure. Specify the relationships between both data divisions. The revised data division is analogous to a userschema.

3-32. What facilities in the conceptual DBMS model satisfies each of the motivators of the database approach?

3-33. How does a comprehensive DBMS meet the objectives of database management? How does it reduce application development effort?

3-34. List and explain each of the means to evolvability provided by a comprehensive DBMS.

3-35. Three types of users can provide supporting facilities for the parametric user. Rank these three alternatives according to two cost factors: human development effort and operational machine time.

3-36. Describe three alternative arrangements of the DBMS and the user programs under the scheduling and control function of the operating system. What are the advantages and disadvantages of each? Which alternative is preferred and why?

3-37. In the placement of functions between the operating system and the DBMS, the DBMS must take over where the operating system stops. What are some examples of limits in the file system of an operating system? Examine the functions of an operating system with which you are familiar.

3-38. Describe how a DBMS interacts with the other functions such as job management, program management, and terminal management within a computer system.

3-39. How is a DBMS used as a tool in building and operating an application system?

3-40. Describe the major components of a database application system and how they interact.

3-41. Why is a DBMS called an "application-independent tool"?

SELECTED REFERENCES

American National Standards Institute/X3, "The ANSI/X3/SPARC DBMS Framework: Report of the Management Systems," edited by D. Tsichritzis and A. Klug, *Information Systems* (3:3), 1978, pages 173-191.

> Presents a DBMS architecture with three data definitions: the *external schema* (corresponding to the userschema in this text); the *conceptual schema* (the logical definition of the database representing the objects in the organization); and the *internal schema* (definition of the stored database or the stored representation of the conceptual schema). The rationale for introducing the conceptual schema is to more explicitly recognize the independence of the logical data structure from its stored physical representation.

BACHMAN, Charles W., "Data Base Management: The Keystone of Applied Systems Architecture," in *Critical Factors in Data Management*, edited by Fred Gruenberger, Englewood Cliffs, NJ: Prentice-Hall, 1969, pages 33-40.

> Makes a good and complete distinction between data management functions and job management functions.

BERRISFORD, Thomas R. and James C. WETHERBE, "Heuristic Development: A Redesign of Systems Design," *MIS Quarterly* (3:1), 1979 March, pages 11-20.

> Recommends building information systems using a DBMS. The process can then iterate with the users with mockups of output reports from sample data *before* fully developing the data input and update mechanisms or fine-tuning the application programs.

CODASYL Systems Committee, *Selection and Acquisition of Data Base Management Systems*, New York: Association for Computing Machinery, 1976.

> See especially Chapter 3 on the functions of database management and Chapter 4 on the hardware and software support environment for a DBMS.

CODASYL Systems Committee, "Introduction to Feature Analysis of Generalized Data Base Management Systems," *Communications of the ACM* (14:5), 1971 May, pages 308-318.

CODASYL, "A Progress Report on the Activities of the CODASYL End User Facility Task Group," Henry C. Lefkovits, Chairman, *Management Datamatics* (5:5), 1976, pages 193-207 (also in *FDT* (8:1), 1976).

CODD, E. F., "Seven Steps to Rendezvous with the Casual User," in *Data Base Management*, edited by J. W. Klimbie and K. L. Koffeman, Amsterdam: North-Holland Publishing Co., 1974, pages 179-200.

CODD, E. F., "Recent Investigations in Relational Data Base Systems," in *Information Processing 74*, Proceedings of IFIP Congress, Stockholm, 1974 August, edited by Jack L. Rosenfeld, Amsterdam: North-Holland Publishing Co., (New York: American Elsevier), 1974, pages 1017-1021.

DALE, A. G., and E. I. LOWENTHAL, "End-User Interfaces for Data Base Management Systems," *The ANSI-SPARC DBMS Model*, Proceedings of the Second SHARE Working Conference on Data Base Management Systems, Montreal, 1976 April, Donald A. Jardine, ed., Amsterdam: North-Holland Publishing Co., 1977, pages 81-99.

LUCAS, Henry C., Jr., "The Evolution of an Information System: From Key-Man to Every Person," *Sloan Management Review* (19:2), 1978 Winter, pages 39-52.

> Presents a "creative, evolutionary" approach to developing information systems. An example illustrates the approach. It puts the user in charge of the design effort resulting in greater commitment to the system and better preparedness for using it. Users design their own input forms, transactions, output reports, and terminal screen formats. When users suggest a new application, the information services department quickly produces some kind of output—a simple model, dummy report, or simulated system—which can serve as a focal point for immediate discussion and user feedback. Evolutionary design provides continuous review and modifications as users react to outputs. Keys to getting a prototype system built quickly are online terminals and a comprehensive DBMS.

NIJSSEN, G. M., "A Gross Architecture for the Next Generation Database Management Systems," in *Modelling in Data Base Management Systems*, Proceedings IFIP Working Conference, Freudenstadt, 1976 January, edited by G. M. Nijssen, Amsterdam: North-Holland Publishing Co., 1976, (New York: American Elsevier), pages 1-24.

> Presents a general DBMS model in which different user views can coexist. A mapping defines the relationship between each user view and the overall database definition ("conceptual schema").

OLLE, T. William, Chairman, "The Large Data Base, Its Organization and User Interface: Transcription of a Panel Session held at the 1968 ACM National Conference, Las Vegas, Nevada," *Data Base* (1:3), 1969 fall, pages 5-17.

FOUR

LOGICAL DATA STRUCTURES

4.1	A TAXONOMY OF DATA STRUCTURES	120
4.1.1	Only What the System Knows	122
4.1.2	The Three ''Great'' Data Structures	122
4.2	SINGLE FLAT FILE DATA STRUCTURE	123
4.2.1	Homogeneous Flat File	126
4.2.2	Composite Flat File	126
4.3	SINGLE HIERARCHICAL DATA STRUCTURE	129
4.3.1	Single-Path Hierarchical Structure	130
4.3.2	Multipath (''Branching'') Hierarchical Structure	132
4.4	MULTIFILE DATA STRUCTURE	133
4.4.1	Multiple, Unrelated Files	135
4.4.2	Multiple, Coordinated Files	135
4.4.3	Multiple, Related Files	135
4.4.4	The CODASYL Database Structure and the Relational Data Model	138
4.5	OBJECT-RELATION DATA STRUCTURE	143
4.5.1	Binary Relational Data Structure	145
4.5.2	Irreducible N'ary Relational Data Structure	147
	SUMMARY	149
	EXERCISES	149
	SELECTED REFERENCES	151
	APPENDIX 4A: Sample Personnel-Organizational Database	153

The previous chapter established a classification of DBMSs based upon functions broadly grouped by user type. This chapter examines and classifies DBMSs based upon the class of data structures which can be defined in and processed by the DBMS. The next chapter classifies DBMSs based upon their user interface and language.

In any evaluation of DBMS it is necessary to consider *both* the types of data structures definable in the system *and* the languages or methods provided for processing those structures. A very rich data structuring capability is useless without comprehensive, high-level languages and facilities for processing and manipulating the data. Conversely, the design of a data language depends partly upon the data structure—a more complex data structure class with several different data constructs requires more operations to be expressed in the language.

4.1 A TAXONOMY OF DATA STRUCTURES

In current DBMS literature, systems are most often classified according to the logical structure of the underlying data "model,"* that is, the class of data structures which can be defined in and processed by a given DBMS. A database is formally defined to a DBMS by writing statements in its Data Definition Language (DDL).

The following paragraphs introduce the taxonomy of data structures by naming and briefly describing various types of structures. At this point the reader should visualize the taxonomy as presented in Figure 4-1. This brief overview provides an initial understanding by placing the pieces of the taxonomy into a consistent, overall picture. Subsequent sections further describe each part of the taxonomy, thus providing a deeper understanding.

Let's start† with the proposition that a database is a collection of information about *entities* (people, organizations, positions, policies, orders, parts, projects, events, etc.). *Attributes* describe entities (e.g., age of person, budget of organization). A particular entity ("instance") is described by the *values* of a set of attributes. (Age of "John Doe" is 41). The database designer selects some set of attributes to describe entities in the database.

The first division in the taxonomy of data structures is based upon whether or not the attributes or data items are grouped into records. (Records represent entities). Historically, most data structures have been record-based. Most people in data processing are familiar with collections of data consisting of files of records. Assuming a grouping of data items at the outset of database design leads to some difficulties in the resulting structures, particularly when they expand to encompass more of the data in an organization. Recognizing these limitations, several authors [notably Abrial (1974); Senko (1976), Nijssen (1976 and 1977), and Kent (1979)] have proposed a class of

---

*The term "model" is widely used although it is somewhat misleading: The phrase "data structure class" is more accurate. Something is a "model" if it bears a likeness to or is an imitation of something else. A defined database is a data model of reality to the users; a DBMS is a data modeling system.

†This is not the only place to start a discussion of data structures. For another see: Tsichritzis and Lochovsky, 1982.

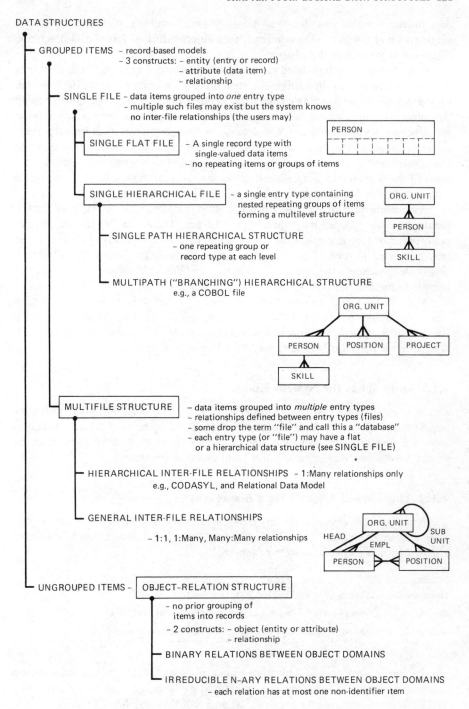

Figure 4-1. A Taxonomy of Data Structures.

data structures which omit the dual notion of entity-attribute, replacing it with the single notion of "object." These are called the **object-relation** class of data structures, explained at the end of this chapter.

Data structures with grouped items can first be divided into single-file structures and multifile structures. In a **single-file structure**, all information in the database can be grouped according to a single entry type. In other words, there is one primary entity connotation for the entire database. Single-file structures are further divided into flat file structures and hierarchical file structures. In a **single hierarchical file structure**, each primary entity may have subentities (that is, the primary record, corresponding to the primary entity, contains nested repeating groups of data items representing attributes of the subentities). Single hierarchical structures are further divided into single path and multipath ("branching") hierarchical file structures or data structures.

A **multifile data structure** consists of multiple, related files. All the data items in the database are grouped into multiple record types. There is no longer one primary entity or record type in the database. Entities may exist independently of each other and may be related to each other. Multifile data structures offer greater flexibility than single-file structures, therefore, enabling greater fidelity in modeling the world of interest to the user(s).

Multifile data structures are further divided into those which only permit a hierarchical relationship between entity types and those which permit a general relationship between entity types. (Multifile data structures are also further divided depending on whether each file must be flat or may be a hierarchical structure.)

4.1.1 Only What the System Knows

In all cases, what can be formally defined in a DDL to a DBMS determines the data structure class. The data structure class is based upon what the *system* knows about the data structure. Generally, the users will know more, *much more*, than the system knows about the meaning of a particular data structure.

4.1.2 The Three "Great" Data Structures

It has become popular to classify DBMSs into three groups based upon the underlying data structure class [Date, 1981; Ulman, 1980]. The understanding of each type is based upon a particular system or proposal:

Hierarchical	IMS from IBM, or SYSTEM 2000 from Intel.
Network	CODASYL DBTG Proposal now embodied in a DDL and DML.
Relational	based on the work of E. F. Codd, now embodied in SQL from IBM.

Language is associated with these examples of each data structure class. It is a common mistake to evaluate the data structure by the language available for processing that structure. Comparing the low-level languages of IMS and the CODASYL DML to the high-level languages defined on the relational data model incorrectly creates a biased judgement of the underlying data structure.

These three classes do not constitute a good taxonomy. While the userschema (or "subschema") for the programming user of IMS is a hierarchical data structure, the overall underlying data structure can be a restricted form of network. To the nonprogramming user of SYSTEM 2000, a database has a hierarchical structure, but to the programming user, the database may be multiple, linked, multipath hierarchical data structures.

Comparing the popular, three-way taxonomy of data structures with Figure 4-1 reveals some important differences. The single flat file is missing, perhaps indicating that some consider it unimportant. However, it is the best place to begin understanding data structures and high-level data languages. Furthermore, several widely used systems process only single flat files (Data Analyzer, Easytrieve, Qwik Qwery, SPSS, and many systems on microcomputers). Both the network, exemplified by CODASYL, and Codd's relational data model are multifile structures restricted to hierarchical relationships between the files (record types or "relations"). They are different in their intrarecord structure—a CODASYL record may contain nested repeating groups ("data aggregates" defined with an OCCURS clause) while records in the relational data model must be flat (a "relation" contains only single-valued or "atomic" domains).

With this brief introduction to a taxonomy of data structures, the following sections define each basic data structure class beginning with the single flat file. Each data structure class is explained using a common example relating to personnel and organizational data.

4.2 SINGLE FLAT FILE DATA STRUCTURE

A **file** is a collection of data about a set of entities which possess some common characteristics. By possessing some common characteristics the entities constitute an entity class. Proper interpretation of the file centers on the *type of entity* it describes. In the example shown in Figure 4-2 the entity is an employee. In general, an entity can be any concrete or abstract object or event in the real world about which we want to collect and store data.

A flat file is conceptually a two-dimensional array. Referring to Figure 4-2, each column corresponds to an **attribute** of the class of entities, and each row corresponds to one particular entity in the class of entities, that is, an **entity instance** (or "occurrence"). An attribute is a named characteristic of entity class. The file describes an entity by the **values** of the attributes in its row. A single row of attribute values is called an **entry**, or "**record**" of the file. The definition of a single **entry type** defines *all* entries in the single file. An entry in the file describes an entity in the real world.

Five characteristics serve to define a file. Each characteristic relates to a particular term or concept.

EMPLOYEE

EMPNO	EMPNAME	UNIT	JOB CODE	LEVEL	TITLE	SEX	BIRTH DATE	PRIMARY SKILL	SSK1	SSK2	SSK3	SSK4	ACTUAL SALARY
45584	PETERSON, N.M.	2000	0110	HEAD	DIVISION MANAGER	M	280607	0110	6130	6625	6040		56000
32579	LYNN, K.R.	2000	5210	EMPL	SECRETARY	F	530121	5210	5520				12000
57060	CARR, P.I.	2100	1110	HEAD	MANAGER DEVELOPMENT DEPT	M	350720	1110	1130	1135	0130	1355	48000
15324	CALLAGAN, R.F.	2100	5210	EMPL	SECRETARY	F	550606	5210	5520	5220			10800
10261	GUTTMAN, G.J.	2110	1110	HEAD	MANAGER SYSTEMS GROUP	M	301110	1110	1130	1135			35000
72556	HARRIS, D.L.	2110	5210	EMPL	SECRETARY	F	550517	5210	5520		1135	0150	8400
24188	WALTERS, R.J.	2111	1110	HEAD	CHIEF PROPOSAL SECTION	M	260202	1110	1120				28000
21675	SCARBOROUGH, J.B.	2111	1120	EMPL	MECH ENGR	M	240914	1120					21000
18130	HENDERSON, R.G.	2111	1130	EMPL	ELEC ENGR	M	340121	1130					23000
91152	GARBER, R.E.	2111	1130	EMPL	ELEC ENGR	M	440707	1330	1130				16400
30793	COMPTON, D.R.	2111	1350	EMPL	COST ESTIMATOR	M	290328	1350	1351	1355	1130		16200
81599	FRIEDMAN, J.M.	2112	1110	HEAD	CHIEF DESIGN SECTION	M	360317	1110	1130				26000
21777	FRANCIS, G.C.	2112	1110	EMPL	SYSTEMS ENGR	M	321111	1110	1130				24000
24749	FAULKNER, W.M.	2112	1120	EMPL	MECH ENGR	M	400621	1120	1130	1330			24000
13581	FITINGER, G.J.	2112	1130	EMPL	ELEC ENGR	M	431216	1130	1355				22000
82802	APGAR, A.J.	2112	1130	EMPL	ELEC ENGR	M	500715	1130	1330				21000
63633	BLANK, L.F.	2112	1330	EMPL	DRAFTSMAN	F	491010	1330					16000
22959	BRIGGS, G.R.	2115	1110	HEAD	CHIEF PROD SPEC SECTION	M	400508	1110	1120				24000
29414	ARTHUR, P.J.	2115	1120	EMPL	MECH ENGR	M	300109	1120					22000
37113	ARNETTE, L.J.	2115	1130	EMPL	ELEC ENGR	M	450729	1130					22000
68840	GODDARD, D.H.	2120	1120	HEAD	MANAGER STDS ENGR GROUP	M	330119	1120	1135				29000
71160	GERRISH, C.S.	2120	5210	EMPL	SECRETARY	F	560331	5210					8000
35401	ANDERSON, R.E.	2122	1120	HEAD	CHIEF SYSTEM STDS SECTION	M	380228	1130	1135				23000
91589	TAUBER, J.S.	2122	1120	EMPL	MECH ENGR	M	451114	1120					19000
80823	STADERMAN, P.K.	2122	1130	EMPL	ELEC ENGR	M	430507	1130					19400
64937	SMITH, R.E.	2123	1120	HEAD	CHIEF COMPONENT STDS SECTION	M	401129	1120	1127				22000
82166	RHODES, J.H.	2123	1120	EMPL	MECH ENGR	M	490303	1120					19000
28654	RAYMOND, H.F.	2123	1130	EMPL	ELEC ENGR	M	341216	1130					20000
17848	HUGHES, J.W.	2123	1330	EMPL	DRAFTSMAN	F	350120	1330					17000
33144	QUINN, S.M.	2123	5520	EMPL	FILE CLERK	F	561115	5520					11000
48464	CHANDLER, W.R.	2130	1120	HEAD	MANAGER COMPONENT ENGR GROUP	M	351015	1120	1135				33000
44432	BERGMANN, R.I.	2130	5210	EMPL	SECRETARY	F	540718	5210					9000
68795	COOPER, J.C.	2131	1120	HEAD	CHIEF ENGR SECTION A	M	290309	1120	1124				24000
39464	BUSTER, A.B.	2131	1120	EMPL	MECH ENGR	M	380719	1120					22000
79935	BOLD, E.W.	2131	1120	EMPL	MECH ENGR	M	460416	1120					21000
62999	NORMAN, H.R.	2131	1330	EMPL	DRAFTSMAN	M	331101	1330					18000
90816	MCCARTHY, J.K.	2132	1130	HEAD	CHIEF ENGR SECTION B	M	431020	1130	1135				23000
36472	MASSARD, L.R.	2132	1130	EMPL	ELEC ENGR	M	201010	1130					21600
10295	SILCOTT, D.N.	2132	1130	EMPL	ELEC ENGR	M	330826	1130					19000
89876	SKINNER, I.P.	2132	1130	EMPL	ELEC ENGR	M	480419	1130					20000
47289	SCHRADER, F.G.	2133	1140	HEAD	CHIEF PROD ENGR SECTION	M	420909	1140	3125	1365			21000
12245	KENT, M.J.	2133	1150	EMPL	PROD ENGR	M	260125	1150	3340				19600
50498	LEGGETT, P.F.	2133	1150	EMPL	PROD ENGR	M	330517	1150	3125	1365			20000
57084	FINERMAN, A.B.	2133	1330	EMPL	DRAFTSMAN	M	500622	1330					17000
21475	FLETCHER, M.W.	2133	1365	EMPL	TOOL DESIGNER	M	320729	1365	3125	3340	7320		19000
26934	HAMMER, C.P.	2135	3125	HEAD	CHIEF MODEL SHOP SECTION	M	200613	3125	3340	3125	1365	3370	20000
15052	BOYD, W.V.	2135	1351	EMPL	MECH TECHN	M	420917	1351	3340	7320	3370		18000
21261	CURTIS, K.R.	2135	1355	EMPL	ELEC TECHN	M	360304	1355	3510	7320			17000
74090	GRAY, S.R.	2135	3125	EMPL	TOOL MAKER	M	230703	3125	3340	7320	1365	3370	19000
87354	DIETERICH, L.J.	2190	1190	CONS	CHIEF SCIENTIST	M	250423	1190	1130	1120	1110	1175	44000
87277	SONNENFELDT, W.R.	2300	0130	HEAD	MANAGER OPERATIONS DEPT	M	230501	0130	3340	7120			44000
61706	FRESCOTT, W.C.	2300	5210	EMPL	SECRETARY	F	540703	5210	5520				10000
61284	MAILLETT, J.R.	2310	0150	HEAD	MANAGER FACTORY OPNS GROUP	M	311126	0150	3340	3740			28000
75683	MELCHERT, F.F.	2310	5210	EMPL	SECRETARY	F	350813	5210	5520				10000
19357	PAYNE, W.F.	2311	3340	HEAD	CHIEF FAB SECTION A	M	330821	3340	3345				20000
32924	LEVITT, P.S.	2311	3340	EMPL	MACHINE OPR	M	440422	3340	3345	3360			16000
42055	LITTLE, E.F.	2311	3340	EMPL	MACHINE OPR	M	380302	3340	3360	3550			17000

Figure 4-2. Example of a Single Flat File.

The data in a single flat file describes a set of entities belonging to the same class. Each entity is described in terms of the values of the set of attributes listed across the top of the columns. (This flat file, extended with organizational data, is the basis for examples throughout this text.)

Source: Thanks to Richard G. Canning who prepared this sample database for the *Second Symposium on Computer-Centered Data Systems*, Santa Monica, Proceedings edited by C. Baum and L. Gorsuch; Santa Monica, CA: Systems Development Corporation, TM-2624 (NTIS: AD 625 417), 1965 December, pages 3-3 to 3-29.

CONCEPT	FILE CHARACTERISTIC
ENTITY:	EVERY FILE HAS A NAME. The name should reflect the class of entities described.
ATTRIBUTE:	A SET OF NAMED ATTRIBUTES DESCRIBES EACH ENTITY. Each column in the two-dimensional representation of a flat file corresponds to an attribute. The attributes are uniquely named within a file. The term *data item* is often used to denote the representation of an attribute in a defined file.
DOMAIN:	ASSOCIATED WITH EACH ATTRIBUTE IS A DOMAIN OF VALUES. In our example, all the values in a given column look alike; they are somewhat homogeneous. The domain for the attribute SEX includes the two values of "M" and "F". The domain of the attribute EMPNO appears to include any five digit number. In general, each domain contains the values of "UNKNOWN" and "IRRELEVANT". For example, TERMINATION DATE would be relevant only if JOB STATUS equaled "RETIRED" or "FIRED". All domains will have a collating sequence defined on the set of values. For some domains, the values will have arithmetic significance, such as with "SALARY".
VALUE:	EACH ENTITY HAS ASSIGNED TO IT ONE AND ONLY ONE VALUE FROM EACH ATTRIBUTE DOMAIN. Looking at the example, there is only one value for each row in each column.
IDENTIFICATION:	ALL ROWS ARE DISTINCT, THAT IS, EACH ENTITY IS UNIQUELY IDENTIFIED BY THE VALUE OF ONE OR MORE OF ITS ATTRIBUTES. COROLLARY: AN ENTITY INSTANCE IS NOT NAMED PER SE. Stated another way, no two rows or entries in the file will have exactly the same set of values. If, in the development of a file, this characteristic is violated, it means that an insufficient number of attributes have been defined to properly describe the entities. One result of this characteristic is that, in general, *any* attribute can be used to identify or select a subset of entities in the file. In some files the relative position of the entity in the file may be necessary for unique identification. This situation can arise when short-lived entities are continually being added to and deleted from the file on either a first-in-first-out basis (or a last-in-first-out), as with a stack of entities. In such cases, it can be argued that rank, or "time of arrival," is an attribute of each entity, and this information is encoded in the relative position of the entry within the file. The attribute is real whether or not it is stored as a data item in the file.

The important concepts and terminology relating to a single flat file are shown in the schematic of Figure 4-3.

Sometimes it is more convenient to represent only the *type* of data in a particular flat file without showing the actual data. A **schema** representation does this as shown in Figure 4-4. At a minimum, the schema for a flat file is essentially just a list of the attributes used to describe each entity in the file. This minimum schema can be augmented with additional information about the flat file such as a description of the type of values for each attribute, the size of each value, the value domain for each attribute either as a range declaration or an enumeration, and a description of the attribute. In general, schema information is any information about the file which can be stated in terms of all the entries in the file. It is the constant or invariant information factored out of each entry (or record). Such information then need only be stored once for the whole file—as the schema.

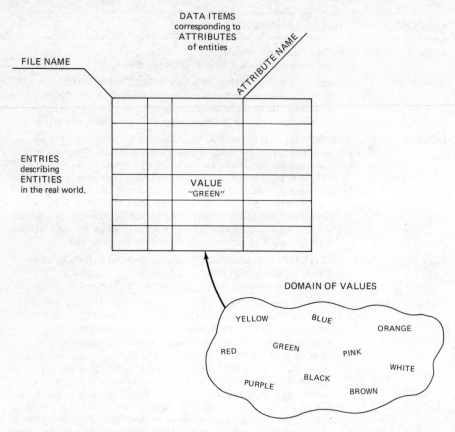

Figure 4-3. Important Data Concepts and Terminology.

With more complex data structures, a minimal schema representation focuses attention on the types of data and the relationships within the structure. This schema representation of a flat file helps describe more complex structures.

4.2.1 Homogeneous Flat File

A homogeneous flat file is a special case of the flat file in which every entry contains the same set of data items and each value appears in a fixed relative position in each entry instance. A homogeneous flat file is generally easier for a user to comprehend and easier for the system to process.

4.2.2 Composite Flat File

A composite flat file results when a user attempts to define a flat file to contain data pertaining to multiple types of entities. The main symptom of a composite flat file

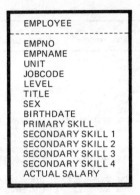

```
EMPLOYEE
---------------------------------
EMPNO
EMPNAME
UNIT
JOBCODE
LEVEL
TITLE
SEX
BIRTHDATE
PRIMARY SKILL
SECONDARY SKILL 1
SECONDARY SKILL 2
SECONDARY SKILL 3
SECONDARY SKILL 4
ACTUAL SALARY
```

```
EMPLOYEE
                         JOB                                    BIRTH  PRIMARY    SECONDARY SKILLS      ACTUAL
EMPNO   EMPNAME    UNIT   CODE  LEVEL  TITLE         SEX  DATE   SKILL  SSK1  SSK2  SSK3  SSK4  SALARY
```

Figure 4-4. Two Representations of a Flat File Schema.
The schema, or definition, of a single flat file is essentially a list of the attributes used to describe each entity instance in the class of entities. In other words, the schema is a list of data items contained in each entry, or "record," in the file. The schema can also include additional information which is common across all entries in the file, such as item value type and size.

is the existence of many IRRELEVANT item values in the entries. An example is shown in Figure 4-5 wherein an entry schema contains both organizational and personnel data.

In alternative 1, the EMPNO data item is used to indicate whether the entry describes an employee or an organizational unit. For an organizational unit entry, EMPNO would be set to a special value (say, 00000) which could not be a valid employee number. The first data item, UNITNO, is relevant for all entry instances; the next three items are relevant only for organizational entities (EMPNO = 00000); the remaining items are relevant only for person entities (EMPNO > 00000). Such a composite file can result in substantial wasted space. (A variation of alternative 1 is to define another data item to contain the values 'ORG' or 'EMP', indicating the type of data record.)

Rather than associate each entry with one specific entity type, each entry could describe a person along with the data pertaining to the organization in which that person works. This results in redundant data since the same organizational data is repeated for each person working in the same organizational unit. This can also present some problems on retrieval. For example, it is no longer possible to sum the BUDGET data item to obtain the total budget for the organization. One alternative is to store the budget data only with the HEAD person of each organizational unit, as shown in alternative 2 of Figure 4-5. Note that the schema representation of these two variants is the same, indicating that additional information is necessary to properly define the semantics of the flat file data structure.

128 EVEREST: DATABASE MANAGEMENT

Schema:

UNITNO	ORGNAME	PARENT UNIT	BUDGET	EMPNO	EMPNAME	JOB CODE	LEVEL	TITLE	SEX	BIRTH DAT...

Instances (Alternative 1):

2000	REPRESENTATIVE DIV	1000	391000	00000						
2000				45584	PETERSON, N.M.	0110	HEAD	DIVISION MANAGER	M	280...
2000				32579	LYNN, K.R.	5210	EMPL	SECRETARY	F	530...
2100	DEVELOPMENT DEPT	2000	323000	00000						
2100				57060	CARR, P.I.	1110	HEAD	MANAGER DEVELOPMENT DEPT	M	350...
2100				15324	CALLAGAN, R.F.	5210	EMPL	SECRETARY	F	550...
2110	SYSTEMS GROUP	2100	264000	00000						
2110				10261	GUTTMAN, G.J.	1110	HEAD	MANAGER SYSTEMS GROUP	M	301...
2110				72556	HARRIS, D.L.	5210	EMPL	SECRETARY	F	550...
2111	PROPOSAL SECTION	2110	87000	00000						
2111				24188	WALTERS, R.J.	1110	HEAD	CHIEF PROPOSAL SECTION	M	260...
2111				21675	SCARBOROUGH, J.B.	1120	EMPL	MECH ENGR	M	240...
2111				18130	HENDERSON, R.G.	1130	EMPL	ELEC ENGR	M	340...
2111				91152	GARBER, R.E.	1130	EMPL	ELEC ENGR	M	440...
2111				30793	COMPTON, D.R.	1350	EMPL	COST ESTIMATOR	M	290...
2112	DESIGN SECTION	2110	132000	00000						
2112				81599	FRIEDMAN, J.M.	1110	HEAD	CHIEF DESIGN SECTION	M	360...
2112				21777	FRANCIS, G.C.	1110	EMPL	SYSTEMS ENGR	M	321...
:	:	:	:	:	:	:	:	:	:	:

Instances (Alternative 2):

2000	REPRESENTATIVE DIV	1000	391000	45584	PETERSON, N.M.	0110	HEAD	DIVISION MANAGER	M	280...
2000				32579	LYNN, K.R.	5210	EMPL	SECRETARY	F	530...
2100	DEVELOPMENT DEPT	2000	323000	57060	CARR, P.I.	1110	HEAD	MANAGER DEVELOPMENT DEPT	M	350...
2100				15324	CALLAGAN, R.F.	5210	EMPL	SECRETARY	F	550...
2110	SYSTEMS GROUP	2100	264000	10261	GUTTMAN, G.J.	1110	HEAD	MANAGER SYSTEMS GROUP	M	301...
2110				72556	HARRIS, D.L.	5210	EMPL	SECRETARY	F	550...
2111	PROPOSAL SECTION	2110	87000	24188	WALTERS, R.J.	1110	HEAD	CHIEF PROPOSAL SECTION	M	260...
2111				21675	SCARBOROUGH, J.B.	1120	EMPL	MECH ENGR	M	240...
2111				18130	HENDERSON, R.G.	1130	EMPL	ELEC ENGR	M	340...
2111				91152	GARBER, R.E.	1130	EMPL	ELEC ENGR	M	440...
2111				30793	COMPTON, D.R.	1350	EMPL	COST ESTIMATOR	M	290...
2112	DESIGN SECTION	2110	132000	81599	FRIEDMAN, J.M.	1110	HEAD	CHIEF DESIGN SECTION	M	360...
2112				21777	FRANCIS, G.C.	1110	EMPL	SYSTEMS ENGR	M	321...
:	:	:	:	:	:	:	:	:	:	:

Figure 4-5. A Composite Flat File.

Every file has a name which should reflect the entity so described. What would you call the entity described by the schema above? A composite entry is defined to contain data about both organizational units and employees. In alternative 1, the data item called EMPNO indicates which type of data is stored in the entry instance: a value of '00000' indicates organizational data making employee attributes irrelevant; a value greater than '00000' indicates employee data in which case the organizational data is irrelevant, except for the UNITNO showing where the employee works. Under alternative 2, the organizational data is stored in the same entry as the person who is the 'HEAD' of the organizational unit. In reality, a composite flat file attempts to contain information about multiple entity classes. To the system, however, it is still a single flat file—because the system does not know about the special meaning of EMPNO = '00000' or LEVEL = 'HEAD'.

One might think of another variant which is to set up a different entry format for each of the two types of entities, as shown in Figure 4-6. Actually, this representation is no longer a single flat file because it cannot be described with a single schema. The particular schema to be used in interpreting an entry depends upon the value in the RECORD TYPE data item. This alternative suggests either a hierarchical data structure or a general multifile data structure.

4.3 SINGLE HIERARCHICAL DATA STRUCTURE

The composite flat file illustrates how organizational data can be added to the personnel data while maintaining a flat file structure. Upon closer examination, the personnel file in Figure 4-2 is not really a flat file either. Each employee entry contains

Schema:

ORGANIZATIONAL UNIT					
RECORD TYPE	UNITNO	ORGNAME	PARENT UNIT	BUDGET	FILLER (if fixed length records)

EMPLOYEE											
RECORD TYPE	EMPNO	EMPNAME	JOB UNIT	CODE	LEVEL	TITLE	SEX	BIRTH DATE	PRIMARY SKILL	SECONDARY SKILLS SSK1 SSK2 SSK3	...

Instances:

```
ORG  2000   REPRESENTATIVE DIV  1000   391000
EMP  45584  PETERSON, N.M.      2000  0110  HEAD  DIVISION MANAGER           M  280607  0110  6130  6625  6040 ...
EMP  32579  LYNN, K.R.          2000  5210  EMPL  SECRETARY                  F  530121  5210  5520             ...
ORG  2100   DEVELOPMENT DEPT    2000   323000
EMP  57060  CARR, P.I.          2100  1110  HEAD  MANAGER DEVELOPMENT DEPT   M  350720  1110  1130  1135  0130 ...
EMP  15324  CALLAGAN, R.F.      2100  5210  EMPL  SECRETARY                  F  550606  5210  6520  5220       ...
ORG  2110   SYSTEMS GROUP       2100   264000
EMP  10261  GUTTMAN, G.J.       2110  1110  HEAD  MANAGER SYSTEMS GROUP      M  301110  1110  1130  1135  0150 ...
EMP  72556  HARRIS, D.L.        2110  5210  EMPL  SECRETARY                  F  550517  5210  5520             ...
ORG  2111   PROPOSAL SECTION    2110   87000
EMP  24188  WALTERS, R.J.       2111  1110  HEAD  CHIEF PROPOSAL SECTION     M  260202  1110  1120             ...
EMP  21675  SCARBOROUGH, J.B.   2111  1120  EMPL  MECH ENGR                  M  240914  1120                   ...
EMP  18130  HENDERSON, R.G.     2111  1130  EMPL  ELEC ENGR                  M  340121  1130                   ...
EMP  91152  GARBER, R.E.        2111  1130  EMPL  ELEC ENGR                  M  440707  1330  1130             ...
EMP  30793  COMPTON, D.R.       2111  1350  EMPL  COST ESTIMATOR             M  290328  1350  1351  1355  1130 ...
ORG  2112   DESIGN SECTION      2110   132000
EMP  81599  FRIEDMAN, J.M.      2112  1110  HEAD  CHIEF DESIGN SECTION       M  360317  1110  1130             ...
EMP  21777  FRANCIS, G.C.       2112  1110  EMPL  SYSTEMS ENGR               M  321111  1110  1130             ...
 :     :        :                :     :     :        :                      :    :      :      :     :     :
```

Figure 4-6. A Single Flat File with Two Entry Types.
With multiple entry types, the entries in a file are not described using a single entry schema. While the system may treat this as a single flat file (by ignoring the contents of an entry), it is no longer a single flat file. Such a structural representation gives rise to either a hierarchical structure or a multifile structure.

multiple skills—one primary and up to four secondary skills. By naming each instance of secondary skill differently, this file *appears to the system* as a single flat file. Not knowing that the four (or five) data items all record the skills of an employee, the system must treat them independently of each other.

The user, knowing more about the stored data than the system, must retrieve, process, and update the file properly. Consider trying to select those employees who possess the skill of electrical engineer. The user must direct the system to look at each of the five skill items independently. Consider adding a new skill to an employee's record. The user must first see which of the data items already contain a skill code and put the new skill code in an unused skill item.

4.3.1 Single-Path Hierarchical Structure

The limitations of the single flat file data structure become evident when trying to design a file to contain data that pertains not only to persons in an organization but also to organizational units and to skills. The basic problem is the need to represent more than one entity in the same data structure. First, the multiple entities are not described according to the same set of attributes. Secondly, there may be relationships between the various entities. In our example, multiple persons may work in an organizational unit, and a person may possess multiple skills. A *hierarchical data structure* is built up from such one-to-many relationships, or *hierarchical relationships*. These terms are defined more precisely after looking at a couple of examples.

Breaking out the three types of entities in our example yields the schema and instance representations of a hierarchical file as shown in Figure 4-7. The data can be stored in a single collection of records. Some call this a file, but it actually contains three types of records. (According to the five characteristics of a file, therefore, it would be *three files* where the three types of records are in a particular relationship to one another.) The hierarchical relationships can be represented implicitly in the sequence of the records. Each ORGANIZATIONAL UNIT record is followed by (logically, at least) all the EMPLOYEE records for those people working in that organizational unit, and each EMPLOYEE record is followed by a list of their SKILLS. It is implicit in a hierarchical structure that an employee must work in one and only one organizational unit (or we artificially make it so by creating redundant copies of employee records for additional units in which they work).

This example is a **single hierarchical file** since, at the top or entry level, the entire data structure has a single entity connotation—that of ORGANIZATIONAL UNIT. An entry in a single hierarchical file consists of one instance of the top record type (ORGANIZATIONAL UNIT), plus all its dependent (EMPLOYEE) records, plus all their dependent records (SKILLS), and so on. A single entry instance is outlined in Figure 4-7. In a single flat file, "entry" and "record" are used synonymously; in a hierarchical data structure, an entry instance may contain multiple record instances which may be from one or more record types. This makes a hierarchical structure much more difficult to manipulate and process than a flat file.

Furthermore, this example is a **single-path hierarchical file** because there is only

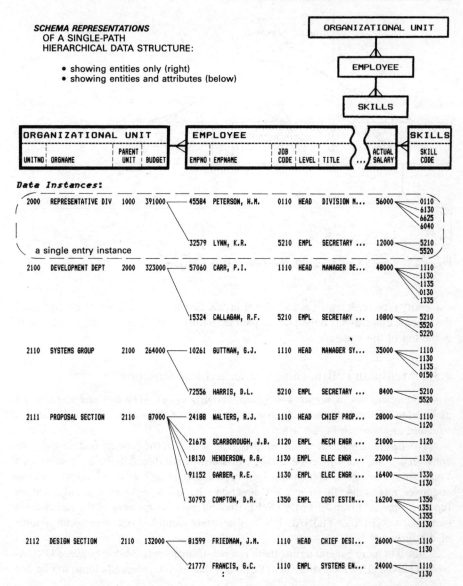

Figure 4-7. Example of a Single-Path Hierarchical Data Structure.

Two schema representations are shown at the top with some instances shown below. Notice the one-to-many parent-dependent relationships shown between ORGANIZATIONAL UNIT and EMPLOYEEs and between an EMPLOYEE and SKILLS. This is the central characteristic of hierarchical data structures and is represented by the "inverted arrows" between entity boxes in the schema representation.

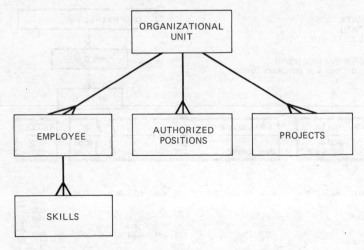

Figure 4-8. Schema for a Multipath Hierarchical Data Structure.

one entity type represented at each level in the data structure schema. Consequently, the schema diagram has only a single path extending down from the entry-level entity at the top of the structure.

4.3.2 Multipath ("Branching") Hierarchical Structure

Adding entities to Figure 4-7 for AUTHORIZED POSITIONS and PROJECTS assigned to an organizational unit creates a multipath or "branching" hierarchical data structure as shown in Figure 4-8.

The parent-dependent relationship is represented in the schema picture using an arc with a "fan," or "inverted arrow." In a downward direction the arc represents a "has" or "contains" relationship—an organizational unit *contains* employees; an employee *has* skills. In an upward direction, the arrow represents a single-valued function, that is, given an EMPLOYEE (the independent variable of the function), a particular ORGANIZATIONAL UNIT is uniquely identified (the dependent variable of the function).*

Stated in more general terms, there is a one-to-many relationship between ORGA-NIZATIONAL UNITS and EMPLOYEE such that each employee belongs to one and

---

*The "contains" or one-to-many relationship is the central idea behind the data structure diagrams described by Charles W. Bachman in "Data Structure Diagrams," *Data Base* (1:2) 1969 Summer, pages 4-10. Nijssen has discussed the relationship between Bachman's data structure diagrams and the notion of a single-valued function in "Data Structuring in the DDL and Relational Data Model," in *Data Base Management*, Proceedings of IFIP-TC2 Working Conference, Cargèse, Corsica, 1974 April 1-5, edited by J. W. Klimbie and K. L. Koffeman, Amsterdam: North-Holland Publishing Co., (New York: American Elsevier), 1974, pages 363-379, and "Two Major Flaws in the CODASYL DDL 1973 and Proposed Corrections," *Information Systems* (1:4), 1975, pages 115-132.

never more than one organizational unit. The arc fanning out is preferable to other notations because it *visually* depicts the one-to-many characteristic of the relationship, without implying the direction of a physical access path.

A **hierarchical relationship** is a one-to-many relationship between two entity classes or types called "parent" and "dependent," respectively, where every dependent entity instance must "belong to" exactly one parent entity instance.

A **hierarchical data structure** consists of a set of different entity types and a set of hierarchical relationships between those entity types combined to form a *tree* in the schema diagram (see Figure 4-8). A *tree* is a rooted, connected, acyclic graph of N nodes (entity types) and N-1 arcs (hierarchical relationships).

- *Rooted* means there is one entity type at the "top" of the tree structure (called the "root" or the entry-defining entity in the hierarchical structure).
- *Connected* means a logical path exists (via one or more arcs) from any given node to any other node in the tree structure.
- *Acyclic* means there is no different logical path back again. In other words, a unique path exists between any two nodes in the tree structure.

An entry (instance) in a hierarchical data structure consists of one instance of the entry-defining entity, plus all instances of dependent entities at all levels down the hierarchical structure.

In the hierarchical data structure, a dependent entity (record) is assumed to have no independent existence apart from its parent. For example, an EMPLOYEE could not exist in the file without being a dependent to some ORGANIZATIONAL UNIT (to ensure this condition is met, we can create a "dummy" organizational unit to provide a home for an employee not belonging to an existing organizational unit). Deleting an EMPLOYEE from the file is assumed to imply that all the SKILL records should also be deleted. Similarly, deleting the ORGANIZATIONAL UNIT associated with an EMPLOYEE would imply deleting all its dependent EMPLOYEES—not always a reasonable assumption. This points up an anomaly which can result from a hierarchical data structure.

Another difficulty arises if an employee can, in fact, work in more than one organizational unit—shoe department in the morning and sporting goods in the afternoon! Also, what if we wish to store more information for each skill code? Or wish to formally represent the fact that employees fill positions *and* work on particular projects?

One way of handling the difficulties of the hierarchical data structure is to let the user be responsible for properly interpreting and processing the data. A better solution is to define multiple, related files to the system—a multifile data structure.

4.4 MULTIFILE DATA STRUCTURE

To realize a true multifile data structure, a system must permit the formal definition of multiple files *and* interfile relationships (that is, multiple record types and relationships between record types). Without this capability, the user must utilize alternative design strategies. We shall first discuss the relative advantages of a single-file structure.

A single-file structure offers several advantages. Organized around a single entity class, *all* the entries can be unambiguously placed in a defined sequence. This permits:

1. using inexpensive serial storage media (punched cards, magnetic tape).
2. efficient batch processing against a sequential file.
3. using the file system facilities in most popular operating systems to create, access, and maintain the file.

This all adds up to a logical file structure which is easy for people to understand, and relatively easy and cost effective to implement.

For the main disadvantage, the single-file structure may not be able to adequately model the real world of the user. It becomes increasingly difficult to incorporate information for multiple entities into a single-file structure—the real world entities may not bear hierarchical relationships to one another so as to fit naturally into a hierarchical data structure.

At this point the designer has four options:

1. squeeze all the data into a single-file structure.
2. establish multiple, unrelated files.
3. establish multiple, coordinated files.
4. establish a multifile data structure.

Of course, the option chosen depends upon the available DBMS capability. For example, with only a single flat file capability, the fourth option is impossible, and the first option would mean squeezing all the data into a single record definition with no repeating data items or groups of items (defining a COBOL file without using an OCCURS clause).

Squeezing all data into a single hierarchical data structure may require any of the following:

- Forcing relationships to be hierarchical even though they're not in the real world.
- Creating artificial relationships or dummy entities.
- Encoding relationships in ways known to the users but not known to the system.
- Ignoring some natural relationships.

Consider the relationship between employees and projects. If an employee may work on multiple projects and a project uses multiple employees, there exists a many-to-many relationship. A hierarchical relationship with employees dependent upon projects can be forced in several ways. Employee records may be duplicated under each project on which they work. This presents problems when updating an employee record. The user must update each copy consistently. Also, gathering statistics on employees is now difficult. A count of employees in the organization does not correspond to the number of employee records in the hierarchical file. Alternatively, each employee record can be stored under only one project with a skeleton employee record stored under other projects on which the employee works. Each skeleton employee record would have to identify the project having the full employee record. Deleting the full employee record or moving it to another project gives the user some special update problems. (The system has insufficient information to handle such situations.)

4.4.1 Multiple, Unrelated Files

Storing multiple files with no explicit declaration of interfile relationships leaves the user responsible for any processing which involves more than one file. The user would first direct the system to process one file, then direct further processing on another file (perhaps the same file) using the results of the first process, and so on. For complex, interfile processing, this procedure could be slow and difficult. Each file would have to contain information the user could interpret (though not the system) to accomplish interfile processing.

4.4.2 Multiple, Coordinated Files

Some systems can process multiple files if they are ordered according to the same criteria. For example, if several files in an organization contained employee identification numbers, then each file can be sorted by employee ID, and a coordinated file system could read entries from each in parallel. By finding a match on employee ID across multiple entries from the parallel files, the system can logically create a composite entry for each employee identifier. In effect, the system can read entries from multiple coordinated files as though there was only one big file. This is the basic mode of operation of several database retrieval systems (Mark IV and ASI-ST which process hierarchical structures; Culprit, Data Analyzer, and Easytrieve which process flat files).

In our example, it would be possible to retain the EMPLOYEE flat file as shown in Figure 4-2 (which includes the employee skills), and construct a separate flat file to contain the organizational data, the top-level record in Figure 4-7. They could be processed as coordinated files by sorting each file on organizational unit number since that attribute is common to both files (see Figure 4-9). Of course, some convention must be established for handling the multiple employees per organizational unit. One alternative is to focus on the employee, adding on the organizational data as each employee record is processed. The other alternative is to focus on the organizational unit and add data for all employees when processing each organizational unit. Choosing the "primary file" depends upon the real world entity the requestor wished to process—employee or organizational unit.

4.4.3 Multiple, Related Files

In the multiple data structure, entities may have an independent existence; in other words, the entries of a file need no longer be considered "nested" or "interleaved" with or dependent upon the entries of a "parent" file. With the data definition lan-

Schema:

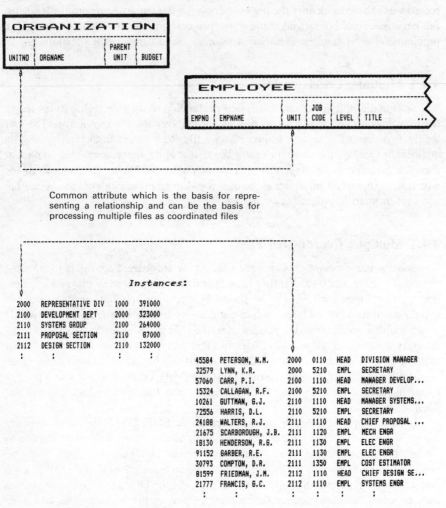

Figure 4-9. A Common Attribute Relates Two Files.

guage, interentity relationships are formally defined to the system. The system maintains them and can access data via the defined relationships.

Interentity relationships, explicitly defined to the system, are the hallmark of multifile data structures. Since a file loses its identity as a separate physical entity, some prefer to drop the term ''file'' and use ''database'' exclusively when speaking of data structures containing multiple, interrelated record types. As used here, ''database'' has a much broader interpretation, and ''file'' has a strictly logical meaning with no intended physical connotation. (Multifile structures have also been called ''network,'' ''plex,'' and ''relational'' structures.)

A relationship of one entity to another always imputes additional attributes of the related entities. If employees work in organizational units, then to database users, "unit number" is a meaningful attribute of an employee. UNIT NUMBER is a *secondary* or *indirect* attribute of EMPLOYEE. It is not an invariant attribute like sex or birthdate because the organizational unit number for a particular employee can vary depending upon where they work. The attribute is still real and meaningful, whether or not the database designer chooses to define the employee record to include a data item for the organizational unit number in which the employee works. Common attributes are the basis for representing *all* relationships between entities. Therefore, it is important to formally define such attributes as part of the relationship definition. If the system does not know the basis and criteria for a relationship, it cannot properly manage and validate the relationship.

A multifile data structure relaxes several limitations of a hierarchical data structure. In the multipath hierarchical data structure, a given entity must have exactly one parent entity (except for the root). In a general multifile structure this restriction no longer applies—a given entity may be related to zero, one, or multiple other entities. In a hierarchical data structure, it is unnecessary to name the hierarchical relationships since no ambiguity can result. In a general multifile structure, however, relationships must be uniquely named since multiple relationships can be defined between any two entity types. Figure 4-10 shows schemas with various interentity relationships.

Sometimes it is desirable to define a relationship where both the parent and dependent are the same entry type—called a "reflexive relationship." For example, an organization unit consists of several subunits. In fact, this relationship was captured in the ORGANIZATION UNIT entry of Figure 4-7 with the inclusion of the PARENT UNIT data item. Also, the same entry type may be the dependent in more than one relationship type with either one parent entry type or multiple parent entry types. The characteristic of multiple parents gives rise to the name "network" data structure.

Combining the primitive relationships shown in Figure 4-10 can build up complex data structures. Since an entry type can simultaneously be a dependent in one relationship and the parent in another relationship, it is possible to construct multilevel structures.

Some multifile systems have restrictions on the types of relationships which can be defined. For example, it is not uncommon to prohibit reflexive relationships or to require all relationships to be hierarchical. Some systems also restrict entry types to be defined as a flat file, that is, containing no nested repeating data items or groups of items (that is, not a hierarchical entry structure).

In addition to representing relationships, the arcs in the schema diagrams may also represent the defined avenues of access. In fact, in some multifile systems, these are the *only* avenues of access to some entry types. The relationship may define two basic avenues of access as direct (using some form of hashing algorithm) or via an instance of the parent entry type. Such access restrictions are *not* inherent aspects of the multifile data structure.

Some multifile data structures do not require stated criteria for the existence of the relationship between instances of entity types. For example, the relationship between ORGANIZATIONAL UNIT and EMPLOYEE would be defined, but the UNIT data item would be omitted from the EMPLOYEE entry—such information would be implicit in the defined relationship. *In this sense the relationship is more than merely an*

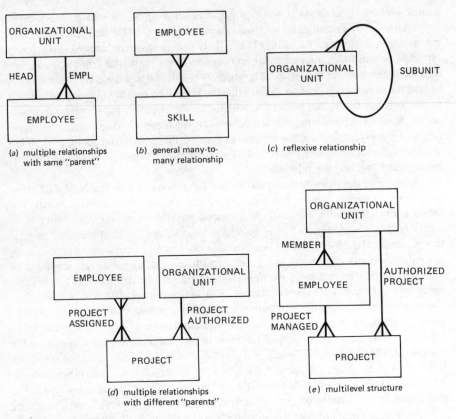

Figure 4-10. Sample Schemas of Multifile Data Structures.
Each schema diagram shows a structure which cannot be represented in a hierarchical data structure. In a multifile data structure, several relationships may be defined between multiple entity types. These simple structures can be combined to form a complex network of relationships among multiple files or entity types.

access path; it carries logical information which is essential to the data structure. Without a UNIT data item in the EMPLOYEE entry, some mechanism must be established (such as a chain, or a set of pointers) to connect the dependent entry instances with their parent entry instance. An explicitly stored UNIT data item would constitute the basis for a relationship without the separate declaration of a connection. The criteria for the relationship would be a match on the values of UNIT in EMPLOYEE entries and UNITNO in the ORGANIZATIONAL UNIT entry.

4.4.4 The CODASYL Database Structure and the Relational Data Model

Two approaches to database structures are singled out for discussion because they are frequently talked about, written about, debated, and compared. Moreover, much confusion surrounds their real similarities and differences.

CODASYL database development began in 1966 under the Data Base Task

Group. After the 1971 DBTG report, the COBOL Committee began to formally incorporate the Data Manipulation Language (DML) into the COBOL programming language. CODASYL also formed the Data Description Language (DDL) Committee to continue development of the Schema DDL independent of any particular host programming language. In 1975 CODASYL began to develop a DML for inclusion in FORTRAN. The *COBOL Journal of Development* includes a subschema definition language and a DML for COBOL; the *DDL Journal of Development* includes the latest language specifications for defining a CODASYL-type database.*

A CODASYL database is a multifile data structure. CODASYL does not use the term "file" in connection with the database facility (although single hierarchical files are still defined within COBOL). A CODASYL database is a collection of records of different types and interrecord relationships called "sets."

A CODASYL database has the following major characteristics (as in the 1978 Journals of Development):

- A record may have a multipath hierarchical structure (by including "data aggregate" defined using an OCCURS clause).
- A record *may* have one or more data items defined as an identifier.
- All interrecord relationships ("sets") are strictly one-to-many.
- Each defined relationship has one "owner" record type and one *or more* "member" record types.
- In a relationship, member record types can be defined as always having an owner ("automatic mandatory") or sometimes existing in the database without a parent ("manual" and/or "optional").
- A relationship may have the same record type as both owner and member (a reflexive relationship).
- Criteria for a relationship *may* be defined (using the "structural" clause), but it is not required to store and identify the common attributes which are the basis for a defined relationship.
- A defined relationship always establishes a "rapid" access path (although this is somewhat up to the implementor).

The **relational data model** as promulgated by Codd† and others is also a multifile data structure. First compare the terminology of the CODASYL and the relational approaches:

---

*CODASYL COBOL Committee, *1978 COBOL Journal of Development*, and CODASYL Data Description Language Committee, *1978 DDL Journal of Development*, both published by the Secretariat of the Canadian Government EDP Standards Committee and available from Materiel Data Management Branch, Department of Supply and Services, Hull, Quebec, Canada; see also T. William Olle, *The CODASYL Approach to Data Base Management*, New York: John Wiley & Sons, 1978, 287 pages, which describes earlier versions of the CODASYL data languages, and also provides insight, rationale, and evaluation of some of the design choices.

†E. F. Codd, "Normalized Database Structure: A Brief Tutorial," *Proceedings of 1971 ACM-SIG-FIDET Workshop "Data Description, Access, and Control,"* San Diego, 1971 November 11, edited by E. F. Codd and A. L. Dean, New York: Association for Computing Machinery, 1971, pages 1-17; E. F. Codd, "A Relational Model of Data for Large Shared Data Banks," *Communications of the ACM* (13:6), 1970 June, pages 377-387; and C. J. Date, *An Introduction to Database Systems*, third edition, Reading, MA: Addison-Wesley Publishing Co., 1981.

	CODASYL	RELATIONAL
File (Entry type):	Record Type	Relation
Entry Instance:	Record (Occurrence)	Tuple
Attribute:	(Elementary) Data Item	Attribute
Repeating group:	Data Aggregate	[not definable]
Attribute Value Set:	[no term]	Domain
Relationship:	Set	Implicit in Foreign Key

The relational data model excludes physical access path information. All relationships are implicit in explicitly defined attributes in the entry types. In our example, UNIT would be included in the EMPLOYEE entry type and that alone would constitute the relationship between employees and organizational units. Additional relationships can be derived in the relational model using the language facilities.

Whereas the CODASYL data structure is defined in terms of multiple record types (each constituting a file) *and* a set of separately defined relationships on those record types, the relational data structure is defined simply as a set of files (called "relations" or tables). The files are interrelated to the extent that they have attributes defined on common domains.

Moreover, the multiple files in a relational data structure must be *normalized flat files*. For every flat file, a key must be defined consisting of a minimum set of attributes needed to uniquely identify the entries of the file. To be in normalized form, every attribute in a flat file must be functionally dependent, on the key, the whole key, and nothing but the whole key.

Referring to our example in Figure 4-7, the hierarchical relationship between ORGANIZATIONAL UNIT and EMPLOYEE must be "flattened" by explicitly storing the UNIT data item in the EMPLOYEE entry. Although most presentations of relational data structures do not show the schema in a graphical form, it is still meaningful to do so with the arc representing the relationship based upon the common attribute.

Figure 4-11 shows the graphical representation of a possible CODASYL schema and a relational schema of part of the sample personnel-organizational database. Several observations on these two representations highlight some similarities and differences.

- The one-to-many relationship between ORGANIZATIONAL UNITs and EMPLOYEEs is represented in the CODASYL schema by a defined "set," and in the relational model by a "foreign key." A foreign key is an attribute in a record type which is an identifier ("key") in another record type. UNIT in the EMPLOYEE record is a foreign key. The CODASYL schema could also include UNIT number in the EMPLOYEE record. Doing so without defining the "set" would still record the relationship but not for the system—the user would have to use that information when processing the database. Doing both would be redundant but useful for simpler processing and greater data integrity. When the parent record identifier is not stored in the dependent record, the relationship defined as a "set"

CODASYL SCHEMA:

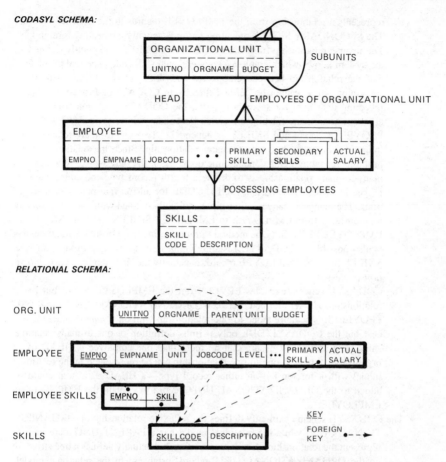

RELATIONAL SCHEMA:

Figure 4-11. CODASYL and Relational Schemas of the Sample Database.
    Both are multifile data structures in which one-to-many relationships can be defined between record types—with a "set" in CODASYL (depicted using an arc with a "fan" on one end), and a "foreign key" in the relational model. A *foreign key* is an attribute in one record type which is an identifier ("key") attribute in another. Neither can represent many-to-many relationships directly. Since the relational model is a collection of flat files, the EMPLOYEE record must be "flattened" by removing the repeating SECONDARY SKILLS data item, a process called "normalization." An additional "linking" record must be defined to capture what is actually a many-to-many relationship between EMPLOYEEs and SKILLs.

carries essential information—the arcs (normally implemented using physical pointers) cannot be removed from the CODASYL schema and a stored database without loss of information. A foreign key in the relational model is logically equivalent to a declared relationship ("set") in CODASYL. However, there is an implicit difference in terms of accessibility. In CODASYL the implied direction of access is from an ORGANIZATIONAL UNIT to its multiple EMPLOYEEs; whereas in the relational model, the implied direction of access is from an EMPLOYEE to his or her uniquely identified ORGANIZATIONAL UNIT.

• The EMPLOYEE record in CODASYL stores SECONDARY SKILLS in a repeating item ("data aggregate" or "vector"), but the system does not know that this represents a relationship from the EMPLOYEE records to the SKILLS records. The SECONDARY SKILLS repeating group is actually a repeating foreign key. The inverse relationship from SKILLS to EMPLOYEES is explicitly defined so the system knows which employees possess each skill code. The real problem is that the relationship between employees and skills is actually many-to-many, something which cannot be defined directly in CODASYL. Instead of using a repeating data item for secondary skills, the CODASYL schema could define another one-to-many relationship called "secondary skills possessed" with EMPLOYEE as parent and SKILLS as dependent. Two one-to-many relationships indirectly represent the many-to-many relationship. Since the relational model prohibits repeating items ("nonatomic domains"), the only way to represent the many-to-many relationship is to define a fourth record type containing the employee identifier EMPNO and SKILL CODE for all relevant pair-wise associations. The many-to-many relationship is indirectly defined with two one-to-many relationships, from EMPLOYEE to EMPLOYEE SKILLS and from SKILLS to EMPLOYEE SKILLS. (This method of representing many-to-many relationships is also possible in CODASYL.) Removing all nested repeating groups, such as SKILLS from the EMPLOYEE record, is actually the first step in the *normalization* process.

- The CODASYL schema excludes LEVEL from the EMPLOYEE record but has a relationship HEAD defined between ORGANIZATIONAL UNIT and EMPLOYEE. It is actually a one-to-one relationship with only *some* of the employees, but the CODASYL DDL only permits definition of one-to-many relationships. The users must ensure that no more than one employee is HEAD of an organizational unit. A one-to-one relationship can be represented in the relational model with a foreign key in either record type—a HEAD data item could be added to the ORGANIZATIONAL UNIT record to contain the EMPNO of an EMPLOYEE.
- The CODASYL schema explicitly defines the reflexive relationship on ORGANIZATIONAL UNIT, while the relational model has a PARENT UNIT data item to represent the relationship. A reflexive relationship actually defines a tree structure on the ORGANIZATIONAL UNIT record instances. In the relational model, PARENT UNIT points "up" the tree, while in the CODASYL schema, the SUBUNITS relationship implicitly points "down" the tree.
- Since JOBCODE is also from the domain of skill codes, the relational model recognizes another relationship between EMPLOYEES and SKILLS (the CODASYL schema also records this information, but it is known only to the users.)

Whereas the CODASYL structure employs the three basic constructs of attribute, entity, and (binary) hierarchical relationship, the relational model employs only the two basic constructs of attribute and relation. The relation construct includes both the entity and the relationship constructs. For this reason, some conclude that the relational data model is simpler than a CODASYL data structure. However, a normalized relational data structure can result in substantially more separate flat files which may make it more difficult for a user to comprehend the *overall* data structure. It is interesting to observe the lack of graphical representations in articles pertaining to the relational data model, yet diagrams can communicate more readily with most people.

The similarities and differences between a CODASYL database structure and the relational data model listed below are based strictly on their logical data structuring capabilities, ignoring any consideration of physical implementation, access paths, or languages used to process the structures.

CODASYL Database Structure versus Relational Data Model

SIMILARITIES:

- Both are multifile data structures.
- Both can define one-to-many relationships (using a "set" in CODASYL and a "foreign key" in the relationship model).
- In a defined relationship, both can declare a parent record to be mandatory or optional for each dependent record (in the relational model by declaring the existence of a value for the foreign key to be mandatory or optional).
- Neither can directly represent a many-to-many relationship. (It is possible in the relational data model if two nonidentifier domains in different relations are explicitly defined in the DDL to be from the same domain.)

MAJOR DIFFERENCE:

- All record types ("relations") in the relational model must be flat files (contain only "atomic domains"), whereas a CODASYL record type may have a multipath hierarchical structure (by defining "data aggregates" with the OCCURS clause).

MINOR DIFFERENCES:

- A record identifier ("key") *may* be defined in a CODASYL structure but *must* be defined in the relational model.
- The attributes which are the basis for a relationship *must* be stored in records in the relational model, whereas they are optional in a CODASYL schema (if stored, a STRUCTURAL CONSTRAINT clause is optional).

The reader must beware of making any value judgments based on the preceding differences. Under the minor differences, the "musts" for the relational model could be construed as undesirable restrictions when they may, in fact, be desirable. They actually represent *more* information which the definer can give the system about a data structure. By allowing greater flexibility to define complex, hierarchical, intrarecord structures, the CODASYL approach may make it more difficult for the user to comprehend a data structure. Furthermore, what good is a rich record structure if the system provides limited facilities for querying and processing the contents of a record? *A formally defined data structure is only as good as the high-level languages available for users to reference and process that structure.*

4.5 OBJECT-RELATION DATA STRUCTURE

The multifile data structure presents some real problems for designing, understanding, and revising the logical structure of a database. Ideally, database design should seek to capture all essential aspects of the real world being modeled without having to specify additional information which is spurious, unnecessary, or premature to the modeling process. The language for defining a data structure is a modeling tool. It should meet these criteria, and should not allow multiple ways of modeling the same phenomenon. The logical database definition language should make it easy to formulate, comprehend, and change database models of the real world.

It is sometimes difficult to distinguish between entities and attributes. In the EMPLOYEE file, the UNIT number is an attribute; in the ORGANIZATIONAL UNIT file, UNIT is the entity being described. For another example, in a file of new cars, color may be an attribute; to the manager of the paint department, color may be the entity of a file with various attributes describing the characteristics of each color: name, how to mix it, what pigments to use, reflectivity coefficient, etc.

Another problem facing the database designer is: how to group the data items into records which describe entities. There are often several possibilities. The choice depends partly on the selected entity types and the attributes to be recorded. It also depends upon how they are retrieved and processed.

The designation of an entry (or record) type depends upon a grouping of real world entities into entity classes and the identification of attributes which describe entities in the class. But the classification of entities is based upon their attributes. For example, the personnel file could be divided into two files—one for the heads of organizational units (LEVEL = HEAD) and one for employees (LEVEL = EMPL), consequently not storing the LEVEL attribute at all. (Presumably the user must know the difference between the two files and interrogate them correctly.) Now there is a one-to-one relationship between HEADs and ORGANIZATIONAL UNITs (which might tempt the designer to include them both in a single record type). All differences or commonalities between entities (of any type) stem from their attributes. Grouping attributes (data items) in records is primarily for the convenience of storing and retrieving data item values in the database; it is not essential to modeling the real world (even though some users may naturally think that way).

The solution is to *reject the notion of a file*, with its grouping of data items into records, representing attributes of a class of entities. Organizational units, persons, skills, and positions are entities but we can also consider dates, names, and dollars to be entities. The value set for any attribute constitutes the set of entity instances. Considering these all to be "objects," there is no need to distinguish between entities and attributes. The entity-attribute-relationship view can be simplified to an object-relation view of data structures.

Objects have attributes only as they *relate* to other objects. Rather than think of employees having a list of attributes, we can think of each relationship separately. If we consider each employee number EMPNO to represent an employee, then we can consider how EMPNO relates to employee NAME, to TITLE, to UNITNO, etc. We note that EMPNO relates to SKILLCODE in three different ways: as a primary skill, a secondary skill, and a job code. Each of these is a *binary relation*, the simplest possible association between two objects (or domains of values).

An object-relation data structure consists of a set of object domains and a set of relations on those domains. Each domain represents a class of objects, and each value is a symbolic identifier of a member of the class. The familiar two-dimensional representation of a flat file is replaced with a graphical representation in which each node corresponds to an object domain and each arc corresponds to a relation between two (or more) domains. A few authors have been strong advocates of this approach to data structures.*

In the formation of an object-relation data structure, each flat file is essentially "chopped up" into its separate columns or object domains. Then binary relations are defined between pairs of object domains. In this way it is often possible to represent more structural information than in the simple flat file, resulting in less ambiguity.

4.5.1 Binary Relational Data Structure

A binary relation is a two-way association defined on two object domains. It defines an attribute on each object. Referring to Figure 4-12, one object serves as a descriptor of the other via the binary relationship.

Instance Picture of a binary relation called JOBCODE:

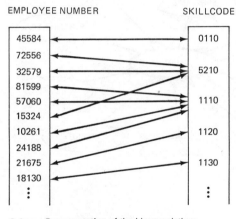

Figure 4-12. Representation of a Binary Relation.

In the instance picture, each valid JOBCODE association of an EMPLOYEE object with a SKILLCODE object is represented by an arc. Each object serves as a descriptor of the other via the binary association. Given the two object domains EMPLOYEE NUMBER and SKILLCODE, the binary relation can be viewed as "employee-number-of-jobcode" or "jobcode-of-employee-number." One JOBCODE attribute of EMPLOYEE NUMBER = 57060 is SKILLCODE = 1110; similarly, one JOBCODE attribute of SKILLCODE = 1110 is EMPLOYEE NUMBER = 57060. The nature of the relationship is written on the arc of the binary relation in the schema diagram. In this case, there is a one-to-many relationship between SKILLCODE and EMPLOYEE NUMBER. Note that EMPLOYEE NUMBER = 81599, 10261, and 24188 are also JOBCODE attributes of SKILLCODE = 1110.

Schema Representation of the binary relation:

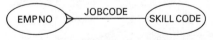

JOBCODE is an attribute of EMPLOYEE NUMBER and EMPLOYEE NUMBER is an attribute of JOBCODE.

---

*See in particular the work of Michael E. Senko, "Data Description Language in the Context of a Multilevel Structured Description: DIAM II with FORAL," in *Data Base Description*, Proceedings of IFIP-TC2 Working Conference, Belgium, 1975 January, edited by B. C. M. Douqué and G. M. Nijssen, Amsterdam: North-Holland Publishing Co., (New York: American Elsevier), 1975, pages 239-258; for a review of several approaches, see the first two papers in *Architecture and Models in Data Base Management Systems*, Proceedings of IFIP-TC2 Working Conference, Nice, France, 1977 January, edited by G. M. Nijssen, Amsterdam: North-Holland Publishing Co., (New York: Elsevier/North Holland, Inc.), 1977; William Kent, *Data and Reality*, Amsterdam: North-Holland Publishing Co., 1978; and William Kent, "Limitations of Record-Based Information Models," *ACM Transactions on Database Systems* (4:1), 1979 March, pages 107-131.

When defining a single binary relation between two object domains, the association names can often be dropped from the schema diagram. From the context of a given object, the name of another object connected via a binary relation can often identify the "attribute" relationship (though not in the case of JOBCODE). The schema representation of our full personnel-organizational data using this abbreviated notation is shown in Figure 4-13, along with a partial instance picture. The heavier ovals represent the

Schema representation:

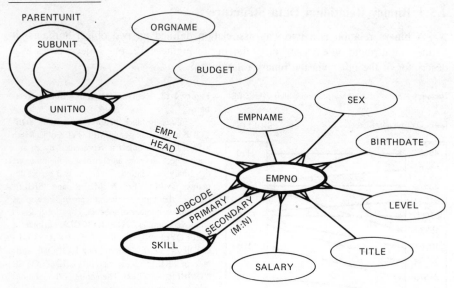

Partial instance picture: (a table for each object)

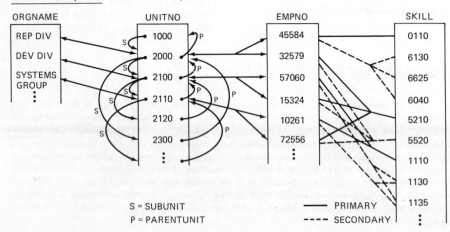

Dual Partial Instance Picture: (a table for each relation)

1 : 1

ORGNAME	UNITNO
REP. DIV	2000
DEV. DIV	2100
SYSTEMS GROUP	2110
PROPOSAL SEC	2111
DESIGN SEC	2112
⋮	⋮

1 : N

PARENT UNITNO	SUB UNITNO	IDENTIFIER
1000	2000	
2000	2100	
2000	2300	
2100	2110	
2110	2111	
2110	2112	
⋮	⋮	

1 : N

UNITNO	EMPNO
2000	45584
2000	32579
2100	57060
2100	15324
2110	10261
2110	72556
⋮	⋮

N : 1

EMPNO	PRIMARY SKILL
45584	0110
32579	5210
57060	1110
15324	5210
10261	1110
72556	5210
⋮	⋮

Adding a Skill Proficiency Rating
yields a ternary relationship:

M : N

EMPNO	SECONDARY SKILL
45584	6130
45584	6625
45584	6040
32579	5520
57060	1130
57060	1135
57060	0130
57060	1355
15324	5520
15324	5220
⋮	⋮

N : 1

EMPNO	SKILL	PROFICIENCY
45584	0110	8
45584	6130	5
45584	6625	3
45584	6040	6
32579	5210	9
32579	5520	9
57060	1110	7
57060	1130	2
⋮	⋮	⋮

Figure 4-13. Example of a Binary Relational Data Structure.
In the schema diagram, an oval represents each object domain and an arc represents each binary relation. A "fan" denotes a "many" side in a relationship. Relation names remove ambiguity when two object domains are related in more than one way. The first partial instance picture shows the values or symbols representing objects in each object domain. The arcs indicate all valid pairwise associations between two object domains. In practice, the arcs would require a data representation equivalent to the *expanded* dual instance picture. Where necessary, a role name is added to the object domain name. A broken underscore indicates the identifier in each binary relation. In a one-to-one relationship, one domain is an identifier; and in a many-to-many relationship, both domains jointly make up the identifier. Adding a skill proficiency rating requires a ternary relation. Such an irreducible n'ary relation has at most one object domain not in the identifier set.

entities identified in the grouped data structure classes discussed previously. The information represented in the arcs between object domains is easier to comprehend if it is shown in tables as in the dual partial instance picture of Figure 4-13 (a table for each relation rather than for each object).

The definition of an object-relation data structure contains the definition of object domains and relationships. An object domain definition characterizes the values or symbols used to identify objects in the domain. This can be done through a data item type declaration or an enumeration of possible values. Each value is a surrogate for the object in the real world. Surrogates often involve an abstraction and can come in various forms. For example, EMPNO represents person, DATE could be year-month-day or some alternate form including a julian date or just the year, SALARY dollars could be expressed monthly or annually, and SKILLCODE represents some package of skill and training that could be possessed by a person or required for a job. Rather than being defined directly, an object domain could be defined as the subset of another domain or as the union of other object domains.

A relation has a name reflecting the reason for the association of the object domains. For example, different relation names are necessary to distinguish the three relations between employee and skills: JOBCODE, PRIMARY SKILL, and SECONDARY SKILLS. Sometimes it is useful to have a different name for each direction of the association. Sometimes the name can be left implicit in the names of the two object domains. Besides identifying the object domains participating in the relation, it may be necessary to specify the *role* each object plays. For example, in the PARENT UNIT-SUBUNIT relation, both domains are the same—role names distinguish the columns from each other.

The definition should also indicate the *identifier* domains in the relation. An identifier domain is one in which all the values are unique. If one of the two domains is unique, the relationship is one-to-many; if both are unique, the relationship is one-to-one; if both domains together are needed to impart uniqueness to each pairwise association, the relationship is many-to-many.

4.5.2 Irreducible N'ary Relational Data Structure

Not all relations are binary relations. Object-relation data structures are divided into those that force all relations to be binary and those that permit irreducible n'ary relations. An n'ary relation is needed when more than two object domains are jointly associated. For example, to add a PROFICIENCY rating for each SKILL possessed by an EMPLOYEE would require a ternary relation on three object domains (see Figure 4-13). SKILLCODE and EMPNO would jointly make up the identifier. In effect, PROFICIENCY rating is an attribute of the relationship between SKILL and EMPLOYEE. An irreducible relation has at most one object domain not part of the identifier. Retaining irreducible n'ary relations is natural to the user but loses the simplicity of a data structure having all binary relations. An n'ary relation can be reduced to (n-1) binary relations. In our example, the binary relation between EMPLOYEE and SKILL would be artificially considered a new object domain, which could in turn be part of a binary relation with PROFICIENCY.

SUMMARY

DBMSs can be classified and understood in terms of their data structures.

The traditional taxonomy of data structures into hierarchical, network, and relational is inadequate. It excludes the popular single flat file and the object-relation data structures; and it puts into separate classes the network and relational structures which are both multifile structures.

The taxonomy of data structures depicted in Figure 4-1 first divides basic data structures into record-based structures and object-relation structures. Record-based structures divide into single-file and multifile structures.

The single-file structures are further divided into flat files and hierarchical structures. A single flat file consists of a set of attributes which describes entities from a single entity class. Each attribute in a flat file structure contains only one value instance for each entity instance. The hierarchical data structure extends the flat file by allowing multiple values for one attribute or a group of attributes to be associated with a single entity instance. In our example, several employees can work in an organizational unit and each employee can possess multiple secondary skills.

The multifile data structure consists of multiple, related files (or record types). Multiple coordinated files are so called because they possess a common attribute (or set of attributes) and can therefore be sorted and processed in parallel as though they constituted a single logical file. Multifile structures are divided into those allowing only hierarchical (that is, one-to-many) relationships to be defined between record types and those allowing more general relationships. Each file in a multifile structure may be a flat file or a hierarchical structure.

The CODASYL and relational data structures are both multifile structures permitting only hierarchical relationships. The only major difference is that the relational data model requires each file (''relation'') to be flat.

The object-relation data structure may consist of binary relations or irreducible n'ary relations. It is formed by explicitly and separately representing the relationship of each attribute with the entity identifier and any other attributes of other entities (files).

The critical factor in determining the data structure class of a DBMS is what the system knows about the structure, that is, what is formally declared to the system in the data definition language (DDL). Users will always know more. For example, in a single flat file system, there may actually be relationships between the records in two files. The system, however, cannot perform searching and processing which is based upon information it does not know.

EXERCISES

4-1. What determines the data structure class of a DBMS in the taxonomy of data structures?

4-2. Why is the term ''data structure class'' to be preferred over ''data model''?

4-3. What is unsatisfactory about the traditional three-way classification of data structures: hierarchical, network, and relational?

4-4. Define "file" as it is used in this text. (Refer back to Chapter 1 to augment your understanding derived from Chapter 4.)

4-5. What are the five characteristics of a single flat file? A flat file is conceptually a two-dimensional array. Relate each of the five characteristics to this conceptual representation.

4-6. What kind of data is typically in a "payroll" file? What is the type of entity being described in such a file? How does this conform to the first characteristic of a file, which says: The name of a file should reflect the class of entities described therein?

4-7. Explain how a flat file might have variable-length records.

4-8. Explain the difference between a homogeneous flat file and a composite flat file. Can the difference be explained in terms of their schema diagrams?

4-9. Carefully define a hierarchical relationship and a hierarchical data structure. Explain the difference between them.

4-10. Define precisely the distinction between a tree structure and a hierarchical data structure.

4-11. What is the major difference between a single-path hierarchical structure and a multipath hierarchical structure? Can the difference be explained in terms of their schema diagrams?

4-12. Given a DBMS which can define and process a hierarchical data structure, is it possible to define a single flat file structure? How?

4-13. If the reality to be modeled in a database contains multiple entry types and interrelationships between them, what options does the database designer have when using a single flat file DBMS? a single-file, multipath hierarchical DBMS? What difficulties will the user face when processing the database?

4-14. Explain why processing coordinated files is essentially the same as processing a single file.

4-15. Describe the basic differences between a multipath hierarchical data structure and a general multifile structure.

4-16. Use the actual organizational data in Figure 4A-3 of the chapter appendix to verify that the reflexive relationships, SUBUNITS, based on the REPORTS to data item, actually creates a tree structure on ORGANIZATIONAL UNIT record instance. Does a reflexive relationship always define a tree in the instance picture?

4-17. Can a DBMS that is designed to handle multifile data structures be used to define a hierarchical data structure? Consider two cases: where each of the files must be flat, and where they need not be flat.

4-18. Compare and contrast the CODASYL database structure and the Relational Data Model. What is the single major difference between them?

4-19. What is the similarity and difference between a CODASYL "set" and a "foreign key"?

4-20. Revise the graphical representation of the CODASYL schema in Figure 4-11 by making the following changes:
a. Remove the SECONDARY SKILLS repeating group from the EMPLOYEE record.
b. Make all four arcs (relationships defined with a "SET") redundant by storing any additional data items in the records.
How does the resulting CODASYL schema diagram compare to the relational schema diagram in the same figure?

4-21. What are the advantages and disadvantages involved in a binary data structure? Is this structure feasible given today's technology? What types of data storage structures make it more feasible?

4-22. Explain why an object-relation data structure is more stable (less disruptive) in response to changes in the logical data structure. Suggest difficult-to-implement changes to the multifile representation of the personnel-organizational database which would be easy to implement in the object-relation schema.

4-23. Suggest a graphical representation for the irreducible ternary relationship on EMPLOYEE NUMBER, SKILLCODE, and PROFICIENCY RATING as shown in Figure 4-13. What problems do you have? Try it with a 4'ary relationship by adding DATE ATTAINED.

SELECTED REFERENCES

ABRIAL, J. R., "Data Semantics," in *Database Management*, edited by J. W. Klimbie and K. L. Koffeman, Amsterdam: North Holland, 1974, pages 1-59.

BACHMAN, Charles W., "Data Structure Diagrams," *Data Base* (1:2), 1969 Summer, pages 4-10.

BILLER, Horst, and Erich J. NEUHOLD, "Semantics of Data Bases: The Semantics of Data Models," *Information Systems* (3:1), 1978, pages 11-30.

CHEN, Peter Pin-Shan, "The Entity-Relationship Model—Toward a Unified View of Data," *ACM Transactions on Database Systems* (1:1), 1976 March, pages 9-36.

CODASYL, *Data Base Task Group Report*, New York: Association for Computing Machinery, 1971 April.

CODASYL Development Committee, "An Information Algebra," *Communications of the ACM*, 1962 April, pages 190-204.

CODASYL Systems Committee, *Feature Analysis of Generalized Database Management Systems*, New York: Association for Computing Machinery, 1971 May, 520 pages.

CODD, E. F., "Relational Database: A Practical Foundation for Productivity," *Communications of the ACM* (25:2), 1982 February, pages 109-117.

CODD, E. F., "Extending the Database Relational Model to Capture More Meaning," *ACM Transactions on Database Systems* (4:4), 1979 December, pages 397-434; (also ACM-SIGMOD Conference Proceedings, 1979 May).

CODD, E. F., "Normalized Database Structure: A Brief Tutorial," *Proceedings of 1971 ACM-SIGFIDET Workshop "Data Description, Access, and Control,"* edited by E. F. Codd and A. L. Dean, New York: Association for Computing Machinery, 1971, pages 1-17.

CODD, E. F., "A Relational Model of Data for Large Shared Data Banks," *Communications of the ACM* (13:6), 1970 June, pages 377-387.

DATE, Chris J., *An Introduction to Database Systems*, Third Edition, Reading, MA: Addison-Wesley, 1983, 536 pages.

EVEREST, Gordon C., "Basic Data Structure Models Explained with a Common Example," *Proceedings Fifth Texas Conference on Computing Systems*, Austin, 1976 October, pages 39-46.

KENT, William, "Limitations of Record-Based Information Models," *ACM Transactions on Database Systems* (4:1), 1979 March, pages 107-131.

McGEE, William C., "The Property Classification Method of File Design and Processing," *Communications of the ACM*, 1962 August, pages 450-458.

NIJSSEN, G. M., "A Gross Architecture for the Next Generation Database Management Systems," in *Modelling in Data Base Management Systems*, proceedings IFIP Working Conference, edited by G. M. Nijssen, Amsterdam: North-Holland Publishing Co., 1976, (New York: American Elsevier), pages 1-24.

NIJSSEN, G. M., "Current Issues in Conceptual Schema," in *Architecture and Models in Data Base Management Systems*, edited by G. M. Nijssen, Amsterdam: North Holland Publishing, 1977, pages 31-65.

OLLE, T. William, "A Practitioner's View of Relational Data Base Theory," *FDT. Bulletin of ACM-SIGMOD* (7:3-5), 1975, pages 29-43.

RUSTIN, Randall, editor. *Data Models: Data-Structure-Set Versus Relational*, part of ACM-SIGMOD Workshop, 1974 May, New York: Association for Computing Machinery, 1975.

SENKO, Michael E., "Information Systems: Records, Relations, Sets, Entities, and Things," *Information Systems* (1:1), 1975, pages 1-13.

SENKO, Michael E., "Data Description Language in the Context of a Multilevel Structured Description: DIAM II with FORAL," *Data Base Description*, Proceedings of IFIP-TC2 Working Conference, Belgium, 1975 January, edited by B. C. M. Douqué and G. M. Nijssen, Amsterdam: North-Holland Publishing Co., (New York: American Elsevier), 1975, pages 239-258.

SHARE Committee on Theory of Information Handling, "Report TIH-1," W. Orchard Hays, Chairman, New York: SHARE, Inc., SHARE Secretary Distribution SSD-71, C-1663, 1959 July 15, 22 pages.

SIBLEY, Edgar H., editor, Special Issue on Data-Base Management Systems, *ACM Computing Surveys* (8:1), 1976 March.
    A collection of six articles covering the evolution of DBMSs; Relational, CODASYL, and Hierarchical DBMSs; and a comparison of the CODASYL and relational approaches.

SIBLEY, Edgar H. and Robert W. TAYLOR, "A Data Definition and Mapping Language," *Communications of the ACM* (16:12), 1973 December, pages 750-759.

TSICHRITZIS, Dionysios and Frederick H. LOCHOVSKY, *Data Models*, Englewood Cliffs, NJ: Prentice-Hall, 1982, 381 pages.

ULLMAN, Jeffrey D., *Principles of Database Systems*, second edition, Potomac, MD: Computer Science Press, 1982.

SAMPLE PERSONNEL-ORGANIZATIONAL DATABASE*

The following diagrams and tables of information describe a sample database of personnel and organizational data. All example data structures, interrogation language statements, and outputs in this text are based upon this sample database.

The sample data pertain to employees and the organizational units within which they work. The partial organization chart in Figure 4A-1 illustrates the normal hierarchical relationships of units within an organization. Figure 4A-2 lists the data pertaining to employees within the partial organizational chart. Figure 4A-3 lists the data for the organizational units shown in Figure 4A-1. These figures are followed by a description of the items of personnel data and the items of organizational data. Additional descriptive information can be gleaned by studying the actual personnel and organizational data. Finally, there is a list of possible job/skill codes and their names.

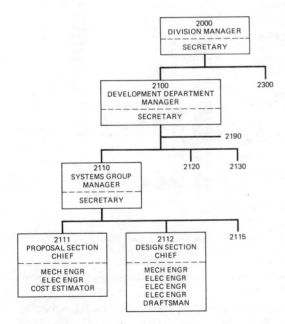

Figure 4A-1. Partial Organization Chart of Representative Division.

*Adapted from a sample database prepared by Richard G. Canning for *The Second Symposium on Computer-Centered Data Base Systems*, Santa Monica, Proceedings edited by Claude Baum and L. Gorsuch, Santa Monica, CA: Systems Development Corporation, TM-2624, (NTIS: AD 625 417), 1965 December 1, pages 3-3 to 3-29.

EMPLOYEE

EMPNO	EMPNAME	UNIT	JOB CODE	LEVEL	TITLE	SEX	BIRTH DATE	PRIMARY SKILL	SSK1	SSK2	SSK3	SSK4	ACTUAL SALARY
45584	PETERSON, N.M.	2000	0110	HEAD	DIVISION MANAGER	M	280607	0110	6130	6625	6040		56000
32579	LYNN, K.R.	2000	5210	EMPL	SECRETARY	F	530121	5210	5520				12000
57060	CARR, P.I.	2100	1110	HEAD	MANAGER DEVELOPMENT DEPT	M	350720	1110	1130	1135	0130	1355	48000
15324	CALLAGAN, R.F.	2100	5210	EMPL	SECRETARY	F	550606	5210	5520	5220			10800
10261	GUTTMAN, G.J.	2110	1110	HEAD	MANAGER SYSTEMS GROUP	M	301110	1110	1130	1135	0150		35000
72556	HARRIS, D.L.	2110	5210	EMPL	SECRETARY	F	550517	5210	5520				8400
24188	WALTERS, R.J.	2111	1110	HEAD	CHIEF PROPOSAL SECTION	M	260202	1110	1120				28000
21675	SCARBOROUGH, J.B.	2111	1120	EMPL	MECH ENGR	M	240914	1120					21000
18130	HENDERSON, R.G.	2111	1130	EMPL	ELEC ENGR	M	340121	1130					23000
91152	GARBER, R.E.	2111	1130	EMPL	ELEC ENGR	M	440707	1330	1130				16400
30793	COMPTON, D.R.	2111	1350	EMPL	COST ESTIMATOR	M	290328	1350	1351	1355	1130		16200
81599	FRIEDMAN, J.M.	2112	1110	HEAD	CHIEF DESIGN SECTION	M	360317	1110	1130				26000
21777	FRANCIS, G.C.	2112	1110	EMPL	SYSTEMS ENGR	M	321111	1110	1130				24000
24749	FAULKNER, W.M.	2112	1120	EMPL	MECH ENGR	M	400621	1120	1130	1330			24000
13581	FITINGER, G.J.	2112	1130	EMPL	ELEC ENGR	M	431216	1130	1355				22000
82802	APGAR, A.J.	2112	1130	EMPL	ELEC ENGR	M	500715	1130	1330				21000
63633	BLANK, L.F.	2112	1330	EMPL	DRAFTSMAN	F	491010	1330					16000
22959	BRIGGS, G.R.	2115	1110	HEAD	CHIEF PROD SPEC SECTION	M	400508	1110	1120				24000
29414	ARTHUR, P.J.	2115	1120	EMPL	MECH ENGR	M	300109	1120					22000
37113	ARNETTE, L.J.	2115	1130	EMPL	ELEC ENGR	M	450729	1130					22000
68840	GODDARD, D.H.	2120	1120	HEAD	MANAGER STDS ENGR GROUP	M	330119	1120	1135				29000
71160	GERRISH, C.S.	2120	5210	EMPL	SECRETARY	F	560331	5210					8000
35401	ANDERSON, R.E.	2122	1120	HEAD	CHIEF SYSTEM STDS SECTION	M	380228	1130	1135				23000
91589	TAUBER, J.S.	2122	1120	EMPL	MECH ENGR	M	451114	1120					19000
80823	STADERMAN, P.K.	2122	1130	EMPL	ELEC ENGR	M	430507	1130					19400
64937	SMITH, R.E.	2123	1120	HEAD	CHIEF COMPONENT STDS SECTION	M	401129	1120	1127				22000
82166	RHODES, J.H.	2123	1120	EMPL	MECH ENGR	M	490303	1120					19000
28654	RAYMOND, H.F.	2123	1130	EMPL	ELEC ENGR	M	341216	1130					20000
17848	HUGHES, J.W.	2123	1330	EMPL	DRAFTSMAN	F	350120	1130					17000
33144	QUINN, S.M.	2123	5520	EMPL	FILE CLERK	F	561115	5520					11000
48464	CHANDLER, W.R.	2130	1120	HEAD	MANAGER COMPONENT ENGR GROUP	M	351015	1120	1135				33000
44432	BERGMANN, R.I.	2130	5210	EMPL	SECRETARY	F	540718	5210					9000
68795	COOPER, J.C.	2131	1120	HEAD	CHIEF ENGR SECTION A	M	290309	1120	1124				24000
39464	BUSTER, A.B.	2131	1120	EMPL	MECH ENGR	M	380719	1120					22000
79935	BOLD, E.W.	2131	1120	EMPL	MECH ENGR	M	460416	1120					21000
62999	NORMAN, H.R.	2131	1330	EMPL	DRAFTSMAN	M	331101	1330					18000
90816	MCCARTHY, J.K.	2132	1130	HEAD	CHIEF ENGR SECTION B	M	431020	1130	1135				23000
36472	MASSARD, L.R.	2132	1130	EMPL	ELEC ENGR	M	201010	1130					21600
10295	SILCOTT, D.N.	2132	1130	EMPL	ELEC ENGR	M	430223	1130					19000
89876	SKINNER, I.P.	2132	1130	EMPL	ELEC ENGR	M	480419	1130					20000
47289	SCHRADER, F.G.	2133	1150	HEAD	CHIEF PROD ENGR SECTION	M	420909	1140	3125	1365			21000
12245	KENT, M.J.	2133	1150	EMPL	PROD ENGR	M	260125	1150	3340				19600
50498	LEGGETT, P.F.	2133	1150	EMPL	PROD ENGR	M	330517	1150	3125	1365			20000
57084	FINERMAN, A.B.	2133	1330	EMPL	DRAFTSMAN	M	500622	1330					17000
21475	FLETCHER, M.W.	2133	1365	EMPL	TOOL DESIGNER	M	320729	1365	3125	3340	7320		19000
26934	HAMMER, C.P.	2135	3125	HEAD	CHIEF MODEL SHOP SECTION	M	200613	3125	3340	3125	1365	3370	20000
15052	BOYD, W.V.	2135	1351	EMPL	MECH TECHN	M	420917	1351	3340	7320	3370		18000
21261	CURTIS, K.R.	2135	1355	EMPL	ELEC TECHN	M	360304	1355	3510	7320			17000
74090	GRAY, S.R.	2135	3125	EMPL	TOOL MAKER	M	230703	3125	3340	7320	1365	3370	19000
87354	DIETERICH, L.J.	2190	1190	CONS	CHIEF SCIENTIST	M	250423	1190	1130	1120	1110	1175	44000
87277	SONNENFELDT, W.R.	2300	0130	HEAD	MANAGER OPERATIONS DEPT	M	230501	0130	3340	7120			44000
61706	FRESCOTT, W.C.	2300	5210	EMPL	SECRETARY	F	540703	5210	5520				10000
61284	MAILLETT, J.R.	2310	0150	HEAD	MANAGER FACTORY OPNS GROUP	M	311126	0150	3340	3740			28000
75683	MELCHERT, F.F.	2310	5210	EMPL	SECRETARY	F	350813	5210	5520				10000
19357	PAYNE, W.F.	2311	3340	HEAD	CHIEF FAB SECTION A	M	330821	3340	3345				20000
32924	LEVITT, P.S.	2311	3340	EMPL	MACHINE OPR	M	440422	3340	3345	3360			16000
42055	LITTLE, E.F.	2311	3340	EMPL	MACHINE OPR	M	380302	3340	3360	3550			17000

Figure 4A-2. Sample Personnel Data in EMPLOYEE File.

Description of Personnel Data

EMPNO: A 5-digit employee number; this number has no reference to job level or alphabetic listing of the names.

EMPNAME: Name of the person up to 25 alphabetic characters, consisting of 1, 2, or 3 initials plus last name.

UNIT: A 4-digit code representing the organization unit to which the person is assigned (see Figure 4A-1).

JOBCODE: A 4-digit code designating the skill specified for the position that this person occupies; it is not mandatory that a person's job code match one of their skill codes.

LEVEL:
A 4-alphabetic-character code: HEAD for head of this particular organization unit, EMPL meaning employees, and CONS meaning consultant.

TITLE:
Title of the position held. For EMPL level, title agrees with the job code name. For CONS level, title is "Consultant". For HEAD level, title is "Chief" for sections, and "Manager" for groups, departments, and divisions. It is up to 30 alphabetic characters.

SEX:
The person's sex, coded M or F.

BIRTHDATE:
The birthdate is a 6-digit field, in the sequence year-month-day (YYMMDD). For some retrievals, it may be necessary to select on any one or two of these three subfields.

SKILL CODE:
A repeated field of 4-digit code(s) designating the person's skills. A person must have a single primary skill, which *usually agrees* with the person's jobcode. In addition, a person may have from 0 to 4 secondary skill codes.

ACTUAL SALARY:
Person's current annual salary in whole dollars.

ORGANIZATIONAL UNIT

UNITNO	ORGNAME	PARENT UNIT	AUTHORIZED COMPLEMENT:				BUDGET
			JOB CODE	UNIT CODE TITLE		AUTH QTY SALARY	
2000	REPRESENTATIVE DIV	1000					459000
			0110		DIVISION MANAGER	1 56000	
			5210		SECRETARY	1 12000	
				2100	DEPARTMENT	1 391000	
2100	DEVELOPMENT DEPT	2000					391000
			1110		MANAGER	1 48000	
			5210		SECRETARY	1 11000	
				2110	GROUP	1 332000	
2110	SYSTEMS GROUP	2100					332000
			1110		MANAGER	1 35000	
			5210		SECRETARY	1 10000	
				2111	SECTION	1 87000	
				2112	SECTION	1 132000	
				2115	SECTION	1 68000	
2111	PROPOSAL SECTION	2110					87000
			1110		CHIEF	1 28000	
			1120		MECH ENGR	1 21000	
			1130		ELEC ENGR	1 21000	
			1350		COST ESTIMATOR	1 17000	
2112	DESIGN SECTION	2110					132000
			1110		CHIEF	1 26000	
			1120		MECH ENGR	1 24000	
			1130		ELEC ENGR	3 64000	
			1330		DRAFTSMAN	1 18000	
:	:	:	:	:		: :	:

Figure 4A-3. Sample Organizational Data.

Description of Organizational Data

UNITNO:	A 4-digit code representing the organization unit; see the organization chart, Figure 4A-1.
ORGNAME:	A 20-alphabetic-character field giving the name of this organization unit.
PARENT UNIT:	A 4-digit code representing the organization unit to which this unit reports.

Authorized complement:

JOBCODE:	A 4-digit code designating a position assigned to this organization unit.
UNITCODE:	A 4-digit code designating a subunit assigned to this organization unit.
	(Note: Each authorized complement record can have a JOBCODE entry or a UNITCODE entry, but not both.)
TITLE:	A 20-alphabetic character field describing the position title (for a jobcode) or the organization name (for a unitcode).
QTY:	A 2-digit field designating the quantity of this jobcode or unitcode authorized for this organization unit.
AUTHSALARY:	A 6-digit quantity field which contains the total authorized annual salaries for this jobcode or this unitcode, in this organization unit.
BUDGET:	A 7-digit field which contains the total of all authorized salaries for this organization unit.

List of Job/Skill Codes and Names (Partial)

CODE	NAME	CODE	NAME
0110	Admin, Division	1330	Draftsman
0130	Admin, Department	1350	Cost Estimator
0150	Admin, Group	1351	Mech Techn
		1355	Elec Techn
1110	Systems Engr	1365	Tool Designer
1120	Mech Engr		
1124	Structures Engr	5210	Secretary
1127	Power Engr	5220	Clerk-Typist
		5520	File Clerk
1130	Elec Engr		
1135	Commun Engr	6040	Reg Sales Mgr
1150	Prod Engr	6130	Branch Sales Mgr
		6625	Salesperson
1175	Metallurgist		
1180	Chemist		
1190	Scientist		

The sample database implies the notion of a "position class." Each organizational unit is authorized to employ some number of different types of people. For example, the design section has an authorized complement of one head, one mechanical engineer, three electrical engineers, and one draftsman—a total of four position classes (or six positions).

More detailed examination of the data reveals several relationships among employees, organizational units, positions, and skills:

- Every organizational unit has exactly one unit as its parent (except the top level).
- Every employee belongs to exactly one organizational unit.
- Several positions are defined within each organizational unit based upon jobcode.
- Multiple employees may be authorized in a "position class".
- Some positions could be temporarily unfilled.
- The salary of some employees may be temporarily unauthorized.
- Each organizational unit has an employee as head.
- Every employee possesses one primary skill (which need not correspond to the jobcode of the occupied position) and zero or more secondary skills.

Some of these relationships are not immediately obvious and present interesting problems in designing a database in an actual DBMS.

Although the database is designed to meet various recurring and ad hoc needs of the personnel department as well as others in the organization, the following output reports illustrate a few types of requests to be satisfied from this database.

1 Employee Job Class Salary Report

For all persons (excluding consultants), generate a report showing their name, organizational unit number, position title, and actual salary. Sort the output in ascending order of jobcode, and calculate the average of the actual salaries for each job class (each unique jobcode value).

Sample Output:

EMPLOYEE NAME	UNIT	TITLE	SALARY	JOB CODE	AVG SALARY
PETERSON, N.M.	2000	DIVISION MANAGER	56000		
				0110	56000
CARR, P.I.	2100	MANAGER DEVELOPMENT DEPT	48000		
GUTTMAN, G.J.	2100	MANAGER SYSTEMS GROUP	35000		
WALTERS, R.J.	2111	CHIEF PROPOSAL SECTION	28000		
FRIEDMAN, J.M.	2112	CHIEF DESIGN SECTION	26000		
FRANCIS, G.C.	2112	SYSTEMS ENGR	24000		
				1110	32200
SCARBOROUGH, J.	2112	MECH ENGR	21000		
FAULKNER, W.H.	2112	MECH ENGR	24000		
				1120	22500

2 Demand Report of Special Electrical Engineers

Print the employee name, employee number, organizational unit number, age, and skills (both skill code and skill name) for each person in the organization satisfying the following criteria:

- The employee has [any] skill of 1130 (electrical engineer),
- The employee has at least two skills recorded in their record,
- The employee is not at the level of HEAD, and
- The employee was born between 1927 and 1940 inclusive.

Sort and print the output in increasing order of age (decreasing birthyear) and secondarily by employee name.

Sample Output:

```
EMPLOYEE NAME     EMPNO   UNIT   AGE   SKILLS
-------------     -----   ----   ---   -------------------------------
APGAR, A.J.       82802   2112   43    1130   ELEC ENGR
                                       1130   DRAFTSMAN
GARBER, R.E.      91152   2111   49    1330   DRAFTSMAN
                                       1130   ELEC ENGR
FITINGER, G.J.    13581   2112   50    1130   ELEC ENGR
                                       1355   ELEC TECHN
FAULKNER, W.M.    24749   2112   53    1120   MECH ENGR
                                       1130   ELEC ENGR
                                       1330   DRAFTSMAN
    :
```

3 Periodic Section Report

Combine the personnel data and the organizational data to prepare a report showing the authorized complement (budget) compared to the actual complement of salaries for sections where they do not match. For each section, print the unit number, name, and head of the organizational unit; then print jobcode, position title, authorized quantity and salary, and actual quantity and salary, calculating any differences; and then print the sum of the authorized salaries, the sum of the actual salaries, and any deviation from budget. Print each report on a separate page so that the output can be bursted and each report sent to the appropriate section chief.

Sample Output:

```
UNIT:   2111
NAME:   PROPOSAL SECTION
CHIEF:  WALTERS, R.J.
                                 AUTHORIZED    ACTUAL
                                 -----------   -----------
JOBCODE   TITLE                  QTY  SALARY   QTY  SALARY   DEVIATION
-------   -----                  ---  ------   ---  ------   ---------
1110      CHIEF PROPOSAL SECTION  1   28000     1   28000
1120      MECH ENGR               1   21000     1   21000
1130      ELEC ENGR               1   21000     2   39400    18400
1350      COST ESTIMATOR          1   17000     1   16200     -800
                                 ---  ------   ---  ------   ---------
                                  4   87000     5  104600    17600
                                 --------------------------------------

UNIT:   2112
NAME:   DESIGN SECTION
CHIEF:  FRIEDMAN, J.M.
                                 AUTHORIZED    ACTUAL
                                 -----------   -----------
JOBCODE   TITLE                  QTY  SALARY   QTY  SALARY   DEVIATION
-------   -----                  ---  ------   ---  ------   ---------
1110      CHIEF DESIGN SECTION    1   26000     1   26000
1110      SYSTEMS ENGR                          1   24000    24000
1120      MECH ENGR               1   24000     1   24000
1130      ELEC ENGR               3   64000     2   43000   -21000
1330      DRAFTSMAN               1   18000     1   16000    -2000
                          TOTAL:  6  132000     6  133000     1000
                                 --------------------------------------
```

USER INTERFACE, LANGUAGE, AND DBMS OPERATION

5.1	EVOLUTION OF THE USER INTERFACE	160
5.1.1	The User Comes Online	160
5.1.2	The Microcomputer Environment	161
5.1.3	New Dimensions of Online, Interactive Dialogue	162
5.2	PRINCIPLES OF DIRECT MANIPULATION	163
5.2.1	Continuous, Visual Representation of the Object of Interest	163
5.2.2	Physical Actions Instead of Complex Language Syntax	164
5.2.3	Rapid, Incremental Operations Immediately Visible	166
5.2.4	Keyboarding versus Voice Recognition	167
5.2.5	Layered Approach to Learning	167
5.3	TYPES OF ONLINE USERS: BY USAGE MODE AND DIALOGUE STYLE	168
5.3.1	System-Driven Dialogue with Menus and Prompts	168
5.3.1.1	Dialogue Levels	170
5.3.2	User-Driven Dialogue with Command Language	174
5.3.2.1	High-Level Data-Oriented Command Languages	174
5.3.2.2	Syntactic Styles of Command Languages	178
5.3.3	Coexistence of Different User Interfaces	179
5.4	ADDITIONAL ONLINE SUPPORT	181
5.4.1	Help Facilities	181
5.4.2	Menu Handling Facilities	182
5.4.3	Facilities for the System Developer	185
5.5	TYPES OF DATA LANGUAGES: DEFINITION, MANIPULATION, AND MAPPING	186
5.6	DATA LANGUAGES ON DATA STRUCTURES	187
5.7	DBMS MODES OF OPERATION	188
5.7.1	Sequential DBMSs	189
5.7.2	Online, Interactive DBMSs	190
5.7.3	Inverted Data Structures	190
5.7.4	Generated Procedures versus Interpretive Execution	191
	SUMMARY	194
	EXERCISES	195
	SELECTED REFERENCES	196

Chapter 3 showed how users access the DBMS functions through some interface. This chapter explores more fully the different ways in which users interface with a system. While these methods are discussed in terms of DBMS functions, the concepts and principles apply to any computer-based system. Topics covered include the evolution of the user interface to online interactive dialogue, principles of direct manipulation, menu-driven versus command-driven interfaces, levels of dialogue, facilities for the system builder including deferred execution of command files, and different types of data languages. The last section discusses various modes of DBMS operation.

5.1 EVOLUTION OF THE USER INTERFACE

Dramatic changes in the operating relationship between the user and the system have significantly influenced the development and use of computer systems during the past two decades. Users have moved from being *offline* to being *online* and operating *interactively* with the system.

All the early DBMSs were designed to operate in a "batch processing" mode. Use of this mode is quite understandable. Given the large capital investment required for hardware, the industry concentrated on efficient use of the hardware—it operated with users offline and data on sequential storage media, later on direct access devices. The collection of functions associated with the DBMS was rather limited—most viewing DBMSs as augmented capabilities for the application programmer. By and large, DBMSs on minicomputers suffered the same batch mentality and narrow functionality.

With users offline, they had to prepare their job requests in advance and send them to the computer for deferred execution. Nearly all DBMSs were used by creating programs, filling in forms, or preparing a file of commands.* These were submitted to the big, expensive computer to be run at its convenience! Since earlier computers and today's large mainframe computers cost considerably more than people, the need for machine efficiency outweighs considerations of people efficiency. Processing batches of requests and sorted batches of transactions sequentially through a file yield more efficient machine operation.

5.1.1 The User Comes Online

Declining hardware costs and rising personnel costs stimulated the search for more efficient personnel utilization. Rather than have the user come to the machine and submit a job to be run, machines have come to the users. First with Remote Job Entry (RJE) terminals, then printing terminals, dumb display terminals, intelligent terminals,

---

*In its 1980 survey of 135 query languages (none of which were for microcomputers), the British Computer Society Query Languages Group found 120 to be exclusively command driven, 6 dominantly command driven with partial dialogue capabilities, leaving only 9 (or 6.7 percent) being predominantly interactive dialogue. Furthermore, of those, 7 used *forms*—"dialogue-driven using fixed formats to specify queries." *Query Languages: A Unified Approach*, London: Heyden & Son (also Philadelphia, PA), 1981, Appendix 2, pages 78-83.

and finally, the microcomputer. These all served to get the user online. With the last one, the computer moved to the user. This trend has made computers more easily and readily available to users at *their* convenience.

The microcomputer is causing a revolution in the delivery of computing and information services to users. The main point of access to computing power is via the desktop workstation—whether that is a terminal to a host computer, or a stand-alone microcomputer. The microcomputer as a multifunction workstation is rapidly becoming the dominant vehicle for access to computing.

5.1.2 The Microcomputer Environment

What's different about the world of microcomputers? Several factors are having a profound impact on the design and use of DBMS tools.

Microcomputers are Smaller and Cheaper

Of course, this goes without saying. The consequence is that organizations no longer have the same obsession to optimize the efficiency of the machine. That which cost over $1 million and filled a large room 15 years ago now costs a few thousand dollars and fits on a desk! Organizations are beginning to focus more attention to optimizing the productivity of humans rather than the machine. Just as with phones and typewriters, lower costs and improved human performance will dictate having a professional workstation (microcomputer) at nearly everyone's elbow, even if it is idle 80 percent of the time!

Software is Cheaper and Off the Shelf

A mainframe DBMS costs from $20,000 to $200,000, and that price generally includes several days of training for several people. Most DBMSs for microcomputers are sold by mail or off the shelf of a computer retailer for under $1000. The resulting margin of a few hundred dollars cannot support any meaningful level of training. Therefore, successful microcomputer software must be self-teaching. Microcomputer software developers have generally paid more attention to ease of use.

There are More Novice and Impatient Users

With the cost so low, we are witnessing an exploding proliferation of microcomputers—many more than there are people who understand how they work. The industry now sells many more microcomputers each year than the total number of mainframe and minicomputers installed worldwide. Thus there are now increasing numbers of novice users who will not tolerate low-level, awkward languages filled with jargon and peculiar syntax.

Software is becoming much easier to use and more integrated. Software is now available that can be used without even reading the manual (though it is heresy to suggest). The systems operate with menus and provide online documentation and help screens.

The User is Inherently Online

Probably the most significant factor is that the user of a microcomputer system is inherently online. A system designed to run on a microcomputer must be in constant communication with the user, responding to requests and advising on the status of actions. The emerging principles of human-machine interaction are gradually being applied to mainframe systems—but they are mandatory to successful microcomputer systems.

Most microcomputer software developers have paid much more attention to the screen interface, keeping the user appraised of what is happening, providing menus and help screens, and letting the user be more in control of the processing steps. It is expensive to redesign existing mainframe DBMSs to operate effectively online. The vendors are having a difficult time breaking out of the "batch processing syndrome." In fact, the developer of a DBMS for micros may be better off never having known the big-systems world. It is very different to write a program knowing that the user is there every moment during execution.

Not only are the end users online, with ad hoc usage of the system but the system developers are also online.

User is Both End User and Developer

In the world of microcomputers there is a whole range of user types. Unlike the mainframe environment, where there is substantial specialization of labor in data processing, the various user types become blended into one on the microcomputer.

At one extreme is the novice end user who needs to be lead through ad hoc use of the system.

At the other extreme is the system developer who needs a tool for building a turnkey system for a specific application environment, such as a doctor's office, architect, real estate sales, or a church. They must be able to set up a system to be used by an ad hoc novice end user. They need to prestore definitions of menus, input screens, and output reports, and to write their own special processing routines.

As the novice end user becomes more experienced, they may want to begin setting up their own stored procedures for deferred execution. In fact, with microcomputers the distinction is increasingly fuzzy. The person at the terminal is the end user, the developer, the operator, the data entry clerk, and the installation manager—all together!

5.1.3 New Dimensions of Online, Interactive Dialogue

The user's being online has opened up a whole range of possibilities in designing the user interface. When the user came online, programs designed to run in an offline, batch mode could be invoked from the terminal. The user would simply set up the job—preparing the input parameters, and submitting the request to the program. The user would have no interaction with the program while it was in execution. Early online systems merely simulated a batch processing environment. Some DBMS systems today do little more than simulate a batch processing environment.

Even though the ability for a user to be online has existed for over a decade, the industry is just beginning to learn the full meaning of interactive dialogue. Principles are beginning to emerge. The user must be able to interact with the program during execution—experiencing immediate execution of commands, monitoring its operation, conditionally following different paths through its processing logic, and responding to error or exception conditions.

Interactive dialogue is much more than just having a terminal interface and good screen design. It involves various levels of dialogue, menu- and command-driven dialogues, effective use of defaults, online help and tutorial facilities, and immediate detection and reporting of errors for on-the-spot correction. The system responds to a request while it is still fresh in the user's mind. This leads to greater effectiveness for the user and greater accuracy in the process.

5.2 PRINCIPLES OF DIRECT MANIPULATION

Shneiderman has pulled together several concepts relating to interactive systems under the term "direct manipulation."* He noted that certain systems had enthusiastic users. He then sought to discover what features produced such satisfied and delighted users. After describing some typical examples from full screen text editors, spread sheet programs like Visicalc, and video games, he outlined some emerging principles of direct manipulation which seemed to produce pleased users.

1. Continuous, visual representation of the object of interest
2. Physical mechanisms, instead of complex language syntax, to position a cursor and manipulate the object
3. Rapid, incremental operations immediately display the effect of the actions

Video games provide an exciting, well-engineered, and certainly successful illustration of direct manipulation. The users know the precise point or object which is to be manipulated, and they see an immediate response to their directives. "The strong attraction of these games contrasts markedly with the anxiety and resistance many users experience toward office automation equipment."

5.2.1 Continuous, Visual Representation of the Object of Interest

Some representation of the object the user is currently viewing or manipulating should always be visible on the display device. The user should also be able to see immediately the effect of any operations or modifications on the object of interest.

---

*Ben Shneiderman, "Direct Manipulation: A Step Beyond Programming Languages," *Computer* (16:8), 1983 August, pages 57-69.

The chosen representation should be natural and lead to unambiguous interpretation by the population of intended users. The use of a graphic icon may be clear to a designer but may lead to greater confusion. A graphic representation may be an analogy which leads the user to make incorrect assumptions about permissible operations on the object.

Within a DBMS, the objects to be represented include records, data item values which make up a record, and relationships between records. The system could display a data structure graphically showing data files as boxes or file drawers, and relationships as arcs between boxes. Different arcs could represent relationships with different characteristics. The user could move over the structure to select the file(s) and relationships of interest. Within a file, the system could graphically portray "thumbing through the entries or records in a file" by displaying overlapping boxes or file folders with the search keys written across the top of each folder. The user would be able to move back and forth through the file, deleting records, opening up a record (folder) for closer examination and possible update, or tagging records for further collective action on the tagged set or the untagged set. Before moving through the file, the user could specify which key or keys to search on (implying the order in which the records are to be presented), which data items to display on the top of each folder (the userschema), and which records to include in the scan (based upon Boolean selection criteria).

5.2.2 Physical Actions Instead of Complex Language Syntax

When users must write a command statement in some language to direct the actions of a system, they must first learn the command structure, semantics, and syntax of the language. They must learn how to put the command sequences together to perform a particular task. They must also write the commands correctly or risk getting a syntax error. The amount of initial learning required before using the system is a significant barrier to acceptance and use.

Furthermore, the syntax of languages tends to be somewhat arbitrary, as in selecting the keys or letters to invoke particular actions. While some designers try to choose command letters for their mnemonic value, inconsistencies across systems are inevitable and annoying—for example, "K" meaning Keep in one system and Kill in another! Syntactic knowledge is acquired through rote memorization, making it easily forgotten unless frequently used.

The solution is to utilize physically obvious and naturally intuitive mechanisms for positioning, and labeled buttons for actions. The interactive user interface involves:

- *Positioning* a cursor over the object of interest—menus, text, data fields, or a graphic image.
- *Actioning* (specifying actions) to manipulate the object—accept a menu option, cut or copy text, etc.
- *Entering* text or numeric values. Keyboarding, that is, typing numbers and characters, etc., is required for entering text, data names when defined, and data values.

Physical mechanisms for positioning a cursor:

ARROW KEYS

Four keys to indicate up, down, left, and right movement. It is desirable to have some way to specify *slow movement*, one character or line at a time, *fast movement*, jumping over several characters or lines perhaps one screen at a time, and *extremity movement* to the beginning or end of the object. This can be done with a modifier, such as a shift key with the arrow key for fast movement.

JOY STICK

Simulates the arrow keys with a vertical lever on the keyboard (or a separate box) which can be pushed in four directions. Joy sticks may be *linear* for uniform movement speed, *two-stage* with fast movement indicated by pushing the stick farther in the desired direction, or *exponential* where the movement speed increases as the stick is held in a particular direction.

TRACKBALL

The operator rolls the top of a ball which is embedded in the keyboard (or a separate box). Unlike the arrow keys or joy stick, horizontal and vertical movement can be specified simultaneously by rolling the ball on a diagonal. Speed of movement can also depend upon the speed with which the ball is rolled. The trackball can be a very efficient and naturally intuitive mechanism for users.

MOUSE

Like an inverted trackball where the user moves the ball holder, called a "mouse," over the table beside the keyboard or display device. This mechanism requires a dedicated flat surface over which to move the mouse—a distinct disadvantage. Since movement is always relative to the current position of the cursor, the mouse can be used anywhere on the flat surface.

GRAPHICS TABLET

Uses an auxiliary surface or tablet and a companion device, like a pencil, for pointing to a spot on the surface. Positioning is relative to the boundaries of the tablet. Used primarily for graphics applications where resolution greater than individual characters or lines is required.

LIGHT PEN

Uses the display screen as the tablet with a special light pen with which the user can go directly to a position on the screen. The computer can sense the position of the light pen on the screen. Also used for graphics applications.

TOUCH SCREEN

Similar to the light pen except that the system senses the position of one's finger on the screen—thus eliminating the need for a separate external pointing device. This mechanism is not suitable for high resolution applications; even isolating the position of a finger to a single line can be difficult. It is most natural and efficient for gross, absolute positioning by humans.

AUDIO RECOGNITION

Substituting voice commands for the preceding physical mechanisms may be even more natural for users, although considerably more research and experimentation is needed to develop efficient and effective designs. One drawback is that the device must be programmed to recognize the voice of each person using the workstation, and reprogrammed when they have a cold! Recognition of discrete spoken words or phrases is being successfully used in applications where people do not have the use of their hands—taking inventory, guiding the movement of heavy materials or equipment, or quadriplegics.

The preceding mechanisms are used to position the cursor over the material displayed on the screen. With a standard screen being 80 columns by 24 lines, sometimes the material requires more space—a file may have more than 24 defined data items; a data item name plus value may exceed 80 characters. Therefore, the display screen becomes a *window* through which to view the data or text. When the cursor reaches an edge of the window, continued cursor movement instructions cause the material to be scrolled vertically or panned horizontally "behind" the window. Some systems may also allow scrolling or panning independently of cursor movement.

Once the cursor is properly positioned, the user then specifies an **action**. In the simplest case, the action is simply to *choose* from among a list of items, as in a menu. Another action could be to begin entering or editing value character strings at the position of the cursor. Additional commands (keys) may specify insert mode, delete characters or whole field values, center or justify values in a field, underline or boldface, etc. It is even easier if specially labeled keys are available on the keyboard for the more frequent actions or commands. The labeled keys act as a permanent selection menu of frequent commands, thus obviating the need for learning any special syntax.

The techniques of direct manipulation argue against instructions which say "UP6" to move the cursor up six lines, or typing in a letter or number to indicate a menu selection. Since the user can enter an invalid menu selection number or make a mistake typing a command, the system must validate the input, display a message (and beep) if an error is detected, and obtain a correction from the user.

If there is no command, letter, or number to type, there is no language syntax; and therefore *syntax errors are impossible*. The user should be able to move the cursor directly over the lines or menu choices. Being restricted to the displayed items, users cannot make an invalid choice. If they attempt to move the cursor too far, it simply stops at the edge of the material (the last or first entry). The user could then simply use the natural inverse operation to move the cursor in the opposite direction (or the system could automatically cycle back to the opposite edge).

When editing an existing data item value, the user should edit directly over the old value, inserting, changing, and deleting characters. The system should immediately display the effect of the action. Use of a separate editing line is less effective. It should also be possible for the data item value to be wider than the display window. In this case, the user can pan the wider value back and forth behind the window while editing.

5.2.3 Rapid, Incremental Operations Immediately Visible

After performing an operation, users ought to be able to see the effects immediately on the screen. They should not have to wait for the system to redisplay or repaint the whole screen. They certainly should not have to explicitly request a display or print to see and verify the effect of the operation. Errors are immediately apparent.

Inserting characters in a data value should be possible without retyping the whole value. The existing characters would be shifted over as the new characters were entered. Deleting characters from a string, the system would shift the remaining characters to fill in the space. After deleting a line, the system would move the subsequent lines up.

Operations should be easily *reversible*. Typing mistakes can be easily corrected by backspacing and retyping or deleting an extraneous character. An UNDO command key could return the system to the state prior to the previous command. Easy reversibility, using natural inverse operations or UNDO, is essential to reducing user anxiety about making mistakes or destroying some data.

5.2.4 Keyboarding versus Voice Recognition

The physical mechanisms for positioning and actioning are not convenient for entering original text or data values. To the computer system, they are essentially arbitrary strings of characters. To utilize the screen would mean displaying the 26 characters and 10 digits (plus some special characters) and asking the user to position a cursor to select characters in a sequence—keyboarding on the screen, obviously less efficient than an experienced typist at a keyboard!

Even with widespread use of physical mechanisms for positioning and actioning, there is still a need to enter strings of characters in the original creation of data names, data values, and text. This will be done predominantly through keyboarding for the next several years. The penetration of computer workstations into more jobs in the working world dictates that all children learn keyboarding in school.

In the future, voice recognition may be able to replace keyboarding for original data/text entry. Today, reasonably inexpensive and effective systems are available which utilize a small vocabulary of a few hundred *discrete* words or phrases, spoken by particular persons. Such systems are "programmed" by a user speaking each word one or more times. The system forms an "average" digital image of the word and associates it with a given character string (input via a keyboard). When that user later speaks to the system it looks up each discrete word in a table and selects the character string associated with the closest matching digital voice image. The character string substitutes for the command or menu response.

Recognizing a small number of discrete words from a particular user is a long way from processing continuous speech using a large, natural vocabulary. The computer must break the sounds into phonemes, reassemble them into words based upon a dictionary, and assemble the words into meaningful sentences using the rules of grammar. Recognizing *and understanding* what the user is saying is now a much bigger task. Experimental systems take massive amounts of memory and processing time. It will be several years before such systems become practical, reliable and economical, on a computer workstation.

5.2.5 Layered Approach to Learning

With the principles of direct manipulation, novice users should be able to use the system immediately with a minimum of knowledge. They are led through the use of a small yet useful set of commands or capabilities. As they gain confidence and master the core of the system, they can gradually expand their knowledge of other features and special techniques.

Applying these principles of direct manipulation leads to the following advantages:

- Novices can learn basic functionality quickly through a self-running tutorial or demonstration by an experienced user.
- Experts can work rapidly.
- Knowledgeable intermittent users can retain operational concepts.
- Error messages are rarely needed.
- Users can immediately see if their actions are furthering their goals, and if not, they can change their actions.
- Users experience less anxiety with a comprehensible system and easily reversible actions.
- Users gain confidence and mastery because they initiate action, feel in control, and can predict system responses.

5.3 TYPES OF ONLINE USERS: BY USAGE MODE AND DIALOGUE STYLE

When the user is online, the system should operate through an interactive dialogue with the user. The dialogue may be *user driven* through the use of a command language, or it may be *system driven* through a series of menus and prompts. A system-driven dialogue can take place at several *levels of dialogue*.

The online user may be an *end user* who desires an immediate execution or response to an ad hoc request, or he or she may be a *system developer* needing to set up a particular request or sequence of actions for *deferred* execution. Rather than having the system execute a request immediately, the planned/deferred mode of use involves setting up a sequence of commands which can be stored and later invoked for execution. This is particularly important when the sequence of actions is to be performed repeatedly.

Putting the two usage modes together with the two styles of dialogue produces four main types of online users and also indicates the types of systems which should be provided for them (see Figure 5-1). Novice end users need to begin with the system asking them what they want to do. As users gain experience, they tend to migrate to the command style of dialogue and eventually to setting up systems for other novice end users (or for themselves) for frequent, deferred execution.

5.3.1 System-Driven Dialogue with Menus and Prompts

The novice end user needs a system-driven dialogue using menus and screens for data entry, data display, ad hoc query (by forms), and helps, plus a comprehensive report generator. The system controls the dialogue; the user need only respond to the messages or prompts initiated by the system. The sequence of prompts is contextually determined by the path of the preceding dialogue and the user responses.

In a database environment, the system can step the user through:

- The definition of a data file and the characteristics of data items.
- The entry of data to create or update records.
- The examination of (whole) records (or data from multiple records) on the screen one record at a time.

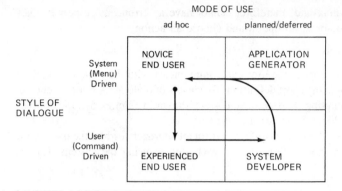

Figure 5-1. Types of Online Users.
Putting two modes of use against two styles of dialogue produces four types of online users. Novice end users need to begin with a system-driven dialogue which can gradually direct them in using the various facilities of the system. After gaining some experience, they will know how and will desire to go directly to the operation they wish to execute by issuing commands to the system. The next step is to be able to define and store sequences of commands for frequent, future execution by themselves or other novice end users. An application generator essentially directs the user to specify various parts of an application in developing a system.

- The definition of an output report to display data from several records at once in a columnar fashion.

Retrieving records for display or reports involves:

- Selection based upon a Boolean expression.
- Projection of named data items.
- Calculation of statistics.
- Derivation of additional data items.
- Ordering the retrieved records.
- Formatting the output for readability.

All these activities can be performed through interactive dialogue with the user. For example, when the user wants the output to be sorted, the system can present a menu consisting of all the data items in the record. The user first picks the primary key and whether ascending or descending, then the secondary key, etc., until the ordering criteria is completely specified.

The system conducts the dialogue with a sequence of prompts or requests to which the user responds by hitting certain keys or typing in certain information. Each dialogue action consists of a prompt from the system and one or more responses from the user. Each prompt may be as simple as a single word or may be a screen full of explanatory information. The system may prompt for one response at a time or may prompt for several responses at once. The latter "block prompt" can resemble a table or form on the screen through which the user steps, filling in the blanks.

A *menu* is a special type of prompt in which the system presents the user with a set of choices from which the user picks an alternative. As was just shown under direct manipulation, it is better to present the user with a set of options. Then they do not have any language syntax and, therefore, cannot have an erroneous response. They simply position the cursor to an option and choose an action.

5.3.1.1 Dialogue Levels

In system-driven dialogue, the user can communicate with the system at various levels. Using an example of report definition, five levels of dialogue—tutorial, choice, prompting, block prompting, and command—are shown in Figures 5-2 to 5-6. The command level of dialogue becomes user driven.

For the novice user, the system follows a **tutorial** approach leading the user by the hand, explaining the various alternatives at each step in using the system. Having

```
FUNCTION?
  DEFINE    -TO INPUT THE DEFINITION OF A NEW DATA STRUCTURE
  LOAD      -TO INPUT DATA VALUES TO A PREVIOUSLY DEFINED DATABASE
  RETRIEVE  -TO SELECT AND PROJECT DATA FROM A POPULATED DATABASE
  REPORT    -TO DEFINE AN OUTPUT REPORT FORMAT OR GENERATE A REPORT
  UPDATE    -TO ADD, MODIFY, OR DELETE EXISTING DATA IN THE DATABASE

REPORT


DEFINITION OR GENERATION?
  DEFINE    -TO DEFINE THE CONTENT AND FORMAT OF AN OUTPUT REPORT
  GENERATE  -TO PRODUCE A PREVIOUSLY DEFINED REPORT WITH CURRENT DATA

DEFINE


LINES?
  NN        -AN INTEGER SPECIFYING LOGICAL PAGE SIZE IN LINES PER PAGE;
            STANDARD PHYSICAL PAGE SIZE IS  66  LINES (11 INCHES).

58


COLUMNS?
  NN        -AN INTEGER SPECIFYING LOGICAL PAGE WIDTH
            (DEPENDS ON PRINTER AND ITS SETTING).

80


CONTENT LINES?
  TITLE      -LINE OF TEXT PRINTED AT THE TOP OF EACH PAGE OF THE REPORT
  HEADING    -COLUMN HEADINGS PRINTED AT THE TOP OF EACH PAGE
  DETAIL     -NAMED DATA ITEMS TO BE PROJECTED ONTO OUTPUT REPORT
  STATISTICS-STATISTICAL FUNCTIONS TO BE CALCULATED ON PROJECTED ITEMS
  [RETURN]   -PRESS 'RETURN' KEY (BLANK LINE) FOR NO MORE DETAIL LINES

TITLE "SALARY REPORT"
DETAIL EMPNAME, UNIT, JOBCODE, SALARY.
STATISTICS COUNT EMPNAME, SUM SALARY PER JOBCODE.
[RETURN]

  :
```

NOTE: *Computer prompt in italics;*
User response in normal type.

Figure 5-2. Tutorial Level of Dialogue.
The system asks a question, gives the valid responses, and specifies the meaning of each.

```
FUNCTION?
   DEFINE
   LOAD
   RETRIEVE
   REPORT
   UPDATE

REPORT


DEFINITION OR GENERATION?
   DEFINE
   GENERATE

DEFINE


LINES?
   NN

58


COLUMNS?
   NN

80


CONTENT LINES?
   TITLE
   HEADING
   DETAIL
   STATISTICS
   [RETURN]

TITLE "SALARY REPORT"
DETAIL EMPNAME, UNIT, JOBCODE, SALARY.
STATISTICS COUNT EMPNAME, SUM SALARY PER JOBCODE.
[RETURN]

   :
```

NOTE: Computer prompt in italics;
User response in normal type.

Figure 5-3. Choice Level of Dialogue.
The system asks a question and simply lists the valid responses. The user is assumed to know what each response means.

learned the meaning of the alternatives, a user often finds this approach very slow and verbose and is ready for faster levels of dialogue.

At the **choice** level the system presents only the choices at each step without any explanation (see Figure 5-3). From this menu, the user selects the desired response. Various terminal devices permit selection to be made using a touch-sensitive screen, a light pen or stylus, or a device to position a pointer (called a ''cursor'') on the screen.

Under **prompting**, illustrated in Figure 5-4, the system in effect asks a question or displays a key word to elicit the appropriate response or data input from the user. This level of dialogue takes place line by line, one request followed by a single response, repeatedly. This is the only practical level of dialogue on printing terminals or dumb display devices which can only produce lines sequentially.

FUNCTION?

REPORT

DEFINITION OR GENERATION?

DEFINE

LINES?

58

COLUMNS?

80

CONTENT LINES?

TITLE "SALARY REPORT"
DETAIL EMPNAME, UNIT, JOBCODE, SALARY.
STATISTICS COUNT EMPNAME, SUM SALARY PER JOBCODE.
[RETURN]

:

NOTE: *Computer prompt in italics;*
User response in normal type.

Figure 5-4. Prompting Level of Dialogue.
The system asks a question or displays a key word to elicit the appropriate response or data input from the user.

```
            REPORT DEFINITION

    LINES_____:58
    COLUMNS____:80
    TITLE_____:"SALARY REPORT"
    DETAIL_____:EMPNAME, UNIT, JOBCODE, SALARY.
    STATISTICS_:COUNT EMPNAME, SUM SALARY PER JOBCODE.
    DERIVATION_:
    ORDERED BY_:
       :



  Use ARROW keys to move cursor; then type or change response
  Press ENTER key when definition is complete and correct
```

NOTE: *Computer prompt in italics;*
User response in normal type.

Figure 5-5. Block Prompting Level of Dialogue.
With an intelligent display, the system can prompt with multiple requests at once and then cycle over them for the user's responses.

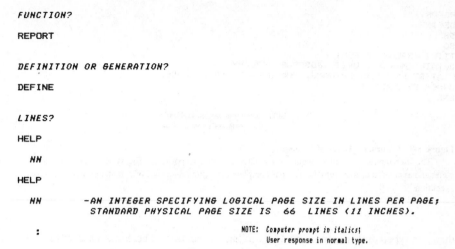

FUNCTION?

REPORT

DEFINITION OR GENERATION?

DEFINE

LINES?

HELP

NN

HELP

*NN   -AN INTEGER SPECIFYING LOGICAL PAGE SIZE IN LINES PER PAGE;
        STANDARD PHYSICAL PAGE SIZE IS 66 LINES (11 INCHES).*

:   NOTE: *Computer prompt in italics;*
                                   User response in normal type.

Figure 5-6. Shifting Dialogue Level with the Help Facility.
At the prompting level, the user may need more information and say HELP or may enter an invalid response. The system can display the set of choices to the user. Saying HELP a second time moves the user to the tutorial level of dialogue. The help facility shifts the dialogue one step toward the tutorial level. The shift in dialogue level could be temporary for the current prompt or made permanent for all subsequent dialogue.

Under **block prompting** (Figure 5-5), the system prompts with multiple requests at once. With intelligent display devices it is possible to display a set of requests or prompts on the screen, then move the cursor back over the prompts, under user control, to accept the user response. The user is presented with a template, or skeleton form, on the screen. The user then fills in the blanks in the form on the screen.

At the tutorial level of dialogue, the system provides a maximum of information to assist the user. At the other levels, a user may need more information in order to continue. Responding with "help," perhaps by pressing a HELP key, the system can move one level of dialogue toward tutorial (see Figure 5-6). This shift in level could be temporary to explain the current prompt or option, or it could be permanent until the user again requests a shift in the level of dialogue.

Conversely, a **skip facility** allows the user to tell the system to move one step toward the command level of dialogue. A temporary skip facility would allow the user to enter a response to the current question followed immediately with the responses to some number of subsequent, anticipated questions. Before asking the next question, the system now checks to see if a response has already been provided.

5.3.2 User-Driven Dialogue with Command Language

At the command level (Figure 5-7), dialogue becomes user driven. With user-driven dialogue, the system merely solicits input with a prompt for the user to enter the next request or command. Commands may be executed immediately as the user enters

```
REPORT
DEFINE
58
80
TITLE "SALARY REPORT"
DETAIL EMPNAME, UNIT, JOBCODE, SALARY.
STATISTICS COUNT EMPNAME, SUM SALARY PER JOBCODE.
ORDER BY JOBCODE
END
```

NOTE: Computer prompt in italics;
User response in normal type.

Figure 5-7. Command Level of Dialogue.
The user inputs a complete sequence of statements or "responses." The system may execute each command as entered or wait until the user has completed entering a sequence of commands and later initiates execution.

them or typed into a command file for later execution. The latter case reduces to one-way communication. The user inputs a complete sequence of statements, commands, or responses without any interruption from the system until the user calls for execution of the command file.

With a command-driven style, the *user* controls the dialogue. A system which is exclusively command driven will present the user with a prompt for a command when the system is first started. For example, dBASE II displays a dot in column 1; SYSTEM 2000 displays a "?". Each waits for the user to enter a command—not very comforting to the novice user! Their only option is to call up a help screen (if the system has one and they know the right command to get it!) or to read the manual (which may not be too inviting!).

In a command-driven style, the system always waits for the user to specify what he or she wants the system to do next. This implies that the user must first study the available commands before using the system. Documented examples showing many different types of processing sequences are essential for the user of a command language.

This level of dialogue assumes a frequent user who knows what command to give to the system. Such users can work rapidly at their own pace.

Many users who start out as novices soon become more sophisticated. They want to be able to bypass the normal menu hierarchy; and to prestore frequently used queries and report definitions. This requires a user-driven command interface.

5.3.2.1 High-Level Data-Oriented Command Languages

The command language of the DBMS should be a high-level *data* language. Such a language provides single commands which operate on the whole file at once, even multiple files. Elements of the language include operations to:

- Select records from a file which satisfy a Boolean expression.
- Project named fields from those records.
- Derive additional values for each of those retrieved records.

- Sort the selected records for output.
- Calculate statistics (count, sum, etc.) on certain fields for the whole file or at "control breaks."
- Present the output with appropriate titles and headings.

In a low-level language, a single statement tends to be semantically simple but more statements are needed to express a processing task. Figure 5-8 provides a vivid comparison of a high-level and a low-level language used to perform exactly the same retrieval request.

With many statements having interdependencies and sequence constraints, a low-level language is more complex making it more difficult to learn and to use. The user must know more details of the processing environment and the data being processed. Using this detailed information, the user can exercise control over time and space efficiency tradeoffs. Once a processing task is written in a low-level language, the proper execution of the process specification probably depends upon the detailed picture used in specifying the process.

By contrast, a single statement in a high-level language implies more underlying processing steps. If the entire user request for processing against the database can be expressed in one comprehensive language statement, there can be no interstatement or procedural dependencies to contend with. The user view of the data structure would consist of the minimum necessary information—at the level of logical names and relationships excluding physical storage and access path considerations. Using such a language provides little control over efficiency tradeoffs. However, assuming less detailed information about the data structure and using a high-level language, the processing specification is easier to write, easier to understand when it is written, and easier to modify.

High-level data languages:

- Allow the user to more closely and directly relate to the problem.
- Can insulate users from physical data storage considerations and machine-level constraints.
- Can reduce application development time by making it easier to define a data structure (or a user view) and to specify processing against that structure.
- Are more readily understood by a user and, therefore, require less training than low-level languages.

These are all the same reasons for the initial development and present widespread use of high-level programming languages such as COBOL or FORTRAN to specify *processes*. Unfortunately, the development of high-level *data* languages for definition and manipulation has lagged far behind the development of high-level programming languages.

Data manipulation languages are used to specify some process or operation on a data structure such as interrogation or update. A low-level data manipulation language provides commands which operate on one record at a time. With the language, a user *navigates* through the data structure. With a high-level data manipulation language the user thinks of processing one file or multiple files at once, often with a single state-

High-Level Language:

```
FROM PERSONNEL-ORGANIZATIONAL DATABASE
PRINT ORGNAME, EMPNAME, COUNT SSKILLS PER EMPLOYEE
WHERE ORGUNITNO BETWEEN 2110 AND 2119 AND
    EMPLOYEE HAS COUNT SSKILLS GT 1.
```

Database Schema: (system)

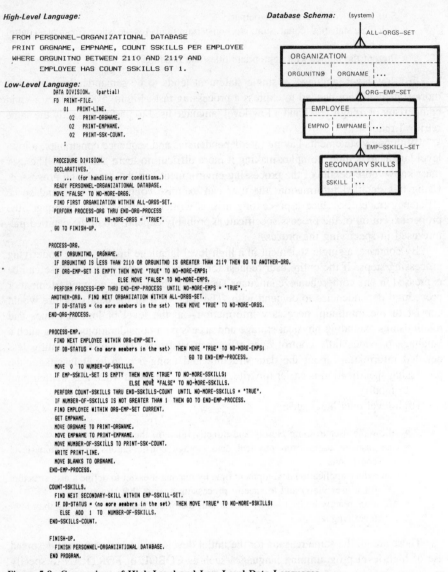

Low-Level Language:

```
    DATA DIVISION. (partial)
    FD PRINT-FILE.
        01  PRINT-LINE.
            02  PRINT-ORGNAME.
            02  PRINT-EMPNAME.
            02  PRINT-SSK-COUNT.
        :

    PROCEDURE DIVISION.
    DECLARATIVES.
        ... (for handling error conditions.)
    READY PERSONNEL-ORGANIZATIONAL DATABASE.
    MOVE "FALSE" TO NO-MORE-ORGS.
    FIND FIRST ORGANIZATION WITHIN ALL-ORGS-SET.
    PERFORM PROCESS-ORG THRU END-ORG-PROCESS
            UNTIL  NO-MORE-ORGS = "TRUE".
    GO TO FINISH-UP.


PROCESS-ORG.
    GET ORGUNITNO, ORGNAME.
    IF ORGUNITNO IS LESS THAN 2110 OR ORGUNITNO IS GREATER THAN 2119 THEN GO TO ANOTHER-ORG.
    IF ORG-EMP-SET IS EMPTY THEN MOVE "TRUE" TO NO-MORE-EMPS;
                           ELSE MOVE "FALSE" TO NO-MORE-EMPS.
    PERFORM PROCESS-EMP THRU END-EMP-PROCESS UNTIL NO-MORE-EMPS = "TRUE".
ANOTHER-ORG.  FIND NEXT ORGANIZATION WITHIN ALL-ORGS-SET.
    IF DB-STATUS = <no more members in the set> THEN MOVE "TRUE" TO NO-MORE-ORGS.
END-ORG-PROCESS.


PROCESS-EMP.
    FIND NEXT EMPLOYEE WITHIN ORG-EMP-SET.
    IF DB-STATUS = <no more members in the set>  THEN MOVE "TRUE" TO NO-MORE-EMPS;
                                            GO TO END-EMP-PROCESS.
    MOVE 0 TO NUMBER-OF-SSKILLS.
    IF EMP-SSKILL-SET IS EMPTY  THEN MOVE "TRUE" TO NO-MORE-SSKILLS;
                           ELSE MOVE "FALSE" TO NO-MORE-SSKILLS.
    PERFORM COUNT-SSKILLS THRU END-SSKILLS-COUNT UNTIL NO-MORE-SSKILLS = "TRUE".
    IF NUMBER-OF-SSKILLS IS NOT GREATER THAN 1  THEN GO TO END-EMP-PROCESS.
    FIND EMPLOYEE WITHIN ORG-EMP-SET CURRENT.
    GET EMPNAME.
    MOVE ORGNAME TO PRINT-ORGNAME.
    MOVE EMPNAME TO PRINT-EMPNAME.
    MOVE NUMBER-OF-SSKILLS TO PRINT-SSK-COUNT.
    WRITE PRINT-LINE.
    MOVE BLANKS TO ORGNAME.
END-EMP-PROCESS.


COUNT-SSKILLS.
    FIND NEXT SECONDARY-SKILL WITHIN EMP-SSKILL-SET.
    IF DB-STATUS = <no more members in the set> THEN MOVE "TRUE" TO NO-MORE-SSKILLS;
       ELSE ADD 1 TO NUMBER-OF-SSKILLS.
END-SSKILLS-COUNT.


FINISH-UP.
    FINISH PERSONNEL-ORGANIZATIONAL DATABASE.
    END PROGRAM.
```

Figure 5-8. Comparison of High-Level and Low-Level Data Languages.

Compared to a high-level retrieval language, a low-level language requires many more statements to accomplish the same task. The low-level language used above is CODASYL-COBOL (1978) augmented with the database manipulation language. The statements are largely self-explanatory, although the detail of the program is unimportant. In the low-level language the user must navigate through the data structure, initializing, incrementing a counter, finding the "next" record, and testing for the end of a set of records in order to take an alternative path in the processing logic. If a user also had available a high-level language, it would seem foolish to go through all the work of using the low-level language. Note that a high-level language could be used from within a COBOL program (though very few vendors offer this capability) or at an online terminal. (Similarly, a low-level, navigational language could be used at a terminal, as some vendors have done.)

ment. A high-level language specifies criteria for selecting a subset of entries from a file, names the attributes to be projected, and defines functions to be performed on the data. A high-level *data* language statement attempts to specify a complete unit or pattern of processing against the data structure directly and succinctly (see Figure 5-8).

Of course, some users may require (or feel more comfortable using) a low-level data language. This may be necessary when they want greater control over data flow, or greater efficiency or generality in processing against a data structure.

The following scenario of *Robert and the Supermarket* illustrates the obvious ridiculousness of *having* to use a low-level data manipulation language, that is, accessing one record at a time.

Robert and the Supermarket

Picture a sunny day when Rob comes home from school and his mother says, "Robert, we need some bread. Would you please walk down to the supermarket on the corner and pick up a loaf?" Being good at following instructions, Rob goes directly to the store. Upon entering, he passes the checkout area and walks down the produce aisle. At the end he turns to walk up the next aisle. After looking at the items on a few more aisles, he comes upon the bread. With loaf in hand, he goes to the front of the store and stands in the shortest line of shoppers. Soon he is at the head of the line, pays the clerk, and leaves the store. Thanks from Mom brings a proud smile on his face.

Then mother says, "Now, Robert, we also need some jam." Reluctantly, but obediently, he returns to the store wondering why mother had not told him about the jam when he got the bread. This time at the store he notices a schema hanging from the ceiling. The sign "JAMS & JELLIES—5A" looks promising. Going directly to aisle 5A he finds the jam and picks out strawberry, his favorite. After a longer wait at the checkout counter, he pays the clerk and returns home.

Greeting him at the door, mother says, "Thanks, Robert, now I would like you to bring home some milk for supper."

Rob's face falls. He wonders why his mother is being so foolish. In exasperation he says, "Mom, why can't you just give me the whole shopping list at once? Then I need to make only one trip; I can pick up the things as I pass them along the aisles in the store, and I don't have to spend so much time standing in line!"

Indeed! The system, Robert in this scenario, can be more efficient when given the full specification all at once for a complete unit of processing. Low-level, one-record-at-a-time data manipulation languages will be intolerable when the "data supermarket" is not just around the corner but across the country—the case with distributed databases and remote file servers in a network.

The large proportion of human interaction with a database can and should use high-level data languages. A user does not always need to know the way data is physically stored within the computer in order to use it. A high-level data language allows the user to interact at the level of the logical data structure, unencumbered by physical details and machine characteristics. The language must facilitate the identification of data within a structure using Boolean expressions and logical data names, and it must permit expression of complete processing operations against the data structure.

5.3.2.2 Syntactic Styles of Command Languages

At the command level, statements to the system have to be more complete. Therefore, it is meaningful to speak of the various forms or syntactic styles of a language. Such language forms apply whether the user is operating online in immediate mode or in deferred mode (that is, entering statements for later execution).

The CODASYL Systems Committee identified four language syntactic styles as narrative, keyword, separator, and fixed position.* Using a data definition example, these four forms are shown in Figure 5-9.

```
NARRATIVE:
     RECORD NAME IS EMPLOYEE WITHIN PERSONNEL DATABASE.
     DATA-ITEM IS EMPLOYEE-NAME, TYPE IS CHARACTER,
     LENGTH IS VARYING WITH MAXIMUM 20, PRIVACY LOCK
     FOR THE DELETE FUNCTION IS PROCEDURE CHECK-USER.

KEYWORD:
     RECORD: NAME = EMPLOYEE, DATABASE = PERSONNEL.
     DATA-ITEM: NAME = EMPLOYEE-NAME, TYPE = CHAR,
     LENGTH = v20, LOCK (DELETE) = CALL (CHECK-USER).

SEPARATOR:
     RECORD EMPLOYEE, PERSONNEL.
     DATA-ITEM EMPLOYEE-NAME, CHAR, v20, , DELETE(CALL(CHECK-USER)).
```

FIXED POSITION:

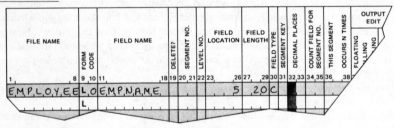

Figure 5-9. Diversity in Language Form or Syntactic Style.
Four styles are illustrated using the example of defining one data item (field) within an employee record.

The most general syntactic style is free-form **narrative**, sometimes called English-like. It usually has a precise syntactic and semantic meaning occasionally resulting in ambiguity and confusion when people try to interpret it in literal English. "Noise words" are sometimes added for clarity but ignored by the system.

Keyword form consists of a sequence of attribute-value pairs. The form is most suitable for a prompting level of dialogue at the terminal. The system generates the attribute name or keyword and the user responds with a value.

Separator form uses a fixed sequence of attributes. A statement usually begins

---

*CODASYL Systems Committee, *Feature Analysis of Generalized Data Base Management Systems*, New York: Association for Computing Machinery, 1971 May, pages 41-42.

with some "context specifier," a keyword, followed by a sequence of attribute values separated by some special character.

Fixed position usually requires a special preprinted form to show where each value is placed. Such forms are particularly useful for inputting large volumes of data. Eliminating the need to scan input makes data entry more efficient, for the machine. The fixed form is also useful in reducing errors in the preparation of input. The template on a screen normally uses fixed-position input in response to prompting.

5.3.3 Coexistence of Different User Interfaces

A community of users generally includes anyone from a first-time novice to an experienced user who is developing sophisticated application systems for other end users. A comprehensive DBMS should provide interfaces appropriate to this broad spectrum of users. Yet there should be uniformity in the underlying DBMS functions and the semantics of the interfaces.

For the same DBMS, it is possible to have several different user interfaces:

- System-driven interface with menus and prompts for the novice users and liberal use of help facilities.
- User-driven interface with an ad hoc command language.
- An extended command language for building command files for deferred execution.
- Natural language interface for the casual user.

The question becomes: Where to focus design and development effort? What can be built on top of what?

From the standpoint of systems architecture, a system-driven dialogue can be built on top of a command-driven interface. Menu and prompting dialogues essentially capture all the necessary information that would otherwise be expressed in one or more commands.

Similarly, a natural language interface for the casual user can be built on top of the command level. The natural language interface is still a user-driven interface but for the intermittent user. They are not assumed to be able to correctly formulate a command to the system. Therefore, dialoguing facilities are provided which allow the user to express a command in their natural language (say, English) with all its ambiguities and contextual dependencies. The system then attempts to interpret the command, asking the user to resolve ambiguities and provide missing information. The output from the natural language processor is a correctly formulated command which can be executed by the formal command processor of the DBMS.

There is some question whether novice or intermittent users should have a natural language interface where they attempt to initiate dialogue with the system, or a system-driven interface where they are led through the use of the system by a series of menus and prompts. The latter may prove to be easier and more efficient for such users.

Since all other user interfaces essentially construct a command for the user (see Figure 5-10), it is important to design and implement a complete and comprehensive command language first.

For a comprehensive DBMS, all user modes should be supported. Furthermore, a

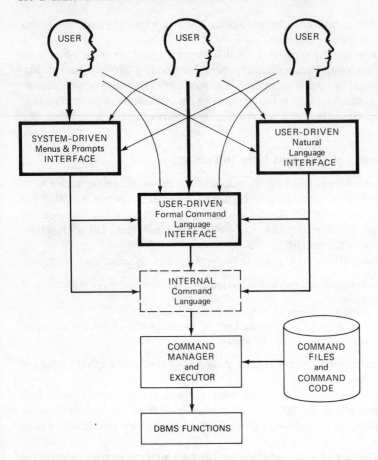

Figure 5-10. Building Multiple User Interfaces on a Common Command Language.
Three types of user interfaces to a DBMS can coexist. They would be built on top of the common formal command language, either a human-efficient narrative style or an underlying machine-efficient internal format. Users should be able to freely move from one type of interface to another depending on their level of experience in general and with respect to the specific function being performed.

user should be able to change interfaces as appropriate depending on their general level of knowledge of the system and their experience with the particular function being performed. Any request should be expressible either as a command or using system-driven prompts and menus.

For human efficiency, the command language should have a narrative syntactic style. However, for machine efficiency, the command language should be fixed position with encoded command verbs. Therefore, it is desirable to have an intermediate command language into which all other interfaces are translated before being stored or executed. The intermediate command language would store commands in a condensed (appearing cryptic), fixed format. Of course, the language would still be a high-level, structured, *data* language.

The user interfaces manage all dialogue with the user. This includes scanning and parsing the input, syntax checking, and messages for syntax errors. The command manager receives syntactically correct commands, loads the appropriate program code to execute the command (if necessary), and initiates execution of the command, that is, the DBMS function.

The preceding discussion is intended only to give a brief glimpse into a possible architecture for accomplishing the objective of separating the user interface modes from the DBMS functions, and of a user's being able to freely move among the different interfaces. The following discussion of menu handling gives specific ideas on the integration of commands and menus.

In choosing between menu driven or command driven, this text usually demonstrates a DBMS functional capability using an illustrative command language statement. Furthermore, the emphasis is on the semantics of the language statement rather than the particular syntax. This is done recognizing that menus and prompts can be built on top of the command language to capture all the information and parameters required to perform the function.

5.4 ADDITIONAL ONLINE SUPPORT

Additional facilities may be provided by a DBMS to support the online user or system developer. Online help facilities enable the user to obtain more detailed information on the meaning and use of a command, a menu, or a function within the system. A tutorial could be constructed from a sequence of help screens. For the person developing a system for online users, the system should provide facilities for defining and handling menus, data screens, and tailored help screens.

5.4.1 Help Facilities

As computers are used by more and more people, proportionally more users will have little background in and a low tolerance for computers. Computer professionals tend to be much more forgiving when using computers and more willing to study the documentation to solve some problem in using the system (largely because *they* have experienced the difficulty in building a ''user-friendly'' system). New novice users are much more impatient and demand to be able to get their job done with a minimum of prior effort, such as reading the documentation. Hence, the motivation for online help facilities.

Shifting the level of dialogue toward tutorial provides additional help for the user (see Figure 5-6).

At the prompting level, if the user does not know the acceptable responses or enters an invalid response, the system can display the set of choices or range of choices. For example, when entering a value for a data item, the system can display the data item type, a set of coded values, or ranges if these have been defined to the system.

At the choice level or menu level, the user can position the cursor at one of the options and press the HELP key to get to the tutorial level for a further explanation of the meaning of that option. A user presented with a sequence of menus is operating at the choice level of dialogue. Several systems offer a help screen to accompany each menu screen. With this facility, the new user could step through the help screens to begin learning about the system.

Even if a system operates in a strict command-driven mode, the online user could request help on any command using the HELP command (or help key), for example:

HELP LIST

and receive an online tutorial on the meaning, use, and syntax of the LIST command, including some examples. This could simply be a sequence of one or more text screens. To get the user started, the system could have a command:

HELP HELP

to explain the use of the help facility, and perhaps

HELP COMMANDS

to get a list of all the commands available in the system. In response to an error, the user might issue a command

HELP error

to receive an explanation of the error, what caused it, and how to correct and recover from the error.

A simple *tutorial* could be constructed by cycling through all the help screens in some logical sequence which the user might follow in using the system. This could be augmented with:

- Some initial screens to give an introduction and overview to the system.
- An explanation of certain features such as the use of special keys on the keyboard.
- How to perform certain functions such as copying files or building a command file.

Another helpful facility is to be able to take an aside from any current processing activity and look at the current status of things in the system, for example, to see:

- A list of defined files (record types) in the current database.
- The definition of a file (record type).
- The defined characteristics of a particular data item including some examples of valid values for the item.
- The current value for some system variables such as DATE.

A more sophisticated help facility provides a response appropriate for the immediate context—for example, positioning the cursor at an option in a menu and pressing the HELP key to receive an explanation for that option.

5.4.2 Menu Handling Facilities

A menu is a prompt from the system which presents the online user with a set of choices. The principles of direct manipulation suggest that the user have some physical mechanism for positioning the cursor to one of the options and then selecting an action.

If the normal operation with a menu involves only positioning and actioning keys, anything typed in by the user could be interpreted as a command. This is a very convenient method of allowing the user to freely move between system-driven menu dialogue and user-driven command dialogue. (Requiring or allowing the user to type in a number or a letter to indicate their choice makes it more difficult for the system to distinguish a command from a menu response. Perhaps the user would first tell the system that the next thing to be typed is a command rather than a menu choice.)

Every menu should be treated as another command within the system. One menu would be the initial menu to be invoked when the system is first started. The user can then:

- Follow along through the menus.
- Issue the name of some other menu where the user knows they can immediately begin the desired processing.
- Issue a system command with all of its required parameters.
- Issue a system command by itself and let the system initiate prompting for the parameters required to execute the command.

As should now be evident, there is no need to have the menus displayed in a strict hierarchy as is the practice in so many systems. If the user ever gets to a point in the system where they are calling for a command and the system does not have all the information it needs, it simply initiates some additional dialogue to obtain the missing information. Of course, the system should use all reasonable *defaults*, or states previously set by the user, before resorting to prompting for additional information. For example, unless stated otherwise in this command or previously, the output from a retrieval request would go to the screen.

A developer of online systems must be able to define menus. While it is always possible to use a low-level language for constructing menus, it is undesirable to do so. A menu definition and handling facility would allow the developer to more directly specify a menu without worrying about details of format and placement on the screen, and without writing procedural code to prompt for, test, and act on the user response. Figure 5-11 contains a schematic showing the various parts of a simple menu.

In one type of menu, all options are literals which can be prespecified and stored. The set of options is invariant. This would be the case, for example, after a user had opened or activated a particular file and the system prompts with the following menu options:

```
DISPLAY FILE DEFINITION
REVISE FILE DEFINITION
DISPLAY RECORDS
INSERT NEW RECORDS
CHANGE EXISTING RECORDS
DEFINE A REPORT
GENERATE A REPORT
```

Each choice would lead to a specified action.

A user developing a system for recording and reporting the contributions for a nonprofit organization may specify a menu such as:

```
ENTER A BATCH OF CONTRIBUTIONS
VALIDATE AND POST A BATCH OF CONTRIBUTIONS, PRINTING AUDIT TRAIL
SUMMARY REPORT OF CONTRIBUTIONS BY TIME PERIOD, BY DEPOSIT, BY FUND
PERIODIC REPORT TO CONTRIBUTORS
AGED ANALYSIS REPORT OF CONTRIBUTORS
MAINTENANCE OF FUND ACCOUNTS
GENERATE SUMMARY POSTINGS FOR GENERAL LEDGER
YEAR END PROCEDURES FOR SUMMARIZING, ARCHIVING, AND MAINTENANCE
```

Each menu option presumably leads to a user written procedure or another menu.

Another type of menu involves a set of choices which may vary for each time of usage. For example, when a user desires to open a file, the system can read the disk directory and display a list of all available files in the form of a menu. The action in this case would be to merely record the user's choice. In the command mode, if the user types "OPEN" without specifying a file name, the system would again respond by displaying the names of all available files.

A variable menu list would also be displayed whenever the user needed to pick one, or a series of, data items from a file. This would be the case, for example, when specifying a userschema for a file; a selection, projection, or sort operation on a particular file; or the calculation of statistics on a file.

Several variations are possible in the specification of menus. One would be to allow the menu definer to specify a variable name in one of the title lines or choice lines. For example, after opening a particular file, the developer may wish to display the name of the chosen file on subsequent menus. More generally, the system could

```
MENU NAME                                  ESCAPE TO:  MENU NAME

                        MENU TITLE
        Zero or more lines of descriptive information
        explaining usage, cautions, etc.

   OPTION ONE                       [ACTION ONE]

   OPTION TWO                       [ACTION TWO]

   OPTION THREE                     [ACTION THREE]
        :                                 :


Choose an option using ARROW keys; then press ENTER or HELP
```

Figure 5-11. Generic Form of a Simple Menu Screen.

Each menu has a name by which it is invoked. Each menu contains a set of choices, and actions associated with each choice. The action could be to invoke another menu or a command. A menu should be treated like another command, capable of being invoked as an immediate command, or from within a command file. Likewise, taking a choice in a menu invokes another command or set of commands. On any menu option, the user would press a key (RETURN or ENTER) to confirm the selection, or press the HELP key. Further, the user should be able to bypass the menu entirely by typing in a command directly allow the developers to literally *paint* their menus. The system would display a blank screen and the developer would move the cursor to spots on the screen to type what they desired to have displayed on the menu, specially marking variable names to be displayed, and commands to be invoked for each menu option.

One interesting approach to menu selection was reported by Joyce and Warn from the General Motors Research Lab. In their Regis DBMS, menus are all defined in a file. Each menu option is supported by one or more command files. Instead of going through the menus hierarchically, the user has the option of entering "a keyword (or character string) that is thought to be present in one of the menus. The system automatically creates a dynamic menu which includes all the selections containing that keyword. These selections may actually be from several different menus."*

5.4.3 Facilities for the System Developer

If a system has a command language, the next logical step is to be able to store sequences of commands in a file which can be invoked for execution at a later time. This is the basic facility needed to develop an application system for use by novice users (thus completing the cycle in Figure 5-1). The command file is named and becomes another command which is invoked by its name. Not all systems having a command language allow commands to be issued for immediate execution *and* stored in a file for deferred execution.

When building command files, additional commands are needed to control the flow of processing: IF . . . THEN . . . ELSE, DO . . . WHILE, DO . . . UNTIL, etc. The system also requires the use of variables and a mechanism for passing parameters between procedures.

In practically all cases, systems developers should use a high-level data language to build application systems. Rarely should any consideration be given to writing any procedures in a conventional programming language such as BASIC, PASCAL, or COBOL. Such languages, even augmented with a Data Manipulation Language (DML) like that proposed by CODASYL, are *low-level* languages *with respect to data processing*. The user "navigates" through a data structure, retrieving and processing one record at a time. Using languages at this level to build application systems should be the avenue of *last* resort. On a microcomputer, it is even questionable to have exits to user-written code—such a facility is often an escape for the DBMS developer who didn't do what should have been done in the first place.

The system developer needs to be able to create all the sorts of facilities which are used by the novice end user. The developer needs to be able to define:

- DATA FILES to store information.
- MENUS and the actions to be invoked for each choice.
- SCREENS to display data records and capture data values for storage.
- REPORTS for retrieving and manipulating stored data.
- HELP SCREENS tailored to the application.

*John D. Joyce and David R. Warn, "Human Factors Aspects of a Modern Data Base System," *Information & Management* (6), 1983, page 33.

All three types of programming users described in Chapter 3 are system developers. They are distinguished by the type of language facility used. If the DBMS does not provide a self-contained language for defining the five elements just listed, the developer must resort to using a conventional programming language augmented with only some of the basic DBMS functions.

5.5 TYPES OF DATA LANGUAGES: DEFINITION, MANIPULATION, AND MAPPING

Three basic types of data languages relate to the following three *functions*:

1. *Defining* a data structure.
2. *Manipulating* a data structure by specifying some process or operation on that structure.
3. *Mapping* one data structure onto another to serve as the basis for data translation or conversion.

The preceding sections of this chapter have already contained examples of definition and manipulation languages.

Data Definition Languages (DDLs) are used to write:

- A schema (the definition of a stored database).
- A userschema (a user view of data which is derivable from or mapable into the stored database).
- The definition of an input data transaction.

A low-level data definition language would define a data structure in terms of physical record layouts. A high-level language would define a data structure in terms of entities, named attributes of those entities, characteristics of those attributes, interentity relationships, and semantic constraints (or validation criteria), but it would not be encumbered with physical storage or access information. Of course, before actual data can be stored and retrieved, all types of definitional information must be provided to the system—logical structure, physical storage, and access path information. This is a more detailed, lower level of language for use primarily by the data administrator. A high-level data definition language permits a higher degree of abstraction in viewing a data structure, and allows users to focus on the important aspects of the structure.

Data Manipulation Languages (DMLs)* specify some process or operation on a data structure such as searching, retrieval, or update. A DML may also be a low-level or a high-level language as vividly illustrated in an earlier section of this chapter (see Figure 5-8).

---

*This text takes a rather broad interpretation of DML. Other authors restrict its meaning to the set of statements used to manipulate a database and which augment, or are embedded within, a host programming language such as COBOL. This is the original meaning established by the CODASYL Data Base Task Group in their reports of 1969 and 1971.

Data mapping languages are used to specify a mapping between two data structures: a userschema to a database schema, an input data transaction to the database, an old database to a revised database, or a stored database to an output report. One form of mapping relates the data items in one structure to the data items in another structure simply by equating corresponding data names. For example:

```
EMPNO  = EMPLOYEE_NUMBER
NAME   = EMPLOYEE_NAME
UNIT   = ORGANIZATIONAL_UNIT_NUMBER
SALARY = ACTUAL_SALARY / 12
     :
```

could be used to specify some convenient short names in a userschema and relate them to the full names in the database schema. The last mapping statement shows a conversion from annual salary to monthly salary. With this simple mapping, it is possible to rearrange the order of data items and to omit unused data items. Mapping statements such as the preceding ones could also be embedded in a manipulation language statement to temporarily redefine the name of a data item.

In the data translation operations of some systems, the mapping is implicit in the use of common data names from one data structure when defining another structure. Common data names create an undesirable degree of dependence between the two defined data structures (or a stored data structure and the implicit data structure of a data manipulation process).

There can be common language elements across these three types of data languages. For example, the use of Boolean selection expressions, which provide the criteria for identifying a subset of data within a data structure, may be common to a userschema definition language, a query language, and a mapping language. Within these basic language types, additional languages may be identified in terms of the related function, for example, validation language or access authorization language.

5.6 DATA LANGUAGES ON DATA STRUCTURES

Some semantic elements and the overall syntactic construction of high-level data languages depends, in part, upon the underlying data structure class. Some logical data structures must be known or assumed by the user. A language statement is written and interpreted in the context of *some* data structure. The user cannot be blind with respect to that data structure.

A user must and always will have some logical structure and definition in mind when interacting with and referencing a database. If it is not a picture of the stored database, then it must be some other picture. A userschema formally expresses an alternate and probably partial view of a database. It is a fallacy to suggest that a user can reference a database without having *any* logical view in mind. Both the system and the user must have a consistent understanding of the logical structure of the portion of the database being referenced in a processing task.

An understanding of high-level data manipulation languages begins with lan-

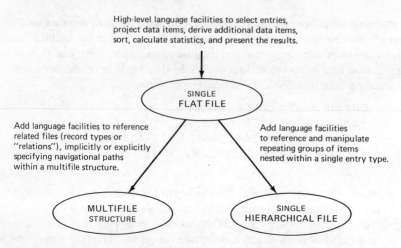

Figure 5-12. High-Level Data Languages on Basic Data Structures.
High-level languages to reference and manipulate single hierarchical or multifile data structures can be understood as extensions of a language for a single flat file. A composite language with both added facilities would be used on a data structure of multiple hierarchical files.

guages on a single flat file. Flat file languages provide a base for building high-level languages to reference a single hierarchical data structure or a multifile structure (see Figure 5-12).

A language for a single flat file provides facilities to select and manipulate subsets of entries in a file. Extending to more complex data structures, the high-level language must provide facilities to reference multiple record types in the same statement, whether across levels of a hierarchy or different record types in a multifile structure.

A language for a multiple hierarchical file structure would combine the facilities for the single hierarchical file and the multifile structures. Such a language would be more complex, reflecting the added complexity of the underlying data structure.

A userschema can partially insulate the user from such complexity by defining only the entities, attributes, and relationships needed by the user. This permits the user to have a simplified view of a portion of the overall database structure. The userschema view of a multifile structure can be restricted to fewer files with fewer relationships, to a single hierarchical structure, or even to a single flat file view. This approach is commonly taken in the design of generalized languages to query multifile data structures.

5.7 DBMS MODES OF OPERATION

One extreme mode of operation is the DBMS which makes the database available on a batch basis, that is, the user submits a request to a central computer facility, which executes the request and delivers the results some time later. This was the dominant mode of operation in most earlier DBMSs. The following approaches can achieve higher degrees of availability either in speed of response to the user or in increased throughput:

- Put the database online by using direct access storage devices.
- Put the user online at a terminal connected directly to the computer system.
- Use inverted file structures for faster database search.
- Generate program code for frequent user requests rather than interpretively executing user requests.

The following subsections discuss each of these approaches. These approaches suggest alternative classifications of database management systems. Of course, the mode of operation at any particular installation is determined by the operating environment—the hardware, the operating system and other system software, the secondary data storage devices, and the terminal devices and their communication links to the computer.

5.7.1 Sequential DBMSs

A sequential DBMS always operates by processing a database sequentially. Since a given processing run must be based on a single defined ordering, a sequential DBMS can process only a single file at a time (either a flat file or a hierarchical file) or a set of coordinated files (which conceptually become one big file). Such systems are sometimes called "file management systems" because they sequentially process one file at a time.

Since the system passes over the entire file to process a single user request, several user requests are normally batched for more efficient processing. Retrieval and update requests can both be included in a processing run against the file. It is an external administrative responsibility to ensure that the requests are properly sequenced in the processing run.

With multiple requests, the system retrieves entries from the file one at a time. While looking at one entry, the system cycles through each of the requests asking if the entry is to be retrieved or updated. In this way the system can build several output reports simultaneously. On the first pass the system generates output lines for the various reports requested. These lines are intermixed, but each is associated with a particular requested report. After the file is processed, the system simply sorts the output lines using "report identifier" as the primary sort key. In this way the output lines for each report are collected together for further processing, sorting, and output.

The database for a sequential DBMS may be stored on a sequential medium, such as punched cards or magnetic tape, or on direct access storage devices. In either case, the database is still processed sequentially. A sequential DBMS may also permit online access. Unless the database is very small, the system may take several minutes or longer to respond to a user request. Under such circumstances, the user will normally initiate a request at the terminal and then have the output delivered later when the processing is completed.

A great many database management systems available today operate by sequentially processing a single file.

5.7.2 Online, Interactive DBMSs

With an online, interactive DBMS, the user enters a request to the system from an online terminal and waits for a response from the system. With the exception of large, complex retrievals, an interactive DBMS should respond within a matter of seconds. The response may be either a direct answer to the request or a request for additional or clarifying information from the user.

The database in an online, interactive DBMS must have multiple external access points, not just one as is the case with a sequential file. This implies an access method which can directly locate individual entries or subsets of entries in the single file or the multiple files of a database. In the simplest case, the system provides an external accessing mechanism based upon the primary entry identifier of a file. With a hierarchical file, the system may provide the external access mechanism only at the top level of the entry, or it may provide external access at any level of the data structure (a substantially more complex capability).

With a sequential DBMS the user request is expressed at the command level of dialogue. Online, interactive operation makes possible other levels of dialogue—tutorial, choice, and prompting. Of course, it is possible to interactively generate a request which is subsequently processed by a sequential DBMS.

Full interactive operation accepts both retrieval and update requests from multiple locations at any time the system is in operation. One common variation allows retrieval only during the busy day, with updates being performed at night. Such a procedure results in better response to daytime inquiries, greater control over update operations, and more efficient processing of update requests which can now be batched. For many organizations, it is adequate to operate with a database which is current for the opening of business in the morning but which loses currency during the day as update transactions occur.

If it is important to reflect changes to the database during the day, it is possible to flag any entry that changes during the day and record the change in a special file which can be referenced by retrievals later in the day. At night or periodically, the main file is updated. Such an arrangement is useful in an environment where a small proportion of the file is subject to modification during any given day. This might include inventory applications or customer service applications (utilities, banking, etc.).

5.7.3 Inverted Data Structures

The discussion of basic data structures did not consider how the data would be accessed. For most users, access path information is secondary to logical data structure information. At this logical level, the user knows the data structure and can use the language to identify subsets of the data for processing; the user is not concerned with the process of isolating and extracting the identified subsets of data from the entire database.

User requests may require access to a file using data items other than the primary entry identifier. A knowledge of the processing activities against a database may indicate that certain subsets are retrieved or certain data items are used for retrieval more frequently than others. In this case, it may be desirable for the database administrator to declare these preferred avenues of access to the system. Then the system can establish additional mechanisms to enable faster search for certain retrievals.

With the database stored on a direct access storage device, it is possible to narrow the search to the relevant portion of the stored database. For example, it is possible to construct an index on any one of the data items (attributes) in a file (see Figure 5-13). A file is then said to be *inverted* on each of its indexed data items.

Although inverted file structures are sometimes considered the basis for classifying DBMSs, it is important to recognize that they do not represent a different logical data structure. Inversion is a variant which can be added to *any* of the basic data structures. The sole purpose of inversion is retrieval efficiency. An inverted file structure enables faster retrieval of records in a file (assuming that the items used as the basis for selection are indexed). On update, inversion will enable faster access to the record(s) to be changed, but then it may also be necessary to update some of the indexes as a result of updating the file.

5.7.4 Generated Procedures versus Interpretive Execution

In constructing a DBMS, two alternative approaches can be followed. Under interpretive execution, user input requests are directly executed by a generalized program. The executing program parses and interprets the user request in its original form. Under the generative approach, a compiler or translator generates machine language object code from the user request (or some intermediate code which is later interpreted). The generated object code can be executed directly by the computer. A generative approach is most practical when the user request will be executed repeatedly in the future and speed of execution must dominate flexibility for ad hoc usage.

A generative DBMS takes user requests or user programs along with the definition of a database and generates object programs with built-in subprocesses tailored to performing the specified processing against the defined database. A generative approach results in much more efficient processing of repeated requests in a database environment. In a fully generative approach, there is no run-time system to control the execution of the user procedures other than the job management routines in the operating system. With no run-time database control system, it is difficult if not impossible to coordinate concurrently executed user procedures as they interact with the database.

In practice, neither philosophy is used in its pure form. At compile time, the system usually performs some initial processing of the data definition or user request in its original input form before it is stored. Then, when a user request is executed, the run-time system can access the previously stored information and invoke any previously stored, generated pieces of object code. Compile-time processing can entail parsing of the input data definition or user request into its semantic elements and storage in a compact, machine-readable form. The compiler or translator can also perform some validation on the initial input; for example, a userschema can be compared to its schema to ensure its compatibility.

A user preparing a request expects either immediate or deferred execution. In either case, the system may use a generative or an interpretive approach. For immedi-

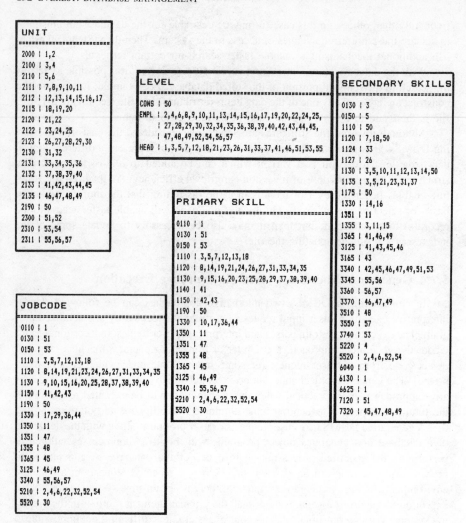

```
UNIT
=============================
2000 : 1,2
2100 : 3,4
2110 : 5,6
2111 : 7,8,9,10,11
2112 : 12,13,14,15,16,17
2115 : 18,19,20
2120 : 21,22
2122 : 23,24,25
2123 : 26,27,28,29,30
2130 : 31,32
2131 : 33,34,35,36
2132 : 37,38,39,40
2133 : 41,42,43,44,45
2135 : 46,47,48,49
2190 : 50
2300 : 51,52
2310 : 53,54
2311 : 55,56,57
```

```
LEVEL
=================================================
CONS : 50
EMPL : 2,4,6,8,9,10,11,13,14,15,16,17,19,20,22,24,25,
     : 27,28,29,30,32,34,35,36,38,39,40,42,43,44,45,
     : 47,48,49,52,54,56,57
HEAD : 1,3,5,7,12,18,21,23,26,31,33,37,41,46,51,53,55
```

```
SECONDARY SKILLS
==============================
0130 : 3
0150 : 5
1110 : 50
1120 : 7,18,50
1124 : 33
1127 : 26
1130 : 3,5,10,11,12,13,14,50
1135 : 3,5,21,23,31,37
1175 : 50
1330 : 14,16
1351 : 11
1355 : 3,11,15
1365 : 41,46,49
3125 : 41,43,45,46
3165 : 43
3340 : 42,45,46,47,49,51,53
3345 : 55,56
3360 : 56,57
3370 : 46,47,49
3510 : 48
3550 : 57
3740 : 53
5220 : 4
5520 : 2,4,6,52,54
6040 : 1
6130 : 1
6625 : 1
7120 : 51
7320 : 45,47,48,49
```

```
PRIMARY SKILL
========================================
0110 : 1
0130 : 51
0150 : 53
1110 : 3,5,7,12,13,18
1120 : 8,14,19,21,24,26,27,31,33,34,35
1130 : 9,15,16,20,23,25,28,29,37,38,39,40
1140 : 41
1150 : 42,43
1190 : 50
1330 : 10,17,36,44
1350 : 11
1351 : 47
1355 : 48
1365 : 45
3125 : 46,49
3340 : 55,56,57
5210 : 2,4,6,22,32,52,54
5520 : 30
```

```
JOBCODE
=================================================
0110 : 1
0130 : 51
0150 : 53
1110 : 3,5,7,12,13,18
1120 : 8,14,19,21,23,24,26,27,31,33,34,35
1130 : 9,10,15,16,20,25,28,37,38,39,40
1150 : 41,42,43
1190 : 50
1330 : 17,29,36,44
1350 : 11
1351 : 47
1355 : 48
1365 : 45
3125 : 46,49
3340 : 55,56,57
5210 : 2,4,6,22,32,52,54
5520 : 30
```

Figure 5-13. Multiple Indexes on a Single File.

An index is essentially another file with an entry for each unique value of the data item being indexed. Associated with each data item value in the index is a list of pointers to the records in the main file containing that value for the data item. In a file, there will be one index for each data item declared to be indexed.

EMPLOYEE: (the file to which the indexes point)

EMPNO	EMPNAME	UNIT	JOB CODE	LEVEL	TITLE	SEX	BIRTH DATE	PRIMARY SKILL	SSK1	SSK2	SSK3	SSK4	ACTUAL SALARY
1: 45584	PETERSON, N.M.	2000	0110	HEAD	DIVISION MANAGER	M	280607	0110	6130	6625	6040		56000
2: 32579	LYNN, K.R.	2000	5210	EMPL	SECRETARY	F	530121	5210	5520				12000
3: 57060	CARR, P.I.	2100	1110	HEAD	MANAGER DEVELOPMENT DEPT	M	350720	1110	1130	1135	0130	1355	48000
4: 15324	CALLAGAN, R.F.	2100	5210	EMPL	SECRETARY	F	550606	5210	5520	5220			10800
5: 10261	GUTTMAN, G.J.	2110	1110	HEAD	MANAGER SYSTEMS GROUP	M	301110	1110	1130	1135	0150		35000
6: 72556	HARRIS, D.L.	2110	5210	EMPL	SECRETARY	F	550517	5210	5520				8400
7: 24188	WALTERS, R.J.	2111	1110	HEAD	CHIEF PROPOSAL SECTION	M	260202	1110	1120				28000
8: 21675	SCARBOROUGH, J.B.	2111	1120	EMPL	MECH ENGR	M	240914	1120					21000
9: 18130	HENDERSON, R.G.	2111	1130	EMPL	ELEC ENGR	M	340121	1130					23000
10: 91152	GARBER, R.E.	2111	1130	EMPL	ELEC ENGR	M	440707	1330	1130				16400
11: 30793	COMPTON, D.R.	2111	1350	EMPL	COST ESTIMATOR	M	290328	1350	1351	1355	1130		16200
12: 81599	FRIEDMAN, J.M.	2112	1110	HEAD	CHIEF DESIGN SECTION	M	360317	1110	1130				26000
13: 21777	FRANCIS, G.C.	2112	1110	EMPL	SYSTEMS ENGR	M	321111	1110	1130				24000
14: 24749	FAULKNER, W.M.	2112	1120	EMPL	MECH ENGR	M	400621	1120	1130	1330			24000
15: 13581	FITINGER, G.J.	2112	1130	EMPL	ELEC ENGR	M	431216	1130	1355				22000
16: 82802	APGAR, A.J.	2112	1130	EMPL	ELEC ENGR	M	500715	1130	1330				21000
17: 63633	BLANK, L.F.	2112	1330	EMPL	DRAFTSMAN	F	491010	1330					16000
18: 22959	BRIGGS, G.R.	2115	1110	HEAD	CHIEF PROD SPEC SECTION	M	400508	1110	1120				24000
19: 29414	ARTHUR, P.J.	2115	1120	EMPL	MECH ENGR	M	300109	1120					22000
20: 37113	ARNETTE, L.J.	2115	1130	EMPL	ELEC ENGR	M	450729	1130					22000
21: 68840	GODDARD, D.H.	2120	1120	HEAD	MANAGER STDS ENGR GROUP	M	330119	1120	1135				29000
22: 71160	GERRISH, C.S.	2120	5210	EMPL	SECRETARY	F	560331	5210					8000
23: 35401	ANDERSON, R.E.	2122	1120	HEAD	CHIEF SYSTEM STDS SECTION	M	380228	1130	1135				23000
24: 91589	TAUBER, J.S.	2122	1120	EMPL	MECH ENGR	M	451114	1120					19000
25: 80823	STADERMAN, P.K.	2122	1130	EMPL	ELEC ENGR	M	430507	1130					19400
26: 64937	SMITH, R.E.	2123	1120	HEAD	CHIEF COMPONENT STDS SECTION	M	401129	1120	1127				22000
27: 82166	RHODES, J.H.	2123	1120	EMPL	MECH ENGR	M	490303	1120					19000
28: 28654	RAYMOND, H.F.	2123	1130	EMPL	ELEC ENGR	M	341216	1130					20000
29: 17848	HUGHES, J.W.	2123	1330	EMPL	DRAFTSMAN	F	350120	1130					17000
30: 33144	QUINN, S.M.	2123	5520	EMPL	FILE CLERK	F	561115	5520					11000
31: 48464	CHANDLER, W.R.	2130	1120	HEAD	MANAGER COMPONENT ENGR GROUP	M	351015	1120	1135				33000
32: 44432	BERGMANN, R.I.	2130	5210	EMPL	SECRETARY	F	540718	5210					9000
33: 68795	COOPER, J.C.	2131	1120	HEAD	CHIEF ENGR SECTION A	M	290309	1120	1124				24000
34: 39464	BUSTER, A.B.	2131	1120	EMPL	MECH ENGR	M	380719	1120					22000
35: 79935	BOLD, E.W.	2131	1120	EMPL	MECH ENGR	M	460416	1120					21000
36: 62999	NORMAN, H.R.	2131	1330	EMPL	DRAFTSMAN	M	331101	1330					18000
37: 90816	MCCARTHY, J.K.	2132	1130	HEAD	CHIEF ENGR SECTION B	M	431020	1130	1135				23000
38: 36472	MASSARD, L.R.	2132	1130	EMPL	ELEC ENGR	M	201010	1130					21600
39: 10295	SILCOTT, D.N.	2132	1130	EMPL	ELEC ENGR	M	430223	1130					19000
40: 89876	SKINNER, I.P.	2132	1130	EMPL	ELEC ENGR	M	480419	1130					20000
41: 47289	SCHRADER, F.G.	2133	1150	HEAD	CHIEF PROD ENGR SECTION	M	420909	1140	3125	1365			21000
42: 12245	KENT, M.J.	2133	1150	EMPL	PROD ENGR	M	260125	1150	3125				19600
43: 50498	LEGGETT, P.F.	2133	1150	EMPL	PROD ENGR	M	330517	1150	3125	1365			20000
44: 57084	FINERMAN, A.B.	2133	1330	EMPL	DRAFTSMAN	M	500622	1330					17000
45: 21475	FLETCHER, M.W.	2133	1365	EMPL	TOOL DESIGNER	M	320729	1365	3125	3340	7320		19000
46: 26934	HAMMER, C.P.	2135	3125	HEAD	CHIEF MODEL SHOP SECTION	M	200613	3125	3340	3125	1365	3370	20000
47: 15052	BOYD, W.V.	2135	1351	EMPL	MECH TECHN	M	420917	1351	3340	7320	3370		18000
48: 21261	CURTIS, K.R.	2135	1355	EMPL	ELEC TECHN	M	360304	1355	3510	7320			17000
49: 74090	GRAY, S.R.	2135	3125	EMPL	TOOL MAKER	M	230703	3125	3340	7320	1365	3370	19000
50: 87354	DIETERICH, L.J.	2190	1190	CONS	CHIEF SCIENTIST	M	250423	1190	1130	1120	1110	1175	44000
51: 87277	SONNENFELDT, W.R.	2300	0130	HEAD	MANAGER OPERATIONS DEPT	M	230501	0130	3340	7120			44000
52: 61706	FRESCOTT, W.C.	2300	5210	EMPL	SECRETARY	F	540703	5210	5520				10000
53: 61284	MAILLETT, J.R.	2310	0150	HEAD	MANAGER FACTORY OPNS GROUP	M	311126	0150	3340	3740			28000
54: 75683	MELCHERT, F.F.	2310	5210	EMPL	SECRETARY	F	350813	5210	5520				10000
55: 19357	PAYNE, W.F.	2311	3340	HEAD	CHIEF FAB SECTION A	M	330821	3340	3345				20000
56: 32924	LEVITT, P.S.	2311	3340	EMPL	MACHINE OPR	M	440422	3340	3345	3360			16000
57: 42055	LITTLE, E.F.	2311	3340	EMPL	MACHINE OPR	M	380302	3340	3360	3550			17000

ate execution, generated program code can be executed immediately. Using an interpretive approach, a user request can be stored as is for deferred execution. When making a request for immediate execution, the user must provide *all* the information needed to complete the processing. Deferred execution means that the information is supplied at two different times. First the user request is stored and labeled. Then it can be later retrieved from a library of stored requests, have the remaining information added to the request and executed. In preparing requests for deferred execution, users desire additional capabilities in the language: looping, conditional execution, and the use of intermediate variables to be valued at execution time.

SUMMARY

DBMSs can be classified and understood in terms of their user interfaces, languages, or modes of operation.

In studying DBMSs, it is insufficient to look only at the definable class of data structures. It is also necessary to look at the languages used to define and process a data structure, and to convert one data structure to another. Most users most of the time should use high-level data languages. A comprehensive DDL permits a user to focus on the essential meaning and structure of a database, without concern for its manipulation and storage, and provides more power per statement. The user can specify processes on the database with fewer statements, perhaps even one, making it easier to write, understand, and modify application processes.

DBMSs evolved from an offline, batch orientation to online, interactive use, reaching full bloom in the microcomputer environment. Principles of direct manipulation suggest that the user should have continuous, visual representation of the object of interest; that physical actions (using arrow keys, joy stick, trackball, mouse, light pen, or touch screen) replace complex language syntax; and that rapid, incremental operations be immediately visible.

Users can be classified by usage mode, ad hoc or planned/deferred, and by dialogue style. The novice, ad hoc end user needs a system driven dialogue using menus and prompts, including a tutorial level of dialogue and help screens. A more experienced user with a command language can engage in a user driven dialogue. A command language should be high-level with respect to *data* processing with the user conceptualizing actions on whole files. Low-level languages require much more writing and limit the system's ability to optimize processing. Menus and natural language interfaces can be built on top of a common command language. Command language syntax style may range over narrative, keyword, separator, and fixed form.

DBMSs operate in various modes with differing responsiveness to user requests. In sequential mode, the DBMS passes over every record in a file. Efficiency results from processing several requests at a time. To operate interactively with a user, the DBMS must have direct access to individual records in its files. Inverted file structures provide access based upon multiple, indexed data items. Any type of data structure may have varying degrees of inversion for faster search (but perhaps slower update).

EXERCISES

5-1. Describe five characteristics of the microcomputer user environment which contrast with a mainframe computer environment.

5-2. What are the implications of the statement "Today's microcomputer users are inherently online" for the design and operation of DBMSs and other software?

5-3. What merit is there in the statement "The developer of a DBMS for microcomputers may be better off never having known the world of large, mainframe computers"?

5-4. What are the principles of direct manipulation? Illustrate how these principles are violated in systems of today with which you have had some experience. What advantages stem from applying these principles?

5-5. What does the phrase "layered approach to learning" mean in the context of a user interface to a DBMS?

5-6. Describe several different physical mechanisms for positioning a cursor on the screen. Why are they preferred to commands such as "UP 6 LINES" or "3" when making a selection from a menu?

5-7. Types of online users can be distinguished by mode of usage and style of dialogue. What facilities are most likely required by each type of user. Write the most appropriate levels of dialogue (tutorial, choice, prompting, block prompting, and command) in each of the four quadrants of Figure 5-1. There may be more than one in each quadrant.

5-8. Describe the essential characteristics of a high-level data definition language and a high-level data manipulation language. Why is it important for most usage of a DBMS to be through high-level data languages? What are the chief benefits of a high-level data language? What is lost by the use of a high-level data language?

5-9. Contrast low-level and high-level data definition languages as they define data structures. Who is (should be) the main user of a low-level data definition language?

5-10. In studying DBMSs, why is it insufficient to look only at the definable class of data structures?

5-11. Describe the nature and purpose of an online help facility.

5-12. What should a menu handling facility do for the user who is developing an application system for novice, ad hoc users? What additional features does a system developer need in a DBMS command language?

5-13. What are three types of data languages? Contrast the purpose of each and give an illustrative statement for each type.

5-14. Discuss why it is necessary for a user to have some knowledge of the logical definition and structure of a database. Must this view be the same for all users? Explain.

5-15. Describe the operation of a sequential DBMS. What changes are needed to support an online, interactive user?

5-16. What is the main purpose of inverting a data structure, that is, of building indexes for a data structure? Explain why this does not constitute another class of logical data structures.

5-17. In constructing a DBMS, there are two approaches to executing user directives: interpretive execution or generated procedures. Although these two approaches may be used in combination, describe each in its more or less pure form. What are the advantages and disadvantages of each approach, especially in terms of:
   a. the time it takes to perform a user request with lots of internal repetitive operations, for example, performing the same process on many record instances.
   b. the time it takes to set up and begin processing the user request.
   c. the time it takes to revise a defined user process.
   d. the appropriateness of the approach for an online, interactive user.

SELECTED REFERENCES

BRITISH COMPUTER SOCIETY Query Languages Group, *Query Languages: A Unified Approach*, London: Heyden & Son (also Philadelphia), 1981, 105 pages.

HAREL, Elie C. and Ephraim R. McLEAN, "The Effects of Using a Nonprocedural Computer Language on Programmer Productivity," *MIS Quarterly* (9:2), 1985 June, pages 109-120.

> Conducted an experiment to compare COBOL and FOCUS (a higher-level data language) in terms of programmer productivity and program efficiency. *Real*, professional programmers developed *real* administrative applications; three were simple and three were not so simple. The applications involved report generation from pre-existing VSAM and sequential files. All programmers were online to the same computer in the same organization; some were beginners and others experienced. Overall, the FOCUS programmers took one-third the time to design, code, and test their programs than the COBOL programmers. For beginning programmers, FOCUS was five times faster. By contrast, the COBOL programs executed significantly faster in terms of CPU time.

MARTIN, James, *Application Development Without Programmers*, Englewood Cliffs, NJ: Prentice-Hall, 1982.

MEHLMANN, Marilyn, *When People Use Computers, An Approach to Developing an Interface*, Englewood Cliffs, NJ: Prentice-Hall, 1981.

MORLAND, D. Verne, "Human Factors Guidelines for Terminal Interface Design," *Communications of the ACM* (26:7), 1983 July, pages 484-494.

MOZEICO, Howard, "A Human/Computer Interface to Accommodate User Learning Stages," *Communications of the ACM* (25:2), 1982 February, pages 100-104.

REISNER, P., "Human Factors Studies of Database Query Languages: A Survey and Assessment," *ACM Computing Surveys* (13:1), 1981 March, pages 13-31.

SHNIEDERMAN, Ben, "Direct Manipulation: A Step Beyond Programming Languages," *Computer* (16:8), 1983 August, pages 57-69.

WELTY, C. and D. STEMPLE, "Human Factors Comparison of a Procedural and a Non-procedural Query Language," *ACM Transactions on Database Systems* (6:4), 1981 December, pages 626-649.

> Studied two high-level languages, SQL and TABLET, which differed primarily in their degree of procedurality. Students without programming experience who studied the procedural language wrote difficult queries better than those who studied the non-procedural language. The experiment did not measure the time to develop and write the queries.

ZLOOF, Moshe M., "Office-by-Example: A Business Language that Unifies Data and Word Processing and Electronic Mail," *IBM Systems Journal* (21:3), 1982, pages 272-304.

DATABASE DESIGN AND DEFINITION

6.1	THE PROCESS OF DATABASE DESIGN	198
6.1.1	The Database: A Model or Image of Reality	199
6.1.2	Designing the "Natural" Data Structure	199
6.1.3	Logical Database Structure Design	201
6.1.4	Schema Diagram—Graphical Representation of a Database Structure	203
6.2	THE PROCESS OF DATABASE DEFINITION	205
6.2.1	Data Definition Language—Linear Representation	205
6.3	DATABASE DEFINITION INFORMATION	213
6.3.1	Characteristics of Data Items	215
6.3.1.1	Name and Description	215
6.3.1.2	Value Type: Numeric, String, Special	215
6.3.1.3	Units of Measurement	217
6.3.1.4	Length and Format	217
6.3.1.5	Value Set: Ranges, Enumeration, and Encoding	218
6.3.1.6	Fixed and Controlled Value Sets	218
6.3.1.7	Role Dependent Characteristics: Existence, Uniqueness, etc.	219
6.3.2	Groups, Entries, and Records	221
6.3.2.1	Characteristics of Repeating Groups	222
6.3.3	Characteristics of Relationships	223
6.3.3.1	Exclusivity	224
6.3.3.2	Exhaustibility (or Dependency)	226
6.3.3.3	Degree	228
6.3.3.4	Criterion	229
6.3.3.5	Representing Relationships	231
6.3.3.6	Representation in CODASYL and Relational Data Structures	236
6.3.4	Validation Criteria and Semantic Constraints	239
6.3.5	Storage and Access Information	240
6.4	IMPORTANCE OF FORMAL DATABASE DEFINITION	242
6.5	LOGICAL DATABASE DESIGN	244
6.5.1	Database Design Methodologies	244
6.5.2	Entity-Attribute-Relationship versus Object-Relation Approaches	245
6.5.3	Rules to Guide Logical Database Design	246
	SUMMARY	250
	EXERCISES	251
	SELECTED REFERENCES	254

Database design and definition are the first steps in setting up a database to serve the needs of users in an organization. Subsequent processes discussed in later chapters include creation, update, retrieval, revision, restructure, reorganization, and, ultimately, retirement.

Database establishment involves the following steps:

- *Design* of a database to model the real world and to meet the user's information requirements.
- *Definition* of a database using the data definition language of some DBMS to formally express the structure, semantics, and constraints of a database.
- *Creation*, that is, collecting actual data and storing it according to the definition.

Once established, a database is available to users for retrieval and update. Update processes are used to keep the database contents a current and accurate representation of the user's world. The database administrator is responsible for establishing databases—for overseeing, controlling, and assisting in the design, definition, and creation of databases to meet the collective needs of all interested users and application processes in the organization.

Every DBMS has or assumes particular conventions regarding the physical storage of data. Newly collected or previously existing data (that is, existing external to the DBMS) is not likely to conform to the system storage conventions. Therefore, it is necessary to convert the external source data into the system's internal representation. The conversion process involves the two steps of database definition and database creation. The prior process of database design specifies *what* data should be collected and stored, and the logical structure of data items, groups, and relationships.

After an established database has been in use for a time (perhaps even before it is installed), organizational and environmental pressures for *revision* begin to arise. Revising an established database involves:

- Redefining the database *schema*.
- Restructuring and reorganizing the *stored data*.
- Changing defined *processes* on the revised database.
- Changing the way some *people* view and interact with the database.

The revision process is discussed in Chapter 11.

This chapter describes the facilities of a comprehensive data definition language. Such a language enables the user to define many characteristics of the data to be stored. Without a comprehensive data definition, the DBMS is less able to *manage* the data. If the users know something about the stored data but cannot declare it to the system, they bear the burden of ensuring that the data conforms to the undeclared characteristics.

6.1 THE PROCESS OF DATABASE DESIGN

Database design seeks to develop a detailed description of a database that will meet the needs of all users and application processes expected to use the database now or in the future. Since both anticipated and future unanticipated uses of the database should influence the design, the requirements of the dominant, immediate user should not unduly bias the process of logical database design. If not the needs of the "big user," then what should provide the basis for developing the logical design of a database?

6.1.1 The Database: A Model or Image of Reality

The most important basis for developing the logical design of a database is the real world of the using environment. The central objective of the logical database design process is to model the collective user perceptions of the real world. The database reflects an image of the real world; an image which governs the behavior of people and application processes in the organization. Conversely, the behavior of the organization depends upon the image recorded in the database. This characterization of the database as the image of an organization is based upon the work of Boulding wherein the analogy can be carried much further.*

The starting point for database design is the organization—its environment, its central mission, its basic operations and activities, and the main products, services, people, and other organizations with which it deals. The logical database structure should model selected aspects of the operations, entities, and events as they really exist or happen. This design approach leads to a more stable and understandable database structure than alternative approaches.

The steps in the process of database design and definition are shown in Figure 6-1, along with the primary inputs and outputs of each step. Experienced database designers find it helpful to separate the design process into a series of distinct steps.

6.1.2 Designing the "Natural" Data Structure

At the beginning of the design process, it is important to capture the essential aspects of the environment to be modeled without concern for how the resulting data structure might be represented within any particular database system. The designer identifies the real world *entities* about which information is to be collected and stored, the *attributes* of those entities, and the *relationships* among the various entities and attributes.

The logical structure of a database primarily reflects the relationships in the real world being modeled. Relationships are the key, the very essence of logical database structure. This logical structure can be represented in a graph, called a *schema diagram*, where a node represents an entity and an arc represents a relationship. Often the graphical schema diagram of the natural data structure is very complex. At this stage in the design process, it is important to capture *all* the relevant information about entities and the characteristics of the inter-entity relationships. (The "natural" data structure is also called a "conceptual" data structure.)

*Kenneth E. Boulding, *The Image: Knowledge in Life and Society*, Ann Arbor, MI: University of Michigan Press, 1956 (Ann Arbor Paperback, 1961), pages 6ff.

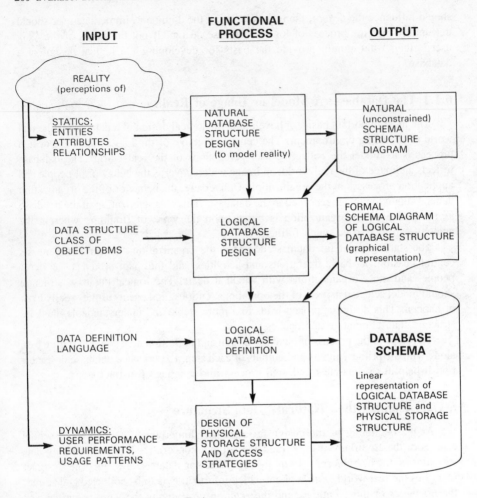

Figure 6-1. The Process of Database Design.
There are four distinct steps in designing a database and formally expressing that design to a DBMS:

- Graphically representing the data and its structure in a way that most naturally models the users' reality.
- Preparing a second graphical representation which molds the natural, unconstrained data structure into a structure which is definable in the DBMS used to implement the structure.
- Formally specifying the logical database structure by writing statements in the data definition language of a DBMS.
- Completing the formal definition by adding specifications of user performance requirements, storage structures, and access strategies. (In many systems this information is integrated with the logical data definition. If so, the database designer must not let physical storage and access information unduly influence the design of the logical data structure.)

Figure 6-2 is a schema diagram of the natural data structure relating to the personnel and organizational data introduced in Chapter 4. The reader should look back to the various designs (flat file, hierarchical, etc.) introduced in Chapter 4 and note how they differ from the natural data structure presented here, particularly noting what is missing in the designs constrained by each data structure class.

The later discussion of relationships includes a full explanation of the notation. Upon closer examination, some relationships are not easy to characterize due to less-than-obvious relationships in the real world. In this example, the relationship between EMPLOYEE and POSITION is not straightforward. A POSITION can relate to one *or more* EMPLOYEES and an authorized salary is assigned to the multiple. One clue is to determine the information necessary to uniquely identify each instance of POSITION. In this case, it would be the ORGANIZATIONAL UNIT NUMBER *and* the POSITION JOBCODE. Furthermore, it is possible to have an unfilled position as well as a hired employee whose salary is not authorized. This leads to the non-exhaustive, 1:N relationship shown.

In preparing the natural data structure, the designer's only concern is to accurately and completely model the reality of interest; the reality in which users operate and make decisions. The designer should not be constrained by what DBMS will be used to implement the final database, indeed, not even think about the DBMS or the computer, only about formally describing the real world.

6.1.3 Logical Database Structure Design

With a reasonably complete representation of the natural structure, the database designer can begin to design a data structure that will "fit" the DBMS used to implement the database. For any DBMS, there is a class of data structures which are definable to the system.

The **data structure class** of a DDL is reflected in the *structural elements* (such as data items, nonrepeating groups, repeating groups, hierarchical relationships, or more general relationships) available for defining a data structure, and *composition rules* for assembling these structural elements (such as maximum number of levels of nested repeating groups, or minimum and maximum number of occurrences of a repeating group).

As a general rule, there will be some aspects of a natural data structure which cannot be directly represented in a given system. The database designer often finds it necessary to "mold" the natural data structure into the data structure class of the object DBMS. For example:

- Omitting direct representation of some relationships to arrive at a hierarchical data structure—the EMPLOYEE-POSITION relationship in Figure 6-2, for example.
- Flattening a natural hierarchy to yield a single record schema in a flat file system.

It is usually possible to convert the natural data structure into the logical data structure class of a DBMS without loss of information *to the user*. It may, however, result in greater data redundancy and more difficult retrieval and maintenance operations on the

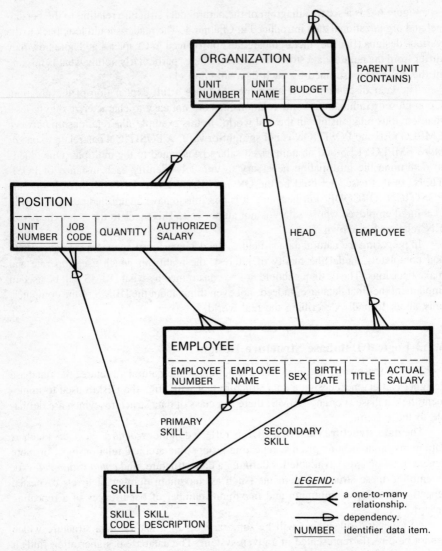

Figure 6-2. Natural Data Structure Schema Diagram for the Sample Database.

The sample database contains four entities—ORGANIZATION UNIT, POSITION, EMPLOYEE, and SKILL. Each entity is described by several attributes (in practice the number of attributes would be much larger). There are several relationships between the various entities:

- Every organizational unit has exactly one unit as parent (except the top level).
- Every employee belongs to exactly one organizational unit.
- Several positions are defined within each organizational unit based upon jobcode.
- Multiple employees may be authorized in a position.
- Some positions could be temporarily unfilled.
- The salary for some employees could be temporarily unfilled.
- Each organizational unit has an employee as head.
- Every employee possesses one primary skill and zero or more secondary skills.

constrained logical data structure. Adding UNIT NUMBER and JOBCODE to EM-PLOYEE captures the relationship with POSITION. Sometimes it is necessary to make some unnecessarily constraining assumptions about the real world entities and relationships in arriving at the logical database structure. For example, we must assume that each EMPLOYEE works in exactly one ORGANIZATIONAL UNIT in order to fit the natural structure into a hierarchical structure.

The objective in designing the natural data structure is fidelity in modeling the real world of the using environment; the objective in designing the logical database structure to be formally defined in the DDL of a DBMS is user simplicity and ease of use subject to a feasible representation within the system. Logical database design necessarily involves some measure of compromise. The extent of compromise depends upon the richness in the data structure class of the target DBMS.

The output from the logical database design process is another schema diagram.

6.1.4 Schema Diagram—Graphical Representation of a Database Structure

The graphical form of a schema diagram is primarily intended for human communication and understanding. A person can comprehend a database structure much easier and faster through some form of pictorial representation than through the data definition language (DDL) statements used to formally define a database to a DBMS. The schema diagram is precisely analogous to the program flowchart used to represent the structure and flow of control in a program. The graphical representation can give an overall picture which separates the macro features from the less relevant detail.

The schema diagram is actually an abstraction of the stored database. Although there will be many *instances* of a record type (representing many entities in the real world), each record type is only defined once in the schema. The schema can contain any information which is constant across all instances of data in the stored database.

There are various methods for preparing the pictorial representation of a database structure. Each DBMS tends to evoke a particular method of drawing database structures if one is not clearly established in the system documentation. The graphical representation used depends on the types of structural elements provided by the system. For example, a system may only permit the definition of items and repeating groups in a hierarchical structure. As Figure 6-3 shows, a simple scheme of representing items with a box and repeating groups with a circle is sufficient to draw a picture of a given database structure. Alternatively, all the data items at a given level and under the same parent could be shown together in one big box, as shown in Figure 6-4. Equivalently, the group name and its contained items may be shown in a single box, as in Figure 6-5. This last representation or abstractions thereof is generally preferred. It is more concise with each box corresponding to an entity type.

Without the ability to define *non*repeating groups, the designer is faced with choosing between not defining the group at all (for example, BIRTHDATE is a nonrepeating group of BIRTHYEAR, BIRTHMONTH, and BIRTHDAY) or defining it as a group which the system would allow to repeat. Figure 6-6 depicts a possible represen-

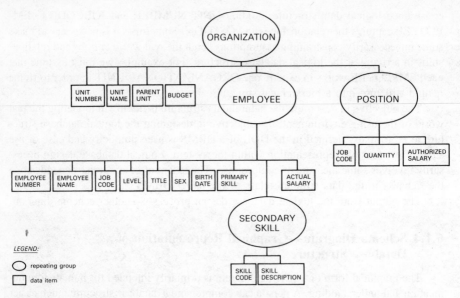

Figure 6-3. Logical Definition of a Hierarchical Data Structure.

tation of the same database structure in terms of items, nonrepeating groups, and repeating groups. In this picture the tree is turned on its side.*

McGee suggested a graphical schema representation containing more information than the preceding illustrations. A sample database definition is provided in Figure 6-7.† In this case, the relationship of each element of the structure to its parent structure is represented in the form of (n:m) written on the arc joining the two structures. When the dependent element is optional, m = 0. When a variable number of elements, either parent or dependent, are permissible, the m or n is shown as a "v". When multiple arcs (relations) exist between the same two structural elements, they are distinguished with unique names, as in the case of EMPLOYEE to SKILL.

When the number of items and groups in a database structure begins to get large, it is desirable to omit or condense the detail information in the graphical representation, such as showing only repeating groups. When this simplification is applied to the data represented in Figure 6-3, the resulting database structure would appear as in Figure 6-8. The similarity between Figure 6-8 and 6-5 is immediately evident. With this

---

*For a more detailed description of this method of a graphical representation see Paul J. Dixon and Jerome Sable, "DM-1—A Generalized Data Management System," *AFIPS Spring Joint Computer Conference Proceedings*, Volume 30, 1967, pages 185-198; and David K. Hsiao, "A Generalized Record Organization," *IEEE Transactions on Computers* (C-20:12), 1971 December, pp. 1490-1495.

†For a more complete discussion of this schema representation, see William C. McGee, "File Structures for Generalized Data Management," in *Information Processing 68*, Proceedings of IFIP Congress, Volume 2, Edinburgh, 1968 August 5-10, edited by A. J. H. Morrell, Amsterdam: North-Holland Publishing Company, 1969, pages 1233-1239.

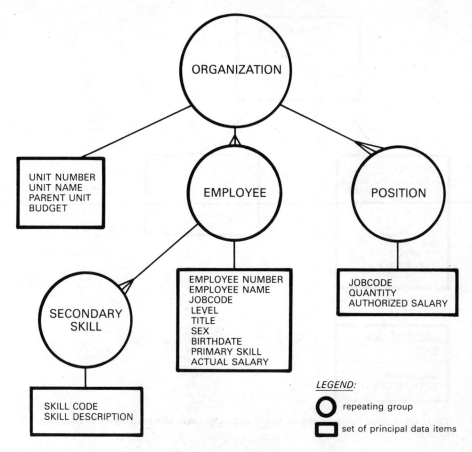

Figure 6-4. Logical Definition of a Hierarchical Data Structure with Data Items Grouped.

abbreviated representation, larger and more complex database structures, including multifile structures, can be represented fairly simply, as shown in Figure 6-9.

6.2 THE PROCESS OF DATABASE DEFINITION

"Database definition" refers to both the process of describing a database and the product of the process—a formalized description of a database. Working from the schema diagram resulting from the database design process, the database definer prepares a description of the database in a form suitable for machine processing.

6.2.1 Data Definition Language—Linear Representation

A database definition language (DDL) is used to write the definition of a database. A set of DDL statements is the formal expression of a database definition. The DDL

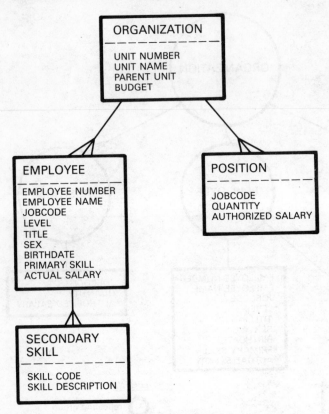

Figure 6-5. Logical Definition of a Hierarchical Data Structure with Items Shown in Their Repeating Group.

produces a linear representation of the database structure. Figure 6-10 shows two examples of DDL statements defining database structures shown in earlier schema diagrams.

A set of DDL statements is input to a DDL processor which validates and translates the statements, and generates an object version, which can be conveniently stored in the machine.

The overall process of database definition is shown in Figure 6-11. The database definition process accepts all the necessary information *for the system* to be able to create and maintain a stored database, and creates a stored representation of that information.

Schema refers to either the source or the object version of a given set of DDL statements. The distinction between a source and an object version of a database definition is precisely analogous to the distinction between the source and the object code of a computer program. Most systems today retain the database definition in some stored object form.

The process of database definition and the resultant stored database definition

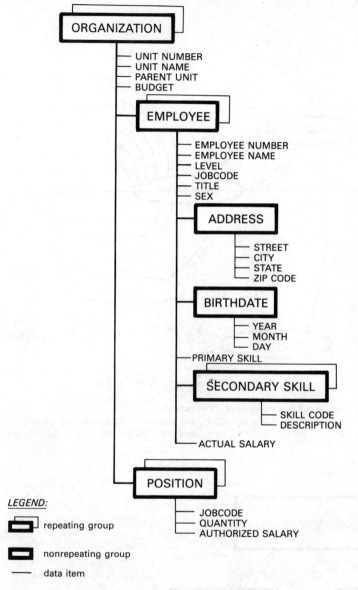

Figure 6-6. Logical Definition of a Hierarchical Data Structure with Repeating and Nonrepeating Groups.

PERSONNEL-ORGANIZATIONAL FILE

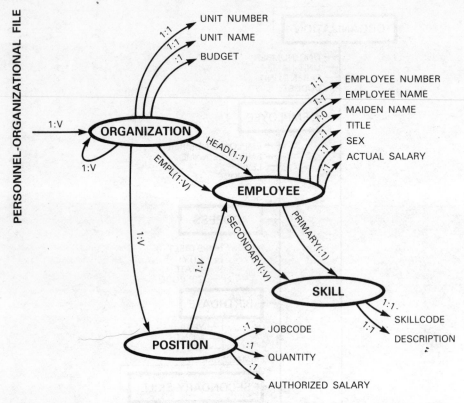

Figure 6-7. Another Graphical Representation of a File Schema.

The arcs represent relationships between the entities. The notation on the arc indicates whether the relationship is one-to-one (1:1), one-to-many (1:V), or optional (1:0). Multiple relationships between the same entities must be named.

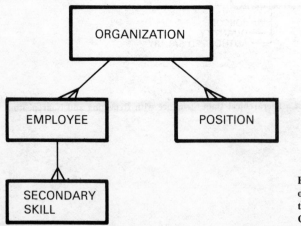

Figure 6-8. Logical Definition of a Hierarchical Data Structure Showing Only Repeating Groups.

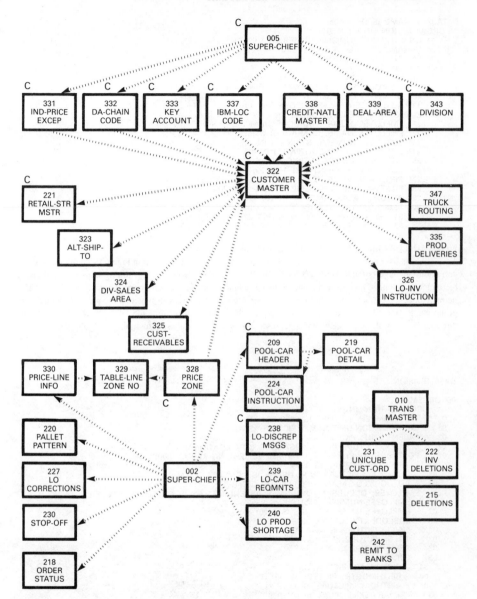

Figure 6-9. Graphical Representation of a Large Multifile Database.

should be separate and independent of any programs and of the actual data. If the definition is an integral part of the program, then after program compilation the definition information is buried in the program. The system is not cognizant of the definition, and, therefore, the proper interpretation of the stored data is strictly under control of the program. It should be possible to access and manipulate the stored database definition independent of the user programs or the stored data.

```
DATABASE NAME IS ORGEMP
0* ORGANIZATION UNIT (ENTRY)
    1* UNIT NUMBER (UNIQUE NUMERIC STRING 4)
    2* ORGANIZATION UNIT NAME (CHARACTER STRING)
    3* PARENT UNIT (NUMERIC STRING 4)
    4* BUDGET (MONEY)
   10* AUTHORIZED POSITIONS (REPEATING GROUP IN 0)
       11* JOBCODE (UNIQUE NUMERIC STRING 4 IN 10)
       12* QUANTITY (INTEGER IN 10)
       13* AUTHORIZED SALARY (MONEY IN 10)
   20* EMPLOYEE (REPEATING GROUP IN 0)
       21* EMPLOYEE NUMBER (UNIQUE NUMERIC STRING 5 IN 20)
       22* EMPLOYEE NAME (CHARACTER STRING IN 20)
       23* JOBCODE (NUMERIC STRING 4 IN 20)
       24* LEVEL (ALPHABETIC STRING 4 IN 20)
       25* TITLE (ALPHABETIC STRING IN 20)
       26* SEX (CHARACTER STRING 1 IN 20)
       27* BIRTHDATE (DATE IN 20)
       28* PRIMARY SKILL (NUMERIC STRING 4 IN 20)
       29* ACTUAL SALARY (MONEY IN 20)
       30* SECONDARY SKILLS (REPEATING GROUP IN 20)
           31* SECONDARY SKILL (NUMERIC STRING 4 IN 30)
           32* SKILL DESCRIPTION (CHARACTER STRING IN 30)
```

Figure 6-10(a). Linear Representation of a Database Structure.

This database definition is a linear representation of the schema diagram in Figure 6-5 written in a data definition language (similar to SYSTEM 2000). It defines data items and repeating groups in a multipath hierarchical structure, giving each a unique name, a unique number, and defining the type and size of data items. Notice the explicit representation of the hierarchical structure by designating the parent of an item or group using "IN 20" for example. Depending on the nature and form of the DDL, there may be many different but logically equivalent linear representations of this database structure.

```
DATA DIVISION
FILE SECTION
FD ORGEMP
01    ORGANIZATION-UNIT
    02    UNIT-NUMBER; PICTURE IS 9999
    02    ORGANIZATION-UNIT-NAME; PICTURE IS A(25)
    02    PARENT-UNIT; PICTURE IS 9999
    02    BUDGET; PICTURE IS Z(8); USAGE IS COMPUTATIONAL-1
    02    POSITIONS; OCCURS 1 TO 9 TIMES ASCENDING KEY IS JOBCODE
        03    JOBCODE; PICTURE IS 9999
        03    QUANTITY; PICTURE IS 9; USAGE IS COMPUTATIONAL
        03    AUTHORIZED-SALARY; PIC; USAGE COMP-1
    02    EMPLOYEE; OCCURS 1 TO 9 TIMES ASCENDING KEY IS EMPLOYEE-NUMBER
        03    EMPLOYEE-NUMBER; PICTURE IS 9999
        03    EMPLOYEE-NAME; PICTURE IS A(20)
        03    JOBCODE; PICTURE IS 9999
        03    LEVEL; PICTURE IS A(4)
        03    TITLE; PICTURE IS A(15)
        03    SEX; PICTURE IS A
        03    BIRTHDATE
            04    BIRTHYEAR; PICTURE IS 99
            04    BIRTHMONTH; PICTURE IS 99
            04    BIRTHDAY; PICTURE IS 99
        03    PRIMARY-SKILL; PICTURE IS 9999
        03    SECONDARY-SKILLS; OCCURS 0 TO 4 TIMES
            04    SKILL-CODE; PICTURE IS 9999
            04    SKILL-DESCRIPTION; PICTURE IS A(20)
        03    ACTUAL-SALARY; PICTURE IS ZZZZZZ; USAGE IS COMPUTATIONAL-1
```

Figure 6-10(b). A CODASYL-COBOL Database Definition.

A linear representation of our sample database written in the CODASYL-COBOL Data Definition Language. It uses a narrative form with explicit level numbers. In contrast to the previous definition, this one is dependent on the physical sequence of the lines—if each line is on a separate card and the deck is dropped, it would be impossible for the system to rebuild the data structure. Both languages build the data structure from the top down.

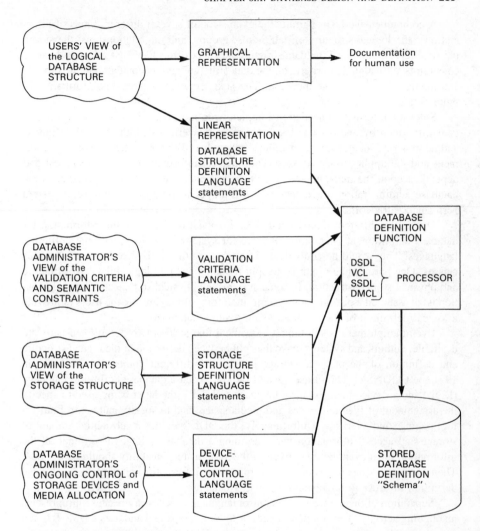

Figure 6-11. The Process of Database Definition.
    The process of database definition accepts a variety of information from a variety of sources expressed in multiple languages, collectively called the Data Definition Language, or DDL, then validates and stores this information in the form of an object schema.

    In some systems the stored database definition can be created and accessed like any other file in the system using the normal functions of creation, retrieval, and update. Nevertheless, due to the potentially widespread disruptive effects of changes to the database definition, it is necessary to retain greater control over updates to the definition than to the data. While the retrieval and update mechanisms may be the same, they are considered to perform different functions when acting on a definition than when acting on a database.

A comprehensive DDL permits the expression of several different kinds of information—the logical structure of data items, groups, and the relationships; the stored physical representation of the data structure and access mechanisms; various semantic constraints and validation criteria on the data structure and its content; and the devices and media used to store the database. The next section discusses this information in more detail.

Since the information needed to completely define a database is so diverse it is not generally given by one person. Users are more concerned with the logical definition and naming of data elements, since those relate directly to the external using environment and the application processes. The physical information is more technical and dependent upon the machine and, therefore, is better provided by a specialist in the database administration organization giving proper recognition to the users' desired performance tradeoffs.

Due to the different motives and skills involved in providing the information for database definition, it is common practice for systems to provide multiple definition languages. This would be equivalent to partitioning the DDL statements into various classes. One partitioning might be to split the language into logical database structure and physical storage structure. In some systems the physical storage structure information is all assumed a priori by the system, therefore, only requiring the users to provide a logical definition of the database using a single language.

Even though there is substantial agreement that at least two definitional parts are desirable, authors and systems make the split between definition of the logical structure and definition of the physical storage structure at different points. For example, in 1971 the CODASYL Data Base Task Group proposed a database definition language (DDL) and a device-media control language (DMCL), the latter being used to specify the assignment of files to devices and media space, and to specify and control buffering, paging, and overflow. Unfortunately, the DDL specifies a substantial amount of storage and access information when defining a database.* Recognizing that all the information must eventually be given to the system, responsibility should be divided. Then most users need only know the minimum information relating to the logical definition in order to understand and use a database.

Separation of the device-media control language is necessary because it represents an ongoing activity. The computer operator mounts a tape reel and uses a DMCL to tell the system the number of the tape drive. With a DMCL an installation can control the disk drive on which a particular file is to be stored. The device-media control language

---

*The physical association of records is defined using the concept of "area" [pages 83ff and 123]; the access method and criteria for selecting a record occurrence are defined in the "location mode" clause [page 104]; the method of access to member records in a group relation or set is defined using the "mode" clause [page 133]; the ordering of members of a set is defined with the "order" clause [page 136]; the method of indexing to members of a set occurrence is defined with the "search key" clause [page 142]; and the rules governing the selection of the appropriate occurrence of a set for the purposes of inserting an occurrence of a member record, or accessing a desired member record are defined using the "set occurrence selection" clause [page 145]; CODASYL Database Task Group Report, 1971 April. Some of these problems were corrected in subsequent actions of the CODASYL Data Definition Language Committee.

instructs the system on how to establish and maintain the physical location of the stored database. The language provides the mechanism by which the database administrator can exercise control over the assignment of the entire database to physical storage devices. In many database management systems this function is performed using the job management language of the operating system.

A single program module or separate modules make up the database definition function, which accepts and processes statements in the various definition languages and stores the information in an object schema. So far, no data has entered the system. In fact, the definition process must be completed before data can be entered into the system and stored in the database—the function of database creation.

The next section details the kind of information captured in a comprehensive DDL.

6.3 DATABASE DEFINITION INFORMATION

In the evolution of computer-based data processing, there is a definite trend toward defining more about the data to the system. A system which is only cognizant of storing many physical records, each consisting of a string of characters, cannot possibly do an effective job of managing the data—parsing input streams of data, validating its structure and content, and searching based upon value content. Unfortunately, too many systems today do not know very much about the data being stored, retrieved, and managed.

The objective in database definition is to tell the system as much as possible concerning the logical structure, contents, and semantics of a stored database. Much of this information is already known to the using environment because it directly relates to the entities, their attributes, and their relationships in the real world. *If a system does not capture this information, fully and formally expressed, it cannot effectively manage the data. A full database definition is a prerequisite to good database management.* This section details the types of database definition information that a comprehensive DBMS needs.

During the early development of computer systems, the user's view of the data was essentially a physical view. The user reviewed the data in its physical layout. Since the logical structure corresponded to the physical view, one definition was adequate for describing data. Furthermore, the data was described within programs. In the evolution of programs and their data, it became desirable to physically represent more of the structure logically inherent in the data. One approach was to define a file with multiple record types, each type identified by a code in a common location in the record. While the system viewed the data as a sequence of physical records, often variable in length, the user was able to view a richer data structure. The user's view of the data included more information than the system's view.

With the development of systems which could handle and recognize hierarchical data structures, it became necessary to implement two views of data. Stored data is ultimately represented by a sequence of physical blocks, each block being a linear sequence of characters. In such an environment, a logical view of the hierarchical structure is possible without knowing its linear stored representation. In many cases, omitting the details of physical storage is necessary for people to comprehend a data structure.

In addition to permitting a *richer* view of data, which transcends its storage structure, the dominant rationale for separating the definition of data into its logical and physical components is to permit the user to have a *simpler* view of the data, unencumbered with the details of physical storage and access mechanisms. In some systems, it is possible for the user to be cognizant only of the name and type of each data item, how the items are grouped, and the hierarchical relationships among the groups (as shown in Figure 6-10). This level of information is sufficient for a user to reference and manipulate the database.

Of course, before any data can be physically stored in the database, considerably more information must be *given* to the system, or, alternatively, additional information must be *assumed* by the system. Whatever the stages of information and whether it is externally given or internally assumed, the database definition must be complete. Ultimately, sufficient information must be available to the system to physically store data and to properly access and interpret the stored data. The stored database definition serves as a blueprint or template governing the storage of data and all access to data. DBMS functions and privileged user programs use the stored definition to properly access and process the database. This relates directly to the integrity objective of maintaining the correspondence between the stored data and its definition.

Often, not all the information is made available to the system at the time of database definition. Nevertheless, the definition must at least establish the mechanism by which the database can be properly stored, accessed, and interpreted. For example, the database definition may include a definition of indexes, even though they cannot be created until actual data is stored. As another example, it may not be possible to know the length of some item values until the data values are actually stored. In this case, the database definition would indicate "variable length" for such data items.

The information given to a DBMS via a DDL (or assumed by the system) can be divided into four categories (as shown in Figure 6-11 and defined in subsequent sections):

1. *Structural information* specifies the content and logical structure of the database in terms of data items, groups of items (or "records"), and relationships. These three basic structural elements (or variations thereon) are used to build up the structure of a database. Each structural element is defined in terms of a particular set of characteristics. This information is most important in defining a database to the system and to users. The purpose of this information is to model reality in the database.

2. *Validation criteria and semantic constraints* provide the system with information needed to ensure a given level of quality in the stored data. This information supplements the basic structural information above.

3. *Physical storage and access information* specifies how the system is to physically represent the stored data values, the logical structure of the data, and the access mechanisms. The objective in supplying (or deriving) this information

is efficient machine processing and storage space utilization—in sharp contrast to structural information.

4. *Device-media control information* specifies the storage location of data—what devices and its placement on the media. It is increasingly common for DBMS's today to rely on the functions of the operating system to manage secondary storage areas and allocate files to available space according to built-in algorithms. An installation exercises control over device-media placement by using the operating system job control language. Device-media control information is highly dependent upon the particular DBMS being used and the computer operating system environment; therefore, it is not discussed in any further detail. Most users are completely insulated from this level of information, except perhaps from knowing whether the records in a file are directly accessible (a performance consideration).

6.3.1 Characteristics of Data Items

A data item is the lowest level structural element used to build up a database structure. All other structural elements are built up from data items. Up to this point in the text, some of these characteristics have been illustrated implicitly and defined intuitively. This section provides a more complete description of many characteristics which can be defined for data items.

6.3.1.1 Name and Description

Name is a common characteristic of all structural elements in a database. Names may be alphabetic, numeric, or both, depending upon the particular DBMS in use. A data item may have an external name used in communication with people, as well as an internal code for efficient use by the system. Multiple external names (synonyms or aliases) may be defined to refer to the same data item. Most systems limit the length of data names. Some do not permit embedded blanks in data names but will allow some other special character(s) as a separator in data names.

Description provides additional information about the nature of the data item.

6.3.1.2 Value Type: Numeric, String, Special

Value is the most significant characteristic of a data item. Values in a database always correspond to data items in the definition. Associated with each data item is a set or domain of values. Each instance of a data item in the database is represented by a single item value taken from this domain of values. The value domain may be defined in a general way by designating a value class or type, or in a specific way by enumerating the acceptable values of the data item.

The common approach to defining the value attribute for a data item is to specify the **value class** of the item with a **type** designation. The basic class designations are numeric, string, or special.

For **numeric** item types, the item value has an arithmetic interpretation. For example, if the item type is "numeric octal integer" the value would be more than simply a string of numerical characters; it would have the arithmetic interpretation

$$361_8 = 3 \times 8^2 + 6 \times 8^1 + 1 \times 8^0 = 241_{10}$$

A numeric item type may be integer, proper fractional (between 0 and 1), or have fractional parts and thus be labeled fixed or floating point, decimal or exponential. Some systems set the maximum sized number which can be represented in each type. For numbers with a decimal point (fractional part) it is necessary to specify the number of positions to be maintained after the decimal point. (Alternatively, the system could maintain maximum precision in all stored numbers, truncating or rounding to a set number of decimal positions only on output). If numbers are actually stored as strings of digits, it may be necessary to specify the maximum number of digits used to represent the values for a data item. Very large or very small numbers can be stored as a mantissa, m, and an exponent, e. Assuming a base of 10, the value of such a stored number would be:

$$m \times 10^e$$

Either m or e could be negative. This type of numeric representation has been called REAL.

Precision is an important characteristic of stored numeric values in a DBMS. Precision depends on the number of digits used to represent a value—more digits yield greater precision. In REAL numbers the precision is in the mantissa; the exponent represents the magnitude. Some systems offer double precision forms of numeric items which double the number of digits used to store the numeric value. Increased precision is important when performing arithmetic operations.

String item types are simply interpreted as a string of characters. Special types of strings may be designated as numeric, alphabetic, alphanumeric, or bit strings. In the personnel file, EMPLOYEE NUMBER, ORGUNITNO, and SKILLCODE are all numeric string item types. Some systems provide a long textual item which could be used to store several lines or even pages of text associated with an entry in the file.

Special item types include Boolean items which can contain only a true (1) or false (0) value, dates, complex numbers, and geographical location coordinates. The variety of type designations is unlimited. For example, a variation on the decimal numeric type would be a "money" item type which always has two positions after the decimal point and is always printed with a monetary symbol (such as $ or £).

The type designation of a data item serves two functions—it indicates the *form* for the stored values and the rules for interpretation, and it indicates *permissible operators* on values of the data item. Sometimes a PICTURE designation (as in COBOL) is used to define acceptable formats for the values of a data item.

It is not yet commonplace in database management systems to explicitly define the **permissible operators** which might act upon a defined data item. Nevertheless, it is clear that the designation of item type often implies something about permissible operators. For example, it would be meaningless to perform substring or string concatenation operations on the binary representation of an arithmetic number.

Similarly, it would be meaningless to apply arithmetic operators to a numeric string such as EMPLOYEE NUMBER—the type designation should preclude such a possibility. Unfortunately, many systems allow only a general designation of 'character string'. A user desiring to limit a string to numerics is tempted to define it as 'integer' which means that the system will allow arithmetic operations, perhaps even totalling all numeric items automatically on reports!

Numeric data items may be further classified by the quantitative relationships among the values in the value set.

- *Cardinal* (or ratio) numbers have a natural zero point and a value scale with equal intervals. All common arithmetic operations (add, subtract, multiply, divide, exponentiation, and compare operators) can be applied to cardinal numbers.
- *Interval* numbers are on a scale which has no zero point, such as date, time, and temperature. It is meaningful to add, subtract, and compare, but not to multiply or divide interval numbers. However, multiplication and division *are* meaningful on intervals of an interval scale (for example, a period of time, such as from 1985 January 1 to 1985 July 19).
- *Ordinal* (ranked) numbers can be matched (EQual, NE-Not Equal) and compared (Less Than- $<$, Greater Than- $>$, $<=$, $>=$) but the magnitude of the difference between two values $(+,-)$ is meaningless.
- *Nominal* values are simply numeric codes and no arithmetic or comparative operations are meaningful. Such values are actually a string data item.

6.3.1.3 Units of Measurement

What is being measured and the units of measurement may be important to define for some data items. The following are some examples:

Temperature	Celsius, Fahrenheit
Distance	meters, inches, yards, miles
Area	hectares, square meters, acres, square feet
Volume	cubic centimeters, liters, ounces, gallons, barrels, bushels
Weight	kilograms, ounces, pounds, tons
Currency	U.S. dollars, Canadian dollars, British pounds, Deutschmarks, Francs, or Kopeks

As the United States moves toward the international system for units of measurements or SI units (commonly called the "metric system"), the explicit recording of units of measurement will become increasingly important in database systems. Without this facility, users are forced to define a second data item to record the unit of measurement for another data item. The consequence is that the system does not know of the unique relationship between the two items. It can do no validation of input data nor check for correct operations on the data. The users are responsible for properly managing and processing the data, and the system is doing less data management!

6.3.1.4 Length and Format

Data items are also defined in terms of a **length** or size attribute. The length attribute combined with the value-class attribute serves to define a range of values that can appear for a data item. For example, if the value of a data item is defined to always be four decimal digits, the implied range of acceptable values is 0001 (or 1000) to 9999. The length may be specified as fixed or variable. If variable, there must be an assumed or specified mechanism for determining the length of each value. The mechanism may be to read a length field or to scan for a delimiter. Even if an item is variable, an indication of maximum length may be desirable.

Sometimes it is useful to define default item value **format** and editing rules and item column headings to be used whenever the data item is specified for output. Though not necessary to convey logical database structure, it is reasonable to include this information in the schema because it is constant across all value instances. This information would be used on output in the absence of user defined formats.

6.3.1.5 Value Set: Ranges, Enumeration, and Encoding

In addition to declaring the type and size of a data item, the domain of acceptable values may be further constrained by an explicit value **range**. For example, a four digit number may also be limited to the range from 1111 to 3999.

Value enumeration is the most specific definition of the domain of values for a data item. This simply consists of declaring each possible value of the data item and is only feasible for a small number of values. Value enumeration is often desirable when the data item represents a classification coding scheme. In such a case, it is desirable to define the code and associate an externally meaningful value with each coded value. The following examples illustrate the use of value encoding:

SEX	SALARY CODE	STATE	SKILL CODE
M = MALE	0 = $0–999	AK = Alaska	0110 = administrator
F = FEMALE	1 = $1000–1999	AL = Alabama	1110 = systems engineer
	2 = $2000–2999	AR = Arkansas	1120 = mechanical engineer
	:	AZ = Arizona	1127 = power engineer
		CA = California	1130 = electrical engineer
		:	:

Whenever possible, use existing, generally accepted coding schemes such as the two-character state codes developed by the U.S. Postal Service, and the "year, month, day" (YYYYMMDD) or "year, day" representation of dates as adopted by the American National Standards Institute and the International Standards Organization (both in 1969). Interestingly, most systems which offer a date type do not offer this standard as one of the formats for date!

6.3.1.6 Fixed and Controlled Value Sets

Sometimes it is useful for the database definer to indicate the degree to which the value set can expand. If a value set is *fixed*, no new values will be accepted. In other words, whenever users enter a value for the data item during data entry and update, it must be one of the predefined set of values, otherwise it will be rejected. A **controlled value set** will not automatically be extended during data entry and database update, but new values can be added by modifying the definition of the database. A variation would be to issue a warning message at the time of data entry and ask the user if the new value should be added to the defined value set. For an *open* value set, any value satisfying the type designation (and other validation and semantic constraints) would be acceptable.

An encoded, controlled value set would be desirable for data items such as position job titles, skills, schools attended, countries, or local cities and municipalities. The names can vary widely in size and be subject to many acceptable forms. If the same entity is recorded with different names, for example, West Germany and Federal Republic of Germany and other possible abbreviations, it is much more difficult to select all those records from the same country. It is very important to consistently enter the same name or code for each country or other entity. If the system maintains a controlled list of codes and their meanings for a value set, the user can enter the code (and the system check that it is valid) or can request a review of the controlled value set at time of data entry to find the correct code. If the value is not there, the user could add a new code to the controlled value set.

A **cross reference** data item takes on a value which must exist as an identifier in some other file. For example, when entering the UNIT number for an employee, the system would check to ensure that the user enters a valid organization unit number, that is, for an entry which already exists in the ORGANIZATION file.

6.3.1.7 Role Dependent Characteristics: Existence, Uniqueness, etc.

Some data item characteristics, such as existence and uniqueness, depend upon the *role* the data item plays in describing a particular class of entities. Assuming such a distinction, **domain** refers to a set of values independent of any particular data attribute of an entity class, and **data item** refers to a domain as it relates specifically to a particular entity class. Most present-day systems do not explicitly include the concept of a domain. The value-related characteristics of a data item (discussed above) are not generally dependent upon the role of the data item in describing an entity. If the same data value domain appears in several roles with respect to several entity classes, it is necessary to give each domain role a unique name. For example, DATE would be a domain with a well-defined set of value characteristics (which is why it is a predefined data item type in many DBMSs). When used as an attribute of an entity, the name must reflect the role of the domain, such as BIRTHDATE or DATE HIRED.

Role dependent characteristics of data items include existence, default values, uniqueness, serialized values, and number of value occurrences.

The **existence** of a data item value in a group or record may be mandatory or optional. Declaring an item to be mandatory would say that a record or group instance cannot be created or retained without a value for that item. The opposite of mandatory existence is *irrelevance*. In between is *unknown*, when the value is currently missing for a data item which is relevant but not mandatory. The common practice of 'NULL' values does not distinguish 'unknown' from 'irrelevant.' An operator looking at the data on the screen does not know when to ask a customer on the phone for some missing data. Knowing which items are irrelevant avoids appearing foolish by continuing to request missing data.

Sometimes mandatory existence or irrelevance are conditional upon other data item values in the record. This could be specified using a Boolean expression. Here are some examples:

```
EMPNAME MANDATORY
UNIT MANDATORY IF LEVEL EQ "HEAD"
DRAFT_STATUS IRRELEVANT IF SEX EQ "FEMALE"
```

Existence can be related to length. It is possible to interpret fixed length items as mandatory unless specified as optional and, similarly, to interpret variable length items as optional (length of zero) unless specified as mandatory.

Defining a **default value** for a data item can be useful if one particular value occurs most of the time. For example, 'EMPL' could be defined as the default value for LEVEL since most people in the company are employees rather than HEAD or CONSultant.

The **uniqueness** characteristic of a data item specifies that no two entities in the same entity class can have the same value for that data item. Such a data item is called an **identifier** data item or simply an identifier (sometimes also called a primary key). The ability to make such a declaration on a data item can be most important for data quality control. Sometimes it is desirable to be able to declare that other data items are to be unique; for example, both EMPLOYEE NUMBER and SOCIAL SECURITY NUMBER would be unique in an EMPLOYEE file. In other cases, it may take multiple data items to uniquely identify an entry in a file.

A **serial data item** is one that takes on a default value which is always one greater than the value assigned to the last entry added to the file. Such a data item guarantees uniqueness in the file. It also ensures that all created entries can be accounted for later. This type of data item is most useful in numbering accounting transactions such as invoices, purchase orders, deposits, or cheques.

Multivalued items may be useful when the entity described by an entry (record, or group) can logically take on multiple values from the domain of the data item. For example, the entity BOOK can have associated with it multiple SUBJECT DESCRIPTIONS. Similarly, an EMPLOYEE may possess multiple SKILLS. Multivalued items are useful for representing one:many and many:many relationships within the stored database. One important characteristic of a multivalued item is the number of values that can be associated with a given entity. In fact, this can be coupled with the existence characteristic in a declaration of 0, 1, or MULTIPLE occurrences of the data item value with a fixed number or some range on the number of occurrences. The multivalued item is actually a special case of the repeating group which is discussed in the next section.

The underlying message through all this discussion is that there is much which users can tell the DBMS about their data. Unfortunately, all DBMSs fall substantially short of capturing all this information. What the system does not know about the data, it cannot manage, and a greater burden of responsibility falls on the community of users to ensure that correct and consistent data is stored and that data is properly manipulated.

6.3.2 Groups, Entries, and Records

Most DBMSs require that individual data items be explicitly grouped into records as part of the definition. Consequently, most people design databases in terms of collections of records. In the simplest case of flat files, data items are grouped into records only at one level. If a system permits hierarchical record structures then groups of data items can be nested within records, or entries, and perhaps other groups.

In the traditional approach to defining a database structure, data items are usually grouped together such that a given grouping provides the basis for describing a particular class of entities. The design activity focuses on identifying and describing classes of entities. Each data item corresponds to an attribute of an entity class. An entity instance is described by values for each of the data items associated with that class of entities. If there are groups defined within groups, the collection of data item values in the top-level group in the structure and the data items in all of its subordinate groups is called an *entry*.

A **group** is a collection of named attributes which may be considered as a unit. In some systems, a group may contain other groups, allowing the nesting of groups, theoretically to any level. A nonrepeating group has at most one value for each item in each parent instance. A repeating group (or *"rgroup"*) can have multiple instances within a parent instance.

A group can actually be considered another entity type. It is like a subentity with a subordinate relationship to the entity within which it is defined. The subentity is presumed not to have an existence independent of its parent entity. That is, the parent instance must exist before a related instance of the dependent (group) can exist. If the parent entity instance is deleted, so will all contained groups or subentities. It is also presumed that the attributes of the subentity must be interpreted in the context of the parent entity. (This corresponds to the hierarchical relationship defined later.)

The value of a group (without subgroups) consists of the values of each constituent data item. For example:

the employee attribute	the value of
ADDRESS	ADDRESS
defined as a group of items:	for one entity instance:
APARTMENT NUMBER	B2
STREET NUMBER	1678
STREET NAME	LAPPAND AVENUE
CITY	MILLERSVILLE
STATE	VIRGINIA
ZIP CODE	23771

The second column is called an instance (or value) of the group defined in the first column above.

Nonrepeating groups establish a naming hierarchy—an alternative naming mechanism to enable a user to reference the whole address or to reference parts of an address. It may also be desirable to define different groups over the same set of data items. For example, LOCATION may be just CITY and STATE. Furthermore, a group could be formed by alternatively defining ADDRESS as consisting of: APARTMENT, STREET NUMBER, STREET NAME, LOCATION, and ZIP CODE, where the group LOCATION contains CITY and STATE. Similarly, the nonrepeating group BIRTHDATE may consist of the three data items: BYEAR, BMONTH, and BDAY.

A **repeating group** (''rgroup'') can have multiple instances for a particular parent entity instance (analogous to a multivalued item). Rgroups establish a data hierarchy—a significantly different construct than the nonrepeating group. A compound repeating group can contain nested repeating groups. In effect, a repeating group defines a little file within each parent entity instance.

An rgroup is used whenever multiple instances of something relate to a parent entity—dependents, past job positions, or skills of an employee, for example. If a system permits rgroups in a record, then one definition is sufficient for multiple instances, just as there is one definition for all records of the same entity type. If the system knows about the existence of repeating groups, the user can reference instances by sequence, existence, or any general selection criteria on the values of the contained data items.

6.3.2.1 Characteristics of Repeating Groups

The definable characteristics of a repeating group of data items, whether constituting a primary entity or nested within a parent entity, include: criteria for inclusion, number of instances, the identifier data item (or items), and a possible ordering on the instances.

One important but often neglected characteristic of an entry type or entity class is the **criteria for inclusion**—the special properties an entity must possess to be included in the entity class. For example, the EMPLOYEE entity class may include all currently employed individuals, but not applicants or retirees.

Number of instances indicates the number of entities included in an entity class, and therefore the number of entries that should exist in the database. For a repeating group, the number of instances is expressed in terms of the parent group or entry. It may be specified as a single fixed integer or a range. The sample EMPLOYEE file implicitly shows space for up to 4 secondary skills. At a minimum, it is generally desirable to specify the maximum number of instances of a repeating group for any given parent entity instance so the system can better allocate storage space.

Even more information is provided by a frequency distribution on the number of instances of the repeating group for an instance of the parent entity. For database establishment, the database designer may wish to estimate the information regarding number of instances. After the database is implemented and used, the system can monitor this characteristic and perhaps even automatically initiate some form of reorganization if changes become significant. A repeating group defined within an entry actually establishes a special type of relationship between the two entities represented, called a hierarchical relationship (which is discussed later).

One (or more) items will serve as an **identifier** for the entries in a file or the instances of a repeating group within a parent entity. It is the identifier which imparts uniqueness to the entity or group instances.

Sometimes an externally meaningful **ordering** is defined on the instances of a repeating group based upon a ranked set of the contained data items. If the ordering is based upon position, it usually means that an attribute is not explicitly represented in a data item, most often the time of addition to the database.

When database design attempts to group data items into records, it necessarily involves some presumptions about relationships—relationships among the data items being grouped into the same record or entry, and relationships between those groups and other data items not included in the group. Modern approaches to database design suggest carefully examining the relationships between individual data items *before* attempting to group them into records. This is the basic idea behind the object-relation data structure class discussed at the end of Chapter 4. In fact, grouping data items into records first may obscure the real relationships among the contained data items.

6.3.3 Characteristics of Relationships

A relationship is a correspondence or association between entities. Entities are related in the real world and the defined database structure should reflect these relationships. A relationship is defined between two (and perhaps more) entity classes or types, that is, between two entities or records.

A relationship is described in terms of five *characteristics*: name, exclusivity, exhaustibility (or dependency), degree, and criterion.

In general, a relationship has a **name**. Different names may be used depending on the direction of reference. Directionality may be implied when a user addresses the data structure in a query language. The relationship is generally interpreted in the context of one entity or the other. Hence, the need for two names, depending upon the context of the query. For example, with EMPLOYEE and SKILL entities, the user may be interested in the skills of a particular employee (or set of employees), in which case EMPLOYEE is the context. Alternatively, the user may be interested in those employees possessing a particular skill. These two segments in a query could refer to the relationship as SKILLS-OF-EMPLOYEE or EMPLOYEES-WITH-SKILL, respectively. If, during the parsing of a query, the context is known unambiguously, then a single name for the relationship will suffice.

Figure 6-12 illustrates the basic graphical schema representation of a relationship. A box represents each entity class (or entry type) and is labeled with the name of the entity. An arc between the two boxes represents a relationship between two entity classes. The form of the arc depends upon the characteristics of the relationship between the entities (as discussed in succeeding sections). The arc is labeled with the name of the relationship, but may be omitted if no ambiguity results.

Different methods of formally *representing* relationships in a defined data structure give rise to various data models—most notable are the hierarchical, network, and relational models. The representation of relationships and the associated data model is of less importance to the user than the relationship itself and its characteristics. It is actually a secondary design choice which is not part of the basic exogenous information needed from the user in the specification of a natural data structure. The user should provide a generic definition of entities, attributes, and relationships unencum-

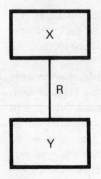

Figure 6-12. Basic Graphical Representation of a Relationship.
X and Y are entity classes (objects or record types) and R is some relationship between X and Y.

bered by any particular view or representational form. (Of course, the mere writing of the next few pages will develop another representational form, but hopefully it will be closer to the way the user thinks and more directly relatable to the real world being modeled in the database structure.)

All relationships are *reversible*. Given two entities, X and Y, if X is related to Y then Y is related to X´, even if it is not explicitly represented in the database structure. All relationships are inherently *bidirectional*. Furthermore, there is no necessary dependence between physical access paths and logical relationships. If a relationship exists and is known to the system, then it can be a basis for accessing entities in the database whether or not access paths (indexes, chains, pointers, hashing algorithms, etc.) have been explicitly defined. Since some widely used systems cannot access records unless a "relationship" is explicitly defined, we have become conditioned to combine and confuse the notions of access path and relationship. The bidirectionality of relationships and the separation of logical relationships from physical access paths have both been further confused by the common practice of using an arrow to represent a "relationship."* In the absence of defined access paths, if a relationship is formally defined and known to the system, then entries or records can be accessed even if it requires an exhaustive search of the entire database. There is only an effect on performance, not on logical feasibility of access.

6.3.3.1 Exclusivity

The exclusivity characteristic of a relationship indicates whether an instance of one entity class (X) is related to *at most one* or more than one instance of another entity class (Y). If an X is related to at most one Y, then the X-Y relationship is said to be exclusive on Y. In set theoretic terms, such a relationship is a *function* from X into Y, that is, given an X, a unique Y is determined (or perhaps no Y, but that

---

*See Charles W. Bachman, "Data Structure Diagrams," *Data Base* (1:2), 1969 Summer, pages 4-10; and John K. Lyon, *An Introduction to Data Base Design*, New York: Wiley, 1971 (Section 3).

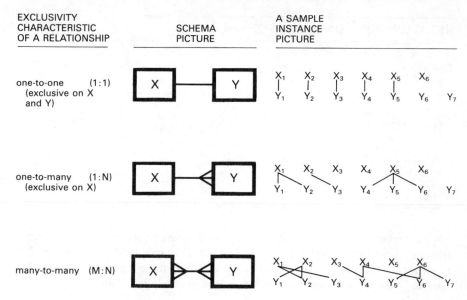

Figure 6-13. Exclusivity Characteristic of a Relationship.

depends upon the exhaustibility characteristic). A function is a special case of a relationship. We say that the function maps or transforms X into Y .

Not only must a relationship be defined in terms of its exclusivity on Y but it must be defined in terms of its exclusivity on X . If a relationship is exclusive on both entity classes, it is a *one-to-one* (1:1) relationship. In general, there are four possibilities for the exclusivity characteristic of a relationship: one-to-one, one-to-many, many-to-one, and many-to-many. Three are shown in Figure 6-13 along with their graphical representations and sample instance pictures.

The fanning out of the arc visually communicates the inherent nonexclusivity characteristic of a relationship. As such it is preferred to the use of alternative graphical notations such as the arrow. The arrow can be misleading because it inherently communicates directionality and implicitly depicts an access path.

If a relationship is nonexclusive on either entity class, it is desirable (for better storage space allocation) to provide some information concerning the size or cardinality on the "many" side(s) of the relationship. For example, the relationship may be better characterized as "one-to-a-few" or "one-to-at-most-four" or "one-to-between-two-and-four." To the extent possible, the database definer should provide information concerning the cardinality of the relationship which is known or can be estimated. If the "many" is variable, the file design process is even better served by specifying a frequency distribution on the cardinality of the relationship in each direction. For a one-to-many relationship, such a cardinality frequency distribution might be as shown in the table on the next page.

RELATIONSHIP: 1:N between X and Y

NUMBER OF Y's FOR AN X n	NUMBER OF X's WITH n Y's f(n)
0	300
1	750
2	975
3	500
4	250
5	200
TOTAL NUMBER OF X's	2975

As a second-order behavioral characteristic it would be useful to know the direction and rate of shift in this frequency distribution. For example, if the number of Y's is growing, where are the new ones being added? If the number of X's remains constant, then the mean of the distribution is most surely increasing.

6.3.3.2 Exhaustibility (or Dependency)

The exhaustibility characteristic of a relationship indicates whether *all* or just some of the instances of one entity class (X) are related to instances of the other entity class (Y). In other words, it indicates whether or not the relationship exhausts the members of an entity class. From the opposite perspective, if the relationship exhausts the set of X's then every X must be related to *at least one* Y, and X is said to be *dependent upon* Y. The terms exhaustibility and dependency are used synonymously; an exhausted entity is dependent upon another related entity.

If a relationship between X and Y is a function of X into Y, and the relationship exhausts X, that is called a *total function*; otherwise it is a *partial function*. Notice that whether a function is total or partial on X implies nothing about whether or not the relationship exhausts Y. The exhaustibility characteristic of a relationship independently applies to each of X and Y. Therefore, there are four possibilities: some of X are related to some of Y, all X to some Y, some X to all Y, and all X to all Y.

There are several possible ways to graphically represent the exhaustibility or dependency characteristic of a relationship. The one recommended here is to add the letter ''D'' on the arc of the relationship close to the dependent entity. If the relationship is mutually dependent, add the letter ''D'' at both ends of the arc. Since exhaustibility or dependency is the more restrictive condition on a relationship, it is selected as the one for explicit notation in the graphical schema diagram. The less restrictive nonexhaustibility characteristic is the default if no notation is added to the arc representing a relationship. Some selected relationships are graphically shown in Figure 6-14.

The all or exhaustive characteristic is a more restrictive condition on the data structure and its behavior. With a *one-to-one relationship* between X and Y which

(a) one-to-one (1:1) relationship between X and Y,
    with Y exhausted or dependent:

(b) one-to-one (1:1) relationship between X and Y,
    mutually exhausted or dependent:

(c) one-to-many (1:N) relationship between X and Y,
    with Y exhausted or dependent:
    (called a HIERARCHICAL relationship)

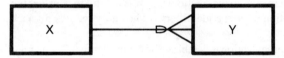

(d) one-to-many (1:N) relationship between X and Y,
    with X exhausted or dependent:

(e) one-to-many (1:N) relationship between X and Y,
    with mutual dependence:

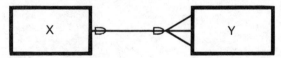

Figure 6-14. Graphical Representation of Exhaustibility or Dependency in a Relationship.

exhausts the Y's , that is, with Y dependent upon X (Figure 6-14a) there must be at least as many X's as there are Y's . A Y cannot exist or be added without an X , and an X cannot be deleted without first deleting the dependent Y's . If the one-to-one relationship is mutually exhaustive on X and Y , that is, X and Y are mutually dependent upon each other (Figure 6-14b), there must be exactly the same number of X's and Y's . With mutual dependence, an X and a Y must be added or deleted simultaneously.

With a *one-to-many relationship* between X and Y which exhausts Y , that is, Y is dependent upon X (Figure 6-14c), an X cannot be deleted without first (or simultaneously) deleting all of its dependent Y's . If a Y is added, it must be related to an existing X or else a new X must first (or simultaneously) be added. This relationship is very common and is given the special name of *hierarchical relationship*. The hierarchical data structure is built up from a set of hierarchical relationships.

If a one-to-many relationship exhausts both X and Y (Figure 6-14e), the number of Y's must remain greater than or equal to the number of X's . With such mutual dependence, the addition of an X requires the simultaneous addition of (at least) one Y , and the deletion of an X requires the simultaneous deletion of all dependent Y's . Addition (deletion) of a Y requires the addition (deletion) of the X if the Y is the first (last) of the dependents of X .

In capturing information about a relationship that is nonexhaustive, it is helpful for the definer to indicate what proportion of the entities in the nonexhausted class do not participate in the relationship.

6.3.3.3 Degree

The degree of a relationship consists of the number of pieces of information needed to represent the relationship. The minimum is two pieces of information corresponding to the two entities participating in the relationship. It is helpful to consider the two minimum pieces of information to be the identifiers of the entity records for each arc in an instance picture.

From the sample personnel-organizational database shown in Figure 6-2, one relationship would be represented by the two data items: employee number (EMPNO) and organizational unit number (UNITNO). It is a many-to-one relationship which exhausts the set of employees, that is, every employee must be assigned to exactly one organizational unit. The set of all instances of the employee-organization relationship can be represented by the table:

EMPNO	UNITNO
45584	2000
32579	2000
57060	2100
15324	2100
10261	2110
:	:

Another relationship exists between organizational units within the hierarchy of an organization. Such a relationship is *reflexive* since it relates entities from the same entity class. The two items which represent the relationship are UNITNO and the organizational unit number of the parent. The reflexive one-to-many relationship with dependency on the "many" side effectively constructs a tree of organizational units. The "D" on the arc indicates that each organizational unit must have a parent. For a reflexive relationship, this dependency rule must be relaxed slightly to say that each organizational unit *except one* must have a parent unit, that one being the top level organizational unit or the root of the tree.

A third relationship exists between employee and skill which can be represented by the pair: EMPNO and SKILLCODE. In fact, there are two such relationships between employee and skill which is why they must be separately named. Each employee must have exactly one skill which is his or her primary skill. Secondary skills is a many-to-many relationship and is nonexhaustive on either the employee or the skill entities. There is actually a third relationship between employee and skill. It is indirect through the jobcode attribute of position. Usually, but not always, the employee primary skill will match the skill required for the position (jobcode).

Notice that primary skill is a total function into skill. This means that, given an employee record, a unique skill is determined for the relationship. As a consequence, it is rather simple to represent each instance of this relationship by storing the SKILLCODE (the identifier of the skill entity) in an appropriately named data item within the employee record as shown. (The organization UNITNO could similarly have been stored within the employee record to represent the organization-employee relationship.) The secondary skills relationship is more difficult to represent as will be shown later.

All of the relationships discussed so far have been binary relationships. Now, consider extending the definition of the database to include additional attributes associated with a relationship, for example, a proficiency rating for each skill possessed by each employee. Such a relationship is ternary and would consist of three pieces of information: employee identification, skill code, and the proficiency rating. The degree of a relationship refers to the number of individual pieces of information required to represent it.

6.3.3.4 Criterion

Every relationship must have some criterion or rule which provides the basis for an association between two entity instances. The criterion is generally stated in the form of a Boolean expression on the value of at least one attribute from each of the entities participating in the relationship. The following paragraphs describe the various types of criteria. Figure 6-15 depicts five types of criteria based on one data item in each record and relates them to the exclusivity characteristic.

Common identifier. Two records (or entities) which possess the same common identifier are automatically related. For example, an organization may consider one entity type to be active employees currently on the payroll and another entity to be all personnel ever associated with the organization, including applicants never hired and those on leave or retired. In both files, the entities may be identified by some personal identifier (such as the U.S. Social Security Number or the Canadian Social Insurance Number). A simple matching of the value of the identifier for each entity establishes an association between two entities. In fact, a match probably indicates that the related records represent the same actual entity in the real world. This criterion is only possible for one-to-one relationships.

Mutual identifiers. With mutual identifiers, entities in two files are related because there is a one-to-one relationship between the identifiers. For example, one file may have organizational unit number as an identifier and another may have organizational unit name as an identifier. As a second example, one file of motor vehicles might be identified by a Vehicle Identification Number (VIN) while another file is identified by a license number. Since names and numbers, or VIN's and license numbers, are

1:1 Relationship

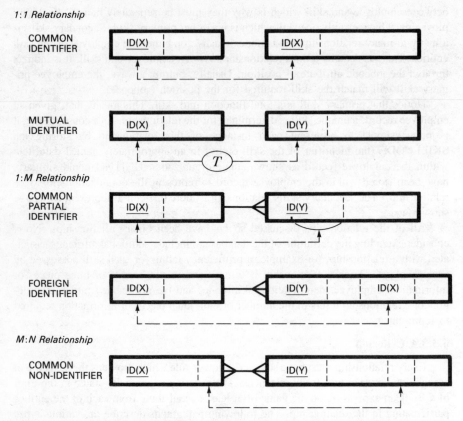

Figure 6-15. Criterion for a Relationship and Exclusivity.
The criterion for a relationship is, in general, a Boolean expression on at least one logical data item from each record. These diagrams show five different types of criteria (there are more) as they relate to the exclusivity characteristic. These examples all show a relationship based on the equality of a single data item in each record.

assigned uniquely to the entities, there will be a one-to-one correspondence. In most cases, such files essentially describe the same real-world entities. Defining a relationship based upon mutual identifiers requires some representation which relates each value in one set of identifiers with each value in the other set of identifiers. This criterion is only possible with one-to-one relationships.

Common partial identifier. Two entities are related if they have a common partial identifier, in other words, part of the identifier (which is a ranked set of data items) of one entity corresponds to the identifier (all or part) of another entity. For example, part of the identifier of a position is organizational unit number. Therefore, organizational unit relates to one or more positions. The other part of the position identifier is jobcode which is from the skill domain, so each skill relates to one or more position entities. In each case, the relationship is based upon a match of the appropriate data item values in the related entities. When the whole identifier of one entity relates to part of the identifier of another, there is a one-to-many relationship between the entities. A common partial identifier in both entities implies a many-to-many relationship.

Foreign identifier. Two entities may be related through a foreign identifier, that is, one entity possesses a non-identifier attribute which is actually the identifier for another entity. For example, the organizational unit within which an employee works is an attribute of the employee and is also the identifier of some other ('foreign') entity, organizational unit. The foreign identifier establishes a one-to-many relationship between organizational units and employees.

Common non-identifier domain. Two entities can be related through a common non-identifier domain. If two entities have an attribute which is based upon the same domain, they are related, although such a relationship may not always be meaningful. For example, position has an AUTHORIZED SALARY attribute and employee has an ACTUAL SALARY attribute; therefore, these two entities are related through the salary values. For a second example, entities in a customer file could be related to entities in a salesperson file through the common attribute of LOCATION indicating the city where they are located. This relationship through a common non-identifier domain could be quite meaningful and useful. Such a relationship is automatically established as soon as the system knows that the two data items in the two files are from the same domain, even if they are named differently. Two entity instances would be related if the values are equal in the common domain. In general, such a relationship would be many-to-many.

Except for mutual identifiers, all of the above criteria establish the relationship between two entities based upon a data item value in one entity instance being equal to a data item value in the other entity instance where the two data items are from a common domain. In general, the criterion for a relationship can be any Boolean expression in which the operands are data items from both entity classes. The mutual identifier is a simple example of such an expression which is a one-to-one transformation from the identifiers in one set to identifiers in the other set.

Sometimes a relationship may exist between three or more entity classes. In this case, one entity class must be designated as the parent (various other terms used include master, header, or owner) and the others are dependent entity classes (detail, trailer, or member). Such a relationship requires that there exist a common domain across all the dependent entity classes. If there is no common domain, there can be no single criterion upon which the relationship is based. As an alternative, a separate relationship can be defined between the parent and each dependent entity class.

6.3.3.5 Representing Relationships

As seen in the previous section, a relationship is always based upon an equality (or other more general functional relationship) between values of data items in each of the entity classes participating in the relationship. Although such data items are real attributes of the entities represented, they need not always be explicitly defined within the formal database structure.

A relationship may be represented in the data structure using one of three forms:

1. *Explicit data items* as defined by the user and stored in each of the entity records participating in the relationship, sometimes called "symbolic pointers"
2. *Physical pointers*—chaining or an array of pointers in the many direction of the relationship (for example, from "parent" to "child," terminology which assumes a hierarchical relationship), pointer in the one direction to an exclusive member of the related entity class (for example, from child to single parent)
3. *Physical contiguity*—storing member records with parent records (not completely possible in a multifile structure where a child can participate in multiple relationships and, therefore, have multiple parents)

More than one form can be used simultaneously, resulting in greater redundancy and greater reliability.

A **one-to-one relationship** can be represented by a data item value in one entity being equal to (or otherwise functionally related to) a data item value in the other entity. There can be no relationship between two entities unless there is some common domain on which to base the relationship (or a defined correspondence between two domains).

The second representational form uses a physical pointer in one record to point to a related record instance. In the third representational form, one of the two entity types could be designated as "parent" with the other entity instance physically stored "next" to the parent entity instance. With physical pointers or physical contiguity, it is no longer necessary to explicitly store the data item values of the common domain.

The problem with the last two representational forms is that the proper recording of the relationship is dependent upon the correctness of the physical pointer or physical contiguity. If the (unstored) attribute value in the dependent entity instance changes (the employee moved to a different organizational unit), the person updating the database must identify *both* the *old* and the *new* instances so that the system can appropriately update both physical pointers, or the change must be reflected in a physical move of the entity record. Also, the pointer and physical contiguity representational forms imply a directionality and access path which must be known and adhered to on the part of the user. It is more difficult (and sometimes impossible) to access dependent entity instances independent of parent entity instances.

It is generally more desirable to store the data item explicitly, and then let the use of pointers or physical contiguity be dictated solely by the need for more rapid access or better utilization of storage. At the very least, the user should be insulated from these physical considerations. Defining the database structure should initially be concerned only with the relationship and not its representational form—that is a matter for physical storage structure design.

Figure 6-16 shows four possible representations of a *one-to-one relationship* based upon a foreign identifier or a mutual identifier. The relationship is represented by adding a data item to one record. It contains the identifier of the related record from the other entity class. Either the identifier of X is stored in the records of type Y or vice versa. Doing one or the other has some access efficiency implications. If the identifier

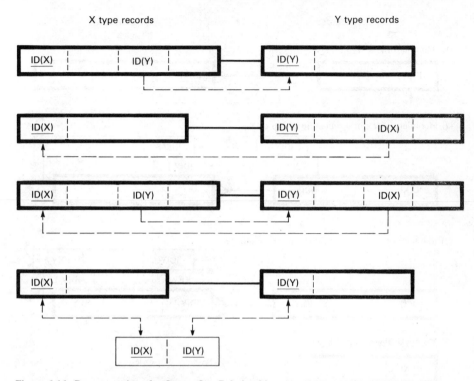

Figure 6-16. Representation of a One-to-One Relationship.
     For relationships based upon a mutual or foreign identifier, record X can contain the identifier for
record Y , or record Y can contain the identifier for record X . For greater reliability and redundancy,
each can contain the identifier for the other. The fourth alternative represents the relationship in a separate
table (or file) with an entry for each valid association of X and Y . For relationships based upon common
data items, whether identifiers, non-identifiers, or partial identifiers, no additional data items are required—
the relationship is fully represented in the existing data items. The *solid arc* between entities depicts the
logical relationship; the *thin broken arcs* show various physical representations of the relationship.

of Y is stored in the records of type X , then finding the record of X that corresponds to a given record of Y is not obvious. Such retrieval, however, is feasible
since it is always possible to scan all the records of X until one is found with the
matching identifier of Y . Alternatively, the records of X may be indexed on the
data item containing the identifier of Y . The fourth representational form stores the
matching pairs of identifiers of X and Y together in a separate table.
     A **one-to-many relationship** between X and Y can be represented by storing
the identifier of X in each instance of Y , storing a set of identifiers of Y in a
repeating group within each instance of X , or storing the identifier for the *first* Y in
X and having the rest of the Y's chained together. These choices are shown in Figure 6-17. In these three cases it is possible for the foreign identifiers to be replaced
(or augmented) by physical pointers. The fourth representational choice is to store
the Y's physically contiguous with their related X . A variation of the third choice

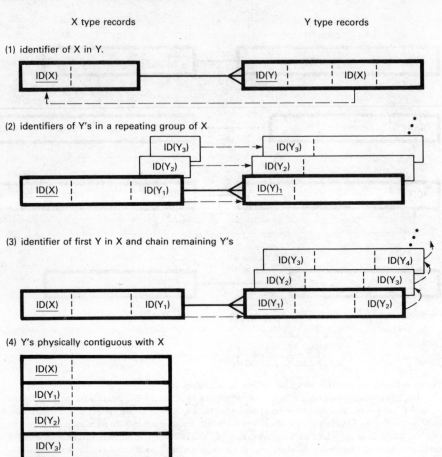

Figure 6-17. Representation of a One-to-Many Relationship.
For a one-to-many relationship between X and Y , we can store (1) the identifier of X in each instance of Y , (2) the set of identifiers of Y in a repeating group within each instance of X , and (3) the identifier of the first Y in X with the rest of the Y's chained together, or (4) the Y's physically contiguous with each X . In the first three, physical pointers can replace (or augment) the foreign identifiers.

would be to store the Y's of an X remote from X but physically contiguous with each other.

The first representational form is the basis for the relational data model while the second and third are the basis for the network data model. There is an implicit directionality from many-to-one (Y to X) in the relational data model and a directionality from one-to-many (X to Y) in the network model. Neither one of these directions is inherent in the relationship to be defined and captured in the stored database. The particular representational form chosen depends upon the behavioral characteristics of the database—how it is used and the more frequent avenues of access. It is obviously possible to store sufficient information to permit efficient access in either direction. The X records can be indexed on the identifier of the Y's and the Y records can be indexed on the identifier of X . Each form shown in Figure 6-17 is a minimal set of information for representing the relationship.

Many-to-many relationships can be represented using the basic forms in Figure 6-17 looking in the "many" direction. Forms 1 and 4 are impossible since there is no exclusive X record. Either the X records or the Y records can contain a repeating group of pointers or the head of a chain of pointers to the related records of the other type. A third alternative is to set up a special linking record type to contain two data items: an identifier of X and an identifier of Y . This is shown in option 4 of Figure 6-16 noting that the identifier of this linking record is now the *combination* of both the X and Y identifiers (drawn with a single solid line under both data items). The file of linking records contains all relevant pairs of identifiers.

If a relationship exhausts an entity class, a value is mandatory for the foreign identifier in that exhausted entity record. Without the exhaustibility condition, some foreign identifier data items may be null.

When the degree of a relationship is greater than binary, its representation is straightforward for one-to-one and for one-to-many relationships. In a one-to-one relationship, the attributes of the relationship can be added to the records of either entity class. This is because the records are both essentially describing the same class of entities or at least one set of entities is a subset of the other. In a one-to-many relationship between X and Y the extra attributes of the relationship would always be added to Y , the entity on the "many" side. This is because an entity of Y can have at most one parent.

With higher degree, many-to-many relationships, the extra attributes of the relationship can be added to the repeating group of foreign identifiers in either the X or the Y record. Alternatively, the extra attributes can be added to the special linking record. This last alternative is the only one permitted in either the network or the relational data models (unless the full nature of the relationship is not explicitly defined to the system, and therefore its maintenance is the responsibility of the users). Ideally, the user should not be involved with definitions at this level of representation. It should be sufficient to declare two entity classes, a relationship between them, the characteristics and criteria of the relationships, any attributes of the relationship, and the behavioral characteristics of the relationship.

A full data item representation of the sample Personnel-Organizational database from Figure 6-2 is shown in Figure 6-18. All relationships are represented by storing foreign identifiers or mutual identifiers as data items within the entity records.

In the EMPLOYEE entity record, the following data items were added:

- UNIT NUMBER, to represent the one-to-many relationship between organizational units and employees.
- The combination of JOBCODE and UNIT NUMBER, to relate an employee to the position s/he fills (if any, since it is not an exhaustive relationship with respect to employees).

ORGANIZATION

UNIT NUMBER	UNIT NAME	BUDGET	REPORTS* TO

POSITION

UNIT NUMBER	JOB CODE	QUANTITY	AUTHORIZED SALARY

EMPLOYEE

EMPLOYEE NUMBER	EMPLOYEE NAME	SEX	BIRTH DATE	TITLE	ACTUAL SALARY	JOB* CODE	UNIT* NUMBER	LEVEL*	PRIMARY* SKILL	SECONDARY* SKILL-1	SS-2	SS-3

SKILL

SKILL CODE	SKILL DESCRIPTION

Figure 6-18. Full Data Item Representation of the Sample Database.
    In a full data item representation, all relationships are represented by storing foreign identifiers or additional data items (*) in entity records. Compare with Figure 6-2 and find all the relationships.

- LEVEL, to indicate if the employee is the HEAD of the organizational unit.
- PRIMARY SKILL, to store the code of the primary skill of the employee.
- SECONDARY SKILL repeating group, to store all the secondary skill codes for an employee.

Note that SKILL CODE, JOBCODE, PRIMARY SKILL, and SECONDARY SKILLs are all from the same domain of values.

6.3.3.6 Representation in CODASYL and Relational Data Structures

    The CODASYL data structure, also called a *network* data structure, was originally proposed in 1971 [CODASYL-DBTG]. In 1978, after continued refinement, the American National Standards Institute began work on a standard Network Data Language [ANSI, NDL, 1984]. The CODASYL proposal and ANSI draft NDL standard essentially take a COBOL file structure (single file, multipath, hierarchical structure) as the basic building block for a network data structure, thereby remaining upward compatible (in theory, at least) with COBOL. To this they add the ability to formally declare relationships among the files.

The fundamentally new construct in the (CODASYL) network data structure is the *set*. A set defines a relationship between two (or more) record types. A set instance ("occurrence") consists of one "owner" record instance and multiple "member" record instances (from one or more record types).

Conditions on membership are declared in the "insertion" and "retention" clauses which are part of the definition of a record type as the member of a set. Together these clauses define the exhaustibility characteristics of the relationship.

The *insertion* clause governs when adding new records to the database:

```
          / AUTOMATIC                                                      \
INSERTION : STRUCTURAL <member record item> = <owner record id> [AND...] :
          \ MANUAL                                                        /
```

- Manual insertion—member records are associated with owner records only when the user issues an explicit CONNECT statement.
- Automatic insertion—the user must first make current (by some action such as READ-ing) some instance of the owner record type. This must be done for *all* sets in which the member record type participates as an automatic member. Then the system automatically associates or "connects" the newly added member record to the current owner record instances in each set type. Notice that the system cannot check the validity of the resulting relationship since it has no join criteria.
- Structural insertion—the correct owner record instance is selected by the DBMS as satisfying the Boolean expression given in the insertion clause. The value of the specified data item(s) in the member record must match the value of the data item(s) in the owner record. Note that the data item in the owner record type must be a unique identifier.

The *retention* clause governs when deleting records from the database or disconnecting them from membership in a set:

```
            / FIXED     \
RETENTION : MANDATORY :
            \ OPTIONAL  /
```

- Fixed retention—a member record instance, once having been "connected" to an owner record, remains related to that owner record until deleted from the database. A member record instance cannot move from one owner to another.
- Mandatory retention—a member record instance, once having been "connected" to an owner record, must thereafter remain a member of *some* owner. In this case, a member record may move from one owner to another.
- Optional retention—member records may be disconnected, using a DISCONNECT statement, at any time.

All relationships in a (CODASYL) network data structure are exclusive on the owner, that is, a member record can have at most one owner in each relationship. Relating to the previous concept of exhaustibility, automatic or structural insertion coupled with fixed or mandatory retention specifies a dependent relationship.

In a **relational data structure**, relationships between record types (called "relations") are not explicitly declared, usually. They are implicit whenever a join criterion is given, such as in a query language statement. In the draft proposed ANSI standard [ANSI,RDL,1984], referential constraints can be declared.

The definition of a data item within a record ("table") definition includes optional declarations:

```
ITEM  < item-name >   < item-type >          [ NOT NULL ]        [ UNIQUE ]
                                             / CASCADE  \        / MODIFY \ ]
     [ REFERENCES  < ref-item-name >         | NULLIFY  |         \ ERASE /
                                             \ RESTRICTᵈ /
```

- NOT NULL indicates that this data item must always have a value in a record. No record instance can be added to the database if this data item does not have a value, and the value for this data item in existing records can never be set to NULL. Specifying NOT NULL defines a dependent relationship.
- UNIQUE specifies that the values in this data item are to be unique within this table (or file).

The REFERENCES clause specifies constraints or conditions on the insertion, modification, and deletion of records of this file based upon records in another file. The < ref-item-name > is the data item in a related file. If the referenced item name is ambiguous in the database, then it must be qualified with the name of the related file. If there is a match of the value of this data item with the value of a referenced data item in a related file, then the referential constraint clause is satisfied. If the data item value is NULL, the referential constraint is not invoked. The referenced data item must be declared *unique* in the related file.

One of three levels of constraint can be specified for either modifications (MODIFY) or deletions (ERASE), or both, to the related file. If the referenced data item (in the related file or "table") is modified or its (unique) record instance deleted, then:

- CASCADE—modify the corresponding data item, or delete the corresponding record instances in the referencing file.
- NULLIFY—set to NULL the value of the data item in the corresponding record instances in the referencing file.
- RESTRICT—do not perform the modify or delete of the related record in the referenced file. This is the assumed default if a REFERENCES clause only specifies a referenced item name.

Since the item in the referenced file must be unique, the relationship between the referencing file and the referenced (related) file must be many-to-one. Thus the relationship is exclusive on the referenced file, just as a CODASYL "set" is exclusive on the "owner." The CASCADE and RESTRICT options imply that the referencing records are dependent upon the referenced records, otherwise the NULLIFY option indicates no dependency.

Notice that it is not possible to declare a many-to-many relationship directly, nor to declare dependency on the "one" side of a relationship. This is true of both the (CODASYL) network data structure and the relational data structure as proposed by ANSI (and in practically all implementations).

As illustrated above, the exhaustibility characteristic relates directly to the mandatory characteristic of the data items which are the basis (criterion) of the relationship. The relationship between organizational unit and employee can be represented by storing the unit number in the employee record. If a value for unit number is mandatory in the employee record, the relationship exhausts employees and therefore employees are dependent upon organizational units.

The exclusivity of a relationship correlates directly to the items in the criterion of the relationship which are identifiers. If both entities are related by their whole identifiers, the relationship is one-to-one. If only one is the whole identifier, and the other is a partial identifier or a non-identifier, the relationship is one-to-many. If neither relates to the whole identifier, the relationship is many-to-many.

6.3.4 Validation Criteria and Semantic Constraints

Validation criteria and semantic (or consistency) constraints relating to the stored database are actually an extension of the database definition. A semantic constraint defines the acceptable value domain for an attribute or a consistency relationship between several attribute values—for example, the net pay for a period should equal the gross pay (which is hours worked multiplied by the hourly rate for regular and overtime) less deductions for income tax withheld, pension, insurance premiums, etc.

In the example of net pay, the database designer may define net pay as a *derived data item* to be calculated whenever requested. In this case, the expression becomes the derivation rule. Alternatively, net pay could be explicitly defined, stored, and maintained in the database. Now the expression becomes a validation rule used to check the consistency of the values in the database. Due to the dependency, whenever any gross pay or deduction data is entered or modified, the net pay must be modified simultaneously. The designer clearly faces a tradeoff in choosing to explicitly store the data item or to derive its value when necessary. Nevertheless, with either alternative, the user must specify the semantic information as part of the data definition process. If these semantics are not defined to the system such that it *knows* what the data should look like, the users are collectively responsible for ensuring that the values in the database remain consistent.

Some argue that validation criteria and semantic constraints should not be part of the database definition (and, indeed, in many systems today they are not). The difficulty with such an argument is in determining where definitional information ends and validation information begins. Validation involves comparing stored data to some expression of what the stored data *should* look like. In fact, all database definition information provides a basis for validation. To define an item as numeric integer means that a value containing any alphabetic or special characters must be rejected as being invalid for that item. Other parts of the database definition information provide semantic rules for screening out unacceptable values or operations in the database: enumeration of values or ranges on a value set, limitations on the number of instances of an item or repeating group, declaring a data item to be mandatory in a record or unique across entities in a class, or exclusive or dependent characteristics of a relationship.

The viewpoint here is that validation is a process, not a set of criteria. It is a process which compares data to its definition. The data may be stored in the database or in update transactions (perhaps interactively captured on a screen display). The validation criteria may be stored as part of the database definition or the update transaction definition, or it may be embedded in the validation program or in the transaction processing program. Ideally, it should be part of the stored database definition so that it can be enforced at all avenues of access which update the stored data. The more complete and comprehensive the definition, the more effective can be the validation process.

The process of validation requires the specification of three pieces of information:

- *Validation criteria* or semantic constraints.
- *Condition* under which the database is to be tested against the criteria.
- *Action* the system is to take in response to a detected violation.

If the database were static, there would be no need for the second piece of information; the database would (theoretically) be checked continuously and would always satisfy the stated validation criteria. The database does change, however, as update processes act upon it. If an update process consists of multiple steps, the database could temporarily pass through an invalid state. This would happen, for example, between the posting of a debit and its corresponding credit in an accounting transaction. Specifying when to apply validation criteria can avoid testing a database during a temporarily invalid state.

Chapter 13 provides a more detailed discussion of data validation, including several different types of validation operations and times for invoking validation processes.

6.3.5 Storage and Access Information

Although the structural information discussed previously may be sufficient for a user to comprehend and reference the database, it does not provide sufficient information to enable the system to store and subsequently access the stored data. Whereas the structural definition serves to build up a data structure, the storage structure information defines how the system is to break down the structure, map it onto storage media and devices, and subsequently access it.

The characteristics of the secondary storage devices must be defined or assumed by the system. This includes such information as the physical block size, the devices and volumes used to store the data, and how to partition the database to fit onto the volumes. The dominant characteristics of storage devices are that they consist of a linear sequence of physical blocks, each consisting of a linear sequence of character spaces. Therefore, it is necessary for the system to know, by definition or convention, how to **linearize and partition the data structure** so as to map it onto the medium of the secondary storage device.

In contrast to the process of logical database design, the objective of physical storage structure is efficient use of storage space and processing time. The following categories of information are necessary to achieve this objective: item value encoding, data compression, delimiters, ordering, access paths, generations, and media allocation.

In terms of data item values, it is often desirable to define an **internal coded representation** corresponding to each external value representation. Having two forms of value representation decouples an external form, which is designed for effective human communication, and an internal coded form, designed for efficiency of machine processing and storage utilization. For example, the item SEX has the values MALE and FEMALE, which may be internally coded as M and F or 1 and 2. Item values input to the database are encoded using a value set table. Before item values are printed or otherwise output they are decoded. This is called an encode/decode facility.

Data compression further reduces the space needed to store data. Individual item values can be replaced with a fixed (or variable length - "Huffman") binary code. Whole record compression techniques include: replacing a string of one character with a special flag, a count and the repeating character; or replacing a recurring string of characters with a special (shorter) code which is then retrieved from a common string table.

There may be varying degrees of correspondence between instances of defined structural elements and the physical blocks of storage. The structural information in the data definition is natural and helpful to the user but the storage structure need not necessarily mirror the logical data structure. The only requirement is that it be possible to map from one to the other.

Once the data structure has been mapped into physical blocks the system must know, by definition or convention, how to **delimit item values and group instances** within the physical blocks. This is a natural consequence of having linearized (and compressed) the data structure. The structural information and replication information is retained through some form of delimiter mechanism. In this way, the system is able to recreate the structure from the stored representation.

The storage structure definition specifies how items are to be ordered in a group, how group instances are to be ordered, and how entries are to be ordered in a file. The **orderings** may be reflected in physical contiguity, or logically through the use of pointers (chains) in the stored data.

Storage structure definition includes the specification of **internal and external access paths** to the stored data. Access paths are established in addition to those inherent in the logical data structure. External access mechanisms are set up to be able to establish a starting point for a search within a file or data structure. This involves the definition of various forms of indexes, identifier ("key") transformation algorithms, or access via an instance of a related entity. Internal access paths are used to search within a given structure—searching over physically contiguous elements or searching along a chain of pointers.

An additional aspect of storage structure definition is the designation and control of **generations or versions of data**. This may be done by assigning dates or version numbers to files or file partitions. Alternatively, it is possible, though expensive, to attach a date and time to each data item value and group instance.

Storage structure definition finally specifies the **storage devices** to be used and how the media space is to be allocated to the actual data to be stored. This information must be available on a continuing basis and may be explicitly provided via some form of Device-Media Control Language.

In contrast to logical data structure definition, it is common practice to permit little or no control over the definition of storage structures and access mechanisms. In many generalized DBMSs, most of the storage structure and access conventions are established *a priori* and built in to the design of the system. Some other systems take no defaults and require the user to define all the necessary storage characteristics and access mechanisms, an expensive burden particularly for small and simple applications. The ideal would be to combine both approaches: allow the user to be insulated from any concern for storage structure definition, in which case the system must take some default design choices, and allow the user to selectively override any of the default choices to obtain a desired performance in the operation of the database system.

6.4 IMPORTANCE OF FORMAL DATABASE DEFINITION

A database must be formally defined to the system which will process and manage the data. Formally defined means that the definition of a database is explicit, approved by the database administrator, permanently stored within the computer system, and separate from all using processes. All processes access, manipulate, and interpret the stored database in terms of the stored definition or schema.

The concept of a stored database definition is as important to processing and managing data as is the concept of a stored program to running a computer—with stored programs a computer can run itself, and with a stored database definition the system can automatically manage the stored data. The effectiveness of that management of data is limited to the extent that the formal database definition does not capture all the essential semantics of the stored database, that is, the essential semantics of the real world being modeled by the database.

Information which is not explicitly defined to the system must be implicitly assumed or ignored by the system. The extent to which definitional information is assumed *a priori* by the system is the extent to which the users are unable to make tradeoffs based upon *their* criteria of optimality. In assuming some definitional information, the system assumes a particular position in the classic tradeoffs of:

- Processing time versus storage-space utilization.
- Batch processing (high activity ratio) versus one-at-a-time processing.
- Retrieval efficiency versus update efficiency.
- Machine efficiency versus people efficiency.
- Present performance efficiency versus future evolvability.

Consider an example of extreme tradeoff positions relating to frequency of update versus frequency of retrieval. A database consisting only of national census data is updated once every few years but may be the subject of retrieval several hundred times a day in response to queries to produce output reports. At the other extreme, a database containing information about suppliers and their hardware and software products would be updated with each new product announcement, perhaps in weekly batches. Actual retrieval may take place only once a year when the entire database is printed to publish an annual directory.

When certain definitional alternatives are **assumed**, the system and its users are locked-in to a prescribed assessment of the optimal choices in the tradeoffs. For example, a system may assume that all defined groups may repeat a variable number of times. If a particular group should always repeat exactly three times, it is a user responsibility to ensure that the data always conforms to this characteristic; the system cannot do it. For another example, a system may assume all item values to be variable in length resulting in greater flexibility and better storage space utilization at the cost of reduced processing efficiency. Alternatively, a system may assume all item values to be fixed length and allocate storage space for all instances whether or not value is present. The resulting tradeoff is reversed. For a third example, the system may automatically maintain indexes for all data items resulting in retrieval efficiency at the cost of update efficiency.

The extent to which definitional information is **ignored** by the system is the extent to which the using environment is responsible for knowing, conforming to, and maintaining the definition. For example, a system may accept length as the only attribute related to the value class of a data item. Consequently, as far as the system is concerned, any string of characters of the prescribed length is acceptable. Since the system does not know what should be in the value set of an item, it cannot validate incoming item values. Of course, such a system will operate more efficiently than one which does validate item values—more efficiently, that is, in terms of machine processing as opposed to people processing. The system operates more efficiently because it does less.

In these situations, the users are entirely responsible for maintaining the definition of item values and items within a group. They are also entirely responsible for maintaining the validity of the stored values. Furthermore, virtually all users must agree on the proper interpretation of the stored data. If any user inadvertently or intentionally modifies the stored data so that it no longer conforms to the definition commonly agreed upon, the system cannot detect the change. The users are left to discover the nonconformity for themselves. The result is that all users will (or should) validate all stored data prior to using it; that is, the user (program) should check all data retrieved from the database before using it. The cost of such a procedure is prohibitive yet, because it is buried in the cost of applications development or direct data usage, it is being incurred in many installations today.

Even more unforgivable is for a system to accept a definition and then promptly ignore that definition in subsequent operations. Such a policy is actually being followed in some commercially available systems and is a flagrant violation of an important integrity objective—ensuring the conformance of data to its definition. Such a policy deceives users and administrators into believing that if you can define it to the system, the system will maintain it.

If an organization uses a database management system which maintains only a sketchy database definition, and if that organization desires to maintain a high level of database integrity, there must be strict standards and procedures for enforcing those standards in user processes which create and maintain the stored data. Additional mechanisms must be incorporated into the user application processes to maintain the database in conformance to the additional semantics which are not formally known to the DBMS. This presents a tremendous administrative and processing burden on the data processing organization—a burden which is all too prevalent today.

In addition to data integrity, the objective of evolvability is also much less achievable in a system which maintains an incomplete definition of the stored database. One of the primary mechanisms for achieving evolvability is the easy and automatic conversion of data from one form to another—between a schema and a userschema, or in performing database revision. The system cannot perform such conversion processes if it does not know the full semantics of the data as stored and as it should be after conversion. Again, such systems place a heavy burden on the using organization when the database has to be revised or if processing requirements change.

6.5 LOGICAL DATABASE DESIGN

Logical database design uses several rules or concepts which are reasonably well understood and accepted. Disagreement arises in formulating a particular methodology—the place to start and the sequence of steps to follow in applying those rules. After a brief discussion of database design methodologies, this section presents several concepts, principles, or rules which are generally recognized and applied regardless of the particular methodology used.

6.5.1 Database Design Methodologies

A *database design methodology* specifies a sequence of steps to follow in developing a "good" database design—one that meets user needs for information and that satisfies performance constraints. Each step consists of the application of a set of techniques or rules which may be formalized to varying degrees and embodied in software tools. A methodology should be (1) usable in a wide variety of design situations and (2) reproducible in different designers. The second objective implies that the methodology be teachable, and that those trained in applying the methodology would arrive at the same end result. This is not evident in the present state of the art. Logical database design remains very much an art.

Teorey and Fry [1982] outline a database design methodology consisting of four steps:

1. *User Information Requirements*—involving the users in analyzing organizational needs, setting the scope of interest, investigating what people do (organizational tasks; usage patterns), and determining the data elements needed to perform those tasks.
2. *Conceptual Design*—developing a high-level diagrammatic representation of a

logical data structure; a structure which includes object domains, events, entities, attributes, and relationships; a structure which seeks to model the users' world.

3. *Implementation Design*—refining the conceptual design, checking for satisfaction of user needs and for consistency, and adjusting it to meet processing and performance constraints in a particular computer and DBMS environment.

4. *Physical Design*—developing record storage designs, clustering, and establishing access paths.

The techniques and rules in the steps of a methodology are applied iteratively in the process of unfolding, growing, and refining a database design. For a starting point, some suggest applying the methodology to individual user application areas or local views. Different user views may contain related complementary parts or overlapping parts. Multiple local views are then consolidated into a global logical structure or conceptual schema. The process of consolidation seeks to resolve inconsistencies, and to integrate related pieces. Even within a local view, there may be redundant, overlapping, and inconsistent parts. The rules of a methodology are intended to assist the designer in asking the right questions and representing the data structure in a coherent and consistent way regardless of the scope of the design activity, and regardless of whether it begins with individual local views or a global perspective. The product of the design activity will grow as it unfolds over the area of interest; and it will be refined as the rules are applied to focus attention on particular aspects of an infinitely complex reality and to resolve ambiguities and inconsistencies in the developing database structure.

6.5.2 Entity-Attribute-Relation versus Object-Relation Approaches

Perhaps the most significant difference among methodologies or approaches to logical database design is found in the point at which data items are clustered or grouped into records. The top division of the taxonomy of data structures presented in Chapter 4 reflects this division. The number of basic constructs distinguishes the two approaches: Those which presume an early clustering are often called "Entity-Attribute-Relation" or "E-A-R" approaches; the alternative is called the "Object-Relation" or "O-R" approach.

Historically data processing has always worked with records. Programming languages such as COBOL and FORTRAN cluster data items into records. The formation of records as a contiguous set of data items is necessary for efficient data processing. A record is the unit of access for getting data in and out of programs. Data is moved to and from secondary storage in blocks of records. Earlier data processing systems forced a "unit record" view, that is, all data for an application had to reside in a single sequence of records (this reflected the technology of the day, which used what was called "unit record equipment"). Even today, with DBMSs supporting a multifile data structure, data exists in the form of records in most organizations. Users are very familiar and comfortable with a record-oriented view of their data. Most designers today use an E-A-R approach to logical database design.

The major problem with the E-A-R approach to logical database design is that it allows the relationships among data items within a record to be hidden. It does not force the designer to explicitly consider and define intrarecord structures. This accounts for the recent emphasis in the literature on record decomposition and normalization based on an analysis of functional and multivalued dependencies. These techniques are all aimed at uncovering and making explicit the relationships among individual data items within records. The end result of repeatedly applying record decomposition rules is irreducible n'aries (see section 4.5)—at which point there exists *at most one* non-identifier data item within each record. By then the designer will have considered all interitem relationships.

At the implementation or physical level, data items must be clustered into records for efficient data processing. Even at the logical level, it is still relevant and useful to think of attributes which cluster around and describe entities, whether the attribute items are considered as part of entity records or as individual object domains. It is relatively unimportant whether the design activity starts with records which are decomposed to analyze interitem relationships, or starts with object domains which are clustered to form records. In practice a designer will do both. It is important that certain rules and concepts be applied in the design process. Early formation of records is dangerous only if it inhibits the designer from properly analyzing intrarecord relationships among data items, and from considering alternative groupings of items into records.

Ideally, the formation of records should be part of the implementation phase of database design since it is done primarily for system convenience and processing efficiency. In fact, it is desirable to have software tools to perform the clustering [see Carlis and March, 1983 and 1984], leaving the designer to concentrate on defining the individual data objects, relationships, and performance factors and constraints.

In a strict application of the object-relation approach to logical design, all object domains are treated equally. In the E-A-R approach, attention is initially focused on entities, then on the attributes of those entities which may turn out to be other entities. In fact, the distinction between attributes and entities is often confusing and arbitrary (as described in Chapter 4). Again, regardless of the approach taken, it is important for the designer to focus attention on the more important parts of the users' world being modeled in the data structure. This is automatically done in the E-A-R approach but can also be done in the O-R approach. The designer needs a high level of abstraction when developing a data structure and may start out by representing the main entities as boxes labeled with a name only (as shown in Figures 6-8 and 6-9).

6.5.3 Rules to Guide Logical Database Design

Even though there is no widespread acceptance of any particular design methodology, there is general recognition of many underlying rules and concepts used in logical database design. They relate to conceptual design and part of implementation design. A good database designer will generally know these rules and apply them, often intuitively, wherever they are relevant in the process of developing, checking, and refining a database design.

The following rules are presented here in a reasonably logical order, but there is no implication that they should be applied in any strict sequence. There is also no implication that these rules are sufficient or complete for the database design task. While progress is being made in formalizing the principles and process of database design, it still depends heavily on human intelligence and experience. Even experienced designers can arrive at different database designs which purport to model the same user environment. [Various restatements of some of these rules, more detail, and additional rules can be found in Vetter and Maddison, 1981; Curtice and Jones, 1982; and Teorey and Fry, 1982].

ENTITY: *Clearly identify the entities to be represented in the database.*

An entity is any object (person, place, thing), event, or abstract concept within the scope of interest about which data is collected. An entity is the object of decisions and actions within an organization. Entities are the pivotal elements in a data structure and must be well defined. Start out by focusing on the main entities, gradually expanding the logical data structure view to include related entities. When looking at an existing database, clearly define the primary entity which is described in each file (record type).

INCLUSION: *Specify the criteria for including (or excluding) entity instances from a defined class of entities.*

The ENTITY rule names a class of entities and the INCLUSION rule specifies the conditions for membership in that class. For example, does the EMPLOYEE entity class include managers, job applicants, rejected job applicants, those fired or laid off, those who quit, or employees on definite or indefinite leave? Consideration of these other "EMPLOYEES" may suggest broadening the name of the entity class, or it may give rise to another entity class. Narrowing (subsetting) or broadening the definition of the entity class represents movement along the generalization hierarchy [see Smith and Smith, 1977].

ATTRIBUTE: *Identify the attributes of each entity.*

Initially focus on the major attributes of each entity. Some will be clear and obvious, some will seem to be artificial, and some may also relate to other entities. Include all attributes which assist in understanding the nature of the entity being described. Include at least one attribute from each set of similar attributes.

ATTRIBUTE CHARACTERISTICS: *Define the characteristics of each attribute.*

Clearly define the characteristics of each attribute (as described in section 6.3.1). Initially focus on name, type, (size), existence, uniqueness, and some indication of the nature of the value set. When describing an existing database, specify any encoding of data item values. Description of other characteristics can be deferred until later in the database design process. Eventually plan to describe one attribute per page in the final database documentation.

DERIVED ATTRIBUTE: *Identify and define derived attributes.*

The values of an attribute may be derived from the values of other attributes in the database. Specify the derivation rule, which may be an expression for a derived item or a statistical calculation across instances of an entity type or a repeating group.

IDENTIFIER: *Designate the attribute(s) which uniquely identify entity instances in each entity class.*

An entity identifier may be a single attribute (EMPNO) or multiple attributes (UNIT and JOBCODE for POSITION). There may be multiple identifiers for the same entity (EMPNO and SOCIAL SECURITY NUMBER). Indicate if the identifier is not guaranteed to be unique. The identifier can be a good clue to understanding the nature of the entity described in an existing file.

RELATIONSHIP: *Identify the primary relationships between entities.*

RELATIONSHIP CHARACTERISTICS: *Define the characteristics of interentity relationships, particularly exclusivity and exhaustibility (or dependency).*

Exclusivity refers to whether instances of one entity type can be related to at most one or more than one instance of another entity type. Since it is defined in both directions there are four possibilities: 1:1, 1:Many, Many:1, Many:Many. Exhaustibility (also called dependency or optionality) specifies whether or not an instance of one entity type must be related to an instance of another entity type. Indicate if there is some condition on the dependency of a relationship. Also indicate if there is some minimum or maximum cardinality on the "many" side of a relationship. (See section 6.3.3 for more detail on these characteristics.)

FOREIGN IDENTIFIER: *Indicate the basis for each relationship by including, as an attribute in one entity type, the identifier from each related entity type.*

Every relationship is based upon common domain(s) in the related entity records. At the logical level, it is necessary to include the identifier of a related entity as a foreign identifier. In the storage structure, if the common domain is not explicitly stored in a related record, then some form of physical pointer is necessary to represent the relationship.

DERIVED RELATIONSHIPS: *Suppress derived relationships.*

The logical database design should not include relationships which can be derived from other relationships. For example, it is reasonable to think of organizational units as possessing a pool of skills. Furthermore, such information can be retrieved from the database. However, such a relationship should not be defined since it is derived from the ORGANIZATION-EMPLOYEE relationship and the EMPLOYEE-SKILL relationship. An organizational unit only possesses skills because it has employees who possess skills.

REPEATING GROUP: *Isolate any multivalued data item or repeating group of data items within a record.*

This rule ensures that a record only contains atomic (single-valued) data items, thus allowing only flat files. This is also called first normal form. The real importance of this rule is to force the designer to explicitly recognize a "something-to-many" relationship and possibly a new entity type. If a repeating group of data items becomes a new entity record type, the identifier of its parent record must propagate down into the new record. If the relationship was actually many-to-many, the propagated identifier becomes part of the identifier of the new record; if the relationship was one-to-many, the propagated identifier becomes a foreign identifier in the new record (but not part of the identifier). Multivalued data items or nested repeating groups of data items may be included in the storage structure of a record (as they are in a hierarchical data structure).

PARTIAL DEPENDENCY: *Each attribute must be dependent upon the whole record (entity) identifier.*

An attribute which is dependent upon only part of the identifier should be removed from the record, and placed in a record where that part of the identifier is the whole identifier. Suppose we had a record with the following data items: EMPNO, SKILLCODE, SKILL DESCRIPTION, and PROFICIENCY. The identifier would have to be the first two data items jointly since PROFICIENCY relates to both of them together. However, DESCRIPTION relates only to the SKILLCODE and, therefore, should not be in this record. A record with no partial dependencies is said to be in second normal form.

TRANSITIVE DEPENDENCY: *Each attribute within a record must be directly dependent upon the entity identifier.*

Any attribute which is not directly dependent upon the record identifier should be removed from the record, and related directly to the object on which it is functionally dependent. For example, if the EMPLOYEE record contained UNIT and BOSS, and the employee was moved to another organizational unit, it would not be sufficient to update the employee's UNIT—the BOSS data item would also have to be changed. The update anomaly results because BOSS is directly dependent upon UNIT and not EMPNO. BOSS does not belong in the EMPLOYEE record *even if processing is faster and easier*; it belongs in the ORGANIZATIONAL UNIT record. A record with no partial or transitive dependencies is said to be in third normal form. Restated: An attribute should be dependent upon the identifier, the whole identifier, and nothing but the identifier.

Application of the previous three rules to arrive at third normal form requires an examination of every attribute in a record. A record not in third normal form produces undesirable update anomalies. To identify these anomalies, the designer can ask: If a given attribute is updated, what other attributes must change, or if another attribute is updated, what effect will it have on the given attribute?

NAMING: *Assign names to entities, attributes, and relationships using a consistent, well-defined naming convention.*

When describing an existing database, watch for naming inconsistencies—different names for the same object, or the same name used to refer to different objects. (See section 15.5.3 for a discussion of naming conventions.)

STORAGE & ACCESS: *Suppress any consideration of physical storage structures and access mechanisms in describing the logical structure of the data.*

This includes any stored ordering on the records in a file, and whether or not a data item is indexed (see section 6.3.5 for information to ignore). Do not be concerned with questions of how to find or access a particular record in a file, perhaps along a relationship. Remember, all relationships are inherently bidirectional.

SUMMARY

The functions of database design, definition, creation, and revision, relate directly to data per se. Definition and creation serve to initially establish a database whereas revision is the ongoing incremental re-establishment or structural evolution of a database.

Database design begins with perceptions of the real world of the users and attempts to model the relevant objects and events in a database structure. The design process focuses on identifying basic entities, their attributes, and relationships between entities. Schema diagrams are a graphical aid to recording the natural database structure and the logical database structure to be formally defined to the DBMS using a Data Definition Language.

Definitional information encompasses logical data structure information about entities, attributes, groups, and relationships; nonstructural information such as validation criteria and semantic constraints; physical storage structure and access mechanisms; and device-media control information. Definitional information is expressed in a graphical form for communication to humans and in a linear form for communication to the machine. The data definition language (DDL) statements defining a given database are processed by the database definition function, like a DDL compiler, to generate a stored or object version of the data definition or schema.

It is important that the data definition language of a DBMS be comprehensive. It should enable the designer to specify all user-meaningful characteristics and constraints on the data to be stored. What the system doesn't know about the data, it cannot manage. The extent to which definitional information is not given to or used by the DBMS is the extent to which programmers and users of the database must be responsible for properly interpreting the database definition and ensuring the conformance of stored data to its definition.

While there is no wide-spread agreement on any particular database design methodology, there are some generally accepted rules and concepts to guide logical database design. The rules are not necessarily applied in any particular sequence. The design process can take an Entity-Attribute-Relationship approach, focusing on the normalization and decomposition of records containing several data items. Alternatively, the design can focus on object domains and relationships, clustering data items into records in the implementation phase of the database design methodology. Many of the rules suggested in this chapter are often applied by experienced database designers, sometimes intuitively. The objective of logical database design is to produce a good model of the users' world of interest. Initially it should be natural, that is, unconstrained by the DBMS and computer used to implement the data structure, and by considerations of physical storage structure and access mechanisms.

EXERCISES

6-1. Describe the three steps required to establish a database making it available for users to retrieve and update stored data.

6-2. What is the difference between a schema diagram and an instance diagram? Give an example of each.

6-3. What is the key difference between a natural data structure design and a logical data structure design? Why is it important to carefully document the natural data structure first? Why do you think many organizations skip the natural data structure design?

6-4. Briefly describe the four distinct steps in the process of database design. What is the central objective in performing each step? Stated another way, what criterion would be used to judge each step?

6-5. Why is it important to separate the definition of the logical structure view of data from the physical view of data? What are some of the benefits which result from this separation?

6-6. What are the major characteristics of data items? of groups?

6-7. Discuss at least two ways of expressing the value set for a data item.

6-8. A relationship is best described as which: directional, nondirectional, or bidirectional? Explain.

6-9. Describe the five characteristics of a relationship. Illustrate each possible state of each characteristic with a real world example.

6-10. Show the impossibility of a reflexive relationship with dependency on the 'many' side of the relationship. What can you say about a one-to-one reflexive relationship—can it contain any cycles? How many?

6-11. For the frequency distribution of the number of X's with n Y's shown in section 6.3.3.1, there were 2,975 X's . How many instances of Y are there?

6-12. Draw the schema diagram for an M:N relationship (say between EMPLOYEE and SKILL for primary skill) as it must be implemented in a system which does not allow the direct representation of such relationships. HINT: you must introduce a special linking record. Clearly designate the contained data items and the identifier of the new linking record type. Also clearly indicate the nature of all primary (not derived) relationships among the three record types.

6-13. Given an EMPLOYEE file and a SKILL file and a many-to-many relationship between them, add a PROFICIENCY LEVEL data item to record the level of proficiency at which a given employee possesses a particular skill. Sketch a data structure diagram to depict this ternary relationship. Then add the DATE ATTAINED to represent the date on which the employee attained that proficiency level (making it a 4-ary relationship). What problems do you have in graphically depicting relationships of higher order than binary? Draw the logical data structure diagram assuming a system which permits only binary relationships between entities.

6-14. Describe the three major forms for representing relationships in a database. What are the main advantages/disadvantages of each?

6-15. List some of the tradeoffs involved in computer-based data processing, some or all of which can be affected by the choice of storage of data?

6-16. What types of information relate to the storage structure of data?

6-17. What three types of information must be specified (explicitly or implicitly) for the process of validation?

6-18. Should validation criteria be part of the database definition? Explain.

6-19. Discuss the consequences of using a DBMS which maintains an incomplete definition of the database. What is the main advantage of having a schema which contains as much information as possible about the stored database?

6-20. Why is it undesirable for a DBMS to accept a definition of stored data and then ignore that definition in subsequent processing?

6-21. Describe the process of database definition. What are the inputs? the outputs?

6-22. Describe the form of database definition which is most suitable for human use.

6-23. Carefully study the natural data structure of the personnel-organizational database introduced in Appendix 4A and as shown in Figure 6-2 and its representation in Figure 6-17. Compare this to the logical database designs constrained to various data structure classes in Chapter 4:
   a. Single flat file (Figures 4-2, 4-4)
   b. Composite flat file (Figure 4-5)
   c. Single-path hierarchical file (Figure 4-7)
   d. Multipath hierarchical file (Figure 4-8)
   e. Multiple hierarchical files (Figure 4-11, top)
   f. Multiple flat files or "relational" structure (Figure 4-11, bottom)
For each constrained logical database design, discuss the approaches to and difficulties in representing *all* the information in the data structure (data on organizational units, employees, and skills, as well as data on projects which was added in Figure 4-8). Identify the information which exists in the natural database design but which is difficult or impossible to formally define in each of the constrained logical database designs.

6-24. An organization sends weekly mailings to its 10,000 members, periodic mailings to selected subsets of members, and desires to be able to contact members by phone in important or emergency situations. They have asked you to propose and analyze alternative designs for recording name, address, and phone information. The problem is that a given member may have multiple addresses and/or phone numbers, temporarily or permanently.

For mailings, only one address would be considered active at any given time. Each address entry should have an optional line to contain a building, organization, or "in care of" name. Student members often have a "permanent" home address (parents) and a local address. A legislator often has a home address, and another address in the city which is the seat of government. Some members may have a temporary address while on an extended vacation. In such cases as a summer home at the lake, the address information should remain in the system and not be reinput each time the member switches to the summer home. When a member switches to an alternate address, the system should record the date, if any, after which the address should not be used—mailings would be redirected to some default permanent address. The organization would not want to record an alternate address unless it would be used to receive mail over a period of multiple weeks (for example, they would not record a travel itinerary where the member moved every few days).

For phone calls, multiple locations (say, home and office, or home and neighbor or relative) could be valid. The system would record the phone number at each address location, if known. By contrast, it would not be desirable to record the address of each phone number. However, the system should identify the nature of alternate phone numbers (parent, sibling, child, other relative, neighbor, friend, guardian, overseeing physician, etc.).

It is assumed that the member is responsible for advising the organization of any changes in addresses or phone numbers, and of any change in the active status of addresses.

Develop a natural data structure design to represent name, address, and phone information for members of this organization. Then, assuming that the system will be implemented on a microcomputer with 10 Mbytes of hard disk, design a logical database structure which is restricted to multiple flat files.

6-25. The government of Jaromasa, a developing nation, desires to establish a system for collecting and reporting seaport statistics. This information would be used to improve port utilization and management, forecast future needs, and analyze foreign trade patterns, as well as to support the traditional function of monitoring the flow of goods into and out of the country. You have been assigned the task of designing the database for the docking facilities/activities portion of the overall port information system. Other parts of the database include details on cargos, usage of berth handling and storage facilities, and on persons working the docks.

The single seaport in Jaromasa consists of several docks. Some docks are special purpose permitting only one ship of a specialized type to be berthed at a given time. Others are general purpose facilities which can berth one large ship or several smaller ones. Ships are of various types and come into port for various reasons including loading, unloading, maintenance, and storms. Ships arrive and depart at various times; some have a regular schedule and others are "tramps" arriving at irregular intervals. A ship may stay varying lengths of time at zero or more berths while in port.

The following data will need to be stored:

- Date and time of a ship's arrival into and departure from the port area.
- Type of ship: passenger, split bulk cargo, tramp cargo, tanker, natural gas, bulk carrier, container, barge carrier, roll on/off.
- Ship characteristics: length, beam (width), draft (depth in water both empty and full), deadweight (empty) tonnage, gross weight tonnage (maximum loaded weight).
- Date and time of docking at each berth, if any, while in port.
- Type of activity while berthed: unloading, loading, both, refueling, maintenance, other (such as passenger only, or storms). Empty ships must be distinguished from those with cargo.
- Berth characteristics: location (which dock), type (passenger, general cargo, oil, coal/ore, grain, timber, container, mixed purpose, vehicles roll on/off), berth length, water depth, age, materials handling facilities (by ship type and/or cargo type), handling capacity, storage facilities, storage capacity.

a. Develop a preliminary design for the natural database structure to represent the above information (which can then be carefully integrated with the designs of other parts of the overall database). Identify and define carefully the basic entities involved, all the *primary* relationships among the entities, the characteristics of each relationship, the identifier for each entity type, and the major attributes of each entity. Do not try to list all possible attributes for each entity, but do resolve the meaning, representation, and entity-association of any ambiguous ones. Graphically represent the natural data structure with a schema diagram using notational methods developed in the text. Discuss any assumptions made and difficulties encountered.

b. Now design a logical database structure for a DBMS in which all the data must be represented in a single file, multipath hierarchical data structure (refer back to Chapter 4). Draw the graphical schema diagram to contain as much of the information as possible from the natural data structure. Try to minimize the distortion of reality in the logical structure. Discuss any compromises made, and describe any information about the real world which is no longer directly or explicitly represented in the data structure.

c. Assuming you have a DBMS in which only single flat files can be defined and processed, suggest an appropriate logical database design for the docking facilities/activities information contained in your natural database design. Discuss compromises and lost information as in b.

SELECTED REFERENCES

American National Standards Institute (ANSI), *(Draft Proposed) Network Database Language*, (X3H2-84-23), 1984 March, 143 pages.

American National Standards Institute (ANSI), *(Draft Proposed) Relational Database Language*, (X3H2-84-24), 1984 March, 106 pages.

BACHMAN, Charles W., "Why Restrict the Modelling Capability of CODASYL Data Structure Sets?" *AFIPS National Computer Conference Proceedings* (Volume 46), 1977 June, pages 69-75.
   Argues that the CODASYL "Set" should include recursive relationships, multiple entity types as "members" in a relationship, and multiple entity types as "owners" in a relationship. Introduces the notion of a "fork" set to accomplish the first, and the notion of a "record role" to accomplish the next two.

BACHMAN, Charles W., "Data Structure Diagrams," *Data Base* (1:2), 1969 Summer, pages 4-10.
   Presents a now widely used notation for drawing schema diagrams of logical data structures. Inter-entity relationships are shown with an arrow. In earlier systems (e.g., IDS) they were also access paths.

BENCI, E., F. BODART, H. BOGAERT, and A. CABANES, "Concepts for the Design of a Conceptual Schema," in *Modelling in Data Base Management System*, Proceedings of the Conference IFIP Working Conference, Freudenstadt, Germany, 1976 January 5-8, edited by G. M. Nijssen, Amsterdam: North-Holland Publishing Co., (New York: American Elsevier), 1976, pages 181-200.
   Discusses many facets of modelling the real world and capturing its representation in a formally defined conceptual model, that is, a logical data structure.

CARLIS, John and Sal MARCH, "Computer-Aided Physical Database Design Methodology," *Computer Performance*, 1983 December.
   Gives an overview of an experimental system which takes a logical database structure in the form of object domains and binary relationships and produces a set of records (clustered data items) and file access mechanisms.

CARLIS, John and Sal MARCH, "Multi-level Model of Physical Database Design Problems and Solutions," *Proceedings of IEEE Compdec Conference*, Los Angeles, 1984 April.
   Provides details of the inputs and outputs of the model described above.

CHEN, Peter Pin-Shan, editor, *Entity-Relationship Approach to Systems Analysis and Design*, Amsterdam: North-Holland, 1980.

CHEN, Peter Pin-Shan, "The Entity-Relationship Model—Toward a Unified View of Data," *ACM Transactions on Database Systems* (1:1), 1976 March, pages 9-36.
   Develops a methodology for representing the logical structure of a database using a schema diagram with a separate "diamond" symbol for inter-entity relationships.

CLIFFORD, James and David S. WARREN, "Formal Semantics for Time in Databases," *ACM Transactions on Database Systems* (8:2), 1983 June, pages 214-254, 48 refs.

CODASYL Data Description Language Committee, *Data Description Language Journal of Development*, June 1973, Washington, DC: National Bureau of Standards, Handbook 113 (U.S.GPO #C13.6/2:113), 1974 January, 155 pages.

CODASYL Development Committee, "An Information Algebra," Phase I Report—Language Structure Group, *Communications of the ACM*, April 1962, pages 190-204.
   An earlier and seminal discussion of the nature of a data structure and of the high-level operations on such a structure.

CODASYL Programming Language Committee, *Data Base Task Group Report*, New York: Association for Computing Machinery, 1971 April, 273 pages.

CODASYL Systems Committee, *Feature Analysis of Generalized Data Base Management Systems*, New York: Association for Computing Machinery, 1971 May, 520 pages.

CODD, E. F., "Relational Database: Practical Formulation for Productivity," *Communications of the ACM* (25:2), 1982 February, pages 109-117.

CODD, E. F., "Extending the Database Relational Model to Capture More Meaning," *ACM Transactions on Database Systems* (4:4), 1979 December, pages 397-434.

CODD, E. F., "Normalized Database Structure: A Brief Tutorial," *Proceedings of 1971 ACM-SIGFIDET Workshop "Data Description, Access, and Control,"* San Diego, 1971 November 11, edited by E. F. Codd and A. L. Dean, New York: Association for Computing Machinery, 1971, pages 1-17.
    Perhaps the easiest paper to read to obtain an initial understanding of the relational data model.

CURTICE, Robert M. and Paul E. JONES. *Logical Data Base Design*, New York: Van Nostrand Reinhold, 1982.
    Presents a very workable approach to the database design process including a reasonably comprehensive notational scheme for representing data items, identifiers, indexed items, repeating groups, and relationships, and a form for documenting the characteristics of particular data items. The design approach focuses on individual record or entry types. One weakness is that the view of relationships is always from one record type. The design approach makes it difficult to depict the overall structure showing relationships as inherently bidirectional.

FAGIN, R., "Multivalued Dependencies and a New Normal Form for Relational Databases," *ACM Transactions on Database Systems* (2:3), 1977, pages 262-278.

FLAVIN, Matt, *Fundamental Concepts of Information Modeling*, New York: Yourdon Press, 1981.

KENT, William, "A Simple Guide to Five Normal Forms in Relational Database Theory," *Communications of the ACM* (26:2), 1983 February, pages 120-125.

KENT, William, "Fact-based Data Analysis and Design," *Proceedings Third International Conference on Entity-Relationship Approach*, Anaheim, CA, 1983 October.
    By focusing on the facts to be maintained in a database, the author obtains a methodology for data analysis and design which is both simple and powerful, more systematic and less dependent on intuition.

KENT, William, *Data and Reality*, Amsterdam: North-Holland, 1978.

LARSON, James A., "Bridging the Gap Between Network and Relational Database Management Systems," *Computer*, 1983 September, pages 82-92.

LYON, John K., *An Introduction to Data Base Design*, New York: Wiley-Interscience, 1971, 81 pages.

McEWEN, Hazel E., editor, *Management of Data Elements in Information Processing*, Proceedings of a Symposium Sponsored by the American National Standards Institute and by the National Bureau of Standards, Washington, DC: U.S. National Bureau of Standards, 1974 April, 490 pages, (available from NTIS).
    A wide-ranging collection of papers on the management and standardization of data items, names, and value codes in several application areas. A rich resource book.

McGEE, William C., "On the Evaluation of Data Models," *ACM Transactions on Database Systems* (1:4), 1976 December.
    Looking at the data structure independently of the language used to process it, this paper puts forth criteria for evaluating data models. User criteria include learning, use in modeling the real world, and ease of defining and writing procedures against the database; implementation criteria address the effort to implement a model and the performance of the implemented model.

NIJSSEN, G. M., editor, *Architecture and Models in Data Base Management Systems*, Proceedings IFIP Working Conference, Nice, France; Amsterdam: North-Holland Publishing, 1977.

SMITH, John Miles and Diane C. P. SMITH, "Database Abstractions: Aggregation and Generalization," *ACM Transactions on Database Systems* (2:2), 1977 June, pages 105-133.

A very thoughtful paper on two basic methods of abstraction which are used in database design. Aggregation is an abstraction which turns a relationship between objects into an aggregate object (or entry), for example, pulling together the objects ("attributes") employee number, employee name, sex, birthdate, primary skill, etc. to form an aggregate object called EMPLOYEE. Generalization is an abstraction which turns a class of objects into a generic object which can be thought of as a single named object, for example, taking all the persons employed in an organization and thinking of them as belonging to a class of a single entity type, EMPLOYEE, even if some are truck drivers, some clerks, and others managers.

TEOREY, Toby J. and James P. FRY, *Design of Database Structures*, Engelwood Cliffs, NJ: Prentice-Hall, 1982.

Presents a wide range of topics relating to database design. Takes a predominantly physical view of database design.

TSICHRITZIS, Dionysios and Frederick LOCHOVSKY, *Data Models*, Englewood Cliffs, NJ: Prentice-Hall, 1982.

VETTER, M. and R. N. MADDISON, *Database Design Methodology*, London, England: Prentice-Hall International, 1981, 306 pages.

Brings together various theories and techniques into a comprehensive, systematic procedure for logical database design. Explains how to develop a natural data structure (called a "conceptual data model") which reflects the inherent properties of the information, independent of applications, hardware, software, and the DBMS. Chapter 1 provides a comprehensive and strong conceptual foundation and introduces terminology for the book. The book is well written, easy to understand, filled with examples, and accurate. Each chapter includes references and exercises (with solutions in an appendix).

YAO, S. Bing, editor, *Principles of Database Design, Volume 1: Logical Organizations*, Englewood Cliffs, NJ: Prentice-Hall, 1985, 416 pages.

A collection of 10 papers by specialists covering structures, methodologies and techniques, current research, and practical applications of theory to logical database design problems.

SEVEN

DATABASE RETRIEVAL: FLAT FILES

7.1	STEPS IN THE RETRIEVAL PROCESS	258
7.1.1	A Simplified View of the Retrieval Process on a Flat File	259
7.1.2	Overall View of the Retrieval Process	260
7.1.3	Uses of Retrieval	262
7.1.3.1	Reversion: Generating a "Foreign" File	264
7.2	SELECTION	265
7.2.1	Operands, Operators, and Delimiters	265
7.2.2	Boolean Selection Expressions	267
7.2.2.1	Overcoming Prohibited Use of Parentheses	270
7.2.3	Anticipated Volume of Output	272
7.3	PROJECTION AND DERIVATION OF DATA ITEMS	273
7.3.1	Derivation Rules for Additional Data Items	274
7.4	ORDERING, CONTROL BREAKS, AND STATISTICS	275
7.4.1	Calculation of Statistics	276
7.5	FORMATION AND PRESENTATION OF OUTPUT RESULTS	280
7.5.1	Output Media and Presentation Modes	280
7.5.2	Record-at-a-time Presentation	281
7.5.3	Report Output in List Mode	282
7.5.3.1	Handling Page Width Limitations	283
7.6	A GENERAL FLAT FILE RETRIEVAL LANGUAGE	287
7.6.1	Sample Retrieval Language Statements	287
7.6.2	Catalogued Retrieval Requests for Deferred Execution	292
7.7	GRAPHICAL PRESENTATION OF STATISTICAL OUTPUT	293
7.8	NATURAL LANGUAGE QUERY SYSTEMS AND ARTIFICIAL INTELLIGENCE	299
	SUMMARY	303
	EXERCISES	304
	SELECTED REFERENCES	305

A database management system provides mechanisms to enable people to access and update the contents of an established database. In general, a person uses an established database directly through system-supplied, functional modules, or indirectly through user-written programs. Retrieval and update are the two distinct functions performed. They may be performed with two (or more) separate languages or modules or, since they share several common elements, they may be combined into one module using one language. Retrieval, also called interrogation, encompasses both query and report generation.

The previous chapter on database design and definition described the first steps in establishing a database. The next step would be to enter data into the defined database either through a creation utility or by updating an empty database. These functions are described in Chapter 9. Once some data is entered into a database it can be the object of retrieval.

This chapter describes the use and manipulation of data through high-level languages—the generalized retrieval function. The careful reader should be able to formulate queries and understand what they mean. Retrieval is discussed before update since the function is better understood. Then the update function is discussed in terms of its unique aspects and how it relates to retrieval. Use of the database through user-written programs is discussed in the chapter following update—the programming user interface—noting the similarities and differences with system-supplied, functional modules. The languages with which programming users and nonprogramming users access and update the database are similar in many respects, as will be argued at the end of that chapter.

A good retrieval language depends only upon the logical definition of data; not how that data is stored or accessed. For example, it should not be necessary to restrict your search criteria to only those data items which have been indexed. Developing a comprehensive data definition language, which separates logical from physical characteristics, is a prerequisite to the development of a good retrieval language.

7.1 STEPS IN THE RETRIEVAL PROCESS

Retrieval is a process of query and response, of asking a question and receiving an answer in terms of the contents of the database. The question may be simple or complex and the answer may, independently, be simple or complex. Complexity encompasses both extensive processing and large volumes of output. Examples of simple and complex questions and answers are shown in Figure 7-1. A question expressed in natural English would represent an extreme in complexity due to the great difficulty in parsing and processing the question by machine.

A retrieval request is expressed in a retrieval language. The language statement is processed by a retrieval module, which may incorporate subfunctions common to other processing modules. The retrieval is formulated without detailing the procedural steps used to access the database, extract the required data, and present the results. Every retrieval involves a reasonably well understood series of steps. Therefore, a retrieval language normally consists of a set of parts or clauses. Although it may be

- *Simple Question:*
  PRINT NAME OF EMPLOYEE WITH EMPLOYEE NUMBER EQ 45584.

  Simple Answer:
  PETERSON, N.M.

- *Complex Question:*
  COUNT, AVERAGE ACTUAL SALARY OF EMPLOYEES IN UNITS 2113 AND 2115.

  Simple Answer:
  9.
  11166.67

- *Simple Question:*
  LIST EMPLOYEES.

  Complex Answer:

EMPNO	EMPNAME	UNIT	JOB CODE	LEVEL	TITLE	SEX	BIRTH DATE	PRIMARY SKILL	SSK1	SSK2	SSK3	SSK4	ACTUAL SALARY
45584	PETERSON, N.M.	2000	0110	HEAD	DIVISION MANAGER	M	280607	0110	6130	6625	6040		56000
32579	LYNN, K.R.	2000	5210	EMPL	SECRETARY	F	530121	5210	5520				12000
57060	CARR, P.I.	2100	1110	HEAD	MANAGER DEVELOPMENT DEPT	M	350720	1110	1130	1135	0130	1355	48000
15324	CALLAGAN, R.F.	2100	5210	EMPL	SECRETARY	F	550606	5210	5520	5220			10800
10261	GUTTMAN, G.J.	2110	1110	HEAD	MANAGER SYSTEMS GROUP	M	301110	1110	1130	1135	0150		35000
72556	HARRIS, D.L.	2110	5210	EMPL	SECRETARY	F	550517	5210	5520				8400
24188	WALTERS, R.J.	2111	1110	HEAD	CHIEF PROPOSAL SECTION	M	260202	1110	1120				28000
21675	SCARBOROUGH, J.B.	2111	1120	EMPL	MECH ENGR	M	240914	1120					21000
18130	HENDERSON, R.G.	2111	1130	EMPL	ELEC ENGR	M	340121	1130					23000
91152	GARBER, R.E.	2111	1130	EMPL	ELEC ENGR	M	440707	1330	1130				16400
30793	COMPTON, D.R.	2111	1350	EMPL	COST ESTIMATOR	M	290328	1350	1351	1355	1130		16200
81599	FRIEDMAN, J.M.	2112	1110	HEAD	CHIEF DESIGN SECTION	M	360317	1110	1130				26000
21777	FRANCIS, G.C.	2112	1110	EMPL	SYSTEMS ENGR	M	321111	1110	1130				24000
24749	FAULKNER, W.M.	2112	1120	EMPL	MECH ENGR	M	400621	1120	1130	1330			24000
13581	FITINGER, G.J.	2112	1130	EMPL	ELEC ENGR	M	431216	1130	1355				22000
82802	APGAR, A.J.	2112	1130	EMPL	ELEC ENGR	M	500715	1130	1330				21000
63633	BLANK, L.F.	2112	1330	EMPL	DRAFTSMAN	F	491010	1330					16000
22959	BRIGGS, G.R.	2115	1110	HEAD	CHIEF PROD SPEC SECTION	M	400508	1110	1120				24000
29414	ARTHUR, P.J.	2115	1120	EMPL	MECH ENGR	M	300109	1120					22000
37113	ARNETTE, L.J.	2115	1130	EMPL	ELEC ENGR	M	450729	1130					22000
68840	GODDARD, D.H.	2120	1120	HEAD	MANAGER STDS ENGR GROUP	M	330119	1120	1135				29000

Figure 7-1. Simple and Complex Questions and Answers.
Retrieval may involve simple or complex questions and answers. Simple questions are relatively easy for the user to formulate and comprehend. Greater complexity implies more machine time to parse and process a request or larger volumes of output data.

difficult to identify these parts in any given retrieval language, an attempt to do so will greatly facilitate one's understanding and use of the language. The first step, then, is to understand the parts of the retrieval process.

7.1.1 A Simplified View of the Retrieval Process on a Flat File

Before discussing all parts of a retrieval, it is necessary to make a simplifying assumption. Every retrieval is made against a database. This chapter assumes that the database is a flat file. The next chapter treats the retrieval process on hierarchical and multifile database structures. All retrieval languages on more complex data structures build on the basic constructs for a flat file language. Therefore, the reader must first understand flat file retrieval languages before adding the complexity of querying hierarchical and multifile structures. Also, most commercially available DBMSs provide a query language which only operates on a single flat file.

A flat file consists of only one record type which contains no nested repeating items or groups of items. A flat file is conceptually a matrix where the columns are named data items representing attributes, and the rows are entries or records representing entities in the real world. Each element of the matrix contains a single value of the attribute for the entry. A single flat file is shown at the top of Figure 7-2.

In a simplified form, the basic pattern of the retrieval process is as follows:

from a   *named file*

      select a set of entries meeting some selection criteria,

      project a set of attribute values from each,

and   *present* the results in an output report.

The *selection* process uses a Boolean expression containing the names of data items from the file. The data items are variables in the expression. In the selection process the system ''looks'' at the entries in the file one at a time. For each entry, the values for the data items named in the selection expression are plugged into the expression and the expression is evaluated. If the resulting value of the Boolean expression is 'true,' the entry satisfies the selection criteria and is selected for further processing. After all entries have been considered the file is partitioned horizontally to form a subfile, a subset of entries in the original file containing those entries which satisfy the selection expression. Figure 7-2 illustrates this process.

In the *projection* process, a named set of attributes is extracted from the subfile resulting from the selection process. In this case, the file is essentially partitioned vertically to form a subfile, a subset of the previous subfile.

The combination of selection and projection applied to the file is called retrieval. The product of this retrieval process is again a file which can be manipulated, copied, and printed as any other file using the normal DBMS facilities. The resulting file is logically a subfile, which may or may not be physically generated. The result could be formatted and sent directly to the screen or printer. In this simplified view of the retrieval process, all that remains is to print out the logical subfile. Figure 7-2 conceptually illustrates the overall simplified process.

7.1.2 Overall View of the Retrieval Process

The full retrieval process on a single flat file involves more steps than presented in the simplified view. The overall process can involve the steps or subfunctions shown on page 262.

FLAT FILE:

EMPLOYEES

Attributes

EMPNO	EMPNAME	UNIT	JOB CODE	LEVEL	TITLE
=======	=========	======	==========	=======	=======
:	:	:	:	:	:
24188	WALTERS, R.J.	2111	1110	HEAD	CHIEF PROPOSAL SECTIO...
21675	SCARBOROUGH, J.B.	2111	1120	EMPL	MECH ENGR ...
18130	HENDERSON, R.G.	2111	1130	EMPL	ELEC ENGR ...
91152	GARBER, R.E.	2111	1130	EMPL	ELEC ENGR ...
30793	COMPTON, D.R.	2111	1350	EMPL	COST ESTIMATOR ...
81599	FRIEDMAN, J.M.	2112	1110	HEAD	CHIEF DESIGN SECTION ...
21777	FRANCIS, G.C.	2112	1110	EMPL	SYSTEMS ENGR ...
24749	FAULKNER, W.M.	2112	1120	EMPL	MECH ENGR ...
13581	FITINGER, G.J.	2112	1130	EMPL	ELEC ENGR ...
82802	APGAR, A.J.	2112	1130	EMPL	ELEC ENGR ...
63633	BLANK, L.F.	2112	1330	EMPL	DRAFTSMAN ...
22959	BRIGGS, G.R.	2115	1110	HEAD	CHIEF PROD SPEC SECTI...
29414	ARTHUR, P.J.	2115	1120	EMPL	MECH ENGR ...
37113	ARNETTE, L.J.	2115	1130	EMPL	ELEC ENGR ...
68840	GODDARD, D.H.	2120	1120	HEAD	MANAGER STDS ENGR GRO...

Entries (labeled to the left of the data rows)

QUESTION:

LIST EMPNAME, UNIT, LEVEL OF EMPLOYEES WHERE TITLE EQ "ELEC ENGR"

SELECTION:

TITLE EQ "ELEC ENGR"

EMPNO	EMPNAME	UNIT	JOB CODE	LEVEL	TITLE
=======	=========	======	==========	=======	=======
:	:	:	:	:	:
24188	WALTERS, R.J.	2111	1110	HEAD	CHIEF PROPOSAL SECTIO...
21675	SCARBOROUGH, J.B.	2111	1120	EMPL	MECH ENGR ...
→ 18130	HENDERSON, R.G.	2111	1130	EMPL	ELEC ENGR ...
→ 91152	GARBER, R.E.	2111	1130	EMPL	ELEC ENGR ...
30793	COMPTON, D.R.	2111	1350	EMPL	COST ESTIMATOR ...
81599	FRIEDMAN, J.M.	2112	1110	HEAD	CHIEF DESIGN SECTION ...
21777	FRANCIS, G.C.	2112	1110	EMPL	SYSTEMS ENGR ...
24749	FAULKNER, W.M.	2112	1120	EMPL	MECH ENGR ...
→ 13581	FITINGER, G.J.	2112	1130	EMPL	ELEC ENGR ...
→ 82802	APGAR, A.J.	2112	1130	EMPL	ELEC ENGR ...
63633	BLANK, L.F.	2112	1330	EMPL	DRAFTSMAN ...
22959	BRIGGS, G.R.	2115	1110	HEAD	CHIEF PROD SPEC SECTI...
29414	ARTHUR, P.J.	2115	1120	EMPL	MECH ENGR ...
→ 37113	ARNETTE, L.J.	2115	1130	EMPL	ELEC ENGR ...
68840	GODDARD, D.H.	2120	1120	HEAD	MANAGER STDS ENGR GRO...

PROJECTION:

EMPNAME, UNIT, LEVEL

EMPNO	EMPNAME	UNIT	JOB CODE	LEVEL	TITLE
=======	=========	======	==========	=======	=======
:	:	:	:	:	:
24188	WALTERS, R.J.	2111	1110	HEAD	CHIEF PROPOSAL SECTIO...
21675	SCARBOROUGH, J.B.	2111	1120	EMPL	MECH ENGR ...
18130	HENDERSON, R.G.	2111	1130	EMPL	ELEC ENGR ...
91152	GARBER, R.E.	2111	1130	EMPL	ELEC ENGR ...
30793	COMPTON, D.R.	2111	1350	EMPL	COST ESTIMATOR ...
81599	FRIEDMAN, J.M.	2112	1110	HEAD	CHIEF DESIGN SECTION ...
21777	FRANCIS, G.C.	2112	1110	EMPL	SYSTEMS ENGR ...
24749	FAULKNER, W.M.	2112	1120	EMPL	MECH ENGR ...
13581	FITINGER, G.J.	2112	1130	EMPL	ELEC ENGR ...
82802	APGAR, A.J.	2112	1130	EMPL	ELEC ENGR ...
63633	BLANK, L.F.	2112	1330	EMPL	DRAFTSMAN ...
22959	BRIGGS, G.R.	2115	1110	HEAD	CHIEF PROD SPEC SECTI...
29414	ARTHUR, P.J.	2115	1120	EMPL	MECH ENGR ...
37113	ARNETTE, L.J.	2115	1130	EMPL	ELEC ENGR ...
68840	GODDARD, D.H.	2120	1120	HEAD	MANAGER STDS ENGR GRO...

ANSWER:

EMPNAME	UNIT	LEVEL
=========	======	=======
HENDERSON, R.G.	2111	EMPL
GARBER, R.E.	2111	EMPL
FITINGER, G.J.	2112	EMPL
APGAR, A.J.	2112	EMPL
ARNETTE, L.J.	2115	EMPL

Figure 7-2. A Simplified View of the Retrieval Process on a Single Flat File.
From a named file, *select* a set of entries (rows) meeting the selection criteria, *project* a set of attribute values (columns) from each, and *present* the results in an output report. Viewing the flat file as a matrix, these two basic operations effectively isolate designated rows and columns, thus retrieving the data at the intersection.

from a *named file*

   select a set of entries satisfying the selection criteria,

   project a set of attribute values from each entry,

   derive additional data item values for each entry,

   order the entries of the resulting subfile,

   calculate statistics on data items across all selected entries,

   format and edit any extracted or derived data,

and *present* the results of the retrieval process.

Each of these processes is more fully described in this chapter with particular focus on the inputs and output of each step. Figure 7-3 shows the steps in the retrieval process with their inputs and showing the effect of each on a flat file. Although listed in a specific sequence, some of the steps may be interleaved, repeated, or performed in parallel in any particular implementation.

7.1.3 Uses of Retrieval

Besides simply asking questions of a database and delivering the answer to a human, there are other uses of retrieval facilities. Each step in the retrieval process, being basic to file processing, stands alone as a separate self-contained function and can be embedded in other major database management functions—file writing, update, programming user facilities, and integrity control—all of which are discussed in later chapters.

The independence of each subfunction stems from the fact that the form of the output is the same as the form of the input, namely, a file. Given a file, the retrieval process may be entered after any step which produces a file as output. Alternatively, one can consider the retrieval process to consist of all the steps with each step having a well-defined default action. Default for the selection process is "select all instances;" default for projection is "extract all items;" default for data item derivations is "none;" and default for sort is "no sort."

An implication of the independence of subfunctions is that users may enter the retrieval process with their own file, specially processed and prepared for output, and let the system produce the required output presentation. This approach is desirable if some complex processing is required which cannot be performed using the conventional retrieval functions. The user writes the special-purpose program which generates an intermediate file for output. Since the intermediate file is still managed by the DBMS, the generalized output presentation facilities can be used. In this way, the programmer is relieved of the output task and can concentrate on the unique aspects of the special processing. It may even be desirable for the programmer to specify that the temporary, intermediate file can be destroyed or dumped to backup after completing the output presentation.

The use of Boolean selection expressions is fundamental to the management and use of a file or a database. Files, data attributes or items, and groups of items are always *named* in the definition of a data structure. Entries or group instances are never

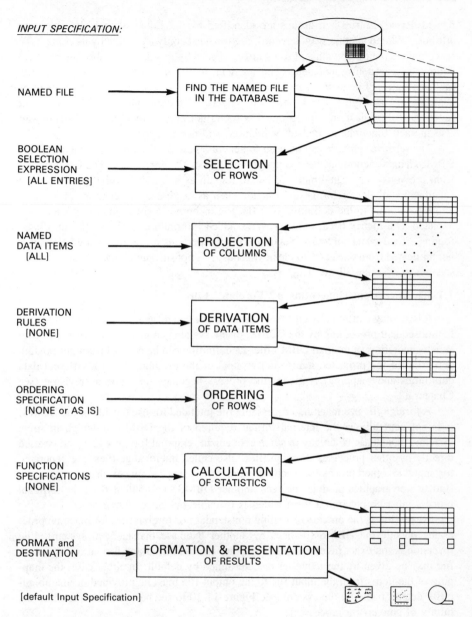

INPUT SPECIFICATION:

NAMED FILE

FIND THE NAMED FILE
IN THE DATABASE

BOOLEAN
SELECTION
EXPRESSION
[ALL ENTRIES]

SELECTION
OF ROWS

NAMED
DATA ITEMS
[ALL]

PROJECTION
OF COLUMNS

DERIVATION
RULES
[NONE]

DERIVATION
OF DATA ITEMS

ORDERING
SPECIFICATION
[NONE or AS IS]

ORDERING
OF ROWS

FUNCTION
SPECIFICATIONS
[NONE]

CALCULATION
OF STATISTICS

FORMAT and
DESTINATION

FORMATION & PRESENTATION
OF RESULTS

[default Input Specification]

Figure 7-3. Steps in the Overall Retrieval Process.
The input to each step is shown on the left with the [default action] taken in case of no explicit input. The effect of each step on a flat file is shown schematically on the right. *Selection* and *projection* cross out rows and columns, respectively; *derivation* adds new data items to each entry; *ordering* rearranges the rows; *calculations* produce statistics across all selected entries; and *formation and presentation* adds information to make the output more readable (or processable) by the recipient, whether human or machine. In any implementation, these steps would not necessarily be processed in this sequence. Some could be interleaved or done in parallel.

named per se. Entries and groups are identified by the values of their data items or attributes. Stated another way, a record, *to the user*, is only identified by its contents— its contained data item values. (To identify a record by its relative or absolute physical address is a system convenience and artificial to the user.) A selection expression includes names of items in an entry and specifies values or conditions on those items as a means of identifying which entries to select. As a consequence of the important function of the selection expression, it is found not only in the retrieval function but also in such functions as update, validation, and access control.

The retrieval process can be used to generate new files within the database of the DBMS. This function has been called *file writing* or *file generation*. The file resulting from previous steps can simply be left to remain as a file within the system. When calculated statistics or format information such as headings are added to a file, it no longer conforms to the definition of a flat file of homogeneous records. It cannot be depicted as a matrix because it may have added information such as title, headings, footings, totals, and subtotals. Such information pertains to the file as a whole and is not replicated from one entry to the next. Thus, it is not sufficient to have a single entry schema to describe all the data.

7.1.3.1 Reversion: Generating a "Foreign" File

File writing can actually take two forms—a file can be generated in internal format for subsequent processing by the DBMS, or the system can generate a "foreign" file. When generating an internal DBMS file, its definition can be derived from the existing definition of the projected items (and groups) of the original file. If a different data definition (and mapping) is given, the process becomes the same as revision (see Chapter 11).

A *foreign file* is a machine-processable file intended for use outside of the DBMS. It is not generally in the internal format required of the DBMS, although in some systems, a database is already in some convenient, external format which can be used directly by other processes. Foreign files, also called interchange files, are generated for input to other processes, such as word processing, a spread sheet program, a statistics or graphics module, or even another DBMS. The output from the retrieval process must be put into a form which is readable by the receiving process.

Reversion is the process of writing nonstandard or foreign files for machine processing outside the DBMS (perhaps by another database management system). File reversion is the exact inverse of file creation. The definition and format of the output file may be given by the requester or determined by default. In either case, the mapping of the items from the input file to the output file must be provided or unambiguously determinable by the system (see Figure 11-10 to see how reversion fits into the family of conversion processes).

A viable process of file reversion or database reversion becomes vital when an organization installs a new DBMS or a new computer hardware system. When moving from an environment without a DBMS, the reversion process can be expensive, especially if the existing mechanized files cannot be read directly by the new DBMS. Furthermore, when moving to a new DBMS from one that has an inadequate reversion facility or that does not retain item-level data definitions, the database reversion process can be even more expensive. The costs of *data* conversion in the future may well dwarf the costs of *program* conversion incurred in the industry in the past.

7.2 SELECTION

The selection process identifies a subset of the entries in a file. The *inputs* to the process are a named file and a Boolean expression which provides the criteria used in selecting the entries in the named file. The Boolean selection expression must contain at least one named data item from the entry as a variable operand. The selection expression must be a Boolean expression so that it produces a Boolean result, that is, a TRUE or FALSE. The result indicates whether or not the entry should be selected.

The *outputs* from the process are a file (a subset of the entries in the original file) and, secondarily, some communication or understanding with the requester concerning the anticipated volume of output. In any given implementation, the output file need not be physically created even though it is logically defined. The output file may be represented by a set of entry pointers. This is particularly convenient if all the data items named in the selection expression are indexed.

7.2.1 Operands, Operators, and Delimiters

An expression consists of operands, operators, and delimiters, combined according to certain construction or syntax rules. For example:

SALARY GT 20000 AND (PSKILL EQ 1130 OR JOBCODE EQ 1130)

The operands are the "nouns" of the expression. For a given entry instance, the operands possess values which are acted upon by operators, the "verbs" of the expression. The delimiters, parentheses, are used to override the normally accepted precedence ordering of binary infix operators and to delimit the operands of prefix and suffix operators.*

An **operand** may be a constant, such as 1130, or a variable, such as JOBCODE. In the case of a constant, the value of the operand is included directly in the expression as a literal. A variable represents one level of indirectness in obtaining a value. It is a data item name which references or points to the value to be acted upon by the opera-

---

*Prefix, infix, and suffix are used to denote whether an operator precedes, lies between, or follows its operands, respectively. This is illustrated with a few examples:

unary prefix operator:	−22	(minus 22)
binary prefix operator:	+ A B	(add A to B)
binary infix operator:	A + B	"
binary suffix operator:	A B +	"
unary suffix operator:	N!	(factorial)

An infix operator is usually a binary operator, that is, having two and only two operands.

tor. Generally, the data item is in the named file and a value can be obtained for it from each entry in the file. The expression is evaluated for each entry in the file. Whenever the expression is being evaluated, one and only one entry in the file is the object entry. Variables may also be data items from an entry other than the object entry (in which case special designations are needed in the expression), they may be from a temporary data item (see the section on derived items), or perhaps from another file. In addition, special operands may be used to designate system data items such as current date, time, or other variables set up by the user. For expression evaluation, the value of each operand must be of a designated type—such as string, numeric, Boolean, or geographic.

Operators in an expression specify the actions to be carried out on certain operands. Each operand must be unambiguously identified with a particular operator. To satisfy this, an expression must be constructed such that each operator is properly positioned with its operands. This rule puts expressions in the class of precedence grammars for which efficient scanning and evaluation techniques exist. Certain operators require operands of a particular type. The execution of an operator produces a value which can then be an operand for another operator. The type of the value produced is determined by the operator and, in some cases, the type of the operands.

When multiple infix binary operators appear in an expression, there exists a high degree of ambiguity in determining which operands an operator is to act upon, for example:

$$\text{SALARY} + \text{OVERTIME} * \text{RAISE} - \text{DEDUCTION} / 12$$

Therefore, an arbitrary but widely accepted precedence ordering has been established for all binary infix operators.

OPERATOR	COMMON NOTATION	RANK
arithmetic: exponentiation	** or ^	1
arithmetic: multiply, divide	* /	2
arithmetic: add, subtract	+ −	3
comparative: Greater than, Less than or Equal to, Not Equal, . . .	GT LT GE LE EQ NE > < > = < = = < > !=	4
Boolean: and	AND or ^	5
Boolean: or	OR or v	6

All delimiters and prefix and suffix operators take precedence over any binary infix operator. Delimiters are used to override the accepted precedence ordering; to clearly define the order of execution of operators.

As shown in the table, there are three major types of operators:

- *Arithmetic operator*—requires numeric operands and produces a numeric result.
- *Comparative operator*—requires arithmetic or string operands, both operands being of the same type, and produces a Boolean result.
- *Boolean operator*—requires Boolean operands and produces a Boolean result.

In the hierarchy of operator execution, once a comparative operator is encountered, all subsequent evaluation of the expression is in the realm of Boolean. (There is no generally accepted operator which takes Boolean operands and produces a numeric result, although some systems interpret a Boolean result as a numeric 0 or 1 when acted upon by an arithmetic operator.)

Besides acting on item *values*, operators may be provided to test the existence, length, or type of a data item. Other operators may act on several values to produce a MIN, MAX, SUM, AVERAGE, or other statistical result. Special data item types often require special operators, for example, DISTANCE and AREA operators to act on geographical data.

7.2.2 Boolean Selection Expressions

The selection of records is based upon a Boolean expression. A Boolean expression consists of one or more Boolean conditions. This section describes such expressions, extended operators, and the typical restrictions often found on the construction of selection expressions in DBMSs.

In general, a Boolean selection expression is a linear sequence of operands, operators, and delimiters put together using a consistent set of construction rules (similar to those used in constructing a FORTRAN or BASIC expression). Such rules normally allow the use of parentheses nested to any level, an assumed order of execution of infix operators having the same precedence ordering (usually designated as a left-to-right or a right-to-left scan). The action graph in Figure 7-4 summarizes a generally accepted set of rules for the construction of an expression. The detail to distinguish different types of operands has not been included. Operators are distinguished in terms of prefix, binary infix, and unary suffix. Suffix operators of higher degree are not included (furthermore, it is a nontrivial task to include them). A legend is included to interpret the symbology of action graphs.*

A Boolean expression is built up from one or more Boolean conditions. A **Boolean condition** is a minimal expression which produces a Boolean result. It could be a single Boolean variable operand or an expression with a single binary comparative operator or a single suffix operator.

A simple example of the second case is a comparison of a single data item against a single constant value (the object):

    item-name   comparative-operator   value

an example being

    TITLE   EQ   ELEC ENGR.

It is not uncommon for systems to require the object of the Boolean condition to be a literal value as shown in the above example.

---

*For a more complete explanation with illustrations see: Mark Resnick and Jerome Sable, "INSCAN: A Syntax-Directed Language Processor," *Proceedings ACM National Conference*, 1968 August, pages 423-432.

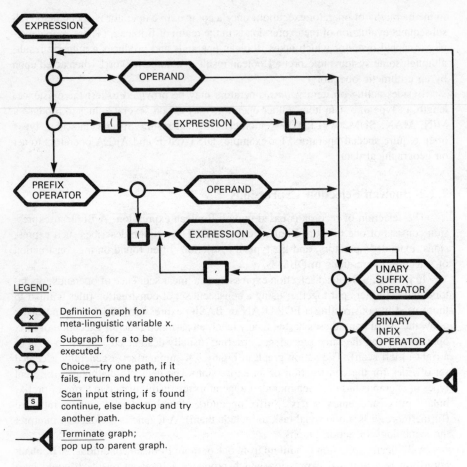

LEGEND:

Definition graph for
meta-linguistic variable x.

Subgraph for a to be
executed.

Choice—try one path, if it
fails, return and try another.

Scan input string, if s found
continue, else backup and try
another path.

Terminate graph;
pop up to parent graph.

Figure 7-4. Syntactic Construction Rules for an Expression.
An "action" graph defines the allowable sequences of language elements when forming, in this case, a Boolean Selection Expression. The Legend explains the meaning of each of the symbols in the graph.

Another restriction sometimes found is that all literal values, or perhaps just string literals, must be enclosed in quotation marks. This restriction makes it easier for the system to unambiguously parse a selection expression (although it is not usually necessary), and places an additional burden on the user.

In general, the operands on either side of the binary comparative operator can be expressions with one containing at least one data item name as a variable. For example,

$$\text{JOBCODE} \quad \text{EQ} \quad \text{PRIMARY SKILL}$$

Also

$$\text{(ACTUAL SALARY)}/12)*1.15 \text{ GT } 2000$$

selects those who would be earning over $2,000 per month after a 15% raise.

For another example:

(ACTUAL SALARY − AUTHORIZED SALARY / QUANTITY)
/ ACTUAL SALARY GT .10

selects employees whose salary differs from their authorized salary by more than ten percent (assuming the authorized salary to be equally divided among those with the same JOBCODE in the same UNIT). The expressions may be arithmetic or string (not Boolean) and they must reduce down to a common value type, such that the two operands are comparable.

Another case has the general form of:

item-name   suffix-operator

where the suffix operators could include EXISTS, FAILS (that is, a value is absent), IS or IS NOT NUMERIC, ALPHABETIC, POSITIVE, NEGATIVE, ZERO, BLANK, or NULL. NULL would take on the user-defined null value or the system default null value for the named data item.

Binary Boolean operators then connect multiple Boolean conditions to form a **Boolean expression**. Parentheses may be added to override the normal sequence of operator execution. For example:

LEVEL EQ HEAD AND ACTUAL SALARY GT 30000.

SALARY GT 20000 AND (PRIMARY SKILL EQ 1130 OR JOBCODE EQ 1130).

Special notation may be developed to specify a combination of operators in a short form. For example, the "between" operator in

item-name   BT   a   AND   b

is actually a tertiary operator where it is understood that the item to be tested appears before it and the two range designators appear after. Some convention must be established concerning which value is high and which is low and whether or not the range is inclusive or exclusive of the end points. The above notation is short form for (assuming an inclusive range):

item-name   GE   a   AND   item-name   LE   b.

Using prefix notation the ternary "between" operator becomes:

BT (item-name, a, b)

An explicit range notation might be:

item-name   [NOT]   (WITHIN)   RANGE a, b
                    (OUTSIDE)

For another example of short form notation:

item-name   EQ   ANY OF   (a, b, c, d)

may be used to avoid rewriting the item name for several OR conditions:

item-name EQ a   OR   item-name EQ b   OR   item-name EQ c   OR. . .

In prefix notation this "equal-or" operator could be written as:

EOR (item-name, a, b, c, d).

As an alternative, for a missing operand plus comparative operator, the system could carry forward from the last complete Boolean condition as follows:

| (subject) operand | comparative operator | (object) operand | Boolean operator | (object) operand | Boolean operator | (object) operand. |

where the underlined portion must be reinserted into the expression at each asterisk (*). For example,

PRIMARY SKILL EQ 1130 OR 1120 OR 1135

Carrying only the subject operand forward would permit the use of different comparative operators:

| (subject) operand | comparative operator | (object) operand | Boolean operator | comparative operator | (object) operand. |

For example:

PRIMARY SKILL EQ 1130 OR   1135 AND   NE 6625 AND   GT 1100

7.2.2.1 Overcoming Prohibited Use of Parentheses

One restriction sometimes found in current systems prohibits the use of parentheses. This is generally accompanied by the rule that the expression must be in either disjunctive or conjunctive form. To be in disjunctive form, the highest level operators (the last ones to be executed) in the operator hierarchy of the expression must be disjunctions, that is, Boolean OR's. In conjunctive form the AND's are executed last. This puts a significant burden on the person writing the selection expression. It now becomes necessary to manipulate the desired expression in order to eliminate the parentheses. This can be done by repeatedly applying the *distributive law*:

A AND (B OR C) = A AND B OR A AND C

or *DeMorgan's law*:

NOT (A AND B) = NOT A OR NOT B.

(Both of these examples assume AND ranks higher than OR.)

Sometimes a seemingly simple query can turn into an extended task, even an impossible task for some users, when the system requires selection expressions to be in disjunctive or conjunctive form and prohibits the use of parentheses. The following side box illustrates this point.

A SIMPLE QUERY TURNED INTO A NIGHTMARE

Consider the following query against the EMPLOYEE flat file in Figure 7-1:

Find all employees who are either skilled as electrical engineers (skill code = 1130) and have an annual salary over $20,000 or are skilled as mechanical engineers (skill code = 1120) and have an annual salary of $22,000 or more.

Each employee has one primary skill (PSKILL) and up to four secondary skills (SSKILLi) recorded. Using parentheses the above query would be written as:

```
PRINT EMPLOYEE NAME WHERE
    (( PSKILL EQ 1130 OR SSKILL1 EQ 1130 OR SSKILL2 EQ 1130
       OR SSKILL3 EQ 1130 OR SSKILL4 EQ 1130 )
       AND ACTUAL SALARY GT 20000 )
OR (( PSKILL EQ 1120 OR SSKILL1 EQ 1120
     OR SSKILL2 EQ 1120 OR SSKILL3 EQ 1120 OR SSKILL4 EQ 1120 )
     AND ACTUAL SALARY GE 22000 ).
```

To convert this Boolean selection expression to *disjunctive form* without parentheses, a useful first step is to substitute a short form for each Boolean condition in the expression and to substitute a short symbol for each operator (OR = v, AND = ^) with the last executed OR symbol larger when converting to disjunctive form. The above query becomes:

```
((Pe v S1e v S2e v S3e v S4e) ^ A20) ᴠ ((Pm v S1m v S2m v S3m v S4m) ^ A22)
```

substituting
'Pe' for Primary Skill EQ 1130, the electrical engineer;
'S2m' for Secondary Skill2 EQ 1120, the mechanical engineer;
and 'A22' for Actual Salary GE 22000)
Applying the distributive law to remove the innermost parentheses yields:

```
(Pe ^ A20 v S1e ^ A20 v S2e ^ A20 v S3e ^ A20 v S4e ^ A20)
ᴠ (Pm ^ A22 v S1m ^ A22 v S2m ^ A22 v S3m ^ A22 v S4m ^ A22).
```

Now the outer parentheses can simply be removed and the expression is in disjunctive form. Expanding back, the query becomes:

```
PRINT EMPLOYEE NAME WHERE
        PSKILL   EQ 1130 AND ACTUAL SALARY GT 20000
   OR   SSKILL1  EQ 1130 AND ACTUAL SALARY GT 20000
   OR   SSKILL2  EQ 1130 AND ACTUAL SALARY GT 20000
   OR   SSKILL3  EQ 1130 AND ACTUAL SALARY GT 20000
   OR   SSKILL4  EQ 1130 AND ACTUAL SALARY GT 20000
   OR   PSKILL   EQ 1120 AND ACTUAL SALARY GE 22000
   OR   SSKILL1  EQ 1120 AND ACTUAL SALARY GE 22000
   OR   SSKILL2  EQ 1120 AND ACTUAL SALARY GE 22000
   OR   SSKILL3  EQ 1120 AND ACTUAL SALARY GE 22000
   OR   SSKILL4  EQ 1120 AND ACTUAL SALARY GE 22000.
```

Converting the original query into *conjunctive form* requires that the AND's be executed last. First, make the following substitution for the set of Boolean conditions which test skills:

```
Se := Pe v S1e v S2e v S3e v S4e
```

Then, beginning with

$$(\ Se \ ^\wedge \ A20 \ ) \ \cup \ (\ Sm \ ^\wedge \ A22 \ )$$

and applying the distributive law to remove the middle OR yields four terms, each a pair of Boolean conditions:

$$Se \ \cup \ Sm \ ^\wedge \ Se \ \cup \ A22 \ ^\wedge \ A20 \ \cup \ Sm \ ^\wedge \ A20 \ \cup \ A22.$$

This expression is in conjunctive form but can be further simplified. Referring to the fourth term, if A22 is true, A20 will always be true: to be selected, an employee must have an actual salary greater than $20,000 regardless of any other conditions. If A20 must always be true for an employee to be selected, then the third term is redundant. The first term ensures that the employee has one of the two desired skills; the second term reflects the differential salary between mechanical and electrical engineers. Thus, the conjunctive form of the query reduces to:

$$Se \ \cup \ Sm \ ^\wedge \ Se \ \cup \ A22 \ ^\wedge \ A20.$$

and expands to:

```
PRINT EMPLOYEE NAME WHERE
     PSKILL EQ 1130 OR SSKILL1 EQ 1130 OR SSKILL2 EQ 1130 OR
     SSKILL3 EQ 1130 OR SSKILL4 EQ 1130 OR
     PSKILL EQ 1120 OR SSKILL1 EQ 1120 OR SSKILL2 EQ 1120 OR
     SSKILL3 EQ 1120 OR SSKILL4 EQ 1120
AND ACTUAL SALARY GE 22000 OR PSKILL EQ 1130 OR SSKILL1 EQ 1130 OR
     SSKILL2 EQ 1130 OR SSKILL3 EQ 1130 OR SSKILL4 EQ 1130
AND ACTUAL SALARY GT 20000.
```

7.2.3 Anticipated Volume of Output

A secondary output from the selection process is some communication or understanding with the requester concerning the anticipated volume of output. Under some circumstances it may be desirable for the system not to continue with the retrieval process if the execution of the selection expression results in a very large number of selected entries. Often the requester is looking for a few but not a large number of entries which satisfy the selection expression. The requester, knowing that a large number of entries were selected, may want to apply more restrictive conditions to reduce the volume of output.

There are several ways in which this communication with the requester can be accomplished. Operating in batch mode, the system may have a default maximum or be given a maximum by the requestor *a priori*. If more than the selected maximum number of entries are selected, the system will abort the retrieval. Operating in online mode, the system can tell the requester the number of selected entries immediately after the selection process and then wait for either a signal to proceed or the input of another selection expression.

If the retrieval expects only one entry to satisfy the selection expression, this can be communicated to the system with

PRINT UNIQUE NAME, OF EMPLOYEE, WHERE EMPNO EQ 44584.

If the employee number is not unique, the system would issue an error message. This facility is particularly important for update statements. Similarly, the requester can specify the maximum number of responses to be printed if a large number is selected.

For a requester who is interacting online with the system, it is desirable to be able to perform **incremental selection** of record subsets. For example, having selected a subset of records and observing the results, such as number selected, the requester may want to incrementally change the Boolean selection criteria. The incremental retrieval could serve to extend (with OR) or further restrict (with AND) the previous selection criteria:

User:	COUNT EMPLOYEES WITH TITLE EQ ELEC ENGR.
System:	*184*
User:	DITTO AND AGE GT 38.
System:	*23*

At this point the user may want to retrieve specific data for the selected employees:

User:	PRINT EMPLOYEE NAME, ORGANIZATIONAL UNIT WHERE SAME.	
System:	HENDERSON	2111
	FITINGER	2113
	ARNETTE	2115

Using SAME instructs the system to repeat the Boolean selection expression from the previous statement (or only consider those entries selected up to this point).

Random sampling is another method of selection particularly suited to the needs of auditors. Auditing a database does not always require exhaustive examination of every entry in a file; it is sufficient to be able to pick a random subset. The auditor-interrogator would specify what proportion of the file to select, say, a 10% sample. Then the system should *randomly* select entries based upon a random number generator. It would be possible to select the first 10% or every tenth entry but such a simplistic procedure may produce a biased sample—something the auditor does not want.

7.3 PROJECTION AND DERIVATION OF DATA ITEMS

The projection process projects or extracts named data items from the object file. The named projected items are those which the requester wants to see.

In addition to the items the user wishes to see, there may be others which the system must see temporarily in order to select entries, derive additional data items, calculate statistics, or sort the output. They too would have to be projected from the records but not output to the user. For example, the requester may wish to see AGE which the system derives from the stored BIRTHDATE. There is no reason why the requester must explicitly project BIRTHDATE from the file as long as the derivation rule is explicitly defined to the system.

EVEREST: DATABASE MANAGEMENT

The *inputs* to the projection process are a named file (perhaps implied by a prior command) and the names of data items whose values are to be projected from the selected entries. The *output* is again a file containing the named data items.

The default is normally to project all the items from the records. Language expressions such as PRINT ENTRY . . . or PRINT ALL . . . can be used. In this case, the structure of the output file is identical to the input file.

7.3.1 Derivation Rules for Additional Data Items

At this step in the retrieval process, the requester specifies that the values for additional data items be derived and added logically to the selected records. In addition to the file resulting from the projection process, the *input* consists of the formula or rule for deriving each additional data item value. The *output* is again a file with the values for derived data items added to each record, in effect, adding columns to the file.

A *derived item* may be actual or virtual. An *actual derived item* is stored in the record. If the value for one of the operands changes, the value for the actual derived item must be recalculated. A *virtual derived item* is not explicitly stored in the database. (If the users can independently modify an actual "derived item," then it really isn't derived and the derivation rule becomes a validation rule.)

In general, the value for the derived data item results from the evaluation of an expression. If the data item is numeric, the expression is likely an arithmetic expression. The operands in the expression may be literals, data items from the object entry, or data items from some or all of the other selected entries. A temporary data item variable which is updated with each new entry, may also be an operand.

TYPE OF DERIVATION	EXAMPLES
one operand plus a literal	MONTHLY_RAISE : = ACTUAL_SALARY*.05/12 LENGTH_CENT : = LENGTH_INCH*2.54
one operand plus a system variable	AGE : = SYSTEMDATE − BIRTHDATE
two operands in the same entry	POS_AUTH_SAL : = AUTHORIZED_SALARY/QUANTITY UNAUTH_SALARY : = ACTUAL_SALARY − AUTHORIZED_SALARY
operands from object entry and previous entry (in order)	Assuming an ordering on ACTUAL SALARY: ACT_SALARY_DIFF : = ACTUAL_SALARY − PREV ACTUAL_SALARY where "PREV" is a system key word.
operand dependent on all selected entries	SALARY_RANK : = RANK (ACTUAL SALARY) where "RANK" is a system defined function which sorts (logically but not necessarily physically) the selected entries and then consecutively assigns integers to them beginning with one.

Another way to specify a derivation rule is with an arbitrary function. An *arbitrary function* associates a value with each value or range of values of an operand. It can be represented by a table with two values for each entry. One value is the search argument (the operand) and the other is the function value corresponding to each value of the search argument. The value of the operand is compared to the search arguments. When a match is found, the corresponding function value is retrieved. This is sometimes called a table-look-up and is often used to decode values in the stored file. The decode capability is used to substitute a human readable value for an internal coded representation of a data item, for example, to substitute the values MALE and FEMALE for the value '1' and '2' for the attribute SEX. The internal encoded value may or may not be retained in the resultant file.

Often it is desirable to derive an item value based upon the value of a stored data item. For example, the requester may desire salary ranges rather than exact salary values. The derivation rule, actually a set of conditional rules, could be expressed as follows:

SALARY CLASS = A IF ACTUAL SALARY BETWEEN 1, 10000.

SALARY CLASS = B IF ACTUAL SALARY BETWEEN 10001, 20000.

SALARY CLASS = C IF ACTUAL SALARY BETWEEN 20001, 40000.

SALARY CLASS = D IF ACTUAL SALARY GT 40000.

As another example, a negative value for UNAUTHORIZED SALARY can be avoided by adding the output condition:

UNAUTHORIZED SALARY = '-' IF UNAUTHORIZED SALARY LT 0.

When a data item is named in an expression it is considered a variable, and, by convention, the *value* attribute of the item is retrieved and substituted for the data item during the evaluation of the expression. Data item attributes other than the value attribute could also be retrieved by explicitly using a unary function operator. For example, if EMPLOYEE NAME produced the value 'PETERSON', LENGTH(EMPLOYEE NAME) would produce the value 8, the number of characters in the name.

Sometimes a selection step must logically *follow* a data item derivation. This would happen if the derived item were an operand in the selection expression. Such examples indicate the necessity of analyzing a retrieval request before it is executed and the file is read.

7.4 ORDERING, CONTROL BREAKS, AND STATISTICS

The ordering step in a retrieval request specifies the sequence in which the requester desires to see the entries presented. It does not refer to any additional sorting which the system may have to perform in order to properly satisfy the retrieval request.

The *input* to the ordering process consists of the file from the preceding step and a defined ordering on the file. The *output* consists of the same file content with the sequence of the entries rearranged according to the defined ordering. No new data is added to the file as a result of the ordering process, only resequencing of the entries occurs.

An *ordering* is defined by:

1. A ranked set of data item names, collectively called the sort "key",
2. An assumed or understood collating sequence on the value set of each data item, such that a transitive arrangement of the item values can be established, and
3. An ascending or descending indicator for each named data item (descending could be designated using a minus sign before the data item name).

If any item named in the sort key is a derived item, the derivation must take place before the sort is performed.

Several subsequent specifications in the retrieval request may depend upon the defined ordering. For example, the requester may want to produce subtotals of a data item for each group of entries possessing the same value for the sort key. The requester may also want to add extra spaces, insert a subtitle, print subfootings, or eject to a new page each time the value of a sort key changes. Such a value change is called a *control break*. Each data item in the sort key can cause a control break at which time any number of statistics calculations and formatting options may be invoked. Figure 7-5 shows an output report with control breaks.

7.4.1 Calculation of Statistics

Statistical data, sometimes called longitudinal data, vertical data, file-level derivations, or "image" functions, is data calculated *across* the entries in a file. Such data consists of various statistical measures applied to the set of values occurring for named data items. The calculation of statistics provides analysis of one (or more) attributes of a set of selected entities, or, conversely, it provides an analysis of a selected set of entities in terms of one (or more) attributes.

Each column or data item in the file, resulting from some previous step in the retrieval process, can be viewed as a variable. As such, it is meaningful to:

- Speak of a frequency distribution of data item values.
- Set up intervals of values in order to condense the information.
- Give a graphical representation of the frequency distribution.
- Calculate statistical measures of the frequency distribution.
- Speak of the relationship between two (or more) data items in terms of a joint frequency distribution and the calculation of multivariate statistics.

The frequency distribution of the values of a single data item can be represented in a tabular form, in a graphical form, or in a summarized form by using statistics which reflect certain characteristics of the frequency distribution. Common statistics calculated from the set of values of a single data item include:

COUNT the number of occurrences of a value for the item
  (the zeroeth statistical moment; a measure of size)

SUM the item values

AVERAGE or MEAN = SUM / COUNT
  (first moment; a measure of location)

EMPNAME	UNIT	JOB CODE	ACTUAL SALARY
=============	====	====	=====
PETERSON, N.M.	2000	0110	56000

```
=== JOBCODE = 0110
=== CNT EMPNAME = 1
=== AVG SALARY = 56000
```

CARR, P.I.	2100	1110	48000
GUTTMAN, G.J.	2110	1110	35000
WALTERS, R.J.	2111	1110	28000
FRIEDMAN, J.M.	2112	1110	26000
FRANCIS, G.C.	2112	1110	24000
BRIGGS, G.R.	2115	1110	24000

```
=== JOBCODE = 1110
=== CNT EMPNAME = 6
=== AVG SALARY = 30833
```

SCARBOROUGH, J.B.	2111	1120	21000
FAULKNER, W.M.	2112	1120	24000
ARTHUR, P.J.	2115	1120	22000

```
=== JOBCODE = 1120
=== CNT EMPNAME = 3
=== AVG SALARY = 22333
```

HENDERSON, R.G.	2111	1130	23000
GARBER, R.E.	2111	1130	16400
FITINGER, G.J.	2112	1130	22000
APGAR, A.J.	2112	1130	21000

```
=== JOBCODE = 1130
=== CNT EMPNAME = 4
=== AVG SALARY = 20600
```

ARNETTE, L.J.	2115	1330	22000
BLANK, L.F.	2112	1330	16000

```
=== JOBCODE = 1330
=== CNT EMPNAME = 2
=== AVG SALARY = 19000
```

COMPTON, D.R.	2111	1350	16200

```
=== JOBCODE = 1350
=== CNT EMPNAME = 1
=== AVG SALARY = 16200
```

LYNN, K.R.	2000	5210	12000
CALLAGAN, R.F.	2100	5210	10800
HARRIS, D.L.	2110	5210	8400

```
=== JOBCODE = 5210
=== CNT EMPNAME = 3
=== AVG SALARY = 10400
```

Figure 7-5. Sample Report with Control Breaks.
This report presents data for all employees, ordered by jobcode. There is also a control break each time the value of jobcode changes. At the control break the system prints out the number of employees with the same jobcode and their average salary. Note that the control break must be on the same attribute as the ordering.

MODE, the most frequently occurring value
  (another measure of location)

MEDIAN, the value at the 50th percentile
  (another measure of location)

STANDARD DEVIATION or VARIANCE
  (second moment; a measure of dispersion)

MINIMUM value for the item across all entries

MAXIMUM value

RANGE = MAXIMUM − MINIMUM (another measure of dispersion)

From a joint frequency distribution of two variables, that is, when considering the sets of values for two data items, statistical measures such as correlation (the correlation coefficient) and covariance can be calculated. With two or more data items, multiple regression can be performed.

In some cases, it may be desirable to classify or partition the set of values of one data item according to the values of a second data item, called the *control variable*, before calculating some statistics. This has the result of dividing the set of values into subsets. Then, for each subset, it is possible to calculate any of the single-variable statistics listed above. For example, using JOBCODE as a control variable on the file shown in Figure 7-1, it may be desirable to know the AVERAGE SALARY PER JOBCODE. For each unique value of the control item, JOBCODE, the statistic, AVERAGE, is calculated on SALARY, as shown in Figure 7-5.

In general, the control variable may be the concatenation of more than one data item, provided none of the data items are unique identifiers. Often, it is necessary to perform a prior sort on the data items which make up the control variable. When the value of a control data item changes from one entry to the next, a *control break* is said to occur. The level of the control break corresponds to the rank of the item in the defined ordering. For example, if the output were ordered first by UNIT and then by JOBCODE within UNIT, UNIT is the major break and JOBCODE is secondary. A control break on UNIT forces a simultaneous control break on JOBCODE.

When there are multiple control items, the statistics for a data item must be associated with a particular control item, that is, a particular control break level. The calculation of subtotals exemplifies this idea. When a control break occurs at a given level, all lower level subtotals are "rolled into" the higher level total, the process eventually culminating in a grand total for the entire file (of selected entries) for this attribute.

An output report which contains actual data item values extracted from the database is a *detail report*. A detail report may also contain summary information based upon calculated statistics. By contrast, a *summary report* only contains statistics with no detail data corresponding to individual stored entries (unless, of course, a selected set had only a single entry).

AN EXAMPLE. Figure 7-6 illustrates the several steps in a retrieval process by showing the parts of a request and the results produced in an output report.

Retrieval Request:

```
LIST FROM EMPLOYEE FILE
    EMPNAME, JOBCODE, ACTUAL SALARY,
    AGE = SYSTEMDATE - BIRTHDATE,
    RAISE8 = ACTUAL SALARY * .08
    RAISE9 = ACTUAL SALARY * .09
    COUNT EMPNAME, AVERAGE ACTUAL SALARY,
    SUM RAISE8, SUM RAISE9, AVERAGE RAISE8, AVERAGE RAISE9,
    ORDER BY EMPNAME,
    WHERE TITLE EQ ELEC ENGR.
```

Output Report:

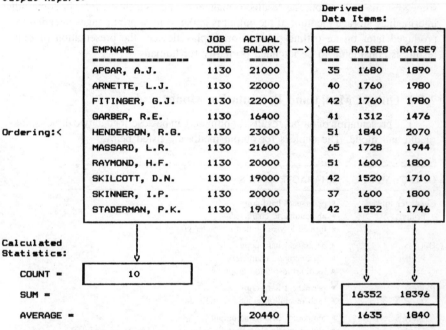

			Derived Data Items:		
EMPNAME	JOB CODE	ACTUAL SALARY	AGE	RAISE8	RAISE9
APGAR, A.J.	1130	21000	35	1680	1890
ARNETTE, L.J.	1130	22000	40	1760	1980
FITINGER, G.J.	1130	22000	42	1760	1980
GARBER, R.E.	1130	16400	41	1312	1476
HENDERSON, R.G.	1130	23000	51	1840	2070
MASSARD, L.R.	1130	21600	65	1728	1944
RAYMOND, H.F.	1130	20000	51	1600	1800
SKILCOTT, D.N.	1130	19000	42	1520	1710
SKINNER, I.P.	1130	20000	37	1600	1800
STADERMAN, P.K.	1130	19400	42	1552	1746

Ordering:<

Calculated Statistics:

COUNT = 10

SUM = 16352   18396

AVERAGE = 20440   1635   1840

Figure 7-6. Illustration of Steps in the Retrieval Process.
The above retrieval request on the Employee file of Figure 7-1 produces the output report as shown. The personnel manager is gathering data to use in salary negotiations with the Association of Electrical Engineers. Identify each of the parts within the retrieval request, and then observe the result in the output report.

7.5 FORMATION AND PRESENTATION OF OUTPUT RESULTS

While the dual processes of formation and presentation are conceptually distinct, the format specifications are so highly conditioned by the selected mode of presentation as to preclude any separation of discussion. Format specifications include such things as titles, headings, editing of data item values, spacing, page size, pagination, scaling on vertical and horizontal axes, and plot characters. The presentation of output results may be in the form of a report to be printed or displayed on a cathode ray tube, or in the form of a file intended for subsequent machine processing.

The presentation of output results basically takes one of two forms. This section discusses presentation intended primarily for humans. Section 7.1.3 discussed the delivery of results intended primarily for subsequent machine processing. Even though some systems may output the results to magnetic tape, punched cards, or some other intermediate storage medium, if the output is in the form of print images intended to be produced later on an offline printing or display device, the presentation of output results is considered to be intended primarily for humans.

7.5.1 Output Media and Presentation Modes

The presentation of output results for humans can be described in two dimensions—media and mode. The choices for output media are listed below.

OUTPUT MEDIA	CHARACTERISTICS
Character Impact Printer	• permanent hard copy • alphanumeric characters • limited low resolution character graphics
Dot Matrix Printer	• permanent hard copy • alphanumeric characters • medium resolution graphics
Plotter	• permanent hard copy • high resolution graphics, and color
Display Screen	• temporary (transient) output • alphanumeric characters • graphics if dot addressable screen
Audio Response	• temporary (transient) output • often used to supplement visual output • limited to small output volumes
Microform (fiche or film)	• reduced onto a transparency requiring special equipment to read • may be alphanumeric or graphic

Some format specifications, such as page size, are most dependent on the choice of output media.

Normally, a system will deliver the results where the request originated. Sometimes it is desirable to be able to override such default action. The override could be in the form of a different verb or a modifier in the retrieval request. A requester, expecting a lot of output and able to wait for it, can say PRINT OFFLINE rather than tie up system resources in getting the output immediately at the terminal. Alternatively, the destination for the output could be another terminal or another processing site in a distributed processing environment.

The three major **modes of presentation** are:

Record   displaying or printing one record or entry at a time
Report   based on a simple listing of all projected and derived data item values
Graph   based on the frequency distribution of selected data item values

7.5.2 Record-at-a-time Presentation

A simple mode of presentation is to display one entry at a time from the selected subset of records. The system pauses after each displayed entry waiting for the user to say continue. The user steps or "pages" through the selected entries one at a time.

Besides being able to move forward, the user could be given the ability to freely move around within the selected set of entries:

NEXT   - move forward to display the next entry
PRIOR   - step back to the previous entry
FIRST   - to beginning of file
LAST   - to end of file
NEXT n   - skipping forward over n entries
PLACE n   - for absolute positioning at the nth entry
PLACE * + n   - to skip forward over n entries (same as NEXT n)
PLACE * − n   - skipping back over n entries (or 'PRIOR n')

To display the contents of each record, the simplest approach is to display one data item per line with the value following the data item name. If the total number of items exceeds the size of the display screen (usually 24 lines; less if there are system reserved status lines, and less if some data item values are longer than one line) the system can pause after each screenful waiting for the user to "turn the page" by hitting some specified key. The system must allow the user to be unambiguous between "more of this record" and "go to the next record" when "paging" through a set of (selected) records which have more than 24 data items.

An alternative to defaulting to one data item per line would be to give the user the option of defining a tailored screen format. The user must essentially be able to specify the row and column location on the screen at which to display a specified data item value or a literal (for easier reading). This would make it possible to display multiple item values per line and to place information on the screen in a more readable and natural arrangement. For larger records, the user may still desire to define multiple screens over which to display the data. By defining their own screens, users should also be able to omit certain data items (that is, do a projection) and even specify derived data items. (The derivation rules could be stored as part of the schema.)

Rather than specifying the row and column locations of displayed information, some systems let the screen-defining user literally "paint" the display screen. Presented with a blank screen, the user moves the cursor to the desired location and then indicates what is to be displayed at that location. It may be a literal label which the user types, a data item from the object data record, or a system variable. Then the system saves the painted screen (which may be converted to row and column locations for each item). At display time the system retrieves the current value for each data item and the system variables.

7.5.3 Report Output in List Mode

Report output in list mode presents the data in columns. Figure 7-1 illustrates a columnar report presentation of the EMPLOYEE file. Reports are the conventional and sometimes the only mode of output presentation available in a DBMS, particularly those with a batch mode of operation.

Up to this point in the retrieval process, only data in the stored file or derivations therefrom have been generated. Format specifications for a report include rules or constraints on the output and new information to be added. The new information is generally added to enhance the readability of the output results. It consists of literals or constants interspersed in the output data:

- Cover page information.
- Titles.
- Column headings—data item names or labels.
- Row headings or stubs.
- Footings.
- Data about the requester.
- Distribution lists.
- Labels indicating restricted distribution.
- Pagination—automatic generation of page numbers.
- Date and time, or period to which data applies.
- Date and time of report preparation.

In addition to the literal or constant information, the format specifications include rules for preparing the output:

- Editing of data item values—dollar sign, handling negative values, decimal places, commas, leading zero suppression, etc. This is often specified using a 'mask', such as in COBOL.
- Relative placement of item values in a line of the report.
- Blocking—the relative place of lines and groups of lines.
- Page size in terms of a maximum number of characters horizontally and a maximum number of lines vertically.
- Conditions for beginning a new page—for example, for each new value of a named data item.
- Relative and absolute spacing, both horizontal and vertical, for extracted and derived data, and for the literal or constant information specified above. Spacing rules determine the placement of various elements in the report.

All the format specification information can come from three sources: data provided and stored with the data definition, from the request, or automatically selected by the system in default of no information being provided. In some cases, it may be useful to supply certain information at the time a data item is defined to the system. This could include an external, human-oriented column heading, and value editing rules for data items.

In general, a system should be prepared to find default information or take a default action whenever specific information or directives are not supplied at report definition time or at request time. For example, the default for a column heading could be the data item name; the default for the title could be the name of the file from which the data was originally extracted, along with the selection criteria used, if any. Any format specification provided at request time would override the corresponding format specifications as previously stored or as determined by default.

With little output from a retrieval request, the system can print the results on separate lines with a name or description as a stub associated with each value. For example,

PRINT COUNT, AVERAGE SALARY, OF EMPLOYEES.

would be output as:

```
COUNT EMPLOYEES = 247,
AVERAGE SALARY = 22,334,00
```

Similarly,

PRINT UNIQUE EMPNAME, UNIT, TITLE, PRIMARY SKILL, OF EMPLOYEE,
WHERE EMPNO EQ 45584.

would produce:

```
EMPNAME = PETERSON, N,M,
UNIT = 2000
TITLE = DIVISION MANAGER
PRIMARY SKILL = 0110
```

In LIST mode this output would appear as:

EMPNAME	UNIT	TITLE	PSKILL
PETERSON, N.M.	2000	DIVISION MANAGER	0110

If the same type of data is to be printed multiple times, it is desirable to LIST it in a columnar form with the data item name at the top of each column of values. With two different verbs, such as PRINT and LIST, the requester has control over the preferred mode of output.

7.5.3.1 Handling Page Width Limitations

A common problem in the formation and presentation of output records is the limitation of page width. Invariably, a requester desires to present more data across a page than space permits. A generalized report writing system can take several approaches to this problem. Some systems simply do not permit the aggregate of column widths and horizontal spaces to exceed the page width. In this situation users must produce multiple output records or compress data values by encoding or truncation before printing.

There are several viable system solutions to the page width limitation including column overflow, column value truncation, repeating value suppression, vertical overflow, horizontal wrap around, and user-defined reports with multiple lines per entry.

With *column overflow*, if a data item is too long for the specified column width, then the system can print the value on multiple lines within the same column. With *column value truncation*, the system would only print as much of the value as would fit on a single line within the defined field width. For example, printing EMPLOYEE NAME with a column width of 10 characters would produce the following output:

```
Column Overflow:          Column Value Truncation:
                          (10 char field)            (12 char field)

EMPNAME        UNIT       EMPNAME       UNIT         EMPNAME       UNIT
----------     ----       ----------    ----         -----------   ----
PETERSON,      2000       PETERSON,     2000         PETERSON, N/2000
N.M.                      LYNN, K.R.    2000         LYNN, K.R.    2000
LYNN, K.R.     2000       APGAR, A.J    2112         APGAR, A.J.   2112
APGAR, A.J     2112       ARNETTE, L    2115         ARNETTE, L./2115
,                         SCARBOROUG    2111         SCARBOROUGH/2111
ARNETTE, L     2115          :            :             :            :
,J.
SCARBOROUG     2111
H, J.B.
   :             :
```

Column overflow preserves the complete value for the data item but produces uneven vertical line spacing and looks messy. Column value truncation looks neater but does result in the loss of some information. Sometimes it is a reasonable tradeoff for the user in formatting a report to be able to get neat, compact output. It may be desirable to allow the user to specify that a special character be printed at the end of the field whenever a value is truncated (as shown in the third column above).

When the output is ordered by certain data items and they are projected first, it is possible to use repeating value suppression or vertical overflow. Under *repeating value suppression* the values of the data items are only printed when they first change in the ordered sequence of output entries. This makes it easier for the user to see the logical grouping of entries on the output report.

Vertical overflow is an extension of repeating value suppression designed to condense the width of the output report in exchange for a longer report. If the ordering on the employee information is defined by UNIT, LEVEL, and JOBCODE, in that order, the report on the following page illustrates vertical overflow on these three data items.

	EMPNO	EMPNAME	TITLE	PSKILL
	-----	--------------	----------------	------
UNIT = 2115				
LEVEL = HEAD				
JOBCODE = 1110				
	22959	BRIGGS, G.R.	CHIEF, PROD SPE	1110
LEVEL = EMPL				
JOBCODE = 1120				
	29414	ARTHUR, P.J.	MECH ENGR	1120
JOBCODE = 1130				
	82802	APGAR, A.J.	ELEC ENGR	1130
	37113	ARNETTE, L.J.	ELEC ENGR	1130
UNIT = 2120				
LEVEL = HEAD				
JOBCODE = 1120				
	68840	GODDARD, D.H.	MANAGER, STDS E	1120
⋮				

Notice how the vertically overflowed data item does not print until the value changes. Vertical overflow is particularly suited to data in which there are natural groupings within groupings. Of course, the output data would have to be ordered according to vertical overflow data items. The above output would be sorted by UNIT,LEVEL,JOBCODE.

With *horizontal wrap around*, the system prints strings of values for an entry of the report on multiple lines, including the column headings. The output then appears to be staggered across the page.

EMPNO	EMPLOYEE NAME	UNIT	JOB CODE	LEVEL
-----	--------------	----	----	-----
	TITLE		SEX	SALARY
	--------------------------	---	---	------
45584	PETERSON, N.M	2000	0110	HEAD
	DIVISION MANAGER		M	56000
32579	LYNN, K.R.	2000	5210	EMPL
	SECRETARY		F	12000
57060	CARR, P.I.	2100	1110	HEAD
	MANAGER, DEVELOPMENT DEP		M	48000
⋮				

Such a report can be difficult to read, especially if the system simultaneously permits column overflow.

Rather than letting the system default to horizontal wrap around a user should have the ability to explicitly specify *multiple output lines per entry*. Of course, another solution to the page width limitation is to give the user the ability to specifically define multiline output for each entry, as in the previous case of a display screen format. The report definition would first give the overall logical page size (columns wide and lines deep); then give the line and column number where each projected item value should be printed within the logical page. The user would need the option of suppressing column headings entirely (rather than taking system defaults) and of adding literals to be printed with each value to aid readability (as in screen definitions).

The ability to define reports with multiple lines per record facilitates such outputs as mailing labels, and name and address directories. For example, the output report definition to produce mailing labels could be as follows:

```
FORM WIDTH = 40 characters
FORM DEPTH =  6 lines
TITLE SUPPRESSED
HEADINGS SUPPRESSED
LINE     COLUMN     ITEM
____     _____     ____
  1         1       TITLE
  1        11       FIRST NAME
  1        26       LAST NAME
  2         1       ADDRESS-C/O
  3         1       ADDRESS-STR
  4         1       CITY
  4        20       STATE/PROV
  4        32       MAIL CODE
  5         1       COUNTRY
```

with the 6th line left blank (for 1″ labels). The output of a record might appear as follows:

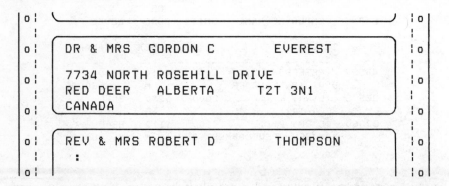

Notice the undesirable appearance of spaces before the last name, between city and state, and the blank line in the middle of the address label. Rather than give absolute line and column positions for output fields, it is desirable to specify an increment relative to the previous data item or line. For example,

LINE	COLUMN	ITEM NAME/LITERAL
1	1	TITLE
1	S1	FIRST NAME
1	S1	LAST NAME
2	1	ADDRESS-C/O
S1	1	ADDRESS-STR
:		

where the column specification "Si" means leave i spaces after the previous value, rather than tab to an absolute position. A similar specification could be used to suppress blank lines. The space used to print each record could be fixed, as with the mailing labels, or variable as might be desired in printing a name and address directory with only one blank line between entries and blank lines suppressed.

7.6 A GENERAL FLAT FILE RETRIEVAL LANGUAGE

Each step in the overall retrieval process has its own input information and a default action in the case of no input. A general retrieval language is made up of these various inputs—each part becomes a *clause* in the language. An examination of the language for any generalized retrieval package reveals these same essential parts. For example, Figure 7-7 shows the Report Request Form for Data Analyzer, a commercially available generalized retrieval package. The user writes requests in a keyword-style language, with the help of the form. These language statements operate on a single flat file.

A narrative retrieval language against a single flat file has the general form as shown in Figure 7-8. This general language excludes formation and presentation specification. A preferred way to add such information is to augment the projection specification, that is, augmenting the "what" with the "how."

7.6.1 Sample Retrieval Language Statements

Using the general retrieval language for a flat file described in Figure 7-8, the following retrieval language statements are made against the EMPLOYEE file in Figure 7-1. There is no implication that these statements would be acceptable to any given system. They are intended to show the features which could be part of a general flat file query language.

1. List the name, jobcode, and title of all persons in the company.

   LIST EMPNAME, JOBCODE, TITLE, OF EMPLOYEES.

2. List the employee number, name, unit number, sex, and birthdate for J. B. Olson, ensuring that there is only one such employee:

   LIST UNIQUE EMPNO, EMPNAME, UNIT, SEX, BIRTHDATE,
   OF EMPLOYEES, WHERE EMPNAME EQ "OLSON, J.B.".

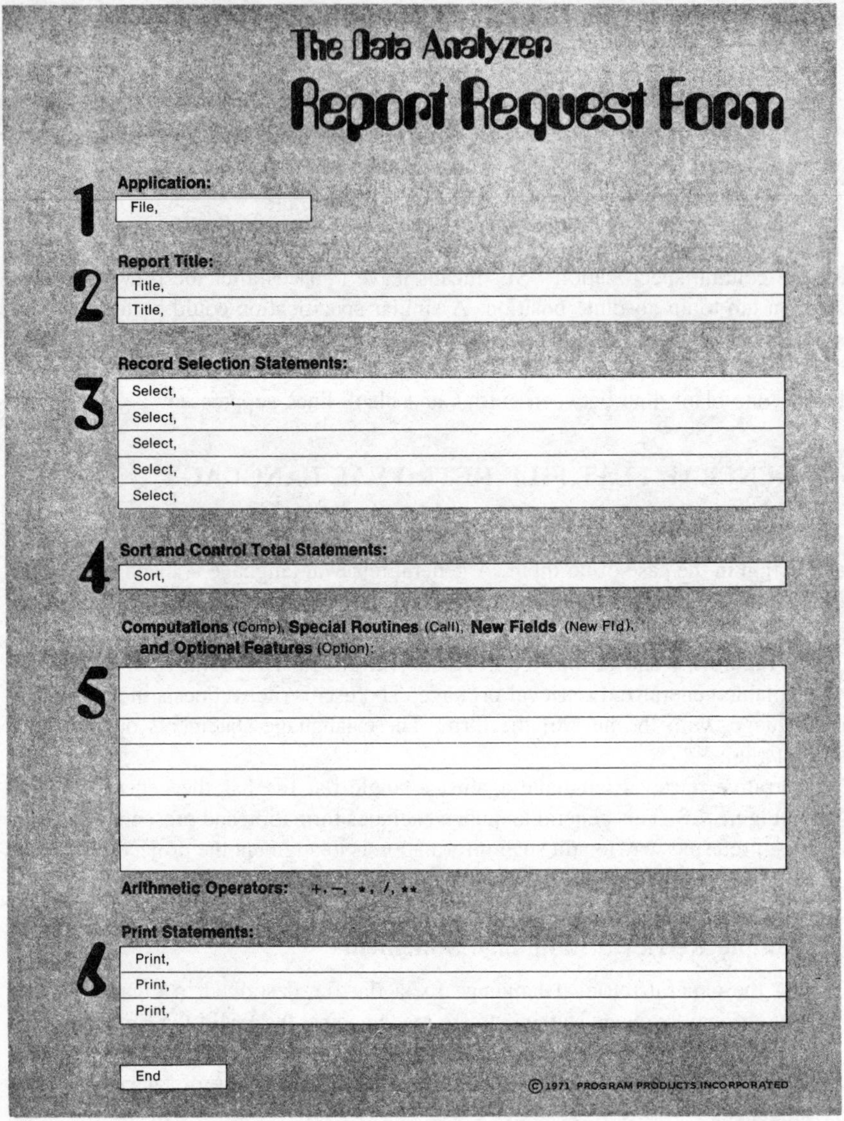

The Data Analyzer
Report Request Form

1 Application:
File,

2 Report Title:
Title,
Title,

3 Record Selection Statements:
Select,
Select,
Select,
Select,
Select,

4 Sort and Control Total Statements:
Sort,

5 Computations (Comp), **Special Routines** (Call), **New Fields** (New Fld), **and Optional Features** (Option):

Arithmetic Operators: +, −, *, /, **

6 Print Statements:
Print,
Print,
Print,

End

© 1971 PROGRAM PRODUCTS INCORPORATED

Figure 7-7. Sample Retrieval Request Form.
This sample form illustrates the basic parts of any generalized retrieval language against a flat file:

- From a named file (1).
- Select records which satisfy a set of selection criteria (3).
- Project named data item values from each record (6).
- Derive new data item values and calculate statistics (5).
- Order the output records (4).
- Print the output report with a title (2).

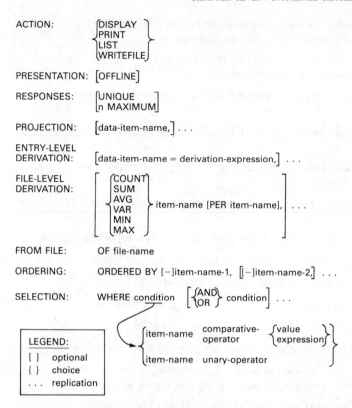

ACTION:
$$\left.\begin{array}{l}\text{DISPLAY}\\\text{PRINT}\\\text{LIST}\\\text{WRITEFILE}\end{array}\right\}$$

PRESENTATION: [OFFLINE]

RESPONSES:
$$\left.\begin{array}{l}\text{UNIQUE}\\\text{n MAXIMUM}\end{array}\right]$$

PROJECTION: [data-item-name,] . . .

ENTRY-LEVEL
DERIVATION: [data-item-name = derivation-expression,] . . .

FILE-LEVEL
DERIVATION:
$$\left[\left\{\begin{array}{l}\text{COUNT}\\\text{SUM}\\\text{AVG}\\\text{VAR}\\\text{MIN}\\\text{MAX}\end{array}\right\}\text{item-name [PER item-name],}\right] \ldots$$

FROM FILE: OF file-name

ORDERING: ORDERED BY [−]item-name-1, [[−]item-name-2,] . . .

SELECTION: WHERE condition $\left[\left\{\begin{array}{l}\text{AND}\\\text{OR}\end{array}\right\}\text{condition}\right]$ . . .

LEGEND:

[ ] optional
{ } choice
. . . replication

item-name comparative-operator $\left\{\begin{array}{l}\text{value}\\\text{expression}\end{array}\right\}$

item-name unary-operator

Figure 7-8. General Flat File Retrieval Language.
Each component of the general language provides the input for a step in the retrieval process. This figure only illustrates the general nature of a free-form narrative language for querying a single flat file. A retrieval statement is built up from a combination of the above phrases, generally written in the sequence shown, and some of which can appear multiple times. The meaning of each of these components and the effect of different phrases in a statement are discussed in this chapter. No attempt is made to be precise at the detailed level. Of course, the language for any actual system will have precise syntax and semantics.

3. List the name and unit number of up to five electrical engineers who were born after 1958 January 01:

   LIST 5 MAXIMUM EMPNAME, UNIT, OF EMPLOYEES,
   WHERE TITLE EQ ELEC ENGR AND BIRTHDATE GE 580101.

4. List name, jobcode, and title of all those who are electrical engineers or in a position where electrical engineer (skill code of 1130) is the primary skill (jobcode) of the position:

   LIST EMPNAME, JOBCODE, TITLE, OF EMPLOYEES, WHERE
   TITLE EQ ELEC ENGR OR JOBCODE EQ 1130

5. List name, unit number, jobcode, and primary skill for all those whose primary skill does not correspond to the primary skill (jobcode) of the position they fill:

   > LIST EMPNAME, UNIT, JOBCODE, PRIMARY SKILL, OF EMPLOYEES,
   > WHERE JOBCODE NE PRIMARY SKILL.

   Notice that the selection expression here includes two data items as variables and no literal value.

6. List the name, jobcode, and primary skill for everyone in the company and order the output by jobcode:

   > LIST JOBCODE, EMPNAME, PRIMARY SKILL, OF EMPLOYEES,
   > ORDER BY JOBCODE

7. Find the average salary for all persons in the company holding the title of electrical engineer:

   > PRINT AVG SALARY, OF EMPLOYEES, WHERE TITLE EQ ELEC ENGR.

8. Find the total number of employees in the company and the total annual salary:

   > PRINT COUNT EMPNO, SUM SALARY, OF EMPLOYEES.

9. Calculate the average salary for those persons in each jobcode skill class:

   > PRINT AVERAGE SALARY PER JOBCODE, OF EMPLOYEES.

   (In this case the system, by default, should also print out each unique jobcode value.)

10. For all employees, list name and unit number, grouping them by jobcode and then ordering them by salary within each jobcode beginning with the highest salary:

    > LIST JOBCODE, SALARY, EMPNAME, UNIT, OF EMPLOYEES,
    > ORDERED BY JOBCODE, −SALARY.

11. What is the median salary of nonsupervisory employees whose primary skill is electrical engineer but who are not employed in that capacity?

    > PRINT MEDIAN SALARY, OF EMPLOYEES, WHERE PRIMARY SKILL EQ 1130 AND JOBCODE NE PRIMARY SKILL AND LEVEL NE HEAD.

12. What are the names, unit numbers, and skills of supervisors who make over $30,000?

    > PRINT EMPNAME, UNIT, PRIMARY SKILL, SSK1, SSK2, SSK3, SSK4,
    > OF EMPLOYEES, WHERE LEVEL EQ HEAD AND SALARY GT 30000.

13. List name, unit, jobcode, and primary skill for all employees, and print an asterisk beside those whose primary skill does not match their jobcode:

    > LIST EMPNAME, UNIT, JOBCODE, PRIMARY SKILL,
    > SKILL DIFFERENCE = "*" IF JOBCODE NE PRIMARY SKILL
    > ELSE " ", OF EMPLOYEES.

14. Calculate the additional monthly cost of 8% salary increase to everyone in the company:

    > PRINT TOTAL SALARY INCREASE = SUM SALARY * .08 / 12,
    > OF EMPLOYEES.

15. What is the average age and the minimum and maximum age of supervisors?

> PRINT AVG (SYSTEMDATE − BIRTHDATE),
> MIN (SYSTEMDATE − BIRTHDATE),
> MAX (SYSTEMDATE − BIRTHDATE), OF EMPLOYEES,
> WHERE LEVEL EQ HEAD.

The following queries are more complex and require more powerful features in the query language. They also show that it may be difficult or impossible to formulate a query in response to a meaningful and apparently straightforward question. In any practical situation, the user of the retrieval facility will encounter difficult queries. The user should not give up if a single query cannot be found to give exactly the desired response. Use the system as far as possible to come as close as possible to the answer. If it takes multiple queries, some manual calculation, or some scanning of partial results, that is not a problem. Make maximum use of the system to assist people in the quest for answers, and fill in manually where necessary.

16. What job pays the most on average? First we must decide on how "job" is to be determined. Let's choose JOBCODE. Essentially, we must find the maximum of the average salaries for each jobcode.

> PRINT JOBCODE, MAX (AVG SALARY PER JOBCODE)

This would require the system to first generate an *array* of values within the parentheses and associate a JOBCODE with each average salary in the array. If this syntax is not permissible, the user would just

> PRINT AVG SALARY PER JOBCODE

and scan the printout for the highest average salary.

17. Who has the minimum and maximum salary among supervisors? To answer this question directly would require that the statistical functions be included in the selection expression:

> PRINT EMPNAME, OF EMPLOYEE, WHERE
> (SALARY EQ (MIN SALARY OF EMPLOYEES WHERE LEVEL EQ HEAD)
> OR SALARY EQ (MAX SALARY OF EMPLOYEES WHERE LEVEL EQ HEAD)).

From the system viewpoint this would imply two "passes" of that file—one to find the MIN and MAX, and the second to find a match. Alternatively, the user could print out the MIN and MAX salary statistics (and optimally all supervisor names and salaries). Then a second query could look for a match of salary with the known MIN and MAX salaries.

18. Who supervises the draftsman named Hughs or Hughes? The connection between employee and supervisor is through a common organizational unit number. This query requires two steps, one to find the unit number of the draftsman, and the second to find the supervisor.

> PRINT EMPNAME, OF EMPLOYEES, WHERE LEVEL EQ HEAD AND UNIT EQ
> (UNIT WHERE (EMPNAME EQ HUGHS OR EMPNAME EQ HUGHES)
> AND TITLE EQ DRAFTSMAN).

The result of executing the part within the parentheses is a list of zero, one (or more) unit numbers, which are then used in the selection expression. Presumably, the evaluation of the

'UNIT EQ ()' would be true if UNIT equalled *any* one of the numbers found in the second part of the query.

19. What is the name of boss of Henderson whose ID is 18130?

> PRINT EMPNAME WHERE LEVEL EQ HEAD AND UNIT EQ (UNIT,
> OF EMPLOYEES, WHERE EMPNO EQ 18130 AND LEVEL EQ EMPL)

If Henderson were already at the level of head, this query would not work. The requester would have to notice that, in the organizational hierarchy, the number of a superior unit has one more zero than its subordinate units. Looking for Guttman's boss, first find Guttman's unit number—2110. Then find the name of the head of unit 2100. In this case the requester must use some knowledge of how the unit numbers are coded to properly query the database.

20. How many supervisors are paid less than any one of their direct subordinates?
    This query requires grouping the employees by organizational unit, calculating the maximum salary in each group, comparing that with the salary of the head of each unit, and counting the number in which the supervisor's salary is less than the group maximum.

21. Get information about supervisors of units with 10 or more direct subordinates.

> PRINT EMPNAME, SALARY, AGE = SYSTEMDATE − BIRTHDATE, UNIT,
> OF EMPLOYEES, WHERE LEVEL EQ HEAD AND UNIT EQ (UNIT WHERE
> (COUNT EMPNO PER UNIT) GE 10).

22. What is the correlation of age to salary level? How does the pattern compare in male and female employees? To answer this question essentially requires a two dimensional plot of AGE vs SALARY, one for males and one for females. Alternatively, the system could provide a statistical function to calculate the correlation coefficient on two variables.

23. What percentage of female employees in the firm have a salary which exceeds the average salary for all employees? This query requires nesting two count functions within a larger arithmetic statement.

> PRINT 100 * (COUNT EMPNO WHERE SEX EQ FEMALE AND
> SALARY GT (AVG SALARY)) / (COUNT EMPNO), OF EMPLOYEES.

The system must first (conceptually) scan the entire file to calculate the average salary for all employees since that is used as a comparator when the system looks at all the salaries of females. If the system does not allow nesting in this way, it is always possible for the user to first find average salary, then do the two counts, then calculate the percentage. Some systems may provide for temporary variables and a procedural language (i.e., the sequence of statement execution matters):

> X = AVERAGE SALARY OF EMPLOYEES
> Y = COUNT EMPNO WHERE SEX EQ FEMALE AND SALARY GT X
> Z = COUNT EMPNO
> PRINT 100 * Y / Z

Although this may offer more flexibility, it looks more like programming in a procedural language, something not every requester is willing or able to do.

All the above queries are done on a single flat file. Such a query language can be very rich and complex. With a powerful query language, a single flat file DBMS can provide a great deal of useful information to users.

It is interesting to note that the prevailing view of "three great data models"—hierarchic, network, and relational—does not even recognize the lowly single flat file. Yet, the single flat file and its query language is the backbone of present data processing and the place to begin when learning high-level query languages.

7.6.2 Catalogued Retrieval Requests for Deferred Execution

If the same retrieval request is used repeatedly, it is desirable to be able to prestore it in the system and give it some identifier with which to invoke it in the future. This is particularly true if the retrieval language request statement is long, thus making it tedious to re-enter each time and to do so accurately. If the requested output is highly formatted with specifications for titles, headings, and vertical and horizontal spacing, it is most desirable to be able to enter a tentative retrieval request, try it, and then incrementally modify it to arrive at a suitable screen definition or report definition.

In fact, it is desirable for the system to maintain a library of stored retrieval requests and report definitions. Furthermore, it is desirable for the system to store them with some formal parameters which must be inserted at the time of invocation. By cataloging the following retrieval request (excluding the format information):

CATALOGUE SKILL REPORT (LIST EMPNAME, UNIT, BIRTHDATE,
PRIMARY SKILL, SALARY, AVERAGE SALARY, OF EMPLOYEES,
WHERE JOBCODE EQ <1>).

a user could later invoke the stored request by entering:

GENERATE SKILL REPORT (1130).

which would substitute the value 1130 for the formal parameter <1> in the stored retrieval request. This type of facility is essential for a parametric user.

When the system accepts the retrieval request statement, it can be parsed, validated, and "compiled" before being stored in the library of system data. This process is shown in Figure 7-9. At one extreme, the retrieval request, which includes both the query and the report definition, can be simply copied into the library of stored report definitions without any processing or validation. At the other extreme, the retrieval request may actually be compiled into object code and tightly bound to the definitions of data in the schema of the stored database. In the former case, all the work is performed interpretively at execution time, that is, when the system receives a request to generate a report according to a stored definition. In the latter case, the system does as much processing and validation as possible at the time the retrieval request is stored. In this case, there is no generalized report generator—only a skeleton process which identifies a request for a report and then initiates execution of its tailored report generator. This latter approach can make good use of system resources with little degradation of system evolvability. Ideally, the users should be able to designate which reports are requested frequently enough to warrant compiling object code for a tailored report generator.

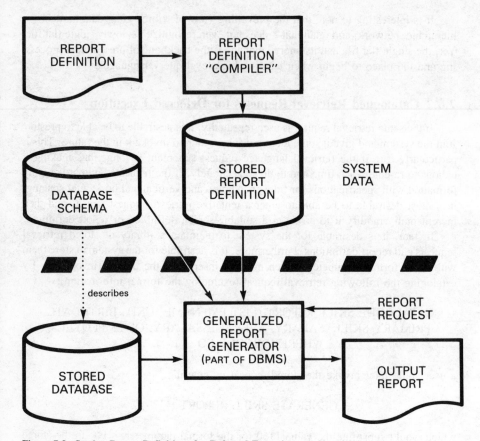

Figure 7-9. Storing Report Definitions for Deferred Execution.
    If a user desires to produce the same report several times (even while iterating to an acceptable report layout), it is useful to be able to store the definition. The system may:

1. Store the report definition as given without checking.
2. Validate the definition against the stored database schema (for example, do data items named in the report actually appear in the database definition?).
3. Generate object code to produce the defined report.

The second approach is preferred to the first, especially since the system generally accesses the stored database definition to find default formatting information anyway. The user should be able to choose between options 2 and 3.

7.7 GRAPHICAL PRESENTATION OF STATISTICAL OUTPUT

A graphical presentation is based on the frequency distribution of one or more data items. The statistics of a frequency distribution essentially summarize certain characteristics of the distribution, thus facilitating comparisons with other distributions and enabling a faster comprehension of the frequency distribution. The graphical mode of presentation uses the entire frequency distribution and theoretically presents *more* information to the user.

JOBCODE	FREQUENCY COUNT
0110	1
1110	6
1120	3
1130	4
1330	2
1350	1
5210	3
	––
	20

Figure 7-10. Tabular Representation of a One-Dimensional Frequency Distribution.
Rather than list each instance of a jobcode value, a frequency distribution shows each unique value only once along with the number of instances of that value.

The simplest case to consider is a *one-dimensional frequency distribution*, that is, pertaining to only one data item or one column of the output file resulting from the previous retrieval process. The basic information of the frequency distribution concerns the number of times each data item value occurred. If the data item is unique, that is, each value occurs only once, then the values must be grouped prior to presenting a frequency distribution. (The process of grouping into value intervals is discussed later.)

Although a frequency distribution is normally presented in a graphical mode, it can also be presented in a tabular mode. For a single data item, the tabular representation of the frequency distribution consists of two columns, the first containing each unique value of the item and the second showing a count of the number of occurrences of each unique value. Figure 7-10 shows the tabular representation of the frequency distribution of JOBCODE values for the first twenty entries from Figure 7-1. Note that while the actual value for JOBCODE was shown for each occurrence in Figure 7-1, each value appears only once in Figure 7-10 along with a count of the number of occurrences.

The basic frequency data, shown in tabular form in Figure 7-10, is used to generate other forms of frequency related information. Representing the set of values for the data item only requires one dimension, the vertical dimension; therefore, the horizontal dimension of the two-dimensional page can be used to graphically represent the frequency information. A graphical representation can enhance visual interpretation of the data and enable a person to quickly judge how the values of a data item are distributed.

Figure 7-11 shows the use of the horizontal dimension to represent the magnitude of the frequency of each unique value of the data item. The frequency distribution is drawn using a solid line connecting the frequency points on the scale for each JOBCODE. If the space between the vertical axis and each plotted frequency point is filled in (using asterisks in Figure 7-11), the resulting graph is called a *histogram* or *bar chart*. Two additional variations of the frequency information are shown in Figure 7-11. First, the cumulative frequency distribution is tabulated and plotted.* Second, for either the frequency distribution or the cumulative frequency distribution, the percentage of total for each item value is shown.

It may be desirable to *group the values* of a data item into value intervals if the

---

*In this particular example, the cumulative frequency distribution may not be too meaningful if there is no ordinal relationship among the JOBCODE values, that is, no meaningful ranking of JOBCODE values.

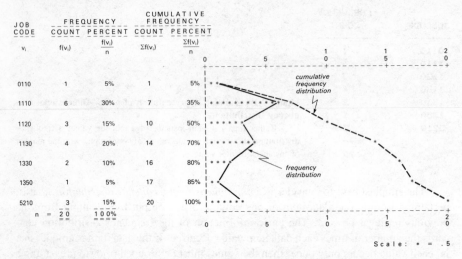

JOB CODE	FREQUENCY		CUMULATIVE FREQUENCY	
	COUNT	PERCENT	COUNT	PERCENT
v_i	$f(v_i)$	$\dfrac{f(v_i)}{n}$	$\Sigma f(v_i)$	$\dfrac{\Sigma f(v_i)}{n}$
0110	1	5%	1	5%
1110	6	30%	7	35%
1120	3	15%	10	50%
1130	4	20%	14	70%
1330	2	10%	16	80%
1350	1	5%	17	85%
5210	3	15%	20	100%
n =	20	100%		

Scale: * = .5

Figure 7-11. Graphical Representation of a One-Dimensional Frequency Distribution.
The horizontal rows of asterisks represent the frequency occurrence of each unique JOBCODE value. The output can also show the cumulative frequency distribution and the percentages of each. The lines connecting the ends of the bars of the frequency distribution and the points on the cumulative graph were drawn in by hand.

value set is larger than 10 or 15, or if the data item has unique values. This will generally be true if the data item is inherently a continuous variable. Condensing the data in this fashion serves to make it easier for a person to comprehend. Referring to the first 20 entries in Figure 7-1, the salary values range from $9,600 to $56,000. If SALARY is to be meaningfully represented in a graphical mode it is necessary to divide the range of values into a reasonably small number of intervals, say 0 to $7,999, $8,000 to $15,999, and so on, yielding eight interval groupings.

In the above example, SALARY is both the basis of the classification (the control variable) and the item whose values are counted. In some cases, it is desired to count or calculate some statistic on one item, based upon the values or value intervals of another. For example, Figure 7-12 tabulates the count, sum, and average SALARY for each JOBCODE. Such a distribution is called a *marginal frequency distribution*. Notice that the frequency distribution of COUNT SALARY PER JOBCODE is exactly the same as the previous frequency distribution of COUNT JOBCODE PER JOB-CODE shown in Figures 7-10 and 7-11. This is because there is a one-to-one correspondence between occurrences of SALARY and occurrences of JOBCODE.

The previous example of SALARY statistics per JOBCODE is an intermediate step to a two-dimensional or joint frequency distribution where the frequency of a particular value of one variable jointly with a particular value of the second variable is considered, that is, the frequency per SALARY per JOBCODE. The tabular form of this joint frequency distribution, often called a cross tabulation or a two-way table, can be represented in two dimensions, as shown in Figure 7-13. As with the one-dimensional representation, it is possible to also tabulate the cumulative frequency distribu-

JOBCODE	COUNT SALARY PER JOBCODE	SUM SALARY PER JOBCODE	AVERAGE SALARY PER JOBCODE
0110	1	$ 56,000	$ 56,000
1110	6	185,000	30,833
1120	3	67,000	22,333
1130	4	82,400	20,600
1330	2	38,000	19,000
1350	1	16,200	16,200
5210	3	31,200	10,400
	20	$475,800	$ 23,790

Figure 7-12. Tabular Representation of a Marginal Frequency Distribution.
A marginal frequency distribution is used to calculate statistics on a variable from selected records which are grouped according to the unique values of some other variable. In this example, statistics are calculated on SALARY for each unique value of JOBCODE.

SALARY classes	0110	1110	1120	1130	1330	1350	5210	TOTAL
$56,000–63,999	1 100% / 100% 5%	0	0	0	0	0	0	1 / 5%
48,000–55,999	0	1 100% / 17% 5%	0	0	0	0	0	1 / 5%
40,000–47,999	0	0	0	0	0	0	0	
32,000–39,999	0	1 100% / 17% 5%	0	0	0	0	0	1 / 5%
24,000–31,999	0	4 80% / 66% 20%	1 20% / 33% 5%	0	0	0	0	5 / 25%
16,000–23,999	0	0	2 22% / 67% 10%	4 45% / 100% 20%	2 22% / 100% 10%	1 11% / 100% 5%	0	9 / 45%
8,000–15,999	0	0	0	0	0	0	3 100% / 100% 15%	3 / 15%
0– 7,999	0	0	0	0	0	0	0	
TOTAL	1 5%	6 30%	3 15%	4 20%	2 10%	1 5%	3 15%	20

JOBCODE (column header spanning 0110–5210)

LEGEND: contents of each cell

Joint Frequency	Percent of Row Total
Percent of Column Total	Percent of Grand Total

Figure 7-13. Tabular Representation of a Two-Dimensional Frequency Distribution.
This method of presentation is also called a cross tabulation or two-way table. Notice the marginal frequency distributions—COUNT SALARY PER JOBCODE across the bottom, and COUNT JOBCODE PER SALARY down the right side of the table.

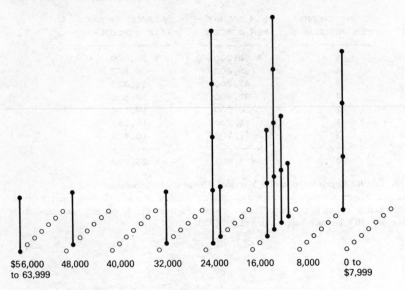

$56,000 to 63,999   48,000   40,000   32,000   24,000   16,000   8,000   0 to $7,999

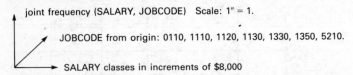

joint frequency (SALARY, JOBCODE)   Scale: 1″ = 1.

JOBCODE from origin: 0110, 1110, 1120, 1130, 1330, 1350, 5210.

SALARY classes in increments of $8,000

Figure 7-14. Graphical Representation of a Two-Dimensional Frequency Distribution.
Such a representation is only feasible if there are a small number of classes of values on each of the two dimensions.

tion and percentages in terms of row totals, column totals, and a grand total, as shown in Figure 7-13.

A graphical representation of a two-dimensional frequency distribution would require three dimensions, the third being the frequency count. If the number of values or value intervals is small, it is possible to represent three dimensions in two as was demonstrated by Curtis Jones.* A similar picture is shown in Figure 7-14.

An examination of Figure 7-11 shows that it would be possible to plot more than two data items on the same graph. One data item would be designated the control variable to appear vertically on the page, while the rest would be plotted on the horizontal axis. In this case the system or the user would have to select different "hit" characters to plot the graph of each variable on the horizontal axis. Also, a convention is needed when two or more variables are to be plotted at the same character position. Figure 7-15 illustrates a machine-generated character plot of multiple variables.

The *format specifications for graphical output* are similar to a conventional report with the addition of information such as, for each axis, naming the data item, the scale factor, location of the origin, the value intervals, whether the values are to be ascend-

*Curtis H. Jones, "At Last: Real Computer Power for Decision Makers," *Harvard Business Review* (48:5), 1970 September-October, page 88.

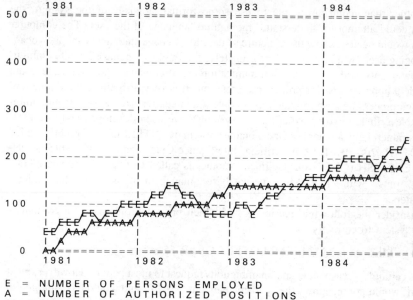

E = NUMBER OF PERSONS EMPLOYED
A = NUMBER OF AUTHORIZED POSITIONS
2 = Common Symbol for both E and A.

Figure 7-15. Graphical Representation of Multiple Variables.
A single character mnemonic is used to plot each variable on the graph. For added readability, a person can connect the symbols for each variable with a line, even using different colors.

ing or descending, and whether or not to print percentage and cumulative figures. For histograms, you may be able to select the shading pattern or color of the bars, and the width of the bars.

7.8 NATURAL LANGUAGE QUERY SYSTEMS AND ARTIFICIAL INTELLIGENCE

The query languages discussed in this chapter so far have implicitly required users to state their questions precisely in the formal query language. Most systems with a formal query language are quite intolerant of incorrect syntax or ambiguous formulations of a query. Users must tolerate responses such as "SYNTAX ERROR," "TRY AGAIN," or simply "?"—not very "user-friendly."

With a formal query language requesters must use only those entity, attribute, and relationship names which have been formally defined to the system (along with any aliases). The structure implicit in their queries must correspond to the structure of the database, or at least the system must know how to relate the two. User queries must also conform to the encoding of data item values. For example, using "ELECTRICAL ENGR" or "N.M. PETERSON" as the comparative value in a selection expression would not find a match with the stored values of "ELEC ENGR" or "PETERSON, N.M.", respectively.

Rather than requiring people to use some formal language of the system, the system could attempt to 'understand' the natural language of the user. The computer system would need to know the structure of natural language statements and the vocabulary being used by a requester. Unfortunately, the English language is quite ambiguous. Statements made in human communication are often vague and open-ended, and dependent upon context for proper interpretation. It is very difficult to build a natural language processing system which uses context and can resolve vagueness and ambiguity. Nevertheless, some experimental systems have been developed and a few are now commercially available. One notable system is INTELLECT, formerly called ROBOT [Harris, 1978], from Artificial Intelligence Corp. and also available as ON-LINE ENGLISH (OLE) from Cullinet. Another is called CLOUT, from MicroRIM, which runs with R:BASE, a database management system for micro-computers.

Consider the following queries, all of which present problems for a computer-based system to correctly interpret:

[1]   LIST ALL MALE EMPLOYEES OVER 55.

This is certainly a reasonable and unambiguous request to most people. However, most systems would not recognize the syntactic element 'MALE' and would have nothing to which to associate the number '55.' The problem is that the relevant data item names are missing—there are no subject operands in the implicit Boolean selection expression. A correct statement would be written as:

LIST EMPNAME, OF EMPLOYEES, WHERE SEX = MALE
AND SYSTEMDATE − BIRTHDATE > 550000.

The system needs to be given the two attribute names, SEX and BIRTHDATE, the derivation formula for calculating age (assuming that AGE is not formally defined as a derived data item), and the value for age which is consistent with the way dates are represented in the system.

[2]   LIST EMPLOYEES WHO WORK AS ELECTRICAL ENGINEERS.

This query is ambiguous since the value 'ELECTRICAL ENGINEER' may relate to either JOBCODE (1130) or TITLE.

[3]   LIST EMPLOYEES FROM WASHINGTON.

This query is also ambiguous since 'WASHINGTON' could refer to Washington state, Washington, DC, or Washington county (in Minnesota at least).

[4]   WHICH MANAGERS HAVE TURNED DOWN PROJECTS
BECAUSE THEY HAVE TOO FEW GOOD WORKERS?

The meaning of this query can be quite different depending on whether 'THEY' refers to managers or projects. An "intelligent" processor such as a human would use context to aid in interpreting the query.

The key to building a natural language processor is for the system to engage the user in dialogue to resolve ambiguity and vagueness. Figure 7-16 [adapted from

Assuming the following Database "Schema" (of which the user has a vague idea):

ENTITY: ATTRIBUTES: *IDENTIFIER

SUPPLIER: | SUP#* | SNAME | SCITY | RATING |

PART: | PART# | PNAME | QTY-ON-HAND | QTY-ON-ORDER |

PROJECT: | PROJ# | PJNAME | PJCITY |

SHIPMENT: | SUP# | PART# | PROJ# | SHIPDATE | QTY-SHIP |

Illustrative dialogue between the system and a Casual User:

USER: Give me a list of the part numbers,
         quantities, and suppliers of Houston
         parts

SYSTEM: You are requesting (among other
           things) a listing of quantities of
           parts. Do you want:
           1. quantities on hand
           2. quantities on order
           3. quantities shipped ?

USER: I want quantities on order

SYSTEM: Fine! Now, with regard to "Houston
           parts", do you mean:
           1. parts supplied by Houston
              suppliers
           2. parts supplied to Houston
              projects
           3. parts associated with Houston in
              some other way ?

USER: I mean item 2

(Note: nothing prevents the user from responding in a manner
which is incomprehensible to the system—for example, "le
deuxieme"—but if he does, the system tightens up the dialog
by: "Please reply by means of one of the numerals 1 or 2 or 3".)

SYSTEM: Good! I need one more piece of
           information. In the listing of part
           numbers, quantity on order, and
           suppliers, how do you want suppliers
           to be identified:
           1. by number
           2. by name
           3. some other way ?

USER: By name and by city

SYSTEM: O.K. This is what I understand your
           query to be: "Find all combinations
           of part number, quantity on order,
           supplier name, and supplier city
           such that the supplier supplied the
           part to a project located in
           Houston".

(We now follow two possibilities.)

(Case 1: the user is satisfied)

USER: Yes

SYSTEM: Do you want the listing to be
           ordered in any special way?

USER: Yes, by part number and then by
         supplier number

This ends the dialog in Case 1. The system now proceeds to
interpret the user's query—a formula that it has been synthe-
sizing in its store, partly from the original statement by the
user, and partly from the succeeding dialog.

(Case 2: the user is not satisfied)

USER: I have changed my mind

(Note: the system does not understand this idiom, but is fully
aware of its inability to understand, so it tightens up the dialog
as follows)

SYSTEM: Please select item 1 or 2 below:
           1. the re-statement is satisfactory
           2. the re-statement is not
              satisfactory

USER: 2

SYSTEM: If your intent can be expressed by
           making minor changes in my
           re-statement, please type it in with
           your changes incorporated. If your
           change is major, you may re-state
           your query in your own terms.

This is where we leave the dialog in Case 2.

Figure 7-16. Dialogue to Resolve Ambiguity in Natural Language Queries.

Codd, 1974] illustrates a hypothetical dialogue in which the system requests additional information from the user or asks the user to pick from multiple possible interpretations of an ambiguous query.

The natural language processor is like a front end to the formal query processor (see Figure 7-17, adapted from Codd, 1974). The user first expresses a query in the natural language. The system then attempts to scan and parse the query. It asks the user to resolve any ambiguity. Finally, the system reformulates the user's original query in the formal language of the system. With the user's approval, the formal query is forwarded to the DBMS for processing.

The natural language processor needs several different types of information when attempting to interpret user queries.

1. Database definition, providing names of entities, attributes, relationships, and their characteristics.

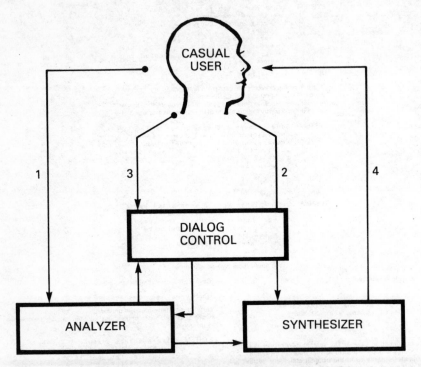

Figure 7-17. Structure of a Natural Language Query System.

1. User makes an initial statement of his query in unrestricted English.
2. System interrogates the user to resolve ambiguities and to obtain information which is missing or hidden in language the system does not understand.
3. User responds with choices and additional information.
4. System restates user's query in system English (in a very precise way, based on the underlying formal query language).

2. Structure and rules of syntax for the natural language (English).
3. Vocabulary of the domain of discourse. This includes all possible values, their aliases and variants, which can appear for the attributes defined in the database.
4. Rules of inference within the domain of discourse which are used to deduce additional facts from those stored explicitly.

Items 1, 2, and 4 represent domain-dependent information which must be given to the system each time it is installed for a particular database in a community of users. Kaplan [1984] suggests that the substantial effort of entering this semantic information is a major reason why natural language database query systems have not found wide application.

A natural language interface is intended primarily for the casual or novice users. With a minimum of training, they would be able to begin asking questions of the database. Their initial formulation of questions would soon improve as they saw the system restate their queries in the formal query language of the system. Perhaps even the early frustration of extended dialogue to resolve ambiguity would encourage new users to learn and use the formal query language.

SUMMARY

The retrieval process (on a single flat file) consists of several distinct, self-contained steps or functions—selection, projection, data item derivations, sort, calculated statistics, and output formation and presentation. Except for statistics and output presentation, these functions have the same form for input and output, namely, a file. Retrieval produces output for humans or for subsequent machine processing.

Selection partitions the file horizontally into two sets of records, those which satisfy a given Boolean selection expression and those which do not. Projection specifies named items from the selected records for further processing, in effect partitioning the file vertically. Data item derivations add additional data item values to each entry in the subfile from the previous step. Sort rearranges the sequence of entries according to a defined ordering. Calculation of statistics produces data derived across the entries in a file such as count, sum, average, and measures of dispersion.

Output results are formatted and presented on various output media and in various output modes. The simplest form is to print or display one record at a time. This mode can be used by the online user to browse through a file. List or report mode is a straightforward printing of the entries generated by the prior steps in the interrogation process along with appropriate titles, headings, editing, and so forth.

When output focuses primarily on the frequency distribution of item values, the output mode can be tabular or graphical. Tabular output is like the list output except that values or defined value intervals of each data item only appear once. Output may be in a tabular or graphical form for one-dimensional or two-dimensional frequency distributions, marginal frequency distributions, or multivariate frequency distributions. The latter two require the designation of a data item to serve as the control variable.

Enhanced user interface can occur on the output with the use of graphics, and on the input through the use of natural language query systems. It is usually easier for a human to absorb and comprehend information when presented in graphical rather than tabular form. The ability of a system to accept and process queries in the natural language of the user can make it easier for casual and novice users to begin obtaining information from a database. In the process, they will subtly learn how to formulate their requests closer to the unambiguous, formal query language of the system.

EXERCISES

7-1. List the sequence of steps in the interrogation process and identify the inputs and outputs of each step.

7-2. Why can each step in the retrieval process stand alone as a self-contained function?

7-3. The retrieval process can also be used for file generation. Define "foreign file" and the process of reversion.

7-4. A file is conceptually a matrix in which each column corresponds to an attribute and each row corresponds to an entity instance. This file is named and each column is named but each row is not named per se. How is an entity instance identified? What assumed characteristic of a file makes this identification possible?

7-5. It has been said that Boolean selection expressions are fundamental to the management and use of a data file. Explain the reasoning behind such a statement.

7-6. What are the nouns and verbs of an expression?

7-7. Why is it necessary to establish a precedence ordering for all binary, infix operators used in an expression?

7-8. What is the generally accepted precedence ordering for operators in an expression? Include prefix and suffix operators as well as infix operators.

7-9. What data item types are required as operands for comparator operators? for Boolean operators? for arithmetic operators? What data item type is produced by each of these three operators?

7-10. What operator takes Boolean operands and produces a numeric result?

7-11. What is the difference between conjunctive form and disjunctive form of an expression?

7-12. Convert each of the following expressions into disjunctive form and remove any parentheses by applying the distributive law or DeMorgan's law:

    a. LEVEL EQ HEAD AND (JOBCODE EQ 3500 OR PSKILL EQ 1150).
    b. (LEVEL EQ HEAD OR UNITNAME EQ DEPT) AND (JOBCODE EQ 3500 OR PSKILL EQ 1150).
    c. PSKILL EQ 3340 AND NOT (SSKILL1 FAILS AND SSKILL2 FAILS AND SSKILL3 FAILS).

7-13. What is wrong with the following selection expression?

$$((\text{ A LT 500 AND B EXISTS }) \text{ EQ 22}) \text{ OR X NE EMPL}$$

7-14. There are a total of 140 employees in the company. If 100 employees are working on project A, 50 on project B, and 20 employees are working on both projects (A ^ B = 20), how many employees would be selected which satisfy the following selection criteria:

$$\text{NOT A AND NOT B}$$

7-15. Define "projection" and contrast it with data item derivation.

7-16. Distinguish between "actual" and "virtual" derived items. When would you prefer to use one or the other?

7-17. Is an "arbitrary function" really a binary relation? Explain.

7-18. How is an ordering on a file defined? What is the purpose of a defined order in the retrieval process? Contrast this with the purpose of an ordering defined on a stored file.

7-19. Explain how the use of control breaks can make report output more readable.

7-20. Explain why the addition of calculated statistics and formation and presentation information to a file produces output which is no longer strictly a flat file.

7-21. Describe various choices of media for the presentation of output results to humans. When would you prefer to use each one?

7-22. Why does the output presentation of a two-dimensional frequency distribution on two data items in a file often yield significant information to a decision maker?

7-23. What are the major advantages of a natural language query system? Why have such systems not yet come into widespread use?

7-24. What information beyond that normally available to a DBMS, is required by a natural language query system?

7-25. Discuss the applicability of relevance and recall ratios (see Appendix 2A) to database retrieval.

SELECTED REFERENCES

BLANNING, Robert W., "Conversing with Management Information Systems in Natural Language," *Communications of the ACM* (27:3), 1984 March, pages 201-207, 47 refs.
> Describes several different types of ambiguities in natural language and gives some interesting illustrations. Goes on to describe a query translator to interface with an MIS model base.

BRITISH COMPUTER SOCIETY Query Languages Group, *Query Languages: A Unified Approach*, London: Heyden & Son (also Philadelphia), 1981, 105 pages.

CODASYL Systems Committee, *Feature Analysis of Generalized Data Base Management Systems*, New York: Association for Computing Machinery, 1971 May, 520 pages.

CODD, E. F., "Seven Steps to Rendezvous with the Casual User," in *Data Base Management*, edited by J. W. Klimbie and K. L. Koffeman, Amsterdam: North-Holland Publishing Company, 1974, pages 179-200.
> Described some experimental work and a hypothetical dialogue in which the system sought to clarify ambiguity in a user query.

CODD, E. F., "A Relational Model of Data for Large Shared Data Banks," *Communications of the ACM* (13:6), 1970 June, pages 377-387.

HARRIS, L. R., "The ROBOT System: Natural Language Processing Applied to Database Query," *Proceedings ACM National Conference*, 1978, pages 165-172.
> Describes a system now commercially available as INTELLECT from Artificial Intelligence Corporation, and also as On-Line English from Cullinet Corporation.

HENDRIX, G. G., E. SACERDOTI, D. SAGALOWICZ, and J. SLOCUM, "Developing a Natural Language Interface to Complex Data," *ACM Transactions on Database Systems* (3:2), 1978 June, pages 105-147.

KAPLAN, S. Jerrold, "Designing a Portable Natural Language Database Query System," *ACM Transactions on Database Systems* (9:1), 1984 March, pages 1-19, 23 refs.
> Discusses several issues involving the portability of natural languages interfaces to database systems. One barrier to acceptance is the substantial installation effort required for each new database. Presents the approach taken in CO-OP, a natural language system that provides cooperative responses to English questions.

KAPLAN, S. J., "On the Difference Between Natural Language and High Level Query Languages," *Proceedings ACM National Conference*, 1978, pages 27-38.

Describes how natural language questions enable a wider range of appropriate responses (due to the vagueness and ambiguity in the language) than do formal queries, and how natural language questions provide conversational and contextual clues for selecting among those responses that are generally absent from formal languages.

MARTIN, James, *Application Development Without Programmers*, Englewood Cliffs, NJ: Prentice-Hall, 1982, 350 pages.

Chapter 8 discusses "languages for end users," and Chapter 9 discusses "data-base user languages." Might be better titled "Application Development Without *COBOL* Programmers."

McGEE, William C., "Generalized File Processing," in *Annual Review in Automatic Programming*, Volume 5, edited by Mark I. Halpern and Christopher J. Shaw, Oxford, England: Pergamon Press, 1969, pages 77-149.

An early article describing high-level language operations on generalized file structures.

McLEOD, Dennis, "A Prescriptive Database Interface Methodology for End-Users," *Information Systems* (7:3), 1982, pages 253-262, 39 refs.

SHNEIDERMAN, Ben, "Improving the Human Factors Aspect of Database Interactions," *ACM Transactions on Database Systems* (3:4), 1978 December, pages 417-439.

STOHR, E., J. TURNER, Y. VASSILIOU, and N. WHITE, "Research in Natural Language Retrieval Systems," in *Proceedings Fifteenth Hawaii International Conference on System Sciences*, edited by W. Riddle, K. Thurber, P. Keen, and R. Sprague, Jr., 1982 January, pages 785-794.

TENNANT, H., *Natural Language Processing*, New York: Petrocelli, 1981.

WALLACE, Mark, *Communicating with Databases in Natural Language*, New York: Wiley & Sons, 1984, 170 pages.

Describes a natural language interface to a relational database. Includes an introduction to PROLOG and a worked example of a PROLOG program.

WALTZ, D., "An English Language Question Answering System for a Large Relational Database," *Communications of the ACM* (21:7), 1978 July, pages 526-539.

WINOGRAD, Terry, *Understanding Natural Language*, New York: Academic Press, 1972.

EIGHT

DATABASE RETRIEVAL: HIERARCHICAL AND MULTIFILE STRUCTURES

8.1	DEVELOPMENT OF RETRIEVAL LANGUAGES ON HIERARCHICAL DATA STRUCTURES	308
8.1.1	Hierarchical Data Structures	308
8.1.2	Early Development of Hierarchical Query Languages	308
8.1.3	Low-Level Approaches to Querying a Hierarchy	310
8.2	QUERYING A SINGLE-PATH HIERARCHICAL DATA STRUCTURE	311
8.2.1	Sample Queries on a Single-Path Hierarchical Structure	311
8.2.2	Brooms and the Process of Qualification	313
8.2.3	Answers to Sample Queries on a Single-Path Hierarchy	314
8.3	QUERYING A MULTIPATH HIERARCHICAL DATA STRUCTURE	323
8.3.1	Sample Queries on a Multipath Hierarchy	325
8.3.2	Alternative Query Languages on a Hierarchical Structure	326
8.3.3	Presentation of Results from a Multipath Hierarchy	328
8.4	RETRIEVAL FROM A MULTIFILE DATA STRUCTURE	330
8.4.1	Approaches to Querying a Multifile Data Structure	330
8.4.2	Multifile Retrieval Language	331
8.4.3	The JOIN Operation on Two Files	331
8.4.4	Sample Queries in a Multifile Retrieval Language	333
8.4.5	Presentation of Results from Multifile Retrieval	334
	SUMMARY	334
	EXERCISES	335
	SELECTED REFERENCES	336

High-level languages to query hierarchical and multifile data structures are a direct extension of the language to query a single flat file. Additional elements must be added to reference and manipulate the more complex data structures. With a solid grasp of a high-level single flat file query language, it is easier (though not easy) to learn and use the more complex retrieval languages.

8.1 DEVELOPMENT OF RETRIEVAL LANGUAGES ON HIERARCHICAL DATA STRUCTURES

This section first presents alternative hierarchical designs for the personnel-organizational database introduced in Chapter 4. The queries in the previous chapter were all made on a single flat file for employees. Now we add data about organizational units and projects. Notice that the information on secondary skills was already in the file although the formal definition did not indicate that they constituted a nested repeating group.

8.1.1 Hierarchical Data Structures

The general schema for a flat file is simply a list of data item names. Each entry of the flat file contains at most one value for each of the data items named in the schema. If any data item or group of data items can contain multiple values within any given entry, the file becomes a hierarchical data structure. The central characteristic of a hierarchical data structure is the replication of data within the entries of the file. Furthermore, the replicated data has no meaning outside the context of the containing entry.

Using the characteristics of relationships discussed in Chapter 6, if the entry corresponds to the entity X and the contained repeating group of data items corresponds to the subentity Y, there is a one-to-many relationship between X and Y with Y dependent upon X. This special combination of relationship characteristics is called a hierarchical relationship; and X is called the parent of Y.

A hierarchical data structure is built up from a set of entity types (nodes) and hierarchical relationships (arcs) between various pairs of entity types such that the resulting nodes and arcs form a tree in the schema diagram.

There are several hierarchical design choices for representing the personnel-organizational data structure introduced in Chapter 4. Some of these choices are shown in Figure 8-1 using a single-path hierarchy. Figure 6-5 showed one possible representation as a multipath hierarchical structure with Position and Employee at the same level. Subsequent discussion of retrieval languages on a hierarchical structure make references to either the single-path hierarchy in Figure 8-1(d) ignoring the Position-related data, or to the multipath hierarchy of Figure 6-5.

8.1.2 Early Development of Hierarchical Query Languages

One of the first attempts to develop a high-level language on a hierarchical data structure was TDMS at System Development Corporation, Santa Monica, California.

(a) FLAT FILE, the basic entity being EMPLOYEE-POSITION; replicating organizational data and storing maximum number of secondary skills.

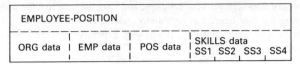

(b) Separate dependent repeating group for Secondary Skills.

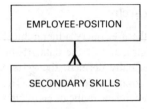

(c) Separate parent repeating group for Organization data.

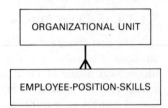

(d) Combine (b) and (c).

(e) Separate Employee and Position.

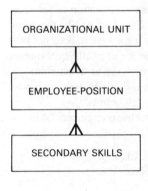

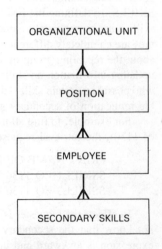

Figure 8-1. Alternative Single-Path Hierarchical Designs for Sample Database.

Robert Bleier [1967] gave an early discussion of the problem and how it was handled in the development of the system. Subsequent to that paper, Al Vorhaus, in commenting on the most expensive feature in implementing the system, said:

"First and foremost of things that have caused expense, that is, programming design and production expense, is the hierarchical capability—the tree structure that the user can declare to the system. This little gadget, which all kinds of people ask for, caused us many months of design, worry, struggle, and effort. . . . We added four words to the language of TDMS and it took us months to figure out what those words should do. . . . People are asking for [tree structuring capability but] do not really know what they are letting themselves in for. These tree structures, in large masses of data, can get very complex, and I am not sure that the people who will be using the data bases will be able to understand what they are doing, just because of the extreme complexity. It was very expensive. I hope it is worth it. I am not sure."*

Later, Paul Fehder described another hierarchical query language called HQL [Fehder, 1974], a forerunner in style to SQL on multifile data structures [Chamberlin, et al, 1976] and Foral on Binary relational structures [Senko, 1975].

8.1.3 Low-Level Approaches to Querying a Hierarchy

The first condition for the system to be able to help the user query a hierarchical structure is that the system must know the hierarchical structure of the data. If the hierarchical nature of the data structure has not been formally defined, the system cannot properly process or manage the nested repeating groups within the data. The user is entirely responsible for referencing *each* of the dependent replications within the structure and for navigating up and down the levels in the structure.

In the previous chapter, the EMPLOYEE file was assumed to be a flat file, but upon closer examination, each record contains a set of up to four SECONDARY SKILLS. In defining the EMPLOYEE file as a flat file, each replication of secondary skills must be separately named, say SSKILL1, SSKILL2, and so on. To the system they are completely different data items within the record. If the system does not know about the repeating group of skills, the user is responsible for correctly querying and updating information on skills. This is most evident when trying to select employees who possess a certain skill—the retrieval statement must explicitly include each possible replication of secondary skill, because each is separately named.

For example, to find all those employees skilled as electrical engineers (skill code of 1130), the retrieval request would be:

PRINT NAME OF EMPLOYEE WHERE PSKILL EQ 1130 OR
SSKILL1 EQ 1130 OR SSKILL2 EQ 1130 OR
SSKILL3 EQ 1130 OR SSKILL4 EQ 1130.

In effect, the requester is doing all the work; the system cannot help since it does not know that the secondary skills actually form a repeating group. The selection expression is awkward and unnatural when dealing with repeating data. Ideally, we want to define the repeating nature of the data to the system and let it examine each value to see if *any one* is 1130.

The problem for the user is further illustrated in updating. Suppose another skill code is to be added for a given employee. The user cannot determine where to store it without first looking at the secondary skills already stored. This is because the update

*In T. William Olle, Chairman, "The Large Data Base, Its Organization and User Interface: Transcription of a Panel Session held at the 1968 ACM National Conference, Las Vegas, Nevada," *Data Base* (1:3), 1969 Fall, pages 12-13.

request must explicitly reference *one* of the four available slots for storing secondary skill codes.

Even if a system knows the hierarchical nature of the data, the language may still provide little or no help in querying the structure. In some database management systems today, selection of entries from the file can only be based upon nonrepeating data items. In other systems, a single retrieval language statement can only reference one record type at a time. This means that the user must navigate from one record type to another issuing multiple retrieval requests to the system. This is a very low level of capability, and that which is found in programming languages such as COBOL, FORTRAN, BASIC, PASCAL, and ADA.*

The next step in improved retrieval language capability is to be able to address multiple entities at different levels in the hierarchy in the *same* retrieval language statement. Even with this level of capability, some systems are highly restrictive. For example, Boolean conditions can only be on entity identifiers, one for each level in the hierarchy, thus ensuring that a unique instance of each entity or record type is selected at each level. The system then concatenates the Boolean conditions together with AND's. At this point, the system can flatten up or down unambiguously (see Chapter 11) and, in reality, has only a flat file for further processing. Such a retrieval language produces a set of paths through the hierarchical structure, each path containing exactly one entity *instance* at each level in the hierarchy.

A high-level retrieval language on a hierarchical structure provides a single language statement to reference any data items within multiple entities or record types at different levels in the hierarchy, whether a single-path or a multipath hierarchy. At this level, the language is fully handling the nested replication of data which is the central characteristic of a hierarchical data structure.

8.2 QUERYING A SINGLE-PATH HIERARCHICAL DATA STRUCTURE

Picking up on the example of EMPLOYEES and SKILLS, if the system knows that multiple skills can be associated with each employee (the first one being the primary skill and the others being secondary), the user could write the retrieval statement:

LIST EMPNAME OF EMPLOYEES WHERE SKILL EQ 1130.

without regard to the number of skills recorded for an employee.

8.2.1 Sample Queries on a Single-Path Hierarchical Structure

Suppose the actual data in the database appeared as shown in Figure 8-2.
Now consider the queries on the following page against the database. Formulate a

---

*These languages are often called high-level languages. While they may be high-level *process* specification languages, they are low-level *data* processing languages.

ORGANIZATION NAME (ORGNAME)	EMPLOYEE NAME (EMPNAME)	SKILL
PROPOSAL	WALTERS	1110
		1120
	GARBER	1330
	COMPTON	1350
		1330
		1130
DESIGN	APGAR	1330
	ARNETTE	1130
		1330

Figure 8-2. Abbreviated Single-Path Hierarchical Database.

general retrieval language statement and suggest an answer for each. Make note of any problems you had in arriving at any answer. Think about the general rules that the system will use in processing these queries. DO THIS BEFORE READING THE DISCUSSION WHICH FOLLOWS THE QUERIES. Each query is carefully chosen to illustrate a principle or a problem when querying a single-path hierarchical data structure.

1. Find the organization to which Apgar belongs.
2. Find the employee(s) belonging to the Design organization.
3. Print the skill codes for the Design organization.
4. Find the organizations with skill code 1330.
5. Find employees in organizations with skill code of 1330.
6. Find the employees in the Proposal organization who have skill 1330.
7. Find the organization where everyone has skill 1330.
8. Find all employees with at least two skills.
9. Find employees whose primary skill is 1130.
10. Find the organizations where skill is 1130 *and* employee is Apgar.
11. Find the organization where skill is 1130 *or* employee is Apgar.
12. Find the employee with skill of 1330 *and* skill of 1110.
13. Find employees with skill not equal to 1330.
14. Find employees satisfying the Boolean condition: NOT skill equal to 1330.
15. For any employees with skill 1330, list organization name, employee name, and skill code.
16. List employee name and primary skill of employees with skill 1130.
17. List all organization names and the number of employees in each.
18. List organization name, employee name, and skill code with each line of output ordered by skill code and by organization within each skill code.

Having attempted the above queries, it should be evident that more language constructs and more general rules of interpretation are needed than we had for flat file queries. Selection is no longer a simple matter of taking each entry, plugging in values for each named data item (now there may be multiple values), evaluating the Boolean selection expression, and accepting or rejecting the whole entry. Sometimes we want to accept part of an entry and reject other parts. Now we find that data items in the selection expression can be at any and multiple levels in the hierarchy as can projected data items. In sorting and printing the output, there can be multiple instances of the same value which leaves the problem of what to do with the repetition. New language elements are needed to specify "how many" since there may now be multiple dependent repeating group instances in each parent.

8.2.2 Brooms and the Process of Qualification

Consider each level in the single-path hierarchy to be a separate repeating group (rgroup) type, then each Boolean condition in the selection expression selects rgroup instances (often of the same rgroup type) within each entry. For example, the Boolean condition, SKILL EQ 1330 , selects four rgroup instances from the skill rgroup type. The question is: what about instances of other rgroup types, such as employees or organizations? It seems obvious that if we wish to print any data about employees or organizations based upon a Boolean selection condition on skills, the selection process is not finished.

Based upon selected rgroup instances, the **qualification** process identifies or *qualifies* additional rgroup instances to be included in the resultant subfile, a subset of the original file. The additional rgroup instances are generally of a different rgroup type than the selected rgroup instances (although under certain circumstances they could be the same). The additional rgroup instances are qualified based upon certain standard rules for qualification. The resultant subfile may be either a flat file or a hierarchical file.

The process of qualification can be better understood and more rigorously defined by introducing the concept of a "broom." A **broom** is a set of rgroup instances within a hierarchical file and is uniquely defined by specifying a particular rgroup instance. The broom of a given rgroup instance contains:

a. The given rgroup instance,
b. All rgroup instances on the path from the given rgroup instance up to the root of the tree (that is, all ascendant rgroup instances, at any level, of the given rgroup instance), and
c. All rgroup instances contained in the subtree for which the given rgroup instance is the root (that is, all descendant rgroup instances of the given rgroup instance).

Figure 8-3, where each box labeled by a number corresponds to an rgroup instance, illustrates the brooms of various rgroup instances. The term broom is meaningful since the set of qualified rgroup instances looks like a broom with the defining group instance at the bottom of the handle where the straw begins to fan out.

In the retrieval process, the selection expression is satisfied by selected rgroup instances. The qualification process qualifies (or additionally selects) the rgroup instances in brooms of the selected rgroup instances. Referring to Figure 8-3 if 10, 12,

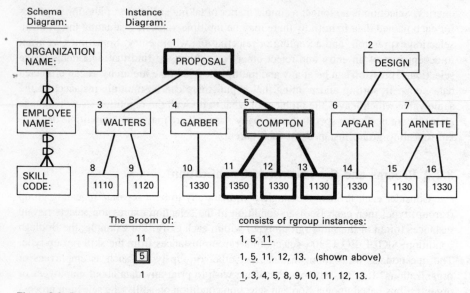

Schema Diagram: Instance Diagram:

The Broom of:	consists of rgroup instances:
11	1, 5, 11.
5	1, 5, 11, 12, 13. (shown above)
1	1, 3, 4, 5, 8, 9, 10, 11, 12, 13.

Figure 8-3. Brooms in an Instance Diagram.
   The broom of a given repeating group (rgroup) instance within a hierarchical data structure is always unique and consists of the given rgroup instance, all of its ascendant rgroup instances on the path to the root, and all of its descendant rgroup instances down all levels in the subtree. The term "broom" conveys a visual image appropriate for the concept.

14, and 16 are selected, then the resulting subfile contains four entries consisting of the following rgroup instances:

$$
\begin{aligned}
\text{first entry} &= (1, 4, 10) \\
\text{second entry} &= (1, 5, 12) \\
\text{third entry} &= (2, 6, 14) \\
\text{fourth entry} &= (2, 7, 16)
\end{aligned}
$$

If data is then projected from level one of the structure, two copies each of (1) and (2) will be printed. A more detailed and rigorous treatment of retrieval from a hierarchical structure using the notion of a broom is found in Lowenthal.*

8.2.3 Answers to Sample Queries on a Single-Path Hierarchy

   This rather lengthy section leads the reader progressively to a sound understanding of the elements of query languages on a single-path hierarchical data structure. This

---

*Eugene I. Lowenthal, "A Functional Approach to the Design of Storage Structures for Generalized Data Management Systems," Austin: University of Texas, Computation Center, UTEX-CC-TSN-34 (doctoral dissertation, 1971 August), 1973 February, 69 pages.

(and later sections on multipath and multifile queries) must be studied carefully to fully appreciate the nuances and complexity of such languages. Then the reader will understand that substantial effort is required to learn how to properly use a high-level language—*any* high-level language on more complex data structures. Many organizations acquire a DBMS with high-level query languages and unrealistically expect that novice users, even experienced programmers, will be able to correctly formulate high-level language queries. If you currently hold such a view, even a little bit, study the following queries until your intuition and expectations begin to change.

Carefully studying all the queries in this section will not make you fully trained in the language. The purpose is only to drive you to an understanding and appreciation of the complexity of high-level query languages on more complex data structures. Read carefully as far as you need to gain that understanding—at least through query 5.

The notion of a broom is a useful construct to logically explain the meaning and results of a query on a hierarchical data structure. The form of the query is generally (though not always) that of the TDMS family of systems, including SYSTEM 2000. Keep Figure 8-3 in hand while reading the explanation of each query. The numbers in parentheses refer to rgroup instances in that figure.

1. PRINT ORGNAME WHERE EMPNAME EQ APGAR.

   The single Boolean condition selects only one rgroup instance (6) thus qualifying (2) and (14) on its broom. The projection from level one of this broom results in the output of:

   ORGNAME = DESIGN

   Since the relationship between employee and organization is many-to-one or exclusive on organization (that is, it is a function of employee into organization) with employee dependent on organization, i.e., employee is exhausted by the relationship, there is *exactly one* organization for each employee. Therefore, if the selection expression identifies only one employee, exactly one organization will be projected.

2. PRINT EMPNAME WHERE ORGNAME EQ DESIGN.

   This query reverses the roles of employee and organization. The Boolean condition selects one rgroup instance (2) on level one and qualifies two others on level two (6 and 7) in the broom of (2). The relationship is not exclusive on employees so multiple employees could result, in this case:

   EMPNAME = APGAR
   EMPNAME = ARNETTE

   Note that the item name need only appear as a stub on the first of a set of values printed in a column, or it could appear as a column heading (using LIST).

   In trying to extend conventional flat file retrieval languages to handle this situation, the designer faces the problem of multiple responses—what should he or she do? Pick one? Which one? The first one? And let the requester ask for another? Try to print them all? What if the request is from a program and the result is to be placed in the program buffer—but it only holds one record at a time? These are problems facing the system designer. From a strictly logical perspective, multiple answers result from the query; the system and user must understand that fact and act accordingly.

3. LIST SKILL WHERE ORGNAME EQ DESIGN.

   Here the single Boolean condition selects one rgroup instance (2) and its unique broom qualifies two at level two and three (14, 15, and 16) at level three in the hierarchical structure. Thus, the output becomes:

```
SKILL
----
1330
1130
1330
```

but this is perhaps not what was expected. The problem is what to do with the duplicate values for skill 1330. While skills are unique for each employee and employees are unique for each organization, skills are not unique within organizations. It is not acceptable to say that the query does not make sense—if it is asked, the system must be able to produce a "correct" result, at least a result which is consistent with a set of rules understood by the users. In fact, the query may be trying to get a profile of skills within an organizational unit. The fact that 1330 appears in two different employee records may or may not be significant. The system must not presume to know which is correct. Additional language elements are needed for the user to explicitly call for the elimination of duplicates, otherwise the user must have been interested in obtaining a one-dimensional frequency distribution of SKILLS PER ORGANIZATION WHERE ORGNAME EQ DESIGN.

4. LIST ORGNAME WHERE SKILL EQ 1330.

This query reverses the roles of selection and projection from the previous query. This time the selection condition applies to the third level of the hierarchy. Four rgroup instances satisfy the condition (10, 12, 14, and 16) thus defining four brooms. Projecting the organization name from the first level in each of these brooms yields:

```
ORGNAME
--------
PROPOSAL
PROPOSAL
DESIGN
DESIGN
```

clearly not the expected answer. In fact, would this ever be an expected result? The system can handle this in one of two ways: assume this is never a valid result and therefore suppress the printing of the repeated values, or add a new element to the language for the user to explicitly specify repeat suppression. One approach would be to allow the user some explicit control over the level of the broom-defining node. Instead of being at the third level (skill) by default since that was the level of the Boolean selection condition, let the user explicitly *raise* it to the first level in the hierarchy. Vorhaus added the 'HAS' operator ("scope modifier") to the TDMS language for just this purpose. Restating the query:

LIST ORGNAME WHERE ORGANIZATION HAS SKILL EQ 1330.

causes the system to reduce the four brooms defined on level three to two brooms defined on level one:

```
1; 4, 5;  10, 11, 12, 13,
2; 6, 7;  14, 15, 16,
```

The HAS operator is a binary operator with the first operand being the name of an rgroup type and the second operator being a Boolean condition used to select rgroup instances. The HAS makes the first operand the broom-defining rgroup type, rather than the rgroup type implied by the Boolean condition. The first operand must be at a higher level in the hierarchy than the rgroup type implied by the Boolean condition. The use of HAS causes additional rgroup instances to be qualified by the condition. Consequently, the use of HAS results in a loss of selectivity at the lower levels—sometimes negating the effect of a previous Boolean selection condition. In the precedence ordering of operators, the HAS is below the comparative operators and higher than the Boolean operators AND and OR.

5. LIST EMPNAME WHERE ORGANIZATION HAS SKILL EQ 1330.

Without the HAS operator, one is hard pressed to find any query statement which expresses the intent of this query. It would not be correct to simply find the employees with a skill of 1330. The meaning of this query is that if an organization has *any* employee with a skill of 1330, then print out *all* the employees in that organization, even if they do not have skill 1330. The Boolean condition selects four rgroup instances as before, the HAS moves the level of the broom-defining rgroup up to organization, and, implicitly, the projection specification moves it back down to level two where there are now five broom-defining rgroup instances (3, 4, 5, 6, and 7) thus producing the output:

```
EMPNAME
-------
WALTERS
GARBER
COMPTON
APGAR
ARNETTE
```

6. LIST EMPNAME WHERE ORGNAME EQ PROPOSAL AND SKILL EQ 1330.

The query is very similar to the last one except that a Boolean condition explicitly applies to the organization at level one. There are two approaches to logically analyzing this query. The condition on organization selects one rgroup (1) and the condition on skill selects two rgroups (10 and 12) within the broom defined by (1). Alternatively, the condition on skill selects four rgroup instances, two of which satisfy the second condition on organization. In either case, with Boolean conditions at different levels of the hierarchical structure, the broom-defining rgroup is placed at the lowest level by default (and can be raised explicitly with HAS if necessary for the logic of the query). The result is two brooms defined on (10) and (12) producing the output:

```
EMPNAME
-------
GARBER
COMPTON
```

So far the queries have looked at the data such that if *any* one of the dependents satisfy the condition, then select the parent. However, there are other ways of referring to the set of dependents under a parent: "every one," "at least two," or "the first one" are just a few examples handled in the next few queries. In all cases, additional language elements are needed to handle the "how many" or "which one(s)."

7. LIST ORGNAME WHERE ALL EMPLOYEES HAVE SKILL EQ 1330.

Without the ALL modifier, this query would select an organization if *any one* of its employees had skill 1330. The ALL specifies that *every* employee in an organization must meet the subsequent selection condition before an organization will qualify. As a result this query outputs the Design organization.

8. LIST EMPNAME WHERE EMPLOYEE HAS MINIMUM OF 2 SKILLS EXISTS.

This form of the query places a numerical requirement on the number of skills selected for each employee. This is just one of several possibilities for expressing the condition on number of replications. An alternative expression of this query (if the language elements are available) is:

LIST EMPNAME WHERE EMPLOYEE HAS COUNT SKILLS GE 2.

Here a statistics function is used in the selection expression. The application of such a function on any dependent set implicitly produces an attribute value for the entity of the parent rgroup instance. In this case, the count of skills results in the answers 2, 1, 3, 1, 2 across the five employees, selecting the first, third, and fifth, and producing the output:

```
EMPNAME

-------

WALTERS
COMPTON
ARNETTE
```

It is evident from this example that the distinction between derived data items and calculated statistics becomes confused when dealing with a hierarchical structure. Actually, a statistic is any function calculated across multiple value, entity, or rgroup instances. If the calculation is not at the top level of the hierarchy (that is, across all entities in a file), the resulting derived value becomes an attribute of the parent entity or rgroup instance.

9. LIST EMPNAME WHERE EMPLOYEE HAS SKILL(1) EQ 1130.

Finding the primary skill requires an understanding between the user and the system that there is an ordering on the stored skills for each employee and that the first skill can be interpreted as the primary skill. There are several alternatives for referencing elements in a sequence, such as the subscript shown above. A subscript of 'n' (or '0') could be used to reference the last member in the sequence. In this case, Arnette satisfies the query.

10. LIST ORGNAME WHERE SKILL EQ 1130 AND EMPNAME EQ APGAR.

With Boolean conditions on two different levels, the brooms are defined at the lower level, or skills in this case. Two skill rgroup instances are selected (13 and 15) and neither of their brooms include Apgar; therefore, the logical result is that no organization satisfies the selection expression as stated. This may not be the desired result. The confusion stems from not knowing explicitly what is the object of the selection. Writing ORGANIZATION HAS in front of the skill condition would make it clear that any organization is to be selected if *any* employee meets the skill condition. Now the system would respond with the Design organization.

11. LIST ORGNAME WHERE SKILL EQ 1130 *OR* EMPNAME EQ APGAR.

The condition on skill selects two rgroup instances and the condition on employee selects one. Combining these three brooms and projecting organization from them gives:

```
ORGNAME

-------

PROPOSAL
DESIGN
DESIGN
```

without making any assumption about the suppression of repeating values.

12. LIST EMPNAME WHERE SKILL EQ 1330 AND SKILL EQ 1130.

    The first condition selects the brooms on four rgroup instances (10, 12, 14, 16) and the second condition selects brooms on two rgroup instances (13, 15). Since there is no intersection of these two sets, no employees satisfy the selection criteria as stated. The problem is that a skill rgroup instance cannot be both 1330 and 1130 at the same time. The corrected query:

    LIST EMPNAME WHERE EMPLOYEE HAS SKILL EQ 1330 AND SKILL EQ 1130.

    specifies that the object of the selection is actually employee and must therefore raise the level of the broom-defining rgroup.

13. LIST EMPNAME WHERE SKILL NE 1330.

    Every skill rgroup instance is tested against this condition and five satisfy. With repeat suppression (perhaps by adding EMPLOYEE HAS) the result is:

```
EMPNAME

-------

WALTERS
COMPTON
ARNETTE
```

    Notice that a value comparison cannot take place without a value—first a value must exist, then it must not be 1330. An employee is selected if *any* existing skill is not 1330.

14. LIST EMPNAME WHERE NOT EMPLOYEE HAS SKILL EQ 1330.

    The query is substantially different from the previous one. The condition on skill selects four brooms and, therefore, four employees. The NOT eliminates the selected employees from the total set of employees in the database leaving as a result:

```
EMPNAME

-------

WALTERS
```

    These last two queries show that NE and NOT do not, in general, have the same interpretation. The unary Boolean operator NOT will often produce unexpected results and is also expensive to execute, requiring the system to scan the set of all existing instances. Therefore, its use should be avoided.

15. LIST ORGNAME, EMPNAME, SKILL WHERE SKILL EQ 1330.

    This query is intended to illustrate some of the choices in presenting the result. The Boolean condition qualifies four brooms of the four selected skill rgroup instances. If the requester wanted to get all skills of the selected employees, the query would have to be:

    LIST ORGNAME, EMPNAME, SKILL WHERE EMPLOYEE HAS SKILL EQ 1330.

    The total selection expression would identify four brooms at the level of employee. The lowest level in the projection specification is at the third level, the skill rgroup, which becomes the level of the broom definition and the query now identifies seven brooms. With no repeat suppression, these would appear as follows:

```
ORGNAME          EMPNAME          SKILL

-------          -------          -----

PROPOSAL         GARBER           1330
PROPOSAL         COMPTON          1350
```

```
              PROPOSAL        COMPTON        1330
              PROPOSAL        COMPTON        1130
              DESIGN          APGAR          1330
              DESIGN          ARNETTE        1130
              DESIGN          ARNETTE        1330
```

If the data items from the higher levels of the hierarchical structure are listed first, repeat suppression can and should be used to produce more easily readable reports.

If the system knows the maximum number of skills for any employee, and it is small enough to fit across the page, the following presentation form could be used (with repeat suppression):

```
ORGNAME         EMPNAME        SKILLS
-------         -------        --------------------
PROPOSAL        GARBER         1330
                COMPTON        1350      1330      1130
DESIGN          APGAR          1330
                ARNETTE        1130      1330
```

As with flat files, it is still possible to have vertical overflow in the presentation of these results:

```
         ORGNAME = PROPOSAL
              EMPNAME        SKILLS

              -------        --------------------
              GARBER         1330
              COMPTON        1350      1330      1130
         ORGNAME = DESIGN
              APGAR          1330
              ARNETTE        1130      1330
```

or alternatively:

```
         ORGNAME
         -------
              EMPNAME        SKILLS
              -------        --------------------
         PROPOSAL
              GARBER         1330
              COMPTON        1350      1330      1130
         DESIGN
              APGAR          1330
              ARNETTE        1130      1330
```

16. LIST EMPNAME, SKILL(1), WHERE EMPLOYEE HAS SKILL EQ 1130.

To retrieve the primary skill, assumed to be the first skill recorded, it is necessary to use the positional criterion in the projection specification. The answer would be:

```
         EMPNAME             PRIMARY SKILL
         -------             -------------
         COMPTON             1350
         ARNETTE             1130
```

17. LIST ORGNAME, COUNT EMPLOYEES PER ORGANIZATION.

This query illustrates the use of a statistic which is conditional on another entity. The resulting output would be:

ORGNAME	COUNT EMPLOYEES
PROPOSAL	3
DESIGN	2

In a flat file query language, the statistics could only be calculated on one item based upon another item. In a hierarchical structure, these derivations can also be based upon the existence of entities. In this example, it is the number of employee entity instances being counted for each instance of an organization entity. Since the count is PER ORGANIZA-TION, the derived values become new, or rather explicit attributes of the organization entity. A count of employees alone is implicitly a count of employees PER FILE, in other words, across all entries in the file, even though it is not the entry-level entity. The query:

PRINT COUNT EMPLOYEES.

would give the response:

COUNT EMPLOYEES = 5,

18. LIST ORGNAME, EMPNAME, SKILL, ORDERED BY SKILL, ORGNAME.

This query illustrates the use of the ordering criteria. The resulting report would be:

ORGNAME	EMPNAME	SKILL
PROPOSAL	WALTERS	1110
PROPOSAL	WALTERS	1120
DESIGN	ARNETTE	1130
PROPOSAL	COMPTON	1130
DESIGN	APGAR	1330
DESIGN	ARNETTE	1330
PROPOSAL	GARBER	1330
PROPOSAL	COMPTON	1330
PROPOSAL	COMPTON	1350

Normally, the data items are listed across the page in the same order as listed in the projection specification. In this case, the resultant report is somewhat confusing. Suppression of repeating values makes little sense and would be even more confusing. As a general rule, *if the output is ordered, the first set of data items should correspond to the items in the defined ordering*. In this way, the output report reflects the implied hierarchical structure in the defined ordering. It then makes sense to suppress repeating values and to use vertical overflow. Restating the above query:

LIST SKILL, ORGNAME, EMPNAME, ORDERED BY SKILL, ORGNAME.

yields the following output suppressing repeated values:

SKILL	ORGNAME	EMPNAME
1110	PROPOSAL	WALTERS
1120	PROPOSAL	WALTERS

```
1130        DESIGN        ARNETTE
            PROPOSAL      COMPTON
1330        DESIGN        APGAR
                          ARNETTE
            PROPOSAL      GARBER
                          COMPTON
1350        PROPOSAL      COMPTON
```

Since the projected data items can be from any level in the hierarchical data structure, it may be desirable for the requester to explicitly indicate the nesting of levels. For example,

LIST ORGNAME (EMPNAME (SKILL)) . . .

would force the sequence of data items to appear in hierarchical order and, therefore, suppression of repeating values can be explicit and unambiguous. If the defined ordering places the data items in a different implicit "hierarchical" relationship, the same notation could be used:

LIST SKILL (ORGNAME (EMPNAME)), ORDERED BY SKILL, ORGNAME.

Repeat suppression could also be explicitly controlled by the PER modifier in the retrieval statement. Without explicit declaration, a statistics function is assumed to be PER FILE. For a hierarchical structure, if the level of broom-definition is down in the hierarchy, the results may not be as expected or desired. For example, the query:

PRINT SKILL, COUNT SKILL, EMPNAME.

will set the broom-defining rgroup at level three (SKILL) and produce:

```
SKILL = 1110
COUNT SKILL = 1
EMPNAME = WALTERS
SKILL = 1120
COUNT SKILL = 1
EMPNAME = WALTERS
        :
```

The requester probably wants to write:

LIST NAME, (COUNT SKILL, SKILL) PER EMPLOYEE.

which raises the level of the broom-defining rgroup from the default of level three to level two (EMPLOYEE) and produces the output:

EMPNAME	COUNT SKILL	SKILLS		
WALTERS	2	1110	1120	
GARBER	1	1330		
COMPTON	3	1350	1330	1130
APGAR	1	1330		
ARNETTE	2	1130	1330	

As another example,

PRINT COUNT ORGANIZATION, COUNT SKILLS.

would produce:

```
COUNT ORGANIZATION = 9
COUNT SKILLS = 9
```

because the system identifies 9 brooms, the broom-defining rgroup being at level three, SKILLS. To remedy the situation, the requester would write:

PRINT COUNT ORGANIZATIONS PER FILE, COUNT SKILLS.

to raise the level of broom definition to level zero, the whole file.

With the default level of broom definition being the lowest level of the projected items, the system defaults to producing a flat file on output. This is preferred since it is easiest to handle even though it may result in excessive data redundancy in the output. To avoid redundancy, the requester could:

- Use the nested parentheses,
- Use the PER modifier to explicitly raise the level of the broom-defining rgroup,
- Use an explicit REPEAT SUPPRESS declaration, or
- Have some implicit understanding with the system when suppression of repeating values is to take place, as, for example, on the items in a defined ordering.

Retrieval from a single-path hierarchical data structure produces either a flat file or a hierarchical file. A flat file results if all the projected data items are from the same level within the hierarchical structure, or if the projected data items are from multiple levels and the broom-defining rgroup is at the bottom level of the projected items, that is, the hierarchy is "flattened down."

Besides being printed out in a listing mode, the results of the retrieval can generate a flat or hierarchical file which remains within the DBMS for a time. The retrieval results could also be output in graphical mode although the inclusion of embedded rgroup instances within each major line of output (analogous to rgroup instances within an entry of a file) becomes problematic. Unambiguous output is possible in some restricted and well-defined cases such as producing a frequency distribution on repeating data item values per entry instance.

8.3 QUERYING A MULTIPATH HIERARCHICAL DATA STRUCTURE

Querying a multipath hierarchical data structure is substantially more complex than querying a single-path structure, both for the system to perform and for the user to comprehend. For this reason, most systems with a hierarchical or multifile structure will only process queries directed at a single-path hierarchy. Some are even more restrictive than this.

Brooms can also be used to interpret a query against a multipath hierarchical structure. The sample database shown in Figure 8-4 provides the basis for explaining several selected queries against a multipath hierarchical data structure. It is similar to

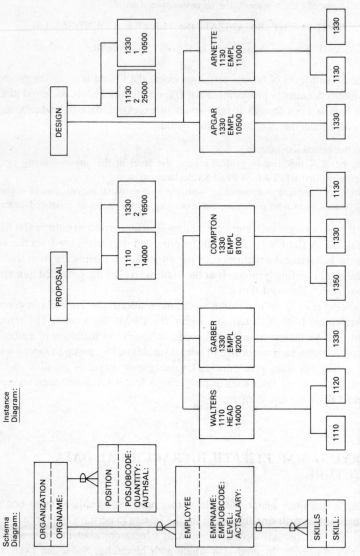

Figure 8-4. Sample Multipath Hierarchical Data Structure: Schema and Instance Diagrams.

The ORGANIZATION-EMPLOYEE database is expanded with POSITION data to illustrate queries against a multipath hierarchical data structure.

Figure 8-2 with the addition of a POSITION rgroup type on the same level as EMPLOYEE and the addition of a few more data items.

8.3.1 Sample Queries on a Multipath Hierarchy

The following queries illustrate selection and/or projection operating on different or multiple branches of a multipath hierarchical data structure. The major difficulty is in establishing the correct intended association between rgroup instances on the separate branches.

1. PRINT EMPNAME WHERE POSJOBCODE EQ 1110.
   With this query, presumably, the requester wishes to see the names of all employees in organizational units which have at least one position recorded with a jobcode of 1110. The selection condition identifies one Position rgroup instance and qualifies one organization rgroup instance on its broom. The request to project employee name from this broom fails because no employee rgroup instances have been selected or qualified and the retrieval produces no output—probably not what was expected! The solution is to use HAS to raise the level of broom definition after the selection and before the projection:

   PRINT EMPNAME WHERE ORGANIZATION HAS POSJOBCODE EQ 1110.

   which would produce the names of the three employees in the Proposal organization. The significance of this query is that the requester can project data from one schema path of the hierarchy based upon selection criteria on another path in the schema diagram of the multipath hierarchy. In systems permitting a query to address only one path in the schema, this would require the use of multiple query statements.

2. PRINT EMPNAME WHERE EMPJOBCODE EQ 1130 AND POSJOBCODE EQ 1130.
   This query might be a first attempt to apply selection criteria to two paths in the hierarchy and then project data from one of those paths. Unfortunately, it produces no output because employee jobcode and position jobcode are on brooms which have no common rgroup instances at level two. This problem is solved using the HAS operator on one branch:

   PRINT EMPNAME WHERE EMPJOBCODE EQ 1130
   AND ORGANIZATION HAS POSJOBCODE EQ 1130.

   producing:

   EMPNAME = ARNETTE

3. PRINT EMPNAME WHERE EMPLOYEE HAS SKILL EQ 1130
   AND ORGANIZATION HAS POSJOBCODE EQ 1130.
   This is an alternate query selecting employees based upon skills rather than employee jobcode. With the sample database, it would produce the same result. (The first Boolean condition selects *two* employee rgroup instances in this case.)

4. PRINT EMPNAME WHERE ORGANIZATION HAS EMPJOBCODE EQ 1130
   AND POSJOBCODE EQ 1130.
   This query produces no output illustrating that the requester must be careful in choosing where to place the HAS operator. In System 2000, the broom-defining rgroup type, which is moved to the same level across the entire selection expression, defaults to the lowest level. In this case, POSJOBCODE is at the lowest level so the broom-defining

rgroup is POSITION, thus excluding all rgroup instances previously selected or qualified on other paths in the schema diagram of the hierarchical data structure.

5. PRINT EMPNAME WHERE ORGANIZATION HAS EMPJOBCODE EQ 1130
AND ORGANIZATION HAS POSJOBCODE EQ 1130.

Adding a HAS operator to *both* selection conditions on the two schema paths results in a loss of selectivity on the second level of the hierarchy. The above query produces:

```
EMPNAME = APGAR
EMPNAME = ARNETTE
```

delivering *all* employee names for every organization selected, which may or may not be the desired result.

6. LIST EMPNAME WHERE EMPLOYEE HAS SKILL EQ 1350.

Queries on a single-path hierarchy can also result in a loss of selectivity when raising the level of broom definition. The above query produces:

```
EMPNAME
-------
COMPTON
```

Raising the level of broom definition to ORGANIZATION:

LIST EMPNAME WHERE ORGANIZATION HAS SKILL EQ 1350.

produces:

```
EMPNAME
-------
WALTERS
GARBER
COMPTON
```

Under the System 2000 "natural" language, which has been the basis for much of the discussion so far, it is not possible to project from two paths while still retaining selectivity on both paths of the hierarchy. Sometimes it is desirable to select on criteria at low levels in the hierarchy, raise the level of broom definition to higher levels to qualify rgroup instances on other paths in the hierarchy, and then *selectively* project from the resulting brooms. For example, consider printing the name and actual salary of employees with a jobcode of 1330. Similarly, consider printing the name and actual salary of employees along with the quantity and authorized salary of the position to which the employee relates. The employee-position relationship is based upon a match of their respective jobcodes.

The difficulty here is that the hierarchical structure is "pruned" on the basis of more than one broom-defining rgroup type. The concept of a broom only permits pruning at the level of the broom-defining rgroup, selecting *all* rgroup instances at lower levels in the subtree of the rgroup.

8.3.2 Alternative Query Languages on a Hierarchical Structure

Fehder [1974] has also defined a language, called HQL, with which to query a multipath hierarchical data structure. With HQL it is possible to select data on multiple paths in the hierarchy because it is possible to include selection expressions within the projection specification. Having selected organizations which have some positions with a jobcode of 1330 and some employees with a jobcode of 1330, the projection specification can print only those employees and positions with a jobcode of 1330 (note that in HQL the selection expression precedes the projection specification):

>   FOR EACH ORGANIZATION
>   HAVING POSJOBCODE EQ 1330 AND EMPJOBCODE EQ 1330:
>   LIST ORGNAME, (EMPNAME, ACTSALARY
>   FOR EACH EMPLOYEE HAVING EMPJOBCODE EQ 1330),
>   (AUTHSAL FOR EACH POSITION HAVING POSJOBCODE EQ 1330);

The HAVING followed by a selection expression effectively prunes the tree at levels below the organization rgroup type.

HQL is interesting for another reason. Rather than having the system implicitly moving the broom-defining rgroup type within the structure with the user overriding with HAS to raise the level of broom definition, in HQL the user must explicitly declare each movement of the broom-defining rgroup. The initial

>   FOR EACH rgroup HAVING selection-expression : projection ;

establishes a global focus for all broom definitions. The selection expression following HAVING can contain conditions on items in the immediately preceding rgroup or any of its subordinate rgroup types. The level of broom definition is moved up by including an IN phrase:

>   FOR EACH rgroup IN superior-rgroup HAVING selection expression . . .

and the selection expression can now contain conditions on the items or subordinate rgroups in the superior rgroup. This explicit movement up and down within the hierarchy makes the retrieval clearer by always designating the context of a selection expression. This in turn aids user understanding at the expense of additional verbosity in the query language. The verbosity stems from the redundant specifications in a query language; it is redundant to always have to declare the context of a selection expression within a query statement because, with a hierarchical data structure and appropriate defaults, there is no ambiguity. No ambiguity, that is, to the system—there may still be considerable confusion in the mind of the user concerning the precise meaning of a complex query, or any error diagnostic produced in response to a complex query.

Kim [1979] performed an empirical test of these two types of hierarchical query languages.* He trained two groups of subjects, one group for each language. They each constructed queries and interpreted queries in their respective languages. He then measured the accuracy of the constructions and comprehensions. He found that, when the query was very simple (i.e., against only one or two rgroups in the hierarchical structure), the language with automatic downward context setting (SYSTEM 2000)

---

*Sung-Woo Kim, ''An Investigation of the Effects of Some Variables on Users in a Database Management System Environment: The Use of High-Level Data Languages,'' Unpublished doctoral dissertation, University of Minnesota, Management Information Systems area, 1979.

resulted in greater accuracy and shorter times to completion. When the queries became more complex, the implicit movement of context became confusing, and the explicit context setting language (HQL) produced greater accuracy.

8.3.3 Presentation of Results from a Multipath Hierarchy

The presentation of results from a multipath hierarchy can add another level of complexity to the retrieval process. When querying a multipath hierarchical data structure, the projection specification may produce a single flat file structure or a single-path hierarchical structure (as discussed before), or a multipath hierarchical structure. With the latter, the user desires to present data items from two parallel repeating groups, that is, on the same level of the hierarchical structure. One approach is to simply print the results vertically with one item value per line:

```
ORGNAME = PROPOSAL
    EMPNAME = WALTERS
    EMPJOBCODE = 1110
        SKILL = 1110
        SKILL = 1120

    EMPNAME = GARBER
    EMPJOBCODE = 1330
        SKILL = 1330

    EMPNAME = COMPTON
    EMPJOBCODE = 1330
        SKILL = 1350
        SKILL = 1330
        SKILL = 1130

    POSJOBCODE = 1110
    QUANTITY = 1

    POSJOBCODE = 1330
    QUANTITY = 2

ORGNAME = DESIGN
    EMPNAME = APGAR
    EMPJOBCODE = 1330
        SKILL = 1330

    EMPNAME = ARNETTE
        :
```

To aid readability in this presentation, a blank line was inserted before printing the item values from an rgroup instance if (1) the preceding rgroup was at a lower level in the hierarchy or (2) the preceding rgroup instance was at the same level and two or more items were printed from it. This mode of presentation prints selected data item values according to a top-down, left-to-right, family order tree traversal of the instance diagram in Figure 8-4.

When printing the results in a columnar listing, the problem is how to treat the parallel repeating groups. The set of instances for each rgroup could be presented side-by-side (with rgroup names added for readability):

ORGANIZATION	EMPLOYEE		POSITION	
ORGNAME	EMPNAME	EMPJOBCODE	POSJOBCODE	QUANTITY
PROPOSAL	WALTERS	1110	1110	1
	GARBER	1330	1330	2
	COMPTON	1330		
DESIGN	APGAR	1330	1130	2
	ARNETTE	1130	1330	1

The problem with the side-by-side presentation is that it sets up a *spurious association* between the employee rgroup instance and position rgroup instance appearing on the same line of output. To the casual reader, this mode of presentation is misleading. In general, there is no association between instances of parallel repeating groups within a multipath hierarchical data structure. (Nevertheless, in our sample database, there is a legitimate association between employee and position based upon a match on job-codes. In the above output, the result is correct for the Proposal section but the lines are improperly matched for the Design section.) Without explicit directives in the report definition, there can be no assurance of correctly matched output.

Perhaps a better presentation alternative is to separate the set of instances for each rgroup vertically.

ORGNAME	EMPNAME	EMPJOBCODE	POSJOBCODE	QUANTITY
PROPOSAL	WALTERS	1110		
	GARBER	1330		
	COMPTON	1330		
			1110	1
			1330	2
DESIGN	APGAR	1330		
	ARNETTE	1130		
			1130	2
			1330	2

This may not be particularly easy to read, but it is the least ambiguous presentation alternative. This is a desirable facility and there are times when users need it; they just need to be cautious in using it.

If only one value is to be projected from each of two parallel rgroups, then presentation side-by-side does not result in any ambiguity providing the values are also printed horizontally rather than vertically:

ORGNAME	EMPNAME(S)	POSJOBCODE(S)
PROPOSAL	WALTERS, GARBER, COMPTON	1110, 1330
DESIGN	APGAR, ARNETTE	1130, 1330

The system could even add an 's' to the data item name in the heading to more accurately reflect the multiple values appearing in the column.

8.4 RETRIEVAL FROM A MULTIFILE DATA STRUCTURE

A multifile structure describes multiple types of entities in separate logical files, that is, an entry (or record) type corresponds to each entity class. All meaningful relationships are formally defined to the system. In a multifile model, the defined inter-entity relationships need not be only hierarchical relationships (as they are in a hierarchical data structure). Every entity class relates to at least one other entity class within the multifile data structure. Thus, a multifile schema diagram with nodes corresponding to entity classes and arcs corresponding to relationships would be a connected graph. Each of the files in a multifile structure could be a flat file or a hierarchical file (single-path or multipath).

Figure 6-18 is a multifile data structure schema diagram for our sample database with all relationships represented explicitly in stored data item values within the entity record types. With the addition of a fifth record to store all valid "employee-secondary skill" associations, this becomes a multiple *flat* file data structure, commonly called a "relational data model" [Codd, 1970].

8.4.1 Approaches to Querying a Multifile Data Structure

Just because a system offers the ability to define and create multifile data structures (often called network or relational structures) is no guarantee that it also provides a high-level language capability for querying such structures. In fact, to do so is the exception in today's marketplace for database management systems.

One common approach is to provide a one-record-at-a-time language with verbs added to or hosted in a conventional programming language. (This is discussed more fully in Chapter 10 on Programmer Facilities.) In such host-language systems, the programming user is completely responsible for logically navigating through the database from one record type to the next via particular defined relationships. With a one-record-at-a-time language, the system identifies or delivers at most a single record instance in response to any user request. A user desiring a subset of the records in a file must repeatedly request "get next" after getting the first instance in the desired subset.

A useful extension of this approach is to identify or deliver multiple record instances (of the same record type) in response to a single user request containing a Boolean selection expression.

Some systems have even made this record-level language facility available to the online, interactive user—thus providing for *online navigation*! Some vendors have misleadingly called this a "natural, user-oriented" retrieval facility. Whatever the description, it is still a low-level approach to retrieving from a multifile structure.

Another approach requires the user to view only a hierarchical data structure within the multifile structure. This is possible by suppressing some relationships and assuming the rest to be hierarchical relationships. The perceived hierarchical structure may be multipath, but is more often only a single-path hierarchy. The userschema is an appropriate vehicle for defining a user's hierarchical view within a multifile data structure.

A variant of this approach allows the user to declare a different hierarchical view immediately before issuing the retrieval request in terms of that view. Thus, the hierarchical view can change from one query to the next. Against such a restricted view of the database, the system can now provide a high-level retrieval language as described earlier. This is a common approach to providing some high-level language capability against a stored database which is actually a multifile data structure.

8.4.2 Multifile Retrieval Language

A desirable goal is to provide a high-level language which can reference two or more files using a *single* language statement. Since there may be more than one relationship between any two entity classes, the language must make explicit provision for naming the relationship to be used as part of the language statement. When only one relationship exists between two entity classes referenced in a query, the system can unambiguously determine what entity instances of one class are related to instances of the other class. The relationship must be defined on at least one data item or domain in each file. The criteria for establishing the relationship may be simple equality on the values of these data items. Whether or not the data item values are actually stored, the relationship must be based upon logical attributes of the respective entities which can be derived from the stored database.

How the system actually relates entity instances from the different entity classes depends upon the characteristics of the relationship. (It does not depend upon the existence of indexes, pre-established access methods, or chains—these are merely efficiency replacements for a full scan of a file in response to a query.) For a one-to-one relationship between X and Y, the system takes each instance of Y and adds its associated instance of X (which is uniquely determined). There is a slight problem if the relationship does not exhaust either one of the sets of entities. Some convention must be established when there is no entry in one file to match an existing entry in the other file. Somewhat more complex is a many-to-many relationship.

8.4.3 The JOIN Operation on Two Files

In general, two related files can be joined to form a single composite file structure using the JOIN operation. If the two files are both flat files, the resultant file is a flat file. If there is a one-to-many relationship between the two flat files, the join operation implicitly "flattens down"; that is, the resultant file has one entry for each entry in the file on the "many" side of the relationship. If either file has a hierarchical structure, the resultant file will have a hierarchical data structure. The number of entries in (the cardinality of) the resultant file will be greater than or equal to the larger of the two files being joined. The join operation is based upon a known or assumed relationship between the two files.

A join of ORGANIZATION and EMPLOYEE record types on the common domain of organizational units produces essentially an expanded EMPLOYEE record augmented with the descriptive attributes of the organizational unit to which the employee belongs. The join operation is simply a flattening down of the hierarchical relationship. Figure 8-5 illustrates the results of two other join operations: EMPLOY-

```
EMPLOYEE                              SKILL
-----------------------------         -------------------------
EMPNO   EMPNAME ...  SKILL            SKILLCODE   DESCRIPTION
=====   =======      =====            =========   ==============
24188   WALTERS      1110             1110        SYSTEMS ENGR
  "        "         1120             1120        MECH ENGR
91152   GARBER       1330             1130        ELEC ENGR
30793   COMPTON      1350             1150        PROD ENGR
  "        "         1330             1330        DRAFTSMAN
  "        "         1130             1350        COST ESTIMATOR
82802   APGAR        1130
  "        "         1330
37113   ARNETTE      1130
```

JOIN OF EMPLOYEE AND SKILL ON SKILL OF EMPLOYEE EQ SKILLCODE OF SKILL:

```
        EMPLOYEE.SKILL
        ------------------------------------------
        EMPNO   EMPNAME ...  SKILL   DESCRIPTION
        =====   =======      =====   ============
        24188   WALTERS      1110    SYSTEMS ENGR
          "        "         1120    MECH ENGR
        91152   GARBER       1330    DRAFTSMAN
        30793   COMPTON      1350    COST ESTIMATOR
          "        "         1330    DRAFTSMAN
          "        "         1130    ELEC ENGR
        82802   APGAR        1130    ELEC ENGR
          "        "         1330    DRAFTSMAN
        37113   ARNETTE      1130    ELEC ENGR
```

Figure 8-5 (a). Sample JOIN Operation on Two Files.

The JOIN of two files X and Y produces a single file, denoted by X.Y , by linking up record instances from each file to form a composite record. The JOIN is based upon a condition on one (or more) data items within each record type.

The JOIN in (a) is based on a match of skill code and produces a hierarchical file since EMPLOYEE is a hierarchical file. The effect of this operation is to append the skill description with each skill code in the employee file.

EES and SKILLS on SKILL CODE, and POSITIONS and EMPLOYEES on organizational UNIT number and JOBCODE.

All the previously discussed operations on flat or hierarchical files—selection, projection, ordering, etc.—acted on a single file and produced a single file. Although there are several new operations when dealing with a multifile structure, the JOIN is the most significant. With a join it is possible to produce a file which is more complex and has a richer structure than either of the two input files.

EMPLOYEE

EMPNO	EMPNAME	JOB CODE	UNIT	ACT SALARY
45584	PETERSON	0110	2000	56000
32579	LYNN	5210	2000	12000
24188	WALTERS	1110	2111	28000
91152	GARBER	1330	2111	16400
30793	COMPTON	1330	2111	16200
82802	APGAR	1330	2112	21000
37113	ARNETTE	1130	2112	22000
24749	FAULKNER	1120	2112	24000

POSITION

UNITNO	JOB CODE	QUANTITY	AUTHSAL
2000	0110	1	56000
2000	5210	1	12000
2111	1110	1	28000
2111	1330	2	33000
2112	1130	2	50000
2112	1330	1	21000
2112	1350	1	26000

```
JOIN OF EMPLOYEE AND POSITION ON
UNIT OF EMPLOYEE EQ UNITNO OF POSITION AND
JOBCODE OF EMPLOYEE EQ JOBCODE OF POSITION:
```

EMPLOYEE.POSITION

EMPNO	EMPNAME	ACTSALARY	UNIT	JOBCODE	QUANTITY	AUTHSAL
45584	PETERSON	56000	2000	0110	1	56000
32579	LYNN	12000	2000	5210	1	12000
24188	WALTERS	28000	2111	1110	1	28000
91152	GARBER	16400	2111	1330	2	33000
30793	COMPTON	16200	2111	1330	2	33000
24749	FAULKNER	24000	2112	1120	-	-
37113	ARNETTE	22000	2112	1130	2	50000
82802	APGAR	21000	2112	1330	1	21000
-	-	-	2112	1350	1	26000

Figure 8-5 (b). Sample JOIN Operation on Two Files.
The JOIN in (b) is based on a match of *both* organizational unit number and jobcode.

Notice that not every entry instance in each file had a match in the other file. Sometimes the user wants to preserve all data in both files; in other cases, only entries with a match in the other file are to be selected. An OR-JOIN retains all entries in both files, as shown in (b); an AND-JOIN excludes entries in each file for which there is no match in the other file as shown in (a)—only the user can determine which type of JOIN is the meaningful one in a given query. (The result of an AND-JOIN has also been called "normalized.")

8.4.4 Sample Queries in a Multifile Retrieval Language

1. For all employees, list their names and the name of the department in which they work.

   LIST EMPNAME OF EMPLOYEE, ORGNAME OF ORGANIZATION
   WHERE UNIT OF EMPLOYEE EQ UNITNO OF ORGANIZATION

   This query produces data item values from both employee records and related organization records. The selection expression provides the basis for the relationship. Note that a join operation underlies the execution of this query. Since there are multiple files addressed in the single query statement, the data item names must be qualified with a file name, or be unique across all files active at the time of the query.

2. Find the name and organizational unit number of the boss of GARBER.

PRINT EMPNAME, UNIT, OF EMPLOYEE, WHERE UNIT EQ
(UNIT OF EMPLOYEE WHERE EMPNAME EQ GARBER)
AND LEVEL EQ HEAD

This query illustrates the nesting of retrieval statements. The inner statement directs the system to find the organizational unit number for a particular employee, then the outer part directs the system to find the employee who is the head of the organizational unit just found.

This query has exactly the same form as the "nested" queries on a single flat file which required searching through the *same* file multiple times. With a multifile structure, the query can reference *different* files in the nested parts.

3. For each organizational unit produce a report showing the name, actual salary, and jobcode of each employee as well as the quantity and authorized salary for the associated positions, then sum the actual and authorized salaries calculating the difference for each unit.

LIST EMPNAME, ACTSALARY, JOBCODE, OF EMPLOYEE, QUANTITY,
AUTHSAL, OF POSITION, TOTACT = SUM ACTSALARY PER UNIT,
TOTAUTH = SUM AUTHSAL PER UNIT, SALDIFF = TOTAUTH − TOTACT,
ORDERED BY UNIT, JOBCODE, WHERE UNIT OF EMPLOYEE EQ UNITNO OF
POSITION AND JOBCODE OF EMPLOYEE EQ JOBCODE OF POSITION.

This query makes use of the join illustrated in Figure 8-5(b) and produces a report based upon the resultant single flat file along with calculating statistics per organizational unit.

The high-level language on a multifile data structure is very similar to a *comprehensive* query language on a single flat file except that the query can now refer to multiple, different files. If multiple files are referenced, the system must implicitly perform a join on the files, or logically search through one file then another as it processes the inner nested parts of the query. If the multifile data structure includes hierarchical files, then the query language must have additional syntax as discussed earlier in this chapter. Such a high-level query language would be very complex, which explains its absence from the marketplace. In fact, some would argue that you do not need, even should not have, hierarchical records in a multifile data structure. The data structure should be redefined to pull out all the nested repeating groups within the hierarchical files making them separate flat files. This is the first step in "normalization" to produce a "relational data structure."

8.4.5 Presentation of Results from Multifile Retrieval

If a multifile query produces a single file, whether a flat file or a single-path or multipath hierarchy, the presentation alternatives are those discussed previously. In fact, the results of a multifile query must always be a single (flat or hierarchical) file; to produce multiple files would imply two disjoint reports which would then have been requested using separate retrieval language statements.

SUMMARY

Query languages on data structures with multiple record types or repeating groups are substantially more complex than query languages on a single flat file. Users should be wary of thinking that such languages are easy to learn and use. The sample queries in this chapter progressively led the reader through an understanding and appreciation of the complexity of high-level query languages on more complex data structures.

Retrieval languages on hierarchical or multifile data structures build on the basic language elements for a single flat file query language.

For hierarchical queries, the language includes the additional step of qualification. Qualification serves to qualify for selection additional group instances which are parent or dependent of the selected group instances. The concept of "brooms" aided the analysis and understanding of hierarchical queries.

The user must be conscious of moving or "navigating" up and down within the hierarchy. In partial context setting languages, the system defaults down to the lowest referenced level in the hierarchy. The language then provides explicit syntax (HAS and BY operators) for the user to *raise* the level of the broom defining node. In explicit context setting languages, the requester had to explicitly move *up or down* in the hierarchy using specific elements in the language.

Presentation of output results was straightforward from a single-path hierarchical structure. Presentation of output from a multipath hierarchy presented a distinct problem—how to place the values from multiple, unrelated group instances so as not to produce a spurious association between two rgroups at the same level in the logical data structure.

Most systems with a multifile data structure do not have high-level query language facilities for retrieving and presenting data from multiple related files. They either offer a low-level, one-record-at-a-time navigation language, or they restrict the user view of the query to a single-path or multipath hierarchy in the data structure.

The additional construct to handle multiple files in a high-level query language is the underlying JOIN operation. This allows the user to implicitly (or explicitly) join two files across a defined (or assumed) relationship, thus forming a single (flat or hierarchical) file which is used to produce the output from the query. The join criterion is expressed in a Boolean expression with one or more operands from each of the related files. An OR-JOIN includes record instances even if there is no match in the related file; an AND-JOIN does not.

EXERCISES

8-1. Under what conditions is the qualification step necessary?

8-2. Explain the concept of a broom as used in qualification. What is the significance of the broom-defining node? What additional nodes are selected in the qualification process?

8-3. Explain why it is sometimes necessary to redefine the broom after the selection phase of a query and before the projection phase.

8-4. Explain how raising the level of the broom-defining node can result in a loss of selectivity.

8-5. Illustrate how repeating group instances within an entry can be presented on a printed output report. Show at least two different approaches.

8-6. What is the most important new element which must be added to an interrogation language against a hierarchical data structure? a multifile data structure?

8-7. Define the join operation and explain its significance in multifile retrieval.

8-8. Distinguish between an OR-join and an AND-join.

8-9. How would the output change by applying an AND-join instead of an OR-join to the files in Figure 8-5(b)?

8-10. If the criteria for a relationship between two files involves nonidentifier data items from both files, the files will be in a many-to-many relationship to each other. If this relationship is used to perform a join of the two files, what can you say about the number of record instances in the join file? In particular, will it be less than, equal to, or greater than the number of record instances in the larger of the two files?

8-11. A join operation can be applied to two files to physically produce a third file—the join. If the two files are large, the resultant join file will be very large. If the only reason for performing the join is to produce an output report with data from both files, discuss how it might be possible to generate the report without actually producing the join file. Some have called this a "dynamic join."

8-12. Within each organizational unit of our sample database, at most one employee is designated as HEAD. The second multifile query (Q2) requested the name of the boss of Garver, who is not the head of his organizational unit. How would you write a query for the name of the boss of someone who is the head of their organizational unit?

SELECTED REFERENCES

AHO, A. V., C. BEERI, and J. D. ULLMAN, "The Theory of Joins in Relational Databases," *ACM Transactions on Database Systems* (4:3), 1979 September.

BRITISH COMPUTER SOCIETY Query Languages Group, *Query Languages: A Unified Approach*, London: Heyden & Son (also Philadelphia), 1981, 105 pages.

BLEIER, Robert E., "Treating Hierarchical Data Structures in the SDC Time-Shared Data Management System (TDMS)," *Proceedings of the 22nd ACM National Conference*, 1967, pages 41-49.

CHAMBERLIN, D. D., et al., "SEQUEL 2: A Unified Approach to Data Definition, Manipulation, and Control," *IBM Journal of Research and Development* (20:6), 1976 November, pages 560-575.
　　Describes comprehensive, high-level language facilities for query, data definition, manipulation, and control of a database consisting of multiple flat files (that is, a relational data model). SEQUEL 2 is the main external interface of System R, an experimental database management system, now marketed by IBM as 'SQL'.

CODD, E. F., "A Relational Model of Data for Large Shared Data Banks," *Communications of the ACM* (13:6), 1970 June, pages 377-387.

DATE, C. J., *An Introduction to Database Systems*, third edition, Reading, MA: Addison-Wesley, 1981, annot. refs.
　　Includes several chapters with extended discussions and examples of languages for hierarchical (IMS), relational, and network (CODASYL-DBTG) data structures. Also includes a chapter on the UDL.

DATE, C. J., "An Introduction to the Unified Database Language (UDL)," *Proceedings Sixth International Conference on Very Large Data Bases (VLDB)*, 1980 October.
　　Presents data definition and manipulation languages which purport to support hierarchic, network, and relational data structures in a uniform and consistent manner. It is intended to be embedded in some host programming language. It provides both [low-level] record-at-a-time and [higher-level] set-at-a-time operations.

DATE, C. J., "An Architecture for High-Level Language Database Extensions," *Proceedings ACM-SIGMOD Conference*, 1976, Washington, D.C., 1976 June 2-4, edited by J. B. Rothnie, New York: Association for Computing Machinery, 1976, pages 101-122.
　　Develops a data definition language which clearly shows the differences between the commonly accepted data models—hierarchical, network, and relational. Also describes a high-level data manipulation language for a programmer. The paper contains several noteworthy ideas.

CHAPTER EIGHT: DATABASE RETRIEVAL: HIERARCHICAL AND MULTIFILE STRUCTURES **337**

FEHDER, Paul, "HQL: A Set-Oriented Transaction Language for Hierarchically-Structured Data Bases," *Proceedings ACM National Conference*, 1974, page 465.

Describes a high-level query language on a hierarchical structure; a forerunner of SQL [Chamberlin, 1976, and FORAL, Senko, 1975].

GOTLIEB, L. R., "Computing Joins of Relations," *Proceedings ACM SIGMOD Conference on the Management of Data*, 1975.

Describes and compares several algorithms for implementing the "natural" (equality) join.

HARDGRAVE, Walter Terry, "Theoretical Aspects of Boolean Operations on Tree Structures and Implications for Generalized Data Management," Austin: University of Texas, Computation Center, TSN-26 (doctoral dissertation), 1972 August, 108 pages.

Provides an examination of the schemes that might be used for qualifying additional nodes [group instances] other than the selected nodes. Distinguishes between a set theoretic scheme and a "tree-theoretic" schema. A significant contribution toward a solid theoretical foundation for retrieval operations on a hierarchical data structure.

HEINDEL, L. E. and J. T. ROBERTO, "ARPL—A Retrieval Process Language," *The Computer Journal* (17:2), 1974 May, pages 113-116.

Describes a retrieval language for hierarchical data structures, focusing on file-level derivation functions. Selection expressions relate to one record type at a time, thus requiring the user to "navigate" through the hierarchy.

HOUSEL, Barron C. and Nan C. SHU, "A High-Level Data Manipulation Language for Hierarchical Data Structures,"*Proceedings of Conference on Data: Abstraction, Definition, and Structure*, Salt Lake City, Utah, 1976 March 22-24, (published by ACM, New York, in *FDT* (8:2), 1976), pages 155-169.

McGEE, William C., "File-Level Operations on Network Data Structures," *Proceedings ACM-SIGMOD Conference on Management of Data*, San Jose, California, 1975 May 14-16, edited by W. F. King, New York: Association for Computing Machinery, 1976, pages 32-47.

Proposes an approach to developing a language with operators which act on sets of record instances including whole files, and illustrates several different operations using such a language—file creation, update, processing, and report generation.

MORLING, S. C. R. and Donald H. SUNDEEN, "ASI/INQUIRY—An Advanced IMS DB/DC Query Language," presented at the GUIDE 40 meeting, Miami, Florida, 1975 May 21, 29 pages.

PARSONS, Ron G., A. G. DALE, and C. V. YURKANAN, "Data Manipulation Language Requirements for Database Management Systems," *The Computer Journal* (17:2), 1974 May, pages 99-103.

Proposes extensions to a Data Manipulation Language (such as CODASYL DBTG) for processing hierarchical data structures and more complex network structures. The extensions are in the form of additional verbs (ADJUST, QUALIFY, SELECT, and LOCATE) made available to the user who navigates through the structure.

SENKO, Michael E., "Data Description Language in the Context of a Multi-level Structured Description: DIAM II with FORAL," in *Data Base Description*, Proceedings of IFIP-TC2 working conference, Belgium, 1975 January, edited by B. C. M. Douqué and G. M. Nijssen, Amsterdam: North-Holland Publishing Co., (New York: American Elsevier), 1975, pages 239-258.

Describes a high-level retrieval language against a binary relational data structure.

SINOWITZ, Norman R., "DATAPLUS—A Language for Real Time Information Retrieval from Hierarchical Data Bases," *Proceedings AFIPS Spring Joint Computer Conference*, Volume 32, 1968, pages 395-401.

An early discussion of patterns of processing a hierarchical structure. Discusses elements of the query language and introduces the concept of the "raised level variable" and PER qualifier.

TSICHRITZIS, D., "LSL: A Link and Selector Language," *Proceedings ACM-SIGMOD Conference on Management of Data*, Washington, D.C., 1976, edited by James B. Rothnie, New York: Association for Computing Machinery, 1976, pages 123-133.

Describes a simple language for interrogating a multiple flat file data structure. A *selector* is a named Boolean selection expression and a *Link* is a named relationship based upon defined criteria on data items from the two linked record types.

ZLOOF, Moshe M., "Query-by-Example: Operations on Hierarchical Data Bases," *Proceedings AFIPS National Computer Conference* (45), 1976.

ZLOOF, Moshe M. and S. Peter de JONG, "The System for Business Automation (SBA): Programming Language," *Communications of the ACM* (20:6), 1977 June, pages 385-396.
    Offers a unique approach to querying a multifile data structure. This article is descriptive of a nonprogrammer oriented system and contains several interesting examples.

NINE

DATABASE CREATION AND UPDATE

9.1   DATA CAPTURE AND MECHANIZATION   340

9.2   DATABASE CREATION   341
9.2.1   The Process of Database Creation   342
9.2.2   Database Creation Using the Update Function   345
9.2.3   Database Creation with a User-Supplied Program   345

9.3   TRANSACTION PROCESSING AND DATABASE UPDATE   346
9.3.1   Update by Individual Records   346
9.3.2   Update by Transactions   348
9.3.3   The Process of Transaction-Oriented Update   349
9.3.4   Characteristics of the Update Function   352

9.4   GENERAL UPDATE OPERATIONS   354
9.4.1   Item-Level Update Operations   354
9.4.2   Record-Level Update Operations   355
9.4.3   File-Level Update Operations   356

SUMMARY   356

EXERCISES   357

SELECTED REFERENCES   358

After formally defining a database to the DBMS and before any retrieval can take place, data must be entered into the database. Database definition specifies what the data will look like once it is collected and stored. Data can be entered into a database in one of two ways:

Creation is the process of loading data, which already exists in machinable form, into a defined database.

Update is the process of adding, modifying, or deleting data from the database through transaction processing or direct processing of the records. The objective of update is to maintain the database in a current state.

If the data does not already exist in a machinable form, it is necessary to capture or collect the data and put it into a machine-readable form—a process called *mechanization*.

The creation and update functions discussed in this chapter relate to the nonprogramming user. A special, self-contained command language provides the communication with these functions. Language facilities hosted in a programming language to serve the needs of the programming user are discussed in the next chapter.

9.1 DATA CAPTURE AND MECHANIZATION

The complete process of establishing and maintaining a database extends beyond the boundaries of the DBMS. The data definition reflects the data required by the users in an organization. The next step is to get the data into a form which is processable by the DBMS.

When a decision is made to put certain data into the database, one of two situations will exist: either the data is already in a mechanized form or it is not.

Often the data already exists in a mechanized form, perhaps because it was previously collected and entered in an earlier version of the application system or in a previously installed DBMS. The data may already exist in the files of a conventional programming language, such as COBOL. Already mechanized data is rapidly becoming the prevalent situation as organizations increase their use of computers and as application systems penetrate into more and more activities and functions.

With data already mechanized, the organization seldom has to go through the task of rekeying the data. Nevertheless, it still has the sometimes difficult task of converting this foreign file into a form acceptable to the system. General conversion utilities may be available; or it may be necessary to write a special conversion program. The previously installed DBMS may have a facility to "export" files, that is, to generate an output file according to some standard external format. At the same time, the new DBMS may have an "import" facility to load files from a standard external format into the internal format of the new DBMS. For large files, the conversion process may take several hours or even days. Then it may take months to change the procedures that operate on that file and to retrain the people who maintain and use that file, all the while trying to keep the organization running smoothly.

If the data is not already mechanized, appropriate strategies and procedures must be set up to capture the data and get it into machine-readable form. The organization is able to exercise some discretion and control over the mechanization process and the design of input data transactions.

Nearly all manual data entry today is accomplished by human keyboarding. When the data is keyed it may be first stored on punched cards or magnetic tape for subsequent processing by the computer, or it may be entered directly into the computer from online terminals or microcomputer workstations. Some limited forms of data entry may be accomplished using direct manipulation methods—choosing from a menu of options using a touch screen, light pen, or a mouse. The future will see increased use of voice input of data as voice recognition devices become more reliable and less costly.

If the data does not exist even in a manual form, appropriate data gathering mechanisms, such as forms and questionnaires, must be developed.

Often the required data exists in several places and with varying degrees of quality. The organizational process of locating the data and getting it into the system can be a very long and arduous task. It is at this point that people suddenly realize how sloppy and incomplete their manual record keeping systems really are. While it may take only a few days to acquire and install a DBMS, it can sometimes take many months to enter the data, create the database, and make it available to the users. People in the organization must have a lot of patience during this process.

Keyboarding of data presents one of the biggest problems in the development and use of computer-based information systems. Data entry is most subject to error when the people doing the keyboarding are remote from the environment in which the data is generated. Being unfamiliar with the operations, they have little basis on which to judge the correctness of the data being entered. This is generally the situation in specialized organizational units set up with highly trained keyboard operators to perform efficient, high-volume data entry. While sometimes this approach is necessary and satisfactory, every effort should be made to capture data close to the source and have it entered by persons who have some knowledge of the situation and operations.

Data entry is a highly repetitive and time-consuming task. It is often viewed as drudgery necessary to making data available. All too often the effort required to create the database initially or to keep it current is substantially underestimated. Users can get caught up in the excitement of having a system which provides the data they need without realizing the burden of keeping the data up to date (and, therefore, useful). Sometimes applications are infeasible and abandoned because the effort required for data entry and/or maintenance is simply too high.

9.2 DATABASE CREATION

Database creation refers to the initial creation of an internal, system-defined database from external (to the DBMS) machinable data. Creation of an initial instance of the database is often referred to as "populating" the database definition. Basically, database creation is the process of getting raw data or foreign files into the standard, internal format required by the DBMS for subsequent processing.

There are basically three ways to accomplish the initial creation of the database, each using a particular system function or module:

- Creation function module, like a file load utility.
- Update facility, which assumes that update can begin processing with an empty file.
- Special-purpose program supplied by the user, which assumes a programming user interface to the DBMS.

The first two are discussed in this chapter. The third alternative is accomplished using the programming user facilities described in the next chapter.

9.2.1 The Process of Database Creation

The database creation process using a special creation function or load utility is depicted in Figure 9-1.

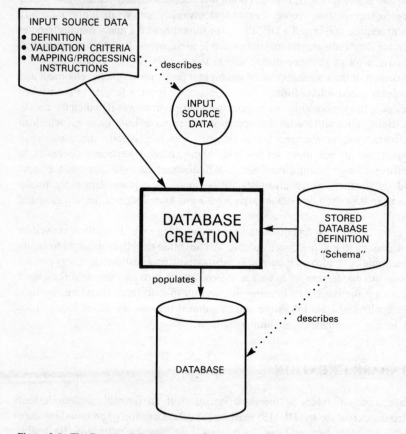

Figure 9-1. The Process of Database Creation.
The database creation process accepts mechanized input data, its definition, and processing instructions, and populates (or creates) a stored database according to its database definition or schema.

The major *inputs* to the creation process are:

- Stored definition of the database to be created (or portion thereof).
- Input source data.
- Definition of the input source data.
- Instructions for how the input data is to be mapped into the database.

The **input source data definition** covers the entire range of definitional information from logical structure through storage structure to device and media allocation. If the data structure class for the input source data is the same as for the stored database, the same data definition language can be used. It is not uncommon, however, to define the input source data using a more restricted data structure class.

In fact, some database management systems prescribe the format for input source data. The users are not at liberty to define their own input data formats in an attempt to maximize efficiency or minimize errors in the data collection process. When the system prescribes the input format, the source data file must be specially prepared—unless, of course, the data collection and mechanization process is designed to produce data in the system-prescribed format. If the data already exists or is prepared by someone else, it must be converted to the system-prescribed format before it can be entered into the system and stored in the database. This process is shown in Figure 9-2. The conversion may be accomplished using a special-purpose program or, alternatively, a generalized conversion program. The input to the generalized conversion program is not only the input source data but also its definition and mapping instructions. This brings us back to where we started from except that the input data is now processed twice, a needless expenditure of effort.

The **validation criteria** are applied to the input data before transformation and storage in the database. Validation of the input data supplements the information in the database definition which is (or should be) used to validate the data after it is stored in the database.

The **mapping information** defines the correspondence between the input data definition and the stored database definition. The mapping used to transform the input data before storage in the database is often very simple. The simplest transformation is a one-to-one mapping where the input data is copied directly into the database. Various forms of transformation can be applied including encoding item values, changing intra-record structures, or applying algorithms to derive new item values. If a system allows some differences between the schema and a userschema, the input data could be placed into a buffer by the creation module with the database control system performing the implied transformation upon writing the data into the database.

The input data used to create a file in the database could come from within the system, that is, it may already be stored in the database in some form. This is not within the scope of database creation as previously defined. Creation results in the storage of *new* data within the database and not the transformation of data which already exists within the database. The new input source data is external or foreign to the DBMS. The process of taking existing data within the database and generating another internal, system-defined file is a variation of the restructure process and is discussed under database revision in Chapter 11.

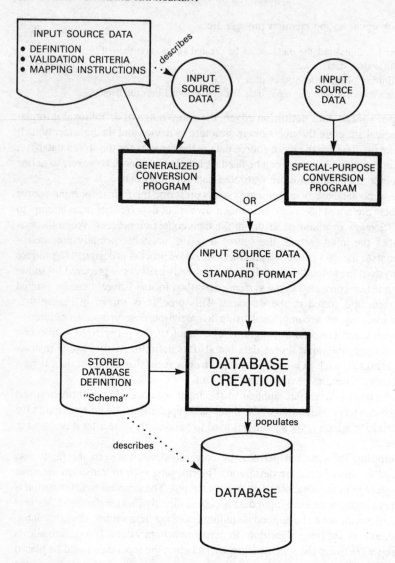

INPUT SOURCE DATA
- DEFINITION
- VALIDATION CRITERIA
- MAPPING INSTRUCTIONS

describes

INPUT SOURCE DATA

INPUT SOURCE DATA

GENERALIZED CONVERSION PROGRAM

SPECIAL-PURPOSE CONVERSION PROGRAM

OR

INPUT SOURCE DATA in STANDARD FORMAT

STORED DATABASE DEFINITION "Schema"

DATABASE CREATION

populates

describes

DATABASE

Figure 9-2. Database Creation Process with Prescribed Input Data Format.

When the creation function of a DBMS expects the input source data to be in some standard format, users must preprocess the input data using a generalized conversion program (if available) or by writing their own special-purpose conversion program.

Many variations in the database creation process stem from the two figures for the creation process. A system need not even have a separate database creation function if it provides either a programming user interface or an update function that can begin writing into an empty file.

9.2.2 Database Creation Using the Update Function

A defined database can be initially created using the update function to populate an empty file. Even if the update function cannot begin writing into an empty file, it may be possible to start with a dummy entry.

Several similarities and differences can be noted between the creation function and the update function.

- Both functions process and store external or foreign input data.
- A specification of validation criteria and transformation processing is required in both functions.
- While the mapping in the creation function is often minimal, the amount of processing and transformation of input data in the update function is usually more extensive.
- Whereas the creation function only adds data to the database, the update function adds, changes, and deletes data in the database.

While creation can be considered a file-level function and update can be considered a transaction or record-level function, the distinction is quickly blurred. Creation is a one-time operation of putting an input file into the database. A file is a set of entries or records, or can even be considered a set of input data transactions. Update is an ongoing activity of processing transactions against the database, either one at a time or in batches. Since a batch of transactions is analogous to a file, the difference between creation and update becomes one of degree.

Finally, the creation function is generally more efficient than update, particularly if the update function requires data in a standard, prescribed format or if it cannot handle batches of input data transactions.

9.2.3 Database Creation with a User-Supplied Program

When the user writes a special program to perform database creation, the system is not cognizant of the source or form of the input data. It is a user responsibility to recognize, validate, and properly process the input source data. In effect, the user has to do all the work. To the system, the user program is like any other program which is reading and writing the database. A system that permits some differences between the userschema and the schema can provide some assistance to the user. Even if the system provides a database creation function, it may still be desirable or necessary to use special purpose programs to satisfy more extensive mapping or validation requirements on some data input tasks.

9.3 TRANSACTION PROCESSING AND DATABASE UPDATE

The update process is similar to the retrieval process except that input data is usually involved and that a successful update action always results in a change to the database. Update action only changes the *content* of a database. Changes in structure, including item-level attributes such as length, are accomplished using the redefinition facilities and restructuring the stored data.

As defined here, generalized update facilities do not include facilities available to programming users who use conventional programming languages to write their own program to change the content of the database. Of course, after the user program is written it can be considered another language facility or "system-supplied" functional module that can be used by nonprogramming users to accomplish update. This suggests that the distinction is somewhat spurious and, indeed, it does become fuzzy especially when considering the person performing various database activities from a terminal. Nevertheless, the distinction will be employed as long as it is useful to an understanding of the various processes involved.

The update process can be viewed in two ways: by focusing on the change to the database, or by focusing on the input data causing the change. In the first case, update is done by creating and modifying individual records of a single file. The second, more complex case uses transaction processing to accomplish database update.

9.3.1 Update by Individual Records

In perhaps its simplest form, updating is driven by the record definitions only. At a given update session, the user specifies which file is to be the object of update for that session. Then the user declares whether he wishes to create and insert new records, or modify existing records. To create new records, the system accepts a value for each data item in the record definition. If the user is online, the system can prompt with the data item name and optionally display the maximum length and type of the data item. When the user enters a value for the data item value, the system can check it for conformance to its definition, including any validation checks. Errors could be corrected immediately by the online user.

Upon entering values (or no value) for all the data items, the user can scan over the screen for one last check before telling the system to accept and store the newly created record. This process continues until the user indicates no more records to be input. A single update session would apply only to a single file.

To update existing records, the user must specify to the system which records are to be modified, or deleted. In the simplest case, the user simply steps through the records one at a time. In general, the records to be updated are specified using a Boolean selection expression, exactly as in the process of retrieval. If a given selection expression identifies a subset of records in the file, the user can still step through the subset of records, changing values in one record at a time. The system would first display all the values in a selected record. The user first determines whether or not any values are to be changed; if so, moving the screen cursor to the desired item value and making the change. As in record creation, the user indicates when a record is correctly updated. Then the system can accept and store that record and display the next (selected) record until there are no more records or the user says 'done.'

Of course, if the updating is done in a deferred batch mode, the user input to the process would have to unambiguously identify the record(s) to be the object of the update action.

During record creation or modification, the user may not need to see and be prompted to update every data item in the record. This requires the user to provide a projection specification, naming the data items to be displayed or updated. The projection serves only to identify certain data items in the record, not to actually extract the values as in the retrieval process.

For those data items not projected, the system would have to follow some convention for placing a value in those items when creating new records. Preferably, this would be indicated by a default value for the item provided as part of the data definition. Otherwise the system could store a standard default value. Such default values are generally based upon the data item type—blank for character strings, zero for arithmetic items (unless the system can actually store nothing for the data item).

Regarding form of presentation, the system can simply display the data items one per line, as shown in Figure 9-3.

If a record contains more data items than there are available lines on the display device, the system can use multiple "pages" or screens to display and capture the input data for a record. Alternatively, the system could provide a facility for the users to define their own tailored screens. In this case, they could:

- Place the data item values at any spot on the screen, including several on a single line.
- Include more user-understandable labels for the data items, such as ACTUAL SALARY or EMPLOYEE NAME in Figure 9-3.
- Omit certain data items from the display.
- Specify that certain data items are for display only, not to be changed (such as the record identifier).

The same user-defined screen facility for retrieval could be used for record update, with the addition of a facility to add or change data item values.

Once the user tells the system to accept the values for a record, the system designer has several options for actually storing that record in the file.

1. The most secure but time consuming option would be to write each record to the file on secondary storage immediately upon acceptance by the user.
2. Alternatively, the system could write the created or updated records to secondary storage each time the internal system buffer is full (or the user ends an update session).
3. Thirdly, the system could write the whole records to an intermediate "transaction" file to be later merged in with the records of the main file. This option would automatically provide a rudimentary audit trail of changes to the database if the intermediate files were saved after the merging process.

```
FILE:  EMPLOYEE                           RECORD UPDATE

EMPNO............:45584
EMPNAME..........:PETERSON, N.M.
UNIT............:2000
JOBCODE.........:0110
LEVEL...........:HEAD
TITLE...........:DIVISION MANAGER
SEX.............:M
BIRTHDATE.......:280607
PSKILL..........:0110
SSKILL1.........:6130
SSKILL2.........:6625
SSKILL3.........:6040
ACTSALARY.......:56000

ARROWS move cursor to change values; RETURN to accept.
```

Figure 9-3. Updating One Record at a Time.
The simplest form of update for the online user is to prompt for and accept data items values for one record at a time to a single file. Only the record definition is needed to guide the system in the update process.

9.3.2 Update by Transactions

The disadvantages of individual record update driven by the stored file definition are:

- The update action can only apply to one record at a time, in one file at a time.
- The record must be viewed exactly as defined.

Sometimes it is desirable to decouple the way the user "sees the record" from the way it is actually represented within the system, and to decouple the process of capturing input data from the process of updating the database. A transaction can now contain data items and have a structure independent of any particular record, and can be targeted to update multiple records at once, or even multiple record types.

This view draws attention to the definition and processing of transactions. It is the basis for the notion of transaction-oriented or transaction-driven systems. The notion of transaction is apt for it implies that some event or exchange has occurred in the environment. Such an event generates a transaction consisting of data concerning the event. If the database is to remain an accurate reflection or image of the external environment, the transaction must be posted to change the stored data making it correspond to the changed environment.

In addition to the information required for the above processes, the update function requires as input the actual transaction data and the definition of the transaction. The *transaction definition* information includes:

- Description of the structure and format of the transaction.
- Edit and validation criteria which the transaction must satisfy.

- Mapping specifications between transaction data and the database.
- Processing actions such as add, modify, or delete.

This, combined with a selection expression, "projection" specifications, derivation formulas, and other processing actions, makes up the complete spectrum of input information for the update process.

9.3.3 The Process of Transaction-Oriented Update

The designer of a general-purpose update facility faces a variety of design choices. The variety of approaches to designing the update facility seems to be greater than for retrieval. Many systems take a rather simplistic approach to data input and file update. Perhaps this reflects relatively less understanding of the update process than of retrieval. The update process has proven difficult to generalize; and attempts to generalize often produce greatly increased complexity.

One particular dimension of design choice is based upon *when* the input information is given; a second is based upon *where* the prior information is stored. These two dimensions are depicted in Figure 9-4.

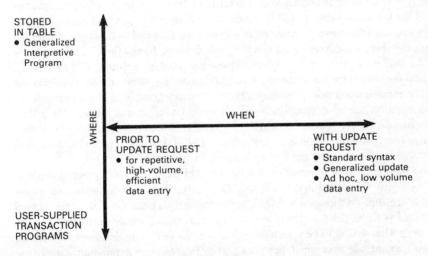

Figure 9-4. Update Transaction Information: When Entered and Where Stored.
Information required as input to a general update transaction process includes:

- Definition of transaction structure and format.
- Input edit and validation criteria.
- Mapping of transaction data to the database.
- Processing action (insert, modify, delete).
- Projection and selection criteria indicating the object of the update action.
- Update data—the actual data to be added to the database.

In a generalized update language, all of this information would be part of the update request. However, for efficient processing of high-volume repetitive requests, some of this information can be supplied in advance and stored in the system. It would be used upon receipt of each request for that type of update.

At one extreme on the **'when' dimension**, all the information needed for the update process (described previously) could be given at the time an update request is made. In this case, the update program module would be highly generalized to permit a wide variety of update actions. All update requests would have to conform to a standard language syntax, albeit perhaps a highly generalized syntax. This includes a standard syntax for the input transaction data within the update request.

The syntax of the transaction data could actually be standardized at two levels—at the level of the data, or at the level of the description of the data, that is, at the meta-data level. In the first case, the user is not free to format the input data in just any way. It must be formatted according to the standard syntax. Examples of standard input data syntax rules might be:

- The length of all item values must be indicated by a particular ending delimiter.
- Each item value must be preceded by its name.
- Item values must be input in a consistent top-down left-right sequence relative to the hierarchical structure of the defined database.

If the syntax is standardized at the meta-data level, that is, the level of the data definition language, the user is free to format the input data as long as the format can be properly defined using the standard data description language. In this case, the description of the transaction data would be given to the update function immediately before the transaction data in every update request. Since the data and its description enter the system together, some have called this the "self-defining transaction." Such a facility may be useful when a single update request can contain a batch of transactions.

Moving toward the other end of the 'when' dimension, some common information could be input immediately preceding a batch of transactions. Rather than provide *all* the information needed to completely specify an update request at the time the update transaction data is given to the system, it may be desirable to provide some of the more stable or constant information in advance. Such *a priori* information can be catalogued and stored for later use by the update process.

By supplying some information in advance, such as transaction format, it is possible to simplify the actual update request. Generally, the minimum information provided at the time of the update request is the transaction data. One exception occurs when data is to be deleted. Even in this case, parameters would normally be given indicating what data is to be selected for deletion. As this example shows, the update request may include data which becomes part of the selection expression, rather than being directly stored in the database. By simplifying the update request and requiring less information at request time, the system begins to serve the parametric nonprogramming user. Such users can simply invoke a prestored update request and supply the missing data as parameters.

Presumably, if some update request information is stored in advance, the system maintains a library of information relating to several different types of transactions. Each catalogued transaction type must be uniquely identified and each incoming transaction must contain one of these unique identifiers. Then, when the transaction is processed, the update program is able to retrieve the previously stored information when needed to complete the update request. An overview of the update process is shown in Figure 9-5.

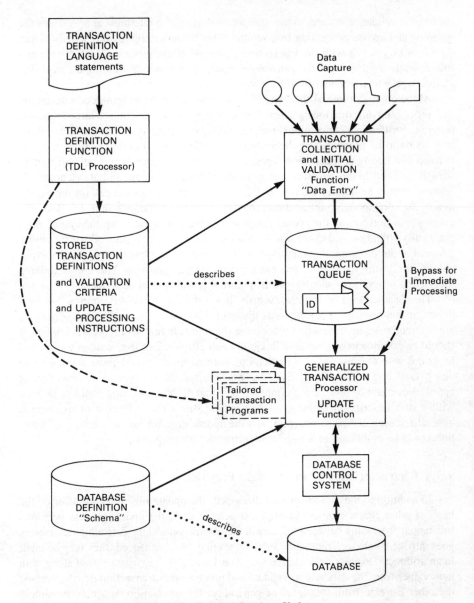

Figure 9-5. The Process of Transaction-Oriented Database Update.

When some information is stored in advance, the **'where' dimension** concerns where or in what form the stored information is kept. The previous discussion implied that any prior information would be stored as data in a library. When the transaction is received for processing, the generalized update program retrieves the stored data which then directs the update processing. The generalized update module interprets the stored transaction definition in order to scan and parse the incoming transaction data, it applies the validation criteria to the transaction data, and it interprets and executes the mapping and update processing instructions. This process roughly corresponds to that shown in Figure 9-5 with the transaction definition being processed and stored, and subsequently used to guide the generalized update function in processing a transaction of that type when received by the system.

At the other extreme of the 'where' dimension, the *a priori* transaction definition and processing information is embodied in a transaction program. One transaction program, written in a conventional programming language, is tailored for each type of transaction to be processed by the system. A single transaction type may actually be defined as a family of transaction types. A transaction program is specially written by the DBMS user. In this situation, the generalized update program all but disappears. It remains merely to identify the type of the incoming transaction and call for the execution of the corresponding transaction program to process the transaction. In effect, the entire job of performing the update function is delegated to the users; the system does practically nothing to aid in the update process. On the positive side, all the flexibility inherent in the programming language used to write the transaction program, is available in specifying the update process for each transaction type. The use of tailored transaction programs is also shown in Figure 9-5 with the broken lines.

The disadvantage of relying exclusively on the use of tailored transaction programs, is that sooner or later the users discover that many of the operations performed are common to many transaction processing situations. In fact, as Figure 9-5 implies, it should be possible to combine the flexibility and efficiency of user-written transaction programs with the descriptive simplicity of a stored transaction definition library into one overall update capability. Even for a single transaction type, a combination of approaches could be used. For example, the format of the transaction could be defined with a data description language, which would direct the execution of a common generalized scan and parse program, and the update mapping and processing information could be embodied in a user-written transaction program.

9.3.4 Characteristics of the Update Function

In addition to the factors already discussed, the update function can differ on the basis of other characteristics. In the most general case, the update process performs substantial processing between the data in the transaction and the data which ultimately goes into the database. Transaction item values may be resequenced, they may be input to an arithmetic expression to derive new data values, or they may be used along with item values from the database to validate and process other transaction item values. At the other extreme from this level of generality, the transaction data may be simply transferred to the database and stored as a string exactly as written in the transaction. From the standpoint of update processing this is much simpler, but it means that the format of the input transaction data must correspond exactly to the defined structure of the database (similar to Updating by Individual Records as discusssed earlier). This may pose a severe limitation on the definition of input transactions. Obviously, both methods are desirable.

On another dimension, the update function may process a transaction immediately upon receipt, or batch transactions for later processing. Batching transactions by type minimizes the swapping or loading of transaction definition and processing instructions. Batching transactions according to target 'master' file and then sorting the batch to correspond to the file ordering can yield greater efficiency, if the master file is stored sequentially or partly so. Also, certain validation criteria will apply to the batch level, for example, control totals. Both immediate processing and batching in a transaction queue are shown in Figure 9-5.

Besides immediate or deferred processing of transactions, it is possible to have immediate or deferred update of the database. While update requests and input transactions can be processed immediately, they need not result in immediate update of the stored database. Various strategies can be used to keep track of the updates while deferring the actual database update to a later time.

It can be very expensive for every update request to be *immediately posted* to the stored database. As records are physically added, deleted, and changed in size, the stored database (and its indexes) can become significantly disorganized. If the stored records in a file are kept in some physical order (according to some key), the system must take appropriate steps to maintain that order. As the stored database becomes increasingly disorganized, access efficiency may decline. Some systems attempt to maintain file organization and access efficiency after each update (which can slow down the update process); others require the user (or database administrator) to periodically invoke a reorganization utility to clean up the stored database. Also, since a copy (or dump) serves as the primary backup for a file, it is desirable to leave the physical file unchanged and post the new or updated records in a separate storage area.

The essential idea behind deferred file update is to separately record and keep track of all changes to a stored database. Then, when it is convenient or efficient, those changes can be folded back or merged into the main stored database. Several options are possible. In each case, increased access time and complexity is traded for reduced update and backup effort.

- The system maintains a table or index which contains a pointer to each record in the file. Initially, all records are stored in a single, well-organized, and perhaps ordered physical file. As records are added, modified, or deleted, they are stored in a separate file area or even appended to the original file. The table or index would be modified after each update, but the original stored file would not be changed until the updates were actually folded in.
- Rather than maintain a system index to all the records, both old and new, the system can first search the separate file of new or changed records. If not found, the system can search the main file.
- Severance and Lohman [1976] describe a filtering mechanism for determining whether or not a desired record *might* be in the "differential file." If the filter says "probably," the system searches the differential file. If the record is not found (a possibility which can be kept quite low), the system would search directly in the main file. This scheme avoids the need to *always* search through the differential file before searching through the main file.
- One organization maintains a master file on tape. Each morning it is loaded onto disk ready for online access during the day. Updates are memo posted to the database on disk which becomes increasingly disorganized. The updates are immediately

available for subsequent retrievals during the day. Updates are also recorded in a separate update transaction file for "official" posting to the master file on tape during the evening. Next morning the newly updated database is reloaded to the disk.

Ultimately, the update function involves capturing data, converting it to a mechanized form, and entering it into the system. In this sense, it involves all the same activities as the creation function. In fact, if the update process can begin with an empty file, define any general format for a transaction, and batch incoming transactions, then it can eliminate the need for a special creation module. One exception to this similarity of the update and creation functions, is that often the capture of input data transactions is accomplished online. Data transactions captured online will be handled by a terminal management and communication system. With the online capture of data it is possible to perform various levels of validation, for example, the transaction could be validated against data stored in the database. When data transactions enter the system in a general message processing environment, some global function would have to examine all messages to discriminate update transactions from other requests entering the system. Such a message discrimination function is not the same as the simple 'update' function which decides which transaction program to invoke.

Additional update function characteristics include allowing one transaction to update more than one file, and surveying the state of the database after the posting of a transaction to determine whether or not to initiate further action or to generate, internally, a new transaction. For example, if a withdrawal of stock from inventory reduces the level below the reorder point, the update function could generate a new transaction to initiate an order for additional stock.

9.4 GENERAL UPDATE OPERATIONS

General update operations apply at various levels in a database: item, record, and file.

9.4.1 Item-Level Update Operations

Within the context of a particular record, the simplest form of item-level update operations is a *replacement statement*. The specifications of a value or expression on the right determines the value used to replace the data item in the object record instance. A literal value can be used to replace the data item in the object record instance. A literal value can be used directly whereas, with an expression, all operands must be resolved (that is, given a value) in context and the expression evaluated.

Examples of implicitly specified (that is, without using an explicit verb) item-level updates include:

1. item-name ← value
2. item-name ← expression
3. item-name ← item-name + c
4. item-name ← NULL

The first two are direct (value independent) item-value replacement operations, the third is a value dependent modification of the currently stored data item value, and the last operation effectively deletes any existing value for the data item. Increases and decreases are two simple, value-dependent operations.

The distinction between value dependent and value independent item-level update actions is extremely important to backup and recovery operations. In a value dependent operation, the resulting data item value depends upon its previous value. Proper recovery requires recording both before and after values, or one of those plus the change (say '+10') to the old item value.

Update actions using explicit verb specifications provide added integrity. For example, one verb would assign a value to an item only if it was previously null, while another verb would assign a value only if the data item was previously valued, and a third verb could operate either way. The implicit update specified with a replacement statement (as discussed earlier) is equivalent to the third case—and is unable to distinguish the first two. To accomplish the first two would require a condition to be associated with the replacement statement. It could be of the form:

$$\text{IF condition THEN item-name} \leftarrow \text{value}$$

where, for example, the condition might be defined as:

$$\text{condition} : = \text{item-name IS NULL}$$

9.4.2 Record-Level Update Operations

Record-level update operations act upon a single object record instance. To modify or delete an existing record instance, the update request must name the record type and identify a particular record instance. Then record modification is simply a collection of item-level operations. Sometimes the update language does not allow the user to directly express the modification of records. Rather, the user must first read the current record into a buffer, change it in the buffer using some local commands or statements in a programming language, then request the system to use the modified record from the buffer to replace the record as stored.

Creating a new record instance requires assembling a set of data item values, either by a series of item-level operations, or by stringing together all the values for all the items in the record. Record creation (and modification) must be done in a manner consistent with the definition of the file. All mandatory data items must have a value in the record instance, otherwise the operation should not be executed. Moreover, if the new record identifier already exists in the file, the update action should not take place. For the online user, a request to create a new record instance could initiate a series of prompts whereby the system would print each data item name and the user would enter a value in response.

Deleting a record implies deleting all the data item values which exist in the object record instance. It is important to distinguish the deletion of data items and the deletion of a record instance. Even though all data items in a record are deleted, the record instance still exists (assuming no mandatory data items) until an explicit record-level delete command is issued. For the online user, it is good practice to display the entire record instance before finalizing the delete action.

The proper execution of an item-level operator may depend upon the role of the object data item in the entity record. For example, changing the value of an item upon which the records are physically ordered implies that the object record be moved in storage to maintain the defined ordering. Similarly, the value of an identifier may change the entity (say, a part number) and, therefore, such action should be disallowed, or at least restricted to a well-defined set of semantic constraints. Other instances of changing the identifier may not indicate a change in the entity, for example, changing an employee maiden name to a married name, or reassigning part numbers. Changing an identifier may also affect the representation of relationships with other entities in the database, since other records may store this identifier as a foreign key. Such consequent update actions should be (but seldom are) looked after by the system.

9.4.3 File-Level Update Operations

File-level update operations imply that some (or all) record instances in a file are to be modified based upon a Boolean selection expression. It is more important with update than retrieval that the user clearly indicate to the system how many record instances are expected to be the object of an update section, particularly if it is only one. If a large number of record instances are involved the update action can be very costly. Nevertheless, there are times when such a multiple record update facility is extremely convenient and worth the cost. If multiple update language statements are needed to perform some complex processing against the several record instances, it would be useful to have a DO loop facility for which one record instance is the object of each iteration. A Boolean selection expression could be associated with the record DO statement.

Due to the complexities of updating multiple files at a time, most systems permit a single update language statement to reference only a single file. However, for a hierarchical data structure, additional update statements may be available to insert, modify, and delete a record instance *and* its subordinate record instances. In this case, the data for the multiple records (or nested repeating group instances) would have to be entered in a particular sequence enabling the system to unambiguously create rgroup instances with the proper parent-child relationships.

SUMMARY

Database creation is the process of taking new data and storing it within the database according to its definition. If the creation function requires data in a standard format, it may be necessary to write a special conversion program to allow the input of existing mechanized files. The creation process is one of a family of conversion processes, which includes mechanization, update, revision, schema-to-userschema mapping, and revision.

If the data for a defined database is not already mechanized, that is, in machine-readable form, the organization must go through a process of gathering the data manually and entering it into the system. Data entry is accomplished by human keyboarding, a process which is prone to error if the data is not entered by people who are close to the operating environment in which the input data is generated. Keyboarding is required for initial data entry and ongoing maintenance of the database. The required level of keyboarding effort is often underestimated in new applications, even to the point where it exceeds the benefits of the system and renders a project impractical.

Update is the process of changing the content but not the structure of an established database—adding new entries, and deleting or changing old entries. The update process involves defining transactions in terms of structure and format, edit and validation criteria, instructions for mapping transaction data into the database structure, and specification of the processing actions. Transaction definition and processing instructions may be stored in a library to be executed upon receipt of the defined transaction type. Alternatively, the transaction processing information may be embodied in a user-written transaction program which is invoked upon receipt of that transaction type. Furthermore, both alternatives could be provided in a single update capability.

Update may be accomplished one record at a time with the system automatically generating data capture screen(s) based upon the definition of the file. A system may also allow user-defined data entry screens, perhaps even capturing data which will update multiple files simultaneously. In a command language, the system can provide facilities which operate on individual data items within existing records, and which create and destroy individual records. With a Boolean selection expression, the system can perform global updates on the set of records satisfying the criterion.

EXERCISES

9-1. When setting up a database within a new DBMS, which situation is likely to entail more effort for an organization: Most of the data already exists in COBOL files, or the data has already been captured and recorded manually? Explain what remains to be done in each situation.

9-2. Why is keyboarding data entry one of the biggest stumbling blocks to the development and operation of information systems?

9-3. What are the three basic ways of accomplishing database creation? What conditions attach to each?

9-4. Discuss the consequent problem of requiring input source data to be in a standard format for the creation process?

9-5. Compare the database creation process with update.

9-6. The CODASYL Systems Committee has defined the creation function somewhat more broadly than has been done here [CODASYL, 1971, pages 337 and 349]: "Creation . . . is the process of making known to the database management system a set of entries on which it can perform other functions." Accordingly, a file may exist within the system before it is defined to the system, that is, existence before definition in contrast to the normal sequence of definition before creation. Quoting again from CODASYL, creation "may mean nothing more that entering a data definition . . . for a file which already exists in machine processable form. . . . The population of the master file or data base can be achieved by the simple means of defining an existing file in such a way that it becomes acceptable to the system as a file or data base."
What threat does this procedure pose to the integrity of the database so created?

9-7. To organizations heavily involved in mechanized data processing, why might data conversion in the future prove more costly than program conversion has in the past?

9-8. In general, what are the inputs to the update process? When supporting high-volume, repetitive updates, which of those inputs are most likely to be provided in advance and stored in the system?

9-9. Identify some of the various design approaches which can be used in designing the update function.

9-10. What are the disadvantages of using a tailored (user-written) transaction program rather than a generalized database update function?

9-11. How does the update function relate to transaction-driven systems?

9-12. Describe the differences in the facilities needed to support low-volume, ad hoc ("quick fix") updates and high-volume, repetitive updates.

9-13. What are the advantages and disadvantages of immediately accepting and processing update requests and input transactions but NOT posting them directly to the main stored database until sometime later, say when sufficient changes have accumulated or periodically during times of slow processing?

9-14. Describe the basic differences among item-level, record-level, and file-level update operations. How do they work together to provide a general update facility for users?

9-15. When inserting and deleting records in a hierarchical or multifile data structure, what special problems are created by dependency (exhaustibility) relationships? How do the insertion and retention rules proposed by ANSI for the network and relational data languages solve this problem (see section 6.3.3.6)?

SELECTED REFERENCES

CODASYL Systems Committee, *Feature Analysis of Generalized Data Base Management Systems*, New York: ACM, 1971 May.

> Includes separate chapters on creation and update, and reviews how 10 systems performed each of those functions.

MORLAND, D. Verne, "Human Factors Guidelines for Terminal Interface Design," *Communications of the ACM* (26:7), 1983 July, pages 484-494.

> Includes a discussion of defaults and editing on data entry.

SCHUELER, B.-M., "Update Reconsidered," in *Architecture and Models in Data Base Management Systems*, edited by G. M. Nijssen, Amsterdam: North-Holland Publishing, 1977.

> A very thought-provoking paper. The author argues that stored data should never be destroyed by update operations which delete or overwrite existing data. All new data and modifications to existing data are strictly *added* to the database. Deleting results in setting logical delete flags rather than physical destruction. Every piece of data (items or records) is perceived as a chronologically ordered stack. The last value added is on the top of the stack with older values "pushed down" in the stack. Each entry is time stamped and all entries are retrievable from the database. The author claims that such a scheme can dramatically simplify the structure of a database system (in such areas as recovery, auditability, locking, archiving, understandability, and usability) and hence reduce system costs and ease limitations on performance. Moreover, the availability of new, cheap, high-capacity, write-once storage media, such as optical (laser) disk, may make such a scheme practical to implement.

SEVERANCE, Dennis G. and Guy M. LOHMAN, "Differential Files: Their Application to the Maintenance of Large Databases," *Transactions on Database Systems* (1:3), 1976 September, pages 256-267.

TODD, S. J. P., "Automatic Constraint Maintenance and Updating Defined Relations," *Proceedings IFIP Congress*, 1977.

PROGRAMMING USER FACILITIES
FOR SYSTEM DEVELOPMENT

10.1   METHODS OF PROGRAM ACCESS TO A DATABASE   361
10.1.1   Access to Data Directly; Bypassing the DBMS   361
10.1.2   Access to Data Using DBMS Facilities   362

10.2   COBOL INPUT-OUTPUT STATEMENTS   362

10.3   PROGRAM COMMUNICATION WITH THE DBMS   364
10.3.1   Action   364
10.3.2   Object Data   365
10.3.3   Selection Criteria   366
10.3.3.1   Content-based Selection   366
10.3.3.2   Position-based Selection   367
10.3.3.3   Selection by Unique Internal Record Identifier   368
10.3.3.4   Dependence on Indexes or Other Access Mechanisms   368
10.3.4   Userschema Definition and User Program Buffer   368
10.3.5   Error and Exception Conditions   369
10.3.6   Access Authorization   371

10.4   FORM, TIME, AND SCOPE
         OF PROGRAM-SYSTEM COMMUNICATION   371
10.4.1   Call Form and Verb Form of Communication   371
10.4.2   Time and Scope of Program-System Communication   373

10.5   ADDITIONAL FACILITIES FOR
         THE DBMS SYSTEM PROGRAMMER   375

10.6   CONVERGING FACILITIES FOR PROGRAMMING AND
         NONPROGRAMMING USERS   376
10.6.1   The Six Elements of Program-System Communication Revisited   376
10.6.2   Some Higher-Level Functions   378

         SUMMARY   380

         EXERCISES   381

         SELECTED REFERENCES   382

A programming user develops procedures which are stored for deferred execution. These procedures are written in some programming language. As described in Chapter 3, there are three types of programming users, distinguished by the languages they use to write the procedures:

1. DBMS language programmer using the self-contained command language of the DBMS.
2. Conventional application language programmer using programming languages such as COBOL, FORTRAN, BASIC, PASCAL, ALGOL, 'C', or Assembly language.
3. DBMS system programmer could use either of the above programming languages *if* they permit a high degree of generality.

Most of the earlier DBMSs were accessed through a conventional programming language. The programmer would write a program, say in COBOL, and use special verbs or calls to invoke the facilities of the DBMS. In this sense the DBMS was *hosted* in the programming language, and generally could not be used without the host. Such DBMSs have come to make up the greatest proportion of systems used in organizations today on mainframe and minicomputers. More recent is the self-contained DBMS command language, sometimes called a 'fourth generation language' to distinguish it from the host language DBMSs. The self-contained DBMS language is the norm on microcomputers; with relatively few systems offering an interface to a host language.

Programming user facilities are needed to set up a process which is to be run repeatedly in the future. After performing the same sequence of commands over and over again, an end user soon desires the ability to prestore that sequence of commands. Similarly, a system developer desires to write and store a whole set of processes to create an application system for novice end users.

A program consists of a sequence of commands or statements, usually written into a text file. The text file may be called a program, a command file, a procedure file, or some other name chosen by the vendor. The stored, executable form of the program may be:

1. The text, exactly as entered by the programmer.
2. Tokenized, that is, with the command keywords and perhaps the variable names replaced with short codes or 'tokens' to conserve on storage space. PASCAL systems often store programs in p-code, and Microsoft (MS) BASIC replaces command words with a single byte token.
3. Compiled code, generated by preprocessing the source code text and producing 'object' program code in some programming language, usually assembler or machine language.

In the first two cases above, the computer cannot execute the program directly. There must be another program in memory to read the statements, full text or tokenized, interpret them (scan and parse), and then execute them. This is called *interpretive execution*. Compiled code is generally much faster since it can be executed directly by the computer, *after* having been preprocessed by the compiler.

The simplest facility for the programming user would be the ability to place ad hoc commands or module calls into a procedure file. However, they generally need additional facilities in the language to:

- Position and display output data or literals (messages, prompts) on the screen for the user.
- Capture data or a user's response at the keyboard.
- Conditionally execute commands—IF . . . THEN . . . ELSE.
- Repeatedly execute commands—DO WHILE, DO UNTIL.
- Define and manipulate memory variables.
- Macro replacement of parts of a command string using memory variables.
- Define, allocate, and reference data buffers (can be the same as memory variables).

These facilities are normally available in a conventional programming language. Therefore, the developer of a host language DBMS does not have to provide them for the programming user. However, a well-designed, self-contained DBMS command language must have all these facilities added to the normal facilities of searching, accessing, and manipulating data.

If the database resources are to be shared by the full spectrum of user types, and if the database management system is to evolve in meeting the needs in the using environment, facilities must be provided to enable *programming users* to use the database.

This chapter deals with the facilities of a DBMS which are available to those users or system developers who want to set up prestored procedures to reference and manipulate the database. It covers the nature of the interface and the forms of communication between the system and the programming user. The primary focus is on host language DBMSs due to their historical dominance and also because a self-contained DBMS command language would generally have the same types of facilities.

10.1 METHODS OF PROGRAM ACCESS TO A DATABASE

Programs may access the stored database *through* the DBMS or *around* the DBMS. Bypassing the DBMS means accessing the data directly.

10.1.1 Access to Data Directly; Bypassing the DBMS

Some DBMSs do not provide an explicit means to access stored data through a user written program. This is particularly true for many systems available on microcomputers today. Nevertheless, it may still be possible for the user to write a program which operates independently of the DBMS. Such a program would access the data directly through the access methods available in the programming language. The programmer is not able to use the facilities of the DBMS to assist in accessing the data manipulating the data, or controlling the integrity of the data. The programmer would have to know the stored form of the data.

Each programming language has its own special storage representation(s) for stored data. For example, for sequential files, (Microsoft)BASIC stores records with variable length field values separated by commas and a 'carriage return, line feed' at the end of each record. Any field value containing a space or special character is enclosed in quotation marks. For direct access (or 'random' access) files, BASIC stores each record in a fixed number of bytes, the field values still variable length and separated by commas. FORTRAN generally stores data values in fixed length fields in fixed length records. If the DBMS documentation does not explicitly describe the stored form of the records, the user is left the difficult task of discovering the stored form, particularly the use of special characters and delimiters.

A far bigger problem with accessing the data directly is that the programmer bypasses the integrity controls of the DBMS. If the program is read only, there is no threat to the integrity of the data. When programming users go around the DBMS, they are potentially able to do anything with the stored data. This could change the stored data so that it no longer conforms to its definition or its validation criteria. Furthermore, if the data is changed and the DBMS does not know about the changes, it may make it impossible for the DBMS to correctly process the stored data file.

10.1.2 Access to Data Using DBMS Facilities

When the DBMS provides facilities for the programming user, access to the stored database is *through* the DBMS. The normal DBMS functions can be used to assist in accessing and manipulating the data, and can maintain the integrity of the stored database. This is clearly the preferred mode of interface to the database for the programming user.

The importance of providing facilities for the programming user relates directly to the objective of evolvability. A programming user facility makes it possible to extend and modify the capabilities of the system to perform certain processing functions in a more general way, in a more specialized way, or in a more efficient way than by using the system-supplied functional modules.

The most visible aspect of the facilities provided to a programming user are the language statements used to read and write a database. These input-output statements make up part of the programming language available to the programming user. It is becoming widely accepted to refer to the set of input-output statements dealing with secondary storage devices as database manipulation language (DML) statements. Although programming languages have always had input-output statements, the capabilities of database manipulation language statements are considered more sophisticated. COBOL input-output statements are examined in the next section and provide a baseline of comparison for the extended capabilities for processing a database.

10.2 COBOL INPUT-OUTPUT STATEMENTS

A discussion of the COBOL facilities to handle data on a secondary storage device provides an initial understanding of the rudimentary aspects of a database manipulation language. It also serves as a basis of comparison with the (usually) more powerful and complex capabilities of DBMS.

Early versions of COBOL only handled sequential files, that is, files stored on a sequential storage medium, and provided the programmer with four verbs. The mass storage facility was later added to COBOL to enable handling files stored on a direct access device. Starting in 1966, the CODASYL COBOL Committee began to develop proposals to extend the facilities of COBOL to handle databases with a much richer and more complex data structure. Toward this end the Data Base Task Group (DBTG), in their April 1971 report, proposed a data definition language for defining a database and a data manipulation language giving the programmer fourteen verbs with which to manipulate the database. A modification of this proposal was approved and incorporated into subsequent issues of the COBOL Journal of Development.

In dealing with sequential files, the COBOL programmer uses four verbs: OPEN, READ, WRITE, and CLOSE. The OPEN signals the intention to begin processing a named file, and CLOSE signals the end of any further processing of a named file. Along with the OPEN statement, the programmer specifies whether the file is to be used for INPUT or for OUTPUT. READ statements can only be issued for an INPUT file and WRITE statements can only be issued for an OUTPUT file. READ causes a single record, the next one in sequence, to be accessed from secondary storage and placed in the user program buffer. If no more records exist, the system returns an 'end-of-file' message. WRITE causes a new file to be created with records transferred from the user program buffer to the secondary storage device. The user must construct a record in the buffer area prior to issuing a WRITE statement. To update a file, the programmer transfers modified records from the program buffer associated with the INPUT file to the OUTPUT file buffer before issuing a WRITE. Such a procedure creates a new version or generation of the file. Not transferring the record to the OUTPUT buffer effectively deletes the record from the file.

With the development of direct access storage devices, a fifth verb, SEEK, was added to the COBOL language. In the previous case the record to be read is implicitly identified as the next one in sequence. With the SEEK facility, the programmer is able to identify a record on a logical rather than a physical basis by providing a value for the data item serving as the record identifier. In the File Control Paragraph of the Environment Division, the programmer must declare which data item is to be used as the identifier for each file stored on a direct access storage device. Once declared, a different data item cannot be designated as an identifier or used as an identifier without redefining and reorganizing the file.

Before issuing a READ or WRITE against a direct access file (the action of the SEEK verb was later incorporated into these two verbs), the programmer must place a value for the declared identifier, the search argument, in a specially designated part of the user program buffer. Upon issuance of the READ or WRITE, the system selects the record or finds the spot for a record with a value equal to the search argument. If the system cannot find a record with the same identifier value as the search argument, or if the search argument is outside the environmental limits defined for the file, the system returns an 'invalid key' message.

The READ and WRITE statements always address one whole record of a named file. In dealing with sequential files there must be a mutual understanding between the programmer and the system concerning the physical sequence of records on the file. Each READ depends upon the current position of the system with respect to the file, such currency having been established by prior READs issued against the file.

10.3 PROGRAM COMMUNICATION WITH THE DBMS

The preceding discussion illustrates how a programmer interfaces with files on secondary storage using the input-output language facilities of the COBOL language. The programmer uses language statements consisting of verbs and associated modifiers to reference the files. In addition, the language statements are issued and interpreted in a context of assumed conventions, and explicit prior communications, some of which are of a global nature. Along with issuing language statements and transferring data in and out of the user program buffer, the programmer has to be cognizant of a file sequence or provide a data item value to serve as a search argument, and he or she has to specify what action the system should take when it reaches end-of-file or if it is given an invalid identifier.

The following scenario further illustrates the interaction and intercommunication between a program and a DBMS. Recognizing that there is considerable diversity among host language systems, this scenario is intended to be generally representative of current systems, and is, therefore, somewhat more sophisticated than would be found using COBOL.

Assuming the programmer wishes to read data from a file, she must first obtain security clearance to access the desired parts of the database. To do this she may provide her name, a password, or some other means of identification. Then she can issue a command to open the file(s) or portion of the database in which she is interested. Upon issuing the read request, made in terms of the userschema, the system translates the request into schema terms. The system searches for and locates the requested data by using the user-supplied selection criteria and whatever index and access mechanisms have been established. The system transmits the relevant blocks of the stored database from secondary storage to a section of main memory, called the DBMS buffer. By comparing the schema to the userschema, the system further selects, converts, and otherwise transforms data as it is being transmitted from the system buffer to the user program buffer. The system resets the currency pointers, reports any error or exception conditions, and transfers control back to the requesting program.

The program and the DBMS communicate in terms of six types of information:

- Action
- Object data names.
- Selection criteria.
- Userschema definition and user program buffer location.
- Response on detection of error or exception condition.
- Access authorization.

In addition to *what* information is communicated, are the dimensions of *how* the information is communicated and *when* the information is communicated. All three of these are discussed in succeeding sections.

10.3.1 Action

The action information refers to the verbs which the programmer uses to tell the DBMS what to do. Action statements include two types: retrieval statements which do not change the contents of the database, and modification statements which do change the content of the database.

Retrieval statements may be provided to:

- *Locate* data in the database to determine its existence or to prepare for further processing. This often results in data being brought into the DBMS buffer, but does not make it available to the user program.
- *Access* data, that is, move located data from the system buffer to the user program buffer, performing any required schema to userschema conversions in the process.
- *Locate and access* data.

In systems which permit multiple user programs to concurrently access the database, it is desirable for programmers to be able to indicate their intention to subsequently modify data at the time they request its retrieval. Such notification would effectively instruct the system to lock out any intervening attempts to modify the retrieved data by another user program. Some systems provide modifiers to the action verbs to communicate such holding action.

Modification statements may be provided to:

- *Add* new data to the database.
- *Change* existing data.
- *Delete* existing data.

In addition, some systems provide statements to reorder the entries in a file or instances in a repeating group, and statements to "connect" or "disconnect" group instances from certain group relations.

Deletion of data from a hierarchic or a multifile database structure always raises the problem of how to handle the dependent or subordinate data. It is often desirable for the system to provide modifiers to be used with the delete verb. Such modifiers could be used to say: delete all dependent data regardless of any other relationship, delete dependent data only if it has no other parent relationships and therefore would be left dangling if this parent were deleted, or do not delete the named data if it has any dependent data in which case the programmer must delete the dependent data, from the "bottom up."

A common practice in the design of database manipulation language statements is to combine an action with a frequently occurring selection criteria to form a special purpose verb. Such verbs include 'read parent,' 'read next' as contrasted with 'read starting from the beginning of the file,' 'read next within parent,' or 'read last.'

10.3.2 Object Data

The second type of information to be communicated to the DBMS conveys the names of elements in the database structure which are to be the object of the action part of the statement. In general, the programmer will name files, groups, and data items. To the extent that names are not unique within a database, the programmer will have to provide additional qualifying names to resolve any possible ambiguity of reference. Where only one file can be addressed at a time, the file name may be determined globally or by default. Similarly, where the system always retrieves or writes a complete entry of a file (as with COBOL), it is not necessary to name any groups or data items to identify selected portions of an entry.

With a system which permits a programmer to reference more than one file at a time and also permits referencing a subset of the data within a file, the naming of object data may take the form:

$$\text{group-name IN file-name}$$

or

$$\text{item-name IN group-name IN file-name}$$

If all item names are unique within a file and the programmer wishes to reference multiple items at once, the naming of object data may take the form:

$$\text{item-name-1, item-name-2, item-name-3, IN file-name;}$$

or

$$\text{file-name (item-name-1, item-name-2, item-name-3).}$$

Many variations are possible in naming the object data in the database structure. These depend on such factors as the types of data structure elements which can be defined and the rules for choosing names for those elements.

10.3.3 Selection Criteria

A file consists of many records of a single record type, that is, conforming to a single definition. In any database, there will generally be many instances of the named object data. The selection criteria information identifies which instance(s) of the object data are to be selected.

The basis for the selection criteria may be either position or content.

10.3.3.1 Content-based Selection

In content selection, the criteria is expressed in terms of the contents of the named object data instances. This may range from a simple criterion, such as the equality of a predeclared key data item with a search argument value (as in COBOL), to a full Boolean expression. The Boolean selection discussed under Retrieval (Chapter 7) represents the fullest form of content selection and is equally applicable in the context of programming user facilities.

Both programming users and nonprogramming users must be able to identify selected instances of repeating data structures (such as records). The normal and most natural way (natural, that is, from the user's viewpoint) to identify instances of a repeating data structure is on the basis of criteria applied to the content of that data structure and expressed in the form of a Boolean expression. Since the function is the same, the mechanisms should be the same for both types of users. This idea is in direct opposition with that expressed by the CODASYL Data Base Task Group, which stated in their 1971 proposal, "The DML is not an inquiry language and does not provide for selection criteria in the form of Boolean expressions." Unfortunately, most vendor "implementations" of the CODASYL-DBTG proposal do not offer content-based Boolean selection expressions or offer only a restricted capability.

When selection is expressed in terms of criteria on the content of the database, that is, the values of data items or the values of other attributes of any data structure element, there is no inherent dependency on the ordering of a file, on the sequence of processing the entries in a file, or on the physical access mechanisms.

10.3.3.2 Position-based Selection

Position selection depends upon an existing or assumed sequence on the instances of the object data. Both the programmer and the system must have a common understanding regarding the sequence of records in a file. The positional criteria are expressed using such phrases as 'first,' 'last,' 'nth from the first' or 'nth from the last.'

Additional positional criteria may be based upon the concept of **currency**. Once the system has successfully executed a database manipulation language statement which names object data and locates or selects particular instances of the object data, there will exist, in effect, if not in fact, a pointer into the database. The pointer "remembers" the most recent place in the database that the system looked or acted, hence, the concept of currency and currency pointers. A currency pointer is analogous to a book mark. The system may maintain several currency pointers to remember the most recent instance of each type of database structure element that the system referenced for a given user program.

Coupling the concept of currency with an understood sequence, the programmer may express positional criteria relative to a currency pointer using such terms as 'next,' 'prior,' 'nth instance back,' 'nth instance forward,' 'parent,' or 'first dependent.' If there is an implicit 'next' in a read verb, it may be desirable to have a 'reread' verb, which also depends upon a currency pointer for its proper execution (though not an assumed sequence).

With the ability to express positional selection criteria, the system may also permit the use of clauses with the various action statements to update, or suppress the update, of the currency pointers after the successful execution of the action statement. Additional statements may also be provided to save the currency pointers and to reset the currency pointers to some previously saved position.

Under sequential processing, it is possible to select on both position and content criteria. Under random processing, some nonpositional criteria must be used for selection. In general, position and content criteria can be used in combination in a given DML statement. Positional criteria can be incorporated into the Boolean selection expression by such phrases as

READ. . . WHERE group-name AT 3

identifying the third instance of the named group, or

READ. . . WHERE group-name AT N-1

identifying the second last instance of the named group.

If a system does not provide a full Boolean selection expression capability which can reference multiple levels or multiple parent-dependent relationships simultaneously, then it leaves to the user the responsibility for traversing the paths in the tree or network in search for the desired data in the database. If the responsibility for record selection is left to the programming user, the system must provide positional selection criteria which uses the concept of currency. In this way, the programmer is literally able to navigate or step through the database selecting the desired data and acting on it.

10.3.3.3 Selection by Unique Internal Record Identifier

A third basis for selection criteria is some form of unique internal identifier assigned to each record or group instance when it is put into the database. Since this selection criteria is more "physical" and therefore more artificial to the user, it should have restricted usage. Furthermore, since the unique internal identifiers may change during a reorganization of the database, their use as selection criteria should be limited to a single execution of a user program.

10.3.3.4 Dependence on Indexes or Other Access Mechanisms

The use of selection criteria often constitutes a point of significant dependence of the database manipulation language on the database definition language. The definition may specify which data items are to be keys (so that indexes can be constructed for efficient retrieval), and it may specify the access methods or paths to be used in accessing each type of data structure element. For example, if records are defined to be stored at an address calculated from a transformation on certain key items, it may thereafter always be necessary for the user to supply the values for those particular key items prior to every reference to the file. The real question here is, can the user, not having the key values, still access records in the file based upon other criteria?

The decisions embodied in the database definition are made at a point in time, considering all anticipated patterns of usage. If someone makes a request using criteria that do not conform to the search mechanisms established in the definition, they should only have to pay the price of inefficiency, not infeasibility. Many systems today freeze the modes of access and selection at database definition time. This severely restricts the programmer from using the most natural method of selection—identification based upon content, any content—referenced within some Boolean selection expression.

10.3.4 Userschema Definition and User Program Buffer

Every program which references the database must have one or more userschemas associated with it. The userschema is a definition of a data structure as the programming user sees it when writing a program, and, therefore, as the program expects to see it during execution. The userschema provides the definition and the structural context for the data names as the object of the action and for the data named in the selection criteria.

The userschema is actually made up of three parts—a logical data definition, a physical storage or buffer definition, and a mapping.

The **logical data structure definition** provides the names, other defining attributes, and structure, of the data as seen by the program. Since actual data will be delivered to the program during execution, the logical definition must ultimately have a

physical representation. Such a representation will be made manifest in one or more areas of main memory, collectively called the user program buffer. The user program buffer receives data transferred by the system from the database to the user program in response to a retrieval statement. Similarly, it is the place where the user places data prior to issuing a statement to transfer it to the database. The definition of the user program buffer and the allocation of space for it in main memory derive from the userschema definition. As such, the programmer can reference the data in the program buffer logically, based upon the userschema definition, even though he or she knows that physical data is being referenced and moved.

The **buffers** associated with the userschemas can be set up at compile time or during execution when the program first signals its intent to begin processing a file or portion of the database (perhaps with an 'open' statement). Generally, a buffer would be set up for each userschema. Furthermore, if the system allows the programmer to give a buffer address as one of the parameters with each statement or call issued to the DBMS, it is possible for multiple buffers to be associated with a userschema at any given time. In this way the programmer is able to set up a subfile, that is, several instances of a group or entry, in main memory during execution. When user program buffers are set up and allocated by the compiler, there is usually only one per userschema. However, this restriction can be circumvented by essentially performing a double move when data is transferred to or from the database. The INTO and FROM capability in CODASYL-COBOL takes this approach by allowing the programmer to name a second area of main memory where data will also be placed.

The third part of the userschema defines the **mapping** or correspondence between elements in the userschema and elements in the schema. Often the correspondence only requires associating the names of data items, groups, and files in the userschema with their counterparts in the database schema. From that correspondence definition the system will generally be able to determine what mappings, transformations, and conversions are required when data is transferred between the user program buffer and the database. Further mapping information is needed if there is not a one to one correspondence between data elements in the userschema and the schema. This may occur, for example, with a virtual item in the userschema which requires a formula defining how its value is derived from items in the schema. It may also occur if a group of the userschema consists of data items taken from more than one group in the schema.

10.3.5 Error and Exception Conditions

The fifth type of communication relates to the error and exception conditions that the system may encounter while attempting to execute a database manipulation language statement. *Exception conditions* include reaching the end of a sequential file and not finding a group or entry satisfying the selection criteria. *Error conditions* include invalid syntax in the DML statement, unidentified data names, truncation or other conversion error on transmitting data item values, and no currency pointer established.

If the user program is to operate properly even under most abnormal conditions, there must be a clear understanding between the programming user and the system concerning the communication and response to detected error and exception conditions. Some aspects of this communication and understanding will be established *a priori* by convention (or by decree of the system designers). The programmer may tell the system how to respond to abnormal conditions before issuing a statement to the system. The programmer must ensure that all types of abnormal conditions are handled properly—first by understanding what the system will do, and then by incorporating appropriate response procedures into his or her own program.

When the system detects an error or exception condition it can either return control to the program or not. After doing whatever is appropriate with respect to the detected condition the system can communicate the condition to the program in a special communication item which the program can inspect, and then return control to the requesting program. The return might be made immediately following the point in the user program at which the system was called or it could be made to a different error return location designated by the programmer. If the error condition is severe enough to warrant a termination of the requesting program, the error and associated facts would be communicated to the user through the operating system or the system operator.

When the user program regains control it must first ask of the system "how did you make out with my request?" If the system in effect responds, "I did what you asked me and everything turned out as expected," then the program can continue in the normal stream of processing. If the system responds, "I tried to do what you requested but encountered some difficulty. The abnormal conditions I detected have been communicated to you. Please look at . . . ," this signals the program to interrupt the normal stream of processing to see what can be done in response to the abnormal situation.

In addition to understanding what condition was detected by the system, the programmer must understand how the system left things, such as the status of the currency pointers and the transfer of data. Was everything reset back to the same state as before the request was issued or did the system make an attempt to complete the request as best it could? Note, too, that the program's response must be programmed in advance. To the extent that the condition cannot be handled, the program must seek additional help from the external using environment in an effort to correct the situation.

Proper and full communication between the system and the user program can contribute significantly to the integrity of the program and the application process of which it is a part. Responsible handling of all detectable error and exception conditions can enhance the integrity of the overall information system and gives users greater confidence in using the system.

Responsible handling of error and exception conditions means that the system must initially make an assumption about the user. In the extremes, the system can assume the user is naive or very sophisticated. The **naive user** is assumed not to check for the occurrence of error conditions. Even doing so, the naive user would not be assumed to know how to respond to the abnormal condition, except for the obvious case of end-of-file. Furthermore, the naive user is not generally interested in taking the time to figure out what to do. Under the naive user assumption the system should terminate execution of the user program.

The **sophisticated user** does not want his or her program to be terminated except in the case of totally unrecoverable error conditions. Such users prefer to be told what happened so that they can try to correct or properly respond to the condition. They will include all the necessary procedures in their programs to test and respond to conditions. Under the sophisticated user assumption, the system must return information and return control to the user program. In addition, the system should be able to police the fact that the user responded to the condition. This could be done, for example, by requiring that the user program reset the flag error before the DBMS will execute the next request.

Rather than the system blindly making the naive or the sophisticated user assumption, the user can declare which type of user he wants to be. The user simply tells the system whether or not he is going to try, to the best of his ability, to handle all error and exception conditions. Alternatively, the system can give the users a terminate option when they declare how the system should respond to an error or exception condition. The users can write in their program, in effect, 'do this, and if you cannot, do that' or the user might give the system more than one choice by saying, in effect, 'do this, and if you encounter error type A, do that, and if you encounter error type B, do the other.'

10.3.6 Access Authorization

In the sixth type of communication, the programmer must supply sufficient identifying information so that the system can check its access authorization tables to ensure that the programmer has received clearance to do what he is asking to do.

Access authorization includes identification of the user, identification of the data to be accessed, and an indication of the action requested on the data. The identification of the user may be explicit in the form of a name or other identifier, or it may be implicit in the name of the program being executed. In the latter case, the initial steps of security clearance are performed by the job management system. The data to be accessed may be identified in terms of a whole database, a file, a group type, a set of group or entry instances satisfying a given selection expression, or individual items. The requested action against the identified data may be controlled in terms of retrieve only, add only, retrieve and add, or modify.

There are many ways to accomplish access authorization. Whatever the established procedure, the programmer must apply the appropriate information and satisfy that authorization procedure before being permitted to access the database.

10.4 FORM, TIME, AND SCOPE OF PROGRAM-SYSTEM COMMUNICATION

The previous six types of communications between a program and a DBMS covered *what* information is communicated. This section discusses *how* and *when* the information is communicated.

10.4.1 Call Form and Verb Form of Communication

Form concerns *how* information is communicated. The two basic forms of program-system communication are the "call" form and the "verb" form.

In the **call form** of communication, the programmer's request to the DBMS is written in the form of a subroutine call statement. The call statement includes a parameter list containing some or all of the types of information discussed in the previous section. The syntax of the call statement and the parameter list would conform to that of the host programming language. The syntax of the actual parameters would not have to conform to the host programming language syntax, making it relatively easy to use the facilities of the DBMS from several host programming languages. The called subroutine may be a single control module which interprets the request and transfers control to the appropriate function modules, or the call may be made directly to the function modules. Each host programming language may have its own central control module to be called.

The **verb form** incorporates new database manipulation language verbs directly into the host programming language. The information to be included in the request is written in a free form narrative style using verbs, modifiers, phrases, and clauses. Generally, the syntax of the DML statement must conform to the general syntax rules of the host programming language, making it more difficult to incorporate the facilities of the DBMS in several host programming languages.

The narrative verb form is easier and more natural for people to use, whereas the call form of communication tends to be less natural for the human user due to the separator or fixed form of the calling parameter sequence. On the other hand, the relative fixity of the call form tends to be more efficient from a machine standpoint. The narrative verb form requires a character-by-character scan of the request.

In the call form no modification of the compiler is necessary. In the verb form either the compiler must be modified to recognize and generate code for the new statement types or a special precompiler has to be written. The precompiler method is more frequently chosen since it leaves the compiler inviolate. However, it sometimes leads to awkward and inefficient object code. The greater effort in using the DBMS from several host programming languages results from the need to modify the compiler or write a precompile for each host language.

The verb form, whether handled in the compiler or a precompiler, fixes the request in the object code. During execution it is seldom feasible for the program to modify a DML statement. On the other hand, the call form is inherently interpretive. The values of parameters in the calling sequence are set and can be changed during execution. This permits the program to loop on a request, changing some of the parameters on each iteration.

An intermediate solution is to combine the two forms of communications resulting in maximum flexibility for the programmer. A call form can be used as a skeleton with one of the parameters (perhaps the only one) pointing to a DML statement written in a narrative verb form. In this case, the DML statements can have a common syntax across several host programming languages, thus necessitating only one program module to scan and interpret the DML statement.

The greater flexibility of this intermediate solution is not without its cost. Since the narrative DML statement is a parameter in the call statement, it will pass right through the compiler. Instead of being scanned and interpreted once, at compile time, the DML statement must be scanned every time it is encountered during execution. In some situations this can result in a significant reduction in machine efficiency . . . and a significant improvement in people efficiency. Since the DML statement is scanned and interpreted each time it is encountered, it is possible to modify the same statement between issuances. This could be a most powerful capability within a processing loop.

10.4.2 Time and Scope of Program-System Communication

So far, the discussion has focused on the actual action request. However, all the information needed to properly interpret and execute a request need not be given at one time. Some of the information may be provided in explicit prior statements or declarations which preset certain conditions, and some may be assumed implicitly through an understood system convention. When information is constant over several successive requests, it is desirable to allow the programmer to give a one-time global declaration. Such a procedure is simpler for the programming user and more efficient for the DBMS.

Normally, a DML statement is issued and interpreted within a context. The statement context can be established at several prior points in time:

- Immediately prior to the request when data is placed into the buffer, or when some communication variables are set, such as search key,
- Prior action statements which, for example, establish the currency pointer,
- Prior control statements such as open,
- When the userschema is defined, or
- When the system is built, in which case the condition or context is established by convention (or decree).

All prior information communicated to the DBMS establishes a context which both the system and the programmer must remember when a DML statement is issued.

It would be impossible to present all the ways in which information could be given in advance or assumed by the system. The following paragraphs will, therefore, only be representative.

Open and close statements are often used to signal the intention of the programmer to begin and cease processing of a named file. Issuance of the open statement gives the system the opportunity to initiate some preparatory actions, such as read the userschema, allocate memory space for user program buffers, and ensure the online availability of the named file. The close enables the system to finalize all updates issued against a file and to release buffer space. Without an explicit open statement, the activity associated with an open is carried out upon the issuance of the first action statement against a particular file.

An initial **declaration of processing mode** is required by most DBMS. One distinction made is between sequential and random processing. If the system knows in advance that the programmer only intends to process sequentially through a file, greater processing efficiency can be realized. Similarly, if the system knows that the programmer intends to process randomly, it always knows that it must obtain some content-based selection criteria. The processing mode declaration can also be an aid to the programmer. For example, under sequential processing, statements which would cause the system to move backwards in the file would not be permitted. A file stored on a sequential medium cannot usually be processed randomly.

Another type of processing mode declaration relates to input, output, and update. Under input mode, the programmer intends to only retrieve from the file. Any statement which calls for a modification of the data would not be executed. Output mode indicates the intention to add data to the database, often starting from scratch to create a file. Update mode incorporates both input and output. Under random processing, update mode would indicate the programmer's intention to update in place. Updating a sequential file requires that a new copy be created. In this case, the system could automatically declare an output file with the same definition as the input file, or it could disallow the combined declaration of random and update modes of processing. The input, output, and update mode declaration is useful to the system in controlling the operation of concurrent processes.

Both types of mode declaration (sequential or random; input, output, or update) are usually made at open time. Alternatively, the declaration may be associated with the userschema definition, or perhaps the declaration could be changed between an open and a close. It may also be desirable to give mode declarations for portions of data within the object data named in an open statement. For example, a programmer could declare modes of processing for each group type or record type to be processed.

For maximum flexibility a **user program buffer** area would be named with each DML action request. Alternatively, a single user program buffer can be associated with each defined userschema so that the buffer location is implicit in the name of the file or group within the userschema. Normally, the data to be put into the database with a modification statement is not included directly with the request. It is usually placed in the buffer prior to issuing the modification request.

The location for the **error or exception** condition code can be given at request time or it can be established earlier—declared at the beginning of the user program or by convention. It may also be possible to declare to the system that on the detection of certain specified conditions, it is to take a particular course of action, such as execute a named subroutine, until further notice.

Information for **access clearance** is generally supplied earlier than at request time. It can be given when the execution of the program is requested, when the userschema is defined, or when the open statement is issued.

When one considers supplying the **selection criteria** in advance of the actual action request, several interesting processing possibilities arise. Suppose that the programmer wishes to process a set of records, entries, or group instances in a similar fashion. One possibility is to assume sequential processing and issue a statement of the form:

READ NEXT IN file-name WHERE selection-expression.

Such a statement would be included in a processing loop and the loop would be exited upon reaching end of file. Each time the system executes this statement it must process the selection expression. An alternative would be to give the selection expression to the system only once thereby establishing a subset of the file for further processing. For example, the statement might appear as follows:

LOCATE RECORDS IN file-name WHERE selection-expression

followed by the statement:

READ NEXT

within a processing loop.

Carrying this one step further, a variation of the DO-loop could be used:

DO READ file-name WHERE selection-expression.
    < processing statements >
                :
    ENDDO

where the selection expression is provided with the DO statement. The DO statement would cause the system to read another record satisfying the selection expression, for each iteration of the processing statements between the DO and the ENDDO statement. Upon reaching end of file, the system would branch to the statement immediately following the ENDDO.

Carrying this still further, a selection expression could be provided with the open statement to indicate that the programmer was interested in looking only at records satisfying that condition. Similarly, a selection expression could be associated with the userschema definition. The effect would be the same except that the selection expression would be fixed in the userschema definition rather than the open statement. If the selection expression passed through the compiler for the system to scan and interpret during execution, greater flexibility would be derived by having the selection expression with the open statement.

10.5 ADDITIONAL FACILITIES FOR THE DBMS SYSTEM PROGRAMMER

The DBMS programming user requires facilities that will assist in writing more generalized or more efficient programs. The DBMS programmer is assumed not to know what part of the database is to be processed until their program is in execution and receives its input data. This distinguishes the DBMS programming user from the conventional application programming user.

There are three consequences of not knowing *a priori* what data is being processed. These consequences indicate the facilities needed by the DBMS programming user in addition to those provided for the application programming user. The DBMS programming user must be able to:

- Access the stored database definition at execution time.
- Defer definition of the user program buffer until execution time.

- Construct, at execution time, the statements which call upon the facilities of the DBMS. This requirement is facilitated by having a fixed form or machine-oriented interface with the system rather than the narrative form.*

It may also be safe to assume that the DBMS programming user is more knowledgeable and hence less error prone than an application programming user. Since application programming users may not always be cognizant of the full implications of their actions, it may be reasonable to terminate their programs for all but the simplest of errors. On the other hand, the system should fully communicate any detected errors back to the DBMS programming users under the assumption that they will test the conditions and know what to do in response. The system should make the "sophisticated user" assumption for DBMS programming users.

10.6 CONVERGING FACILITIES FOR PROGRAMMING AND NONPROGRAMMING USERS

The retrieval and update facilities for nonprogramming users and the facilities for the programming user have been discussed. This last section takes a comparative look at the two classes of facilities. The 1971 CODASYL Systems Committee report [page 359] stated that "the facilities provided by a system for the programming user represent capabilities which are distinctly different from the functions of Data Definition, Interrogation [Retrieval], and Update." While this statement may be true historically, it bears closer examination in the light of what has been described so far.

10.6.1 The Six Elements of Program-System Communication Revisited

The facilities for programming users and nonprogramming users are examined on several different dimensions. The first six correspond to the six types of program-system communication discussed in section 10.3.

The **actions** which each type of user performs against the database are very similar. The programmer accomplishes retrieval with such verbs as READ, FIND, SEEK, or GET while the nonprogramming user issues such commands as PRINT, LIST, QUERY, or REPORT. The *functions* at this level are essentially the same—involving input or output. Other parameters and the context of the command must be examined to more readily distinguish between the two classes of facilities.

In terms of **object data**, there appears to be a significant difference between the two classes of users. While both users may name data items, groups, records, entries, or files, the nonprogramming user thinks in terms of files whereas the programming user thinks in terms of records. The nonprogramming user is often selecting a subset of the file for retrieval. The programming user is often restricted to using positional selection criteria, or content selection criteria consisting of a unique key for each

---

*A fuller discussion of these points can be found in CODASYL, *Feature Analysis*, pages 437-440 ("Facilities for system programmers").

record type. Such a restriction practically assures that only one (or perhaps no) record will be retrieved.

In fact, there is no reason why a programming user cannot think in terms of files and issue selection criteria which will result in multiple selected records. By restricting the selection criteria, the programming user is responsible for finding and dealing with the multiple records satisfying a selection expression—a selection expression which is not communicated to the system. Most present-day host language DBMSs force the programming user to think in terms of records. Many do not allow retrieval of parts of a record or data from multiple records with a single command, yet these facilities should be just as available to the programming user as the nonprogramming user. A programming user should have available all the logic and generality associated with file-level processing. Some systems are beginning to offer file-level facilities to programming users, thus attesting to the validity of this statement.

Most host language DBMSs offer very restricted facilities for expressing **selection criteria**. As mentioned in the preceding paragraph, they are often limited to positional criteria or content selection based upon a unique key, or perhaps a secondary key. The section on programming user facilities argued that this is an unnatural and unnecessary restriction. The uniquely natural way to identify records in files, whether a programming user or a nonprogramming user, is in terms of a Boolean selection expression, containing multiple data items (even from multiple record types) as operands. Database management systems are beginning to appear which offer a reasonably full Boolean selection expression capability to the programming user, thus supporting our contention.

Programming users normally reference a **buffer** explicitly or at least must always be cognizant of its existence. The nonprogramming user, by thinking in terms of a file, conceptualized a complete processing step when issuing a command to the system. There was no explicit thought of navigating through the data structure record-by-record, or of moving records in and out of a buffer. This was clearly evidenced in the first five steps of the retrieval process where the input and the output were of the same form, namely, a file. In fact, the "buffer" could actually be considered the output screen or the printed page! For the programming user, the buffer serves to break up a complete processing pattern; it is a form of intermediate storage. By thinking in terms of file-level processing, programming users would have less need for the concept of a buffer. Actually, they would think of variables defined in a userschema which have values assigned to them by the programmer before a write, and by the DBMS after a read operation.

If nonprogramming users constructed a procedure using a sequence of high-level data language statements, they, too, would begin to need the concept of a buffer. The results of executing one statement could be some intermediate data which would be held temporarily (in a buffer!) for input to subsequent statements in the sequence. This is becoming more common as DBMSs provide the ability for users to construct their own database procedures to perform a whole sequence of individual DBMS commands. In fact, this facility, coupled with statements for building, displaying, and capturing information on the screen, building menus, etc., has been called an Application Development Facility or system.

The discussion of the programming user interface always assumes the existence of a **userschema**. On the other hand, the functions of retrieval and update do not often include the concept of a userschema. Since the purpose of a userschema is to represent a user view of a portion of the database and to restrict that user to only that portion of the database, its use has equal validity for nonprogramming users to simplify their view and provide a measure of integrity control. It is entirely reasonable to have a whole class of nonprogramming users query the database in terms of a given userschema rather than the global view of the database. The database administrator could provide the same generalized retrieval facility with different userschemas to different groups within the organization.

Communicating **error and exception conditions** is actually a meta-level of communication. Commands from a nonprogramming user are relatively self-contained. Upon seeing the results, the user knows whether or not the system satisfied the request. When operating "online" the user has no need for a meta response from the system saying "I did it" or "I didn't do it and here is why." Programming users are not around when their programs are being executed and, furthermore, the next command is usually highly dependent upon an expected or normal response to the previous command. They must allow for all possibilities in advance if their programs are to operate with maximum integrity. Therefore, they must always test to see if the system responded as expected. The alternative is for the system to terminate their program upon detection of the first error condition or the passing of the first untested error or exception condition.

Security conditions, the last type of program-system communication, are the same for both classes of users.

10.6.2 Some Higher-Level Functions

The nonprogramming user effectively accomplishes **file generation** at each of the first five steps in the retrieval process, that is, conceptually, if not actually, the system generates a subfile from the named file. With a full Boolean selection expression capability, the programming user would essentially be able to accomplish file generation as well.

Similarly, there is no reason why programming users should not be able to define a report format, and then select, qualify, project, derive items, and sort data to be output according to that **report definition**. They should also be able to invoke a previously stored report definition. In fact, the ability to define and generate a report exists within the COBOL language notwithstanding that such a facility is uniquely a data-oriented function rather than a programming language function.

Continuing to look at the typical nonprogramming user facilities, there is no reason why a programming user should not be able to generate an input data transaction and invoke the generalized **update** function. One commercially available system on microcomputers uses a single command, which can be embedded in a DBMS command file, to perform data entry and file update. The single command:

- Invokes a standard screen for a named file.
- Prompts the online user to enter values for the data items.
- Validates the entered data according to criteria given previously in the file definition.

- Notifies the user if an error is detected and seeks a correction.
- Requests user confirmation that the entered data is correct.
- Writes the record to the data file on disk.
- Continues accepting data and writing records to the datafile until the user indicates there are no more records to enter.

All with a single command!

Both programming and nonprogramming users must know and should be able to **access the data definition** of the data they are processing. The application programming user and the nonprogramming user need to refer to it at the time they formulate their request to the system, the latter doing it in terms of the userschema when writing a program. On the other hand, DBMS system programmers do not know what data their programs will need until they are in execution. Therefore, they must be able to write commands in their programs to access the database definition. It is of little help for them to obtain a hard copy of the database definition from the database administrator prior to writing their programs.

Some may be tempted to distinguish between programming users and nonprogramming users in terms of the **degree of procedurality** in formulating their requests to the system. Some self-contained DBMSs are very procedural offering such facilities as branching, conditional branching, loop control, temporary and local variables, definition of subroutines, subroutine calls, and arithmetic computation. All of these facilities are distinctly part of a conventional, procedural programming language. In fact, with all this procedurality, nonprogramming users may have to think of records a good part of the time. They are "programmers" in the fullest sense of the term but are not writing in a conventional programming language—they could be writing in a high-level, data language, building procedures to operate against a database. Such a system would require a data language compiler or interpretive processor for the self-contained DBMS command language.

In most host language DBMSs, users must often think quite procedurally; but, as has been argued, they could be less so by avoiding positional selection criteria, by having file-level actions, and by having automatic iteration over multiple selected records. One thing is distinctly different—programming users generate programs in some conventional programming language (which is precisely why they are called programming users). The database manipulation language statements are handled in one of three ways—by a precompiler, by extensions to the programming language compiler, or by a run-time interpreter.

All this seems to say that the data-oriented facilities for each class of user are very similar; it is the nature of the interface which is different. That difference is further obscured when looking at a person, online, operating in conversational mode, using the DBMS facilities. The real distinction then becomes whether the users have each request executed immediately, line-by-line as they "converse" with the system, or have a "one-way conversation" which is stored for deferred execution.

With all these database management facilities and this high degree of similarity, we can conclude that indeed it is *one* system serving two (or more) classes of users, the only difference being in the form or language of the interface—the front end.

Others have expressed the design goal of producing one underlying system of database management facilities. The following statement says it well. It comes out of the DIAM Project at IBM when they were developing a Representation Independent Language:

> "In contrast to a 'data sublanguage' [DML], it has been our intent that RIL be complete and self-contained. That is to say, RIL should, in and of itself, provide a user with the facilities necessary to specify any reasonable query or transaction—without recourse to procedural statements written in some 'host' programming language. Although certain statement-types from RIL might, with appropriate syntactic modification, be embedded in or interfaced with an existing programming language (e.g., COBOL, PL/I, etc.), our goal has been to develop a language that can be used by those persons who have neither the need nor inclination to master the subtleties and intricacies of computer programming."*

To summarize, facilities for the programming user and the nonprogramming user are not and need not be that different. The basic database management functions are the same inside, and the differences are in the packaging of those functions for different classes of users operating in different modes and in different environments. Being able to tailor a system at the boundary, that is, at the user interface, the evolvability of the system is enhanced. Various user types work at various levels to extend the system for users up the hierarchy from DBMS programming user to parametric user.

Fortunately, we are beginning to see systems which have one underlying, high-level, comprehensive command language which can be used for immediate, ad hoc execution, or written into a command file or program for deferred execution.

SUMMARY

In addition to generalized retrieval and update facilities for the nonprogramming user, a database management system should provide facilities for programmers to write their own programs to access the stored database. While writing programs, a programmer always has some conception of the structure of the database being used. The programmer's view of data is formalized in the userschema—the definition of data the way a program expects to see it.

A programmer communicates with a DBMS (through a program) in terms of the action to be performed, object data to be acted upon, data selection criteria, userschema definition and program buffer location, error and exception conditions, and access authorization. The selection criteria may be based upon content or position. Content selection requires some form of Boolean selection expression which includes named data items and their related values. Position selection depends upon an assumed sequence on the occurrences of the object data and on a pointer or "bookmark" to remember the current (or some previously established) position in the database.

Communication between the program and the DBMS can be expressed in call form

---

*Paul L. Fehder, "The Representation-Independent Language, Part 1: Introduction and the Subsetting Operation," San Jose: IBM Research Laboratory, DIAM Project, Report RJ 1121, 1972 November, page 2.

or in verb form. The call form is more efficient for the machine. Since it passes through the host language compiler, the call statement is interpreted and, hence, modifiable at execution time. The verb form is easier for people and must conform to the syntax of the host language. Since the verb form must be recognized and processed by a precompiler or an extended host language compiler, the data manipulation language commands are generally unalterable at execution time.

Program system communication can occur at several points prior to the final action request—immediately before the request when supplying update data or the value for a search key, in a prior locate or error control statement, at open time, or at the time of userschema definition. Earlier and more global declarations of processing intent yield more efficient communication and make possible more efficient execution of requests.

The role of DBMS programming user is important for writing generalized or more efficient programs to extend the functional capabilities of the DBMS. The DBMS programming user is not assumed to know what part of the database is to be processed until the program is in execution and receives its input data. Therefore, special facilities are needed at execution time to access the stored database definition, to define and allocate the buffer, and to construct the request to the DBMS.

Although there is little evidence in present day DBMSs, a comparison of facilities for programming and nonprogramming users suggests a future convergence. The underlying DBMS functions remain the same for both types of user; the difference is in the packaging—how the user interfaces with the DBMS. The trend is also away from record-at-a-time DBMS facilities hosted in a conventional language, to high-level self-contained DBMS languages which can be used by DBMS programmers and novice interactive users alike. Some languages have the high-level functions discussed in this text along with the necessary facilities to control logic flow, screen displays, and perform character manipulation. This trend is even more noticeable for DBMSs on microcomputers.

EXERCISES

10-1. Some database management systems are self-contained in that they do not provide a programming user interface. Discuss the importance of programming user facilities.

10-2. What are the three types of programming users?

10-3. What are the two main methods of program access to a database?

10-4. What are the implications of accessing the stored database by going around the DBMS rather than through the DBMS?

10-5. Identify the six types of information used in communication between a programmer (in a program) and the DBMS.

10-6. How is content-based selection expressed?

10-7. How is position-based selection expressed? What does position selection depend upon?

10-8. Explain the concept of "currency" for the programming user who manipulates a data file one record at a time.

10-9. Why should record selection based upon a unique internal record identifier have restricted usage in a database environment?

10-10. What are the two assumptions a system can make regarding the user when communicating about and handling error and exception conditions? What are the conditions for each assumption? Is one assumption necessarily better than the other?

10-11. Under the naive user assumption, the system normally terminates the program when an abnormal or exception condition occurs, except for one particular situation. What is that?

10-12. What is the difference between exception conditions and error conditions that a system may encounter when trying to execute a data manipulation statement?

10-13. Contrast the call form and the verb form of program system communication. List the advantages and disadvantages of each.

10-14. Describe an intermediate form of program system communication which has most of the advantages of the call form and the verb form.

10-15. What three facilities does a DBMS system programmer need in addition to those provided for the application programming user?

10-16. Should programming users and nonprogramming users have the same facilities? Why? What are the key differences?

10-17. Regarding the suggested convergence of programming user and nonprogramming user facilities, examine each of the following and explain why convergence is possible or impossible:

- Actions performed.
- Identification of object data.
- Selection criteria—content and position.
- Userschema.
- Buffer definition and location.
- Error and exception conditions.
- Security clearance.
- File generation.
- Report definition.
- Inputting transactions to the generalized update function.
- Access to the database definition (schema).
- Degree of procedurality.

SELECTED REFERENCES

BACHMAN, Charles W., "The Programmer as Navigator," *Communications of the ACM* (16:11), 1973 November, pages 653-658.
    Based upon his Turing Award lecture, Bachman argues that programmers want and will always need the ability to navigate through a database structure from record to record. The evolution of DBMS languages and commercially available DBMS products since then has shown this argument to be less and less true, as also suggested in this chapter.

CODASYL Data Base Language Task Group, *COBOL Data Base Facility Proposal*, Ottawa, Canada: Government Department of Supply and Services, 1973 March, 140 pages.

CODASYL Programming Language Committee, *Data Base Task Group Report*, New York: ACM, 1971 April, 273 pages.

CODASYL Systems Committee, *Feature Analysis of Generalized Data Base Management Systems*, New York: ACM, 1971 May, 520 pages.

CODD, E. F., "A Relational Model of Data for Large Shared Data Banks," *Communications of the ACM* (13:6), 1970 June, pages 377-387.

EVEREST, Gordon C. and Edgar H. SIBLEY, "A Critique of the GUIDE-SHARE Data Base Management System Requirements," *Proceedings of the 1971 ACM-SIGFIDET Annual Workshop, "Data Description, Access and Control,"* San Diego, California, 1971 November 11-12, edited by E. F. Codd and A. L. Dean, New York: ACM, 1971, pages 93-112.

FEHDER, P. L., "The Representation-Independent Language. Part 1: Introduction and the Subsetting Operation," San Jose: IBM Research Laboratory, DIAM Project, Report RJ 1121, 1972 November 2, 39 pages.

GUIDE-SHARE Database Requirements Group, *Data Base Management System Requirements*, New York: SHARE, Inc., 1970 November 11, 132 pages.

McGEE, William C., "Application Program Data Structures in the Data Base Environment," paper presented at the New York University Seminar on "Data Base Systems—Current Theoretical and Pragmatic Issues," New York, 1970 January 26-29, 33 pages.

OLLE, T. William, "UL/1: A Non-Procedural Language for Retrieving Information from Data Bases," *Information Processing 68*, Volume 1, Proceedings of IFIP Congress, Edinburgh, 1968 August 5-10, edited by A. J. H. Morrell, Amsterdam: North-Holland Publishing Co., 1969, pages 572-578.

SU, Stanley Y. W., Hsu CHANG, George COPELAND, Paul FISHER, Eugene LOWENTHAL, and Stewart SCHUSTER, "Database Machines and Some Issues on DBMS Standards," *AFIPS National Computer Conference Proceedings*, 1980, pages 191-208, 53 refs.
Argue that low-level languages, such as the CODASYL DML which has been the primary focus of ANSI standardizaton efforts, are inappropriate as the interface to an efficient backend database management machine, because they generate a high volume of communication with the host computer.

DATA INDEPENDENCE, DATA CONVERSION, AND DATABASE REVISION

11.1	HISTORICAL EVOLUTION OF THE PROGRAM-DATA RELATIONSHIP	387
11.2	DATA INDEPENDENCE	390
11.2.1	Program-Data Independence	392
11.2.2	Relationship between Schema and Userschema	394
11.2.3	Physical Data Independence	395
11.2.4	Other Facets of Data Independence	398
11.3	BINDING, DATA INDEPENDENCE, AND EVOLVABILITY	398
11.3.1	Components of the Binding Process	400
11.3.2	Binding Times	403
11.3.3	Cost of Late Binding	405
11.3.4	Benefits of Late Binding: Data Independence and Evolvability	405
11.3.5	Early Binding for Greater Efficiency	408
11.4	DATA CONVERSION PROCESSES	409
11.4.1	The Family of Data Conversion Processes	409
11.4.2	Levels of Mapping in Data Conversion	412
11.4.2.1	Data Item Mappings	412
11.4.2.2	Intra-Record Mappings	413
11.4.2.3	Inter-Record Relationship Mappings	414
11.4.2.4	File-Level Mappings	416
11.5	DATABASE REVISION	416
11.5.1	The Ongoing Structural Evolution of a Database	417
11.5.2	Approaches to Database Revision	418
11.5.3	Changing Userschemas, Process Specifications, and People	419
	SUMMARY	421
	EXERCISES	422
	SELECTED REFERENCES	423

Once a database is established (defined and populated) and processes set up to use the database (including prestored queries, report and transaction definitions, and user-written programs) the demand for change becomes relentless (see Figure 11-1).

One of the greatest underlying fears of system developers and users is being locked in to their first solution, that is, the initial design of a database and associated processes. Developers often spend agonizing days seeking to ensure that the initial design is "correct." In fact, it can never be correct or complete. It is impossible to think of everything; impossible to build it all at once; and impossible to foresee all future needs, some of which will be externally imposed.

Change is inevitable. The real question is how will an organization respond to the need for change. There are only two choices—do it or not. All too often an organization is forced to forego making the change because the cost and disruption is simply too high.

The ability to readily adapt to change depends upon both:

- The degree of evolvability in the initial design and the DBMS. This means a high degree of data independence.

Figure 11-1. "I Just Installed the Perfect System, and Now the Department Head Wants to Change It."

- The tools available to accomplish the change, including, for example, a facility to redefine the database and a utility to convert the stored data.

Probably the most significant aspect of database management is the separation of the definition of the database from the processing of the database, that is, the degree of insulation between processes (programs and users) and the database. When many application programs interface with the database, it is highly desirable for changes in either the database structure or in any program to cause a minimum of disruption in the system. If attention is seriously focused on the data resources of an organization, then control of that resource must be vested outside the application programs. The database must be defined and exist apart from the programs which operate on it. This separation is called data independence. The concept of data independence is fairly simple to understand but rather difficult and costly to achieve.

The term "data independence" is an often used and much misused and misunderstood term today.* Some authors say that it can be completely achieved; some systems claim to offer complete data independence. For example, the manual for one states that "one of the key facilities provided by the system is data independence. This means that the application program is insulated and not affected by physical changes to the database or any data set within the database." While all the benefits of a high degree of data independence are presented, the costs are usually ignored.

The concept of data independence can perhaps better be understood by examining the evolution of the relationship between programs and data.

11.1 HISTORICAL EVOLUTION OF THE PROGRAM-DATA RELATIONSHIP

While this section discusses the relationship between programs and data, the same principles apply to the relationship between data and *any* processes which interact with the data, including predefined queries, the DBMS, and users.

Five stages in the evolution of the program-data relationship are shown in Figure 11-2.

Stage I: It was not too many years ago when the definition of a data file was buried within the program or programs which processed it. (This is still true in languages such as FORTRAN.) This was a natural consequence of an almost obsessive focus on programs. The file was often seen as an adjunct to the program and was designed as a derivative of the program. Outside of the program the file had little or no meaning; the physical file could seldom be interpreted and understood on its own. It had no independent meaning or value. Data independence began to appear when file transport devices were symbolically referenced in the program and resolved immediately prior to each

---

*For a glimpse at various opinions and arguments see Richard G. Canning, "The Debate on Data Base Management," *EDP Analyzer* (10:3), 1972 March, pages 10-12.

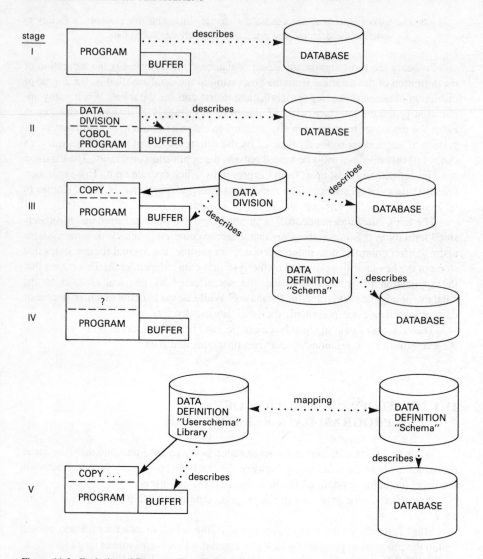

Figure 11-2. Evolution of Program-Data Independence.
   Early programming languages dispersed the data definition within the program (I). In 1960, COBOL introduced the DATA DIVISION to collect the data definition information in one place (II). This could be stored in a shared library so several programmers would use the same data definition (III). The industry remained in this state for over a decade, struggling to maintain application programs in the face of frequently revised files (IV). Finally, we began to recognize that one definition of data actually describes data in two different places—the database and the program buffer. The solution, then, is to establish two independent yet related definitions of data within the system—the schema describing the stored database, and the userschema describing a user's view of data.

execution. It also began to appear in a decoupling of record lengths between the storage medium and the buffer within the program. Some intermediate input-output control system would handle the blocking and deblocking of records. These features represented the primitive beginnings of file-level and record-level independence, respectively.

Stage II: A significant step forward in program-data independence was taken in the development of the COBOL programming language. The definition of the data within the program was brought together and formalized in the DATA DIVISION which was set apart and distinct from the PROCEDURE DIVISION. At least now it was possible to find, *in one place,* all the information defining the data.

Stage III: In the next stage of evolutionary development the DATA DIVISION of the program was stored in a library of DATA DIVISIONs. When the program was compiled, a COPY statement in the DATA DIVISION would cause the prestored DATA DIVISION to be copied into the program as a first step in compilation. This stage of development enabled multiple programs or programmers to share the same definition of a data file thus achieving, in a rudimentary way, the database management objective of sharability. Furthermore, this stage enabled central control to be exercised over the definition and redefinition of a data file thus achieving, in a rudimentary way, the objective of control over a facet of database integrity. It is interesting to note that this stage of development was reached rather early. COBOL-1961 contained the COPY statement.

Stage IV: This stage represented a period of questioning with no significant advances in program-data independence. The problem was this: data physically existed "out there" in files and the DATA DIVISION in the library described those files. During program execution, data also physically existed in the buffer of the program. Since the DATA DIVISION was copied from the library prior to compilation, *the same data definition was used to describe the data as it physically existed in two different places.* Of course, the emphasis on this statement can only be provided in retrospect.

So far there still remained (and does to a large extent even today) an absolute physical dependence between the programs and the data. The two objectives of sharability and evolvability were severely hampered. Files were designed in conjunction with the development of an application. If others subsequently wanted to use the same data file, they would have to view it exactly as did the previous application developer. Sharability demands that, ideally, different users be allowed to view the data in a way that is most natural and convenient to them.

If, subsequent to initial file design, a change in the definition of the data is required, virtually all programs which invoked that DATA DIVISION would have to be, at least, recompiled. That can sometimes be such a time-consuming task that the change never gets made and the data file becomes less available and less responsive to the need of the users. Unfortunately, this is still the case in the vast majority of organizations today. Sometimes the changes *have* to be made due to external forces beyond corporate control. Depending upon the nature of the change it may be necessary to undertake considerable reprogramming.

By the mid 1970's, the industry began to recognize how the need for data independence could be met. Some commercial database management systems had begun to offer a measure of program-data independence.

Stage V: Separate data definitions are needed to provide an initial and meaningful degree of program-data independence. Also needed is a database control system at execution time which can convert and transform the data as it is transferred between the data buffer in the program, and the system buffer associated with the database on secondary storage. Two separate definition processes are required to produce a definition of the database, called a schema, and a set of definitions of data as it is to appear in the several program buffers in the system, such a definition is called a userschema. The userschema not only defines the data as it appears in the program buffer but it must also provide the definition of the correspondence or mapping between the data in the program and the data in the database. Using both the schema and the userschema, the database control system is potentially able to perform the required conversions as defined by the mapping (or recognize when it is impossible). A more comprehensive picture of Stage V is shown in Figure 11-3.

11.2 DATA INDEPENDENCE

Use of the term "data independence" seems to have two shades of meaning in the literature. If the central focus is on programs, then data independence means the independence of programs from data—both as logically defined and as physically stored. If the primary focus is on the database, the shift in focus implied by the Copernican revolution in data processing, then data independence means independence of the database from everything else:

- From programs.
- From the definition of the database.
- From its physical storage structure and access methods.
- From storage media, machines and devices.
- From user-written, application programs.
- From predefined queries and reports.
- From update data transactions.
- From screen definitions.
- From the DBMS.
- From the design and operation of application systems.
- From users and managers.
- From the organization!

The phrase *program-data independence* denotes the relationship between the logical definition of data in the program and the logical definition of the data in the database. *Physical data independence* refers to the relationship between the definition of the logical structure of the database and the physically stored data in the database.

Ultimately, the relationship between the data processed in a program and the data physically stored in a database involves both program-data independence and physical data independence. The relationship divides into these two components of data independence—the logical to logical mapping of program-data independence and the logical to physical mapping of physical data independence.

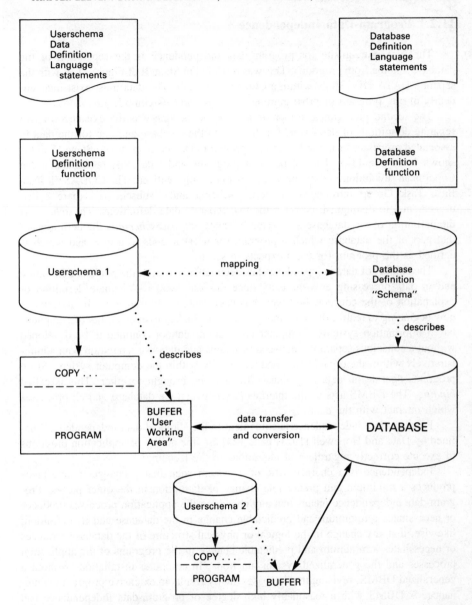

Figure 11-3. Program-Data Independence.
The fundamental prerequisite for program-data independence is to have two separate streams of data definition—one produces the "schema," the definition of the stored database, the other produces "userschemas," the definition of data the way the user wishes or expects to see it, whether in a program buffer or on a display screen.

11.2.1 Program-Data Independence

The first prerequisite for program-data independence is the separation of the database schema from programs. This was reflected in Stage II of Figure 11-2, with the separate DATA DIVISION within a COBOL program. The data must exist independently of any program or programming language (and its compiler).

The second prerequisite for program-data independence is the existence of two separate definitions of data—one for the data in the database and one for the data in associated processes or in the buffer of a program. This corresponds to Stage V and is shown in Figure 11-3. The tie between programs and data must be broken if the Copernican revolution in data processing is to be fully realized. The CODASYL Data Base Task Group introduced the terms schema and "subschema" (here called userschema) to distinguish between the two separate data definitions. The *schema* is the definition of the database as it actually exists; the *userschema* is the definition of that part of the database which a program (or user) intends to access and which is defined as the program (or user) expects to see it.

The subject of data independence has been talked about in the published literature and in data processing environments since the late 1960's. Adequate definition or explanation of the concept, however, has been lacking. Fortunately, the industry is now beginning to realize that data independence is the key to evolvability of computer-based information systems. Computer applications cannot continue to be developed without a conscious separation between programs and data—a separation both administratively within the organization and technically within the computer system. Since programs operate on data they must ultimately be brought together. This is called *binding*. The DBMS acts as the intermediary between the database and all processes which interact with the data.

Program-data independence is equivalent to the "logical data independence" defined by Date and Hopewell [1971, page 124] as "the ability of application programs to execute correctly regardless of alterations to the [schema]."

Independence is a characteristic of a system such that a change in one piece produces a minimum and predictable change or disruption in the other pieces. Program-data independence means that any change in the application processes produces or necessitates a minimum and predictable change in the database and its definition; likewise, that any change in the logical or physical structure of the database produces or necessitates a minimum and predictable change in the programs of the application processes and the generalized system functions. In computer installations without a generalized DBMS, revising the database usually results in extensive program maintenance. A DBMS with a reasonably high degree of program-data independence can significantly reduce the effort required for program maintenance caused by changes in the definition of the database. The benefits, and costs, of program-data independence are discussed further in the section on binding.

Changes in the database or the application processes are reflected in a redefinition of the schema or the userschema, respectively. A change in either data definition may be accompanied by a change in the mapping. As the database evolves, the schema and the userschema may diverge and the required mapping may get increasingly complex. Eventually, the mapping may become very inefficient or impossible to perform. At that point reprogramming would be required. In this sense, program-data independence is never completely achievable.

Data independence is a desirable ideal to approach but it is never completely possible. To even suggest that it is, does a great deal of harm because it sets up a false expectation in the minds of present and future users of database management systems.

In what sense is program-data independence never completely achievable?* To begin with, the "logical record" or userschema record must have a physical stored representation within the application program. Its definition may be explicit, as in the WORKING STORAGE section of a COBOL program, or it may be implicit as with some FORTRAN programs. Each data item delivered to the application program is physically stored in memory.

For an obvious example of the impossibility of complete data independence, consider the deletion of a data item from the database. If a program was originally written to read that data item, the next time it is run it will not be able to execute correctly. It will be asking for a data item which is no longer stored in the database.

Suppose that a numeric field is represented by a maximum of n characters in both the userschema and the database. Suppose further that, with our evolving database, the numeric field has had to be increased to n + 1 characters (our gross sales just reached $100,000,000 for the first time so we have to increase our field size). For programs that reference the expanded field, an overflow will eventually occur in transferring the data to the working area of the program. Only the program (or its compiler) could have handled such a situation by having anticipated the possibility of increased field size, tested for overflow, and taken appropriate corrective action. Only very sophisticated programmers (or compilers) could handle this situation. Therefore, it is unfair to suggest that *all* programmers and their programs will be unaffected by changes in the database definition.

Although the concept of program-data independence is generally discussed in the context of user-written, application programs, it actually applies to all programs which interface with the database. Program-data independence relates to the degree of isolation between any process and the definition and structure of the database. It applies to generalized DBMS program modules for retrieval and update as well as to application programs. Often generalized programs are written to address the entire database, which is consistent with the philosophy of being generalized. Nevertheless, under some circumstances it may be desirable to include a userschema with the generalized program. This may be done to insulate the program from changes in the database or to permit the user of the generalized program to have a simplified view of the database. For example, when the database is a complex network structure and the user desires to query multiple "levels" of the structure, he or she may have to use a userschema to invoke a view of the database which ignores some relationships defined in the database, thereby viewing only a hierarchical structure.

---

*This discussion is largely drawn from Everest and Sibley [1971].

11.2.2 Relationship between Schema and Userschema

The schema is a complete description of the entire stored database. The description is formally expressed in written statements of a database definition language (DDL). The userschema is a description of a portion of the database as it is to be made available to or accessed by a program or a user. It describes the data as it exists in the program (or on the user's screen).

Although the userschema must be consistent with and understandable by the programming language used to write the program, the userschema can be "compiled" or processed and stored separately from the program. There are several conditions on the relationships among schemas, userschemas, and programs:

- Each database has only one schema but may have several userschemas.
- Each userschema is uniquely named with respect to a given schema.
- The userschemas are independent of each other.
- Userschemas may overlap, that is, they may describe common portions of the database.
- A program or user would not be allowed to use two overlapping userschemas on the same schema.
- The same userschema may be invoked by several programs.

A significant degree of program-data independence is achieved by merely allowing a program to access or be bound to a portion of the database. The program is simplified by not having to be cognizant of the entire database. Also, the program is independent of the unreferenced portion of the database (that part of the database to which the program is *not* bound, called the *unbound* portion). In other words, the program is insulated from any changes in the unbound portion of the database. Not only is the program independent of the unbound portion of the database, it is expressly prohibited from referencing any portion of the database to which it is not bound. This guarantees the integrity and privacy of the unbound portion of the database with respect to that particular program.

An early CODASYL DBTG Report [1973, page 18] stated that the userschema must be "a consistent and logical subset of the schema from which it is drawn." Considerable confusion has since been created concerning the meaning of this statement. To begin with, it must be possible to identify the set of which the userschema is a subset. Any attempt to define the schema as a set would be a gross oversimplification. It consists of many different things having many complex inter-relationships. In fact, the only condition required is to be able to perform the mapping between the userschema and the schema. No other condition is needed. If a mapping is possible, the userschema is valid. The DBTG Report implicitly clarifies the meaning of subset by indicating that a userschema is valid if a correspondence or conversion procedure exists between the schema description and the userschema description of the data.

Some authors, and particularly DBMS vendors, suggest that being bound to only the relevant portion of the database is all that is meant by the term data independence. However, the concept involves much more. In particular, the concept of program-data independence also involves the relationship between the program's userschema and the *bound* portion of the database. Ideally, a program would be insulated from changes to the portion of the database to which it is bound.

Permitting a userschema to differ from the definition of the portion of the database to which it relates provides an increased degree of program-data independence. While some data characteristics are fixed in the schema definition, other data characteristics can be modified in the userschema definition. This implies that the physical existence of the data in the database differs from the physical existence of data in the program. Therefore, a conversion or mapping is required when data is transferred between the database and the program buffer. When the bound portion of the database is changed, the recompilation and rewriting of programs is reduced. Programs may run less efficiently or not at all, but the conversion procedure tries to ensure that they will at least run.

The data structure class of the programming language is reflected in the userschema definition. To the extent that it is different from the data structure of the database schema, some transformations and perhaps exclusions are needed. For example, if a schema data structure class does not include the direct equivalent of a three dimensional FORTRAN array, some system convention must be established for transforming one into the other. Potentially, there may be certain cases where a mapping is not defined for a particular structure in the userschema or a particular structure in the schema. McGee [1970] has explored in more detail the problem of accommodating the data structure classes of multiple programming languages to a single database structure, and the notion of a correspondence definition.

11.2.3 Physical Data Independence

Physical data independence is the other half of the independence of programs from the stored, shared database. The first half is logical independence as previously discussed—two separate logical definitions of data, a necessary condition for program-data independence. A necessary condition for *physical* data independence is the separation of the definition of the logical data structure from its physical definition and stored representation.

A parallel does *not* exist between the separated definitions in program-data independence and the separated definitions in physical data independence. This idea is illustrated in Figure 11-4. It essentially relates the two types of data independence to the database definition process shown in Figure 6-11. A complete definition of the data in a stored database consists of all three kinds of information—logical data structure, physical storage structure, and device-media information. The physical information can only be interpreted in the context of the logical information, that is, the physical information does not meaningfully stand alone. The reverse, however, is a different matter.

The logical definition of the data does provide complete communication for certain purposes such as to human users and to the logical definition of the data in a program buffer. Therefore, *if* the logical definition of the database can be looked at separately and independently of the physical definition, *then* program-data independence relates

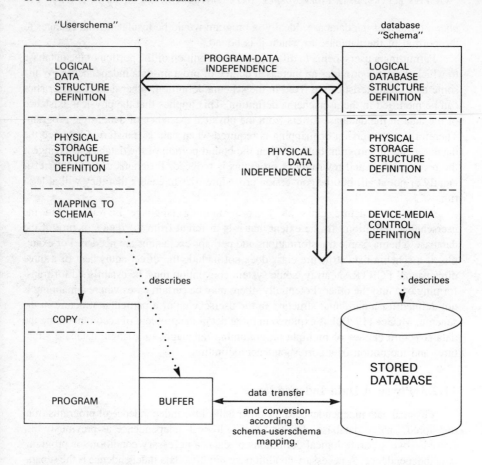

Figure 11-4. Orthogonality of Program Data Independence and Physical Data Independence.

The schema describes the stored database in terms of its logical structure and physical structure; a userschema describes the data the way the user sees it. The userschema also defines both logical and physical structure, and specifies the mapping between the userschema and the schema. Physical data independence refers to the separation of the logical database definition from its physical definition. Ideally, it should be possible to view the stored database only in terms of its logical structure, remaining insulated from any physical or access characteristics and from any changes in these defined characteristics. Program-data independence refers to the separation between the defined logical structures of the database and the user view. Some measure of physical data independence is a prerequisite to any meaningful level of logical data independence; otherwise, the user is more dependent upon the defined physical storage structure and access mechanisms of the stored database. This is all summed up in the diagram by noting the perpendicular or orthogonal relationship between program-data independence and physical data independence.

to the two separate *logical* definitions of data as it exists in two different places. Some degree of physical data independence is prerequisite to a meaningful degree of program-data independence. To be sure, the logical definition information is not sufficient to actually access and properly interpret the stored data. To do that requires the other component of information making up the complete definition of the stored data.

In the early use of computer systems, the user's view of data corresponded to the physical layout of the records. Having two definitions of data, logical and physical, permitted a richer and logically simpler user view. One early distinction referred to the logical and physical definitions as data structure and storage structure, respectively. The *storage structure* is the way the data is physically stored. The *data structure* is the user's view of the data without regard for any transformation that the data may undergo prior to storage. This assumes that the data structure provides a picture of the data which remains invariant as the underlying storage structure of the database changes. The independence of programs from data depends upon this assumption. A necessary condition for program-data independence is the ability for application programs to execute correctly regardless of the physical storage structure chosen to represent the logical data structure and the methods used to access it. There are many possible physical storage representations for a given logical data structure. The underlying storage structure may vary considerably without compromising the aim of physical data independence.

The distinction between data structure and storage structure often seems fuzzy. (By drawing the line between the two on the basis of a particular system, as has been the practice, the resulting distinction is subjective.) This is evident in the common practice of defining the data structure as the user's view of the data. In fact, the user's view of the database is highly conditioned on what the system decrees the user must know. The designers of a DBMS make their own decisions concerning what the user needs to know to reference the database. If they decide that the user should be given lots of flexibility to select the given level of performance desired, the user's conception of the data structure will include some information relating to the physical storage structure and access methods. Furthermore, having made those choices in setting up a database, the user must thereafter remember them and is dependent upon them.

What is needed now is a normative view, unbiased by any existing system, asking what the user *should* have to see. Depending on the requirements, this can range from a very simple and strictly logical view of the data, to a very detailed view including the physical organization to facilitate making tradeoffs for performance efficiency. Since the range is broad, it might be useful to introduce more than two levels of definitions to clear up the fuzziness between data structure and storage structure.

The important task is to pick a line separating logical definition information from physical considerations such that the logical definition can remain invariant across a reasonably large number of physical organizations. In this way users can have confidence that they need depend on no more than the logical definition. As was shown earlier, the CODASYL DBTG proposal and systems based on it draw the line to include a substantial amount of physical information in the schema, of which the user must be cognizant. Consequently, programmers in a CODASYL network environment must be quite sophisticated and their programs will be significantly dependent upon the physical organization of the database. To the extent that storage structure or access method information is in the schema, the userschema will be dependent upon it. Fortunately, more recent decisions by the ANSI X3H2 committee developing a standard DDL have separated out some.elements of physical storage and access from the logical data definition language specification.

Maximal data independence is achieved when the users and programs are dependent on a minimum of information concerning the database. Therefore, the highest level of database definition should be kept as simple as possible, only including the minimum of information needed by using processes to logically and naturally reference the database. Then the programs need be dependent only on this minimum logical definition, unless the programmer wants to assume further information to obtain greater efficiency or flexibility.

11.2.4 Other Facets of Data Independence

The preceding discussion has focused on two main aspects of data independence—program-data independence and physical data independence. While these are the most widely discussed facets of data independence, several other interpretations have appeared in the literature.

Lyon argues that a database should be independent of management:

> "Recognizing that management turnover is a fact, it is only logical to provide a database which is broad enough to cover the desires of any management, and which leaves the 'tailoring' of information to the process.
> "As a matter of fact, the data which describe a company and its relationship to its environment is essentially independent of management. It is only the information that is produced from the database that reflects the personality of management."*

In discussing the need for a data dictionary system to complement many existing DBMSs, Plagman and Altshuler identify a form of data independence between the database definition and the DBMS. If the system stores its own database definition, then the database is dependent upon the DBMS. They argue that the database definition (dictionary and directory) should be established and maintained separately from the DBMS so that, ideally, when there is a need to evolve to a different DBMS, a new one can be plugged in without having to make any changes to the stored database or its definition.†

11.3 BINDING, DATA INDEPENDENCE, AND EVOLVABILITY

Binding is the act of bringing together two sets of information, testing for compatibility, and setting up some form of correspondence which is assumed to hold true thereafter. Since the two sets of information are generally a program and data, binding

---

*John K. Lyon, *An Introduction to Data Base Design*, New York: Wiley-Interscience, 1971, page 3.
†Bernard K. Plagman and Gene P. Altshuler, "A Data Dictionary/Directory within the context of an Integrated Corporate Database," *AFIPS Fall Joint Conference Proceedings* (volume 41), 1972, page 1135.

is the formal association of a program with the data on which it will operate during execution. More precisely, binding is the formal association of data as the program expects to see it, with the way it exists in the stored database.

A common-place analogy may lend further understanding to the concept of binding. Once a year a person's name, address, and phone number are "bound" together and published in the phone book. Thereafter, we will refer to the phone book (assuming no other data store) to obtain a phone number. Furthermore, we may copy down the phone number into our personal "little black book"—another binding process. Thereafter, we will continue to use the number in our personal book until we have reason to believe it is in error. This practice could get us into trouble if it were not for the traditional protocol of both parties to a call identifying themselves before beginning the conversation.

The best way to avoid a wrong number would be to assume no information *a priori* and go back to the most reliable and timely source of information each time a phone number is needed—that is, call the telephone operator for directory assistance. Admittedly, this is less efficient, but it does reduce the possibility of making an erroneous and perhaps embarrassing phone call.

Of course, phone numbers change, reflecting the evolutionary nature of our telephone system. It would be unthinkable to assume that we could mandate that phone numbers never change or that if they do change, every phone book printed and every little black book would have to be updated at the moment of each change. Yet this is too often precisely what happens when a data definition is changed. All the referencing programs must be changed before they will execute correctly against the revised database. As argued before from the standpoint of evolvability, the programs and the database must be allowed to change somewhat independently. Then, each time they are brought together, a binding process takes place to compare, testing for compatibility between the program's view of the database and the actual definition of the database. If all detected differences can be resolved or mapped, run the program—perhaps inefficiently but at least it will run.

In the binding process many differences can be tested for compatibility in advance of execution. When a program is compiled, the compiler may make reference to the userschema to ensure that all data names used in the program are defined with each data element having compatible attributes. Similarly, when a userschema is processed or "compiled," it can be checked against the schema to ensure compatibility, that is, to ensure that the mapping can be performed. If this is all that were done during compilation, the process would simply be called testing or debugging.

Binding involves not only testing for compatibility, but also taking certain preparatory actions based upon any detected differences. For example, if a data item is of a different type in the userschema than in the schema, item value conversion routines could be compiled inline in the program object code with item type and size information built in. If action is taken, conversion routines established, or data description tables constructed, binding has taken place based upon the assumed characteristics of the data. The detection process will not be repeated at any future time including at program execution time.

In any computer system, programs and the data ultimately come together; ultimately, the two are very dependent and, therefore, complete program-data independence is impossible. Programs read, process, and produce data, but a program cannot access data until the data is bound to the program. There are actually three stages to the program-data relationship: testing for compatibility, binding, and finally, data transfer with any consequent transformation.

11.3.1 Components of the Binding Process

The whole framework of the program-data relationship has become formalized in the concept of the schema and userschema. If the schema and userschema are the same, there is a direct one-to-one mapping and a single definition of data is sufficient (see stage III in Figure 11-2). Traditionally, the single data definition (DATA DIVISION in COBOL) is compiled with the program into a single executable load module. This is shown schematically in Figure 11-5.

With the concept of a userschema, there are four components of the binding process: schema, userschema, program, and data. Data is added to this list because the binding process is not complete until the actual data is accessed, tested for compatibility, and transformed based upon any detected differences. With both a schema and a userschema, there are a variety of ways to accomplish the binding process. The important point is that some independence exists in compiling the first three components. The schema may be 'compiled' independently of any user program or userschema and the userschema may be 'compiled' independently of any user program.

In **serial binding**, the schema is compiled first, the userschema is compiled next using the object version of the schema, and finally, the program is compiled incorporating the object version of the userschema. In the serial binding of data to the program, shown in Figure 11-6, the information in the schema and userschema are all bound together in the object program. If any changes occur in the database schema, recompilation must be performed in a cascading fashion from the schema to the programs.

In **parallel binding**, the schema and userschemas are compiled independently. The objective of data independence is to achieve a separation between the stored database and the programs which act on it. Therefore, the separation between the schema and the userschema is more important than the separation between the userschema and the program. Also, at the time the program is written the application programmer must have some explicit picture of the data being processed. The picture is merely formalized in the userschema definition. Figure 11-7 shows the userschema and the program being bound together at compile time and the schema being compiled and stored independently. Of course, when the userschema is compiled it should be checked against the schema—checked but not bound, for the checking procedure would be carried out again at execution time.

Serial binding provides the potential for maximum machine operating efficiency; parallel binding provides maximum data independence. The most significant part of this whole discussion is a recognition that the user should be able to have a choice of binding strategy. This provides greater flexibility in responding to processing tradeoffs.

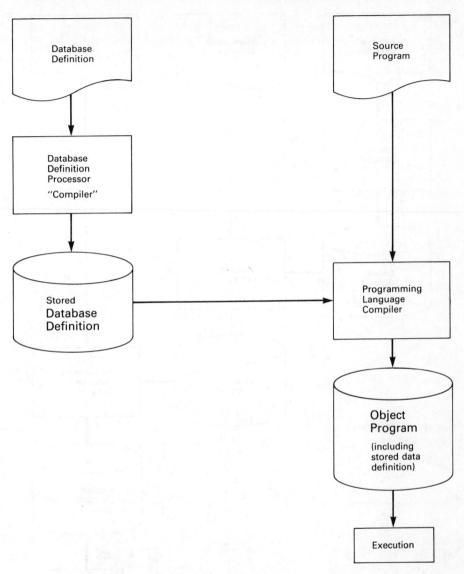

Figure 11-5. Compile-Time Binding of Data Definition.
All data references are written in the program in terms of the schema, and the program is compiled with reference to the schema. There is no userschema. The binding of the programmer's view of the data to the schema actually takes place in the mind of the programmer before the program is written. The programmer or user must change their view of the data to conform to the view reflected in the schema.

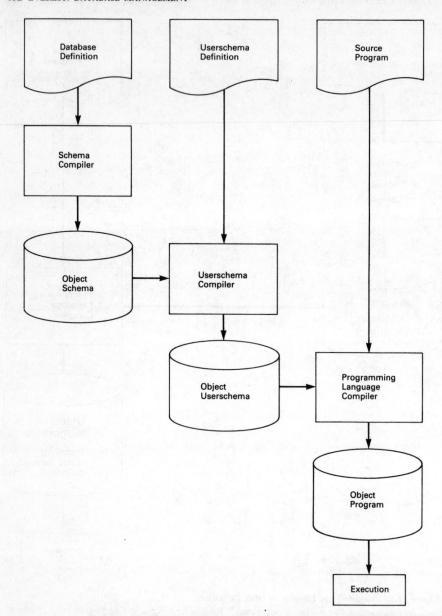

Figure 11-6. Serial Binding of Program and Database.
The userschema is bound to the schema when "compiled" and the user program is bound to the userschema when compiled. Thus the program is tightly coupled to the schema and any changes to the database schema require recompilation of the userschema and the program. However, not all of these changes are made by human effort, as they were in compile-time binding. The machine is able to assist in the process simply because the userschema was made explicit.

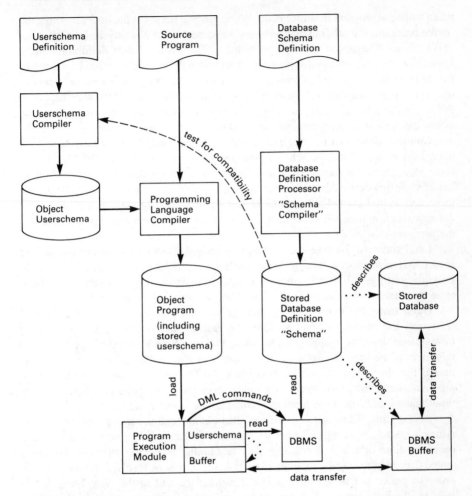

Figure 11-7. Parallel Binding of Schema and Userschemas.
While the program is bound to the userschema at compile time, neither are bound to the schema until run time. The userschema can be checked for compatibility but not bound to the schema. At execution time the DBMS reads both the userschema (generally embodied in the object program) and the schema, checks for differences and converts the data upon transfer according to the implicit or defined mapping.

11.3.2 Binding Times

The discussion in the previous section indicated that binding can occur at different times. In fact, various phases of binding can occur at five different times, identified as source, compile, load, open, and access. Just as there is the concept of levels of data independence so there is the corresponding concept of binding at each of those levels. Different levels and various attributes of data can be bound at different times.

Source code time: The earliest binding takes place in the mind of the programmer when writing a program in source code. When binding occurs at the time of writing the source program, the programmer assumes the same logical and physical definition of the database as exists at the time of writing. The assumed data definition can be implicit or explicit. Successful program execution will depend upon the constancy of the database definition and its stored representation. No mapping is required between the expression of the data definition in the program source code and the way the data is defined in the schema. A single definition serves both purposes. This level of binding offers the least data independence and potentially the highest execution efficiency.

Compile time: During program compilation, the compiler may look at and act upon information in the userschema (and perhaps even the schema, directly or indirectly through the userschema). When the compiler detects differences it may set up buffer correspondence tables or it may compile conversion routines inline. By taking these actions the compiler is assuming that the detected differences will also exist during execution time when the data is actually transferred between the database and the program.

Load time: At the time the object program and its subprograms are loaded, the loader may also link or bind to some attributes of the data. This may include, for example, setting up buffer locations and sizes in main memory and setting up correspondence tables of pointers to data elements in those buffer areas.

Open time: If the program is selective in what portion of the database it will reference, the binding actions of setting up buffers and setting up correspondence tables based upon the mapping information may best be performed at open time. At this time, or perhaps at load time, the system can ensure the online existence of the named file. In an online realtime environment where the database is online and the programs are in execution over many hours, even days, the difference between open time binding and load time binding becomes more significant.

Access time: The latest possible time that binding can occur is when the program issues a DML command to access the database. Access time binding is also called execution-time or run-time binding. Any remaining differences between the actual stored data and the way the program expects to see it must be resolved at access time in order to get or put the right data in the right place and in the right form. While inter-record differences will generally be resolved at earlier stages of binding, item value conversions cannot be performed until access time when the system has the actual data.

Except for the actual transfer of data, it is possible for all the attributes of the database to be incorporated into the object code of the program. The programmer writing the source program may have a view of the data which differs from the database schema view. Nevertheless, the compiler, loader, or open module can look at the schema and build all the required transformation and conversion routines into the object code load module. In effect, the object program during execution only sees data according to the schema definition—the structure and attributes of the stored database are all assumed by the object program. This is what is meant by full binding at some time prior to access time. With full compile-time binding, if part of the schema changes between compilation and execution, the object program could be rendered inoperative and have to be recompiled.

11.3.3 Cost of Late Binding

Lower machine operating efficiency (both time and space) is the only cost of late binding. Though late binding may render an application economically infeasible, it will never render an application process technically or humanly infeasible. The increase in machine time is required because the data definitions and program instructions are more frequently interpreted in the process of testing for compatibility and acting on detected differences. The magnitude of the cost of binding depends upon the lateness and frequency with which the binding process is performed.

Considering the five possible binding times as a hierarchy, the frequency of processing increases as one proceeds down the hierarchy to later binding times. At each possible binding time, the binding process is carried out multiple times for each execution of the binding process at the next higher level in the hierarchy. For example, a program is written once but may be compiled many times after that (perhaps with minor modifications). Similarly, the object code resulting from a single compile may be loaded for execution many times after that. Also, a program can be expected to issue many reads and writes against a file once the file is opened. Comparing compile time and load time binding, if all binding is done at load time, then all the binding activity is carried out every time the program is loaded for execution rather than once for each time the program is compiled or recompiled. Repeated interpretive processing required at the later end of the hierarchy of binding times contributes to the high cost of data independence.

11.3.4 Benefits of Late Binding: Data Independence and Evolvability

Under source-time binding, the earliest time binding can take place, the schema and the userschema are the same. There is, in effect, one data definition for all programs accessing the file. Source-time binding represents a minimum of data independence. When the database is redefined and restructured, all programs must be at least recompiled and possibly rewritten before they can be run against the revised database. Such a condition results in very high resistance to database revision. When the database is revised (as is often dictated by nondiscretionary external forces), the effect on the organization can be traumatic. The conversion effort requires substantial human resources and the redefinition, data conversion, and program conversion (for those needed regularly) must be accomplished in a very short time span.

The present-day practice of developing computer-based information systems is to select a set of applications, design a solution for that applications portfolio, and then implement the solution in a way that is somewhat optimal over the applications set. As the system is used, two kinds of forces will influence its modification. The first is a desire to have the system do what it does more efficiently. The second is a desire (or need) to have the system extended to do something new. The first force generally dominates because it is usually more immediate, more clearly defined, and less risky than changes of the second kind.

The danger in allowing efficiency forces to dominate is that in making some problem solutions efficient (optimal) some new problem solutions are made infeasible.

It becomes increasingly difficult and expensive to enhance an installed system. The future availability or evolvability of the system is seriously impaired. This is undesirable when the system is operating in and intended to serve a dynamic environment of growing users and new problems.

Later binding yields a higher degree of data independence. Full binding at access time would provide the fullest possible degree of data independence, other things being equal. Binding at any time later than source time requires the existence of two separate definitions of data—the schema and the userschema. Binding at load time or open time provides a substantial measure of data independence resulting in a significant reduction in human effort to effect system modification and enhancement. Binding at compile time provides some degree of data independence and a saving, chiefly of machine time, to effect system modification and enhancement.

Data independence through late binding makes it possible to enlarge the set of applications for which feasible solutions are possible. The parts of the system which provide the solution to the current applications set are not so intimately tied together. Therefore, subsequent changes are not so disruptive.

Independence between programs and data means that one can change without adversely disrupting the other, which in turn means that one can be designed independently, with no undue or unnatural bias from the other. Application processes can be designed and programs can be structured without being tied to a particular data structure or storage structure. Conversely, the structure and definition of the database can be designed without any undue bias toward the patterns of processing in the current set of applications, or toward the current styles and problem concerns of the managers in the using environment. The database can be designed based upon the inherent nature and structure of the data.

With a reasonable degree of data independence, the stored physical representation of the database can be changed causing little or no change in the logical data definition or the programs which reference it. The database administrator can reorganize the physical storage structure when necessary for greater processing efficiency or greater storage efficiency.

With a reasonable degree of data independence, a change in the database definition reduces the change or conversion required in the programs. Some, but not necessarily all, programs would be rendered inoperable due to changes in the database definition. The remaining programs could still be executed, initially accepting some machine inefficiency and then applying available human resources to the conversion effort based upon priority of need. Since the conversion of some programs can be deferred, the whole conversion effort is more gradual. Conversion need not be a traumatic event. At least there should be no more massive conversion efforts due to changes in the structure and definition of the database. Reducing the conversion effort increases the evolvability of the database.

With late binding and permitted differences between the schema and the userschemas, what is the mechanism for effecting a change in the database definition? The database in any management information system is dynamic. Changes in the database are reflected in changes to the schema. The userschema can remain static over a much longer period than the schema. As the schema continues to change and evolve, it will grow increasingly different from various userschemas within the system. The mapping may become more complex and the binding process may become more difficult, leading to less efficient execution of the programs associated with the userschemas. The process of redefining the database and possible degraded performance in the execution of programs can continue until it becomes impossible to perform the schema-userschema mapping with the algorithms built into the system.

A proposed change to the definition of the database will lead to one of several situations for each userschema associated with the schema. The six outcomes are described in Figure 11-8.

With this analysis it becomes evident how to respond to a proposed change to the schema. For userschemas falling into the first two categories, no redefinition of userschemas and no rewriting of programs is required to accomplish the change in the

	1	2	3	4	5	6
Userschema in changed part of schema:	No	Yes	Yes	Yes	Yes	Yes
Change in userschema required:	No	No	Yes	No	Yes	No/Yes
material adverse impact on performance:	No	No	No	Yes	Yes	can't map or inoperable
THEN CHANGE THE PROGRAM:	No	No	No	Optional	Optional	MUST!

Figure 11-8. Possible Impacts of a Changed Schema.
A change to a database schema leads to one of the following situations, as summarized in the above table:

1. The userschema does not reference the changed part of the schema.
2. The userschema references the changed part of the schema but no change is required in the userschema; it remains logically feasible with no material adverse effect on the using programs.
3. A change is required in the userschema but it remains logically feasible and does not adversely affect the execution performance of the using programs; for example, change the name of an item in the schema and only the mapping information in the userschema needs to be changed.
4. No change is required in the userschema to maintain logical feasibility but the change in the schema materially and adversely affects the execution performance of the programs using the userschema.
5. A change in the userschema is required to maintain logical feasibility and even with the change the performance of using programs is adversely affected.
6. The proposed change to the schema renders the program inoperable; the userschema must be changed and all using programs must be examined and appropriately rewritten to accommodate the change in the schema.

In the first three cases, there is no performance effect so no modifications are required to the programs. In the fourth and fifth, management has the option of modifying the program to improve performance. Only in the last case must changes be made to the program to enable continued execution after changing the database schema.

schema. Category (3) userschemas require modification with no effect on using programs.

With userschemas falling into categories (4) and (5), the only effect of the schema change is less efficient execution of the programs using the userschemas. The cost of this inefficiency in repeated processing can be weighed against the cost of reprogramming. This allows the organization to make a tradeoff between machine time resources used in inefficient processing, and human resources needed to accomplish the reprogramming. The central point is that the using organization has a choice. It can apply its human and machine resources to priority needs with some freedom in future scheduling. Frequently run programs with many references to the database will call for more frequent reprogramming. Seldom used programs may never call for reprogramming due to inefficiencies in the mapping.

Of course, programs falling into the last category (6) would have to be rewritten before they could be run again. In response to a proposed change to the database, many if not all the programs will not have to be rewritten before they are run again. The overall need for reprogramming will be reduced. By contrast, with source-time binding (stage III in Figure 11-2) *all* programs must at least be recompiled using the revised data definition, and many may have to be rewritten depending upon the proposed change to the data definition.

A set of cross reference tables can help to determine the impact of a proposed change to the database definition. A table could be maintained to show the names of the userschemas which reference or depend upon each database element such as item, group, or file. This is often provided in a data dictionary system. Alternatively, it may be possible to develop a tool to analyze each userschema and determine the impact of a proposed change to the schema.

11.3.5 Early Binding for Greater Efficiency

From the standpoint of evolvability it is desirable to bind as late as possible, but from the standpoint of efficiency it is desirable to bind as early as possible. An environment which permits late binding need not preclude early binding. To achieve maximum database processing efficiency in a program, the userschema could be defined to be a copy of the relevant portion of the schema. Furthermore, the system would have to be told that fact so that it would assume exact correspondence *a priori* without testing for compatibility. During set-up and execution, the system would not perform any conversion or transformations on data transfer.

Copying the schema as the userschema would work correctly until the schema changed. To preserve the integrity of both the process and the database it is necessary to record in the userschema the date or version number of the schema copied. The whole schema or perhaps parts of it would have an associated date of last change or latest version number. Just before execution, a comparison of these two dates or version numbers would reveal any potential incompatibility. Alternatively, when a change is made to the schema, all potentially affected userschemas could be flagged. At that point, it would be necessary to examine the identified userschemas and the using programs to determine the difference and the consequent impact on the programs, if any.

As before, if the change to the schema only has an efficiency impact, it may be desirable to continue to execute the program with a fully defined userschema, omitting the fact that it was a copy of the (old) schema. The system would operate normally, testing for incompatibilities and performing any required conversions and transformations. The less efficient execution would be an interim solution until the program could be rewritten as priority demands on the human resources would permit. Again, the central point is that the using organization has a choice, based purely on economic grounds—the cost of running inefficiently versus the cost of reprogramming in order to run more efficiently in the future.

11.4 DATA CONVERSION PROCESSES

A data conversion process takes data in one machine readable form and converts into another form. Data conversion takes place during database creation, update, and in the schema-userschema mapping discussed earlier in this chapter. These processes are all members of a family of data conversion processes.

Referring to Figure 11-9, a general data conversion process takes as *input*:

- Existing mechanized data (in a database, an external file or a program buffer) called "source" data for the conversion process.
- Its complete definition, which may be separate and explicit, may be buried in a special-purpose conversion program, or may be assumed in a general conversion program which expects the existing data to be in a prescribed format and structure.
- The definition of the new "target" data to be generated by the conversion process. The target data definition may be complete or it may be incremental to the source data definition. Also, the mapping between the two definitions may be completely implicit or partly explicit where the conversion process cannot infer the association.

The conversion process produces as *output*:

- A new collection of data (in a database, external file, or program buffer) which conforms to the target data definition.

11.4.1 The Family of Data Conversion Processes

The family of data conversion processes includes mechanization, creation, update, revision, reversion,* and the schema to userschema conversion. These functions are shown in Figure 11-10 as they relate within the family. For clarity, the source and target data definitions required of each conversion process are not shown.

In a DBMS it is highly desirable for data conversion to be performed by the same underlying modules in the database control system. The availability of rich data conversion facilities in each of the members of the family of conversion processes determine the degree of overall data independence exhibited in the system, thus contributing

---

*Also called file writing or file generation (see section 7.1.3).

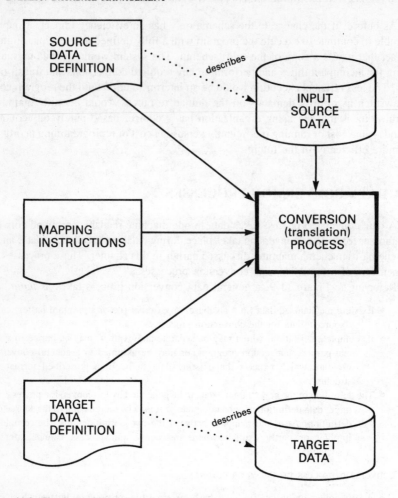

Figure 11-9. The General Data Conversion Process.
The general data conversion process takes data, its old definition, and a new definition as input and converts the old data into a form which conforms to its new definition.

to the evolvability objective. Rich data conversion facilities will span various levels of mapping between the source and target data.

In assessing the degree of data independence, the first step is to identify the data characteristics which could possibly vary between the source and the target. Not only do all of the differences have to be identified, they have to be handled by the conversion process in transferring data between the source and the target. It is unreasonable to assume that such a state of omniscience could ever be achieved such that *all* differences could be handled. There will generally be certain structural characteristics of the source definition which the target definition cannot modify.

When speaking of program-data independence in the previous section, the source and the target definitions are the schema and userschema. Even if a system provides

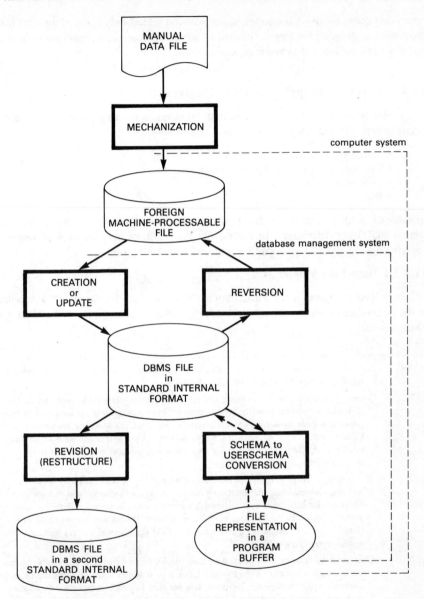

Figure 11-10. The Family of Data Conversion Processes.

some program-data independence at all four levels, it is still important to determine how much difference a system will tolerate, that is, be able to map or convert, before rendering an application program unable to execute correctly.

Some data conversion operations are *data preserving* while others are *data reducing*. A data preserving conversion retains all the information in the source data when generating the target data. Database creation, update, and revision are generally data preserving conversions. A data reducing conversion selects only some of the data from the source to generate the target. Schema to userschema and reversion (retrieval to an internal file) are often data reducing conversions.

11.4.2 Levels of Mapping in Data Conversion

Differences between the source data definition and the target data definition can occur at four distinct levels:

- Individual data items.
- Intra-record, that is, groups of items or records.
- Inter-record relationships.
- Files.

In some cases the system can perform the required data conversion just by knowing the source and target definitions. In others, the system must have an explicit mapping specification in order to perform the required data conversion.

11.4.2.1 Data Item Mappings

Item level mappings relate a data item in the source data definition with a data item in the target data definition. Item level mappings relate to changes in various data item characteristics:

NAME   Renaming a data item in the target data definition always requires an explicit mapping to relate it to an item in the source data definition.

TYPE   Some type conversions do not make any sense; and the conversion on those that do can generally be inferred from the two definitions. Most systems will set up a type-to-type conversion table indicating which conversions are legal and how they are performed. Conversions between numeric data items from one physical representation to another are usually straightforward, allowing for such steps as truncation or conversion from decimal to integer.

SIZE   The size of a data item can often be changed without any specific mapping specification, with the understanding that truncation may occur on size reduction and that padding will occur on size expansion with assumed left to right value justification. Explicit mapping directives could be used to override built-in defaults. If data item values are always stored in variable length, then a difference in field sizes between source and target would present little difficulty.

SCALE   Change in the scale or units of measurement require explicit mapping instructions unless the conversion process "knows" the relationship. It would be useful to predefine to the conversion process the rules for converting between certain common data item values, such as between Fahrenheit and Celcius, between various representations of linear, area, volume, or weight measures, and between the SI units of measurement and the different British and American units.

VALUE   Change in the representation of values was implied by several of the above conversions but additional value conversions may be specified with an explicit encode-decode table in which a new value is listed for each existing value in the source data. The value conversions may be many-to-one—for example, substituting salary ranges for actual values.

Changing only a data item name in a schema-userschema mapping would not require any changes to the program, other than changing the mapping in the userschema. Changes in other characteristics which could not be handled in the mapping specifications would require modifications to the program.

If data item values are always stored in variable length, then a difference in field sizes between source and target would present little difficulty.

Very few systems offer any measure of item-level independence. While repeated conversion on transfer of data item values is expensive in terms of operating performance, the lack of item-level independence may prove to be even more costly in the future when items within existing groups must be redefined in the database. The consequent cost of reprogramming could be extremely large.

11.4.2.2 Intra-Record Mappings

Record-level mappings relate to the contents of a group or record, and the relationships between data items within each instance of a repeating group or record type. Data items may be rearranged, added, or deleted. Rearranging requires an explicit naming sequence of data items. Deletion can be implicit in the omission of a data item name or explicit in a mapping instruction. Addition requires the specification of a derivation rule. A conversion which changes the physical size of a record may be explicit or derived from size changes in contained data items.

Again, deleting an item in the database will clearly have repercussions on every program which is bound to the item. Such programs would have to be rewritten to remove all references to the deleted item.

When performing record-level mappings, it is quite common for systems to require the data item names to be the same in both the source and the target definitions. In this way, no explicit mapping statements are needed to accomplish the conversion. In a separate redefinition it may be possible to change the names of data items.

In addition to item level independence, many systems today do not offer any significant level of intragroup-level independence between the schema and userschema. This is largely due to the fact that the systems are not cognizant of the definition of the contents and format of a group, except for perhaps a key data item. Under these circumstances a program must view the data items within the group exactly as stored in the database. In fact, all programmers referencing the same group must view it in precisely the same way. Furthermore, if the system is not cognizant of the definition of a group, all responsibility for maintaining the commonly understood group definition rests solely with the programmers and users. In many organizations today this is an increasingly intolerable situation which poses a serious threat to database integrity. With no intragroup or item level independence, any change to the definition of an existing group will lead to recompilation of all programs bound to that group and may lead to extensive reprogramming.

If a program's userschema can omit, from the group, some data items which are stored in the database, it is possible for the database administrator to add data items to existing groups or records without affecting any existing programs. New data items may be included in the userschema even though they do not explicitly appear in the database. Such items are called virtual items and are derived by applying a definition rule to data item values existing in the database.

In addition to the group level mappings (discussed above) which relate one-to-one between two instances of similar group types, other group level mappings may involve more than one repeating group or record type. For example, the items in a target record may come from different record types in the source data. For another example, a target data item may be derived from the sum of data item values across several instances or another group, perhaps a subordinate repeating group. Obviously, these types of conversions are much more difficult to implement.

One interesting situation arises when a program is only bound to some but not all items within a group and that program adds new instances of that group to the database. The missing data item value must be explicitly recorded by the system. Only in this way can the integrity of the database be maintained when a subsequent program calls for the values of those same data items. Furthermore, the system must check to see that the unbound data item is not a mandatory item, that is, an item which must always have a value in every group instance. In this situation, the database administrator should not approve a userschema unbound to a mandatory item of a group which the program intends to write to the database. This case is further complicated when a program reads an existing group instance, is only bound to a portion of the group, modifies the group, and rewrites it to the database. During this process the system must preserve the values of the unbound data items.

11.4.2.3 Inter-Record Relationship Mappings

Inter-record level mappings change the relationships between multiple record types by omitting record types, inverting inter-record relationships, or combining or splitting record types within the structure. Some mappings involving a single path hierarchical structure are shown in Figure 11-11. Additional mappings can be defined which involve a multipath hierarchical structure and which combine separate structures. In particular, see Navathe and Fry [1976].

Program-data independence at the level of inter-record relationships assumes the whole record to be the indivisible structural element. If the system permits a program to view *some* (rather than having to be bound to all) records (or groups) within the database, then a measure of inter-record independence is achieved. In this case, new records (or groups) can be defined to the database without affecting the existing programs. Similarly, the redefinition of records or groups *to which the program is not bound* will not affect the program. Of course, the deletion of a record (or group) will affect all programs which reference that record type.

A measure of program-data independence is provided when a program can view groups in a different relationship to each other than actually exists in the database. This includes, for example, the situation where a program userschema can change the parent-dependent relationship among groups in the database.

This is one of the most difficult levels of program-data independence to achieve. Codd [1970, page 378] calls a lack of independence at this level "access path dependence—Many of the existing formatted data systems provide users with tree structured files or slightly more general network models of the data. Application programs devel-

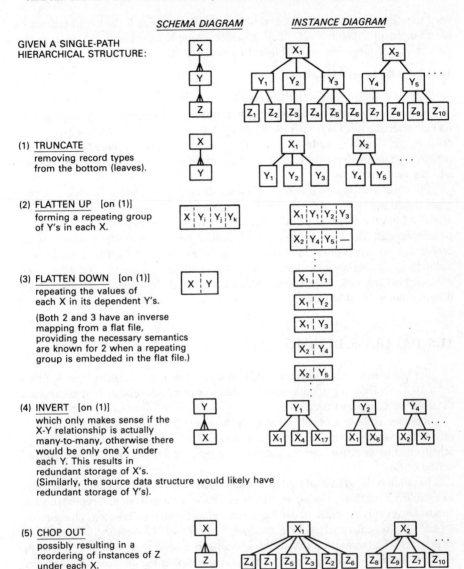

Figure 11-11. Inter-Record Level Mappings with a Single Path Hierarchical Structure.

In these diagrams, a box represents a record, X represents a record type, and X_i represents an instance of record type X. Flatten up, flatten down, and invert are information preserving mappings, while truncate and chop out are information reducing mappings.

oped to work with these systems tend to be logically impaired if the trees or networks are changed in structure.'' He then provides a simple example to demonstrate the dependence of programs on established hierarchical structures.

11.4.2.4 File-Level Mappings

File-level mappings act on the record instances of a file as a collection rather than independently of each other, as in group or record level mappings. File-level mappings include selecting records from a file based upon a given Boolean selection expression, ordering the records in a file given a defined ordering, and, at a more physical level, creating and destroying indexes to the file and merging records from an overflow area into the main file area.

File-level independence concerns actions dealing with a file as a whole. A program should not be affected if a new file is added to the database. Clearly the deletion of a file from the database would make it impossible to execute any program which referenced that file. Prior to taking such action, the database administrator should ensure that no active programs depend upon the existence of the file to be deleted. Splitting or combining logical files are file-level changes, as in the JOIN operation discussed in Chapter 8. A situation in which a program could reference different files at different times could be construed as file-level independence.

11.5 DATABASE REVISION

Several words such as revision, redefinition, restructure, and reorganization have been used to refer to a particular set of facilities or processes relating to databases and database management systems.

Revision is the process of changing the logical structure or physical storage structure of a previously defined and created database. Revision is the process of changing a schema and its database after the database has been established (and often used for a period of time).

Revision is not to be confused with update—the process of changing the *content* of an established database. Update is content evolution, a normal, well-accepted function almost universally provided in database management systems. Revision, changing the logical or physical structure of a database is *structural evolution*. Since structural changes can be more disruptive to the system and its using environment, use of the revision function should be under the exclusive control of the database administrator.

When an organization desires (or is forced) to revise an established database, several consequent activities must be taken into account. The first and simplest step is *redefinition*, to modify the stored database definition. That immediately requires a conversion of the stored database to bring it into conformance with the revised definition. If only the physical storage structure is changed, database *reorganization* is required.

The *restructure* conversion process is needed if the logical structure of the database is changed. Next, it is necessary to examine and possibly change each of the processes which act upon the revised database, including user application programs, catalogued queries, stored report definitions, stored transaction definitions with their update processing instructions, profiles of authorized users, and any associated userschemas with their mapping instructions. Finally, it is necessary to change the image of the database in the minds of people who use the revised database. This may involve revising user manuals and human-oriented database documentation, sending out change notices, and conducting training sessions. It's no wonder that most organizations simply do not revise their established databases except under extreme external pressure!

Redefinition is simply changing the database definition, a conceptually straightforward process. The problem is in doing everything else implied by the redefinition such that the integrity of the database is maintained. Altering the definition of a previously established database can result in invalid data; that is, data previously stored in the database is rendered invalid under the revised definition. The stored database may no longer conform to its definition.

Restructure is the process of converting the stored database so that it is in conformance with its new definition. The redefinition may involve a change in content (new or deleted), a change in the structure of existing content, or a change in the physical representation of existing content. The revision may take place at any of the levels of mapping and may involve addition, modification, or deletion.

Depending on the degree of dependence between the logical definition of the database and the physical storage structure, some cases of redefinition may not require any restructure. This would be the case with strictly additive changes such as adding a new record type or perhaps adding a new data item to a group.

Reorganization is considered a special case of restructure wherein the logical structure and content remain constant while the physical storage structure is changed. Reorganization of the database may be required after a period of use involving numerous insertions and deletions—just like rearranging merchandise on the shelves of a store after a period of heavy activity. The sole purpose of reorganization is improved performance of database processing or improved storage space utilization. Reorganization should have no effect (although in some systems it does) on the people and processes in the using environment beyond the performance aspect.

Reorganization includes such operations as purging the storage space of logically deleted records, integrating data in overflow areas with the main file, modifying physical pointer mechanisms, creating or destroying indexes, and sorting stored data.

11.5.1 The Ongoing Structural Evolution of a Database

The revision of an established database is often treated lightly in many organizations. Several database management systems do not even mention a revision capability. In those systems which do, the revision process is often very awkward, providing few system facilities.

Once the major files of a corporate database are established and reasonably complete, the importance of database definition (that is, the definition of new databases) diminishes. Structural evolution through revision becomes the dominant functional capability of the DBMS. Revision is no longer a supplemental activity but a central activity in the life of the using environment. The organization, its people, and the DBMS settle in to a pattern of mutual growth and evolution. Once a database is established, evolutionary change becomes the name of the game. If the DBMS has no ability to change it will die. Many corporations have not yet reached this stage of development. Nevertheless, movement in the direction of a corporate database must be rooted in the *going concern assumption*. This demands a shift in emphasis from definition to revision, from establishment to structural evolution.

The importance of the revision function and the structural evolution of the database cannot be overemphasized. Revision is necessary to accommodate new technology (particularly in storage devices), new application processes, new data, and to improve storage utilization and performance characteristics. All data requirements and processing needs cannot be foreseen. Furthermore, it is only practical to establish the database in stages.

Some early observations on the revision process were made at a 1968 ACM panel session.* Howard Bryant said, "I have never seen a file design that lasted more than three or four months before some change in structure had to be made. . . ." Charles Bachman, in speaking about the development of a restructure capability, observed that the "system takes a number of passes and really a number of processes to get from one format to another. Our goal has been to take what might have been a 200 or 300 hour process and get it down to something that we could do over the weekend." These two quotations point out the ever-present need for structural revision of a database, and that the task of restructure can be extremely difficult and time-consuming. Al Vorhaus summed up the importance of revision by saying, "We have to—absolutely have to—build flexibility into these new systems. That is what they are for." These observations from some DBMS pioneers are equally valid today.

11.5.2 Approaches to Database Revision

Existing database management systems take several different approaches to database revision. In some cases, the revision is accomplished using other system facilities.

When revising an established database, one approach is never acceptable— manually rekeying all the data. This was sometimes the dominant alternative with very early DBMSs on large computers. Unfortunately, it is re-emerging as a suggested alternative on some less sophisticated DBMSs on microcomputers.

At the very least a system should provide for deleting a definition so that a revised definition may be entered in its place. With this minimal capability, the revision procedure is to dump the old file to external format, delete the old definition, enter the new definition, and go through the database creation or update process. This may involve defining the old file to the creation function, or writing a special purpose program to convert the old file into the required format of the creation or update module or into the required structure of the new definition. This approach ignores the past since it requires

---

*T. William Olle, "The Large Data Base, Its Organization and User Interface: Transcription of a Panel Session Held at the 1968 ACM National Conference, Las Vegas, Nevada," *Data Base* (1:3), 1969 Fall.

a complete repetition of database definition and creation. Unfortunately, it is the approach taken in too many contemporary database management systems. It is clearly an unacceptable approach to achieving evolvability in the database.

A similar approach is to revise the old definition to form a new definition and then run a special program which checks the conformance of the old database to the new definition and reports any nonconformities in the form of diagnostics. Presumably, the responsibility for bringing the data back into conformance, that is, the responsibility for restructure, falls on the external using environment. This approach is only a slight improvement over the previous approach in that the database remains in internal format.

Another approach, similar to the previous two, is possible when the system provides the capability to rename a database definition. In this case, the revision procedure is to enter the new definition with a new name, restructure the stored database from the old definition to the new definition, delete the old definition and the old database, and finally change the name of the new definition back to the old name. The restructure process may be performed by a functional module provided by the system or by a special user program. This approach is preferred to the previous one because both the database and the two definitions remain within the DBMS.

An extension to the above approach would be to incrementally change the old definition. The system would hold the change in limbo while the restructure function is run against the affected portion of the database. When the restructure is completed, the redefinition is finalized.

For a system which stores data both online and offline, and which stores a copy of the definition with every offline file, it is possible to redefine the online definition and wait. When the offline file is brought online the definition stored with it is compared to the online definition. This comparison can be on the basis of a date of last change or a unique version number. Any difference is a signal that a restructure may be required. Alternatively, it may be possible to continue to process the old file using its old definition. In fact, it may be possible to accomplish the restructure as a natural byproduct of an update run performed in sequential mode with the input file read according to the old definition and the output file written according to the new online definition.

A final approach, giving full recognition to the going concern assumption and the importance of evolvability, is to enter all database definition on an incremental basis. The objective of evolvability is enhanced with incremental database definition and with automatic restructuring.

A reasonably comprehensive approach to database revision is illustrated in Figure 11-12. The two-step approach involves redefinition followed by restructure in the general case. The optional mapping instructions may be required if the restructure module is unable to infer the conversion needed to bring the established database into conformance with the revised definition—for example, a name change requires explicit association of the old name with the new name.

11.5.3 Changing Userschemas, Process Specifications, and People

So far only the stored database and its definition have been changed in response to new and changing needs of the using environment. However, several other compo-

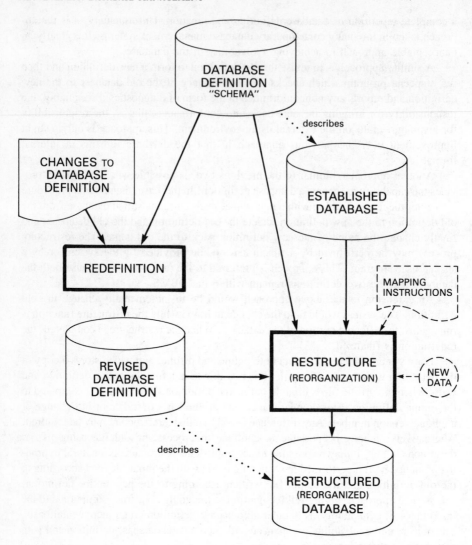

Figure 11-12. The Process of Database Revision.

nents of the database environment may no longer operate correctly or efficiently against the revised database.

First, it is necessary to examine all programs which interact with or map onto the changed portion of the revised database. The redefinition may have changed the characteristics of the mapping between a userschema and the schema, thus rendering some programs inefficient or inoperative. In some cases it will be sufficient to change the data definition in the userschema, and in still others it may be necessary to change the data references and procedural logic of the program. In addition, catalogued queries, report definitions, and transaction definitions with their update processing instructions must be examined and possibly changed if they reference the changed portion of the revised database.

Ideally, the DBMS should indicate which userschemas, programs, and other process specifications would potentially have to be changed in response to a proposed revision to the database. Although beyond the scope of most DBMS's today, this is just what some data dictionary packages attempt to do for the using environment (see Chapter 15). Some data dictionaries break down the process specifications into modules of programs of application systems and then permit their association with data items, groups, record types, relationships, and databases. With all the associations recorded, it is possible to produce a listing of those processes which are potentially affected by a proposed revision to the database.

After changing all affected processes, the task of database revision is still not completed. It is necessary to revise the database documentation which is available to the users. Ultimately, the mental images people have formed must be changed to conform to the revised database! With a data dictionary package which includes the people in the using environment, the process of database revision would be even better served.

SUMMARY

Once a database is established (defined and populated) and user processes developed, the demand for change is inevitable. Data independence and data conversion facilities can ease and assist the process of change.

Data independence refers primarily to the separation of data from its definition, from its stored representation, and from its representation to processes. Program-data independence refers to the degree of separation between the program userschema and the logical database definition embodied in the schema. Physical data independence refers to the degree of separation between the logical definition of data and its stored physical representation.

A high degree of data independence is achieved through the following steps:

- Separate the data definition from the application programs.
- Separate the logical structure from the physical storage representation.
- Add userschema definitions for each program or user process interacting with the database to separate the user views from the global system (schema) view.
- Provide a comprehensive database schema definition language.
- Provide a mapping between the database schema and the userschemas which handles a wide range of differences between the structures, even allowing differences on the bound portion of data.

Data independence seeks to minimize the disruptive effects of changes to programs or the database. Data independence is reflected in the ability of programs to execute correctly and efficiently regardless of revisions made to the logical data structure or the physical stored representation of the database. A high degree of physical data independence is necessary for any significant degree of program data independence. For greater data independence, a program must be insulated from changes in the portion of the database to which it is bound as well as the unbound portion.

The role of a DBMS is central to achieving a high degree of data independence. Upon transferring data between the stored database and the program, the DBMS converts and transforms the data based upon a comparison of the schema and the userschema, and any mapping instructions provided.

Binding is the act of examining the schema and the program userschema, testing for compatibility, and setting up some form of correspondence which is assumed to hold true thereafter. A compromise approach to binding compiles the userschema information into the object version of a program. Attributes of data in the userschema and the schema are then bound at various times—source, compile, load, open, or execution.

Late binding incurs a cost in terms of machine efficiency. The later the binding time the more frequently binding must take place. Late binding increases data independence which results in greater evolvability in the database and the DBMS. With a reasonably high degree of data independence, revisions to the schema will not always require program modification and recompilation. In many cases, the effect is only one of efficiency, thus giving management a choice of when to convert affected programs. The choice is made solely on economic grounds. Early binding can result in greater machine efficiency at the cost of lower evolvability.

The family of conversion processes includes mechanization, creation, update, reversion, schema-to-userschema mapping, and revision. Differences between a target data structure and a source data structure can occur at four levels—file level, intergroup relation level, intragroup level, and the data item level.

Revision is the process of changing the structure of a previously established database. Revision constitutes the ongoing or incremental re-establishment or structural evolution of a database. Redefinition may lead to the necessity to restructure the stored data so that it conforms to its new definition. This can be a very difficult and time-consuming process and is handled very inadequately in many DBMSs. At the same time, as an organization establishes a greater proportion of its data resources in the DBMS, the process of revision begins to dominate with the development of new applications. Reorganization is a special case of revision wherein the physical storage structure is changed while the logical database structure remains constant. The revision process is really not complete until interacting userschemas and process specifications have also been examined and changed if necessary, and people using the revised database have been notified and retrained.

EXERCISES

11-1. Describe the stages in the evolution of the relationship between programs and data.

11-2. Define data independence.

11-3. Describe how the use of userschemas can provide data independence.

11-4. With program-data independence the programmer (or user) no longer needs to know what is in the database schema. Explain why this is true.

11-5. What are the benefits of data independence? the costs?

11-6. Explain why complete data independence is never possible. Give an example at the data item level. At the intergroup relation level.

11-7. Contrast between program data independence and physical data independence.

11-8. How does the concept of program data independence differ between self-contained systems and host language systems?

11-9. Program data independence is being independent of changes to the bound portion of the database as well as the unbound portion. Explain.

11-10. What is the effect of a user being able to select a binding strategy—source, serial, or parallel?

11-11. What is the cost of late binding? the benefit?

11-12. What are the costs and benefits of early binding?

11-13. Is it possible to have late binding and early binding in the same database management system? How?

11-14. It has been argued that greater processing efficiency can be achieved through early binding and that the following constraints will permit early binding.

- Fixed record formats, that is, each data item value appears in a fixed position in each record.
- Fixed data item attributes, for example, fixed length, type, and access authorization.

To what do these constraints relate? At what time is early binding being suggested? In the environment suggested above, is it possible for some users to experience a high degree of data independence while other users (of the same data) obtain greater efficiency? Why or why not?

11-15. Define the following terms: revision, redefinition, restructure, reorganization, and indicate how they relate to each other.

11-16. Why is it important to separate the definition of the logical structure view of data from the physical view of data?

11-17. Describe some approaches to the process of database revision.

11-18. How does revision differ from update?

11-19. Describe the importance of revision to the future of data processing in an organization.

11-20. Describe the revision process in a database management system with which you are familiar.

SELECTED REFERENCES

ASTRAHAN, Mort M., E. B. ALTMAN, P. L. FEHDER, and M. E. SENKO, "Concepts of a Data Independence Accessing Model," *Proceedings of 1972 ACM SIGFIDET Workshop on "Data Description, Access and Control,"* Denver, 1972 November 29 - December 1, edited by A. L. Dean, New York: Association for Computing Machinery, 1972, pages 349-362.

BERG, John L., editor, "Data Base Directions—The Conversion Problem," Washington, DC: U. S. National Bureau of Standards, Special Publication 500-64, 1980 September, 167 pages.

CANNING, Richard G., "The Debate on Data Base Management," *EDP Analyzer* (10:3), 1972 March, 16 pages.

CODASYL Data Base Language Task Group, *COBOL Data Base Facility Proposal*, Ottawa, Canada: Government Department of Supply and Services, 1973 March, 140 pages.

CODASYL Programming Language Committee, *Data Base Task Group Report*, New York: Association for Computing Machinery, 1971 April, 273 pages.

CODASYL Stored-Data Definition and Translation Task Group of the CODASYL Systems Committee, *Stored Data Description and Data Translation: A Model and Language*, James P. Fry, et al., published as a special issue of *Information Systems* (2:3), 1977, pages 95-148.

A very substantive work by several individuals over several years. It develops a model for the process of converting or translating data stored in one computing environment to another environment, and a language to direct such a process. A Stored-Data Description Language (SDDL) is used to define both the source data and the target data, and the structural and encoding conversions to get the data to and from a standard internal form. Contains a useful taxonomy of inter-record conversions.

CODASYL Systems Committee, *Feature Analysis of Generalized Data Base Management Systems*, New York: Association for Computing Machinery, 1971 May, 520 pages.

CODD, E. F., "A Relational Model of Data for Large Shared Data Banks," *Communications of the ACM* (13:6), 1970 June, pages 377-387.

DATE, Christopher J. and Paul HOPEWELL, "File Definition and Logical Data Independence," *Proceedings of 1971 ACM SIGFIDET Workshop on "Data Description, Access and Control,"* San Diego, 1971 November 11-12, edited by E. F. Codd and A. L. Dean, New York: Association for Computing Machinery, 1971, pages 117-138.

DATE, Christopher J. and Paul HOPEWELL, "Storage Structure and Physical Data Independence," *Proceedings of the 1971 ACM SIGFIDET Workshop on "Data Description, Access and Control,"* San Diego, 1971 November 11-12, edited by E. F. Codd and A. L. Dean, New York: Association for Computing Machinery, 1971, pages 139-168.

EVEREST, Gordon C. and Edgar H. SIBLEY, "A Critique of the GUIDE-SHARE Data Base Management System Requirements," *Proceedings of the 1971 ACM-SIGFIDET Annual Workshop, "Data Description, Access and Control,"* San Diego, California, 1971 November 11-12, edited by E. F. Codd and A. L. Dean, New York: Association for Computing Machinery, 1971, pages 93-112.

FEHDER, P. L., "The Representation-Independent Language. Part 1: Introduction and the Subsetting Operation," San Jose: IBM Research Laboratory, DIAM Project, Report RJ 1121, 1972 November 2, 39 pages.

LUM, Vincent Y., N. C. SHU and B. C. HOUSEL, "A General Methodology for Data Conversion and Restructuring," *IBM Journal of Research and Development* (20:5), 1976, pages 483-497.

McGEE, William C., "Application Program Data Structures in the Data Base Environment," paper presented at the New York University Seminar on "Data Base Systems—Current Theoretical and Pragmatic Issues," New York, 1970 January 26-29, 33 pages.

McGEE, William C., "Data Description for Data Independence," *fdt. Journal of ACM SIGFIDET* (1:2), 1969 December, pages 3-10.

NAVATHE, Shamkant B. and James P. FRY, "Restructuring for Large Databases: Three Levels of Abstraction," *ACM Transactions on Database Systems* (1:2), 1976 June, pages 138-158.

An important, well-written article dealing with the logical restructuring of one multipath hierarchical data structure into another. Eight inter-record level mapping operations are discussed: "renaming," "compression" (FLATTEN DOWN) and its dual "expansion," "assembly merging" and its dual "assembly partitioning," "instance merging" and its dual "instance splitting," and "inversion" (same as INVERT). These are all information preserving mapping operations and constitute the first level of abstraction. The second and third levels of abstraction simply describe the steps necessary to carry out each of these inter-record level mapping operations.

SHU, N. C., B. C. HOUSEL, R. W. TAYLOR, S. P. GHOSH and V. Y. LUM, "EXPRESS: A Data Extraction, Processing, and Restructuring System," *ACM Transactions on Database Systems* (2:2), 1977 June, pages 134-174.

Discusses the design and implementation of a comprehensive and generalized data conversion system, utilizing high-level languages to define the source and target files (there may be more than one of each), and to specify the mappings to be performed between them. All user views of source files must conform to a hierarchical representation. The CONVERT language has nine generic mappings which can be nested.

SOCKUT, Gary H. and Robert P. GOLDBERG, "Data Base Reorganization—Principles and Practice," *ACM Computing Surveys* (11:4), 1979 December, pages 371-395, 79 refs. (also NBS Sp. Pub. 500-47).

   Defines reorganization as changing the way in which a database is arranged *logically or physically*, which contrasts with the definition in this text being only physical rearrangement. Discusses why reorganization is necessary and classifies types of reorganization into several levels. Also covers pragmatic issues such as reorganization strategies, survey of commercially available products, case studies, and database administration considerations.

SWARTWOUT, D. E., M. E. DEPPE, and J. P. FRY, "Operational Software for Restructuring Network Databases," *Proceedings AFIPS National Computer Conference* (46), 1977, pages 499-508.

TAYLOR, R. W., J. P. FRY, B. SHNEIDERMAN, D. C. P. SMITH, and S. Y. W. SU, "Database Program Conversion: A Framework for Research," *Proceedings Fifth International Conference on Very Large Data Bases*, New York: ACM, 1979 October, pages 299-312.

TEOREY, Toby J. and James P. FRY, "Reorganization," Chapter 17 in *Design of Database Structures*, Englewood Cliffs, NJ: Prentice-Hall, 1982, pages 387-407.

   Calls the overall process of revision "reorganization" and calls reorganization "reformatting." Discusses various aspects of logical restructuring and several strategies for physical reorganization, particularly involving general multifile ("network") data structures.

TUEL, W. G., Jr., "Optimum Reorganization Points for Linearly Growing Files," *ACM Transactions on Database Systems* (3:1), 1978 March, pages 32-40.

YAO, S. B., K. S. DAS, and T. J. TEOREY, "A Dynamic Database Reorganization Algorithm," *ACM Transactions on Database Systems* (1:2), 1976 June, pages 159-174.

TWELVE

DATABASE INTEGRITY: BACKUP AND RECOVERY

12.1	OVERVIEW OF INTEGRITY CONTROL FUNCTIONS	428
12.2	THE PROCESSES OF DATABASE BACKUP AND RECOVERY	430
12.3	BACKUP STRATEGIES	431
12.3.1	Dual Recording of the Database	433
12.3.2	Periodic Dumping	433
12.3.3	Logging Input Data Transactions	435
12.3.4	Logging Changes to the Database	437
12.3.4.1	Logging versus Dumping	437
12.3.4.2	Information Recorded in a Logging Action	.437
12.3.4.3	Logging "Before" Images	438
12.3.4.4	Logging "After" Images	438
12.3.4.5	Logging Both "Before" and "After" Images	439
12.4	SUMMARY CHART OF TRADITIONAL BACKUP AND RECOVERY STRATEGIES	439
12.4.1	Problems with Traditional Backup Strategies	440
12.5	RESIDUAL DUMP BACKUP STRATEGY	441
12.5.1	Variations in the Residual Dump Strategy	442
12.5.2	Performance of Residual Dumping	443
12.6	VARIABLES IN THE BACKUP PROCESS	444
12.7	PROCESS CHECKPOINT AND RESTART	446
	SUMMARY	448
	EXERCISES	450
	SELECTED REFERENCES	450

Database integrity functions of backup and recovery, quality control, and access control are covered in the next three chapters. This first chapter of the three begins with an overview of all the integrity control functions. The selected bibliography includes items which cover all the integrity control functions.

12.1 OVERVIEW OF INTEGRITY CONTROL FUNCTIONS

The discussion of integrity control functions in these three chapters focuses on the technical mechanisms which can be implemented within a DBMS. Part III of the text concerns Database Administration and focuses on the administrative controls which may be used to maintain integrity.

The DBMS usage functions of retrieval, update, and programming user facilities should all be subject to the same set of database integrity controls. Since integrity controls are pervasive, they must underlie and support the direct availability functions. Such underlying support functions generally reside in the database control system (or default to the facilities in the operating system).

The underlying integrity control functions of a DBMS provide the tools with which the database administrator can carry out his or her responsibility for maintaining database integrity. Various facets of database integrity are discussed in connection with the functions of database administration and in connection with the integrity objective of database management.

The use of computers to manage organizational data resources offers far greater potential for controlling the integrity of the data than was ever possible under manual systems. Administrative procedures to control data integrity depend upon human diligence, making them weak and difficult to apply consistently. Computerized controls, once defined and in place, will be invoked consistently. The computer is not intimidated by threats or influenced by a persistent requester.

Providing data integrity control mechanisms within a computer system, however, does not eliminate the need for administrative control procedures. Administrative controls are needed to ensure that a potential intruder does not obtain information about the security system itself.

There are three levels of mechanisms for maintaining database integrity:

- *Legal* mechanisms are external, governmentally imposed laws, rules, and regulations.
- *Administrative* mechanisms are the internal policies and procedures adopted unilaterally, often in response to legal or public pressure.
- *Technical* mechanisms are those incorporated into the computer system.

The three Database Integrity chapters focus on technical mechanisms and their administrative implications, while chapters in Part III discuss legal and administrative mechanisms.

The technology is here, and with computer technology, the economics are substantially more in favor of greater security. The problem is the will to expend resources commensurate with the security need and consistent with enhanced availability. Additional security functions in a computer system have a direct degrading effect on performance, which perhaps accounts for the relatively low level of technical integrity control existing in many of today's information systems.

Some DBMS and computer vendors take the view that data quality is a user's responsibility. While that is ultimately true, it should not be an excuse for not providing appropriate tools and controls in the DBMS to facilitate data integrity. The vendor has a responsibility to provide adequate tools; the user is responsible for applying those tools.

Two factors add great complexity to the maintenance of data integrity. Geographically remote access systems are more vulnerable, more open to penetration, and more susceptible to security violations than single location or batch processing systems where all access to the system is physically controlled through humans. The second factor is the provision of a programming language capability at the remote locations, rather than parameter-driven canned programs. The greater flexibility of programming languages increases the need for security controls.

Data security is a subset of computer security. The subject of computer security has taken on new dimensions and an increased urgency in recent years. The evidence is seen in the increased volume of literature recently, increased attention from the experts, a rise in the number of companies specializing in computer security, and the expanded levels of funding from the federal government and private industry. Hopefully, in a few years, substantially better data security controls will be available to the average business computer installation.

These chapters do not cover the physical security of a computer center, protection against natural environmental hazards such as fire and flood, or human hazards such as vandalism. The database management system has virtually no role to play in controlling physical access to the computer center, placing the computer system underground in a basement, responding to detected intrusions with locks and alarm systems, or providing insurance to compensate for irrecoverable losses. Nevertheless, backup, validation, access control, and monitoring measures can be exercised by a DBMS to maintain some level of integrity and enable some form of recovery after a physical, environmental, or human threat to security materializes, resulting in the loss or destruction of data.

The underlying integrity control functions discussed in these chapters relate to the data integrity objectives as follows:

DATABASE MANAGEMENT INTEGRITY OBJECTIVE	DATABASE MANAGEMENT SYSTEM UNDERLYING INTEGRITY CONTROL FUNCTIONS
Existence	Database Backup and Recovery
Quality	Data Validation
	Update Control
	Monitoring and Audit Trail
Privacy	Data Access Control
	Encryption
	Monitoring and Audit Trail

The three Database Integrity chapters correspond to these three integrity objectives and describe the technical mechanisms for achieving those objectives.

12.2 THE PROCESSES OF DATABASE BACKUP AND RECOVERY

Backup and recovery seeks to protect the existence of the physical database and to re-create the data whenever loss or destruction occurs. The possibility of loss always exists. The use of backup and recovery procedures depends upon an assessment of the risk of loss and the cost of applying the procedures. Data loss should be expected and therefore plans made for recovery.

In order to recover from loss or destruction of data, it is necessary to store data redundantly and preferably remotely from the primary location. *Backup* is the process of maintaining an historical record of any of the following:

1. Past states of the database	DUMP
2. Changes to the database	IMAGE LOG
3. Transactions which caused a change in the state of the database	TRANSACTION LOG

The data stored for backup is generally some combination of periodic dumps, input data transaction logs, and logs of before and after images of a portion of the database each time it changes. Backup enables reconstruction of all or part of the database in the event of loss or destruction of data.

Re-creation or *recovery* of a database can take one of two forms:

1. Recovering the lost current state of the database.
2. Recovering a valid prior state of the database.

The first involves "bringing forward" a valid prior state of the database by redoing or reinstating the update processing since recording (dumping) the prior state. The extent of damage may entail restoration of the entire database or it may be localized and only require restoration of a few records.

The unsuccessful completion or erroneous action of an update process necessitates the second form of recovery. This involves "rolling back" from the current erroneous (contaminated or otherwise unstable) state of the database by undoing or reversing the changes back to the point at which the update processing began (or some logically acceptable intermediate point). Selective rollback may be required if two or more processes were updating the database concurrently when one of them failed. In general, each change to the database must be identified with:

- Its associated update program.
- The input transaction causing the change.
- The user requesting the change.
- The terminal from which the change was requested.
- The time of the change.

The "redundant" backup data is subject to the same physical and administrative security measures used on the main database. Furthermore, for maximum protection the backup data should be stored immediately on permanent storage media remote from the database. The remote storage requirement is needed to protect against a common disaster destroying both copies of the database.

If the database definition can change in the interval between backup and recovery, all data stored as backup must be associated with a particular version of the database definition. Alternatively, the backup data and its definition could be stored together. Full dumps of the database and archival storage in particular should be accompanied by a copy of the definition in effect at the time of writing to backup. Of course, the database definition should be subject to backup.

Some people suggest that a good backup program can also satisfy the need for archival data storage. While the same backup and recovery mechanisms can be used for archival storage, the archival data is not stored redundantly so it is not backed up—a procedure which may not be acceptable in the light of certain legal and governmental requirements for records retention.

12.3 BACKUP STRATEGIES

Various strategies such as:

- Dual recording of data
- Periodic dumping of data
- Logging input transactions
- Logging changes to the data

can be used to back up a database. The method of recovery is highly dependent upon the particular backup strategy selected. The database administrator selects a backup strategy based upon a tradeoff between the necessity or difficulty of reconstructing the database and the cost of performing the backup operation.

The *cost of backup* is measured in terms of:

- Interruption of database availability.
- Degradation of update efficiency.
- Storage of redundant data.

More frequent and extensive backup results in easier, faster, and more accurate recovery. These tradeoffs are considered in the discussion of the various strategies.

Selection of a backup strategy is actually a matter of selecting when and how much data to copy to backup storage. The "when" can extend from every few seconds, or upon every change to the database, to weekly or monthly or more. The "how much" generally ranges from individual group instances or records to the entire database. Although there are two dimensions to the backup strategy, there is, practically, only one continuum ranging from "logging a little bit quite frequently," to "dumping a lot periodically." Identifying a continuum is not meant to imply that the extremes are mutually exclusive. On the contrary, a good backup strategy generally involves picking a balance of two points along the continuum. Figure 12-1 illustrates the continuum

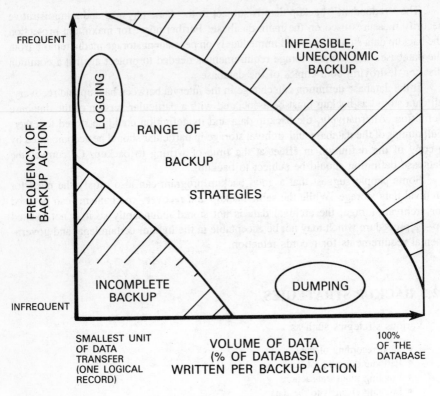

Figure 12-1. Logging and Dumping: A Continuum of Backup Strategies.
The database administrator can choose a backup strategy along the continuum from logging a little bit frequently, to dumping a lot periodically. Often a chosen strategy involves multiple points along this continuum.

of backup strategies between logging and dumping. A single backup action is an act of copying something from the database to backup storage while disallowing a concurrent update process to intervene. Updates are permitted between backup actions.

When the database is stored on a sequential storage medium such as magnetic tape, a substantial degree of backup is achieved as an automatic (unavoidable) by-product of the sequential update process. The sequential update process requires all transactions to be sorted on one input file, and always produces a new copy of the updated file, leaving the old file available for backup. The input transaction files and the father and grandfather versions of the ''master'' file constitute complete backup of the current ''master'' file.

The new optical recording media can only be written once and cannot be overwritten. Therefore, past copies of a file are never destroyed. As with sequential storage media, update always creates a new copy and the old copy becomes the automatic backup.

The remainder of this discussion concerns data stored on magnetic direct access storage devices. Only with magnetic recording media is it possible to overwrite the prior copy when updating. Therefore, explicit strategies are required to provide backup protection against possible loss or destruction of data.

12.3.1 Dual Recording of the Database

One backup strategy involves maintaining two complete copies of the database online and updating both simultaneously. This dual recording strategy is particularly useful when recovery must be accomplished in a very short time, say a few minutes. Such a strategy offers good protection against disk failures but no protection against events which damage or make unavailable the data on both disks, such as power failure or a faulty update program. Storing the copies in physically separate locations (two rooms, two buildings, or one in the basement) offers additional protection. Even greater protection is afforded if one copy of the database is stored on a more stable medium and device. For recovery, if one database goes down, the system can set a few status switches and operate with the other while the defective database is recovered and brought forward to current status [see Yourdon for a fuller discussion]. The limited backup protection generally entails substantial costs in doubling storage device capacity and channel capacity. This strategy can be extended to include dual computer processors as well, each updating its own copy of the database. Such a duplexed system configuration offers greater backup protection at a considerably greater cost.

12.3.2 Periodic Dumping

The second and perhaps most common strategy involves taking a periodic dump of all (or part) of the database. The status of the database or some part of it is saved at a point in time by copying it onto some backup storage medium—magnetic tape, removable magnetic disk pack, or optical disk. The dumps may be made on a regularly scheduled basis, triggered automatically by the system at fixed intervals, or triggered externally by database administration personnel—say, at the end of each day, week, or month, or after periods of heavy updating. This presumes that updates are generated concurrently from several sources. If updates are administratively collected and periodically performed through a single person or organizational unit, then an appropriate strategy is to backup the database after each update session.

Since the dump is a record of the status of the database, update operations on the whole database or the portion being dumped must be inhibited during the dumping process. For large disk files, dumping may take several hours, making such a procedure unacceptable in some environments.

A disk dump may be performed on a logical or a physical basis. A *logical dump* copies logical records in their logical sequence. A *physical dump* copies physical blocks or tracks in address sequence. A physical dump is generally faster than a logical dump, particularly when dumping the same amount of information, but makes selective recovery more difficult.

A physical dump applies to a whole volume on the storage device, or perhaps some contiguous portion (in the address space) if the device can be partitioned such that no file can span a partition. A physical dump is not selective—all files in the volume are copied to the backup medium whether or not they have changed since the last dump. Writing from the disk can take place at disk rotation speed to a streaming tape drive (it does not stop and start between blocks).

Recovery with physical dumps is somewhat more difficult. If some information on a volume is lost or damaged, the backup dump must be reloaded onto the volume of the active storage device. If there is only one storage volume or if the system requires that the physical dump be reloaded only to the volume from which it was copied, reloading the backup will destroy the current copies of the files. Therefore, it is necessary to follow the following steps:

1. Take a physical dump of the current contents of the volume.
2. Reload the prior backup copy.
3. Recover the lost or damaged file(s) by *logically* copying them to another device.
4. Reload the current dump made in step 1.
5. Copy the recovered file(s) to the current active volume.

There are several possible variations on this sequence of steps. With a stand alone microcomputer having only one hard disk, backup by physical dumping (say, to a streaming tape cartridge) generally requires the above sequence of steps for recovery. Step 3 would involve copying to a floppy disk. If a system has multiple volumes of the same size and characteristics, it may be possible to load the prior backup copy onto a different volume. Then the recovery operation would simply copy the lost or damaged file(s) from the loaded backup volume to the current volume. Copying between online volumes is generally possible with multiple disk drives, each having a removable cartridge or disk pack.

With logical dumping, an installation can be selective in the files which are copied to the backup media. Only the files which have changed since the last backup action need be copied. If this is substantially less than the total contents of the volume, the logical dump may actually be faster than a physical dump. If a file is lost or damaged, only that file need be reloaded in a recovery operation rather than all the files in the volume. This makes recovery much faster and more flexible with logical dumps than with physical dumps. Furthermore, it is possible to recover selected records from the logical dump, rather than attempting to restore the entire file.

With physical dumping, the database should not be physically reorganized between dumps. If it is, selective recovery of records from the backup copy would not be possible. Any physical reorganization of the database must be accompanied by a physical dump immediately after the reorganization.

Logical dumping permits physical reorganization of the database between dumps. Logical dumping assumes no physical addresses are stored as pointers (inter-record links) in the records. (Reorganization includes recovering space from logical deletes, merging overflow areas into the main file, rearranging records in storage, balancing a search tree with a consequent shifting of records in storage, physical sorting of the records, expansion of a hashing area, re-establishing the optimum percentage of excess capacity in each block, equalizing chain lengths, and many more strategies designed to improve performance efficiency.) Recovery may be fast with logical dumps or fast with physical dumps depending on the nature of the loss. Since reorganization for performance efficiency will become increasingly important, subsequent discussion and analysis assumes logical dumping and copying to backup storage.

Periodic dumping does not by itself provide complete backup of the database. All changes to the database since the last dump are lost. The amount of work lost and, therefore, the cost of the recovery operation depends upon the frequency of the periodic dumps. In some environments the loss of some work can be tolerated. The effect is that users must keep a record of all work done in order to know what has to be redone in the event of a loss. However, this can still present a dilemma if a daily dump is desired and it takes several hours to perform the dump! A more comprehensive backup strategy is required to provide a complete backup of all changes to the database. With a very large database, perhaps only a small fraction of it changes each day.

12.3.3 Logging Input Data Transactions

A third option in selecting a backup strategy involves logging the input data transactions which cause changes to the database. Normally this is coupled with a periodic dump. Recovery to restore a totally destroyed database means reloading the last dump and reprocessing the transactions which have been logged since the last dump. In the event of localized damage, a recovery program (or the system operator) could attempt to restore only the damaged records.

Input data transactions can be logged at various stages in their processing, as shown in Figure 12-2. When *logging transactions immediately upon receipt* by the system (a necessary practice in maintaining an audit trail), care must be taken during the reprocessing for recovery. The recovery program must bypass those transactions which were not successfully processed the first time, or else inhibit the communication of transaction reject or error messages back to the user for a second time. It would be confusing to the user to receive two undifferentiated notices to correct the same error.

The problem of dealing with rejected transactions during the recovery process can be avoided by *logging only transactions successfully processed*. (Of course, this no longer meets the accountant's need for an audit trail unless all rejected messages are also logged, probably on a separate but coordinated backup file.)

Rather than have special recovery programs, the recovery process could be carried out by the normal update programs in which a "recovery flag" is set to modify their normal mode of operation. Large reports output as a result of a normal update processing run could be inhibited as could the regeneration of error messages regarding rejects. Instead, the recovery mode could verify the restoration action using control totals, etc. produced by the normal update processing done earlier.

Repairing localized damage to a database is very difficult and sometimes impossible to accomplish with a recovery program utilizing logged transactions only. With no information concerning the prior contents of a record, it is often impossible to determine whether or not a transaction was completely processed just before the damage occurred. This is particularly true if the transaction was incrementing or decrementing the contents of a numeric field in the record.

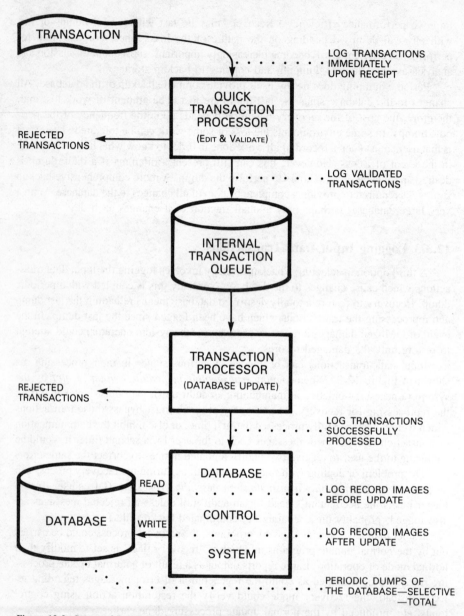

Figure 12-2. Stages of Logging for Database Backup.

For audit trail reasons, incoming data update transactions should be logged immediately upon receipt into the computer system. For backup purposes logging may take place at any point in the processing stream—validated transactions, successfully processed transactions, the before and/or after images of changed records, or periodic dumps of part or all of the database.

Given the difficulty and sometimes impossibility of repairing localized damage, the recovery process must fall back on reloading the last dump and reprocessing all subsequent transactions. Such a recovery process can be very costly if a large database dump has to be reloaded, if a large number of transactions must be reprocessed, or if it takes a relatively long time to reprocess each transaction. This would also be an impractical recovery strategy if damage occurred frequently.

12.3.4 Logging Changes to the Database

The fourth backup strategy involves copying a record each time it is changed by an update action. The changed record can be logged immediately before the update action changes the record, immediately after, or both. The choice affects the ease of various types of recovery. As evidenced in Figure 12-2, this backup strategy is at another stage in the continuum of transaction processing and database update.

12.3.4.1 Logging versus Dumping

Several comparisons can be made between logging and dumping.

LOGGING	DUMPING
• Only write changed records	• Write all database records
• Complete backup protection *if* a complete history of changes is recorded (practically infinite)	• Incomplete backup since changes between dumps are lost
• Concurrent update actions are inhibited only with respect to each record as it is being updated and logged	• Concurrent update actions must be inhibited during the dumping operation
• Degrades efficiency of the update action	• No degradation of update efficiency but makes the database unavailable for update during dumping
• For small databases and large transaction volumes, recovery is more complex because all changes must be scanned selectively to determine the cumulative effect of the changes	• If the database is small, recovery by reloading a dump can be fast. Recovery time is independent of the volume of transactions
• For large databases, recovery time is relatively independent of total number of records	• For large databases, may be infeasible
• Permits selective recovery of the database and repair of localized damage	• Does not permit repair of localized damage (generally)

12.3.4.2 Information Recorded in a Logging Action

In general, each change to the database must be identified in terms of several pieces of information, information which might be needed to perform the recovery operation.

1. A copy of the logical *record* being changed. The copy may be a before image, an after image, or both.
2. Indication of *insert or delete* if update action was not a change.
3. An identification of the *physical location* of the logical record before and/or after the update action, including block identification and the physical device location of each block. (This information better belongs in record location tables which should also be backed up.)
4. The *update program* which performed the update action, including job identification.
5. The *date* and precise *time* the update action took place. The time must be recorded with sufficient precision to permit a strict time sequencing of update actions.
6. The unique identifier of the input *transaction* causing the change.
7. The *source* of the transaction, generally the unique identification of the *user* requesting or initiating the change. May also include the *terminal* from which the change was requested (if relevant and if it provides additional information).

The above collection of data would constitute a single entry on the backup log. After some loss of data, an assessment may isolate the damage to a single logical record, a physical block, a runaway update program, or an erroneous or unauthorized transaction. With a knowledge of the time period in which the damage occurred, the recovery process can utilize the above information to repair the damage.

12.3.4.3 Logging "Before" Images

One variation in logging changes to the database involves copying the record to be changed (or some other unit of data) *before* the change takes place. Logging such "before" images facilitates rollback since the recovery process can replace the current copy with the before image on the backup file. Moreover, the rollback can be accomplished selectively based upon the additional information tagged to each backup file entry.

Bringing forward a wholly or locally damaged database is not possible when only before images are logged because a backup copy of the most current version of each record is not maintained. Therefore, to obtain complete backup protection it is necessary to couple the logging of input data transactions with the logging of before images. Then it is possible to bring forward the database by recovering the backup copy of the second version of each record (the latest before image recorded on the backup file), and reprocess the associated input transaction to restore the lost current version. At most one transaction per record will have to be processed making recovery under this backup strategy faster than if only input transactions are logged.

12.3.4.4 Logging "After" Images

Writing copies of a record to the backup file *after* a change is made facilitates bringing forward the database. The last dump and the so called "after" image backup file are scanned to extract the latest version of each record in the database, or each record in a local region of damage. Rollback is a little more difficult since the previous version of a record must be obtained by searching back (in time) in the after image backup file to find the after image of the change before the last change. This backward look may involve going to the last dump if none or at most one update action has taken place against a record since the dump. It is also necessary to distinguish those after images which resulted from an insert action that created a new record. In such cases, there is no after image of a previous change. Notice that it is not necessary, for the purposes of backup protection, to log the input data transactions along with after images to obtain complete backup protection.

12.3.4.5 Logging Both Before and After Images

This combined backup strategy yields the advantages of both before and after image logging to improve the efficiency of the recovery process. It is relatively easy to perform a total or partial restoration of the database or to rollback to a prior valid state of the database (that is, backout selectively on the basis of the tagged information on the backup file entries). In both cases, the logging of input data transactions lends no further support to the backup and recovery operation (although it is absolutely necessary to the maintenance of an audit trail). Obviously, this strategy involves redundant logging—the after image of one change will be the same as the before image of the next change. Such a procedure provides greater flexibility and reduces the recovery time; it does not increase the completeness of the backup or the accuracy of the recovery process.

12.4 SUMMARY CHART OF TRADITIONAL BACKUP AND RECOVERY STRATEGIES

The table in Figure 12-3 presents various recovery processes under each of seven backup strategies:

1. Periodic dump only.
2. Logging input transactions and/or changes only.
3. Periodic dump plus logging input transactions.
4. Periodic dump plus logging before images.
5. Periodic dump plus logging input transactions and before images.
6. Periodic dump plus logging after images.
7. Periodic dump plus logging both before and after images.

Three basic types of recovery operation are included in the table: bringing forward the entire database in the event of major loss or damage, bringing forward to repair localized damage to the database, and rollback or backing out the effects of selected update actions against the database. The table then shows whether each type of recovery operation is easy, possible (marked "YES") but more difficult, incomplete, or impossible, for each of the seven backup strategies. Only three of the seven backup strategies provide for complete recovery of a lost or damaged database.

BACKUP STRATEGY	1	2	3	4	5	6	7
Periodic Dump	DUMP		DUMP	DUMP	DUMP	DUMP	DUMP
Log Input Transactions		TRANS &/or	TRANS		TRANS		
Log Before Images } change		BEFORE &/or		BEFORE	BEFORE		BEFORE
Log After Images } file		AFTER				AFTER	AFTER
—Complete Backup	NO	NO*	YES	NO	YES	YES	YES
RECOVERY OPERATIONS							
Total Bring Forward	COMPLETE	IMPOSSIBLE*	YES	INCOMPLETE	YES or	YES, EASY	YES, EASY
• reload dump	X	•	X	X	X / •	[X]	[X]
• select from dump	•	•	•	•	• / X	X	X
• reprocess trans	•	•	X	•	X / X	•	•
• process change file	•	•	•	X	• / X	X	X
Local Bring Forward	NO	MAY BE INCOMPLETE	YES BUT EXPENSIVE	INCOMPLETE	YES	YES, EASY	YES, EASY
• reload dump		•	X	•	•	•	[X]
• select from dump		•	•	X	X	X	X
• reprocess trans.		X	X	•	X	•	•
• process change file		X	•	X	X	X	X
Rollback	NO	MAY BE IMPOSSIBLE	MAY BE IMPOSSIBLE	YES, EASY	YES, EASY	YES, BUT DIFFICULT	YES, EASY
—Complete recovery	NO	NO	NO	NO	YES	YES	YES

*theoretically, yes, but impractical unless small, involatile file.

Figure 12-3. Recovery under Various Backup Strategies.

For each of seven backup strategies, the table shows the three basic types of recovery operations: bringing forward the entire database in the event of major loss or damage, bringing forward to repair localized damage to the database, and rollback or backing out the effects of selected update actions against the database.

The table lists the four types of available backup information under the bring forward recovery operations. Then, under each backup strategy, an 'X' is shown opposite those types of backup information that would be used in the recovery process. In the first, the entire last dump is loaded at the start of the recovery operation; in the second, only certain records need be selected from the last dump during the recovery operation. Processing the change file involves the use of the before and/or after image backup file. An [X] in square brackets indicates an alternative though generally less desirable choice in the bring forward operation.

Under the first four backup strategies, complete backup and recovery is not always possible. In other words, if complete backup and recovery protection is necessary, only the last three offer viable strategies. The fifth strategy may involve some expensive reprocessing of input transactions in order to bring forward to restore a damaged database. The sixth strategy is somewhat more difficult for rollback. The last strategy involves substantially more redundancy in the backup files but produces greater flexibility and efficiency in the recovery operation. In the table, "easy" is meant in a relative sense noting that most forms of recovery are definitely not easy.

12.4.1 Problems with Traditional Backup Strategies

Assuming that an environment requires complete database backup protection, the selected strategy must include some combination of both periodic dumping and some form of logging between dumps. Logging alone is insufficient. Under the traditional backup strategies, some periodic dumps are needed to avoid the potential "infinity problem." That is, without a dump, the recovery process would have to examine *all* entries in the backup log file since the original creation of the database. This is most impractical even with moderate transaction volumes. Taking a dump makes it unnecessary to look back at any logs taken before the dump. Obviously there is a tradeoff between the cost of periodic dumps (which increases as the frequency increases) and the cost of the recovery operation taking into account the risk of damage. Finding the optimal balance between the fixed cost of the dump and the incremental cost of logging between dumps has been analyzed using the Renewal Reward Theorem [see Loman and Muckstadt].

During each dump operation, concurrent updates must be inhibited since a dump is a snapshot of the database at a single point in time.

The backup data exists in two different forms—one for the dump and one for the log. Moreover, a record which is updated since the last dump will be backed up during the update operation (logged) and will again be backed up during the next dump operation. This can result in a significant amount of redundant backup particularly if a substantial portion of the file is updated between each dump operation.

In some cases, the database may be so large as to prohibit taking a complete dump at any time. An alternative backup strategy would be to dump partitions of the database on a round robin basis. Yourdon calls this a differential disk dump [p. 345]. Although this reduces the size of a continuous period during which updates are inhibited, it still involves the same amount of effort to obtain a complete dump and additionally complicates the recovery process. The backup data still exists in two forms.

12.5 RESIDUAL DUMP BACKUP STRATEGY

The residual dump backup strategy is presented as an alternative to the traditional backup strategies in situations requiring complete backup of a database stored on a direct access storage device.

If a "date of last change" being equivalent to the date of the last backup, is recorded with each stored record in the database, it is possible to avoid a full dump. Periodically, a residual dump is taken. All stored records are scanned and those that have not been backed up (that is, have not changed) since the last (or some previous) residual dump, are logged on the backup file. Each record log is flagged to indicate that the log was triggered by a residual dump action rather than a record update action (change) and, therefore, the before and after images are the same.

A residual dump does not have to inhibit concurrent updates against the entire database, because it is not a snapshot of the status of the database at a point in time. The residual dump operation is actually a logging operation and can be spread out and performed during idle periods. During a residual dump, concurrent updates need be locked out only with respect to the current record being logged. This is in contrast to the lockout of concurrent updates against the entire database (or database partition) when taking a periodic dump. Stated another way, a record should not be logged as part of a residual dump between the before and after images of a record being updated. Such control of concurrent update processing can be handled by the normal record-level lockout mechanism which is (or should be) available on any sophisticated database management facility.

A residual dump can be performed during periods of idleness, without delaying any new work when it arrives. This is possible because the residual dump can act on as few or as many records as the length of the idle period permits. Furthermore, the interval between residual dumps can vary. The residual dump job can remain an active process in the system and be given the lowest priority in the system (subject to a maximum time interval between residual dumps).

Under a residual dump strategy, recovery involves going back to (but not including) the *second last* residual dump, rather than the last dump. Since the logging operation of a residual dump is spread out, some bookkeeping is required so the recovery process knows how far to go back to obtain a complete copy of the database.

A total bring forward recovery operation uses all the records on the log file back to the point at which a complete copy of the database is obtained. The log file contains records logged as a result of a residual dump as well as before and after images of records logged as a result of update actions.

The recovery process is simplified by a prior sort of the logged records. The primary sort key is the unique internal record identifier, and the secondary sort key is the time the record was logged. If the system does not maintain or does not make available any unique internal identifiers, the logged images are sorted, first by record type, then by the combination of data items in the record type which imparts uniqueness to each record instance, and thirdly, by the time the record was logged. Since the key values themselves may have been changed, the sort would be performed on the before or after images depending on whether the recovery process was rolling back or bringing forward the database, respectively. Then the lost current state of the database simply takes the latest copy of each unique record.

A selective rollback operation, caused by, for example, the failure or pre-emption of an update process, can use the before images of logged records *bypassing* any logs due to a residual dump.

12.5.1 Variations in the Residual Dump Strategy

Assuming for a moment the theoretical limit in which the residual dump (R_i) takes place in a single moment of time, the following diagram results:

```
complete backup interval
..............................
 :                            :
 :                            :
----------------------------------------------/-------------------> time
     R₁                        R₂      L
```

Updates are assumed to take place at any time. If a database loss occurs at **L** , then all the records logged back to R_1 including R_2 but not including R_1 must be scanned in the recovery operation. The interval from immediately after R_1 up to and including R_2 constitutes a complete backup of the database. That is, during the time interval every record is logged at least once. Furthermore, a record will be logged more than once only if it is updated more than once during this time interval.

But a residual dump cannot occur in a single moment of time. It must occur over a time interval, from R_i to S_i in the following diagram:

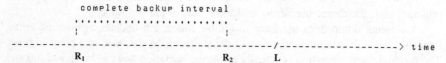

```
---------+===================+==============/-------------> time
    :    :                :    :            L
    R₁   S₁               R₂   S₂
```

Taking the residual dump at R_2 involves logging all those records not changed (and therefore not logged) since the time of the last residual dump. The time of the last residual dump would be taken as S_1. Thus, all records not logged since S_1 (due to an update action) will be logged at R_2.

The residual dump at R_2 could consider logging all records not backed up since R_1. Then the complete backup interval would span two residual dumps—from R_1 to S_{i+1}. In this case the first residual dump after initial database creation or a complete recovery would have to log only *half* the records, leaving some for the second residual dump.

During a residual dump, the "date last backed up" of *all* records must be examined. If this time is substantial compared to the time to log a record, splitting the records over multiple residual dumps is probably less efficient than having a single residual dump.

It is interesting to consider these two cases when residual dumping is a continuous process, that is $S_i = R_{i+1}$. If records older than $S_1 (=R_2)$ are logged in the second residual dump, the complete backup interval coincides with the period of the residual dump. This is like a round robin dump of portions of the database, where the portion is a record instance.

Traditional dump-and-log systems require a large and continuous block of time dedicated to dumping to the exclusion of updating, whereas residual dumping does not. For environments which experience unpredictable surges in critical, undeferrable updates, residual dumping is preferred. A residual dump can be temporarily suspended at any time to permit updates to take place. Traditional dumping inhibits updates and does not allow backup activity to take place during varying sized periods of idleness.

In an application environment, if there are periods during which there are no updates or updates can be deferred, and these periods are predictably long enough and frequent enough, then residual dumping is not likely to be the preferred backup strategy. It is likely to be periodic *physical* dumps and logging between dumps since physical dumping is considerably faster than logical dumping.

Since all backup data is uniform under residual dumping, and since changes to the database must be logged on a logical basis, the backup logging during a residual dump must be done on a logical record basis.

By logging both changes and residual dumps on a logical basis, physical reorganization of the database can occur without affecting the backup strategy. This may be a longer-run advantage of the residual dump backup strategy in environments requiring a high degree of evolvability in the database system. If physical location is one of the tagged parameters during record logging, and this information is not backed up during or after physical reorganization (an unlikely occurrence), then the moved records would have to be logged to the backup file as a result of the reorganization activity.

12.5.2 Performance of Residual Dumping

The graph in Figure 12-4 shows the reduction in the proportion of records backed up under a residual dump strategy compared to the 100% of all records under periodic dumping.

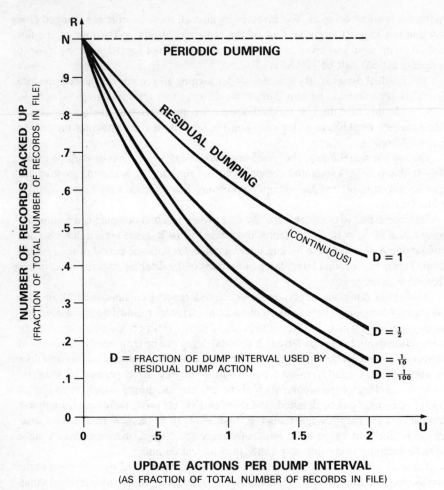

Figure 12-4. Proportion of Records Dumped per Dump Interval.
Under periodic dumping, all records are written to the backup file on each dump regardless of intervening updates. Since records are normally backed up when updated, residual dumping need only log the records *not* changed since the last residual dump. The more records updated per dump interval, the lower the proportion of residually dumped records. Further, if the residual dump time **D** (as a proportion of the dump interval) is smaller, the proportion of residually dumped records falls even further. (These graphs assume that insertions and deletions balance out so file size is constant. They also assume that the probability of a record being updated is uniform across all records and independent of other records.)

12.6 VARIABLES IN THE BACKUP PROCESS

In addition to the various backup strategies, further flexibility can be available in defining the operation of the backup process (see Figure 12-5). The backup copy may initially be written to another part of main memory, to a direct access storage device, or directly to a more permanent and removable storage medium such as magnetic tape.

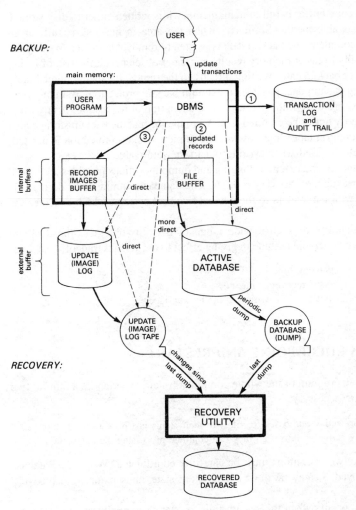

Figure 12-5. Data Movement in the Backup and Recovery Processes.

Users or user programs generate update transactions which are given to the DBMS. The DBMS performs three actions:

1. Logs receipt and disposition of the transaction.
2. Sends new or updated records back to the data file stored on secondary storage. Record updates would be preceded with a read.
3. Logs before and/or after images of record changes.

The record updates and the image logs may be held in memory until the buffer is filled with a block of records, or sent directly to secondary storage for greater backup protection. For even greater backup protection, the image logs may be written directly to more permanent and removable media, such as magnetic tape or optical disk. Periodically the database would be dumped to another file stored on disk or more permanent media. The recovery process uses the image logs and the last periodic dump to restore a database.

When the backup copy buffer is full in main memory it is written either to disk storage or directly to removable media. Similarly, when the area in the disk is full, or an update process is complete, the backup data is written to removable media. Writing the backup copy initially to faster memory results in greater efficiency at the risk of losing up to a buffer full of backup data. Writing directly to the removable media immediately prior to performing each update provides maximum backup protection. With anything less than maximum protection, the user can have the option of requesting, at any time, that the main memory buffer be emptied to disk or tape, or that the backup storage area on disk be written out on tape. In cases where complete backup protection is needed, no buffering should be used when writing out to the removable media.

Defining the timing and extent of logging and dumping actions provides additional flexibility in the backup and recovery process. The database administrator defines the backup strategies with parameters to the database control system, which executes the strategy.

With the availability of such a wide range of backup strategies, the database administrator has considerable latitude in giving effect to the various tradeoffs, such as:

- Dump time versus log time.
- Backup time versus recovery time.
- The degree of buffering in writing to the backup tape.

12.7 PROCESS CHECKPOINT AND RESTART

When a running program or the whole computer system experiences a failure, two types of actions are necessary:

- *Recover* any active *databases* (or files) to their status just prior to the failure.
- *Restart* any active *processes* so they can continue processing the database.

Furthermore, these two operations must be carefully coordinated. While the database may not be destroyed, it may be in an inconsistent state, thus requiring a recovery operation.

System failure occurs when the system fails to operate normally or ceases operation altogether. Recovery and restart may occur automatically within the system with little or no interruption of service, or it may require some outside investigation, intervention, and correction. For example, if erroneous reports or billings have been printed and distributed or mailed, external action is necessary. Some form of recovery must be possible regardless of the nature of the failure, and however unlikely the contingency.

A simple approach to restart would be for the human operator to go back to some known starting point and redo all processing since then. Where considerable work (processing, data entry, etc.) has been done, this method needlessly requires extra work. This solution is feasible in a batch processing environment (where batches of transactions are sorted and processed against a master file, and perhaps related secondary files). Even if transactions are not batched, the master files can be left unchanged by only memo posting online, leaving the real posting for later (at night), or by recording changes in a differential file. In such an environment it is not necessary to recover the online database since it is not changed.

In systems which interact with the external world by accepting transactions as they come and updating files in place, the solution of rerunning all the processes from the beginning is not only very wasteful, but infeasible and intolerable in the disruption to human activity. We no longer have 'generations' of master files, with sorted transaction files.

To accomplish recovery and restart, the system needs some mechanism for knowing the state of affairs around the time of the failure and the events leading up to the point of failure. This requires active monitoring of various types of activities, coordinated over time. Recovery of databases requires backup in the form of periodic dumps and logs of changes between dumps. Restart requires periodic snapshots of the state of the system and logging of activities between snapshots. Such a snapshot is called a checkpoint (also synchpoint or breakpoint).

A **system checkpoint** (or global checkpoint) is a static picture or "snapshot" of the state of processing at a fixed point in time. The system notes the state of each active process, where each is in its processing sequence, and the value of all its variables, including buffers and queues. This could include dumps of portions of main memory.

A checkpoint must be associated with a particular state of the database. Furthermore, it must be possible to recover a database to its state at a checkpoint using dumps and logs. A checkpoint performs the following operations:

- Force the database update buffers and image log buffers to be emptied to secondary storage.
- Write a special 'checkpoint record' to the log tape (update log tape and transaction log tape) so that subsequent database recovery could be coordinated with the checkpoint. The checkpoint record itself must identify all active processes which were interacting with the database at the time of the checkpoint.
- Write (to disk) the position of the checkpoint record within the log tape to facilitate finding the location of the last checkpoint record, thus speeding recovery.

In the event of a failure, the system first recovers the database to its state at the time of the checkpoint. The system then locates the checkpoint record on the log tape, and searches forward to identify those processes which were completed after the checkpoint and need to be 'redone,' and those processes which were not completed and must be 'undone' and restarted. When the recovery process gets to the end of the log tape (the point of failure) it goes back undoing the incomplete processes, then, after reaching the checkpoint record, it goes forward again, redoing the completed processes (that is, bringing forward the database from the checkpoint to the point of failure).

Several different criteria may be used to determine when a checkpoint should be taken. Typically a checkpoint would be taken every 5-10 minutes, or somewhat longer on smaller systems. Alternatively, it could be taken after a certain amount of work has been done or number of transactions have been processed, or at the request of the operator (just before a scheduled dump operation, file reorganization, or even when the system is not busy).

The above procedure implies that the system makes some arbitrary choice regarding where to break an active process. A much better solution is to have the process specify when it is at a logical breakpoint or *quiet point*. Such a point may occur between reading transactions, or after doing some identifiable 'unit of work.' The interval between quiet points, that is, the duration of a unit of work, should range from a few seconds to a few minutes.

If a process is long running, it will be desirable to perform a **program checkpoint** (or local checkpoint) at each quiet point. This may be nothing more than recording (on disk or tape) the last transaction successfully processed, or the last record read from the primary file. It also means recording the current value for running counts or totals. A process may be interrupted, either involuntarily due to failure or voluntarily (had to go to lunch or someone else took priority in the use of the machine). To restart, the program first looks for the recorded information on disk to decide where to begin processing again. In the absence of anything being recorded, the program would begin from the start. (Of course, when the program reaches successful completion, it must erase the program checkpoint information). An alternative would be for the program to display its current position in the processing sequence. The operator would note this information in the event of a voluntary or involuntary break, and give it back to the program when it was restarted. When the operator initiates a voluntary break, the program should continue to its next quiet point.

With program checkpoints, system checkpoints can be performed differently. When a system checkpoint is triggered, the system suspends execution of each process at its next quiet point. When all processes are suspended, the system takes a global checkpoint, including program checkpoint information which is now much easier to determine. Notice that this requires additional discipline on the part of those developing and writing applications. The program would indicate the beginning of a unit of work (sometimes called a "transaction," though not to be confused with the use of that term in this book). All updates would be held in limbo, the system being able to easily roll them back. When the unit of work is completed, the program issues a COMMIT command, saying that the updates should be finalized and made accessible to other requesting processes.

SUMMARY

Maintaining database integrity is driven at three levels:

- Legal requirements external to an organization.
- Administrative mechanisms implemented within an organization but external to the computer system.
- Technical mechanisms implemented internal to the computer system, and preferably within the DBMS, though not all DBMSs have all the integrity control mechanisms.

Internal database integrity controls should reside within a DBMS and underlie all avenues of access to a database.

Database integrity encompasses the existence, quality, and privacy of data. The next three chapters cover mechanisms for achieving these three objectives.

Backup strategies seek to protect the existence of data and facilitate recovery in the event of loss or destruction of data. Backup entails making a copy of data and storing it in some secure, preferably remote, location. Possible backup strategies include:

- Simultaneously recording all updates to two copies of the database.
- Periodically dumping, i.e., making a copy of, the entire database.
- Logging before and/or after images of all changes made to the database.
- Logging transactions which cause a change to the database.

Dumping and logging strategies lie on a continuum from recording a lot infrequently to recording a little bit frequently, respectively. These strategies are generally used in combination for more complete and rapid recovery.

A logging action not only keeps a copy of the record, but also identifies the transaction causing the update, the action taken (insert, change, or delete), the source of the transaction (user, terminal, program), and the date and time of the update action. The record may be copied before and/or after the change is made to the record. After images facilitate bringing forward a prior dump of the database when the current database is destroyed or unreadable. Before images facilitate rolling back the database to undo recent changes which were found to be incorrect or should not have been posted.

There is a distinct tradeoff between backup and recovery. The more work done during backup (copying more data, more frequently, and in different forms—all of which slows down the update process), the faster recovery can be. A simple (and incomplete) form of backup is to periodically take a *physical* dump of the storage media containing the database. Copying a device track by track can be much faster than copying the database record by record, called a logical dump. Recovery entails reloading the whole database—it is practically impossible to merge the records to be recovered from the physical dump with the still good, updated records from the current database.

Both dumping and logging have their disadvantages. During a dump, for example, all updates must be suspended in order to copy the whole database in a consistent state. The dump can take a long time for larger databases and backup is still incomplete unless changes are logged between dumps.

The residual dump backup strategy solves many of the problems of traditional approaches to backup and recovery. First, all records must be tagged with the time they were last logged as a result of an update action (or a previous residual dump action). The residual dump utility periodically cycles through all records of the database, logging those records which have *not* been backed up since the last residual dump. Now all backup is in the form of logs. A residual dump only logs one copy of a record since the before and after images are the same. Updates to the whole file or database do not need to be suspended during a residual dump. In fact, the residual dump can be spread out over time with records being logged only during periods of low retrieval and update activity. Residual dumping results in fewer total record copies than conventional backup using dumps and record image logs. Recovery entails going back on the record image log file to the last residual dump (or second last depending on the logging rule), and rebuilding the database from the single log file.

Restarting programs which were active at the time of database loss or destruction must be coordinated with the database recovery operation. One approach is to record the status of each program at its program checkpoint—that is a point at which the program is at a lull and can be conveniently interrupted, for example, between processing transactions. These program checkpoints can be coordinated with global system checkpoints, at which time the system flushes out memory buffers, logs the status of the database and system tables, and writes a checkpoint record on all database log files.

EXERCISES

12-1. Name and describe the three levels of mechanisms for maintaining database integrity.

12-2. State the three database integrity objectives. What are the internal DBMS technical control mechanisms for achieving each of them?

12-3. Describe the backup strategy of maintaining two active copies of the database and dual recording of update transactions. What are the advantages and disadvantages of this strategy? What type of threats to database integrity are not covered by dual recording?

12-4. Differentiate between dumping and logging backup activities.

12-5. Simply making a copy or 'dump' of the database periodically is not sufficient to provide complete backup protection. Why not? What additional actions must accompany periodic dumping to provide complete database backup?

12-6. Explain why logging changed records alone, without taking a periodic dump, is an impractical backup strategy.

12-7. Describe the differences in terms of recovery strategies between logging after images and logging before images. Explain why it might be desirable to do both.

12-8. Briefly explain the tradeoff between difficulty of reconstructing a database and the cost of performing the backup operation. Is there an optimal strategy? Outline how you might formulate a decision model to find the optimum.

12-9. Periodic dumps plus logging before and after record images provides complete backup protection and relatively easy recovery. Why then might an organization want to log input transactions?

12-10. Explain the difference between logical and physical dumping. What are the relative advantages and disadvantages of each?

12-11. Contrast periodic dumping and residual dumping.

12-12. What are the benefits of following a residual dump backup strategy? What are the tradeoffs involved?

12-13. Describe the application environments which are particularly suited to each of the backup strategies—dual recording of the database, periodic dumping only, periodic dumping plus logging before and after images of changed records, and residual dumping.

12-14. Design a database backup and recovery plan for a large bank having a large database and many transactions. Discuss the tradeoffs you make.

SELECTED REFERENCES

AGHILI, Houtan and Dennis G. SEVERANCE, "A Practical Guide to the Design of Differential Files for Recovery of On-Line Databases," *ACM Transactions on Database Systems* (7:4), 1982 December, pages 540-565, 16 refs.

DATE, Chris J., "Recovery," Chapter 1, *An Introduction to Database Systems*, Volume II, Reading, MA: Addison-Wesley, 1983.
     This comprehensive and detailed chapter on backup and recovery also outlines the methods followed in particular systems, and includes an annotated bibliography.

EDELBERG, Murray, "Data Base Contamination and Recovery," *1974 ACM SIGMOD Workshop Proceedings*, Ann Arbor, edited by Randall Rustin, New York: Association for Computing Machinery, 1974, pages 419-430.

GRAY, J. N., et al., "The Recovery Manager of the System R Data Manager," *ACM Computing Surveys* (13:2), 1981 June.

LOHMAN, Guy M. and John A. MUCKSTADT, "Optimal Policy for Batch Operations: Backup, Checkpointing, Reorganization, and Updating," *Transactions on Database Systems* (2:3), 1977 September, pages 209-222.

Develops a model balancing the cost of update with the cost of recovery based upon the Renewal Reward Theorem.

MARTIN, James, *Security, Accuracy, and Privacy in Computer Systems*, Englewood Cliffs, NJ: Prentice-Hall, 1973.

SAYANI, Hasan H., "Restart and Recovery in a Transaction-Oriented Information Processing System," *1974 ACM SIGMOD Workshop Proceedings*, Ann Arbor, 1974 May 1-3, edited by Randall Rustin, New York: Association for Computing Machinery, 1974, pages 351-366.

SEVERANCE, Dennis G. and Guy M. LOHMAN, "Differential Files: Their Application to the Maintenance of Large Databases," *Transactions on Database Systems* (1:3), 1976 September, pages 256-267.

Suggests setting up a separate file to hold all new and changed records separate from the main database, which can remain invariant. This differential file starts out much smaller than the main file and is, therefore, easier to update and backup. When retrieving a record, the system may find the latest copy in the main file, or in the differential file if the record has been changed. The article describes three algorithms for deciding whether or not to look in the differential file first. Periodically the differential file is folded in with the main file.

VERHOFSTAD, Joost S. M., "Recovery Techniques for Database Systems," *Computing Surveys* (10:2), 1978 June, pages 167-195.

A reasonably comprehensive classification and survey of the major database recovery techniques used or proposed in the literature.

YOURDON, Edward, "File Recovery for On-Line Systems," Chapter N, *Design of On-Line Computer Systems*, Englewood Cliffs, NJ: Prentice-Hall, 1972, pages 340-353.

THIRTEEN

DATABASE INTEGRITY: QUALITY CONTROL AND CONCURRENT UPDATE

13.1	DATA VALIDATION	454
13.1.1	External, Manual Validation	455
13.1.2	System Validation of Input Data and Stored Data	457
13.1.3	Conformance of Stored Database to its Definition	459
13.1.4	Elements of a Validation Criteria Language	460
13.1.4.1	Transitional Validation Criteria	462
13.1.4.2	Levels of Validation	463
13.1.5	Response to a Validation Failure	465
13.2	UPDATE AUTHORIZATION	465
13.3	CONCURRENT UPDATE CONTROL	466
13.3.1	Transaction: A Set of Read and Write Actions	466
13.3.2	Concurrent Updates Threaten Database Integrity	468
13.3.3	Process Integrity Loss: The Appearance of Database Integrity Loss	470
13.3.4	The Solution: Lockout	470
13.3.4.1	Serializability of Update Transactions	470
13.3.4.2	Lockout Preserves Database Integrity	471
13.3.4.3	Lockout Preserves Process Integrity	471
13.3.4.4	Lockout Leads to Deadlock	472
13.3.5	Deadlock Solution Criteria and Approaches	473
13.3.5.1	Overview of Deadlock Solution Strategies	474
13.3.5.2	Desirable Criteria for Choosing a Solution	476
13.3.5.3	Data as the Object of Resource Allocation	476
13.3.5.4	Granularity of Locks on Data	477
13.3.5.5	Identifying the Data to Be Locked	479
13.3.6	Locking Mechanisms	480
13.3.7	Conditions for Deadlock	485
13.3.8	Specific Deadlock Solution Strategies	485
13.3.8.1	Presequence	487
13.3.8.2	Pre-empt	488
13.3.8.3	Preclaim	491
13.3.8.4	Preorder	492
13.3.8.5	Timestamping	493
13.4	UPDATE SYNCHRONIZATION	496
	SUMMARY	498
	EXERCISES	500
	SELECTED REFERENCES	502

The second set of database integrity control functions seeks to maintain the quality of data in an information system. Data quality refers to data being:

- *Accurate*—the data actually recorded is correct, when compared to stored validation criteria.
- *Current*—the recorded information is up-to-date (this requires storing the date of last update or verification in each record).
- *Complete*—knowing what data is relevant and should be recorded.

Mechanisms are needed within the DBMS to ensure that update actions are performed in accordance with the stated rules, by authorized processes or persons, and that the results of the update actions are properly recorded.

There is a direct correlation between the level of data quality in a system and the level of user confidence in the system. Low user confidence translates into low system usage or skeptically tolerated system usage—the end result being less effective user/manager behavior and decisions. Data validation is all too often bypassed or deferred in the interests of getting the system developed faster. The results of poor data quality are very subtle; they insidiously undermine user confidence and thwart the original objectives of management information and decision support systems.

Database quality control is accomplished by the following functions, each of which is discussed in this chapter.

1. Data validation
2. Update authorization
3. Concurrent update control
4. Update synchronization

13.1 DATA VALIDATION

The fundamental basis for validation is some idea or expression of what the data *ought* to look like, or not look like. The process of data validation cannot be performed without having some validation criteria. It is impossible for the system or a person to look at data and determine its validity without knowing what the data *should* look like—what tests to perform, what comparisons to make. All data validation is conditional upon having a prior expression of validation criteria.

The validation process cannot produce error-free data. Sometimes it is humanly impossible to express or even to know the validation checks to be performed. More often, we know what should be checked but the system does not provide a convenient means for formally expressing or performing those checks. Moreover, even if the system could perform some validation checks, we may decide that it is economically unjustified. Certain checks may be operationally infeasible because they take too long for the system to perform, or the burden on humans is too great to externally review and correct the system-detected 'errors.' Nevertheless, as we compromise data quality, users become less confident in the results obtained from the system.

Data validation can be performed external to the system by people or within the system based upon formally stated validation criteria. Validation may be performed on input data, stored data, or output data (see Figure 13-1).

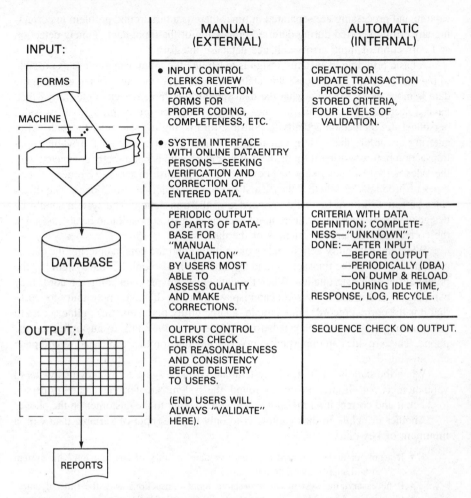

INPUT:	MANUAL (EXTERNAL)	AUTOMATIC (INTERNAL)
FORMS / MACHINE	• INPUT CONTROL CLERKS REVIEW DATA COLLECTION FORMS FOR PROPER CODING, COMPLETENESS, ETC. • SYSTEM INTERFACE WITH ONLINE DATAENTRY PERSONS—SEEKING VERIFICATION AND CORRECTION OF ENTERED DATA.	CREATION OR UPDATE TRANSACTION PROCESSING, STORED CRITERIA, FOUR LEVELS OF VALIDATION.
DATABASE	PERIODIC OUTPUT OF PARTS OF DATA-BASE FOR "MANUAL VALIDATION" BY USERS MOST ABLE TO ASSESS QUALITY AND MAKE CORRECTIONS.	CRITERIA WITH DATA DEFINITION; COMPLETE-NESS—"UNKNOWN", DONE:—AFTER INPUT —BEFORE OUTPUT —PERIODICALLY (DBA) —ON DUMP & RELOAD —DURING IDLE TIME, RESPONSE, LOG, RECYCLE.
OUTPUT:	OUTPUT CONTROL CLERKS CHECK FOR REASONABLENESS AND CONSISTENCY BEFORE DELIVERY TO USERS. (END USERS WILL ALWAYS "VALIDATE" HERE).	SEQUENCE CHECK ON OUTPUT.

REPORTS

Figure 13-1. Location of Validation Processes.
Validation processes can be performed external to the system by people, or automatically within the system. They can be applied to input data, stored data, or output data. For each of these, the above chart gives a brief indication of the types of validation which can be performed.

13.1.1 External, Manual Validation

In every system, data is subject to a certain amount of human validation, on both input and output data. In fact, a good validation program will depend substantially on people, assisting them as much as possible by checking against predefined validation criteria and seeking verification at various stages in the operation of the system. Manual validation can be performed on input data, stored data, or output data.

Input data validation can be performed at different stages from initial data capture to final database update. When some validation is performed concurrent with data capture, the system can immediately ask for a correction of any detected errors. When capture and processing are separated in time, there is a turnaround problem in correcting any errors detected during deferred processing of the input data. Timely detection and correction of input errors enhance database integrity.

A basic principle in systems design is to capture the input data as close as possible to the source. This can increase the quality of input data since the person entering the data is more likely to know what the data should look like. For example, rather than have a secretary or clerk in the sales department enter orders brought in by sales personnel, let the person actually responsible for making the sale enter the data. After entering an order, the system can request a final visual check on the whole input transaction before writing it to the database. A clerk who is not directly connected with the sales activity is not likely to know whether this customer usually orders certain types of products, or whether they usually place big orders or small ones. The direct sales person will have firsthand knowledge of the transaction. The system should be designed to seek verification from those persons in the best position to be able to judge the correctness and appropriateness of the data.

When the data entry activity takes place online and the person entering the data is a firsthand party to the transaction (and the database is also online), the system has the potential for high data quality. When the data entry person is updating a record, they can first request it and the system can display it, giving them an opportunity to verify that it is the correct record. For example, a large utility that maintains online access to customer records, can display it before the clerks as they talk to customers on the phone. This provides an opportunity to verify *any* data on the record and to complete any missing data.

When the data is entered, the system can check it against any previously stored validation criteria. If any 'errors' are found, the system can alert the data entry person to check it and correct it *on the spot*, even while talking to the customer on the phone.

Another principle in data capture is to only require input of variable data with a minimum of key entry.

- If a new or updated record contains the 'date of entry or last revision,' the system should supply that date automatically.
- If necessary, the system can timestamp input transactions with the time of entry.
- If entry records are to be numbered serially for control, the system should automatically enter a value which is one more than in the last record entered.
- If a data item can only take on one of a small, fixed set of values, the system should display the allowable values and have the user pick one (like check-off boxes on a manual form) rather than keying in a value.
- Turn around documents and plastic badges or cards should be read as part of the data entry task to avoid the introduction of errors upon rekeying.

With the advent of microcomputers, some of the validation processing can be 'downloaded' from the central computer. The local microcomputer could obtain the validation criteria from the central computer. The data entry personnel use the micro to perform input data capture, editing, and validation. The system would accept, process, and validate the data, and seek verification and correction of errors detected. This would all be done without bothering the central host computer until one or a batch of validated transactions are ready to be transmitted.

Some input validation may be performed outside the system before key entry. Data collection forms can be manually reviewed for completeness, proper coding, and reasonableness before being converted into machine readable form. **Validating stored data** is just as important as validating input data. It is impractical to rely on input validation alone to maintain data quality. Since it is never possible to guarantee the complete accuracy of stored data, it is always meaningful to solicit evaluations of quality from the users. There always remains one criterion of quality: the credibility of data to its users.

Various mechanisms can be used to obtain feedback from users on data quality. The simplest is to periodically print out portions of the database and send it to the prime user for review. This is similar to the auditor's practice of sending a statement out to debtors to verify their recorded level of indebtedness to the organization. In this way, the auditor obtains a quality check on the inventory of accounts receivable. Similarly, the organization can obtain a most important quality control check on the data stored within the database.

If the data happens to pertain to individuals outside of the organization it may be desirable (indeed, advisable in the light of the due process provision of privacy laws— see Chapter 16 on Data Privacy) to send them a copy of the information currently stored. Such communication would have to include some explanation of the individual data items and the meaning of any codes used. The organization would then ask for verification and correction of their information.

Output data validation is commonly seen in the manual inspection of output reports. This, of course, is always done by the end user upon receipt of the data. Within the Data Processing Organization, the task of output control clerks is to check output data for reasonableness and consistency before the data is delivered to the users. This is a relatively easy point at which to establish quality control measures and a relatively important one from the standpoint of user confidence. The image of data processing diminishes when a user receives a stack of printouts in response to a requested report, only to discover that the system aborted the job and produced a memory dump!

13.1.2 System Validation of Input Data and Stored Data

While it is tempting to refer to system performed validation as 'automatic' validation, it is no more automatic than anything else done on the computer. In fact, no validation gets done unless the system is first given some formally stated criteria against which to check the data.

Validation requires that the system have some information (that is, validation criteria) in addition to the data already stored. In a sense, this is redundant data serving the purpose of improving data quality. The validation criteria can be stored as an integral part of the validation program, with the data or transactions, as part of the definition of the data or transactions, or separately from all of these.

One alternative for accomplishing data validation is for the users to write their own validation programs. When building a validation processor, it is desirable to make it generalized. In fact, it is most desirable for the DBMS to provide generalized validation functions as part of the major functions of the system. Rather than have the validation checks built-in or the validation criteria stored in tables compiled with the validation program, the validation processor should use information stored with the data (input transactions or database) and its definition. Of course the design of the validation processor dictates the form (syntax) and meaning (semantics) of the criteria to be formally expressed. For batches of input transactions, some of the validation criteria can be in a header record.

Validation processing can be applied to incoming data used to update the database, or to the stored data. The primary distinction is the object of the validation process. Validation criteria can be associated with either the input data or the stored data, or both. In fact, the means for expressing validation criteria would apply equally to input data and stored data.

Many systems make the mistake of expressing the validation criteria in terms of input data transactions and concentrating validation activity with the transaction processing and update function. Unfortunately, there are usually other avenues of access to the database through which data can be added or modified, for example, the programming language interface. These avenues of database update usually bypass the validation criteria expressed in the update function. End users can no longer be confident that expressed validation criteria are always enforced. Data validation degenerates to an 'honor' system where people are individually responsible for checking data quality.

This is not to say that input data validation is not important. On the contrary, that is the point at which most errors should be detected. But, the validation checks should be based substantially on criteria associated with the definition of the stored database. Validation criteria associated with the input data should never be a replacement for comprehensive validation criteria associated with the definition of the stored database.

Is input data validation sufficient? It is impossible to check all input data completely (as noted earlier). Furthermore, even if it were, it would be unwise to assume that other errors could *never* be introduced into the stored database. We should always assume that things will go wrong, that errors can crop up out of nowhere and propagate through the database.

> A mechanism for a systematic flushing out of errors should be established. Its function is analogous to that of kidneys in an animal organism. If the system poisons are not constantly being eliminated, the system gets sicker and sicker until it dies eventually, i.e., deteriorates to the point of uselessness.*

By analogy, it is not sufficient for us to check the purity of all the food we eat—we should still have a periodic physical health checkup. Therefore, it is important to periodically check the validity of our stored databases—to run a validation utility which checks the stored data against all stored validation criteria, to follow the chains to ensure that all records are accounted for, etc. Database validation could be incorporated into file dump or file load utilities since these are normally run during relatively idle times.

---

*Joseph Orlicky, *The Successful Computer System: Its Planning, Development, and Management in a Business Enterprise*, New York: McGraw-Hill, 1969, page 186.

13.1.3 Conformance of Stored Data to its Definition

Every DBMS retains a description of the database. This is necessary to enable the system to properly interpret the bits, bytes, and blocks physically recorded on the storage media. The system must employ appropriate mechanisms to ensure that the stored database always conforms to its definition. This is particularly important after database update. Whenever the database definition changes, the physical data affected must be changed (revision and restructure). If ever the database definition does not accurately reflect the physically stored data, data integrity is lost, perhaps to the point where continued processing would produce garbage.

One very simple approach to this problem is for the system to provide a utility program which will scan over all the stored data, check the data against its definition, and issue a report on any deviations found. At least the users are made aware of corrections which should be made. If some online users cannot tolerate the time it takes to check all the data entered, they can do quick and dirty data entry and run the validation utility after a period of heavy update. Placing users on their honor to run the validation checks can lower data quality. Clearly it is preferred to check the data before it is entered into the database.

This aspect of integrity may seem self-evident but it is occasionally forgotten. For example, one DBMS permits the user to define a stored ordering on a file. Then, when a user establishes a pointer into the file to insert a new record, the values of the ordering key fields are not compared against the key values in the prior and next records to ensure that the ordering is maintained. Furthermore, it is possible to change key field values when updating an existing record. To maintain integrity the system should either reject the insert or update, or else insert the new or modified record into the correct place in the ordering sequence.* For another example, one commercially available system accepts the definition of item types such as hexadecimal, packed decimal, or alphanumeric but never checks to ensure the conformance of a stored field value with its definition.

Whether a system stores a sketchy database definition or a comprehensive definition is immaterial here. A skeleton definition simply makes it easy for the system to check for conformance! Users are responsible for testing additional conditions which should be satisfied for the data to be valid. This could be very expensive for the users. If fifty user-written programs use a particular data item expecting it to be numeric between 1000 and 9999 and the system does not check it, then this simple validation check will have to be written into 50 different programs and performed every time any one of them is executed. The DBMS vendor may be happy because he sold a system that was fast. Unfortunately, the savings in processing time is lost many times over in the application processes written to work with the DBMS.

Proper data validation begins with a comprehensive definition of the data to be validated. A comprehensive definition means more work for the system but also means less work for the user-developer, and higher quality data.

---

*The argument that the system should not allow the user to define orderings in the storage structure may be valid but is not germane here. If the system permits the definition of an ordering on the stored records, it should maintain that ordering.

The distinction between data definition information and validation criteria is fuzzy; there is considerable overlap. For example, defining a data item to be a numeric integer with a fixed length of four digits represents an expression of validation criteria. Any value received or stored for this data item which contains an alphabetic character or is more or less than four characters long should be rejected by the system. The minimum definitional information of field size (or assumed delimiter or count if variable length) is needed to properly scan and parse individual data item values from the stored (or input) data. After that, additional definitional information actually serves primarily to validate the data.

13.1.4 Elements of a Validation Criteria Language

Statements in a validation criteria language define the criteria used to detect invalid data. The statements may be part of the creation function when entering new data, the update function when processing input data transactions, or the data definition function to be used to validate stored data, new data, or update data.

All of the information concerning the definition of data items, groups, and relationships described in Chapter 6 would serve as the basis for validation.

Numeric and string types must be clearly distinguished in a validation criteria language. In both cases, the item value may be *represented* as a string of characters. If the item type is string then no further interpretation need be imposed on the value representation. If an item type is numeric, then an arithmetic interpretation is imposed on the character string representing the value. Putting it another way, the sequencing of values of string items is determined by the collating sequence of the characters (which in turn is determined by the bit representation of the characters), whereas the sequence of values of numeric item type is determined by the position of the item's arithmetic value interpretation on the line of real numbers.

The following table describes the more common types of validation checks on data items.

TYPE	A data item value should first be validated according to the defined type for the item. The more types offered by a DBMS the better for data quality.
SIZE	Defining the minimum and maximum size of data item values. Although the definition may contain a size, this is often the maximum size only of the field to contain a value for this data item.
RANGE(S)	Providing one or more ranges within which the data item must fall or must NOT fall. Applies to both numeric and string item types.
VALUES	Providing a list of acceptable values or NOT allowable values for the data item. Also applies to both numeric and string item types.
MANDATORY	Indication of whether a value for this data item (in this record type) is mandatory or optional. This could also be accomplished by excluding or including 'NULL' as a permitted value.
UNIQUE	Whether or not the stored values for this data item (in this record) must be unique. This declaration is needed for items which serve as identifiers.
FORMMASK	Providing a pattern of allowable characters which define the permissible formats for the item values.

The VALUES and RANGE(S) declarations can be conveniently combined into a single language specification of the general form:

$$\text{VALUECHECK item-name } [\text{ NOT }] v_1 [\text{ THRU } v_2], \ldots$$

where there may be any number (indicated by the ellipsis . . .) of single values or ranges of values (connected by THRU) all intermixed. It is often desirable to require the values v_i be constantly increasing as you scan the statement left to right. The prior type declaration on the 'item-name' determines whether the check is performed on an arithmetic or a string (collating sequence) basis. The **NOT** is used to designate a list of values or ranges (perhaps enclosed in parentheses) which are not allowable for the data item value. Special symbols could be used to designate the 'NULL' value, and the minimum or maximum possible values consistent with the item definition (say, '*'). Additional semantic rules are needed to indicate whether the range is to be inclusive or exclusive of the end points.

An operand (v_i) of the VALUECHECK statement could be written as:

- *Constant literal.*
- *Variable* consisting of a single named data item from the rest of the record or input transaction, from a stored record of a different file type, from a memory variable or table, or from a system variable (such as today's date).
- *Expression* which reduces to a value of a type consistent with the type of the item being tested. Expression operands in turn could be constant literals or variables as before.

The designation of the MASK to check the FORM of a data item value depends on the specification of allowable sets of characters that can appear in each character position of the field containing the data item value. For example,

X := any characters with alphabetics uppercase only.

m := alphanumeric only (A-Z, a-z, 0-9).

M := as m, alphabetics uppercase only (A-Z, 0-9).

a := alphabetic only, upper or lower case (A-Z, a-z).

A := alphabetic, uppercase only (A-Z).

D := numeric digits only (0-9), no decimal point or sign.

I := signed integer only (0-9, +, −).

F := floating point decimal number (0-9, +, −, .).

E := exponential number (as 'F' with trailing 'Enn' 'E+nn' or 'E−nn').

B := Boolean (0 or 1 only).

$:= floating dollar sign may appear at the beginning of the number.

-,/ := special characters may appear as themselves as constants.

It would be possible to allow the definition of additional character sets as the union of two or more of the above.

The general syntax of this statement could be:

$$\text{FORMCHECK item-name } [n_1] a_1 [[n_1] a_1] \ldots$$

where the a_1 specifies an alphabet from the list on the preceding page, and n_1 is the number of contiguous character positions to which it applies. The n_1 is assumed to be one if omitted. If all n_i are omitted, the FORMCHECK specification corresponds to a 'picture' of the field for the data item value. A special label for the count (say 0) can be used to indicate all (remaining) character positions in the field.

Another type of validation statement may be of the general form:

$$\text{CHECK Boolean-expression : response}$$

where the Boolean-expression contains operand(s) from the record type being validated, plus additional operands as noted earlier. If the result of evaluating the expression is true the check passes, otherwise one of the operands must be invalid. If there are multiple operands from the record, there is no way to tell which data item is in error.

The validation of a data item using any of the above check may be conditional upon the value of some other data item(s):

```
/ MANDATORY  \
| OPTIONAL    |
| VALUECHECK |  . . .  WHEN [NOT] Boolean-expression
| FORMCHECK  |
\ CHECK      /
```

To check a database for *completeness* requires that, when a data value is absent, a method be provided for distinguishing whether a data value should be present or a value for the data item is irrelevant. When a value is irrelevant no effort need be spent in acquiring the missing data. In general, the set of possible values for a data item should contain two additional values, 'unknown' and 'irrelevant,' that can be assigned to any given data item. From the viewpoint of completeness in database integrity, the use of a single 'null' value to indicate missing values is ambiguous. Zeros or blanks used to represent the null value may be perfectly relevant values in some situations. In fact, when calculating statistics, the system must be able to distinguish 'no value' from 'zero' value.

Sometimes it is also desirable to check stored data for *consistency*. For example, consider the different ways of referring to the State of Pennsylvania—in full or abbreviated as Penna, Penn, Pa, or PA with or without a period following.

13.1.4.1 Transitional Validation Criteria

Validation criteria may be specified to control the valid value transitions that may occur for a data item. For example, only the following transitions would be valid for the data item called MARITAL STATUS:

SINGLE	→ MARRIED
MARRIED	→ SEPARATED / DIVORCED / WIDOWED
SEPARATED	→ DIVORCED / MARRIED
DIVORCED	→ MARRIED
WIDOWED	→ MARRIED

For another example, validation criteria may specify that an employee can only move up through the job ranks one step at a time, or that, when salary changes, the new salary must not be less than the old salary. This could be expressed as

$$\text{NEW SALARY} \; > = \; \text{OLD SALARY}$$

where **NEW** and **OLD** are keywords of the language.

13.1.4.2 Levels of Validation

Validation criteria can be categorized according to the scope of reference.

ITEM LEVEL	if the validation is performed only looking at the target data item value and the information in the validation criteria statement.
RECORD LEVEL	if the validation is made with reference to values of multiple data items within the same record or input transaction.
BATCH LEVEL	if the data validation is made with reference to a set or batch of input data transactions.
DATABASE LEVEL	if the validation is performed with reference to some data stored in the database.

These four levels of validation for transactions are illustrated in Figure 13-2.

An example of record level (or inter-item) validation would be ordering a car with air conditioning which also means you must order the heavy duty front end suspension. Batch level validation may relate to:

- Ordering of a set of data transactions.
- Count of the number of transactions in the batch.
- Sum of a named data item within the batch.

The sum is meaningful on an arithmetic field, for example, a total of cash receipts. A sum would not be meaningful on items such as employee number or jobcode, even though they might be defined as numeric. A "hash" total is the same as a sum except that it is on a field (non-arithmetic) for which a sum has no meaning to the user. A good example of batch level validation is from accounting where the sum of the credits must equal the sum of the debits for all the transactions in the batch. If a batch level validation criteria fails, all the transactions in the batch would be rejected.

Database level validation is performed using some values taken from the database. The reason for calling out this level of validation is that, unlike all prior levels, this one requires a direct reference to the stored database. Database level validation cannot be performed without the required database files being online and accessible at time of validation processing. Examples include, ensuring that an employee is assigned to work in a valid department; ensuring that a valid skill code is recorded for an employee; ensuring that only one employee is designated as the leader of a project. Database level validation would be performed to ensure that the insertion and deletion of records would not violate the defined characteristics of any inter-record relationships involved.

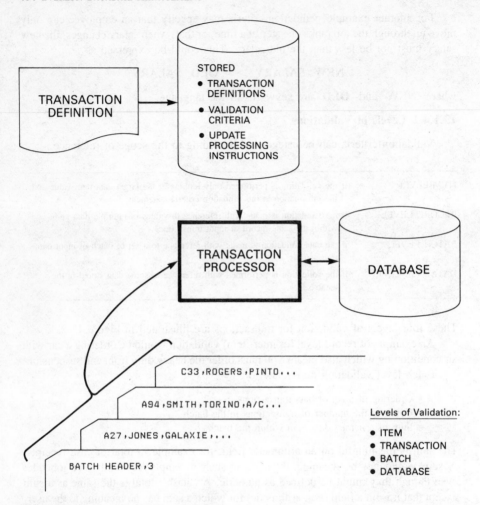

Figure 13-2. Levels of Transaction Validation.
Validation criteria for processing transactions can be expressed as part of the transaction definition.
Item level validation is done with reference only to the data item—one alpha and two numerics in the first
field. Transaction level validation is performed with reference to multiple data items in the same transaction—
ordering heavy duty suspension if you order air conditioning in a car. Batch level validation is performed
across all transactions in the batch—a count, or sum. Database level validation is done with reference to the
database—a valid model number, or the employee is assigned to a valid organization.

Some of the validation checks mentioned previously may be made with reference
to a table, rather than a literal, or a list of values. For example, the VALUECHECK
statement could specify a table lookup where the table is part of the validation procedure or is stored in the database.

For additional generality, it would be desirable for the system to provide a means
for including user-written procedures in the validation process.

13.1.5 Response to a Validation Failure

Data quality control does not end with the application of validation processes. Whenever an error or deviation is detected, some form of response is required. *Response rules* need to be given to the system along with the validation criteria—perhaps appended to the validation criteria statement, or an address/label to go to when a violation is detected. The response rules can vary widely. Types of responses might include:

- Stop everything and abort.
- Reject immediately the erroneous data record or transaction.
- Continue validating the erroneous data record or transaction with ultimate rejection.
- Make a note of the error and continue processing.
- Do nothing except to begin a different validation procedure.
- Surveillance condition detected; print out a message and continue processing.
- Let the system attempt to correct the error and continue processing if it can.
- Let the system attempt to correct the error and print out an error message.

If a DBMS does not allow the specification of a type of response to a detected validation condition, it must be taking some default action. Automatic error correction is only possible in limited cases with the user specifying what actions need to be taken.

A log should be kept of all errors detected. Errors requiring external corrective action can be flagged for the attention of the database administrator who may in turn delegate the corrective action to a user. The system should maintain a record of all unresolved errors and continue to report to the external environment until some disposition is made of each error. The logged history of errors can be analyzed to detect patterns and draw generalizations. This may help to localize problem areas in data, calling for additional validation checking, or in processes, indicating that additional program checkout or program modification may be necessary.

13.2 UPDATE AUTHORIZATION

Update processes change the contents of the database. If not properly controlled, they can diminish the quality of the database.

Three special aspects of update control are:

1. Update authorization
2. Concurrent update control
3. Update synchronization

Not everyone in an organization should be permitted to freely update the database. Some responsible authority must tell the system *who* is permitted to initiate *what* update operations. The system must check every requested update action to ensure that it is properly authorized.

The update authorization mechanism within the DBMS is the same as the *access* control mechanism used to ensure data privacy. Access authorization must be extended to include additional privilege categories. The control mechanism may lump all update actions into a single privilege, or break them out for greater control:

- ADD new records, or data values to previously unvalued data items.
- MODIFY existing data in existing records.
- DELETE existing records, perhaps even whole files.

Merely adding data to a database is not generally as disruptive as changing the existing data. Tighter controls may be needed on processes which delete data, particularly whole records or files.

13.3 CONCURRENT UPDATE CONTROL

When updating a database, most users implicitly assume that their actions are performed in isolation. Users should not have to worry about or even know about others who may be using the data. Users will also assume that multiple updates are performed serially. If the DBMS is to serve multiple users, there are two possibilities. Either the users must schedule themselves to take turns using the system, or the system must explicitly provide mechanisms to handle multiple user requests received concurrently from multiple workstations. Such a system is called a *multiuser* DBMS.

Mechanisms are needed to coordinate the actions of multiple users who want to access the data at the same time. Obviously, this is necessary in large systems serving dozens or hundreds of users simultaneously. It is also necessary in a local area network connecting multiple microcomputers. It is not sufficient to merely provide communications between the workstations and a multiuser operating system—the DBMS (and there may be more than one) must also have built-in mechanisms for controlling concurrent processes such that the integrity of the database is preserved.

When a process updates a database concurrently with another update process, the integrity of the database is threatened. For example, many agents selling airline tickets may sell the same seat twice. Similarly, the integrity of a reading process is threatened by a concurrent update process. Loss of process integrity can give the appearance of database integrity loss. Use of a lockout mechanism is the obvious solution but that can lead to deadlock. Several approaches to handling deadlock have been suggested, and all are less than ideal. This section expands on these ideas from the unique perspective of data resources.

The problems of concurrent update are addressed primarily from the standpoint of maintaining database integrity. Solution approaches are viewed from the perspective of data management rather than job management (the operating system responsible for scheduling and controlling the execution of processes).

13.3.1 Transaction: A Set of Read and Write Actions

The concurrency control problem can be described in terms of multiple update processes acting on multiple data objects. An update process is usually more than just a single write action. For example, to post the transfer of funds from one bank account to another requires the following steps:

1. READ the balance of the source account to see that there are sufficient funds; if not, abort the transaction.
2. SUBTRACT the transfer amount from the source account.
3. WRITE the new balance of the source account back to the database.
4. READ the balance of the receiving account.
5. ADD the transfer amount to the balance.
6. WRITE the new balance of the receiving account back to the database.

We assume that a database is kept in a consistent and correct state as a result of the quality control mechanisms (discussed in the previous section). To properly understand and implement concurrency control mechanisms, it is necessary to define updates to the system as a *set* of operations which constitute a complete, self-contained unit of processing. Such a set of operations is commonly called a transaction.

A **transaction** is a sequence of actions, including reads and writes to the database. A correct transaction transforms the database from one consistent state to another. An update process may consist of one or more transactions, for example, a program which posts multiple journal entries into a general ledger file. During the execution of a transaction, the database may be in an inconsistent state, for example, between steps 3 and 6 above. The proper execution of the transaction depends upon no interference from another concurrent update process which might change the value of an account balance between the READ and the WRITE (1 and 3, or 4 and 6 above). A transaction should also be defined such that no resources, such as data, need be held between transactions. This would imply that the time between transactions is a quiet point as described in section 12.7. All subsequent discussion assumes correct transactions which preserve the integrity of the database when executed in isolation.

One useful way to classify transactions is based on the dependence of the update action on prior values in the database.

REPLACE	No dependency on prior values within the database. E.g., recording a new phone number for an employee.
REPLACE with BASE VARIABLES	Dependency on values in the database *other than* the one(s) being replaced; for example:
	$$PAY = RATE * HOURS + 0.5 * RATE * (HOURS - 40)$$
	which calculates pay with time-and-a-half for overtime.
MODIFY	Dependency on the prior value of the data being replaced; for example:
	$SALARY = SALARY * 9\%$ ... for a pay raise.
	$BALANCE = BALANCE - AMOUNT$ ... for a withdrawal.
MODIFY with BASE VARIABLES	Dependency on base variables, some of which are modified and others read only.

Clearly, when executing the transaction, the retrieval of values from the database to go into the equation and the storage of the calculated value(s) must not have any interference from concurrent update processes.

A concurrency control mechanism disallows the interleaving of actions within transactions which would not guarantee consistency in the database.

13.3.2 Concurrent Updates Threaten Database Integrity

The independent and uncontrolled execution of concurrent update processes can threaten the quality of the database. In a shared database environment, several programs can interact with the database. At a primitive level, two or more users (or processes) can share the same data by taking turns. They use the data sequentially rather than concurrently. This poses no threat to database quality (if properly authorized) and avoids the problem of concurrent update. The sharing processes are controlled outside of the system.

In a large, ongoing database environment where job requests are being initiated continually, automatically, and from many diverse locations, such external control may be impossible to administer and may cause long delays for users wishing to access a database. Allowing multiple processes to operate on the same database simultaneously achieves greater sharability and availability.

Uncontrolled concurrent updates can result in the "lost update" problem or the "phantom record" problem. For example, concurrent users could sell the same seat in an airline flight twice.

To illustrate the *lost update*, suppose that two concurrent processes, **S** for SALE and **R** for RECEIPT, desire to update the same record, **A** for PART A, at the same time. Since all requests to access the database are funneled through a single process or function (the DBMS) such requests are ultimately handled sequentially. Remember the data cannot be updated directly on secondary storage; it must first be read into main memory. Now suppose that the following sequence of events is allowed to take place (refer to Figure 13-3):

1. Process **S** requests and receives a copy of record **A** in its buffer.
2. Process **R** also requests and receives a copy of record **A** in its buffer.
3. Process **S** modifies record **A** in its buffer.
4. Process **S** requests that modified record **A** be written back into the database.
5. Process **R** then modifies its copy of record **A** in its buffer.
6. Process **R** requests that modified record **A** be written back into the database.

As a result of **R**'s action, the update of **A** performed by **S** is lost forever. In effect, **R** acted without "seeing" the output results of **S**. The database reflects 90 units of part A27 in stock when it should be 80. Unable to account for the discrepancy with a physical inventory count, an auditor might write off the difference as "loss due to theft!"

Unfortunately, the lost update problem leaves no tracks. An examination of the audit trail records of the two processes would reveal that the transaction was actually received and successfully processed. All evidence would indicate that no problem

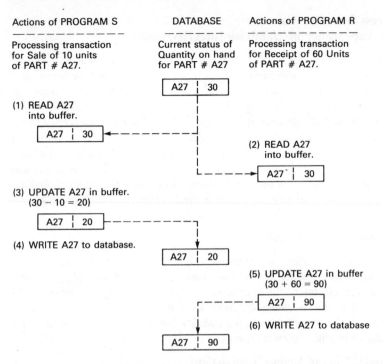

Actions of PROGRAM S	DATABASE	Actions of PROGRAM R
Processing transaction for Sale of 10 units of PART # A27.	Current status of Quantity on hand for PART # A27	Processing transaction for Receipt of 60 Units of PART # A27.

Figure 13-3. Concurrent Update Destroys Database Integrity.
Since all updating of data must take place in the main memory of the computer (not directly on secondary storage), the updates of two processes on the same piece of data can result in the update of one overwriting the update action of the other. In this figure, the time flow of events is shown down the page; the sequence of events are numbered. What should the inventory records say for Part A27 after processing the one sale and one receipt transactions above? The sequence of the two 'modify and write' actions could be reversed with **R**'s action being posted *before* **S**'s action. What would the inventory records show now? The answer is different but still wrong.

occurred, yet an update was still lost when looking at the final balance. No problem did occur as far as the two processes were concerned. The problem stemmed from the uncontrolled interaction of two update processes—their individual read and write actions were interleaved so as to destroy the integrity of the database.

The above scenario demonstrates the problem of concurrent processes and the need to control their interaction to protect database integrity and ensure the validity of user actions.

The *phantom record* problem occurs when an update process is acting on a *class* of records, and a new member is added to that class by a concurrent update process. For example, while giving a 7% raise to the set of all employees whose POSITION TITLE equals ELECTRICAL ENGINEER and calculating the total increase in the annual salaries budget, the update process will produce inconsistent results if an intervening process adds new ELECTRICAL ENGINEERs to the database and some get the raise while others do not.

13.3.3 Process Integrity Loss:
The Appearance of Database Integrity Loss

When concurrent updates are allowed to interfere with the retrieval and processing of data, the integrity of the reading process may be destroyed and give the appearance of lost database integrity. To illustrate, consider a process designed to produce an accounting trial balance. It operates by successively printing the current balance of each account in the chart of accounts. If a process is allowed to post transactions to the accounts while the trial balance is being prepared, it is possible that the debit of a transaction is posted in time to be included in the trial balance while the corresponding credit is not. The resulting trial balance would be out of balance!* The problem is that the interfering update transaction put the database into an inconsistent state, and another process was allowed to read the database while in that inconsistent state.

13.3.4 The Solution: Lockout

The solution to the problem of concurrent updates involves some form of exclusion of processes from accessing or modifying data at the time of their request. Processes may be suspended, rescheduled, or restarted. Some techniques use actual exclusionary locks on data objects; others are based upon timestamps placed on processes and data. The underlying concept of serializability helps us to understand how the various techniques produce 'correct' results.

13.3.4.1 Serializability of Update Transactions

A correct update transaction is a complete unit of processing which transforms a database from one consistent state to another. It follows that *any serial execution* of multiple correct updates will still be correct and produce a consistent database. A serial execution performs the update transactions one after another, in series. The problem of concurrent updates results from *interleaving* the separate actions of multiple update transactions.

Eswaran [1976; and described in DATE, 1983] introduced the notion of serializability (by a different name) as a formal criterion for the correctness of executing concurrent updates. A given interleaved execution of concurrent update transactions will be considered correct if it is serializable, that is, if it produces the same result as *some* serial execution of those same transactions. The result in the database must be just as if the update transactions were executed serially. Locking and timestamping schemes can be set up to ensure serializability.

Note that if the result of concurrent execution matches *any* serial execution results, it is considered serializable and, therefore, correct. The operation of a concurrency

---

*Of course, the organization should externally establish a cutoff date and time for producing the trial balance and other accounting statements. All transactions to be included in the current period must be entered before that cutoff point. Nevertheless, with data entry occurring at multiple, dispersed locations, some clerks may still try to slip some transactions in just after the deadline. Whatever happens, the system should ensure correct operation *in spite of* the actions of users.

control mechanism assumes that transactions are independent. If they in fact are not, the users must ensure that they are given to the system in the correct sequence. For example, an employee's new pay rate for the period should be entered, and the update verified, *before* entering the hours worked and having the system calculate the pay amount. The proper serial order can only be determined externally. Often it will not matter, as in the transaction examples of Figure 13-3.

13.3.4.2 Lockout Preserves Database Integrity

The obvious solution to the problems described above is that a process must be able to declare that concurrent processes not be permitted to update the data it uses until the processing is completed. Stated another way, any process must be able to request *exclusive use* of a resource *with respect to updates*.

In the example of updating the inventory, process R must not be permitted to acquire resource A until process S is finished using it (see Figure 13-4).

> WRITER RULE: When a process is *updating* part(s) of a database, then the entire sequence of actions essential to the update process *must* be protected from any interference by another process which would attempt to update the same part(s) of the database.

Note that the updating process must declare its intention to update the data at the time of the read request, whether or not it actually updates the data later. The system must *lockout* concurrent updates. Lockout preserves the integrity of the database by reserving a part of the database for the exclusive use of at most one writing process at a time.

If there were several processes, all requesting exclusive use of the same data resource, some may wait a long time depending on the order in which the requests are satisfied. It is analogous to the person back in the line with everyone cutting in ahead. Such a condition is called *livelock*. You may have experienced a similar situation trying to call a busy telephone number (such as a radio talk show call-in). An alternative is to provide an automatic queuing mechanism (''rotary'') for the phone which puts you on hold, as the airlines do for handling reservations. It is important that all requests for a single data resource be queued and serviced using a FIFO (First In First Out) discipline if livelock is to be avoided.

The ''phantom record'' problem is solved if lockout can be specified on the basis of a *class* of data objects, as defined, for example, by a Boolean selection expression. The system must then disallow the addition of new objects to the class.

13.3.4.3 Lockout Preserves Process Integrity

Solving the problem of lost process integrity involves a similar rule:

> READER RULE: When a process is *reading* part(s) of the database but not changing it, then that process *may* require protection from any interference by another process which would attempt to update the same part(s) of the database.

Whether a process is reading or writing a database, a lockout request will inhibit concurrent updates. Concurrent processes are permitted only to look at the data, but not change it.

It is popular to refer to the writer rule as ''exclusive control'' and the reader rule as

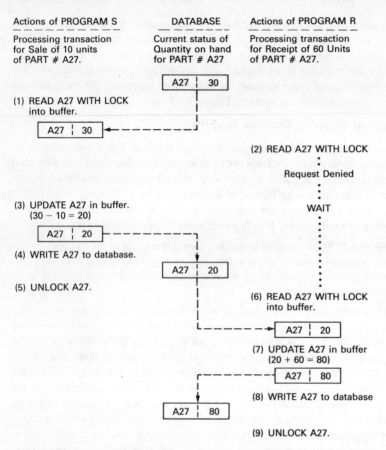

Actions of PROGRAM S

Processing transaction
for Sale of 10 units
of PART # A27.

(1) READ A27 WITH LOCK
    into buffer.

(3) UPDATE A27 in buffer.
    (30 − 10 = 20)

(4) WRITE A27 to database.

(5) UNLOCK A27.

DATABASE

Current status of
Quantity on hand
for PART # A27

Actions of PROGRAM R

Processing transaction
for Receipt of 60 Units
of PART # A27.

(2) READ A27 WITH LOCK

    Request Denied

    WAIT

(6) READ A27 WITH LOCK
    into buffer.

(7) UPDATE A27 in buffer
    (20 + 60 = 80)

(8) WRITE A27 to database

(9) UNLOCK A27.

Figure 13-4. Concurrent Update with Lockout Preserves Database Integrity.
The above chart shows the sequence of actions of two processes, (S)ale and (R)eceipt, attempting to update the same record concurrently. Unlike Figure 13-3, here they use a lockout mechanism to preserve the integrity of the database. Their sequence of actions progresses over time down the page. What could process R do while it waits?

"shared control." As commonly interpreted, when a process gains exclusive control no other process is allowed to update *or read* the locked data. With shared control, concurrent processes are allowed to read but not change the data. As will be argued later, this popular interpretation is misleading. Note that, from the standpoint of database integrity, lockout need only refer to the exclusion of concurrent *update* processes, not the exclusion of both concurrent readers and writers.

13.3.4.4 Lockout Leads to Deadlock

Unfortunately, the use of a lockout mechanism leads to the possibility of an even more difficult problem—deadlock. The possibility of deadlock arises when concurrent processes are allowed to hold resources exclusively while requesting exclusive use of additional resources.

In the simplest case, process **P** holds resource **A** while requesting **B**, and process **Q** holds resource **B** while requesting **A** (see Figure 13-5). All such processes will wait indefinitely for requested resources.

When a process is told that the requested resource is "busy," that is, currently locked, there are two options. The system can place that user's request into a queue waiting for the requested resource to become available. Alternatively, the system can return an exception code to the requesting process indicating that the resource is busy and to try again later.

13.3.5 Deadlock Solution Criteria and Approaches

For most computer installations, deadlock has not been a major problem, but the factors which increase the probability of deadlock are on the rise in newer, modern computer installations:

- Higher investment in the total pool of shared system resources.
- Larger number of online users demanding realtime response.
- Trend toward larger, online, shared databases.

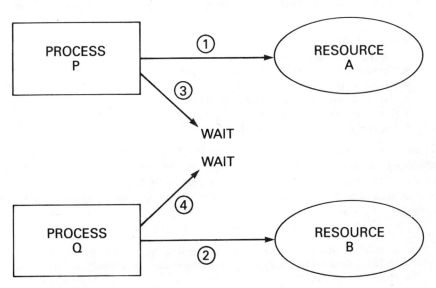

Figure 13-5. Simplest Case of Deadlock.
Consider the following sequence of events:

1. Process **P** requests and acquires exclusive use of resource **A**.
2. Process **Q** requests and acquires exclusive use of resource **B**.
3. Process **P** requests exclusive use of resource **B** but is told it must wait until **Q** is finished with it.
4. Process **Q** requests exclusive use of resource **A** but is likewise told it must wait until **P** is finished with it.

At step 3, there is no deadlock since **Q** is able to finish with **B** and then **P** will be able to use it. Deadlock cannot be detected until step 4 (unless there is some prior analysis of **P** and **Q** before initiating execution). **P** and **Q** are now waiting for each other and will wait indefinitely.

Considerable effort has been spent recently seeking effective ways to control concurrent processes. Unfortunately, most approaches seek efficient resource allocation and process scheduling. From the standpoint of database resources, no ideal solution exists; they all impose penalties and require compromise. The threat to database integrity resulting from the concurrent execution of processes has largely been handled by gross internal measures, such as lockout on the basis of a whole file, or handled by external administrative procedures, such as scheduling jobs to avoid conflicting resource usage. While these solutions may be acceptable for batch operations, they are unsatisfactory for online systems with several people and processes manipulating the database on demand.

The lockout and deadlock handling mechanism relate to the use of *any* system resource—data communication, programs, disk space, tape drives, main memory, or a central processor. This makes the solution mechanisms more difficult because it requires coordination between a DBMS and the general resource management functions within an operating system.

13.3.5.1 Overview of Deadlock Solution Strategies

The strategies for handling concurrent update processes are outlined in Figure 13-6.

- If there is shared data, and
- If there are multiple update processes, and
- If concurrent operation is to be permitted, and
- If database integrity is to be preserved,
- Then there must be a lockout mechanism; and
- If there is a lockout mechanism,
- Then the possibility of deadlock exists.

Of course, one strategy is to require that processes be presequenced externally before requests for execution are submitted to the system. The problem with this approach is that the system has no way of *guaranteeing* that conflicting processes will not be initiated such that they execute concurrently. Some lockout mechanism is still required.

Then the question is: How to handle deadlock? The basic choices are to:

- IGNORE deadlock within the system and let it be discovered externally.
- DETECT deadlock internally and *pre-empt* conflicting processes.
- PREVENT deadlock by:
  - requiring processes to *preclaim* required resources before using them.
  - *preordering* the sequence in which resources may be requested.
  - internally *presequencing* the execution of processes.

Note that deadlock should be impossible among read only processes. It can arise, however, if they are allowed to obtain exclusive use of a resource with respect to *all processes, both readers and writers.*

To **ignore deadlock** within the system means that it can only be detected externally—by an astute machine operator, a programmer waiting to get a job back, or a user waiting to get a response back from the system. In an online environment, the

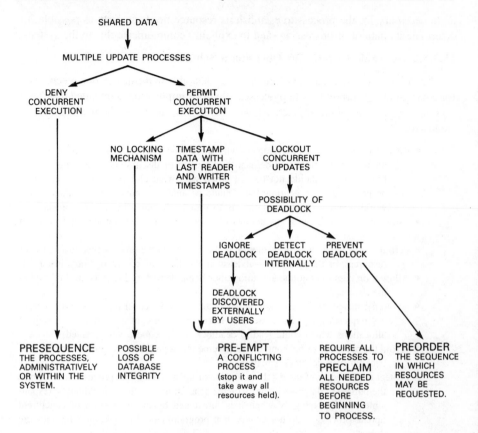

Figure 13-6. Strategies for Handling Concurrent Update Processes.

deadlocked users may eventually call up the computer operations center asking if the machine is down! Within the computer system, it is possible to discover deadlocked processes by observing two or more processes waiting for input or output operations to be completed while the system is idle. Waiting processes can also be discovered internally by a timeout mechanism.

To **detect deadlock**, whether externally or internally, requires that the operator or the system pre-empt one of the deadlocked processes (users). Pre-empting a process involves aborting its execution, releasing (unlocking) all of the resources it held exclusively, and taking steps to gracefully undo and redo its processing. If this does not permit the remaining processes to continue, then another process must be pre-empted. The real problem with this solution is the difficulty of *gracefully* backing out of the deadlock condition while maintaining the integrity of the data and the pre-empted process(es).

While it may be more desirable to **prevent deadlock**, it exacts a price on the users of the system. They must be disciplined in following a specified protocol when interacting with the system. In writing programs to interact with a database, it is increasingly necessary for the process to establish its resource needs as early as possible, to determine its pattern of processing, and to explicitly communicate this to the system.

13.3.5.2 Desirable Criteria for Choosing a Solution

The following criteria are put forth as being desirable in the design of a mechanism for controlling concurrent update processes. No prior implication is intended that these criteria are all attainable. In fact, as will be shown, some of them are mutually exclusive.

- Keep it simple for the programmers who write process specifications; place a minimum of restrictions and demand a minimum of discipline on the programmer. Ideally, users should not be concerned with what else is going on when their programs are in execution; they should be able to assume they are alone in the world making simple declarations to protect the integrity of their processing.
- Allow a process to request any number of resources as needed and release them when no longer needed.
- Permit a reasonable level of resolution in the data when the process specifies its use of resources in the database—at least at the level of record or entry instances.
- Allow a process to continue execution after being denied exclusive control of data in the database.
- Avoid permanent block, a condition where the scheduler consistently bypasses a process requesting exclusive use of a resource because of a continuous stream of allocations which could lead to deadlock if the request were granted.
- Avoid the necessity of backout; do not assume that a programmer knows what to do to backout of a deadlock situation.
- Protect the integrity of the database in spite of the actions of the process; do not place the burden of database integrity on the programmers—they should not be responsible for data integrity when it is threatened by the interaction of concurrent update processes; do not assume that programmers always know what they are doing.
- Do not depend upon external administrative procedures for sequencing the execution of processes so as to avoid conflict and thereby maintain database integrity; such a dependence is intolerable in an online, realtime database environment.

From the standpoint of data resources, an ideal solution does not exist which meets all of the above criteria.

13.3.5.3 Data as the Object of Resource Allocation

In attempting to characterize data as the object of resource allocation to concurrent processes, it is useful to classify all types of resources.

The first distinction is made between consumable and reusable resources. Once a **consumable resource** is assigned to a process, it is consumed and no longer available for reallocation. This would include card images from a card reader, and messages and signals such as "ready-to-send," "ready-to-receive," and "receipt acknowledged" transmitted in interprocess communication.

A **reusable resource** can be reassigned to another process when released by a using process. Reusable resources are further divided into those that follow the law of conservation and those that do not because they can be reused an unlimited number of times.

A **conserved resource** is usually a physical resource which inherently can have only one owner at any point in time. For a conserved resource, lockout is inherent in its allocation to a process. For example, it is physically impossible for a printer to print two lines of output simultaneously. Similarly, a clocking mechanism is used to resolve conflicting references to main memory, using read-followed-by-write as an indivisible operation. Undesirable interaction of processes cannot destroy the integrity of a conserved resource because simultaneous use is impossible. Alternatively, if the internal state of the reusable resource can be modified during use, it is a conserved reusable resource only if it is always initialized upon assignment to another task.

Stored data is a reusable, unconserved resource and differs in some fundamental respects from conserved resources. Lockout is not inherent in the allocation of data to a process. (Lockout is inherent with respect to the physical access mechanism but not the data being accessed.) The same stored data can be accessed over and over again. If lockout is not imposed when the process intends to update the data, the integrity of the database may be threatened.

Unlike processes which use conserved resources, processes which use an unconserved resource must be distinguished by what they intend to do with the resource. It is absolutely necessary for a process to declare its intention to either read only or modify the data resource. If it intends to modify, all other processes which intend to modify that same object data must be locked out until the first process is finished with the object data.

If a process only intends to read the object data, it must still have the *option* of locking out all other processes which intend to modify the data it is reading. A process which only wants to read some object data always has the option of reading, whether or not the object data is locked by some other process. Furthermore, it is impossible for a concurrent update process to make the lockout decision (exclusive versus shared control) for the reading process. Data can be read concurrently by any number of processes but can only be modified by one process at a time. These ideas are sometimes obscured when authors discuss the control of concurrent access to data.

Whereas pre-emption may be an option with conserved resources, it is never a desirable option with data undergoing modification by a process. Pre-emption means that a previously allocated resource can be taken away from a process before the process voluntarily releases it. In other words, a process must be prepared to release on demand a previously allocated resource. Such a resource is called a pre-emptive resource.

13.3.5.4 Granularity of Locks on Data

The granularity of a lock refers to the amount of data locked, or the size of the data objects locked. *Coarse* granularity means large data objects such as whole files; *fine* granularity means small data objects such as individual records. In between, the system can lock on the basis of logical groups of records, or physical blocks of records.

The designer of a concurrency control mechanism has a choice of granularity in the unit of data to be locked. The resulting tradeoff is between concurrency and overhead. *Concurrency* is the ability of processes to interact with the data without encountering interference from concurrent processes. If the probability of interference is low, then the level of concurrency is said to be high. Increased concurrency translates into increased sharability and availability.

	COARSE GRANULARITY	FINE GRANULARITY
Size of data object	large	small
Number of data objects	few	many
Housekeeping overhead	low*	high
Probability of interference	high	low*
Level of concurrency	low	high*

*desirable characteristic.

With coarse granularity, say a file, a requester must lock the whole file in order to update or read even a single record. If another process wanted to access a different record, it would be locked out *even though there is no threat to data integrity*. This could be considered a false alarm. At this level of granularity the system has relatively few data objects to manage. Therefore, the overhead of the locking mechanism is low. Coarse granularity yields reduced concurrency (increased probability of interference), and low overhead costs.

Generally, when the responsibility for concurrency control rests with the operating system, it allocates data objects at the file level. In some cases a process can only request lockout on one file at a time with the result that data integrity is threatened when the process must update more than one file in a single transaction. If the operating system permits a process to separately issue exclusive requests on multiple files in succession, the possibility for deadlock exists.

In environments which share a large database, perhaps even one large master file, lockout control at the file level in unacceptable. It must be possible for a process to request lockout on a smaller subset of the database.

Fine granularity, say at the record level, yields increased concurrency. It is desirable to lock small amounts of data—only what is needed—so requesters will not have to wait. However, fine granularity greatly increases the overhead burden of managing many more (smaller) data objects. Fine granularity also makes it difficult for a process to specify, in advance, its needed set of data resources. When a process is written, the programmer usually knows which files are to be used, but does not usually know which specific records will be processed until the program is in execution and receives its input parameters.

For different transactions, different granularities may be appropriate, rather than performing lockout at exclusively coarse or exclusively fine granularity.

If a transaction accesses a small portion of the database (say less than 1% or a few records), then fine granularity is preferred. Also, if locks are held for extremely long times, fine granularity is preferred. Long locking periods may result from a process prompting users online for input parameters, as they wait for a customer to make up their mind on the telephone, for example.

If a transaction accesses many records in a file, it will be much more efficient for it to request a file lock once, rather than many individual record locks. This would be the case for a process printing out a trial balance in an accounting system—it would have to lock every record in the file (with a non-zero balance)!

It is desirable to be able to request locks at multiple granularities—on either whole files or individual records—as dictated by the nature of the process.

13.3.5.5 Identifying the Data to Be Locked

The following table indicates how data would be identified for locking:

UNIT OF LOCKING	METHOD OF IDENTIFICATION
Whole file	File name
Individual record	Record identifier (value)
Logical subset of records	Boolean selection expression

In between one individual record and the whole file, a process may desire to lock a *logical subset of records* based upon a Boolean selection expression. For example, one process may be giving a raise to electrical engineers:

CHANGE SALARY = SALARY * .09 WHERE TITLE = "ELEC ENGR"

while another may be calculating the total salary for those in a range of departments:

PRINT SUM SALARY WHERE UNIT BT 2110 AND 2115

Each of these commands should be processed completely without interference from concurrent updates. They will conflict if there are any electrical engineers in any department with a unit number between 2110 and 2115. If the processing were more complex (requiring multiple commands and a looping mechanism, say) it might be necessary for the process to isolate and lock the required subset of records in a separate command. Such a read-with-lock command would have the same selection expression for its predicate.

If the system maintains a list of selection expressions for locked records, that is called predicate locking. When processing a record for *any* transaction, it would be necessary for the system to test it against every active predicate lock before proceeding. This is necessary because the predicates may identify overlapping sets of records. Alternatively, upon receiving the predicate lock request, the system could search for all records satisfying the selection expression and set their record locks on, thereafter ignoring the predicate. The latter strategy is easier to implement but it does not solve the phantom record problem.

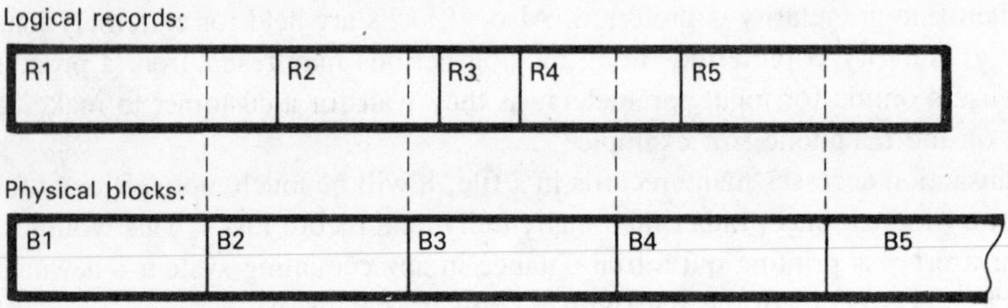

Logical records:

R1		R2		R3	R4		R5	

Physical blocks:

B1	B2	B3	B4	B5

Figure 13-7. Locking Physical Blocks Instead of Logical Records.
Suppose that variable length logical records are stored and the system allows them to span physical blocks. In the above example, a lock on record **R4** will result in a lock on blocks **B3** and **B4**. This would mean that records **R2**, **R3**, and **R5** are also locked. The system can safely lock more than requested. The effect may be a reduction in the level of concurrency (an increase in the probability of interference).

When implementing a locking mechanism, the system can safely lock more than the amount of data requested. It is not uncommon for a system to lock physical blocks or pages of memory, rather than logical records. A block may hold more than one record, or a record may span multiple blocks (see Figure 13-7).

13.3.6 Locking Mechanisms

A necessary condition for controlling concurrent processes and maintaining data integrity is that there exist some mechanism to delay or deny the requests of some processes if they actually or potentially conflict in their use of resources. The common approach in centralized systems is for each process to declare to the system that *other* processes which update the database must be locked out from modifying the identified object data. An alternative, which holds out greater promise in distributed systems, is based upon the notion of timestamping each transaction and ensuring that they are posted serially against the data. This alternative is discussed at the end of this section.

A lockout request is mandatory if the requesting process intends to update the identified object data. Notice the distinction here—the process is not requesting that a particular data resource be assigned exclusively to the process, rather the process is requesting a lockout of all attempts by concurrent processes to *update* the object data while it is being used.

If the requesting process only intends to read the object data, it has the *option* of requesting that concurrent update processes be locked out. Since the integrity of a reading process can be threatened when concurrent update is allowed, the reading process must be able to request that certain identified object data will not undergo any modification until the process is finished reading. To the system, lockout requests from reading and writing processes always have the same meaning—concurrent updates are to be excluded. They are not requesting full exclusive control of the object data, only *exclusive control with respect to update actions*.

One proposal is to provide explicit LOCK and UNLOCK commands:

LOCK identified-object-data

    . section of code
    · from which concurrent update
    ' is to be locked out.

UNLOCK [identified-object-data]

The LOCK command would instruct the system to test for the existence of a lock on the object data held by some other process. If the lock is set, the system can put the requesting process into a wait state and keep testing the lock until it is unset. The waiting processes would queue up for the use of each requested resource, and be served on a FIFO basis to avoid livelock.

Alternatively, the system could return control to the requesting process with a "busy signal" indicating that the lock was set, and to try again later. This approach gives the process an opportunity to do some other processing in the interim instead of waiting idle. It is interesting to speculate what the process would do while waiting. Few programmers have ever considered such a processing sequence (let alone have the ability to do it in their programming language).

Nevertheless, returning control has some merit if the process is executing with the user waiting online. The user could be notified of the delay and given the opportunity to do something else for a time. Even better would be to queue up the request anyway, and let the user know when the needed resources become available. This would require multitasking at the user's workstation.

If none of the object data is locked by another process, the LOCK statement would set a lock and return control to the requesting process. The TEST and SET functions of the LOCK command must be indivisible. That is, the system must not initiate execution of another LOCK command from a concurrent process until after it completes the test and set sequence for the requesting process. To do so would destroy the integrity of the lock—a problem of concurrent update processes again!

Between the LOCK and UNLOCK commands would be commands to read and/or write the identified object data. If the LOCK matching the UNLOCK is unambiguous, the object data need not be identified with the UNLOCK command. There could be several LOCK-UNLOCK pairs, even nested, within a single update transaction. A COMMIT command at the end of the transaction would be an implicit UNLOCK ALL command.

Unfortunately, a simple LOCK-UNLOCK mechanism is insufficient. The system also needs to know whether the requesting process intends to update the object data or not. If one reading process sets a lock on some object data (which it does not want to change during the process), the system should not exclude a second reading process from requesting the data with lockout of concurrent updates.

To solve this problem, the system could provide two types of lock commands: LOCKR and LOCKU. The suffix would indicate whether the requesting process intended to Read or Update the object data. Note that it is not sufficient for a process to "read with lock" or "read hold" without the system knowing whether the process intended to update.

Alternatively, the system could accept some prior declaration of processing mode, read or update, and automatically set the appropriate type of lock on each read of the data. The read or update declaration would be made for each set of object data to be processed. The prior declaration could conveniently be in the OPEN command. Some systems actually set the LOCK at the time of the OPEN command. This is undesirable if the process intends to actually use only a small proportion of the opened data. Such coarse granularity increases the likelihood of interference and reduces concurrency. Of course, if the process intended to use all the opened records, it is most desirable to lock them all at once and avoid the need to lock records as they are individually read.

The matrix in Figure 13-8 indicates permitted concurrent usage.

It has become prevalent for systems to provide "shared" control (relating to the reader rule) or "exclusive" control (relating to the writer rule). See, for example, the ANSI proposal in Figure 13-9. As commonly interpreted, when a process gains exclusive control, no other process is allowed to update *or read* the locked data. While shared and exclusive control is the result, it is wrong to infer that readers and writers alike should be allowed to *declare* whether they desire shared control or exclusive control. As generally implemented, exclusive readers will be unnecessarily denied concurrent access, and "shared writers" will be wrongly permitted access (threatening the integrity of the data). Of course, shared readers would be prohibited from updating

	READ ONLY WITH NO LOCKOUT OF CONCURRENT UPDATES.	READ ONLY WITH LOCKOUT OF CONCURRENT UPDATES.	READ WITH INTENT TO UPDATE (MANDATORY LOCKOUT).
PROCESS 1: → PROCESS 2: ↓	NO LOCK	LOCKR	LOCKU
NO LOCK	YES	YES	YES
LOCKR	YES	YES	NO
LOCKU	YES	NO	NO

Figure 13-8. Compatibility Matrix of Permitted Usage Modes.

A process reads data in one of three modes. When two processes request to read the same object data, the matrix indicates when they will be permitted concurrent access (YES) and when not, depending on their usage modes.

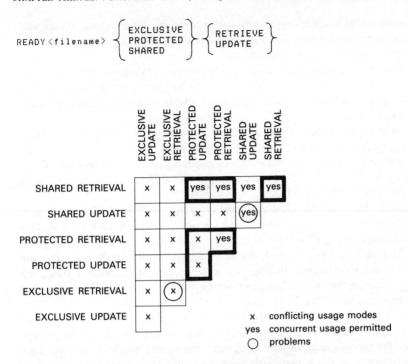

Figure 13-9. Compatibility Matrix for the CODASYL/ANSI Proposal.

The compatibility matrix in the Network Database Language proposal (X3H2-1984-23, page 96) of the American National Standards Institute (ANSI) is essentially the same as originally proposed by the CODASYL Data Base Task Group in their 1971 report. When READYing a file for use, the programmer declares the share mode as EXCLUSIVE, PROTECTED, or SHARED, and the access intent as RETRIEVE or UPDATE. Depending upon how other users opened the same file, this READY request may be granted or denied. The above 6x6 matrix shows conflicting usage modes and permitted modes for all combinations of two programs requesting use of the same file. Note the needless denial of two exclusive readers, and the integrity-threatening approval of two shared writers, who are then responsible for properly reading, locking, and updating the shared data. Compare this with the simplified compatibility matrix in Figure 13-8. In short, the three-way share mode declaration can be reduced to a single exclusive option if the access intent is retrieve. It is also interesting to note that the CODASYL/ANSI proposal forces a pre-emption strategy for handling concurrent updates.

the object data. From the standpoint of database integrity, lockout need only refer to the exclusion of concurrent *update* processes, not the exclusion of both concurrent readers and writers.

To summarize: a writer must always be exclusive (with respect to concurrent updates) and a reader must never be exclusive (with respect to concurrent readers). Furthermore, a writer should never be able to exclude a reader who does not care about concurrent updates.

It should *always* be possible for a reader to browse through the database without interference, with no explicit intent to update. This becomes increasingly important as the locking granularity becomes coarser. Reading without concern for concurrent update may be desirable when taking a quick look at only one piece of data. It may also be acceptable when performing a statistical analysis or sampling process on the data where complete accuracy is not required.

If the database is divided into mutually exclusive units of data such as files, logical records, or physical blocks, it is possible to associate the locking information with each unit of data. At a minimum, the system must know whether the unit of data was locked by a reader or an intended writer. If a writer, the system must identify which process holds the exclusive write lock on the data. If readers only, the system must keep track of how many readers have a lock on each data object at any point in time. Each granted lock adds one to the count; each released lock subtracts one. This means the system must keep track of the locks held by each process so the correct data objects can be identified when the locks are released.

If the locks are not maintained on mutually exclusive units of data, the system must maintain a table showing the selected data which is locked by each process. This could even involve storing each Boolean selection expression. The table would have to be checked for each new lock request, and all of the potentially overlapping selection expressions would have to be evaluated. Again the process of checking, testing, and setting any locks on the object data must not be interrupted by another process of checking, testing, and setting locks.

Another approach to handling concurrency is to not set any locks at read time. The system would read the data when requested and store it in a non-changeable buffer. Then, when the process issues a write command, the system would reread that same data and compare to what was previously read. Any difference would indicate that the data had been changed since the previous read and the update action would not be performed. The process would have to go back to reread the new data and redo the update processing.

Unfortunately, the update may be dependent upon the constancy of some other data as base variables. If so they would all have to be reread, too. Furthermore, *all* the data as base variables and as data to be modified must be reread, compared for no change, and the update written, all in a *single indivisible action*—impossible in any practical implementation. The purpose of locks is to divide the transaction into smaller actions which the system can guarantee will be indivisible. Thus, it is not feasible to ignore locking at read time.

An updating process must read and lock all data on which the update action depends, and hold those locks until the update action is completed. Some systems place a limit on the number of data objects which can be locked by a writer at any one time. One commercially available system allows the users to only hold a lock on one file at a time. In such an environment, it will be impossible to guarantee the integrity of those updates which depend upon data in multiple files. This example implies a caution: just because a system provides a locking mechanism does not mean that it adequately protects the integrity of data under concurrent processing.

By now you may be wondering why all this discussion about locking. Unfortunately, locking mechanisms are not always implemented correctly in commercially available DBMS. It is important for the prospective buyer/user to look carefully at how locking is handled in candidate systems. Do not be misled by the mere mention of a locking mechanism. This discussion is also helpful for developers and vendors of DBMS as design guidelines or indications of where their system needs correction or improvement.

Some mechanism is required to control concurrent processes if database integrity is to be preserved. The mechanisms involve monitoring the actions and status of processes. The mechanisms use information provided by the process (requests issued and processing intentions) or information about the process (when it started execution of a transaction).

13.3.7 Conditions for Deadlock

Five conditions must simultaneously hold true for deadlock to be able to occur. They are summarized in the following table:

CONDITION FOR DEADLOCK	SOLUTION STRATEGY
LOCKOUT: a process can obtain exclusive control of resources (with respect to update).	(none)
CONCURRENCY: multiple (update) processes compete for exclusive control of multiple resources.	PRESEQUENCE
COMPLETION: a process is allowed to hold resources until processing is completed.	PRE-EMPT
ADDITIONAL REQUEST: a process can request additional resources while holding exclusive control of other resources.	PRECLAIM
CIRCULAR WAIT: a circular chain of processes exists such that each holds a resource being requested by the next process in the chain.	PREORDER

Each solution to the deadlock problem stems from relaxing one of the above conditions. Relaxing the first condition, by not providing a lockout mechanism, threatens the integrity of the database and therefore is not considered a viable solution. The following section describes the four specific solution strategies plus timestamping.

A traffic jam analogy can provide an intuitive understanding of the deadlock problem arising from the above five conditions, and the four viable solution strategies (see Figure 13-10).

13.3.8 Specific Deadlock Solution Strategies

All viable strategies for handling concurrent processes involve some form of exclusionary or locking mechanism. Then deadlock can be handled by detecting it and pre-empting resources used by one (or more) of the deadlocked processes. Alternatively, deadlock can be prevented by requiring the processes to follow a particular protocol when interacting with the concurrency control mechanism.

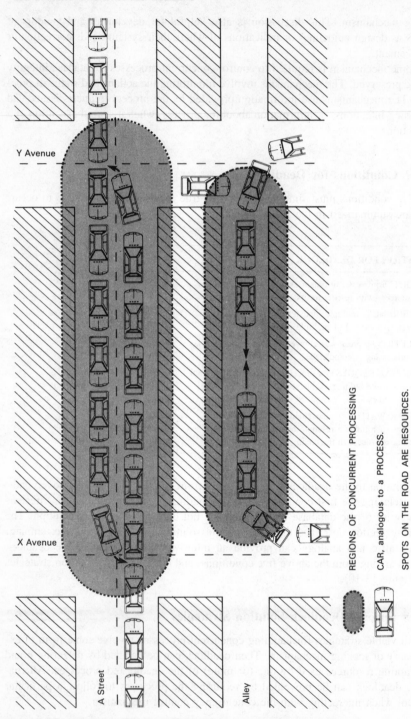

REGIONS OF CONCURRENT PROCESSING

CAR, analogous to a PROCESS.

SPOTS ON THE ROAD ARE RESOURCES.

The remaining sections describe the various solution strategies in more detail.

- Presequence, by denying concurrency.
- Pre-empt, a detection strategy.
- Preclaim, a prevention strategy.
- Preorder, a prevention strategy.
- Timestamping, an important variant of pre-emption.

All solution strategies impose some conditions or some protocol on the processes as they interact with the concurrency control mechanism. The condition may relate to when a process will be permitted to perform. A protocol is a restriction on the sequences of steps which a transaction may perform. Under a protocol restriction, the processes must follow some rules or discipline when specifying processing actions against the database.

13.3.8.1 Presequence

For those processes which potentially compete for exclusive use of the same object data, deadlock can be prevented if they are simply not executed concurrently. This solution strategy can be administered externally as well as implemented internally. Date refers to the presequence strategy as transaction scheduling [1983, page 107].

In the simplest case requiring no prior analysis, *no* processes are permitted to run concurrently. This solution is automatically imposed in computer systems which can only run one task at a time, such as in many desktop personal computers.

To be more selective in applying this solution strategy requires a prior analysis of processes to determine which do and which do not conflict with each other. This information would have to be recorded in a conflict matrix (see Figure 13-11) showing all processes on both dimensions.

If only some processes are analyzed for potential conflict, then any other process would have to be analyzed against all those previously included before being scheduled for execution (or else not run concurrently with any of them).

Figure 13-10. Traffic Jam Analogy of Deadlock.
The diagrams on the preceding page depict classic traffic jams; one on a two-lane, two-way street with the lead car in each direction attempting a left turn, the other a single lane alley with cars entering at each end. Consider each car to be a process requiring resources which are the spaces on the road. The cars are using the road (several resources) concurrently. The regions of concurrency are on **A** street and the alley between **X** and **Y** avenues inclusive. Each car uses a resource exclusively (lockout), must hold it while requesting additional resources (the spot ahead), cannot be arbitrarily removed from the spot it occupies, and requests resources in any desired sequence (resulting in a circular wait pattern).

Study the above situations carefully pretending that you are a traffic cop, or a traffic or road engineer. What can you do to solve the problem of deadlock now (detection and pre-emption), and what can you do in the future to prevent (absolutely) this situation from ever happening again? Your solutions must allow each driver to go where they desire, in so far as possible. Thus, saying that the lead car must go straight ahead is undesirable—it is like telling the payroll program, "You are going to stop printing cheques and start processing withdrawals from inventory!" There is a fairly clean analogy for solving the traffic jam corresponding to the relaxation of each of the four conditions for deadlock. All (except one) appear commonly in actual driving situations. Come up with your own suggestions *before* reading the next section. You will gain a substantial understanding of the deadlock problem and the viable solution strategies.

PROCESSES

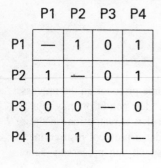

Figure 13-11. Process Conflict Matrix.
A conflict matrix indicates which processes conflict with each other. A one (1) entry at the intersection of two processes would indicate a potential conflict, while a zero (0) entry would indicate no conflict. With the sample matrix shown above, process 4 could not be run concurrently with processes 1 or 2. Process 3 could be run anytime since it has no conflicts with other processes. Such a conflict matrix could be maintained externally, or within the computer system.

What is the basis for determining a conflict? Clearly, it is if the two processes wish to have exclusive use of the same data (or other resources). This analysis would normally be done on the basis of a database or individual files. Performing a conflict analysis at any finer granularity would generally be impractical, if not impossible. In fact, if information is kept with each process indicating which data files it uses, the person controlling the execution of tasks simply makes sure that no other processes are currently using the required data files before running the process. Note that a conflict matrix is no longer needed. In effect, this is applying a preclaim strategy to control update processes and prevent deadlock. If it is done externally (and always guaranteed!), then there is no need for an internal locking mechanism.

Presequencing processes is a most prevalent solution strategy used outside the system. It may be acceptable in a batch processing environment where all jobs are normally run in some sequence. It is not acceptable in an online, multiprogramming, shared-database environment. Nevertheless, even in a dynamic processing environment, presequencing, or at least sequencing according to strict time limits, may be necessary. For example, all of the accounting transactions for the month must be processed before the books of account are closed. Similarly, all of the deposits and withdrawals for a given period must be posted to bank savings accounts before calculating earned interest.

In the traffic-jam analogy, the extreme of presequencing would correspond to having only one car within the block between **X** and **Y** avenues at a time. Placing coordinated lights at each end of the block would effect a solution and permit multiple cars to pass through at a time. A green light at one end would permit cars to enter and pass through the block (region of concurrency) while a red light stops traffic from entering at the other end. Both would be red for a time, allowing all the cars within the block to clear out before cars at the other end are allowed to enter the block. This solution is often seen on single lane bridges in rural areas.

13.3.8.2 Pre-empt

In the pre-emption strategy, a mechanism is set up to detect when deadlock occurs. Then a particular procedure is followed to pre-empt the use of locked resources by one (or more) of the deadlocked processes. This is the solution suggested by Murphy [1968].

Externally, deadlock can be detected by users who find themselves waiting too long for a request to be processed. They can then voluntarily abort their request, or a central operator can abort one of the deadlocked processes.

Internally, the system can construct a wait-for graph to record which processes are waiting for which processes (see Figure 13-12). Each active process is a node in the graph, and each arc indicates a wait. If process **P** holds resource **A** and process **Q** requests **A**, a directed arc (arrow) would be drawn from **Q** to **P** in the graph. Each time a process requests a resource, exclusive with respect to updates, the system can check the wait-for graph to see if a deadlock would result. Manipulation of the wait-for matrix (as shown in Figure 13-12) reveals the deadlocked processes.

Which of the deadlocked processes should be pre-empted? There are several possible criteria:

- The process holding the fewest locked resources.
- A process which has not issued any updates yet, making rollback easier. This strategy implicitly gives priority to writers since a reader could experience livelock.
- The process with the lowest priority; priority levels must be established in advance for each process.
- The most recently started process.
- The oldest starting process (used in timestamping).
- The last process to request exclusive use of a resource.

The simplest approach to pre-emption is to stop the selected process in the middle of what it is doing, thereby releasing all the resources it held exclusively. If appropriate steps are not taken, this may leave the data files in an inconsistent state and may produce undesirable or duplicated results when the process is rerun.

An intermediate approach is to return control back to a special entry point within the pre-empted process. This requires the programmer or online user to take appropriate action to backout the process gracefully, and perhaps resume at some earlier point. One vendor's DBMS gives users the option of adding a "rollback paragraph" to their program. The only difficulty is in discovering where the process was when pre-empted and determining what to do to recover!

A better solution is for the system to roll back the process, that is, the transaction, just as if it had never started. Each transaction should be processed on an all or nothing basis. All updates from a transaction must be held in limbo until the transaction reaches completion. Completion is indicated by a quiet point, an explicit COMMIT command in the process, or the process exits. Upon completion, all update actions can be posted permanently to the database in one atomic action (the two-phase commit). If the process does not complete successfully, its requested changes to the database must not be posted, or if they are posted, they must be backed out. Process rollback involves *selective* rollback of the database. Successful concurrent updates should be retained. Note that the same underlying functions used in recovery can also be used in concurrency control using a pre-emption strategy.

While in limbo, all updates must not be made available to other processes. Some authors suggest exclusion from *all other processes*. Actually the exclusion need only

WAIT-FOR Graph:

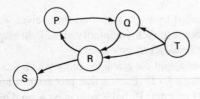

NODE: represents a process
ARC: represents one process waiting for another,
for example, P waits for Q.

WAIT-FOR Matrix:

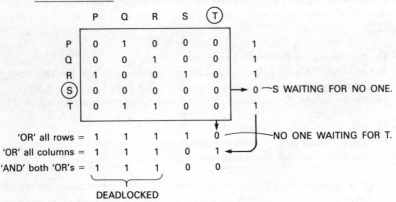

DEADLOCKED

Figure 13-12. Wait-For Graph and Matrix to Detect Deadlock.

In the wait-for graph, a deadlock only occurs when a process requests a resource that would result in a directed cycle within the graph, as with **P**, **Q**, and **R** above. In the matrix representation of a wait-for graph, a **1** indicates the process on the left is waiting for the process on top.

1. Combining all *columns* with a Boolean 'OR' reveals that process **S** is waiting for no one, and could run to completion (releasing its resources) if it requests no locked resources in the meantime.
2. Combining the *rows* with a Boolean 'OR' reveals that process **T** is not involved in the deadlock because no other process is waiting for it.
3. Combining the row and column vectors with a Boolean 'AND' leaves processes, **P**, **Q**, and **R**.
4. Cross out the rows and columns for the eliminated processes, **S** and **T**, and repeat the procedure from step 1. above until no processes are eliminated.

Since no further processes are eliminated, **P**, **Q**, and **R** are deadlocked in a circular wait. One of these would have to be pre-empted.

Notice that pre-empting **P** will not help in the short run since **R** would still be waiting for **S**. Notice also that in pre-empting **Q** the released resource must be given to **P**, a process involved in the circular wait. Giving it to **T** would immediately produce deadlock again, even if **T** requested it before **P** (the FIFO allocation rule must be suspended here).

apply to other processes requesting a lockout of concurrent updates; a reader who does not care, should be permitted to see updates even if in limbo. A writer must not release locked resources, on which the correctness of the update depends (base variables or modified variables), until all the updates in the transaction have been issued.

The preceding discussion of the pre-emption strategy presumes that the first process to request exclusive use of a resource gets it if it would not lead to deadlock. Timestamping, discussed later, uses the opposite approach but is still considered a pre-emption strategy.

In the traffic-jam analogy, pre-emption requires that the needed resource (spot on the road) be physically separated from the car. One gets a vision of a big crane moving in and lifting the car out of the traffic jam! The car (process) is prevented from continuing as it originally intended. Requiring one of the lead cars to go straight ahead instead of turning left might also be interpreted as a pre-emption strategy (though it would not work in the case of the one-lane alley).

13.3.8.3 Preclaim

Preclaim is a preventative strategy which requires all update processes to request-with-lock all resources needed to successfully complete a transaction (both base and modified variables), such a request to be made and satisfied *before the process issues any update commands*. This solution strategy was first explored in detail by Habermann [1969] in the context of general system resources. It was further explored in the context of data resources by Frailey [1973] and by King and Collmeyer [1973].

Under a preclaim protocol, the transaction to post a transfer of funds from one bank account to another (see section 13.3.1) would have to be rewritten as follows:

1. READ balance of the source account.
2. READ balance of receiving account (was step 4).
3. SUBTRACT transfer amount from source account, and abort transaction if insufficient funds (was step 2).
4. ADD transfer amount to receiving account (was step 5).
5. WRITE new balance of source account to database (was step 3).
6. WRITE new balance of receiving account to database.

In a pure preclaim strategy, a process requests all needed resources at one time. That is, the set of requests (steps 1 and 2 above) is considered indivisible (may be difficult to implement). If all the requested resources are available, the system locks them all. If there is a conflict with concurrent processes, the system can queue the requesting process until needed resources are free, or return control to the requesting process. The latter approach could lead to livelock—the process being denied exclusive use of requested resources indefinitely. With a pure preclaim protocol strictly followed, processes can experience interference and delays, but deadlock will never occur.

One problem with the pure preclaim strategy is that the specific resources needed may be determinable only after reading, analyzing, and manipulating other data resources. For example, if the boss of a particular employee is to get a year-end bonus, the update process would first have to read the employee record and get the organizational unit number to know which boss employee record to read and lock. A process may need to request needed resources incrementally.

If all the needed resources are not requested in a single indivisible command, then the preclaim strategy becomes more like the pre-emption strategy. The system must now maintain a wait-for matrix to detect potential deadlock. The difference is that the process must still request all needed resources before updating any data (as in the above example). When deadlock does occur, the requesting process, or any other deadlocked process, can simply be restarted since there are no updated data files to roll back.

One way to enforce the incremental preclaim protocol is for the system to deny any requests to lock a resource after the process issues its first update command. Further requests for exclusive use of resources will not be honored until after the process releases all resources held exclusively, such as at COMMIT time. Performing *all* reads before *any* writes means that a process may have to calculate what the effect of an update would be without actually performing the update, in order to determine what additional data must be read.

The two-phase locking protocol [Eswaran, et al., 1976; Date, 1983, page 102] is a variation of the preclaim strategy. A process acquires a lock on a data object before updating it; and it also acquires all the locks, on both base variables and modify variables, needed to complete processing a transaction before releasing any locked resources. This forces a *growing* phase of acquiring locks, and a *shrinking* phase of releasing locks. This protocol guarantees all interleaved executions of concurrent update transactions to be serializable.

In the traffic-jam analogy, a preclaim strategy requires a car to not enter the intersection unless it can see that it can get through. In other words, there must be a spot on the road on the other side of the intersection where the car can go without being caught in the middle. In fact, this rule is embodied in the traffic laws of most states and many countries. In the single lane road, a car must not enter the alley unless it is clear to the other end, that is, the driver can see that the way is clear to get back out again. The driver, in effect, preclaims all needed spots on the road (resources) to get through the intersection or the narrow alley or bridge before beginning to use them. If a driver entering at the other end followed the same procedure, deadlock would not occur.

13.3.8.4 Preorder

Preorder is a deadlock prevention strategy which requires establishing an arbitrary ordering on all system resources which are nonpre-emptible and used under exclusive control. All resource requests from each process must be issued according to the preordering. Assuming that resources are requested from a high to a low preordering, the next resource a process requests must be lower in the preordering than any of the resources it currently holds. Havender [1968] proposed this solution strategy in the context of operating systems. He imposed a global ordering on all resources.

The linear preordering of all system resources ensures that a circular chain of processes both holding and requesting resources is impossible.

A preordering scheme would be very difficult to implement in a database environment with:

- A large number of lockable units (records or blocks).
- A changing set of data units (insertions and deletions).
- Indirectly referenced data units (using a Boolean selection expression).
- Hierarchical and multifile interrecord relationships. Programs will generally access in either direction across a relationship, but preordering would dictate one direction only.

When considering all of the different ways of dividing a database into resource units, the preordering strategy for preventing deadlock is practically infeasible. Even considering resource allocation at the file level, it may be impossible to establish a preordering across all of the files in the database such that all processes could operate properly by requesting the files according to the preordering. In any case, it would impose a severe, and perhaps unnecessary, discipline on the programmer.

One multiuser operating system on a microcomputer has implemented a preorder strategy with a twist. Users or processes must request exclusive use of data resources according to an established preordering. Locks must be requested on files in the same order as they appear in the directory of shared files, and released in reverse order. Suppose a user does not follow this ordering, say requesting locks on file 1, 4, then 2. Rather than deny a request for a resource (2) higher in the preordering (than 4), the system releases, automatically and without notice, the locks held on any resources (4) lower in the preordering than the level of the resource currently being requested. In such an environment, programmers must be very alert to avoid compromising the integrity of the database.

In the traffic-jam analogy, a preorder strategy corresponds to making the street or the alley one-way, thus prescribing the order in which resources (spots on the road) can be requested for exclusive use. This solution is also commonly implemented when the traffic becomes very congested in a downtown area. It means you must plan ahead the route you will take (processing) to get to your destination.

13.3.8.5 Timestamping

All of the above deadlock solution strategies assume that there is some central point of control which receives requests for resources, knows what processes hold what resources, and enforces protocols. In other words, there exists a central point of global intelligence. The advent of distributed systems has stimulated a search for alternative control mechanisms which do not depend upon a central point of control and still guarantee that concurrent processes will not threaten data integrity.

Most proposals for controlling concurrent processes in a distributed environment (they are equally applicable to a centralized environment) use some sort of globally unique identifier which establishes the sequence in which the transaction processes are initiated. For an initial understanding, it is useful to think of the identifier as the start time of a transaction—hence, timestamping.

Strategies based upon timestamping are pre-emption strategies since they force a process to restart (pre-empting any resources held) based upon a comparison with the timestamps of conflicting processes. With the rollback and restart done automatically by the system, the users only experience a delay. Since the users do not see the pre-emption, some consider timestamping to be a different strategy.

In the solution suggested by Rosenkrantz, et al., [1978] each update transaction or process is given a globally unique timestamp when the process begins execution (of a transaction). When process **P** requests a lock on data which is already locked by process **Q** , then **P** waits if it is older than **Q** , otherwise **P** dies. To die is to be pre-empted—all resources locked by **P** are released, and **P** is rolled back to begin execution again. Keeping the original timestamp raises the chance that **P** will be able to execute successfully the next time—thus avoiding a livelock because **P** would eventually be the oldest process in the system. This is called the Wait-Die protocol. (They also had a Wound-Wait protocol which simply reversed the priorities for pre-emption. It pre-empted the older process which would not protect against livelock.)

The Wait-Die strategy effectively applies a preordering to the processes rather than the resources. The preordering is based upon the time each process initiates execution of a transaction. The time then becomes the basis for establishing priorities under the pre-emption strategy. Hence, it is not a deadlock prevention strategy at all, as some have suggested. The strategy detects a potential deadlock, and automatically pre-empts and restarts the younger (older) of the conflicting processes.

The Wait-Die protocol is actually stronger than necessary. Suppose **P** and **Q** held exclusively resources **A** and **B** , respectively. If **Q** then requests **A** , it will Die (be pre-empted) if it is younger than **P** . Yet deadlock would not occur until **P** requested resource **A** , which it may never do. The Wait-Die protocol is a special case of timestamping.

First, a general outline of the timestamping strategy. Every transaction is assigned a globally unique timestamp when it is started. A restarted transaction is assigned a new timestamp. Updates must be held in limbo (not physically posted to the database) until a transaction comes to successful completion, as is characteristic of the pre-emption strategy. Every data object in the database carries the timestamp of the latest transaction to read it, and the timestamp of the latest transaction to update it. Now for the pre-emption conditions:

- When a process issues a **read** of a data object, it will be pre-empted and restarted if its timestamp is *earlier* than the timestamp of the latest process to update the data object.
- When a process issues an **update** of a data object (which can only happen at commit time), it will be pre-empted and restarted if its timestamp is *earlier* than the timestamp of the latest process to read the data object *or* the latest process to update the data object. In other words, the updating process must be younger than the youngest process to read *and* the youngest process to update the data object.

The timestamping strategy has less overhead and does not require a central point of control and intelligence. It does not keep track of which resources are currently assigned to which processes, nor maintain a wait-for graph to detect deadlock. The decision to pre-empt a process can be made locally at any node in the network. Some suggest that it does not use locks. However, the mechanism which excludes a process from using a resource is equivalent to a lockout.

In a centralized system, timestamps are easy to implement. Of course, the system must ensure that the clock is incremented between each pair of consecutive events at that site. In a distributed network, the timestamps must be unique across all data objects residing at all sites. To guarantee global uniqueness, the local clock reading is augmented with a unique site identifier. To coordinate the clocks, every time a receiving site gets a message from a sending site, the receiver checks to see that its clock is greater than or equal to the timestamp on the received message. If not, the clock at the receiving site must be set to equal the timestamp on the received message. The clocks do not have to record real time, as long as they are incremented according to the rules above. This technique [suggested by Lamport, 1978] imposes a global ordering on all events in the system.

The timestamping strategy outlined above is much stronger than it needs to be. It often pre-empts and restarts a process when there is no threat to data integrity and no imminent deadlock. The pre-emption condition presumes that a reading process always wants concurrent updates excluded from all its base and modify variables, even if it is a read only process. The rule ensures that there are no other processes in the entire system or network that started after this process and had any update activity on what is read, nor any read or update activity on what is to be updated. A process is pre-empted and restarted if it tries to read data already updated by a younger process, or if it tries to update data already read or updated by a younger process.

Not only does the timestamp strategy pre-empt processes more often than necessary, it will repeatedly restart a longer running process if shorter processes keep interfering, like cutting in front in the line to use common data resources. The younger, shorter processes effectively have priority and the longer running processes will experience longer delays in periods of higher database activity. The locking and Wait-Die strategies effectively give priority to the older processes. They satisfy processes on a FIFO basis whereas timestamping uses a LIFO scheme.

The strong condition of timestamping results in needless loss of concurrency—needless, of course, only if we are able to devise better strategies. Considerable work is being done and remains to be done to achieve high levels of concurrency while still guaranteeing data integrity and avoiding deadlock [see Date, 1983, for a discussion of some attempts at improvement]. The need is particularly acute in distributed systems.

Reread verification is an interesting variation of the timestamping strategy. In one system this is done when single records are updated in an online environment. First, the record to be modified is read and displayed to the online user. No lock is placed on the record and the system retains an extra copy of the record in memory. After making the changes locally, the user says 'save the record to disk.' The system rereads the record and compares it to the original copy in memory. If it has been changed by some concurrent update process, the user must begin the update process all over again. If it has not been changed, the modified record is written back to the file. Of course, the reread and the following write must be atomic so that no other update process interferes; the system must effectively lock the record between the reread and the write. If the update depends on some other records containing base variables, this scheme is considerably more difficult since the base values would also have to remain unchanged between the first read and the final write.

13.4 UPDATE SYNCHRONIZATION

A distributed data processing environment consists of a set of computing sites connected with some communication facility. There may or may not be a central host site along with multiple local sites. In addition to concurrent updates, other factors further complicate the update process:

1. Update transactions may originate from multiple sites.
2. The base and modify variables for an update transaction may reside at different sites—partitioning.
3. Multiple copies of parts of the database may be stored at various sites—replication.

The preceding sections have discussed the problems of maintaining the integrity of a single copy of data while processing multiple updates. Partitioning and replication can improve performance and availability of data. With a distributed system it is possible to store, maintain, and make available data closer to the local sites where it originates or is used.

Assuming that the system can always communicate between nodes, **partitioning** presents no greater problem than has already been discussed. The system reads-with-lock the base and modify variables, gathers or calculates the new values, replaces the modified records in the database, and releases the locked resources. If the needed data is unavailable (because it is locked or the system is down), the update transaction cannot be executed, at that time. With partitioned data in a distributed network, data may also be unavailable because a site is down, or the communication link to a site is severed.

On the other hand, **replication** presents a new problem which makes data integrity even more difficult to maintain. Maintaining multiple copies of data requires synchronization of updates to all the replicas. Besides the obvious cost of additional storage space, the major cost of data redundancy is in synchronizing updates (or tolerating inconsistent data!). These costs must be weighed against the benefits of increased availability of data, faster response to requests for data, and better recovery with the redundant data serving as backup.

The most popular and easiest solution is to designate one copy of each replicated data object as the *dominant copy*. All updates from any site must be directed to the site of the dominant copy. There the update transaction is executed and concurrency controlled as though it were a single copy. All base and modify variables must be read from, and all locks must be placed on, the dominant copy. An update transaction is final when committed on the dominant copy. Successful changes are then forwarded to all replicas for posting. Bringing all copies into conformance becomes a matter of time and persistence. Note that the update transaction is not reprocessed on the replicas. Rather, the changes are simply posted with an add, replace, or delete action.

Rather than send the update transaction to the site of the dominant copy, it could be executed by the DBMS at the originating site. The reading and locking must still be performed only on dominant copies, globally within the network.

To ensure that the replicas eventually reflect the changes to the dominant copy, the site responsible for executing the update transaction must receive a message back from each replica site confirming that the update took place. (Each replica site could also send confirmation when the update request is received). Since a site may be unavailable, the dominant copy site can keep track of replica sites yet to confirm, and persist in forwarding the update request. Alternatively, the dominant copy site (or some other site) could record all unposted updates pending notification that a previously unavailable site is now available to receive past updates.

The dominant copy may be maintained at any local site or a central host site, and it may change dynamically. If the dominant copy site becomes unavailable, a replica site could be designated as the new dominant site for that data object. The switch could be initiated by any other site noticing that the site of the dominant copy is no longer available.

A simplified form of the dominant copy is for the system to make no attempt to synchronize the replicas. All replicas are copies (dumps) of the data object at a point in time. Even though no attempt is made to keep the copies up to date, it may be satisfactory for some, perhaps many, retrieval requests. Most commercial banks, for example, work with a set of account balances that were up-to-date at the end of the preceding business day. The phone book is a copy taken once a year! It is extracted from the master file to create read only copies. If you want the latest information, call "Directory Assistance" where they will read from the dominant copy. Many organizations make copies of data files, or extracts or summaries thereof, available to be downloaded to local microcomputer workstations for manipulation or analysis. A user needing more recent data could simply extract and download a more recent copy. Obviously, local copies would not be the object of updates.

To some, the notion of a dominant copy is as undesirable as the notion of a central host site exercising control over some functions within the network. They argue that a truly distributed system must decentralize all control functions. Suppose that two sites, with copies of the same data, are available but the communication link between them has been severed. How can an update transaction processor ensure that it is reading the latest values for the base and modify variables? Furthermore, some updates could be directed at one site and another set of updates directed at the other. When the communication link is restored, consider the problem of synchronizing the global set of updates on the two copies. One could conceive of updates continually flowing through the network, pending processing at various sites, with all copies of the data lagging behind the virtual latest copy—a real latest copy never existing. So far, no viable proposals have emerged to synchronize updates. Even the dominant copy model is inadequate in the face of lost communication links, continued database access to the latest copy, and automatic switching of the dominant copy.

Update synchronization problems are not unique to distributed processing systems. Consider the case of redundant data within a single database stored at a single site. For example, UNIT NUMBER may be stored as the key in the record for each organizational unit. It may also be stored in each employee record. While this data is redundant, it is used to record the relationship between employees and organizational units. Now when a unit number is changed, perhaps as part of a reorganization, it must be changed in multiple places to properly reflect the new state of the organization and its employees.

The most popular solution to this problem requires users to issue multiple update requests to change all occurrences of the same logical data. If there is no way of formally declaring redundant data as part of the definition of a database, the system can do nothing to synchronize the update of all occurrences in response to a single update request, or even to warn the user that inconsistent data may result if an update request is processed.

A prerequisite for the system to synchronize updates of redundant data is for all redundancies to be known to the system (perhaps through the data definition language). Then the system can locate redundant data and perform the update processing at *all* locations. Since all updates ultimately occur serially (or asynchronously) there will always be a time lag between updates of each copy of the same logical data. This becomes a significant problem when multiple copies of the same data are stored at geographically dispersed sites. Update synchronization across replicated data is a very real problem in data management, still looking for practical and efficient solutions.

SUMMARY

After protecting the existence of data through backup and recovery mechanisms, the second objective of data integrity is to maintain the *quality* of stored data. Accurate, current, and complete data instills greater user confidence. Data quality is diminished when inputs and updates are not checked against stored validation criteria, are not properly authorized, and are not controlled when concurrent execution could threaten data integrity.

The process of data validation first requires some criterion for correct data. These are not always easy to express. People can examine input forms, checking data for reasonableness and accuracy. Validation can be performed manually at the time the data is first entered into the system, say, at a computer terminal or workstation. To be most effective, the validation should be performed close to the source by someone most likely to recognize errors—preferably someone who is a party to the transaction being recorded. Data quality is further exhanced by having knowledgeable persons periodically examine a printout of portions of the stored database.

If the validation criteria are formally communicated to the system, then the DBMS (or user-written programs) can perform the validation checks. Checking input data against stored criteria is important, though not sufficient. It is still important to check the stored database against validation criteria, just as we periodically have a physical health checkup for our bodies.

Every DBMS has information which defines the data. This information provides an initial basis on which to validate incoming or stored data. Whether the definitional information is comprehensive or sketchy, the system should ensure that the stored data always conforms to its definition.

For data item values, the system can validate for such characteristics as type, size, ranges of values, enumerated values, mandatory values, uniqueness, or form mask. The formal validation criteria may be expressed in the data definition language or a separate validation criteria language. Elements of the language include checking a value against a set of valid/invalid values or ranges of values, checking form against a set of defined alphabets and masks, and checking item values in a general Boolean expression. Checks may be conditional on the value of other data items in the file. Validation criteria may also control the transitions of data items values.

The system response to a detected violation of validation criteria can vary from "stop everything and abort" to printing an advisory message and continuing. The language can give the user the option of specifying the system response to each validation check.

Concurrent updates can threaten the integrity of the database. Interleaving the read and write actions of update transactions can result in a *lost update*. Even a read-only process can give the appearance of lost data integrity if concurrent updates are allowed.

The solution is some form of lockout mechanism to ensure that a process has exclusive use of data resources, that is, exclusive with respect to updates. Solution strategies must explicitly consider the nature of data—an unconserved, reusable resource. It can be "allocated" concurrently to requesting processes an unlimited number of times (unlike a printer). If a process intends to update data, all other update processes must be locked out and all read processes have the option of reading or not. Unfortunately, the solution leads to an even greater problem—deadlock—where two or more processes are waiting to use resources currently held by other processes in a circular fashion. For deadlock to occur, a process must be allowed to hold resources exclusively, as long as needed, and be able to request additional resources in any order.

The system can be set up to ignore, detect, or prevent deadlock. Ignoring deadlock leaves it to be discovered externally, say, by a user waiting for a response from the system. Upon detecting deadlock internally the system must pre-empt a conflicting process, that is, take away all resources held and roll back the process as though it had not performed any updates. The system can prevent deadlock using a preclaim, preorder, or presequence strategy. Unfortunately, the deadlock prevention strategies impose some discipline on the users, which may account for the widespread preference for the detection—pre-emption strategy.

Granularity refers to the amount of data locked in a locking action. Coarse granularity, such as locking whole files, results in low housekeeping overhead but reduced levels of concurrent use. Locking smaller pieces such as individual records is fine granularity and increases concurrency but with greater housekeeping overhead. In between, subsets of records can be identified for locking with a Boolean expression.

In the presequence strategy, process execution is sequenced externally or within the system so that processes do not, in fact, execute concurrently. In pre-emption, the system maintains information in a state graph to detect if granting a new lock request would lead to deadlock. If so, one of the deadlocked processes is pre-empted. The preclaim strategy requires each process to request all needed resources before updating any. The preorder strategy requires all processes to request the exclusive use of resources in a particular order. Timestamping is a variation of pre-emption which detects deadlock by comparing the start time of a requesting process with the start time of the process holding the requested resource.

Besides having multiple processes attempting to read or update the same data concurrently, there may also be multiple copies of the data. Establishing a dominant copy is one strategy for synchronizing updates to replicated data. Which copy is dominant may shift dynamically as the network configuration changes over time.

EXERCISES

13-1. Identify the four functions which contribute to maintaining data quality.

13-2. At what points in time or in the data processing cycle is data validation performed?

13-3. Describe the people who are in the best position to perform manual validation (both input data and stored data) outside of the system.

13-4. In what sense is redundant data required be a database validation process? Give two examples.

13-5. Where can the criteria for validating data be stored—in what language, or associated with what processes, functions, or data? Which approach is superior and why?

13-6. What is the relationship between the richness of the data definition language and the extent of the validation checks which can be applied to the data (without conventional applications programming)?

13-7. What are the real serious consequences of a system which permits the definition of certain characteristics of the data but does not enforce those definitions to ensure that data conforms to the definition?

13-8. Outline and describe the validation checks which can be applied to data item values.

13-9. Explain what is meant by transitional validation criteria. Give another example different from the one in the text.

13-10. What are the four levels of validation? Why is database level validation of input data so much more difficult and time-consuming than the others?

13-11. If all input data is properly validated there is little need to validate data read from the database. Do you agree or disagree? Explain.

13-12. Describe a possible range of responses to a validation failure.

13-13. The corporate controller recently issued a directive that all financial data shall be completely checked for 100% accuracy before entering the system. Is this reasonable? Explain.

13-14. What four problems stem from the uncontrolled execution of concurrent updates? What is the basic approach to solving these problems?

13-15. Describe the problems of the 'lost update' and the 'phantom record.'

13-16. Define deadlock and livelock. Use an everyday situation to illustrate each.

13-17. Under what circumstances, if any, should a writing process be permitted to exclude concurrent readers?

13-18. The scenarios in Figures 13-3 and 4 involved a MODIFY type of update transaction. Construct a similar scenario of concurrent update without and with a locking mechanism for the other types of updates (Replace, Replace with Base Variables, and Modify with Base Variables). What is the impact on the integrity of the database in each case? What is the effect of the lockout mechanism?

13-19. Explain the difference between detecting deadlock and preventing deadlock.

13-20. What are the desirable criteria in choosing a mechanism for controlling concurrent update processes?

13-21. What makes data different from other resources to be allocated to and used by processes within a computer system? Other resources include transmitted messages, devices such as a printer, or memory space. Contrast data with these other resources. Indicate how concurrency control is different with respect to data resources.

13-22. Contrast coarse and fine granularity of data locks with respect to concurrency level and overhead. Does a system need to provide both options? Describe an example database accessing or updating situation which would prefer coarse data locking, and a situation preferring fine data locking.

13-23. Describe the five conditions which must simultaneously hold true for deadlock to be possible. Identify the deadlock solution strategy for each and briefly explain how each works.

13-24. What are the major advantages and disadvantages of each of the four deadlock solution strategies?

13-25. In a pure preclaim strategy, can the system queue each of the individual resource requests rather than queuing up the processes? If yes, explain how it would work; if not, why not?

13-26. For each Wait-For matrix below, which processes are deadlocked? Draw the Wait-For graph for each.

a.

	P	Q	R	S	T
P	0	0	1	0	0
Q	1	0	0	1	0
R	1	0	0	0	0
S	0	0	1	0	1
T	0	0	1	0	0

b.

	P	Q	R	S	T	U
P	0	0	0	1	0	0
Q	1	0	1	0	0	0
R	0	0	0	1	1	0
S	0	0	0	0	0	1
T	0	1	0	0	0	0
U	0	0	0	0	1	0

c.

	P	Q	R	S	T	U
P	0	0	0	1	0	0
Q	1	0	1	0	0	0
R	0	0	0	1	1	0
S	0	0	0	0	0	1
T	0	1	0	0	0	1
U	0	0	0	0	0	0

13-27. Given an initial balance of 9000 shares outstanding, a Sale transaction which records the sale of 1000 shares of stock (adding to the shares outstanding), and a Split transaction which records a two-for-one stock split (doubling the shares outstanding), what results are obtained from each of the two possible serializations of these transactions? What can you say about the correctness of each serialization?

13-28. In *The Design of On-Line Computer Systems*, Ed Yourdon says that use of a locking mechanism in an online system is fraught with problems such as vulnerability to deadlock, to extended lockout by a long process, and high overhead. While this is true, he concludes that "locking is *not* a useful concept if all of the users are sharing a common database, where an extended delay in their ability to access or update the data base is an intolerable nuisance. In short, then, the concept of locking in useful in a scientific or university time-sharing environment, but is not useful in a centralized information retrieval system, or in most other forms of 'dedicated' systems.'' [page 327] Do you agree or disagree? Explain your answer.

13-29. What is update synchronization? When is it needed?

SELECTED REFERENCES

American National Standards Institute, *(Draft Proposed) Network Database Language*, New York: ANSI, X3H2-84-23, 1984 March, 143 pages.
   Draft of the proposed standard for a database definition and manipulation language for network data structures. It is based upon the 1978 Journal of Development from the CODASYL COBOL Committee.

BAER, J. L., ''A Survey of Some Theoretical Aspects of Multiprocessing,'' *Computing Surveys* (5:1), 1973 March, pages 31-80.
   Discusses several variations of lockout.

BERNSTEIN, Phillip A., D. W. SHIPMAN and James B. ROTHNIE, Jr., ''Concurrency Control in a System for Distributed Databases (SDD-1),'' *ACM Transactions on Database Systems* (5:1), 1980 March, pages 18-51.

BERNSTEIN, Phillip A. and Nathan GOODMAN, ''Concurrency Control in Distributed Database Systems,'' *ACM Computing Surveys* (13:2), 1981 June, pages 185-221.
   Presents the state of the art in distributed database concurrency control and surveys 48 techniques for solving the two major subproblems (read-write and write-write synchronization). Discusses how to determine whether an order of interleaved actions of multiple transactions is a correct order. An order is correct if it is serializable.

CODASYL COBOL Committee, ''Proposal for a Validation Facility,'' proposal number BCS-80001.01, 1980 May 01.
   Provides a detailed specification for enhancing COBOL with a validation facility. All the validation criteria are contained in the DATA DIVISION [the right place for them]—including optional, mandatory, valid, invalid, values or range(s) of values, optionally from a table, all positively or negatively conditional on an expression based on values of other data items. The validation process is invoked for a named data item with a VALIDATE statement in the PROCEDURE DIVISION.

CODASYL Programming Language Committee, *Data Base Task Group Report*, New York: Association for Computing Machinery, 1971 April, 273 pages, (in Europe: British Computer Society, London, England, or IFIP Administrative Data Processing Group, Amsterdam, Netherlands).
   Contained the original proposed conflict matrix (7 x 7) which appears essentially the same in the 1984 ANSI Network Data Language proposed standard.

COFFMANN, E. G., Jr., M. J. ELPHICK and A. SHOSHANI, ''System Deadlocks,'' *Computing Surveys* (3:2), 1971 June, pages 67-78.

DATE, Chris J., *An Introduction to Database Systems*, Volume II, Reading, MA: Addison-Wesley, 1983, 383 pages.
   Devoted to advanced topics in database management—Chapter 3 is on concurrency, and Chapter 7 discusses concurrency, synchronization, and other topics relating to distributed databases.

ESWARAN, K. P., J. N. GRAY, R. A. LORIE and I. L. TRAIGER, ''The Notions of Consistency and Predicate Locks in a Database System,'' *Communications of the ACM* (19:11), 1976 November, pages 624-633.
   Introduces the notion of serializability. Also discusses the phantom record problem and shows that locking records based upon a Boolean expression ('predicate') can solve this problem.

EVEREST, Gordon C., ''Concurrent Update Control and Database Integrity,'' *Data Base Management*, proceedings of IFIP Working Conference, Cargèse, Corsica, 1974 April, edited by J. W. Klimbie and K. L. Koffeman, Amsterdam: North-Holland Publishing Co., 1974, pages 241-270.

FRAILEY, Dennis J., "A Practical Approach to Managing Resources and Avoiding Deadlocks," *Communications of the ACM* (16:5), 1973 May, pages 323-329.

An early excellent discussion of the preclaim strategy as it applies specifically to data resources.

GALLER, Bruce I., *Concurrency Control Performance Issues*, University of Toronto, Computer Systems Research Group, Technical Report CSRG-147, 1982 September, 170 pages.

Presents a brief and understandable description of several concurrency control methods in both centralized and distributed environments. Then develops a model for determining optimal granularity, and optimal performance of the various methods. In a distributed environment, the basic timestamp ordering scheme with the Thomas write rule was found to be superior in most cases [see BERNSTEIN and GOODMAN, 1981; similar to the timestamping technique described in this text].

GARCIA-MOLINA, Hector, "Using Semantic Knowledge for Transaction Processing in a Distributed Database," *ACM Transactions on Database Systems* (8:2), 1983 June, pages 186-213.

Suggests a scheme for better performance of transaction processing in a distributed environment. It relaxes the strict serializability criterion using information given by the users. The nonserializable schedules of transaction processing still preserve database consistency but burden the users with the classification and analysis of transactions.

GRAY, J. N., "Notes on Database Operating Systems," in *Operating Systems: An Advanced Course*, edited by R. BAYER, R. M. GRAHAM and G. SEEGMULLER, Lecture Notes in Computer Science, Volume 60, Berlin (and New York): Springer-Verlag, 1978.

Consolidates and amplifies earlier published material.

GRAY, J. N., R. A. LORIE and G. R. PUTZOLU, "Granularity of Locks in a Shared Database," *Proceedings International Conference on Very Large Data Bases*, Framingham, MA, 1975 September 22-24, New York: ACM, 1975, pages 428-451.

HABERMANN, A. Nico, "Prevention of System Deadlocks," *Communications of the ACM* (12:7), 1969 July, pages 373-377, 385.

An early detailed description of the preclaim strategy from the perspective of operating system resources.

HAVENDER, J. W., "Avoiding Deadlock in Multitasking Systems," *IBM Systems Journal* (7:2), 1968, pages 74-84.

Proposed and described in detail the preorder strategy for deadlock prevention from the perspective of operating system resources.

KING, Paul F. and Arthur J. COLLMEYER, "Database Sharing—An Efficient Mechanism for Supporting Concurrent Processes," *AFIPS National Computer Conference Proceedings*, 1973, pages 271-275.

An early description of the preclaim strategy involving data resources.

KOHLER, Walter H., "A Survey of Techniques for Synchronization and Recovery in Decentralized Computer Systems," *ACM Computing Surveys* (13:2), 1981 June, pages 149-183.

KORTH, Henry F., "Deadlock Freedom Using Edge Locks," *ACM Transactions on Database Systems* (7:4), 1982 December, pages 632-652.

A deadlock detection scheme, using pre-emption, which handles a variety of lock modes—locks at multiple granularities; locks on files, pages, records, or indexes; and locking when reading or writing. Utilizes locks on arcs ('edges') as well as nodes in the wait-for graph.

KUNG, H. T. and John T. ROBINSON, "On Optimistic Methods for Concurrency Control," *ACM Transactions on Database Systems* (6:2), 1981 June.

Locking mechanisms are pessimistic because they assume maximum contention among concurrent transactions. This paper proposes optimistic concurrency controls that do not actually lock data. Updates occur on a *private copy* of the object data and are checked at commit time to see if there are in fact any conflicts. If not, the updates are written to the database; if so, the transaction is rolled back and restarted. In environments dominated by read-only transactions or where the probability of conflicting concurrent updates is very low, such a scheme may be preferred.

LAMPORT, L., "Time, Clocks, and the Ordering of Events in a Distributed System," *Communications of the ACM* (21:7), 1978 July, pages 558-565.

MOREY, Richard C., "Estimating and Improving the Quality of Information in a MIS," *Communications of the ACM* (25:5), 1982 May, pages 337-342.

Describes three types of error rates—transaction reject rate (those rejected), intrinsic transaction error rate (those that are truly in error), and the stored MIS record error rate (the probability that a given stored record is in error for any reason). Then the author develops a model for estimating these three error rates, which in turn can be used to determine the relative cost effectiveness of various error reduction strategies and pick the best way to reach some given accuracy goals.

MURPHY, James E., "Resource Allocation With Interlock Detection in a Multi-task System," *AFIPS Fall Joint Computer Conference Proceedings* (volume 33), 1968, pages 1169-1176.

Proposed and described in detail the pre-emption strategy for deadlock resolution from the perspective of operating system resources.

OBERMARCK, Ron, "Distributed Deadlock Detection Algorithm," *ACM Transactions on Database Systems* (7:2), 1982 June, pages 187-208.

Extends the deadlock detection scheme using a wait-for graph to a distributed environment. Suggests each site maintain a local wait-for graph augmented with a node, called 'external', to represent other sites in the network. A potential deadlock at one site, where the cycle contains an external node, requires communication of deadlock information from other nodes.

RIES, Daniel R. and Michael R. STONEBRAKER, "Locking Granularity Revisited," *ACM Transactions on Database Systems* (4:2), 1979 June, pages 210-227.

Extended an earlier simulation study varying the level of granularity. The results shifted from preferring coarse granularity (files) to finer granularity (records or blocks) under certain conditions, e.g., if all transactions are randomly accessing small parts of the database. Also found that a preclaim strategy produced better machine utilization than a 'claim-as-needed' strategy.

ROSENKRANTZ, D. J., R. E. STEARNS and P. M. LEWIS, II, "System Level Concurrency Control for Distributed Database Systems," *ACM Transactions on Database Systems* (3:2), 1978 June, pages 178-198.

ROTHNIE, J. B. and Nathan GOODMAN, "A Survey of Research and Development in Distributed Database Management," *Proceedings International Conference on Very Large Data Bases*, 1977, pages 48-62.

THOMAS, Robert H., "A Majority Consensus Approach to Concurrency Control," *ACM Transactions on Database Systems* (4:2), 1979 June, pages 180-209.

Suggests an algorithm to synchronize updates to multiple copies in a distributed database environment.

ULLMAN, Jeffrey, D., "Concurrent Operations on the Database," *Principles of Database Systems*, Chapter 11, Potomac, MD: Computer Science Press, 1982, pages 369-408.

A good tutorial discussion of concurrency with emphasis on serializability and the two-phase protocol.

WEBER, Wolfgang, Wolffried STUCKY, and Jakob KARSZT, "Integrity Checking in Data Base Systems," *Information Systems* (8:2), 1983, pages 125-136.

Deals with methods for efficiently testing semantic integrity assertions, that is, validation criteria. Provides an excellent classification on multiple dimensions of validation criteria—state, prestate, and transition criteria; immediate, delayed, and user-invoked testing; abort, warning, and self-correcting responses; and single-file or multifile references in the criteria.

YOURDON, Edward, "The Problem of Simultaneous Access to the Data Base," *Design of On-Line Computer Systems*, Englewood Cliffs, NJ: Prentice-Hall, 1972, Chapter L, pages 310-339.

A most understandable and detailed discussion of the problems of simultaneous access and simultaneous update.

FOURTEEN

DATABASE INTEGRITY:
ACCESS CONTROL AND ENCRYPTION

14.1	DATA ACCESS CONTROL POLICIES AND APPROACHES	508
14.2	A GENERAL MODEL OF DATA ACCESS CONTROL	510
14.2.1	The Object Profile Model: One Password Per File	510
14.2.2	Multiple Passwords Per File	511
14.2.3	The User Profile Model of Data Access Control	512
14.2.4	General Model of the Data Access Control Process	512
14.3	USER IDENTIFICATION AND AUTHENTICATION	515
14.3.1	Users and User Surrogates	515
14.3.2	Authentication	516
14.3.3	Authentication by Remembered Information	517
	Password Selection, Lifetime, Characteristics, Size, Protection and Administration; Dialogue Schemes	
14.3.4	Identification by Possessed Objects	523
14.3.5	Identification by Personal Characteristics	523
	Fingerprints, Voiceprints, Hand Geometry, Signatures, etc.	
14.4	AUTHORIZATION	529
14.4.1	Authorization Matrix	530
14.4.2	User Access Privileges	531
14.4.3	Granting Privileges	533
14.4.4	Data-Dependent Authorization	533
14.4.5	Multilevel Classification and Need-to-Know Schemes	535
14.4.6	Implementing Authorization Mechanisms	536
14.5	CONTROLLING INFERENCES FROM STATISTICAL DATA	538
14.5.1	Approximate, Supplemental, and Indirect Disclosures	540
14.5.2	The Problem and Methods of Statistical Inferencing	540
14.5.3	Distortion Techniques and Random Sample Queries	542
14.5.4	Summary of Defenses Against Statistical Inferencing	543
14.6	ENCRYPTION	544
14.6.1	Variable Storage, Value Encoding, and Data Compression	548
14.6.2	Traditional Methods: Transposition and Substitution	549
14.6.3	Stream Encryption for Data Communications	552
14.6.4	Block Encryption for Stored Data	553
14.6.5	The U.S. Data Encryption Standard (DES)	554
14.6.6	Public-Key Cryptosystems	556
14.6.7	Secure Key Distribution and Management	560
14.7	THREAT MONITORING AND AUDIT TRAIL	562
14.7.1	Unauthorized Access Threat Monitoring	563
14.7.2	Logging Receipt of Incoming Transactions	564
	SUMMARY	565
	EXERCISES	566
	SELECTED REFERENCES	568

Access control and encryption are internal computer techniques used to prevent the unauthorized or inadvertent disclosure of information. These techniques contribute to data security—the protection of data from unauthorized disclosure, alteration, or destruction. Backup and recovery techniques enable recovery of data *after* loss or destruction (see Chapter 12). Access control techniques seek to *prevent* unauthorized access and update, including destruction.

The primary focus of this chapter is on techniques for controlling or limiting the dissemination of data to authorized users. Controlling information transfers is not restricted to physical data movement. For example, authorized retrieval of statistical data can be the basis for *inferring* information about specific individuals, disclosure of which may be unauthorized.

The term *access* in the context of data access control can include both retrieval and modification. Essentially the same control mechanisms are used in each case. Including update control in access control simply enlarges the set of possible user actions. Controlling data retrieval contributes to maintaining data privacy. Controlling data modification contributes to improved quality and accuracy of data.

Threats to data security can be intentional or accidental. People can exploit loopholes or abuse privileges to intentionally or maliciously gain access to confidential data. Accidental disclosures can result from hardware, software, or human failures, or natural disasters. For example, a hardware failure in the middle of running a program could leave confidential data in the computer memory which could subsequently be retrieved by a snooper.

Access control mechanisms will not avoid all unauthorized accesses. In fact, over half of all reported abuse involving a computer resulted from insiders abusing their access authority. Moreover, most abuses involved breaches of external security, rather than internal security, which uses controls implemented within the computer system [see Parker, 1976].

Access control becomes more important in an environment where data resources are shared and not all users are privileged to access and modify all data. Sharability demands some mechanism to control who does what to what data.

Direct access uses the established avenues of access to data. A general model of direct access control involves the following steps:

1. Identification of a user.
2. Authentication to verify a user's purported identification.
3. Authorization of certain actions on certain data objects.

Passwords schemes are most popular and provide a simple method of direct access control. A more general mechanism uses authorization tables to associate with each user the data they are authorized to access, the actions or functions they can invoke, and the conditions which must be satisfied.

Once the users are identified, their access privileges defined, and authorization tables set up, the database management system can enforce the access control policies. Most systems have some ability to control access, an ability which must be exercised by the database administrator. When the database administrator makes a decision to control access to data and defines certain authorizations, the database control system can carry out those decisions.

Indirect access involves the following control activities:

4. Flow controls on data movement from one place to another.
5. Inference controls on statistical outputs from confidential data on individuals.
6. Encryption of transmitted or stored data.
7. Monitoring of system activities and user interactions.

People can use indirect avenues of access to circumvent the controls on the normal avenues of access. For example, encryption techniques scramble the data to thwart someone's attempts to gain access to data indirectly—by stealing a tape from the library, or by tapping in on the communication line between the computer and an authorized user at a terminal.

The above seven internal security mechanisms are described in this chapter. The reader should not expect to find many of these data security controls in current computer systems and database management systems. There still exists a large gap between what is technically feasible and what is commercially available. Concerned buyers and users should take every opportunity to demand that vendors implement these control measures in future DBMS products.

A total security program involves controls external to the computer system (physical and administrative), and computer security controls outside the scope of database management. Such controls include:

- Personnel screening in hiring.
- Fences, walls, and perimeter surveillance systems.
- Physical access controls at entrances to secured facilities—computer rooms, tape and disk libraries, terminal rooms.
- Locks on computer terminals and work stations.
- Uninterruptible power supplies (UPS) and line surge protectors.
- Radiation shielding.
- Fire and flood detectors and inhibitors.
- Operating system controls.
- Application program controls.

In general, the subject of access control includes access not only to data, but also to terminals, to the computer system, and to programs. From this broader perspective, considerable literature has been generated in recent years. This chapter focuses on data access control, drawing upon the literature from the broader context whenever appropriate. Several items in the bibliography cover computer security and external controls [see particularly Hemphill, 1973; Hoffman, 1977; Hsiao, 1979; Martin, 1973; and Parker, 1981].

The task of controlling access to data has often been relegated to the operating system. Several differences between operating systems security and data security make it impractical to extend operating systems to control access to data objects.

- There are more objects (such as, records) to protect in a database.
- Data has a longer lifetime than other operating system resources.

- Database security must operate at various levels of granularity—controlling access on the basis of whole files is unacceptable considering the dual objectives of availability and integrity.
- Data security must go beyond just physical characteristics and include semantics.
- Data objects are complex, overlapping, logical structures, multiple of which can map to the same physical object.
- Data can be used in several modes, not tied to its allocation to a process.
- Sensitivity of data is inherent in the data rather than programs or the computer.

Therefore, data security should be the responsibility of the database management system rather than the operating system or application programs. [Similarly argued by Wood, 1980, page 239ff.]

The principle of a database control system being the single avenue of access to the database is particularly important for access control. A single, fully controlled access path to the data can better protect the data from unauthorized access due to anomalies which may result from the combined use of multiple access paths by a clever intruder.

14.1 DATA ACCESS CONTROL POLICIES AND APPROACHES

This section discusses some of the basic policies and premises for designing a data security system. Such policies are expressed as high-level guidelines. They influence the choice of, but are distinct from, security control mechanisms. Control mechanisms implement and enforce the policies. User needs, risk-loss assessments, application environment, institutional regulations, and legal constraints all influence the selection of particular security policies and mechanisms. [See Parker, 1981, page 170 for an expanded list of 20 safeguard selection principles.]

CENTRALIZED OWNERSHIP AND CONTROL

The authority to grant data access privileges rests with some central authority, such as a database administrator or security officer. Ownership of files is presumed to be corporate and the DBA is the agent of the organization and the users. This contrasts with a policy where the definer/creator of a file is the owner and has the sole authority to grant access privileges to others. Such decentralized control is characteristic of most operating systems and timesharing systems, which make them inappropriate models for *data* security.

DENY ACCESS UNLESS AUTHORIZED

With a default of no access, users must justify their needs (to some central authority) and privileges must be explicitly assigned before access is granted. The contrasting policy is to permit open access, thus maximizing sharing, unless specifically forbidden. This may be suitable for statistical or research databases where confidentiality is of minor concern.

LEAST PRIVILEGE

Users or programs operate with the least privilege needed to perform their functions. The least privilege may be based upon levels of authority, as in the U.S. military classification system, or upon need to know, or both.

SPECIFYING ACCESS CONTROL RULES

Several policies concern the method of identifying data objects and the conditions for granting access.

- *Granularity* refers to the size of data objects—whole files, named data items, or individual records.
- *Action privileges* specify what actions a user is allowed to perform on specified data objects—read only, append, change.
- *Data-dependent access* controls are based upon data content of the records. For example, a manager may have access to the salaries and performance evaluations of employees in his or her division if the salary is less than $30,000 per year.
- *Context-dependent access* controls specify which data items can or cannot be disclosed together—for example, a user may be able to access and analyze individual salary or age data but not when associated with identified individual employees. Such controls are easy to circumvent without the next rule.
- *History-dependent access* controls utilize a log of past accesses when granting new requests from a user. This is particularly important in minimizing disclosure of individual data from statistical databases.

DIVISION OF RESPONSIBILITY

For greater security, access can be set up to require the collusion of multiple people in order to gain access to confidential data or to perpetrate a fraud. For example, the system can require two passwords from two different people, each not knowing the password of the other, before granting access. This forces an external system of checks and balances. Few DBMSs implement division of responsibility controls.

COMPLETE MEDIATION

Every access request is checked for proper authorization at request time. This allows changes in the authorizations with assurance that they will be effective when entered into the system. Complete mediation requires access control checking at run time not compile time.

USER ACCEPTABILITY

Any security system must be acceptable to the users, or they will find ways to circumvent the controls. Acceptable implies simple, efficient, natural, and easy to use.

14.2 A GENERAL MODEL OF DATA ACCESS CONTROL

This section starts by describing the simplest model for data access control, based upon object profiles, then extends it to a more general model. The models progress from one password per file, to identify users with the data objects they can access, the permitted actions on those data objects, and the conditions on the access privilege.

14.2.1 The Object Profile Model: One Password Per File

The object profile model for data access control simply associates some alternate identifier with each data object—for example, a password for each file. To gain access to the file, a user simply gives two parameters to the system—the file name, and its password. When a file is initially created, the system can optionally be given a password. The password is easily stored along with the file name in the file directory (see Figure 14-1). This is the basic access control model for most operating systems.

In the simplest object profile model, there is no explicit identification of authorized users of a file.* The password is an attribute of the file, not the user. This leads to several problems which are discussed later, along with ways to overcome some of these problems. The simple password schemes of operating systems are discussed here because it is not uncommon for a DBMS to defer to the operating system when providing data access control facilities. Such facilities are generally quite inadequate.

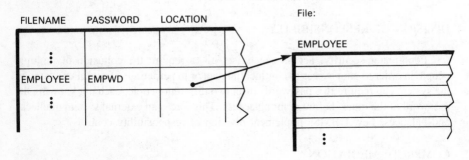

Figure 14-1. Object Profile Access Control Model: One Password Per File.
When defining a file, the owner may optionally specify a password for the file. When a user desires access to such a file, they must supply the correct password along with the file name. One extension is to have two columns in the table to store two passwords for each file—a read-only password, and a write password for modifying the data. Using a data object profile such as this is the basic access control model for most computer operating systems.

---

*A typical operating system does, however, keep track of user accounts, have a password on each account, and associate private files with each user account. The user of that account is considered the owner of any files created under that account. The user-owner can assign a password to any file, and can usually grant other user accounts permission to access particular files on this account.

14.2.2 Multiple Passwords Per File

One password per file gives 'all or nothing' authority—a user with the correct password can take any action on the file. Also, the system cannot distinguish among users. One extension to the simplest model is to allow multiple passwords per file.

The multiple passwords could relate to permitted actions—for example, Figure 14-1 can be extended by having a read-only password and a write password. The passwords are still associated with the file and can be stored in the file directory.

The problem with multiple passwords is that the users must remember more passwords—one for each privilege for each file. The problem gets worse when passwords are assigned to control access to parts of a file (subsets of data items or records). Remembering can be impossible with many, long, randomly generated passwords. If users must do all this remembering, what is the computer for? Users are increasingly forced to write down the passwords, thus compromising the main benefit of using passwords.

Alternatively, the multiple passwords could be associated with multiple users or groups of users, as shown in Figure 14-2. This could ultimately be extended to one password for each individual user. With many possible users, the storage structure of the file directory would have to accommodate high variability in the number of passwords per file. It may even be possible to use the same password for the same user (or user group) across several files. This would reduce the number of passwords a user would have to remember.

The obvious next extension is to decouple the password information from the file directory, and organize it according to the users. This leads to the user profile model for data access control.

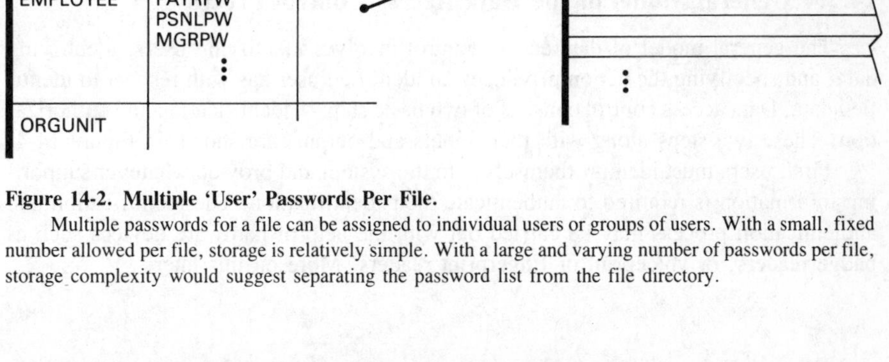

File Directory:

File:

FILENAME	PASSWORDS	...
⋮		
EMPLOYEE	PAYRPW PSNLPW MGRPW ⋮	
ORGUNIT		

EMPLOYEE

Figure 14-2. Multiple 'User' Passwords Per File.
Multiple passwords for a file can be assigned to individual users or groups of users. With a small, fixed number allowed per file, storage is relatively simple. With a large and varying number of passwords per file, storage complexity would suggest separating the password list from the file directory.

User Profile and Authorization Table:

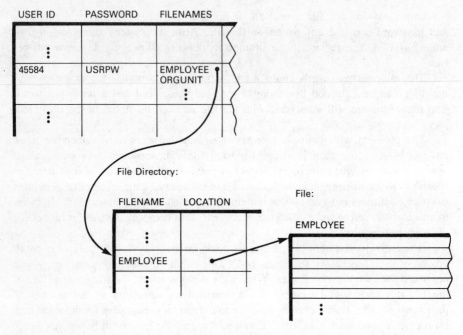

Figure 14-3. User Profile Model of Data Access Control.
A separate user profile and authorization table contains each user's password and the names of data objects which each user can access. The basic authorization table can be extended with restrictions on mode of access (read-only, write, etc.) and conditions on the access privilege.

14.2.3 The User Profile Model of Data Access Control

A user profile model for data access control simply associates data objects (such as files) with authorized users. This information would be stored as tuples in a user profile and access authorization table (see Figure 14-3).

14.2.4 General Model of the Data Access Control Process

The general model of data access control involves identifying users, identifying data, and specifying the action privileges an identified user has with respect to identified data. Data access control consists of two basic steps—identification and authorization. These two steps along with their inputs and outputs are shown in Figure 14-4.

First, users must identify themselves to the system and provide whatever supporting information is required to authenticate their identification. The identification and authentication process may be carried out with the help of hardware devices such as badge readers, or voiceprint or fingerprint readers. More on this later.

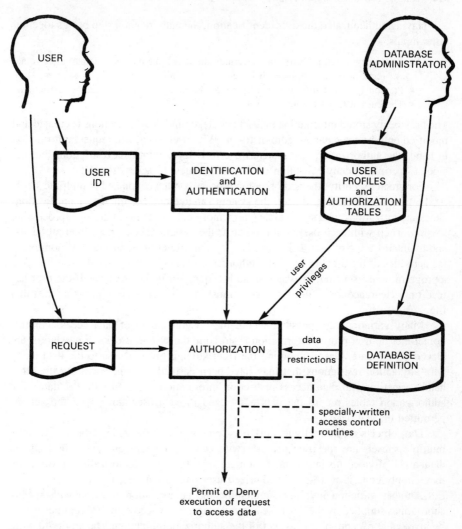

Figure 14-4. General Model of the Data Access Control Process.
    The database administrator or some security officer defines the access restrictions on the database. The authorizing person also provides a profile of users and the data objects to which they have specified access rights. At request time, users identify themselves and provide parameters to gain access clearance. The system authenticates that identification with information from the user profiles. Then the system checks the user's privileges (data objects, actions, and conditions) against the restrictions in the database to make a permit or deny decision. For data-dependent authorization, the system must actually retrieve the requested data before deciding to grant access to the user. In some systems, the generic authorization mechanism can be supplemented with special user-written access control routines.

Having authenticated the user identification, the authorization step brings together three inputs:

- Previously stored information concerning the users, the data each is permitted to access, and the actions each is authorized to initiate.
- Previously stored information relating to the database, such as access restrictions.
- The current request from the users.

The previously stored information on user privileges and data restrictions is created and modified only by the database administrator. With user, data, and request information in hand, the authorization step matches user privileges with data restrictions and decides to permit or deny execution of the user request to access the data.

For greater security, the authorization process is often conducted in multiple steps. At the time of initial user contact, the system can authenticate the user identification, check authorizations, and set up tables in memory to be referenced during a processing session. Then with each user action request, the system checks these internal tables, and maintains a log of user activities. The log constitutes an audit trail for monitoring the activities of the user. In general, authorization is performed when the user invokes a program, a userschema, or issues an ad hoc query or update request. If the user has read-only clearance for a file, the system must inhibit all update requests against that file.

Many variations are possible within the general model of data access control. Sometimes no user profile information is stored in the system. Locks or passwords are placed on the data. Users supplying the right key are given access to the data along with any action restrictions that may have been defined with the lock. On the other hand, sometimes no data access restriction information is stored with the data. The authorization tables record the data authorized to each user along with the actions permitted on that data.

Data objects are normally identified as some subset of the entire database. Usually multiple subsets are specified per user with action privileges on each subset. If the database is divided up into a small number of pieces, the authorization information may simply consist of a list of authorized user names with each piece.

Another variation involves augmenting the authorization function with special subroutines supplied by the database administrator. Such access control routines would be invoked at execution time as part of the authorization function. The ability to write special routines to augment the authorization function provides increased flexibility in the definition of access controls. The routines can make a permit-or-deny decision based upon a wide variety of inputs—time of day, database contents, or a dialogue with the user—in fact, anything that can be written in the program code. The control routines may also be invoked when certain defined conditions obtain, such as a particular database manipulation language verb being issued by the user, or a particular type of data structure being referenced in the database. The execution of special access control routines corresponds to the "database procedures" specified in the DBTG proposal and the "formularies" as defined by Hoffmann.*

---

*CODASYL, Data Base Task Group Report, 1971 April, page 64; Lance J. Hoffmann, "The Formulary Model for Flexible Privacy and Access Controls," *AFIPS Fall Joint Computer Conference Proceedings* (volume 39), 1971, pages 587-601.

14.3 USER IDENTIFICATION AND AUTHENTICATION

Data access control begins with some identification of the user, sometimes called the 'subject' of access control. This may be direct identification of a human user, or some intermediate user surrogate such as a terminal or a program.

An identifier is the first piece of data which the system receives from a requester. It may be a name or a number. The identifier enables the system to locate the corresponding entry in the stored user profiles or authorization tables.

To detect random entry of numeric identifiers by a possible intruder, a *check digit* can be appended to the number. The following is a possible procedure for calculating a check digit:

1. Multiply each digit by its position from the right.
2. Sum the products.
3. Take the sum modulo 8, that is, divide the sum by 8 and take the remainder.
4. Append the digit to the end of the number.

An example illustrates the procedure for the number 74782:

$$
\begin{aligned}
7 \times 5 &= 35 \\
4 \times 4 &= 16 \\
7 \times 3 &= 21 \\
8 \times 2 &= 16 \\
2 \times 1 &= \underline{2} \\
\text{sum} &= 90 \\
90 \text{ modulo } 8 &= 2
\end{aligned}
$$

The resulting identifier is 747822.

Until authenticated, the user-supplied identifier is only a *claimed identity*.

In the object profile model, the system requires the name of the desired data object (file) in order to look up the password since the stored password is associated with the data. In this case, the password is not actually serving to authenticate a user identification.

14.3.1 Users and User Surrogates

The preferred approach to data security is to identify individual persons as users, rather than groups of users or user surrogates. In this way the authenticating information can be specific to the person. Also, each person can be held accountable for proper access to and use of data.

In organizations with a large number of users, the user profiles and authorization tables can get quite large. One simplification is to control access on the basis of affiliation with a *group of users*. Each group is uniquely identified to the system. Authentication information, such as passwords, would have to be known to all members of the group.

Serious problems result from group-assigned passwords (or other authenticating information). Every time a group password is changed, all affected users in the group must be notified before they can gain access to the data (or system). Passwords should be changed whenever illegal use is suspected. Also, the only way to revoke the access privilege from someone who leaves the group is to change the password for those users remaining in the group. Furthermore, no single user can be held responsible for loss or misuse of the group password (except, perhaps, someone who has direct authority over the group). Incidentally, the association of passwords with data objects rather than individual users suffers the same problems.

Sometimes the user, as seen by the database management system, is not always a person. The user may simply be identified as a terminal or a program. Although the terminal or program may serve as a surrogate user, any privilege ascribed to the program or terminal, derives from privileges of the population of human users invoking the program or operating at the terminal. In this situation, proper identification of the user becomes the responsibility of the operating system or the terminal management system. Since terminals or programs cannot be held accountable for their behavior (which is neither malevolent nor benevolent), every request must ultimately be tied to a responsible individual.

For added security, the identification of specific programs or terminals can be used as additional conditions to be satisfied by the user to obtain access to the database. The authorization conditions relating to the user could be passed through the program and added to the authorization conditions for the program. Such a procedure is particularly necessary for generalized programs designed to access any part of the database.

14.3.2 Authentication

With the identifier, the system goes through a process of *authentication*—using additional information to verify the purported identity of the user. The system attempts to match additional information supplied by the intended user with information previously stored in the user profile. For added security, the system may perform multiple such matches to increase confidence that the user is not an imposter. If all tests are successful, the system assumes that the requester is an authorized user.

Authentication mechanisms, some are illustrated in Figure 14-5, can be divided into three classes:

1. Something the person *knows*—remembered information.
2. Something the person *has*—possessed objects.
3. Something the person *is*—personal characteristics.

Information a person can remember includes name, account number, password, or lock combination. The computer could even engage in some question-answer dialogue with the user. Possessed objects include a badge, plastic card, or key. Personal characteristics include fingerprint, voiceprint, hand size or geometry, or signature. In combination, these mechanisms can provide greater security. For example, automated teller machines (ATMs) require the use of a possessed plastic card and a remembered personal identification number (PIN).

Initial identifying information is generally included in one of the first two catego-

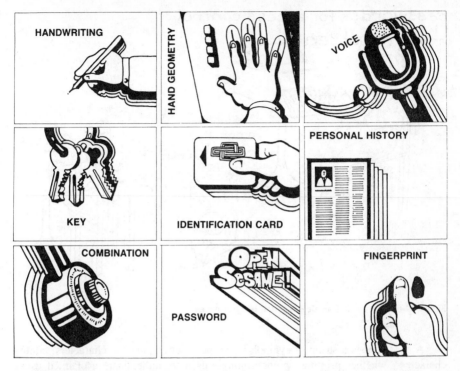

Figure 14-5. Sampling of Ways to Authenticate a Claimed User Identification.
Several different methods can be used to authenticate the claimed identification of a user. Classify the methods illustrated into:

- Something a person *knows*—remembered information.
- Something a person *has*—possessed objects.
- Something a person *is*—personal characteristics.

ries. The second and third categories require special purpose devices to capture the information and put it into a convenient digital form for transmission and comparison. Each of the three classes of information has its inherent weakness:

- Remembered information can be forgotten or guessed (see Figure 14-6).
- Possessed objects can be lost or stolen.
- Personal characteristics are difficult to measure and compare with high accuracy.

14.3.3 Authentication by Remembered Information

Passwords represent the simplest and most widely used data access control technique today. Password schemes are inexpensive to develop and operate. They do not require any special equipment. If properly administered, a password scheme can contribute significantly to data security. Unfortunately, principles of secure password systems are not widely practiced.

Figure 14-6. Passwords Can Be Forgotten or Overlooked!

A *password* is a string of symbols—numbers, letters, special characters, control characters, whether printing or nonprinting—used to authenticate a claimed user's identity.

To be effective, passwords must be:

- Easy for the user to remember.
- Difficult for an intruder to guess or discover.
- Frequently changed.
- Well-protected.

A well-designed password scheme must consider:

- Method of selection.
- Lifetime.
- Characteristics, such as size.
- Distribution and administration.
- Protection within the computer system.

These topics are discussed in the following sections.

14.3.3.1 Password Selection

Passwords may be selected by the user, the database administrator, or automatically generated by the system.

Users tend to pick passwords which have some personal significance, such as birthdates, name of spouse or child, address, room number, or project. User-selected passwords are easier to remember but also easier for others to guess. Passwords picked by some other authority will generally lack personal significance but may still be relatively easy for the user to remember.

The use of obvious passwords can greatly reduce the time to conduct a successful trial and error search. There are many examples of successful penetration by intruders simply knowing something about the user and guessing likely passwords. Selecting passwords which are actual words reduces the search to the more common words found in a dictionary. Furthermore, the search would probably be limited to the maximum length of a password, generally 5 to 8 characters.

A system can generate random character sequences for use as passwords. Such passwords are much more secure since they are difficult to guess and it would take longer to exhaustively try all possible combinations. Unfortunately, system generated passwords are much more difficult for users to remember. When passwords are hard to remember, users are more likely to write them down, thus defeating the original purpose for using passwords.

In an effort to select passwords which users are less likely to forget, sometimes passwords are selected with mnemonic significance, or with an ability to be pronounced. Gasser [1975] describes a random word generator which forms pronounceable syllables and concatenates them to create 'words.' Hyphens are added to the following examples to help the user separate the syllables:

> qua-vu
> ri-ja-cas
> te-nort
> oi-boay

14.3.3.2 Password Lifetime

For enhanced security, it is obviously desirable to change passwords frequently. In all too many systems, passwords remain in effect indefinitely. This gives a potential intruder ample time to discover a valid password through exhaustive testing. Such systems rely on users or the administrator to initiate password changes. When passwords are associated with individual users, they can change passwords whenever they choose. Group passwords are more resistant to change since notification must be sent to all members at once.

A variety of techniques can be used within the system to promote more frequent password changes. Each time a user requests access, the system can supply the date and time of the last successful access. This could reveal a prior fraudulent access. After a prescribed interval, say one month, the system can force the user to change his or her password the next time they access the system.

When an authorized user is first set up on a system or their password is reset, the assigned password can be limited to the first access. At that time, the user is expected to change their password. This scheme can keep passwords unknown even to the data security administrator.

In the extreme, passwords may be discarded after each use, both the system and the user working from a list of passwords. When desiring access to the system, the user selects the next password on the list and the system compares it to the next one on its list. Upon successful access, they both cross the used password off their respective lists. One drawback to the use of one-time passwords is the cost and difficulty associated with the distribution of lists to many users. Also, users who get 'out of step' must go to the database administrator or security officer to obtain a new list of passwords.

14.3.3.3 Password Characteristics and Size

Longer passwords constructed from a large set of characters (upper and lower case letters, numbers, special characters) increase the total number of possible passwords. Passwords so constructed take longer to discover through exhaustive testing. Longer passwords are also more difficult to remember—illustrating again the inherent tradeoff between data security and user convenience.

A password consists of a sequence of **S** characters, each taken from an alphabet of **A** characters. The total number of possible passwords is:

$$N = A^S$$

For five character passwords using upper case letters and numbers, the total number of possible passwords would be:

$$N = 36^5 = 60,000,000 \text{ approximately}$$

Restricting the possible passwords to randomly generated pronounceable syllables, Gasser [1975] found the total number of passwords was about 2.5 percent of the total possible, or about 1,500,000 passwords in the above example.

The total number of possible passwords influences the expected time it would take to guess a password. The expected time would also depend upon the speed of transmission to a remote computer. Suppose that:

R = Rate of transmission = 100 baud = 10 cps = 600 char per minute
E = number of characters Exchanged in a clearance request = 20

then the time required to try each password would be E/R or 2 seconds, and the expected time to guess a password, the expected 'safe' time, would be (assuming around-the-clock attempts):

$$T = \frac{1}{2} \times N \times E/R$$
$$T = \frac{1}{2} \times 60,000,000 \times 2 \text{ seconds} = \text{nearly 2 years.}$$

This time could be increased to nearly 12 years by introducing a 10 second forced delay after every unsuccessful access clearance request.

A lower bound on the probability **P** that an interloper can find a password is:

$$P = (\text{ number of characters one can transmit in M months } / \text{ E }) / N$$

$$P = \frac{43,200 \text{ minutes per month} \times R \times M}{E \times A^S}$$

Suppose we wished to establish a password size **S** such that the probability of an interloper finding a password in **M = 3** months of systematic testing would be no greater than $P = .01$. In the above example,

$$P = .01 = \frac{43,200 \times 600 \times 3}{20 \times 36^S}$$

isolating **S**

$$36^S = 388,800,000$$

which gives **S** between 5 and 6. Therefore, the required password size is 6 characters.

Several other characteristics of passwords can be used to improve security. The greater security of more complex methods must be weighed against increased computer time and user inconvenience of simpler methods.

One effective modification adds nonprinting characters, such as space, backspace, or control characters to the password. Then the passwords:

$$f \ K \ C \ B \ T \ L \ b \qquad R \ N \ \hat{\ } S \ B \ Z$$

where **f** is a forward space, **b** is a backspace, and $\hat{\ }$**S** is a control-S, would appear on the printer or screen as:

$$K \ C \ B \ T \ L \qquad R \ N \ B \ Z$$

thus thwarting any potential interloper.

14.3.3.4 Password Protection and Administration

One difficulty with a password scheme is that unauthorized users may be able to obtain passwords by trial and error, by looking over the shoulder of an online user, or by looking at discarded card decks, printouts, or terminal typewriter ribbons. Besides external administrative procedures such as keeping unauthorized users out of the authorized user area and locking up job card decks with passwords punched in the job cards, various system-based measures can be implemented.

When passwords are first assigned, the security officer should follow procedures to ensure proper identification of intended recipients. Also, the distribution mechanism should be secure. Passwords can be given in person or by registered mail. Users should report at once if they receive new passwords in an opened envelope which should normally be sealed. The user identifier should never accompany passwords recorded for distribution. Anyone who stumbles upon or intercepts a distributed password would not possess the identification information which the user must supply with the password to gain access to the system.

The system should never print out or display passwords. The system should attempt to hide or obscure a password when the user enters it. On printing terminals, the system can preprint a combination of characters in each print position before the user overtypes the password in the same print positions. Since this is impossible on video display terminals, the system should not echo the password back to the terminal.

Unsuccessful access clearance attempts should be logged by the system. The system should respond with a single message such as "unsuccessful" or "improper login" regardless of the nature of the error—improper identifier, account number, password, or file name. After a given number of attempts, say three, the system should abort the user and notify some authority.

Most access control schemes store passwords in tables within the computer memory. Passwords and all other authenticating information should never be stored or transmitted in clear text form. They should be encrypted before storage, preferably using a one-way (irreversible) encryption technique. There is never a reason to decrypt a stored password. The system can encrypt a user password *before* matching it with the previously stored (encrypted) password. If a password is forgotten, a new one is assigned. Safeguards are also needed to ensure that the encryption algorithm and a table of encrypted passwords are not simultaneously available. Together, it would be possible to exhaustively test clear text passwords attempting to find a match in the encrypted form.

When a stored program or procedure file serves as a user surrogate, passwords should not be permanently written into the procedure. Someone may be able to list the program and obtain the user passwords. If initiated online, the procedure should be set up to prompt the user for a password each time it is executed. For a batch procedure, the required password should be supplied as an input parameter each time it is executed.

14.3.3.5 Dialogue Schemes

Greater security is possible by storing more authentication information. The dialogue method of authentication, also called 'handshaking,' offers unlimited possibilities. Several have been described in the literature; a few are outlined here.

- Several pieces of personal user data could be stored and used by the system to conduct a dialogue—mother's maiden name, birthdate and place, facts about children, and educational history. When the user requests access, the system could randomly ask questions relating to the stored information and compare the user responses. The chosen set of facts should be easy for the user to remember but with a small chance that someone else would know all the facts.
- Another form of dialogue uses an algebraic function known to both the user and the system, say $3x + 2y + 5$. When the user desires access, the system supplies values for the variables, say $x = 2$ and $y = 4$, and the user responds with the resulting value of the algebraic function, in this case 19.
- The system asks the user for selected letters from the password:

Real password:	THEGOODLORDABOVE (not displayed)
System request:	enter characters 8, 6, 15, and 3, please.
User responds:	LOVE

thus never revealing the whole password at one time.

- The system supplies a number chosen at random. The user responds with the result of applying a prearranged transformation to the given number. Suppose the transformation was:

Transformation:	(sum digits in odd positions)squared + hour of the day.
System presents:	74783925
User responds:	376 (at 3:15 p.m. using 24 hour time)

  In this case, the authenticating information is the transformation which must be kept secret, rather than the transmitted numbers which are all an eavesdropper would see.
- Rather than going through the system, the dialogue could be conducted *around the system*. After receiving a user identification, the system hangs up and calls back to the terminal, or a security guard could phone back to the terminal area to verify that the identified user is in fact there.

14.3.4 Identification by Possessed Objects

The use of objects which a user must possess in order to gain access clearance can significantly increase the level of security when used in combination with remembered information. Terminals and microcomputers are available today with special features to assist in access control—keyed locks, plastic card readers, and a unique hardware identifier. Access control can be based upon information in the card, the access location, or the time. This information can also be logged for both authorized accesses and for unauthorized access attempts.

Possessed objects may be used to open or activate hardware devices or they may have information recorded on them. The information may be stored and read mechanically, optically, or magnetically, and transferred to the system. Magnetically encoded information can be read quickly, cannot be read by the possessor of the object, and can be updated by the system. With a badge or card reader on the terminal, the user places the (concealed) card next to a sensor or inserts it into a slot and the computer reads the identifying information.

If the system detects a lost card or an unauthorized user, the terminal can refuse to eject the card and signal a guard to go to the terminal location and investigate. Since cards can be lost or stolen, administrative procedures must require the immediate reporting of missing cards, so that the system can inhibit their use and detect a possible offender.

14.3.5 Identification by Personal Characteristics

Remembered information and possessed objects can be made unique through administrative procedures. The authentication decision is essentially binary—the requester either knows or does not know, has or does not have, what was previously established to obtain access. Authentication by personal characteristics depends upon the accuracy of the information capture and comparison operations. Personal physiological characteristics are measured; thus introducing measurement error, the need for a tolerance to intrapersonal measurement differences, and the need to set acceptance and rejection thresholds.

The technologies relating to such personal characteristics as fingerprints, voiceprints, signatures, and hand geometry, though technically feasible today, are not yet in widespread use for data access control. Greater complexity results from the sophisticated pattern matching operations required. Personal characteristic methods are more likely to reject an authorized user due to the margin of error in the matching algorithms. Nevertheless, when used to authenticate user identification, these methods are much harder to subvert and, therefore, offer the potential for much greater security.

The authentication process compares a measured "live" print (finger or voice) with a previously stored reference print and obtains a measure of the likelihood that they are from the same individual. The resulting value is compared to a preset threshold value for granting or denying access to the individual.

Two factors are important in judging the effectiveness of the matching system—how well it recognizes the correct user, and how well it discriminates against imposters. Due to the difficulty of performing precise and repeatable measurements, two types of errors can occur:

I. Rejection of an authorized individual—called an "improper rebuff" or a "false alarm" since the individual is falsely accused of being an imposter.
II. Acceptance of an imposter—a "successful invasion."

These are inversely related; and their relative magnitude depends upon the threshold established for declaring two prints to be a match. The four possible outcomes are shown in Figure 14-7. Increasing the tolerance to variation in intrapersonal measurements also increases the tolerance to variation in interpersonal measurements; thus increasing the probability of an imposter being accepted. The threshold can be adjusted depending on the relative concern for improper rebuffs versus successful invasions. Another possibility is to establish a threshold range within which further authentication steps will be taken, perhaps even repeating the measurement of the print.

In actual practice, a rejected requester will be allowed a small number of repeated attempts to gain access. This dramatically affects the probabilities for an improper rebuff and a successful invasion, and it will, therefore, influence the chosen threshold. A .10 probability of improper rebuff becomes .001 ($=.10^3$) allowing three attempts. However, a .10 probability of successful invasion becomes .27 ($=1-(1-.10)^3$) in allowing three attempts. The first is decreasing exponentially while the second is increasing approximately linearly. Thus, with repeated attempts, the matching threshold should be set much higher.*

---

*These calculations assume independent access attempts which is certainly not true. Therefore, the probability of improper rebuff is something greater than .001 and the probability of successful invasion is something less than .27.

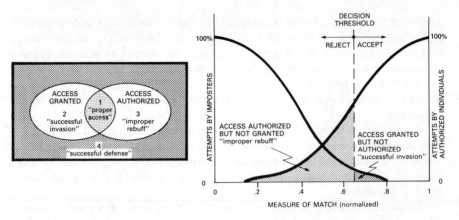

Figure 14-7. Print Matching: Successful Invasion versus Improper Rebuff.
When matching prints (finger or voice), the system may grant or deny access. The requester may be an authorized user or an unauthorized intruder. The four possible outcomes are shown using a Venn diagram. A high matching threshold will minimize "successful invasions" (region 2) but increase "improper rebuffs" (region 3) making legitimate users unhappy. A low matching threshold will do just the opposite. An ideal system would produce a very small percentage of both "successful invasions" and "improper rebuffs" (making regions 2 and 3 nearly empty).

Several criteria for evaluating personal identification systems are suggested by the U. S. National Bureau of Standards [FIPS PUB 48, 1977, pages 18-20].

- Resistance to deceit.
- Ease of counterfeiting an artifact.
- Susceptibility to circumvention.
- Time to achieve recognition and permit or deny access.
- Convenience to the user.
- Cost of recognition device and its operation.
- Interfacing of device for intended purpose.
- Time and effort involved in updating (adding and deleting users, issuing new passwords, keys, changing combinations).
- Processing required in the host computer system to support the identification and authentication process.
- Reliability and maintainability.
- Cost of protecting the device from destruction and theft.
- Cost of distribution and logistical support.

14.3.5.1 Fingerprints

A fingerprint consists of ridges in a loop, arch, or whorl pattern on the tip of each finger. No two fingerprints have ever been found to be identical in minute detail. Furthermore, the minute details or minutiae of a fingerprint never change throughout the normal life of a finger. Theoretically, this makes fingerprints an ideal means for uniquely identifying individuals.

In manual systems, fingerprints are recorded in person, using a finger-on-ink-on-paper method. Each fingerprint is classified into one of a dozen or so general patterns. Law enforcement organizations have used fingerprints for several decades to successfully identify people. With a fingerprint taken from the scene of a crime, investigators can manually search through the files looking for a match. For less serious crimes, the search is not undertaken unless a suspect is known to the investigator. It takes several person-days to manually search through the prints on file within the general pattern category.

Several police agencies have installed computer-based fingerprint matching systems around the country and world since their introduction in the mid 1970s. Now it is possible to search and compare one million prints per hour using systems costing a few hundred thousand dollars. The system outputs a list sorted in descending order of match probabilities.

Fingerprint matching is done on the basis of minutiae which are points where a ridge ends or branches into two ridges (a bifurcation), as shown in Figure 14-8. The system captures a fingerprint using a high-resolution television camera and then scans the image to identify and record the minutiae, along with the center location.

The use of fingerprints to authenticate a user identification does not involve comparison with a library of fingerprints, only a single comparison with the reference fingerprint stored for the identified user. If the comparison is reasonably close, it would serve to authenticate the user identification.

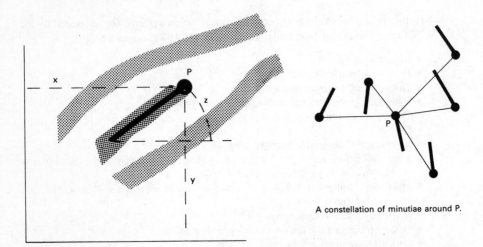

Recording x-y location coordinates
and angle z of minutia at P.

A constellation of minutiae around P.

Figure 14-8. Elements of Capturing and Matching Fingerprints.
A single minutia is either a ridge ending (shaded) or a bifurcation (light). For each minutia, the system records the **x-y** location of the vertex and the angle, **z** , of the orientation of the ridge or valley. A single rolled fingerprint has about 100 minutiae, or about 300 recorded values. Matching is done using complex mathematical formulas which compare the relative distances and relative angles of the minutiae in selected constellations of two prints. A match on as few as six minutiae is sufficient for positive identification. [Wegstein, 1968; Lawson, 1977]

One main problem has inhibited the use of fingerprints for access control—the cost of the equipment needed to capture and digitize information about a fingerprint from the user at the terminal. In 1984, Fingermatrix, Inc., of North White Plains, NY, announced the "Ridge Reader" and the Personal Touch Verification (PTV) system. The PTV attaches inline between the local terminal or workstation and the computer network or central host computer. The file of reference prints is stored on the host computer. To obtain access, a user's identification is sent to the host and the corresponding reference print is sent back to the local PTV scanner for comparison. The system has the following charcteristics:

- The reader box is about one cubic foot and contains an optical scanner.
- 3-5 minutes to enroll a new authorized user.
- Records a constellation of 8-15 minutiae from any 2 fingerprints per user and stores that information in 500-800 bytes.
- Throughput is 5 seconds or less per requested access.
- Automatically "heals" broken ridges in a damaged print; operates under a variety of finger conditions—flat ridges, wet, contaminated, or pitted.
- Type I error rate (initial false rejection) less than .1%
- Type II error rate (imposter admission) less than .0001%
- Will optionally capture and store the full fingerprint of an imposter.
- Cost is currently about $6,000 for the scanner reader in quantity one.

The most difficult (and proprietary) aspect of the system is finding a stable constellation of minutiae from a digitized print—the matching algorithm is relatively easy.

When matching an imposter's fingerprint with the single stored print of an authorized user, it is extremely unlikely that they would even come close. Therefore, fingerprint matching has the potential to be a very effective means for authentication in data access control.

14.3.5.2 Voiceprints

Although neither fingerprint nor voiceprint matching systems are at the point of commercial viability or widespread availability, the use of voiceprints may offer greater promise than fingerprints.

Voice recognition devices are now readily available at a modest cost for computer terminals and microcomputer workstations. There are systems for under $1,000 which can have a few hundred discrete utterances (words or short phrases) active at one time, and have multiple such utterance tables in auxiliary storage.

Until 1971, the courts and most experts agreed that voiceprints were not reliable enough to be used in evidence. Then, Dr. Oscar Tosi, a professor of Audiology at Michigan State University, reversed his position and began to testify in favor of voiceprint evidence. Several tests verified to him the reliability of voiceprints as a means of corroborating identification.*

---

*"Speak, Voiceprint," *Time*, 1972 January 10, page 59. For further information see "Voiceprint Concept Supported by Government-Sponsored Test," *Communications of the ACM* (14:6), 1971 June, pages 434-435; and a contrary response by William Squire, "Voice Identification by Spectrograms Not Reliable," *Communications of the ACM* (14:11), 1971 November, page 751.

Unlike fingerprints, voiceprints may vary for the same speaker according to the speaker's health or the time of day. We sound different when we first get up in the morning or when we have a cold. Also, different speakers can sound alike. There are also problems in measurement, comparison, and time registration of spectrographs. Fortunately, the differences in pronunciation on the part of a single individual are insignificant compared to the major differences between individuals.

First, the security control officer has an authorized user speak a specified word or phrase into the system. The system stores a digital form of the audio signal (or perhaps the 'average' of multiple utterances of the same word). A recorded voiceprint consists of sampled *amplitudes* (loudness), in different *frequency* ranges (pitch), taken at very short (100 millisecond) *time* intervals. Figure 14-9 shows a picture of a digitally recorded voiceprint. One system records a voiceprint using about 4,000 data values and performs a match test in 50 microseconds.

A user requesting access to the system would speak into a device at the terminal or workstation. This device would have to capture the analogue audio signal and convert it to a digital signal. The voiceprint would then be compared to the one on file for the

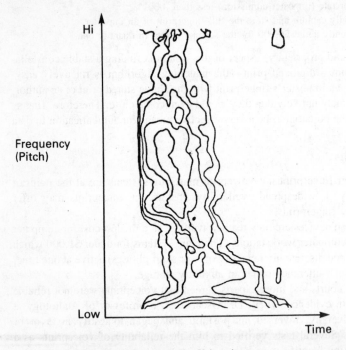

Figure 14-9. Digital Representation of a Voiceprint.
     This illustrates the contour form of the word 'you.' The word starts starts at the left and extends right over time. Low frequency sounds (pitches) are at the bottom with high frequencies at the top. Greater intensity of sound at each frequency for a particular time is shown with peaks in the contour lines. This form of the voiceprint is easily recorded and analyzed with a computer. [Reprinted with permission of Dr. L. G. Kersta.]

identified user. The tradeoffs in setting a matching threshold are the same as for fingerprints.

An imposter may be able to gain access to a system using a recording of an authorized user's voice. To counter this threat, the system can randomly select a sequence from a *set* of previously stored words. The user would then have to speak selected words or phrases in the specified sequence. The potential number of permutations is large enough to thwart an intruder from trying to use a recorder to rearrange the sequence within the time allowed for a user response, or to prerecord all sequences in advance. For example, there are 64 possible permutations of up to four words, and 325 permutations of up to 5 words.

Several manufacturers now offer voice recognition attachments for microcomputers (Votan, Fremont, CA; Texas Instruments, Dallas, TX; The Voice Connection, Irvine, CA; and Keytronic, Spokane, WA) [see *PC Magazine*, 1984 June 26, pages 170-179]. Most systems set up a speaker-dependent, active vocabulary of 50-500 discrete phrases. Some come on a board which plugs into an expansion slot of the computer, others are built into the keyboard, and all come with a microphone and associated software. They primarily act as a substitute for the keyboard, accepting input commands which are converted to a string of predefined keystrokes and sent to the computer just as though they had been typed on the keyboard. Some modification would be required for these systems to satisfy the need for access control.

14.3.3 Hand Geometry, Signatures, etc.

A third method of identification using personal characteristics relies on **hand geometry** and size. IDentimat from Stellar Systems senses the lengths of the fingers, translucency of the web between the fingers, and the curvature of the finger tip. These measurements are reduced to digital form and stored. When access is desired, the user's hand is placed in a special device which measures the distances from the webs between the fingers to the tips of the fingers and compares the results to previously stored hand measurements. These factors were found to be remarkably dissimilar among people and thus could serve as the basis for authentication.

Authentication based upon **signatures** is also possible using the dynamics of motion which occur during the actual signing process—speed, acceleration, and pressures. These characteristics are much more difficult to detect and duplicate than the static signature image.

Another suggestion is based upon looking at the blood flow in the retina of a person's eye.

14.4 AUTHORIZATION

Data access authorization is the process of permitting users (whose identity has been authenticated) to perform certain operations on certain data objects in a shared database. Permitted relationships between users and data, and permitted usage privileges are defined by the database administrator or data security officer and enforced by the database control system. The authorization process compares the restrictions placed on information with privileges of users requesting access to this information. The authorization information can be extended to include conditions on the access privileges.

14.4.1 Authorization Matrix

The basic user profile model of data access control depicted in Figure 14-3 combined authorization information with user profile information, such as passwords, used to authenticate the identification of users. Profile information is one-to-one with users while authorization information is many-to-many between users and object data. Good database design would suggest normalizing or splitting the structure into two files—the user profile, which will not be discussed any further, and the authorization table.

The basic design for an **authorization table** or file consists of triplets of the form:

USER ID	OBJECT DATA	ACCESS PRIVILEGE

where *both* USER ID and OBJECT DATA together serve to uniquely identify entries in the table. The value in USER ID relates the authorization triplet to an entry in the user profiles, the value in OBJECT DATA identifies some part of the database, and the value in ACCESS PRIVILEGE specifies the functions or actions the identified user can perform on the identified data.

In the most general case, there could be multiple entries in the authorization table for any given user (perhaps accessing in different roles or from different locations). The "users" in the table could be any *subjects* which are the source of actions on objects—people, groups, programs, or terminals. The *objects* can include resources other than data—programs, memory pages, or peripheral devices. Access privileges or *rights* can include read, write, allocate, execute, or grant privileges to others.

The general authorization table can be viewed as an **authorization matrix** as sketched in Figure 14-10. The rows represent subjects or users and the columns represent data objects. The access privilege information is recorded in the cells of the matrix, one cell at the intersection of each user with each data object. The objects accessible by a subject, together with the access privileges and conditions, are sometimes called the *capabilities* of the subject. Lampson [1971] gave one of the earliest descriptions of the authorization matrix; Graham and Denning [1972] extended it; and Conway, Maxwell, and Morgan [1972] called it a "security matrix." The authorization matrix has been one of the most influential and widely used models for data access control because of its simplicity and generality, and because it allows a variety of implementation techniques.

Columns of the authorization matrix correspond to data objects. Simply naming data files would yield a relatively small number of nonoverlapping data objects for the authorization matrix. Such coarse granularity of the data objects keeps the matrix to a manageable size.

OBJECT
(data, program, or other protected resource)

O_j

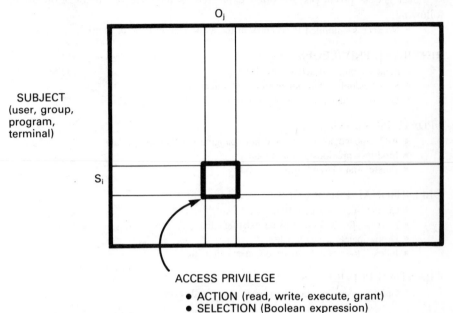

SUBJECT
(user, group,
program,
terminal)

S_i

ACCESS PRIVILEGE

- ACTION (read, write, execute, grant)
- SELECTION (Boolean expression)
- CONDITION (time, location)

Figure 14-10. Authorization Matrix for Access Control.
Each column represents an *object* such as data, program, or other resource to be protected. Each row represents a *subject* such as user, user group, program, or terminal which is the source of actions on protected objects. A cell in the matrix contains the authorized actions or access privileges (capabilities, rights) which the corresponding subject has on the intersecting object along with any limiting conditions. The matrix is a convenient way to visualize the authorization information, but is not likely the method of implementation.

Finer granularity enables access control to be more precisely limited to the data actually needed. For finer granularity, a data object could correspond to subsets of named data items or subsets of records, even to individual data items or records. Finer granularity results in greater overhead with many more columns in the matrix. Considering the naming of different data structures and the values for data items that can be used in the Boolean selection expression, the number of different data objects (columns) is practically unlimited.

Naming files or data items as the objects of access control provides authorization which is *independent* of stored data values. Expressing data independent authorization rules is similar to the projection specification in a retrieval language. The authorization decision can be made without reference to the database and, therefore, can be made before execution time, for example, at compile or open time.

14.4.2 User Access Privileges

User access privileges are often expressed as any one or combination of the following:

- No access—implied if no entry in the authorization table or matrix.

RETRIEVAL PRIVILEGES
- Read—applies to actual stored data.
- Statistics only—but not reading individual data.
- Selection—using data items in the selection expression.

UPDATE PRIVILEGES
- Add, append, or insert—but not changing existing stored data.
- Modify—previously stored data.
- Delete—an extreme form of modify.

DEFINITIONAL PRIVILEGES
- Create—define a new file.
- Revise—the definition of an existing file.
- Drop—delete a whole file.
- Index—to create an index on an existing file.

GRANTING PRIVILEGES
- Grant—assign privileges to other users (and revoke).

Most systems do not have such a broad choice of access privileges. Often there are only two—READ and WRITE, where 'write' implies all forms of update.

The same access control mechanism can be used to protect other system resources, such as programs. This requires additional privileges, such as 'execute.' Privileges to list (read) and modify can be extended to programs as though they were files.

If the above privileges are treated as independent of each other, one or more would be specified for each user of each data object. In this case, having one privilege would not imply having another. For example, one system provides four combinations of two privileges:

00. no access
01. read only
10. alter only
11. read and alter

Having 'alter only' permission without being able to 'read' is equivalent to 'add' or 'append' permission. Sometimes it is desirable to have an 'append only' privilege for data entry clerks who would have no need to access all previously entered data or to see the aggregate of charitable contributions from an individual, for example. 'Read and alter' permission would include append and modify privileges. This could be extended to a general 'bit vector' with each bit position corresponding to a different privilege.

Some systems define certain privileges to subsume others. For example, 'update' privileges would imply 'read' privilege. Several privileges may be ranked—READ, APPEND, MODIFY, REVISE—such that having a higher order privilege implies having all the lower order privileges. The privilege to 'revise' (define or redefine a data object) includes the privileges to read and update. The 'revise' privilege may be further divided into 'appending' new data items to the definition, and 'modifying' the definition of existing data items which is potentially more destructive.

Some systems have an all inclusive privilege category such as OWNER, MASTER, or DBA. This privilege may be limited to a single user, or to a single user for each data object. The privilege could apply to particular data objects, or to *all* data objects in the system.

One particularly troubling avenue of gaining access to sensitive information relates to the *flow* of data from one data object to another, where the receiving data object has differing or lesser restrictions. Consider the following example:

- User **A** is authorized to read file **X** .
- User **A** is authorized to write or append to file **Y** .
- User **B** is authorized to read file **Y** but not file **X** .

Both users can collude with user **A** copying sensitive information from file **X** to file **Y** , which user **B** then reads, thereby gaining unauthorized access. Controlling the flow of data is very difficult in the access matrix model. Some ranking of privileges is needed as in the multilevel model discussed later.

14.4.3 Granting Privileges

In the centralized view of database management, one person, such as a database administrator or data security officer, grants (and revokes) privileges to users. The system merely keeps track of who has what privileges on what data objects. This is the one-owner-model for access control. An alternative view, adopted by most operating systems, considers the creator of a file to be the owner who possesses all the privileges of ownership, including who else should be granted access to the file.

The emergence of distributed systems and the proliferation of microcomputer workstations has increased the pressure for greater decentralization of access control authority. In a shared data environment, additional users could be granted the privilege of granting privileges to other users—called the 'grant' privilege. This would allow the DBA to delegate some authority for data security.

If the 'grant' privilege includes granting the 'grant' privilege to another user, the chain of authority could spread out indefinitely. For accountability and to later revoke privileges, it may be desirable for the system to keep track of who granted the grant privilege to a particular user. Suppose **X** granted a privilege to **Y** who in turn granted it to **Z** . If **X** subsequently revokes the privilege granted to **Y** , should **Z** also lose the privilege? What if **Z** independently received the same privilege from **W** ? These are interesting policy questions for data security with significant consequences for implementation [see Griffiths & Wade, 1976].

14.4.4 Data-Dependent Authorization

Data-independent authorization would simply permit or deny access to, say, employee salary data. Sometimes it is desirable to have more selective or conditional control over access. Data-dependent access rules identify data objects using a Boolean selection expression. For example, a user may be allowed to access

SALARY WHERE LEVEL EQ EMPL

thus excluding salary data on anyone at the level of HEAD. Alternatively, a user may be allowed to access data only on employees below a certain salary level:

ALL ITEMS OF EMPLOYEE WHERE SALARY LT 25000

A third example permits managers to access data only on employees in their department:

... WHERE UNITNO = (UNITNO WHERE EMPNO = <user> AND
LEVEL = HEAD)

where <user> is a system variable. At execution time, its value would be the employee number of the currently identified user (which could be obtained from the user profile file). Note that a requester not at the level of HEAD would not gain access since the second selection condition within the parentheses would evaluate to false, and the embedded query would not retrieve a valid UNITNO.

Data-dependent access control requires that the authorization decision be made at execution time when actual data values can be retrieved from the database and plugged into the Boolean expression. Since excluded confidential data is transferred from secondary storage to main memory, care must be taken against unauthorized disclosure—by tapping in on the channel, or accessing the data residing in memory buffers after user job termination or system malfunction.

Implementing data-dependent access controls is fairly simple. The data-dependent access condition(s) can be ANDed to any selection expression on the user's request before the query is executed. Stonebraker and Wong called this access control by *query modification* [1974]. If a user only had access to data on EMPLoyees, the query:

PRINT EMPNAME, SALARY, . . . WHERE TITLE EQ ELEC ENGR.

would be modified as follows:

PRINT EMPNAME, SALARY, . . . WHERE TITLE EQ ELEC ENGR AND
LEVEL EQ EMPL.

Note that the user is receiving only part of the data requested. Users must realize that partial satisfaction of a request is possible with this form of access control.

If a user does not have access to salary data, allowing selection based upon salary can have the same effect. With the following query:

PRINT EMPLOYEE NAME WHERE SALARY GT 50000

a user would be able to determine very specific salary information about named employees. The user should at least have read privileges on salary before it is permitted in a selection expression.

Selective access control can be conditional on factors other than stored data. System variables such as date, day-of-the-week, time-of-day, and terminal identification can be used for access control. The privilege can be expressed as an allowed range of days or times for access. An access privilege can have an expiration date. Specifying terminal IDs effectively controls access based on the physical location of the user (or possession of an authorized terminal).

14.4.5 Multilevel Classification and Need-to-Know Schemes

Another approach to access control is based upon classification levels. The U. S. military uses the following levels:

- UNCLASSIFIED
- CONFIDENTIAL
- SECRET
- TOP SECRET

Every document is *classified* into one of these categories, and every user is assigned a *clearance* level corresponding to one of these categories. A user is authorized access to any document with an equal or lesser classification than the user possesses. For example, a user with SECRET clearance could see documents classified as SECRET or CONFIDENTIAL, but could *not* see documents classified as TOP SECRET.

Multilevel classification can be combined with need-to-know [an earlier version of this model was proposed by Bell and LaPadula, as described in Landwehr, 1981]. An expression of need-to-know and authority-to-know provides a link between user profiles and data definition without an intermediate authorization table. As shown in Figure 14-11, the user information is extended to include an authority level for each user and a set of need-to-know classes, and the definition of each data item is extended to include a minimum authority level and the sets of need-to-know data classes to which it belongs.

Access privileges based only upon authority levels would give a user permission to access any data classified at the user's clearance level or lower. Access permission based upon a need-to-know provides an additional degree of security. The need-to-know classes are established on the basis of homogeneous groupings of users, homogeneous groupings of data, or some balanced combination of the two. User groups can be defined on the basis of commonality in function or in organizational unit. The need-to-know classes are completely unrelated and they need not be mutually exclusive with respect to either users or data items. They can be considered an arbitrary means of linking data to users.

Users seeking to access data must satisfy both the authority level and the need-to-know classes of authorization.

It is important to note that the dual scheme for access authorization based upon authority level and need-to-know does not permit the expression of data dependent access criteria. No provision was made for the storage of Boolean selection expressions. One alternative to remedy this weakness would be to associate one or more Boolean selection expressions with the userschema assuming that the user is being constrained to view only that data which is defined in the userschema. If the user is retrieving or updating using a generalized functional module which can address the

Extended User Profile:

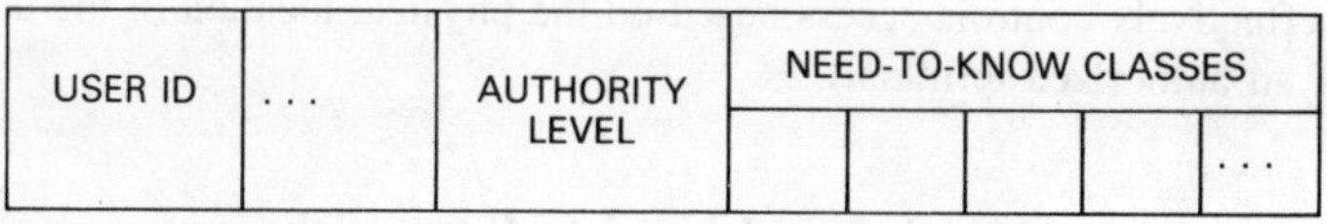

USER ID	. . .	AUTHORITY LEVEL	NEED-TO-KNOW CLASSES				. . .

Extended Data Item Definition:

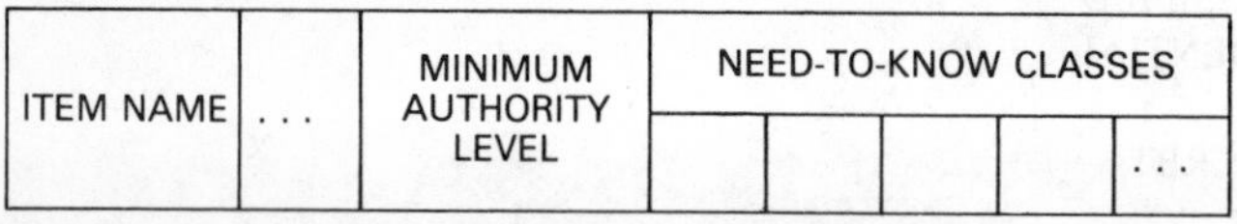

ITEM NAME	. . .	MINIMUM AUTHORITY LEVEL	NEED-TO-KNOW CLASSES				. . .

Figure 14-11. Multilevel plus Need-to-Know Model for Access Control.
Each user is assigned an authority level and classes of data which they have a need to know. Each data object is assigned to a set of need-to-know classes and given a minimum authority level. The authority levels could be numbers, say between 0 and 15. A user must possess an authority level equal to or higher than the minimum authority level assigned to each of the data items to be accessed, AND the user must be assigned a need-to-know class which includes the desired data.

entire database, some additional mechanism is needed to couple the flexibility of the dual-criteria authorization scheme with the ability to express data-dependent conditions on accessing the database.

14.4.6 Implementing Authorization Mechanisms

Except for the multilevel classification model, a matrix provides a good conceptual view of an authorization mechanism. In actual implementations, a strict matrix is seldom used because it would be too large, sparsely populated, and the information in a cell can be varied and complex—with multiple access privileges, contextual conditions, and a Boolean selection expression.

To appreciate the potential size of the authorization file or the authorization matrix, suppose an organization has 1,000 users and 1,000 separately identified data objects (a rather small database). The authorization matrix would have one million cells and the authorization file would have a potential of one million entries. That is a data management problem in itself! The real challenge in providing a feasible authorization mechanism is to bring the problem of recording authorization information down to manageable proportions.

Several practical alternatives are possible. One is to reduce the size of the *user dimension* by defining homogeneous groups of individual users. The user profile table still includes one entry for each authorized user with their authentication information. Each user is also identified as belonging to a particular user group. All members of a user group have the same authorization privileges. The authorization matrix has one row for each user group.

The *data dimension* can be reduced by clustering data items, or by identifying data at higher levels such as repeating group types or record types. The subsets of data may be mutually exclusive or overlapping. If overlapping, there would be potentially more data objects (columns) in the authorization matrix.

Storing each cell of a sparse matrix wastes storage space. The alternative is to go back to the basic design for an authorization table introduced in section 14.4.1. The triplets (the first three below) can be extended as follows [see Wood, 1980]:

- User Subject or user group (the grantee).
- Data Object—file, rgroup, data items, or clusters of items.
- Access Privileges.
- Boolean expression on the data object for data-dependent control (called a *predicate* on the data object).
- System Conditions using date, time, day, or terminal ID (may be coupled with the data-dependent Boolean expression).
- Authorizer (grantor) who created this access rule—sets up an accountability mechanism; can be used to restrict who is able to revise or revoke an authorization permission.
- Grant Privilege—whether this user is authorized to grant their privilege to another user (can be recorded as an additional access privilege).
- Response to a denied access request—log, notify security officer, abort user, message to user.

Lack of certain access privileges implies that certain commands cannot be issued by the user. For example, with read-only privilege, the user would be prohibited from executing any update commands. Without being the 'owner' of a file, the user could not revise or destroy the definition. Without being the DBA or 'master' password holder, the user would be unable to grant, revise, or revoke access privileges. Certain privileges give the user the ability to execute certain commands.

There are several ways of expressing access privileges and authorizations to the system through a command language. Some systems combine profile information (such as passwords) with authorization information:

ASSIGN <password> TO <user> FOR <privileges> ON <data object>.

The problem here is that the user is assigned multiple passwords corresponding to the various authorizations received. It is better to separately specify passwords and other authentication information:

ADDUSER <userid> [<password>] . . .

ASSIGN <password> TO <user>.

ASSIGN <password>.

and then specify authorization rules:

GRANT <privileges> TO <user> ON <data object> WHERE <selection>.

where the data object can be a file name or a list of data items. The command to assign a password would be issued by the current user to change his or her password after having supplied the correct (old) password. Only someone with grant authority would assign a password to another user. A DROPUSER command goes along with ADD-USER, and REVOKE <privileges> FROM. . . goes along with the GRANT command. Of course the person issuing these commands must have the proper authorization.

Certain policies can be enforced within the system to control the actions of the DBA, data security officer, or anyone taking action to enter or modify authentication or authorization information.

- Delay action for a day—a 'cooling off' period.
- Require duplicate action or approval from another authorized person—thus requiring collusion to break security.

All action requests would be logged on an audit trail. The delay would allow someone to review the logged actions and take countermeasures if necessary.

Information stored in user profiles and authorization tables must be kept secure. The stored information can be encrypted. The ability to read authentication information such as passwords, must be carefully controlled. The ability to change authorization information must also be carefully controlled. If the security files are considered additional data objects, then read and modify privileges can be controlled using the same mechanisms described in this section.

14.5 CONTROLLING INFERENCES FROM STATISTICAL DATA

Applying statistical functions such as COUNT, SUM, AVERAGE, MINIMUM, and MAXIMUM to the individual values in a database produces statistical data. Individual personal data may be confidential and subject to strict access control. Statistical data can satisfy various research and management needs and should be more widely available, that is, subject to less strict access control. Such data is not used to make evaluative judgments about individuals or to take action which directly affects an individual. Research-oriented output may be used to appraise the condition of a group of individuals with respect to some social theory or the effectiveness of a program in which the group is involved.

It is often thought that the confidentiality of individual data can be preserved if output is restricted to statistical results. Some even believe that deleting all personal identifying information such as name, account numbers, and addresses will ensure the privacy of individual data. The following scenario illustrates how personal facts can be obtained or closely approximated from a data bank allowing only statistically aggregated output. *Compromise* occurs when a requester deduces, from the responses of one or more queries, confidential information which was previously unknown.

Suppose that we wish to determine whether John Doe earns over $50,000 per year. We already know some of his personal characteristics and can use them to obtain "statistical" data from a data bank in which we know his record is stored. (Of course we would need to know how to access the data bank and something of the data definition, at least data item names and how values are recorded.)

PRINT COUNT OF EMPLOYEES	WHERE	AGE = 39
	AND	EDUCATIONAL LEVEL = LLB
	AND	SEX = MALE
	AND	COUNT OF CHILDREN = 4
	AND	CITY = NEW YORK
	AND	PROFESSION = LAWYER.

Suppose the system responds with "57."

Now we query the system again augmenting the above with a salary condition:

PRINT COUNT WHERE SAME AND SALARY GT 50000.

If the system responds with "57" again, we have learned that John Doe earns over $50,000 a year. Furthermore, we can incrementally increase the salary amount in the query to arrive at a minimum when the count goes down. The smaller the count, the more likely we are able to infer personal data about John Doe. Consider what personal data we would be able to obtain if the system had responded with a count of "1"! We could incrementally add conditions to the query—if the system responds with "1" they are true for John Doe; and "0" would indicate false.*

Individual identifiers are needed for both update and retrieval when data is used to make administrative judgments or take action with respect to single individuals. In the social research function, individual identifiers are only needed on update to serve as an accounting device. Identifiers are needed on research data to be able to track the changes in individuals over time, a requirement of so-called "longitudinal studies." If no administrative function is served by the individual data there are several strategies which can be used to isolate individual identifiers from the data pertaining to those individuals.†

The real difficulty arises when the data serves both an administrative and a research function. Access controls of the type discussed so far can be applied to retrieval of individual data. Additional control mechanisms are needed to permit retrieval of statistical data without violating the privacy of individual data. The problem is that some individual information can always be inferred from statistically aggregated data. For example, if the maximum age in a sample of individuals is 62, no one in that sample is older. Similarly, if the monthly rentals reported in my census block are all within 10% of each other, I can infer with reasonable precision the rental that my neighbors are paying. The real question is not to guarantee absolutely that no individual data can be inferred but rather that precautions are followed to limit disclosures to a reasonable level.

---

*This example is taken from Lance J. Hoffman and W. F. Miller, "Getting a Personal Dossier from a Statistical Data Bank," *Datamation* (16:5), 1970 May, pp. 74-75.

†Robert F. Boruch, "Security of Information Processing—Implications from Social Research," *AFIPS Fall Joint Computer Conference Proceedings* (volume 41), 1972, page 426; and Alice M. Rivlin, Chairman, Committee on Federal Agency Evaluation Research, *Protecting Individual Privacy in Evaluation Research*, Washington, DC: National Academy of Sciences, 1975.

14.5.1 Approximate, Supplemental, and Indirect Disclosures

Morris Hansen [1971], then an administrator at the U. S. Bureau of the Census, presents various methods that can be used to limit approximate disclosure, supplemental disclosure, and indirect disclosure of individual data from a statistical databank.

Approximate disclosure can result when the classes used to group data values are too small and the user can infer magnitudes too accurately. He proposes a rule where the upper limit of any given class is at least twice its lower limit, for example,

NUMBER OF EMPLOYEES
> under 5
> 5-9
> 10-24
> 25-49
> 50-99
> 100-199
>   :

Supplemental disclosure results from collusion when one can subtract known individual data (perhaps his own) from the aggregation and infer something about the other respondent(s). Supplemental disclosure can be inhibited if at least three nontrivial cases are aggregated in a cell so that, for example, a business respondent will not know his competitor's response. Small sample cells should either not be reported or combined with adjacent cells.

For an example of an *indirect disclosure*, suppose a small county has six hardware stores, and that a city within the county has four of them. If retail sales are published for the county, and also for the city, an indirect disclosure occurs. Each of the two stores in the balance of the county could directly determine the competitor's sales by taking the difference between the county statistics and the city statistics.

14.5.2 The Problem and Methods of Statistical Inferencing

Inferring confidential data on individuals from legally obtained statistical data is difficult to control. Controlling this type of disclosure requires monitoring all statistical retrievals from the database. The system must record each retrieval in an audit trail. When processing a request, the system must analyze the history of retrievals for that user to determine if the response to the current request could be combined with the results of prior requests to compromise the confidentiality of individual data.

Response to a single isolated request presents a relatively minor threat to data security. The problem stems from repeated requests. Furthermore, to counteract users who conspire by pooling their collective responses, the system would have to analyze past requests from *all* users!

One should not assume that it is easy to deduce confidential information by inference from statistical data. The methods of compromising a database with statistical results are nontrivial. However, they must be taken seriously because the benefits of compromise may far outweigh the cost. For example, medical history and financial data might be very valuable to certain authorized users, such as political opponents. The objective of inference controls is to make the cost of obtaining confidential information unacceptably high.

The example of obtaining John Doe's salary showed that compromise is easy when the selected set of records is small, particularly so when the query isolates the single record for the targeted subject. It is equally easy when the selected set is just slightly less than the total number of records in the file—since the query can be restated using the complement (WHERE NOT . . .) of the expression of known conditions.

The suggested countermeasure is not to report small counts on repetitive, similar queries. Of course, this may be precisely the data the legitimate researcher needs, so the countermeasure reduces the richness of the database system. Even this countermeasure can be subverted if the system permits the user to add new dummy entries to the database. The user simply adds fictitious entries with the same characteristics as known for John Doe until the count is above the threshold of 'small.'

The following example illustrates how to obtain individual data from statistical results. Suppose we were only allowed to obtain average salaries from the employee file and that the system will not respond if fewer than M records are selected. To find John Doe's salary, we must find a selection expression which will retrieve more than M records and will exclude John Doe and myself (or include, but I must know which). It could select on any combination of data items. Schlörer [see Denning, Denning, and Schwartz, 1979] called it a *tracker* expression. Now we issue the following three queries and obtain the responses:

PRINT AVG SALARY WHERE <tracker>.
AVG SALARY = 30000
PRINT AVG SALARY WHERE <tracker> AND EMPNAME EQ "DOE, JOHN".
AVG SALARY = 35000
PRINT AVG SALARY WHERE <tracker> AND EMPNAME EQ <my-name>.
AVG SALARY = 32500

From this we can build three simultaneous equations, using the general form of 'average $\times$ count = sum,' with three unknowns:

N = the number of employees selected with the tracker expression
S = the total salary of those employees
D = John Doe's salary
50000 = my salary

$30000 \times N = S$
$35000 \times (N + 1) = S + D$
$32500 \times (N + 1) = S + 50000$

Solving for D , we learn that John Doe's salary = 70000! Note that if we had permission to obtain sums rather than averages, we could have deduced John Doe's salary with just two queries.

Notice that the system does not allow queries on small sets, which avoids supplemental disclosure. In fact, M can be arbitrarily large and this unauthorized disclosure can still occur. The problem lies in the ability to ask multiple queries which are almost the same. This suggests that the system must not only restrict the *size* of the selected set, but also the size of the *intersection* of two selected sets. Using this technique, the disclosure of individual data can be made arbitrarily difficult.* Unfortunately, application of the technique is costly, requiring a comparison of every new query with a history of past queries and determining the size of the intersection set.

The above example is called an "individual" tracker. Denning and Schwartz [1979] extended the concept to "general" and "double" trackers [see Date, 1983, page 163 for a readable example of a general tracker]. Many possible queries in a database system are general trackers and thus apt to be easily discovered by guessing. Denning and Schlörer [1980] describe a fast procedure for finding a tracker. It assumes that the user knows or can approximate the value sets for each data item of interest in the database. This is a reasonable assumption since the user must have some knowledge of the value sets to construct valid selection expressions. Although the number of queries required to find a tracker is at most of order $\log_2 S$, where S is the size of the cartesian product of the value sets of interest, their experiments showed that the procedure often finds a tracker with just one or two queries.

Existing designs for query systems do not adequately prevent disclosure of confidential data by combinatorial inference. Recent literature has revealed a myriad of inference techniques, indicating that compromise is much easier than once thought. Many suggested controls are too restrictive, impractical to implement, or easy to subvert. For example, controls to limit overlap of selected sets may unduly restrict results needed for legitimate research—comparison of statistics for subgroups of a population and the population as a whole. Also overlap controls are extremely costly to implement since they require comparing each new query with all previous queries to determine if there would be too much overlap.

Much of the recent literature on statistical inferencing has shown how and how easy it is to compromise a confidential database. Little is known how to effectively and efficiently counter the threats posed by statistical inferencing. At the very least, when a database contains sensitive information, all retrieval requests should be monitored and logged.

14.5.3 Distortion Techniques and Random Sample Queries

The dominant characteristic of the above attacks is the degree of user control over the selected set of records. Also, system responses are presumed accurate. Another class of protection strategies is based upon deliberately distorting the system responses. This may be an acceptable tradeoff to users of the statistical results, in return for greater safeguards over the disclosure of accurate information on individuals.

---

*Jeffrey D. Ullman, *Principles of Database Systems*, Second edition, Potomac, VA: Computer Science Press, 1982, page 359.

Rounding controls modify the exact answer to a query by a small amount before the system reports it to the requester. The change should not be determined randomly since the correct answer could be deduced by averaging a sufficient number of responses to the same query. The system should use a pseudorandom value that depends on the data. Then a given query always produces the same result.

In *error inoculation*, the values in the records are randomly modified before calculating the requested statistics. Error inoculation and rounding controls both reduce the quality of the reported statistics.

The use of *random sample queries* [Denning, 1980] seeks to avoid disclosure of accurate data by denying the requester complete control over the selected set of records used to calculate the statistics. When a record satisfies the user's selection criteria, the system uses pseudorandom techniques to determine whether or not to include it in the sample of the selected set of records. Statistics are then computed from the sample of selected records. As before, a response is denied if the true selected set is too small or too large (close to the total number of records).

Denning [1980] reports on an experiment using a simulated database. With a probability of 0.9375 of accepting a selected record into the sample, the random sampling technique estimated counts and sums of answerable queries to within 1% of their true values. At the same time, the estimates of counts and sums using trackers contained errors of several hundred percent. This is because the requester must calculate small counts (or sums) by taking the difference between large counts (and sums). In the individual tracker example above, John Doe's salary was found to be 70000. With an assumed error of 1% on the calculated averages, the error on Doe's salary would be 8.6%—and that small only because the selected set size (N) was 7. Larger N would produce greater error in the deduced data.

14.5.4 Summary of Defenses Against Statistical Inferencing

When the user access privilege is 'statistics only,' various system controls may be used to minimize the disclosure of confidential data on individuals:

- Deny response to any single query that selects only one record from the file, whether on the identifier data item, or some combination of attributes, since statistics such as SUM or AVG SALARY will be exact if the selected set size is one. (Responding when there are *no* selected records is also a problem since negative information may also be used to infer individual data.)
- Deny response to any query if the count of selected records is less than some minimum M (say 3), or greater than N − M where N is the total number of records in the file.
- Deny response to any query if the size of the intersection of selected records with a prior query is small. The designer of the control mechanism must decide how many past queries to examine—from the same user, same user group, or all users; and how far back to go. Unfortunately, no technique has yet been devised to efficiently make such comparisons with past queries.
- Distort the statistical answers to queries by a small, pseudorandom amount; or distort the data before calculating the statistics.

- Random sample the selected records and calculate the statistics on the sample. This technique coupled with the denied response on small selected set sizes appears to offer substantial protection against deduction of confidential information by inference, especially when the requester is using a general tracker selection expression.
- Log all queries on a audit trail to enable subsequent investigation of potential security threats.

14.6 ENCRYPTION

Access control is only applied to the established avenues of access to the database. Clever people using clever instruments may be able to access the data by circumventing the controlled avenues of access. Also, innocent people who passively stumble upon an avenue of access may be unable to resist the temptation to look at and perhaps misuse the data so acquired. To counteract the possibility that either active or passive intruders obtain unauthorized access to sensitive data, it is desirable to obscure or hide the meaning of the data accessed.

Encryption techniques complement access controls. Access controls are ineffective if:

- A user leaves a listing in the work area or in the trash.
- Passwords are written down and found.
- Offline backup files are stolen.
- Confidential data is left in main memory after a job has completed.
- Someone taps in on a communication line.

When a data system is geographically dispersed, physical security measures become less practical and less effective against intrusion because the system is more open and vulnerable to penetration at more points. If the computer system and all the sensitive data are maintained in a single, isolated environment into which a user must be admitted before access to data is permitted, little need for encryption exists. An increased need for encryption comes with the increased tendency for systems to reach out into the using environment and become more available to the users.

Encryption is any sort of transformation applied to data (or text) prior to transmission or prior to storage, which makes it more difficult to extract information content or meaning. The word 'cryptography' comes from the Greek meaning 'hidden or secret writing.' Rein Turn [Petersen & Turn, 1967] has used the term *privacy transformation* to connote the use of encryption techniques in civilian and commercial systems, in contrast to military intelligence.

The basic encryption scheme is shown in Figure 14-12. Original *plaintext* is transformed by an *encryption algorithm* using an *encryption key* to produce *ciphertext*. An inverse *decryption algorithm* transforms the ciphertext using the same (or related) key to reconstruct the plaintext.

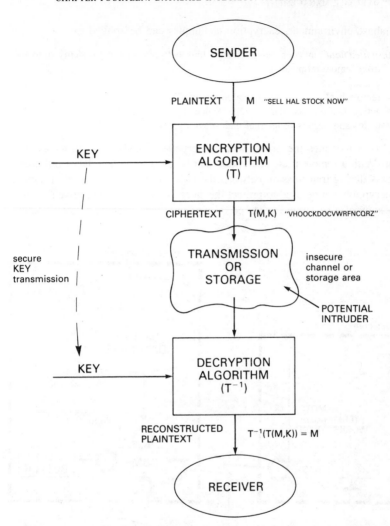

Figure 14-12. Basic Encryption/Decryption System.
An encryption algorithm (T) transforms a sender's plaintext message (M) using a key (K) to produce ciphertext. Plaintext is in a form recognizable by humans (or computers). The encrypted message or data can be transmitted through an insecure channel or stored in an insecure area since a potential intruder would only see a scrambled message. Using the same (or related) key, the decryption algorithm applies an inverse transformation (T^{-1}) to the ciphertext to reconstruct the original message (M). Transmission of the key to the decryptor must be kept secure, since knowing the decryption key and the encryption algorithm makes it easy to decrypt or decipher a message, thereby disclosing sensitive information.

In a database environment, encryption techniques can be applied to:

- *Transmitted data* sent over communication lines between computer systems, or to and from remote terminals (1).
- *Stored data*:
  - remote backup data on removable media (2).
  - active data on secondary storage devices (3).
  - tables and buffers in internal main memory (4).

Figure 14-13 indicates the points where encryption can be used in a database environment. With a remote user, encryption can be used to protect data from unauthorized access during transmission between the user and the system. With a remote database, encryption can be used to protect the stored data from unauthorized access. The backup copy of a sensitive file stored on magnetic tape in some remote location

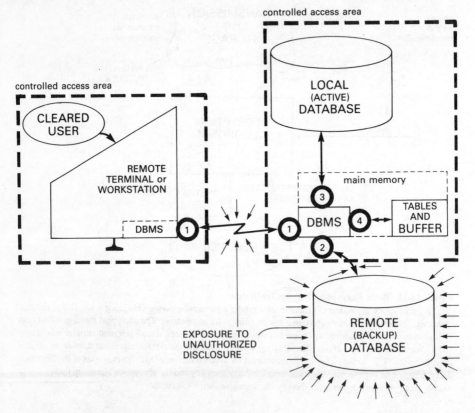

Figure 14-13. Encryption in a Database Environment.
Encryption techniques can be used in the transmission or storage of data. The stored data may be remote backup data on removable media, active (updated) data on secondary storage devices, or tables and buffers in internal memory. Sensitive data outside of a secured area is more exposed to unauthorized disclosure and therefore encryption can contribute significantly to greater security.

may be a good candidate for encryption. The remote "user" may be a person at an online remote terminal or another computer system in a different location.

Encryption methods can be classified according to:

1. The nature of the **algorithm**:

   • *Transposition*, or *permutation* in general.
   • *Substitution*, either mono-alphabetic or polyalphabetic.
   • *Product*, combining permutations and substitutions.

2. The nature of the **key**:

   • *Private-Key*, requiring independent, secure key distribution from sender to receiver, includes most transposition and substitution ciphers, and the U.S. Data Encryption Standard (DES).
   • *Public-Key*, actually a dual key system in which everyone can have everyone else's public key, and each receiver can keep their private key wholly private. The security of both private and public key systems depends entirely on the security of the keys; it should be possible to reveal the algorithm or process.

3. The nature of the **material** to be encrypted:

   • A contiguous *stream* of characters or numbers.
   • A *block* of characters or numbers.

Cryptographic techniques have been widely used in military and government intelligence activities for centuries but due to the secretive nature of the subject, very little has been published until the last few decades. [For more details see Gaines, 1939; Shannon, 1949; Kahn, 1967; Sinkov, 1968; Mellon, 1973; and Hoffman, 1977.]

The increased potential for more sophisticated encryption and cryptanalysis through the use of computers, coupled with the increased concern for data privacy, has generated a great surge of interest in the past decade or two. There has been substantial published literature on the use of encryption in computerized database systems. The U.S. Government has adopted a data encryption standard. Unfortunately, these modern techniques have not yet been widely implemented in organizations.

Choosing an encryption method depends upon the cost, what is available, and the level of user need. The object of any particular method is to raise the work factor high enough to discourage anyone from breaking the code. The cost of the chosen method must be commensurate with the level of risk and the degree of security desired. Even fairly modest and simple encryption methods can render transmitted messages and stored data secure from all but the most persistent penetrators. In many present day situations, *some* protection would be better than none.

Hoffman [1977, page 67] conducted some experiments to determine the *encryption time coefficient* of selected encryption algorithms—the ratio of the time to fetch, encrypt, and send/store over the time to simply fetch and send/store data. He found that some methods resulted in coefficients of nearly one, meaning the time cost of encryption was negligible. He also found significant differences with the same method on different machine architectures, particularly word size and memory cycle time.

14.6.1 Variable Storage, Value Encoding, and Data Compression

Several functions relating to data storage also provide a measure of encryption. These include:

- Omitting identifying information.
- Variable length fields.
- Item value encoding.
- Data compression.

Although each item above has some other primary purpose, such as more efficient usage of storage, they also serve to obscure the meaning of data. The data may be stored in some encoded form which is not immediately and obviously readable by a human without having additional information or without knowing the encoding rule.

Stripping off or not storing information which identifies the item type or the magnitude of the value can provide a measure of protection. Examples include data item names, decimal points, dollar signs, or any indication of the unit of measurement. Such information is normally stored as part of the database definition rather than with the data values. This implies that controlling access to *both* the data and its definition is much more important than controlling separate access to either the database or its definition.

Storing data in variable length fields, encoding item values or compressing stored data are done primarily to economize on storage space, and to reduce processing time or data transfer time. Nevertheless, all three techniques contribute something to data privacy. When data values are stored in variable length fields, the boundaries between values are less easily discerned than if the values were stored in fixed length fields.

With item value encoding the external, human-oriented values for a data item are replaced by shorter, fixed length codes. For example, LEVEL may be encoded as follows:

EXTERNAL VALUE	INTERNAL CODE
HEAD	1
EMPLOYEE	2
CONSULTANT	3
UNKNOWN	0

Although item value encoding is used to avoid having to store longer item values many times in the database, it can sometimes provide a meaningful degree of protection. The protective value of this technique depends upon the degree of access control placed on the database definition where the value encoding table is often stored.

Greater protection results when the codes do not have any mnemonic significance as in the above example. Of course, depending upon the nature of the data and any known contextual information it may be possible to infer the meaning of the codes. In a typical organization, the above example might show the value '2' appearing several times more often than '1'. With a modal distribution of values, the most frequent coded value can often be inferred. Depending upon the needs of the using environment, item value codes can be picked not only with economy in mind but also with privacy in mind.

Under some circumstances, data compression techniques can provide an increased measure of security. Compression can be accomplished by removing consecutively repeated characters, usually blanks and zeros, by packing more characters into the storage cell normally used to contain a single character, or by replacing common character strings with codes and storing them only once for the entire database.

A most efficient data compression scheme replaces each uniquely occurring value with a variable length binary code, also called a Huffman code.* The length of the code is inversely related to its frequency of occurrence.

14.6.2 Traditional Methods: Transposition and Substitution

Historically, transposition and substitution have been the two major classes of encryption techniques. They were applied manually to encrypt streams of text prior to transmission. The earliest techniques relied on the secrecy of the method. Permutations and substitutions serve as the basis for some present-day computerized methods, and therefore are covered here briefly.

Transposition techniques permute the ordering of characters in the data stream according to some rule. For example, if the transposition pattern or rule is to transpose each consecutive pair of characters, the phrase

$$\texttt{database management systems}$$

would appear as

$$\texttt{ADATABESMbNAGAMENEbTYSTSMEbS}$$

obviously not very secure. An example of a general permutation would be to form blocks of, say, four characters and permute 1234 to 3124, padding the end to make the message an even multiple of four. The phrase would now appear as:

$$\texttt{TDAASBAEAbMNEAGMTENbSSYTSEMb}$$

With a correct guess of the length of the permutation block, only a few trials are needed to break the code.

Substitution techniques retain the relative position of the characters in the original plaintext but hide their identity in the ciphertext. By contrast, transposition techniques retain the identity of the original characters but change their position.

---

*D. A. Huffman, "A Method for the Construction of Minimum Redundancy Codes," *Proceedings IRE* (vol. 40), 1952 September, page 1098. If p_i is the probability of occurrence of the ith value, then $-\log_2 p_i$ is the minimum number of bits required in a variable length binary code to represent that value. Of course, the codes assigned to each value must be an integral number of bits. Huffman presents a method for constructing a set of uniquely decipherable variable length binary codes. It essentially consists of a 'code mobile' in the form of a binary tree with the sum of the probabilities (weights) at each branch of the tree being as nearly balanced as possible.

A simple example is the *Caesar Cipher* which substitutes the nth letter away from the plaintext character in the alphabet. This is applied 'modulo 27' (includes a blank), that is, if you count past the end of the alphabet, cycle back to the beginning. The plaintext message in Figure 14-12 was encrypted using a Caesar Cipher. The n is the key indicating the alphabet shift. Did you know that the name of the computer, HAL, in the movie *2001: A Space Odyssey* was also the result of a Caesar Cipher? Such a simple cipher is very easy to break.

A general **mono-alphabetic substitution** cipher replaces characters in the plaintext with characters from some other alphabet, called a cipher alphabet, which becomes the key. For example:

Plaintext alphabet:	a b c d e f g h i j k l m n o p q r s t u v w x y z
Ciphertext alphabet:	G O R D N C H A L E S Z Y X W V U T Q P M K J I F B
Transforms the Plaintext:	d a t a b a s e m a n a g e m e n t s y s t e m s
Into the Ciphertext:	D G P G O G Q N Y G X G H N Y N X P Q F Q P N Y Q

Assuming that the plaintext message is written in natural English using 26 letters, mono-alphabetic substitutions are susceptible to frequency analysis of single letters, letter pairs, and reversals. The analysis is increasingly accurate for larger messages—the letter frequencies in the message would approach the characteristic letter frequencies for the language. In English, the most frequently occurring letters are E,T,A,O,N,R,I,S,H. Some people can even read such ciphertext directly! Some computers have built-in machine instructions to perform substitutions between two alphabets (needed for ASCII-EBCDIC code conversion), thus enabling faster exhaustive analysis of mono-alphabetic substitutions. Cryptanalysis techniques based upon assumed letter frequencies in the input character stream are much less relevant and less useful when encrypting streams of *data*.

A **homophonic cipher** [Stahl, 1973] provides the obvious solution to attacks based on letter frequencies. It substitutes multiple characters in rotation for the frequently occurring characters in the plaintext.

Plaintext alphabet:	a b c d e f g h i j k l m n o p q r s t u v w x y z
Ciphertext alphabet:	G O R D N C H A L E S 9 8 7 6 Z Y X W V U T Q P M K
	5 4 3 21 J
	I F
	B
Plaintext:	d a t a b a s e m a n a g e m e n t s y s t e m s
Ciphertext:	D G V 5 0 I W N 8 G 7 5 H 4 8 F 2 J W M W V B 8 W

This encryption technique makes the relative frequency of letter occurrences more uniform, effectively eliminating frequency analysis as a tool for the code breaker.

Polyalphabetic substitution uses multiple alphabets cyclically according to some rule. Each character of the plaintext is replaced with a character from a different ciphertext alphabet, thereby obscuring the frequency characteristics of the characters in the plaintext alphabet.

The classic Vigenère tableau (adding a blank = b) provides a standard sequence of cipher alphabets:

```
                 1111111111222222
        0123456789012345678901234556
        ────────────────────────────
        bABCDEFGHIJKLMNOPQRSTUVWXYZ
        ABCDEFGHIJKLMNOPQRSTUVWXYZb
        BCDEFGHIJKLMNOPQRSTUVWXYZbA
        CDEFGHIJKLMNOPQRSTUVWXYZbAB
        DEFGHIJKLMNOPQRSTUVWXYZbABC
        EFGHIJKLMNOPQRSTUVWXYZbABCD
        ++++++++++++++++++++++++++++
        ZbABCDEFGHIJKLMNOPQRSTUVWXY
```

It consists of all possible shifts in the Caesar Cipher. A key is used to select the alphabet for each character in the plaintext. The following example uses the key 'GORDNCHALES' to produce a substitution cipher with 11 alphabets:

Plaintext: d a t a b a s e   m a n a g e m e n t   s y s t e m s
Cipher Key: GORDNCHALESGORDNCHALESGORDN
Ciphertext: KPLEPDbFLRTUPYIbHVULXQZHWQF

The character for the ciphertext is found at the intersection of the plaintext and the cipher key characters in the table. The cipher key character effectively specifies the offset in the alphabet for each plaintext character. By assigning a number to each character corresponding to its position in the alphabet (blank=00, A=01, B=02, . . . Z=26) the Vigenère substitution can be expressed as:

$$\#(\text{ciphertext char}) = [\#(\text{plaintext char}) + \#(\text{cipher key char})] \text{ modulo } 27$$

and it is no longer necessary to refer to the Vigenère tableau. The decryption algorithm is expressed as:

$$\#(\text{plaintext char}) = [\#(\text{ciphertext char}) - \#(\text{cipher key char})] \text{ modulo } 27$$

The work factor for substitution algorithms increases with longer keys. The above example has a key periodicity of 11. By applying a second encryption using a key of, say, 13 characters, the periodicity of the composite key is 143 (= 11 × 13). For even greater security, ciphertext alphabets should be randomly generated, rather than simply a shifting of the alphabet.

The number of possible ciphertext alphabets used in a substitution scheme indicates the effort needed to analyze an intercepted encrypted message and, therefore, indicates the amount of protection provided. However, as Mellon [1973] points out:

> Simple substitution is trivial. . . . Under the rules of simple substitution, there are 25! possible "keys," or roughly 1.5×10^{25} possibilities. . . . At the rate of [one key trial per microsecond, a computer] would take 170,000,000,000,000

years to run through the list. . . . Yet most people can solve this sort of newspaper puzzle in a few minutes. Some can "sight-read" them. . . . The moral to be gained here is that one ought not be awed solely by large numbers. When a data-encryption device is promoted as having 10^{xx} different keys, the cautious system designer will repress the proclivity to regard this huge number as an unchallengeable figure of merit. It is not. [page 570]

In the above techniques, the permutation order or the ciphertext alphabet is considered the key. In the polyalphabetic substitution, a key determines which cipher alphabet to use for each character position. The longer the key the longer the periodicity of the cipher. If the key is longer than the plaintext (and the user discovers no fragment of the plaintext), a cipher is theoretically unbreakable. A good pseudorandom number generator* can be used to generate a key of potentially infinite length. However, even if the key is kept secure, knowing which of the above methods was used can help in breaking a given ciphertext. More recent techniques rely solely on the security of the key, allowing the algorithm to be published.

Computer implementations of the traditional methods can ignore constraints stemming from the need to have error-free manual calculations. The first step converts the message into a numeric form, replacing each letter with its position in the alphabet or with its binary ASCII code. Instead of using only 26 letters of the alphabet, a Vigenère tableau could use the 96 binary ASCII codes (excluding control characters) for encrypting computer-stored information. Then the manipulations can be performed numerically using the arithmetic registers in the computer.

A binary version of the Vigenère tableau uses a binary key to perform an "Exclusive-OR" on each block of binary 'plaintext.''

Plaintext: 01001110 10010100 11011100
Key: 11011101
Ciphertext: 10010011 01001001 00000001

An encryption algorithm can be made substantially stronger by repeatedly applying permutation and substitution transformations. Such a transformation, called a "product cipher," is the basis for modern, computerized cryptographic systems.

14.6.3 Stream Encryption for Data Communications

The traditional encryption techniques were originally applied to *streams* of text for transmitting messages through insecure channels. They provide a measure of end-to-end, sender-to-receiver security. The same basic techniques can be used for communication within computer networks. Most modern stream encryption algorithms are based on the Vigenère scheme (that is, a varying, key-determined offset to each digit

*The pseudorandom number generator is perhaps the most important tool in computerized cryptography. It must be pseudorandom, otherwise the encryption algorithm would not be reversible. The receiver must be able to reproduce the (infinitely) long encryption key. The generator must be carefully chosen to be assured of long periodicity and random characteristics [see discussion in Hoffman, 1977, Chapter 6].

position within the 'plaintext' alphabet) using long key-strings from a pseudorandom number generator. Today, a pair of end point devices can be obtained for under $500. Encryption/decryption may be performed at one of several points using hardware devices or software routines:

- On the output from the modem.
- Inside the modem.
- A separate box between the modem and the computer.
- In the computer system, either in hardware or software.

14.6.4 Block Encryption for Stored Data

Stream encryption techniques require a known starting position, normally the beginning of the message. Decryption of any part of the message requires starting from the beginning and decrypting the whole message. However, with stored data, it should not be necessary to decrypt an entire file to get an individual record, it should not even be necessary to decrypt an entire record to get an individual data item. It should be possible to encrypt only the sensitive items within a record [see Davida, 1981].

Block encryption techniques operate on individual blocks of data (or the message) independent of all other blocks. This allows decryption of a single block of data for retrieval or update, followed by re-encryption prior to storage again. Neither time nor position synchronization of encryption/decryption operations is necessary.

Figure 14-13 shows three types of stored data. If a whole file is transferred to a remote location for backup (2), stream encryption would be satisfactory. This presumes that recovery would operate on the file as a whole; no operation would be performed on part of the remote backup file. Active files on secondary storage (3) are normally the object of selective retrieval and update operations. This requires block encryption; stream encryption is impractical. Similarly, sensitive information stored in tables or buffers in main memory (4) would require block encryption.

Encryption of stored data also provides solutions to some of the access control problems discussed in the previous section. If plaintext data is never delivered to or from the DBMS or residing in memory buffers, problems of data leakage by someone else accessing buffers or tapping in on the data channels can be reduced. Also, a person not knowing how to encrypt stored data will be unable to create records which appear to be legitimate when decrypted by an authorized user.

Access control passwords stored in tables (which are moved in and out of main memory) represent a unique situation. They should be stored using an irreversible encryption technique, that is, with no easy method of decryption. Then, even if one had the encrypted password file and knew the encrypting algorithm, it would be very difficult to work backwards to obtain the plaintext encryption key or password. Passwords and encryption keys should never appear in plaintext form within the system except at the point of encryption/decryption.

An interesting difference arises when comparing encryption with a remote terminal and encryption with stored data. With a remote terminal, the encryption and decryption operations are performed at two different locations, therefore, requiring secure key transmission. Since encrypted data in a stored file would never be in its original form, both the encryption and decryption operations are performed within the computer system (the DBMS). For stored data the key is only needed in one place. Though the key does not have to be transmitted, it must be saved and kept secure as long as encrypted data is stored.

In a network environment, shared data may be stored at one node and accessed from multiple nodes. In some cases, the DBMS local to the database would be allowed to decrypt the local data. However, for security reasons, it may be desirable to pass the data through in encrypted form to a requester at a remote node. Then, all the users sharing the same remote database would require the same key to decrypt the data. This requires a means for secure key transmission. An alternative would be to have the local DBMS decrypt the local stored data, then re-encrypt it prior to transmission to the remote site.

The use of encryption techniques on stored data makes it important to funnel all data access through the single door of the database control system. For example, when concurrent processes are reading and writing data on the database, the encryption and decryption activities must be coordinated and controlled.

14.6.5 The U. S. Data Encryption Standard (DES)

In 1977 the U. S. National Bureau of Standards adopted a standard for data encryption, called the DES, based upon earlier work at IBM [See Feistel, 1973; an experimental hardware implementation was called "Lucifer"]. The U. S. standard is intended for unclassified, non-defense government communications where encryption is required. The U. S. government also intended that the standard specifications be easily and equitably available to all users and suppliers in the private sector at a reasonable cost.

The DES is an iterative product cipher, repeatedly applying permutation (transposition) and substitution operations to 64 bit blocks of data or text. The key is also 64 bits long. Every 8th bit of the key is a parity bit so only 56 bits are used for encryption. Figure 14-14 details the steps in the algorithm. The abridged flow diagram and the explanation are intended only to give the reader a feel for how the algorithm operates, not a complete understanding. [For further details see NBS FIPS PUB 46, 1977].

The U. S. Data Encryption Standard has several advantages, some real, others claimed:

- Usable for data transmission or data storage, since it is a block encryption technique.
- A product cipher, combining both substitution and transposition (permutation) operations.
- Every bit is a function of all data bits and all key bits, that is, a change in any *one* input data bit produces some probability of change in each of the output data bits.
- Protection depends only on the key; not on keeping the algorithm secret.
- Economical to implement in either software or hardware.
- Efficient to operate; a hardware implementation can operate at high transmission speeds.

Not everyone regards the DES as a highly secure system, perhaps indicated by its recommendation for U. S. non-defense application only. Hellman [1979; Diffie and

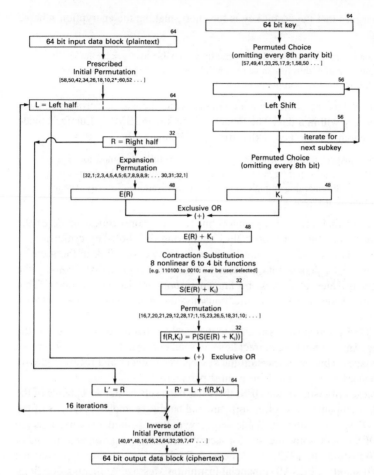

Figure 14-14. U. S. Federal NBS Data Encryption Standard (DES).

The DES algorithm works independently on 64 bit blocks of plaintext, either stored data or transmitted data or text. It is a product cipher using a series of permutations and substitutions on the plaintext block and the key. Except for one user-definable contraction substitution, all substitutions and permutations are prescribed as part of the algorithm. Referring to the initial permutation, for example, bit 1 becomes bit 58, bit 2 becomes bit 50, . . . bit 8 (marked with an asterisk) becomes bit 2; and in the inverse permutation, bit 2 (also marked with an asterisk) becomes bit 8. Both the data block and the key are given an initial permutation, and then run through 16 iterations of the main algorithm.

On each iteration, the right half of the data block is expanded to 48 bits and exclusively ORed with a 48 bit permutation of the key. Each iteration uses a different 48 bit permutation of the initially permuted key (omitting every 8th parity bit). A contraction substitution is applied to the result with a user selected 6 to 4 bit nonlinear function. That result is permuted and exclusively ORed with the left half of the data block to become the right half of the data block for the next iteration. The right half at the beginning of the iteration becomes the left half of the data block for the next iteration.

Finally, the inverse of the initial permutation is applied to the result of the 16th iteration giving a 64 bit output data block.

Decryption uses the same procedure but applies the 16 subkeys in reverse order to produce the plaintext from the ciphertext.

Hellman, 1977] argues that the 56 bit key is too short, making the encryption scheme too easy to break.

> The NBS Data Encryption Standard "is currently vulnerable to attack by the intelligence community and within fifteen years it will be rendered totally insecure due to the rapidly falling cost of computation."*

For a few million dollars, he claims that a computer system could perform an exhaustive search for the key within a day. The longer 128 bit key in IBM's "Lucifer" made it impossible to search for the key, exhaustively or heuristically.

> "Some critics suspect that this coding system was carefully designed to be just secure enough so that corporate spies outside the government could not break a user's code and just vulnerable enough so that the [U.S.] National Security Agency (NSA) could break it."†

Proponents point out that applying the algorithm two (or more) times increases the effective key size to 112 bits (or more); thus countering the short-key criticism.

The size of the key, however, is not likely to be the weakest link in the security chain. The DES is strictly dependent on secure key management and distribution—the key must be kept private yet it must be known to *both* sender and receiver. That necessarily requires some form of secure transmission or communication between sender and receiver.

Finally, the DES provides no assurance to the receiver that the actual sender is the purported sender. Anyone with the correct key can send encrypted messages or receive and decrypt messages. Having to transmit the key between sender and receiver greatly increases the chances of revealing it to a third party.

In spite of these criticisms of the DES, there has been substantial acceptance of the standard. Several companies now offer software and hardware implementations of the standard; and a DES chip is now available for a few dollars.‡ Many organizations are now using the DES to gain some measure of security in the transmission and storage of confidential information. In 1982, the American Banking Association approved the DES-based ANSI standard FIMAS (Financial Institution Message Authentication Standard) for protecting the electronic transfer of funds in EFTS.∮

14.6.6 Public-Key Cryptosystems

Hellman [1976] introduced the notion of a cryptographic system where a subscriber would place, in a public directory, the procedure required to encrypt messages

---

*Whitfield Diffie and Martin E. Hellman, "A Critique of the Proposed Data Encryption Standard," *Communications of the ACM* (19:3), 1976 March, page 164.

†Gina Bari Kolata, "Computer Encryption and the National Security Agency Connection," *Science* (197), 1977 July 29, page 438.

‡See Oldehoeft and McDonald, 1984; "Encryption Boards May Lure More Users," *Electronics* (50:14), 1977 July 7, pages 40, 42; and a description of IBM software and hardware product implementations of the DES in Konheim, et al., 1980.

∮Michael B. Schwartz, "Safeguarding EFTS," *Datamation*, 1983 February, pages 148-160.

others wished to send to him. His corresponding decryption procedure would be kept wholly private. This requires a simple means for subscribers to generate their own encryption and decryption procedures or keys. The public disclosure of the encryption procedure must not compromise the decryption procedure. That is, the derivation of the decryption key from the public encryption key must be computationally intractable.

In general, a public-key cryptosystem derives the public encryption key (u) from the private decryption key (v):

$$u \leftarrow f(v)$$

It is called a "one-way" function if it is difficult to solve for **v** given **u** ; that is, the inverse function

$$v \leftarrow f^{-1}(u)$$

is computationally infeasible. The function **f** is a *trapdoor* one-way function if f^{-1} is easy to compute only if certain "trapdoor" information is known.

Using the public key of the intended receiver, the sender applies the encryption procedure (U_R) to a message (M) which generates the ciphertext (C):

$$C \leftarrow U_R(M)$$

The receiver, using his own private key, applies the decryption procedure (V_R) to **C** to reproduce the original message:

$$M \leftarrow V_R(C) = V_R(U_R(M))$$

If **U** and **V** are cummutative, that is, they can be applied in reverse:

$$M \leftarrow U_R(V_R(M)) = V_R(U_R(M))$$

then it also provides for signature authentication. (The private "decryption" key **V** is now used for encryption, and the public key **U** is used for decryption.)

The big advantage of a public-key cryptosystem is that it does not require secure transmission of keys between sender and receiver. There need be no prior private communication between them before sending encrypted messages, except to authenticate each other's identity.

Various public-key cryptosystem implementations have been proposed [see Lempel, 1979, for descriptions of some]. Merkle and Hellman at Stanford proposed an implementation using a *trapdoor knapsack* encryption key. It is based upon the classic knapsack problem:

> Given a knapsack of fixed capacity, choose a subset from a given set of **N** things such that the knapsack is exactly filled. Stated another way, given a set of **N** numbers and a sum, find a subset of the numbers which adds up to the given sum. The best known method for solving this problem is not much better than trying all 2^N possible combinations of things or numbers, yet a guessed solution can be checked with no more than **N** additions.

The proposal from Rivest, Shamir, and Adleman [1978] at MIT depends upon the difficulty of factoring large numbers. Finding the correct set of prime numbers is very difficult, yet only a few multiplications are needed to check a proposed solution. It also inherently provides signature authentication.

The following description illustrates the basic idea of a public-key cryptosystem with signature authentication, similar to the RSA scheme.

Let V_S = the private key procedure of the sender
U_S = the public key procedure of the sender
V_R = the private key procedure of the receiver
U_R = the public key procedure of the receiver

The private key V is derived from a set of large prime numbers and the public key U is the product of those numbers. Finding V by factoring U, suggested to be at least 200 digits long, would take a very long time (billions of years on a fast computer performing an exhaustive search), yet deriving U from V is comparatively easy.

In the simple case without signature authentication, the sender encrypts the message with the intended receiver's public key. Only the receiver with the correct private key can decrypt the ciphertext message. This scheme does not require any secure key distribution between sender and receiver. The simple scheme also does not provide the receiver with any guarantee concerning the supposed sender since anyone can access the intended recipient's public key and send an encrypted message. Diffie compares this scheme to a bank's night-deposit box: anyone can put money in, but only authorized employees can take it out.

To provide *signature authentication*, the sender encrypts the message using *both* his own private key and the intended recipient's public key:

$$C \leftarrow U_R(V_S(M))$$

The receiver decrypts the ciphertext using the purported sender's public key and his own private key:

$$M \leftarrow U_S(V_R(C))$$

The $V_S(M)$ computed by the sender is like a signature which is dependent on both the message and the sender (a normal paper signature is dependent only on the sender). In this scheme, the signature provides two-way authentication. Communication is successful only if the intended and actual recipients are the same, and if the purported and actual senders are the same. The receiver can be sure that the received message actually came from the sender, and the sender can be sure that no one will be able to attribute to him a message he did not send. An imposter without the correct private key at either end will make the communication impossible.

To secure stored data, in contrast to transmitted data, the user need only apply his own public encryption key prior to storing the data. Upon retrieval, the private decryption key is used to recover the plaintext data. This could be strengthened by using a two-key scheme similar to the signature scheme described previously.

The five years after the first paper on public-key cryptosystems witnessed considerable optimism. Since the proposals depend upon the intractable computational complexity of solving certain mathematical problems, they were felt to be uncrackable. Nevertheless, there is still no proof that these schemes are as hard to break as the proponents claim. In fact, in 1982 the Stanford scheme was cracked, and in 1984 the RSA scheme from MIT was seriously threatened (see box). What is needed is a means to certify the degree of security offered by any particular scheme, perhaps based upon combinatorial complexity theory.

PUBLIC-KEY CRYPTOSYSTEMS: OPTIMISM TURNS TO REALITY

In 1978, *Time* magazine reflected the current optimism with the headline:

An Uncrackable Code?
The snoops may finally have met their match

". . . Ciphers that are for all practical purposes unbreakable can be produced easily. Says *Scientific American* Mathematics Columnist Martin Gardner: 'The breakthrough bids fair to revolutionize the entire field of secret communication.'. . ." [1978 July 3, page 55.] The Hellman team at Stanford and the Rivest team at MIT each offered a $100 bet to the first mathematician who could crack their respective coding schemes.

In 1982, *Time* ran the headline:

Opening the "Trapdoor Knapsack"
An Israeli mathematician cracks a formidable code

". . . To the surprise of all concerned, however, the Stanford scheme sprang a leak this year, putting $100 in the pocket of a determined young Israeli theoretician and raising troublesome, and potentially costly, questions about whether computers can ever be made to keep their secrets. . . . The demonstration of a code's vulnerability inevitably has worrisome implications for the way banks and multinational firms do business. . . . The Stanford code, . . . was thought to be so fiendishly complex that even the world's most powerful computers could not crack it. But Shamir [originally of the MIT team] proved otherwise. Exploiting recent advances in an obscure branch of number theory, he bore into the trapdoor knapsack system and revealed that the secret decoder could in fact be unraveled by analysis of the encoder that was published. . . . The real security problem for the electronic age may be that no computer can be made completely safe from intruders determined to break in." [1982 October 25, page 88]

In 1984, *Time* ran another headline:

Cracking a Record Number
Mathematicians solve a three-century-old puzzle in 32 hours

Mathematician Gustavus J. Simmons and his colleagues at Sandia National Laboratories ". . . announced that they had factored a 69-digit number, the largest ever to be subjected to such numerical dissection. Their triumph is more than an intellectual exercise. It could have far-flung repercussions for national security. . . . Until recently, mathematicians despaired of factoring any number above 50 digits. . . . [Then Simmons learned that] the internal workings of the Cray [computer] were especially suited to factoring, which is essentially done by a process of trial and error. . . . When RSA was first proposed, its inventors suggested using 80 digit numbers on the assumption that they were too big to be factored. Obviously, with researchers at Sandia closing in on ever larger numbers, even RSA could eventually fall to the code breakers." [1984 February 13, page 47]

14.6.7 Secure Key Distribution and Management

Regardless of the particular cryptographic scheme used, the keys must be properly managed. This area represents a big problem for organizations and is a major weakness in security systems. Since the algorithms are usually published and since finding the key by exhaustive search is computationally impractical, an intruder's most promising means of penetration is to gain access to the key. Therefore, key management must be the main focus of attention in maintaining secure systems.

Encryption keys should be:

- Changed frequently and at unpredictable times.
- Stored securely at the local site, temporarily in a protected area of computer memory only as long as needed. Long term storage of keys is needed when encryption applies to stored backup or archive data.
- Never printed out.
- Picked randomly from the full range of possible choices, not related to any other entity.
- Statistically independent with a uniform probability of occurrence.
- Protected and kept private when being input to the system, whether by setting manual switches, plugging in a ROM module, inserting a magnet stripe card, or key-boarding on a computer.
- Handled only by a few privileged employees.

Many of these management guidelines are similar to those for passwords. All aspects of the key management system should be kept secret.

With both public-key and private-key encryption systems, it is necessary to secure the private keys. With private-key systems, including the DES, keys must be separately and securely transmitted between sender and receiver. Sending by registered mail or special courier is increasingly unacceptable. In a network or distributed environment, keys must be transmitted along the same channels used for messages and data. Additional system requirements to validate the keys, to authenticate the identity of users, and to obtain digital signatures necessitate secure transmission of keys and messages in *both* types of encryption systems. Popek and Kline [1979] argue that "once the system implications are understood, public-key algorithms and conventional algorithms are largely equivalent" [page 354], a somewhat surprising conclusion but one which they adequately support.

The sidebox outlines suggested communication protocols between sender and receiver when a central authority node distributes new private keys for a conventional private-key system or maintains current public keys in a public-key system. Other communication protocols are possible. This is intended to illustrate that *some* protocol overhead is needed to ensure the identity and currency of other users before engaging in private communication; some protocol is needed to foil an impostor or an eavesdropper [see Denning, 1984]. A central, trusted authority is also needed to keep a record of old keys to adjudicate conflicts over old signatures.

Communication with the central authority could be reduced if each user stored public and private keys locally. Communication would then be needed whenever a key is changed or revoked. The problem is that such a change will not be known until a user experiences unsuccessful communication with another user, or the central authority

Communication Protocols Between Sender, Receiver, and a Central Authority

For a more secure *private-key system*, the encryption key should be changed for each communication session. Assume that the sender (S) and the receiver (R) each have a private key (K_S and K_R) known only to themselves and some central authority node (A) within the network. The sender requests from the central authority a new key (K_N) to communicate with the receiver:

$$S \rightarrow A: REQUEST, TID$$

where **TID** is some random identifier which is unique each time a node communicates with the central authority. The sender receives (in encrypted form) a new key (K_N) from the central authority.

$$A \rightarrow S: K_S(K_N, TID, REQUEST, K_R(K_N, S))$$

where the last element is a message which **S** can send to **R** to establish the connection and prove **S**'s identity. Upon successfully decrypting the message from **A**, **S** knows it is genuine, and if the **TID** is the same, **S** knows that the communication is current and not a replay of a prior request. Upon receiving and successfully decrypting the message from **S**, **R** knows the new key and the identity of **S**. However, **R** does not know that the message just received is not a replay of a prior message. Therefore, **R** must send some **TID** to **S** encrypted with K_N. Then **S** performs some operation on **TID** and returns the result to **R**, who now knows that **S** is current. They are now ready to communicate, each being assured of the identity and currency of the other.

The security of a *public-key system* depends critically on the correct receiver's public key being used by the sender and on the proper management of changes in the public keys. The public keys must be protected against unauthorized alteration since a key could be changed to something which an imposter receiver could decrypt. Since keys can and should be changed periodically, updates need to be controlled, probably at some central directory. With the public keys kept in a central directory, users still need assurance that they receive the correct and current key for the proposed receiver. This requires secure, encrypted communication with the directory node.

The communication protocol begins by assuming that each user has a public key known only to the authority (previously distributed public keys may have been changed), and the authority has a public key known by all users. First, a sender (S) requests of the authority (A) the current public key (U_R) of an intended receiver (R).

$$S \rightarrow A: REQUEST, TIME$$

where TIME is a current timestamp. The authority responds with:

$$A \rightarrow S: V_A(REQUEST, TIME, U_R)$$

encrypted with the authority's private key. Upon successfully decrypting this message using the authority's public key, **S** verifies the source of the message, the timestamp ensures it is not an old message and that the public key of **R** is current, and the copy of the request permits **S** to verify that the original request was not altered. These two steps essentially represent an authentication protocol.

Sender **S** is now ready to communicate with **R**:

$$S \rightarrow R: U_R(S, TID_S)$$

sending his name plus some random identifier which is separately chosen for each communication. After decrypting with his private key, **R** now repeats the first two steps to obtain the public key of **S** from the authority with the directory, and uses it to communicate back with S:

$$R \rightarrow S: U_S(TID_S, TID_R)$$

adding another random identifier. Upon decrypting with his private key, **S** can verify that **R** is current. Finally, **S** must encrypt and send back the TID_R to **R** so **R** can verify that **S** is current.

sends out a change notice. (This is similar to the problem of telephoning someone when they have moved and their phone number has changed.)

The public-key cryptosystem suffers a serious flaw in its signature capability. Any sender of messages can disavow or repudiate his signature at any time by divulging his private key, or otherwise causing it to be disclosed. Whether done accidentally or intentionally, all previously signed messages are invalidated since the private key *could have been used* by another. The signature is guaranteed only as long as the private key remains secure. Furthermore, the guarantee can be removed by the very person who should not hold that right—the author. One important purpose of a signature is to fix responsibility for originating a message such that it cannot be later disavowed. Further, an author can divulge *any* past private key! One partial defense is to change keys frequently and timestamp all uses. Another defense is to include a trusted third party in the communication between a sender and receiver, analogous to a notary public who ensures the identity of both parties and timestamps and encrypts with his own private key all messages between them. A third defense may be to prohibit a sender from actually seeing his private key—it is used and changed within the system but never need be revealed to the person.

Breaking a cipher and discovering the key is often easier if the intruder can obtain some plaintext and its corresponding ciphertext. Therefore, it is desirable to avoid repetitive strings of data or text. This may occur in common headings to memos or in common field values in data records. One method of attack appends some text to a message or appends another record to a file. A countermeasure is to use a different key for each memo or part of a memo, and to use a different key for each data record. Then finding a key for the dummy appended record does not compromise the keys for the other records.

An even better defense is to use a different key for each block (64 bits in the case of the DES). The starting key for each data record can be dependent on some invariant characteristic of the record, such as its unique internal identifier. The key for each subsequent block of the record can be dependent on the prior block. This method of successive data-dependent encryption has been called block chaining and resembles a stream encryption technique. [See Konheim, et al., 1980, for details of such a system.]

14.7 THREAT MONITORING AND AUDIT TRAIL

All the security mechanisms discussed so far cannot guarantee the security of confidential, sensitive, private data. Monitoring and recording information on an audit trail is the final line of defense against threats to the integrity and security of the database. Threat monitoring involves examination of audit trail logs for unusual activity patterns, such as repeated unsuccessful requests for access clearance or repeated similar queries.

Active threat monitoring can itself serve to deter potential intruders, provided everyone knows that activity logs are kept and monitoring actually takes place. The mere existence of a monitoring facility threatens exposure of illegal activity.

An *audit trail* is a chronological record of all events that take place within a system. Keeping an audit trail is a system-wide function. Since some of the events relate to database integrity, the database management system will generate messages to be logged using the system-wide facility. In some cases, the monitoring and audit trail functions may be undertaken by the database management system because of inadequate facilities in the operating system.

Keeping track of activities and events serves two purposes—realtime monitoring, and post analysis and investigation. Realtime monitoring involves an examination and analysis of events as they are recorded. After that, the chronological record of events is often referred to as an audit trail. An audit trail enables later investigation and detection of undesirable events.

With a monitoring function the system can continually examine the chronological record of events and initiate corrective action or some other form of response in realtime. It may involve blocking an access attempt, invoking some special internal procedure, or signaling the operator or a security officer.

Since it is impossible to prevent all intrusions and threats to database integrity, the audit trail provides "what happened" information to enable an after-the-fact reconstruction of events. It enables the database administrator to go back and verify the actions of the system by retracing its steps to investigate suspected errors and integrity violations after the fact, and it aids in settling disputes involving a combination of actions in the external environment and actions internal to the system.

Although not the primary purpose of an audit trail, some of the logged information provides backup which may assist in realtime recovery. If so, it is important to write the logged information on a permanent storage medium without buffering or blocking (see Chapter 12).

If the needed data has been recorded, manual or mechanized processing of the audit trail can provide various forms of analysis. In fact, the DBMS facilities for interrogation and presentation of statistical results could be used to aid in the analysis.

The ability to chronologically record events within the system is a general-purpose tool. Some events will be recorded all the time. Others will only be recorded for selected periods of time to permit the database administrator to concentrate on gathering data pertaining to a particular problem area. The system should provide the facility to selectively turn on and turn off the logging of events. The system should also permit new events and new data to be recorded. In this way, it is possible to log more information and monitor it more closely in an area of current management concern.

Since the audit trail and monitoring facility is a general-purpose tool, an unlimited array of event information can be recorded. The audit trail could log errors occurring within the system, deadlock and backout actions, all authorized accesses to the database, and all unauthorized attempts to access the database. Only two are discussed here: threat monitoring and logging all incoming transactions.

14.7.1 Unauthorized Access Threat Monitoring

Threat monitoring is intended to complement data access control to provide greater data security. If a user requests and is denied access to the database that fact could be important. For each access to the database, the data access control facility should log:

- User identification.
- Job or program identification.

- Transaction identification, if any.
- Time.
- Whether access was permitted or denied.

With such a record of events, the system can monitor the access activity. Repeated unsuccessful attempts to access the database can be brought to the attention of the operator or a security officer so that follow-up action, enforcement, and possible apprehension can be initiated. While a security officer is dispatched to the scene of the threat, the system can respond with dummy data or continue as though no violation of access authorization had been detected, much the same as a telephone conversation with a person can be prolonged while the call is traced.

The monitoring facility also looks for attempts to extract private individual data from a statistical databank. The system can attempt to monitor for repeated requests where the selection expression is only modified slightly from one request to the next. Of course, if the repeated interrogations are several hours or days apart, it would be more difficult for the monitoring function to detect a threat.

Realtime threat monitoring reduces the time available for an intruder to penetrate system security.

14.7.2 Logging Receipt of Incoming Transactions

Logging all incoming transactions provides a record of the starting point for one type of audit trail through the computer system. It verifies receipt of a transaction from the using environment, a fact which may itself be in dispute. Each incoming transaction is uniquely identified by assigning some form of serial number. The serial number can be constructed using the time and date of receipt and a code for the source of the transaction. Then it is possible to relate subsequent events with particular incoming transactions, events such as logged before and after images of modified data, and rejected transactions due to detected errors. The eventual disposition of each transaction is also logged whether it was successfully processed or was sidetracked to an error file for correction and subsequent disposition. Every transaction should be traceable from original receipt in the system to final disposition.

All input data transactions received and processed by the generalized update function can be logged by the system since the existence of the transaction is known. On the other hand, transactions received and processed by user programs are not normally known to the system. All the system receives is a request to update the database. In fact, no updates should be applied directly to the database (say, from user programs) without going through the DBMS with its validation, logging, and monitoring functions. The update function should be used to create a transaction file which is subsequently processed by a user program if the complex processing logic is beyond the general capabilities of the update function.

The serialized logging of incoming transactions would not normally serve as backup for the modified database. Periodic dumps and logs of before and after images of the database provide the primary backup. Input transaction logging, however, could be considered secondary backup to the primary backup mechanism.

SUMMARY

Data security is the third facet of database integrity—controlling access to sensitive data, limiting disclosure of individual data from statistical output, encryption of transmitted and stored data, and finally, threat monitoring and an audit trail.

Threats to data integrity stem from persons intentionally attempting to gain access to sensitive information, or persons who accidentally obtain access through some hardware, software, or human error, or natural disasters.

A set of policy areas govern the approach to data access control:

- Centralize ownership and control of data.
- Deny access unless specifically authorized.
- Give people the least privilege required to perform their duties.
- Divide responsibility to require collusion to subvert the controls.
- Complete mediation of access clearance at each request.
- Specify control rules in terms of granularity of data objects, types of action privileges, and data-, context-, and history-dependent access control rules.

An access control mechanism uses information about who is authorized to perform what actions or privileges on what data objects. The authorization information can be associated with the objects, such as passwords with a file. Better is the user profile model which stores information about authorized users separate from the data objects.

In the general model of access control, users first identify themselves to the system, then respond to the system with additional information or actions which serve to authenticate their identification. Authentication information can be based upon what a person knows (passwords), what a person has (possessed objects such as keys or plastic cards), or what a person is (personal characteristics such as fingerprints or voiceprints). Once satisfied that the identification is correct, the system compares what the user is requesting to do with what that user has been authorized to do, permitting or denying access to the requested data.

The authorization table or matrix is one of the most widely used models for access control. The simplest matrix records user subjects (individuals or homogeneous groups) on the side and data objects (files, or data items) across the top. The elements of the matrix indicate the action privileges a user has with a data object. These include statistics only, read only, append, update, revision, or granting privileges.

Data-dependent authorization is based upon the actual data values in the file. For example, a manager may be able to only look at salaries under $30,000 or for employees in his or her department. Context-dependent authorization is based upon additional conditions such as the id (location) of the terminal, or the time of day. History-dependent controls look at the past record of queries from the same user or all users to guard against incremental statistical queries from which a requester can infer information pertaining to individual records. Multilevel and need-to-know schemes can also be used for access control.

Even though individual data may be confidential, it is often desirable to permit wider access to statistical information from a file. Unfortunately, this presents a very real risk that individual information can be inferred from the strictly statistical output. Output controls must guard against approximate, supplemental, and indirect disclosures. The system must not produce statistics based upon small sets of selected records, or when the overlap between two selected sets is small, through the use of a 'tracker.' Random sampling on the selected set can produce relatively small errors in the aggregate statistics but rather large errors when someone attempts to infer individual data.

Encryption techniques are used to hide the meaning of transmitted or stored data. Storing variable length data, encoding data values, and data compression all serve to obscure the meaning of data, though their primary purpose is efficient utilization of storage space. The traditional methods of encryption—transposition or permutation, and substitution—are primarily used for stream encryption of messages for transmission. Encryption of stored data requires a block encryption. The U.S. Data Encryption Standard (DES) is a block encryption technique, implementable in hardware or software, which uses a product cipher, that is, an iterative combination of permutations and nonlinear substitutions.

Public-key crypto systems have been developed to overcome the limitations of private-key systems, including the DES, which require secure distribution of the encryption key. It is a dual key system in which the sender encrypts a message with the receiver's encryption key, which can be published in a directory. The receiver decrypts the message using their decryption key which has a special mathematical relationship to the public encryption key, such that derivation of the decryption key from the encryption key is computationally intractable. Some public-key systems have the added benefit of signature authentication—the receiver cannot decrypt the message unless it was from the correct sender, and messages cannot be falsely attributed to the sender.

Monitoring the interactions with users and events within the computer system is the final line of defense against threats to data security. The audit trail provides a chronological log of events which can be used to investigate and analyze actual or suspected intrusions and unauthorized disclosures. Two aspects include monitoring repeated attempts to gain access to the system and to the data, and logging of incoming transactions.

EXERCISES

14-1. Explain why it is impractical to extend the typical security controls in operating systems to provide access control to data objects.

14-2. Describe and explain the importance of each of the following access control policies: centralized ownership and control, deny access unless authorized, least privilege, granularity, data-dependent and context-dependent controls, division of responsibility, complete mediation, and user acceptability.

14-3. Contrast the object profile model and the user profile model for providing access control. Which is preferred and why?

14-4. Outline the information needed by a DBMS to enforce access control policies.

14-5. The basic sequence of steps in access control is identification, authentication, and authorization. Briefly describe each step.

14-6. Individual users can be identified by three means. Name the three, give examples of each, and describe the weaknesses of each.

14-7. Given the check digit rule: add to each digit its position from the right, sum the results modulo 9, and append the answer to the end of the original number. What is the new number resulting from 74882?

14-8. What accounts for the widespread use of password schemes? Is their use likely to diminish in the future? Explain.

14-9. What are the major weaknesses of password systems for access control and what can be done to make the use of passwords more secure?

14-10. Give four advantages of assigning passwords to individual users rather than accounts, files, or homogeneous groups of users.

14-11. What is the percent increase in the total number of possible 5 character passwords (a) by increasing the alphabet size from 36 (in the text) to 40 characters; or (b) by increasing the size of the password to 6 characters (keeping a 36 character alphabet)? Assuming a transmission rate of 1200 baud and 20 characters exchanged per access clearance request (using a 5 character password as before) what is the expected time to guess a password (assuming continuous trials)? Now suppose you desired a probability of .0001 that an interloper could find a password in three months of systematic testing. How long would the password have to be (constructed from a 36 character alphabet)?

14-12. What are the advantages of a dialogue scheme for authentication over the simple use of passwords. Give examples of three different dialogue schemes.

14-13. Although the technology appears to be feasible, fingerprints and voiceprints have had little impact on authentication for data access control. Suggest some reasons for this.

14-14. To thwart an imposter using a recording of an authorized user's voice to subvert voiceprint authentication, a system can specify a random sequence of words to be spoken from a given set of prerecorded words. How many different permutations of words are possible using from 1 to 6 words selected from 6 prerecorded words?

14-15. Describe the basic authorization matrix model for data access control and some of its extensions. What are some of the action privileges which may be given to authorized users? What is the 'granting privilege' and how is it used and controlled?

14-16. What is meant by data-dependent access control? Give two examples of a data-dependent access rule.

14-17. Describe the multilevel and need-to-know schemes for data access control.

14-18. What steps can be taken to reduce size and complexity when implementing an extended authorization matrix model?

14-19. Describe the countermeasures which can be taken to minimize approximate, supplemental, and indirect disclosures of individual data from a statistical database.

14-20. Given the abbreviated EMPLOYEE file introduced in the appendix to Chapter 4, illustrate how you might attempt to find out the salary of a particular employee when you are authorized to obtain statistics only from the data file. Find a tracker selection expression and illustrate how it can be used to isolate the salary of a single employee, even though the system does not respond to queries having fewer than four selected records.

14-21. Explain the use of random sample queries for controlling inferences of unauthorized data from a statistical database. What is the key advantage of this scheme?

14-22. Some DBMS functions intended primarily to improve the utilization of storage space, also serve to obscure the meaning of data. Describe three techniques.

14-23. Define encryption. Describe four major types of data encryption algorithms giving an example of each.

14-24. Using the Vigenère tableau and the cyclic key SECURITY, decrypt the following ciphertext:

X HLPI MGICYTVLYXSFLPYMQSYKZRAMMJJGUVJMY

14-25. What are the main advantages and disadvantages of the U.S. Data Encryption Standard (DES)?

14-26. Explain how a public-key crypto system works.

14-27. What is meant by a signature capability on a public-key crypto system? Explain how it works and what it does for the sender and the receiver in a system which transfers money debits and credits over a computer network. How can a signing author repudiate past signatures?

14-28. Contrast the functions of threat monitoring and an audit trail. What is the main purpose of monitoring? What are the main reasons for maintaining an audit trail in a DBMS environment?

SELECTED REFERENCES

AKI, Selim G., "Digital Signatures: A Tutorial Survey," *Computer* (16:), 1983 February, pages 15-24.
> Suggests appending an encrypted signature to every message. Discusses private key and public key systems for signatures.

BECK, Leland L., "A Security Mechanism for Statistical Databases," *ACM Transactions on Database Systems* (5:3), 1980 September, pages 316-338, 25 refs.
> Shows that any protection scheme which gives "statistically correct" results is vulnerable to penetration. Presents a general model of user inference, and shows that the number of queries required to compromise a database can be made arbitrarily large by accepting moderate increases in the variance of responses to queries. Includes a numerical example to illustrate the technique.

BECKER, Hal B., *Information Integrity: A Structure for its Definition and Management*, New York: McGraw-Hill, 1983, 237 pages.
> With a broad definition of information integrity, including data, program, and system concepts, the author develops a classification scheme for integrity issues. It is not a detailed list of integrity control measures. The book focuses on the two dimensions of resources (system, information, personnel, support services) and threats (onsite retrieval, alteration, loss, remote usage).

BROWNE, Peter S., "Computer Security—A Survey," *AFIPS National Computer Conference Proceedings*, 1976, pages 53-63, 134 refs.
> This good overview paper highlights the major subtopics relating to computer security, with an extensive, annotated bibliography.

BUSSOLATI, U. and G. MARTELLA, "Towards a New Approach to Secure Database Design," *Computers & Security* (2:), 1983, pages 49-63, 35 refs.
> Describes access control using an extended authorization matrix.

CONWAY, R. W., William L. MAXWELL, and Howard L. MORGAN, "On the Implementation of Security Measures in Information Systems," *Communications of the ACM* (15:4), 1972 April, pages 211-220, 19 refs.
> An early discussion of implementing data-dependent access controls within an authorization matrix.

DATE, Chris J., *An Introduction to Database Systems*, Volume II, Addison-Wesley, 1983, 383 pages.
> Chapter 4 (35 pages) on data security covers authentication, authorization, statistical databases, encryption, and brief examples from existing systems, most notably System R. Good examples of statistical queries and the use of a general tracker. Extensive annotated bibliographies with each chapter, 36 in Chapter 4.

DAVIDA, George I., David L. WELLS, and John B. KAM, "A Database Encryption System with Subkeys," *ACM Transactions on Database Systems* (6:2), 1981 June, pages 312-328, 18 refs.
> Discusses the need for database encryption which independently encrypts individual fields in a record. Proposes such a system based on the Chinese Remainder Theorem.

DeMILLO, Richard A., David P. DOBKIN, Anita K. JONES, and Richard J. LIPTON, editors, *Foundations of Secure Computation*, Academic Press, 1978, 404 pages.

Papers on security research presented at a 3-day workshop, Atlanta, 1977. First two sections on data security and encryption; the rest on operating system security.

DENNING, Dorothy E., "Digital Signatures with RSA and Other Public-Key Cryptosystems," *Communications of the ACM* (27:4), 1984 April, pages 388-392, 11 refs.

Points up the fundamental importance of encryption protocols. It is not enough to have an algorithm that is computationally hard to break; the procedures for using the algorithm must also withstand attack. Describes a potential weakness in the RSA public-key cryptosystem, then presents an improved signature scheme.

DENNING, Dorothy E., "Secure Statistical Databases with Random Sample Queries," *ACM Transactions on Database Systems* (5:3), 1980 September, pages 291-315, 37 refs.

Presents a defense against statistical inference in which the user does not control the selected set of records used to calculate statistics. Instead statistics are based on a pseudorandom sample of the selected set. Random sample queries, when coupled with minimum query size control, effectively protect against compromise, particularly the use of a general tracker.

DENNING, Dorothy E. and Peter J. DENNING, "Data Security," *ACM Computing Surveys* (11:3), 1979 September, pages 227-249, 102 refs.

A good general introduction to four types of security controls: access, flow, inference, and encryption. Discussion of each includes illustrative threats, policies, examples of control mechanisms, and limitations.

DENNING, Dorothy E., Peter J. DENNING, and M. D. SCHWARTZ, "The Tracker: A Threat to Statistical Database Security," *ACM Transactions on Database Systems* (4:1), 1979 March, pages 76-96.

DENNING, Dorothy E. and Jan SCHLÖRER, "A Fast Procedure for Finding a Tracker in a Statistical Database," *ACM Transactions on Database Systems* (5:1), 1980 March, pages 88-102, 16 refs.

Describes a method for finding a general tracker easily and experiments which often find a tracker with just a few queries.

DIFFIE, W. and Martin E. HELLMAN, "Exhaustive Cryptanalysis of the NBS Data Encryption Standard," *Computer* (10:6), 1977 June, pages 74-84.

Outlined the cost of breaking the DES using present-day computer technology through exhaustive search. Argued that the 56 bit key is too short.

DIFFIE, W. and Martin E. HELLMAN, "New Directions in Cryptography," *IEEE Transactions on Information Theory* (22:6), 1976 November.

An excellent discussion of problems in the area of cryptography. Introduces the concept of public-key encryption which responds to some of these problems.

EHRSAM, W. S., S. M. MATYAS, C. H. MEYER, and W. L. TUCHMAN, "A Cryptographic Key Management Scheme for Implementing the Data Encryption Standard," *IBM Systems Journal* (17:2), 1978.

Proposes a set of protocols (for both database and data communications) that use a 'master key' to encrypt all other keys, thus reducing the problem to protecting a single key. Other keys are changed frequently, while the master key and encryption/decryption algorithms are kept in nonvolatile, protected storage.

FEISTEL, Horst, "Cryptography and Computer Privacy," *Scientific American* (228:5), 1973 May, pages 15-23.

Describes development at IBM of a block encryption algorithm suitable for data transmission and storage using computers. Hardware implementation by Smith and Nolz was called 'Lucifer.' Forerunner of the U.S. Data Encryption Standard.

FERNANDEZ, Eduardo B., Rita C. SUMMERS, and Christopher WOOD, *Database Security and Integrity*, Addison-Wesley, 1981.

FISHER, Royal P., *Information Systems Security*, Reading, MA: Prentice-Hall, 1984, 240 pages.

Focuses on safeguarding and organization's information and data assets in the interactions between people and computers. Includes concrete procedures, tables, and questionnaires for identifying security exposures. The reader is systematically led to focus on control points, assessing risks and selecting cost-effective controls. Seven contributed appendices illustrate aspects of corporate policies related to data security.

GAINES, Helen Fouché, *Elementary Cryptanalysis*, A Study of Ciphers and Their Solution, Boston: American Photographic Publishing Co., 1939, 230 pages; republished in paperback as *Cryptanalysis*, New York: Dover Publications, 1965.

One of the earliest competent tutorials in English on cryptanalysis—the methods of solving encrypted messages.

GASSER, M., *A Random Word Generator for Pronounceable Passwords*, Bedford, MA: The Mitre Corporation, (U. S. National Technical Information Service, AD-A017 676), 1975 November, 183 pages.

Presents details of a random generator of pronounceable words for use as easier-to-remember passwords. Provides implementation details (on Honeywell's Multics system), and an analysis of the algorithm.

GRAHAM, R. S. and P. J. DENNING, "Protection—Principles and Practice," *AFIPS Spring Joint Computer Conference Proceedings* (vol. 40), 1972, pages 417-429.

Extended the authorization matrix proposed by Lampson.

GRIFFITHS, P. P. and B. W. WADE, "An Authorization Mechanism for a Relational Data Base System," *ACM Transactions on Database Systems* (1:3), 1976 September, pages 242-255.

Describes an authorization mechanism originally proposed for System R being developed by IBM. Particularly good discussion of granting and revoking privileges.

HANSEN, Morris H., "Insuring Confidentiality of Individual Records in Data Storage and Retrieval for Statistical Purposes," *AFIPS Fall Joint Computer Conference Proceedings*, (volume 39), 1971, pages 579-585.

An administrator from the U.S. Census Bureau describes approximate, supplemental, and indirect disclosures from statistical data and suggested countermeasures.

HELLMAN, Martin E., "The Mathematics of Public-Key Cryptography," *Scientific American* (241:2), 1979 August, pages 130-139.

Discusses the problems with conventional private key encryption. Provides details of the Diffie-Hellman, and the Rivest-Shamir-Adleman (RSA) public-key cryptosystems, using examples (which the reader must work through to really understand the techniques).

HEMPHILL, Charles F., Jr. and John M. HEMPHILL, *Security Procedures of Computer Systems*, Homewood, IL: Dow Jones-Irwin, 1973, 251 pages.

HIGHLAND, Harold Joseph, *Protecting Your Microcomputer System*, New York: Wiley, 1984, 272 pages.

Practical steps on how to safeguard your microcomputer from unauthorized use or theft of programs and computerized data; what to look for in buying protection and encryption equipment; and limiting access to information to authorized users in networking and timesharing systems.

HOFFMAN, Lance J., *Modern Methods for Computer Security and Privacy*, Prentice-Hall, 1977, 255 pages, 202 refs.

Separate, well-written chapters on authentication, authorization, encryption, statistical databanks, and logging; also operating systems and machine architecture, and administrative and legal aspects of computer security.

HOFFMAN, Lance J., "Computers and Privacy: A Survey," *Computing Surveys* (1:2), 1969 June, pages 85-103, 69 annot. refs.

This earlier classic paper surveys the problems of access control and privacy in computer systems, and reviews a number of suggested legal and administrative safeguards.

HSIAO, David K., Douglas S. KERR, and Stuart E. MADNICK, *Computer Security*, Academic Press, 1979, 299 pages.

> One chapter on data security and one on encryption, as well as chapters on operational, operating system, hardware, and physical security. Extensive annotated bibliographies with each chapter.

JACOBSON, Robert V., William F. BROWN, and Peter S. BROWNE, *Guidelines for Automatic Data Processing Physical Security and Risk Management*, Washington, DC: National Bureau of Standards, FIPS PUB 31, 1974 June.

> Guidelines for federal organizations to use for the physical security of computer systems. Treats security analysis, natural disasters, supporting utilities, system reliability, procedural measures and controls, off-site facilities, contingency plans, security awareness, and security audit.

KAHN, David, *Kahn on Codes—Secrets of the New Cryptology*, New York: Macmillan, 1983, 343 pages.

> A collection of selected articles by Kahn covering his historical research, and effective insights into the modern use of cryptography. The use of computers has greatly increased both the complexity of codes used to encrypt information and the ability to break those codes. Excellent nontechnical overview.

KAHN, David, *The Codebreakers*, The Story of Secret Writing, New York: Macmillan, 1967, (London: Weidenfeld and Nicholson, 1966), 1164 pages.

> Provides a fascinating account of the history of cryptography going back 2500 years. His goal was to narrate the development of the various methods of making and breaking codes and ciphers, and how these methods have affected men.

KOCH, Harvey S., "Online Computer Auditing Through Continuous and Intermittent Simulation," *MIS Quarterly* (5:1), 1981 March, pages 29-41.

> Describes an auditing process which operates in parallel with a regular DBMS application, simultaneously receiving all input data transactions and output data. The article is as much about input data transaction validation as it is about auditing. The article describes the methods of transaction validation in an application specific environment, rather than how the validation checks would be expressed in general.

KONHEIM, A. G., *Cryptography, A Primer*, New York: Wiley, 1981.

KONHEIM, A. G., et al., "The IPS Cryptographic Programs," *IBM Systems Journal* (19:2), 1980, pages 253-283, 29 refs.

> Describes the data-dependent, block chaining encryption system based on the DES which has been implemented and widely used within IBM.

LAMPSON, B. W., "Protection," *Proceedings Fifth Annual Princeton Conference on Information Sciences and Systems*, 1971 March, pages 437-443; reprinted in *ACM Operating Systems Review* (8:1), 1974 January, pages 18-24.

> An early presentation of the authorization matrix for access control.

LANDWEHR, Carl E., "Formal Models for Computer Security," *ACM Computing Surveys* (13:3), 1981 September, pages 247-278, 80 refs.

> Surveys existing and proposed models, with emphasis on multilevel classification schemes used in the military, and from the broader perspective of computer security rather than data security. Discusses the access matrix model and the Bell and LaPadula model.

LAWSON, Herbert G., "Police Use Computers to Trace Fingerprints of Suspects in Crimes," *The Wall Street Journal*, 1977 July 8.

> Describes first use of the Rockwell International system (now from De La Rue) by San Jose Police Department, and other aspects of computerized reading and matching of fingerprints for criminal investigations and employee-access control.

LEMPEL, Abraham, "Cryptology in Transition," *ACM Computing Surveys* (11:4), 1979 December, pages 285-303, 47 refs.

> Cryptography has moved from manual and mechanical devices to large computers, from statistical uncertainty to computational complexity, from private-key systems to public-key systems. This excellent survey briefly outlines classical cryptology, principles underlying present schemes, the data encryption standard, public-key systems, and the problematic concept of cryptocomplexity.

MADNICK, S. E., *Computer Security*, New York: Academic Press, 1979.

MARTIN, James, *Security, Accuracy, and Privacy in Computer Systems*, Prentice-Hall, 1973.

MELLON, G. E., "Cryptology, Computers, and Common Sense," *AFIPS National Computer Conference Proceedings*, 1973, pages 569-579, 16 refs.
  A readable introduction to the main methods of encryption and those applicable to computer systems. Gives a reasonably comprehensible explanation of how computers can be used to decrypt text which has been encrypted with a key whose periodicity is longer than the plaintext.

MEYER, Carl and Stephen MATYAS, *Cryptography: A Guide for the Design and Implementation of Secure Systems*, New York: John Wiley & Sons, 1982, 624 pages.
  Describes the design, development, and implementation of cryptographic systems based upon the DES.

MOULTON, Rolf T., "A Practical Approach to System Security Devices," *Computers & Security* (3:2), 1984 May, pages 93-99.
  Covers a wide range of hardware and software security techniques and devices.

MOULTON, Rolf T., "Data Security is a Management Responsibility," *Computers & Security* (3:1), 1984 February, pages 3-7.
  A practitioner outlines guidelines for planning and implementing an effective security program. Looks at commitment of personnel and financial resources, and the development of control policies and procedures.

MURRAY, W. H., "Security Considerations for Personal Computers," *IBM Systems Journal* (23:3), 1984, pages 297-304.
  Practical suggestions for protecting the computer itself, its data, and its application programs, as well as procedures for controlling access to host sites.

National Bureau of Standards, *Data Encryption Standard*, Washington, DC: NBS, FIPS PUB 46, 1977 January.
  Describes a block encryption (and decryption) technique to be used when cryptographic protection is required for data maintained by U.S. federal organizations.

National Bureau of Standards, *Guidelines on Evaluation of Techniques for Automated Personal Identification*, Washington, DC: NBS, FIPS PUB 48, 1977 April 1, 23 pages.
  Excellent overview of the basic methods for verifying identification, particularly those based on physiological characteristics. Outlines 12 evaluation criteria and system considerations.

National Bureau of Standards, *Guidelines for Implementing and Using the NBS Data Encryption Standard*, FIPS PUB 74, 1981 April.

National Bureau of Standards, *DES Modes of Operation*, FIPS PUB 81, 1980 December.

National Bureau of Standards, *Guidelines and User Authentication Techniques for Computer Network Access Control*, FIPS PUB 83, 1980 September.

OLDEHOEFT, Arthur E. and Robert McDONALD, "A Software Scheme for User-Controlled File Encryption," *Computers & Security* (3:1), 1984 February, pages 35-41.
  Describes an easy-to-use technique based upon the NBS Data Encryption Standard for encrypting stored data files.

PARKER, Donn B., *Computer Security Management*, Reston, VA: Reston Publishing, 1981, 308 pages, 31 refs.
  A balance of theory, concepts, and practice, based on the author's research on computer abuse, and experiences with many companies in conducting computer security reviews. Computer security is primarily a people problem, and the book emphasizes behavioral, organizational, and managerial issues and approaches.

PARKER, Donn B., *Crime by Computer*, New York: Charles Scribner's Sons, 1976, 308 pages.
  This highly readable book, based on hundreds of investigated cases, discusses the motivations and methods of criminals where computers were involved, legal entanglements, violations of personal privacy, computer 'intimidation,' and the future of white-collar crime.

PETERSEN, H. E. and R. TURN, "System Implications of Information Privacy," *AFIPS Spring Joint Computer Conference Proceedings*, 1967, pages 291-300.
This classic article provides an excellent classification and analysis of threats to data security, corresponding countermeasures, and systems implications of providing a secure environment.

POPEK, G. and C. KLINE, "Encryption and Secure Computer Networks," *Computing Surveys* (11:4), 1979 December, pages 331-356.
Comprehensive discussion of encryption in a computer network or distributed environment, including protocols for secure communication, key management, user authentication, and signatures.

REGHBATI, H. K., "An Overview of Data Compression Techniques," *Computer* (14:), 1981, pages 71-75.

RIVEST, R. L., A. SHAMIR, and L. ADELMAN, "A Method for Obtaining Digital Signatures and Public-Key Cryptosystems," *Communications of the ACM* (21:2), 1978 February, pages 120-126, 14 refs.
Presents a more easily realizable public-key system (now called RSA) than the original Diffie-Hellman scheme, and it inherently satisfies the need for a sender's signature.

SEVERANCE, Dennis G., "A Practitioner's Guide to Data Base Compression," *Information Systems* (8:1), 1983, pages 51-62, 80 refs.
Data compression techniques can obscure the meaning of data as well as improve performance by reducing database size. This paper assists practitioners desiring compression of commercial databases. Reviews a wealth of literature, and presents facts and guidelines to select compression techniques appropriate for the needs, and to evaluate the costs and benefits of data compression.

SHANNON, Claude E., "Communication Theory of Secrecy Systems," *Bell System Technical Journal* (28:4), 1949 October, pages 656-715.
Set down a theory of cryptology which is still used today.

SINKOV, A., *Elementary Cryptanalysis*, A Mathematical Approach, New York: Random House, 1968.
Provides an outstanding tutorial for the post-computer age.

STAHL, Fred A., "A Homophonic Cipher for Computational Cryptography," *AFIPS National Computer Conference Proceedings*, 1973, pages 565-568.
Explores the use of mono-alphabetic substitution ciphers in computer systems. A homophonic cipher cyclically substitutes multiple characters for the frequently occurring characters in the plaintext to obscure the characteristic letter frequencies.

STONEBRAKER, Michael and Eugene WONG, "Access Control in a Relational Data Base Management System by Query Modification," *ACM National Conference Proceedings*, 1974, pages 180-186.
An early paper which discusses the implementation of a data-dependent access control mechanism within Ingres.

WEGSTEIN, J. H., "Automated Fingerprint Identification," Washington, DC: U.S. Government Printing Office (C13.46:538), National Bureau of Standards, Technical Note 538, 1970 August, 28 pages.

WEGSTEIN, J. H., J. F. RAFFERTY, and Walter J. PENCAK, "Matching Fingerprints by Computer," Washington, DC: U.S. Government Printing Office (C13.46:466), National Bureau of Standards, Technical Note 466, 1968 July, 13 pages.
These two papers describe some of the earlier work on computerized fingerprint recording and matching. Methods were developed and experiments conducted in conjunction with the U.S. Federal Bureau of Investigation (FBI).

WOFSEY, Marvin M., editor, *Advances in Computer Security Management*, volume 2, New York: John Wiley & Sons, 1983, 268 pages.
Several good, current articles, particularly ones on legal implications of computer security, and the management view of computer security.

WOOD, C., E. B. FERNANDEZ, and R. C. SUMMERS, "Data Base Security: Requirements, Policies, and Models," *IBM Systems Journal* (19:2), 1980, 27 refs.
Good survey of several models of access control mechanisms; covers the access matrix model in some depth. Concerned with implementation in a DBMS.

WOOD, Helen M., *The Use of Passwords for Controlled Access to Computer Resources*, Washington, DC: National Bureau of Standards, Special Publication 500-9 (also U.S. Government Printing Office, C13.10:500-9), 1977 May, 59 pages, 79 annot. refs.

An excellent, comprehensive discussion of various password schemes for authentication, including issues of password selection, construction, protection and administration. Includes a glossary and annotated bibliography.

WOODS, Charles C., "Effective Information System Security with Password Controls," *Computers & Security* (2:1), 1983 February, pages 5-10.

Contains many practical suggestions for selecting passwords, and for implementing and administering a password system.

FIFTEEN

DATABASE ADMINISTRATION
ORGANIZATION, FUNCTIONS, AND TOOLS

15.1	HISTORY OF AND NEED FOR DATABASE ADMINISTRATION	576
15.2	DATABASE ADMINISTRATION WITHIN THE ORGANIZATION	576
15.2.1	Sharing, Conflict, Mediation, and Compromise	577
15.2.2	Information Systems within the Organization	578
15.2.3	Organizational Evolution of Database Administration	579
15.2.4	Data Administration versus Job and System Administration	579
15.2.5	Database Administration and System Development	582
15.2.6	Database Administration and Users	584
15.2.7	Building Management and User Confidence	585
15.2.8	Controlling the Database Administrator	585
15.3	ORGANIZATION OF THE DATABASE ADMINISTRATION FUNCTION	586
15.3.1	Data Administration versus Database Administration	587
15.3.2	Advising and Controlling versus Doing	588
15.4	FUNCTIONS OF DATABASE ADMINISTRATION	589
15.4.1	Define, Create, Redefine, and Retire Data	590
15.4.2	Provide Availability Tools	592
15.4.3	Inform and Assist Users	593
15.4.4	Maintain Database Integrity	595
15.4.5	Monitor Operations	599
15.5	DATABASE ADMINISTRATOR TOOL: THE DATA DICTIONARY	601
15.5.1	Providing a More Complete Definition of Data	602
15.5.2	Uses of a Data Dictionary	603
15.5.3	For Systems Analysis and Design	604
15.5.4	Data Item Naming Conventions	605
15.5.5	The 'OF-language'	607
15.5.6	Data Dictionary Management Systems (DDMS)	608
15.6	DBMS PERFORMANCE MONITORING AND USAGE STATISTICS	610
15.6.1	Monitoring Sizes in the Stored Database	611
15.6.2	Monitoring Dynamic Activity	611
15.6.3	Logging Activity on an Audit Trail	613
15.7	ORGANIZATIONAL RESPONSE TO A DATABASE ADMINISTRATION ROLE	613
	SUMMARY	614
	EXERCISES	615
	SELECTED REFERENCES	616
	APPENDIX 15A: Commercially Available Data Dictionary Systems	620

The database administrator (DBA) plays a key role in achieving the database management objectives of data availability and the maintenance of data integrity. The database administrator is the external human agent who is responsible for the control and use of an organization's data resources as represented in the database.

This chapter describes organizational arrangements for database administration, the functions of database administration, and the tools of database administration. It is difficult to separate organization and function. The organizational choices set boundaries on the functions ascribed to database administration. By contrast, organizational units often subdivide functionally and, therefore, organizational considerations depend upon the discussion of functions.

15.1 HISTORY OF AND NEED FOR DATABASE ADMINISTRATION

Early, major database management systems did not explicitly conceive of the role of database administrator during the development or initial use of the system [see CODASYL Systems Committee, 1971, pages 442-444]. One exception was in conjunction with the development of SC-1 at Western Electric. The role of database administrator was established early in the development of their DBMS. In fact, they assigned central responsibility to a single manager to coordinate the definition of the corporate database—the naming and structuring of data elements. Furthermore, they set up a "school" for database administrators before a prototype version of the DBMS was operational.

In organizations using DBMSs, the functions of database administration were usually dispersed, through "delegation by default," to users, programmers, and computer system operators. The maintenance of database integrity relied upon external, manual procedures. As the database becomes increasingly vital to the operation of an organization, however, better mechanisms are needed to maintain database integrity.

As the sharing of data becomes more widespread, there is a growing awareness of the need for both coordination and conflict resolution among those who share the data. The responsibility for various administrative functions must be centralized to achieve coordination and mediation of conflicting demands and to achieve a greater measure of global optimization. For example, in determining the content and structure of the database, it is necessary to make design choices based upon all the needs in the organization, both present and foreseen, to resolve any conflicting differences, and to balance the needs against the available resources. Recent literature suggests that the role of database administrator has become widely accepted today, in theory, if not in practice. Nevertheless, considerable diversity of opinion exists concerning the functions to be performed in that role and how the role should be incorporated into the organization.

15.2 DATABASE ADMINISTRATION WITHIN THE ORGANIZATION

Discussion of database administration involves its position within the overall organizational structure, and the internal structure of the database administration unit. In discussing database administration within the overall organization, it is initially assumed that the DBA functions are centralized into a single organizational unit.

Once an organization gives formal recognition to the existence of data which is common across applications, functions, or organizational units, the next necessary step is to appoint an agent to be responsible for the creation and maintenance of this common resource. Such an agent is called the database administrator, or information resource manager. The appointment can be made by either top management or the community of users.

If data is considered to be a valued corporate resource, then the chief executive officer is ultimately responsible for its availability and integrity. To discharge this responsibility, the CEO may delegate the task to an appropriate subordinate. Alternatively, when data resources are shared, the community of users may elect to have a single person responsible for managing those resources.

The role of database administrator is an ambivalent one, reflecting both dictator and slave. On the one hand, the DBA is subservient to and works for using organizational units, while on the other hand, the DBA has authority over several using organizational units. This is not unlike the personnel manager who serves other units in the organization but is directly responsible to top management. Should any conflict arise in the performance of the personnel or the database management function, it is up to top management to resolve it.

15.2.1 Sharing, Conflict, Mediation, and Compromise

Consider the chain of events:

SHARING

produces CONFLICT

necessitating MEDIATION

resulting in COMPROMISE for one,

but yielding GLOBAL OPTIMA for all.

Sharing produces conflict, for example:

- Users may disagree in the choice of data item names and the naming conventions used.
- A shared data file will necessarily contain the superset of data needed by all users. A user needing only some of the data may be burdened by having to view all the data (unless the system offers a userschema capability) and by having to wait for all the data to be transferred when it is being read from the disk.
- The major user of a database may experience degradation of performance when secondary indexes and pointers (which have to be maintained) are added to satisfy the needs of other users.
- Some users may require more extensive quality control measures (validation, etc.) than others, resulting in slower operation and greater "nuisance" for those other users. For example, data entry in the receiving and inspection department may be subject to greater validation controls which are required by users responsible for inventory control and order entry.

- Allowing concurrent update to common files places a burden and additional discipline on all users of the data.

Database administration is fundamentally a people-oriented function. The key responsibility of the database administrator is to coordinate and resolve conflicting needs and desires of users in their diverse application areas as they relate to the data resources. Furthermore, there must be a mechanism whereby each of the affected users will be bound to a mediated decision. While not necessarily having direct authority over the using organizational units, the DBA must be able to appeal to the authority of a manager who does. Similarly, whether the database administrator's decision is arrived at democratically or autocratically, a user must have the right to appeal to a higher authority for a review of the decision.

By centralizing the database management function, the database administrator can seek a globally optimal solution to such things as the logical and physical design of the database and the related efficiency of the applications accessing and maintaining the database. Furthermore, these decisions can be made and revised, based upon the changing needs and patterns of usage in the using environment.

15.2.2 Information Systems within the Organization

Database administration exists within the information systems area of an organization. Historically, information systems emerged where people were first pushing for the installation of computers—most often within the financial area for accounting. This organizational position had the potential for bias in favor of accounting applications, and also lacked authority. Some organizations resolved the bias problem by creating information systems as an independent staff function, however, that still lacked credible authority. As information systems matured and increased in importance, it was set up as a line function in more and more organizations. Today, information systems reports directly to top management in the majority of organizations, rather than through some functional area.

The organizational approach suggested here also reflects the corporate-wide scope of information needed to give unbiased service to all organizational units, and it confers organizational status. In the event of a dispute, the Director of Information Systems should report to an executive who is at a higher level than any of the disputing parties.

Frederic G. Withington describes alternative locations for the data processing function in the parent organization. After discussing placement in the financial organization, in some other user department, in a service unit outside of the organization's structure, or in a staff position reporting directly to central management, Withington concludes that the only viable place left is to establish the data processing activity as a separate functional division. In addition to achieving impartiality and status, he argues that this gives proper recognition to data processing as a line function and puts it on a coequal basis with such divisions as manufacturing, marketing, and finance. Withington [1972] does caution, however, that the data processing function must *earn* a position of such importance. In many organizations today such stature is not deserving.

15.2.3 Organizational Evolution of Database Administration

The early appearance of a separate database administration function grew out of systems development (see Figure 15-1). As development projects began to overlap in the data used, organizations recognized the need to coordinate the definition and use of common data files across application systems. Someone had to resolve conflicts in use and maintain common data resources. That necessitated giving up some autonomy in systems development.

It was further discovered that the DBMS tool could assist developers in becoming more productive in building information systems. Since a DBMS can be very complex, difficult to select from those available, and require substantial training to use effectively, developers began to look to those who had mastered the use of DBMS for assistance in building systems.

In some organizations, database administration is placed along with other technical support functions under operations. Such a position tends to emphasize control over the physical and operational aspects of databases.

As database administration matures, the need for coordination and control extends beyond systems development into operations and directly to end users in other parts of the organization. This calls for raising the level within the information systems organization to report directly to the chief information officer, independently of development and operations (see Figure 15-2). It may be placed alongside other support functions such as planning, communications, and quantitative methods.

The position of database administrator should not be imposed on users. Users must first see the need for such a position. This may require a series of meetings and orientation sessions. When the position is established, users need to encounter a positive and helpful attitude, and experience some beneficial results when interacting with the database administrator. This reinforces their new roles and helps prevent the users from reverting back to their old behavior patterns, thereby undermining the DBA's authority and responsibilities.

Looking within the information systems department, it is necessary to examine the various kinds of activities before suggesting how they might be organized. The following discussion focuses on the separation of functions between the database administrator and the rest of the information systems organization.

15.2.4 Data Administration versus Job and System Administration

A major organizational problem arises from the relationship between programs and data, in particular, the execution of programs or jobs and data. Some authors want to give the database administrator responsibility for controlling the operation of the entire computer system including scheduling jobs, assigning priorities, being a program librarian, and restarting the system when it fails.

The CODASYL Systems Committee [1971, pages 441-442] began their discussion of data administration functions by indicating that, even though "the role of data administrator could frequently be merged with that of the systems administrator . . . it is possible to identify a meaningful division of responsibility between these two." In

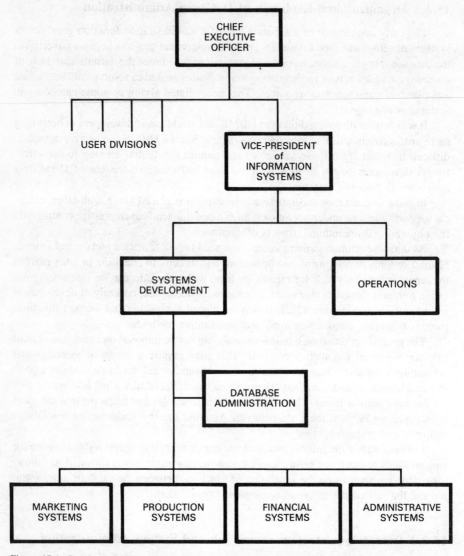

Figure 15-1. Database Administration Serving Systems Development.
When system development projects overlap in the data used, it is necessary to coordinate and control common data files. Furthermore, DBMS tools can assist in building information systems. Both of these factors point to the need for a separate database administration staff to serve several application development areas.

their view, the structure and content of the database have significant meaning to the database administrator. However, "to the systems administrator, the data base is merely a large quantity of stored representations, which as far as he knows may possibly be data, possibly programs, ..." As was noted earlier, the Committee ascribed to the database administrator the responsibility for storing permanent programs, for

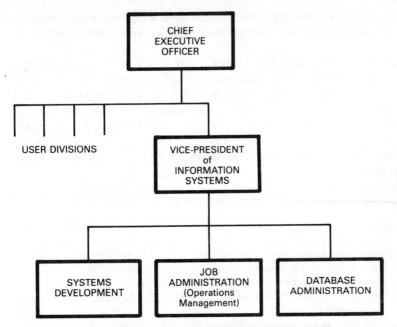

Figure 15-2. Mature Database Administration within the Organization.
As database administration matures it must coordinate and control common data across systems development areas, operational aspects of databases, and the access and interpretation of data by end users directly.

scheduling jobs, and the priorities assigned to programs which act upon the database. After defining the role distinctions in this way it is not surprising to find in the report the statement that "the clearer separation one identifies between the data administrator and the system administrator, the closer the role of the latter merges into every day machine room supervision."

Good role definition requires a clear statement of the object of role responsibility. In Figure 15-2 the objects to be administered are jobs and data. When requested, jobs are assigned computational resources, scheduled, and executed on the computer. Within the system, a software module called a job manager acts as the internal agent of the job administrator in carrying out his policies and prescribed procedures. From this viewpoint, there is an obvious parallel between job management and database management. Job management is responsible for the jobs within the system and the computational resources used in their execution; whereas, data management is responsible for the data resources.

The confusion between job management and data management may stem from the current concept of an operating system. The operating system within a computer is that massive collection of software which operates, that is, stimulates and coordinates the actions of all the pieces of a computer system. The operating system is commonly thought of as a monolith performing a single function, when, in fact, it performs many functions. It manages such objects and resources as data, jobs, programs, messages, terminals, and memory devices. Bachman is careful to distinguish these functions in an excellent discussion of how the various management activities interact with each other.*

Since programs act on data, there is often a high degree of interdependence between job management and data management. Several points of interaction can be identified, and each point of interaction at the functional level implies a potential conflict at the organizational level. Better role definition could result from studying corporations that have established some definite organizational division of responsibility. Setting up and observing an organizational separation of job and data administration would provide a vehicle for actually testing the degree of independence between the two functions.

Varying degrees of interaction between data and programs or between the database administrator and the job or system administrator are found in the following activities:

- Creating and maintaining a cross reference table showing what data elements are referenced by what programs and how (read, create, or modify data values).
- Approving userschemas (that is, the definition of the data as the program expects to view it) to ensure compatibility with the defined database.
- Providing a testbed of data for use in debugging programs.
- Authorizing programs to act on parts of the database after they have been thoroughly tested and debugged.
- Servicing requests for data access received from jobs in execution.
- Mounting and demounting offline files.
- Authorizing programs from the standpoint of data privacy to reference certain parts of the database.
- Monitoring program-data interaction and providing a record in the form of an audit trail.
- Providing for backup to the database in the event of destruction.
- Restarting the system after a breakdown. This involves restoring both the data and the programs before jobs can be restarted.

To clarify organizational roles, a definite assignment of responsibilities must be made relative to each of these activities.

15.2.5 Database Administration and System Development

Another interface exists between database administration and system development. System development includes the planning, analysis, design, and implementation of application processes. The database administrator would participate in the design effort and determine technical and economic feasibility in seeking to satisfy the data requirements of the application processes. The data requirements of new systems may be satisfied by using data already collected and stored, or by extending the definition of the database to include new data requirements.

---

*Charles W. Bachman, "Data Base Management: The Keystone to Applied System Architecture," in *Critical Factors in Data Management*, edited by Fred Gruenberger, Englewood Cliffs, NJ: Prentice-Hall, 1969, pages 33-40.

One of the more difficult tasks facing the DBA is to get the systems development personnel to use the new DBMS tools in building application systems. Tremendous inertia exists in favor of the old familiar system-building tools, such as COBOL, even if augmented with the (low-level) data manipulation language of a DBMS. With the higher-level tools of a comprehensive DBMS:

- Developers can be much more productive in building application systems.
- A new approach can be taken in the development cycle of application system development.
- Users are more likely to get a system which better satisfies their needs.

In a DBMS environment, the traditional life cycle of systems development gives way to a more experimental or heuristic approach.

1. Make available the data which is required by the new application system. It may already be mechanized and in the database. If the required data is not in the internal format of the DBMS but exists in a mechanized form, bring that data into the DBMS using the data definition and creation facilities. Prefer to use real data, though not necessarily up-to-date data. Also, it is not necessary to use all the available data. For example, it is sufficient to use a small subset of a customer file containing one million records.

2. Utilize the general-purpose, high-level facilities for query, report generation, and screen management to develop a prototype interface for the end users. Have them try to use the prototype system to obtain output from the database established in step 1 above, and give feedback on how well it meets their needs. This is not the time to be concerned about clean or timely data.

3. Iterate with the users, revising the database definition, presentation screens, queries, and output reports until they are satisfied with the results. Notice, this new development approach does not require the users to specify completely and in advance their system requirements and information requirements (a practically impossible task for them anyway). The requirements are determined iteratively through a process of experimentation.

4. Once the data requirements and output presentation mechanisms are known and agreed upon, the development process turns to the design and implementation of the "backend"—data collection, entry, validation, and database update. This part of the system seeks to satisfy the need for timely and accurate data.

This approach to systems development is similar to that suggested by Berrisford and Wetherbe [1979] which they called "heuristic development."

In this new environment, database administration is not doing the systems development work. They are responsible for providing the tools, for training developers (which may be the end users themselves) and encouraging them to use these tools, for providing assistance and support in the use of these tools, and for establishing conventions and controls in the use of these tools.

15.2.6 Database Administration and Users

Although responsible for the content and structure of the database, for making it available, and for controlling its integrity, the database administrator does not operate in a vacuum. The only way these responsibilities can be properly executed is through communication with the relevant users. In cooperation with users, the database administrator seeks to determine what data to collect and store and the criteria used in validating input data and stored data.

It has been suggested that the correctness of data is the responsibility of the user, while the protection of data is the responsibility of the database administrator. A Diebold research report notes a trend toward "placing responsibility for data accuracy, validity, and so forth, in the hands of the user who will be served by the data base." The report suggests the appointment of a "Prime Responsible Authority" (PRA) for each database from its primary user division. . . . The PRA interfaces with all users on one side and with the 'Data Base Administrator' on the other. [Diebold, 1971, page 43] To reiterate, the "prime responsible authority," working in a user division rather than the database administrator's organization, would be responsible for the content, integrity, and use of the database with respect to *all* users within the organization, both within and outside of his own using organization.

Although the database administrator must interface with the users, the division of responsibility suggested in the Diebold report could lead to increased conflict, suboptimization in database design, and partiality in the satisfaction of user needs for database services. Such a separation of responsibility is feasible only if a single user is associated with or has any interest in the database or a given part of the database. When multiple users share any part of the database, and sharing is assumed to be the normal case, they must agree on who will have the responsibility for its correctness. It could be the primary using organization, as suggested by the Diebold report, but if there are any other using organizations they would tend to receive second priority consideration.

Another difficulty is presented if the data collection activity is within an organizational unit different from the primary using organization. A database administrator, with the requisite level of authority, may be the best one to have responsibility for the availability and integrity of the database. Where a database administrator does not exist in an organization, the appointment of "prime responsible authorities" may be a good *interim* solution.

Even with a fully authorized database administrator, the concept of "prime responsible authorities" within each user organization is a good idea—provided that their responsibility focuses on the users represented rather than on a database. They would serve as liaison between a relatively homogeneous cluster of users and the database administrator. They would be knowledgeable in the functions of their user group and would represent their needs before the database administrator. On questions of database design, expansion, and restructure, the database administrator would bring together and enlist the help of all concerned "prime responsible authorities" in attempting to reach a mutually agreeable compromise.

15.2.7 Building Management and User Confidence

The database administrator is the key link in establishing and maintaining management and user confidence in the database and in the system facilities which make it available and control its integrity. They have a person to receive both requests and complaints. As with any organization, the degree of confidence is determined by the extent to which the database administrator and the DBA staff listen and are responsive to management and users.

15.2.8 Controlling the Database Administrator

Even a cursory examination of the functions of database administration shows the DBA to have considerable authority and power in an organization. This power can be used beneficially, or it can be abused. Centralizing certain functions improves communication, coordination, and control in a database environment. On the other hand, vesting substantial power in a single organizational position runs contrary to the fundamental principles of sound internal control. The auditor must be aware of the control weaknesses resulting when a database administration position exists and the remedial measures which are available to reduce the potential effects of these weaknesses.

The DBA can abuse vested power by improper actions in that role. Two aspects of the DBA role represent direct threats to data and system integrity. First, the breadth of functions vested in the DBA role violates the traditional control principle of separation of duties. Second, the DBA has available global knowledge of the database environment. The database tools available to the DBA, though necessary for the performance of various functions, can also be used to override established controls. For example, the DBA can set up valid passwords for access to confidential data. Typically, the DBA also has related tools to find out the various user passwords, even if a user is authorized to change their own password.

Several remedial measures are available to counteract the control weaknesses inherent in the position of database administrator:

- Assignment of appropriate seniority to the position.
- Separation of duties to the extent possible.
- Training and rotation of duties.
- Maintenance of logs.

The database administration position presents many of the same control problems which exist with any senior position in an organization. Primary emphasis must be placed on a set of administrative controls over the DBA. However, some technical controls can also be used in the form of activity logs kept by the DBMS or the operating system.

The DBA must occupy a **senior position** in the organization and be capable of remaining independent of the users. The responsibilities assigned to the position dictate that it be held by a person with proven competence and who is considered trustworthy. Individuals in the position should be subject to the same scrutiny which applies to all senior personnel.

Traditional **separation of duties** is used to prevent any one individual from having sufficient power to be able to perpetrate a fraud by themselves. With appropriate separation of duties, fraud requires the collusion of two or more individuals. Separation of duties serves as a check on the performance of each person's duties. As systems become more complex, the number of interfaces with other systems increases and separation of duties can cause rather than prevent control problems. Control is increased by simplifying processes and decreasing the number of system interfaces. The problem is determining the point at which further separation of duties will cause a degradation in control.

The role of DBA is a response to the problems of control in a complex set of organizational activities. Channeling communication and coordination through a single point increases control. The anomaly is that it also decreases control because there is a decreased scope for an independent check on the correct performance of functions.

Careful thought must be given to the way in which the duties of the DBA can be separated without impairing the satisfactory performance of functions. For example, assigning or changing passwords and authorizations to control access to or update of data could require the joint approval of the DBA and the user's manager. Even if the DBMS does not have such a dual authorization scheme, it can be implemented administratively using manual approval forms which can then be independently audited against the actual functioning of the DBMS. Similarly, the DBA could have permission to store, retrieve, and move application system programs without permission to execute them.

Training and rotation of duties can also contribute to increased control. If the size of the database environment warrants a group of people in database administration, control can be exercised by training each member of the group in different duties and rotating duties amongst the group members. This increases the chance of exposing fraud and makes it more difficult for a member of the group to perpetrate a fraud using a single technique.

Maintaining logs, either manual or machine, serves to record the activities of all personnel, including the DBA. While the DBA may have permission to run certain database utilities, such as assigning passwords, he should have no authority over the logging of system activities—that authority should rest with operations. The fact that passwords were assigned or changed and by whom would be clearly evident in the system activity log. Where possible, machine logs should supplement or provide an independent check on manual logs. Periodically the auditor should examine the manual and machine logs and check for unauthorized or questionable activity and for correspondence between logs.

15.3 ORGANIZATION OF THE DATABASE ADMINISTRATION FUNCTION

A role is defined in terms of a set of expectations, a set of functions, and a set of relationships with other roles. The relationship of database administration with other roles was discussed in the previous section and the functions are discussed in the next section. Roles materialize within an organization when "mapped" onto people, or conversely, when people are actually assigned to the roles.

Until the past decade, the role of database administrator in most organizations was diffused among several people. The effective management of shared data resources, however, demands that a central authority be assigned the responsibility for coordinating certain administrative functions. Responsibility for data administration functions must be separated from responsibility for other activities within the information systems department. The central administrative role may be assigned to a person who also has other responsibilities, it may be assigned to a single person who performs all and only the functions of data administration, or it may be assigned to a group of individuals, one of whom has the full responsibility for database administration. The choice between one or more individuals depends largely on the size of the organization.

15.3.1 Data Administration versus Database Administration

Some authors have made a distinction between data administration and database administration, perhaps based upon IBM's distinction between data management and database management, the latter being the lower-level, more technical function within a computer system. The following table, adapted from Durell [1985, page 6] contrasts these two roles:

	DATA ADMINISTRATION	DATABASE ADMINISTRATION
PRIMARY ORIENTATION	Administrative	Technical
PRIMARY LIAISON	Management	Programmers, analysts
HORIZON	Long-term data planning	Short-term database development and use
SCOPE OF DATA	All databases, both mechanized and nonmechanized	Database specific
DATA DESIGN	Logical information architecture	Physical design and implementation
FOCUS OF WORK	Metadata Data Dictionary Data Analysis DBMS independent	Data Database Data design DBMS specific

In many organizations, the person with the technical orientation is probably easy to identify—the management oriented role may not even exist yet. In this text, the term "database administration" encompasses both positions described in the preceding table.

Some larger organizations have established two places for the database administration function. One provides a direct interface with users in determining their information needs, development of userschemas, and global database design and long-range planning to meet collective user needs. The other unit is responsible for actual implementation in the DBMS, the formal definition and creation of databases, monitoring and fine tuning performance, and providing specific technical support.

15.3.2 Advising and Controlling versus Doing

In assigning role responsibilities, it is important to distinguish the "doing" from the "control over doing." While the responsibility for control and coordination of activities relating to database administration is centralized in the role of database administrator, the actual "doing" can be decentralized. The "doing" may be delegated to persons directly responsible to the database administrator, or to persons within the using organizations.

The definition of a data structure, for example, can actually be generated by an application programmer. This is done today whenever a COBOL programmer writes a DATA DIVISION. When the data identified in the DATA DIVISION is common within the organization, that is, multiple programs in more than one application area are referencing the same data structure, then the database administrator is needed to ensure compatibility between the programmer's DATA DIVISION and the definition of the data as it is or will be stored in the database. The database administrator would be required to sign off or authorize the cataloguing of the DATA DIVISION.

In addition to being the central authority, the database administrator gives guidance and counsel to others in the organization. When methods and techniques are transferable, the knowledge and methods of applying them can be developed within the database administration organization and made available to those with a need. For example, the database administrator can establish guidelines and standards to aid the process of designing a data structure, or of naming data items.

More than one dimension can serve as the basis for organizing the database administration function. The basis of organization will normally be highly dependent upon the assigned functions. If an organization is large and consists of reasonably autonomous units, each organizational subentity may have its own information systems department with its database administrator. Similarly, if independent collections of data resources can be identified, they could be separately managed. In this case, each independent collection of data can be considered a database. Both of these approaches present a problem because at some point some of the data will have to be brought together for top level management. Multiple database administrators would have to report to one overall data administrator. The situation is similar to multiple regional sales managers reporting to one overall national sales manager.

In summary, while the "doing" of database system development may be centralized or decentralized, the planning and control of database systems should be centralized at the corporate level. This corresponds with the findings of a Diebold research team which stated that "*at least* planning for data base systems should be at the corporate level; there is no other way to ensure the potential integration of functional data bases for providing consistent, coherent information at successively higher levels [of management]." They concluded with a recommendation that "data base development be *centrally coordinated*, whether or not centrally developed'' [Diebold, 1971, page 41].

The question of centralization of the database administration function is actually independent of the DBMS tool(s). The tools can be applied to a using environment of any scope. The only requirement is one of feasibility or justification. Nevertheless, it seems evident that it requires several applications and a medium to large-sized organization to justify one of the more sophisticated systems available today.

Any further discussion of the database administrator's organization would be derivative of the functions considered to be a DBA responsibility. Before discussing DBA functions, it may be useful to identify some of the positions that might be found in today's organizations and which might be contained within the database administration organization of the future. These might include tape librarian, input-output control clerk, machine operator (when mounting and demounting offline files), forms designer, forms control clerk, file designer, and security officer. An examination of functions in the next section will necessarily lead to the creation of additional titles as part of the collective administrative role.

Database administration may include any of the following:

- Logical database design and definition.
- Physical database design and implementation.
- User support: systems development, data requirements, and userschemas.
- Integrity, security, recovery, and operations monitoring.
- Database development, planning, and evolution (revision).
- Database standards and documentation.
- Maintenance of a data dictionary.
- DBMS and related software support: installation, training, and documentation.
- Data entry equipment, collection procedures, and error correction.

15.4 FUNCTIONS OF DATABASE ADMINISTRATION

This section provides an overall view of the functions associated with database administration. It emphasizes functions rather than techniques for performing those functions, even though it is sometimes difficult to avoid bringing in the latter.

Internally, the database administration unit may be organized according to function. This gives rise to subroles of database administration such as tape librarian or input-output control clerk.

Although the role of database administrator is often associated with generalized DBMS, most of the functions are relevant whether or not such a system is available in the organization. For example, it is still necessary to control the definition and (future) redefinition of shared files. The emergence of DBMS technology simply brings to light more of the problems of database management and, hopefully, offers some help in their solution.

Some authors discuss the database administration role in terms of activities rather than functions. This does not mean to imply that a clear distinction can be drawn between functions, and activities carried out with respect to those functions. The span of activities which generally relate to each function includes:

- Definition of the function, policies, standards, etc.
- Informing those concerned of the definition.
- Carrying out the defined function in operations.
- Monitoring to measure compliance during operations.
- Detection of deviations and either enforcement of the definitions or adaptation of the system to a changing environment.
- Revision of the definition.

In this dimension, there is a sequence of performing the defined function, monitoring what has been defined, and responding to the results of the monitoring activity. For each function the acts of defining, performing, monitoring, and responding can be accomplished using ad hoc methods. Once the function is better understood, the methodology can be formalized in automatic tools. In this development stage, it is important for embryonic database administrators not to simply do these functions but also to attempt to develop methodologies and tools to aid in their accomplishment.

The natural set of responsibilities of any manager includes the personnel, policies and procedures which relate to his or her own organization. To the extent that these are not unique to database administration, they are not discussed.

The unique functions of database administration are:

- Defining, creating, redefining, and retiring data.
- Making the database available to the using environment.
- Informing and assisting users.
- Maintaining database integrity.
- Monitoring operations and performance.

Each is discussed in the following subsections with a focus on functions rather than on activities.

15.4.1 Define, Create, Redefine, and Retire Data

The data resources in an organization constitute the central responsibility of database administration. The scope of responsibility may be limited to mechanized data resources, or further limited to the data defined within the DBMS tool(s). Ensuring that needed data is available to users may involve getting data into a mechanized form, using a conversion utility or writing a special conversion program, and perhaps establishing a communication link between two computers if the data currently resides on a different machine.

The process of data definition begins in response to stated data requirements from the using environment. New data may be needed to satisfy a request from top management or from a user organization or to satisfy the data requirements of a new application under development.

The first step in the definition process is to design the logical data structure, incorporating as much as possible of the natural structure inherent in the data. In a sense, the logical data structure should model the real world of interest. The design should not have a "runs" or process orientation but instead should model selected aspects of the operations and entities as they really exist. When a data structure already exists in an organization the new data must be incorporated into existing databases in a way that is compatible with the logical structure of the existing data.

During the past decade, there have been a few suggestions of formal methodologies to aid in the process of database design. However, most corporations still approach the design task in an ad hoc manner. Databases are being designed every day. The process needs to be carefully studied so that general principles can be learned. In a rudimentary way, the process of data structure design is essentially one of identifying and naming structural elements of data, grouping data items, and relating the groups.

Once the logical data structure is developed, it is formalized in the data definition language (DDL) of the particular database management system being used in the organization. Since every system has a permissible class of data structures which can be defined, it is generally necessary to modify the "natural" data structure so that it will be acceptable to the system. For example, some systems permit the definition of tree structures with only two levels in the hierarchy. If the inherent relationships in the data suggest more levels, the natural hierarchy must be partially collapsed or modified in some way to arrive at a database structure acceptable to the system.

The data structure, in addition to being formally defined to the *system*, should be fully documented in a master catalogue for the use of *people* in the organization. This suggests a form of graphical representation for easier comprehension.

Since the data described in the logical data structure will eventually be stored physically within the computer system, the system usually needs some guidance in how to linearize and partition the logical structure. The process of linearization and partitioning produces physical blocks which can be conveniently mapped onto and transferred to and from the storage devices. This definition of a storage structure may include the specification of block size, storage devices, data compression, access strategies, indexes, and orderings. Some and perhaps all of these features may be selected by default within a particular DBMS. The fewer choices that are made available within a system, the less the database administrator is able to give effect to tradeoffs in satisfying differing requirements. Such choices can have a direct impact on the responsiveness and efficiency of the system.

Whether the design activity is conducted by the database administrator or by a user, the resulting formal data definition and user-oriented documentation must be approved by the database administrator before the data becomes a part of the corporate database. The design process generally entails substantial interaction between the database administrator and the various user organizations who have an interest in the data being defined. The database administrator:

- Solicits user expressions of the meaning of data being defined.
- Seeks to obtain user agreement and resolve any data conflicts which arise.
- May establish certain standards and procedures which must be followed in the design process.

With specialized knowledge, the database administrator would presumably be more closely involved with the definition of the storage structure. Ideally, the DBA seeks to arrive at a storage structure which is optimum with respect to all uses of the database, present and foreseen, taken collectively.

Having defined some data to the system, the next step is to set up the mechanisms to acquire the new data and to bring it into the system. The creation process refers to capturing data and storing it within the system according to the logical and physical structures previously defined. The creation process is often accompanied by extensive editing and validation of the incoming data.

The tasks of definition and redefinition go together. Modification of an existing data structure may be motivated by such factors as new data needs or changes in the current pattern of usage. When a logical data structure is modified, it necessitates a reorganization of the storage structure and notification of the using community, and it may involve a recompiling and perhaps rewriting some application programs. With a cross-reference listing of programs and data, the database administrator should ideally be able to predict the effect of a proposed change in the data structure. The DBA needs to be able to detect those programs (or rather userschemas) rendered inefficient or inoperative by a change in the data structure. Since it is probably impossible to predict all effects, some sort of checking mechanism would have to be invoked during the initial phases of program execution.

Finally, the last step in this process is to execute management policies regarding data retention. The value of data diminishes over time so it is desirable to aggregate older data, store the detail in offline archival files, and eventually retire all the old data to archival files.

15.4.2 Provide Availability Tools

To achieve the objective of availability, the database administrator provides the facilities and tools with which the users can query and update the database in a manner suitable to their needs. Meeting this responsibility involves acquiring (or developing) appropriate database management tools. Such tools can be extended and augmented to further enhance the facilities in response to increased diversity of requirements. The DBA should strive to acquire and make available common generalized functions. Pooling top talent to develop functional tools can often result in better use of human resources and the development of better software and systems for database use. When new system software tools are developed they must be validated by the database administrator and approved for use in production.

Availability tools are not only needed for the end users (query, report generation, update) but also for the system developers. They need to be able to develop tailored screen definitions for both retrieval and data entry/update, tailored menus for the end user, and set up predefined processes which interact with the stored database. DBMSs with these enhanced capabilities for the system developer are sometimes called application development tools.

When there are several database management tools available in an organization, the DBA should maintain comparative information on the strengths and weaknesses of each, and the appropriate situations and necessary conditions for using each.

The database administrator should keep abreast of the latest database technology and commercially available database management products, as well as what other organizations are doing. A useful way to exchange information is through local and national professional organizations. In some cities an association of database administrators has been formed.

15.4.3 Inform and Assist Users

It is not sufficient to simply acquire DBMS tools and then expect that they will be used. People must accompany the tools to foster their use. Many organizations have made the mistake of acquiring a new DBMS without assigning someone the responsibility to learn how to use the system and be in a position to encourage and assist others in using the new tool. Every tool needs a shepherd.

The database administration function is fundamentally a service function within the organization. The central part of a database administrator's responsibility is to relate to the people who use the data resources and the database management system tools. The DBA is the servant and agent of the persons who make up the diverse user community. The DBA informs and services people in user departments, top management, and programmers and analysts in other parts of the information systems division. Often the DBA offers assistance to a user who is in the process of attempting to solve problems and develop applications.

The database administrator interacts with the user community on a broad spectrum of communication levels from passive to highly interactive:

PASSIVE
- Inform

- Educate and train

INTENSIVELY INTERACTIVE
- Help, assist, advise, and counsel

Informing refers to regular or when-needed communication from the database administrator to the using community in the form of published memoranda, documentation and manuals made available on demand, and broadcasts over an online user terminal facility. In this mode of communication, there is no two-way interaction between the database administrator and the user, and in that sense the user is passive. Education and training entail more active user involvement in a learning situation in which students and teacher interact in a group setting. The documentation and manuals mentioned above can serve as the basis for this instruction. At the other end of the spectrum is the tailored personal help given to a user with the primary focus being a specific application or problem of the moment.

The database administrator has the responsibility to keep the users fully informed regarding many aspects of the database environment. First, the database administrator must maintain up-to-date documentation on the structure and contents of the database itself. Such documentation describes what data is kept in the database, what it means and how it is to be interpreted (not simply a listing of the codes that can be stored for a data item), how to access it, a dictionary of data names with cross references to similar or related data elements, a pictorial representation of the data structure intended for human understanding, and the more detailed and precise definition needed to accurately reference the database. The database documentation would be made available to users on demand, assuming no privacy restrictions and that they had a need to know. The appropriate users also need to be automatically notified when any changes are made to the database definition.

The database administrator is responsible for making available reference manuals and user manuals on how to use the facilities and languages of the database management tools such as retrieval, report generation, and update. The DBA may also conduct special training sessions based upon these manuals and on the proper application of these tools to solving particular problems. When a new database management tool is developed or otherwise acquired, it should be placed in the program library for general use and the users informed about its existence and how to use it.

Users need to be informed of potential or actual loss of integrity of the database, for instance, when an update process goes out of control or data is lost or destroyed. When data is found to be in error, the using community needs to be notified in case prior actions were taken based upon the erroneous data. For example, the price for a particular product may have been wrong, causing billings to be sent to customers with the wrong figures. The error is now beyond the control of the system, and the only recourse is to send out correction notices. The database administrator could go back to the audit records to find out when the wrong price was entered and notify the users, particularly those who might have used the price data.

As with any operation, there are the usual administrative notices, communicated to the users of the resources under control of the database administrator. These would include procedures relating to the control and use of the database and the database management system, changes in the status of the system, and standards.

Responding to the questions and problems of users constitutes the interactive form of communication provided by the database administrator. The database administrator responds to user problems concerning the use of the system and its tools, and responds to questions concerning the understanding of the data. Often some data, especially highly specialized data, requires interpretation. For example, it is sometimes difficult to properly interpret accounting data. Allowance-for-depreciation data is handled differently in the context of income determination than in the context of cash flow. Also, statistical data is often difficult to interpret properly. If the database administrator is not trained in these areas and the database documentation supplied by the specialists is not complete, the DBA should at least know where to send the questioning user.

The database administrator receives and attempts to respond to the data requirements of new and improved applications. Interaction with the user helps to provide assistance and direction in the economical development and use of the database. Conversely, the user may develop application processes and data definitions without the assistance of the database administrator. In either case, the database administrator verifies proposed definitions or solutions as to feasibility, suitability to the application, and expected economy in operation. In certain cases, the DBA gives formal approval to the proposed definition or solution. This process of assistance, verification, and approval is applied to the definition of userschemas, additions to the database, update data transactions, and output reports. For example, when a user needs a new report, the database administrator can verify the requirements by asking if the data is in the database, if it can be easily derived, or if existing reports can be used with some modification.

During the development of application systems the database administrator can assist in providing a testbed of data for program testing. To allow undebugged programs to be tested using the live database could pose a serious threat to database integrity. For program testing, the database administrator can provide a pseudo-database environment. When a set of application programs is thoroughly checked out, the software package and its associated userschemas are approved for cataloguing and use within the system in interaction with the database.

15.4.4 Maintain Database Integrity

The goal of implementing integrity procedures is reduction in the incidence of degradation or failure, and reduction in the cost of recovering from or repairing a loss of integrity. Complete integrity protection is never possible, but if it is deemed important enough (and the level of importance can usually be reflected in cost consequences), substantial resources can be applied to enhance and maintain a high level of integrity.

There are several procedures or controls which can be used in maintaining database integrity. Some or all of them can be implemented to varying degrees depending upon the expected benefit to be derived, or more accurately, depending upon the expected cost of not implementing them. This section discusses several integrity control measures which could be invoked by the database administrator. What is actually done in any given situation will depend upon the requirements of the using environment and upon the results of a cost-benefit analysis.

Integrity protection measures involve both *preventative* and *curative* aspects. The actual establishment of any control procedure requires setting up certain information, *definitions*, or parameters. For example, to validate data requires, first, an explicit expression of what constitutes valid or "right" data. This provides some standard against which to compare existing data. The preventative aspects of a control procedure involve *monitoring* and *regulation* to ensure that defined integrity measures are being enforced or carried out, and to detect and report any deviations. The curative aspects relate to the *recovery* or corrective action taken in response to detected errors or deviations.

Existence Control seeks to ensure the physical existence and well-being of the database. This can be accomplished by instituting a wide variety of security measures including isolation of facilities and control over such physical conditions as temperature and humidity. Such measures are preventative and are usually externally administered, that is, administered outside of a DBMS.

The curative aspects of existence control are generally referred to as *backup and recovery*. Backup refers to the regular storage of parts of the database redundantly, and, preferably, remotely. This is usually done by *logging* incoming transactions or before and after images of changes to the database, or by periodically *dumping* all or part of the database. Recovery is the process of using the backup data to re-create a lost or destroyed portion of the database. Besides safeguarding the existence of data, the backup mechanism can be used to recover from loss of integrity due to faulty update or a decline in data quality.

Definition Control seeks to ensure that data always conforms to its definition. This applies especially after any update action and after any form of redefinition or reorganization of the data. In reality, this must be a mandatory integrity procedure. The database administrator must seek to ensure that no database management system software would ever destroy the correspondence between the database and its definition as it accesses either one. Definition control is actually the most primitive form of quality control or validation.

Quality Control seeks to detect and correct errors in data and to maintain and improve the quality of data in the database. Data quality refers to the accuracy, completeness, and consistency of data. Analysis of recurring patterns of reduced data quality can lead to improvement in the processes which input, store, process, and retrieve data.

The scope of a data quality control program depends on the sensitivity of the value of data to varying levels of quality. For example, data pertaining to bank accounts, payroll, and accounts receivable generally demands a high level of quality. On the other hand, marketing intelligence data may be fragmentary and based on hearsay. It may still be very meaningful, but its value is not very sensitive to level of quality. As with other integrity control measures, the extent of implementation should be determined by a cost-benefit analysis.

In one system to process medical claims, several straightforward edit and validation checks were defined. When the new system began processing claims, the reject rate was 55 percent! This was much higher than in the previous system. Since there was insufficient personnel to manually review all the rejects, management decided to turn off some of the validation checks. They were gradually turned back on again as the staff was able to handle the volume of rejects, and as those preparing the claims made fewer errors.

Quality control is always based upon redundant information. One cannot just look at data and validate it without having some prior notion of what it should look like. The validation process is only as good as the validation criteria used. There is nothing absolute about validation. It is simply the comparison of data with other data. The quality of validation is limited by our inability to formally express exactly what constitutes good quality data. It is also limited by choice due to such factors as cost and efficiency.

Some quality control concepts and procedures used in accounting (auditing) and production engineering are readily transferable to data quality control. These include, for example, keeping an audit trail of errors, inventory verification procedures, and sampling techniques. Much can be learned by viewing the data processing activity as a production factory which takes in raw material (input data), processes and stores it in finished goods or parts inventory (the database), and produces assemblies (reports) based upon standing orders or on demand.

In a factory production environment, quality control is often instituted in response to customer demands for particular levels of quality or tolerances for error. Buyers often demand certain testing procedures and a report of test results as a condition of a contract between manufacturer and supplier.

By contrast, the response of the EDP technician has too often been a complaint that the users are entering bad data which showed up on the output reports as garbage— the common maxim: Garbage In, Garbage Out! Given enough garbage, these data customers become disillusioned with the computer as a tool and enemies of the Data Processing Department. The DBA must provide a program of data quality control, not to remove all error, but to indicate that a serious attempt is being made to reduce error, to improve both the product and the process.

Managers cannot repeatedly blame bad decisions on bad data. They are paid to make good decisions based on whatever data they can get. Data processing technicians are paid to generate data that managers can trust. Managers turn to engineers for quality control techniques to insure the credibility of manufactured products in the eyes of the customer. Managers must similarly depend on the EDP technician to support the credibility of data with a quality control program.

The validation process may be applied to incoming data, to the inventory of stored data, and to output data. The process may be performed manually outside the system, or within the system by programs which check the quality of data against previously stored validation criteria (see Chapter 13).

Sometimes it is necessary or desirable to check stored data for *consistency*. For example, consider the different ways of referring to the State of Pennsylvania—in full or abbreviated as Penna, Penn, Pa, or PA with or without a period following. If data item values are not stored according to a consistent, standard coding scheme, it is very difficult to formulate retrieval requests. Consider finding all those employees from a national database who work in Pennsylvania when data entry allows any of the above abbreviations.

Two questions relate to the validation of the database—*what* validation information is stored, and *when* the database is checked against the validation criteria. The stored validation criteria can be applied on input, after update, on output, or periodically. If periodic, the validation process may be initiated by the database administrator, by the user, or automatically by the system.

Validation of the database after update seeks to ensure that any update action results in a database which is still valid according to the validation criteria. Validation of the database on output involves checking the stored data *before* it is retrieved for display or inclusion in a report in response to an output request.

Validation processes can be initiated by the database administrator periodically or when a need arises. This could be considered a year-end or month-end inventory check. It is made even though the database is apparently healthy, just as people have an annual medical checkup even though they are apparently healthy.

It is never possible to store complete validation criteria. Some validation criteria are intuitive and difficult to formalize; it may be possible to express other criteria but perhaps the system is limited in what it can accept; other validation criteria may be left out for reasons of economy or performance. Whatever the reason, it is always possible to solicit quality evaluations from the users. There is one foremost criterion of value:

the credibility of data to its users. It should also be noted that data users are seldom the same as data providers. However, it is the providers, those who enter the data into the system, who are in the best position to check the quality of stored data and enforce validation rules. It is a responsibility of the DBA to tell the data provider to perform data quality control checks to the level required by other users in the organization.

Various mechanisms can be used to obtain feedback from users on data quality. The simplest is to periodically print out portions of the database and send it to the prime user for review. This is similar to the auditor's practice of sending a statement out to debtors to verify their recorded level of indebtedness to the organization. In this way, the auditor obtains a quality check on the inventory of accounts receivable.

It is important to note that if the system does not perform quality control checks and they are important, then the checks must be done by the users, written into their procedures. It is a responsibility of the DBA to ensure that such quality control procedures are enforced.

Update Control seeks to ensure that a user who requests an update to the database has received prior authorization to do so. The same regulatory mechanism used in access control can be used for update control. There are two forms of update which imply two levels of authorization. The first involves adding data to the database without changing any data that already exists. The second form of update involves the modification or deletion of existing data. In some situations it may be desirable to distinguish these two forms of update and impose tighter control on modification and deletion.

The database administrator, in approving system or application software for regular production use, may want to set stronger program testing requirements for programs that add or modify the database. Certifying that software is "correct" and properly handles all possible input conditions is a major technical problem. It is one thing to establish that software will do what it is supposed to do. It is even more difficult to prove that it does not do what it is not supposed to do.

Concurrency Control seeks to control the concurrent execution of programs which update* the database thus protecting the integrity of the update action and the resultant database. While some systems employ a lockout mechanism at the level of files, record types, or file partitions, this cannot be considered a satisfactory long-run solution. Ideally, lockout should occur at the level of individual record instances. Most DBMS's provide no control over the method used to control concurrent updates. In some systems, the method is very obscure, if concurrent update is permitted at all. Furthermore, it may be practically impossible for users to know how to function correctly in a given concurrent update environment. All this points to the need for the database administrator to carefully evaluate any candidate DBMS to ensure that con-

---

*If the concurrent programs are all retrieving or only one of them is updating, there is no threat to the integrity of the database. However, there is a threat to the integrity of any one of the retrieval programs. That is, there is a threat to process integrity but not to data integrity. Also notice that the output resulting from a retrieval program may give the *appearance* of database integrity loss when in fact that may not be the case.

current updates are adequately controlled and that the documentation makes it clear what the users must do in that environment.

Access Control seeks to protect data from inadvertent or unauthorized disclosure to unauthorized persons or for unauthorized purposes. Some access control is realized in the use of physical security measures. Some form of restricted access is usually required since all data cannot be considered completely open to outsiders or even to all persons inside the organization. There is often a need to protect individual and corporate privacy and to control the interpretation of certain data.

The mechanism for access control requires the database administrator to set and periodically reset access authorizations on both users and objects of data to be controlled (sometimes called privacy locks and keys). At the time of an access request, the system can seek to identify requesters and check their authorization (which has been previously defined to the system) against their request. The system can monitor unsatisfied requests in an attempt to detect a potential breach of security. In addition, a record or audit trail may be kept of all accesses to the database to permit a followup investigation in case of a suspected breach, perhaps by an authorized person but for an unauthorized purpose.

Another measure for access control is encryption or the encoding of confidential data before it is stored or transmitted.

Although the database administrator needs a privileged mode of access to the database, it cannot be a blanket authorization. Internal control procedures are still required to set up appropriate checks and balances on the actions of personnel within the database administration organization.

15.4.5 Monitor Operations

Finally, as a fifth function, the database administrator is generally responsible for the data-related aspects of operations. This includes:

- Keeping things in operation.
- Controlling operations related to the database.
- Striving to obtain maximum efficiency in operations against the database.
- Keeping a recorded history of data-related events which can be reviewed when problems arise.

The database administrator needs to receive feedback of operations information in order to better inform and advise users, to improve the integrity control procedures, and to reorganize the database for better performance.

A subrole within database administration is directly responsible for performing data-related tasks during operation of the system. Such a subrole could be labeled the *database operations supervisor*—the onsite representative of the database administrator. The database operations supervisor executes (or oversees to ensure the proper execution of) policies and procedures established by the database administrator. This includes such functions as:

- Backup logging and dumping of the database.
- Recovery of the database when it is lost or destroyed.
- Controlling usage of the database during recovery and periods of degraded performance.
- Ensuring compliance with standards.
- Monitoring security authorizations.
- Transferring data from offline storage in preparation for online processing (mounting) and for removing data to offline storage (demounting).

The last function is normally assigned to the tape or disk librarian. The database operations supervisor is required to work very closely with the machine room supervisor. In fact, some difficulty arises in defining the two roles distinctly enough to clearly separate their duties.

No one set of users should be allowed to optimize the performance of the system for their own operations if it adversely impacts the performance for other users. Conflicting performance demands require mediation by the DBA.

Users and data processing management often fear that installing a new DBMS will result in an overall degradation in the performance of other jobs on the computer. This is not unreasonable since a DBMS is generally trying to do more for the users than was being done without the DBMS. It takes machine time to perform more functions for the user. The alternative may be to have the users perform the functions themselves, such as extra data validation during update processing. More likely, the functions would not be performed at all.

It is important for the DBA to first acknowledge that performance may suffer and to take steps to monitor the performance of the new system. Monitoring the pilot applications can provide the basis for projecting performance of larger applications later. As applications are added the DBA can monitor the usage mix over time, noting what jobs are running concurrently when performance diminishes. Rescheduling the times for running certain jobs may lead to improved performance for everyone. Poor performance may indicate the need for additional hardware—more disk storage space or a bigger CPU.

The database administrator needs to monitor the usage of the database and gather performance statistics to periodically assess the appropriateness of the existing database to the current population of users. The information gathered can serve as the basis for changing the logical or physical structure of the database in response to changing patterns of usage. The database administrator constantly seeks to optimally serve the using environment, which means constantly seeking to balance the changing needs of the individual users. For each user or application, the volume of data and frequency of usage can change. When it does change, and sometimes the change is gradual, the database administrator must monitor operations to be aware of the changing pattern of usage and then attempt to respond to it.

15.5 DATABASE ADMINISTRATOR TOOL: THE DATA DICTIONARY

Several computer-based tools have emerged to satisfy various functions of database administration. These include tools for:

DATABASE INTEGRITY MAINTENANCE

- Backup and recover (dump and load) data.
- Check the stored data to ensure that it conforms to its definition and satisfies defined validation criteria.
- Analyze monitoring and audit trail logs for evidence of any suspicious activity or problem trends.
- Trace all chains in the stored data to ensure that all pointers are valid and that all stored pieces are connected.

DATABASE REVISION

- Redefine a stored database.
- Restructure the database to conform to the new definition.

PERFORMANCE MONITORING AND IMPROVEMENT

- Analyze monitoring logs for changing trends in database usage.
- Determine storage space utilization and recover space left by logically (but not physically) deleted data.
- Reorganize stored data by folding in data from overflow areas and physically reordering stored records.
- Reorganize file search and access mechanisms; rebalance indexes.

DATABASE DESIGN

- Check a proposed design for consistency.
- Generate a graphical data structure diagram from a proposed definition.
- Provide estimates of file size and performance.

Most of these tools require information about the database. From a broader perspective, the database administrator, users, and the DBMS all require information about the database. Ideally, such information should be stored in one central place. This is the role of the data dictionary, or dictionary/directory. A data dictionary is the main tool of database administration.

A *dictionary* provides definitions of things.

A *directory* tells you where to find them.

A *data dictionary/directory* contains information (or data) about data.

More recently, data dictionaries have been extended to provide information on other entities as they relate to data—programs, external input transactions and output reports, userschemas, and users. The phrase *information system resource dictionary* has been used to reflect this broader perspective. Allen, Loomis, and Mannino [1982] simply dropped the limiting designation of "data" and used the phrase "integrated dictionary/directory." Furthermore, the term "catalogue" is sometimes used to better reflect the broader perspective than is implied by the traditional notion of a dictionary. Nevertheless, the term *data dictionary* still persists and is used here to encompass an information system resource catalogue.

The information system resource catalogue, or simply "data dictionary," is a DBA tool for an organization to maintain information relating to the various resources used in information systems—data, input transactions, output reports, programs, application systems, and users. The information about nondata entities is maintained primarily as they relate to the data entities.

Historically, data dictionary systems evolved to satisfy the need for *more complete* information about data stored in a database than was provided by the database schema. Some early DBMSs provided a very sketchy definition of a database—sufficient for machine access and processing but not sufficient for the people who had to use and manage the data [see Cahill, 1970; Uhrowczik, 1973]. There was (and is) also a need to provide a repository of data about data to support the systems analysis and design process, *before* formally defining the data to a DBMS (or in application programs).

15.5.1 Providing a More Complete Definition of Data

When the database definition is formalized in the database definition language (DDL) of a DBMS, it contains sufficient information to enable machine processing. For the people in the using environment, the DDL statements and graphical representation usually contain *in*sufficient information. The DDL only needs to be complete enough for the *machine* to be able to store data and subsequently retrieve it. Many DDLs contain substantially less information than was discussed in Chapter 6. They only give the tip of the iceberg of "data about data."

Nevertheless, the more complete the formal database definition, the less the need for a data dictionary to "complete" the definition of the data within the system. A data dictionary supplements a database definition; it is like a "super" database definition. Conversely, the database definition is (or should be) a subset of the information in the data dictionary. That is, all the information required for the formal database definition should be derivable from the information in the data dictionary.

This is the critical element of the data dictionary/directory system proposed by Plagman and Altshuler [1972]. They argue that an integrated corporate database system be driven by one central definition for both people and processes, including the DBMS. When a system contains both a stored database definition and a mechanized data dictionary which are separate and largely independent, there is no assurance that the definitional information in the two will be consistent. The database definition informational needs of the DBMS should be derived from the data dictionary/directory. This reduces the dependence on the currently installed DBMS.

The following points indicate the kinds of information that could be stored in a data dictionary. The list goes substantially beyond the database definition information discussed in Chapter 6 to include information needed for database administration. Although the primary focus is on data about data items (or data "elements"), some information pertains to other structural elements.

- Name—short name, full name, and name aliases or synonyms as used in the DBMS or in programs (e.g., names in COBOL). May include long forms of the name perhaps developed from some hierarchical classification scheme or highly structured naming scheme (see following section for an outline of one such scheme called the 'OF-language').
- Description or explanation; meaning, interpretation rules and guidelines; purpose of the data item and why it is kept.
- Owner—delegated responsibility for creation, maintenance, and integrity of the data item values.
- Date of creation and date of last update of this dictionary entry.
- Value set designation by type, ranges or enumeration of values, the meaning of attribute values and codes, and values for the null states of unknown and irrelevant.
- Internal format and size.
- External display format, and default column heading on reports.
- Unit of measurement.
- Derivation rule or algorithm, if applicable.
- Validation criteria and editing rules.
- Subjective expression of reliability or validity of the data.
- Conditions for existence or relevance; mandatory or optional.
- Frequency of generation and change; useful life.
- Where the data is stored and how to get it; based on relationships.
- Relationship to other data in the database—from a common domain of values.
- Relationship to other entities in the system—computer installations, application systems, programs, files (record types), external data collection forms and input transactions, output reports, userschemas.
- How the data is used (created, added, read, modified, deleted) by related process entities (programs).

Providing a more complete database definition, the data dictionary serves several purposes. It is used by the DBA to support design activities and control responsibilities. It can be used by consumers (users) of data to find out what data is available, what the data means, and where and how to get it.

15.5.2 Uses of a Data Dictionary

A comprehensive data dictionary provides the definition of data items, how they fit into a data structure, and how they relate to other entities in the information system environment. The types of entities can be classified as follows:

- Data—data item, record type (group, segment), database.
- Processes—computer installation, application system, program, module.
- External inputs and outputs—transaction, form, report, display screen, userschema.

- Users—individual, group, organizational unit, terminal—any of which may be the source or user (destination) of data, or the point of responsibility for the creation and maintenance of data.

The foundation of the data dictionary is information about data items. With a comprehensive base of information, the data dictionary can serve several useful purposes. These purposes span the whole spectrum of planning, determining information requirements, design and implementation, operation, and revision.

- Documentation—providing reports of data about data. The data dictionary can be used to generate a graphical representation of the database structure similar to automatic program flowcharting.
- Data availability—a data map for end users to discover what data exists in the organization, what it means, where it is stored, and how to access it. May be provided using a facility for browsing through a data dictionary.
- Design—a tool to support the processes of database design and systems analysis and design. A data dictionary can contain the latest proposed contents of a database as a design evolves.
- Schema generation—automatic generation of the DDL for a target DBMS to serve as the vehicle for implementing a database.
- Change control—setting and enforcing standards; evaluating the impact of proposed changes and implementing those changes.

In a general sense, the data dictionary is a vehicle for managing size and complexity in a database environment. In a typical, single-function organization (not a mixed conglomerate) the individual data items will number in the several thousand. The data items appear in hundreds of files (record types) which are interrelated, and in hundreds of input transactions or data capture screens and output reports. In fact, these numbers tend to be relatively independent of organization size; at least they are not linearly proportional to organization size.

15.5.3 For Systems Analysis and Design

For purposes of systems analysis and design, the data dictionary results from taking inventory of all the data in an organization (or a particular application system). This inventory of existing data can be refined, and it can be extended with new data requirements.

In building a data dictionary, the primary focus is a description of *existing* data, that is, the collection of data about *all* existing data within an organization whether mechanized or not. The process of collecting data about data is a necessary step in the analysis of an existing system to discover:

- Data flows, sources, and destinations.
- Redundant data within the system.
- Multiple descriptions of the same data and similar descriptions for different data.
- Something about the tasks which create, process, use, move, and store data.

The methodology of inventorying data usually revolves around the groupings of data on input forms, in manual and mechanized files, and on output reports, all of which can be called "records." Records are identified, their contained data items are described, and their flow through a system of processes is charted. This information can then be analyzed in various ways to infer things about the system and lead to increased mechanization or improved design.

Several formal techniques for building and analyzing a data dictionary have been developed. Some are manual while others are mechanized tools, and in some formalizations, the data dictionary concept is part of a more comprehensive approach to systems analysis and design. Formalized techniques, which are or include the development of a data dictionary, include SOP and TAG from IBM, ADS from NCR, BISAD from Honeywell, AUTOSATE from the RAND Corporation, and more ambitious attempts in ISDOS from the University of Michigan, and ARDI from Philips in Europe.*

Some would argue that inventorying all the existing data in an organization is a useless and never-ending task. It represents the epitome of the bottom-up approach to systems design. At some point, it is necessary to be normative, to ask what all this data is used for, to set priorities on systems development, and to select the data needed in the priority areas of the organization. The alternative is to *incrementally* establish a corporate database to meet the priority needs in an organization.

15.5.4 Data Item Naming Conventions

Since so many people can be involved with a database, programmers and end users accessing and referencing data, it is critical to establish standard names and abbreviations for all data items within the databases. Readability of programs, input screens, and output reports depends heavily on the choice of data names.

For names to be consistent and somewhat predictable requires the use of naming conventions. Standard naming conventions throughout an organization will increase the probability that people will arrive at the same formal name when constructing a name for the same data item, or arrive at similar interpretations for the same named data item. Lack of consistent data naming standards makes it difficult, even for the experienced user, to remember the names; and makes it impossible to construct new data names (since existing names will appear to be arbitrary).

The first step is to make a list of all the full English words that are or will be used to make up data names. Then for each decide whether to use the full word or a standard abbreviation. A naming convention primarily provides guidance in the selection of abbreviations.

Carter [1982] has suggested a series of rules for forming abbreviations:

1. *There should be at most one abbreviation per word.*

   NUM and NO should not both be allowed as abbreviations for "Number."

---

*More detail and bibliographic references can be found in: Richard L. Nolan, "Systems Analysis for Computer Based Information Systems Design," *Data Base* (3:4), 1971 Winter, pages 1-10; and Daniel Teichroew, "A Survey of Languages for Stating Requirements for Computer-Based Information Systems," *AFIPS Fall Joint Computer Conference Proceedings* (volume 41, part II), 1972, pages 1203-1224.

2. *Once defined, an abbreviation should be used consistently in place of the full word.*

   Consistent use helps people get used to the abbreviation.

3. *Form abbreviations by dropping trailing letters, not by dropping letters from the middle.*

   LOC is better than LCTN for "location." It is easier to remember, spell, and pronounce (over the phone!) complete syllables.

4. *An abbreviation should be at least three letters shorter than the full word.*

5. *Multiple words should not have the same abbreviation.*

   ACC could stand for "access," "account," or "accumulate."

6. *An abbreviation for one word should not be a possible abbreviation for another word.*

   CURR for "currency" could also be for "current."
   CHG could be for either "change" or "charge."

7. *One abbreviation should not be another full word.*

   ADDR is okay for "address," but not ADD.

Of course, it is never possible to follow these rules all the time. Minimizing the exceptions can lead to greater consistency and readability.

Having selected a set of abbreviations, the next problem is putting them together to form data names. They may be simply concatenated together, or separated by some system-allowed special character (often an underscore or hyphen). Most systems only permit the use of upper-case letters. If a mixture is possible, the first letter of each part could be capitalized. An example of these alternatives is given below:

NAMELAST   NameLast   NAME_LAST

Next it is necessary to have a convention for sequencing the terms in forming a data name. It is often possible to identify parts that indicate the broad context, other parts that are specific, and still other parts that indicate type or class. Experience indicates a preference for putting the broadest context indicator first, and putting the type designation, if any, last. For example:

EMP_NAME_LAST   EMP_NAME_FIRST   EMP_NAME_TITLE   EMP_NAME_SUFFIX

EMP_ADDR_CARE   EMP_ADDR_STR   EMP_ADDR_CITY   EMP_ADDR_STATE

Sometimes it is desirable to establish a short, 2 or 3 letter code for each record type in a database, and then prefix each data item name with the record code. This is less desirable if data names must be short, if records can contain many items, or if the system establishes interrecord relationships based upon common data item names.

15.5.5 The 'OF-language'

The 'OF-language' was developed by IBM and is now incorporated into their Data Dictionary/Directory System. It assigned to each data object a series of words separated by connectors in a hierarchical fashion from the most general term to the most specific. The most general term is "name" since it can distinguish among entities. Asking the question "name of what?" we answer "name of customer." Finally, we know something about the name of customer—it is abbreviated. Putting this in the proper sequence yields "name, customer, abbreviated." Inserting some carefully chosen connectors completes the data object name in the 'OF-language' as follows:

NAME (of) CUSTOMER (which is) ABBREVIATED.

In general, the first term of the language designates the *type* of data object: data item (called "element"—which is the default type), nonrepeating group, or repeating group (called "array"). The next term designates the *class* of the data object as one of the following eleven classes:

CLASS WORD	SYMBOL	DEFINITION
Name	N	An alphabetic entity instance *identifier*.
Number	#	A numeric entry instance *identifier*.
Code	C	Data which identifies classifications of entities.
Quantity	Q	The number or quantity (including fractions) of anything except monetary amounts.
Amount	$	The quantity of monetary amounts.
Date	D	Actual calendar date.
Text	T	Data having relatively undefined content.
Flag	F	A binary code (limited to two conditions).
Control	X	Information used for control of other information during processing.
Constant	K	Data which does not change value from one transaction to another.
Percent	%	Ratios between other data values expressed as a percentage.

Subsequent terms relate to the specific nature or description of the data object being named based on key words appropriate for the application. The first is the prime word which is followed by zero or more increasingly restrictive modifier terms.

The terms in the name are connected using one of six connectors:

CONNECTOR	SYMBOL	DEFINITION
Of	(blank)	A blank between terms designates "of."
Which is/are	*	Indicates further qualification or attribute of the preceding descriptor term.
Hyphen	-	Connects two or more words to become a single word or phrase.
Or	!	Indicates coequal descriptor terms.
And	&	Indicates combined descriptor terms.
By/Per/Within	/	Indicates a domain or basis for a descriptor.

The following examples illustrate the application of the 'OF-language' in assigning names to data items from our sample personnel-organizational database.

EMPLOYEE NUMBER		# [of] EMPLOYEE
SKILL CODE		C [of] SKILL
PRIMARY SKILL		C [of] SKILL [of] EMPLOYEE * PRIMARY
BIRTHDATE		D [of] BIRTH [of] EMPLOYEE
	or	D [of] EMPLOYEE * BIRTH
ACTUAL SALARY		$ [of] SALARY [of] EMPLOYEE * ACTUAL / YEAR
QUANTITY		Q [of] POSITION / ORGANIZATION-UNIT / JOBCODE
REPORTS TO		# [of] ORGANIZATION-UNIT * PARENT [of] ORGANIZATION-UNIT
SECONDARY SKILLS		ARRAY [of] C [of] SKILL [of] EMPLOYEE * SECONDARY

15.5.6 Data Dictionary Management Systems (DDMS)

A data dictionary management system (DDMS) is a software package (or set of system utilities) used to create and maintain a data dictionary, and to provide query and report output from a data dictionary. If the data dictionary is defined as another database, then the DBMS serves as the DDMS, too. A data dictionary system built with a DBMS becomes a set of DDL statements to define the dictionary and a set of predefined reports.

Examples of the types of reports typically provided by a DDMS include the following:

- Listing of all data items within each defined record type (or report, display screen, program, etc.) along with (selected) other characteristics of those data items.
- Alphabetical listing of data item names, indicating where each data item appears (in records, transactions, reports, display screens, and userschemas) or is used (programs).
- Key-Word-In-Context (KWIC) listing of data item names (see sidebox).
- Listing of users and the data items (or reports, input source documents, etc.) received by or owned/controlled by each user.

With all of the cross reference information in a comprehensive data dictionary, the variety of reports is endless. This points out the importance of using a general-purpose report writer and allowing ad hoc retrieval of information from the data dictionary.

KWIC Index of Data Item Names

```
                              *ACTUAL SALARY
                              *AUTHORIZED SALARY
                              *BIRTH DATE
                              *BUDGET
                 EMPLOYEE JOB *CODE
                 POSITION JOB *CODE
                        SKILL *CODE
                        BIRTH *DATE
                        SKILL *DESCRIPTION
                              *EMPLOYEE NAME
                              *EMPLOYEE NUMBER
                              *EMPLOYEE JOB CODE
                     EMPLOYEE *JOB CODE
                     POSITION *JOB CODE
                     EMPLOYEE *NAME
          ORGANIZATIONAL UNIT *NAME
                     EMPLOYEE *NUMBER
          ORGANIZATIONAL UNIT *NUMBER
                       PARENT *ORGANIZATIONAL UNIT
                              *ORGANIZATIONAL UNIT NAME
                              *ORGANIZATIONAL UNIT NUMBER
                              *PARENT ORGANIZATIONAL UNIT
                              *POSITION JOB CODE
                              *POSITION TITLE
                              *PRIMARY SKILL
                              *QUANTITY
                       ACTUAL *SALARY
                   AUTHORIZED *SALARY
                      PRIMARY *SKILL
                              *SKILL CODE
                              *SKILL DESCRIPTION
                     POSITION *TITLE
       PARENT ORGANIZATIONAL *UNIT
             ORGANIZATIONAL *UNIT NAME
             ORGANIZATIONAL *UNIT NUMBER
```

The following is a list of features and capabilities which might be found in a data dictionary system:

- Stands alone or requires the use of a particular DBMS.
- Is *active*, that is, the data dictionary is referenced during execution of the DBMS and associated user processes, particularly during data update. With an active dictionary, there is at least the potential of enforcing definitional and validation criteria on the stored data. The alternative is a *passive* dictionary which is not referenced during execution of the DBMS and user access to the database. A passive dictionary can mislead users into believing that, because the data is defined a certain way, those definitional characteristics will be enforced on the stored data.
- Permits the description of other entity types—programs, application systems, reports, transactions, userschemas, and users, in addition to data objects (items, groups, records, files).
- Allows online browsing through the data dictionary.
- Produces output reports providing various indexes and cross reference listings to the descriptions of selected objects in the database system environment.
- Provides security features to control access to the data dictionary.
- Generates its own skeleton entries in the data dictionary from pre-existing definitions in COBOL or one or more DBMSs. Other information could then be added to the entries in the data dictionary.
- Generates the stored database schema definition (or DDL statements) for one or more existing DBMSs (and perhaps a COBOL Data Division or the DECLARE statements for PL/I programs). DDMSs which stand alone and operate independently of any particular DBMS should have a schema generation facility, otherwise the database administrator is responsible for ensuring the consistency of definitions in the database schema and the data dictionary.
- Generates test data for debugging programs which will interface with the stored database.

A review of the above capabilities indicates that it would be very desirable to use a comprehensive DBMS (with powerful reporting capabilities) to establish and maintain the data dictionary.

A selected list of commercially available data dictionary systems is given in Appendix 15A.

15.6 DBMS PERFORMANCE MONITORING AND USAGE STATISTICS

Monitoring the performance of the DBMS and operations on the database by gathering usage statistics is essential to improved performance and enhanced availability. DBMS performance monitoring is part of the broader context of systems performance monitoring.

Performance monitoring and evaluation should be directed toward specific objectives. The objective might be to improve a poor response time to particular types of user requests, or to project the growth in storage space utilization. Expression of the objectives will determine the data to be gathered during system operation.

For example, performance and usage statistics can be used to signal the need to reorganize and perhaps revise the database structure in order to balance the tradeoff between update and retrieval performance. By collecting usage statistics, the system is able to detect and adjust to changing usage patterns either under the initiation and control of the DBA or automatically. For another example, user response time statistics may be used to counter or support user claims of a poor level of service.

Many factors can be monitored and the variety of statistics which can be gathered is unlimited. The DBA will gather statistics on particular aspects of performance that are of interest. Since the act of gathering statistics results in some degradation of performance, it should be possible to turn the monitoring function on and off with respect to selected statistics.

15.6.1 Monitoring Sizes in the Stored Database

Database sizing information can be useful for a variety of purposes. The following information provides a static profile of a stored database.

- Number of different files or record types.
- Size of each file, measured in blocks.
- Number of record instances in a file.
- Distribution of records sizes for a file with variable length records.
- Proportion of logically deleted records, which can indicate when it is time to run a utility to reclaim the unused storage space.
- Number of unique values for each data item.
- Range of data item value sizes, perhaps a frequency distribution of the length of values for a data item, or even the distribution of actual values (useful in setting up value codes for a data item).
- Number of indexed data items and the size of each index.
- The degree to which a search mechanism (ISAM or other indexing scheme, or hashing algorithm) is out of balance.
- Distribution of the number of occurrences of one record type (or nested repeating group) which is related to another record type.
- Number of orphaned records in a defined, non-exhaustive relationship with another record type.

Monitoring changes in this information over time provides trends which can be useful in projecting future needs for physical storage space and additional secondary storage devices. Some systems require a prior declaration of space to be allocated for each file. As the actual file size begins to fill up the allocated space, the system may cease to operate efficiently. Some systems even fail to operate properly when the actual file size exceeds the allocated space. In this case, it becomes very important to monitor changes in file size and send warning messages to the user or DBA when the allocated space is nearly full.

15.6.2 Monitoring Dynamic Activity

Besides profiling the database for sizes and monitoring for trends in those sizes, it is desirable to monitor the activity against the database and the DBMS.

Size is generally a major determinant of the time it takes to perform particular operations in a database environment. However, the access method can also have a substantial influence on response time. Direct addressing through the use of a hash addressing algorithm is the fastest way to retrieve individual records. If properly set up, the time to access a record is independent of file size. At the other extreme, scanning a whole file to access individual records (or a selected subset of records) will perform in time which is directly proportional to file size, that is, the number of records in the file. In between are a variety of indexing schemes, which, if properly set up and "balanced," will perform a record search in time which is proportional to the log (base 2) of the number of records in the file.*

Though external accessing schemes, such as indexing and hash addressing, can yield much faster access, they must also be maintained and updated when records are inserted, deleted, or modified. If there are periods of substantially more update activity than retrieval activity on the file, it may be desirable to suspend index updating (or destroy the indexes and recreate them later) during the update activity. Since the benefit of faster access using indexes is offset by the cost of maintaining them, statistics on the frequency of use of each index should be gathered.

For the online user at a terminal, the performance of the system will be a function of the terminal, the speed of the communication links, the number of other active terminals, the teleprocessing monitor, the operating system, the secondary storage device, the file access methods, and finally, the DBMS. Nevertheless, the performance of the DBMS may be a major determinant of the overall performance experienced by the end user.

With respect to the direct interface to the DBMS, the following types of statistics may be collected for each "call" to the system [adapted from Krinos, 1973]:

- Elapsed time from call to response.
- Type of function requested—control, retrieval, update.
- CPU time.
- Number of disk accesses.
- Disk input-output time.
- Name(s) of the file(s) accessed.
- Identification of the calling program.
- Identification of the user.
- Identification of error type if an abnormal condition is encountered.

Each time an index is accessed, the following types of statistics may be collected:

- Name of the index (or the indexed data item/s).
- Value criteria used to search the index.

Having gathered these statistics, they can be used to calculate averages and trends. For example, for each type of transaction, summary statistics could be calculated for

---

* To appreciate the difference, assume a file of 50,000 records. Using a sequential scan to find a record would require the system to examine 25,000 records on the average. Using a balanced index search (which simulates a binary search) the system would have to examine ($\log_2 50,000 =$) 16 records on the average— substantially fewer than 25,000!

frequency of occurrence, average number of disk accesses, and average CPU time to process. It can be useful to calculate the average time from call to return for control requests, retrieval, and modification requests, and to know the relative frequency of occurrence of each type of request. Statistics on the usage of data items and indexes for selection are useful to determine which items should be indexed and which need not be indexed to balance the performance between retrieval and update requests.

Krinos [1973] was one of the first published articles to report performance statistics relating specifically to DBMS. In his system, all accesses to the database must be made through the DBMS which accounted for 60% of all CPU activity. The average time from call to return was 5.6 seconds. Retrieval requests took an average of 5.9 seconds to satisfy and accounted for 55% of the demand, whereas modification requests took an average of 13.2 seconds to satisfy and accounted for 8% of the demand. Thus Krinos concluded that the database structure and organization offered a reasonable balance between retrieval and modification performance. Since improving the performance of the DBMS depends upon gathering statistics, more attempts like that of Krinos must be made and published so that the industry can improve the level of service to the using environment. Such published data could also provide some benchmarks for comparison.

The database administrator may also need to monitor the binding of program data structures (userschemas) and the actual structure of the database (schema) to determine the occurrences of binding errors and the frequency and types of mappings between userschemas and the schema.

15.6.3 Logging Activity on an Audit Trail

Besides internal monitoring and gathering of statistics, some information relating to database operations will be recorded on the *audit trail*. The term audit trail comes from accounting and refers to the ability to retrace the steps through the system and reconstruct the sequence of events that occurred. The audit trail is actually a chronological record of events that happened in the system. The events recorded on the audit trail can serve different people responsible for the system and its operation. For the database administrator it may be the means for monitoring such things as potential breaches of privacy and the occurrence of errors. In some cases, it can be used as the vehicle for backup and gathering statistics. The raw data of an audit trail usually needs to be summarized and analyzed before it can be a meaningful basis for action. There is no limit to the uses for an audit trail. It is another important tool available to database administrators to better carry out their responsibilities.

15.7 ORGANIZATIONAL RESPONSE TO A DATABASE ADMINISTRATION ROLE

Definitions of the role of database administrator have appeared in the literature over the last several years. Several companies today have or have had a position called database administrator. Few have created a full-fledged database administrator with the authority required to fully discharge the responsibility. A growing number of firms do have someone they are quick to point to when asked, but upon further investigation, it is often a glorified input-output control clerk or the supervisor of many such clerks, or a narrow technical person responsible for physical data definition and maintenance. Perhaps the DBA is responsible for the existence but not the content of the database. These are certainly parts of the responsibility of a database administrator, but not all.

Any detailed discussion of the database administrator role at this time is speculative and should be considered tentative until tested in several organizational environments. Organizations with the willingness to experiment are needed now, to take these various statements of the database administrator role, postulate a job description, and appoint someone to operate in that role. Several organizations need to experiment so the industry can begin iterating toward an effective role definition and organizational arrangement. For many of the proposed database administration functions, organizations will be using ad hoc methods for some years to come. Hopefully, some organizations will have the courage to experiment so that formal procedures and automatic tools can evolve from the ad hoc methods.

Once some corporate experience has been realized from these experiments, it needs to be studied and reported so that the industry can begin to establish some guidelines in developing organizational arrangements for the corporate database administration function.

Some organizations have had and now discontinued the position of database administrator. In most cases, the incumbent was not successful due to lack of authority, too technical an orientation, too low down in the organization to have any visibility, poor people skills, or an inability to negotiate compromise out of conflict. As long as there are shared data resources, there will be a need for the role of database administrator, or what has come to be called the information resource manager.

SUMMARY

Acquiring a DBMS is not sufficient for successful data management. The role of database administrator provides the human focus of responsibility to make it all happen. The DBA role may be filled by one person or several persons.

Whenever people share the use of a common resource such as data, the potential for conflict exists. The database administrator role is fundamentally a people-oriented function—to mediate the conflicts and seek compromise for the global good of the organization.

Within an organization, database administration generally begins as a support function within the systems development unit. Sometimes it is in a technical support unit associated with operations. Eventually, it should be separate from both development and operations, residing in a collection of support functions reporting directly to the director of information systems. Such a position has some stature, some independence, and can work directly with users to capture their data requirements. Database administration works with development, operations, and users to coordinate the response to data needs. The database administrator is the key link in establishing and maintaining management and user confidence in the database and in the system facilities which make it available and control its integrity.

While the 'doing' of database system design and development can be decentralized to several development projects in the Data Processing Department or the user organizations, planning and control of database development should be centralized. In this way an organization can provide more consistent and coherent information to successively higher levels of management.

The functions associated with the role of database administration include:

- Definition, creation, revision, and retirement of data formally collected and stored within a shared corporate database.
- Making the database available to the using environment through tools such as a DBMS and related query languages and report writers.
- Informing and advising users on the data resources currently available, the proper interpretation of the data, and the use of the availability tools. This includes educational materials, training sessions, participation on projects, and special assistance.
- Maintaining database integrity including existence control (backup and recovery), definition control, quality control, update control, concurrency control, and access control.
- Monitor and improve operations and performance, and maintain an audit trail of database activities.

The data dictionary is one of the more important tools for the database administrator. It is used to maintain information relating to the various resources used in information systems (hence sometimes called an information resource dictionary)—data, input transactions, output reports, programs, application systems, and users. It can:

- Assist the process of systems analysis and design.
- Provide a more complete definition of the data stored in the database (than is maintained by the DBMS).
- Enable an organization to assess the impact of a suggested change within the information system or the database.
- Help in establishing and maintaining standards, for example, of data names.
- Facilitate human communication through more complete and accurate documentation.

Several data dictionary software packages are commercially available.

The DBA should also have tools to monitor the performance of the database system to indicate the need for reorganization or revision of the database.

EXERCISES

15-1. Discuss the human-oriented and technical dimensions of database administration. Which one should dominate?

15-2. Historically, many organizations acquired a DBMS before establishing the position of database administrator. Why might this have happened? Is this a good practice? Explain the advantages of reversing the sequence. What are the costs of reversing the sequence?

15-3. Give an example of the process of sharing, conflict, mediation, and compromise.

15-4. Argue to the Vice President of Information Systems why there should be a database administration function.

15-5. Describe two or three ways in which the position of DBA might evolve and grow to greater levels of authority within the information systems organization.

15-6. Why should database administration be organizationally independent of systems development and operations, and have an equal level of authority?

15-7. How does database administration differ from job administration or systems administration? What activities force them to interact with one another?

15-8. What are the different levels of interaction and communication between database administration and the end user community (outside of data processing)?

15-9. Identify five major functions of database administration.

15-10. List some of the areas of responsibility which could be assigned to a database administrator.

15-11. What is it that a DBA does that would require a high level of skill in dealing with people?

15-12. If you were a newly appointed DBA in an organization which never had one before (and several people within the information systems organization are not sure there is really a need for one!) what would you try to accomplish first?

'5-13. Discuss the difficult task of maintaining a high quality of data and how the role of database administration can achieve this goal?

15-14. How do the functions of database administration support the database approach discussed in Chapter 6? How do specific DBA activities relate to the conceptual model of a DBMS?

15-15. What is likely to be the most difficult job of a database administrator in a large corporation?

15-16. Suppose you were writing a 'position available' advertisement for a database administrator. What qualifications would you state? During the interview, what personality traits would you look for?

15-17. Looking at the job of a database administrator, what might be the likely entry points into an organization and the career path to DBA?

15-18. As the DBA staff grows and the use of high-level DBMS tools increases, some have suggested that the need for systems and programming personnel decreases. Why might this be so? Is it likely? Where would people with such talents go?

15-19. What are some of the purposes of a data dictionary?

15-20. A data dictionary contains information on what types of entities? What information is common across all these entities?

15-21. What information on data items would often be found in a data dictionary but not likely found in a DBMS?

15-22. Carefully review the seven suggested rules for forming abbreviations to be used in naming data items. Are there any with which you would disagree? Explain. What other rules might you add?

15-23. What do you identify as the advantages and disadvantages of the 'OF-language.'

15-24. Try to obtain the manual for a data dictionary software package and compare its features with those discussed in the text.

SELECTED REFERENCES

ALLEN, Frank W., Mary E. LOOMIS, M. V. MANNINO, "The Integrated Dictionary/Directory System," *Computing Surveys* (14:2), June 1982, pages 245-286, 40 refs.
   A compehensive article based on a detailed survey of several commercial dictionary/directory systems.

BERRISFORD, Thomas R. and James C. WETHERBE, "Heuristic Development: A Redesign of Systems Design," *MIS Quarterly* (3:1), 1979 March, pages 11-20.

BRATHWAITE, Kenmore S., "Resolution of Conflicts in Data Ownership and Sharing in a Corporate Environment," *Data Base* (15:1), 1983 Fall, pages 37-42.

Suggests a corporate data ownership philosophy, a model for data sharing, and a user group to arbitrate and mediate in data sharing conflicts. Resulting benefits can be greater control over the data resource, increased auditability of the data, and a reduction in the number of systems developed mainly to get around problems created by the user's inability to access data from the corporate database.

British Computer Society, "Data Dictionary Systems Working Party Report," *Data Base* (9:2), 1977 Fall, and *SIGMOD Record* (9:4), 1977 December, pages 2-24.

CAHILL, John J., "A Dictionary/Directory Method for Building a Common MIS Data Base," *Journal of Systems Management* (21:11), 1970 November, pages 23-29.

Discusses the IBM approach to building and using a data dictionary system.

CANNING, Richard G., "The 'Data Administrator' Function," *EDP Analyzer* (10:11), 1972 November, 14 pages.

CARLSON, Eric D., editor, "Database Administration, Selected Papers from the Database Week Conference, San Jose, 1983 May," in *Data Base* (15:1), 1983 Fall.

CARTER, Breck, "On Choosing Identifiers," *ACM SIGPLAN Notices* (17:5), 1982 May, page 54.

Presents a very practical set of guidelines for data naming conventions.

CODASYL, British Computer Society, "Data Base Administration Working Group, June 1975 Report," London, England.

CODASYL Systems Committee, *Feature Analysis of Generalized Data Base Management Systems*, New York: ACM, 1971 May.

Contains a chapter on the role and responsibilities of the database administrator.

CURTICE, Robert, "Data Dictionaries: An Assessment of Current Practice and Problems," *Proceedings 7th International Conference on Very Large Databases*, New York, NY: ACM, 1981.

CURTICE, R. and E. DIEKMAN, "A Survey of Data Dictionaries," *Datamation* (27:3), 1981 March, pages 135-158.

DEARNLEY, P., "Monitoring Database System Performance," *The Computer Journal* (21:1), 1978.

Diebold Research Program, *Organizing for Data Base Management*, New York: The Diebold Group, Inc., Document Number S16, 1971 December, 94 pages.

DURELL, William R., *Data Administration: A Practical Guide to Successful Data Management*, New York: McGraw-Hill, 1985, 203 pages, 10 refs.

Very practical discussion of approaches to the many tasks of data administration with concrete examples and solutions. Since a data dictionary is considered the essential tool for data administration, much of the book focuses on the nature and use of a data dictionary. Extended discussion of data naming standards. A whole chapter on selling DBA in your organization.

GUIDE, "Establishing the Data Administration Function," Chicago, IL: Guide International, 1977.

KAHN, Beverly K., and Eunice W. LUMSDEN, "A User-Oriented Framework for Data Dictionary Systems," *Data Base* (15:1), 1983 Fall, pages 28-36, 34 refs.

Presents a framework for selecting a data dictionary package based upon the needs and environment of the organization, rather than on an idealized feature list. Identifies four operational control activities of data administration:

- Control systems maintenance and documentation.
- Enforce systems and programming standards.
- Enforce control of integrity and security of corporate data.
- Aid in systems analysis and design.

KRINOS, John D., "Interaction Statistics from a Database Management System," *AFIPS National Computer Conference Proceedings*, 1973, pages 283-290.

LEFKOVITS, Henry C., *Data Dictionary Systems*, Wellesley, MA: Q.E.D. Information Sciences, Inc., 1976.

    Begins with an introductory discussion of data dictionary systems and their features, then describes six commercially available systems (Lexicon, CINCOM TOTAL Data Dictionary, IBM DB/DC Data Dictionary, DataManager, Data Catalogue, and UCC TEN), and ends with a critical and comparative evaluation and a look to the future of data dictionary systems.

LEONG-HONG, Belkis W. and Beatrice MARRON, *Technical Profile of Seven Data Element Dictionary/ Directory Systems*, Washington, DC: U. S. National Bureau of Standards, Special Publication 500-3, 1977 February, 45 pages.

    The seven: Data Catalogue, DD/D (IBM), Total Dictionary, DataManager, Lexicon, UCC TEN, and IBM's DB/DC Data Dictionary.

LEONG-HONG, Belkis W. and Bernard K. PLAGMAN, *Data Dictionary/Directory Systems: Administration, Implementation, and Usage*, New York: John Wiley & Sons, 1982, 328 pages

LONG, Larry E., *Design and Strategy for Corporate Information Services*, Prentice-Hall, 1982.

LYON, John K., *The Database Administrator*, New York: John Wiley & Sons, 1976, 170 pages.

    The first book to be published on database administration. Focuses on the design of network (CODASYL) structured databases. Cursory treatment of organization and functions of database administration.

MARTIN, James, *Managing the Data-base Environment*, Englewood Cliffs, NJ: Prentice-Hall, 1983.

McCRIRICK, Ian B. and Robert C. GOLDSTEIN, "What do Data Administrators Really do?" *Datamation* (26:8), 1980 August, pages 131-134.

    Surveyed 555 large computer users in Canada in both the public and private sectors. Of those, 253 responded and 71 claimed to have data administration functions—only 28%. They tended to be in the larger, older organizations with more mature data processing departments. The database administrators with a computer science background outnumbered those with a business background by 2:1 implying that most were primarily techicians. 80% of the organizations with DBA had five or fewer employees. 70% said less than 25% of the data resources were shared. 93% had a DBMS, 20% had two, and 65% had a data dictionary. 70% said the DBMS came before the DBA.

McEWEN, Hazel E., editor, *Management of Data Elements in Information Processing*, Proceedings of a Symposium Sponsored by the American National Standards Institute and by the National Bureau of Standards, Washington, DC: U.S. National Bureau of Standards, 1974 April, 490 pages, (available from NTIS).

    A wide-ranging collection of papers on the management and standardization of data items, names, and value codes in several application areas. A rich resource book.

National Bureau of Standards, "Prospectus for Data Dictionary System Standard," Washington, DC: NBS Special Publication 80-2115, 1980.

NOLAN, Richard L., editor, *Managing the Data Resource Function*, St. Paul, MN: West Publishing Co., 1974, 394 pages.

    A collection of 20 readings relating to the broader information systems organization, which Nolan prefers to call the 'data resource function,' thus recognizing the centrality of data in the activities of an MIS organization.

PATTERSON, Albert C., "Data Base Hazards," *Datamation*, 1972 July, pages 48-50.

    A very readable piece still relevant today. Out of his own experiences, the author discusses comparing the costs in money and talent with the expected benefits to the organization before leaping into DBMS. Organizational politics and resistance will initially preclude any large scale data sharing and data integration.

PLAGMAN, Bernard K. and Gene P. ALTSHULER, "A Data Dictionary/Directory System within the Context of an Integrated Corporate Data Base," *AFIPS Fall Joint Computer Conference Proceedings* (Volume 41), 1972, pages 1133-1140.
Motivated by the use of a DBMS with a skeleton database definition and by the needs of a large organization, the authors describe the central importance of a repository of "data about data," called the Data Dictionary/Directory, which is then available to the users, the database administrator, and to the database management system. With such a facility, the organization might even be able to become independent of its DBMS! The authors then describe the design objectives, functional requirements, information content, and implementation of a Data Dictionary/Directory system.

ROSS, Ronald, *Data Dictionaries and Data Administration*, New York, NY: AMACOM, 1981.

ROSS, Steven, "Who is the Data Security Officer?" *Bank Administration* (vol. 58), 1982 October, pages 52-58.
Reports on a survey of the new role of data security officer in banks—their backgrounds and experiences. Suggests that data security will move away from a technical data processing function to a "professional" role in the organization.

SCHUSSEL, George, "The Role of the Data Dictionary," *Datamation* (23:6), 1977 June, pages 129-142.
A practical discussion of what a data dictionary is and should be, what it can do for an organization, and a listing of eight major commercially available systems.

TILLMAN, George D., "Data Administration versus Data Base Administration—There is a Difference," *InfoSystems* (31:), 1984 February, pages 98-102.
Discusses a widely held distinction within database administration. The DBA uses technical expertise to install, monitor, and maintain the DBMS and related software products such as the data dictionary. The DA is a broader role with a management focus. The DA works with end users and provides non-software services to the organization—determining information needs, logical database design, setting policy on database use, and setting standards for database design, database-related programs and procedures, documentation, and data naming conventions.

UHROWCZIK, P. P., "Data Dictionary/Directories," *IBM Systems Journal* (12:4), 1973, pages 332-350.
Provides a comprehensive discussion of a Data Dictionary/Directory system, its nature, objectives, and capabilities, including its use by users, administrators, and the database management system. The author views a DD/D system as the single repository of *all* data about data, its storage, and its use. It also contains descriptions of transactions, programs, and application systems within a database environment.

VAN DUYN, Julia, *Developing a Data Dictionary System*, Englewood Cliffs, NJ: Prentice-Hall, 1982, 204 pages.
A step-by-step guide for an organization to develop their own data dictionary. Includes a comparison of some software packages and the criteria for selecting one. Contains several examples.

WEBER, Ron and Gordon C. EVEREST, "Database Administration: Functional, Organizational, & Control Perspectives," *EDPACS* (6:7), 1979 January, pages 1-10, 4 refs.

WELDON, Jay-Louise, *Data Base Administration*, New York: Plenum Press, 1981, 250 pages.
Presents the general findings from several surveys of data processing organizations and their organization and practice of database administration. Quite broad based in describing functions, organization, and staffing. Short chapters arranged by database organization, planning, design, operation and control, and managing the user interface. Includes a brief survey of ten data dictionary systems.

WITHINGTON, Frederic G., *The Organization of the Data Processing Function*, New York: Wiley-Interscience, 1972, pages 57-67.

COMMERCIALLY AVAILABLE DATA DICTIONARY SYSTEMS

A selected list of commercially available data dictionary systems is given below along with a brief description of each. The purpose of this appendix is to give some idea of the features and limitations of commercially available data dictionary products. For more detail see the comparative tables at the end of Allen, Loomis, and Mannino [1982]. Note that these systems are experiencing continual evolution and enhancement of capabilities (or may be withdrawn from the market). Therefore, a prospective user should seek the latest information.

SYSTEM NAME VENDOR NAME LOCATION	BRIEF DESCRIPTION
ADABAS Data Dictionary Software ag Reston, Virginia	Requires ADABAS; passive; generates schema definitions for ADABAS; approximately 1000 users.
Application Management System (AMS) TRES Computer Systems Dallas, Texas	Does not require the use of a DBMS; provides more facilities than data dictionary—program generation from decision tables, extensive system documentation, monitoring and performance statistics.
Data Catalogue 2 TSI International San Jose, California (formerly Synergetics, Bedford, Mass.)	Does not require the use of a DBMS; generates data definitions for IMS, TOTAL, ADABAS, DMS 1100, DM IV, MARK IV, COBOL, and PL/I; Approximately 250 users; free form input to describe programs and systems as well as data; general browsing and interrogation facilities with indexes and cross reference reports.

SYSTEM NAME VENDOR NAME LOCATION	BRIEF DESCRIPTION
Data Dictionary (DDS) Sperry Corp (UNIVAC) St. Paul, Minnesota	Requires the use of DMS 1100 and generates schema definitions for DMS 1100.
Datadictionary Applied Data Research Princeton, New Jersey	Requires the use of DATACOM/DB; generates schema definition for DATACOM; active dictionary for DATAQUERY.
DataManager Management Systems and Programming, Ltd. London, England Lexington, Massachusetts	Does not require the use of a DBMS; generates data definitions for several DBMS's and programming languages; approximately 600 users; can describe wide range of data structures as well as systems and programs; can define extensive data validation and access controls; comprehensive retrieval and reporting capabilities.
DB/DC Data Dictionary International Business Machines	Requires the use of IMS; generates IMS data definitions and userschemas; can also define system objects; very limited definition of data integrity controls; extensive and complicated output reports generated online or in batch mode.
EDICT Infodata Systems	Operates independently of a DBMS or uses INQUIRE; generates an INQUIRE schema definition; approximately 150 users.
Integrated Data Dictionary (IDD) Cullinet Corp. Westwood, Massachusetts	Requires the use of IDMS; active dictionary supplies schema definitions for IDMS.
Integrated Data Dictionary (IDD) Intel (formerly MRI) Austin, Texas	Requires the use of SYSTEM 2000; supports the definition of SYSTEM 2000 databases (and conventional files), userschemas, schemas, programs, and reports; produces standard reports on interrelationships between entities, "what if" modification impact reports, plus tailored reports using SYSTEM 2000 output languages.
Lexicon Arthur Anderson & Co.	Does not require the use of a DBMS; generates data definition for IMS, TOTAL, IDMS, and several programming languages; describes broad set of data structures as well as programs and systems; extensive edit and validation controls; provides query language and various output reports.
PRIDE-Logik M. Bryce & Associates New York	Part of the PRIDE system development methodology; does not require the use of a DBMS; generates schema definitions for IDS II, IMS, COBOL, and PL/I; approximately 300 users.
TIS Directory Cincom Systems, Cincinnati, Ohio	Requires the use of TOTAL DBMS; supports the definition of TOTAL databases and conventional files excluding data items; can also define transactions, reports, users, programs, and systems; limited security on the dictionary information; produces a set of standard output reports.
UCC TEN University Computing Co. Dallas, Texas	Requires the use of IMS and only generates data definitions for IMS and for COBOL or PL/I programs; limited definition of data integrity controls; flexible reporting capability.

SIXTEEN

DATA PRIVACY
AND FAIR INFORMATION PRACTICES

16.1	PRIVACY AND PERSONAL DATA	624
16.1.1	Growing Public Concern	624
16.1.2	Role of Computer Technology	626
16.1.3	Emergence of Laws	626
16.2	THE THREE BASIC RIGHTS	628
16.2.1	Personal Privacy	628
16.2.2	Personal Access and Due Process	629
16.2.3	Public Access	630
16.2.4	Conflict—None of These Rights Are Absolute	631
16.2.5	Government-Held versus Privately Held Personal Data	632
16.2.6	Personal versus Nonpersonal Data	633
16.3	ORGANIZATIONS, INDIVIDUALS, AND PERSONAL DATA	633
16.3.1	Primary Disclosure	635
16.3.2	Limiting Intrusiveness in Data Collection	635
16.3.3	Importance of Purpose in the "Contract"	635
16.3.4	Selective Disclosure	636
16.3.5	Secondary Disclosure	636
16.3.6	Need for Additional Data from Third Parties	637
16.3.7	Data as a Surrogate for the Individual	637
16.3.8	Individual Access to Personal Data	638
16.3.9	Data Retirement: Shaking One's Past	639
16.3.10	Fallacy of Statistical Databanks; Research Data	639
16.4	LEGISLATIVE APPROACHES TO FAIR INFORMATION PRACTICES	640
16.4.1	The Need for Legislation	640
16.4.2	Scope of Legislation—The Need for Uniformity	642
16.4.3	Typical Provisions of Fair Information Practices Laws	645
	Rights of Data Subjects; Responsibilities of Data Handlers;	
	Enforcement, Penalties, and Remedies	
16.4.4	Some Inappropriate Solutions	652
16.5	ORGANIZATIONAL RESPONSE	653
16.5.1	Assign Responsibility	655
16.5.2	Principles Must Permeate Systems Development and Operations	656
16.5.3	Notice, Personal Access, and Dispute	657
16.5.4	Control Dissemination to Third Parties or for Other Uses	660
16.5.5	System Implemented Data Integrity and Audit Trail	661
16.5.6	Implementation Strategy: A Call to Creative Action	663
	SUMMARY	664
	EXERCISES	665
	SELECTED REFERENCES	667

Discussing the functions of database management assumes that an organization would naturally want to implement features to improve accessibility, data integrity, data quality, and access controls. That has not always been the case. While such features may be good for an organization, they also carry costs of implementation. An organization may decide that implementation costs exceed benefits to the organization.

Besides those within an organization, other parties have an interest in the policies and practices of data management—other organizations, universities and research institutions, government, the general public including the press, and private individuals. Their concern may relate to records retention and destruction, accuracy, accessibility, access control, backup, and logging sources and uses of data. In many cases, an organization will behave with these outside interests in mind—as long as it is relatively easy and inexpensive to do so.

Sometimes the outside party has sufficient standing that the organization will want to respond to their wishes. A government can require an organization to do certain things (such as record keeping for tax purposes, or providing information to public stockholders).

While there are several external impacts on database administration, this chapter focuses on the basic rights underlying the notion of data privacy, reviews legislative approaches to embody principles of data privacy and due process, and explores organizational responses to these principles.

When the data pertains to individuals, an organization has some added responsibilities with respect to the collection and dissemination of personal data. The basic rights have always existed. Increased public concern has led to legislation which embodies these rights and places additional responsibilities on organizations which maintain files of personal data.

16.1 PRIVACY AND PERSONAL DATA

Growing public concern over the new computer technology and the potential (sometimes actual) abuse of individual rights has led to the emergence of laws to protect those rights and to circumscribe the behavior of organizations and government agencies which collect personal data.

16.1.1 Growing Public Concern

One area of substantial ignorance, and growing abuse, is in the collection and use of personal data on individuals. This is true in both the public sector (government) and the private sector (business and industry). Such organizations usually set up records containing personal data and then behave as though they were the only party with an interest in that data. Concern for data quality, access control, and use often takes a back seat to the admittedly difficult task of getting computer systems to run correctly at all. Nevertheless, individuals on whom data is collected, whether by private businesses or governmental agencies, do have a substantial interest in what happens to "their" data.

Figure 16-1. **"Really Now, This Fuss the Americans Make About Computers and Privacy."**

Some people ask, "Why all the Fuss?" The British Younger Commission Report (1972) essentially said there was no problem (prompting the cartoon in Figure 16-1) and that present laws in Britain were adequate. But there is a real problem.

The mood of the people is one of increasing concern as frustration grows and as abuses increase, and more people experience or hear first hand about abuses. Problems encountered include:

- Denial of access to data pertaining to oneself.
- Inability to discover the sources of adverse data.
- Inability to have data corrected.
- Continued dissemination of incomplete, old, or erroneous data.
- Use of data for secondary purposes without the person's knowledge or consent.
- Inability to exercise control over disclosure of personal data to third parties.

A 1983 Harris opinion poll found that the American people are greatly concerned about threats to their personal privacy—77% of the respondents expressed concern, up from 64% five years earlier which was doubled from 10 years earlier. In 1971 a joint *TIME* Magazine and AFIPS survey found 38% of Americans felt that computers represented a real threat to people's privacy. Similarly, a 1972 Canadian survey found one-third of the people felt that computers threatened their personal privacy. In the short span of a decade, public concern has increased dramatically. This concern is pervasive throughout society and the world.

16.1.2 Role of Computer Technology

One factor contributing greatly to this rise of concern is the increasing use of computers for data processing. The computer permits greater efficiency, more data gathering, faster retrieval selectively and remotely, and cross referencing of files. With computers, organizations are able to do much more with one's data, including wider sharing and dissemination. This all raises the specter of privacy invasions with a system which people don't even know about, let alone have any control over.

Computers *per se* do not invade privacy—people do. In their zeal to use computers for improved responsiveness and efficiency, governmental and business organizations have generally ignored the potential for harm. They have responded to an irresistible temptation to use the technology in support of pressing social problems; to consolidate data and circulate it to all appropriate agencies in both the public and private sectors. People who develop, operate, or use computers can inadvertently or knowingly invade one's personal privacy. Computers simply change the economics of threats and abuses. Computers shape *how* people can invade privacy by breaking down the traditional barriers of inefficiency.

Fortunately, the computer also affords greater ability to protect privacy, to limit access to authorized users, to deny unauthorized disclosure, and to maintain higher standards of data quality.

Even though computers change the complexion of the problem, they have not changed the problem. The basic rights and responsibilities existed and were violated before the computer. With its greater potential for harm, the computer has added a profound sense of urgency to reaffirm those basic rights.

Society needs countermeasures—both legal and technical—to protect the human rights of individuals. Protective measures are now seen in laws. They must be carried out in the administrative procedures and technical safeguards implemented by organizations maintaining personal data.

16.1.3 Emergence of Laws

Public officials and elected representatives reflect this mood of concern. States and countries around the world conducted studies and governmental hearings which led to new laws during the 1970's.

1970	Data Protection Act, State of Hesse, West Germany; world's first law to specifically regulate government's automated data systems.
1970	U.S. Fair Credit Reporting Act (PL91-508); applies only to credit reporting agencies.
1972	Younger Commission Report; Great Britain.
1972	*Privacy and Computers*, Joint task force report of Department of Communication and Department of Justice, Canada.
1973	Data Law, Sweden; requiring all data banks in both government and private sectors to be licensed.
1973	U.S. Department of Health, Education, and Welfare; study and report on Automated Personal Data Systems.

1974	Privacy Act, Minnesota (Sec 15.16); first omnibus, public sector, privacy law in the United States.
1974	Privacy Act, United States (PL93-579), relating to personal data held by the federal government.
1974	Family Educational Rights and Privacy Act (FERPA), United States; relating to personal data held by educational institutions.
1977	Report of the U.S. Privacy Protection Study Commission.
1978	Right to Financial Privacy Act, United States (PL95-630); relating to personal data held by financial institutions.
1978	Human Rights Act, Canada.
1980	U.S. Privacy Protection Act (PL96-440); placing controls on government search and seizure of documents.
1980	OECD Guidelines Governing the Protection of Privacy and Transborder Flows of Personal Data, Paris.
1980	Uniform Fair Information Practices Act, United States.

So far, privacy laws have been enacted in over a dozen states in the U.S., and in Germany, France, Austria, Norway, Switzerland, Canada, and New South Wales (Australia), with others, undoubtedly, since this book was published.

Some people have even passed a constitutional amendment, such as that in South Carolina:

> The right of the people to be secure from unreasonable invasions of privacy shall not be violated.

Similarly, the United Nations includes individual privacy in their Declaration of Human Rights. Unfortunately, such statements provide little guidance to organizations seeking to develop specific policies and procedures for handling personal data. Guidance depends upon future uncertain court decisions to define the limits of actions which violate an individual's right to privacy.

The earlier term of "data privacy" is giving way to the term "information practices." In 1980 the National Conference of Commissioners on Uniform State Laws (Chicago) adopted the Uniform Information Practices Code, recommending adoption by the states of the U.S. The new label recognizes that legislative concerns relate to:

- Data privacy.
- Individual right to due process.
- Rights of personal and public access.
- Intrusiveness in data collection practices.
- Fairness in an organization's dealings with individuals.
- Standards in the operation and security of personal data systems.

The main purpose and rationale for such laws is *to establish the basis for an open, honest, and fair relationship between organizations and individuals* on whom data is collected, maintained, and used. Disclosure of data to others must be considered in the light of this relationship.

People are concerned; laws are being enacted, often in direct response to abuses and organizational shortsightedness (or irresponsibility). There will be more and they will get tougher. Some organizations are under the jurisdiction of one (or more) laws now; for others, legislation is pending. Data privacy issues can no longer be ignored by organizations collecting, maintaining, and using personal data.

What are those issues? What are the principles and what actions should an organization take in response? An examination of the various laws reveals considerable commonality. Whether or not an organization presently faces a privacy or fair information practices law, principles of behavior are emerging. There still remains the difficult task of working out the details of *how* to comply most effectively and economically. Any responsible organization must creatively seek ways to be responsive to the principles embodied in the new fair information practices laws. These principles and their impact on organizations provide the focus for the remainder of this chapter.

16.2 THE THREE BASIC RIGHTS

The central motivator behind the heightened public concern is the inability of individuals to control the circulation of information relating to themselves. This is the heart of data privacy, but let's start with the notion of privacy.

Privacy as a separate right was first enunciated eloquently and profoundly in a paper by Warren and Brandeis [1890] as the right to be let alone. Privacy is the freedom from unwarranted intrusion upon oneself, into one's private affairs, home, family, and relationships. The common law right of privacy extends to the person (physically and psychically) and the space (territory and property) around the person. The 1939 Restatement of the Law of Torts included violation of privacy as a new tort: a person who unreasonably and seriously interferes with another's interest in not having his affairs known to others or his likeness exhibited to the public is liable to the other.

The notion of *data privacy* extends the right of privacy from individuals to *data about* individuals. It derives from the assumption that all information about a person *belongs*, in a fundamental way, to that person, *regardless of who possesses that information*. Misuse or abuse of personal data can violate the privacy rights of individuals.

Three basic rights underlie a comprehensive information policy regarding personal data: personal privacy, personal access, and public access. All privacy laws or fair information practices codes seek to embody these three basic rights.

16.2.1 Personal Privacy

Personal privacy is the right to determine what information about oneself shall be communicated to other persons and for what purposes. This makes it necessary for a holder of someone else's personal data to guard against inadvertent or unauthorized disclosure to unauthorized *persons* or for unauthorized *purposes*.

Until the advent of privacy laws, the individual to whom the data pertains had no control over how that data was used. Holders were free to do as they wished with personal data, without regard for the privacy or due process rights of the individual. The U.S. Constitution is silent on the subject of privacy. Some argue that a right to privacy was so obvious that it was overlooked. The U.S. Supreme Court moved one step closer with an opinion in 1965:

> "Various guarantees create zones of privacy. The right of association contained in the penumbra of the First Amendment is one. The Third Amendment in its prohibition against the quartering of soldiers 'in any house' in time of peace without the consent of the owner, is another facet of that security. The Fourth Amendment explicitly affirms the 'right of the people to be secure in their persons, houses, papers and effects, against unreasonable searches and seizures.' The Fifth Amendment in its self-incrimination clause enables the citizen to create a zone of privacy which the government may not force him to surrender to his detriment. The Ninth Amendment provides: 'The enumeration in the Constitution, of certain rights, shall not be construed to deny or disparage others retained by the people.'" [Griswold v. Connecticut, 381 U.S. 497 (1965), 484.]

The constitutional roots for a right of privacy are even more tenuous regarding data privacy. Examining the Fourth Amendment, we have torts of assault on persons, trespass on houses, and theft on effects, but none relating to "papers." By separating papers from effects, the original framers of the Constitution must have had more in mind than just the physical papers—perhaps the information on the papers!

The weak constitutional and judicial support for a right of privacy relating to one's personal data made it necessary to clearly establish such a right by statute. That was accomplished in 1974 in the U.S. and has been accomplished in several other countries.

16.2.2 Personal Access and Due Process

The right of personal access is the right of an individual:

- To know that a record of their personal data exists or is to be created.
- To know and have interpreted the contents of their data record.
- To dispute that data and have it amended if it is inaccurate or incomplete.
- To know the sources and disclosures of their personal data.

The right of personal access is rooted in the principle of *due process*. For personal data held by the federal government or by a state government, this principle is expressed in the Fifth and Fourteenth Amendments to the U.S. Constitution, respectively: "No person shall be deprived of life, liberty, or property, without due process of law." The due process clause affords protection against arbitrary and unfair procedures in judicial or administrative proceedings (before the government) which could affect the personal and property rights of a citizen. Note that there are no constitutional roots for a right of personal access when personal data is held in the private sector.

Due process takes place in three steps:

1. Timely and adequate *notice* of a hearing or trial and of charges against an accused.
2. A fair *hearing* before an impartial judge or jury to present evidence in one's own behalf and to challenge the accuser.
3. Presumed innocent until proven guilty by *legally-obtained evidence* with the verdict supported by the evidence presented.

The first step is the foundation upon which to begin exercising one's rights. Adverse data floating around about you is implicitly a charge against you. Whether or not it's true, you must first know about it before you can take further steps to protect your individual rights, and request a hearing. How can one face their accuser without access to the data which is the basis for the accusation?

16.2.3 Public Access

A strong democratic society depends upon the free flow of information and the public right to know. A right of public access is needed to:

- Maintain the health, safety, and national security of society.
- Monitor and evaluate the activities of government, to hold elected officials accountable to the people.
- Perform research, transfer technology, make better decisions regarding the use of resources and carry out activities in an increasingly complex society.

While there are no constitutional roots, the right of public access finds expression in:

- The First Amendment freedom of the press (note that this is freedom of *output* for the press, not freedom of *input*, i.e., not access to anything the press wants).
- Recent freedom of information laws or public records laws allowing private access to government held data.
- Certain acts, such as the National Labor Relations Act, which provide for private access to data held in the private sector.
- Certain other acts, such as the Bank Secrecy Act of 1970 [PL.91-508] and criminal justice laws, which provide for government access to data held in the private sector.

With regard to personal data, public access means access by anyone other than the individual to whom the data pertains. This clearly stands in conflict with the right of personal privacy. The right of public access to government held data was clearly established with passage of the U.S. Freedom of Information Act in 1966 [section 552, USC] (most states have similar laws). Prior to this the relative inaccessibility and decentralized nature of government data, and bureaucratic reluctance to disclose data to outsiders afforded a measure of privacy to personal data. The 1966 act coupled with the use of computers quickly opened up government data and called for countervailing protections of personal data. Since 1974 both rights have been stated in U.S. law with the balance often tipping in favor of disclosure. To illustrate a confusion, most people view the Freedom of Information Act as the appropriate vehicle for obtaining access to their *own* data—failing to recognize a key intent of the 1974 Privacy Act to assert a right of personal access.

Prior to the Freedom of Information Act, requesters had to have an "interest" in the data stemming from their position or intended use. Unfortunately, disclosure now is to *anyone* for *any purpose*, and the person to whom the data pertains has no right to be informed of the disclosure. An agency can decide unilaterally, without hearing from the individual, to disclose personal data or may determine that disclosure would constitute a "clearly unwarranted invasion of personal privacy" and deny a third party request.

16.2.4 Conflict—None of These Rights Are Absolute

An inherent conflict exists between privacy and access. Three distinct areas of conflict relate to:

* Personal access to data supplied by another person.
* Public access.
* Personal access to sensitive information about oneself.

When one person provides a recommendation or evaluation of another person's character, performance, or works, *not* disclosing the source and content of the statement to the individual to whom it pertains violates their right to due process. The statements may be misleading, half truths, or outright lies. Neighbors may give adverse information to a private investigator simply because they dislike you. An individual is, in effect, charged guilty without an opportunity of a hearing to defend oneself.

On the other hand, to reveal the source of the statement violates the evaluator's or informant's right to privacy. An appropriate compromise is to reveal the information content but not the source (which only works if the source cannot be inferred from the information). Some argue that bland (or no) statements would result from a practice of revealing sources, undermining the whole evaluation process. One obvious solution is for the evaluator to voluntarily provide the subject with a copy of the evaluation, thus giving the evaluated person an opportunity to "face their accuser." Unfortunately, not everyone is mature enough to risk such exposure.

Soliciting a letter of recommendation can produce an interesting conflict of interest. Consider the case of a job applicant. The prospective boss requests a letter of recommendation from the applicant's current boss. For a good worker, the current boss is tempted to provide a poor recommendation so as to be less likely to lose the employee. Conversely, the current boss might write a favorable recommendation in an effort to get rid of a poor worker. A word of advice: do not rely on or seek data from anyone who has an interest in the outcome stemming from the use of that data. Likewise, refuse to give information when faced with such a conflict of interest.

Adoption provides a further example of the conflict between individual privacy and access. Most societies consider adoption to be permanent and legally prohibit the adoption agency from revealing the identity of the adoptive parents to the natural parents or the identity of the natural parents to the adopted child. When the adopted child reaches maturity a disinterested party, such as the government, could reveal such identities providing that all three parties give their informed consent. Giving access to one party can invade the privacy of another. Therefore, an intermediary must obtain agreement from all interested parties.

The second area of conflict is between personal access and the mental health and stability of an individual unable to act in his or her own best interests. This is of particular concern regarding medical data, especially psychiatric records. Access to such information may be destructive to the individual. A qualified, trained professional must judge whether and the extent to which information should be disclosed to the individual. It is common practice to permit access only with the permission of a doctor and then often only in the presence of the doctor who can provide appropriate explanation and interpretation of the information or test results.

A clear public interest in access to personal data may override an individual right of privacy.

- Law enforcement officials gather all sorts of personal data in seeking to protect the public from criminal elements.
- A doctor who diagnoses a serious communicable disease (especially venereal disease) is expected, and in some states required, to report it to public health officials. They can then determine the magnitude and perhaps control the spread of the disease by locating, isolating, and treating infected individuals.
- An automobile manufacturer should have access to government files of registered owners to provide notice of safety-related defects in a recall campaign.
- Increasingly, elected and appointed public officials must give up some individual privacy as a condition of the job.
- The media persistently penetrates into the private lives of celebrities (sports figures, entertainers, etc.) claiming an insatiable public interest in their lives, activities, and thoughts.

In these examples of public access, the information is often obtained from organizations or individuals other than the individual to whom the data pertains.

As a general rule, all access to personal data should seek to balance the individual right of privacy with the other interests stemming from the disclosure. This balancing should consider:

- *Consequences* of invasion—potential economic loss, deprivation, or mental anguish to the individual.
- *Motive* for the disclosure—benefit to the individual, some social good, or malicious destruction.
- *Method* of access—secret, misrepresentation, or illegal and whether or not the individual is notified and gives their permission.

16.2.5 Government-Held versus Privately Held Personal Data

Personal data held in the private sector is generally considered private unless there is an overwhelming public interest in its disclosure (or a self-interest in the possessing organization). In this case access to the public (government, media, other organizations or individuals) should be carefully circumscribed so as to preserve the right of personal privacy. In the U.S., government access to personal data in financial institutions is controlled by the 1978 Right to Financial Privacy Act which requires a copy of the subpoena for personal data to be simultaneously served on the individual to whom the data pertains. The financial institution is then required to delay two weeks before delivering the data. Of course, there are exceptions if the advance notice would jeopardize a criminal investigation, national security, or human life. This law is still the exception. In many areas and in most countries, the government can compel disclosure of personal data without regard for any rights of the individual to whom the data pertains.

Just the opposite is true in the public sector. Personal data held by a government is considered freely accessible to the public unless it would constitute "a clearly unwarranted invasion of personal privacy." While it is desirable to hold private organizations accountable to society, it is essential to a free democratic society that the government be held accountable to the people. This is best accomplished by free access to information about governmental activities.

The problem with freedom of information laws which embody the principle of public access to government-held data is that they fail to give adequate recognition to the right of privacy in personal data. At least the law should state each right with equal force.

Our society is entering a new era of respect for the individual which includes governmental respect for data pertaining to individuals. Nothing is absolute—not public access to government-held data nor privacy of the individual. Yes, the public needs a free flow of information to monitor the activities of government, but we also need to respect the privacy and due process rights of individuals where personal data is involved.

16.2.6 Personal versus Nonpersonal Data

The discussion so far relates only to personal data, that is, data which pertains to specific, identifiable individuals rather than to things or organizations. Examples of nonpersonal data include elevator inspection certificates, oil well pumping figures, product evaluations, a register of lakes and bridges, and weather statistics. For such data no individual right of privacy or personal access exists because there is no identifiable individual to whom the data pertains. Also, if it is impossible to retrieve data on identifiable individuals even though the database contains personal data, it is the same as nonpersonal data (however, be aware of the possibility of statistical inferencing, see section 14.5). Thus, the right of public access dominates for government-held data. In the private sector, the desire to protect proprietary or competitive interests dominates because, again, there are no individual rights at issue.

16.3 ORGANIZATIONS, INDIVIDUALS, AND PERSONAL DATA

This section explores the relationship between individuals and organizations, and examines the flows of data relating to the conduct of affairs in that relationship. Figure 16-2 depicts various aspects of the record-keeping relationship between individuals and organizations. Several concepts emerge in this section: limiting data collection, selective disclosure, purpose of disclosure and the implied contract, primary versus secondary disclosure of third party sources, data as a surrogate for the individual, personal access, and shaking one's past.

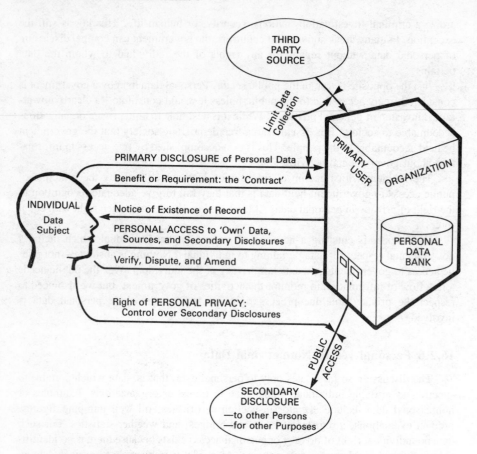

Figure 16-2. The Record Keeping Relationship Between Individuals and Organizations.

This figure portrays various aspects of an open and fair relationship between individuals and organizations maintaining personal data banks. The arrows generally show flow of data. The individual makes a primary or direct disclosure of personal data to obtain some benefit in goods or services or to meet some legal requirement. The intended recipient and 'authorized' user are part of the 'contract.' Since organizations often require supporting evidence from third parties and sometimes establish personal data records wthout direct involvement of the data subject, individuals need notice that a record for them exists, and they need to be able to access and amend 'their' data. Secondary disclosures allow public access by other persons or for other purposes, which could also be within the organization maintaining the personal data. Secondary disclosures are made in the person's interest, that is, for the direct benefit of the individual data subject, or in the public interest, to protect or benefit society. The data subject has an interest in knowing the sources and secondary disclosures of personal data. Individuals should have control over secondary disclosures when there is no overriding public interest in such disclosure.

In 1977 the U.S. Privacy Protection Study Commission published a most substantive and informative report relating to personal privacy. "The Commission's findings clearly reveal an overwhelming imbalance in the record-keeping relationship between an individual and an organization, and its policy recommendations aim at strengthening the ability of the individual to participate in that relationship" [page 30].

16.3.1 Primary Disclosure

In dealing with organizations, individuals necessarily disclose *some* information about themselves. Personal data exists because a person chooses to be somewhere, to do something, or to give information to another party. Primary disclosure emanates firsthand from an individual.

In order for individuals and organizations to conduct their affairs adequately and honestly, selected personal data must be divulged to selected persons or organizations. For example, a lender or employer must obtain data from a prospective borrower or employee. For another example, it was not too many decades ago that women would go to a medical doctor, refuse to disrobe, and expect the doctor to make an accurate diagnosis of their problem. As citizens, we expect our government to perform certain duties, yet we often hear complaints when the government tries to gather the data required to satisfactorily execute its responsibilities, as in a periodic population census.

16.3.2 Limiting Intrusiveness in Data Collection

It is unrealistic to suggest prohibitions on the collection of data on individuals. At the same time, we need limits on the degree to which an organization can intrude into the lives of individuals in their data collection practices. Organizations should only collect information needed to facilitate their relationship with the individual or to responsibly carry out their publicly mandated purposes and programs.

16.3.3 Importance of Purpose in the "Contract"

An individual usually reveals personal data in exchange for some consideration. The disclosure is part of a transaction to obtain goods or services, or a legal requirement of the government. Some *purpose* is always present in disclosing some data to someone else. There is an implied, if not explicit, *contract* between the person revealing the data and the person or organization using it. The emerging theory of social exchange suggests a balance of obligations between parties to the exchange. The primary disclosure is assumed to be made for a specific set of uses implied by the "contract."

In some transactions involving personal data, an individual may refuse disclosure thereby foregoing the benefit being sought. In other transactions, such as income tax and census, the individual is legally required to disclose personal data. In any situation, the individual should be able to know the consequences of refusing disclosure.

Unfortunately, not all parties who have access to privileged information, use it for the purpose originally intended. We hear of the clerk who used personal information to provide contacts for selling insurance on the side, the phone company that gives out the details of your long distance phone calls, the credit card company that keeps sending you "special merchandise" offers, or the membership list used to solicit unrelated charitable contributions. The primary recipient can turn around and misuse the personal data; use always encompasses the possibility of abuse.

The sensitivity of personal data to invade privacy may be dependent upon its use. Efforts to establish a sensitivity classification on data without regard for use are in vain. The association of address and phone number is innocuous enough, but that may be all a thief needs to make a phone call before breaking in to a home. People should have the choice of not having their address and phone number appear together in phone books, employee directories, membership lists, etc. Data may be considered private in one context and not in another.

16.3.4 Selective Disclosure

The term "private" generally means not public, secluded, secret, withheld from public view, or unknown to the public. Traditionally, law and the courts have interpreted privacy as all-or-nothing. Wishing to keep something private, a person must not reveal it to *anyone*. Disclosure to someone else, however limited (except for privileged communications), assumes you no longer desire privacy of the matter, and opens it up to the world, unlimited and forever.

Today, such a notion is unrealistic. Under the principle of selective disclosure, giving information to selected parties does not automatically mean that it is available thereafter to anyone for any purpose. Individuals rightly assume the existence of a middle ground between being wholly private and wholly public.

16.3.5 Secondary Disclosure

After a primary disclosure of personal data, an individual has a continuing interest in what happens to the data—an interest in controlling its subsequent disclosure and use. Any disclosure or use beyond that which was originally intended may be considered an invasion of privacy; a breach of contract. The recipient of primary disclosures, anticipating any secondary disclosures or uses, should advise individuals at the time of primary disclosure or later obtain their consent before the secondary disclosure takes place. In certain cases, an individual may consent to secondary disclosures but retain the right to receive notice (but not to control) each instance of secondary disclosure.

The basic right of personal privacy means that the individual has control over secondary disclosures and uses of personal data. It means that there is a middle ground in which selective and limited disclosure can take place.

By analogy, corporations control trade secrets by formal contract. When making a primary disclosure for which they desire to limit secondary disclosures, a corporation may require the recipient of the trade secret to sign a nondisclosure agreement specifying the conditions under which the secret can and cannot be used.

The law in many states and countries already recognizes areas of *privileged communication* where an individual retains absolute control over secondary disclosures. These rights are recognized in such relationships as:

attorney	—	client
doctor	—	patient
accountant	—	client
priest	—	penitent
husband	—	wife

In these cases, the communication is protected as though known only by the individual. The attorney, doctor, etc., cannot legally be compelled to disclose any information received from the client, patient, etc. without the consent of the individual. Of course, the privilege does not hold when illegal acts or grave danger to the public are involved.

When making a primary disclosure, individuals have some control over their personal data and the uses made of it. Once a person's data gets into an organization's records, they often have little or no opportunity to verify (and correct) that information, or control its subsequent uses. After several secondary disclosures, such opportunity virtually disappears.

The primary recipient of personal data who makes a secondary disclosure should know the secondary recipient's intended use for the data, and perhaps receive written certification. Also, disclosure to third parties should be limited to that which is requested or required, even if it would be easier to deliver a copy of the whole record. The secondary recipient must also be held responsible if personal confidential data is obtained under false pretenses.

16.3.6 Need for Additional Data from Third Parties

From the standpoint of the recipient of the primary disclosure, the data obtained from the individual may be inadequate for making a decision. A lender must have confidence that the ability of the borrower to pay back exceeds some minimum threshold of risk. When the borrower is unknown, the lender must gather more information about the borrower in order to raise his confidence level above the threshold. The lender will go to third parties to obtain additional personal data on the individual. Such data may have been obtained by some other organization directly from the individual; from a general pool of data on many individuals and intended to serve any potential creditor or lender; by surveillance of the individual; or from present or former friends, neighbors, and employers.

An organization seeking to engage in a relationship with an individual cannot be expected to rely solely on the information obtained directly from the individual. Most people will only divulge that which places them in the best light. Everyone is prone to exaggerate, bend the facts, tell half the story, and some even lie, if it appears to be in their own best interest. When dealing with individuals some organizations (credit, employers, insurers, government) will go to great lengths to seek out any adverse data on an individual. Finding none corroborates the "good" information they may have received directly from the individual. However, "bad" data which is old, incomplete, inaccurate, misleading, or irrelevant can harm an individual. Of course, the whole truth, whether good or bad, should be brought to bear on the dealings with an individual, assuming it is pertinent to the relationship.

16.3.7 Data as a Surrogate for the Individual

Many important relationships which individuals have with organizations today are based upon records—credit, insurance, medical care, employment, education, and social services. Each requires individuals to divulge information about themselves.

This, coupled with increasing reliance on data from third parties, usually leads to some evaluation or judgment regarding the individual.

As organizations get larger and more complex, they must substitute personal data for face to face contact with individuals. The data becomes a surrogate for the individual. Decisions greatly affecting individual lives are made daily with increasing, sometimes exclusive, reliance on *data* about the individual. The judgment may matter much to the individual but too often they have no substantial or procedural protection. The law often ignores the strong interest individuals have in records about themselves.

As records continue to supplant firsthand contact, there has been no compensating tendency in organizations or in law to give individuals the same control over the collection, use, and dissemination of personal data as they would normally have in face to face contacts. In personal relationships, people choose how much of themselves to reveal depending on their degree of trust in the recipient. Many organizations today have squandered that trust, resulting in widespread public distrust of our institutions, businesses, and government.

16.3.8 Individual Access to Personal Data

As individuals become increasingly separated from their data, as data becomes the predominant basis for decisions affecting those individuals, and as more data comes from third parties, it becomes imperative that the individuals have access to data about themselves. The data may be old, incomplete, misleading, or just plain inaccurate. Changed circumstances may render the data misleading. Without access to their own data, the individuals may be adversely affected or implicitly charged guilty on the basis of false or misleading evidence. The result might be no credit, no job, or denial of services. Therefore, it is important that the individuals have access to data about themselves to verify its accuracy, completeness, and the context of its understanding, and to defend themselves.

A similar situation may ensue when the individuals do not come into direct contact with the person or organization making a decision affecting them. They may not even know that a decision is being made. The decision may be based on data obtained through surveillance—involuntary disclosure. Such data is often incomplete, misleading, and hearsay. The individuals should receive notice of the existence of data about them. Only in this way can they know to access the data and verify its quality.

Having access to personal data, an individual may find it to be inaccurate and will therefore seek to have it corrected, updated, or deleted. In addition, the individual may want to know the source of the data. If the holder of the personal data refuses to respond, the individual must be able to have a hearing at which both sides of the dispute are presented before an impartial judge.

Responding to an individual's interest in their data also means that an organization will at least allow an individual to know who has received information from their record and for what purpose. Sometimes this would only be appropriate for information disclosed outside the organization or for non-routine uses. Furthermore, when there is no compelling public interest, disclosure to other persons or for other purposes than originally intended should not take place without the consent of the individual.

16.3.9 Data Retirement: Shaking One's Past

One danger with widespread automated personal data systems is that individuals find it increasingly difficult to shake their past. The efficiency and capacity of computers make it easier to remember past information. In fact, most organizations find it easier to simply keep records that have been generated, thus avoiding the risk of not having the information when it might be needed in the future. It is much harder to selectively retire records.

No one really wants to live in a world where every facet of their life becomes a subject of organizational data recording. Yet organizations feel compelled to gather more personal data for greater efficiency and to make better decisions.

Our society lives with a paradox: For whatever a man sows, that he will also reap [Galatians 6:7 (RSV)]. On the other hand, people should be able to have the slate wiped clean and make a fresh start. Increased organizational data collection and retention is moving us toward more "remembering" and less "forgiving."

There is precedence for releasing individuals from their past. Bankruptcy laws permit a fresh start economically, by forgiving past debts. Our laws often include the notion of a statute of limitations in which legal action cannot be taken after a specified period of time. Christianity carries the promise of forgiveness of sins to those who truly repent (turn away) from their past ways. Most governments follow a practice of sealing records of juvenile offenders after a period of no further offenses. "With the advent of systematic record-keeping, a man needs the chance, which a businessman has, to go into economic bankruptcy and obtain a discharge from the past."* People do hope for a tolerant forgiveness to overlook past sins, errors, and foolishness. To ignore the Christian notion of forgiveness and redemption would ultimately destroy life and society.

Organizations should not blindly assume that people can't, don't, and won't change. Specific mechanisms are needed to discount the value of old data; to retire and purge data which is no longer needed. Past misdeeds never forgotten are effectively never forgiven. "Systematic 'forgetting' of peoples' pasts, even when troublesome from the standpoint of bureaucratic efficiency, may reflect a social value of considerable importance."†

16.3.10 Fallacy of Statistical Databanks; Research Data

Personal data is not always collected and maintained to make administrative decisions regarding particular individuals. Sometimes personal data is used for research or management purposes requiring only statistically aggregated data. Where personal data serves both needs, it is desirable to allow broader access to statistical summaries than to individual records.

Some people have argued that allowing only statistical results to be obtained from

---

*Senator Sam J. Ervin, Jr., "The First Amendment: A Living Thought in the Computer Age," *Columbia Human Rights Law Review* (4:1), 1972 Winter, p. 42.

†James B. Rule, *et al.*, *The Politics of Privacy*, Westport, CT: Greenwood Press, 1980.

a collection of individual personal records poses no threat to personal privacy. The discussion of section 14.5 on statistical inferencing illustrates how personal facts can be obtained or closely approximated from a data bank allowing only aggregated output.

An alternative strategy for protecting personal privacy is to aggregate the data *before* it is entered, storing only statistical summary data. Of course this would be unacceptable if administrative decisions had to be made on particular individuals or if a researcher desired to perform follow-up (longitudinal) studies on individual data subjects.

Research and program evaluation depends upon the free flow of data from individuals. When a primary disclosure of personal data may result in a threat to personal privacy through secondary disclosures, individuals are more reluctant to respond to survey questions. Researchers must adopt rigorous procedures to ensure that collected data about individuals are kept strictly confidential and are not used for purposes other than originally intended or in any way that permits identification of individuals.

Even following the best security safeguards a researcher cannot, in fact, guarantee the confidentiality of personal data. In most countries, there is no legal basis for refusing to reveal information subpoenaed by the courts or the government or others in the process of discovery, that is, searching for evidence in a legal suit. Some have suggested establishing a legal basis for protecting researchers and the confidential data they collect.* If researchers are really serious about protecting individual privacy of the respondents, they must physically destroy the collected data as soon as it is no longer needed (something most researchers are loath to do).

16.4 LEGISLATIVE APPROACHES TO FAIR INFORMATION PRACTICES

Actual or potential abuses of the principles of fair information practices has led to legislation. This section explores the need for legislation, the possible scope of legislation, typical provisions, and some inappropriate approaches to legislation.

16.4.1 The Need for Legislation

Perhaps the first question to ask is why we need legislation at all. Are not the technical and administrative measures available to an organization sufficient? Technical measures include system mechanisms such as access control, identification, authorization, monitoring, and encryption. Administrative protection measures include physical security and isolation, personnel screening, standard operating procedures, and insurance.

Technical and administrative measures chiefly provide on-the-scene regulation and control. They come into play at the moment of request or attempted intrusion to permit

---

*See Committee on Federal Agency Evaluation Research, Alice M. Rivlin, Chairman, *Protecting Individual Privacy in Evaluation Research,* Washington, DC: National Academy of Sciences, 1975.

access only to those who have been previously authorized. Using technical measures, a system can be made as secure as management wants, and is willing to pay for. Very high levels of data integrity can be very expensive and can degrade performance efficiency. This discourages implementation of technical and administrative measures.

Most abuses of personal data involve insiders—persons within the organization who have an inherent right to access the data as part of their normal duties. Examples include the policeman who gives information on arrest records to requesting employers or the tax preparer who sells your income data to local merchants. While most people may be sincere in their desire to protect personal data from misuse, some can be fooled by an imposter who says one thing but does something else with the data, and others can be bribed. Technical measures can never stop an authorized person from making or being party to unauthorized use of personal data. Hence the need for legislation.

Legal measures are needed to deter before the fact and provide remedies after the fact of breach of an individual's rights of privacy and due process. Access control and data quality control are administrative responsibilities. Management must *choose* to apply the technical measures. Since technical measures are costly, there is a negative economic incentive to implement them. Some managers view the need for privacy protection and the right of access as an organizational nuisance. Sometimes the need for effective technical measures is not even recognized, either by systems designers or managers. Even though information system managers are becoming increasingly aware of the importance of technical measures, some force must be set up to counterbalance the negative economic incentive against the costs of implementing technical measures. Responsible action can be encouraged through legislation which defines the basic rights and responsibilities of individuals, databank operators, and data users, and which incorporates penalties for violations of those rights and responsibilities.

As the cartoon in Figure 16-3 indicates, we need both legal and technical legislation from the legal community and technical and administrative solutions from the data processing community to attack "the privacy problem." With the principles of fair information practices spelled out in the law, technology provides the means of compliance, and the law specifies penalties for noncompliance.

Some industry groups and professional societies argue that they can control their own members by encouraging responsible, ethical behavior. Since the strongest sanction is generally expulsion from membership, such a solution depends upon moral suasion and voluntary compliance. Furthermore, it would be virtually impossible to obtain consistency across industries or professional groups.

The cartoon in Figure 16-4 shows the holder of (computerized) personal data banks promising to make their own unilateral decisions regarding the use of such data. In fact, three years after the cartoon was published, evidence emerged that the U.S. Defense Department was still using the same domestic files of personal surveillance data they had previously promised to destroy. Self-control, whether by individual organizations or by industry groups, is laudable but inadequate. Legislative guidance is still required.

Another reason for legislation is to bring some consistency and assistance in the implementation of data practices. Legislation seeks to set down principles or guidelines regarding the rights and obligations of data subjects, data collectors and holders, and

Figure 16-3. "It Seems to Be Getting Ahead of Us."
   Both the technical/administrative data processing community and the legal community are needed to attack the data privacy problem. Technical and administrative measures provide the means of compliance; legal measures provide penalties for noncompliance. Technical and administrative measures can furnish increasing levels of on-the-scene control at an increasing cost, but they can never stop authorized access. Legal penalties encourage responsible action.

data users. Such guidelines are needed by organizations involved in designing or operating personal data systems, and by those who must adjudicate disputes.

   The extreme opposite of legislation is no legislation. Some would argue that individuals make their own records and should have nothing to hide or fear if they have behaved appropriately. This suggestion assumes that record keeping is a neutral process, that only the truth gets stored, and that all records are objective and can be independently verified. Such assumptions are not always true. The truth can be used, misused, abused, and half-used.

   Again, the primary purpose of "privacy" legislation or a fair code of information practices is to establish an open and fair relationship between individual data subjects, and those who gather, maintain, and use personal data.

16.4.2 Scope of Legislation—The Need for Uniformity

   Specific pieces of legislation may apply rather narrowly or cover a broad segment of society. Some laws are targeted at specific abuses in specific industries, such as the 1970 U.S. Fair Credit Reporting Act. Some laws cover all agencies of the government

Figure 16-4. "Don't Worry, We Won't Use Him Again Unless We Decide It's Necessary."
Even though many would argue that self-control is important to achieving more open, honest, and fair information practices, it can never guarantee compliance. Some organizations will simply not be moved to respond to the principles of fair information practices without laws and regulations that apply penalties for noncompliance. In fact, three years after this cartoon was published, that very same databank emerged again, apparently being used for some questionable purposes.

or all segments of the private sector. Such legislation is called omnibus legislation. The U.S. has one omnibus "privacy" statute which applies to all federal government agencies.

In the U.S. it has been easier and perhaps more appropriate to pass legislation aimed at the public sector first. That represents the government, in effect, taking a look at itself and seeking to put its own house in order before extending rules to the private sector, where they would be met with greater resistance. The public sector also poses the larger potential threat due to their ability to compel disclosure coupled with the power of enforcement. The Privacy Act of 1974 is an omnibus law which applies uniformly to all federal government agencies.

In covering the private sector, the trend in the U.S. has been to seek legislation which focuses on specific sectors or industries. While specific legislation was proposed for insurance, medical, personnel, and research records, only the 1978 Right to Financial Privacy Act has passed, covering financial institutions. With a policy of minimizing government regulation of the private sector, subsequent U.S. administrations have not actively sought further legislation covering other areas of record keeping.

Several individual states have passed omnibus, public sector laws covering the executive branches of government, and perhaps even the legislative and judicial branches (though less common). Narrowly defined or applied state laws proliferate in such areas as: criminal history records, education records, medical records, personnel records, insurance records, credit reporting agencies, tax returns, government surveillance, use of social security numbers, public access to government records, and oversight or regulatory commissions.

There are also significant differences at the international level. In contrast to the United States, European countries have tended to:

- Cover only computerized data.
- Include organizations (legal persons) as well as individuals (natural persons) as data subjects whose privacy needs protection.
- Establish a registrar of databanks to oversee compliance.
- Cover both public and private sector organizations with omnibus legislation.

In addition, the European approach to privacy legislation is enmeshed in economic concerns and feelings of nationalism. They fear that some organizations will maintain data banks outside their country, perhaps to avoid obligations and controls imposed by the new laws. Concern for transborder data flows dominated in the late 1970's.

Some observers suggest that economic protectionism is the real basis for many of the laws which are passed under the guise of privacy protection. They believe that Japan, Canada, and a number of European countries passed laws to ward off domination by U.S. computer telecommunications vendors.

The state of New South Wales in Australia has taken a unique approach. Rather than establishing specific legal guidelines, it set up a commission with broad powers to handle the privacy problem. The commission works with individual sectors or industries to draw up mutually acceptable policies and procedures to be followed in their information handling practices. The agreed upon provisions are widely disseminated. In large measure due to the effectiveness of the commission head, this nonadversary approach has achieved greater success than countries with specific laws.

States and countries acting independently are bound to produce laws with different provisions, particularly in the area of privacy where the issues are complex. Individuals face a patchwork of expressed rights depending on the type of organization or the type of personal data held. Faced with nonuniform laws, individuals may have to follow one procedure when dealing with state and local government, another procedure when dealing with federal government agencies, and still many more when dealing with financial institutions, educational institutions, medical institutions, or any other institution. The current multiplicity of laws, and the anticipated further fractionation will present some real problems for individuals wishing to exercise their basic rights of personal privacy, personal access, and public access.

Organizations seeking to comply with privacy-related laws face a bewildering array of rules and regulations—sometimes with directly conflicting provisions. Many organizations conduct their affairs across state boundaries and across international boundaries, perhaps with high speed, computer-to-computer transmission of data. The data may pass through multiple jurisdictions yet be controlled by a single computer system.

Organizations providing equipment, software development, or consulting services, or educational institutions training people to operate data processing functions would also have to be aware of any differences in laws. Legislative differences can occur geographically, across data types, and across areas in the private or public sector.

In 1980 two modest attempts at uniformity emerged. On the international scene, the Organization for Economic Cooperation and Development (OECD, Paris) issued guidelines for individual countries to follow in data privacy protection and resolving international differences.

In the United States, the National Conference of Commissioners on Uniform State Laws (Chicago) adopted a proposed Uniform Information Practices Code to be promulgated among the state legislatures. The suggested Uniform code is quite comprehensive and should be seriously considered by the states in the 1980's.

Fortunately, most legislation in the U.S. has followed the "fair code" approach, rather than alternative approaches.

- *Constitutional amendment*—provides little specific guidance to organizations seeking to establish policies and procedures, and to adjudicators seeking to resolve disputes. They must wait for a (sometimes patchwork) set of judicial decisions to emerge. Such decisions characteristically only chip away at the periphery of the real issues.
- *Enabling legislation*—establishes a regulatory body charged with some mission and given general objectives, guidelines, a scope of jurisdiction, and discovery and enforcement powers. In theory, this approach can be more responsive. Unfortunately, past experience shows that such bodies soon begin to serve those who are regulated more than the public interest they were originally established to protect. Such an approach also leaves the parties without any specific guidance until specific regulations are issued.
- *Specific, detailed laws*—attempt to deal with all possible cases which might arise. Unfortunately, such laws are difficult to write, even more difficult to pass since everyone can find something objectionable in a proposed law, often passed in haste, prone to compromise, and slow to change once passed. Britain tried unsuccessfully for many years to pass this type of legislation.
- *Fair code*—attempts to spell out the rights and responsibilities of data subjects and "dealers" without getting bogged down in detailed laws which apply to specific situations. A fair code approach seeks to lay down fair practices, thus encouraging desirable behavior, and makes undesirable behavior costly. It provides specific and immediate guidance in the formulation of policies and practices, and in the adjudication of disputes.

It is useful to look at the various laws passed in the U.S. and categorize them according to the three basic rights and where the data is held (see Figure 16-5).

16.4.3 Typical Provisions of Fair Information Practices Laws

The typical provisions found in privacy laws or fair information practices laws relate to the rights of data subjects, the responsibilities of data handlers, and enforcement mechanisms for detecting and responding to violations.

	PERSONAL DATA HELD BY AN ORGANIZATION IN:		
	Public Sector		*Private Sector*
BASIC RIGHT:	Federal Government	State & Local Government	Organizations
Personal Privacy	Limited right expressed in PL 93-579 [Omnibus] "Privacy Act of 1974"	Limited right expressed in Omnibus legislation in several states	Limited Federal legislation in selected areas, e.g., PL 95-630, "Right to Financial Privacy Act of 1978"
Personal Access	Due Process Rights of 5th Amendment reflected in PL 93-579	Due Process Rights of 14th Amendment reflected in state privacy laws	Limited Federal legislation in selected areas, e.g., PL 91-508, "Fair Credit Reporting Act," and FERPA
Public Access by Government (federal or state)	Yes, for law enforcement, public health and safety, and national security		Otherwise, in specific areas such as PL 91-508, "Bank Secrecy Act"
by private sector (includes the media)	U.S. Freedom of Information Act (§552, USC)	Similar FOI or Public Records Laws in most states	Some Federal Laws in specific areas, e.g., National Labor Relations Act grants access to UNIONs if there is a grievance

Figure 16-5. Array of U.S. Laws Arranged by Basic Right and Sector Holding the Data.
Various laws are referenced in the figure to shown places where each of the three basic rights is embodied respecting data held in the public and private sectors. One interesting observation: individuals tend to seek access to their data held by the U.S. government via the Freedom of Information Act rather than the due process provisions of the Privacy Act.

SOURCE: Gordon C. Everest, "Nonuniform Privacy Laws: Implications and Attempts at Uniformity," in *Computers and Privacy in the Next Decade*, edited by Lance J. Hoffman, New York: Academic Press, 1980, page 144.

Whatever the specifics of legislation or regulation, it should not restrict the effective operation of legitimate information systems. Such systems are increasingly necessary to enable public institutions and private organizations to perform efficiently and to fulfill their social responsibilities.

Also, legislation should not require organizations to retrofit current computer-based information systems to meet some of the more difficult provisions. Changes are best implemented as systems come up for major revision. Every effort should be made to encourage organizations to infuse the principles of privacy and due process in any redesign or any new system involving the storage and dissemination of personal data.

16.4.3.1 Rights of Data Subjects

Provisions regarding the rights of data subjects relate to notice, access, and dispute procedures.

PUBLIC RECORD

All databanks shall be a matter of public record. This is the first step for people to know about the possible existence of data about themselves. The public record should include the following information:

- Identification of the databank.
- Criteria or circumstances under which a person is likely to be included in the databank.
- Type of data which is stored in it.
- Intended uses and users of the data.
- Sources of the data.
- Name and address of the person responsible for the system and to whom questions, requests for access to data, and disputes may be directed.

This requires some place where people can go to get this information or some place where it is published. The U.S. law requires annual statements to be published by each federal agency in the *Federal Register*. By contrast, the Minnesota statute requires each state and local government agency to compile this information and make it available whenever asked (the law originally required a filing with the state Commissioner of Administration).

NOTICE

There must be some reasonable mechanism whereby individuals are told or become aware that they are the subjects of data in a databank. The notice requirement is obviously met in the case of a primary disclosure. Of greater concern is the compilation of personal data from third parties which will be used to make decisions affecting the individuals. Such notice can be provided upon initial collection of data or when material changes are made to the data; it can include a copy of the personal data, its sources, and recent disclosures of the data. This information may be given unsolicited or upon request. If an organization only provides this information upon request, there must be some mechanism by which individuals receive notice of the existence of a record on them and of their right to request access!

PERSONAL ACCESS

There must be some mechanism for individuals to gain access to data stored about themselves, how it is used (purposes), the sources of the data, and recent disclosures of the data (to whom and for what purpose). This often requires some explanation, particularly if the data is coded. Since individuals and groups can harass an organization or agency with repeated requests, they should be limited to one request every few months (unless there has been a material change in their record). It is also not unreasonable to charge a *nominal* fee for access to one's record to discourage unnecessary requests. Such a fee should not be established to cover the cost of providing access.

PERSONAL PRIVACY

Since individuals have an inherent interest in the data stored about them, they must have the ability to control the purposes for which the data will be used; to limit secondary disclosures to other persons for other purposes. Such disclosures should require their informed consent. If there is an overriding public interest in the disclosure, individuals should at least receive notice that the secondary disclosure did or will take place (including what data, to whom, and for what purpose).

DISPUTE

There must be a way for individuals to correct or update data stored about themselves. If there is compelling reason for the data holder not to modify the data, the individual should at least be able to submit a statement explaining the disagreement. Such a statement would be included with subsequent disclosures of the data in dispute.

16.4.3.2 Responsibilities of Data Handlers

Organizations which receive, store, use, and disseminate personal data have a responsibility to limit collection and disclosure to agreed purposes; to maintain the accuracy, timeliness, and completeness of the stored data; and to maintain an audit trail of sources and disclosures of personal data.

LIMIT DATA COLLECTION

Organizations should limit the data they collect from individuals to that which is required for their purposes, to administer programs, and to maintain the relationship with the individual.

NOTICE OF USES

At the time of collecting data from individuals (primary disclosure), an organization should clearly state the purpose(s) for which the data is collected, how it will be used, who will use it, for how long, etc. This information is particularly important if it is not obvious to the individual; or if usage is by others outside the organization or for other purposes.

REFUSAL CONSEQUENCES

The individual should be told of any legal requirement to disclose certain data, and of the consequences of refusing to supply requested data.

CONTROL DISCLOSURE

Disclosure of data on individuals should be made only to authorized persons and used only for authorized purposes. This requires some mechanism for properly identifying individuals requesting data, whether on themselves or on others. It also requires that recipients (such as employees) be fully informed of the authorized uses and the consequences of misuse.

MAINTAIN DATA QUALITY

An organization has an obligation to ensure that the stored data is accurate, complete, and current as required for fairness in making decisions respecting the data subjects. An excellent way to check the accuracy of the stored data is to send a copy to the individual on whom it pertains! This also satisfies the notice requirement!

AUDIT TRAIL

An organization should keep a record of sources of data so that its accuracy can be checked in the event of a dispute. It should also keep a record of recent disclosures, including what data, to whom and for what purpose, so that corrections can be sent if the data is subsequently found to be inaccurate or in dispute. An audit trail is particularly necessary for external, nonroutine sources and disclosures; it may not be necessary for routine, internal maintenance and dissemination.

RETIRE DATA

When data is no longer pertinent or timely to the purpose(s), it should be retired, that is, destroyed or archived so as to be unavailable for routine use.

16.4.3.3 Enforcement, Penalties, and Remedies

According to the 1983 Harris opinion poll, both the public and leaders had some strong feelings regarding enforcement. By wide margins, they favored federal laws which would:

- Make it a criminal offense for data-collecting organizations to violate personal privacy.
- Require that any data from a computer that might be damaging to people be double-checked before use.
- Impeach public officials who abuse privacy.
- Punish those responsible for computer errors that harm individuals.
- Put companies out of business if they violate privacy by sharing data.
- Set federal regulations on combining a person's data with other information about the same individual.

A fair information practices code may be enforced through the initiative of individual data subjects—self-protection—or by setting up a body to administer and enforce the provisions of the law.

Data privacy demands some different legal constructs than have been used in the past. Seeking redress through the conventional court system can be slow and costly. Furthermore, seeking relief further invades privacy through the normal discovery procedures.

SELF-PROTECTION

Many argue that the main responsibility for protecting individual privacy rights should rest with the individual and not a third party, such as a government agency or an independent tribunal. Individuals take it upon themselves to see that only pertinent data is collected, and to vigorously defend their civil rights of privacy and due process. Individuals would be given certain rights and remedies and would have defined procedures to follow.

This approach has several weaknesses. Many records are invisible to the person. One often learns of their possible existence only after being adversely affected or facing a crisis. Some people are apprehensive about exercising their rights; they do not want confrontation. Furthermore, it takes time and effort to investigate and fight. An individual refusing to disclose information risks giving up something—employment, a loan, insurance, or medical services. If a government is the data collector, the individual may risk loss of services, a fine, or jail.

At a very minimum, individuals need to have some place to go if they have a problem. They need to know what to do when they are refused access to data about themselves, when disputed data is not corrected or a statement is not filed to accompany subsequent disclosures, and when data is not used for authorized purposes or by authorized persons.

PENALTIES

Data is not property. This was an early and is a continuing confusion in judicial decisions. Warren and Brandeis [1890] enunciated an independent right to privacy based, not on property rights, but on human rights. The value of data resides with the user in the *use* of the data, not in the data itself.

Property follows the law of conservation, that is, when it is transferred, the previous owner no longer possesses it and obtains no value from it. Therefore, damages may be assessed based upon replacement cost and financial loss.

Data is not conserved on transfer. A 'loss' is irreversible and forever! Thus, damages based upon costs or economic loss are inappropriate. Data 'theft' or misuse is a crime with a victim; a crime against the person. Invasion of one's privacy through unauthorized disclosure or use is a violation of one's person. Therefore, prevention not remedies must be the primary point of the law.

The law would prescribe criminal penalties, such as a misdemeanor, to violators. Funds can be withheld from organizations or agencies which do not comply with the law. An organization must take affirmative action to inform its employees of the relevant provisions of applicable laws, and of internal policies and procedures to comply with those laws. An organization can take disciplinary action, suspension, or discharge, against any officer or employee who knowingly (and willfully?) violates provisions of the law.

Penalties must be applied equally to the holder/discloser and the recipient/user of personal data. A recipient may obtain data under false pretenses or bribery, for example, by putting on a white smock and walking into a hospital, or by promising to use requested data for one purpose but then using for another.

REMEDIES

An aggrieved individual may take action to compel disclosure of data pertaining to himself or herself, or obtain an injunction to prohibit certain secondary disclosures.

ADMINISTRATIVE, REGULATORY, REVIEW BODY

So far in the U.S., little has been done to set up separate bodies to administer the information practices laws and enforce compliance. This is different from other countries in Europe, Canada, and Australia. European countries have generally set up a registrar of databanks to set standards of conduct, license operators after hearing their justification for a databank, inspect for compliance to the standards and then relicense, enforce individual rights, and investigate complaints. Such mechanisms can be overly intrusive and very costly. They often become seemingly arbitrary and myopic, and become less able to properly weigh the potential threat to individual rights against the social and economic advantage of personal databanks.

A 1978 Harris poll conducted in the U.S. found that 46% of the general public and over 75% of business and government leaders opposed the creation of a National Privacy Protection Agency. However, 81% of the public felt it important to have an independent body or agency to handle complaints about violations of personal privacy by an organization, while a majority of the leaders felt it was not important at all. This indicates a sharp disagreement between the leaders and the public.

A reasonable approach is to provide an administrative mechanism to:

- Disseminate information to individuals about their rights.
- Assist individuals in exercising their rights.
- Handle complaints and mediate disputes.
- Investigate possible violations of fair information practices.
- Assess the impact on personal privacy of new or modified systems.
- Monitor, review, and recommend changes to compliance procedures.
- Assist organizations and agencies in complying with the law.
- Recommend new policies or changes in policy.

Such a mechanism would function as an ombudsman. It could sensitize government agencies, private organizations, and the general public regarding the issues of data privacy, due process, access to data, the abuses which can stem from record keeping practices, and the principles for responsible and fair information practices. It can provide the individual with an avenue of recourse short of the courts. Such a body could have limited discovery powers to gather information when resolving disputes. When this avenue fails, an aggrieved party would have access to the courts.

16.4.4 Some Inappropriate Solutions

In the legal quest for dealing with the 'privacy problem' some inappropriate solutions have been suggested.

FIRST SPECIFY WHAT IS PERSONAL DATA

Such a task would never end and widespread agreement would be impossible.

PROHIBIT DATA COLLECTION

While some data may be needlessly collected, a total ban on data collection ignores the reality of today's society. Some exchange of data is needed to conduct our affairs adequately and honestly. A lender needs data from the borrower. A government needs data to discharge its responsibilities, for example, census data, law enforcement, and defense. The fact that data exists is not the problem per se. Problems more often stem from secondary disclosures.

Going one further step backward, some even suggest eliminating big government, big organizations, and the use of computers. The problem is not solved by eliminating the agents involved; they are here to stay and so is the need for data.

COLLECT DATA ONLY FROM THE DATA SUBJECT

This would only work if people were totally trustworthy to tell the truth, the whole truth, and nothing but the truth. But we don't always tell the whole truth. Therefore, organizations must seek corroborating evidence from third parties.

CLASSIFY CERTAIN DATA AS PERSONAL AND PRIVATE

This usually begins with the premise that all data held by a government is public unless classified as private (the approach taken in Minnesota). Specific pieces of data are then declared as private without regard for how it is to be used. Is one's address and phone number private? Perhaps yes if the recipient plans to call first before burglarizing your home. If I register a list of valuables with the police and the government has not classified such data as private, it follows that the police are obliged to disclose it to any requester. A priori classification is a trap—the government has the impossible task of deciding what data to classify, and the whole thrust of legislation is diverted from the central issues.

PROHIBIT THE USE OF SOCIAL SECURITY NUMBERS

The rationale here is that identification of individuals in and across data files is made easier. It ignores that, for proper database design and unambiguous file references, *some* unique identifier is required. (Of course, it is still wise for an organization to avoid using the Social Security Number as an identifier, if not for a federally mandated purpose.)

PROHIBIT DATA SHARING AND INTEGRATION

This approach would deny one government from sharing data collected by another agency. Such a policy can lead to great inefficiency and thwarts a central advantage of computer technology. Moreover, an individual can tell different stories to different agencies if it suits their self-interest. What about the driver who claims a blind exemption on his income tax return? What about the abandoning father who fails to pay child support but files a sizeable income tax return? Such data sharing *should* be performed by a government . . . *but only if the individual knows in advance that such comparisons will take place.* Due process requires that individuals know the rules of the game in advance. Not to compare such data is to foster the image of a big, blind, blundering bureaucracy.

The primary and proper point of control is on output:

- NOT *what* data to collect.
- NOT *whether* or not to collect data.
- NOT *where or from whom* to collect data.
- NOT how data is *classified.*
- NOT how to *identify* data.
- NOT how to *process* data.

but WHO uses the data . . . PERSONS
and WHY . . . PURPOSES.

16.5 ORGANIZATIONAL RESPONSE

Existing legislation imposes some specific responsibilities on certain organizations which collect and maintain personal data. Even if an organization is not under the direct jurisdiction of some law, there is still a need to be responsive to the spirit of the law. Moreover, it may place an organization in a better position to be compliant with any future laws.

The principles relating to data privacy and embodied in fair information practices codes demand a response from organizations. Many of the provisions actually represent good management practice. They should be seriously considered for implementation by all organizations . . . even without the added stimulus of legislation.

Today, many organizations feel under great pressure to develop new applications

Figure 16-6. "Crush to the Rear of the Bus, Please."

needed by users and to maintain existing application systems in the face of demands for change, sometimes externally imposed. Management often feels that the requirements of privacy legislation just place another burden on the data processing operation with no obvious gains in productivity or economic returns to the organization (see Figure 16-6).

It is precisely because of the heavy demands on data processing that organizations need additional motivation to be responsive to the principles of fair information practices. When resources are limited and demands are high, organizations often place considerations of data privacy and integrity on the back burner—to be implemented in 'phase two' of the project. Retrofitting data integrity mechanisms into an existing system can be very costly. Legislation with penalty provisions can change the economic balance among the choices management faces when deciding how to allocate resources. With legislation and a raised awareness, perhaps more resources will begin to be devoted to concerns of data privacy, data integrity, and the relationship between individuals and their personal data.

Some have argued that the marketplace will produce a change toward greater responsiveness to the principles of fair information practices. If one organization's record keeping and dissemination practices ignore the interests of individuals, let them take their business elsewhere. Such a position is entirely too glib. It is not that easy to go out and get another job, to find another local telephone company, or to move to another state. 'Taking your business elsewhere' may not be possible or practical, especially with a public sector agency.

Organizations must become more responsive in implementing fair information practices. Some organizations will require the external force of legislation. Some organizations have already taken significant initiatives on their own (see, for example, the advertisement from Aetna Life & Casualty, Figure 16-7).

16.5.1 Assign Responsibility

The first step of response is to assign responsibility within the organization. This person or office would be responsible for overall corporate information policy, including fair information practices, data integrity policies, and implementation. Responsibility must be fixed in some person who can be held accountable and who has the authority to commit the organization to act in response to the principles reflected in the laws. Various responsibilities can be assigned to the Database Administrator, others on the information systems staff, or the corporate legal counsel. In fact, the legal staff should play a role in monitoring legislation and overseeing compliance. In the end, the principles of fair information practices must become a charter for the computer professional—for only insiders can effectively enforce the provisions of legislation.

Because these questions worry so many Americans today, Ætna wants to tell you how we are committed to doing business when you come to an Ætna agent or broker for personal insurance:[1]

We'll ask you for the information we need, and no more. We'll tell you what data we're after, how we intend to get it and from whom. If we turn you down, we'll tell you *why.* (And we *won't* turn you down just because someone else has.)

If you think we have misinformation, just ask what we've got. We'll tell you the nature and substance of all underwriting information in your file. (Except medical information which we'll give your doctor.) If you say some part of it is wrong, we'll reinvestigate—and respond.[2]

And we'll go out of our way not to pass on information about you without permission.[3]

By openly discussing our policies on privacy, we hope to encourage action among governmental and private organizations. And to insure this, we support both voluntary and legislative measures as recommended by the federal government's Privacy Protection Study Commission.[4]

Today the burden of proof rests upon business and government to show that we deal fairly and openly with private citizens. Don't underestimate your own influence in helping to protect your personal privacy. Use it as we are trying to use ours.

Ætna
is protecting your privacy.

"**Just one more question for our files, Sir.**"

At what point do corporations' requests for personal information become an unwarranted invasion of our privacy?

How many of the questions they ask (and answers they demand) are really necessary? How much information do they already have about us? Where did they get it? How accurate is it? And how freely do they exchange it among themselves?

[1] When any state law requires us to act differently, naturally, we must comply.
[2] "Respond" means: If we are wrong, we'll correct the error by informing our source and any one else you request who received the misinformation from us in the past two years. If we conclude our information is correct, we'll tell you so. If you ask, we'll even put your disagreement in the record. We'll also distribute that statement of disagreement in the same way as we would correct an error.
[3] Occasionally, sound business reasons dictate exceptions (and we let you know what they are in advance). For example, Ætna will provide information needed by those selling or servicing our policies, for fraud prevention, or when required by law.
[4] The Federal Privacy Act of 1974 which established controls over the federal government's use of personal information, also created the Commission to explore the need for similar restraints on local governments and businesses. Ætna's President, William O. Bailey, served on this commission and the conclusions it arrived at are the basis for Ætna's privacy policy.

Ætna Life & Casualty,
151 Farmington Avenue,
Hartford, CT 06156

Figure 16-7. "Just one more question for our files, Sir."

16.5.2 Principles Must Permeate Systems Development and Operation

The principles of fair information practices must permeate the whole process of systems design, development, and implementation, right from the initial feasibility study. An organization must begin with a plan to effect change toward accomplishing the goal of implementing fair information practices.

FROM OWNER TO STEWARD OF PERSONAL DATA

Who owns the personal data maintained within an organization? If people in an organization really begin to behave as though the personal data in their systems belonged to the individual, some attitudes and practices would change. No holder of personal data should assume an absolute right to use it as they desire. Accepting the premise that personal data belongs to the individual means that the organization becomes a *steward* of data which is owned by someone else.

Employees who handle personal data must understand the principles of fair information practices. Developers, operators, and users must be informed of the policies and procedures relating to personal data. They should be required to sign a statement that they agree to abide by those policies and procedures, and that they understand the consequences and penalties resulting from failure to do so.

Most organizations seek to demonstrate to the public that they are socially responsible. The activities and established procedures relating to fair information practices can be included as part of their overall social responsibility program.

PRIVACY IMPACT STATEMENT

As a first step, an organization should examine its existing data files and seek to answer the following questions. For proposed new or revised information systems, the feasibility study can include such an evaluation of the privacy and due process implications.

- What types of personal data are or will be collected and stored in the data files? This calls for compiling a comprehensive and formal definition of the data.
- What is the real need for the data? Is it pertinent to the purposes of the system and the organization?
- What are the interests and rights of data subjects? How are they being satisfied in the current or proposed system—for example, notice and access rights?
- How might the data subject be adversely affected by the use, misuse, or inaccuracy of the stored data? Catalogue the possible damages a person might suffer as a result of the normal operation of the system, including unintended disclosures, neglect, and intentional misuse.
- In case of misuse or inaccuracy, what is the risk and probable loss to the organization?
- What is the degree of access control for secondary disclosures?
- What are the physical security mechanisms, operating controls, audit trails, etc.?
- What is the retention period for the personal data?

With answers to these questions, a manager is in a better position to assess levels of risk and decide how resources should best be allocated.

16.5.3 Notice, Personal Access, and Dispute

An organization must take affirmative action to advise individuals regarding data on file—when a new record is created or whenever it is materially changed. Periodically, there must be *some* unrequested communication from the organization to all individuals on file. At a minimum, such notice would indicate that a record exists (or may exist) and how to gain access to the data. In addition, the notice could include:

1. A complete copy of the data currently stored for the individual.
2. An explanation of the data—its definition and the meaning of value codes.
3. The purposes and uses of the data.
4. The general sources of the data.
5. The specific sources of the actual data for this individual.
6. Recent recipients of the data about this individual, indicating who received what data and why, if known. Recent can mean the past several months to a few years.

This requirement for notice may seem like a costly burden for organizations, and for some it can be depending upon how it is accomplished. Rather than arguing that they can't provide notice because it is too costly, organizations should creatively seek ways to provide notice to individuals. The notice requirement need not be an economic burden, if an organization honestly searches for alternative notice mechanisms. Wherever possible, notice statements should be coupled with other forms of communication with individuals.

The first place to include notice is on or with the forms used to collect data directly from individuals. Such notice would indicate the purpose for collecting the data, and all intended uses and users of the requested data. It should also clearly indicate what data is optional and the consequences of not disclosing the mandatory data. See Figure 16-8 for sample statements from the U.S. and Minnesota income tax returns. At the very least, every form an organization uses to collect data from individuals should have some statement regarding the purpose and intended uses/users of the data, particularly for those uses/users which would be unobvious, unexpected, or nonroutine for most individuals filling out the form.

Giving notice of uses at the time of primary disclosure, will persuade some individuals to be more truthful in their responses and to refrain from undesirable or unlawful behavior. For example, knowing that the claim of blind exemption on the income tax return will be checked against the existence of a valid driver's license, may discourage some individuals from claiming the blind exemption. The due process principle of knowing the rules of the game in advance can produce more desirable behavior and perhaps significantly reduce the magnitude of a problem.

Other than giving notice at the time of primary disclosure, a good approach is to couple the notice with other forms of regular communication with the individuals actually (or potentially) on file. Simply preparing and mailing the information is a significant cost. For example, with one million individuals on file and assuming it costs $.50 in postage, materials, and handling, the total cost comes to $500,000 for

U.S.-1984:

The Privacy Act of 1974 and Paperwork Reduction Act of 1980 say that when we ask you for information, we must tell you:

a. Our legal right to ask for the information.
b. What major purposes we have in asking for it, and how it will be used.
c. What could happen if we do not receive it.
d. Whether your response is voluntary, required to obtain a benefit, or mandatory under the law.

For the Internal Revenue Service, the laws include:
• Tax returns and any papers filed with them.
• Any questions we need to ask you so we can:
  Complete, correct, or process your return.
  Figure your tax.
  Collect tax, interest, or penalties.

Our legal right to ask for information is Internal Revenue Code sections 6001 and 6011 and their regulations. They say that you must file a return or statement with us for any tax you are liable for. Your response is mandatory under these sections. Code section 6109 and its regulations say that you must show your social security number on what you file. This is so we know who you are, and can process your return and papers.

You must fill in all parts of the tax form that apply to you. But you do not have to check the boxes for the Presidential Elections Campaign Fund.

We ask for tax return information to carry out the Internal Revenue laws of the United States. We need it to figure and collect the right amount of tax.

We may give the information to the Department of Justice and to other Federal agencies, as provided by law. We may also give it to States, the District of Columbia, and U.S. commonwealths or possessions to carry out their laws. And we may give it to foreign governments because of tax treaties they have with the United States.

If you do not file a return, do not provide the information we ask for, or provide fraudulent information, the law provides that you may be charged penalties and, in certain cases, you may be subject to criminal prosecution. We may also have to disallow the exemptions, exclusions, credits, deductions, or adjustments shown on the tax return. This could make the tax higher or delay any refund. Interest may also be charged.

Please keep this notice with your records. It may help you if we ask you for other information. If you have questions about the rules for filing and giving information, please call or visit any Internal Revenue Service office.

U.S.-1975:

The principal purpose for soliciting tax return information is to administer the Internal Revenue laws of the United States. . . .

The routine uses which may be made of tax return information include disclosure to the Department of Justice in connection with actual or potential criminal prosecution or civil litigation; to other Federal Agencies; to States, the Commonwealth of Puerto Rico, or possessions of the United States to assist in the administration of their tax laws; to other persons in accordance with and to the extent permitted by law and regulations; and to foreign governments in accordance with treaties.

MN-1984:

USE OF INFORMATION

All Information on your return, by state law, is private. It cannot be given to others without your consent except to the Internal Revenue Service, other states which guarantee the same privacy, certain commissions, municipalities, state and county agencies and persons performing services on behalf of the Department of Revenue. Information about persons who owe a debt to a state or county agency may be given to that other agency. Information about parents who appear to have deserted their children may be given to the Commissioner of Public Welfare. [Information about persons who claim to be blind may be given to the Commissioner of Public Safety for comparison to drivers licenses]. Information about persons who received unemployment compensation may be given to the Commissioner of Economic Security. Information about persons who have been found by a court to be delinquent in making child support payments may be given to the court. Information about persons holding a license issued by the Minnesota Racing Commission or a horse owner may be given to the Minnesota Racing Commission. Information about persons applying for a liquor license may be given to a county or municipality. Information about persons participating in enterprise zones may be given to the Commissioner of Energy and Economic Development or a municipality receiving an enterprise zone designation.

Your name, address and social security number are required by law for identification. Your income, deductions, credits and marital and residency status are required by law to determine your correct tax or refund. If you fail to provide the information necessary to determine your tax, your form may not be accepted, the processing of your forms and issuance of any refund may be delayed, deductions and credits may be disallowed and you may be subject to civil and criminal penalties for failure to file a return.

The only information requested on your return not required by law is your occupation, telephone number, former name, address or marital status if changed, the county and city or township you live in and the telephone and identification numbers of your tax preparer, if any. Your occupation will be used to determine if certain deductions are allowable and to analyze income levels by occupation. Your telephone number will be used to contact you, if necessary. The county and city or township you live in will be used for research, evaluation of the tax structure and to determine distribution of the state elections campaign fund. The information about your preparer will be used to identify and contact him or her, if necessary. The information on your return may be compared with other information you may have furnished the Department of Revenue.

Figure 16-8. Notice Statements on U.S. and Minnesota Income Tax Returns.

This information is given to individuals along with the forms and instructions used to file an income tax return. Adding these few paragraphs gives some notice at a minimum of additional cost. Contrast the relative specificity of the Minnesota statement, with the obviousness and blandness of the U.S. statement, particularly in 1975 just after the U.S. Privacy law was passed. Is there anything left in the 1975 U.S. statement which could be considered a 'nonroutine use'? Clearly, the Minnesota statement is more in keeping with the spirit of the law.

each mailing! This may exceed the annual net revenues for the organization! If the notice statement can be included in other normal mailings to the individuals, the incremental costs can be almost negligible.

A newsletter or other general mailing sent periodically to members could contain a general statement that personal data records are maintained and that individuals have a right to ask if a record exists and to get a copy of their record. The newsletter would indicate where an individual would go and what they would have to do to gain access to the data on file. The newsletter could also contain a description of the purpose for the existence of various data files and the intended uses of the data. None of the information in such a general mailing would be specific to the individual since the same information is duplicated and sent to everyone.

Some organizations fear that telling individuals that they may have access to their data will generate a flood of requests. In fact, actual experience indicates otherwise. One credit reporting agency with some 60 million people on file argued against passage of the U.S. Fair Credit Reporting Act stating that requests from an estimated 1% of those on file would be a severe economic hardship. As it turned out they had fewer than .01% or 6,000 request access to their records in the first year. Of course, no specific notice was mailed to the individuals on file indicating their right to ask and where to make their request (such a mailing would obviously be prohibitive). People only knew of this right through knowledge of the federal law.

The next level of information would be to provide individuals with a printout of the specific data on file about them. The cost could be kept low by including this information with some other regular communication with the individual—monthly billing or periodic statement of account, the subscription renewal request, annual statement of contributions to a church or charitable society, registration materials for the next school session, confirmation of a reservation, etc. This is one area where an organization can exhibit some imagination in meeting the notice requirement while keeping costs to a minimum.

A reasonable cost estimate of providing a copy of personal data to individuals runs about $.01 per line per person per mailing, exclusive of postage (assuming it can be coupled with some other mailing). This includes equipment and labor costs of printing, collating, and stuffing.

Generally data is encoded when stored in computer files. Therefore, it is necessary to include some explanatory information with which the individual can decode the data and comprehend its meaning. This would include the definition of each data item in the record, the meaning of the values which can be recorded for each item, and the conditions under which a value should or should not be recorded.

When an organization shares the data it has on file with the individuals, they are affirming that people are important and that they desire to have an open and fair relationship with those individuals. Of even greater importance is the increased data accuracy and completeness which can result from this sharing.

Besides the specific data about the individual, the organization can include references to the sources of data, where relevant, and secondary disclosures to third parties or for nonroutine uses. This information would come from the audit trail of disclosures maintained by the organization (see section 16.5.5).

Some organizations do not have any regular contact with the individuals on whom they collect data. Such organizations generally serve businesses in a particular industry. For example, the Medical Information Bureau, Inc. (MIB) maintains medical information on anyone who has applied for an insurance policy through one of their participating insurance companies. Insurance companies submit to MIB the information they get from medical providers when processing an application for insurance. They also see if any other information is on file about an individual who is applying to them for insurance. MIB is a central repository of medical data for use by companies in the insurance industry.

For many years, people outside the insurance industry did not know of the existence of MIB. If incorrect data is recorded, an individual may be denied insurance by *any* company from whom they seek to acquire a policy. Even though organizations such as MIB have no direct contact with individuals, they have no less a responsibility to give notice to those individuals that a record exists and to provide them access to their data. Such organizations still need to find appropriate avenues for giving notice to individuals. One way would be to work through the participating insurance companies who *do* have direct contact with the individuals on file. In fact, it is in the best interests of MIB to establish specific policies and procedures to be followed by the member companies as they relate to individuals, in particular, to tell them about the existence and purpose of MIB, and how they can obtain access to their records.

Even if an organization periodically, say annually, gives some form of notice to individuals on whom they have data, they must still be prepared to respond to a specific request from an individual for access to their data. This may be necessary if the personal data is too sensitive or confidential to be sent through the mail, risking an invasion of privacy if the data would fall into the wrong hands, intentionally or unintentionally.

When an individual initiates the action for personal access, it is important for the organization to have some means for verifying the identity of that individual. This is often done by having the individual reveal other information which is kept on file. For example, the credit industry has used your mother's maiden name—something even your close friends are unlikely to know! The need to identify individuals brings in the whole discussion of access control mechanisms discussed in Chapter 14.

After reviewing their data, an individual may find it to be inaccurate or incomplete. Their first point of appeal is to the operator of the databank who should reinvestigate, verifying with the source of the data. The organization would then make the requested correction or notify the individual that they believed the data to be correct. The individual then files a statement of dispute. The stored record must have provision for indicating that certain data is in dispute so that subsequent disclosures can include or reference the statement of the individual.

16.5.4 Control Dissemination to Third Parties or for Other Uses

Heeding the personal privacy rights of individuals requires an organization to use personal data only for the purposes specified in the notice given to the individuals. That is an assumed part of the understanding or 'contract' with the individuals on whom they collect and store data.

When disclosing personal data to outside parties over whom the holder has little or no control, an organization should obtain written assurances, perhaps in the form of affidavits, that the data will be used only for permitted purposes.

When a new use is contemplated, the intended user should obtain the informed consent of the individuals. Perhaps this means waiting until the next notice cycle to advise individuals of a new intended use and to give them an opportunity to respond or complain. A better plan would be to include a return card on which to indicate they do not wish to have their data used in particular ways. We are now starting to see magazine resubscription and membership renewal forms which give individuals an opportunity to check a box if they do NOT wish to receive promotional advertising materials. The Direct Mail Marketing Association now provides the opportunity for individuals to get *off all* mailing lists of member organizations (through voluntary compliance). They also have a form by which you can get *on selected* mailing lists—an interesting, and self-serving inconsistency.

Uses which are foreseeable by the organization should be included in the notice of uses given at time of data collection. Some uses will be required and central to the purpose of the organization. Other uses will be incidental to the organization. For example, states will register cars and boats and tax them through a licensing fee. Most states will also sell the list of all registered boat owners to others trying to sell you marine insurance or a bigger boat! These are incidental uses and should not be permitted if the individual boat owner says no—using a negative check-off ('yes' unless specifically 'no,' rather than 'no' unless specifically 'yes').

Individual control over disclosure to third parties and for new uses is not absolute. Sometimes such disclosure or use is justified by an overriding public interest such as the health and safety of others, or the conduct of criminal investigations. For example, there is a clear public interest in giving automobile companies access to owner information of registered cars which have been recalled for safety related defects. In fact, it would even be reasonable for the state to suspend driving privileges until the defect was fixed. Even when disclosure in the public interest does take place, the individual should be notified, unless it would materially interfere with the purpose of the disclosure, as, for example, in a criminal investigation.

Sometimes it is difficult to find the delicate balance between an individual's right of privacy and the public need to know, the balance between the risks to/rights of the individual and the benefits to society. Nevertheless, we must constantly seek a balance between these two in many and varied situations.

In response to this principle an organization must first inform all accessors and users of data about the proper uses. Then the system must implement an access control mechanism to limit access only to authorized users. Within the system, it is impossible to completely limit access to permitted uses since an authorized user can receive the data and use it for a different purpose.

16.5.5 System Implemented Data Integrity and Audit Trail

It may go without saying that organizations which collect and maintain personal data should keep the data accurate, current, and complete, particularly if it is to be the

662 EVEREST: DATABASE MANAGEMENT

basis for making decisions affecting individuals. Unfortunately, inadequate attention
and resources devoted to maintaining data integrity is too often the norm.

Part of the problem is the inadequacy of the DBMS tools used to manage data. If
a system does not provide easy and direct facilities for declaring data validation criteria, the checks may not be performed at all and data quality suffers. If the system does
not provide an easy and direct avenue for capturing updates, then the timeliness of the
data may suffer. In selecting a DBMS, organizations should give more weight to data
integrity mechanisms, and make more demands on vendors to provide needed
capabilities.

Besides validation performed internal to the DBMS, the data can also be given to
those in the best position to judge its accuracy. In the case of personal data, that is the
individual on whom the data pertains. The individual recipient is asked to verify
the information, to correct errors, and to fill in any missing data. It is helpful for
the organization to include a 'date last reviewed' in each record of personal data. The
organization can then record if and when an individual last reviewed their record.

Data which reflects badly on an individual, whether true or false, will lead people
to make negative judgments about that individual. The individual is judged guilty,
even though our constitution says that an individual shall be considered innocent until
proven guilty. Due process says that an individual shall have notice of charges against
him and be given an opportunity for a hearing to defend oneself, admitting only legally
obtained evidence. This makes it all the more important to maintain accurate data, to
be able to verify sources, and to give notice to the individual of any adverse data which
is stored about them.

The completeness criterion requires an organization to explicitly seek to gather all
the relevant information about an individual. When arrest information is front page
news it is easy for organizations to capture and record such data in their personal
databanks. Are organizations as diligent in capturing information about the disposition
of the arrest? Again, there is a strong tendency to judge a person guilty merely because
they were arrested. The charge may have been later thrown out but that information
will be buried in the newspaper, if it is published at all (it doesn't make news which
sells newspapers!).

While giving individuals the right to inspect and correct personal data can improve
data accuracy, it does not *guarantee* accuracy. The fact that an individual does not
challenge the information supplied to him must not be accepted as evidence supporting
the truth or accuracy of the data.

Maintaining an audit trail of sources and uses of data represents good management
practice whether or not it is required by law. If the individual or anyone else challenges
the accuracy of data, it is desirable to be able to go back to the source to verify its
accuracy, and trace how it got into the system. This is particularly important for data
obtained outside of the organization. A source audit trail would record some of the
following information:

- Name and location of the source—may be a person, an outside organization, or a
  transaction program.
- Date created, last changed, or last verified.
- Authority for the update.

An output audit trail records all disclosures to recipients of data outside the organization or for nonroutine uses. The U.S. Privacy Act of 1974 requires databank operators to first divide all uses into routine and nonroutine. Then the law exempts disclosures for routine uses from having to be logged. Unfortunately some agencies have defined routine uses so broadly as to preclude any nonroutine uses (see, for example, the 1975 statement of the IRS in Figure 16-8).

A log of disclosures would include some of the following information:

- Name, organization, and location of the recipient.
- Date and time of the disclosure.
- Purpose and intended use of the disclosed data.
- What data was disclosed.

Various laws require the disclosure log to be kept for 6 months to 5 years back. An audit trail of disclosures is needed to advise the individual who has received data about them. It is also needed for the organization to go back and advise past recipients if the individual disputes the data or it is materially changed.

16.5.6 Implementation Strategy: A Call to Creative Action

All these suggestions can be overwhelming for an organization. A good place to start implementing fair information practices is with personnel records. It is easier to contact individuals who are your own employees and therefore easier to meet the notice requirement. With an explanation of what the organization is trying to accomplish and an honest solicitation of comments and suggestions, employees may be more open and free to share their ideas and concerns. Furthermore, such an approach can sensitize employees to privacy and due process issues, and can change employee attitudes when they see how it affects them personally. A news reporter who demands the right of public access to personal data on others may be more understanding when they experience demands from others for their own personal data. A clerk may be more sympathetic to others seeking access to their own data when they have been refused access to their own data.

The laws cannot possibly deal with all possible situations; they have generally sought to spell out some broad principles and guidelines. Now organizations must be diligent in seeking out creative responses to those principles. Only by trying various approaches can we gain more experience and assess the costs of responding to fair information practices laws.

So far the laws passed in the U.S. and around the world include relatively weak enforcement and penalty provisions. Up through the early 1970's, organizations gave little attention to data privacy and due process. They were excused because the principles had not been well stated and there was little public concern. As concern increased, laws were passed to give some guidance and direction. General principles and guidelines are reasonably well understood and accepted today. Now all organizations, in both public and private sectors, have been put on notice that they had better take some affirmative steps toward implementing fair information practices.

Organizations must work out specific approaches to provisions of fair information practices laws. They must creatively seek out appropriate, economical responses. Organizations that rely solely on the specifics of state or federal legislation, that wait for laws to be passed for them, or that operate at a minimum level of compliance will be at greater risk.

The days of grace are running out. As public concern increases, more and tougher legislation is likely, with stiffer enforcement and higher penalties. An organization can no longer claim ignorance or lack of resources. There has now been sufficient publicity of the issues and directions for solution. It is time for action.

SUMMARY

Privacy is an issue between the individual and organizations which maintain data on individuals. Many facets of fair information practices legislation seek to reaffirm the basic rights of individuals and to place a burden of responsibility on organizations. Remedying the imbalance of power between individuals and organizations begins with the right of individuals to know about the possible existence of data records pertaining to them (notice) and to access their data.

In response to the growing public concern and increased use of computer technology, the 1970s saw special government hearings and enactment of laws relating to data privacy, due process, public access to personal data. They sought to affirm and balance the three basic rights of personal privacy, personal access (and due process), and public access. By 1980 the focus had broadened to fair information practices which additionally dealt with intrusiveness in data collection, fairness in an organization's dealing with individuals, and standards in the operation and security of personal data systems.

Privacy concerns the right of individuals to be left alone; the freedom from unwarranted intrusion into one's private affairs. The notion of *data privacy* extends the right of privacy to *data about* an individual.

Several issues are important concerning the record-keeping relationship between individuals and organizations:

- Limiting intrusiveness in data collection by collecting only data which is needed.
- The importance of purpose in the "contract" when personal data is given to an organization.
- Primary disclosure versus secondary disclosure.
- Selective disclosure of personal data to authorized users for specified purposes.
- Making decisions based upon data about an individual, the data becomes a surrogate for the individual.
- The need for third party data and the consequent responsbility to at least consider revealing the source to the individual.
- The importance of planned retirement of data to allow individuals to shake their past, and gain a reprieve from past mistakes.

The purpose of fair information practices laws is to establish the basis for an open, honest, and fair relationship between individuals on whom data is collected, and organizations, both government and private sector. Disclosure of personal data to others must be conditioned by this relationship.

Legislation is required to counterbalance the negative economic incentives to implementing organizational policies, operational procedures, and technical control measures for safeguarding personal data. Legislation is necessary because self-control is not always effective. Legislation provides deterence and remedies to the misuse and abuse of personal data.

Typical provisions relating to the rights of data subjects include:

- All personal databanks shall be a matter of public record.
- Individuals shall have notice that data is being collected, that they are or may be included in a person databank, and the purposes for which that data will be used.
- Individuals shall have access to data about themselves and an explanation of its meaning.
- Individuals should have some control over secondary disclosures.
- Individuals shall have a means to dispute, correct, or update data about themselves.

Typical provisions relating to the responsibilities of data handlers include:

- Limit data collection to that which is needed.
- Provide notice to individuals regarding data maintained and intended uses.
- Notify individuals of consequences of refusal to disclose personal data.
- Control disclosure of personal data to authorized third parties and for authorized purposes.
- Maintain quality of data to be complete, accurate, and current.
- Maintain an audit trail of sources and disclosures of data.
- Retire data when no longer needed.

In response an organization must look beyond the current demands on data processing. First, they must assign responsibility within the organization. Principles must permeate systems development and operation. One idea is to prepare a privacy impact statement for all newly proposed application system development projects. Organizations must be creative in seeking efficient ways to give notice to individuals concerning the data which is collected and maintained. The computer system can assist in controlling dissemination of personal data to authorized third parties, in maintaining the quality of the stored data, and in maintaining an audit trail of sources, disclosures, and changes to the data.

EXERCISES

16-1. What are some of the problems which are creating public concern and frustation over the use of computers to collect, maintain, and disseminate personal data?

16-2. Define each of the three basic rights which underlie a comprehensive information policy regarding personal data.

16-3. None of the three basic rights are absolute. Give an example of a conflict between public access and personal privacy, between privacy and personal access to data supplied by another person, and personal access to sensitive data about oneself.

16-4. What are the three steps of due process?

16-5. Chapter 15 on database administration argued that data, such as personnel records, belongs to the whole organization. Under the principles in this chapter, who owns such data stored in a corporate database? Give reasons to support your answer.

16-6. There is a definite trend in organizations to substitute data about individuals for face-to-face contact; data becomes the surrogate for the individual. What effect has this trend had on data collect practices?

16-7. Some would argue that the best way to handle private data is to not disclose *any* such data to *anyone* else. What is the difficulty with this viewpoint?

16-8. What is meant by "primary disclosure"? Explain the meaning and implications of secondary disclosure. What are some of the typical primary disclosures which individuals generally make without considering the possibility of secondary disclosures?

16-9. What is the legal difficulty with extending the concepts of privacy to data?

16-10. Describe the privacy rights of individuals under the fifth and fourteenth amendments of the U.S. Constitution.

16-11. When an organization collects and stores personal data, what are some of the rights of individuals with respect to the data stored about them?

16-12. What is the difference in data access rights between data held in the public sector (government) and data held in the private sector?

16-13. Describe some of the abuses which can occur if individuals are denied personal access to data about themselves maintained by organizations.

16-14. Why is there a need for legislation regarding data privacy and fair information practices? Why are administrative and technical measures insufficient for dealing with the "privacy problem"?

16-15. What are the major differences between privacy legislation enacted in the United States and in Europe?

16-16. Outline several responsibilities of data handlers who collect, maintain, and use personal data, responsibilities arising out of the principles of fair information practices.

16-17. What is the fundamental distinction between property and data? What does this difference imply in assessing damages or penalties for violations of a fair information practices law?

16-18. What is the most significant, fundamental principle which should underpin the attitudes, policies, and procedures within an organization that handles personal data?

16-19. How can social science researchers guarantee the confidentiality of personal data collected from interviews or questionnaires?

16-20. Briefly outline an implementation strategy that an organization might follow to ensure the privacy of individual personal data.

16-21. Explain how the computer can be both part of the problem and part of the solution to data privacy concerns. How does the computer afford a greater ability to protect the privacy of individuals in the data maintained about them?

16-22. What are the important questions an organization must answer in developing policies for fair information practices?

16-23. How does a data retirement policy pertain to data privacy?

16-24. Consider the following situation: You apply for a credit card and are required to list several references including your bank. The bank subsequently reveals your credit status to the credit card company, including loan size and payment records. From a data privacy viewpoint, did the bank act properly in conducting their affairs, or should they first have requested your permission to disclose this information? Support your answer.

SELECTED REFERENCES

Canada Departments of Communications and Justice, *Privacy and Computers*, A Report of a Task Force established jointly by Department of Communications/Department of Justice, Ottawa, Canada: Information Canada, 1972, 236 pages.

EVEREST, Gordon C., "Nonuniform Privacy Laws: Implications and Attempts at Uniformity," in *Computers and Privacy in the Next Decade*, edited by Lance J. Hoffman, New York: Academic Press, 1980, pages 141-150.

GERBERICK, Dahl A., Chairman, Los Angeles Chapter Ombudsman Committee on Privacy, *Privacy, Security, and the Information Processing Industry*, New York: Association for Computing Machinery, 1976, 187 pages.

GOLDSTEIN, Robert C., "The Costs of Privacy," *Datamation*, 1975 October, pages 65-69. Based upon the author's doctoral dissertation funded and published by Honeywell, Brighton, MA, 1975. Details of the computerized cost model also published in *A Methodology for Evaluating Alternative Technical and Information Management Approaches to Privacy Requirements*, Washington, DC: National Bureau of Standards Technical Note 906 (available from U.S. Government Printing Office), 1976 June, 72 pages.

GOLDSTEIN, Robert C. and Richard L. NOLAN, "Personal Privacy versus the Corporate Computer," *Harvard Business Review* (53:2), 1975 March-April, pages 62-70.

HANSEN, Morris H., "Insuring Confidentiality of Individual Records in Data Storage and Retrieval for Statistical Purposes," *AFIPS Fall Joint Computer Conference Proceedings* (vol. 39), 1971, pages 579-585.

HARRIS, Louis, & Associates, Inc. and Alan F. WESTIN, *The Dimensions of Privacy: A National Opinion Research Survey of Attitudes Toward Privacy*, sponsored by Sentry Insurance, Stevens Point, WI, 1979 May, 104 pages.

HOFFMAN, Lance J., editor, *Computers and Privacy in the Next Decade*, Proceedings of a Workshop Sponsored by AFIPS Special Committee on the Right to Privacy, Asilomar, CA, 1979 February, New York: Academic Press, 1980, 215 pages.

    Contains papers on the issues of privacy in the use of personal computers, in Electronic Funds Transfer Systems (EFTS), in preserving individual autonomy, in the protection of public order, in transborder data flows (from OECD representative), and research into the cost of privacy.

MILLER, Arthur R., *The Assault on Privacy: Computers, Databanks, and Dossiers*, Ann Arbor, MI: University of Michigan Press, 1971, 333 pages.

National Conference of Commissioners on Uniform State Laws, *Uniform Information Practices Code*, with prefatory note and comments, Chicago, IL: National Conference . . . , 1980 July, 61 pages.

Organization for Economic Co-operation and Development (OECD), *Recommendations of the Council Concerning Guidelines Governing the Protection of Privacy and Transborder Flows of Personal Data*, Paris, France: OECD, 1980 October, 33 pages.

PACKARD, Vance, *The Naked Society*, New York: Pocket Books, 1965.

Privacy Protection Study Commission, Davis Linowes, chairman, *Personal Privacy in an Information Society*, Final Report, Washington, DC: U.S. Government Printing Office (Y3.P93/5:1/977), 1977 July, 654 pages.

PROSSER, William L., "Privacy," *California Law Review* (vol. 48), 1960, page 383.
    Classic treatment of the legal status of the notion of privacy.

RIVLIN, Alice M., Chairman, Committee on Federal Agency Evaluation Research, *Protecting Individual Privacy in Evaluation Research*, Washington, DC: National Academy of Sciences, 1975, 126 pages.

RULE, James B., McADAMS, STEARNS, and UGLOW, *The Politics of Privacy*, Westport, CT: Greenwood Press, 212 pages. (See book review in *Datamation*, 1981 August, page 161.)

SCHNEIDER, Daniel B., "Plain Talk on Privacy: What Do We Gain by Ignoring Issues? and Policymakers Only Concerned About 'Use and Misuse,'" *Computerworld*, 1974 October 23 & 30.

SMITH, Robert Ellis, "Privacy: Still Threatened," *Datamation*, 1982 September, pages 297-305.

STIBBENS, Steve, "Privacy: A Nagging Problem," *Infosystems*, 1982 August, pages 49-53.

TARVER v. SMITH, 29 L. Ed. 2d 1966, 1971.
> The U.S. Supreme Court refused to hear a case in which a welfare mother was denied access to her own file. Her caseworker had filed a highly critical report including derogatory comments, allegations of child neglect, and a recommendation that she be permanently deprived of the custody of her children. Another caseworker had told her that the file contained false information about her. In arguing why the case should be heard, Justice Douglas noted that the petitioner apparently has no rights to a hearing to correct the report even if they are total lies. And it appears that she will never be informed prior to transmittal of her file to various 'authorized' groups. Douglas argued that the case should be heard because it presented an important question of procedural due process under the Fourteenth Amendment.

TURN, Rein, "Cost Implications of Privacy Protection in Databank Systems," *Data Base* (6:4), 1975 Spring, pages 3-9.

U.S. Congress House Committee on Government Operations, *Oversight of the Privacy Act of 1974*, Hearings before the Subcommittee on Government Information, Justice, and Agriculture, 98th Congress, First Session, 1983 June 7-8, Washington, DC: U.S. Government Printing Office, 655 pages.
> Contains a wealth of information, opinions, letters, prepared statements, newspaper reprints, articles, and reports, all of which are used by the Congressional committee to write their report (see next entry).

U.S. Congress House Committee on Government Operations, *Who Cares about Privacy? Oversight of the Privacy Act of 1974 by the Office of Management and Budget and by the Congress*, Eighth Report by the Committee on Government Operations together with Separate Views, Washington, DC: U.S. Government Printing Office, 1983 November, 58 pages.

U.S. Senate Committee on the Judiciary, *Federal Data Banks, Computers, and the Bill of Rights, Part I*, Hearings before the Subcommittee on Constitutional Rights, 92 Congress, First Session, 1971 February 23-March 17, Washington, DC: U.S. Government Printing Office, 1971, 1045 pages.

U.S. Public Law 93-579, *Privacy Act of 1974*, Title 5, U.S. Code, section 552a, enacted 1974 December 31, 15 pages.

WARE, Willis H., "Information Systems Security and Privacy," *Communications of the ACM* (27:4), 1984 April, pages 315-321.
> Outlines the need for security of information system and issues a call for action by the Federal Government.

WARE, Willis H., "Records, Computers, and the Rights of Citizens," *Datamation* (19:9), 1973 September, pages 112-114.
> Summary of the DHEW report below.

WARE, Willis H., et al., *Records, Computers, and the Rights of Citizens*, Report of the Secretary's Advisory Committee on Automated Personal Data Systems, Washington, DC: U.S. Department of Health, Education and Welfare, DHEW Publication No. (OS) 73-94, 1973 July, 346 pages (reprinted by MIT Press, Cambridge, MA).
> This very important report laid the foundation for modern data privacy laws in the United States.

WARREN, Samuel C. and Louis D. BRANDEIS, "The Right to Privacy," *Harvard Law Review* (4:5), 1890 December 15, pages 193-220.
> Classic; enunciated a right of privacy separate from property rights.

WESTIN, Alan F., "New Eyes on Privacy," *Computerworld* In Depth (vol. 17), 1983 November 28, pages 10-18.
> Surveyed 100 leading users of CRT terminals. In 90% of the firms, management was not addressing the policy questions regarding privacy and confidentiality arising from use of microcomputers. He argues that privacy principles and fair information practices must be extended from data processing to office automation.

WESTIN, Alan F., *Computers, Personnel Administration, and Citizen Rights*, Washington, DC: U.S. National Bureau of Standards, 1979 July, 439 pages.

WESTIN, Alan F., *Computers, Health Records, and Citizens Rights*, Washington, DC: National Bureau of Standards, monograph 157 (available from U.S. Government Printing Office), 1976 December, 401 pages.

WESTIN, Alan F., *Privacy and Freedom*, New York: Atheneum, 1967.

WESTIN, Alan F. and Michael A. BAKER, *Databanks in a Free Society*, New York: Quadrangle Books, 1972, 522 pages.

WHALEN v. ROE, decision of the U.S. Supreme Court, 429 U.S. 589 (51 L.Ed 2nd 64), 1977 February 22.
Argued that the state of New York had the right to compel pharmacists to file reports when certain potentially harmful but legitimate drugs were sold. They were concerned that lawful drugs were being diverted into unlawful channels. The required report form identified the prescribing physician, dispensing pharmacy, drug and dosage, and the patient's name, address, and age. Such information was not a public record and was to be destroyed after five years. Appellees felt it violated the privileged doctor-patient relationship.

YOUNGER, Kenneth, Chairman, *Report of the Committee on Privacy*, London, England: Her Majesty's Stationery Office, 1972 July, 350 pages.

Your Right to Federal Records: Questions and Answers on the Freedom of Information Act and the Privacy Act, joint publication of the U.S. General Services Administration and the Department of Justice, Washington, DC: U.S. Government Printing Office (329-551/8129), 1981 January, 18 pages.

SEVENTEEN

DBMS SELECTION AND ACQUISITION

17.1	BEGINNING THE SEARCH AND EVALUATION PROCESS	672
17.1.1	The Evaluation Team	672
17.1.2	Schedule of Activities for DBMS Evaluation and Selection	673
17.1.3	Assessing Organizational Needs	675
17.1.4	DBMS Concepts Education	677
17.2	ACQUISITION ALTERNATIVES	679
17.2.1	Make: Inhouse Development	681
17.2.2	Have Made: Contract for Outside Development	682
17.2.3	Modify or Enhance an Existing Package	683
17.2.4	Lease: An Existing DBMS Package	683
17.3	DBMS EVALUATION PROCESS	685
17.3.1	Asking Questions and Obtaining Answers	685
17.3.2	Simplified Evaluation Methodologies	686
17.3.3	A Cost-Benefit Evaluation Methodology	689
17.4	INVESTIGATING DBMS PACKAGES ("Getting Answers")	693
17.4.1	Genesis and Development of DBMS Software	693
17.4.2	Searching for Available Systems	694
17.4.3	Gathering More Information on Candidate Systems	695
17.5	SELECTION CRITERIA ("Asking Questions")	697
17.5.1	What Type of DBMS?	698
17.5.1.1	Host-Language, Self-Contained, or Both	698
17.5.1.2	Proliferating Database Definitions	698
17.5.1.3	Circumvented Database Integrity Controls	699
17.5.1.4	Select a Full-Function DBMS with Integrated Facilities	699
17.5.2	Efficiency versus Functionality	699
17.5.3	Suggested Technical Evaluation Criteria	703
17.5.4	Administrative Criteria	703
17.5.5	The Path from Efficiency to Profitability	704
17.6	FINAL SELECTION, CONTRACT NEGOTIATION,	
	AND ACQUISITION	704
17.6.1	Making the Final Selection	706
17.6.2	Economics of the Software Market	707
17.6.3	Contract Negotiation and Terms	708
17.6.4	Protecting Proprietary Software	712
17.7	INSTALLATION AND USE	714
17.7.1	Selecting the First Application	714
17.7.2	Charge Out Schemes Inhibit DBMS Use	715
	SUMMARY	716
	EXERCISES	716
	SELECTED REFERENCES	717
	APPENDIX 17A: Technical and Administrative Selection Criteria	720
	APPENDIX 17B: Software Listing Services	727

Sooner or later people will desire tools for storing, accessing, and managing data, and for building data intensive application systems. From a manual system, the first plateau in satisfying this need involves a computer system. However, using programming languages is a primitive way to do *data* processing—low level building blocks are very resistant to change once the procedures are developed.

Sooner or later people will desire *better* tools for accessing and managing data. The second plateau involves a DBMS, but not just any DBMS. Simply augmenting a programming language still does not get "data to the people." Even with an installed DBMS, the pressure for enhanced capabilities and improved performance continues unrelentlessly.

This chapter guides an organization through the steps to acquiring a DBMS. Most of the discussion presumes acquisition of a commercially available system. This must be a serious if not the dominant alternative to inhouse development (more on this later). The steps entail:

> **Learning** about DBMS,
> **Evaluating** available systems against organizational needs,
> **Selecting** the best DBMS,
> **Acquiring** it through contract negotiation.

17.1 BEGINNING THE SEARCH AND EVALUATION PROCESS

The move to develop or acquire enhanced database management capabilities formally begins with the appointment of a person or a team:

- To assess the organizational needs.
- To educate appropriate persons within the organization concerning the nature of database management, the fullness of solution alternatives, and the fundamental tradeoffs in those solutions.
- To search out, evaluate, and select a solution alternative appropriate to the organizational needs. This process often results in the acquisition of a DBMS.

It is most appropriate that the Database Administrator be the focus of responsibility for carrying out the search and evaluation process. With an evaluation team, the DBA may be chairperson, member, or director of the team support staff.

17.1.1 The Evaluation Team

For a successful selection and acquisition process, some person or persons must be given the responsibility and authority to carry it out. Someone must have the sense of responsibility or assigned duty to initiate and follow through on the search and evaluation activities. They must also have the commensurate authority to command a response from everyone in the organization who is or would be involved in data collection, processing, or use.

At a minimum, the evaluation could center on a single individual who obtains cooperation from others in the organization. Such an informal approach may be appropriate for a smaller organization. Larger organizations may wish to formally establish an evaluation team. The composition of the team may change during the evaluation process as the different activities take place. Initially, the users and management dominate in the assessment of organizational needs. Later, data processing technicians seek to evaluate the technical capabilities of several candidate systems. Finally, financial or accounting personnel review cost estimates, payment alternatives, and any tax consequences, and legal personnel enter the picture during contract negotiation.

It is important that a representative cross section of users have a voice in the assessment of organizational needs and information system requirements. This includes:

- End users, such as analysts, ad hoc users, recipients of output reports, and data entry personnel.
- System analysts who design and implement user application systems utilizing shared organizational data resources.
- Top management and their supporting staff are also users.

User groups should be represented based upon both current and potential needs for organizational data resources. Care must be taken not to bias the evaluation process in favor of any single user, however large or dominant, so as to preclude effectively meeting the needs of other users.

The data processing technicians within the information systems division are on the evaluation team to understand the system capabilities needed to meet certain user requirements and to assess the degree to which candidate DBMSs provide those capabilities. Users are not expected to understand the technical details of various database management systems. A common problem in many organizations is to have the evaluation team consist largely of data processing technicians, the systems and programming personnel. This often results in the selection of a system which they understand and feel comfortable with but at the expense of not meeting the needs of the end users. End users need direct data capturing, retrieval, and reporting facilities, and high-level, user-oriented languages.

Sometimes an organization will engage outside advisors or consultants to help in their data processing activities. Such individuals can be particularly useful in educating the organization about database concepts, a comprehensive approach to data management, and computer-based facilities for managing data. Outside consultants can also be helpful in suggesting candidate DBMSs and in providing technical evaluations of various candidate systems. A few hundred dollars here can save weeks of digging on the part of inhouse personnel.

17.1.2 Schedule of Activities for DBMS Evaluation and Selection

The selection of a database management system is a most important decision for an organization in providing computer data processing facilities. It is second only to the initial selection of the hardware and its associated operating system. A poor decision can have long-range consequences for the use of computers in an organization, the level of confidence in users and management, and the effectiveness of the operational activities and management decisions. Therefore, the initial stages of the selection process should be carried out with deliberate planning and adequate time and resources. It should involve the talented and key individuals in the organization. Most important, it must have the full, informed support of top management.

The major tasks for the evaluation team are shown in Figure 17-1. Even before the formal establishment of the evaluation team, some recognition of organizational needs and exploration of possible solutions will have already taken place. Particular problems identified in Chapter 2 will have motivated certain individuals to pursue the possible improvement or enhancement of data management capabilities.

It is not uncommon for some people to assume the selection and acquisition proc-

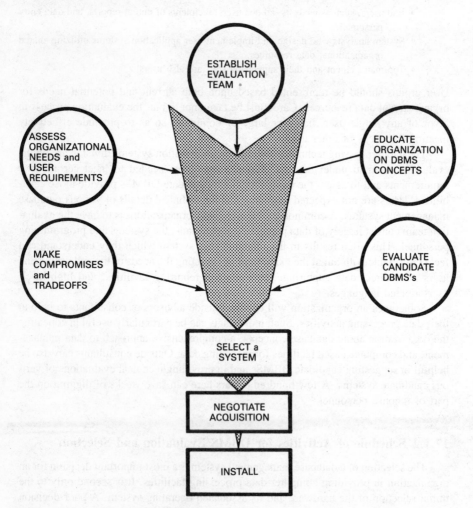

Figure 17-1. Major Steps in DBMS Evaluation, Selection, and Acquisition.

ess to be relatively straightforward. It is not. It takes time and patience. Two situations can lead to trouble: making a decision without adequate study and planning; or making a decision under pressure. A crisis may be looming as the deadline for implementation approaches, and perhaps some key systems development personnel have just quit. A new and unfamiliar DBMS should not be considered the way out. Resist the temptation to cut short the acquisition process. More importantly, an organization must allow time for people to become familiar with the capabilities of an acquired DBMS and to learn how to use it effectively.

The overall selection and acquisition process should take from three months to a year depending upon the size and nature of the organization and the perceived extent of the impact on the organization. An organization should not skimp on the allocation of time and resources to the evaluation and selection process. Furthermore, the greatest share of effort should be directed at the first two steps in Figure 17-1, assessing the organizational needs and DBMS concepts education. Only then is the organization in a position to intelligently evaluate the available systems and choose the appropriate compromises in seeking to satisfy those needs.

17.1.3 Assessing Organizational Needs

Movement toward the database approach to data processing is not for every organization now. Discerning the right time requires an assessment of organizational need, capacity, and readiness.

Several factors may motivate the move to acquire a DBMS:

- The need for more comprehensive data selection and retrieval capabilities.
- Faster response to ad hoc queries.
- Faster application development.
- Reduced data redundancy.
- Transferability across hardware.
- Reduced program maintenance.
- Increased ability to respond to changing requirements.
- More consistent data values.
- Increased security.
- Better audit facilities.
- More reliable backup and recovery.
- Reduced operating costs.

Whatever the reasons, they should be clearly documented. This serves to set priorities on the objectives and provides the basis for making tradeoffs among conflicting objectives and in the selection of various DBMS features.

Sometimes the characteristics of an organization make it very difficult to move toward the database approach. If the basic nature of the operations require high data processing throughput with high volumes of data and fast response times, the organization will have developed a stability in its operating procedures and the types of requests that can be handled by the system. Machine efficiency dominates the desire for flexibility. On the other hand, some organizations may experience a high degree of diversity in their operations, high turnover in employees, and a measure of instability or unpredictability in operations. This requires an evolvable system which is easy to learn and use and can be modified in the face of diversity and change. Such an organization cannot tolerate long lead times to get an application up and running because the situation may have changed and may not require extensive fine tuning for processing efficiency.

The database approach is much more than simply installing a DBMS. It involves a substantial shift in the focus and attitude of an organization:

- From programs and application systems to data as a corporate-wide resource.
- From single-use files to multipurpose, shared data.
- From data processing professionals to users.

An organization with strong departmental walls around autonomous units controlling key data resources must be willing to release control and cooperate in the maintenance of those common data resources. Whether centralized or decentralized, the degree of interdependence between organizational units will determine the degree of data sharing required. If this shift in focus has not or is not taking place, the organization must question its readiness for the database approach to data processing.

No one division or application area should dominate the determination of organizational needs. Organizational requirements should develop from a corporate perspective. Out of that should come a master plan for the development of data resources. Such a plan needs to be coordinated with the master plan for application systems development but should receive separate organizational attention and management.

In developing a statement of organizational needs, an organization must not be led astray by zealous data processing technicians who wish to be on the forefront of new developments, particularly those who want the experience of building their own "more advanced" DBMS. At the same time, there are technical developments in DBMS which are sound and can be of great benefit to an organization. All this requires a careful assessment of needs and a matching of capabilities to needs.

Similarly, an organization must be cautious of the overly enthusiastic user who wants all the additional features even though they might be of marginal utility to the organization. At the same time, the biggest danger is in buying a system that does too little for the organization. Many well-known systems are popular due to marketing effort and not due to technical superiority or functional comprehensiveness.

Finally, it is necessary to assess the organizational capacity to acquire and utilize a DBMS. Does the organization have talented technical people who are available to participate in the evaluation and subsequent application of a DBMS? Is management willing to support the evaluation effort by giving direction and allocating sufficient time and resources? Is the money available? Will the current (or planned) hardware and software environment support a move to a DBMS?

After investigating these various questions, the organization will ask: Should we go with a DBMS or wait? If the organization does not have the capacity or does not demonstrate the readiness, acquisition of a DBMS may be ineffectual at best and a disaster at worst. But to wait is to forego the opportunity to grow toward better management and utilization of organizational data resources—a direction in which all organizations must eventually move. To wait is to prolong and intensify the data conversion problem, to continue to tolerate the lack of consistency and integrity in the data, and to not learn how to cooperate and share in the maintenance of common data resources.

With or without a DBMS, an organization can begin to develop greater central control over data resources and foster the sharing of data. Without converting existing independent files to an integrated database, an organization can acquire a generalized retrieval and reporting package and begin to excite users about new possibilities for data accessibility. The organization can begin to lay the groundwork for an integrated database by developing a global logical design for common data resources. Users can be brought together to agree on common views of data, common definitions, and a common structure for the database. The important point is that some manageable step should be taken toward the goal of a database approach. What the step is depends upon the current status of data processing, on the current organizational structure, and on the readiness of talented people to make it a reality.

17.1.4 DBMS Concepts Education

Paralleling the assessment of organizational needs is the education of users, managers, and data processing people in the organization about DBMS concepts. The objectives of this education are:

- To learn what kinds of solutions are possible.
- To learn about the tradeoffs in providing data management capabilities.
- To learn how to distinguish the important concepts from the less important.

One obvious place to learn about DBMS concepts is from a vendor. Perhaps the hardware vendor also offers some DBMS package(s). The problem here is that without a comprehensive picture of DBMS concepts, a vendor can paint a glowing picture for prospective customers. Often the vendor begins with an overview of concepts and why, *in general*, DBMS is good for your organization. The presentation can be biased to stress the points which are also the strengths of their system.

One common approach in vendor presentations is to spend considerable time on the methods of structuring and accessing data, spending less time on what the system will do for you in processing that data. Of course, if the system only offers you general low-level manipulation commands, the systems will *let* you do many things in processing the data—will let *you* do it! That is a polite way of saying that the system does *not* do it for you, or does not have a high-level language capability. Unfortunately, many systems fail on this point. Fancy data structuring capabilities are relatively useless if the system does not provide comprehensive, high-level language capabilities for processing the data. Such capabilities include high-level and comprehensive data definition languages, ad hoc query languages, report definition, update transaction definition, user-defined screens for data entry and display, and validation criteria specification. If the system does not offer these facilities, users must do it themselves. Users must compensate for the lack of system facilities through extra checking and extra programming.

To counteract the bias of a single vendor, an organization can listen to the presentations of several vendors. Most people, however, will have great difficulty in relating the concepts and terminology of one vendor to the next, resulting in confusion. A few people will be able to synthesize the information content of multiple presentations and come away with a more comprehensive picture of what database management is all about.

A better approach would be to seek a comprehensive understanding of DBMS concepts first, then listen to several vendor presentations. Now the people will understand more, will be able to ask more meaningful questions, and will be able to find out what a system does *not* do for its users, to discover its weaknesses, its limitations, and how its developers made some of the basic tradeoffs in designing and implementing the DBMS. Too many organizations are *sold* their DBMS. Understanding DBMS concepts, they can be knowledgeable and discerning *buyers*.

With a comprehensive understanding of DBMS concepts, data management problems come into sharper focus. The previous section spoke of taking a manageable step forward. It will only be "forward" if it is moving toward a comprehensive solution to the problem of managing organizational data resources. Some prominent vendors are trying to sell systems which create more overhead for an organization without any significant movement toward better database management. One way to recognize this is to become educated in the data management concepts and the capabilities of a comprehensive DBMS.

The following points suggest how an organization can obtain expertise and educate its people in DBMS concepts.

- **Read this book** which seeks to 'arm' users—to provide them with sufficient education in the concepts, functions, and administrative aspects of database management to be intelligent buyers and users of DBMS.
- **Discover own employees** who continually seek to educate themselves through reading and attending professional society meetings and conferences. Such individuals can be extremely valuable to an organization. Unfortunately, experts are seldom recognized in their own organization.
- **Hire knowledgeable individuals** working for another organization or graduating from a university—individuals who already possess the necessary expertise. Several universities are now educating students in the relevant DBMS concepts, both in business schools and in computer science.
- **Encourage employees** to read the literature, subscribe to relevant journals in the field (*ACM Transactions on Database Systems, Information Systems, Information & Management,* and *Data Base,* for example), participate in activities and meeting seminars of local professional societies, join special interest groups of professional societies (such as SIGMOD on Management of Data, and SIGBDP on Business Data Processing, both of ACM), and join special DBMS committees of hardware vendor user groups. Encouragement can be in the form of picking up the tab for meetings, subscriptions, or dues.
- **Send employees** to university for specific courses, to national conferences which often have DBMS-related sessions, or to intensive seminars of a few days to a week. This alternative costs from $500 to $2,000 per attendee.
- **Bring in professional consultants or educators** to conduct seminars for a group of employees or perform tailored training activities. Seminars may range from half a day to several days and cost from $500 to several thousand dollars, still less expensive than sending out more than a few attendees.

In summary, it is very difficult to obtain an unbiased, comprehensive DBMS concepts education from vendors only. An organization needs to obtain an understanding of what constitutes a comprehensive solution to the problem of managing organizational data resources. No DBMS capability will ever be the ideal solution, but an organization cannot assess the degree of compromise in a particular DBMS without first having some expression of the fullness of database management. That is what this book is all about!

17.2 ACQUISITION ALTERNATIVES

An organization can acquire DBMS capability by building its own system, having someone else build a system for them, or obtaining a system which is already built and available in the software market. Figure 17-2 depicts these three major acquisition alternatives as *make, have made*, and *lease*. Three additional acquisition alternatives result from the pair-wise combinations of the major three.

Whether an organization plans to build its own DBMS or to acquire some commercially available system, it must still have some understanding of the user application environment within the organization—the internal market for a DBMS—and some idea of what constitutes a comprehensive solution to the data management problem. These are the first two activities of the evaluation team as shown in Figure 17-1. Unfortunately, it is all too common for organizations to embark on DBMS acquisition without paying adequate attention to these first two activities. This is particularly true for inhouse development. Once built, many organizations discover that the system is too narrow in its functional capability. Going outside to acquire a DBMS requires some additional activities such as searching for commercially available systems, evaluating vendors and their offerings, and assessing how well a DBMS meets the needs of the organization.

Up until the early 1970s the market for DBMS software was practically nonexistent. Most systems available in the 1960s were developed on a "have made" basis for large organizations or governmental agencies. Until the late 1960s, it was common practice for hardware vendors to bundle hardware and systems software, including DBMS, in one price. Having bought the hardware, the software was "free." This effectively excluded from the market independent software vendors who had to charge for their products. In the face of threatened legal action, IBM unbundled in 1969, establishing separate prices for its software. Burroughs, Univac, and Honeywell are still largely bundled today which, in part, accounts for the lack of independently supplied DBMS software on these systems. With the unbundling of software by hardware vendors, independent software vendors began developing DBMS packages, not for a particular user, but primarily for selling to a large number of users. With marketability as a major concern, developers paid more attention to generality, good documentation, training, user support, and continued enhancement of both functional capability and performance efficiency.

Today, acquiring a commercial DBMS must always be a seriously considered

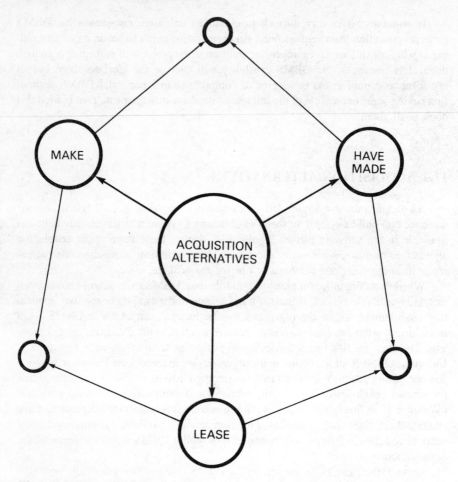

Figure 17-2. DBMS Acquisition Alternatives.
There are three major acquisition alternatives plus three more consisting of the pair-wise combinations of the major three. The selection of an alternative depends upon the availability of talent, the urgency of needs, the initial and operating costs, and the need to tailor the result or accept a compromise solution.

alternative. Unless there are some special needs such as high processing throughput, an organization can generally find acceptable alternatives in leasing a commercially available DBMS. This chapter focuses on outside acquisition.

Then why are many organizations reluctant to look outside and beyond their hardware vendor in the search for a DBMS? One reason is the NIH syndrome, a common malady among systems and programming personnel—"if it was *Not Invented Here*, that is, developed inhouse (see Figure 17-3), then it is not good enough to satisfy the unique needs of our data processing environment."

Another reason is that the software market for software products was slow to become visible and viable. Mechanisms exist for bringing buyer and seller together.

Figure 17-3. The NIH Syndrome.

Several vendors have been actively marketing their products long enough to have a good track record of stability and of standing behind their products.

For a third reason, even if an organization conducts a detailed cost estimate, some costs are often missed—indirect administrative costs, preparation of *good* documentation and training aids, ongoing maintenance costs, and the cost of a lost (or delayed) opportunity to have the system development personnel working on needed new application systems.

17.2.1 Make: Inhouse Development

For an organization to build its own DBMS requires good technical people with an understanding of:

- Functions and features of a comprehensive DBMS.
- Inherent tradeoffs involved in designing a DBMS.
- Techniques for implementing various features of a DBMS.

It is still difficult to find a person or persons with the requisite knowledge and skills. This text only provides part of this understanding. Even with talented people, an organization is well advised to make some use of knowledgeable, perceptive consultants to serve as a source of ideas and design direction, and to test DBMS design conceptions.

Organizations contemplating inhouse development will often underestimate the magnitude of the task. As a rough guideline, it will take from six months to several years, and from a few hundred thousand to several million dollars to build a reasonably comprehensive DBMS. In addition, since DBMS is more complex than a typical application system, successful development requires the use of sound principles of software engineering—a small technical design team, strong project leadership, use of top down design and structured programming techniques, periodic design reviews, and the maintenance of good documentation throughout the development process. Any imposed time pressure for completion generally produces a system of poor design and unreliable performance. Brook's Law states that adding more manpower to a late software project makes it later.*

Building your own DBMS is not really a serious option anymore, except for large organizations with very special processing needs. Back in 1973, Canning emphasized that inhouse development will take longer, cost more, and do less than originally planned—with high continuing maintenance costs. It is too risky. If you must spend money to solve the problems of database management, support research in the field!†

The singular advantage of building your own DBMS is the opportunity to tailor the design to best fit the particular situation and needs of the organization. Sometimes an organization will search out the marketplace and find no acceptable system. The available systems may be lacking in functional capability, they may be too inefficient to handle the high volume or rapid response requirement, or they may not offer enough data integrity controls.

An organization should not be deluded into thinking that its problems are unique and therefore not amenable to solution with available systems. Inhouse development often "reinvents the wheel" at great cost. An application considered unique by one company is often quite similar to the requirements of other organizations in the same industry. Similarities far outweigh the differences. Most organizations have much to gain by utilizing available technology to grow toward the database approach and to do it at less cost.

17.2.2 Have Made: Contract for Outside Development

If an organization finds that its requirements cannot be satisfied by any available DBMS package and that it does not have and cannot hire the necessary technical talent, then it can consider having a software development firm build a system to meet the need. The organization is thus in a position to influence the direction of the design.

Contracting for outside development passes on the headaches and the risk of failure to another organization but only if the organizational requirements are clearly defined and the needed capabilities of the system are clearly written into the contract. A contract to simply provide technical assistance will not pass on the risk. This is a

---

*Frederick P. Brooks, Jr., "Why is the Software [Always] Late?" in *The Mythical Man-Month: Essays on Software Engineering*, Reading, Massachusetts: Addison-Wesley Publishing Company, 1975.

†Richard G. Canning, "The Cautious Path to a Data Base," *EDP Analyzer* (11:6), 1973 June, page 8.

combination of "make" and "have made." A contract for a product must clearly specify the deliverables (source code, system reference manual, user manual, etc.) and must contain measurable criteria for determining when the job is done, that is, an acceptance test. The better defined the problem and the product, the more satisfactory will be the experience in dealing with outside professionals. (In fact, the same holds true in dealing with an internal systems group.)

Of course, an organization will pay more when an outside firm accepts the risk of development. One way to reduce costs is to share through some form of joint venture. Several organizations in the same industry or with similar needs can get together and jointly contract for the development of a system to meet their collective needs. If the system turns out to be more widely marketable, the firms in the joint venture can share in the dividends from future sales.

17.2.3 Modify or Enhance an Existing Package

If an available DBMS comes close to meeting the need, an organization can obtain the system and modify, tailor, or expand the system to make it acceptable.

The modification can be done internally in which case the organization must obtain complete documentation for the system and the source code, which many vendors are reluctant to supply. Having made the modifications, the organization must now maintain the system and the documentation for internal users. Alternatively, the organization may contact with an outside firm to perform the required modifications and enhancements. A third alternative is to have the vendor perform the required modifications. The vendor presumably understands the internals of the system and would be in the best position to make the changes at a lower cost. If the changes would enhance the marketability of the product the vendor may make the changes without additional cost.

Before seriously pursuing this acquisition alternative, the organization must ensure that the package is well documented, that the program code is clear and modular, and that the system represents a viable base from which changes can be made. A common misconception is that an organization can acquire a host language DBMS and build on top the facilities for generalized ad hoc retrieval, report writing, and generalized update transaction processing as required by nonprogramming users. *Most host language database management systems do not constitute a feasible base upon which to add high-level language facilities for the nonprogramming user.* One basic reason is the incompleteness of the database definition.

17.2.4 Lease: An Existing DBMS Package

For most organizations the best alternative is to acquire an existing DBMS package. Today there is a viable market for software products. During the past 20 years, over three hundred generalized DBMSs have been developed. More recently, another hundred or more have appeared on microcomputers. While perhaps only one quarter are commercially available today, the market for software products has come of age and must be a considered alternative. ICP annually reports software products achieving a cumulative gross revenue in excess of one million dollars.* There are over 400 such products with a total cumulative gross revenue of over two billion dollars. Database management systems and related products account for roughly 20 percent of the products and 25 percent of the total dollars.

When leasing an existing system, the most significant advantages and disadvantages are:

LEASING AN EXISTING SYSTEM

ADVANTAGES	DISADVANTAGE
Short time to install	Less than an ideal solution; lacking some capabilities
Lower initial cost	
Reduced maintenance effort	

With respect to any particular system, there will be additional advantages and disadvantages.

Most DBMSs can be installed in a matter of hours or perhaps a few days. One vendor of a comprehensive system will mail a tape and install the system remotely using an online terminal! For microcomputers, systems can be acquired 'off the shelf.' This is considerably less time than the months or years required for inhouse development. The short installation time makes it possible to begin immediate development of application systems with the technical staff using the DBMS. Inhouse development can tie up key technical people for several months.

Since an existing package is available immediately, there need be no uncertainty concerning its operability or its capabilities. With adequate documentation and an informed vendor representative a potential buyer can get answers to questions about the system.

The acquisition cost of an existing DBMS is generally less than 10 percent of what it would cost for inhouse development; in some cases much less. The vendor is able to spread the development costs over several users and apply some of the acquisition proceeds to documentation, user support, system enhancement, and marketing. For systems on microcomputers, sales of a single system have reached tens of thousands, thus justifying prices less than $1000. Some systems on micros are functionally equivalent to their mainframe siblings, yet cost 30 times less!

Often, the real burden of inhouse development is the need for continued support, maintenance, and enhancement of the system. Acquiring an existing package effectively spreads these costs over several users. Furthermore, the vendor has much greater motivation to maintain the system and its documentation and to continually enhance the capabilities and performance of the system. It is much more effective to have the maintenance responsibility focused in one place. This is particularly true for an inhouse product.

The most significant disadvantage of acquiring an existing DBMS package is that

---

*"The ICP Million Dollar Awards," *ICP Interface, Data Processing Management* (Indianapolis, Indiana: International Computer Programs, Inc., Larry Welke, Publisher).

it will fall short of a total solution to the problem, sometimes involving a heavily compromised solution. Sometimes it is better for potential users to revise their system design for a new application so they can use an existing software package. Of course, an organization which builds its own DBMS still accepts a compromise solution. The difference is that with an existing system the degree and points of compromise can be known before acquisition.

The degree of compromise can be known in advance only if an organization has some understanding for a comprehensive approach to database management. Recognizing the degree of compromise is essential to a successful acquisition—it avoids creating false expectations and the dissatisfaction which follows. When looking at an existing system, it is most difficult to determine what you are *not* getting.

Even though outside acquisition may result in a heavily compromised solution, it will still probably be better than inhouse development. An existing system must meet the needs of several users on a continuing basis if it is to be successfully marketed. An existing system will be the embodiment of accumulated knowledge and experience in the use of the system in several environments over a period of time. An inhouse system is usually narrow and inflexible once built (an outside system can be too if it was originally built for a particular using environment).

There are a lot of good packages available today, but it requires a sophisticated user to select a good package. It almost takes sharper people to buy software than to build or sell software! An organization is well advised to seek independent, outside assistance in DBMS evaluation and selection.

17.3 DBMS EVALUATION PROCESS

The word, eVALUation, means to determine the value of something. The acquisition of a DBMS only results in a cost to an organization. Value stems from applying or using the system in the solution of a problem or in the development of a user application system. Solving a problem means setting priorities, making choices, and allocating costly resources to the means for solution. Value derives from a problem solved, not a DBMS acquired.

What does it mean, then, to evaluate several candidate systems? Looking at one system versus another is only a process of *comparison*. Independent studies and surveys can only describe and compare available systems. Evaluation results from comparing a particular system to a particular problem environment. Database management systems cannot be *evaluated* without reference to a particular problem environment. An organization cannot just look at available systems to make a selection. It must look at its own needs to evaluate available systems.

17.3.1 Asking Questions and Obtaining Answers

The process of evaluation is one of asking questions and obtaining answers. The using environment of an organization is the source of questions; information about available systems is the source of answers.

Based upon the needs of the using environment, the evaluation team can establish technical and administrative criteria and from this construct a *feature list*. Organizational requirements must be analyzed to construct a list of DBMS features which will satisfy those requirements. The items in the feature list form the basis for gathering information on available systems. The list of technical and administrative criteria indicate the system capabilities and characteristics which are deemed important to the organization.

At this point, the evaluation team should clearly segregate those features which are *mandatory* for meeting the immediate and longer term needs of the organization. While a mandatory feature is seldom a simple 'yes' or 'no' for a candidate system, together they provide a means to screen the available systems. The remaining features are at various degrees of "desirable" or "nice to have." Here is where compromise is acceptable; where an organization is willing to sacrifice in the final selection.

For some organizations, particularly governmental units, the process of asking questions and obtaining answers must be highly formalized in order to be fair and give equal opportunity to all potential vendors. Procurement procedures will call for a formal, written Request for Proposal (RFP) or Request for Bid (RFB). The formal request document describes the user application environment, the special requirements for a DBMS, a detailed list of features and capabilities to be evaluated in the selection process, and sometimes a statement of evaluation criteria and methodology. Actually, this is nothing more than what the evaluation team should do regardless of the need for a formal, written request. They should carefully document the organizational needs and user requirements. The request document contains the questions, and the responding vendors provide answers in their bid proposals.

Sometimes an organization is seeking to acquire a DBMS to operate on their existing hardware, thus restricting the set of candidate systems. An organization seeking to acquire a new computer system is in a unique position to select comprehensive DBMS software. The availability of comprehensive DBMS software is becoming an increasingly significant factor in the selection of computer hardware. Mused one bundled hardware vendor, "When you acquire our DBMS for $400,000.00, you get the hardware free!"

When acquiring hardware it is difficult to involve the independent software vendor. In response to a Request for Proposal, hardware vendors will only bid their own DBMS packages, and most independent software vendors are unable to respond with a hardware bid. In many cases, a DBMS from an independent software vendor is superior to the offerings of the hardware vendor.

One solution is to make two separate acquisitions, one for hardware and one for software. This makes it difficult for an organization to evaluate the integrated effects of a DBMS on a particular hardware configuration. The organization would like to have the hardware and software vendors cooperate in the evaluation or even collaborate in the preparation of a bid proposal. Another solution is for the organization to contract with an independent third party to solicit proposals and perform an integrated evaluation of various combinations of hardware and software.

17.3.2 Simplified Evaluation Methodologies

An evaluation methodology begins with the feature list. Listing the features down the left side of a page with a parallel column for each candidate system provides the

DBMS FEATURE	:	SYSTEM1	:	SYSTEM2	:	. . .
TECHNICAL CRITERIA:	:		:		:	
1. Complete Data Definition	:		:		:	
2. Integrity Controls	:		:		:	
3. Programmer Interface	:		:		:	
4. High-Level Query Language	:		:		:	
5. Online Update	:		:		:	
6. Selective Indexing	:		:		:	
7. Overall Evolvability	:	Information about each feature				
:	:	for each system			:	
ADMINISTRATIVE CRITERIA:	:		:		:	
1. Required Hardware	:		:		:	
2. Documentation	:		:		:	
3. Vendor Financial Stability	:		:		:	
4. Vendor Support	:		:		:	
5. Cost—Initial	:		:		:	
6. Cost—Ongoing	:		:		:	
:	:		:		:	

Figure 17-4. A Simplified Evaluation Methodology.
The simplest methodology for evaluation lists the DBMS features considered important to meeting the organizational requirements along with a column for each candidate system. Each column contains information about each feature for a system. The evaluator then looks over the completed form in making a selection.

simplest approach as sketched in Figure 17-4. The column for each candidate system is filled in with information about each feature of a system. The features listed in the first column provide the questions, and the subsequent columns contain the answers for each system. If the criteria are cast as yes-no questions, the answers could simply be checkmarks for each "yes."

This simplified evaluation methodology assumes that the features listed are important to meeting the needs of the organizational using environment; unlisted features are not important. Any differences in the level of importance among various features are not made explicit in the simplified methodology.

Once the form is completed, the evaluator can visually scan and compare the information about the candidate system, finally arriving at a selection decision. Even if a final selection is not made at this stage, the simplified methodology can provide an initial screening of possible DBMS packages, eliminating those which do not meet some minimum set of mandatory criteria.

An evaluation methodology using points can rank the candidate systems by the total number of points earned. Each evaluation criterion in the feature list is assigned a maximum number of points reflecting its importance relative to the other criteria in meeting the organizational requirements. Then each system can earn up to that maximum for each feature. Figure 17-5 illustrates this procedure.

Assigning a weighting factor to each feature is an alternative method of recording the relative level of importance of the various features. Making all feature weights sum

DBMS FEATURE LIST	MAXIMUM POINTS	SYSTEM1	SYSTEM2	SYSTEM3
TECHNICAL EVALUATION CRITERIA: (74%)				
Logical Data Structuring	20	10	16	12
Data Definition	60	45	30	50
Integrity Controls	40	25	20	35
Programmer Interface	30	28	22	22
High-Level Query Language	50	45	40	36
Transaction Processing/Update	20	18	12	16
Online Operation	20	14	15	16
Database Revision	40	30	10	20
ADMINISTRATIVE CRITERIA: (26%)				
Hardware, System Software	10	9	6	7
Documentation	40	30	25	20
Vendor Support	30	15	25	20
Cost	20	15	10	17
TOTALS:	380	284	231	271

Figure 17-5. Evaluation Methodology Using Points.
Each feature is assigned a number of points reflecting its relative importance to the organization. Each system is then scored points up to the maximum for each feature. Then the total points for each system are calculated to provide an aggregate basis for comparing the candidate systems.

to one (or 100%) simplifies the arithmetic. Figure 17-6 provides a simplified example using a weighting methodology.

Before applying a weighting methodology, available systems must be screened to ensure that they meet any mandatory requirements or capabilities. For example, does the system run on the current hardware system? Or does it provide facilities for both programming and nonprogramming users? Mandatory conditions may also include characteristics which the system must not possess. Absence of a mandatory feature

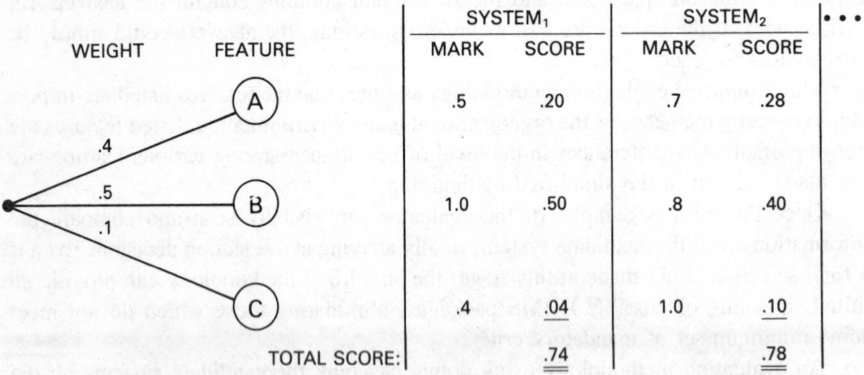

Figure 17-6. A Simplified Evaluation Methodology with Weights.
To each *feature* or need (A, B, C) as expressed in the feature list, the organization assigns a *weight* indicating the relative level of importance of each feature. The weights should sum to one. Then each system is given a *mark* for each feature. The *feature score* for a system is the product of the mark and the feature weight. The overall *system score* is the sum of the feature scores for a system. In this example, SYSTEM2 is the preferred choice over SYSTEM1 unless some intangible factors dictate otherwise.

disqualifies a system from further consideration; presence means that the system meets some minimum requirement and is a candidate for the rating procedure.

The organization determines the maximum points or weighting factor for each feature based upon the needs of the organization, *without reference to the characteristics of any specific candidate system*. Organizational need determines the weights. Determining weights is subjective and should be done by managers, skilled analysts, and users who understand the problem environment. The weighting scheme establishes the importance of a particular feature compared to all other features in the feature list.

Consensus in the weights is desirable and can be obtained using the Delphi Method* whereby key people are asked to give weights to the features. After seeing the resultant average weights, each person repeats the process. Three rounds bring good consensus.

The next step is to assign a mark to each system in terms of each feature. The mark may be assigned on a scale from zero to one. Whatever the scale, it must be consistently applied across all features. For each system, the product of the mark and the weight for each feature, summed across all features, determines the overall system score.

Even though the weighting and marking of individual features may be rather subjective, the methodology can achieve greater objectivity at the macro level. Several micro judgments replace a single global judgment about a system, hopefully reducing the bias in the global subjective judgment.

Weights may be easier to determine using a multilevel scheme, as illustrated in Figure 17-7. It is often easier to determine the relative importance of a few criteria in the same category than to compare completely different criteria at a micro level. The major criteria are at the first level with each one broken down into subcriteria. This forms a multilevel hierarchy of criteria. The weights of subcriteria under the parent criteria would sum to one. The resultant weighting on a single criterion is the product of the weights on all the segments on the path to the top of the hierarchy. This yields a set of weights on the leaf nodes of the criteria hierarchy. They add up to one and the procedure continues as before (in Figure 17-6).

17.3.3 A Cost-Benefit Evaluation Methodology

One weakness of the methodologies discussed so far is that they do not explicitly relate the goodness or benefits of a system to the cost. A system which is twice as good as another system and which costs twice as much should be considered equivalent on the basis of a cost-benefit analysis. A good evaluation methodology should choose the most cost-effective solution to a problem. Such a procedure is outlined in Figure 17-8.†

The cost-benefit procedure differs from the simplified methodology with weights by setting a *nominal mark* for each feature. A nominal or "average" system would receive a rating of one for each feature.

Another difference in the cost-benefit procedure is the use of a *rating function* for

---

*N. C. Dalkey, et al., *Studies in the Quality of Life: Delphi and Decision-Making*, Lexington, MA: Lexington Books, D.C. Heath and Co., 1972.

†Based upon the System Evaluation Methodology developed by Sable [1970].

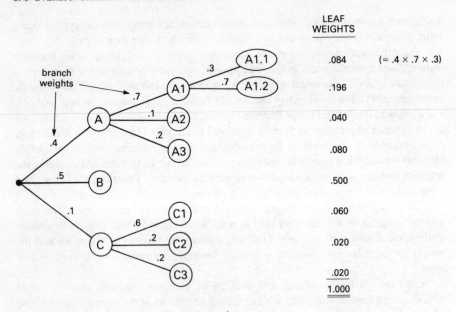

Figure 17-7. Evaluation Methodology with Multilevel Weights.
The hierarchical classification of evaluation criteria makes it easier to assign weights, particularly with a large number of criteria. The weights within the same filial set add up to one. The leaf weights are the product of the weights along that path of the hierarchy. The methodology continues as before with the leaf weights adding up to one.

each feature to normalize the scores. Rather than assigning a mark between zero and one, the mark is measured on a scale which is appropriate to the feature, such as number of terminals supported or amount of main memory required. Some sample rating functions are shown in Figure 17-9. The rating function transforms a system's feature mark into a normalized rating indicating its value relative to a nominal mark for that feature. The nominal mark for each feature has a nominal rating of one.

The use of rating functions is more sophisticated and costly to apply than the simplified methodologies. The greater objectivity and precision obtained must be weighted against the overall benefits of DBMS acquisition and use. Some features will have no appropriate objective scale on which to mark the feature. The analyst could use a five point scale with a linear rating function as follows:

FEATURE EVALUATION	RATING
Excellent	2.0
Good	1.5
Average	1.0 (Nominal)
Fair	0.5
Poor	0.0

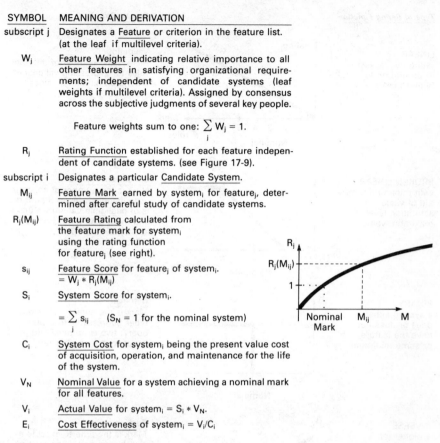

SYMBOL	MEANING AND DERIVATION
subscript j	Designates a Feature or criterion in the feature list. (at the leaf if multilevel criteria).
W_j	Feature Weight indicating relative importance to all other features in satisfying organizational require- ments; independent of candidate systems (leaf weights if multilevel criteria). Assigned by consensus across the subjective judgments of several key people.

$$\text{Feature weights sum to one: } \sum_j W_j = 1.$$

R_j	Rating Function established for each feature indepen- dent of candidate systems. (see Figure 17-9).
subscript i	Designates a particular Candidate System.
M_{ij}	Feature Mark earned by system$_i$ for feature$_j$, deter- mined after careful study of candidate systems.
$R_j(M_{ij})$	Feature Rating calculated from the feature mark for system$_i$ using the rating function for feature$_j$ (see right).
s_{ij}	Feature Score for feature$_j$ of system$_i$. $= W_j * R_j(M_{ij})$
S_i	System Score for system$_i$. $= \sum_j s_{ij}$ ($S_N = 1$ for the nominal system)
C_i	System Cost for system$_i$ being the present value cost of acquisition, operation, and maintenance for the life of the system.
V_N	Nominal Value for a system achieving a nominal mark for all features.
V_i	Actual Value for system$_i$ = $S_i * V_N$.
E_i	Cost Effectiveness of system$_i$ = V_i/C_i

Figure 17-8. A Cost-Benefit Evaluation Methodology.

Variations can expand or contract the rating scale, using a nonlinear rating function, or expand the points in the feature evaluation scale to achieve greater resolution. In extreme cases, the analyst could simply use subjective judgment to arrive at a rating directly, remembering that a feature rating of one applies to a nominal or average system.

Having converted all the marks to ratings, the *system score* is the product of the rating and the weight summed across all features, just as before. The overall score for a *nominal system* would be one (since all weights sum to one and all nominal ratings are one). This is important for determining *cost effectiveness*, the ratio between the value of a system and its cost. The organization first determines the value of a system which earns a nominal mark for all features. This is called the *nominal value*. Then the *actual value* of a given system is the product of the overall system score and the nominal value. The cost effectiveness of a system is the actual value divided by the

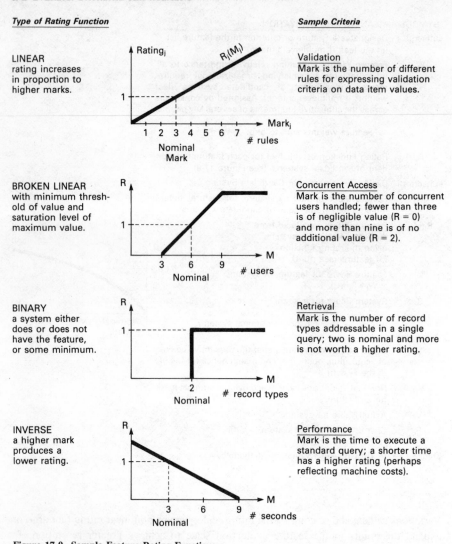

Figure 17-9. Sample Feature Rating Functions.
For each feature, the rating function uses an appropriate and convenient scale of measurement for determining a system's feature mark. The rating function transforms the mark into a standard dimensionless rating scale so that a nominal mark for a feature has a rating of one. Other marks convert to a rating relative to the nominal rating of one. There are combination and variations of these sample rating functions, including smooth, curved functions such as exponential or S-shaped functions.

cost of the system. System cost is the present value cost of acquisition, operation, and maintenance over the estimated life of the system.

With a cost-effectiveness measure for several candidate systems, the organization would tentatively select the system with the highest cost-effectiveness ratio. Intangible factors not included in the formal evaluation methodology influence the final selection as well as the intuitive or political judgments of management.

17.4 INVESTIGATING DBMS PACKAGES ("Getting Answers")

On the path to DBMS acquisition, after an organization has discovered its needs and become educated, it must search for available DBMS packages and gather detailed profile information on candidate systems. This section discusses where to look and what to look for.

17.4.1 Genesis and Development of DBMS Software

Understanding the sources and development patterns of DBMS software can aid the investigation. Manufacturers of early computer systems only sold hardware, programming language compilers, and the time of people to help in their use. In developing their own software, users would identify common functions and often develop generalized software to be used in a variety of situations. User groups sprang up to share approaches to common problems and to share software. Users would be willing to give or trade a software package they found useful but documentation was often spotty and continuing maintenance was nonexistent.

By the mid 1960's, hardware vendors offered rudimentary operating systems, packages of input-output routines, sort utilities, and report generators. These formed the building blocks for developing generalized DBMS. During the seventies, hardware manufacturers began to develop and offer DBMS facilities to their users. Often the vendor built the system under contract with a large user. For example, in the early sixties IBM built DL/1 (which grew into IMS) for North American Aviation as part of the NASA Apollo program. In the early seventies, Honeywell built MDQS (the commercial version of WWDMS), now part of DM IV, as part of the World Wide Military Command and Control System (WWMCCS of the U.S. Government).

During the same period, software companies developed systems under contract for large users. Informatics built GIRLS (Generalized Information Retrieval and Listing Service) for the U.S. Air Force and it grew into Mark IV. SYSTEM 2000 from Intel Commercial Systems Division (formerly MRI) has its roots in TDMS, developed by System Development Corp. for the U.S. Defense Department.

Some users developed systems inhouse primarily for their own use. B. F. Goodrich Chemical Company built IDMS, now available from Cullinet Corp. Most inhouse developments have not been actively marketed due to competing efforts to concentrate on the business.

Spurred by IBM's unbundling of software from hardware prices in 1969, software companies began to develop packages with the express purpose of marketing them. They expected to spread the high development costs over several users. Cincom Systems Inc. developed TOTAL to provide the nucleus for building tailored database-oriented application systems for clients. They soon discovered that the system had more sales potential by itself. Today, the system is available on several different machines. It has more users and has generated more revenue than any other DBMS. Similarly, Mathematica developed RAMIS primarily to meet the need for an inhouse database management capability. Today, it is separately marketed.

Knowing the ancestry of a package can provide important insight into design objectives for the system which are not always made explicit. For example, TDMS was built for accumulating military intelligence data. Fragments of information would come from various sources, which explains why *all* data items are optional in a repeating group. The user also required extensive and powerful retrieval and manipulation facilities. Today, the retrieval language of SYSTEM 2000 (a grandchild of TDMS) is among the most powerful high-level languages on a hierarchical data structure.

Knowing the history of a package may provide some clues concerning its performance efficiency. A system developed on second generation equipment may have become less efficient when converted to a third generation environment. Knowing the background of the developers can also uncover important design objectives. For example, with prior experience in building systems for an online environment, the developers of DATACOM/DB from ADR (formerly Insyste Datacom Corp.) produced a system with a strong online orientation.

Until recently, marketing forces have dominated the DBMS software industry. Marketing and financial success does not necessarily stem from technical superiority. Vendors have been selling to a relatively naive and uninformed market. Many DBMS users today are just plodding along with a heavy administrative burden in using a DBMS and have little time to write about their experiences. Fortunately, this is changing as users spend more time in database concepts education when acquiring a DBMS.

17.4.2 Searching for Available Systems

Until the early 1970's, the DBMS buyer had to search out the sources of systems with fragmentary information. Today, several intermediaries bring together buyers and sellers of software. They include software houses acting as brokers or distributors who promote packages and offer varying degrees of support and maintenance. They also include companies who publish regularly updated listing services and evaluation reports.

First, a user can look to their **hardware vendor**. All major hardware vendors have some DBMS facilities to offer. Acquiring vendor software is an "easy" alternative which eliminates one vendor pointing the finger at another when problems arise. In many cases, however, better software is available from independent vendors, particularly when there is a large base of installed systems making independent software development economical. Some hardware vendors seem to give lower priority to software; perhaps finding hardware easier and more profitable to market.

A major problem is that some hardware vendors still *bundle* their software in the price of the hardware. Others price the software unrealistically low, not reflecting the true cost of development. Such practices make it very difficult for independent software vendors to compete. If the hardware vendor's software is inferior, the users suffer. One recommendation is to avoid that vendor's hardware (a recommendation which comes too late for some!).

An organization that is contemplating or actively pursuing hardware acquisition is in a unique position to let the quality of available DBMS (and other) software influence the selection. Every hardware selection decision today should include criteria relating to the software. Furthermore, this should include the best available software, whether from the hardware vendor or an independent software vendor.

Other sources include subsidiaries of a developer organization created with exclusive marketing rights, joint industry development projects, trade association efforts to foster sharing of common software, software brokers and distributors who market packages developed by some other organization (some will contract to find the "right" package for a prospective buyer). Today, an organization need not ferret out these sources. A good, supported DBMS product will likely be found in one of the listing services.

Several **listing services** publish regularly updated information on various segments of the computer industry. These are mentioned in Appendix 17B recognizing that the information is soon out of date in such a rapidly changing industry.

In all these listing services, there is considerable variation in extent of coverage for each product, as well as overlap in coverage. The more popular systems appear in most of the services. Used in combination, they will identify most available systems suitable to a prospective buyer.

The cost of these services ranges from $50 to a few hundred depending on the use of an independent staff to gather, write, and evaluate the product information. This is still considerably less than the inhouse manpower spent to search and screen available systems. Sometimes listing services will be available at the local public library or your corporate library.

In the listing services, it is common to distinguish first between applications software and systems software. Most classify DBMS products as systems software since they are more like utilities and independent of any particular application area. One word of caution: Do not put much weight on their classification of database-related software. For example, one distinguishes "data*base* management systems" as being for multiple applications, from "data management systems" which are for single applications. Such a distinction is fuzzy and spurious. In fact, they include very comparable systems in each category! In another, systems which provide substantial database management facilities are listed in four or five categories including file management systems, file maintenance systems, storage and retrieval systems, and report writers. Go beyond the labels and look at the program descriptions when searching for systems which might satisfy your needs.

17.4.3 Gathering More Information on Candidate Systems

Having found some DBMSs which appear to be suitable, the next step is to gather more information. As more information becomes available about a system, it is continually being screened against the mandatory requirements. At any point in the process, a candidate system can be excluded from further consideration. Considerable effort goes into searching for available systems and gathering more detailed information on candidate systems. Therefore, a system found not to meet the mandatory requirements should not be the object of further information gathering.

Additional information about a candidate system may come from any of the following:

- Vendor.
- Developer.
- Users.
- Demonstration.

- Introductory course.
- Trial use.
- Benchmark.

The following paragraphs explore these further, indicating their usefulness and pitfalls. These sources of additional information sources are arranged in order of increasing cost to the prospective buyer.

The **vendor** is the obvious first place to obtain more information on a candidate system. The vendor can supply sales brochures and quasitechnical literature to augment the information gathered from the software listing services. If the system looks like a candidate, ask for more substantial technical documentation, such as user manuals and reference manuals. Read these carefully for detailed information on system capabilities; do your homework before calling in the vendor. Follow up with an invitation to the vendor to visit, make a presentation, and respond to technical questions. A good sales person often defers technical questions to competent technical personnel who can be more complete, candid, and impartial in their response. Determine the number of good technical people assigned to the maintenance and enhancement of the system, perhaps with a visit to the vendor headquarters. Does the vendor seem to have a long-term commitment to the support and continued development of the package?

Most vendors will come to your location for a day to make a presentation on their system. Some will even cover their travel expenses. Be sure to have some attendees knowledgeable in DBMS concepts to keep the presentation honest and to ask penetrating questions, even if they are from outside the organization or a hired consultant. As revealed in the tone of the meeting, are the vendor representatives excited about having a good product to sell? Some vendors regularly give public presentations in different cities so ask if there is one soon in your area. The organization could also send people to a course, such as one given annually at the University of California, Los Angeles, Extension Division, where some twenty vendors make their presentations over three days.

The **developer** of the system, if different from the vendor, is an important source of information about the design philosophy of the package. Determine the pedigree and historical development of the system [see Fry and Sibley, 1976], and investigate the background and qualifications of the developer. Did they use a disciplined, top-down approach in the development of the system? What were their main objectives in building the system?

Talk to **users** of the system, particularly those in the same industry who have used it extensively. Learn firsthand of their experiences. Visit existing installations to talk directly with those involved in the installation, maintenance, and use of the system. Users can be an excellent, independent source of information on the capabilities and operation of a candidate system, and the likely compromises and difficulties in its use. Find out which candidate systems they rejected and why.

Ask the vendor for a list of user references, although some may be reluctant to respond. Newly introduced systems may have few users, leaving you with the choice of being an early user of more advanced technology at the risk of encountering some initial operating problems. Some of the listing services annually conduct surveys asking users to rate the proprietary software products they use.

A live **demonstration** of the system shows it to be operational. The vendor may conduct the demonstration or, better yet, see it at some user site. If the system is available on a commercial timesharing service, this provides a convenient means for seeing it in operation. The demonstration is important if there is any doubt that the system is not fully operational. Systems which appear good on paper may never materialize with the stated functional capability and performance characteristics. During the development of such complex software, it is difficult to predict the functional capability and performance characteristics of the system in operation.

Taking the vendor's **introductory course** before making a final selection can give a more intensive exposure to the system, how it works and how to use it, and can provide an opportunity to ask more probing questions than in a sales presentation. Normally, technical personnel conduct such training sessions lasting from two to five days. The sessions will indicate whether or not the vendor can adequately provide training in the philosophy and use of the system. Survey the attendees for their evaluation of the system's ability to meet their needs.

Arrange for a **trial use** of the system on your own computer to test out needed functions and ease of use. Set up a file and experiment with it. Many vendors will install their system on a trial basis, applying part or all of the fee, if any, toward the purchase price. Careful planning is necessary to effectively utilize the trial period. The trial period needs to be three to four months; thirty days is insufficient time to try it against your needs.

Performing a **benchmark test** is mentioned last because it is rarely worth the cost. A benchmark is a standard processing sequence run with several competing systems. A benchmark test provides information which can be used (with varying degrees of accuracy) to project expected throughput levels, response times, and operating costs of the system. A representative problem is used to make estimates of system performance under a full load. A sample benchmark might involve setting up a file (from existing input data), performing some specialized search and update processing, asking some standard queries, and producing a set of reports. Some vendors are willing to contribute substantial time and effort to conducting the benchmark test.

The major problem with benchmark testing is its focus on machine operating efficiency. A benchmark can only test competing systems in an area of common functionality. Since available systems differ widely in functional capability, benchmarking is of limited usefulness, except in situations requiring high throughput or rapid response in the face of large volumes of input or stored data.

17.5 SELECTION CRITERIA ("Asking Questions")

Selection criteria are broken down into technical criteria and administrative criteria. Technical selection criteria relate to the functional capabilities of the DBMS product. Administrative selection criteria include efficiency, ease of use, documentation, acquisition and operating costs, compatibility with the existing organization and data processing facilities, and characteristics of the vendor.

The most important technical criteria concern the basic type of system required and the set of functional capabilities needed to serve the user community.

17.5.1 What Type of DBMS?

17.5.1.1 Host-Language, Self-Contained, or Both

The basic type of system best for an organization depends upon the intended types of users. A *host-language DBMS* is for programmers—anyone wanting to use the system must first write a program (or use one already written) to access the database. A *self-contained DBMS* provides its own languages for querying and updating the database—it is impossible for a programming user to write a program in a conventional programming language, such as COBOL or FORTRAN, to interact directly with the database. Selecting one type of system or the other excludes a whole class of user from interacting directly with the database using the DBMS facilities.

The choice of system type may be unduly influenced by one type of user depending on who makes the selection recommendation or who dominates the evaluation team. Systems and programming personnel are likely to select a host-language DBMS because its facilities are oriented to their skills. Even more important, and more subtle, such a choice gives the programmers job security. The Systems and Programming Department remains in control because everyone in the organization must go through them to use the DBMS. A steering committee of user representatives is likely to select a system which can be used by nonprogramming users—a self-contained DBMS with its own high-level, user-oriented languages. *Management needs to be aware of these inherent biases in the selection of a DBMS.*

When faced with an exclusive choice between the two basic types of DBMS, most organizations select a host-language DBMS with its inherently greater flexibility. They are afraid of getting a system with which they may not be able to do what they want. A self-contained DBMS may leave little opportunity to develop tailored routines to satisfy those special processing requirements that inevitably arise. (The ability to exit to a user-written subroutine is only a partial solution.) With a host-language DBMS you have great flexibility in building an application system, but notice who is doing the work. People in the using organization must build the application system, often with low-level building blocks, that is, using a one-record-at-a-time language.

Once several databases are established and several application systems are built using the "flexible" facilities of the host language DBMS, an organization finds itself locked-in to the original designs. Revisions to a database structure become exceedingly difficult and expensive with most systems. The flexibility of the system turns out to be a trap. The evolvability of a database system is greatly enhanced with a comprehensive definition of the stored data and high-level languages with which to access and manipulate the data.

The next inclination is to select one of each type of system with an interface between them—a system with facilities for a nonprogramming user to query, update, and generate reports from a database, and which interfaces with a host-language DBMS under which the database is defined and maintained. Unfortunately, many such marriages are poor marriages, even from the same vendor.

17.5.1.2 Proliferating Database Definitions

The main reason for poor marriages is the lack of a comprehensive definition of the stored database on the part of many host-language systems. As long as only programmers interact with the database, the system can pass on much of the responsibility for knowing the format of data in the database to the application programmers. A self-contained DBMS interfaced with a host-language DBMS (now it is no longer "self-contained") must have a more complete definition of the stored database. Now, there is another definition of the same stored data. Maintaining consistency across multiple data definitions becomes an administrative responsibility of the external using environment because the "system" does not do it.

Proliferating database definitions can be a real burden to an organization (see Figure 17-10). One solution is to have a single, comprehensive database definition (there could still be internal derived definitions which are automatically generated and maintained). Another solution is to allow a mapping between different definitions and perform dynamic data conversion upon data transfer. This is, in effect, a userchema capability and contributes to greater evolvability.

17.5.1.3 Circumvented Database Integrity Controls

Another reason for poor marriages is that the self-contained DBMS often has better data validation capabilities. However, users cannot depend upon them being enforced because programming users of the host-language interface actually circumvent the validation controls. The validity of the stored data can only be ensured to the extent of the controls in the host-language DBMS (see Figure 17-10). In a good marriage of programming language facilities and nonprogramming user facilities, *all* the integrity controls will underlie *both* user interfaces. Therefore, the validation criteria and semantic constraints must be part of the database definition language of the host-language DBMS.

17.5.1.4 Select a Full-Function DBMS with Integrated Facilities

To serve more people in the using environment, an organization is wise to select a DBMS with well integrated facilities for both programming and nonprogramming users to access a common database. Most application systems can be built using the high-level retrieval and update language facilities of the DBMS with the programming language interface used only when there are special processing requirements for greater generality or greater efficiency.

Many systems are now available with integrated facilities or the result of combining systems (although some of the marriages suffer from the problems noted earlier). Figure 17-11 lists selected systems or combinations from a single vendor. The hardware on which a system operates is given if from an independent vendor and it does not run on IBM hardware. The list also includes the home office location for some vendors, recognizing that they may have branch offices and affiliates throughout the world.

17.5.2 Efficiency versus Functionality

Often the question of speed is the most immediate concern of an organization investigating candidate DBMS. They ask "How fast does it run?" or "How much main memory does it take?" before they ask "What will the system do?" This focus of concern is seen in "benchmarkphobia"—a desire to benchmark a system before using

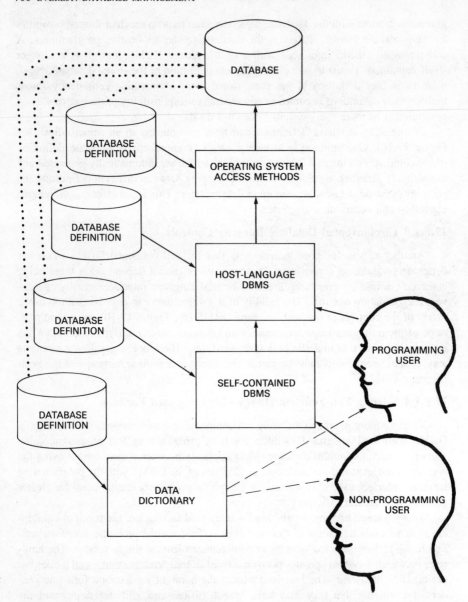

Figure 17-10. Proliferating Database Definitions.
When multiple, independently developed systems are coupled together, each will have its own definition of the database. With no system facility to ensure consistency across these definitions, the responsibility falls on the DBA to ensure consistency. This can be a heavy administrative burden, with success depending on persistent enforcement and cooperative DBMS users. Some suggest adding a data dictionary but if its *full* definition does not *directly* control the operation of the other parts, it merely adds another database definition which an organization must keep consistent with the rest. Note also that if the host-language DBMS operates with a limited definition and few validation constraints on the data, the stored data cannot be guaranteed to conform to any further definitional or validation criteria in the self-contained DBMS or the data dictionary.

ADABAS + ADASCRIPT + ADAWRITER + NATURAL from Software ag, Reston, VA (Darmstadt, West Germany)

AMBASE from AMCOR Computer Corp, Louisville, KY. (on PDP-11)

DATABOSS from Floria Computer, Inc., N. Miami. (on PDP-11)

DATACOM/DB + DATAQUERY + DATAREPORT from Applied Data Research, Princeton, NJ

DATAFLEX from Data Access Corp, Miami, FL. (on micros)

DB2 (as SQL) from International Business Machines

DBASE II, III from Ashton-Tate, Culver City, CA. (on micros)

DBMS-990 from Texas Instruments

DM IV = IDS II + QRP (formerly MDQS) + TP from Honeywell, Inc.

DMRS from Intergraph, Huntsville, AL. (on enhanced DEC VAX)

DMS II + DMINQuiry + REPORTER from Burroughs

DMS 170 + QUERY/UPDATE from Control Data Corp.

DMS 1100 + QLP from Univac

DPL from National Information Systems, Inc., Los Altos, CA. (on DEC 10/20)

DRS from Advanced Data Management (A.R.A.P.), Princeton, NJ

ENCOMPAS + ENFORM from Tandem Computers, Inc.

FOCUS from Information Builders, Inc., New York

IDMS + CULPRIT + OnLine English ++ from Cullinet, Westwood, MA

IMAGE + QUERY from Hewlett-Packard

IM/DM from Control Data (and Battelle Institute)

IMS/VS (or DL/I) + GIS/VS or SQL from International Business Machines

INFORMIX from Relational Database Systems, Sunnyvale, CA. (on micros)

INGRES from Relational Technology, Inc., Berkeley, CA

INQUIRE from Infodata Systems, Falls Church, VA

MAG/base III from Micro Applications Group, Canoga Park, CA (on micros)

MDBS + QRS from Micro Data Base System, Inc., Lafayette, IN. (on micros)

MODEL 204 from Computer corporation of America, Cambridge, MA

NOMAD 2 from National CSS, Inc.

OPTIMUM from Uveon, Denver, CO. (on micros).

ORACLE from Oracle Corp., Menlo Park, CA. (on IBM, DEC, and micros)

Q PRO-4 from Quik 'n Easy Products, Langhorne, PA. (on micros)

RAMIS II from Martin Marietta (formerly Mathematica), Princeton, NJ

R:BASE and CLOUT from Microrim, Bellevue, WA. (on micros)

RELATE/3000 from CRI, Mountain View, CA. (on Hewlett-Packard)

REVELATION from Cosmos, Seattle, WA. (on micros)

SEED + QUERY + REPORT WRITER + TP from Int'l Data Base Systems, Phila. PA

SQL from International Business Machines

SYSTEM 1022/1032 from First Data, Waltham, MA. (on DEC)

SYSTEM 2000 from Intel Commercial Systems Div (formerly MRI) Austin,TX

TIS = TOTAL + SOCRATES + QUERY from Cincom Systems, Inc., Cincinnati, OH

UNIFY from Unify Corp, Portland, OR. (on micros)

Figure 17-11. Selected List of "Full" Capability DBMSs.
Systems or combinations of systems included on this list provide facilities for both programming and nonprogramming users. Recognizing that the list is no sooner published than it is out of date and incomplete, it is not definitive. It is intended primarily to indicate that lots of such systems are commercially available.

other sources of detailed technical information to assess the level of functional capability in a system. After a system is installed and used for awhile, concern for efficiency gives way to concern for lacking functionality, particularly integrity and evolvability functions.

An organization should carefully evaluate the *functional completeness* of candidate DBMSs. How far does the system go in performing basic data-oriented tasks for both application developers and end users? How much does the system do compared to what the users have to do? With machine costs falling and people costs rising, the trend is to let the system do more. If the system does not validate stored data, for example, the users will have to include appropriate routines in the application. A system which is "fast" may be suspect—the fastest way to do something is not to do it! If the system is "fast," people may be burdened with a large share of the data-oriented tasks. *The purpose of a DBMS is to provide these data-oriented services to users; machine efficiency is a secondary concern.*

In fact, it always takes time in the DBMS to do more for the user. Functions relating to integrity and evolvability are diametrically opposed to machine efficiency. Within machine efficiency there is still the basic tradeoff between processing time and space utilization. These multiple objectives of database management systems are shown in Figure 17-12. Considerations of machine efficiency do not lead to effective use of human resources.

Availability, integrity, and evolvability objectives primarily affect human resource utilization. Increased functional capability which makes the database more directly available to users and which provides more powerful, high-level languages leads to reduced human effort in using the system and building application systems. Greater integrity leads to increased user and management confidence in the use of the system and its output. Greater evolvability leads to easier database revision and application system modification in response to changing user demands, thus resulting in more responsive systems. Greater integrity and evolvability means the system has to do more and is, therefore, less efficient in the straight processing of data.

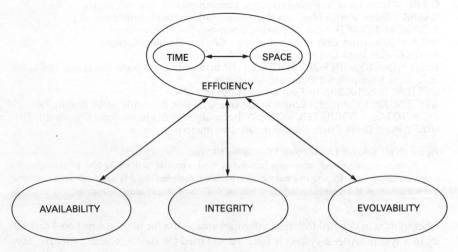

Figure 17-12. Multiple Competing Objectives in Database Management.
An obsession with machine efficiency in selecting a DBMS can short change other objectives of providing greater functional capability to the users.

Management needs to be aware of the inherent conflict between efficiency and functionality in selecting a DBMS.

Decide what you want and know what you are getting.

17.5.3 Suggested Technical Evaluation Criteria

Recognizing that any statement of selection criteria must be tailored to the needs of the organization, certain technical criteria are often overlooked. This book gives a comprehensive picture of the functions of database management. An outline of the various section headings in the chapters of Part II can provide a good basis against which to compare a DBMS for functional completeness.

The major categories of technical criteria for selecting a DBMS are as follows:

MAJOR TECHNICAL CRITERIA

---

1. *Database Definition*, including logical structure and physical storage structure.
2. Generalized *retrieval* capability—asking questions and getting answers.
3. Generalized *Update* capability—to add, delete, and modify the data in the database.
4. *Programmer interface.*
5. Maintenance of *Database Integrity*.
6. *Modes of operation*—online and/or batch, for above functions.
7. *Database revision* and evolvability.

Each of these categories is expanded in Appendix 17A. The outline of features in these categories provides a starting point for an organization to begin an evaluation and selection process.

17.5.4 Administrative Criteria

Selection criteria not relating to functional capabilities are considered administrative criteria. These include the required configuration of hardware and software, operational and performance characteristics, vendor support, documentation, required staff support, and cost. While some technical capabilities (or lack of) have administrative implications, it is desirable not to confuse the technical criteria for evaluation with administrative considerations.

Aside from the system itself, the next most important consideration is the vendor (or developer). Are the people genuinely excited about their product? That is the most important question to ask. Visit their location, mingle with the people in sales and in development, and look into their eyes as they speak of working for this vendor. Are they proud to be on the team? Are they enthusiastic about the future of this vendor and this product? Whether or not it's possible to get that close, a prospective buyer should try to get a feel for these questions about the vendor.

The following lists direct attention to various areas which may be important in evaluating the administrative aspects of a candidate system.

MAJOR ADMINISTRATIVE CRITERIA

---

1. Vendor Characteristics and Product Stability—history, size, financial strength, years since product introduced, record of enhancements, and number of users.

2. Maintenance Support—written agreement and are other users satisfied, responsiveness to user problems.

3. Documentation and Training—readable, updated with changes, training classes and materials available at reasonable cost.

4. Ease of Learning and Use—understandable system architecture, user-friendly interface, and online help facilities.

5. Operating and Performance Characteristics—it actually works (see a demonstration), and will handle the sizes and throughputs required.

6. Supporting Environment: Hardware, Software, and Administrative Staff—the system will "fit" into the organization and the existing (or upgraded) hardware and software environment.

7. Costs—direct acquisition or lease plus changes to existing hardware configuration, installation, training, and documentation.

17.5.5 The Path from Efficiency to Profitability

A DBMS must ultimately be judged by its contribution to organizational profitability through increased effectiveness of users and management decision makers. Figure 17-13 depicts the relationship of selection criteria from DBMS machine efficiency to organizational profitability. Selecting a DBMS involves much more than how fast it runs on a computer. Besides the efficiency (time and space) of a DBMS while executing on the computer, several other factors contribute to organizational profitability. A good DBMS must have a balance of capabilities in all four of the inner circles. When a DBMS is fast, the other factors usually suffer. When a DBMS has more functional capabilities the execution of user applications *with the DBMS* can be more efficient, people can be more efficient in building those application systems and people can be more efficient when it is necessary to revise those applications and the supporting databases. When a DBMS is more responsive to user requests and to changing requirements, then users and managers in the organization can be more effective in their duties.

17.6 FINAL SELECTION, CONTRACT NEGOTIATION, AND ACQUISITION

Having gathered information in answer to the many questions suggested by the technical and administrative criteria, an organization proceeds to make a final selection. Seldom does a clear-cut choice emerge; each of the finalists has some strengths along with some drawbacks.

One of the most difficult tasks is to put all the information together to facilitate making a selection. The various evaluation methodologies presented earlier in this chapter provide a means to assemble the information gathered. Instead of making one

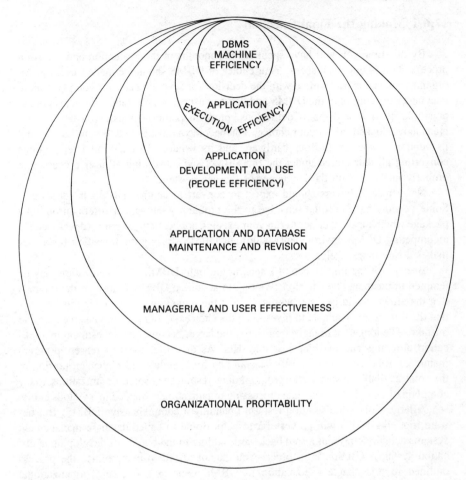

Figure 17-13. DBMS Selection Criteria: Efficiency or Profitability?

big subjective judgment, the methodologies force you to make many small, independent, subjective judgments. Then they mechanically lead you to calculate an aggregate score for each system which takes into account the information on each system and your weighting of importance on the many features and criteria.

With aggregate system scores, you can now focus on the final selection. Close scores (say within 5%) should not be considered significant and the final selection should rest on other less tangible factors. Often at this point, an organization will go back and reflect on some of the weightings and adjust them. "If I was overly optimistic in judging the vendor's commitment to support this product, what difference would it make in the final score?" A word of caution: Do not be overly dependent on the results of the formal evaluation methodology. It is only an aid to making the decision—use it as long as it is useful.

17.6.1 Making the Final Selection

By this time you will have spent several months in the evaluation and selection process. This is time well spent. Your choice of DBMS should be made carefully. An organization can expect to live with the decision for several years. As you place more data under the control of the DBMS and develop user processes (application programs, prestored queries, and report definitions, predefined transactions), you become increasingly "locked in" to your choice. You become almost as tied to your DBMS and its vendor as you are to your hardware and its vendor. To back out later requires converting all data stored under the old DBMS and retrofitting all user processes to properly interface with the languages of the new system.

Nevertheless, buyers should expect to convert to another DBMS in the future. Some vendors have become sensitive to the problem. One vendor offers an optional package which makes it easier to run your existing application programs (developed for a competing DBMS environment) with their DBMS. Easing the transition for a user makes a sale more likely.

Because of the importance of selecting the right DBMS, an organization may be tempted to postpone the decision. Waiting to acquire a DBMS simply on the grounds that the effects could be far-reaching, or that the money is not available this year, or that the time is not available to investigate the choices, could prove to be an expensive mistake. The longer an organization waits, the larger becomes the investment in application programs and machine readable data. As this investment increases, program maintenance becomes more costly, accounting for a higher and higher proportion of the total available systems and programming resources. (Some organizations today complain of 70 to 80%.) The data processing organization is trapped in a vicious circle.

A large part of the solution rests in obtaining a comprehensive DBMS. But beware, not all DBMSs will go very far to help. Some so called database management systems actually represent a step backwards adding to the burden of developing application systems. Caution is in order. You cannot afford to compromise the process outlined in this chapter—education in DBMS concepts, assessing organizational needs, searching for available systems, gathering more information relating to both technical and administrative criteria, then zeroing in on a final choice, installing a system, and finally, working hard to make it work for you.

Choosing to postpone the acquisition of a DBMS will not stretch the organization to move toward the database approach and learn how to share data resources, how to release control of those resources to a common responsible authority, and how to cooperate in the maintenance of those resources. Although the installation of a DBMS is not strictly necessary to move toward that database approach, few managers have the will and the strength to push for such a move. Organizations do not change overnight. If installed and managed with a healthy attitude of cooperation and self-help, a database management system can be the catalyst for a gradual move toward the database approach.

Of course, there is always the possibility that you truly do not find a suitable DBMS. Then an organization can establish and continue to develop the database administration function, and can inventory and document the data items and natural data structures that exist within the organization. It may also be good to acquire a retrieval only package that can extract and report data from existing files. Such a strategy can help to educate users and get "data to the people."

17.6.2 Economics of the Software Market

When shopping for software one notices a wide variation in prices. A look at the relationship between fixed and variable costs provides us with a clue. For a given product, the total cost to a vendor is:

$$\text{TOTAL COST} = D + R * N$$

where

D = the fixed cost to develop, design, and build the product; the total accumulated cost to produce the first unit of the product.

R = the variable cost of reproduction or making an additional unit of the product.

N = the total number of units sold (or expected to be sold).

The unit cost of the product is the reproduction cost plus a proportionate share of the fixed development cost:

$$\text{UNIT COST} = R + D/N$$

which approaches **R** as **N** gets very large.

The unit variable cost, **R** , represents the minimum price which a vendor would set for the product, which is reasonable if **R** is substantial relative to **D** .

For software, almost all the costs are for development, **D** is much much greater than **R** . While it would be typical for the cost of developing a DBMS to be several million dollars, the cost of making another copy to sell to you is perhaps $20, the cost of the magnetic media on which to copy and send it. What the vendor sets as the selling price is particularly sensitive to volume or anticipated number of sales (see Figure 17-14).

This all means that the pricing of software is rather arbitrary. There is little correlation between price and quality or capability. Marketing forces dominate. This means, in theory, at least, the buyer has great bargaining power. Software vendors will often make a deal if it means getting a foot in the door, getting something in return, or if they perceive this sale leading to several more sales. If a vendor is firm in their price quotation, at least you know that it is not for economic reasons.

The problem of pricing software is particularly acute on microcomputer systems. When the hardware costs one quarter of a million dollars and up on the medium to large scale computers, the DBMS software costs in the range of $30,000 to $200,000. But when the hardware costs $10,000 you can hardly charge $30,000 for the software. The cost of developing good software for a microcomputer does not take substantially less effort than for a large scale computer. So what is the vendor to do? One vendor selling their DBMS for $96,000 on a mainframe computer offers essentially the same product for sale on microcomputers at less than $2,000.

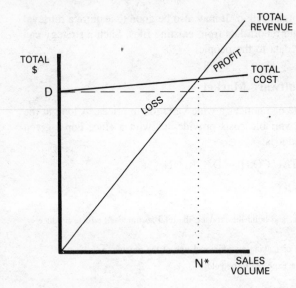

Figure 17-14. Pricing Software: Total Revenue vs Total Cost.

In selling software, the initial development costs are much, much greater than the cost to make and sell another copy. Profit is particularly sensitive to the anticipated volume of sales (N^*). Therefore, setting the price (the slope of the Total Revenue line) is quite arbitrary and the buyer has, theoretically, great bargaining power. Also, the buyer should not expect any relationship between price and quality or capability.

With hardware costs declining and the lack of good software, two things must happen in the industry. First, users must begin to expect software to cost more than the hardware. Secondly, we must establish protection for proprietary software to ensure that economic rewards flow back to the developers (discussed in a later section).

17.6.3 Contract Negotiation and Terms

After narrowing the choice to one system, the next step is to negotiate an acquisition and maintenance agreement with the vendor. At this point you might say, "Don't we just sign on the dotted line, get the system, and pay for it?" Read on!

Blindly signing the vendor's standard contract is making a foolish mistake. You may be signing away all your rights and remedies and signing away any obligation of the vendor. If you are unable to get the system to do for you what you need and expect, you may have no recourse—you may not even be able to get your money back. You must consider all the objectives and risks in acquiring the software, and incorporate these in a written contract which is enforceable in the courts or in arbitration if necessary.

Most vendors have a standard contract form. Assume at the outset that it can be changed. Do not be afraid to be firm in getting terms written in that are to your own advantage. You can be sure that the standard contract was drawn up to protect the vendor. Now it is up to the customer to equalize the agreement. Consider the standard contract to be the vendor's *initial* offer at the bargaining table. Now draw up your own counteroffer, thus establishing the basis for negotiating toward an agreement. Do not be surprised if you lose on most of your demands, but be hard-nosed on those that are really important.

The time to exercise your bargaining power is in negotiating the software contract.

Some vendor terms will be non-negotiable. Some (smaller) vendors may not even have a contract. For the protection of both, you need some written understanding. Both parties will benefit from being explicit in their expectations. The final contract should be the result of arm's length bargaining—to pay an honest price for a system with needed functional capabilities, performance characteristics, and support services.

If you are depending on certain representations, promises, or commitments made by the vendor in sales or technical presentations on the system, get them into the contract so you have some recourse if they turn out to be false or misleading. If the vendor is confident in their product, this should present no problem. Spell out the rights and remedies of the user in case the vendor fails to perform certain obligations. Take nothing for granted. Leave nothing important out of the contract—relying on verbal agreements. The vendor representative may not work for that vendor tomorrow.

Remember that the vendor has probably had lots of experience in negotiating contracts. Get your lawyer involved. Data processing people must not expect to be able to understand the subtle meanings behind the legal phrases in a contract. Trying to review and revise a vendor contract and write in your own terms without legal help is an invitation to disaster. Giving definitive advice on contract terms is beyond the scope of this text. Furthermore, a contract should be tailored to reflect the major concerns in each individual situation. Several good books have been written on data processing contracts and some are included in the bibliography. Your lawyer is well advised to be familiar with these references. If you do not have a lawyer, some firms now specialize in working with clients in negotiating and drafting contracts and related products and services.

Responsibility for overseeing contract negotiations should rest with one person in the acquiring organization. All suggestions for inclusion, and all vendor contacts should go through that person. They are also responsible for ensuring that technical, legal, and financial expertise are brought to bear on the contract.

The biggest problem a user has is thinking of all the areas that need special attention and protection. The user should try to spell out who is responsible for doing what and when, particularly if something goes wrong. If everything goes smoothly, there is little need for a contract. The contract is needed primarily when everything doesn't work out as expected.

The contract cannot cover all eventualities but at least it should cover the major risks and try to clearly set forth the intent of both parties. Even when getting something down in writing is difficult, anything is better than nothing, than relying on a verbal understanding.

The remainder of this section briefly touches various terms that may appear in a contract. This is not intended to be definitive or complete, but to make you aware of some of the terms to look for or to look out for.

WARRANTY. Many vendor contracts specify that the software is licensed on an "as is" basis, with no warranty of "merchantability or fitness for a particular purpose." In short, the vendor does not guarantee that the product will do *anything* useful for the customer! Furthermore, they may not even *guarantee* to fix errors in the program or clear up any problems in using the software. At the same time they may say that the product has been thoroughly tested and that they will *try* to help if any problems arise. The point is that the customer must place much more reliance on the practices of the vendor, and other user experiences with the vendor. How has the vendor responded in the past to user problems? Some vendors will at least agree to correct a product so that it performs in accordance with its documentation which should be specifically referenced in the contract. The customers should seek some contract provisions relating to what they expect the system to do for them. A good place to start is the documentation and sales literature supplied by the vendor. It can be included in the contract by reference.

MAINTENANCE. The vendor should warrant the product and maintenance for a period of time, agreeing to fix problems or errors attributable to the product within a specified period of time. It is reasonable for vendor obligations to end if the user modifies the program.

DELIVERABLES. Be specific about what the customer receives—object code delivered in a particular form, user manuals and system reference manuals (how many), training (specify what you get, how many attendee hours/days, who gets it, when, and who does the training), installation (who does it), operating instruction manuals, test data validation package, and perhaps the source code. The user faces a real dilemma if the vendor does not agree to fix errors *and* will not deliver the source code.

ACCEPTANCE. Delivery can mean dropping the product on your desk; installation can mean merely copying the software to the user's program library on disk. Initial payment should not be based on these, but rather on an acceptance test. Acceptance should be based on satisfactory completion of an objective, operational test. It could be running a vendor-supplied test data validation package. Better yet, base it on the functional and performance characteristics which you require in the system. Get your mandatory criteria in an acceptance test, expressed in precise, measurable terms.

PAYMENT. The transfer of money controls the leverage of the parties. Therefore, make payment conditional on the vendor satisfying certain provisions, such as the product meeting the acceptance test. During a warranty period, the customer should have the right to rescind the contract by returning or destroying all materials acquired and paying only the appropriate license fee for the actual period of use. This protects the user if the product fails to perform and they are unable to satisfy their application needs.

The buyer may acquire the system under a fully paid up license making one lump payment. Continuing maintenance would then be obtained by making additional period payments. Alternatively, acquisition may be under a perpetual license arrangement with payments made on a regular basis as long as the product is in use. It is important that the user obtain price protection such that the perpetual license fee remain constant (or decline) but never increase. The vendor is recovering part of the development costs and they do not change in the future. Of course, the maintenance fee is separate and may increase. One vendor quotes a single fee with the option to raise it upon three months notice. The customer has the option of paying or discontinuing use—an impossible choice once tied in to the use of the package.

LIABILITY. Most vendors start out by saying that they will not be liable for anything— "loss or damages caused or allegedly caused directly or indirectly by the package including but not limited to loss of profits or consequential damages." In short, the user is ultimately responsible to see that the package runs correctly and does what it is supposed to do *before* placing reliance on its use in a vital activity of the organization. The customer should not be discouraged but try to place liability where it belongs (via express warranties and contract remedies). At the same time, the contract should protect both parties from delays or failures in performance resulting from acts beyond their control.

COMPATIBILITY. Vendor should guarantee that the package will operate on the customer's particular hardware/software configuration, including the computer, terminals, storage devices, and other software such as operating system and teleprocessing monitor. If not, the vendor should try to make it work and, if unsuccessful, release the customer from any payment obligations. The user would even like some assurance that the software will continue to operate with future releases of equipment and systems software.

PROPRIETARY RIGHTS. Every vendor will include several terms to protect their proprietary interest in the software product. You never *buy* software, even when you make one lump sum payment, you only acquire, through a "nonexclusive, nontransferrable license," a right to *use* the software under certain conditions for a specified period of time (which may be 99 years!). The vendor retains title and ownership. The vendor can use any combination of patents, copyrights, and trade secrets to protect their interests. The contract should clearly specify the limits on use of the software—on which computers, in which organizations, etc. This can be a tricky part of the contract. What if the customer later sells the computer? Do not assume the software goes with it since the contract is for use by customer only. If you are in a subsidiary of a larger company, have the parent organization sign the contract with the vendor. The contract should spell out the extent to which the customer can make copies of the documentation and the software (for backup purposes). Trade secret provisions require the customer not to disclose any materials to anyone other than those employees who work with the software, and they must comply with the nondisclosure agreement (preferably in writing) even after leaving the employ of the customer. The customer should get the vendor to be specific about what it is that must be kept secret. The contract should seek a balance holding both parties to nondisclosure of proprietary information of material.

INDEMNIFICATION. If the vendor is found to not hold clear title to the software (for example, part of the code came from someone else's program), then a third party may unexpectedly assert rights against the user. For protection, the vendor should indemnify and "hold harmless" the user against any loss, liability, costs, or legal fees arising from the use of the infringing software. During such time, the user should withhold further payments to the vendor, accumulating the monies for possible payment to the adverse claimant. If the vendor is small, the user can require the vendor to post an indemnity bond as a condition of the sale.

VENDOR FAILURE. If the vendor should go out of business, the user would not want to be left without the software upon which they soon become very dependent. A contract term can specify that the user gains unlimited rights of use with no further obligations to the vendor. If source code and detailed system documentation was not originally given to the customer, the contract could specify that these materials be placed with an independent escrow agent to be released to all users upon failure of the vendor. One vendor's contract specifies that title to the software and all materials shall pass to the (well-organized) users' group.

All this sounds like an adversary situation, pitting vendor against buyer—and it is. In most cases, you can file the contract away and forget about it. Most vendors realize that their business success depends on satisfied customers and will bend over backwards to assist a user. BUT . . . in those few instances where things do not work out, the contract is indispensable—it defines the arena in which you will do battle; it defines the rights, remedies and obligations of both parties.

17.6.4 Protecting Proprietary Software

The thorniest problem facing software vendors is how to protect their proprietary interest in their software. Having made the investment to develop the software, they need some assurance that just economic rewards will flow back to them.

A vendor can use any combination of three basic mechanisms to protect software: patent, copyright, trade secret. Each has serious drawbacks, providing limited protection.

The fundamental objective of both patent and copyright law is

"to promote the progress of science and the useful arts, by securing for limited times to authors and inventors the exclusive right to their respective writings and discoveries."*

Widespread dissemination for public benefit promotes progress. Having an exclusive right means that the creator should receive any economic compensation when someone else wants to use their creation. Trade secret protection is obtained through a contract which the law recognizes.

Figure 17-15 summarizes the characteristics of the three protection mechanisms. While patents and copyrights require some form of publication or disclosure, trade secrets protection is only obtained through nondisclosure.

The U.S. *Copyright* Law of 1976 protects the wrong thing—the expression of an idea (or algorithm or flow of processing logic) "fixed in a tangible medium" (i.e., recorded on paper or other media), rather than the *use* of the program to direct the operation of a computer. Interestingly, the copyright law does extend to "public performances" of work. While execution of a program might be construed as a performance, it is hardly done in public. In 1980 the U.S. Congress passed the Computer Software Act which extends copyright protection to computer programs, preventing pirating, unauthorized copying (except needed backup copies), and use.

Patents are slow and costly to obtain, and then the probability of success in an infringement suit is very low (though there has yet been little experience). During the 1970's the U.S. government generally held that software was not patentable. Then, in 1981, the U.S. Supreme Court ruled that machine processes implemented in software are patentable† thus opening the door to software patents, though the battle is by no means won. There is still a reluctance to extend patent protection to software per se, partly because it is not innovative (which is usually true, but is a requirement for obtaining a patent). One vendor has successfully obtained several patents on a combi-

*Article 1, Section 8, of the United States Constitution
†Diamond vs. Diehr, No. 79-1112, March 3, 1981

	COPYRIGHT	PATENT	TRADE SECRET
PROTECTS:	*Expression* of ideas. (not ideas or algorithms)	Innovative (new and unobvious) apparatus or process	Information or knowledge
OBTAINED UPON:	Creation	Acceptance of application (must search all prior patents)	Signing nondisclosure contract agreement
TIME TO OBTAIN:	Immediate	1-5 Years	Immediate
TERM:	75 Years (life + 50 yrs. for individuals)	17 Years	Perpetual
COST TO OBTAIN:	$10	Many $1,000s	$1,000
COST TO MAINTAIN:	None	None (New contract)	
COST TO ENFORCE:	Moderate	Moderate	Higher
STATUTORY DAMAGES:	Yes (up to $50,000)	No	No
LEGAL FEES FROM INFRINGERS:	Yes	Yes	No
PROTECTION LOST BY:	Gross Neglect	Unsuccessful litigation (probability .95)	Disclosure
DEGREE OF PROTECTION FOR SOFTWARE:	Low-Moderate	Low	Moderate

Figure 17-15. Characteristics of Copyright, Patent, and Trade Secret Protection Mechanisms.

nation of their software *and* a particular computer—together they are an apparatus or process and more clearly fall under the purview of the law.

Given the weaknesses of statutory protection (copyright and patent) most vendors rely on the contractual mechanism of *trade secret*. Its major problem is the cost to obtain and maintain secrecy with every new contract. Furthermore, the vendor has no recourse to a third party who may have illicitly or otherwise obtained a copy of the materials, including software, which was to have been kept secret by every recipient. Problems are compounded when the vendor also seeks copyright and patent protection— they both require some disclosure of the very information to be protected.

Enforcement in all three cases is practically impossible. No wonder the vendors are paranoid at times. Once the software is out and being exchanged it is difficult to trace where it came from, even if you could find those who have a copy without paying for the right to use it. This problem is particularly acute with off-the-shelf software for the millions of small microcomputers in homes and businesses.

Some people feel we need new legal mechanisms (or substantial amendments to existing copyright or patent laws) to explicitly deal with software. The price if we don't is to discourage the development of good quality software; and one of the biggest problems in the computer industry today is the lack of good quality software.

17.7 INSTALLATION AND USE

Once a DBMS is installed, an organization's work has only just begun. Since the initial learning and application development will take some time and effort, it is wise not to schedule the immediate post implementation period in parallel with any major information systems activity (e.g., a reorganization, installing a new computer system, upgrading to a major new operating system, or implementing a big new application system).

If a DBMS is to serve an organization well, people must be aware of its availability, and excited about what it can do for them. Someone must be the shepherd—probably the database administrator—to lead people into the new database approach, to ensure that needed training takes place, and to assist in the decisions people must make to prepare for using the DBMS.

At the same time, these people need to be realistic in their expectations. The DBMS does not provide instant panacea once installed. It takes patience. First some specialists in the organization must become familiar with how to use the new software. A nucleus team is needed to design and implement the first application system. The members should be able to relate to other people and their needs, should have solid technical experience, and have a contagious enthusiasm. The last criterion is probably the most important. Enlist people from anywhere in the organization, within data processing or in user organizations.

17.7.1 Selecting the First Application

It is critical to pick the first DBMS application wisely. It will be the first impression for many in the organization and, therefore, will form a lasting impression. People turned off at these initial stages are hard to get back in support of the DBMS approach.

Pick the first application to satisfy two major objectives:

1. *Demonstrate* to users the feasibility and usefulness of DBMS.
2. *Learn* how to use the DBMS.

The following criteria can guide the selection of the first application. The chosen application should satisfy as many of these as possible.

TO ENHANCE USER'S POSITIVE PERCEPTIONS the application should:

- Be highly visible to the users and easily understandable.
- Do something useful, of real value to the organization, not trivial.
- Do something new that was not done before.
- Emphasize retrieval and presentation of data, preferably online.
- Be important to managers, e.g., ad hoc query with some aggregations and comparisons.
- Target the main motivation for acquiring the DBMS.

TO MAXIMIZE PROBABILITY OF SUCCESS the application should:

- Be simple and straight forward to develop with well-defined requirements.
- Be nonvital to the organization (low risk if it fails).
- Be separable from the mainstream of organizational activity (not tightly coupled to other applications).
- Involve a low volume of data—avoid having to collect and input lots of data before having anything to show.
- Not be dependent on immediate, timely update of data to be useful.
- Focus on satisfying the needs of the "right" user.

The last point may be the most important of all. The "right" user will be a visionary leader, commanding the respect of colleagues. That user should be sympathetic to the potential and struggles of data processing, and an excited advocate. Such a user can do much to bring other users along with their contagious enthusiasm.

An often suitable first application is in the personnel area, perhaps relating to a skills inventory. Unacceptable applications would include payroll to produce pay cheques, inventory control, and order entry. One bank mechanized the records of securities held on deposit in trust accounts. To delay the tide of user demands stimulated by a demonstration, an organization could first pick a project internal to data processing. In most organizations, a suitable application is immediately obvious and probably already in the queue.

The design team of both user and data processing personnel should be small and able to learn fast. They should be somewhat introspective with what they do, concentrating as much on the process of developing the application as on the final product. When the first application is all done, they will constitute the core of people to help others. They will promulgate and foster the use of the system for new applications.

Allow several months for the first application. The development team will struggle at first to learn how to use the system and will make lots of mistakes. What they produce will probably not be very elegant (internally). When it is done, they will see many ways to do it better next time (these should be documented). An organization should even be prepared to scrap the system after it is built (though they probably won't), or at least redesign it substantially. Remember, the main objectives are to learn how to use the DBMS and to demonstrate its usefulness.

17.7.2 Charge Out Schemes Inhibit DBMS Use

Organizations mature in their use of computers tend to charge users for the use of resources and services in systems development and operation. With a newly installed DBMS this could be a defeating policy. Initially, there is a need for people to discover the new DBMS tool and what it can do for them. People need to get excited about the very real potential of this new tool. Use of the DBMS should be free initially, at least until the users try it and can assess its true value in their operations and management.

SUMMARY

The business of evaluating, selecting, and acquiring a DBMS takes substantial time and effort. The task begins with an exploration of organizational needs and user requirements, this along with an education on DBMS concepts. Building your own DBMS is not a realistic alternative with more and more reasonably good commercial systems available. Leasing a system is faster, costs less, and lets someone else maintain the system . . . but perhaps with less capability than you would ideally want.

Needs translate into technical capabilities and administrative criteria. An organization searches for available systems through hardware vendors, software listing services, and other sources. As the list of candidate systems narrows, additional information may come from vendor, developer, users, a demonstration, introductory course, trial use, or benchmarks.

Key technical selection criteria relate to the type of system required and balancing the competing objectives of efficiency and functionality (availability, evolvability, and integrity). Administrative criteria include vendor characteristics, product stability, maintenance support, documentation, training, ease of learning and use, operating performance, supporting environment, and cost. When weighing various criteria, it is important to remember the path from efficiency to profitability. Putting all the gathered information into some comparative form suggested by various evaluation methodologies leads to a preliminary choice. This is mediated by consideration of intangible factors.

In negotiating the acquisition and maintenance contract the buyer has substantial bargaining strength (as indicated by an examination of the economics of the software market). Instead of just accepting the vendor's contract form, a buyer should work with an attorney and consider terms relating to product warranty, maintenance, deliverables, acceptance tests, payment alternatives, vendor liability, compatibility with buyer's existing environment, vendors proprietary rights, indemnification, and vendor failure.

The first application should be selected wisely using a small, nucleus team of technically solid and excited people. The first application serves to demonstrate to users the usefulness of the DBMS, enhancing their positive perceptions. It will also be a vehicle for learning how to use the system. The initial application should be selected to maximize the probability of success and the exposure to users. The success of the first application will leave a strong impression with users.

An organization will live with its chosen DBMS for several years. If the initial study and selection is done with a broad view or organizational needs now and into the future, the choice can enhance data processing's responsiveness to user needs, managerial effectiveness, and organizational profitability.

EXERCISES

17-1. Outline the basic sequence of steps to acquiring a DBMS. What steps are the most important?

17-2. How should a DBMS Evaluation and Selection team be organized? Who should be members on the team? Who should head the team?

17-3. Describe the problems which may arise if the DBMS evaluation team consists entirely of persons from Systems and Programming in the Data Processing Department.

17-4. What are the key factors which condition the choice of a DBMS selection strategy? What factors make it particularly difficult for an organization to move toward the database approach?

17-5. What are the consequences for an organization which delays in taking specific steps to move toward the database approach, and which delays in the acquisition of some sort of DBMS.

17-6. Explain why the database approach is much more than simply installing a DBMS.

17-7. Discuss the central objectives of DBMS Concepts Education. Why is it not sufficient to talk only to DBMS vendors?

17-8. Identify the three main software acquisition alternatives and the three hybrids. Describe the key strengths and weaknesses of each.

17-9. Why should an organization no longer seriously consider building their own DBMS today? What conditions might call for inhouse development?

17-10. Who in the organization would most likely choose a self-contained DBMS and why? A host-language DBMS and why?

17-11. Briefly describe four evaluation methodologies. As described in the chapter, what was the advantage or improvement of each method over the previous method?

17-12. What is implicitly wrong with the following statement: "The most important motive for looking at several DBMSs before acquiring one is to find out what a system does and does not do for its users, to discover its weaknesses and limitations, and how its developers made some of the basic tradeoffs in designing and implementing the system."

17-13. What are the advantages and shortcomings of obtaining information about a candidate system from each of these sources: vendors, current users, demonstration, introductory course, trial use, benchmark, listing services?

17-14. Why should an organization be careful about placing undue reliance on "benchmark" tests in selecting a DBMS?

17-15. What are the major technical criteria for selecting a DBMS? Would they all be important to an organization? Explain.

17-16. The joint use of a host-language DBMS and an independently developed self-contained DBMS to satisfy both programmers and nonprogrammers often results in a poor marriage. Why?

17-17. Explain how the objectives of availability, evolvability, and data integrity compete with the objective of machine efficiency.

17-18. Take a specific system (or two) and describe it (compare them) in terms of the technical and administrative selection criteria presented in this chapter. Use one of the suggested evaluation methodologies.

17-19. Explain why the pricing of software is rather arbitrary and therefore not well correlated with quality or capability.

17-20. Identify and briefly describe some of the terms which should normally be included in a software acquisition contract.

17-21. Compare and contrast the three primary mechanisms for protecting proprietary rights in software. What advice would you give a software vendor?

17-22. Why is it so important to select the first DBMS application wisely? What criteria should be used in selecting this first application?

SELECTED REFERENCES

BENTLY, Trevor J., "Defining Management's Information Needs," *AFIPS National Computer Conference Proceedings* (vol. 45), 1976, pages 869-876.

BIGELOW, Robert P. and Susan H. NYCUM, *Your Computer and the Law*, Englewood Cliffs, NJ: Prentice-Hall, 1975.
> Part four covers the law of contracts, and provides a checklist of contract terms to consider, including specific terms relating to computer software.

BRANDON, Dick H. and Sidney SEGELSTEIN, Esq., *Data Processing Contracts: Structure, Contents, and Negotiation*, New York: Van Nostrand Reinhold, 1976, 465 pages.
> After general material, this book contains 300 pages listing 29 general clauses and 34 possible clauses for software acquisition contracts (and others for software development contracts). Each clause is described in terms of where it is generally used, risk rating, intent and scope of the clause, what it protects against, expression of ideal coverage and then a fall back position, and some standard wording from actual contracts. Not all are applicable in all situations but it is a good place to begin.

BROMBERG, Howard, "Software Buying," *Datamation* (16:11), 1970 September 15, pages 35-40.

BROOKS, Frederick P., Jr., "Why is the Software [Always] Late?" *Data Management* (9:8), 1971 August, pages 18-21.

CANNING, Richard G., "The Cautious Path to a Data Base," *EDP Analyzer* (11:6), 1973 June.

CANTER, Susan J., "Database: The Application Implementation Decision," *Data Base* (15:1), 1983 Fall, pages 4-10.

CODASYL Systems Committee, *Selection and Acquisition of Data Base Management Systems*, New York, NY: Association for Computing Machinery, 1976 March, 252 pages.
> A comprehensive report covering all facets of the selection and acquisition process. Organized into six chapters:
> 1. shift in attitudes toward data and data processing, reasons supporting the use of DBMS, and prerequisite conditions for organizational readiness to install a DBMS;
> 2. characteristics and requirements of the user environment which bear on the selection and use of a DBMS;
> 3. the spectrum of functional capabilities considered to be part of a comprehensive DBMS;
> 4. the relationship of DBMS to other software systems and to computer hardware;
> 5. how various capabilities (in 3 and 4) meet the user requirements (in 2);
> 6. provides a systematic methodology for assembling an evaluation team, for guiding its selection and acquisition activities, including contract negotiation, installation, and acceptance procedures.

CONTU, *Final Report of the National Commission On New Technological Uses of Copyrighted Works*, 1978 July 31, Stanley H. FULD, Chairman, Washington, DC: Library of Congress, 1979, 154 pages.
> Created by the Copyright Act of 1976, the Commission looked at copyright of software, machine-readable databases, and photocopying. They concluded that copyright was the appropriate and adequate means for protection and recommended that the Copyright Act be amended to explicitly include computer programs. These recommendations became the basis for the U.S. Computer Software Act of 1980.

CONWAY, Melvin E., "On the Economics of the Software Market," *Datamation* (14:10), 1968 October, pages 28-31.

COULSON, Christopher J., "Putting the Pieces Together—Solving the Puzzle of How to Buy the Best DBMS for You," *ICP Software Business Review* (vol. 2), 1983 February/March, pages 84-88.

DRAPER, Jesse M., *Costs and Benefits of Database Management: Federal Experience*, Washington, DC: U. S. National Bureau of Standards, Special Publication 500-84, 1981 November.

EVEREST, Gordon C., "Comparative Survey of Database Management Systems on Microcomputers," Fourth edition, Minneapolis, MN: University of Minnesota, School of Management, MISRC Working Paper 84-01, 1983 November.
> Identified over 300 software packages where the combined hardware and software cost was less than $25,000. This edition of the survey included 63 systems. More systems are included in subsequent revisions.

FRY, James P. and Edgar H. SIBLEY, "Evolution of Data-Base Management Systems," *ACM Computing Surveys* (8:1), 1976 March, pages 7-42.

An excellent survey article covering the history and development of DBMS. Presents the significant contributions to technological development of many systems, discussing their ancestry and diagramming the relationships in major families of DBMS. Begins with the objectives of data management and ends with an extensive bibliography categorized by subject.

GLESER, Malcolm H., Judith BAYARD, and David D. LANG, "Benchmarking for the Best," *Datamation* (27:5), 1981 May, pages 127-136.

A reflective look at the actual experience of an organization in going through the DBMS selection process. The article is much broader than the title of "benchmarking" would imply.

GREGURAS, Fred M., "Software Protection: A Step Beyond Copyright," *Computerworld* (17), In Depth, 1983 December 12, pages 25-32.

Suggests using a licensing agreement.

KRASS, Peter and Hesh WIENER, "The DBMS Market Is Booming," *Datamation* (27:10), 1981 September, pages 153-170.

Gives a brief description, including vendor information, on 54 different commercially available DBMSs. Includes some systems on microcomputers. (This issue of *Datamation* included several other articles on DBMS.)

PERRY, William E., *Evaluating the Cost/Benefit of Data Bases*, Wellesley, MA: Q.E.D. Information Sciences Inc., 1982.

SABLE, Jerome D., "System Evaluation Methodology," in *INFORM Data Management System Study*, Auerbach Technical Report AUER-1834-TR-2, 1970 October 20, for the U.S. Forest Service, (available from NTIS: PB 250 423).

SHIVELY, William C., "Packaged Software vs. In-House Programming," *Data Management* (9:9), 1971 September, pages 37-39.

Provides a good discussion of the evolution of the software industry, general administrative criteria in the selection of a software package, and the relative advantages of building your own software versus buying packaged software.

SIBLEY, Edgar H. and Alan G. MERTEN, "Implementation of a Generalized Data Base Management System Within an Organization," *Management Informatics* (2:1), 1973, pages 21-31.

WEISS, Harvey M., "Which DBMS is Right for You?" *Mini-Micro Systems* (14:10), 1981 October, pages 157-160.

Offers a five step process for selecting a DBMS.

YAO, S. Bing, Alan R. HEVNER, and Tom ROMEO, *Performance Evaluation of Database Systems: A Benchmark Methodology*, Washington, DC: U. S. National Bureau of Standards, Final Report NBS-GCR-84-467, 1984 May, 38 pages.

TECHNICAL AND ADMINISTRATIVE
SELECTION CRITERIA

This appendix outlines the major technical and administrative criteria for selecting a DBMS. The criteria listed within each category cover the major considerations, highlighting the capabilities or questions less often considered but important to overall database management objectives. The lists are not intended to be complete; some obvious capabilities are not mentioned.

TECHNICAL CRITERIA

1. Database Definition

- Comprehensive data definition language which captures many data characteristics and clearly separates logical structure from physical storage representation.
- The database definition is provided to the system independent of any program, i.e., there is a separate data definition language (DDL) which is outside of any program and processed by a separate "compiler."
- The database definition includes item definitions with attributes such as name type, size (fixed or variable), mandatory/optional, entity identifier, and validation criteria.
- Repeating group capability, that is, the system allows the definition of multiple record (group) types within a file and, further, these groups can be defined in a hierarchical structure.
- General definition of relationships between entities including all the necessary characteristics.
- Stored data definition available to, and used by, user application programs and the generalized interrogation and update facilities (avoids that proliferation of definitions).

(The following points pertain to storage structure which is primarily an efficiency consideration, and should generally be given less weight than more important functional capabilities.)

- Ability to selectively declare indexes on more than one data item per record.
- Support data stored on direct access device or sequential device (tape).
- Choices available to give effect to efficiency tradeoffs:
  - time vs. space
  - retrieval vs. update
  - online (single request processing) vs. batch
- Storing variable length data values; data compression.

2. Retrieval

- High-level, human-oriented language with which to express:
  - the file(s) to be addressed
  - the records to be selected (selection expression)
  - the attributes (fields) to be extracted
  - the functions, manipulations to be performed on the resultant "subfile"
  - the form of the output
- Generalized Boolean selection expression:
  - to reference any attribute in a record
  - to combine them into an expression using the full power of comparative and Boolean algebra, and including existence and form conditions
  - ability to address multiple levels of a hierarchical data structure or multiple files with a single selection expression
  - available to a user-written program
  - verify the need for long searches with the requester
- Able to select attributes to be printed or otherwise extracted.
- Able to address multiple files at one sitting (one load).
- Able to produce single output with data from multiple files.
- Functions performed on the extracted data:
  - derivation of new data items
  - statistical functions (count, sum, min, max, mean, deviation)
  - sort the output with control breaks
- Generate output reports intended for human consumption:
  - tabular or graphical form
  - using default format and headings
  - or under line-by-line and character-by-character control of the user; needed if using preprinted forms
- Online or offline generation of output.
- Generate file for machine use:
  - for internal system use
  - for external use
- Ability to prestore retrievals in a library and subsequently invoke:
  - as predefined
  - inserting additional parameters (filling in the blanks)

3. Update

- High-level, human-oriented language, especially important for easy online use. Includes action, data, and selection expression.
- Generality in transaction definition and processing specifications:
  - ability to define transaction formats and validation criteria—ability to specify a priori how a predefined transaction is to be processed against the database
  - degree of generality in expressing processing specifications
- Ability to efficiently process sorted batches of transactions where transaction contains all data and processing:
  - specifications expressed in the function-oriented language
  - where the transactions have been predefined
- Ability to populate a null file:
  - using a high-level, human-oriented language
  - using predefined transactions (if this is not possible, the system must offer a generalized file creation or file load module)
- Use of generalized Boolean selection expression in the processing specifications.
- Variety of input media for transactions.
- Incorporate user-written transaction program to perform special update processing.

4. Programmer Interface

- High-level, user-oriented language for application programmers.
- Language hosted in major high-level programming languages, such as COBOL, FORTRAN, PL/I.
- Use of full Boolean selection expression capability (as in retrieval) extract data items from a record.
- Derive new ("virtual") items from extracted data.
- Access to the stored database definition.
- Ability to generate reports using generalized retrieval facility.

5. Database Integrity

- System maintained database definition, that is, the system always ensures that stored data conforms to its full definition.
- Comprehensive validation criteria on stored data included in database.
- Augmented database definition language.
- Separate access/modification authorization procedure.
- Ability to encrypt data for storage.
- Facilities for logging all changes to the database regardless of source.
- Provision for checkpoint, restart, recover, roll back, and bring forward.
- Control of programs which attempt to reference/update the database concurrently, without having to lock up an entire database.

6. Modes of Operation

- Online operation of the previous functions.
- Batch mode operation of the previous functions.

- Multiple user access to same database concurrently, which also requires a common (copy of the) database control system.

7. Database Revision; Evolvability

- Ability to make several types of changes to an established database:
  - add (or delete) a record type
  - change inter-record relationships
  - add, delete, or change a data item within an existing record type
  - change indexes, access methods, or device-media placement of existing files and to make these changes easily with minimum, predictable impact on unchanged parts of the database and on user-written programs, particularly those that reference unchanged portions of the database.
- Userschema capability permitting different user views (for both programming and nonprogramming users) of the stored database; the system performing any required conversion on data transfer. (A comprehensive userschema capability reduces program maintenance effort when revising the database.)
  - allowing inter-record differences
  - allowing intra-record differences
- Ability to incrementally redefine an established database.
- System-supplied restructure and reorganization utilities.

ADMINISTRATIVE CRITERIA

1. Vendor Characteristics and Product Stability

Look for evidence that the vendor will be around for several years and that gives some assurance that the product will continue to be supported.

- History of the organization and length of time in business.
- Size in terms of gross sales and number of employees.
- Profitability, productivity (gross sales per employee), and strength of financial backing to cover initial development, growth, and market penetration.
- Human resources, adequacy and strength of sales, technical and managerial.
- Evidence of pride and excitement in the product and dedication of the organization and its management to continued support and enhancement of the product.
- Examine the past record of releases of product enhancements.
- Number of years this product has been on the market and the number of users. The size of the customer base is one indication of product stability. Look particularly for the number of *active* users (e.g., those still under a maintenance agreement), and the *recent* rate of sales (number of new customers during the last year).
- General user ratings (as published in some of the software listing services), and individual user opinions.
- Existence of a functioning user group—exchanging usage hints, problems, and experiences through a newsletter or periodic conferences, actively supported by the vendor, and influencing the direction of future system development and enhancement.

2. Maintenance Support

Evidence of support can be found by looking at the past record and talking to users.

- Does the vendor have a written maintenance agreement? It is folly to acquire a system without considerable assurance that you can get help when needed, when something goes wrong.
- Assurance that errors in the system will be corrected.
- Quality and speed of response to problems—by telephone and on site.
- Access to future modifications and enhancements, not necessarily free.
- Responsiveness to suggestions for change. Perhaps some needed changes can be made as a condition of your acquisition of the system. Desiring the source code can be a trap. With it, users are tempted to make their own changes. Not being intimately familiar with the overall system and the parts, some users soon find themselves in too deep and seeking help from the vendor. This could be a costly mistake for both. It is much better for users to urge the vendor to make the needed modifications, and for the vendor to be responsive when it actually enhances the product.
- Continuing forum, such as a newsletter, for disseminating usage hints and problem solutions.

3. Documentation and Training

Although part of vendor support, documentation deserves attention due to its vital role in the successful use of a system. Good documentation is essential and is often correlated with the success of a DBMS product.

- Overall quality of system documentation—related to organization, readability, completeness, and usage aids such as indexes and cross references.
- Mechanism for update and frequency of updates.
- Availability of documentation tailored to different needs in a using organization:
  - general information manual to get an overview of system capabilities and operation
  - user manuals for different types of uses, such as application programmers, nonprogramming uses and online retrievals written to get one using the system early and then gradually unfolding the system capabilities
  - reference manual, providing a complete, modular description of the system, used to look up the answer to specific questions or problems
  - database administrator documents on designing, defining, and creating databases, setting up integrity control mechanisms, and operating utilities such as revision and reorganization
- Quality and extent of training provided for users, programmers, maintenance and operations personnel, and database administration; including both introductory courses and advanced design and optimization after a period of use. Availability of on-site courses.
- Availability and quality of training aids, tutorial documentation, and exercises.

4. Ease of Learning and Use

- Ability of people to learn and understand how to use the system easily and quickly depends upon the perceived simplicity of the system, the degree of top-down structure in the external system design, and the quality of the system documentation and user training aids.

- Ease of using the system. Depends upon the robustness of the system languages (for example, through the use of synonyms and multiple input forms), and the extent of natural or user-defined defaults.
- Flexibility in using the system and its ability to adapt to different user skill levels, needs, and modes of interaction.
- Extent to which users can be insulated from the physical storage characteristics and defined access paths in the stored database.
- Tools and support aids for the database administration staff.

5. Operating and Performance Characteristics

- Operational status of the system, i.e., does it work!
- Efficiency of the system in terms of machine time and storage space. Several factors may combine to dictate some form of direct performance evaluation (such as a benchmark): quick response time requirement, high throughput of data, frequent use, high system cost or multiple systems available which are roughly comparable in other respects.
- Extent of compile-time and binding to generate tailored DBMS routines. Interpretive execution can provide greater flexibility but reduces operating efficiency.
- Interface with the machine operator in bringing up and monitoring the operation of the system, including console messages and diagnostics.

6. Supporting Environment: Hardware, Software, Administrative Staff

- Main memory required for storing DBMS nucleus and system buffers.
- Required hardware, operating system software, and peripherals to support the DBMS, noting the differences from your existing system configuration.
- Available interfaces to other software such as teleprocessing monitors, data dictionary systems, generalized report writers, statistical and graphical output packages, generalized transaction edit and validate packages.
- Additional staff personnel required to support the use of the DBMS, to help in the design of application systems using the DBMS, to maintain the system installing fixes and new releases, designing and defining databases in support of the applications portfolio, establishing and enforcing data definition and usage standards, and defining and maintaining integrity controls. Some systems place a substantially heavier administrative burden on a using organization than others.
- Required level of training and technical expertise to install and maintain the system.

7. Costs

- Direct acquisition cost may be expressed in several ways, such as an ongoing monthly lease fee of the system including any extra cost options, a one-time fee for a fully-paid-up lease, a combination of both, or a choice.
- Legal fees for negotiating or reviewing the acquisition contract.
- Any applicable sales or property taxes and investment tax credit. (Some governments want to impose sales and use taxes on software (resisted by the U.S. computer

industry, quite successfully so far), but don't admit that software could be a balance sheet asset and qualify for the investment tax credit).

- Changes to the existing hardware-software configuration including personnel costs, software upgrades, and additional hardware (main memory, peripheral storage devices, etc.).
- Installation fee and related expenses.
- Additional costs for training or documentation.
- Annual maintenance fee, included in a monthly rental fee. (In addition, there are costs of conducting the evaluation and selection, concepts education, gathering information, performing the evaluation, and conducting benchmarks or acceptance tests.)

SOFTWARE LISTING SERVICES

AUERBACH Computer Technology Reports, System Software (Segment J)
Auerbach Publishers Inc., 6560 North Park Drive, Pennsauken, NJ 08109, USA.
$475 per year, updated monthly and well indexed.
DBMS and related products are covered in three sections:
- Data Base Management
- Information Storage and Retrieval
- Report Generators

Each section begins with some general information about the class of products followed by 1-3 page reports on specific products. Each report contains an overview of the package, a general description of functional capabilities, using the system, evaluation comments, and vendor support. The classifications basis is unclear with similar products falling into different sections. Depth of each product report is good but limited coverage of systems (about 75).

AUERBACH Information Management Series, Data Base Management
Auerbach Publishers, Inc. (Address above)
$265 per year; new portfolios added bimonthly.
A collection of portfolios written by individual authors in the field. Topics cover DBMS concepts, planning, historical development, implementation planning, components of a DBMS environment, evaluation and selection, technological aspects, database administration, user/system interfaces, database design, application systems development, current and future directions of development, and DBMS implementation case studies. The last section includes specific product reports (about 20 and growing); content of reports and coverage of systems similar to the System Software (Segment J) reports above.

DATA DECISIONS
20 Brace Road, Cherry Hill, NJ 08034
$480 per year; updated monthly.
A relative newcomer which is rapidly gaining acceptance. Several pages devoted to each product, beginning with an overview and including price charts, detailed descriptions of various features and options, and user ratings. The service makes no attempt to categorize products—all reports are organized by vendor name. The comparative charts and indexes up front make it possible to find the products you are looking for. It is particularly candid in commenting on the strengths and weaknesses of various products, including how they relate to the competition. Fewer DBMS systems covered but relatively comprehensive information on those that are included. Currently in two volumes but sure to grow.

DATAPRO 70, Software (Section E of Volume 3)
Datapro Research Corporation (a McGraw-Hill Company)
1850 Underwood Boulevard, Delran, NJ 08075 USA
(In Europe: Computer Information Service Ltd.,
        286-288 Pentonville Road, London N1 9NY, ENGLAND.)
$540 per year; 3 volumes; updated monthly and well indexed.

Each product report of two or more pages includes substantial technical information on the characteristics, capabilities, and functioning of the system along with a parallel management summary. Limited coverage of DBMS products (about 50); their reports intermingled with other types of software. Product reports include a survey of user reactions. Includes "A Buyer's Guide to Data Base Management Systems" and an annual "User Ratings of Proprietary Software."

DATAPRO Directory of Software
Datapro Research Corporation (see above)
$270 per year; updated monthly and well indexed.

Most DBMS products are covered under DATA MANAGEMENT, which includes "Data Base Management Systems," "File Management," and "Storage and Retrieval," with "Report Writers" included under UTILITIES. One-quarter to one-half a page describes each product with a paragraph or two and some key attributes: vendor company, system functions, hardware, memory and operating system requirements, source language and availability of listings, price, options, maintenance, documentation, training, current number of users, and date first installed. Also includes the "User Ratings" from *Datapro 70*. Broader coverage of systems (about 150) but less information on each than the previous listing services.

ICP Reference Series Software Directory, Vol. 1, Data Processing Management
International Computer Programs, Inc., Larry Welke, Publisher
1119 Keystone Way, Carmel, Indiana 46032 USA
(Also Prodata International GMBH, 6 Frankfurt am Main, Eschercheimer, Landstrasse 60, GERMANY; TechnoSystems Corporation, Yaesu 5-5, Building 5-5. Yaesu, Chou-Ko, Tokyo, JAPAN; and Wennergren-Williams A.B., Nordenflychtsvagen 70, Stockholm, SWEDEN.)

Volume 1 (volume 2 covers applications software) categorizes systems software into:

i. Computer Operations Support Systems
ii. Application Development Foundation Systems
iii. Application Development Support Systems

DBMS products are generally included in the second category although they are spread around with no easy way of finding those products which are closely related. Each product writeup covers one-eighth to one-half a page with a short description and key information about hardware and operating system requirements, price, and vendor name and address. Broader coverage than any of the preceding listing services including several foreign systems. Publisher seems quick to add a system description received from a vendor; some systems are retained even though no longer available.

National Computer Program Abstract Service (NCPAS), Report No. 17
P.O. Box 3783, Washington, DC 20007 USA
$10 membership plus $37 for No. 17; updated quarterly.

Operates as a clearinghouse for over 50,000 products, each described by a short, vendor-written program abstract. Program abstracts are listed free of charge from any source and without any further investigation or evaluation. Paying an annual membership fee, you receive the quarterly Program Index Newsletter. Program abstracts are available by subject area with 210 subjects. The number of abstracts determines the price. Report Number 17 on "Information Retrieval Systems" contains over 1,500 program abstracts covering, "MIS, Data Management Systems, Key Searches, KWIC Index, Abstracting Systems, Data Dictionaries, and DBMS."

Directory of Interactive Data-Base Systems
Association of Time-Sharing Users
75 Manhattan Drive, Boulder, CO 80303 USA
$15 to nonmembers; bimonthly updates to members.

Covers about 50 systems from 35 time-sharing services. For each system, the directory includes the vendor contact, a short general description, a highlight of special features, and the approximate number of current users. The information is prepared by the vendor.

EIGHTEEN

TRENDS TO THE FUTURE
IN DATABASE MANAGEMENT

18.1	DBMS DEVELOPMENT AND USAGE TRENDS	732
18.1.1	Serving Both Programming and Nonprogramming Users	732
18.1.2	Greater Functional Completeness	733
18.1.3	Simpler, Higher-Level User Interface	734
18.1.4	Common Data Definition	734
18.1.5	New Tools for Systems Development	735
18.2	ORGANIZATIONAL RESISTANCE TO NEW DBMS TOOLS	736
18.2.1	Resistance to DBMS Acquisition	736
18.2.2	Resistance to DBMS Use	737
18.3	DATABASES IN A DISTRIBUTED PROCESSING ENVIRONMENT	738
18.3.1	Levels of Interconnectedness	740
18.3.2	Typical Networking Systems	741
18.3.3	The Network DBMS and Network Data Directory	743
18.3.4	Distribution Alternatives for Data-Related Components	745
18.3.5	Distribution of DBMS Functions	747
18.3.6	Linking Personal Computers to Databases on a Central Host	749
18.4	BACKEND DATABASE MANAGEMENT MACHINE	750
18.4.1	Design Considerations for a DBMM	752
18.4.2	Advantages of a Well-Designed DBMM	753
18.4.3	Specialized DBMM Hardware—Parallelism is the Key	754
18.4.4	Commercial DBMM Products	758
18.5	EMERGING STANDARDS IN DATABASE TECHNOLOGY	760
18.5.1	Standards Organizations and Their Activities	760
18.5.2	Advantages and Inhibitors to the Development of Standards	763
18.5.3	The Development of Database-Related Standards	764
18.5.4	Direction of Emerging Standards	766
18.5.5	Development of a Reference Model for Database Standards	770
	SUMMARY	775
	EXERCISES	777
	SELECTED REFERENCES	778

The future of database management is bright. Forecasters anticipate a $1 billion industry by 1990. Recent trends in DBMS, particularly on microcomputers, promise to better serve users with greater functionality, and a simpler, higher-level interface. The newer tools for systems development will greatly improve the productivity of developers and enable an organization to begin to crawl out of the pit of inefficient applications development and heavy program maintenance. Yet there is still some resistance to the use of the new DBMS tools.

This chapter outlines trends in the development of DBMS, the organizational factors inhibiting the acquisition and use of those tools, and steps to overcoming the resistance. The chapter also covers the newer technological issues of databases in a distributed environment, and backend database management machines. The final section examines the development of database-related standards, the advantages and inhibitors to the development of standards, and the direction and likely outcomes of current standards activities.

18.1 DBMS DEVELOPMENT AND USAGE TRENDS

Several trends in the development of DBMS are evident. Some of these have arisen from concerns with the earlier available systems and their use. Each of these concerns has led to a new label being applied to system tools and organizational approaches for managing data:

TOOL CONCERNS

- Need for better tools for application system developers has led to *application development systems* which integrate data, menu, and help screen generators with the normal facilities for access to the database.
- Need for better tools for ad hoc use by end users has led to so called *fourth generation languages*.
- Need for accurate, controlled, and comprehensive definition of data has led to *data dictionaries*.

ORGANIZATIONAL CONCERNS

- Need to provide support for end user computing and access to corporate databases has led to the concept of an *information center*.
- Need to focus on overall management of data as a valued organizational resource has led to the notion of *information resource management*.

All of the tool concerns are part of a comprehensive DBMS, and the organizational concerns are part of database administration, as they have been developed in this book.

18.1.1 Serving Both Programming and Nonprogramming Users

Up through the 1960s, almost all DBMS products were exclusively host-language or self-contained systems—either intended to augment a conventional programming language, or to be used stand-alone by a nonprogramming user.

Then in the early 1970s, developers and vendors of each type of system, and third party vendors, began to add interfaces for the "other" type of user, or added interfaces to systems of the "other" type (see Figure 17-11 for a more complete list of systems).

- Originally self-contained systems, such as SYSTEM 2000, RAMIS, and INQUIRE, added host-language interfaces.
- Vendors of host-language systems added "self-contained" facilities, such as a query language or report writer, to their products, often as separately named, extra cost options: Socrates added to TOTAL from Cincom, Adascript and Adawriter added to Adabas from Software ag, QLP added to DMS 1100 from Sperry (then Univac), and QRP (formerly MDQS) added to IDS II from Honeywell.
- Some vendors already had a report writer and simply built an interface to their host-language DBMS: IDMS plus Culprit from Cullinet, DMS 170 plus Query/Update from Control Data, and IMS plus GIS from IBM.
- Third party vendors of report writers built interfaces to some of the more popular host-language DBMSs: Mark IV, Asi-st, Data Analyzer, and Easytrieve.
- Some systems were developed in the 1970s which explicitly included interfaces for both types of users: System 1022 from First Data, SQL and DB2 from IBM, Focus from IBI, Oracle from Oracle, DRS from A.R.A.P., Ingres from Relational Technology, and Ambase from Amcor.

All these developments have made it possible to acquire a package of DBMS facilities which provide access to common data for both programming and nonprogramming users, thus enhancing the objective of sharability.

18.1.2 Greater Functional Completeness

Many of the earlier DBMSs provided little functionality beyond the definition of data and some facility to access and update the data in a batch mode. A major purpose of this book has been to greatly broaden this view of DBMS. Important additional functionality includes:

- *Comprehensive data definition* which includes much more information about a stored data structure (see Chapter 6).
- *Revision* of a database after it has been created and used for a while (see Chapter 11).
- *Database integrity* functions to meet the demands of increased user dependence on the system and demands external to the organization (see Chapters 12, 13, 14, and 16).
- *Extended retrieval* capabilities, including statistical analysis and graphical output presentation.
- *External interfaces* with other software packages—statistical, graphical, spread sheets, modelling for decision support, word processing, and transfer between microcomputer workstations and central host computers.

One interesting trend is in the development of commercially available application systems such as financial and manufacturing systems, and specific packages for industries such as insurance and banking. More of them are being built using a DBMS as the foundation.

In organizations where the database has become an integral and vital part of operations and the users are increasingly dependent upon the data and its accuracy, management and auditors are increasingly intolerant of low levels of database integrity found in many of their systems. They are beginning to demand greater sophistication in the underlying integrity support functions. Laws relating to data privacy and fair information practices are also forcing greater concern for data integrity.

18.1.3 Simpler, Higher-Level User Interface

The user interface is becoming simpler is several ways:

- *Logical view of the data* without concern for physical representation and access mechanisms (which is why these topics have received cursory treatment in this text).
- *Userschema* through which the users can view parts of the database of interest to them without having to comprehend the whole.
- *Online interface* for ad hoc, interactive use by novice users, both command driven and menu driven, and incorporating the principles of direct manipulation (see Chapter 5).
- *High-level languages* available to both the online user and the programming user, including the new developments in inferential retrieval, artificial intelligence, and natural language processing (see Chapters 7, 8, and 10).

A simpler interface does not necessarily mean a less powerful language. On the contrary, a simplified language can offer considerably more power to the programming and nonprogramming user than do conventional DBMS languages. In fact, many of the newer systems offer a comprehensive, self-contained language for both programming and nonprogramming users. This is particularly true of systems on microcomputers.

18.1.4 Common Data Definition

Early systems evolved with separate packages for different DBMS functions. Each had its own definition of the data to be processed. The resulting proliferation of data definitions has created an administrative nightmare for some organizations— consistency across multiple definitions must be externally maintained. Such proliferation may even exist with multiple packages from the same vendor.

The obvious solution is to have a single data definition for a stored database. Then all the functional modules of the DBMS, even if they were developed independently or from different vendors, would obtain definitional information from the same source. In practice, it is very difficult and expensive to retrofit independently developed modules to work with a common data definition or data dictionary (as witnessed at Cincom with their development of TIS from TOTAL or at Cullinet with their development of IDMS).

The concept of a data dictionary serves to emphasize the separation from the (often inadequate) schema of the DBMS. The data dictionary or directory is a separate and independent repository of information about the database. The dictionary may be *passive*, that is, not referenced at the time of database access. A so called *active* data dictionary is used to control access to the database, enforcing definition and validation rules at the time when requests are being executed. An active data dictionary is functionally equivalent to a comprehensive database schema (which is why it has not been emphasized in this text).

The trend to a common data definition, while evident, is slow to be realized. It depends on commonality of definitional information which implies some commonality or at least correspondence in the basic constructs of the underlying data structure (or data "model"—see Chapter 4). Such commonality would be embodied in a common data definition language. Standardization of a data language is actually the place to begin to achieve a common data definition throughout the industry (see later section in this chapter).

18.1.5 New Tools for Systems Development

With the newer DBMS languages there is less need for having to build an application system by writing programs in a conventional language such as COBOL and accessing the DBMS though special commands. In fact, a higher-level language makes it possible to build application systems in a fraction of the time it takes in COBOL. This is possible because the languages usually include commands which conceptually operate on whole files at a time for selection, projection, item derivations, ordering, calculating statistics, and formatting the output. In response to the newer language facilities, Martin was led to write a book entitled *Application Development Without Programmers* [1982], which should be read ". . . Without *COBOL* Programmers" or the use of other conventional programming languages.

Higher-level data manipulation facilities must be accompanied by more comprehensive data definition facilities. More information about the data allows the DBMS to better manage the data. It also allows the DBMS to do more work for the user. In several new DBMSs (notably on microcomputers) single commands can initiate an extensive stream of processing, such as data entry. The commands can be issued online for immediate execution, or embedded in a program. The important point is that the execution of the command is entirely driven by the information given to the system to define the database.

For example, a single command may be used to update existing records (a selected subset with some data items projected), or to capture whole new records to be added to the database. First the system presents a view of the record showing data item names, field sizes and types, and displayed values if existing records are to be updated. The user then moves a cursor over the data items to enter or modify values. As each new value is entered, the system checks it against the stored definition and validation criteria, or this checking can be done when the user instructs the system to store a completed record. The validation can even include interfile cross references, for example, checking that the value entered for organization unit number in the employee record references a valid (existing) organization unit in the organization file, or that a skill code is from the set of valid codes established by the personnel department. If values are in error, the system issues an appropriate error message and allows the user to enter corrections. When a complete, valid record is stored, the system repeats the process until the user indicates "done."

In the above example, the user did not write a program to:

- Retrieve records from the database.
- Prompt the user and control cursor movement.
- Capture data item values.
- Allow the user to edit data item values.
- Check for validity.
- Issue error messages.

- Display help screens.
- Recycle back for corrections.
- Store the validated records.
- Update any active indexes.
- Iterate until the user had no more records to enter or change.

All these operations were driven by the stored data definition and the DBMS designer's knowledge of the basic activities required for data entry.

Such a comprehensive, powerful, high-level facility is a far cry from doing it all in COBOL—hundreds of lines of user-written code are compressed into one command plus the lines required to define the data file. Similarly, Figure 5-8 vividly illustrated the difference between low-level and high-level query languages. Such powerful commands greatly reduce the time it takes to develop an application system. Then why do so many organizations still persist in using the old, low-level tools for systems development?

18.2 ORGANIZATIONAL RESISTANCE TO NEW DBMS TOOLS

There are several points of resistance to new DBMS tools:

- Resistance to *acquiring* a new tool.
- Resistance to *choosing* to use a new tool.
- Resistance to *learning* how to use a new tool.
- Resistance to *using* a new tool.

18.2.1 Resistance to DBMS Acquisition

The selection and acquisition of a DBMS and related tools is one of the most important computer-related decisions made in an organization. It is also one of the most difficult. There are many systems from which to choose and it is very difficult to obtain the necessary information to make a good decision. Vendors always have great things to say, convincing arguments for their systems, and often many satisfied customers. Published literature and software listing services are too cursory to provide sufficient information on which to base a decision. The mere difficulty in gathering information and making the selection is one point of resistance to acquiring the new DBMS tools.

The initial cost may also be a barrier to acquisition. However, the subsequent investment in training people, developing applications, and entering and maintaining data will be many times more. Selection of an inadequate system can greatly increase these subsequent costs to the point where the initial acquisition cost becomes irrelevant.

In spite of the apparent resistance to acquisition, the projections referenced in the preface are forecasting a multi-billion dollar industry by 1990. Even though an organization may acquire a DBMS, there are still several additional points of resistance to overcome.

18.2.2 Resistance to DBMS Use

Simply having a DBMS does not mean it will be used. Several factors may contribute to the lack of use of new DBMS tools.

- Lack of familiarity with the tool and what it can do.
- System developers used to writing COBOL (or other language) programs prefer to build systems using the tools they already know.
- The pressure to get new application development projects completed dictates using established tools and techniques.
- Systems development personnel have not been thoroughly trained in the use of the new tool.
- The organization has not set up a program to train users of new DBMS tools.
- Users are reluctant to use a new tool because there is no one in the organization to provide advice in its use and to help when problems arise.
- Tool is only known to a few specialists in the data processing organization.
- No one in the organization encouraging, even compelling the use of new DBMS tools.
- DP management is afraid of run away demand on the computing facilities if they allow users to directly access the data on the host computer using an easy to use, high-level retrieval facility.
- Organizational policies which do not demand appropriate justification for the tools chosen (or not chosen) for each system development project.

In the meantime, many data processing organizations are faced with a large and growing backlog of application system development projects. Their best people are always being dragged away to fix or modify existing systems—program maintenance has become a tragic way of life in many organizations. The users also know something is wrong. Data processing has lost its credibility in most organizations today. The hidden backlog of unrequested development projects may be even larger than the known backlog. Users who have repeatedly experienced lack of satisfaction on past requests will feel that it is useless to put any more project requests in the queue. Data processing systems are no longer seen as improving the way of doing business; and the data processing unit is no longer seen as a viable support organization.

How does an organization break out of this cycle of despair, this bog of inefficient development, this quagmire of system maintenance, this thicket of dissatisfied and disgruntled users? I believe that the use of inadequate system building tools is a major contributor to the problem. An organization must seek to acquire some of the more effective DBMS tools, if they do not have them already, and then take specific steps to encourage familiarity and skill with their acquired DBMS tools. Several practical suggestions were offered at the end of Chapter 17.

Every organization needs a DBA who *encourages* the use of the new DBMS tools. Management must set specific goals for developers and users to *learn* the new DBMS tools. This means setting aside specific blocks of time for learning activities—making learning and usage a specific part of their job evaluation criteria. People must become familiar enough with the new tools that they will *prefer* to use them for systems development and database access most of the time. At least they need to be familiar enough to make a balanced decision regarding which tool to use in each situation. This familiarity and experience cannot be gained ''as time permits'' or ''in the employees own spare time.'' Management must make learning an up front priority. The investment will pay off when users and developers become more productive in accessing data and building systems with the new tools.

For systems development, use of the old, comfortable tools such as COBOL should be considered the avenue of last resort. The proposal for a development project must include justification for why the higher-level, people-efficient tools are *not* being used.

Then an organization needs an ongoing forum for users of the new tools to share experiences, usage techniques, problems, and solutions.

18.3 DATABASES IN A DISTRIBUTED PROCESSING ENVIRONMENT

Computers at multiple sites linked together through a communications facility provides the basis for distributed processing. Distributed processing is driven by two main technological factors:

- Lower hardware costs for computer processing and data storage.
- Moderately higher communications costs.

and three main organizational factors:

- More responsive to local user needs by offering faster access and greater autonomy or control.
- Greater reliability through reduced operational dependence on a single, central site for data processing and data storage.
- Increased sharing and coordination in the use of common resources.

Distributed processing is not a panacea for achieving these organizational goals and reducing costs. A distributed processing environment adds complexity to the data management problem compared to a single site environment. In spite of the claims of some vendors of networks or distributed DBMS, substantial problems remain to achieve the full potential of distributed data processing.

A distributed processing environment is characterized by a network of multiple computing nodes connected with some communications facility (see Figure 18-1). A node, like a single site computer, can perform some combination of the following functions: execute programs, respond to a user request, run a DBMS, or store data.

A *communications facility* is the collection of processes and physical facilities which interconnect the nodes. It includes knowledge of the physical location of each node, the physical connections or paths between the nodes, the protocols for sending messages between nodes, and processes which accept a message from one node and deliver it to one or more other nodes. A *network access process* (NAP) exists at every node and is the interface between processes at the node and the communications facility. The NAP is usually some combination of software and hardware. The hardware may consist of a standard input-output port on the computer or a special plugin board to which a network cable is connected. The actual configuration or topology of the net-

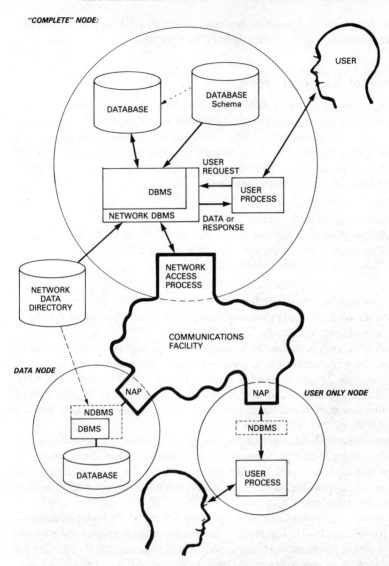

Figure 18-1. Data and Users in a Distributed Processing Environment.
A distributed processing environment consists of multiple computing nodes connected with some communications facility. A network access process (NAP) at each node provides the interface between processes at the node and the communications facility. Nodes may be data only, users only, or both. A data node always has a DBMS; a user node *may* have a DBMS. Without a DBMS, a user process is presumed to know how to access the NAP and direct a request to the appropriate data node. The Network DBMS provides additional data-related functions to operate in the network environment. The Network Data Directory keeps track of what data is where in the network. In a simple scenario, a user request at one node may be forwarded to the DBMS at the data node for processing against the database with the response sent back to the user node for further processing and display to the user. [Adapted from CODASYL, 1982, page 8.]

work and the communication prototcol is secondary—the important point is that any node can communicate with any other node in the network.

18.3.1 Levels of Interconnectedness

Distributed data processing entails much more than just being physically connected and being able to send messages from one node to another. Establishing connections for data communications is one thing, intelligently managing processes and data within the network is another. It is like comparing the existence of highways to having a trucking system for handling commodities.

The four levels of interconnectedness are:

1. Teleprocessing—terminals connected to a host.
2. Communicating—with a network access process (NAP) at each site.
3. Shared Processing—with a network operating system (NOS).
4. Shared Data—with network DBMS (NDBMS).

Teleprocessing with remote terminals connected to a central host computer is not generally considered distributed processing (though it may satisfy some of the objectives as far as users are concerned).

At a minimum, each node must be a general purpose computer (mainframe, mini, or microcomputer workstation) with its own processor(s), memory, and operating system. The node must be able to execute certain processes, such as the NAP, some rudimentary DBMS functions, and user processes. A node initiates the execution of processes, allocates node resources to processes, and manages interaction with the external environment.

At a *communicating* level, a network access process at each node provides the first level of interconnectedness with system-managed communication. Such a network requires user-managed resource sharing and data movement. The nodes operate autonomously; users are responsible for initiating and interpreting internode activity such as message and data transfers.

Shared processing requires a network operating system (NOS) with global intelligence [see Kimbleton, 1981]. The system manages processing capacity and allocates computing resources (processors, memory, peripherals) to processes. By knowing the current node location of unused resources, the system can transfer processes for execution at other nodes in the network. For example, early morning jobs in New York can be sent to California where most people are still asleep. Users need not be aware that their processes may actually be running somewhere else. At this second level, users are still responsible for data movement; users must specify that requests for data and data transfers be sent between user-identified nodes in the network.

Shared data uses network DBMSs to manage data movement in a way that is transparent to the users. Each NDBMS is explicitly aware that data exists at multiple locations so they manage data globally.

Most networking systems provide little beyond the second level of interconnectedness. Considerable additional functionality is required to satisfy the third and fourth levels. The level of shared data requires a network DBMS and a network data directory.

18.3.2 Typical Networking Systems

The communicating level is the baseline for a simple local area network (LAN). Figure 18-2 depicts the components which can typically be connected to a local area network. These include:

- Microcomputer workstations, with or without secondary storage.
- Printer(s) to be used from any node in the network.
- Disk storage devices.
- Gateway to another network, a central host computer, or a modem to communicate with other computers over telephone lines.

A workstation without secondary storage generally depends upon the network being up to load the operating system, application programs, and data files from a shared disk elsewhere on the network. All networks allow multiple users to share printers. Some networks perform *print spooling*, that is, allowing users to send the print image of their output to a disk file (which can be done quickly) after which they can continue working at the computer on other tasks. Then when the desired printer is not in use, the system prints the output from the print queue on disk, effectively by stealing processor cycles when the user process is idle.

The simplest way to share disk is to allocate space to individual users for their exclusive use, perhaps leaving one partition available for public (read-only) use. While this may be sharing the space on the disk device, it is certainly not sharing common data files. If multiple users can access files in the *same* area of the disk, the system should provide some mechanism for controlling concurrent usage. Permitting read-only access is relatively easy to manage since it does not threaten data integrity.

Most network vendors are aware that concurrent update threatens data integrity. A common approach (used in the popular Omninet from CORVUS and EtherSeries from 3Com) is to provide a file of "semaphores." All users in the network agree a priori on the controlled data object(s) to be associated with each named semaphore. Often the data objects are whole files but that is not a necessary restriction. A user desiring to update a data object, first requests a lock on the associated semaphore. A lock is granted if no other user currently holds a lock on the requested semaphore. The user is then free to access and update the data associated with the semaphore. If a requested semaphore is locked, users are *on their honor* not to update the associated data object. Unfortunately, such network systems provide no way of enforcing the prohibition on update. The documentation is usually careful to point out that if users attempt simultaneous access or update to the same data files, the results are unpredictable and data may be destroyed. Data integrity is a user responsibility and the organization

TERMINALS, MICROCOMPUTER WORKSTATIONS, COMPUTER NODES:

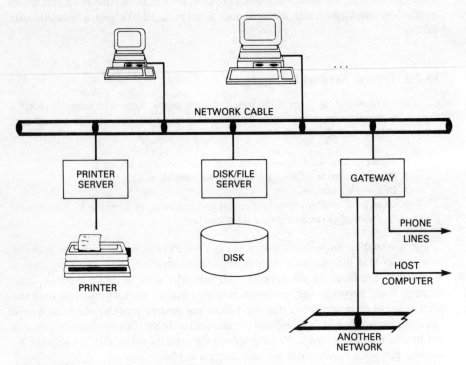

Figure 18-2. Typical Configuration for a Local Area Network.

A local area network (LAN) connects multiple computers or workstations so that they can send messages to each other, share printers, and share disk storage space. The LAN may also provide a connection to phone lines, a host computer, or a gateway to another network. Most networks use a "bus" architecture with each node or device attached to a cable (twisted-pair or coaxial). A few networks provide a *file* server for handling shared data files, in contrast to a disk server which only permits sharing space on a common disk storage device.

must take steps to educate and externally control the activities of users on the network.

Some networks do not require or use a *central file server*. Any user potentially has access (if permitted) to the data files or printers of any other user on the network. Each user defines a local configuration table which specifies the node location of any remote devices or files which will be referenced from the local process. A local user can then lock a file which is at a remote user site. Other users in the network cannot lock that file (or record), including the owner-user at the remote site, until the local user releases the lock. Such a mechanism does indeed guarantee the integrity of the data under concurrent update. Without a central file server, it is very difficult for the system to protect against global deadlock.

Other networks say they can handle *multiple file servers*. If the servers operate independently, global deadlock may also occur. The problem is that proper control of concurrent update requires some point of global intelligence if deadlock is to be detected or prevented (see Chapter 13). This is relatively easy to provide with a single file server. It is also possible if every local process consults *all* other sites before granting a request to lock a data object.

The minimum capability to effectively handle data sharing is for the system to control concurrent updates against the same file to protect the integrity of the data and to prevent, or at least detect and handle, deadlock. This requires some form of global coordination of data requests and locking, whether by some central point of control (such as a file server) or through mutual consultation. There are a few local area networks which properly perform these functions. Nevertheless, there are even more functions needed to achieve the full potential of distributed *data* processing.

18.3.3 The Network DBMS and Network Data Directory

The functions required to control concurrent requests for devices and files originating at several nodes in a network may be implemented in a variety of ways:

- Augmenting the local operating system.
- Building a shell around the operating system to intercept all calls to data (and devices) which might be at some other node.
- Handling concurrent requests centrally in the file server.
- Augmenting the local DBMS.

Usually the functions are implemented using some combination of the above. For purposes of discussion we will assume that some cluster of data management functions exists at each node, whether a user node, a data node, or a central file server.

Ideally, a user process or an online user interacting with a DBMS should not have to be concerned with where data is located in the network, nor should they have to be concerned about protecting data integrity under concurrent updates or handling deadlock. These functions should be handled by the DBMS and the underlying support functions in the local operating systems, the communications facility, and the central file server.

The key components for accomplishing these functions are the network DBMS and the network data directory.

The *Network DBMS* (NDBMS) performs several functions beyond a single-site DBMS. A DBMS generally assumes that all known data is stored locally and that it has exclusive control over all stored data. Figure 3-18 shows the major components and flows within a single-site DBMS. Additional activities or responsibilities of an NDBMS include:

1. Receive and analyze a user request to determine what data is required to form a response.
2. Know how to access the network access process.
3. Access the Network Data Directory to determine where the target data is stored

within the network (or otherwise be able to direct requests to the appropriate data nodes).

4. Interface with all DBMSs within the network.

5. Convert a user request from the language of one DBMS to another if they are different, and convert the form of the data transferred from one DBMS to another.

6. Decompose a user request if the required target data exists at multiple nodes, forward the subrequests to the appropriate data nodes, and re-assemble the responses into a single response for the user. The strategy selected should minimize the volume of communications and maximize parallel processing.

7. Operate network-wide recovery when a data node fails. If a targeted node is down, the NDBMS may be able to forward a retrieval request to another node with a copy of the same data, otherwise processing of the request must be suspended until the node is back online. Updates to a failed node must be saved until the node is back online, at which time the updates would have to be processed before the data is made available to any requesting processes.

Activities 5 and 6 are optional and add considerable complexity to the NDBMS. Handling the heterogeneity implied in 5 is certainly one of the goals of distributed processing but has not been achieved in any substantial measure with today's systems. The operation of most DBMSs in present networks presumes homogeneity within the network.

The *network data directory* maintains information about the various units or collections of data within the network. The information for each data part may include:

- Node location(s) where each data part or "fragment" is currently stored.
- Relationships among the distributed data partitions.
- Which data parts are redundant copies of other parts.
- Current status of data within the network.
- How to access the data, including access restrictions.

If the basic unit of allocation within the network is a file, then the minimum directory would simply list each file and the node at which is resides.

Network directory information may be kept in one central file within the network. The NDBMS uses the network data directory to determine where to send a request. If the information is not all kept together, the NDBMS can route a request to every node or broadcast a request to all nodes simultaneously. Each receiving node would then look at its local directory to see if it has the data needed to process the request. A central network data directory contains some information from all the local data directories. It may even contain complete database schema information.

Information regarding the network topology would be used and maintained by the communications facility. The network access process must be able to determine which nodes are currently online, their identification, and the path to use for routing a message to another node. The information must be dynamically maintained to reflect failures and restorations of nodes or links between nodes.

18.3.4 Distribution Alternatives for Data-Related Components

Besides the actual data, other data-related components in a distributed environment include schemas, userschemas, and the network data directory. For each of these components, there are three distribution alternatives:

- *Centralized*—one copy stored at a central node, such as the host computer or the file server.
- *Partitioned*—one copy but split into disjoint parts and stored at different nodes.
- *Replicated*—multiple copies of any of the parts (stored at different nodes).

A single-site DBMS would represent the completely centralized alternative—all components exist at one central node. Connecting user nodes to the central host would not make it a distributed system unless some of the components were stored at the local sites, that is, distributed.

A basic distributed system would consist of one data node and one user node. Even this seemingly simple arrangement presents some nontrivial design problems. For example, are any DBMS functions performed at the ''user node''? If so, what functions? Where is the userschema? To what extent is the user invoking predefined processes stored at the ''data node''? Is any part of the schema known at the ''user node''?

All the data in a network may be considered one big database which can be distributed within the network by partitioning and replication. As shown in Figure 18-3, partitioning takes some of the files from a central node and stores them at other nodes. Full replication keeps a complete copy of all files at all nodes (not generally a viable choice). Normally, there would be some combination of partitioning and replication.

Individual files can also be partitioned and replicated. As shown in Figure 18-4, a file may be partitioned by entities or by attributes, or both. Then each of the resulting ''logical fragments'' can be replicated and stored at different nodes.

When a database is partitioned, the NDBMS is more likely to have to decompose a query, sending subrequests to multiple nodes, and assembling the responses for the user. When a database is replicated, the NDBMS must choose which copy or copies should be used to respond to a request. For a query, *any* copy will satisfy the request, assuming all copies are kept up to date through update synchronization. However, *all* copies must be the object of an update request.

The particular choices in partitioning and replication depend upon such factors as file size and frequency of use from each of the nodes. The following table gives some very general rules of thumb which can help to understand the basic choices:

EXCEPTION RATE	FILE SIZE	PREFERRED METHOD OF DISTRIBUTION
—	Small	Replicate
Low	Large	Partition
High	Large	Centralize

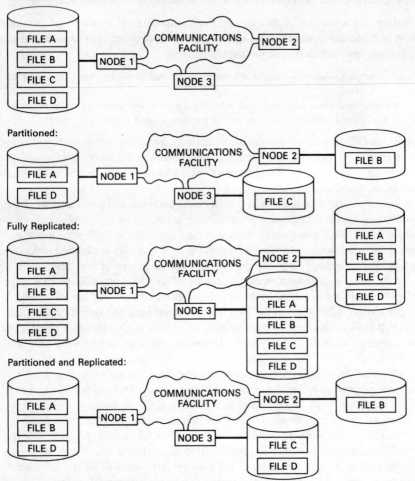

Figure 18-3. Data Distribution Alternatives.
    A centralized architecture maintains one copy of each file at one node, the central host or file server node. The partitioned alternative still maintains a single copy of each file but they may be stored at different nodes. Full replication stores everything at every node. A general data distribution architecture partitions the database and replicates some of the parts, storing them at various nodes in the network.

To begin the design process, allocate data to the nodes where it is most likely to be requested. Then the exception rate is the ratio of the number of requests which cannot be satisfied locally, that is, must be sent to some other node, to the total number of requests. This over simplified decision rule does not consider the need or desire for local autonomy and control, nor the contribution of replication to better reliability and recovery.

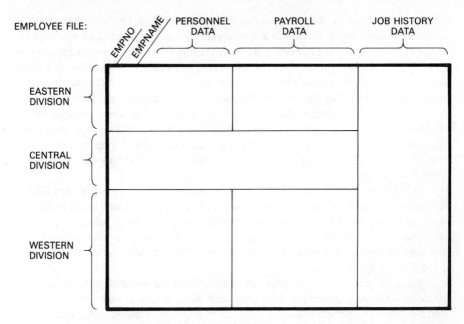

Figure 18-4. Partitioning and Replicating Parts of a File.

A file may be partitioned by entities or by attributes. *Entity partitioning* ("horizontal") might break an employee file into geographical regions—eastern, central, and western divisions. Each entity partition is defined with the same schema but contains a different set of employee records. *Attribute partitioning* ("vertical") might break up the file into personnel data, payroll data, and job history data. Note that each attribute partition must have duplicate identifiers, such as employee number and employee name, to properly relate the data from one record type to another. The fragments in attribute partitioning are not defined with the same schema. A join operation can be used to combine attribute partitions. Any one of the partitions or fragments can be replicated for storage at nodes within the network. For example, headquarters may store personnel and payroll data for all employees, archive services may store job history data for all employees, central division may store personnel and payroll data in one file for all of its employees, and the eastern and western divisions may divide up their employee data into two files—personnel data and payroll data. File size and frequency of use influence the particular choices of partitioning and replication.

The distribution of database schemas will generally parallel the distribution of data. A definition is required wherever data is stored. Definition information (though excluding physical storage information) may also be stored (replicated) at other nodes.

18.3.5 Distribution of DBMS Functions

Wherever there exists a database (or partition) and its definition, there also must exist *some* database management functions. Any process which accesses stored data, reads and interprets a stored data definition, or performs a mapping conversion between a userschema and schema is, by definition, a database management function.

Most attempts to implement a DBMS in a distributed environment have kept the system in one piece and built front-end or back-end interfaces. One simple approach is to have a single copy of the DBMS at the data site and simply forward all user requests to the data site with a tag indicating the node it came from. The opposite approach is to keep the DBMS (replicated) at the user sites, and provide some basic, low-level access routines at the site of the stored database. In both cases, there must be some minimum set of DBMS functions at the data node to perform input-output (at some level) and integrity control. Integrity controls include controlling changes to the database definition and ensuring that the stored data always conforms to its definition, controlling and executing updates, controlling access according to prespecified authorizations, performing backup and recovery operations, and checking the data against validation criteria.

In between these two extremes are many possible ways to partition the DBMS functions between a user node and a data node. The userschema could reside at the user node to enable the DBMS to partially process the user request, converting it into database schema structure and terminology (using the mapping information in the userschema) before forwarding it to the data node. Some access controls could also be implemented at the user site.

There are also some appropriate ways to partition the major steps in the retrieval process—selection, projection, data item derivation, ordering, calculating statistics, and formation and presentation of results—as well as functions associated with update. With no partitioning of functions, the entire request must be processed at either the data site or the user site, either of which may entail transmitting large volumes of data. The functions can be partitioned to minimize the volume of data transmitted. Operations on data may be *data reducing* or *data expanding*.

- Prompting or dialoguing with the user to build a formal request is better done locally, providing that the required base of information (definitions, forms, menus, value sets, inference rules, vocabulary, etc.) can be stored locally.
- Selection and projection are data reducing operations and therefore should be performed at the data site before transmitting data.
- Formation and presentation are data expanding operations and therefore should be performed at the user site after transmitting the data.
- Data item derivations and calculating statistics could be either depending on whether or not the user wants the detail data that goes into the calculations. If the user just wants the average salary for electrical engineers, the calculation is data reducing and should be done before transmission of data.
- Ordering is neither data reducing nor expanding but it requires additional storage workspace so is probably better done at the data site. Furthermore, the calculation of statistics may depend on a prior ordering which will dictate where it should be done.
- Input data validation is better performed locally for faster error detection, notification to the user, and solicitation of correction. Database dependent validation requires access to the database so may be performed at the data site.
- A join operation will be data expanding if the underlying relationship is one-to-many or many-to-many; an AND-JOIN (which excludes entries without a match in the other file) will be data reducing.

18.3.6 Linking Personal Computers to Databases on a Central Host

One area receiving considerable attention lately is the interface between personal computers or microcomputer workstations and a central host computer on which resides corporate-wide databases. Users are demanding such a link, vendors are trying hard to provide one, and central data processing is reluctant to open the flood gates.

Users have been frustrated for years at not being able to get ready access to corporate data. With the advent of the personal computer workstation, they see unlimited possibilities for data manipulation and presentation to provide better information for decision making. A simple approach is to extract information from the central database using the host DBMS and "download" the results to the local workstation. Successful file transfer requires appropriate communications software at both ends and they should be compatible in their error checking protocols. If the data is in one of several standard formats, there is probably some software (data management, spread sheet, statistical analysis, or modelling) which can be used to read the data and give the user some functions to manipulate the data.

Some DBMS vendors have built a special downloading program to run on a personal computer that will interface directly with their central DBMS. The local software may provide some manipulation and presentation functions for the user. Other vendors have succeeded in implementing their mainframe or mini-based DBMS on a microcomputer workstation. It will operate as a powerful stand-alone DBMS and interface with the same DBMS on a host computer. This approach allows them to download files in internal format and then use all the power of the DBMS to manipulate, update, and manage the data.

With read-only access to central databases, the major issue is controlling access to properly authorized users at the workstation. There is considerably more resistance to allowing local users to enter data and update the corporate databases directly. Central data processing is rightly concerned that all the appropriate data validation controls be enforced. A compromise approach is to use the local workstations for data entry and some initial validation. Then a batch of update transactions could be "uploaded" to the central host for update processing against the corporate database *using the existing programs and integrity controls* for performing transaction processing and database update.

The CODASYL Systems Committee report [1982] discussed several technical and administrative issues regarding the design and operation of distributed database systems:

- How best to partition data, what degree of replication, and how to allocate to nodes all relate to data distribution.
- Handling conversion problems in an environment with heterogeneous hardware and/or heterogeneous DBMSs. In most organizations, hardware (particularly microcomputers) and DBMSs have been acquired by several disparate groups. Corporate standards came too late and now they must either try to interface in a heterogeneous environment or replace and retrain people with common hardware and software. Which direction is more cost effective?

- Strategies for controlling concurrent updates and synchronizing updates against multiple copies of a database (see Chapter 13).
- How to maintain continuity of operations when nodes and communication links are down, and what is the best recovery strategy? Several have been discussed in the literature but have not yet been realized in commercially available products.
- How to pick a local area network when most of them do not even offer a minimum level of functionality for data sharing?
- Managing user demand, capacity planning, and deciding who is in control and responsible for data integrity when users are allowed to access common data from local workstations.

Many of these issues are still unresolved and complex to deal with. In some cases technical solutions have been slow in coming. There are several areas in need of some major research effort. Products are beginning to appear with some of the needed functionality but it will be several years before we will be able to realize a good share of the potential in distributed data processing.

18.4 BACKEND DATABASE MANAGEMENT MACHINE

Many organizations are experiencing a bottleneck in throughput performance with their DBMSs running on general purpose computers. Once large numbers of users are introduced to the capabilities of a comprehensive DBMS and the power and ease-of-use of high-level languages, demand increases inevitably and dramatically. Some users are demanding more comprehensive DBMS facilities such as automatic restructuring, data conversion, and better data quality control. Some more mature DBMS installations are experiencing over 50% of their computer capacity devoted to running the DBMS applications. Acquiring a bigger computer or another computer is one avenue of solution but it is quite costly and may not be necessary. A better solution might be to offload database functions to a special purpose machine—a *database management machine* (DBMM), also called *database machine, database processor*, or *data computer*.

The primary motivation behind the concept of a DBMM is improved cost performance. Putting data management functions in hardware should improve performance and lower costs. Putting them on a separate processor should increase throughput since the DBMM can operate in parallel with the host processor. Another motivation is better integrity control by isolating the data storage devices from the host computer and prohibiting user processes from executing on the backend DBMM. This would make it more difficult to circumvent the system controls and access the data directly.

Most DBMSs today are implemented in software on conventional computer systems. Conventional computer architecture has either one central processor or multiple, identical processors. The multiple processors are used to execute independent processes or parallel process steps. They all operate in basically the same way. Also, control in traditional computer systems resides in the operating system. Present-day operating systems actually perform several different functions, one of which is data management, albeit at a low level. Most DBMSs operate with the vendor-supplied operating system unmodified. User processes interact with the DBMS which in turn interacts with the operating system (see Figure 18-5). File access methods and basic input-output control routines are embedded in the operating system. The DBMS gets to the data through the operating system.

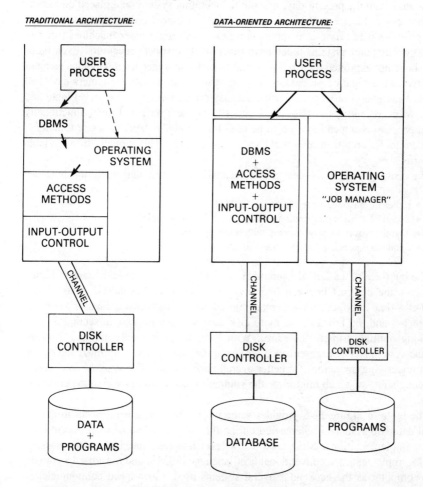

TRADITIONAL ARCHITECTURE:

DATA-ORIENTED ARCHITECTURE:

Figure 18-5. Traditional and Data-Oriented Computer Architectures.

In traditional computer systems, the DBMS operates as another application on top of the monolithic operating system. The operating system still controls all access to the files (data plus programs) on secondary storage devices. Traditional multiprocessor architectures still use identical general purpose processors which are best suited for sequential execution of programs. A better architecture for *data* processing gives the DBMS full control of the entire stream of processing within the computer system—access methods, input-output, buffering, and out to the secondary storage device and its controller. Breaking out the data-related functions of the operating system, combining them with the higher-level functions of database management, and placing them on a separate processor gives rise to the basic notion of a backend database management machine (DBMM).

18.4.1 Design Considerations for a DBMM

The concept of a database management machine requires that the functions of database management, including access methods and physical input-output routines, be separated from the present-day, monolithic operating system, and placed on a dedicated processor. In effect, there is a specialized machine within a computer system which provides data services to application processes run on *other* machines (processors). Few computer systems today have functionally distinct processors. Even those that do have not exploited their full potential to perform higher-level data management functions on the separate processors. For 20 years Control Data computers have had multiple "peripheral processors" (PPs) but they are only used for low-level input and output. More recently, the IBM 308x series computers have multiple, functionally distinct processors which have yet to be used for the higher-level database functions. Future computer architectures should see increased use of functionally differentiable processors.

The central issues in the design of a backend database management machine are:

- Level of language interface to the DBMM.
- Speed of the communications link with the host computer.
- Tightly versus loosely coupled with the host computer.
- Sequential versus parallel processing architecture.

The interface to the DBMM should be equivalent to a high-level language. Figure 5-8 shows the contrast between high-level and low-level languages. A low-level, record-at-a-time interface results in many more interactions between the user's application process and the DBMS, and more disk accesses (see the box in section 5.3.2.1 describing multiple trips to the store). With a single, high-level command from the user, the system is able to resequence, do in parallel, or otherwise optimize the execution of underlying operations for better overall performance. The system can choose a processing strategy which minimizes the volume of data transfers within the computer system.

The table in Figure 18-6 provides some information on several backend experimental database systems implemented during the 1970s, and some more recent commercial implementations. Most used a low-level language interface to the backend DBMM, implementing a conventional host-language DBMS, and most used a conventional computer as the backend. Several systems used a low speed communications link. The result with a low-level language and a low speed link was no significant performance improvement [Maryanski, 1980, page 15]. The commercial ADABAS system used a high-speed, channel-to-channel adapter and reported a 25% performance improvement.

A *tightly coupled backend computer* is dedicated to a single host computer and its interaction is closely controlled by the host operating system. It uses a high-speed communications link, perhaps with synchronous transmission. High-speed communications would be something over 1 Megabaud (1 million bits per second). A tightly coupled backend can exhibit improved performance with a minimum of overhead for

DEVELOPER	DATE	HOST MACHINE	BACKEND MACHINE	DBMS	LEVEL OF LANGUAGE	COUPLING	SPEED OF LINK	COMMENTS
EXPERIMENTAL RESEARCH PROJECTS								
Bell Labs[1] "XDMS"	1972	Univac 1108	META-4 (mini)	DMS-1100 (CODASYL)	low	tight	slow (2000 b)	Demonstrated feasibility. No performance improvement.
Cullinane[3]	1974	IBM 370 mainframe	PDP-11/70 (mini)	IDMS (CODASYL)	low	tight	slow (4800 b)	No performance improvement.
Kansas State University[3]	1976	Interdata (mini)	ITEL AS5 mainframe	TOTAL (Cincom)	low	tight	slow	Little performance improvement.
General Electric "MADMAN" [3]	1978	PDP-11 (mini)	LSI-11 (micro)	(CODASYL)	low	tight	high (bus)	No performance improvement.
Computer Corp of America[2,3] "Datacomputer"	1975	-many-	PDP-10 (large mini)	Specialized "Datalanguage"	medium	loose	slow	Data node for ARPANET.
COMMERCIAL PRODUCTS (all include specially built backend hardware)								
Software ag Reston, VA [4,8]	1980	IBM mainframe	ESP, built by Cambex	ADABAS	low	tight	high (channel)	Hardware/software backend for about $250,000 in minimum config. Only a handful sold.
Britton-Lee Los Gatos, CA [4,6,7,8]	1981	-many- (mainframe, to micro)	IDM-500 (E,X,XL)	relational DBMS	high	loose	slow (232/488)	Database size: 160Mb—32 Gigabytes. End user cost $50,000—$150,000+ 450 sold as of 1985.
Intel Phoenix, AZ (Austin, TX)	1982	-many-	iDBP	relational	high	loose	slow	End user cost starts at about $40,000.
CSSN [4] Boston, MA	1982	DEC,DG PRIME... (minis)	DISPATCH S-1000 MP-1000	MDBS (CODASYL+) others added?	low	loose	slow (232/488)	10-256 Megabytes starting at $30,000 (including 24 Mb drive).
Teradata Corp. Los Angeles, CA [5,8]	1984	-many- (mainframe)	DBC/1012	relational DBMS	high	loose	slow	Base config. 1,800 Megabytes and six processors for $320,000. Seven installed as of 1985/5 [8].

[1] CANADAY, 1974.
[2] MARILL, 1975.
[3] MARYANSKI, 1980.
[4] *Mini-Micro World*, 1981 October, pages 15-17.
[5] *MIS Week*, 1984 August 1.
[6] *MIS Week*, 1985 February 27, page 16.
[7] CARDENAS [1985].
[8] MYERS, *Datamation*, 1985 May 15, page 52.

Figure 18-6. Some Backend Database Management Machines.

Of these experimental systems and commercial efforts, one used a mainframe for the backend, a few used a specially designed higher-level language interface, some used a loosely coupled architecture, and two used a high-speed communications link. All of the experimental systems used a general purpose computer for the backend, while all of the commercial products use a specially built backend computer. Many of these produced little or no significant improvement in performance due to a combination of a low-level language, a low speed link, or use of a conventional computer for the backend machine. Tight coupling implies a single host, whereas loose coupling permits use with multiple hosts or in a distributed network. Loose coupling with a high-level language interface is the preferred design, in which case the speed of the communications link may not have a significant effect on the overall performance.

communications management. It is not necessary to build a completely general communications interface.

A *loosely coupled backend computer* provides greater flexibility but suffers in performance if other design options are not well chosen. Loose coupling enables asynchronous communication but requires additional communications software on both the host and the backend. The backend computer may be connected to multiple host computers directly or through a network. In fact, a loosely coupled backend DBMM is the same as a data node in a distributed processing environment.

18.4.2 Advantages of a Well-Designed DBMM

To realize any significant performance improvement with a *low-level interface*, the backend DBMM must be tightly coupled to the host with a high-speed link. With a *high-level* language interface to the DBMM, a slow speed link may be quite adequate to achieve significant performance improvements, along with the added advantages of a loosely coupled architecture.

The preferred design for a DBMM uses a high-level DBMS language interface to a separate dedicated processor loosely coupled to one or more host computers. This approach opens up new horizons for more efficient and effective database processing. Some of the advantages include:

- Freeing upwards of 50% of the capacity on the host by offloading the DBMS functions.
- Serving multiple hosts, even if different hardware manufacturers, and sharing common data.
- Attaching newer storage devices, such as large mass stores or laser disks, to (perhaps obsolete) mainframe computers for which direct interfaces are not provided for the new devices.
- Upgrading or replacing the host while keeping the backend, and therefore not having to convert existing data.
- Improving the level of database integrity and security.
- Opportunity for building specialized hardware: integrating some data management functions into the disk controller using more sophisticated search logic, and utilizing increased parallelism.

Figure 18-7 illustrates some of these relationships and the basic functional parts of a host processor and a backend database management machine.

The database management machine makes it possible to attain a much higher level of database integrity. All channels to the data on the secondary storage device would be dedicated to the exclusive use of the database management machine. With a single door to the database, it is much easier to control access to the database. Being the single point of access, the database management machine is able to perform all the underlying integrity control functions (according to administrative direction). Such integrity control functions include logging and dumping for backup, validation, ensuring the constant conformance of data to its definition, controlling concurrent update of the database, regulation of access to private data upon user authorizations, encryption of data prior to transmission or storage, monitoring operations, and maintaining an audit trail.

The backend DBMM should probably not be user programmable. That would entail reintroducing the general purpose development tools (compilers, debuggers, etc.) and an operating environment characteristic of conventional computers. Such a general environment makes it more difficult to develop specialized functions for *data* processing and is not very secure, exposing the database to greater integrity violations.

18.4.3 Specialized DBMM Hardware—Parallelism is the Key

The experimental DBMM efforts mentioned above used conventional computers for the backend, perhaps "tuned" for more efficient *data* processing. Conventional computer architecture is best for sequential, numerical computation. Modern general purpose computers, which are all based on Von Neumann principles, are particularly

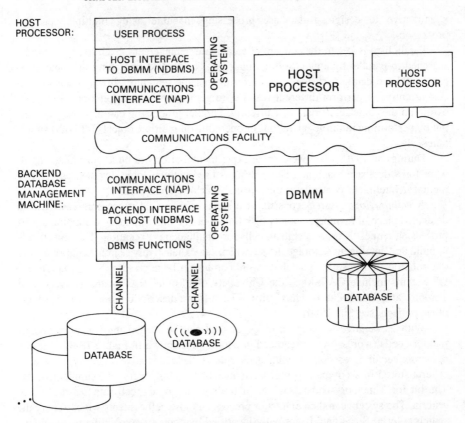

Figure 18-7. A Network of Host and Backend DBMM Computers.

With a loosely coupled architecture a backend database management machine could serve multiple hosts through a general communications facility. In fact, this configuration is a distributed processing network where the bulk of the DBMS functions are performed at the backend, that is, at the data node, with a high-level interface with the host processors. The multiple host processors may be from different manufacturers and may access different backend DBMMs. Each backend computer can be specially built utilizing principles of parallel processing, and can be dedicated to providing improved performance and data integrity. Under tight coupling, the host interface would entail a nominal amount of NDBMS functionality, and the communications interfaces would be much more specialized than a general NAP.

suited to executing programs. A program consists of a set of instructions to be executed sequentially. However, executing a program is fundamentally different from processing data. Conventional, sequential processors are inherently inappropriate and inefficient for searching and processing data.

A fundamental characteristic of data is replication—a set of records which conform to a common definition. *Data* processing is primarily associative and therefore amenable to parallel processing techniques. This was vividly illustrated in the selection and projection operations shown in Figure 7-2. The fundamental nature of data makes it attractive to design a database processing machine using multiple, parallel processors.

Parallelism is key to the concept of a database management machine. Data can be searched in parallel by content (direct matching) or context (matching on some adjacent or related data). A system may perform the same search on different sets of data concurrently, or perform different searches (e.g., multiple conditions) or other processing on the same set of data concurrently. Parallel processing can increase throughput by performing multiple operations or operating on multiple objects (or both) simultaneously.

During the 1970s there were some experimental efforts to build specialized hardware for a database machine. These designs used cellular-logic devices, associative memory, intelligent controllers, and special machine architectures.

A *cellular-logic system* consists of a series of identical processors each with a dedicated piece of memory, notably disk (but could be other memory technologies). A processing request is broadcast to all cells for simultaneous execution. The objective is to build an "intelligent" storage device which can exhaustively search an entire disk in one rotation. Indexes to the database would no longer be necessary. Some experimental systems include CASSM at the University of Florida, RAP at the University of Toronto, and RARES at the University of Utah [for a description of each of these and other projects see Su, 1980].

With *associative memory*, a block of data can be loaded into memory and its memory cells (words, bytes) searched in parallel. As shown in Figure 18-8, a bit in a response vector is associated with each cell of the associative memory. A search criteria stored in a comparand register is matched against every cell simultaneously. The bit for a memory cell is set 'on' if the contents of the cell satisfies the search criteria. The system can then extract or process all those cell contents which satisfy the search criteria. Since data is normally identified by content, associative memory systems are uniquely suited to perform database management functions.

One early effort to develop a commercial product using high-speed associative memory was Staran by Goodyear Aerospace [see Su, 1980 for a brief description and several references]. It contains up to 32 associative processor arrays of 256 x 256 bits. Each array can be searched on 256 bits in parallel (32 bytes). Data must be loaded into an array (8 kilobytes) before performing the very fast parallel search. High cost dictated a small associative memory. Small associative memories can be used economically for searching tables, directories, or indexes where there is high locality of references. However, large database applications create a bottleneck in moving data in and out of the relatively small memory.

Due to the use of small, fixed-size blocks, associative processing may entail some severe constraints on the database—fixed record formats, the entire database divided up into fixed blocks, and perhaps no intermingling of record types. Since databases in business organizations naturally tend to be of large volume, heterogeneous, and variable length, it may be more feasible to just apply associative processing to the indexes. The high cost for associative memory, the time to stage data into associative memory, and the requirement for small fixed-size blocks of data all explain the lack of acceptance of this technology for database management machines.

Comparand Register:

B	21	EM

Mask Register:

00000100000000000000000011100000011

Associative Memory:

Response Bit Vector:

45584PETERSON, N.M.	20000110HE	0
32579LYNN, K.R.	20005210EM	0
57060CARR, P.I.	21001110HE	0
15324CALLAGAN, R.F.	21005210EM	0
10261GUTTMAN, G.J.	21101110HE	0
72556HARRIS, D.L.	21105210EM	0
24188WALTERS, R.J.	21111110HE	0
21675SCARBOROUGH, J.B.	21111120EM	0
18130HENDERSON, R.G.	21111130EM	0
91152GARBER, R.E.	21111130EM	0
30793COMPTON, D.R.	21111350EM	0
81599FRIEDMAN, J.M.	21121110HE	0
21777FRANCIS, G.C.	21121110EM	0
24749FAULKNER, W.M.	21121120EM	0
13581FITINGER, G.J.	21121130EM	0
82802APGAR, A.J.	21121130EM	0
63633BLANK, L.F.	21121330EM	1
22959BRIGGS, G.R.	21151110HE	0
29414ARTHUR, P.J.	21151120EM	0
37113ARNETTE, L.J.	21151130EM	0
68840GODDARD, D.H.	21201120HE	0
71160GERRISH, C.S.	21205210EM	0
35401ANDERSON, R.E.	21221120HE	0
91589TAUBER, J.S.	21221120EM	0
80823STADERMAN, P.K.	21221130EM	0
64937SMITH, R.E.	21231120HE	0
82166RHODES, J.H.	21231120EM	0
28654RAYMOND, H.F.	21231130EM	0
17848HUGHES, J.W.	21231330EM	0
33144QUINN, S.M.	21235520EM	0
48464CHANDLER, W.R.	21301120HE	0
44432BERGMANN, R.I.	21305210EM	1
68795COOPER, J.C.	21311120HE	0
39464BUSTER, A.B.	21311120EM	1
:	:	:

Figure 18-8. Example of Searching an Associative Memory.

A '1' in the mask register indicates which positions of the comparand register are to be compared to each cell in the associative memory. A bit is turned 'on' in the response vector for each cell whose contents matches the masked positions of the comparand register. All memory cells are searched simultaneously in an associative memory. The search criteria in the above example is:

MARK CELL WHERE EMPNAME BEGINS WITH 'B'
   AND FIRST TWO DIGITS OF UNIT NUMBER EQ '21'
   AND FIRST TWO CHARACTERS OF LEVEL EQ 'EM'

Note that the search criteria can only consist of ANDed equality (character match) conditions.

With an *intelligent controller* some of the data management functions can be implemented in the controller. The controller itself is actually a computer with processing logic. A conventional controller, which simply moves data, can be augmented to perform other functions on the data at the same time—selective search, backup and recovery, encryption/decryption, or reorganization. Data reducing operations such as selection and projection are the most likely candidates for an intelligent controller.

Special machine architectures use functionally specialized hardware to achieve efficiency. The hardware can use multiple processors, parallel processing, pipelining techniques, and large high-speed buffers. Experimental research projects include the Data Base Computer (DBC) at Ohio State University [Banerjee, 1978], RAP.2 at the University of Toronto, INFOPLEX at MIT, DIRECT [DeWitt, 1979], MICRONET at University of Florida [for a brief description of each of these projects and references see Su, 1980], and the SABRE project in France [Valduriez, 1984].

18.4.4 Commercial DBMM Products

One significant milestone in database machines is the commercial development of IDM from Britton-Lee [see advertisement in Figure 18-9]. The system is a specially built "box" (only about three cubic feet!) which sits between one or more host computers and up to 32 Giga (billion) bytes of disk storage. The system uses conventional processor and memory components in an architecture which is designed specifically for database processing.

Formed in 1978, Britton-Lee first developed a prototype backend DBMS on a minicomputer but found that it could not handle data very well. The company then developed its own special-purpose machine targeted for the "mid-range" user and priced at $50,000 to $150,000. The IDM 500 has sold over 450 in the first four years after its introduction in 1981. The database consists of up to 32000 different flat files, 2 billion records per file, 250 attributes per file, any of which may be indexed separately or combined. The system maintains B-tree indexes (self-balancing). The database can be stored on up to 16 conventional moving-head (SMD-compatible) disk drives. The minimum configuration handles up to 8 host connections at 19.2 Kilobaud and one controller for 4 disk drives on a 20 Megabits per second bus. The system can search about 30,000 average records per second. A most interesting option is the database accelerator—a 10 million instruction per second (Mips) auxiliary Schottky transistor-to-transistor (TTL) pipelined processor which can increase performance up to ten times. The system can reportedly handle 100 to 2000 transactions per minute.

The DBMS is relational, using a high-level language similar to SQL or the language described in this text. Userschemas can be defined across multiple files, and the DBA can define access controls on the userschemas. It is possible to cancel or backout of any operation. The overall DBMS has a rather high level of functionality. The cost is competitive with the major software-only DBMSs. The performance is reportedly better and users recover up to 50% of their host CPU capacity when the DBMS functions are offloaded to an IDM backend.

For the high-end IBM mainframe market, Teradata began to market the DBC/1012 in 1984 after several years of design and testing. The minimum configuration has six

DBMS In a Box

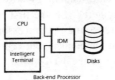

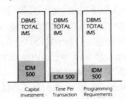

Figure 18-9. The Britton-Lee IDM 500 "DBMS in a Box."
This 1981 advertisement presents the advantages of a "DBMS in a Box."

processors and 4 474Megabyte disk drives and costs $320,000. The high speed and throughput is achieved using parallel processing techniques (up to 1024 processors!). As with the Britton-Lee IDM, the Teradata uses a high-level language interface to the backend database management functions. The seven users as of 1985 are very enthusiastic about the system [Myers, 1985].

A recent development in chip technology was announced by Inmos in Britain [Petre, 1984] called the "transputer." It is the first commercial chip built to incorporate the principles of parallel processing—a processor, memory, and communications circuitry on a single chip. This announcement represents the sort of technological advances needed to produce economical DBMMs.

18.5 EMERGING STANDARDS IN DATABASE TECHNOLOGY

Mention of standards often evokes strong feelings. For some it is what they feel should be the direction and content of a standard, for others it is despair at what is or is not happening in the standards arena. Nevertheless, standards are important to both users and developers of DBMS products. This section reviews the major standards organizations, the what and why of standards, the evolution and current status of activities in the development of database-related standards, and the direction, likely outcomes, and consequences of these current activities.

18.5.1 Standards Organizations and Their Activities

At the international level, standards activities are undertaken by ISO. In the United States they are undertaken by ANSI. (See Figure 18-10 for partial organization charts showing the committees involved with database-related standards.) Other countries also have standards bodies, notably the United Kingdom (BSI), Germany (DIN), and Canada (Standards Council).

In 1969 John Gosden, as chairman of an ANSI/X3/SPARC ad hoc Committee on Data Descriptive Languages, submitted a report to SPARC which in turn recommended to X3 that it appeared premature to start a standardization effort on Data Descriptive Languages. Then in 1972, SPARC again set up an ad hoc study group to investigate the whole subject of DBMS to determine if any candidates were suitable for standardization and to develop a framework for standards. The latter they did in a 1975 interim report [see ANSI, 1977] where they introduced the notions of conceptual schema, external schema, and internal schema. The ANSI/SPARC DBMS Framework, as it is known, is widely mentioned though not widely understood or accepted.

In 1978, following SPARC's recommendation, ANSI directed the COBOL and FORTRAN standards committees to incorporate DMLs to handle databases in their respective programming languages. ANSI also set up a new committee (H2) to develop a standard data definition language based upon the work of the CODASYL DDL Committee. ANSI/SPARC again set up a database systems study group in 1978 to re-examine the DBMS framework, to coordinate the multiple database-related stand-

International:

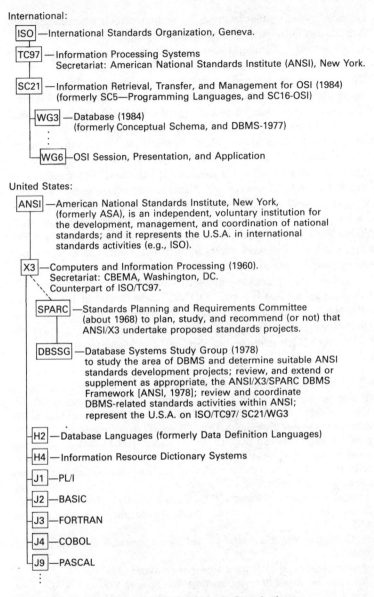

ISO —International Standards Organization, Geneva.

TC97 —Information Processing Systems
   Secretariat: American National Standards Institute (ANSI), New York.

SC21 —Information Retrieval, Transfer, and Management for OSI (1984)
   (formerly SC5—Programming Languages, and SC16-OSI)

WG3 —Database (1984)
   (formerly Conceptual Schema, and DBMS-1977)

WG6 —OSI Session, Presentation, and Application

United States:

ANSI —American National Standards Institute, New York,
   (formerly ASA), is an independent, voluntary institution for
   the development, management, and coordination of national
   standards; and it represents the U.S.A. in international
   standards activities (e.g., ISO).

X3 —Computers and Information Processing (1960).
   Secretariat: CBEMA, Washington, DC.
   Counterpart of ISO/TC97.

SPARC —Standards Planning and Requirements Committee
   (about 1968) to plan, study, and recommend (or not) that
   ANSI/X3 undertake proposed standards projects.

DBSSG —Database Systems Study Group (1978)
   to study the area of DBMS and determine suitable ANSI
   standards development projects; review, and extend or
   supplement as appropriate, the ANSI/X3/SPARC DBMS
   Framework [ANSI, 1978]; review and coordinate
   DBMS-related standards activities within ANSI;
   represent the U.S.A. on ISO/TC97/ SC21/WG3

H2 —Database Languages (formerly Data Definition Languages)

H4 —Information Resource Dictionary Systems

J1 —PL/I

J2 —BASIC

J3 —FORTRAN

J4 —COBOL

J9 —PASCAL

Figure 18-10. International and U.S.A. Standards Organizations.

ards efforts within ANSI, and to recommend any other areas ready for standardization. In 1982 DBSSG submitted a report on Relational Definition Languages [see Brodie, 1982] and ANSI assigned it to X3H2 for further development. In 1984, ANSI/X3/H2 sent out for vote a proposed standard Network Definition Language.

As of 1984, neither ISO nor ANSI had adopted any standards relating to database languages or systems, including the database declaration portion (userschema) and DML of the COBOL and FORTRAN programming languages.

In addition to the "official" international and national standards bodies, other organizations also develop and adopt standards.

The U.S. National Bureau of Standards develops mandatory standards and non-mandatory guidelines for all U.S. government non-military or administrative systems, called Federal Information Processing Standards (FIPS). FIPS-TG24 was established in 1977 to develop database-related standards. Although they apply only to U.S. federal government systems and acquisitions, FIPS standards can have a substantial impact due to the size of the U.S. government in the marketplace.

While compliance with ISO and ANSI standards is voluntary, NBS standards are generally mandatory for the U.S. government. Mandatory standards require a process of validation, compliance testing, and reporting. With voluntary standards, the process of acceptance is left to the goodwill of vendors and the persistent demands of users.

CODASYL has had a major impact on the development of standards. CODASYL is an independent, nonprofit, voluntary organization of users and vendors whose purpose is to develop *common* specifications and languages relating to the design and development of business data processing systems. Committee membership includes people from U.S.A., Canada, and Europe. CODASYL was formed in 1958 out of a COnference on DAta SYstems Languages (hence the name) to develop a common business-oriented language. Their first effort produced the COBOL programming language in 1960. CODASYL has continued to focus on *data* languages within various committees and task groups:

- COBOL Committee, which set up the Data Base Task Group (DBTG) in 1966 to develop extensions to COBOL to handle databases. Its 1971 final report proposed a set of 14 data manipulation language (DML) verbs to be hosted in COBOL. The Data Base Language Task Group (DBLTG) was set up to continue DML development and integration into COBOL. DBTG also proposed a data definition language (DDL) for what has since come to be called "network" data structures. Since the DDL should be independent of any programming language, a new committee was formed.
- Data Definition Language Committee (DDLC, formed 1971), published the *DDLC Journal of Development*, 1978, which became the base document for ANSI/X3/H2.
- Systems Committee, which is more study and research oriented. The Committee has published:
  Feature Analysis of Data Base Management Systems (1971),
  Selection and Acquisition of Data Base Management Systems (1976),
  and *A Framework for Distributed Database Systems: Distribution Alternatives and Generic Architectures* (1982).

Although CODASYL is careful to emphasize that they are *not* a standards-making body, their work has substantially influenced the development of standards. ANSI has not normally given serious consideration to a proposal relating to COBOL, the DML, or the DDL unless it has first been considered and approved by CODASYL.

Since the 1971 CODASYL DBTG report, all major computer manufacturers except IBM (Sperry Univac, Control Data, Honeywell, Burroughs, Digital Equipment, Texas Instruments), have implemented a system based upon those specifications. DBTG adopted all but 2 of some 70 changes suggested by IBM to the 1969 interim DBTG report but still voted against the final 1971 report. IBM had a sound technical position but never produced a counter proposal. Their DBMS products (IMS and GIS) did not (and still do not) stand up to the IBM technical position opposing the DBTG proposal.*

Unfortunately, since CODASYL separated the development of the DML and the DDL, their specifications have drifted apart and become incompatible, despite liaison efforts. Recognizing that the DML depends strongly on the DDL, ANSI suspended further work on the DML in the COBOL and FORTRAN standards committees, and charged the DDL committee (H2) with developing a standard which is independent of any programming language. When a standard is approved for the DDL plus associated DML (semantics only being important), the ANSI/X3/J . . . committees can begin to mold the DML into the syntactic style and rules of their respective programming languages.

18.5.2 Advantages and Inhibitors to the Development of Standards

The main purpose of standards is to foster interchangeability of products by defining standard interfaces and to foster the compatibility or coexistence of products by defining standard interchange formats. Interchangeability allows users to mix and match DBMS and related products. Transferability allows different products to be used together by enabling the transfer of data or other materials between them. Standards accomplish the following desirable goals:

- Guide manufacturers and vendors in the design and development of products. They encourage developers to build systems with common interfaces.
- Open competition to more developers, particularly small ones, when they can build to a standard and when interchangeable parts are available from different vendors.
- Give conforming products an implicit stamp of approval.
- Assist users in choosing from among competing products and result in fewer different products from which to choose.
- Increase portability of software and applications across people, machines, and operating system environments.
- Reduce the cost of training and increase the productivity of personnel who use the standard products.

All of the above assume that each standard is a "good" standard and is generally accepted. People, however, can disagree on what constitutes a "good" standard. The vendors of existing products will not want to see a standard go beyond or be different

*Robert W. Engles, "An Analysis of the April 1971 Data Base Task Group Report," *Proceedings of the 1971 ACM SIGFIDET Workshop on "Data Description Access, and Control"*, San Diego, California, 1971 November 11-12, edited by E. F. Codd and A. L. Dean, New York: Association for Computing Machinery, 1971, pages 69-91.

from the capabilities of their products. Users may feel that a standard does not go far enough to adequately meet their needs.

The major disadvantage of standards is that a premature standard can inhibit innovation in product development and incorporation of the latest technological advances. Other forces will also inhibit the adoption of standards. A vendor which dominates an industry or a particular type of product may delay or disrupt the standards development process, preferring to see their own position or product become a de facto standard (see cartoon in Figure 18-11).

18.5.3 The Development of Database-Related Standards

Standards typically *follow* industry developments, and are therefore strongly influenced by vested interests. A standardization effort begins with some concrete proposal which may be in the form of an operational system or language, or a detailed specification for a system or a language. Furthermore, any proposal should have reasonably wide industry willingness to at least entertain cooperative action toward developing a standard. Wide industry willingness may stem from cooperative industry development of a proposal or from widespread use of an existing system or language.

Clearly the CODASYL-DBTG proposal of 1971 which evolved into the ANSI/

Figure 18-11. 'Gentlemen, Why Decide This Industry Standard Now? You'll Have It in Three Years Anyway, When Our First Unit Is Delivered . . .'

X3/H2 proposed Network Database Language is a candidate for standardization. The DBTG proposal has received vigorous technical attention and debate. It has been widely accepted, described in several textbooks on DBMS, and spawned many commercial implementations, the one notable exception being IBM.

In 1970, Ted Codd, working for IBM, published a paper introducing the relational data model. That paper generated considerable interest, as evidenced in many subsequent papers of primarily theoretical and academic interest, and spawned several experimental system development projects. In 1976 a group working at IBM published a rather complete specification for a high-level, multifile data retrieval language called SEQUEL (subsequently changed to SQL) [see Chamberlin, et al., 1976]. Since then, several commercial database systems have been built which use SQL or a similar language (Oracle, Ingres, Informix, Unify, the Britton-Lee database machine, and other DBMSs promising to build an SQL front-end). As expected, IBM offered its own system called SQL under DOS, and DB2 for MVS on their mainframe computers. It seems clear that SQL and the relational data model are also candidates for standardization.

During the 1970s there was much discussion and debate concerning the relative merits of the CODASYL network approach versus the relational approach. In 1972, Canning* argued that if a common approach were not forthcoming, a tower of Babel would result with the development of many different and incompatible systems. Fortunately, even though a standard has not been adopted, the evolving proposal has remained visible to interested parties. Canning gives a good presentation of the arguments against the DBTG proposal and the rebuttals to those arguments. The 1974 SIGMOD Conference held a debate with Charles Bachman and others arguing the CODASYL network approach and Ted Codd and others arguing the relational approach.†

From the perspective of the data structure (see Chapter 4) the differences are few though not insignificant. The major difference being that the CODASYL network DDL permits nested repeating groups within a record whereas the relational data structure does not. Many people, including those favoring the CODASYL network approach, argue that good database design means flat files in third normal form (at least initially— including nested repeating groups of data items in records for implementation efficiency).

From the perspective of data manipulation (see section 5.3.2.1 and Chapters 7 and 8), the high-level language of the relational approach is clearly superior to the record-at-a-time low-level language of the CODASYL approach.

While there is much diffusion in the support for the relational approach, it is safe to conclude that the two dominant forces in the standards process are IBM along with

---

*Richard G. Canning, "The Debate on Data Base Management," *EDP Analyzer* (10:3), 1972 March, 16 pages.

†Randall Rustin, editor, "Data Models: Data-Structure-Set *versus* Relational," *Proceedings ACM SIGMOD Workshop on Data Description, Access and Control*, Volume 2, Ann Arbor, MI, 1974 May, contains papers by Charles W. Bachman, E. F. Codd, Edgar H. Sibley, Dionysios Tsichritzis, Jim Lucking, and Kevin Whitney, and a transcript of the questions and answers following the debate.

vendors of SQL-like products, and the rest of the industry much of which appears behind the CODASYL "Network" Definition and Manipulation Language proposal. While it is difficult to determine the degree to which IBM may be orchestrating support for the relational approach, if any, it is certainly in their best interests to have a standard for the SQL language. In 1982, ANSI/X3/H2 agreed to use IBM's SQL as the base for developing a Relational Database Language (RDL) standard. In 1984, after two years of refining and extending the RDL, they moved to go back to the original SQL specification, thus increasing the chance of early adoption of a relational standard, albeit the least common denominator of current relational systems. Although currently deferred, the RDL developments are a good indicator of future standards relating to relational database systems.

18.5.4 Direction of Emerging Standards

The first database-related standard to come from ANSI will most likely be the Network Database Language. A 1984 draft proposed standard document has been sent out for public comment. The major features of the proposed standard are clearly evident now and changes, if any, are likely to be minor.

The document essentially consists of four parts:

1. *Concepts*, introducing the pieces, objects, and common elements of the language which is described in the rest of the document.
2. *Schema Definition Language* for declaring a network structured database and its integrity constraints.
3. *Subschema Definition Language* for declaring the user view of a database schema.
4. *Data Manipulation Language* and module language for declaring the executable statements and database procedures for a specific database application.

Implementations of this standard may exist in an environment with:

- Application programming languages.
- End-user and natural language query facilities.
- Report generator and graphics output facilities.
- Data storage definition and device media control languages.
- Access control mechanisms.
- Database copy and reversion ("unload") facilities.
- Schema access facilities for ad hoc users and user-written application procedures.
- Schema manipulation language for revising a database definition.
- Database restructure and reorganization utilities to bring an existing database into conformance with a revised schema.
- Information resource data dictionaries.
- Tools for database design, database administration, and performance monitoring.
- Distributed database facilities in a Network DBMS.
- Interfaces to word processing, spread sheet, decision modeling, and statistical packages.

None of the above are included in the proposed NDL standard [1984]. They may be implementor defined. They may also be covered in subsequent versions of the standard or in separate standards. The document states that a conforming implementation must provide all of those facilities which are described in the standard.

The proposed NDL standard evolved out of the work of CODASYL with some notable changes:

- Removed from the schema definition some information relating to the physical storage and access of data (a desirable move)—inclusion of records in "areas" or "realms" (the user now opens and closes files), relative frequency of direct retrieval and sequential retrieval of records, relative frequency of retrieval versus update of individual data items, set occurrence selection by positioning or navigation, record location mode, and method of set implementation (chain, pointer array).
- Retained the controversial declaration of an ordering on the member records within a set occurrence. The declaration of a stored ordering should be part of the physical storage definition, and the requesting user should separately declare any desired ordering on the *presentation* of data.
- Dropped the ordering verb from the data manipulation language, leaving the application programming user with no way to specify an order of presentation on the members of a set which is different from that defined in the schema. It is preferable that users not have the ability to change the stored ordering of records, but they should be able to declare an ordering for presentation.
- Added the declaration of recursive sets (same record type as owner and member) even though most vendors of such systems did not offer the feature.
- Moved the value-based declaration of the criterion for a relationship ("structural constraint clause") to an option in the insertion constraint. As before, the constraint is enforced at time of record insertion as well as when the value of the data item in the criterion is subsequently modified.
- Retained the READY ("open") declarations of exclusive, protected, and shared, thus inappropriately disallowing concurrent access to exclusive readers, and inappropriately allowing concurrent access to shared writers intending to update the same data (see Figure 13-9).
- Continued to force a pre-emption strategy for resolving deadlock of concurrent update processes.
- Expanded the search condition on a FIND statement to be a general Boolean expression with AND, OR, NOT, parentheses, and comparative ("relation") operators. However, the data items as operands in the expression must all be from a single object record type, and the system only delivers one record for each FIND statement. The user must step through the records satisfying the selection expression with:

  FIND NEXT < record-name > WHERE < condition >

  which will find the FIRST such record when no record has yet been established as current.
- Added a RECONNECT statement to handle the simultaneous disconnect of a record from a set and connect to another set occurrence. Without this feature, a user was forced to temporarily violate the mandatory retention integrity constraint when moving a record from one owner to another.

Now for some global observations about the emerging NDL standard. It has tended to encompass a minimum set of capabilities—those which have already been implemented in the dominant commercially available systems (with the notable exception of recursive sets), or which are more easily implementable. The vendor representatives on the committee are understandably reluctant to approve any addition to the standard which is not in their system. Thus the standard tends to the lowest common denominator. This makes vendors happy since they can say that their system conforms to the (limited) standard. Unfortunately, users are not well served; the standard provides no impetus for vendors to supply the higher-level, comprehensive facilities which many people agree are needed to accomplish the fundamental objectives of database management (as outlined in Chapter 2 and all of Part II).

Besides the previous list of things excluded from the emerging standard (but which could exist in the implementation environment), we could add the need for file-level ("set-oriented") operations, derived data items, simple calculation of statistics on a selected subset of records, global (file-level) update, multifile operations, greater tolerance of differences between the schema and the userschemas and appropriate data conversions (almost unmentioned in the proposed standard but the bedrock of data independence), and more comprehensive facilities for declaring data quality controls (validation, semantic constraints) which are so important to gaining user confidence.

Another serious criticism of the NDL proposal is the inconsistency between the facilities provided the user and the assumption about the user. On the one hand, the proposal provides a great deal of flexibility to the user—flexibility relating to currency, record navigation, the manipulation of unique internal record identifiers ("database keys"), and responding to error returns. All this implies that the system is intended for rather sophisticated programming users. On the other hand, there is no mention of an ability to reference the stored database definition (schema), to dynamically define the userschema and user program buffer, or to dynamically construct a database manipulation language statement. Since these are the facilities required by the DBMS system programmer, we conclude that the proposal is intended to serve the conventional application programmer exclusively. Application programmers will tend to be at the novice end of the programming user spectrum rather than the sophisticated end. Therein lies the inherent inconsistency. To preclude the DBMS system programmer interface is to preclude the possibility of adding the self-contained facilities or "nonprocedural" capabilities for generalized interrogation and update to the existing host-language capabilities.

By focusing only on the low-level interface to a host programming language, the proposed NDL standard deals with a very small part of the total picture in database management. With the increased use of higher-level, self-contained data languages, equally suited for ad hoc interaction and writing procedures for deferred execution, the scope and level of the proposed NDL standard is increasingly unimportant, perhaps even irrelevant. High-level, self-contained data languages (also called "fourth generation languages") generally include (the first two are mandatory for a self-contained language):

- *Declaration of variables*, perhaps as local and global, and including arrays.
- *Control structures* (IF-THEN-ELSE, DO-WHILE, . . .) for conditional, repetitive execution of sequences of commands.
- Full Boolean expression capability for conditional selection of records and execution of processes.
- Built-in system functions and system variables (e.g., Date, time).

- Substring functions to manipulate individual data item values (trim, truncate, concatenate, extract, and convert to upper or lower case).
- User-defined functions, subroutines, and macros.

These facilities are becoming commonplace in the newer, better DBMSs, particularly those on microcomputers. The development of more comprehensive, higher-level facilities reduces the need for low-level, navigational, host-language interfaces. As emphasized in this text, writing application programs in conventional programming languages such as COBOL should be considered an avenue of *last* resort in building application systems.

The Relational Database Language [RDL—1984] is another draft proposal from ANSI/X3/H2. It is not as highly refined as the NDL proposal. Moreover, with X3/H2 falling back to concentrate on the original SQL, the enhanced RDL is several years away from adoption. It attempts to embody much of what is found in DBMSs based upon relational data structures, including high-level, multifile retrieval languages. The proposed RDL includes the following features:

- Explicit declaration of interfile relationships based upon stored data item values, and the constraints on modification and deletion of records (similar to the Insertion and Retention clauses in the NDL proposal).
- Facilities for revising or dropping a file ("table") definition.
- Facilities for granting and revoking access and update privileges.
- A more comprehensive set of operators in the Boolean selection expression (between two values, all/any of a set of values, substring match, and existence). An expression can reference multiple files and can include embedded subqueries which generate a *set* of values for an operand within the expression.
- Derived data items.
- User-declared ordering of records on output.
- Join operation on multiple files, and set operations (union, intersection, difference) on the results of two queries.

With a solid grounding in theory, the relational model has gained substantial support among technical professionals concerned with data structures and management. In contrast to the network data structures defined in the NDL proposal, higher-level languages have already been defined and implemented for relational data structures. The development of higher-level languages on a network structure is much more difficult, though not impossible as can be seen in some newer commercial implementations. Without higher level languages, users must always do their own navigating through the network structured database. Furthermore, the flat files of the relational data structures are inherently suitable for associative processing in hardware.

In many instances, the specifications in the NDL and RDL are functionally equivalent (or at least close) yet they propose substantially different syntax and semantics in their respective languages. Little effort was made to unify the two proposed standards, primarily because they were developed in two different committees. When the RDL report was completed by a subgroup of ANSI/SPARC/DBSSG [Brodie, 1982] ANSI wisely assigned it to the same committee which was working on the NDL proposal (H2). So far the two documents have been treated separately. Since there is a large area of overlap, it would be unfortunate for users in the industry if two separate standards emerged (although this is the most likely outcome—the NDL and the original SQL).

Other ANSI committees are developing standards for programming languages which should be able to interface with or incorporate the data manipulation language statements for dealing with a database. Unfortunately, there is a significant degree of inconsistency and incompatibility between the COBOL, FORTRAN, PASCAL, and PL/I standards and the proposed NDL and RDL standards. ANSI also has a committee on Information Resource Dictionary Systems which will likely produce a proposed standard which is not fully compatible with the efforts in the other committees.

18.5.5 Development of a Reference Model for Database Standards

The development of related but uncoordinated standards is cause for concern. There are several different areas within DBMS technology which are or could be the object of standards development:

- Data structure definition languages which are used to define database schemas and userschemas. Such languages are used in a DBMS, in programming languages, and in Data Dictionaries.
- Integrity control languages to define semantic constraints, validation criteria, access controls, etc.
- Physical storage structures, access methods, and device/media control.
- Data manipulation languages which can appear in a host-language interface to a conventional programming language, a self-contained DBMS language, an ad hoc query language, or a report generation facility. Retrieval and manipulation languages are needed to operate on stored databases but also stored schemas, userschemas, and data dictionaries.
- Data mapping and conversion languages for use in database reorganization, restructure, creation, reversion, and schema-userschema translations.

The development and coordination of standards across all these areas is a massive undertaking. It can only be done in stages; some priorities must be set. A comprehensive data structure definition language seems to be the most important first step, since a given data structure is the object of retrieval, manipulation, and conversion.

To bring some order to standards development, there have been attempts to define a reference model which includes the major modules of a database system. A *reference model* establishes a common framework or background for a class of systems such as DBMS to which people may refer when talking about specific products, product design and development, or standards. It serves as a tool for the development and coordination of standards by identifying major interfaces between component parts of the overall system.

A database system has four major types of interfaces:

- *End user* who is concerned with getting some job done within the organization. End users interface with the various modules or functions of a database system to access database definitions and to retrieve and manipulate stored data, both in writing procedures for deferred execution and in ad hoc, interactive use.
- *Administrative support staff* concerned with the design, development, installation, maintenance, and evaluation of database system products, and the training of end

users. The database administrator needs to create and revise database definitions, to establish integrity controls, and to monitor performance.

- *External interfaces* to other computer system components (non-DBMS) such as the operating system and the network access process.
- *Internal interfaces* between functional parts or modules of the database system.

The first ANSI/SPARC DBMS Framework [ANSI, 1977; Young, 1982] attempted to provide a comprehensive description of a DBMS environment, its major modules and interfaces. They defined the discipline of database management as ". . . records, fields, files, sets, and the descriptions of all these, and all the indices, mapping techniques, access methods, file organizations, and end-user languages . . ." The Framework focused on *interfaces* which the group felt was the appropriate object of any subsequent standards effort. They prepared a large diagram which identified 42 interfaces (see Figure 18-12).

The most essential component of the Framework is the *conceptual* schema. It is the logical or natural "real world" view of the enterprise. It is the basis for integrity and security rules imposed on the users. It is also the common denominator of the multiple user views and the internal stored representation of the database. An *external* schema is a user view of some portion of the conceptual schema used in the development and operation of application processes. The *internal* schema is the machine view of the stored database and its access mechanisms. The report emphasized that the conceptual schema must be described explicitly in machine readable form (and available to the DBMS) in some well defined and potentially standardizable data definition language. The internal and external views of data must necessarily be consistent with (mappable to) the view in the conceptual schema. The triangle in Figure 18-12, commonly called a data dictionary/directory facility, contains the stored representations of all three types of schemas and the mappings with the conceptual schema.

The report identified the enterprise administrator as responsible for developing and maintaining the conceptual schema, the database administrator responsible for the internal schema, and application administrator(s) responsible for external schemas used in various application processes. By contrast, this text has included all these areas of responsibility within the single role of DBA.

ISO/TC97/SC5/WG3 carried the notion of a conceptual schema one step further. They argued that it should contain *all* the relevant static and dynamic aspects of the universe of discourse—all entities, facts which describe and events which can affect those entities, the structure of the data, and permissible retrievals and updates. They called it the "100% principle." The conceptual schema tells us what to record when designing an information system. The important point is that all this information is kept independent of any application processes or programs.

The original ANSI/SPARC Framework has not been pursued further. In 1982, ANSI/SPARC directed DBSSG to extend or supplement the original DBMS Framework and to consider the OSI reference model.

In developing a DBMS reference model, there is concern that it be consistent with the Open Systems Interconnection (OSI) reference model developed by ISO/TC97/SC16 [ISO, 1981]. Their reference model described a seven layer architecture for interprocess communication to be used in distributed networks (see page 773).

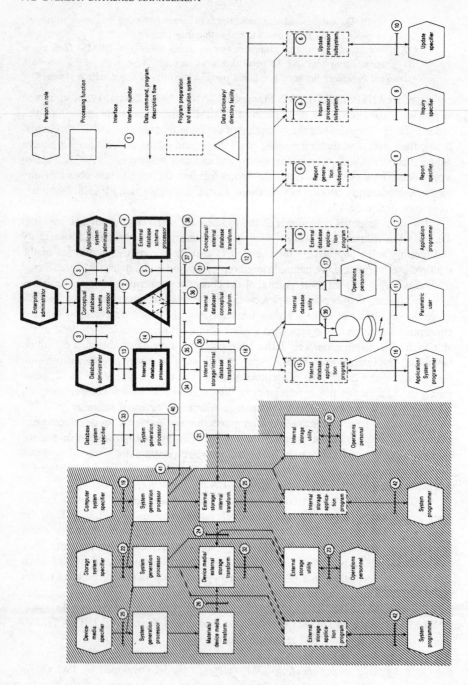

OSI Reference Model
$\begin{cases} \text{7. Application layer} \\ \text{6. Presentation layer} \\ \text{5. Session layer} \\ \text{4. Transport layer} \\ \text{3. Network layer} \\ \text{2. Datalink layer} \\ \text{1. Physical layer} \end{cases}$

The bottom layers 1 to 4 were quite well defined and have been embodied in the standard data communications protocol designated as X.25 and now implemented by several manufacturers. The top three layers were less well defined. The *application layer* provides information services applications—remote file access, basic DBMS functions of data storage and retrieval, and integrity functions such as locking, rollback and recovery. The *presentation layer* organizes information into recognizable formats performing any necessary data conversion such as code or character set translations. This layer handles heterogeneity and manages the entry, exchange, and display of structured data. The *session layer* handles the initiation and termination of transmission sessions, accepting and delivering packets of information.

The DBMS functions are in the application and presentation layers. Unfortunately, they were very poorly defined in the ISO OSI reference model. Bachman (who was on the committee) and Ross [1982] argued that the presentation layer must go beyond simply interprocess communication to include data storage and retrieval, and operations on the data local to the process. Fuller definition is needed for the upper three layers of the OSI reference model and work continues in ISO/TC97/SC21/WG6.

Emerging from the DBSSG efforts is a reference model which treats the schema data similar to the stored application data. The predominant ISO and ANSI thinking to date has implicitly assumed that the schema information is stored separately from user data, and is accessed and manipulated with different functions of the DBMS. The Database Architecture Framework Task Group of DBSSG [ANSI-DAFTG, 1985] outlines an architecture in which the application data, the schema (meta-data), and the schema schema are all stored and manipulated with the same set of facilities. In fact, several commercially available DBMSs do just that. It is more efficient for the DBMS builder to use the same storage, retrieval, and update facilities for both data and schema information. The access control mechanism can be used to limit access to the

---

Figure 18-12. Diagram of the ANSI/X3/SPARC DBMS Framework.
The legend is given in the upper right corner. The figure shows people in particular roles, the various DBMS processing functions, and the major interfaces between and among them. The diagram focuses on interfaces as being the appropriate object of standardization. The top half of the diagram includes definitional components; the bottom includes usage components. The idea of three separate yet related schemas was the most significant contribution of the report (bolder shapes in top center). The *conceptual* schema embodies the "real world" view of the enterprise being modeled in a database. An *external* schema is a user's view of some portion of the database. The *internal* schema is the machine's view of the database as it is stored and accessed. The shaded portion on the left encompasses the storage subsystem and is not discussed further in the ANSI report.

Reproduced from D. Tsichritzis and A. Klug, editors, "The ANSI/X3/SPARC DBMS Framework: Report of the Study Group on Database Management Systems", *Information Systems* (3:3), 1978, page 178.

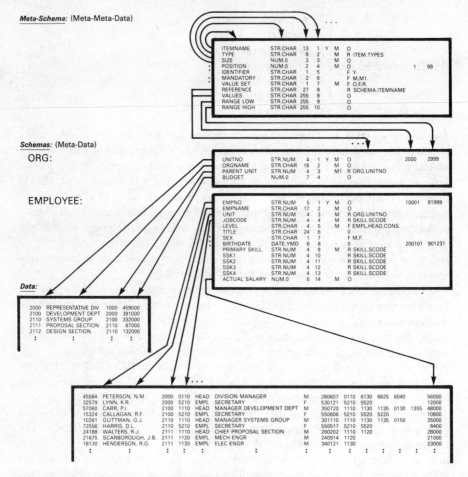

Figure 18-13. Data, Schema (Meta-Data), and Meta-Schema.

The schema information which defines a data file is sometimes called "meta-data" or data about data. The "meta-schema" would be the definition of a schema file. It is desirable to use the same facilities for storage, retrieval, and update whether operating on a data file or a schema file. In either case the system facilities require a description of the data object. When accessing or manipulating a schema, the system uses the meta-schema. Notice that the meta-schema describes itself. Revision of a schema (using the standard update facilities in the DBMS) may require restructuring or reorganization of the associated stored data. This three level scheme assumes a single underlying data structure class ("data model") for all data files. It is possible to add a fourth level to accommodate multiple types of data structures. The top level is self-describing, built-in, and should not be changed. With four levels, revision of the meta-schema may require revision of the schemas *and* their associated data files.

schema. Of course, the system must always know which level of data it is dealing with. Changes to schema data will affect the stored data it describes and therefore must be controlled. Figure 18-13 illustrates three recursive levels of data and meta-data using the personnel-organization database.

SUMMARY

Looking to the future of DBMS, several trends are evident. These trends result primarily from concerns of users to have better tools for application systems development. DBMSs will increasingly serve both programming and nonprogramming users, with a shift from DBMS facilities hosted in a programming language to stand alone data languages for the programming user. Systems are exhibiting greater functional completeness with a single, comprehensive definition of data, revision facilities, database integrity functions, extended retrieval facilities, and integration with other software packages such as word processing and spread sheets. These added or extended facilities are being made available in higher-level languages with better end user interfaces. All of these facilities use a single, central, comprehensive definition of data which is the real key to better database management. The newer generation of DBMS provides greater support for application systems development with built-in facilities for defining and handling data screens, menus, and help screens—all recognizing the inevitable and dominant shift to online development of online systems. All these trends are even more evident in DBMSs on microcomputers.

With these emerging trends in DBMS tools, many organizations still have not moved very significantly to effectively utilize these tools in systems development and ad hoc access by end users. Resistance to acquiring new, advanced DBMS tools may stem from not knowing which ones to select from the hundreds available. There may also be resistance to the initial cost even though the ongoing costs of not acquiring more productive tools can be many times the initial cost.

There is also resistance to using the tools which are available in an organization. This stems from unfamiliarity, lack of training, poor technical support with no inhouse experts, and a preference to use the known and familiar tools. Management must: acquire better DBMS tools; specifically set aside time for people to learn how to use the new tools; develop inhouse expertise in technical support personnel; provide incentives for users to try, learn, and use the new tools; and demand appropriate justification for the tools used and not used for each development project.

Distributed systems are driven by the dramatic reduction in the cost of computers. Distribution promises increased responsiveness and control to local users, and greater reliability through replication and reduced dependence on a central site. Multiple computing nodes are connected through a communications facility to form a network. Each node requires a network access process to interface with the communications facility. A network operating system globally manages system resources and allocates them to processes within the network. Global access to and management of data is provided by a Network DBMS.

Networks generally allow sharing of printers and disk space but few provide adequate facilities for sharing data. These facilities must include global detection of conflicts in concurrent access to common data, and often involve a central file server. A network data directory records what data is stored at what nodes in the network. The NDBMS provides several functions beyond the single-site DBMS—determining the location of requested data, forwarding subrequests to the NDBMSs at other nodes in the network or to the local DBMS, and reassembling the responses for the user. Heterogeneity in the DBMSs may require translation of requests and conversion of data between DBMSs.

Within a network data may be centralized, partitioned, or replicated. Partitioning may be by attributes or by entities. Replication requires synchronization of updates against the multiple copies, a difficult process which must be coordinated over time, and must persist until disabled nodes are back online. Replication is preferred for small databases, partitioning is preferred for large databases with highly localized usage, and centralized storage is preferred for large databases having heavy usage spread throughout the network.

Even the DBMS functions can be distributed. Data reducing functions such as selection and projection are best done at the site of the data. Data expanding functions such as item derivations, statistics, and formatting are better done at the user site. Linking microcomputers to a central host computer provides an opportunity to optimally allocate the DBMS functions to each. Users can download data from the host for local manipulation, and they can do data entry and validation locally before uploading the transactions for updating to the central database.

Placing the DBMS functions in a special-purpose database machine holds the promise of relieving some of the load on mainframe computers. The architecture of conventional general purpose computers and operating systems is inappropriate for *data* processing. With a high-level language interface to a backend database machine, the speed of the communications link with the host computer is less important to throughput performance. A tightly coupled DBMM is dedicated to a single host computer. A loosely coupled DBMM provides greater flexibility with asynchronous communication to multiple host computers—effectively a node in a distributed network. A backend database machine also permits greater data security. Parallelism is the key to the architecture of a database machine, using cellular logic, associative memory, or other special designs.

To date neither the International Standards Organization (ISO) nor the American National Standards Institute (ANSI) have adopted standards relating to database management systems. The first standard likely to emerge is the Network Data Language (NDL) from ANSI/X3/H2 based upon the work of the CODASYL Data Base Task Group. This follows substantial public debate and several commercial implementations of network structured DBMS. Standards can guide system developers in designing their systems and guide users regarding what systems to acquire. Products which conform to standards will interface more easily. Vendors with existing products are more likely to resist anything in the standard which is not included in their system. The resulting standards may make it more difficult to take advantage of new technology.

The proposed NDL standard includes the DDL for a network database structure and low-level, record-at-a-time language verbs to be embedded in a host programming language. This focus excludes many other aspects of database management, some considered to be more important, such as high-level languages. A second proposed standard from ANSI covers relational systems but is further from adoption. It includes some facilities for revision, access control, derived data items, and user-declared ordering on presentation. The most significant aspect of the relational proposal is the high-level set-oriented command language.

Recent activities in the standards community has been directed to developing a DBMS reference model to coordinate standards in several areas—data structure definition, integrity control, physical storage definition, manipulation languages for retrieval and report generation, and data mapping and conversion. A reference model identifies the many components in a DBMS environment and the interfaces with end users, administrative support personnel, external non-DBMS packages, and between functional parts of the DBMS. The latest work in the ANSI/X3/SPARC DBSSG is looking at a reference model which explicitly stores a meta-schema which describes the schemas in the system. In this way the same facilities for storage, retrieval, and update can be used for both data and schemas.

This is written in the hope that vendors, users, and standards developers will all feel stretched—vendors to develop more comprehensive high-level tools, users to think more broadly of the capabilities required to meet their needs, and standards developers to look beyond present-day products to what can really serve the needs of users.

EXERCISES

18-1. What are the major trends in the development of DBMS?

18-2. Explain how an increasing diversity of user types is affecting the evolution of DBMSs and the design of the user interface.

18-3. What are some of the reasons for organizational resistance to the acquisition and use of the newer and better DBMS tools? What specific steps can be taken to overcome this resistance?

18-4. What are the four levels of interconnectedness in a distributed processing environment? What functions are needed to support each level?

18-5. Describe the role and functions of a Network DBMS and a network data directory.

18-6. What are the appropriate criteria for distributing DBMS functions within a distributed network? How should these functions be divided between a local microcomputer workstation and a central host which stores the corporate database?

18-7. Explain the three database distribution alternatives.

18-8. Explain how global deadlock can occur in a network which does not have a file server.

18-9. What are the advantages of using a separate, special-purpose backend machine for database management? How would a dedicated DBMM enhance database integrity?

18-10. What are the main design considerations for a backend database management machine?

18-11. Why is the speed of the communications link between a host and a backend DBMM relatively unimportant with a high-level language interface to the DBMM?

18-12. Explain why the architecture of conventional general purpose computers and their operating systems is inappropriate for a database management machine.

18-13. Although associative memory appears uniquely suited to database management operations it has not achieved any wide-spread use. Why? What are some of the factors limiting the use of associative memories?

18-14. What are the dominant forces which push for or inhibit the development of standards?

18-15. What are the weaknesses of the proposed Network Data Language standard from ANSI/X3/H2?

18-16. Some say that any industry standard will be ineffective if not adopted by IBM due to their dominance in the marketplace. Do you think this is true? Are there any examples which contradict this statement?

SELECTED REFERENCES

American National Standards Institute—ANSI/X3/SPARC Database Architectural Framework Task Group of DBSSG, "Reference Model for DBMS Standardization," Gaithersburg, MD: U.S. National Bureau of Standards, NBSIR 85-3173, 1985 May, 78 pages.

American National Standards Institute—ANSI/X3/SPARC Database Management Systems Study Group, "Framework Report on Database Management Systems," AFIPS, 1978; reprinted as D. Tsichritzis and A. Klug, editors, "The ANSI/X3/SPARC DBMS Framework," *Information Systems* (3:3), 1978, pages 173-191.

American National Standards Institute, "(Draft Proposed) Network Database Language," New York: ANSI, X3H2-84-23, 1984 March, 143 pages.

American National Standards Institute, "(Draft Proposed) Relational Database Language," New York: ANSI, X3H2-84-24, 1984 March, 106 pages.

ASCHIM, Frode, "Data Base Networks—An Overview," *Management Informatics* (3:1), 1974 February, pages 12-28.
   An early paper to describe various database distribution alternatives.

BABB, E., "Implementing a Relational Database by Means of Specialized Hardware," *ACM Transactions on Database Systems* (4:1), 1979 March, pages 1-29.

BACHMAN, Charles W. and Ron G. ROSS, "Toward a More Complete Reference Model of Computer-Based Information Systems," *Computers & Standards* (1:1), 1982, pages 35-48.
   Proposes an ambitious endeavor to develop standards based upon a reference model which explicitly includes the interaction between a DBMS framework and the OSI reference model.

BANCILHON, F. and M. SCHOLL, "Design of a Back-end Processor for a Database Machine," *Proceedings ACM SIGMOD Conference*, 1980.

BANERJEE, J., David K. HSIAO, and R. I. BAUM, "Concepts and Capabilities of a Database Computer," *ACM Transactions on Database Systems* (3:4), 1978 December, pages 347-384.
   Describes the Data Base Computer (DBC) being developed at Ohio State University.

BERRA, P. Bruce, and E. OLIVER, "The Role of Associative Array Processors in Data Base Machine Architecture," *Computer* (12:3), 1979 March.

BOOTH, Grayce M., *The Distributed System Environment: Some Practical Approaches*, New York: McGraw-Hill, 1980.

BRAY, Olin H., *Distributed Database Management Systems*, Lexington Books, 1982.

BRODIE, M. and J. SCHMIDT, editors, "Final Report of ANSI/X3/SPARC DBSSG Relational Task Group," *ACM SIGMOD Record*, 1982 July.
   Developed a comprehensive statement of syntax and semantics for the DML and DDL of relational database systems. It was assigned to ANSI/X3/H2 to develop into a proposed standard.

CANADAY, R. H., R. D. HARRISON, E. L. IVIE, J. L. RYDER, and L. WEHR, "A Back-End Computer for Database Management," *Communications of the ACM* (17:10), 1974 October, pages 575-582.
   A landmark paper describing an experimental system built at Bell Labs using a CODASYL-based system on a minicomputer backend to a Univac 1100 host.

CARDENAS, Alfonso F., "Data Base Machines," Chapter 15 in *Data Base Management Systems*, second edition, Boston, MA: Allyn and Bacon, 1985, pages 615-639, 27 refs.
   Provides a good overview of the rationale for DBMMs, the limitations of conventional computers and operating systems, five DBMM architectures, and a closer look at specific systems (Britton-Lee IDM, RDM-1100 from Amperif, System 2000 FAST 3805 DBAP from Intel, NDX-100, and Tandem).

CHAMBERLIN, D. D., et al., "SEQUEL 2: A Unified Approach to Data Definition, Manipulation, and Control," *IBM Journal of Research and Development* (20:6), 1976 November, pages 560-575.
   Comprehensive specification of a high-level data language on a relational data structure. Provided the basis for several experimental and commercial implementations of relational DBMS.

CHAMPINE, George A., "Backend Technology Trends," *IEEE Computer* (13:2), 1980 February, pages 50-58.

CHAMPINE, George A., "Six Approaches to Distributed Data Bases," *Datamation*, 1977 May, pages 69-72.

CODASYL System Committee, *A Framework for Distributed Database Systems: Distribution Alternatives and Generic Architectures*, New York: ACM, 1982 November, 134 pages, 40 refs.
Following in the trend of reports on database management systems, the committee looks at databases in a distributed processing environment. A landmark study of approaches to and issues in distributed database systems.

CODD, E. F., "A Relational Model of Data for Large Shared Data Banks," *Communications of the ACM* (13:6), 1970 June, page 377-387.

Computer Corporation of America, "An Architecture for Database Management Standards," Washington, DC: U.S. National Bureau of Standards, NBS-SP 500-86, 1982 January.
A detailed DBMS reference model which identifies 79 components and their interfaces, and describes how they fit together. It takes a conventional process or flow orientation.

CONARD, James, "A Primer on Open Systems Interconnection," *Auerbach Data Communications Management*, portfolio 51-20-02, 1983 January-February, 12 pages.

DEPPE, Mark E. and James P. FRY, "Distributed Data Bases: A Summary of Research," *Computer Networks* (1:2), 1976.

DeWITT, D. J., "Query Execution in DIRECT," *Proceedings ACM SIGMOD Conference*, 1979, pages 13-22.

ENGLES, Robert W., "An Analysis of the April 1971 Data Base Task Group Report," *Proceedings of the 1971 ACM SIGFIDET Workshop on "Data Description Access, and Control,"* San Diego, California, 1971 November 11-12, edited by E. F. Codd and A. L. Dean, New York: Association for Computing Machinery, 1971, pages 69-91.

ENSLOW, Philip H., Jr., "What is a 'Distributed' Data Processing System?" *Computer*, 1978 January, pages 13-21, 13 refs.
Provides a comprehensive definition of distributed data processing by looking at the components of distribution. Examines three dimensions characterizing distribution: hardware decentralization, control decentralization, and database decentralization. Suggests what should be included and excluded from the definition of a distributed data processing system.

EPSTEIN, Robert and P. HAWTHORN, "Design Decisions for the Intelligent Database Machine," *AFIPS National Computer Conference Proceedings*, Vol. 49, 1980, pages 237-241.

EVEREST, Gordon C., "The Futures of Database Management," *Proceedings ACM SIGMOD Conference*, Ann Arbor, New York: ACM, 1974.

GLINERT-COLE, "Two Views of the LANscape," *PC Tech Journal*, 1984 January.
A thorough comparison of two of the leading local area networks—3 Com's EtherSeries and Novell's Sharenet.

GOSDEN, John A., "Report to X3 on Data Definition Languages," *fdt. Journal of ACM SIGFIDET* (1:2), 1969 December, pages 14-25.

HAWTHORN, P. and D. J. Dewitt, "Performance Analysis of Alternative Database Machine Architectures," *IEEE Transactions on Software Engineering* (SE-8:1), 1982 January, pages 61-75.

HILL, Marjorie P. and Jo L. WLAKOWICZ, *The World of EDP Standards*, Washington, DC: U.S. National Bureau of Standards, NBSIR 77-1195, 1976 December.
World-wide view of organizations involved in developing and promulgating standards relating to EDP. Covers the organizational structure of committees and groups, areas of jurisdiction, and their goals.

HSIAO, David K., *Advanced Data Base Machine Architecture*, Englewood Cliffs, NJ: Prentice-Hall, 1983.
The first text devoted entirely to database machines.

HSIAO, David K., editor, "Special Issue on Database Machines," *Computer* (12:3), 1979 March.

International Standards Organization, "Information Processing Systems—Open Systems Interconnection—Basic Reference Model," Document ISO/DP 7498 (or ISO/TC97/SC16 N890), 1982 February; published in *Computer Networks*, volume 5, 1981, pages 81-118.

KIMBLETON, Stephen R., "Network Operating Systems (NOS)," AFIPS National Computer Conference Proceedings (vol. 50), 1981.

KOHLER, W. H., "A Survey of Techniques for Synchronization and Recovery in Decentralized Computer Systems," *ACM Computing Surveys* (13:2), 1981 June, pages 149-184.

LOCKE, P. W., "A Guide to DBMS Standardization Activities," *Computers & Standards* (1:2-3), 1982, pages 169-188.

LOWENTHAL, Eugene I., "Data Base Processors: What Can They Do?" *Computerworld* (13:23), 1979 June 4, In Depth, pages 1-12.
    Describes several possible configurations of a backend database machine—single host, chain of DBMMs, storage shared with host, direct front-end link, multiple hosts, intelligent controller, associative controller with multiple data streams, and associative controller with multiple search requests on a single stream of data.

LOWENTHAL, Eugene I., "A Survey—the Application of Data Base Management Computers in Distributed Systems," *Proceedings of Conference on Very Large Data Bases*, 1977 October, pages 85-92.

MACHRONE, Bill, "Battle of the Network Stars," *PC Magazine*, 1983 November, pages 92-104.
    A detailed comparison of the performance of 7 leading (at that time) local area networks—Omninet from Corvus, PLAN 4000 from Nestar, EtherSeries from 3Com, Elan from Tecmar, PC Net from Orchid, and Sharenet X and S from Novell. Also includes a good discussion of the features and operational characteristics of typical local area networks.

MARILL, Tom and D. STERN, "The Datacomputer—A Network Data Utility," *AFIPS National Computer Conference Proceedings* (vol. 44), 1975, pages 389-395.

MARYANSKI, Fred J., "Backend Database Systems," *ACM Computing Surveys* (12:1), 1980 March, pages 3-25, 53 refs.
    This tutorial examines the basic structure of backend database systems, their potential benefits and limitations, and the problems facing developers of such systems. Several prototype systems are described with details of their hardware and software components.

MILLER, M. W., "A Survey of Distributed Database Management," *Information and Management* (1:), 1978, pages 243-264.

MOULDER, Richard, "An Implementation of a Data Management System on an Associative Processor," *AFIPS National Computer Conference Proceedings*, 1973, pages 171-176.

MYERS, Edith, "Database Machines Take Off," *Datamation*, 1985 May 15, pages 52-63.
    Discusses the Britton-Lee and Teradata machines and user reactions.

OLLE, T. William, "IX: Data Base Management Systems," *Computers & Standards* (2:2-3), 1983, pages 119-126.
    Excellent review of DBMS standardization activities from 1979 to 1983 in ISO, ANSI, and other organizations relating to DBMS standards.

PETRE, Peter, "A Computer Chip with a Mind of its Own," *Fortune*, 1984 May 14, page 114.
    Reports on the new "transputer" chip from Inmos which incorporates the principles of parallel processing—processor, memory, and communications circuitry on a single chip.

SCHWARTZ, Joel and Wesley P. MELLING, "Sharing Work and Logic," *Datamation*, 1982 November, pages 113-120.
    Discusses the role of the personal computer in the overall organizational computer network, and the delivery of computing services in an integrated computing strategy.

SMITH, Diane C. P. and John Miles SMITH, "Relational Data Base Machines," *Computer*, 1979 March, pages 28-38, 41 refs.

SU, Stanley Y. W., Hsu CHANG, George COPELAND, Paul FISHER, Eugene LOWENTHAL, and Stewart SCHUSTER, "Database Machines and some Issues on DBMS Standards," *AFIPS National Computer Conference Proceedings*, 1980, pages 191-208, 53 refs.

Describes the limitations of conventional computers for database processing, four types of database machines (cellular-logic systems, backend computers, integrated database machines, and associative memory systems), and the implications of these systems on the development of DBMS standards. They argue that since low-level, record-at-a-time languages are not likely to be used as the interface to a reasonably efficient backend machine (such languages generate a high volume of communication with the host), standardization efforts would better be directed to high-level languages acting on *sets* of records. They admit that low-level languages such as the CODASYL DML (the main object of recent standardization efforts) "have scored high points for feasibility and economy, but that the emergence of DBMM technology may actually reverse this situation in the next few years."

VALDURIEZ, Patrick and Georges GARDARIN, "Join and Semijoin Algorithms for a Multiprocessor Database Machine," *ACM Transactions on Database Systems* (9:1), 1984 March, pages 133-161, 30 refs.

Describes relative performance of experiments on the SABRE database machine to perform joins and semijoins. The paper describes architecture of the SABRE system and several algorithms which have been suggested for processing joins in uniprocessor and multiprocessor environments. Join operations are one of the major factors limiting the performance of relational systems. The results show the value of performing semijoins before joins in a multiprocessor system. (A semijoin only projects data from *one* of the relations or files being joined.)

WAH, B. W. and S. Bing YAO, "DIALOGUE: A Distributed-Processor Organization for a Database Machine," *AFIPS National Computer Conference Proceedings*, 1980, pages 243-253.

WOOD, Helen M. and Stephen R. KIMBLETON, "Access Control Mechanisms for a Network Operating System," *Proceedings AFIPS National Computer Conference*, 1979.

YOUNG, John W., Jr., "Evolution of Industry Standards—The ANSI DB Approach," *AUERBACH Information Management Series: Data Base Management*, Portfolio REV 21-01-04, Philadelphia: Auerbach Publishers, 1982 March-April, 11 pages.

A well-written description and explanation of the ANSI/X3/SPARC DBMS Framework. Updates a previous version written in 1977 by Beatrice YORMARK, a member of the original study group.

INDEX

bold page numbers = major or main discussion.
italic page numbers = definition of term (index serves as a glossary).
see ... = cross reference to preferred term with the same meaning.
see also ... = cross reference to related, more general, or more specific terms.
##*n* = reference is to a footnote only.
##*b* = reference is to a bibliographic entry or an annotation.
##*Fig* = reference is to a Figure or includes a Figure.

A

Abbreviations for data names, 605-606
ABRIAL, J. R., 120, 151*b*
Abstraction, 101, 203, 256*b*
Acceptance test, 683, 710
Access, *506*
  (*see* Database, levels of access to)
Access clearance, 364, 371, 374, 513*Fig*
Access control, 52, **506-538**, 568*b*, 599,
    660
  authorization, 506, 514, 529-538
  data-dependent, 509, 513*Fig,* 533-535,
    568*b*
  facilities not in proposed NDL standard,
    766
  facilities in proposed RDL standard, 769
  general model of, 510-514
  identification and authentication, 515-
    529
  ineffective in some circumstances, 544
  language to define, 537-538
  policies, 508-509
  for privacy laws, 649
  response to denied request, 537
  using passwords, 506, 510-512, 517-
    522, 585

Access methods, 55, 57*Fig*, 59, 331, 734
  monitoring, 612
Access paths, 224, 241
  in multifile structure, 137-138
Access path dependence, 414
  (*see* Program-data independence)
Access privileges, 509, 511-513, **530-533**,
    537-538
Access-time binding, 404
Accountability:
  of machines/programs versus people,
    48, 516
Accounting/Accountants, 52, 596
Accounting trial balance, 470, 479
ACKOFF, Russell L., 22*b*
Acquisition of DBMS, 672-715
  alternatives, 679-685
  contract terms, 708-712
  costs, 681
  now or wait, 676-677, 706
  resistance to, 736
  selecting the first application, 714-715
Action graph (*see* Transition diagram)
Actioning, 164, 166
Active data dictionary, *610*, 734
Actual derived item, *274*

Acyclic graph, *133*
Ad hoc (*see* Retrieval, ad hoc)
ADABAS from Software ag, 23*b*, 26*b*,
    620, 701, 733, 752, 753*Fig*
Adaptability versus evolvability, *44*
Add privilege, 466
ADELMAN, L., 557, 573*b*
Administrative DBMS selection criteria,
    703-704, 708-711, 723-726
Adoption, 631
Aetna Life, privacy ad, 655*Fig*
After image logging, 436*Fig*, 438-439
Aggregation, 256*b*
AGHILI, Houtan, 450*b*
AHITUV, Niv, 67*b*
AHO, A. V., 336*b*
AKI, Selim G., 568*b*
ALLEN, Frank W., 602, 616*b*
ALTMAN, Ed B., 423*b*
ALTSHULER, Gene P., 602, 619*b*
AMBASE from AMCOR, 701, 733
Ambiguity in natural language, 300-302
American National Standards Institute
    (ANSI), 760-769, 761*Fig*
Database Architectural Framework Task
    Group (DAFTG), 773-774*Fig*,
    778*b*
DBMS framework, 116-117*b*, 760,
    771-773, 772*Fig*, 778*b*
date representation, 218
definition of data, 7
definition of information, 9
Network Database Language (NDL),
    236-237, 254*b*, 398, 482-483,
    502*b*, 761, **766-769**, 778*b*
Relational Database Language (RDL),
    238-239, 254*b*, 778*b*
AND-JOIN, 333*Fig*, 748
Application administrator, 771*Fig*
    (*see* Database administrator)
Application development systems, 28,
    377, 732
Application Management System (AMS)
    from TRES Computer Systems,
    620
Application programmer
    (*see* Conventional application
    programmer; Programming user)

Application system design/development:
    DBMS tool in building, **109-113**, 733
    early binding for efficiency, 405-407
    focus on data, 7
    high costs, 32-33
    machine versus human resources, 32-33,
        43, 94
    reducing development effort, **97-98**,
        196*b*
    traditional approach, focus on processes,
        28-31, 97-98
    (*see also* System developer/
        development)
Approximate disclosure, *540*
Arbitrary function, *274-275*
Archival data storage:
    versus backup data, 431
Arithmetic expression
    (*see* Derivation expression)
Arithmetic operators (*see* Operators)
Arithmetic value versus numeric string,
    215-216, 460
Arrow, in representing relationships,
    224-225
Arrow keys, 165
Artificial intelligence, 299, 734
ASCHIM, Frode, 778*b*
ASI-ST, 135, 733
Association for Computing Machinery
    (ACM):
    Special Interest Groups:
        on Business Data Processing
            (SIGBDP), 26, 678
        on Management of Data (SIGMOD),
            26, 678
Associative memory, 756-757*Fig*
Associative processing, 755, 769
ASTRAHAN, Mort M., 423*b*
ATRE, Saku, 22*b*
Attribute, *8*, 120, *123*, *125*-126,
    140
    becomes an entity, 144, 246
    indirect or secondary, *137*
    rule in database design, 247
Attribute partitioning, 747*Fig*
Audio recognition (*see* Voice recognition)
Audio response, 280
Audit trail, 52, 468-469, 538, 613

Audit trail (*Cont.*)
  logging input transactions, 435-436, 439, 445*Fig*
  logging user accesses, 514, 521-522
  of statistical retrievals, 540
  of sources and disclosures, 649, 662-663
  (*see also* Monitoring)
Auditing, 571*b*
  random sampling, 273
Auditor, 468, 733
AUERBACH, 727
Authentication, 506, 516-517
Authority levels, 535-536
Authorization, 506, 514, **529-538**
  dual scheme, 586
  language to assign privileges, 537-538
Authorization table, 506, 512*Fig*, 513*Fig*, 514, *530*, 537
  matrix, 530, 531*Fig*, 536, 571*b*
Availability, of data, **38-44**
  backup and recovery interrupts, 431, 437
  dichotomy violates, 58-59
  functions, 87
  future (*see* Evolvability)
  low versus high, 41
  modes of, 41
  with userschema, 92-94
  versus machine efficiency, 702
Average, 276

B

BABB, E., 778*b*
BACHMAN, Charles W.:
  on CODASYL network data structure, 254*b*, 765
  data structure diagrams, 132*n*, 151*b*, 224*n*, 254*b*
  Integrated Data Store (IDS), 56, 68*b*
  on job management, 116*b*, 582
  on Open Systems Interconnection (OSI) reference model, 773, 778*b*
  programmer as navigator, 382*b*
  on restructure, 418
Backup action, 432
Backup and recovery, 48-50, **430-440**

Backup and recovery (*Cont.*)
  coordinated with program checkpoint and restart, 446-448
  data movement, 445*Fig*
  with data-dependent modification, 354-355
  in a distributed environment, 744
  variables in the process, 444-446
Backup data:
  exposure to unauthorized disclosure, 544, 546*Fig*
  versus archival storage, 431
BAER, J. L., 502*b*
BAKER, Michael A., 669*b*
BANCILHON, F., 778*b*
BANERJEE, J., 758, 778*b*
Bank Secrecy Act (U.S.), 630, 646*Fig*
Bankruptcy, 639
Bar chart (*see* Histogram)
Base variables in update, 467, 484
BASIC programming language:
  stored form of data, 361-362
Batch-level validation, 458, 463-464*Fig*
Batch processing, 134, 160, 188
  mentality, 30
  of transactions, 352-354, 446
  (*see also* Sequential processing)
BAUM, R. I., 778*b*
BECK, Leland L., 568*b*
BECKER, Hal B., 568*b*
BECKER, Joseph, 72*b*
BEER, Stafford, 44*n*
Before image logging, 436*Fig*, 438-439
BELL, Daniel, 22*b*
Benchmarking DBMS, 697, 699-700
BENCI, E., 254*b*
BENTLY, Trevor J., 717*b*
BERG, John L., 423*b*
BERNSTEIN, Philip A., 502*b*
BERRA, P. Bruce, 778*b*
BERRI, C., 336*b*
BERRISFORD, Thomas R., 117*b*, 583, 616*b*
Between operator, 269
Bibliographic systems, *53*, 54, **69-72**
Bifurcation in fingerprint, 526
BIGELOW, Robert P., 718*b*
BILLER, Horst, 151*b*

Binary infix operators, 265-266
Binary relation, *144-145*, 229
Binary relational data structure, *145-148*
Binding, 102-103, 392, ***398-409***
Binding times, 403-404
BLANNING, Robert W., 305*b*
BLEIER, Robert E., 309, 336*b*
Block encryption, 547, 553-554
Block prompting, 169, 172-173
Blocks, locking of, 480*Fig*
Boolean condition, 267-269, 313
Boolean data item, 216, 461
Boolean operators, 266-267
Boolean expression, ***262-272***
  in access control, 534-535, 537
  added to 1984 proposed NDL standard,
    767
  in associative processing, 757*Fig*
  in concurrency control, 471, 479, 484
  criterion for relationship or join, 229,
    231
  for data identification, 125, 479-480,
    534, 537
  in data manipulation language, 366-367,
    377
  in existence condition, 220
  implicit subject operands, 270, 300
  position criteria in, 281, 318, 320,
    367-368
  in retrieval, 260
  in update, 346, 356
  in validation criteria, 462
BOOTH, Grayce M., 778*b*
BORUCH, Robert F., 539*n*
BOULDING, Kenneth E., 61*n*, 199
BRADLEY, James, 23*b*
Branching hierarchical data structure
  (*see* Multipath hierarchical data
    structure)
BRANDEIS, Louis D., 628, 650, 668*b*
BRANDON, Dick H., 718*b*
BRATHWAITE, Kenmore S., 617*b*
BRAY, Olin H., 778*b*
Breakpoint, 447 (*see* Checkpoint)
Bring forward the database, 49, 430,
    438-439, 440*Fig*
British Computer Society, 160*n*, 196*b*,
    305*b*, 336*b*, 617*b*
Britton-Lee, 753*Fig*, 758, 765, 778*b*

BRODIE, Michael, 761, 769, 778*b*
BROMBERG, Howard, 718*b*
BROOKS, Frederick P., Jr., 628*n*, 682*n*,
    718*b*
Brook's Law, *682*
Broom, *313*-314*Fig*, 323
Broom-defining repeating group, 314*Fig*
  explicit designation, 327-328
  movement with HAS operator, 316-317
  movement with IN operator, 327
BROWN, William F., 571*b*
BROWNE, Peter S., 568*b*, 571*b*
BRYANT, Howard, 418
Bubble chart, 146*Fig*
Buffer (*see* Program buffer; System buffer)
Bundled software with hardware, 679,
    693, 694
Burroughs, 679 (*see also* DMS II)
BUSSOLATI, U. 568*b*
BY operator, 335 (*see* PER operator)

C

Caesar cipher, 550-551
CAHILL, John J., 602, 617*b*
Call form of DML, 372
Canada:
  human rights act, 627
  privacy study, 625, 626, 651, 667*b*
CANADAY, R. H., et al., 753*Fig*, 778*b*
CANNING, Richard G., 68*b*, 124*n*, 153*n*,
    387*n*, 423*b*, 617*b*, 682*n*, 718*b*,
    765
CANTER, Susan J., 718*b*
CARDENAS, Alfonso F., 23*b*, 753*Fig*,
    779*b*
Cardinal numbers, 217
Cardinality, 222, 225
CARLIS, John, 246, 254*b*
CARLSON, Eric D., 617*b*
CARTER, Breck, 605, 617*b*
CASSM of University of Florida, 756
Casual user, ***78-80***, 84, 85*Fig*, 104-106,
    302*Fig*
  natural language for, 179-180, 305-306*b*
Catalogued requests, 293-294*Fig*
Cellular logic system, 756
Centralization:
  of database administration, 508
  of databases, 12

CHAMBERLIN, D. D., et al, 310, 336*b*, 779*b*, 765

CHAMPINE, George A., 779*b*

CHANG, Hsu, 383*b*, 781*b*

Change (*see* Revision)

Chargeout for DBMS user, 715

Check digit, 515

CHECK validation statement, 462

Checkpoint, 446-448

CHEN, Peter Pin-Shan, 151*b*, 254*b*

Choice level of dialogue, 171

Chopout mapping, *415Fig*

Ciphertext, *544-545Fig*

Classification for access control, 535-536

Clearance level, 535

CLIFFORD, James, 254*b*

CLOSE in database manipulation language, 363

CLOUT from Microrim, 300, 701

COBOL, 23*b*, 175-176, 196*b*, 423*b*, 502*b*, 735, 770

  file definition, 210*Fig*, 388*Fig*

  input-output facilities, 362-363

  (*see also* Conventional programming language)

COBOL file, 121*Fig*, 134, 236-237, 762

CODASYL organization and committees, 762

CODASYL COBOL Committee, 363, 502*b*, 762

CODASYL Data Base Task Group (DBTG), 92*n*

  on access control, 514

  concurrency control, 483

  DDL includes storage structure definition, 212, 397

  proposed network data structure and manipulation language, 23*b*, 24*b*, 26*b*, 122, 139, 151*b*, 186*n*, 212, 254*b*, 363, 382*b*, 423*b*, 762, 764

  on selection criteria in the DML, 367-368

  on userschema as 'subset' of the schema, 394

CODASYL Data Description Language Committee (DDLC), 139, 254*b*, 760, 762

CODASYL data structure, *139-143*, 236-237, 764-765

  (*see* Network data structure)

CODASYL Development Committee, 151*b*, 254*b*

CODASYL End User Facility Task Group, 117*b*

CODASYL Stored-Data Definition and Translation Task Group (SDDTTG), 424*b*

CODASYL Systems Committee, 762

  adoption of the term 'schema,' 92*n*

  computer system environment of DBMS, 108*Fig*

  on database administration, 576, 579-581, 617*b*

  on database creation, 357

  distributed databases, 739*Fig*, 749, 779*b*

  feature analysis of DBMS, 23*b*, 68*b*, 117*b*, 151*b*, 254*b*, 305*b*, 358*b*, 382*b*, 424*b*

  on host-language and self-contained DBMS, 56, 58

  on language syntactic styles, 178

  on programming user facilities, 376

  selection and acquisition of DBMS, 68*b*, 117*b*, 718*b*

  taxonomy of DBMS functions, 61-64

CODD, E. F.:

  on casual user and other users, 78, 84-85*Fig*, 117*b*, 305*b*

  natural language, 301-302*Figs*

  on program-data access path dependency, 414

  on relational data model, 117*b*, 122, 139*n*, 151*b*, 255*b*, 305*b*, 330, 336*b*, 382*b*, 424*b*, 765, 779*b*

Codes for data values, 218, 241, 255*b*

  serves purpose for encryption, 548-549

COFFMANN, E. G. Jr., 502*b*

Collating sequence, 125, 276

COLLMEYER, Arthur J., 491, 503*b*

Column overflow, 284

Column value truncation, 284

Command-driven dialogue, 160*n*, *173-174*, 182-183

Command file, 360

  (*see* Command language, extended)

  (*see also* Program)

Command language, 174-181, 183
  extended for deferred execution, 82,
      185, 194, 361, 379, **768-769**
  menu as a command, 183
COMMIT command, 448, 481, 489
Common domains:
  basis for a relationship, 136*Fig*, 229-
      232
Communications facility, *738*, 739*Fig*,
      755*Fig*
Comparative operators, 217, 266-267
Compatibility matrix, 482*Fig*, 483*Fig*
Compatibility terms in contract, 711
Compile-time binding, 400-401, 404
Compiled code, 360
  (*see* Generated procedures)
Completeness, *100*, 454, 462, 662
Composite flat file, *126-128*
Composition rules, 201
Compression (*see* Data compression)
Computer and Business Equipment
      Manufacturer's Association
      (CBEMA), 761
Computer security, 429, 507, 573*b*
Computer Software Act of 1980 (U.S.),
      712
Computer systems:
  conventional architecture, 751*Fig*,
      754-755
  data-oriented architecture, 751*Fig*
Computer vendor
  (*see* Vendor of hardware)
Computerized data integrity controls, 428,
      626
Conceptual schema, 199
  ANSI/SPARC DBMS Framework, 116*b*,
      771
  design, 244-245
  (*see* Natural data structure)
Concurrency, *478*
Concurrent update control, 109, **466-496**,
      598-599
  in CODASYL DBTG proposal and
      Network Database Language,
      483*Fig*, 767
  cooperation with job manager, 107-108
  in a distributed environment, 743
  lockout during backup, 441
Conditional update, 355

Conflict matrix, 487-488*Fig*
Conformance of data to its definition, 214,
      243, 362, 419, **459-460**, 596
Conjunctive form of expression, 270-272
CONNECT statement in NDL DML, 237,
      365
Connected graph, *133*
CONRAD, James, 779*b*
Conserved resource, 477
Consistency, 462, 467, 470, 597
Constellation of minutiae, 526*Fig*
Consultants, use of in DBMS acquisition,
      673, 678, 681, 685, 696
Consumable resource, 476
Content searching, *756*
  (*see* Boolean expression)
Context-dependent access control, 509
Context searching, *756*
Context setting in retrieval language,
      327-328
Contract terms, **708-712**
Contracts, 718*b*
Control break, *276*, 277*Fig*, 278
Control Data Cyber computer, 109*n*, 752
Control variable, 278, 298-299
Controlled value set, *218-219*
  at data entry time, 456
  (*see also* Consistency)
CONTU, 718*b*
Conventional application programmer, 78-
      79*Figs*, **82-83**, 104-106, 360,
      375, 768
Conventional programming languages,
      25*b*, 77, **82-83**, 185, 330, 360-
      361
  input-output statements in COBOL,
      362-363
Conversion, 4
  (*see* Data conversion; Program
      maintenance/revision)
CONVERT, 424*b*
CONWAY, Melvin E., 718*b*
CONWAY, R. W., 530, 568*b*
Coordinated files, *135*, 189
COPELAND, George, 383*b*, 781*b*
Copernican revolution in data processing,
      4-7, 390, 392
Copying software, 711
Copyright, 712, 713*Fig*, 718*b*

Correlation, 278
CORVUS network, 741
Cost-benefit evaluation methodology, 689-692
COULSON, Christopher J., 718*b*
COUNT, 276
Covariance, 278
Creation (*see* Database creation)
Criteria for inclusion, 222, 247
Criterion of relationship, 229-231
Cross reference data item, *219*
Cross tabulation, 297*Fig*
Cryptography, *544* (*see* Encryption)
CULPRIT from Cullinet, 135, 701, 733
   (*see also* IDMS)
Cumulative frequency distribution, 295-296*Fig*
Currency:
   position in database, 367-368
Cursor positioning, **165-166**
CURTICE, Robert M., 247, 255*b*, 617*b*

D

DALE, Al G., 117*b*
DALKEY, N. C., et al, 689*n*
Data, *3, 7, 10*
   diversity of, 38-39
   management of, 13-14
   for management, 16
   *M*essages in the 5 *M*'s, 7, 47
   private collections, 12, 31
   problem of, **3-7**
   singular versus plural, 11
   surrogate for individuals, 515-516, 522, 628, 637-638
   surrogate for reality, 19
   unconserved reusable resource, 476-477, 650
   versus database, 14*n*
   versus information, **9-11**
   viewed as a valued resource, 7, 12, 47
Data administration
   (*see* Database administration)
Data aggregate, 139-149
DATA ANALYZER, 123, 135, 287-288*Fig*, 733
Data capture (*see* Data entry)
Data Catalogue from TSI International, 618*b*, 620

Data compression, 573*b*
   for encryption, 548-549
   in storage structure, 241
Data conversion, 4, 33, 340, 405, 409-410*Fig*
   between schema and userschema, 94, 390, 394-395, 768
   data preserving versus data reducing, 411-412, 415*Fig*
   family of processes, 409-411*Fig*
   levels of mapping, 412-416
   versus program conversion, 264-265
   (*see also* Database revision)
DATA DECISIONS, 727
Data definition language (DDL), 92, 120, 186, 200*Fig*, *205*, 394
   common in the reference model, 770
   inclusion of storage structure definition, 397-398, 767
   insufficient information for people, 602
   priority for standardization, 770
   (*see also* Database definition)
Data-dependent access control, 509, 513*Fig*, 533-535
Data-dependent encryption, 571*b*
Data-dependent modification, 354-355
Data-dependent validation, 463-464
Data dictionary, 23*b*, **601-605**, 700*Fig*, 734
   in ANSI/X3/SPARC DBMS framework, 771, 772*Fig*
   independent of DBMS, 398, 602
   Information Resource Dictionary System of ANSI, 761*Fig*, 770
   no facilities in proposed NDL standard, 766
   program-data cross reference, 408, 421, 582, 608-609
   providing a more complete definition of data, 602-603, 732
   use in systems analysis, 604-605
Data Dictionary (DDS) from Sperry (UNIVAC), 621
Data dictionary management system (DDMS), 608-610, 617-621*b*
DATA DIVISION in COBOL, 388*Fig*-389
Data Encryption Standard (DES), 554-556, 555*Fig*
Data entry, 340-341, 351*Fig*

Data entry (*Cont.*)
  access control, 532
  capture at source, 456
  minimizing variable information, 456
  user-defined screen, 347
  validation at time of, 455-458
  (*see also* Mechanization)
Data expanding operations, 748
Data independence, 3-5, 24*b*, **102-104**,
      387, *390*, 398, **404-409**, 768
  (*see also* Program-data independence;
      Physical data independence;
      Binding)
Data-independent authorization, 531
Data integrity, 34 (*see* Integrity of data)
Data item, 11*n*, 125-126*Fig*, 140
  characteristics of, **215-220**, 603
  grouping to form records, 221, 245-246
  validation criteria, 460-461
Data languages, 180, 186-188
  high-level, 32, 83, **175-177**, 176*Fig*,
    734-736
  syntactic styles, 178-179
  versus process specification languages,
    32, 175, 311
  (*see also* Data definition language; Data
      manipulation language;
      Language; Mapping language;
      Retrieval language)
Data management versus database
    management, 587
Data manipulation language (DML), 175-
    179, 186
  call and verb form, 371-373
  common across all user interfaces, 770
  in COBOL, 362-363
  on a data structure, 187
  on rich data structure class, 120, 330,
    677
  six types of information, 364-371
  (*see also* Retrieval language)
Data 'model', 120
  consequences if inadequate, 34
  three 'great', 122-123, 293
  (*see* Data structure class)
Data naming (*see* Naming)
Data preserving/reducing conversion, 411-
    412, 748, 758
Data privacy, 627, *628*
  (*see also* Fair information practices)

Data processing versus program execution,
    754-756
Data processing system
  (*see* Database application system)
Data reducing operations, 748, 758
Data requirements, 7, 244, 583
Data retirement (*see* Retirement of data)
Data security, 48-49, 429, *506-508*
  (*see also* Access control; Encryption;
    Monitoring)
Data structure:
  in bibliographic reference systems,
    69-71
  decomposition, 26*b*, 246
  graphical representation, 203-209, 591
  linear representation in DDL, 205-213
  natural, 199-203, 223-224
Data structure class, 120, 122, 200*Fig*,
    201, 774
  of a programming language, 395
  rich, useless without high-level
    manipulation facilities, 120, 330,
    677
Data systems:
  HAYES taxonomy, 68*b*
  types of, 53
  (*see also* Database application system)
Data to the people, 4*Fig*, 672, 707
Database, *11-12*, 120, *136*
  levels of access to, 58-59, 87*Fig*, 361-
    362
  physical storage structure, changes in,
    103-104
  role in an organization, **18-19**
  versus data, 14*n*
Database administration (the function),
    13-16, **576-584**, *587*
  activity versus functions, 589-590
  backup strategy selection, 431-432*Fig*
  central versus local control, 31, 508
  encourage use of DBMS tools, 737
  functions of, 14, 86-87, 212, **589-601**
  organizational position, **578-581**
  organizational response, 613-614
  provides user support, 584, 593-595,
    737-738
  responsible for data integrity, 47-48,
    428, 506-509, 576, 595-599
  responsible for compliance with privacy
    laws, 655

Database administration (the function)
(*Cont.*)
  select and acquire DBMS tools, 592-
    593, 672, 737
  in systems development, 582-583
  tools for, 601, 770-771
  train users, 593-595, 737-738
  user confidence in, 585
  versus data administration, 587-588,
    619*b*
  versus job administration, 109-110,
    116*b*, 474, 579-582
Database administrator (DBA) (the role),
    13-16
  agent of user community, 577
  appointment of, 19, 577
  control over, 538, 585-586, 599
  DBMS as machine agent for, 14-15
  mediates conflicting needs, 577
  versus enterprise administrator, 771
Database application system, 111-113*Figs*
  four components of, 3-6
  user compensates for low-level DBMS,
    111, 677
Database approach, *12-14*, 19-20, 28,
    676, 706
  building a base of data, 32
  inhibitors, **34-36**
  motivation for, **31-34**
    satisfying the motivators, **97-98**
Database control system (DBCS), *91*, 428,
    90*Fig*, 110*Fig*, 436*Fig*, 529, 554
Database creation, *198*, 213, *340*-345, 357
  compared with update, 345
  in family of conversion processes, 409,
    411*Fig*
  inverse of reversion, 264
  versus using update function, 345, 354
Database definition, *198*, 242-244, 591,
    720
  access to, 84, 211, 375, 379, 773
  common, 699-700*Fig*, 734-735
  comprehensive information, 213, 733-
    736
  consolidation of userschemas, 244
  controlling access to, 548
  DBMS selection criteria, 720
  distribution of, in a network, 745, 747
  evolution of, 213
  extended for access control, 536*Fig*

Database definition (*Cont.*)
  generation from data dictionary, 604
  given, assumed, or ignored information,
    214, 242-244
  impact of changes, 406-408
  incomplete, consequences of, 122, 134-
    135, 213, 217, 220, 239, 242,
    244, 264, 683
  independent from DBMS, 398
  logical and physical, 212, 214
  manipulation as data by DBMS,
    773-774*Fig*
  process of, **205-213**, 211*Fig*
  proliferation of definitions, 698-700*Fig*,
    734
  renaming for revision, 419
  responsibility for versus doing, 588
  revision of in reference model, 774*Fig*
  satisfying all motivators, 97
  separate from programs, 5, 206-209
  serves as validation criteria, 458-460
  stored data conformance to, 214, 243,
    362, 419, **459-460**, 596
  stored with backup data, 431
  (*see also* Data definition language;
    Validation criteria)
Database design, *198-205*, 221, 223, 244,
    590-591
  guidelines or rules, *246-250*, 765
  logical versus physical, 232
  methodology, *244-245*
  tools to support, 601, 604
Database establishment, *198*
  (*see* Database design; Database
    definition; Database creation)
Database integrity (*see* Integrity of data)
Database key, 768
  (*see* Unique internal record identifier)
Database management:
  in context of organizations and MIS,
    16, 54
  objectives, **36-52**
Database management machine (DBMM),
    23*b*, 91-92, 383*b*, **750-760**
  benefits, 750, 754
  commercial products, 753*Fig*, 758-760
  experimental systems, 753*Fig*, 756-758
Database management system (DBMS),
    14-16
  acquisition, xii, 68*b*, 672-685, 707-715

Database management system (DBMS)
(*Cont.*)
 building your own, 20, 672
 classification of, **74**, 120
 commercially available, 20
 concepts education, 674*Fig*, 677-679
 conceptual model, 15*Fig*, **88-91**
 cost, 161, 684, 725-726, 736
 DBA selects and acquires, 592-593,
  672, 737
 dichotomy, **55-57**, 74
  why it must disappear, **58-61**
 environment of, **106-113**
 evolution of, 55-58, 693-694
 full function systems, 699, 701*Fig*
 functional completeness, 111-112, 701-
  702, **733**
 functions of, xii-xiii, 15, **61-64**, Part II,
  84-88, *747*
  in the DBMS model, 90*Fig*
  distributed in a network, 747-748
 future of, 20, **732-736**
 generalized tool, 13, 14*n*, *33*, 56, 106,
  109-111, 100-101
  versus dedicated system, 54, 697
 hardware architecture to support,
  751*Fig*-753
 inhibiting forces, 34-36
 in house development, 679, 680*Fig*,
  681-682, 684-685
 installation, 684, 714
 installed systems, 57
 internal computer environment, 107-108
 machine agent of DBA, 14-15
 market size, xii, 683-684, 732, 736
 on microcomputers, 57, 84, 161-162,
  360-361, 418, 466, 684, 734,
  749, 769
 not an MIS, 109-111
 in a network (NDBMS), 739*Fig*, 740,
  743-744, 747-748
 operating modes, **188-194**, 722-723,
  724-725
 organizational dependence on, 706
 performance monitoring, 610-613
 pricing versus capabilities, 707-708
 resistance to use, 583, **736-738**
 selecting the first application, **714-715**
 selection, **693-707**

Database management system (DBMS)
(*Cont.*)
 tool for building MIS and application
  systems, **109-112**, 733
 types of, 28, **55-58**
 user roles, **74-84**
 (*see also* Host-language DBMS;
  Self-contained DBMS)
DBMS language programmer, 78-79*Figs*,
  82, 104-106, 360
DBMS system programmer, 78-79*Figs*,
  83-84, 104-106, 360
 facilities for, 375-376, 768
Database operations supervisor, 599-600
Database planning, 587-589
Database procedures, 514
Database revision, 103-104, *198*, 264,
  343, 386-387, 405, *416-421*,
  420*Fig*, 592, 733
 DBMS selection criteria, 723
 facilities in proposed RDL standard, 769
 in family of conversion processes, 409,
  411*Fig*
 no facilities in proposed NDL standard,
  766
Database schema, *92*, *125*, 127, 206,
  391*Fig*, *392*
 relationship with userschema, 394-
  395*Fig*
 (*see also* Database definition)
Database standards
 (*see* Standards, database)
Database Systems Study Group (DBSSG)
  of ANSI, 761
DATABOSS from Data Access Corp.,
  701
DATACOM/DB from ADR, 621, 693,
  701
DATAFLEX from Data Access Corp., 701
DataManager from MSP, Inc., 618*b*, 621
DATAPRO Directory of Software, 728
'Dataware,' 7
DATE, Chris J.:
 on access controls, 542
 on concurrency control, 470, 487, 492,
  495
 database integrity, 450*b*, 502*b*, 568*b*
 introduction to database, 22*b*, 23*b*,
  151*b*, 336*b*

DATE, Chris J. (*Cont.*)
  on program-data independence, 392,
    424*b*
  relational data model, 139*n*, 336*b*
  on three 'great' data structures, 122
  universal data language (UDL), 336*b*
Date, standard representation, 218
Datum, 11
DAVIDA, George I., 553, 568*b*
DAVIS, Donald L., xvi
DAVIS, Gordon B., xiv, xvi, 18, 22*b*
DB2 from IBM, 701, 732, 765
DB/DC Data Dictionary from IBM, 618*b*,
    621
dBASE II/III from Ashton-Tate, 174, 701
DBMS-990 from Texas Instruments, 701
DBTG
  (*see* CODASYL Data Base Task Group)
Deadlock, 472-476, 473*Fig*
  conditions for, 474-475, 485
  global, in a network, 742-743
  solution strategies, 474-475, 485-496
DEARNLEY, Peter, 617*b*
Decision support, 19, 109-111
Decomposition:
  of data structures, 26*b*, 246
  of retrieval requests in a network,
    744
Decoupling (*see* Independence)
Decryption, *544-545Fig*
  (*see also* Encryption)
Dedicated database systems, 53-54, 697
Default data item value, 220
Defaults:
  in retrieval request, 262, 283
  in update, 347
  in user definitions, 242
Deferred execution, 168-169, 191-194,
    360
Deferred update, 347, 352-354
Definitional privileges, 532
Degree of a relationship, 228-229, 235
Delete privilege, 466
Deleted records:
  reclaiming storage space, 417
Deliverables, 683, 710
Delphi method, 689
DeMILLO, Richard A., 569*b*
DeMorgan's Law, 270

DENNING, Dorothy E., 541, 542, 543,
    560, 569*b*
DENNING, Peter J., 530, 541, 542,
    569-570*b*
Dependency in a relationship
  (*see* Exhaustibility)
Dependent entity, 133, 226, 237
  (*see also* Parent entity)
DEPPE, Mark E., 425*b*, 779*b*
Derivation expression, 273-275
  stored with schema, 281
Derived data items, 281, 413-414
  in data entry, 343
  in database definition, 239
  not in proposed NDL standard, 766
  in proposed RDL standard, 769
  in retrieval, 262-263*Fig*, **274-275**,
    279*Fig*, 748
  rule in database design, 248
Derived relationship rule in database
    design, 248-249
Detail report, 278
Development (*see* System development)
Device-media control language (DMCL),
    211*Fig*-213, 215, 242
  no facilities in the proposed NDL
    standard, 766
DeWAN, Ed, 11
DeWITT, D. J., 758, 779*b*
Dialogue:
  for authentication in access control,
    522-523
  to resolve ambiguity, 300-302
Dialogue levels, 42, 160*n*, **168-174**,
    182-183
DIAMOND v. DIEHR, 712*n*
Dictionary, *601*
  (*see also* Data dictionary)
Diebold Research Program, 17, 584, 588-
    589, 617*b*
DIEKMAN, E., 617*b*
DIFFIE, Whitfield, 556*n*, 558, 569*b*
Differential disk dump, 441
Differential files, 353, 447, 451*b*
Direct access, *506-507*
Direct Mail Marketing Association,
    661
Direct manipulation, **163-168**, 341
Directory, *601*

Directory of Interactive Data-Base
    Systems, 729
DISCONNECT statement in NDL DML,
    237, 365
Disjunctive form of expression, 270-271
Disk server, 741-742*Fig*
Distributed databases, 23*b*, 177, 745-747
Distributed processing environment, 493,
    496, **738-743**, 739*Fig*
  encryption of data in, 554
Distribution alternatives, 745
Distribution of DBMS functions, **747-748**
Distributive law, 270-272
Division of responsibility, 509, 538,
    585-586
DIXON, Paul, 62-64*b*, 204*n*
DM from Battelle, 701
DM IV from Honeywell, 620, 693, 701,
    733
DMRS from Intergraph, 701
DMS 1100 from Sperry (UNIVAC), 620-
    621, 701, 733, 753*Fig*
DMS 170 from Control Data Corp., 701,
    733
DMS II from Burroughs, 701
DOBBS, Guy H., 62-63*b*
DOBKIN, David P., 569*b*
Document reference retrieval system
    (*see* Bibliographic system)
Documentation of DBMS, 696
  DBMS selection criteria, 724
Domain, *125*-126, 140, 218, *219*
Dominant copy, 496-497
Dominant user, 673, 676
DOUGLAS, William O., Justice, 668*b*
DOWKONT, Anthony J., et al., 62-63*b*,
    84
DPL from National Information Systems,
    Inc., 701
DRAPER, Jesse M., 718*b*
DRS from A.R.A.P., 701, 733
Dual data recording, 431, 433
Due process, 627-630
Dump, 430
  for backup, 430-435
  logical versus physical, 433-434, 443
  residual dump, 441-444
  versus logging, 437
DURELL, William R., 617*b*

E

EASYTRIEVE, 123, 135, 733
Economics of software market, 707-
    708*Fig*
EDELBERG, Murray, 451*b*
EDICT from Infodata, 621
Editing values for output, 282-283
Efficiency
    (*see* Machine efficiency; Human
        efficiency)
EHRSAM, W. S., et al., 569*b*
ELPHICK, M. J., 502*b*
EMERY, James C., xvi, 22*b*, 111
Encode-decode facility, 218-219, 241, 343
ENCOMPAS from Tandem, 701
Encryption, 52, 507, *544-562*
  algorithms, 545*Fig*, 547
  of authentication and authorization
      information, 522, 538, 553
  data dependent, 571*b*
  ensuring identity and currency of sender
      and receiver, 561-562
  key distribution and management,
      545*Fig*, 554, 556, 560-562
  transmitted data versus stored data,
      553-554
End user computing, 732
End users, 168-169, 770
ENGLES, Robert W., 763, 779*b*
English language, 300
  frequently occurring letters, 550
ENSLOW, Philip H., Jr., 779*b*
Entering data, 164
  keyboarding versus voice recognition,
      167
Enterprise administrator, 771
    (*see* Database administrator)
Entity, *8*, 120, 125-126
  entity rule in database design, 247
Entity-attribute-relation (E-A-R) design
      approach, **245-246**
Entity class/type, 12, *123*, 221
  criteria for inclusion, 222
  versus attribute, 144, 246
Entity instance, 120, 123, 221
Entity partitioning, *747Fig*
    221
Entry, *123*, 126, 130-131*Fig*, 210*Fig*,
Enumeration of values, 218

EPSTEIN, Robert, 779*b*
EQUAL-OR operator, *269-270*
Error and exception conditions, 364, 369-
    371, 374, 378
  response rules, 370, 465
Error innoculation, 543
Error log, 465
Errors, in syntax, impossible, 166
ERVIN, Sam J., Jr., Senator, 639
ESWARAN, K. P., 470, 492, 502*b*
European privacy laws versus U.S., 644,
    651
Evaluation, *685*
Evaluation methodology, **686-692**
  final selection, 704-705
Evaluation and selection of DBMS, 672-
    707
EVEREST, Gordon C., 23*b*
  concurrency, 502*b*
  database administration functions,
    619*b*
  futures of DBMS, 779*b*
  GUIDE-SHARE critique, 383*b*, 393*n*,
    424*b*
  objectives of database management, 36
  privacy laws, 646*n*, 667*b*
  survey of microcomputer DBMS, 718*b*
  taxonomy of data structures, 151*b*
Evidence, legally obtained, 629, 640
Evolution:
  of data definition, 213
  of database administration, 576
  of DBMS, **52-64**, 693-694
  of DBMS functions, 61-63
  of program-data relationship, 387-390
Evolvability, **44-46**
  data independence is the key, 392
  dependence on binding time, 405-408
  dependence on data conversion
    processes, 409-410
  DBMS dichotomy violates, 60
  functions, 87
  hampered without userschema, 389
  means to, **99-104**
  for parametric user, 81
  programming user role in, 77, 362
  with sketchy database definition, 244
  with userschema, 92-94
  versus machine efficiency, 702

Exception conditions
  (*see* Error and exception conditions)
Exception rate, 745, *746*
Exclusive control, 471-472, 477, 482-483
Exclusivity of a relationship, 224-226,
    238-239
  implied in relationship criterion, 229-
    231
Executable form of program, 360
Execute privilege, 532
Exhaustibility of a relationship, 226-228,
    235, 237-239
Existence:
  characteristic of data item, 219-220
  operator, 269
  protecting database, 48-49
Existence control, 429, 595-596
  (*see* Backup and recovery)
Explicit context setting, 327-328
Exponential data item, 216, 461
Export, *340*
EXPRESS, 424*b*
Expression
  (*see* Boolean expression; Derivation
    expression)
External access path, 241
External interests in data management,
    624
External schema:
  in ANSI/SPARC DBMS framework,
    116*b*, 772*Fig*
  (*see* Userschema)
External security, *506-507*
Extract and download data, 749

F

FAGIN, R., 255*b*
Fair Credit Reporting Act (U.S.), 642-
    643, 646*Fig*, 659-660
Fair code approach to laws, 645
Fair information practices:
  enforcement, 649-652
  inappropriate solutions, 652-653
  legislative approaches to, 640-645
  organizational response, 653-664
  purpose for laws, 627
  three basic rights, 628-632
  typical provisions in laws, 645-652

Family Educational Rights and Privacy Act (FERPA), 627, 646*Fig*
Family tree order of traversal, 328
Feature list for DBMS evaluation, *685-686*, 687-688*Figs*, 720-726
Federal Information Processing Standards (U.S. FIPS), 572*b*, *762*
FEHDER, Paul L., 310, 326, 380, 383*b*, 423-424*b*
FEISTEL, Horst, 554, 569*b*
FERNANDEZ, Eduardo B., 569*b*, 573*b*
File, *12*, *123-126*, 130, 136
  master, 5, 6*Fig*, 29, 353, 432
  name of, 125
  problem of grouping items, 144
  (*see also* Flat file; Hierarchical data structure)
File directory, 511
File generation, 264, 378
File-level mappings, 416
File-level operations, 57
  for the programming user, 376-377
  (*see also* Languages, high-level; Statistics)
File-level update, 356
File load utility, 342
  (*see* Database creation)
File management system, *189*
File server, *742Fig*-743
Financial Institution Message Authentication Standard (FIMAS), 556
Fingermatrix, Inc., 527
Fingerprint identification, 524-527, 571*b*, 573*b*
First normal form, 249
FISHER, Paul, 383*b*, 570*b*, 781*b*
Fixed-position language syntax style, 178-179
Fixed value set, *218*
Flat file, *123-129*, 259-260, 308
  composite, 126-128
  homogenous, 126
  retrieval languages, 287-293, 334
Flatten up/down, 323, 331, 416*Fig*
FLAVIN, Matt, 255*b*
Flexibility is a trap, 698, 768
Floating point number, 461
Flow controls, 507, 533

FOCUS from Information Builders, Inc., 196*b*, 701, 733
FORAL, 310
Foreign file, *264*, 340, 411*Fig*
Foreign identifier ('key'), 140-141, 231, 249
  rule in database design, 248
Forgiving and forgetting, 639
Format specifications, 218, 262-263*Fig*
  for graphical output, 298-299
  for tabular output, 282-287
Formation and presentation step in retrieval, 263*Fig*, 280, 748
Formatted file/data systems, 11, 53
FORMCHECK validation statement, 461-462
Formularies, 514
FORTRAN, 770
  data definitions buried in the program, 387
  stored form of data, 362
Fourth generation language, xi, 28, 32, 360, 732, 768
Fragment of data, from partitioning, 744-747
FRAILEY, Dennis J., 491, 503*b*
Freedom of Information Act (U.S. FOIA), 630, 646*Fig*
Freedom of the press, 630
Frequency distribution:
  of data item values, 276, 294-299
  of instances, 222
  of a non-exclusive relationship, 225-226
  graphical representation, 296-299*Figs*
  statistics of (*see* Statistics)
  tabular representation, 295-297*Figs*
Frost and Sullivan:
  estimated DBMS market, xii
FRY, James, P.:
  database design methodology, 244, 247, 256*b*
  distributed databases, 779*b*
  evolution of DBMS, 68*b*, 696, 719*b*
  functions of DBMS, 61-63*b*, 68*b*
  program conversion, 425*b*
  restructuring, 414, 424*b*
Function:
  DBMS versus DBA functions, 86-87
  as a relationship, 224

Function (*Cont.*)
 versus mechanism/module, 84-86
Functional dependency, 26*b*, 246

G

GAINES, Helen Fouché, 547, 570*b*
GALLER, Bruce I., 503*b*
Garbage in, garbage out, 597
GARCIA-MOLINA, Hector, 503*b*
GARDARIN, Georges, 781*b*
GASSER, M., 519, 520, 570*b*
General (nonprogramming) user, 78-
 79*Figs*, *81*, 85*Fig*, 104-106
Generality:
 means to evolvability, 100
Generalization, 56, 247, 256*b*
Generalized DBMS
 (*see* DBMS, generalized)
 (*see also* Dedicated database systems)
Generalized programming user, 60
 (*see* DBMS system programmer)
Generated procedures, 191, 194, 293, 360
Generations of data, 241-242
GERBERICK, Dahl A., 667*b*
GHOSH, Sakti P., 23*b*, 424*b*
GIRLS from Informatics, 693
 (*see* MARK IV)
GIS from IBM, 23*b*, 701, 733
GLESER, Malcolm H., 719*b*
GLINERT-COLE, 779*b*
Global checkpoint, 447
 (*see* System checkpoint)
Global update (*see* File-level update)
GOETZ, Martin A., 101
Going concern assumption, 418
GOLDBERG, Robert P., 425*b*
GOLDSTEIN, Robert C., 618*b*, 667*b*
GOODMAN, Nathan, 502*b*, 504*b*
GORRY, G. Anthony, 22*b*
GOSDEN, John A., 68*b*, 760, 779*b*
GRAHAM, Robert S., 530, 570*b*
Granting privilege, 532-533, 537-538
Granularity:
 in access control, 509, 530-531*Fig*
 in concurrency control, 477-479, 503*b*
Graphical representation:
 of a relationship, **223-224**
 of data structure, **203-209**, 591
 of retrieval results, 276, **294-299**

Graphical representation (*Cont.*)
 no facilities in proposed NDL
 standard, 766
Graphics tablet, 165
GRAY, J. N., 451*b*, 503*b*
Great Britain, privacy study, 625, 626,
 645, 669
GREGURAS, Fred M., 719*b*
GRIFFITHS, P. P., 533, 570*b*
GRISWOLD v. Connecticut, 629
Group, 221
Grouping items into records, 120-122,
 144, 223
GUIDE, 617*b*
GUIDE-SHARE, 24*b*, 40*n*, 383*b*

H

HABERMANN, A. Nico, 491, 503*b*
Hand geometry, 524, 529
HANOLD, Terrance, 10-11, 22*b*
HANSEN, Morris H., 540, 570*b*, 667*b*
Hardware vendor
 (*see* Vendor of hardware)
HAREL, Elie C., 196*b*
HARRIS, L. R., 300, 305*b*
HARRIS, Louis, & Associates, 667*b*
 opinion polls, 625, 649, 651
HAS operator, 316-320, 325-327
HASEMAN, William D., 23*b*
Hash total, 463
Hashing (*see* Identifier transformation)
HAVENDER, J. W., 492, 503*b*
HAWTHORN, P., 779*b*
HAYES, Robert M., 68*b*, 72*b*
HAYS, W. Orchard, 152*b*
Header entity record (*see* Parent)
HELLMAN, Martin E., 554-557, 559,
 569-570*b*
Help facility in dialogue, 173, 181-182
HEMPHILL, Charles F., Jr., et al, 507,
 570*b*
HENDRIX, G. G., et al, 305*b*
Heterogeneity in a network, 744, 749
Heuristic development, 117*b*, 583
HEVNER, Alan R., 719*b*
Hierarchical data structure, 121*Fig*-122,
 129-133, 221, 338*b*
 high-level language on, 188, 308-329
 sample multipath queries, 324-326

Hierarchical data structure (*Cont.*)
  sample single-path queries, 315-323
  interrecord-level mappings, 414-415*Fig*
  limitations of, 134, 137
  multipath, 132*Fig*, 206*Fig*, 324*Fig*
  single path designs, 130-131*Fig*, 308-309*Fig*
  updating of, 356
  userview over a multifile structure, 330-331
Hierarchical relationship, 121*Fig*, 130, *133*, 221, 227*Fig*-228 _
High-level language
  (*see* Language, high-level)
HILL, Marjorie P., 779*b*
HIGHLAND, Harold Joseph, 570*b*
Histogram, 295-296*Fig*
History-dependent access control, 509
  (*see* statistical inferencing)
Hit character, 298-299
HOFFER, Jeffrey A., 25*b*
HOFFMAN, Lance J., 507, 514, 539, 547, 552*n*, 570*b*, 667*b*
Homogeneous flat file, *126*
Homophonic cipher, 550
Honeywell, 679
HOPEWELL, Paul, 392, 424*b*
Horizontal overflow, 285
Horizontal partitioning, 747
  (*see* Entity partitioning)
Host-language DBMS, 15, 56-58, 68*b*, 77, 106, 330, 360-361, 698-700*Fig*, 732-733
  for conventional application programmer, 83
  infeasible base for high-level facilities, 683, 768
HOUSEL, Barry C., 424*b*
HQL, 310, 326-328
HSIAO, David K., 204*n*, 507, 571*b*, 778*b*, 779*b*
Huffman code, 241, 549
  (*see* Variable length binary code)
HUFFMAN, D. A., 549
Human efficiency, 160-161, 704-705
Human resources, 702
  consumed in program maintenance, 737
  versus machine resources, 32-33, 408

I

IBM 308x computer, 109*n*, 752
ICP Million Dollar Awards, 683-684*n*
ICP Software Directory, 728
iDBP from Intel, 753*Fig*
Identification of data, 125, 479-480, 534, 537
  (*see also* Boolean expression; Projection)
Identification of users, 506, 515-516, 536-537, 539
Identifier, 147-148, 220, 222, 515
  changes in value during update, 356
  in relationship criterion, 229-231
  rule in database design, 238-239
Identifier transformation, 241
IDM (*see* Britton-Lee)
IDMS from Cullinet, 26*b*, 621, 693, 701, 733, 734, 753*Fig*
IDS from Honeywell, 23*b*, 24*b*, 56, 64, 254*b*, 733
IMAGE from Hewlett-Packard, 701
Image log, 430
Image of reality, **199**, 348
  database for organization, 2, 19, 61*n*
IM/DM from Control Data (from Battelle), 701
Immediate processing:
  of commands, 168-169, 191, 194
  of transactions, 351*Fig*-353
  versus deferred execution, 379
Implicit context setting, 327-328
Import, *340*
Improper rebuff, 524-525*Fig*
IMS from IBM, 23-26*b*, 122-123, 459, 620-621, 693, 701, 733
Inclusion rule, 247
Inconsistent data, 29
Indemnification, 711
Independence, 102, *392*
  (*see also* Data independence; Machine independence)
Indexes:
  on data structures, 54, 235, 241, 331
  maintenance, 353, 416-417
    suspended during update, 612
  monitoring usage of, 612
  (*see also* Inverted data structures)
Indirect access, *507*

Indirect attribute, *137*
Indirect disclosure, *540*, 544
Inference controls, 506-507, 540-544
Inference rules, 303
Inferential retrieval, 734
Infix operator, 265*n*
Information, *9-11* (*see also* Data)
Information center, 732
Information practices
    (*see* Fair information practices)
Information requirements
    (*see* Data requirements)
Information Resource Dictionary Systems
    of ANSI, 761*Fig*, 770
Information Resource Management (IRM),
    xi, 12, 28, 732
    (*see also* MIS)
Information revolution, xi, 22*b*
Information storage and retrieval system,
    11, 53
Information system resource dictionary,
    602
    (*see* Data dictionary)
INFORMIX from Relational Database
    Systems, 701, 765
INGRES from Relational Technology,
    701, 733, 765
Input-output control system (IOCS), 55,
    57*Fig*
    (*see also* Access methods)
INQUIRE from Infodata Systems, 621,
    701, 733
INSERTION clause, 237, 769
Installation of DBMS software, 684, 714
Instance, *9*
    versus schema, 123-127, 203,
        211
    (*see also* Record instance; Entity
        instance)
Instances, number of, 222
Integrated Data Dictionary (IDD) from
    Cullinet, 621
Integrated Data Dictionary (IDD) from
    Intel, 621
Integrity of data, 34, *47*, 476, 733
    Chapters 12-14
    consequences if low, 34
    control functions, 15-16, 58-60, 87,
        428-429

Integrity of data (*Cont.*)
    bypassed by programming user, 362,
        699
    in the database management machine,
        754
    DBCS controls, 91
    database management objective, **46-52**,
        214, 429
    DBMS dichotomy violates, 58-60,
        698-699
    DBMS selection criteria, 722
    dependence on database administration,
        47-48, 428, 506-509, 576,
        595-599
    need for laws, 640-642, 654
    retrofitting mechanisms, 647, 654
    satisfying the objectives of, 99
    threatened by concurrent updates, 466-
        469*Fig*, 482
    a user responsibility, 429, 584, 741-742
    versus machine efficiency, 702
    (*see also* Access control; Backup and
        recovery; Concurrent update
        control; Database definition,
        consequences of incomplete;
        Quality of data)
INTELLECT from Artificial Intelligence
    Corp., 300, 305*b*
Interactive DBMS, 190
Interactive dialogue, 160, 163, **168-173**
Interchange file, 264 (*see* Foreign file)
Internal access path, 241
Internal schema, 116*b*, *771*
Internal security, *506-507*
    (*see also* Computer security;
        Data security)
International Business Machines (IBM):
    influence on standards, 764*Fig*, 765-766
    unbundled in 1969, 679, 693
    (*see also* DB2; GIS; IBM 308x; IMS;
        SQL)
International Data Corp., xii
International Standards Organization (ISO),
    760, 761*Fig*
    date representation, 218
    definition of data, 7, 780*b*
    definition of information, *9*
    Open Systems Interconnection (OSI)
        reference model, 771-773

Interpretive execution, 191, 194, 293, 349*Fig*, 360, 372
Interrecord-level mappings, 414-416, 415*Fig*
Interrogation (*see* Retrieval; Query)
Interval numbers, *217*
Invert mapping, 415*Fig*
Inverted arrow on data structure diagrams, **131-133**, 224-225
Inverted data structures, 24*b*, **190-193**
  (*see also* Indexes)
Involuntary disclosure, 638
Irreducible n'ary relational data structure, 148, 246
Irrelevant value, 148, 219, 462
Isolation, 52
Item (*see* Data item)
Item-level data independence, 412-413
Item-level data validation, 460-461, 463-464*Fig*
Item-level mappings, 412-413
Item-level update operations, 354-355

J

JACOBSON, Robert V., 571*b*
JAROMASA (II Cor 2.15), 253
Job management, 109-110, 466
  versus data management, 116*b*, 474, 579-582
JOIN, 238, 331-333*Fig*, 416, 748, 781*b*
  in proposed RDL standard, 769
Joint frequency distribution, 276, 278, *297-299Figs*
JONES, Anita K., 569*b*
JONES, Curtis H., 298*n*
JONES, Paul E., 247, 255*b*
Joy stick, 165
Journals on database systems, 26, 678
JOYCE, John D., 185
JUERGENS, Hugh F., xvi

K

KAHN, Beverly K., 617*b*
KAHN, David, 547, 571*b*
KAM, John B., 568*b*
KAPLAN, S. Jerrold, 303, 305-306*b*
KATZAN, Harry, Jr., 24*b*
KENT, William, 120, 145*n*, 151*b*, 255*b*
KERR, Douglas S., 571*b*

KERSTA, Larry G., 528
Key (*see* Identifier)
  (*see also* Ordering)
Key transformation
  (*see* Identifier transformation)
Keyboarding, 167, 341
Key-Word-In-Context (KWIC) index, 608-609
Keyword language style, 178, 287-288*Fig*
KIM, Sung-Woo, 327-328
KIMBLETON, Stephen R., 740, 780-781*b*
KING, Paul F., 491, 503*b*
KLINE, C., 560, 573*b*
KLUG, Anthony, 116*b*, 778*b*
Knapsack problem, 557
Knowledge, 10-11
KOCH, Harvey S., 571*b*
KOHLER, Walter H., 503*b*, 780*b*
KOLATA, Gina Bari, 556*n*
KONHEIM, A. G., 556*n*, 571*b*
KORTH, Henry F., 503*b*
KRASS, Peter, 719*b*
KRINOS, John D., 612, 613, 617*b*
KUNG, H. T., 503*b*

L

LAMPORT, L., 495, 503*b*
LAMPSON, Butler W., 530, 571*b*
LANCASTER, F. Wilfrid, 72*b*
LANDWEHR, Carl E., 535, 571*b*
LANGEFORS, Borge, 24*b*
Language:
  dialogue levels, 42
  high-level for database machine, 752
  high-level on rich data structure, 120, 143, 330, 677
  high-level versus low-level, 41, 101, **174-176**
  low-level, 185
  process specification, 32, 175, 311
  syntactic styles, 42, 178-179
  versus function, 86
  (*see also* Process specification languages; Data language; Data definition language; Data manipulation language)
LARSON, James A., 255*b*
Laser disk (*see* Optical recording media)

Late binding, 405-406
LAWSON, Herbert G., 526, 571*b*
Leasing (licensing) software, 679, 680*Fig*, **683-685**
Least privilege principle, 509
LEFKOVITS, Henry C., 117*b*
LEFKOVITZ, David, 24*b*, 68*b*, 618*b*
Legal counsel in contract negotiation, 709
LEMPEL, Abraham, 557, 571*b*
Length of data item values, 217-218
LEONG-HONG, Belkis W., 618*b*
Levels of interconnectedness, 740-741
LEWIS, P. M., II, 504*b*
Lexicon from Arthur Anderson, 618*b*, 620
Liability terms in contract, 710-711
Library systems, 11, 53-54, 69-72
Licensing agreement, 709, 711
Licensing software (*see* Leasing software)
Light pen, 165
Limit data collection, 635, 648
Linear representation of data structure, **205-213**, 210*Fig*
Linking record, to represent M:N relationship, 141-142, 235
LIPTON, Richard J., 569*b*
List mode of output, 282-283
Livelock, 471, 481, 494
Load (*see* Database creation)
Load time binding, 404
Local area network (LAN)
  (*see* Networking system)
Local checkpoint, 448
  (*see* Program checkpoint)
LOCHOVSKY, Frederick H., 26*b*, 152*b*, 256*b*
LOCK command, 481-482
Locking mechanisms, 480-485
LOCKE, P. W., 780*b*
Lockout, *470-473*, 477
  in a distributed system, 742-743
  using semaphores, 741
LOCKR and LOCKU commands, 481-482*Fig*
  for access control, 514, 521-522
  associated information, 430, 438
Logging changes to the database, 430
  for audit trail, 435-436*Fig*
  for backup, 430-432*Fig*, 436*Fig*, 437-440

Logging changes to the database (*Cont.*)
  versus dumping, 437
  (*see also* Audit trail)
Logging errors, 465
Logging input transactions, 431, 435-436*Fig*, 439-440*Fig*, 445*Fig*
Logging system activity, 586
Logging user accesses, 514, 521-522
Logical data independence, 392
  (*see* Program-data independence)
Logical data item (*see* Boolean data item)
Logical data structure
  versus physical storage structure, 212
Logical database design
  (*see* Database design)
Logical dump, *433-434*
LOHMAN, Guy M., 353, 358*b*, 441, 451*b*
LONG, Larry E., 22*b*, 618*b*
Longitudinal studies, 539, 640
LOOMIS, Mary E. S., 602, 616*b*
Lost update, *467-468*
Low-level building blocks, 111, 177, 677
LOWENTHAL, Eugene I., 117*b*, 314, 383*b*, 780-781*b*
LUCAS, Henry C., Jr., 117*b*
LUCKING, Jim, 765*n*
LUM, Vincent Y., 424*b*
LUMSDEN, Eunice W., 617*b*
LYON, John K., 24*b*, 224*n*, 255*b*, 618*b*

M

McCRIRICK, Ian B., 618*b*
McDONALD, Robert, 556*n*, 572*b*
McDONOUGH, Adrian M., 10, 22*b*
McEWEN, Hazel E., 225*b*, 618*b*
McFADDEN, Fred R., 25*b*
McGEE, William C.:
  on correspondence of data structure classes, 383*b*, 395, 424*b*
  functions of DBMS, 61-63*b*, 68*b*
  generalization of DBMS functions, 56, 100, 306*b*
  graphical schema representation, 204, 255*b*
  property, 151*b*
  use of term 'schema', 92*n*
McLEAN, Ephraim R., 196*b*
McLEOD, Dennis, 306*b*

Machine efficiency:
  versus human efficiency, 160-161
  versus functionality, 699-703
Machine independence, 3-5
Machine resources:
  versus human resources, 32-33, 408
Machines not accountable, 48, 516
MACHRONE, Bill, 780*b*
MADDISON, R. N., 247, 256*b*
MADNICK, Stuart E., 571-572*b*
MAGbase III from Micro Applications
    Group, 701
Mailing labels output, 286-287
Maintenance, 61-62
  (*see also* Update; Revision)
Maintenance term in contract, 710
  DBMS selection criteria, 724
Management/managers, 16-17
  confidence in using data, 47
  data independent from, 398
  direct system interface, 40
Management information systems (MIS),
    16-19, 22*b*
  context for DBMS, 16, 54
  DBMS tool for building, **109-113**
  organization or department, 11-12, 45,
    578
  use of term 'information,' 10
  (*see also* Information Resource
    Management)
Management of any resource, 28, 36
Mandatory data item, 219-220, 460
  updating, 355, 414
Mandatory DBMS selection criteria, 686,
    688-689, 695
  in contract, 710
MANNINO, M. V., 602, 616*b*
Manual procedures for data integrity, 428
Mapping:
  in general conversion process, 410*Fig*
  input data to database, 343
  levels of, **412-416**
  userschema to schema, 369, 392-395
Mapping language/instructions, 187,
    420*Fig*, 770
MARCH, Salvatore, xvi, 246, 254*b*
Marginal frequency distribution, 296,
    297*Fig*, 321
  (*see also* PER operator)

MARILL, Tom, 753*Fig*, 780*b*
MARK IV from Informatics, 23*b*, 135,
    178, 620, 693, 733
MARRON, Beatrice, 618*b*
MARTELLA, G., 568*b*
MARTIN, James:
  application development without
      programmers, 25*b*, 196*b*, 306*b*,
      735
  database organization and DBMS, 22*b*,
      24*b*, 25*b*, 618*b*
  security of computers and data, 451*b*,
      507, 572*b*
MARYANSKI, Fred J., 752, 753*Fig*, 780*b*
Mask, 460-461
Mask register, 757*Fig*
Master entity record (*see* Parent entity)
Master file(s), 5, 6*Fig*, 29, 353, 432
Matching threshold, 524-525*Fig*, 527
MATYAS, Stephen, 572*b*
MAXWELL, William L., 530, 568*b*
MDBS from Micro Data Base Systems,
    701, 753*Fig*
MDQS from Honeywell, 693, 733
  (*see* DM IV)
MEADOW, Charles T., 25*b*, 72*b*
Mean, 276
Measurement units, 217
Mechanization of data, 340-341, 409,
    411*Fig*, 590
Median, 278
Medical Information Bureau (MIB), 660
MEHLMANN, Marilyn, 196*b*
MELLING, Wesley P., 780*b*
MELLON, G. E., 547, 551-552, 572*b*
Member entity record
  (*see* Dependent entity)
Memo posting, 353-354
Menu-driven dialogue, 168-173, 179-180,
    183
Menu handling facilities, 182-185
Meta-data, 774*Fig* (*see* Schema)
Meta-schema, 774*Fig*
Methodology, *244*
MEYER, Carl, 572*b*
Microcomputer environment, *161-162*,
    487, 713
  DBMSs in, 57, 84, 161-162, 360-361,
      418, 466, 684, 734, 749, 769

Microcomputer environment (*Cont.*)
  pricing software for, 707
Microcomputer workstation, 741, 749
  access control at, 516, 521, 523, 527
  data entry at, 456, 749
  voice recognition equipment, 527, 529
Microform output media, 280
MILLER, Arthur R., 667*b*
MILLER, M. W., 780*b*
MILLER, William F., 539*n*
Minnesota Data Practices Act, 627, 647,
  652
Minnesota income tax return, 658
Minutiae in a fingerprint, 525-527
Mnemonic data codes, 548
Mode statistic, 278
Model, 120*n* (*see* Data model)
MODEL 204 from CCA, 701
Modeling the real world, 122, 134, 199-
  201, 203
Modification (*see* Update)
Modify action, 365, 467
Modify privilege, 466, 532
Modularity, *100*
Money item type, 216
Monitoring, 52, 599-601
  for integrity threats, 507, 514, 521-522
  for performance, 610-613
Mono-alphabetic substitution cipher, 550
MOREY, Richard C., 504*b*
MORGAN, Howard L., 530, 568*b*
MORLAND, D. Verne, 196*b*, 358*b*
MORRISON, Paul L., Jr., 42
Motivators of database approach, **31-34**
  satisfying the, 97-98
Motivators of DBMS acquisition, 675
MOULDER, Richard, 780*b*
MOULTON, Rolf T., 572*b*
Mouse, *165*
MOZEICO, Howard, 196*b*
MUCKSTADT, John A., 441, 451*b*
Multifile data structure, 121*Fig*-122, ***133-***
  138, 235-236*Fig*, 330
  high-level language on, 188, 330-334
    not in proposed NDL standard,
    768
  limitations, 143-144
Multilevel classification, 535-536
Multilist structures, 24*b*

Multipath hierarchical data structure, **132-**
  133, 206*Fig*, 324*Fig*
  retrieval language, 323-329
Multiple output lines per record, 285-286
Multiuser DBMS, 466
Multivalued dependency, 255*b*, 246
Multivalued item, 220
MURPHY, James E., 489, 504*b*
MURRAY, W. H., 572*b*
MYERS, Edith, 753*Fig*, 760, 780*b*

N

Naive user assumption, 370-371
Name:
  of data item, 215
  of entity or file, 125
  of relationship, 223
Name qualification, 366
Naming convention, 605-608
Naming hierarchy, 221, 366
Naming rule in database design, 250
Narrative language style, 178, 180,
  289*Fig*, 372, 376
National Bureau of Standards (NBS),
  168*b*, 525, 554, 572*b*, 762
National Computer Program Abstract
  Service (NCPAS), 728
National Conference of Commissioners on
  Uniform State Laws, 627, 645,
  667*b*
National Labor Relations Act (U.S.), 630,
  646*Fig*
National Security Agency (U.S. NSA),
  556
Natural data structure, **199-203**, 223-224
  design, 244-245, 590-591
Natural Language, 734
  interface for casual user, 80, 84, 179-
    180, 305-306*b*
  no facilities in proposed NDL standard,
    766
  query, ***299-303***
NAVATHE, Shamkant B., 414, 424*b*
Navigation, 56, 57*Fig*, 185, 311, 330,
  367-368, 377, 768-769
  (*see also* Record-level operations)
Need-to-know access control, 535-536
Nested queries, 291-292, 334
  in proposed RDL standard, 769

Network Access Process (NAP), *738,*
   739*Fig,* 740, 771
Network data directory, 739*Fig,* 740, 743,
   744
Network data structure, 122-123, 136
   based on CODASYL data structure,
      139-143, 236-237, 762
   representation of relationships, 234
   versus relational data structure, 143
   (*see also* Multifile data structure)
Network Database Language (NDL), 254*b,*
   398, 502*b, 761,* ***766-769,*** 778*b*
   candidate for a standard, 764-769
   CODASYL (DBTG) proposal
      differences, 767
   concurrency control, 482-483
   INSERTION and RETENTION clauses,
      236-237
   low-level manipulation language, 765-
      766, 768-769
   serving conventional application
      programmer exclusively, 768
Network DBMS, 739*Fig,* 740, ***743-744***
Network operating system (NOS), 740
Networking system, 741-743, 742*Fig,* 750
   heterogeneity in, 744, 749
   technical and administrative issues,
      749-750
   tight coupling versus loose coupling,
      752-753, 755*Fig*
NEUHOLD, Erich J., 151*b*
New South Wales, Australia, 627, 644
NIH syndrome, 680-681*Fig*
NIJSSEN, G. M., xvi, 117*b,* 120, 132*n,*
   151*b,* 255*b*
Noise ratio, 70-71
Noise words, 178
NOLAN, Richard L., 25*b,* 605*n,* 618*b,*
   667*b*
NOMAD from National CSS, 701
Nominal value/numbers, *217*
Nonprogramming user, 15, 59, **76-79,**
   82-84, 85*Fig,* 89-90
   facilities for, 683, 732-733
      compared to programming user
         facilities, 376-378
   (*see also* Casual user; General user;
      Parametric user)
Nonrepeating group, 203, 207*Fig,* 221-222

Nonroutine uses, 663
Normalization, 140, 142, 246, 249-250,
   255*b,* 334
Normalized JOIN, 333*Fig*
   (*see* AND-JOIN)
NOT Operator, 269-270, 461
   versus NE (not equal), 319
Notice provision in law, 647-648, 657
Novice user, 161, 169, 174, 179, 181,
   185, 303, 734
NULL data item value, 219, 269, 461-462
Numeric data items, 215-217, 460
NYCUM, Susan H., 718*b*

O

OBERMARCK, Ron, 504*b*
Object of access control, 530-531, 537
Object code, 360, 401*Fig,* 404
Object profile model of access control,
   510
Object-relation data structure, 121*Fig*-122,
   143-148, 223, 245-246
Objectives of database management, **36-52**
   meeting them, 98-104
   (*see* Sharability; Availability;
      Evolvability; Integrity)
OF-language, 607-608
Offline, *41,* 160
OLDEHOEFT, Arthur E., 556*n,* 572*b*
OLIVER, E., 778*b*
OLLE, T. William, xvi, 62-63*b,* 117*b,*
   139*n,* 151*b,* 383*b,* 418*n,* 780*b*
OLSON, Margrethe H., 18
Omission ratio, 70-71
Online, *41,* 160-163
OnLine-English (OLE) from Cullinet, 300,
   305*b,* 701
Online navigation, 330
Online users, 41, 162, 168-169
OPEN command, 363, 373, 375, 482
Open Systems Interconnection (OSI)
   reference model, **771-773,** 780*b*
Open time binding, 404
Open value set, *219*
Operands of Boolean expression, 265-266
Operating system, 55, 215, 510*n,* 581-
   582, *750-751Fig*
   file system inadequate, 107

Operating system (*Cont.*)
  inadequate for data integrity control, 91,
    478, **507-508**, 510
  interface with DBMS, 107-110*Figs*,
    752*Fig*, 771
Operators, in expressions, 266-267
  permitted on data items, 216-217
Optical recording media, 432
OPTIMUM from Uveon, 701
Optional relationship (*see* Exhaustibility)
OR-Join, 333*Fig*
ORACLE from Oracle, 701, 733, 765
Ordering, *276*
  generalized sort, 56
  for presentation, 262, 263*Fig*, 275-276,
    279*Fig*, 321, 748
    not in proposed NDL standard, 767
    in RDL proposed standard, 769
    for vertical overflow, 285
  on a repeating group, 318
  of stored data, 223, 241, 353, 416,
    459, 767
    changing the sort key value, 356
Ordinal numbers, *217*, 295*n*
Organization for Economic Co-operation
    and Development (OECD), 627,
    645, 667*b*
Organizational need/readiness for DBMS,
    674-677
Organizations, 16
  dependence on DBMS, 706
  response to DBA, 613-614
  response to fair information practices,
    653-664
  role of database(s) in, 18
  state of database management in, 18-20
ORLICKY, Joseph, 458*n*
ORTON, Jim, 625*Fig*, 642*Fig*, 643*Fig*,
    654*Fig*, 681*Fig*, 764*Fig*
Output format of data item, 218
Output formation and presentation, **280-287**
Output media, 280
Output mode, 281
Output volume anticipated, 272-273
Owner entity record (*see* Parent entity)
Ownership of data:
  in an organization, 37
  stewardship of personal data, 656
  in a time-sharing system, 37

P

PACKARD, Vance, 667*b*
Page width limitations:
  handling, 283-286
Panning, 166
Parallel binding, 400, 403*Fig*
Parallel processing, 752, 754-757*Fig*
Parametric user, *78-81*, 85*Fig*, 104-106
  using catalogued report definition, 293
  using prestored update request, 350
Parent entity, 133, 231-232, *308*
  (*see also* Dependent entity)
Parentheses, in expressions, 265-270
  overcoming prohibited use of, 271-272
PARKER, Donn B., 506, 507, 508,
    572*b*
PARSONS, Talcott, 61*n*, 74*n*
Partial dependency rule in database design,
    249
Partial function, 226
Partitioning, 496, *745*, 746*Fig*, 747*Fig*
PASCAL, 770
Passive data dictionary, *610*, 734
Passive intrusion or disclosure, 544
Passwords for access control, 506, 510-
    512, **518-522**, 585
  encrypted in storage, 522, 553
Patents, 712-713*Fig*
PATTERSON, Albert C., 68*b*, 618*b*
Payment terms in contract, 710
PER operator, 289*Fig*, 290-292, 296-297,
    321-323
  (*see also* Control break; HAS operator)
Performance:
  DBMS selection criteria, 725
  degradation with DBMS, 600
  conflict with evolvability, 99-100
Performance monitoring, 610-613
Permanent block, *476*
Permutation cipher, 547, 549
Personal characteristics for access control,
    517, 523-529
PERRY, William E., 719*b*
Personal access, 629-631, 634*Fig*, 638,
    645
Personal data versus nonpersonal data, 633
Personal identification, 506, 515-516,
    536-537, 539
  system evaluation criteria, 525

Personal privacy, 628-629, 631-632,
634*Fig*, 636, 645
Personnel-Organizational database,
153-158, 201-202, 235-236
in multipath hierarchical structure,
206*Fig*
single-path hierarchical designs, 308-
309*Fig*
PETERSEN, H. E., 573*b*
PETRE, Peter, 760, 780*b*
Phantom record, *469*, 471, 479
Physical data independence, 390, 395-398,
396*Fig*
Physical data structure
(*see* Storage structure)
Physical database design
(*see* Storage structure, design; Database
design)
Physical dump, *433-434*
Physical security, 48-49, 429, 507
PL/I, 770
PLAGMAN, Bernard K., 602, 618-619*b*
Plaintext, *544-545Fig*
Planning and control, 18-19
Plex data structure, 136
(*see* Multifile data structure)
Pointers to represent relationships, 232
Polyalphabetic substitution cipher, 550
POPEK, G., 560, 573*b*
Populating a database, 341-342
(*see* Database creation)
Positional criteria, 281, 318, 320,
367-368, 376-377
Positioning, **164-166**
Possessed objects for access control, 517,
523
Precedence ordering of binary infix
operators, 265-266
Precision, 216
Preclaim, 474-475*Fig*, 485, 487, **491-492**,
503*b*
Precompile, 372
Predicate (*see* Boolean expression)
Predicate lock, 479
Pre-emption, 474-475*Fig*, 477, 483, 485,
487-491
Prefix operator, 265*n*
Preorder, 474-475*Fig*, 485, 487, **492-493**

Presentation of retrieval results, 262-
263*Fig*, 280-283
from multifile structure, 334
from multipath hierarchy, 328-329
from single-path hierarchy, 319-323
Presequence, 474-475*Fig*, **484-488**
Pricing of software, 707-708
Primary disclosure, 634*Fig*-635
notice at time of, 657
Primary key, 220 (*see* Identifier)
Print spooling, *741*
Privacy, *628*
of data, 51-52
mechanisms for ensuring, 52
of unbound portion of database, 394
(*see also* Personal privacy;
Fair information practices)
Privacy Act of 1974 (U.S.), 627, 630,
643, 646*Fig*, 663
Privacy impact statement, 656
Privacy invasion, 626
Privacy laws and studies, 626-627
Privacy Protection Study Commission
(U.S.), 627, 634, 667*b*
Privacy transformation, *544*
(*see* Encryption)
Private, *636*
Private key encryption, 547, 560-561
Privileged communication, *636-637*
Privileges, 466, 509, 511, 513*Fig*, 530-
533
language to assign, 537-538
Problem of data, **3-7**
Procedural language, 292, 379
Procedure, *3n*
Process, *3n*
Process integrity, 370, 598
loss of, 470
Process orientation, 6-7, *28-31*, 97-98
Process specification language, 32, 175,
311
Processing mode declaration, 373-374,
481-482
Product cipher, 547, 552, 554-555*Fig*
Program, *3n*, *360*
executable form, 360
execution versus *data* processing,
754-756

Program (*Cont.*)
  as user surrogate, 516, 522
Program buffer, 364, 368-369, 374
  deferred definition, 375
  programming versus non-programming
    user, 377
Program checkpoint, 448, 467
Program-data independence, *387-395Figs*,
    414-416
  never completely achievable, 393-394
Program-data relationship, 4-5, 582
  cross reference, 408, 421, 582
  evolution of, 387-390, 388*Fig*
Program-DBMS communication, 364-375
  form (call and verb), 371-373
  what, 364-371
  when, 373-375
Program maintenance/revision, 4, 30, 33,
    392, 395, 405, 413, 416-417,
    419-421
  consuming large share of human
    resources, 737
  impact of changed schema, 406-408
  with low-level *data* languages, 706
  versus data conversion, 264-265
Program management, 109-110
Programmer productivity, 196*b*
Programming languages, 3, 55, 311
  data structure class, 395
  impact on data integrity, 429
Programming user, *76-77*, *78-79Figs*, **82-
    84**, 85*Fig*, 89-90, *360*
  as navigator, 382*b*
  role in evolvability, 362
  (*see also* Conventional application
    programmer; DBMS language
    programmer; DBMS system
    programmer)
Programming user facilities, 101-102,
    360-380, 732-733
  convergence with nonprogramming user
    facilities, 376-378
  DBMS selection criteria, 722
  for update, 342
Projection process, 260-261*Fig*, 273-274,
    748
  object data in DML, 365-366
  in update, 347, 349

Prompting level of dialogue, 168-172
Proprietary software protection, 708, 711,
    712-714
PROSSER, William L., 667*b*
PROTHRO, Vivian C., 25*b*
Protocol, *487*
Pseudorandom numbers in encryption, 552
Public access, right of, 630-632
Public concern for data privacy, 624-625
Public-key crypto system, 547, **556-561**
Public records laws, 630, 646*Fig*

Q

Q PRO-4 from Quick'n Easy Products,
    701
Qualification:
  of data names, 366
  in retrieval process, 313-314*Fig*
Quality of data, 50-51, *454*, 596-59ঙ,
    649, 768
  (*see also* Concurrent update; Update,
    authorization; Update
    synchronization; Validation)
Query-by-example (QBE), 23*b*, 338*b*
Query language (*see* Retrieval language)
Query modification access control, 534
Quiet point, *448*, 467
  (*see also* Program checkpoint)
Quota on output, 272-273
QWIK QWERY from CACI, 123

R

RAICHELSON, Eugene, 68*b*
RAMIS II from Martin Marietta, 693,
    701, 733
Random sample queries, 273, 542-543
Range, 269, 278
  validation check, 460-461
  of values, 218
RAP, University of Toronto, 756
RARES, University of Utah, 756
Rating function, 689-690, 691-692*Figs*
R:Base from Microrim, 300, 701
READ command, 363
  with lock, 481-482
Reader rule, *471*, 482-483
READY command, 483*Fig*
REAL data item type, 216

Recall ratio, 70-71
Recommendation letter, 631
RECONNECT statement, 767
Record, 120, 123, 130, 140
 grouping of data items, 144, 221, 245-246
 instance, 9
  identified by content, 263-264, 479
 schema diagram, 9
 storage structure, 9
Record-at-a-time presentation, 281-282
Record-based data structures, 120-121, 245-246
Record decomposition (*see* Decomposition)
Record-level mapping, 413-414
Record-level operations, 57
Record-level update, 355-356
Record-level validation, 463-464*Fig*
Records retention:
 legal requirements, 431
Recovery, 430, 439-440*Fig*
 (*see also* Backup and recovery;
  Bring forward; Rollback)
Recursive relationship, 137-138*Fig*, 139, 201-202*Fig*, 228, 767
Redefinition of database, *416-417*, 420*Fig*, 774*Fig*
 effect on userschemas and programs, 406-407
 (*see also* Revision)
Redundancy, 28-30, 127, 130
 of backup data, 431, 439
 in relationship representation, 232
 update problems, 30, 51, 498
 of validation criteria, 457, 596
Reference model, 770-774
 ANSI/X3/SPARC DBMS framework, 770-772
 Database Architecture Framework Task
  Group, 773-774
 Open Systems Interconnection (OSI) of
  ISO, 771-773
Reference systems, *53*
Referential integrity, 219, 238-239, 463
Reflexive relationship
 (*see* Recursive relationship)
REGHBATI, H. K., 573*b*
REGIS DBMS (General Motors), 185
Regression, 278

REISNER, Phyllis, 196*b*
RELATE/3000 from CRI, 701
Relation, 140, 238 (*see* File)
Relational data model, 23-26*b*, 121*Fig*-123, 136, **139-143**, 151*b*, 330, 334, 765
 with high-level manipulation language, 765-766, 769
Relational Database Language (RDL), 254*b*, 761, 778*b*
 representation of relationship, 238-239
Relational operators
 (*see* Comparative operators)
Relationship, 8, 136*Fig*, 223
 characteristics of, **223-231**
 explicit definition in proposed RDL
  standard, 769
 imputes attributes to entities, 136-137, 144-145
 intrarecord (interitem), 245-246
 naming, 137, 148
 naming in multifile retrieval language, 331
 representation of, 224-225, **231-236**
  in CODASYL Network Data
   Structure, 236-237
  in Relational Database Language
   (RDL), 238-239
 rule in database design, 247
Relevance ratio, 70-71
Remembered information for access
 control, 517-523
Remote access system:
 impact on data integrity, 429
Reorganization, 104, 353, 425*b*, *416-417*, 420*Fig*
 between backup dumps, 434, 443
 monitoring usage to indicate need, 611-612
Repeating group, **221-223**, 308, 765
 rule in database design, 249
 update problems, 310-311
Repeating value suppression, 284, 316, 319-323
Replace action, 354-355, 467
Replication, 496, *745*, 746*Fig*, 747*Fig*
Report definition/generation, 293-294, 378
 no facility in proposed NDS standard, 766

Request for Bid/Proposal (RFB/RFP), *686*
Requirements (*see* Data requirements)
Reread verification, 484, 495-496
Research use of data, 539, 640
Residual dump, **441-444**
RESNICK, Mark, 267*n*
Response rules
   (*see* Error and exception conditions,
      response rules; Access control,
      response to denied request)
Restart, 446-448
Restructure, *416-417*, 420*Fig*
  no facilities in proposed NDL standard,
    766
RETENTION clause, *237*, 769
Retention of records
  (*see* Records retention)
Retirement of data, 592, 640, 649
  of personal data, 639
  (*see also* Records retention)
Retrieval, *258*
  ad hoc requests, 31-32
  anticipated volume of output, 272-273
  catalogued requests, 293-294
  DBMS selection criteria, 721
  decomposition in a distributed
    environment, 744
  extended capabilities, 733
  incremental, 273
  random sampling, 273
  steps in the process, 258-263*Fig*
    partitioning in a distributed
      environment, 748
Retrieval language:
  commands, 365
  on a flat file, **287-292**, 334
  on a hierarchical structure, 188, **308-329**
  on a multifile structure, **330-334**
Retrieval privileges (*see* Privileges)
Reusable resource, 476-477
REVELATION from Cosmos, 701
Reversion, 264-265
  in family of conversion processes, 409,
    411*Fig*
  no facilities in proposed NDL standard,
    766
Revision:
  of programs, 33

Revision (*Cont.*)
  structure versus content, 61, 346, 416
  (*see also* Database revision)
Rgroup (*see* Repeating group)
Ridge ending in fingerprint, 526
RIES, Daniel R., 504*b*
Right to Financial Privacy Act (U.S.),
    627, 632-633, 643, 646*Fig*
RIVEST, Ronald L., 557, 573*b*
RIVLIN, Alice M., 539*n*, 640*n*, 667*b*
ROARK, Mayford L., 68*b*
Robert and the supermarket, 177
ROBINSON, John T., 503*b*
ROBOT, 300, 305*b* (*see* INTELLECT)
ROGER, Craig, xvi
Role:
  of domain, 148, *586*
  of person, 74
Role dependent characteristics of data
    items, 219-220
Rollback, 49, 430, 438-439, 440*Fig*
  of a pre-empted process, 475-476, 489
ROMEO, Tom, 719*b*
Rooted tree/graph, *133*
ROSENKRANTZ, D. J., 494, 504*b*
ROSS, Ronald G., 25*b*, 619*b*, 773, 778*b*
ROSS, Steven, 619*b*
ROTHNIE, James B. Jr., 502*b*, 504*b*
Rounding controls, 543
RSA public-key cryptosystem, 558-559,
    569-570*b*
RULE, James B., 639, 667*b*
Run-time module
  (*see* Database control system)
RUSTIN, Randall, 151*b*, 765*n*

S

SABLE, Jerome D., 204*n*, 267*n*, 689*n*,
    719*b*
SALTON, Gerard, 72*b*
SAMUELSON, Kjell, 24*b*
SAYANI, Hasan H., 451*b*
SC-1 (Western Electric), 23*b*, 64*n*, 576
Schema, *92*, 774*Fig*
  (*see also* Database schema)
Schema diagram, *8-9*, 125, 127, **199-209**
SCHLÖRER, Jan, 541, 542, 569*b*
SCHMIDT, J., 778*b*
SCHOLL, M., 778*b*

SCHUELER, B. M., 358*b*
SCHUSSEL, George, 619*b*
SCHUSTER, Stewart, 781*b*
SCHWARTZ, Joel, 780*b*
SCHWARTZ, M. D., 541, 542, 569*b*
SCHWARTZ, Michael B., 556*n*
SCOTT, George M., xvi
Screen, user defined, 281-282, 347
Scrolling, 166
Searching by content, 756
Searching by context, 756
Second normal form, 249
Secondary attribute, 137
Secondary disclosure, 634*Fig*, 636-637
Security, 506-508
  (*see also* Data security; Computer
        security; Physical security;
        External security; Internal
        security)
Security matrix, 530
  (*see* Authorization matrix)
Security officer
  (*see* Database administration)
SEED from International Data Base
        Systems, 701
SEEK verb in COBOL, 363
SEGELSTEIN, Sidney, 718*b*
Selection criteria:
  content-based, 366-367
  dependent on access mechanisms, 368
  position-based, 281, 318, 320, 367-368,
        376-377
  supplied in advance, 274-275
  by unique internal record identifier, 368
  in user program, 364, 366-386, 377
Selection of DBMS:
  administrative criteria, 703-704, 708-
        711, 723-726
  bias in choice, 698
  final selection, 704-706
  finding available systems, 694-695
  gathering more information, 695-697
  technical criteria, 697-703, 720-723
Selection expression
  (*see* Boolean expression)
Selection step in retrieval, 260-263*Figs*,
        265-273, 748
  (*see also* Boolean expression)
Selective disclosure, 636

Selective dissemination of information
        (SDI), 70-71
Selectivity, loss of, 326
Self-contained DBMS, 15, 56-58, 77,
        106, 698-700*Fig*, 732-733
  for DBMS language programmer, 81
  for general user, 81
  versus host-language DBMS, 83, 360-
        361
Semantic constraints, 211*Fig*, 239-240
  (*see* Validation criteria)
Semaphores for locking data, 741
Semijoin, 781*b*
SENKO, Michael E., 120, 145*n*, 151-152*b*,
        310, 423*b*
SENN, James A., xvi
Separation of duties
  (*see* Division of responsibility)
Separator language style, 178-179, 372,
        376
Sequential processing, 160, 189
  automatic backup, 432
  mode declaration, 373-374
  using positional selection criteria,
        367-368
  (*see also* Batch processing)
Serial binding, 400, 402*Fig*
Serial data item, 220, 456
Serializability, 470-471, 502*b*
SET, in CODASYL data structure, 139-
        141, 237
SEVERANCE, Dennis G., 353, 358*b*, 450-
        451*b*, 573*b*
SHAMIR, A., 557, 573*b*
SHANNON, Claude E., 547, 573*b*
Sharability, **36-38**, 47, **75-76**
  DBMS dichotomy violates, 58-59
  hampered without userschema, 389
  requires access control, 506
  satisfaction of, 98-99, 733
SHARE, 152*b*
Shared control, 472, 477, 482-483
Shared data environment, 676
  in a distributed network, 740
  needs access control, 506
  needs concurrency control, 466, 488
  needs database administrator, 577
  produces conflict, 577-578
SHIPMAN, David W., 502*b*

SHIVELY, William C., 719*b*
SHOSHANI, A., 502*b*
SHNEIDERMAN, Ben, xvi, 196*b*, 306*b*, 425*b*
SHU, Nan C., 424*b*
SIBLEY, Edgar H., 68*b*, 151*b*, 383*b*, 393*n*, 424*b*, 696, 719*b*, 765*n*
Signature, 524, 529, 568*b*
  authentication, 556, 557, **558**
  repudiation, 561-562
Single file data structure, 121*Fig*-122
  advantages of, 134
Single-path hierarchical data structure, 130-132
SINKOV, A., 547, 573*b*
Skip in dialogue, 173
SMITH, Diane C. P., 247, 256*b*, 425*b*, 780*b*
SMITH, John Miles, 247, 256*b*, 780*b*
SMITH, Robert Ellis, 668*b*
Social Security Number, 653
SOCKUT, Gary H., 425*b*
Socrates from Cincom, 701, 733
Software:
  protecting proprietary interests, 708, 711-714
Software engineering, 682
Software market, 680-681, 683, 694
  economics of, 707-708*Fig*
  listing services, 695-696, 727-729
Software vendor (*see* Vendor of software)
Sophisticated user assumption, 370-371, 376, 768
Sorting (*see* Ordering)
Source code time binding, 403-405
South Carolina, privacy amendment, 627
Spacing on output, 282, 286-287
Special data items, 216
Sperry (UNIVAC), 679, 763
SPRAGUE, Ralph H., 22*b*
SPROWLS, Clay, 26*b*
SPSS, 123
SQL (from IBM), 23*b*, 122, 196*b*, 310, 336*b*, 701, 733, 758, 765-766, 778*b*
  (*see also* DB2)
SQUIRE, William, 527*n*
STAHL, Fred A., 550, 573*b*
Standard deviation, 278

Standards, database, **760-773**
  advantages and inhibitors, 763-764
  picking candidates, 764-765
Standards Planning and Requirements Committee (SPARC) of ANSI, 760, 761*Fig*
STARAN by Goodyear Aerospace, 756
Statistical databases, 568-569*b*
Statistical inferencing, **538-544**, 633, 640
Statistics:
  in retrieval, 262-263*Fig*, 276-279*Fig*, 321, 748
  on nested repeating group, 318
  zero value versus missing value, 462
STEARNS, R. E., 504*b*
STEMPLE, D., 196*b*
STERN, D., 780*b*
Stewardship of personal data, 656
STIBBENS, Steve, 668*b*
STOHR, E., 306*b*
STONEBRAKER, Michael R., 504*b*, 534, 573*b*
Storage media/devices, 30, 41, 55, 134, 240, 242, 432-433, 468-469
  shared in a network, 741, 742*Fig*, 743
  (*see also* Device-media control language)
Storage structure, 198
  changes in, 103-104
  DBMS selection criteria, 721
  definition of, 211*Fig*, 214-215, 240-242, 591
  design, 232, 245
  physical versus logical data structure, 212, 397
  of a record, 9*Fig*
  suppression in logical database design, 250
Stored-Data Description Language (SDDL), 424*b*
Strategic Inc., xii
Stream encryption, 547, 549-550, 552-553
Streaming tape drive, *434*
String data item, 216
STRUCTURAL clause, 139, 767
Structural elements in data structure, 201, 214
Structural evolution of a database, 417-418

Structure versus content change, 61, 346, 416

Structured programming, 82

SU, Stanley Y. W., 383*b*, 425*b*, 756, 758, 781*b*

Subject of access control, 530-531*Fig*

Subschema, 392 (*see* Userschema)

Substitution cipher, 547, 549-552

Successful defense, 525*Fig*

Successful invasion, 524-525*Fig*

Suffix operator, 265*n*

Sum, 276

Summary report, 278

SUMMERS, Rita C., 569*b*, 573*b*

SUNGREN, Bo, 26*b*

Supplemental disclosure, *540*

Surrogates:
  data for reality, 19
  for users, 515-516, 522

SWARTWOUT, Donald E., 425*b*

Sweden Data Law, 626

Synchpoint, 447 (*see* Checkpoint)

Synchronization, of updates, 51, 465, 496-498

Symbolic pointer, 232, 236

Syntax errors, 299
  impossibility of, 166

SYSTEM 1022/1032 from First Data, 701, 733

SYSTEM 2000 from Intel, 23*b*, 26*b*, 122-123, 174, 210, 315, 325-328, 621, 693-694, 701, 733

System buffers:
  use in backup, 445*Fig*, 447

System checkpoint, **447-448**

System data:
  versus user data, 111-113

System developer/development:
  compensates for low-level DBMS, 111, 677
  dialogue levels, 168-169
  early focus of database administration, 579
  facilities for, 76, 185-186, 735-736
  fair information practices permeate, 656
  fear of being locked in to initial solution, 386
  heuristic development, 117*b*, 583
  in microcomputer environment, 162

System developer/development (*Cont.*)
  replacing the traditional lifecycle, 583
  use of conventional programming languages as a last resort, 769
  user role, 75-76
  versus database administration, 582-583
  (*see also* Application system design/development)

System-driven dialogue
  (*see* Menu-driven dialogue)

System for Distributed Databases (SDD-1), 502*b*

System R, 451*b*, 568*b*, 570*b*

T

TABLET, 196*b*

Tabular representation of frequency distribution, 276, 295*Fig*, 297*Figs*

TARVER v. SMITH, 668*b*

Taxes on software, 725-726

Taxonomies:
  data structures, **120-123***Fig*
  DBMS, **74**
  functions, 62*Fig*, **86-88***Fig*
  motivators of database approach, 31-34, 97
  objectives of database management, 36-52
  users, 78-79*Figs*

TAYLOR, Robert W., 152*b*, 424-425*b*

TDMS (SDC), 23*b*, 64, 308-310, 315-316, 336*b*, 693-694

Technological change, responding to, 45

TEICHMAN, Ronald, xvi

TEICHROEW, Daniel, *64n*

Teleprocessing, *740*

Teleprocessing monitor
  (*see* Terminal management)

Temporal data
  (*see* Time dimension of data)

TENNANT, H., 306*b*

TEOREY, Toby J., 244, 247, 256*b*, 425*b*

Teradata, 758-760

Terminal (*see* Microcomputer workstation)

Terminal management, 107, 109-110

Ternary relationship, 147*Fig*-148, 229

Test data, 595

Text data item type, 53, 216

Text processing systems, 53, 68*b*
Thesaurus, controlled, in Bibliographic
    systems, 69-72
Third normal form, 249-250, 765
THOMAS, Robert H., 503-504*b*
THOMPSON, Robert D., Rev., 286
Threat monitoring (*see* Monitoring)
TILLMAN, George D., 619*b*
Time dimension of data, 254*b*
Time-sharing systems, 37*n*, 508
Timestamping 438, 441, 470, 480, 485,
    487, 491
TIS (TOTAL) Directory from Cincom,
    618*b*, 701
TODD, Stephen J. P., 358*b*
Topology of a network, 744
TOSI, Oscar, 527
TOTAL from Cincom, 23*b*, 26*b*, 620-621,
    693, 701, 733, 734, 753*Fig*
Total function, 226, 229
Touch screen, 165
Trackball, *165*
Tracker expression, 541-542
Trade secret, 636, 711, 713
Tradeoffs, 242, 353, 408, 721
    in backup and recovery, 446
    data security versus user convenience,
        420
    machine efficiency versus organizational
        profitability, 704-705*Fig*
Traffic jam deadlock analogy, 486*Fig*
Training, 167, 593-595, 724, 737
Transaction, 19, 347
    as a unit of work, 448, *466-468*
Transaction definition, 343, 348-351
    language for, 186
Transaction logging, 430
Transaction processing, 346-352, 436*Fig*,
    464*Fig*
    (*see also* Update)
Transaction program, 349*Fig*, 351*Fig*, 352
Transaction queue, 351*Fig*, 436*Fig*
Transaction scheduling, 487
    (*see* Presequence)
Transaction validation, 343, 571*b*
    insufficient for quality control, 458
Transborder data flows, 644
Transition diagram, 268*Fig*
    to define expression syntax, 367-368*Fig*

Transitional validation criteria, 462-463
Transitive dependency rule in database
    design, 249
Transposition cipher, 547, 549
Transputer, 760, 780*b*
Trapdoor one-way function, 557
Tree, *133*, 228, 308
Tree traversal, 328
Trial balance
    (*see* Accounting trial balance)
Truncate mapping, *415Fig*
TSICHRITZIS, Dionysios C., 26*b*, 116*b*,
    120*n*, 152*b*, 256*b*, 765*n*, 778*b*
TUEL, W. G. Jr., 425*b*
Tuple, *140*
TURN, Rein, 544, 573*b*, 668*b*
TURNER, Jon, 306*b*
Tutorial level of dialogue, 170-171
Two-dimensional frequency distribution,
    296-298*Figs*
Two-phase commit locking protocol, 489,
    492
Two-way table, 297*Fig*
Type conversion, 412

U

UCC TEN from University Computing
    Co., 618*b*, 620
UHROWCZIK, P. P., 602, 619*b*
UL/1 from RCA, 383*b*
ULLMAN, Jeffrey D., 22*b*, 26*b*, 122,
    152*b*, 336*b*, 504*b*, 542*n*
ULMAN, Joseph N.:
    data as a collective noun, 11
Unbundling software from hardware, 679,
    693-694
Unconserved resource, 477, 650
UNDO command, 167
    (*see also* Rollback)
Unified Database Language (UDL), 336*b*
Uniform Information Practices Code, 627,
    645
    (*see also* EVEREST, 667*b*)
UNIFY from Unify Corp., 701, 765
Unique data item, 220, 238 460
    (*see* Identifier)
Unique internal record identifier, 368, 768
Unit record, 245

United Nations, Declaration of Human
Rights, 627
United States Constitution, 629, 646*Fig*,
712
United States income tax return (IRS), 658
Units of measurement, 217
UNIVAC (*see* Sperry (UNIVAC))
Unknown value, 125, 462
UNLOCK command, 481-482
Update, *340-356*
authorization, 465-466, 532
(*see also* Access control)
base variables in, 467, 484
data dependent, 354-355
DBMS selection criteria, 722
degradation due to backup, 431, 437
with dependent entity, 227-228, 237-239
in family of conversion processes, 409,
411*Fig*
generalized function for programming
user, 365, 378-379
generalized language for, 349, 354-356
high-level facilities not in proposed
NDL standard, 768
by individual records, 346-348
inhibited during backup actions, 432-
433, 437, 441
maintenance of indexes during, 363,
416-417, 612
synchronization, 51, 465, **496-498**
with user-defined screen, 347
versus database creation, 345, 354
versus revision, 416
Update control, 506, 598
(*see* Access control)
Update privileges, 466, 532
Update problems, 249
with dependent entity, 227-228, 365
with mandatory data item, 355, 414
with nested repeating group, 310-311
with redundancy, 30, 51, 498
when representing relationships with
physical pointers or contiguity,
232
Usage statistics (*see* Monitoring)
User demands:
responding to changes in, 45-46
User-driven dialogue
(*see* Command-driven dialogue)

User interface, 160
becoming simpler, higher-level, 734
coexistence of different, 179-181
levels of access, 58-59, 87*Fig*
(*see also* Language)
User profile model for access control,
512*Fig*, 513*Fig*, 530
User program buffer (*see* Program buffer)
User roles in DBMS, **74-84**
administrative, 75
direct versus indirect, *74-75*
end user versus system developer, *75-
76*, 162, 168-169
hierarchy of, 79*Fig*
in microcomputer environment, 75-76,
161-162
nonprogramming versus programming,
76-78
roles versus persons, 74
(*see also* Nonprogramming user;
Programming user)
Users of data/DBMS:
changing demands, 45-46
confidence in data, 47, 454, 585, 597
demands versus system capability,
46*Fig*
diversity of, 39-40
frustrated at inaccessibility of data, 749
identification (*see* Identification)
managers as, 40
notified of changes in database
definition, 594
online, 160-162, 734
profile for access control, 512-513*Figs*,
522, 536*Fig*
program as surrogate for, 516, 522
providing support for, 593-595, 737-738
relation to database administration, 584
responsibility for data integrity, 429,
584, 741-742
supportive relationships, 104-106*Fig*
surrogates for, 515, 522
training, 161, 167, 593-595, 724, 737,
763
view of data, 92-96, 211*Fig*, 389, 397,
734
conforming to system's view, 93-94,
400
more than system's view, 122, 213

Userschema, *94-96Figs*, 123, 188, 330-331, 364, 388*Fig*, 391*Fig*, *392*, 734
  approval of, 582, 588, 594
  binding to the schema, 399
  changes due to revised schema, 407*Fig*, 419-420
  consolidation into global schema, 245
  contributes to evolvability, 92-94, 389
  copy of schema, 400, 408
  definition of, 186, 390-391*Fig*
  external schema in ANSI/SPARC DBMS framework, 116*b*, 772*Fig*
  independent of bound portion of schema, too, 394-395
  for nonprogramming user, 378
  parts of, **368-369**
  requires some view of the data structure, 187
  'subset' of the schema, 394-395
  use in data entry, 343
  in user program, 364, 368-369, 378

V

VALDURIEZ, Patrick, 758, 781*b*
Validation of data, **454-465**, 597-598
  of a batch, 353
  controlled in distributed environment, 749
  of input data transactions, 348, 571*b*, 458, 748
  levels, 463-464*Fig*
  manual versus mechanized, 455-459
  response rules, 465
  (*see also* Error and exception conditions)
Validation criteria, 211*Fig*, **239-240**, 454, 597-598
  in batch header, 458
  extension of database definition, 214, 239, 458
  language for, **460-465**
Value class, 215
Value of data, 10
Value of information, 10
Value set, 218
VALUECHECK validation statement, 461
Values of attributes, *8*, 120, 123-126
  characteristics of, 215

Values of attributes (*Cont.*)
  variable length, 214, 218
  coded, 218
VAN DUYN, Julia, 619*b*
Variable length binary code, 244, 549
Variable length fields, 214, 218, 220, 241
  in encryption, 548
Variance, 278
VASSILIOU, Yannis, xvi, 306*b*
VASTA, Joseph, 26*b*
Vendor:
  different terminology, 677-678
  view of standards, 763-764, 767-768
Vendor of DBMS:
  help in DBMS concepts education, 677
Vendor of hardware:
  source of DBMS, 694
Vendor of software:
  characteristics for evaluation, 723-724
  contract provision for failure, 711
  excitement about their product, 696, 703
  independent, 686, 694
  modifications to existing package, 683
  motivation to support, 684
  signing their standard contract, 708
Verb form of DML, 372-373
VERHOESTAD, Joost S. M., 451*b*
Versions of data, 241-242
Vertical overflow, 284-285, 320
Vertical partitioning, 747
  (*see* Attribute partitioning)
VETTER, M., 247, 256*b*
View (*see* Userschema)
Vigenère tableau, 551-552
Virtual (derived) data item, *274*, 413-414
Vocabulary in natural language querying, 302-303
Voice recognition, 165, 167
  for data entry, 341
  devices, 527, 529
Voiceprint, 528*Fig*
Voiceprint identification, 524-525, 527-529
Volume of output anticipated, 272-273
VORHAUS, Al, 309-310, 316, 418

W

WADE, B. W., 533, 570*b*
WAH, B. W., 781*b*

Wait-die protocol, 494-495
Wait-for graph and matrix, 489-490*Fig*
WALLACE, Mark, 306*b*
WALTZ, D., 306*b*
WARE, Willis H., 668*b*
WARN, David R., 185
Warranty, 709-710
WARREN, David S., 254*b*
WARREN, Samuel C., 628, 650, 668*b*
WATSON, Hugh J., 22*b*
WEBER, Ron, 619*b*
WEBER, Wolfgang, 504*b*
WEGSTEIN, J. H., 526, 573*b*
WEISS, Eric A., xvi
WEISS, Harvey M., 719*b*
WELDON, Jay-Louise, 619*b*
WELLS, David L., 568*b*
WELTY, C., 196*b*
West Germany, Hessen Data Protection
      Act, 626
WESTIN, Alan F., 668*b*
WETHERBE, James C., 22*b*, 117*b*, 583,
      616*b*
WHALEN v. ROE, 669*b*
WHINSTON, Andrew B., 23*b*
WHITNEY, Kevin, 765*n*
WIEDERHOLD, Gio, xvi, 26*b*
WIENER, Hesh, 719*b*

Windowing, 166
WINOGRAD, Terry, 306*b*
WITHINGTON, Frederic G., 100, 578,
      619*b*
WLAKOWICZ, Jo L., 779*b*
WOFSEY, Marvin M., 573*b*
WOOD, Christopher, 508, 537, 569*b*, 573*b*
WOOD, Helen M., 574*b*, 781*b*
WOODS, Charles C., 574*b*
WONG, Eugene, 534, 573*b*
Wound-wait protocol, 494
Word processing, 53, 196*b*
WRITE command, 363
Write privilege, 532
Writer rule, *471*, 482-483

Y

YAO, S. Bing, 256*b*, 425*b*, 719*b*, 781*b*
YORMARK, Beatrice, 781*b*
YOUNG, John W., Jr., 771, 781*b*
YOUNGER, Kenneth, 625, 669*b*
YOURDON, Edward, 451*b*, 504*b*
  on backup and recovery, 433, 441
  on locking, 501-502

Z

ZLOOF, Moshe M., 196*b*, 336*b*